IRELAND

1912–1985

IRELAND
1912–1985

❀

Politics and Society

J.J. LEE

Professor of Modern History,
University College Cork

CAMBRIDGE
UNIVERSITY PRESS

PUBLISHED BY THE PRESS SYNDICATE OF THE UNIVERSITY OF CAMBRIDGE
The Pitt Building, Trumpington Street, Cambridge, United Kingdom

CAMBRIDGE UNIVERSITY PRESS
The Edinburgh Building, Cambridge CB2 2RU, UK
40 West 20th Street, New York, NY 10011–4211, USA
477 Williamstown Road, Port Melbourne, VIC 3207, Australia
Ruiz de Alarcón 13, 28014 Madrid, Spain
Dock House, The Waterfront, Cape Town 8001, South Africa

http://www.cambridge.org

First published 1989
Reprinted 1990 (twice), 1991, 1992, 1993, 1995, 1998, 2001, 2004

Printed in the United Kingdom at the University Press, Cambridge

British Library Cataloguing in Publication data
Lee, J. J.
Ireland 1912–1985: politics and society.
1. Ireland. Political events, 1900–
1. Title.
941.5082.

Library of Congress Cataloguing in Publication data
Lee, Joseph, 1942–
Ireland 1912–1985: politics and society / J. J. Lee.
p.   cm.
Bibliography.
Includes index.
ISBN 0 521 26648 3   ISBN 0 521 37741 2 (pbk)
1. Ireland – History – 1922–   . 2. Ireland – History – 1910–1921
1. Title.
DA963.L44 1989.
941.5082 – dc19   88–23763 CIP.

ISBN 0 521 26648 3 hardback
ISBN 0 521 37741 2 paperback

For my wife Anne,
and our children
Amhairgín, Caoilfhionn and
Desmond

CONTENTS

List of maps   *page* ix
List of tables   x
Preface   xi
Acknowledgements   xvi
List of abbreviations   xix
Note on nomenclature   xxi

1   REBELLION: 1912–1922   1
    'Ulster will fight'   1
    Nationalist reactions   14
    The Easter Rising   24
    Sinn Féin   38
    Partition   43
    The Treaty   47

2   CONSOLIDATION: 1922–1932   56
    Civil wars   56
    The Free State inheritance   69
    State-building   94
    Northern Ireland   136
    The Boundary Commission   140
    Fianna Fáil   150
    Church and state   157
    The fall of Cosgrave   168

3   EXPERIMENT: 1932–1945   175
    The impact of de Valera   175
    The 1937 constitution   201
    Triumph   211
    Behind the headlines   217

Fianna Fáil versus the IRA 219
War economics 224
War politics 236
'We are King's men' 253
Plato's cave? 258

4 MALAISE: 1945–1958 271
The conservative resistance 271
The electoral game 293
The first inter-party government 299
Morass 321

5 EXPANSION: 1958–1969 329
De Valera departs 329
Economic change 341
Social change 359
Political change 365
Lemass 371
The Lynch succession 409

6 NORTH: 1945–1985 411
Reform and reaction 411
The fall of Stormont 435
The search for a solution 441

7 DRIFT: 1969–? 458
The Lynch government 458
The Cosgrave government 469
The crock of gold 487
At the end of the rainbow? 506

8 PERSPECTIVES 511
Performance 511
Potential 521
Institutions 540
Intelligence 562
Character 643
Identity 658

Select bibliography 688
Index 731

MAPS

1 Ireland   *page* xxiv
2 Catholics as proportion of the total population in the district council
  areas of Northern Ireland, 1981   681

TABLES

1 Distribution of population by religion in Ulster counties, 1911   *page*2
2 Birth, marriage and death rates, 1922 (selected countries)   70
3 Total number of persons at work in 1961, 1966, 1971 (000)   360
4 Net emigration rates from Northern Ireland, 1937–71   413
5 Current exchequer deficit, 1973–77   471
6 Projected and actual economic indicators, 1981   488
7 Wage increases and inflation rates, 1978–81 (%)   489
8 Balance of payments' deficits, 1978–81   489
9 Current budget deficits, 1979–82   502
10 Government expenditure, 1977–82 (% GNP)   503
11 Population, 1919–84 (selected countries)   512
12 National product per capita, 1910 (selected countries)   513
13 Agricultural machinery (Denmark and Éire)   529

PREFACE

This study was conceived in the tranquil atmosphere of Peterhouse, continued in more turbulent times in Cork, and completed on the serene slopes of Fiesole. I gladly acknowledge my debt to Peterhouse, where I learned much not only about scholarship, but about fellowship. I do not seek, however, to emulate what has 'become the Peterhouse manner – stern, unrefutable and arcane'.[1] If there be stern and arcane passages in this book, their inspiration derives from other sources. And I hope the text remains sufficiently intelligible throughout to be consistently refutable!

The late F. S. L. Lyons lamented nearly twenty years ago that the historian of contemporary Ireland is condemned to make bricks without straw.[2] The supply of straw has greatly increased since then. There has been a massive expansion in the available archival material, and a marked increase in relevant published work, not only by historians but by scholars in cognate disciplines. Yet the present situation contains its own dangers. The avalanche of archival material, only a small fraction of which has been excavated, not only threatens to obscure perspective beneath mounds of detail, but also to lull the historian, starved for so long of any archival sustenance, into complacency concerning the enduring quality of his necessarily provisional conclusions.

One function of the historian is to transcend the fragmentation of perspective characteristic of the contemporary mind. Research is now so specialised that this fundamental objective has become increasingly difficult to attain.[3] In few fields of intellectual endeavour do the means so threaten to subvert the ends. Synthesis thus becomes even more emphati-

---

[1] J.G.A. Pocock, 'Introduction: the state of the art', in J.G.A. Pocock, *Virtue, commerce and history* (Cambridge, 1985), p. 34.
[2] F.S.L. Lyons, *Ireland since the Famine* (London, 1971), p. ix.
[3] D. Thelen, 'The profession and the *Journal of American History*', *JAH*, 73, 1 (June 1986), pp. 9–10, records the widespread unease among American historians at the fragmentation of the subject.

cally the supreme challenge for the historian.[4] Synthesis is always, at one level, premature. It may seem presumptuously premature in the case of recent Irish history, where so much of the necessary monographic research remains to be tackled, and where no satisfactory interpretive paradigm exists. I hope this effort will encourage others with easier access to the source material to pursue the research on which a more satisfactory synthesis can soon be based. If the contemporary historian is not himself to become an agent of yet further fragmentation, he must strive towards total history, not in the futile sense of trying to write everything about everything, but in the sense of seeking to reveal the range of relevant linkages between the varieties of activity with which he is concerned.[5] That is a formidable task, conceptually and technically, even when an author confines himself to the study of public policy. I am painfully aware of how short of that goal this study falls, but I hope that it at least leaves the reader facing in the right direction.

The familiar problems of contemporary history are exacerbated in the Irish case by the shift in perspective imposed by the emergence of statehood. The nature of Anglo-Irish relations has traditionally constituted the main organising principle of Irish historiography. The historian of independent Ireland, however, and to some extent even of Northern Ireland, must focus more on the relationship between the potential and the performance of sovereignty, however much that relationship may be moulded by external influences. Potential and performance are elusive, complex and, in certain respects, subjective concepts. In tentatively probing the layers of the popular psyche that shaped the quality of national performance, I venture occasional meditations on *mentalité*. Critics of this no doubt faltering effort are urged to construct their own more robust interpretive frameworks.

This shift in the angle of approach has inevitable implications for the role of the historian in the wider society. In a work equally impressive for integrity and intelligence, a French thinker has observed that 'Ireland is a country where history is autobiographical and autobiography historical. It is an important indication as to the way in which a man of letters considers his status in the country.'[6] If there can indeed be still a sense in which the Irish historian may consider himself 'the custodian of the entire

[4] For superior expositions of this viewpoint, see B. Bailyn, 'The challenge of modern historiography', *AHR*, 87, 1 (February 1982), pp. 1–24; T. Bender, 'Wholes and parts: the need for synthesis in American history', *JAH*, 73, 1 (June 1986), pp. 120–36.

[5] H. Rothfels, 'Zeitgeschichte als Aufgabe', *Vjh. f. Zeitgesch.*, 1, 1 (January 1953), p. 7; W.J. Mommsen, 'Die Geschichtswissenschaft in der modernen Industriegesellschaft', *Vjh. f. Zeitgesch.*, 22, 1 (January 1974), p. 9; M. Broszat, 'Aufgaben und Probleme zeitgeschichtlichen Unterrichts', *Geschichte in Wissenschaft und Unterricht*, 9 (1957), pp. 535–6.

[6] Maurice Goldring, *Faith of our fathers: the formation of Irish nationalist ideology 1890–1920* (Dublin, 1982), p. 8.

history of his country',[7] he can no longer succumb to delusions of grandeur in this regard. A fine generation of Irish historians had already begun to adopt from the 1930s a more discerning approach towards the role of Viking, Norman, English and Scot in Irish history than had been possible for the protagonists during the protracted struggle for sovereignty. That generation discharged its duty, which was essentially one of inculcating a more mature attitude towards Anglo-Irish relations. Central though the relationship with England remains, the main function of the contemporary Irish historian of a later generation is to evaluate the performance of a sovereign people. The effective discharge of that duty is not destined to win him the affection of all his Irish readers. The market for truth is a distinctly finite one, even in Ireland! In a culture where ambiguity plays so active a mediating role in human relations, anyone venturing to suggest that the Emperor may even occasionally be glimpsed in a state of *déshabillé* risks remonstrance for *lèse-majesté*. The author is already well aware that the slightest lack of reverence for sacred cows arouses intense resentment among the guardians of the bovine faith! An absence of systematic self-appraisal, as distinct from complaint, of which there is ample if incoherent supply, remains characteristic of the Irish intellectual condition. The contemporary historian can be reasonably expected to supply some of the deficiency.

Comparative perspective can illuminate our understanding of the Irish condition. Yet there is no wholly comparable case. Many distinctive features of the Irish experience might be listed. The South, following a highly unusual colonial-type history, achieved a degree of political stability rare for a new state. Northern Ireland, on the other hand, failed to acquire legitimacy in the eyes of a sufficient number of its inhabitants to prevent itself being torn apart by what appears to be a variety of tribal religious war, as if a slumbering monster had writhed out of some primeval slime. The South has succeeded in maintaining military neutrality, but it has succumbed ever more to cultural dependence. It has a unique demographic history, and a most unusual economic history, with the slowest rate of growth of gross national product of any European country in the twentieth century. The North, too, in a rather different way, counts among the striking economic failures of the century. Even this cursory catalogue suffices to remind us that recent Irish historical experience cannot be encompassed within conventional categories of either European or Third World historiography. It is none the worse for that. On the contrary, if comparative perspective can illuminate the Irish scene, an understanding of Irish history may in turn enrich wider historial perspectives. Yet the distinctive nature of the Irish case complicates the challenge confronting the historian.

[7] *Ibid.*, p. 7.

The Irish contemporary historian finds himself in the unusual position of being simultaneously insider and outsider. He cannot pronounce on both Northern Ireland and the Republic from the same perspective, relying on the same silent assumptions. A truly comparative history of North and South has yet to be adequately conceived, much less completed. Southern Irish historians, like myself, are likely to be as ambivalent towards the North as are citizens of the Republic in general. If it was a striking achievement of an impressive generation of Irish historians to 'exorcise passion' from the study of the Irish past,[8] it did so largely by evading the challenge of contemporary history. This book is inevitably written from a Southern perspective. My own preferences are not concealed. But I have tried to assess individuals, North and South, *within* their own traditions. Many an unworthy cause has been worthily served, in Ireland as elsewhere, just as many a worthy cause has, sadly, been unworthily served.

The personalities of Ireland and of Ulster are traditionally defined in historical terms. 'Without history', writes Liam de Paor,

the Irish nation is nothing. It has defined itself by history. Perhaps it is nothing. That remains to be seen. Without history, Ulster is nothing. It is a corner of Ireland, or a corner of the United Kingdom, where infantile behaviour has become tedious as well as dangerous. Perhaps it is nothing. That too remains to be seen.[9]

These are high claims. They may reflect the disenchantment of the mid-eighties, stumbling towards the future with tragedy in the North and gloom in the South. They may reflect too a sense of the unfulfilled potential of self-government. It is usual to aver that the Irish are haunted by history, that they suffer from too much rather than too little historical consciousness. But the modern Irish, contrary to popular impression, have little sense of history. What they have is a sense of grievance, which they choose to dignify by christening it history. History therefore is 'not so much a matter of learning from the past as of stirring old grievances to keep them on the boil'.[10]

How to learn from history is one of the most difficult challenges confronting any people. It is central to my argument that the Irish of the late twentieth century have still to learn how to learn from their recent history. As Gearóid Ó Tuathaigh has observed:

The process of de-colonisation is not simply an exercise in erasing, expunging and substituting. As many new post-colonial states have discovered in this century, the achievement of political-constitutional independence is the beginning and not the

---

[8] A. Clarke, 'Ireland 1534–1660', in J. Lee (ed.), *Irish historiography 1970–79* (Cork, 1981), p. 34.
[9] Liam de Paor, 'Gone with the wind', *Irish Times*, 4 July 1985.
[10] Dick Walsh, *The Party: inside Fianna Fáil* (Dublin, 1986), p. 1.

end of the task of national liberation. These new states may learn valuable lessons from the Irish experience, under the Union and since Independence. So too may the Irish themselves.[11]

[11] M.A.G. Ó Tuathaigh, 'Ireland and Britain under the Union, 1800–1921: an overview', in P.J. Drudy (ed.), *Ireland and Britain since 1922*: Irish Studies 5 (Cambridge, 1986), pp. 19–20.

ACKNOWLEDGEMENTS

I am grateful to all those who have helped over the many years this book has been in preparation.

My first debt is to Cambridge University Press. This volume would not have been contemplated but for the encouragement of Patricia Williams, nor completed without the confidence and patience of William Davies, who has been a model of restraint in the face of prolonged provocation. Sheila McEnery coped imperturbably with a multitude of idiosyncrasies at sub-editorial stage.

The friendly and stimulating Departments of History in the University of Pittsburgh, the European University Institute, Florence, and the Institute for European History, Mainz, provided conditions conducive to scholarly work. University College Cork has provided ideal laboratory conditions for participant observation of the relationship between potential and performance in Irish life.

I am grateful to the Development Fund of University College Cork, and to the Royal Irish Academy, for research support which enabled me broaden my comparative perspective.

Norma Buckley, Orla de Barra, Eileen Fehily, Veronica Fraser, Charlotte Holland, Catherine Long and Margaret O'Connell have contributed greatly to the making of this book. The efficiency, dedication, good humour and grace under pressure of these wonderful secretaries in University College Cork have been a constant reminder of the potential of Irishmen – or at least of Irish women!

The staff of the Boole Library of University College Cork have likewise combined efficiency with fortitude and good cheer in coping with my importunate demands. Jill Crowley and Valerie Fletcher bore the brunt of my direct assaults, while Nora Browne and Finola O'Donovan resolved a variety of difficulties. I want to specially thank themselves and their staffs, for librarians rarely receive the recognition they deserve in Irish universities. I wish too to thank the staffs of the following archives and libraries:

the Auswärtiges Amt, Bonn, the British Library at Bloomsbury and Colindale, the Bundesarchiv–Militärarchiv, Freiburg, Cambridge University Library, the Library of the European Community Office, Dublin, the Library of the European University Institute, the Hillman Library of the University of Pittsburgh, the Library of the Institute for European History, the National Library of Ireland, the Public Record Office, London, the Library of the Royal Irish Academy, the State Paper Office, the Library of Trinity College Dublin, the Truman Library, University College Dublin Archives.

My other obligations are legion. My benefactors include, apart from my mother, a constant source of support, Peter Alter, Christopher Andrew, M. J. Bannon, Garrett Barden, Tom Barrington, T.C.W. Blanning, Bernard Breen, Donal Counihan, Desmond Clarke, Maurice Cowling, Ray Crotty, Dónal de Buitléir, Beatrijs d'Hartogh, R. de Schryver, Tom Dunne, Owen Dudley Edwards, Connell Fanning, Brian Farrell, Desmond Fennell, Aloys Fleischmann, Jack and Barbara Gillingham, Brian Girvin, Ricky Hall, John and Ruth Ann Harris, Bridie Hartnett, Miriam Hederman O'Brien, Peter Hertner, Ann Heskin, Hugh and Kate Kearney, Dermot and Ann Keogh, David Kirby, Matti Klinge, H. Leibundgut, Frank Litton, John Maguire, Ged Martin, the late M.D. McCarthy, Ciaran McCulloch, Deirdre McMahon, Alan Milward, John Montague, John A. Murphy, Edward Norman, K.B. Nowlan, Dónal Ó Brolcháin, Leon Ó Broin, Marion O'Callaghan, J.P. O'Carroll, Gearóid Ó Crualaoich, Siobhán O'Dowd, Diarmuid Ó Giolláin, Cormac Ó Gráda, M.K. O'Leary, David O'Mahony, Seán Ó Murchú, Jennifer O'Reilly, Gobnait O'Riordan, Seán Ó Tuama, Gearóid and Marie Ó Tuathaigh, Gillian Peele, John Pratschke, R.J. Raymond, Joe and Joanne Ronsley, Joseph Ruane, Claus Scharf, Angela Schenk, Edward Shils, Denis and Margaret Smyth, Vibeke Sorenson, Norman Stone, Christopher Thorne, M.G. Valiulis, Martin Vogt, Brian Walker, Jim and Ann Walsh, Conor Ward, Sidney and Gladys Weintraub, Stuart Woolf, and Leonard Wrigley.

I have learned much from my research students in this and related fields, including Daniel Bradley, Kathleen Doyle, Richard Dunphy, Brian Girvin, Patricia McCaffrey, Christine McCarthy, Eileen Magner, Daniel Mulhall, Patrick O'Keeffe and Bernadette Whelan.

Dermot Keogh, Brian Girvin and Richard Dunphy, colleagues in my own department in Cork, have recently published, or will shortly publish, important studies on aspects of the history of twentieth-century Ireland. I owe much to the stimulus of their scholarship and commitment.

Three of my university teachers who profoundly influenced my understanding of Irish history have since died. I recall, with mingled pride, gratitude, and sense of loss, Dudley Edwards, Maureen Wall, and Desmond Williams.

The price of domestic neglect has been borne by my wife Anne and our children. Anne has not only coped resourcefully with the domestic disruption caused by my physical and mental absences, but has sharpened my awareness of the Irish condition with acute observations. On the admittedly debatable assumption that absence has constituted deprivation, this study is dedicated, in gratitude and restitution, to them all.

I alone am responsible for all errors.

ABBREVIATIONS

AA	Auswärtiges Amt
AFT	An Foras Talúntais
AHR	*American Historical Review*
BA-MA	Bundesarchiv–Militärarchiv
CVO	Commission on Vocational Organisation
DD	Dáil Debates
DDI	Documenti Diplomatici Italiani
DGFP	Documents of German Foreign Policy
DO	Dominions Office
EB	Ernest Blythe Papers
EJPR	*European Journal of Political Research*
ESR	*Economic and Social Review*
ESRI	Economic and Social Research Institute
FG	Frank Gallagher Papers
FRUS	Foreign Relations of the United States
IBR	*Irish Banking Review*
IDA	Industrial Development Authority
IESH	*Irish Economic and Social History*
IHS	*Irish Historical Studies*
IMI	Irish Management Institute
IPA	Institute of Public Administration
IRA	Irish Republican Army
ISC	Irish Situation Committee
JAH	*Journal of American History*
JSSISI	*Journal of the Statistical and Social Inquiry Society of Ireland*
NESC	National Economic and Social Council
NIEC	National Industrial and Economic Council
NLI	National Library of Ireland
OKW	Oberkommando der Wehrmacht

PA	Politisches Archiv des Auswärtigen Amtes
PM	Patrick McGilligan papers
PRO	Public Record Office, London
RM	Richard Mulcahy Papers
RUC	Royal Ulster Constabulary
SPO	State Paper Office
StSekr	Staatssekretär
TL	Truman Library
TRHS	Transactions of the Royal Historical Society
UCC	University College Cork
UCD	University College Dublin
UCDA	University College Dublin Archives
UCG	University College Galway
UDA	Ulster Defence Association
UDR	Ulster Defence Regiment
UVF	Ulster Volunteer Force
Vjh. f. Zeitgesch.	*Vierteljahrshefte für Zeitgeschichte*

NOMENCLATURE

Expressions like the Republic, Éire, Northern Ireland, Ulster, the Six Counties, the Twenty-Six Counties, South, North, etc., are normally employed as stylistic convenience dictates, except where a precise constitutional designation is analytically relevant for my purposes. South and North are capitalised when referring to the political entities colloquially subsumed under these terms. Nationalist, Unionist, and Home Rule are capitalised when referring to the relevant political parties: lower case is used for the ideologies involved, or for popular opinion of the relevant persuasion. Government departments are normally referred to by their substantive titles. Thus, the Department of Finance is usually called Finance.

Irish language nomenclature is employed according to colloquial usage in the Republic, as with Taoiseach (Prime Minister), Tánaiste (Deputy Prime Minister), Dáil (the lower house of parliament), Oireachtas (parliament). The police, the Gárda Síochána (Guardians of the Peace), are usually called either the guards or the gárdaí, as in popular parlance.

Map 1 IRELAND

Chapter 1

❁

REBELLION: 1912–1922

'ULSTER WILL FIGHT'

The Parliament Act of 1911 broke the power of the House of Lords to defy the popular will as represented in the House of Commons. By removing the last parliamentary bulwark against home rule legislation for Ireland, this major measure of constitutional reform in the United Kingdom outraged Irish unionists, whose infuriated reaction to the threat of home rule unleashed violence into twentieth-century Irish politics.

Irish unionists, overwhelmingly Protestant, were divided into two main groups. About 250 000 Anglo-Irish occupied a vulnerable position among a Catholic population of 2.55 million in the three southern provinces.[1] Although most of the Anglo-Irish could count socially as no more than respectable middle class, they were well leavened by landed gentry, the higher professions and the more affluent mercantile classes. However subtle their internal gradations of gentility, their culture, at least by relaxed Hibernian criteria, had a patrician veneer, tinged with condescension towards Catholics but pervaded with a faint sense of *noblesse oblige*. By 1911 their wealth and social status far exceeded their political power, sapped since the 1880s by extension of the franchise to the predominantly Catholic lower orders, and by land legislation which had translated the gentry into a largely rentier class.[2]

The 891 000 Protestants in the northern province of Ulster contemplated quite different prospects from the 250 000 southern Protestants.

---

[1] *Census of Ireland, 1911*, HC 1912–13 (Cd. 6051), cxvi, pp. 38–9.

[2] J.C. Beckett, *The Anglo-Irish tradition* (London, 1976), pp. 119–20; P. Buckland, *Irish unionism: the Anglo-Irish and the new Ireland, 1855–1922* (Dublin, 1972), pp. xiv, xx; I. d'Alton, 'Southern Irish unionism: a study of Cork unionists, 1884–1914', *TRHS*, 5th series, 23 (1973), pp. 71–88; I. d'Alton, 'A contrast in crises: southern Irish Protestantism, 1830–43 and 1885–1910', in A.C. Hepburn (ed.), *Minorities in history* (London, 1978), pp. 70–83; D. Fitzpatrick, *Politics and Irish life, 1913–21* (Dublin, 1977), pp. 46–62; B. Inglis, *West Briton* (London, 1961), pp. 9–35; F.S.L. Lyons, *Culture and anarchy in Ireland, 1880–1939* (Oxford, 1980), pp. 18–23, 57–84.

Table 1. *Distribution of population by religion in Ulster counties, 1911*

County	Protestants (%)	Catholics (%)
Antrim	79.5	20.5
Down	68.4	31.6
Armagh	54.7	45.3
Londonderry	54.2	45.8
Tyrone	44.6	55.4
Fermanagh	43.8	56.2
Monaghan	25.3	74.7
Donegal	21.1	78.9
Cavan	18.5	81.5

Source: Census of Ireland, 1911. HC 1912–13 Cd. 6051, cxvi, p. 38.

Fifty years earlier Protestants were a minority in the province. Now they outnumbered the 691 000 Catholics.[3] The denominational distribution by county, however, as recorded in Table 1, was very uneven.

Ulster Protestants, largely descended from seventeenth-century English and Scottish settlers, dominated the good land and the better occupations, but there was little aristocratic about their culture. They were mainly lower middle class and working class in the towns, and farmers in the countryside, with only a relatively light leavening of gentry, professional men or even affluent commercial people.[4] A high proportion, in contrast to the Anglo-Irish, would count socially as no better than the 'poor whites' of a planter community. They were correspondingly anxious to emphasise their social distance from Catholics.

There were religious, social and regional tensions within Ulster Prot-estantism, especially between the two main denominations, Presbyterians and Episcopalians.[5] Nevertheless, the Protestant sense of solidarity in the face of Catholic importunity easily prevailed over internal differences. Their own peculiar institution, the Orange Order, which included two-thirds of adult Protestant males,[6] fostered a sense of community among Protestants and institutionalised the instinct of racial superiority over the conquered Catholics. The Orange marching season in July and August, a ritualistic celebration of conquest in an annual exhibition of communal machismo, served as regular reminder of the supremacy of victor over vanquished. Race and religion were inextricably intertwined in Ulster

---

[3] *Census of Ireland, 1911*, HC 1912–13 (Cd. 6051), cxvi, pp. 38–9.
[4] *Ibid.*, pp. 13–21.
[5] Lyons, *Culture*, pp. 113–45; P. Gibbon, *The origins of Ulster unionism* (Manchester, 1975); H. Patterson, *Class conflict and sectarianism: the protestant working class and the Belfast labour movement 1868–1920* (Belfast, 1980).
[6] P. Buckland, *A history of Northern Ireland* (Dublin, 1981), p. 5.

unionist consciousness. Unionists could not rely on the criterion of colour, for the Catholics lacked the imagination to go off-white, nor on the criterion of language, for the Catholics had unsportingly abandoned their own. It was therefore imperative to sustain Protestantism as the symbol of racial superiority.[7]

The meaning of race in the political vernacular of the early twentieth century requires delicate probing. Only rarely did it carry the full range of subsequent sinister connotations. It was still often used as an innocent synonym for nation or people, though some racist instinct in Britain was already shifting from the robust to the vicious.[8] Even when used derogatorily, racialist references did not necessarily imply genocidal instincts. Not all effusions of contempt for Catholics among early-twentieth-century Ulster Protestants should be axiomatically attributed to racism, red in tooth and claw. But many of these utterances were embedded in a clearly hierarchical concept of race relations as a law of Ulster nature. Semantic purists might protest that racism should be confined to the description of beliefs arising from directly observable physical differences between peoples. But racism has occurred where there were no such observable differences. The dedication with which Ulster Protestants laboured to sustain a sense of racial superiority in these circumstances itself eloquently expressed the racist cast of their minds. The racial imperative proved so demanding that boundaries had to be constructed where none objectively existed. A high degree of physical segregation, reminiscent of the segregation levels in many colour bar communities, reflected and reinforced psychic segregation.[9] Both communities had long learned to cleave to their own ground.

Ulster Protestants fashioned an elaborate set of images to sustain their

---

7 I follow here the general approach of Liam de Paor, *Divided Ulster* (Harmondsworth, 1970), p. 12. There is a large literature on this important and controversial subject. My thinking has been especially influenced by the following studies, even where my conclusions diverge from those of the authors: St John Ervine, *Craigavon: Ulsterman* (London, 1949); E.U. Ession-Udom, 'Tribalism and racism', in L. Kuper (ed.), *Race, science and society* (London, 1975), esp. pp. 235–6; G. Fitzgerald, *Reconciliation in a divided community* (Pittsburgh, 1982), esp. pp. 5–6; D.W. Miller, *Queen's rebels: Ulster loyalism in historical perspective* (Dublin, 1980); S. Nelson, 'Protestant "ideology" considered: a case of "discrimination"', in I. Crewe (ed.), *British Political Sociology Yearbook*, 2 (London, 1975); C.C. O'Brien, 'Northern Ireland: its past and its future: the future', *Race*, 14, 1 (1972); C. Thorne, *Racial aspects of the Far Eastern War 1941–1945* (London, 1982); F. Wright, 'Protestant ideologies and politics in Ulster', *European Journal of Sociology*, 14, 1 (1973).

8 P.M. Kennedy, 'The pre-war right in Britain and Germany', in P.M. Kennedy and W. Mock (eds.), *Nationalist and racialist movements in Britain and Germany before 1914* (London, 1981), pp. 1–20; M. Howard, 'Empire, race and war in pre-1914 Britain', in H. Lloyd-Jones, V. Pearl and B. Worden (eds.), *History and imagination: essays in honour of H.R. Trevor-Roper* (London, 1981), pp. 340–55.

9 A.C. Hepburn, 'Catholics in the North of Ireland, 1850–1921: the urbanisation of a minority', in Hepburn (ed.), *Minorities*, pp. 84–101.

sense of identity. One portrait enumerated in a loving degree of arithmetical precision the characteristics of 'the Belfast man' as 'Determination 98, business capacity 94, courage 91, trustworthiness 90, self-esteem 84, mental vigour 78, hospitality 70, general culture 55, artistic tastes 48, social graces 44.'[10] In vivid contrast to this self-image of sturdy if dour manliness, Irish Catholics conformed in Protestant minds to the classic stereotype of the native which settler races find it psychologically necessary to nurture. They were lazy, dirty, improvident, irresolute, feckless, made menacing only by their numbers and by their doltish allegiance to a sinister and subversive religion.

Ulster Protestants cherished a satisfying sense of individual self-reliance, which they conveniently confused with individualism. Genuine individualism made little impact on the herd mentality within fortress Ulster. Nonconformity flourished more as a religious label than as an intellectual style. Ulster Protestants were prisoners of their condition as a '*Herrenvolk* democracy'. The extension of the franchise in 1884 increased the electoral power of the Ulster Protestant lower classes, while it undermined that of the Anglo-Irish upper classes. In Ulster, as in the American South, 'Where there was progress towards democracy or equality for whites, there was frequently a diminution or limitation of the rights and opportunities of non-whites. Often, the same men were behind both trends.'[11] It was the popular demagogic leaders, like T.H. Sloan with his Independent Orange Order in the early twentieth century,[12] or Ian Paisley more recently, who fulminated most rabidly against Catholicism.

It was this sense of inalienable superiority that made Ulster unionists impervious to the logic of numbers. The Ulster unionist mind saw no incongruity in denying any nationalist right to rule the nine counties of 'Protestant' Ulster on the basis of a 3:1 nationalist majority in Ireland as a whole, while simultaneously insisting on a unionist right to rule Ulster with a 55 per cent Protestant majority. The nine-county province of Ulster was neither an administrative nor a political unit. In so far as there were local administrative or political units at all, they were the counties, the poor law unions, and the electoral districts. By any of these criteria, more than half the area of the geographical province of Ulster had a Catholic majority. From an Ulster unionist perspective, however, tedious territorial considerations of this type all missed the point. Why should a *Herrenvolk* deign to notice numbers? Why should one Protestant be equated with one Catholic? That would be to undermine the whole *raison d'être* of the divine dispensation. Why should mere majorities be taken seriously when,

10 Miller, *Queen's rebels*, pp. 114–15.
11 Kenneth P. Vickery, '"Herrenvolk" democracy and egalitarianism in South Africa and in the US South', *Comparative Studies in Society and History*, 16 (1974), p. 310.
12 J.W. Boyle, 'The Belfast Protestant Association and the Independent Orange Order', *IHS*, 13 (1962), pp. 117–52.

as Thomas Sinclair, 'the most universally respected of Belfast's business-men',[13] put it, 'inherent and ineradicable endowments, of character and aims'[14] distinguished Protestants from Catholics, blessing them with qualities against which mere numbers should not prevail.

'Ulster', like the German 'East', was less a place than a state of mind, however insistently this mentality expressed itself in the idiom of the territorial imperative. 'Ulsterman' was an abstract Protestant ideal untainted by the contamination of a Catholic presence. To the Protestant mind 'Ulsterman' and 'Catholic' were mutually exclusive identities. In contrast to the Proclamation of the Republic in 1916, which at least acknowledged, however grudgingly, the existence of a unionist minority in Ireland, the Proclamation of the Ulster Provisional Government in 1913 adopted a concept of 'Ulsterman' that defined Catholics out of existence. When Randall McNeill described Ulster as characterised above all by 'the will of the people to live together'[15] he was for practical purposes excluding Catholics from membership of 'the people'. Even for McNeill, by no means a rabid racist, Catholics could easily slip into the category of non-people.

Ulster Protestant workers saw little advantage in adopting the class politics becoming gradually more fashionable among British workers. Their reluctance was economically and psychologically rational, at least in the short term. They did better out of race than out of class. Skilled jobs, as well as the better unskilled ones, were disproportionately Protestant jobs.[16] Protestant workers could see little likelihood that class solidarity with poorer Catholic workers would improve their own economic posi-tion. And solidarity with Catholics might imply equality with Catholics, depriving Protestants not only of their relatively privileged economic position, but also of the psychic pleasure of their racial birth right. Class solidarity would threaten status and identity alike.

Ulster unionist MPs therefore represented a united Protestant commu-nity in their hostility to self-government for the mere Irish when they elected Sir Edward Carson as their leader in February 1910, in anticipa-tion of the imminent parliamentary struggle over home rule. 'Sombre, melancholy, a man of notable courage and great forensic ability, he brought to the Orange cause a considerable capacity for organisation, a moral fervour almost fanatical in its intensity and an instinctive feel for high, political drama.'[17] Anglo-Irish rather than Ulster Scot, a Dubliner,

13 R. MacNeill, *Ulster's stand for union* (London, 1922), p. 38.
14 T. Sinclair, 'The position of Ulster', in S. Rosenbaum (ed.), *Against Home Rule* (London, 1912; Kennikat edn, 1970), p. 173.
15 MacNeill, *Ulster's stand*, p. 2.
16 *Census of Ireland, 1911*, pp. 13–21; S.E. Baker, 'Orange and green', in H.J. Dyos and M. Wolff (eds.), *The Victorian city: image and reality* (London, 1973), 2, p. 802.
17 N. Mansergh, *The Irish question 1840–1921* (London, 1965), p. 200.

confident of his own abilities – he had achieved eminence at the Irish and
English bars – Carson did not fear Catholic competition. He succumbed
to neither the siege mentality nor the rabid anti-Catholicism of his Ulster
followers. His was essentially a Junker temperament. There was something of Parnell, his only peer among the Anglo-Irish of his generation, in
his personality and style. He held that home rule would be disastrous for
Ireland and, sharing the widespread illusion that Southern Ireland could
not survive as a viable economic entity without the support of industrial
Belfast, he seized on the Ulster question more to prevent self-government
for Ireland than to achieve it for Ulster.[18] He received formidable support
from Captain James Craig, MP for County Down, nominally his lieutenant but effectively his partner. Craig, wealthy son of a distiller, had proved
his physical courage in the Boer War. Closer to the east Ulster ground than
Carson, Craig was in many respects the real organiser of victory.

Ulster unionists had organised mass movements in 1886 and 1893 to
resist the first and second Home Rule Bills. In 1892 nearly 12 000
delegates affirmed their hostility to home rule at an impressive convention.[19] Under the leadership of Carson and Craig, the Ulster Unionist
Council, founded in 1905 as the central controlling organisation of
resistance to home rule, revived in 1911 the unionist club movement
which had languished since the House of Lords defeated the second Home
Rule Bill in 1893. Carson elaborated on unionist tactics at a monster
meeting at Craigavon in September 1911, warning his listeners that 'we
must be prepared the morning Home Rule passes, ourselves to become
responsible for the government of the Protestant Province of Ulster'.[20]
The UUC appointed at this stage, eight months before the introduction of
the third Home Rule Bill, a committee to draft a constitution for a
provisional government of Ireland,[21] which was to be duly approved in
September 1913.[22] After the Liberals introduced the Home Rule Bill in
April 1912, the vast majority of Ulster Protestant adult males pledged
themselves in September 1912 in the Solemn League and Covenant,
inspired by a sixteenth-century Scottish covenant,[23] to repudiate the
authority of any parliament forced upon them. Unionist women signed a
Declaration to the same effect. Ulster unionists thus threatened to defy

[18] J.C. Beckett, 'Carson – unionist and rebel', in F.X. Martin (ed.), *Leaders and men of the
    Easter Rising: Dublin 1916* (London, 1967), pp. 86–7; F.S.L. Lyons, *Ireland since the
    Famine* (London, 1971), pp. 198–9.
[19] P. Buckland, *Ulster unionism and the origins of Northern Ireland, 1886–1922* (Dublin,
    1973), pp. 52–3; Gibbon, *Origins*, pp. 130–6; Miller, *Queen's rebels*, p. 92.
[20] A.T.Q. Stewart, *The Ulster crisis* (London, 1969), p. 48.
[21] Lyons, *Ireland*, p. 300.
[22] A.T.Q. Stewart, *Sir Edward Carson* (Dublin, 1981), p. 79. The Provisional Government
    was now confined to Ulster only, and no longer intended for Ireland, as was apparently
    originally the case.
[23] Stewart, *Ulster crisis*, p. 61.

public opinion in Ireland and parliamentary opinion in the United Kingdom.

The Home Rule Bill that provoked so indignant a response did not propose anything so extreme as an Irish republic. Responsibility for relations with the crown, defence and foreign policy, custom and excise, and land purchase, was reserved for Westminster. So was control of the police for a six-year period. Much ingenuity was expended on devising safeguards against religious discrimination. A home rule parliament clearly could not exert much immediate authority on Irish, let alone Ulster, affairs. 'Little more, indeed, than glorified local government,'[24] the measure was so limited that it required all the persuasive powers of the Home Rule leader, John Redmond, to allay the chagrin of his followers.

Unionists could nevertheless harbour the legitimate fear that this might be the first step towards complete independence. It was less from this consideration, however, in so far as the historian can wager generalisations about popular mentalities, than from a sense of violated machismo, that the unionist rank and file, outraged by the very notion of a right to self-government for the baser breed, revolted against the bill. Nothing had changed since the *Belfast Newsletter* declared in 1886 that an Irish parliament 'would be the laughing stock of the civilized world'.[25] When as cerebral a commentator as Thomas MacKnight, the Liberal Unionist editor of the *Northern Whig*, did not spurn the description of home rule as 'a slave revolt' in the wake of the second Home Rule Bill[26] the instincts of the less restrained members of the Protestant populace may be imagined.

The Solemn League and Covenant prophesied that 'Home Rule would be disastrous to the material well-being of Ulster as well as to the whole of Ireland.' Ulster flourished relative to the rest of the country during the nineteenth century. Unionists attributed this good fortune as axiomatically to the Act of Union as nationalists attributed the relative decline of the Southern economy to the same omnipotent act. Ulster was in fact far from an economic success story by western European standards. The population of the province had fallen since 1841. It was Belfast, not Ulster, that was the success story. But the rest of Protestant Ulster basked in the reflected glow of Belfast's growth. Ulster unionists might point to the threat of the economic policy of the new Sinn Féin (Ourselves) Party, founded in 1905 by the Dublin journalist Arthur Griffith, who drew on Frederick List's infant industry argument to advocate a protectionist policy. This would have involved the imposition of tariffs in order to protect initially uncompetitive southern Irish industry. These might have

---

[24] F.S.L. Lyons, 'The meaning of Independnece', in B. Farrell (ed.), *The Irish parliamentary tradition* (Dublin, 1973), p. 227.

[25] *Belfast News Letter*, 20 February 1886.

[26] T. MacKnight, *Ulster as it is* (London, 1896), 2, p. 393.

damaged Belfast industries by raising the cost of imported raw materials, and by provoking retaliation, perhaps pricing Belfast's finished products out of their indispensable export markets. Ulster unionists might have pointed to this threat. But they generally did not at this stage. The evidence of their leading economic spokesman, J. Milne Barbour, president of the Belfast Chamber of Commerce, later first Minister for Commerce in Northern Ireland, himself a big linen manufacturer, before the Primrose Commission on the financial situation, is particularly revealing for its vagueness. Barbour did indeed express fears about the possible introduction of protectionism in a home rule state,[27] but was at least as concerned that 'the rural interest might outweigh the manufacturing interest to too great an extent'.[28] His most serious economic objection was that home rule 'might disturb the feeling of confidence that at present exists as far as credits are concerned'.[29] In the light of his relative vagueness on the economic implications of home rule, he had no difficulty conceding that he felt Ulster unionist opposition to be 'very largely religious'.[30]

Few had heard of Sinn Féin, still a mere fringe nationalist faction, in 1912. Unionists made few references to this movement, soon to rival the Pope himself for pride of place in their demonology. Though some spokesmen referred more strongly to tariffs as a threat than had Barbour,[31] unionists did not usually attribute the economic disaster they predicted under home rule to any specific policy, but rather implied it to the sheer incompetence inseparable from the government of an inferior breed. The argument had not fundamentally changed since 1886 when Belfast businessmen resisted home rule on the grounds that 'under an Irish parliament and government there would be no security for life nor property, no fair play to the Loyalists in the north of Ireland, and that utter want of commercial confidence without which Belfast could not continue to prosper'.[32]

The economic argument carried conviction with all sectors of unionist opinion. But it was not basic to unionist rejection of Irish nationalism. 'Home Rule is Rome Rule' was the slogan that touched a really responsive chord in Protestant hearts. Home rule, the covenanters reassured them-

---

[27] *Minutes of evidence taken by the Committee on Irish Finance, with appendices*, HC 1913 (Cd. 6799), xxx, q. 4568.

[28] *Ibid.*, q. 4551.   [29] *Ibid.*, q. 4396.   [30] *Ibid.*, q. 4565.

[31] The issue loomed more prominently later. The question whether an Irish parliament should have the right to impose customs duties proved a major stumbling block to agreement between unionists and nationalists at the Irish Convention in 1918 (H. Plunkett to D. Lloyd George, 8 April 1918, in *Report of the proceedings of the Irish Convention*, HC 1918 (Cd. 9019), x, p. 5).

[32] MacKnight, *Ulster*, 2, p. 380. For a graphic illustration of unionist images of the economic consequences of home rule, see the cartoons in R. Broad, *et al., The Troubles* (London, 1980), p. 67.

selves, would be 'subversive of our civil and religious freedom, destructive of our citizenship and perilous to the unity of the empire'. Revd Samuel Prenter, Moderator of the General Assembly of the Presbyterian Church, captured the essence of these fears:[33]

The contention of the Irish protestants is that neither their civil nor their religious liberties would be safe in the custody of Rome. In an Irish Parliament civil allegiance to the Holy See would be the test of membership, and would make every Roman catholic member a civil servant of the Vatican. That Parliament would be compelled to carry out the behests of the Church. The Church is hostile to the liberty of the Press, the liberty of public speech, to modernism in science, in literature, in philosophy; is bound to exact obedience from her members and to extirpate heresy and heretics; claims to be above Civil Law, and the right to enforce Canon Law whenever she is able. There are simply no limits even of life or property to the range of her intolerance. This is not an indictment; it is the boast of Rome.

Revd Dr Patterson, preacher at the Ulster Hall service attended by Carson on Ulster Day in 1913, was therefore invoking a familiar theme when he reassured his receptive audience that 'under home rule the Pope would be Ireland's ruler and king, for his word was law'. Persecution would inevitably follow, 'and he ventured to say that in 2013 there would not be a Protestant in the British empire who would presume to affirm that Ulster made a mistake in the stand she was now taking against the aggressions of Romanism'. Patterson detected a 'parallel between the people of Israel in those olden days and the people of Ulster at the present time'. He invoked the robust Ulster Protestant self-image of indispensability, of their cherished role as the chosen people, and of their rentier right to eternal English dividends, for 'England owes more to Ulster than to any part of the empire, and she can never pay the debt.'[34] No wonder the covenanters felt that, by definition, opposition to the chosen people must be 'conspiracy', and felt justified in employing 'any means which may be found necessary' to frustrate the nefarious designs of their papist enemies.

Patterson's fears would have appeared overwrought to Southern nationalists, had they taken the trouble to familiarise themselves with the Ulster Protestant psyche. Nationalist ideology was relatively free from the racism that dominated unionist images of nationalists. There were inevitably racist threads woven into the fabric of nationalist thought, which could not remain wholly insulated from imperialist influences. This is not to suggest that the racist tendencies in Irish nationalism, relatively muted though they were, do not deserve closer scrutiny than they have

[33] S. Prenter, 'The religious difficulty under home rule: the non-conformist view', in Rosenbaum (ed.), *Against home rule*, pp. 218–19. This volume contains an able collective presentation of the Ulster Protestant case. It is a careful work, eminently respectable, designed to appeal to the commonsense and intelligence of England. There are several superior contributions, including Carson's.

[34] *Belfast Evening Telegraph*, 29 September 1913.

normally received in nationalist historiography. Nor is it to imply that Irish nationalism was inherently innocent, through some immaculate ideological conception, of the more virulent forms of popular racism. If historically subordinate peoples have only relatively rarely felt as visceral a need to adopt racist ideologies as intense as those of dominant groups,[35] this reflects more the logic of circumstances than the triumph of character. For whatever reason, however, racism was far less central to the ideology of Irish nationalism than to that of Ulster unionism. But Ulster Protestants assumed, indeed were obliged by their own premises to assume, that Irish Catholics would behave as mirror images of themselves once they smashed Protestant supremacy. In the unionist scenario, home rule would place Protestants 'under the feet of Catholics . . . to be governed as a conquered race'.[36]

It was precisely because the bulk of nationalists were not mirror images of unionists in this respect that they failed to fully grasp these Protestant fears. Whereas to most Ulster Protestants, the Catholic Irish were not only different but inferior, to most Irish Catholics, Ulster Protestants were merely different, not inferior.[37] Most Catholics were sufficiently distant from Ulster geographically and psychologically to be more nationalist than racist. To Ulster Protestants the two were indistinguishable, and in strictly *Ulster* terms unionist fears were far from incomprehensible. Sectarian impulses remained pronounced in popular Ulster Catholicism. Ulster Catholics, precisely because of their relative deprivation, remained more heavily dependent than southern Catholics on clerical leadership. Even in Belfast, which had some educated Catholic laity, a clerical party flourished. The prelate in possession, Dr Henry, entertained an exalted sense of his own political dignity. His Catholic Association dominated nationalist politics in Belfast between 1897 and 1907, before lay forces in the Home Rule Party loosened the clericalist grip.[38] And many Ulster Catholics, influenced by local sectarian movements like the Ancient Order of Hibernians, a partial Catholic counterpart to the Orange Order, did think of home rule as establishing their own ascendancy, simply reversing roles with Protestants.[39] Ulster Catholics could hardly escape the contagion of the racist virus, nor help but feel something of

> This bitterness
> I inherit from my father, the
> Swarm of blood
> To the brain, the vomit surge
> Of race hatred.[40]

35 L. Kuper, *Race, class and power* (London, 1974), p. 21.
36 MacKnight, *Ulster*, 2, pp. 381, 401.
37 Hepburn, 'Catholics', in Hepburn, *Minorities*, p. 85.
38 I. Budge and C. O'Leary, *Belfast: approach to crisis* (London, 1973), pp. 120–3.
39 Miller, *Queen's rebels*, pp. 90, 101.
40 John Montague, *The rough field* (Dublin, 1979, 3rd edn), p. 45.

The McCann case in 1910 graphically reminded Protestants of the implications of Catholic power. Mr McCann, a Belfast Catholic, abandoned his Protestant wife, taking his children with him. His initiative followed enforcement by the Catholic hierarchy of the *Ne Temere* decree after 1908, which declared null and void mixed marriages (i.e. between Catholic and Protestant) not solemnised by the Catholic Church. This case, skilfully exploited by unionist propagandists, proved to the Protestant in the street how the papal viper could wriggle its way into the nuptial bed. The Protestant Bishop of Down, Dr D'Arcy, insisted that *Ne Temere* 'is at this moment a burning question. Under home rule it would create a conflagration.'[41] There were in fact rather few potential opportunities of this sort in Ulster, where little mixed marriage occurred. Those who waxed most indignantly at the insolence of Roman claims also refrained most carefully from producing figures to buttress their fears. Nevertheless, however remote the dangers in practice, the implication of the papal claim was something that no Protestant solicitous for the welfare of his family could calmly contemplate. When Catholics prated about the sanctity of the family they apparently meant only the Catholic family. Other families were ripe for the priestly plucking. As Dr D'Arcy did not hesitate to point out, toleration according to Roman teaching was a matter of mere expediency, not a right in itself. The lurking tyrant would pounce once opportunity offered.[42]

Protestant spokesmen also seized on another decree, *Motu Proprio*. As Thomas Sinclair depicted the situation:[43]

The bringing by a Roman Catholic layman of a clergyman of his Church into any civil or criminal procedure in a Court of Law, whether as defendant or witness, without the sanction previously obtained of his bishop, involves to that layman the extreme penalty of excommunication. The same penalty appears to be incurred *ipso facto* by any Roman Catholic Member of Parliament who takes part in passing, and by every executive officer of the government who takes part in promulgating, a law or decree which has helped to invade the liberty or rights of the Church of Rome. This is a matter of supreme importance in our civil life. It was one of the questions which, in the Reformation times, led to the breach between Henry VIII and the Pope. In a Dublin Parliament no power could resist the provisions of this decree from becoming law. As a matter of fact, the liberty of speech and voting attaching to every member of the Roman Catholic majority in a Dublin Parliament would be under the absolute control of their hierarchy.

[41] C.F. D'Arcy, 'The religious difficulty under home rule: the church view', in Rosenbaum, *Home rule*, p. 207. Note in the same volume the references by Carson (p. 27) and Sinclair (pp. 175–6); A.C. Hepburn (ed.), *The conflict of nationality in modern Ireland* (London, 1980), p. 74; MacNeill, *Ulster's stand*, p. 11.

[42] D'Arcy, 'Religious difficulty', pp. 209–10. See also R.M. Lee, 'Intermarriage, conflict and social control in Ireland: the Decree "Ne temere"', *ESR*, 17, 1 (October, 1985), pp. 26–7.

[43] Sinclair, 'The position of Ulster', pp. 175–6.

It was not that Protestants wanted the clergy taken out of politics. Far from it. That would have deprived them of much of their own leadership.[44] The Ulster Loyalist Anti-Repeal Union founded in 1886 hastened to make 'all Protestant clergymen of the province honorary members'.[45] No fewer than eighty-three Irish protestant clergymen acted as election speakers for the Unionist Association of Ireland in the second general election of 1910 in Britain.[46] The Covenant was submitted for approval to Protestant clergy. The Protestant churches gave their blessing to Covenant Day. If the clergyman in politics proved a less derisive bogey than the priest in politics, it was because the Protestant imagined himself immune from clerical influence. His clergy merely represented him, whereas Catholic clergymen dominated their flocks. Protestant images of the contrasting roles of Catholic and Protestant clergy merely provided a variation on the theme of the superiority of Protestant stock.

Ulster Unionists found enthusiastic champions at this juncture in the Conservative Party, led since November 1911 by Andrew Bonar Law, a Canadian Scot, son of a Presbyterian minister with Ulster connections. Bonar Law supplied the cutting edge to Conservative commitment to the union. The electoral situation reinforced Tory convictions. The Conservatives had been out of office for seven years by 1912, the longest consecutive period in half a century that their leaders had been deprived of the privilege of displaying their devotion to the national interest at the highest level.

They sniffed a winning issue in 'the empire in danger', with home rule being 'as much the occasion as the cause' of their 'new style' of violent opposition to the Liberal government.[47] Since the 1910 elections the Westminster scales were nicely balanced between Liberals and Conservatives. However, Labour and Home Rule support gave the Liberal government a clear majority in the House of Commans. Bonar Law was not the man to be daunted by a little local difficulty of this sort. He claimed that home rule had not been a specific election issue in 1910.[48] Therefore, the Liberals had no mandate to implement it. Asquith, the Liberal leader, had indeed preferred to emphasise the House of Lords rather than home rule as the prime election issue.[49] Yet the British electorate would have had to be singularly simple minded not to have appreciated that home rule was implicit in their vote on the future of the Lords. If Asquith had been coy

[44] On the political role of the Protestant clergy see A.J. Megahey, 'The Irish Protestant Churches and social and political issues 1870–1914' (PhD thesis, Queen's University, Belfast, 1969).
[45] Buckland, *Ulster unionism*, p. 9.   [46] *Ibid.*, p. 73.
[47] R. Fanning, '"Rats" versus "ditchers": the die-hard revolt and the Parliament Bill of 1911', in A. Cosgrove and J.I. McGuire (eds.), *Parliament and community* (Historical Studies 14) (Belfast, 1983), p. 191.
[48] R. Kee, *The green flag* (London, 1972), p. 472.
[49] Buckland, *Ulster unionism*, p. 73.

about home rule in the 1910 elections, the Conservatives had not. The Unionist Association of Ireland not only dispatched 324 general election workers to Britain for the January election in 1910, and 381 for the December election, but distributed over 6 000 000 leaflets in Britain warning of the dangers.[50]

Bonar Law retaliated against the election results by denouncing the Liberal–Home Rule alliance as a 'corrupt parliamentary bargain'.[51] The emotional alchemy by which an alliance between the majority of British members and the majority of Irish members was translated into a 'corrupt bargain', while an alliance between a minority of British members and a minority of Irish members was an honourable understanding, may smack, to the simple mind, of special pleading. It was no such thing. That would be to imply identical rules of debate for both sides. The Tory feeling of moral outrage was not assuaged by having the cup dashed, as they persuaded themselves, from their parched lips. They had sensed themselves on the brink of office in 1910 when it appeared that negotiations between Asquith and Redmond might break down. That the Liberal and Home Rule leaders failed to satisfy Tory expectations further confirmed the corruption of their natures.

Bonar Law's demand for a general election on the home rule issue was brilliantly opportunistic. When he told his Ulster Protestant audience of a 100 000 in April 1912 at Balmoral that 'the government by their Parliament Act has erected a boom against you, a boom to shut you off from the help of the British people',[52] he seemed to be equating, in a delightful flight of fancy, the House of Lords with the people. But what if the Liberals were to win the next general election? What if 'the British people' resisted the importunities of their moral creditors? Carson gave his answer in his reply to Asquith's proposal in March 1914 that any Ulster county could vote itself out of Home Rule for six years. Carson countered that 'Ulster wants this question settled now and forever. We do not want sentence of death with a stay of execution for six years.'[53] This reply exposed a certain inconsistency in the unionist case. Asquith selected a six-year period because this should permit at least two general elections in the interval.[54] Six years should suffice to allow even the most mentally relaxed voter to grasp the issue. But the Unionist leaders would not trust the electorate. They were alarmed that the government might raise the 'boom'.

Bonar Law left himself with an escape route from inconvenient electoral

[50] Hepburn, *Conflict*, p. 75.
[51] R. Fanning, 'The Irish policy of Asquith's government and the cabinet crisis of 1910', in A. Cosgrove and D. McCartney (eds.), *Studies in Irish history presented to R. Dudley Edwards* (Dublin, 1979), pp. 279–303.
[52] Stewart, *Ulster crisis*, p. 55.   [53] *Ibid.*, p. 141.
[54] D. Gwynn, *The life of John Redmond* (London, 1932; Freeport, New York, 1971), p. 208.

verdicts. He spattered his demands for a fresh appeal to the electorate with the Bismarckian reassurance that 'there are things stronger than parliamentary majorities'.[55] Lord Esher argued in 1913 that 'it has always been obvious that the Ulster people would not and ought not to yield, even if a general election were to go in favour of the government'.[56] The Ulster Unionist Council denied the right of any people, including the British, to impose home rule on Ulster.[57]

Although some Unionists posited the existence of 'Two Nations' in Ireland,[58] David Miller has powerfully argued that Ulster unionists ideally imagined themselves as a community that enjoyed a contractual relationship with the British crown rather than as a 'nation' in the conventional, if elusive, contemporary sense.[59] They would be loyal to the crown as long as the crown protected their interests. And they, not the crown, would define those interests. This stance – a congenial one for settler peoples – left them with the best of all tactical worlds. They would no more put themselves at the mercy of mere British than of mere Irish opinion. Their sacred egoism enabled them to follow whatever path secured the Protestant ascendancy in Ulster, and to do so moreover with an exquisite sense of their own righteousness. Their self-image glorified their axiomatic honesty and loyalty, in contrast to the equally axiomatic dishonesty and disloyalty of the inferior breed of Irish and, if necessary, of British, especially English. 'Loyalists', a title cherished by Ulster Protestants, meant, in the last ironical resort, loyalty to themselves alone. Unionism was merely a tactical, if highly congenial, variant of loyalism. They owed no primordial allegiance to British interests, nor admitted any ultimate obligation to abide by inconvenient British verdicts. If so stark a choice had ever to be made, their motto might have been 'Live Protestant Ulster, perish the empire.' It was the task of their more sober leaders to ensure that they never found themselves confronted by such a choice.

NATIONALIST REACTIONS

For nationalists, the Ulster question was a very simple one, but they managed to make it very complex. Their confusion did more credit to their hearts than to their heads. They consistently evaded the logical implications of their own position. Ulster unionists rejected the right of

[55] Kee, *Green flag*, p. 469.   [56] Mansergh, *Irish question*, p. 202.
[57] Miller, *Queen's rebels*, p. 102.
[58] MacKnight, *Ulster*, 2, p. 380; Sinclair, 'Ulster', in Rosenbaum, *Home rule*, p. 173; A. Bonar Law, 'Preface', in Rosenbaum, *Home rule*, p. 13.
[59] This is the central theme of *Queen's rebels*. For a critique see D. Mason, 'Nationalism and the process of group mobilisation: the case of "loyalism" in Northern Ireland reconsidered', *Ethnic and Racial Studies*, 8 (1985), pp. 408–25. See also the discussion in B. Girvin, 'National identity and conflict in Northern Ireland', in B. Girvin and R. Sturm (eds.), *Politics and society in contemporary Ireland* (Aldershot, 1986), pp. 110–12.

Irish nationalists to rule them. Nationalists therefore had two logical alternatives. They could concede the Ulster unionist claim or they could reject it. Practical implications naturally followed. If they rejected the claim, how could they impose their own claim? If they conceded the claim, where was the border of 'Ulster' to be drawn?

John Redmond rejected not only unionist claims to imperial control over Ireland as a whole, but unionist claims to self-determination. He denounced the 'two nations' theory as 'an abomination and a blasphemy'.[60] This rhetoric sufficed as denunciation, but scarcely as refutation. Redmond simply insisted that Ulster unionists were part of the Irish nation, and therefore belonged in a home rule parliament, irrespective of their own wishes. He declared himself prepared to make concessions, however, even to the extent of contemplating some version of 'home rule within home rule'.[61] 'There is no demand, however extravagant and unreasonable it may appear to us, that we are not ready carefully to consider, so long as it is consistent with the principle . . . of a settlement based on the national self-government of Ireland.'[62] The Bishop of Raphoe, Dr O'Donnell, Redmond's staunchest episcopal supporter, assured him that 'there is no length to which any of us would refuse to go to satisfy the Orangemen at the starting of our new government provided Ireland did not suffer grievously, and provided also the nationalist minority in the north east did not suffer badly'.[63] But these general expressions of good will do not appear to have been translated into hard proposals. Redmond responded unenthusiastically, for instance, when William O'Brien, the maverick Home Ruler, suggested that 'Ulster' should have a veto in an Irish parliament.[64]

Redmond, like his party in general, devoted little thought to the nature of home rule society and the role of the church within it. Personally tolerant, he could not apparently detect any objective basis for Orange fears, which he therefore tended to dismiss as purely tactical ploys. Catholic incomprehension of the Protestant position was reflected in the fact that little of the debate on the relationship between the claims of Catholic doctrine and the duties of civil legislators, however hypocritical, cynical or grudging at times, that would characterise responses in the Irish Republic when the Ulster question erupted once more after 1968, occurred between 1910 and 1914.[65]

Redmond refused to take the Protestant threat of violence seriously. He assured Asquith in 1913 that 'nobody denies that a riot may be attempted in Belfast and one or two other towns, but nobody in Ulster, outside a

---

[60] Gwynn, *Redmond*, p. 232.   [61] *Ibid.*   [62] *Ibid.*, p. 233.
[63] *Ibid.*, p. 231.
[64] *Ibid.*, p. 238.
[65] As reflected, for instance, in the New Ireland Forum process. See below, pp. 675–9.

certain number of fanatics and leaders, believes in any organised rebellion, active or passive'.[66] Little was therefore done to satisfy objective unionist fears.

Even had Redmond elaborated on the practical implications of 'home rule within home rule', he would have faced a major obstacle. Ulster unionists simply did not want it. Their spiritual leaders dismissed in advance any possible concessions on the grounds, as Dr D'Arcy put it, that 'professions and promises made by individual Roman Catholics and by political leaders, statements which to English ears seem a happy augury of a good time coming, are of no value whatever'.[67] The Protestants, according to D'Arcy,

do not deny that such promises and guarantees express a great deal of good intention, but they know that above the individual, whether he be layman or ecclesiastic, there is a system which moves on, as soon as such movement becomes possible, in utter disregard of his statements ... The guarantees of individual Roman Catholics, no matter now positively or how confidently stated, are of no account as against the steady age long policy of the Roman church.[68]

This contention of the Bishop of Down was reinforced by his Non-conformist colleague, Dr Prenter. 'It is a strange hallucination to find that there are politicians today who think that Rome will change her principles at the bidding of Mr Redmond, or to please hard-driven politicians, or to make Rome attractive to a Protestant empire.'[69] There was, therefore, no safeguard that Redmond could propose that would carry the slightest conviction in the eyes of Ulster unionists. All Catholics were ciphers.

Even if Rome could never change her ways, might it not be just conceivable that nationalist politicians would resist Roman pretensions? However improbable this appeared to the ecclesiastics, Carson, perhaps remembering nationalist indifference to Roman exhortations during the Land League days, moved to guard against this danger with a masterly exhibition of mental gymnastics:[70]

It is not inconsistent to urge, as many of us have urged, that home rule would mean alike a danger to the protestant faith and a menace to catholic power. The immediate result of successful papal interference with civil liberties in every land has been a sweeping movement among the people which has been, not protestant, but anti-christian in its nature. If we fear the tyranny which the Roman Catholic Church has established under British rule in Malta and in Quebec, may we not fear also the reaction from such tyranny which has already taken place in France and Portugal?

There was only one fate worse than papal control of Ireland – successful Catholic resistance to papal control! Ulster Protestants succeeded in constructing and fortifying mental ramparts which did indeed lower the

[66] Gwynn, *Redmond*, p. 236.   [67] D'Arcy, 'Religious difficulty', p. 206.
[68] *Ibid.*
[69] Prenter, 'The religious difficulty', p. 219.   [70] E. Carson, 'Introduction', p. 27.

boom between themselves and the Irish, or even British, threat. If circumstances so required, they could renege on their 'contract' with the British crown, firm in the conviction that it was the crown who had reneged on them. They would remain 'loyalist' to the end, paragons of fidelity in a faithless world. Come all the world against her, 'Ulster' yet would stand alone.

Redmond achieved a measure of understanding with London. He failed, like all his successors as nationalist leaders, to make an impression on Belfast. The summer of 1914 clarified the issues. The House of Lords proposed an amendment to the Home Rule Bill in June to exclude the nine Ulster counties. This amounted to a unionist concession of home rule for the three other provinces. Redmond had now established that 'Ulster' could not sabotage home rule for the rest of Ireland. He next pushed the unionist claim further back, when Carson compromised at the Buckingham Palace inter-party conference in July by restricting the effective demand to six counties. No later nationalist managed to improve on Redmond's performance.

If unionist territorial claims were flexible, few nationalists had the moral courage or the intellectual integrity to apply their proclaimed principles of self-determination to unionist Ulster. One of the few was Fr Michael O'Flanagan, an erratic Sinn Féin priest who did not, on occasion, shirk the implications of self-determination principles. After showing that they applied, by conventional nationalist criteria, to north east Ulster, he concluded that 'England has begun to despair of compelling us to love her by force, and so we are anxious to start where England left off, and we are going to compel Antrim and Down to love us by force'.[71] O'Flanagan did not, of course, say Fermanagh and Tyrone. He demanded consistency, not casuistry, from unionists as well as nationalists. Even the fantasy world of Irish nationalism can sometimes seem to tremble on the verge of logic compared with that of Ulster unionism.

But there was one logic unionists grasped from the outset, the iron logic of violence. When Carson and Craig established the Ulster Volunteer Force in January 1913, partly to keep the physical force unionist elements under political control, the balance of military power in Ireland began to shift significantly. The UVF, under the command of General Sir George Richardson, who had long experience of teaching the natives lessons,[72] soon enrolled about 100 000 men. John Redmond did not grasp the function of force. He was too much a romantic Commonwealth man, too much a genuine Westminster parliamentarian, to conceive that Ulster

71 D.W. Miller, *Church, state and nation in Ireland, 1898–1921* (Pittsburgh, 1973), p. 350. See also J. Bowman, 'De Valera on Ulster, 1919–1920: what he told America', *Irish Studies in International Affairs*, 1 (1979), p. 7.
72 De Paor, *Divided Ulster*, p. 8.

unionists, much less English Tories, so vehement in their protestations of loyalty, could really contemplate rebellion against the king in the king's name. Once Ulster unionists invoked their physical force tradition stretching sonorously back to Derry, Enniskillen, Aughrim and the Boyne, Redmond had either to raise an army of his own, or persuade the British army to impose Dublin rule on the Protestant areas of Ulster. Whether the British army would have obliged if given firm orders to crush resistance to home rule must remain a matter for conjecture, since no such orders were given. The 1911 census recorded only 6400 Catholics among the 26251 soldiers and NCO's stationed in Ireland, and only 304 Catholics among the 2208 army officers. Nevertheless, it is the considered conclusion of a careful recent analysis of Asquith's Irish policy that 'troops would almost certainly have obeyed direct orders to march to Ulster, so long as they were presented with no alternatives' before the Curragh 'mutiny' of 20 March 1914.[73] But, in an episode characterised by confusion and irresolution on the government's part, astute opportunism on the part of the unionist Brigadier Gough at the Curragh, and high but lethal farce on the part of Sir Arthur Paget, Commander-in-Chief in Ireland, the cabinet appeared to allow the army to dictate the terms – the distinctly unionist terms – on which it would be prepared to become involved in Ulster. Whatever about the prospects before the Curragh 'mutiny', it was now clear that the British army would not, and Redmond could not, coerce Ulster Protestants, least of all after 24–5 April 1914, when the UVF landed 24600 rifles and 3000000 rounds of ammunition from Germany.[74]

If Redmond scoffed at the unionist appeal to force as 'playing at rebellion', some other home rulers reacted differently. As Patrick Pearse, a rising young intellectual, tersely observed in November 1913, 'I think the Orangeman with a rifle a much less ridiculous figure than the nationalist without a rifle.'[75] That same month the Irish Volunteers were founded in response to an article, 'The North Began', by Professor Eoin MacNeill, a prominent cultural nationalist, co-founder of the Gaelic League in 1893, urging nationalist imitation of the Ulster Volunteers.[76]

'The North Began' contains in full measure MacNeill's customary combination of insight and illusion. He insisted that the Volunteers were not intended to coerce Ulster unionists. They were simply to bring pressure to bear on England. Pressure to do what? To coerce Ulster unionists. The object of 'The North Began' was to frustrate what the North began. The Irish Volunteers, however genuine MacNeill's protest-

[73] P. Jalland, *The Liberals and Ireland: the Ulster question in British politics to 1914* (Brighton, 1980), p. 240.
[74] Stewart, *Ulster crisis*, p. 246.
[75] P. Pearse, 'From a hermitage', in *Political writings and speeches* (Dublin, 1966), p. 185.
[76] Kee, *Green flag*, pp. 498–9, notes anticipatory local initiatives before MacNeill's article.

ations to the contrary, had ultimately the logical objective of coercing Ulster unionists.

The illusion implicit in this approach would continue to bedevil Irish nationalism for generations. The essential assumption was that Ulster Protestant attitudes were basically the consequence of British duplicity. The unionist mentality was attributed to the divide and conquer policies pursued by Britain. Once the British notified the unionists that their interests would be satisfactorily guarded in a home rule state, the scales would drop from their eyes and they too would enter the promised land. Ulster unionists, on this assumption, were the creatures of Westminster, utterly incapable of objectively assessing their own situation, puppets dangling from British strings.

This simplistic image of Ulster unionism may appear surprising in view of the fact that several of the early Irish Volunteer leaders, including Eoin MacNeill himself, Bulmer Hobson, and Tom Clarke, were Ulstermen. But in the segregated Ulster society, nationalists had little contact with unionists. MacNeill dismissed unionist aspirations with the capacious claim that 'history shows that this present sentiment of theirs is a calculated outcome of persistent and unscrupulous policy of English statesmen pursued purely in "the English interest" . . . The rest of the Ulster difficulty consists of fears and prophecies.'[77] MacNeill, an historian, might have pondered that much history revolves around fears and prophecies. Instead he dismissed the unionist fear that under an Irish government 'the religion and industry of Ulster Protestants will be suppressed' with the triumphant affirmation that 'there is no body of people in the world more free from intolerance in matters of religion than the Catholics of Ireland'.[78]

MacNeill, Hobson and Clarke knew as little of the Shankill, or of the Falls, as of the Dublin slums. Their image of Ulster was one-dimensional. It was as socially conservative as that of the unionist leaders themselves. It differed in this respect from an alternative image of unionism held by an articulate if tiny minority in the Dublin labour movement. The lockout of September 1913, after members of the Irish Transport and General Workers' Union, led by Jim Larkin and James Connolly, had gone on strike to demand recognition of the union from William Martin Murphy, Dublin's most domineering businessman, threw 20 000 men on the streets.[79] It brought even deeper misery into the hideous Dublin slums, and provoked the creation of the Irish Citizen Army in November to help raise the morale of the unemployed. The training of the 1000 strong

---

[77] E. MacNeill, *The Ulster difficulty* (Dublin, 1917), p. 24.　　[78] *Ibid.*, p. 23.
[79] E. Larkin, *James Larkin: Irish Labour leader 1876–1947* (London, 1968 edn), pp. 101–43; D.F. Keogh, 'William Martin Murphy and the origins of the 1913 lockout', *Capuchin Annual* (1977), pp. 130–57.

'army' – ambitiously christened, for the only 'citizen' army in the country at the time was the UVF – was confined to manoeuvres with dummy weapons. It did not extend to more demanding manoeuvres with theory, dummy or otherwise. But the doughtiest Citizen Army leader, James Connolly, had developed a Marxist interpretation of Irish history. He paid more attention to the Ulster unionist bourgeoisie than did MacNeill. To Connolly, the unionist middle class was no dupe of Westminster. On the contrary, it was the sinister business partner of Westminster in duping the Ulster unionist working class. It was only the workers, or rather the Protestant workers, who were the victims of false consciousness, too deluded to comprehend their real interests or their historical destiny. To Connolly's intense irritation Protestant workers were failing to conform to their prescribed role as cannon fodder for his version of Marxist theory. Connolly himself failed to seriously breach the racial barrier during his trade union work in Belfast between 1910 and 1912. His socialist faith triumphed over this reverse. He proved more susceptible to the evidence provided by the outbreak of the First World War, when the working classes of Europe, unimpressed by the inconvenience their behaviour was causing socialist theorists, flocked to slaughter each other for God, king and country. This finally compelled Connolly to reconsider the theory that socialism would bury nationalism. He concluded that if socialism were to come to Ireland at all, it could only come through nationalism, or rather through republicanism.

But republicanism was still a fringe ideology in 1913. The bulk of the Irish Volunteers were simply home rulers. Some, like MacNeill himself, were more firmly committed than Redmond to cultural nationalism. Some, like Patrick Pearse, editor of *An Claidheamh Solais*, the Gaelic League newspaper, envisaged an opposition role for themsleves in a home rule parliament.[80] The Irish Volunteers were come to fulfil home rule, not to destroy it. The more separatist Irish Republican Brotherhood (IRB) did exert some influence behind the scenes. Bulmer Hobson, Denis McCullough, Sean McDermott, Tom Clarke and, after he joined the IRB in December 1913, Patrick Pearse, conspired discreetly to stiffen Volunteer resolve. The threat of partition and the Curragh 'mutiny' stimulated mass enrolment,but the 150 000 members who joined by June 1914 remained largely innocent of the influence of the IRB. So did MacNeill.

Redmond became so alarmed at the rapid growth of the Volunteers that he felt obliged to impose his own nominees to constitute a majority of the Provisional Committee of the Volunteers in June 1914. The IRB members reluctantly acquiesced, convinced that they could not resist Redmond successfully a mere month after the Home Rule Bill had finally completed its trek through the House of Commons. The more republican elements

80 Pearse, 'From a hermitage', p. 155.

did not even split from the Volunteers when Redmond expressed support for Britain in the House of Commons on the outbreak of the European war. It was not until Redmond actually urged his followers at Wooden Bridge, Co. Wicklow, on 20 September, to volunteer for the British army, that the more extreme nationalists felt compelled to repudiate him.

Whatever Redmond's motives, and however far he may have been swayed by a genuine if imaginative conviction that Britain was fighting 'in defence of right, of freedom and of religion',[81] there were strong tactical arguments in favour of his attitude, even from a separatist viewpoint.[82] Any other policy would have played straight into the hands of Ulster unionists. The Home Rule Bill finally went on the Statute Book in September 1914, with the qualification that its operation should be suspended during the war, and that parliament might then make special provision for Ulster. The war, however, was widely expected to last only a few months. An Ireland that had stood by England in her hour of peril could surely then reckon to have laid the bogey of British fears. British public opinion could hardly be expected to lend credence in a postwar general election, anticipated for 1915, to the argument that a home rule Ireland would still pose a threat to British security. Scant sympathy might, however, be expected from a British electorate for a nationalist Ireland that had remained sullenly neutral while Ulster unionists flocked to the flag. Bonar Law would have enjoyed rich electoral pickings in those circumstances. Even Ulster unionists might be reconciled to a home rule Ireland that had proved its steadfast support for the empire, at least if their incantations of loyalty to that empire were genuine.

The objective odds were, no doubt, heavily against Redmond's gamble on unity. Nothing could have induced Ulster unionists into a home rule state. Why should a *Herrenvolk* inflict on itself the psychic shock of surrendering its privileges? Why should Irish support for the war make any difference to the threat from Rome in the eyes of Ulster unionists – or indeed in reality? Home rule remained Rome rule. Pro-British Catholics remained Catholics. Indeed, their support for the war could be presented as merely the clever ploy of those devilishly cunning conspirators against the people of God. Nevertheless, no one genuinely committed to Irish unity could have acted differently from Redmond in the autumn of 1914. The suggestion that a threat of neutrality from nationalist Ireland would have forced the immediate implementation of home rule might just conceivably have some validity for a twenty-six county home rule state, but none at all for a united Ireland. No British government could have imposed home rule on an armed unionist Ulster supporting Britain, at the dictate of an unarmed nationalist Ireland threatening neutrality. The alternative to Redmond's policy would have been to clinch the unionist

[81] Gwynn, *Redmond*, p. 392.   [82] Miller, *Church, state and nation*, pp. 308–10.

case that home rule Ireland would inevitably stab England in the back in her hour of danger. The neutrality mentality was a partitionist mentality.

Redmond's mistake was not his decision to support the war. It was his failure to secure arms once the formation of the UVF in 1913 made paramilitary power crucial. Redmond played his hand well in the light of the balance of probabilities in August 1914. But his hand was an exceptionally weak one, simply because it was the only one with no gun in it. Participation in the war might in fact strengthen his hand in this respect.[83] As the Volunteers were not effectively armed in August 1914, Redmond could not expect his histrionic promise – or threat – to hold Ireland against invasion to be taken seriously. But many Irish Volunteers would presumably return home after the war – probably in 1915 – with some military training and equipment. It was the potential threat lurking in this possibility that made English recruiting officers reluctant to countenance the formation of specifically Irish nationalist divisions as distinct from Ulster unionist ones. The war offered Redmond his only hope of securing a credible paramilitary base, and thus providing himself with some bargaining power *vis-à-vis* both Carson and Asquith.

Redmond's gamble, however astute the calculations on which it may have been based, seemed spontaneous. But it provoked MacNeill to repudiate Redmond's recruiting drive and to split from him. Perhaps only 13 000 of the 188 000 Volunteers joined MacNeill's 'Irish' Volunteers, however, Redmond's majority now becoming known as the 'National' Volunteers.[84]

MacNeill's reasoning was, not for the only time, honourable and muddled. He offered no realistic political alternative to home rule. He simply argued that neutrality would achieve it more quickly by some unspecified route. His split from Redmond was an empty gesture. The Volunteers, Irish or National, had no *raison d'être* unless they could get guns. The Howth gun running in July 1914, a miniature imitation of the UVF exploit, exacerbated tension in Dublin when the British army killed four civilians in a taunting crowd on the way back,[85] but secured only a modest haul of 900 guns and 25 000 rounds of ammunition. Another small landing at Kilcoole went only a short distance towards restoring the balance with the Larne and Donaghadee landings. With Home Rule on the Statute Book in September, the existence of MacNeill's Volunteers, unless they achieved real military strength, seemed to serve little purpose.

The IRB men who joined MacNeill's splinter movement did have the policy he lacked, even if their response to Redmond's gamble was more

[83] Kee, *Green flag*, pp. 524–5.
[84] The figures cited by the various authorities on the subject often differ in detail, but the orders of magnitude are similar.
[85] G. Dangerfield, *The damnable question* (London, 1977), p. 121. Three died on the spot, one later from wounds.

visceral than cerebral. The IRB appointed a military committee in September 1914 to secure effective control over MacNeill's organisation in order to launch a military rising. This committee would still have been at the preliminary planning phase at the end of the war had hostilities ended as quickly as generally anticipated. Much hinged on the length of the war. Its continuation deprived Redmond of his anticipated postwar home rule army, as well as giving the IRB time to actually do something. The stalemate in Flanders salvaged the reputation of the IRB and doomed the remaining hopes of Redmond.

The war led to the formation of a coalition cabinet in May 1915. Carson joined the government as Attorney General. Redmond refused an offer of office. This was consistent with party principles, but inconsistent with his own tactics since August 1914. The logical conclusion of supporting the war in the hope of forging a union of hearts between nationalists and unionists in Ireland was that Redmond should accept office to confirm his stature as a responsible statesman and to increase further the fund of putative postwar goodwill on which he hoped to draw. There was little logical justification for supporting the war but refusing office, even if the acceptance of office would have offered his critics some ammunition. Redmond got the worst of both worlds. By the summer of 1915, after the initial enthusiasm of the previous autumn, associated with the passing of the Home Rule Bill, Redmond was already losing his grip on nationalist Ireland as the war turned into carnage, as home rule receded into an uncertain future, and as Ulster Unionists were widely felt to have out-manoeuvred Home Rulers at Westminster.[86]

The recruitment figures provide a useful, if partial, clue to public opinion. The Irish returns reveal a relatively weak sense of identity with the war effort. It has been calculated that 26.9 per cent of the relevant age group in Scotland served in the army during the war, 24.2 per cent in England and Wales, but only 10.7 per cent in Ireland.[87] The low Irish figure reflects the steep decline in Irish recruiting as the war progressed. But this decline began quite early in the war. Between August and December 1914, 43 000 men enlisted in Ireland and a further 37 000 between January and August 1915. In the next eight months – before the Easter Rising – there were only 12 000 recruits. The number of volunteers in the first year of the war exceeded the total in the remaining three years.[88] Even in the first year, a disproportionate number, about half,

---

[86] F.S.L. Lyons, 'Dillon, Redmond and the Irish Home Rulers', in Martin (ed.), *Leaders and men*, p. 41.

[87] J.M. Winter, 'Britain's "lost generation" of the First World War', *Population Studies*, 31, 3 (1976), 451.

[88] *Report on recruiting in Ireland, 1914–16* (Cd. 8168), xxxix, 525; Kee, *Green flag*, pp. 525, 552, 623; Fitzpatrick, *Politics*, p. 315, n. 38. Recruitment figures cited in the literature are often compiled in a casual manner. They sometimes fail to distinguish

came from Ulster.[89] Leinster supplied more than a quarter, with Munster and Connacht providing relatively few. If one allows for unionist recruits from Ulster and Leinster, and attributes some of the Dublin working-class recruitment to sheer economic necessity, it would seem that enthusiasm for the war was never as widespread in nationalist Ireland as the media, dominated by pro-war elements, suggested. It waned to virtual vanishing point from the autumn of 1915. The evidence goes some way to confirm the claim of Maurice Headlam, a jaundiced but presumably informed Dublin Castle official, that 'we in Ireland knew . . . that . . . the bulk of the population . . . seized any pretext . . . to avoid fighting in France'.[90]

THE EASTER RISING

The surprising feature of the Rising of April 1916, at least in the light of the hallowed republican dictum that 'England's danger is Ireland's opportunity', was not that it took place, but that it took place so late. It was not until May 1915, when the war had generally been expected to be over, that the IRB 'Military Committee' (later called Military Council) actually began to plan an insurrection.[91] Tom Clarke and Sean MacDermott, the two conscious manipulators on the Supreme Council of the IRB, recruited Patrick Pearse, then Director of Operations in the Irish Volunteers, whom they saw as a suitable front man, to this committee, which also ultimately included Éamon Ceannt, Joseph Mary Plunkett, Thomas MacDonagh, and James Connolly. Had the war finished as quickly as expected, the ineffectuality of the IRB would have been even more ignominiously exposed than during the Boer War. The Military Committee grasped this, and hoped initially for a September 1915 rising, but failed to finalise plans. James Connolly also sensed the urgency of the situation. He urged rebellion in the summer of 1915. The IRB had to curb his impetuosity in January 1916 by assuring him of its determination to rise at Easter, and by co-opting him to the Military Council.

The Easter Rising went off at half-cock. Twenty thousand German guns expected to arrive in time were lost when the British intercepted the supply ship, the *Aud*, on the eve of the insurrection. This mishap was compounded when Eoin MacNeill, hearing of the plans at the last moment,

between recruits during the war itself and the total number of Irish enlisted in the army, which included pre-war recruits. Henry Harris, 'The other half million', in O.D. Edwards and F. Pyle (eds.), *1916: The Easter Rising* (London, 1968), pp. 101–15, includes the descendants of Irish emigrants in Britain and the Dominions to reach his total of a half million 'Irish' recruits. See also Fitzpatrick, *Politics*, pp. 109–11.

[89] Ervine, *Craigavon*, p. xi.

[90] M. Headlam, *Irish reminiscences* (London, 1947), p. 149. Headlam was Treasury Remembrancer and Deputy Paymaster for Ireland at the time.

[91] L. Ó Broin, *Revolutionary underground* (Dublin, 1976), pp. 167–9.

cancelled the mobilisation orders issued for Easter Sunday. The hastily rearranged Rising that began on Easter Monday was not, therefore, the intended insurrection. The Military Council had permitted itself the luxury of hoping that the country in general, outside unionist Ulster, with which it had no contact, would rebel. But the Council's plans for a national rising were distinctly vague.[92] The interception of the German arms, and MacNeill's countermanding order, added to the confusion.[93] In the event, the Rising was mainly confined to Dublin. It proved a militarily gallant but hopeless enterprise in the face of superior force, though it was to leave over 400 dead and about 3000 wounded.

In the manifesto he composed shortly before he surrendered to save useless bloodshed, Pearse, who assumed the role of leader as his natural right, no longer content to play the figurehead role designed for him by MacDermott and Clarke, claimed the rebels would have won but for the loss of the German weapons. In the event, the Rising had turned into a blood sacrifice. But it had not been planned that way from the outset. Had the Rising been intended solely or even mainly as a blood sacrifice, it could have been mounted earlier in the war. It was planned to occur when the rebels felt they had the maximum chance of success, however limited this may have appeared in absolute terms. The IRB doctrine that 'England's danger is Ireland's opportunity' was, in objective terms, sheer illusion. The IRB envisaged a military victory, following full-scale war, not the sapping guerrilla campaign that was finally to induce British politicians to the negotiating table in 1921 through its influence on English public opinion. Whatever about England conceding independence when she felt herself completely secure, no great power could afford any risk where not merely her prestige, but her own security, was at stake. It was therefore only in peacetime, not in wartime, that England could contemplate major concessions to Irish claims. Nevertheless, however illusory the IRB doctrine, it was not blood sacrifice doctrine.[94] And however profusely blood sacrifice sentiments spatter the later writings of Pearse and MacDonagh, and however retrospectively relevant they appeared to be in the circumstances, it seems unhistorical to interpret these sentiments as the basis of the actual planning of the Rising.

In view of the hopeless prospects of the Rising that actually occurred, it became psychologically and morally incumbent on the leaders to justify it in terms of saving Ireland's honour. It was therefore obligatory on them to couch their last testaments in terms of blood sacrifice. It seems reasonable to assume that the actual course of the Rising left its mark on the type of

[92] C. Townshend, *Political violence in Ireland* (Oxford, 1983), pp. 297–8.
[93] Kee, *Green flag*, p. 571.
[94] R.W. Dudley Edwards, 'Resurrection of the spirit of independence', *Irish Press*, 16 April 1979.

interpretation that it was felt would carry most historical conviction. Emphasis on calculation of the balance of military probabilities would have seemed ludicrous in the circumstances, and would appear to vindicate the charges of lunacy hurled at the rebels by vociferous critics. On Easter Monday morning many of the leaders must have felt, like James Connolly, that they were going out to be slaughtered. But this does not justify the presentation of the Rising in purely blood sacrifice terms. Connolly himself had hoped for victory almost to the final moment of decision.[95] Many of the rank and file, like Seán MacEntee, had probably not closely calculated the chances of success.[96] Even the vague suggestion during the Rising, that a German prince should become king of Ireland, intimates a clutching at straws rather than unwavering devotion to blood sacrifice doctrine.[97] As far as the forward planning of the Rising was concerned, a balanced appraisal suggests that it was intended that if it should fail, then it should fail not only with honour, but with effect.[98]

Pearse grudgingly accepted the Home Rule Bill in 1912. He became gradually convinced, however, that the UVF appeal to force made the peaceful achievement of home rule impossible. Much of Pearse's glorification of war in 1915 and 1916 was tactical. Indeed, the extent to which Pearse thought tactically tends to be overlooked in the fascination with the more exotic aspects of his character. Nevertheless, his intense nature did rebel against exclusively tactical argument. He therefore exalted force as potentially noble in itself. There are passages in Pearse glorifying bloodshed, at least in theory, passionately though he denounced Redmond for sacrificing 'ı.ish blood 'to England as a peace holocaust' in the First World War.[99] Fashionable as belligerent sentiments were at this time, and restrained though Pearse's rhetoric may sound compared with that of the young Sean O'Casey,[100] he undoubtedly subscribed to the Churchillian dictum that 'there are things worse than bloodshed, even on an extended scale'. As he himself put it, 'There are many things more horrible than bloodshed, and slavery is one of them',[101] a view he shared fully with Carson, Craig and Bonar Law, as well as with a broad stratum

[95] Ruth Dudley Edwards, *James Connolly* (Dublin, 1981), pp. 133, 145. The most thorough study of MacDonagh rejects the 'blood sacrifice' interpretation of his thinking. See Johann A. Norstedt, *Thomas MacDonagh* (Charlottesville, 1980), pp. 141–2.
[96] Radio interview with Seán MacEntee on RTE, 25 January 1977.
[97] *Memoirs of Desmond FitzGerald, 1913–1916* (Dublin, 1968), pp. 139–41.
[98] F. O'Donoghue, 'Ceannt, Devoy, O'Rahilly and the military plan', in Martin, *Leaders and men*, p. 191.
[99] Pearse, 'Ghosts', in *Political writings*, p. 232.
[100] Robert Hogan (ed.), *Feathers from the green crow: Sean O'Casey, 1905–1925* (Columbia, Mo., 1962), pp. 15–17.
[101] Pearse, 'The coming revolution', in *Political writings*, p. 99.

of British and European intellectuals of his generation.[102] He even shared the robust view of Dr D'Arcy, the articulate Bishop of Down, that 'there are things worse than civil war'.[103] In practice, Pearse, a gentle man, was revolted by the sight of blood. He refused to distribute the explosive bullets landed in the Howth gun running because they were against the rules of civilised war.[104] That he may have exaggerated the lethal qualities of the bullets does not detract from his concern.[105] And if he felt it necessary to claim over the grave of O'Donovan Rossa, the old Fenian, in 1915, that 'splendid and holy causes are served by men who are themselves splendid and holy', he was sufficient of a realist to recognise in 1916 the danger that his idealised republican tradition might be prostituted by some of the Volunteers and to include in the Proclamation of the Republic a plea against rebel 'inhumanity'.

Pearse resisted the conclusion of Eoin MacNeill that a rising was morally unjustifiable unless conscription or other unacceptable measures were imposed. MacNeill felt that only if 'the vital principle of nationality' was at stake could a rising be morally justified.[106] Discerning scholars have found MacNeill's reasoning logically compelling. It is possible to take a less benign view. Neither in terms of military tactics nor of democratic ideology were MacNeill's arguments necessarily superior to those of Pearse. MacNeill held that 'unacceptable measures' might be justly resisted, including above all any attempt by British forces to deprive the Volunteers of their handful of weapons.[107] 'Unacceptable measures' – but unacceptable to whom? MacNeill's Volunteers were a private army. MacNeill's view had no more popular mandate than had the actual Rising itself. Nor had MacNeill's contemplated resistance any more objective chance of success than the actual Rising – and it might have claimed many more innocent casualties. MacNeill's insistence on waiting for the enemy to choose his time made little logical or moral sense in the circumstances. The differences between MacNeill and Pearse were less those of moral principle than of tactical opinion.[108]

[102] R.N. Stromberg, 'The intellectuals and the coming of war in 1914', *Journal of European Studies*, 3 (1973), pp. 109–22; D. Kiberd, 'Inventing Ireland', *Crane Bag*, 8, 1 (1984), p. 17.
[103] Megahey, 'Irish Protestant churches', pp. 83–5, discusses the cult of violence among Protestant clergy opposing Home Rule after 1885.
[104] Dangerfield, *Damnable question*, p. 121.
[105] M. Tierney, *Eoin MacNeill* (Oxford, 1980), p. 144.
[106] Lyons, *Ireland*, p. 347. [107] *Ibid.*, p. 348.
[108] J. Lee, 'A Jabobin (sic) after his time', *Irish Press*, 21 April 1977; J. Lee, *The modernisation of Irish society, 1849–1918* (Dublin, 1973), p. 154. MacNeill's *Memorandum* was published by F.X. Martin, 'Eoin MacNeill on the 1916 Rising', *IHS*, 12 (March, 1961), pp. 226–7. MacNeill's arguments have generally been favourably received by historians. There are sympathetic expositions of his viewpoint in Lyons, *Ireland*, pp. 347–9, in Ruth Dudley Edwards, *Patrick Pearse: the triumph of failure* (London, 1977), pp. 248–50, and in Townshend, *Political violence*, pp. 294ff.

It is tempting to speculate on the possible results of resistance *à la* MacNeill. Conor Cruise O'Brien has ventured to reconstruct the possible results of an insurrection in the face of the conscription threat of April 1918. O'Brien postulates that a rising at that stage would have enjoyed massive popular support, that Britain would therefore have had to withdraw troops from the western front to crush it, that mutinies would then have broken out among the Irish troops on the western front, infecting the war weary British and French, perhaps indeed even the Germans, 'though this is more doubtful'. The European proletariat would then have seized the opportunity to overthrow the capitalist order – hardly the scenario Eoin MacNeill envisaged, however it might have gladdened James Connolly's socialist heart.[109] An equally plausible scenario might assume that a rising in response to the conscription threat, with however massive popular support, would have been crushed far more ruthlessly than that of 1916, unless the rebels were incomparably better armed. As at least half the Irish troops on the western front must have been unionists, it is far from certain that any putative Irish mutiny would have spread like wild fire. Even if it had spread among the western allies, it would be much more reasonable to assume, as Dr O'Brien concedes, that the Germans would not have mutinied. In that case, Germany might either have won the war, or at least driven Britain from the continent – and then have turned on Russia with a vengeance to exact a tribute that would have made Brest-Litovsk appear magnanimous. Lenin might then have had second thoughts as to whether the Easter Rising had occurred 'prematurely'!

We may safely surmise that John Redmond had little time to contemplate such cosmic scenarios as the news from Dublin reached him in London. The Rising placed Redmond in a dilemma. It was a stab in the back for his policy of winning home rule through conciliation. The episode of the *Aud* confirmed the claim of German support contained in the Proclamation of the Republic. The insurrection appeared to vindicate traditional unionist assumptions about the congenital 'treachery' of nationalist Ireland. Nevertheless, if Redmond called for the execution of the rebels he might provoke a nationalist backlash. He denounced the Rising on 27 April, temporised over the first executions, then denounced executions from 6 May.[110]

Public opinion in Ireland was reported hostile to the Rising. But the situation was very unclear. It has remained so to this day. The consensus among historians is that an initially hostile public opinion was trans-

---

[109] C.C. O'Brien, 'The embers of Easter, 1916–1966', in Edwards and Pyle, *Easter Rising*, pp. 225–7.

[110] Edwards and Pyle, *Easter Rising*, have a chronology on the Rising and related events, pp. 30–5. Gwynn, *Redmond*, p. 483.

formed by the executions into retrospective support for, and romantici-
sation of, the rebels.[111] This assumption appeals to both supporters and
critics of the Rising. Supporters, anxious to dramatise the blood sacrifice
theme, or to invoke the authority of a heroic elite against mere public
opinion, naturally stress the lack of initial popular support. Critics are
also tempted to develop this theme in order to denounce the entire
enterprise as anti-democratic. The historical consensus is not based,
however, on scholarly review of the evidence. Indeed, in view of the
importance of the issues involved, it comes as a surprise to find that only
one systematic attempt has been made to follow the reporting in some of
the main newspapers.[112] The failure by historians to sift the evidence can
best be explained by the pervasive assumption that we know the answer
already. Even a cursory examination of the conveniently available evidence, however, reveals some of the complexities of an apparently simple
issue. The real historical challenge is to reconstruct reactions *in the light of
the information actually available to the public at the time*. This is not as
simple as it sounds. It is in fact extraordinarily difficult to reconstruct the
public response. This is mainly because little concrete objective information became available to the public during Easter week itself. It is
therefore difficult to know what precisely the public felt it was in fact
responding to.

The Rising began on 24 April and ended on 29 April. No detailed
newspaper reports appeared until early May. The unionist *Irish Times* did
continue publication during the Rising, but local difficulties combined
with the censorship to restrict reporting. The paper frankly confessed it
carried little news of the Rising, and solicitously enquired on the Wednes-
day of Easter week 'how many citizens of Dublin have any real knowledge
of the works of Shakespeare? Could any better occasion . . . be afforded
than the coincidence of enforced domesticity with the poet's tercentena-
ry?'[113] The unionist *Daily Express* reappeared on 3 May, a day earlier
than the two main home rule papers, the *Irish Independent* and the
Freeman's Journal. We therefore have no strictly contemporary newspaper reporting from the actual scene. Dubliners themselves were

---

111 Lyons, *Ireland*, p. 373; Lee, *Modernisation*, pp. 155–6. Hints of a more discriminating
approach can be detected in Fitzpatrick, *Politics*, p. 121.
112 O.D. Edwards, '*The Irish Times* on the Easter Rising' and 'Press reaction to the Rising in
general', in Edwards and Pyle, *Easter Rising*, pp. 241–50, 251–71. Mr Edwards deals in
these appendices with the *Freeman's Journal, Irish Independent, Daily Express*
(Dublin), *Cork Free Press*, and *Cork Examiner*, as well as with some foreign and Belfast
papers. This important pioneering survey has not received due recognition, perhaps
because it is tucked away in appendices.
113 *Irish Times*, 27 April 1916. No doubt every hand in the 20 000 families whom O'Casey
described as 'wriggling together like worms in a putrid mass in horror-filled one room
tenements' eagerly stretched for the *Collected works* on reading this reminder in their
daily *Times*!

deprived of newspaper information during the Rising. Most had little
knowledge of events. Even diarists in the city centre, like James Stephens,
or residents like Redmond's chief lieutenant, John Dillon, had only
limited knowledge of the general situation. Their accounts vividly
convey the atmosphere of uncertainty, close though they were to the
action.[114] Rumour expanded to fill the void.

The most prevalent rumour in Dublin was that the Rising was part of,
or the immediate prelude to, a German invasion.[115] This was not only
the official version, but found widespread credence among the populace.
The Dublin papers, on their reappearance, clung to the German plot scenario, liberally laced with doses of a 'socialist revolt' theory.[116] The interpretation advanced in the home rule papers did not significantly differ
from that in unionist papers. Only their assessment of the consequences,
and their recommendations on future policy, revealed their different
ideological affiliations. The *Freeman's Journal*, the main Redmondite
paper, naturally followed Redmond's line in the House of Commons on
27 April, in presenting the insurrection as a dastardly German plot. The
Irish Independent, the biggest mass circulation daily, was sympathetic to
home rule, but hostile to Redmond on factional grounds. Its proprietor,
William Martin Murphy, the militant Catholic capitalist, still seethed for
revenge against James Connolly, who had refused to bow the knee
during the 1913 lockout. The *Independent* therefore naturally depicted
in lurid terms the 'insane and criminal'[117] Rising, which it eagerly presented as simultaneously a German and a socialist plot. It invoked the
authority of the Proclamation of the Republic, with its reference to
'gallant allies in Europe' to sustain its 'German support for rebels' interpretation.[118] It made it clear that it did not oppose violence in principle.
It called on young Ireland to 'atone for the crime' of the Rising by
flocking to Flanders to 'show the world that Ireland is still sound at
heart'.[119] Lest its lower-middle class and farmer constituency should be
tempted to forget the threat to social stability posed by the Rising,
however, the *Independent* reiterated that 'the backbone of the insurrection was really "Larkinism" and "the citizen army"'.[120] It did print on
8 May the demands for an end to executions from leading English papers
and from the *Irish News* in Belfast, but with Connolly still alive it continued to demand the execution of the 'worst' of the remaining leaders.
When it could finally record on 13 May that Connolly and MacDermott

---

[114] James Stephens, *The Insurrection in Dublin* (Dublin, 1965); F.S.L. Lyons, *John Dillon*
(London, 1968), pp. 369–72.
[115] Stephens, *Insurrection*, p. 28.
[116] The *Express* laboured hard to keep this interpretation alive into mid-May. See the
accounts 9–12 May, and the cartoon on 10 May.
[117] *Irish Independent*, 4 May 1916.   [118] *Ibid.*, 5 May 1916.   [119] *Ibid.*
[120] *Ibid.*, 6 May 1916.

were safely dead it found it expedient to call for a halt to further executions.

Unionists of all shades, whose articulate indignation made them disproportionately visible as 'public opinion' immediately following the Rising, naturally repudiated the rebellion. So, at least as long as the German plot version retained credibility, did many families with relatives serving in France, whose womenfolk drew separation money. These two groups probably accounted for at least one-third of the population, and much more than half the articulate opinion, of Dublin. But it is clear that there was also much sympathy for the rebels, at least while there appeared to be some hope of success. James Stephens reports few of those feelings of 'detestation and horror' which Redmond attributed to Irish public opinion in his House of Commons statement on 27 April. Redmond was at that stage in no position to know what Irish public opinion was. Instead, Stephens records a mood of reticence, even of muted hope, rather than of hostility, at least until the Friday, when it was clear that the insurrection had failed.[121] Another diarist records hostility to the prisoners after the Rising from 'the gents and ladies especially of Francis Steet' [sic], and from soldiers' wives. Among the crowds waiting for passes at Dublin Castle on Friday he found 'some' welcoming news of the surrender, 'but many are murmuring what a pity'.[122] An unwilling witness provides evidence that hostility to the rebels was by no means universal. Sir John Maxwell, the British Commander, accounted for some atrocities by British troops by explaining that 'We tried hard to get the women and children to leave North King Street area. They would not go. Their sympathies were with the rebels . . .'[123]

Many unionists were as anxious as Redmond, if for different motives, to stress the lack of public support for the Rising. The diary kept by Revd Gordon Clements, a Protestant clergyman, concluded that 'the citizens of all classes welcomed the coming of troops from England . . .'. But Clements had recorded on Easter Tuesday that the men in the street were 'not indignant' at the rebels, feeling that 'they were hardy boys, even if they are fools'. By Thursday he began to detect a change in mood, but hardly on ideological grounds. 'The populace is non-committal or angry at the disturbance to their normal mode of life. Moreover, rumour has it that the rest of the country is quiet, especially Cork,' and already

---

121 Stephens, *Insurrection*, pp. 37–8. Stephens confined this view to the men. The women he found hostile to the Rising.

122 R. Kain, 'A diary of Easter Week: one Dubliner's experience', *Irish University Review*, 10, 2 (Autumn, 1980), pp. 206–7.

123 *Irish Independent*, 19 May 1916. Maxwell may have been searching for an excuse. But presumably he sought a plausible explanation.

the people 'sensed the sure defeat, and probably bloody end, of the Insurrectionists'.[124]

John Dillon wrote on 30 April that '*so far* the feeling of the population in Dublin is *against* the Sinn Féiners. But a reaction might very easily be created . . . '. Correct though this comment may have been, it requires sifting in its own right. Firstly, Dillon himself was in no position to know, as his biographer's account makes clear, what opinion in Dublin during the week had been.[125] Dillon simply did not have a sufficiently wide range of day-to-day contact to enable him to generalise about feeling in Dublin throughout the week. It was not merely that Dillon did not know, but that he could not know. He may have been right about feeling on 29 and 30 April, after the Rising had patently failed. But if he thought it would be so easy to create a reaction, even in the then still confused state of information about the participants and their motives, he must have sensed that sentiment was very volatile indeed. The summing-up a month after the Rising by A.M. Bonaparte-Wyse, a hardline unionist, is noteworthy in so far as it reflects less a change of mood compared with that recorded by Stephens and Clements during the early days of the Rising, than a crystallisation of that mood.[126]

The city is quiet now, but there is a very menacing tone among the lower classes who openly praise the Sinn Féiners for their courage and bravery, and there is a lot of abuse of the soldiers. At the same time the latter seem to be popular, at least with the female population. The sympathies of the ordinary Irish are with Sinn Féin. They want independence and their only criticism of the rebellion is that it was *foolish* (not criminal or otherwise wrong), but just foolish because it had no chance of success.

When reactions in Dublin are so difficult to document, it would be rash to hazard generalisations about public opinion in the rest of the country. Nevertheless, a few points can be made. Provincial newspapers appeared as usual during the Rising. 'As usual,' however, normally meant Saturday, 29 April, when the Rising was already virtually over. Even the few papers that appeared during the week were in no position to vouch for the accuracy of their information. Having to rely, in an atmosphere of censorship, on official statements, English newspapers and House of Commons reports for their news, they candidly conceded the difficulty of sifting fact from fiction.[127] Scarcely a paper failed to draw attention to the

---

124 *Daily Express*, 6 May 1916.   125 Lyons, *Dillon*, pp. 369–73 (quotation p. 373).
126 A.M. Bonaparte-Wyse to his brother, 28 May 1916, as published in *Irish Times*, 24 April 1965. Bonaparte-Wyse was Junior Secretary to the Board of Commissioners of National Education at the time. He later became a prominent civil servant in Northern Ireland.
127 My text seeks to build on the foundations laid by Mr Edwards by studying the eleven following provincial newspapers: *Clare Champion, Connacht Tribune, Cork Examiner, Kerryman, Kilkenny People, Leinster Leader, Limerick Leader, Nenagh Guardian, Roscommon Herald, Tipperary Star, Wicklow People*. These were published in ten

uncertain state of information, when editors were once more as dependent on 'despatch man and runner' as during 'the stirring days of Emmet and Lord Edward, and the men of '67 . . . as if we were not living in the days of motor, telephone and telegraph'.[128] Rumour naturally filled the knowledge vacuum in the provinces as in Dublin. The midlands luxuriated in 'the general crop of rumours' and 'all kinds of alarming reports'.[129] In Limerick 'all sorts of rumours, all of a sensational character are afloat . . . ',[130] while across the Shannon, Clare was bewildered by 'the maze of rumours'.[131]

The most popular interpretations sweeping the provinces were, as in Dublin, the 'German invasion' and the 'socialist subversion' theses. The *Cork Examiner* immediately branded the Rising 'a communistic disturbance rather than a revolutionary movement' which was 'made in Germany'.[132] The shopocracy of Galway condemned the rebels as stooges equally of Prussia and of Larkin.[133] Tipperary readers, learning of German support for a Rising by 'Sinn Féiners and the followers of Jim Larkin'[134] were warned that 'the Rising on this occasion was socialistic as well as political . . . '.[135] Having recovered from the shock of hearing that Germans had landed at Galway,[136] they were privileged to share with their Kerry cousins the insight of the Bishop of Kerry that the Rising was manipulated by 'evil-minded men affected by Socialistic and Revolutionary doctrines'.[137] The *Roscommon Herald*, edited by Jasper Tully, who had long before earned his literary spurs as a vitriolic anti-Parnellite in 1891,[138] seized every opportunity to denounce Larkin, stressed that the Proclamation of the Republic purported to establish 'a socialistic republic', compared the Rising with the Paris Commune, and reminded its eager readers of the case of Portugal, where priests and nuns were massacred by 'the Portuguese Sinn Féiners'.[139] As late as mid-May, Tully invoked the Commune analogy again, denounced 'the red week' in Dublin, relying no doubt on his readers' capacious recollection of recent events in Barcelona, and dismissed the Proclamation yet again, having now discovered that 'it is drafted on Suffragette lines, and gives votes

different counties, and their readership ranged over most of the south and west of the country. Only the *Kerryman* and the *Kilkenny People* could be considered sympathetic to republicanism. On the *Kerryman*, see Seamus McConville, 'The Kerryman' in *Kerrymen 1881–1981* (New York, n.d.), pp. 59–62.
128 *Connacht Tribune*, 29 April 1916.   129 *Leinster Leader*, 6 May 1916.
130 *Limerick Leader*, 26 April 1916.
131 *Clare Champion*, 29 April 1916.
132 *Cork Examiner*, 27, 28, 29 April 1916. See also the issues dated 1 May and 4 May.
133 *Connacht Tribune*, 29 April 1916.   134 *Nenagh Guardian*, 29 April 1916.
135 *Tipperary Star*, 6 May 1916.
136 *Ibid.*   137 *Ibid.*, 13 May 1916.
138 Lee, *Modernisation*, p. 137. Age did not mellow Tully. He was to lose a libel case seventeen years later (*Irish Press*, 11 February 1933).
139 *Roscommon Herald*, 29 April, 6 May, 13 May 1916.

equally to men and women, and it also has a lot of other "crank" notions'.[140]

The *Wicklow People* not only immediately denounced German support for the Rising,[141] but felt able to assert as late as mid-May that[142]

The Dublin outbreak was almost entirely the work of *Larkin's* Citizen Army, with Sinn Féin volunteers and Larkin's sympathisers and supporters. Wrecking of property and destruction of every kind is an outstanding phase of *syndicalism*. With the Larkin Citizen Army, the spirit of syndicalism was abroad, hence Dublin suffered so severely by the destruction of our public and commercial buildings and the looting of shops . . . .

The provincial public therefore found itself confronted with at least as wide a range of information and pseudo-information during the Rising itself and the following weeks as the Dublin public. The public was in no position to begin piecing together a coherent picture, of the rebels and their motives, of the origins, or the course, of the Rising, until the first week in May at the earliest. By that stage, with censorship and martial law in operation, with the Rising crushed, the response had to be inevitably to a failed Rising rather than to a potentially successful one. We will probably never be in a position to know the reaction to news of the real Rising as it finally filtered through to individuals across the country. The only generalisation the historian can confidently hazard in these circumstances is that we should be wary of generalisation!

The press, and many local representative bodies closely associated with the Home Rule Party, automatically accustomed to taking their cue from Redmond, initially sought to stress the isolation of the rebels, in order to impress on English home rule supporters how unrepresentative the separatists were in Ireland. This partly explains the reaction to the Rising as 'even more of an attempt to hit us than to hit England'. Condemnation of the Rising, interpreted as a German plot, as Larkinite, and/or as anti-Redmondite, was accordingly widespread. Condemnation of the Rising as a national anti-English revolt also occurred, but far more on tactical than on ideological grounds. The *Connacht Tribune*, in a long and thoughtful leading article, distinguished three groups of Irish people: impractical separatists, deluded Germanophiles, and realistic home rulers. It admitted that it did not know the motives of the rebels and therefore would not condemn them, and above all it urged no revenge: 'Let us not embitter the good by evil or ill-concealed thoughts about these children, who, though errant and rebellious, yet claim our paternal love and affection.'[143] The *Cork Examiner*, scarcely sympathetic to the Rising, advocated amnesty as early as 1 May, two days before the first executions.

---

[140] *Ibid.*, 13 May 1916.   [141] *Wicklow People*, 29 April 1916.
[142] *Ibid.*, 13 May 1916.
[143] *Connacht Tribune*, 29 April 1916.

The *Kilkenny People* expressed horror, but even more sadness, at the futility of the Rising.[144] It lamented that 'the Dublin revolution has ended, as everybody not a sheer lunatic must have known it would, in unutterable disaster, defeat and ruin'.[145] The strongly Redmondite *Clare Champion*, though insisting that home rule was safe, suspended ultimate judgement on 6 May. History must judge the rebellion. It just wanted clemency.[146] The *Leinster Leader* regarded the war, or the coup, as terrible, but it didn't even formally condemn it, and pleaded instead for 'mutual good will'.[147] The *Tipperary Star*, under the heading 'Inexplicable imbecility', bewailed the stupidity of the Rising, but more in sorrow than in anger: 'How any body of men could embark on such a desperate enterprise passes commonsense comprehension . . . The old story – everything lost, nothing gained . . . It is a pity of pities that the leaders of the people did not take the young men of Ireland in hand with kind advice before it was too late.'[148]

Three papers that had otherwise little in common, and that crossed the Dublin/provincial divide, the *Daily Express*, the *Roscommon Herald*, and the *Wicklow People*, took a somewhat unusual line. They denounced the Rising for having, *inter alia*, the wrong leaders. The *Daily Express* ridiculed the rebellion because 'the men who organised it were men of no position, of no reputation for serious effort, of no stake in the country'.[149] The *Wicklow People* approved of the executions partly because 'it would take sensible, level headed experienced men to guide a great agitation; none such were associated with the Sinn Féin agitation. It was guided by feather heads and dreamers, hence only mischief and worse than mischief could attend it'.[150] Jasper Tully warmed to this theme, reminding his readers that the Rising was doomed from the outset because 'it was a Poet's Rebellion with too much literature' about it.[151] Tully had not yet exhausted the literary possibilities of this approach. After a fortnight's ripe reflection, he felt that 'the Crazy Rebellion was the work chiefly of a lot of Crazy Poets. This has surprised people as far away as Chicago' – Tully's contact with civilization apparently extended to America as well as Europe – 'who generally regard poets – crazy or uncrazy – with amused contempt!'[152]

A more representative response, as the weeks passed, was to contrast the treatment meted out to the leaders with the leniency shown to Carson and de Wet, the Boer leader. This theme then became intertwined with the

144 *Kilkenny People*, 29 April 1916.   145 *Ibid.*, 6 May 1916.
146 *Clare Champion*, 6 May 1916.
147 *Leinster Leader*, 6 May 1916.   148 *Tipperary Star*, 6 May 1916.
149 *Daily Express*, 3 May 1916.
150 *Wicklow People*, 6 May 1916.   151 *Roscommon Herald*, 27 May 1916.
152 *Ibid.*, 10 June 1916.

argument that the rebels 'did not take human life wantonly',[153] that they had fought 'a clean and gallant fight'.[154] The executions undoubtedly roused resentment, not only from gut instinct, but because the honourable character of the executed men now began to be stressed. Where the Ennis District Council gave the weight of its authority on 3 May to the view that German gold lay behind the possibly socialist Rising, the Ennis Board of Guardians found itself a week later demanding no more executions of 'the misguided patriotic Irish men' involved in the Rising.[155] But the rebels the District Council condemned on 3 May were the stooges of the Kaiser and of Larkin. The Rising the Guardians contemplated on 10 May was simply a different rising. Even before the executions, newspaper comment, however critical of the Rising, was far less condemnatory than one might deduce from a perusal of the *Irish Independent* or the *Freeman's Journal* on their reappearance in Dublin.

Much probing local research is required to establish a more precise chronology and archaeology of popular sentiment. It is possible that public opinion, in so far as one can pronounce on it confidently at all, was not so much reversed as simply crystallised by a combination of the executions and better information. The first executions took place on 3 May. Hard news concerning the Rising began to filter through simultaneously with news of the executions. Most provincial readers, having been fed on a diet of the Kaiser and Larkin during the Rising itself, began to assimilate hard information concurrently with news of the executions. It may not have been reactions to 'the Rising' that changed so much as reactions to changing perceptions of the Rising, based on more accurate information. The uncertainty, bewilderment, hesitancy and ambiguity that characterised many reactions to the first fragmentary reports were quickly replaced, in the light of new information, by mingled feelings of despair at the folly of the rebels, pride in their gallantry, and contempt for the behaviour of their gaolors, feelings which John Dillon – 'the old John Dillon'[156] – well caught in his defiant House of Commons speech on 11 May.[157]

It would be unhistorical to leave 1916 without adverting to the calibre of the rebels. However many parasites may have battened on the reflected glory of the rebel band, the genuine rebels did include an exceptional number of remarkable people. Three future prime ministers, W.T. Cosgrave, Eamon de Valera and Seán Lemass, all men of stature in their very different styles, participated in the Rising. So did Michael Collins, soon to make his meteoric mark. So did others of future public distinction,

153 *Connacht Tribune*, 13 May 1916.
154 *Kilkenny People*, 20 May 1916, letter from Canon Murphy. See also *Cork Examiner*, 6 May 1916.
155 *Clare Champion*, 6, 13 May 1916.   156 *Kilkenny People*, 13 May 1916.
157 Lyons, *Dillon*, pp. 380ff.

including Desmond FitzGerald, Seán MacEntee, Richard Mulcahy, and Jim Ryan.

Among the signatories of the Proclamation of the Republic there were some intellectual nonentities. But there were also some thinkers of stature. Connolly was in a class of his own by the standards not only of Irish socialist but of Irish capitalist thought of his generation. Pearse, who has been mindlessly revered and mindlessly reviled, may have had the potential to develop into a considerable thinker. Victim of an emotionally stunted background, he nevertheless drew from his radical English artisan father unusual qualities of character and intellect. A prodigious worker, a generous instinct – however frequently masked towards the end by the self-flagellatory intensity of his martial prose – an open and receptive mind, he has strong claims to be considered a major educational thinker, certainly by the standards of educational thought in the Ireland of his time, perhaps even by contemporary European standards.[158] Indeed, it would have been interesting to see how long Pearse could have endured some of his companions – or they him – had fate spared them all. Thomas MacDonagh, a much slighter thinker, nevertheless ranks a clear cut above the average representative of, for instance, the Home Rule Party.[159]

The government interned nearly 2000 prisoners after the Rising. Asquith commissioned David Lloyd George, his most nubile negotiator, to make a renewed attempt to persuade nationalists and unionists to agree on an immediate home rule settlement. All the old problems re-emerged. Redmond now conceded the 'temporary' exclusion of six counties, but Ulster Unionists refused to budge on their demand for their permanent exclusion, though they were now reduced definitively to this territorial claim. The failure of the negotiations ripped aside the veil of illusion in which constitutional nationalists had garbed the 1914 Home Rule Act. Even the most gullible nationalists now grasped that a united home rule Ireland would not emerge at the end of the war. The convic-

---

158 Séamus Ó Buachalla has assembled Pearse's educational writings, hitherto much neglected because of the scattered and often anonymous nature of his prolific output. See Séamus Ó Buachalla, *A significant Irish educationalist* (Dublin and Cork, 1980). For a brief summary see S. Ó Buachalla, 'An Piarsach mar Oideachasóir', *Feasta*, 29, 5 (1976). Sean O'Casey, not the most ecumenical of witnesses, had a lively contempt for most of the 1916 crowd, but paid generous, if grudging, tribute to Pearse in *Drums under the window* (Pan edn, London, 1980), pp. 616–18, 662. Ruth Dudley Edwards, *Pearse*, remains the only historically satisfying biography.

159 Norstedt, *MacDonagh*, confirms that MacDonagh deserves a biography, which is more than can be claimed for many of his Home Rule contemporaries or for ornaments of later parties. For an interpretation of the Rising as a work of art, see W.I. Thompson, *The imagination of an Insurrection: Dublin, Easter 1916* (New York, 1967). F.X. Martin provides an extensive historiographical survey in '1916 – Myth, fact and mystery', *Studia Hibernica*, 7 (1967), pp. 7–126.

tion that Redmond had been out-manoeuvred by perfidious Albion further sapped his authority in Ireland.[160]

SINN FÉIN

If Redmond and Dillon were the main political victims, Arthur Griffith and Eamon de Valera were the main political beneficiaries of the Rising. Griffith did not participate in the insurrection. Nevertheless, the home rule press and the British succeeded in investing Griffith's moribund Sinn Féin with a degree of authority it had never managed to achieve on its own, by the simple device of branding all rebels Sinn Féiners. Little wonder that those more immediately involved resented Griffith's elevation to unprecedented prominence. Count Plunkett, father of the executed Joseph Mary Plunkett, won a Roscommon by-election in February 1917, and made an early bid for the leadership of the emerging separatist movement. But he was quickly eclipsed by the new star, Eamon de Valera, senior surviving commandant of the Rising, who had no intention of brooking any rivals for the leadership after his release from internment in 1917.

De Valera's spectacular victory as a Sinn Féin candidate in the Clare by-election in July 1917 enabled him to repulse the challenge for the leadership not only of Count Plunkett, but of Griffith himself, firmly relegated to the vice-presidency of his own party. De Valera was unanimously elected president of both Sinn Féin and the Irish Volunteers in October 1917, thus blurring the differences between the political and the paramilitary movements. The rejuvenated Sinn Féin was more akin to a popular front resistance movement than to a parliamentary party. To preserve the unity of the fragile coalition, the leadership shelved potentially disruptive issues. This inevitably meant endorsement of the social and economic status quo. That made political sense. The Proclamation of the Republic, in which Pearse and Connolly appeared, however vaguely, to commit the rebels to building a new society, promising equality of social and economic opportunity, would make little appeal to the established interests now shifting to the new Sinn Féin as the best guarantor of their inherited status.[161]

For unionist Ulster the threat appeared at least as perilous in 1918 as in 1912. Sinn Féin, superseding the Home Rule party, seemed poised to launch a two-pronged attack on the identity of the Protestant people, threatening them with subjection to Gaelic culture as well as to Rome rule. Both nationalist parties shared the same attitude, however much their

---

[160] Lyons, *Ireland*, p. 379; M. Laffan, *The partition of Ireland 1911–1925* (Dundalk, 1983), pp. 54–5.
[161] This is a central theme of David Fitzpatrick's *Politics*.

policies might differ in emphasis, towards Ulster Protestants. Ulster unionists must come into a united Ireland and they would come in, if only the conniving British left. The Proclamation of the Republic clung to the orthodox home rule interpretation of Ulster unionism, portraying the unionists as puppets of the crafty British, who had 'carefully fostered' little local differences between minority and majority. Sinn Féin showed supreme insensitivity towards Protestant fears. The manner in which the Catholic hierarchy bestowed its blessing on nationalist resistance to conscription in 1918 supplied further evidence that home rule was Rome rule. So did the manner in which both Sinn Féin and Home Rulers appealed to none other than the Catholic primate, Cardinal Logue, to act as arbiter between them in the case of disputed nationalist seats in Ulster in the general election of December 1918.

Ill-conceived government policy encouraged the growing enthusiasm for Sinn Féin. 'By the sporadic exercise of ill-directed *force majeure*, by interference in public assemblies, arrests, trials and imprisonments, the Castle made heroes out of nobodies . . . '.[162] County Clare, congratulated by its premier newspaper in 1916 on 'its magnificent and unanimous loyalty to Mr Redmond'[163] had already swung into the Sinn Féin camp with de Valera's dramatic election triumph in July 1917.[164] In February 1918 it had to be proclaimed a 'special military area' under the Defence of the Realm Act.[165]

Redmond, his authority crumbling, died in March 1918, shortly before the collapse of a futile Irish Convention devised by Lloyd George in the alleged hope that the Irish could agree on a constitution for their country. Sinn Féin boycotted the convention, which therefore became a largely academic exercise. The Ulster Unionist representatives predictably rejected Redmond's proposals. In immediate political terms, the main contribution of the convention was to show that Southern unionists were now seeking to accommodate themselves to the likelihood of a Southern state and were thus becoming increasingly aware of the differences separating themselves from Ulster unionists. Despite its immediate irrelevance the convention has been unjustly neglected in nationalist historiography. It confronted, at a high level of civility and intelligence, most of the issues that would baffle later generations of Irishmen, not only in terms of unionist–nationalist relations, but in terms of the nature of a nationalist state. That it failed to reconcile conflicting loyalties and interests, within the constraints imposed by the imperial power, reflects

---

[162] *Ibid.*, p. 148. See also Lyons, *Ireland*, p. 386.   [163] *Clare Champion*, 6 May 1916.
[164] The *Clare Champion* duly swung with public opinion. But de Valera's majority of about 3000, compared with predictions of about 1000, clearly surprised the pundits, who normally expected to predict results to within a handful of votes (*Clare Champion*, 7, 14 July 1917).
[165] C. Townshend, *The British campaign in Ireland 1919–1921* (Oxford, 1978), p. 7.

less on the limitations of the convention than on the intractibility of the problems, which have continued to baffle later generations.[166]

If Redmond stood more in the tradition of Butt than of Parnell,[167] the sombre verdict of his successor, John Dillon, that he 'faced great unpopularity and misunderstanding in Ireland in a high-minded and sincere attempt to reconcile the Irish and British people, and to serve the Empire in a time of terrible crisis and danger, and his reward was to be snubbed and humiliated in the face of his own people'[168] captures the dilemma of all Irish statesmen who would seek conciliation by trusting solely in English good will.

Sinn Féin consolidated its position and achieved increasing respectability by vigorous opposition to the counter-productive threat of conscription in April 1918.[169] London's handling of the issue hardly redeemed England's reputation for statecraft in Irish affairs. Leading Sinn Féin figures were arrested on fictitious charges of a 'German plot' in May. In contrast to 1916, Sinn Féin had now, especially since American entry into the war, adopted neutrality as the correct party line.[170] The arrest of de Valera and Griffith gave an opportunity to the more overt advocates of physical force, especially Michael Collins and Cathal Brugha, to thrust rapidly to the fore.[171]

Sinn Féin, organised into 1354 clubs with 112080 members, had largely supplanted the organisational structure of the once proud Home Rule Party by the end of 1918.[172] It captured 73 seats in the general election in December, compared with 6 for the Home Rule Party, reduced from 69 at the dissolution. Unionists won 26 seats, but had the mortification of taking only 2 seats out of 5 in the disputed counties of Fermanagh and Tyrone. The losers naturally sought, in time-honoured tradition, to derive what comfort they could from the polls. Whatever permutations are posited, and however the figures are read, the election marked a decisive endorsement for Sinn Féin in Southern Ireland.[173]

The immediate aftermath of the election exposed strains within the Sinn Féin popular front. A rump parliament, the first Dáil, consisting of the 27 available Sinn Féin members, adopted a cryptic five article constitution as

---

[166] The standard account is R.B. McDowell, *The Irish Convention 1917–1918* (London, 1970).
[167] P. O'Farrell, *Ireland's English question* (London, 1971), p. 259.
[168] Lyons, *Dillon*, p. 432, n. 2.
[169] Fitzpatrick, *Politics*, pp. 151–2.
[170] R.W. Dudley Edwards, 'The achievement of 1916', in Edwards and Pyle, *Easter Rising*, p. 215.
[171] Townshend, *British campaign*, p. 9.
[172] M. Laffan, 'The unification of Sinn Féin, 1917', *IHS*, 17 (1971), pp. 353–79, traces the early organisational development of Sinn Féin.
[173] Lee, *Modernisation*, pp. 158–63. For an account of the campaign as seen by the Home Rule leaders see Lyons, *Dillon*, pp. 444–55.

well as 'The Democratic Programme' in January 1919. A draft 'Democratic Programme' had been prepared by the leaders of the Labour Party, Thomas Johnson and William O'Brien, who had shirked facing the electorate in December. The draft contained too much of Pearse, not to mention Connolly, for the socially conservative elements in the Dáil. Seán T. O'Kelly took care to eliminate the controversial clauses. He had every 'democratic' justification for doing so. The draft was an attempt to foist on the Dáil a programme that had never been presented to the electorate. The actual 'Democratic Programme', finally cobbled together by O'Kelly, did in fact continue to incorporate more of the social doctrine of the Proclamation of the Republic than the electorate could be considered to have sanctioned.[174]

Sinn Féin's policy remained studiously vague throughout 1917 and 1918. It proposed to abstain from Westminster on the grounds that attendance could not further Irish aims, and instead to present the case for independence to the Peace Conference at the end of the war 'where the Bench will not be packed against us'.[175] This may have made some sense while the Germans appeared possible victors. It made no sense at all in December 1918. How the conference was expected to recognise Irish claims, when Sinn Féin traced its new authority to a Rising that had invoked German aid, remained unexplained. The victors may have been hypocritical in claiming the war was fought on behalf of 'small nations', but Sinn Féin, after all, had refused to support the war. Dillon might have a claim on the conscience of the Peace Conference. De Valera could have none. And how was a Peace Conference expected to compel a victorious Britain to withdraw from Ireland, and not least from Protestant Ulster, which had continued to support the war effort down to the end, at a time when nationalist Ireland resisted conscription? It is true that high hopes were staked on American support for Irish claims, and on the Fourteen Points. But Woodrow Wilson, himself of Presbyterian stock, had little instinctive sympathy for the Irish. He would hardly have been the man he was had he taken Irish claims seriously after the 'Nationalist Letter to President Wilson' in June 1918.[176] The case Sinn Féin presented to him in this letter would have been an insult to the intelligence of a lesser mind than that of a president of Princeton University. Nothing illustrates better the collapse of the Home Rule Party than its failure to effectively expose

[174] B. Farrell, 'A note on the Dáil constitution 1919', *The Irish Jurist*, 4 (1969), 127–38. Johnson's draft can be compared with the Dáil version in B. Farrell, *The founding of Dáil Eireann* (Dublin, 1971), pp. 87–9; P. Lynch, 'The social revolution that never was', in T.D. Williams (ed.), *The Irish struggle 1916–1926* (London, 1966), pp. 45–8.

[175] *Clare Champion*, 7 July 1917. On the ethos of Sinn Féin, see D.G. Boyce, '"The Marginal Britons": the Irish', in R. Colls and P. Dodd, *Englishness: culture and politics* (Beckenham, Kent, 1986), p. 245.

[176] McNeill, *Ulster's stand*, pp. 287–95.

the illusions in Sinn Féin's proclaimed policy. The letter gave Ulster unionists a golden opportunity, which they gleefully seized, to despatch a more cerebral 'Unionist letter to President Wilson' in August 1918.[177]

From January 1919 local Volunteer groups began to engage in sporadic assassinations of policemen. It was not until August 1919 that the Dáil attempted to impose its authority, however nominally, on these groups by assuming responsibility for their activity. The British, as if, not for the last time, in collusion with the extremists, drove the elected representatives more into the hands of the gunmen by suppressing the Dáil and Sinn Féin in late 1919. The level of Volunteer activity rose steeply. The IRA, as the Volunteers came to be increasingly called, killed 192 policemen and 150 soldiers in 1920 compared with 13 policemen and 1 soldier in 1919.[178]

De Valera's first cabinet, which he formed in April 1919 after he himself had escaped from Lincoln jail, and the other 'German plot' prisoners had been released, balanced the various factions in the new Sinn Féin. A teacher who claimed the mantle of the educationalist Pearse, de Valera nevertheless conspicuously failed to nominate a Minister for Education, in order to avoid potential tension with the Catholic Church, whose benediction he sought.[179] His appointment of Michael Collins as Minister for Finance did not suffice to exhaust the exuberant energies of the rumbustious young Corkman, successfully though he raised a national loan.[180] Collins, who fought in the Easter Rising, and played an active role in organising the Volunteers and the IRB after his release from detention in 1917, soon emerged as a key figure in the armed struggle. His post as Director of Intelligence in the Volunteers from June 1919 enabled him to paralyse the British information network. During previous agitations the intelligence system kept the government closely in touch with rebel plots. This network decayed during the Liberal administration before 1916. Subsequent attempts to reconstruct it proved difficult as Collins had leading Intelligence agents assassinated. The British only began to achieve success in this respect in early 1921, when General Ormonde Winter weeded out some of Collins's key informers.[181] When de Valera spent from June 1919 to December 1920 in America, soliciting financial and political support, Collins emerged at home as a powerful political as well as military figure. This gave some semblance of coherence to the locally fragmented Volunteer/Sinn Féin movement.

There was scarcely even the semblance of coherence on the British side. Lloyd George was so reluctant to acknowledge the scale of the revolt that he refused to either declare, or wage, full-scale war.[182] While British

---

[177] *Ibid.*, pp. 296–9.   [178] Kee, *Green flag*, pp. 671–2.
[179] Miller, *Church, state and nation*, p. 441.
[180] L. Ó Broin, *Michael Collins* (Dublin, 1980), p. 38.   [181] *Ibid.*, pp. 74–5.
[182] Townshend, *British campaign*, p. 40.

forces never enjoyed as free a rein as the IRA, the government for its part lacked any clearcut political design, and muddled through 'by means which no systematic planner would have countenanced'.[183] There may be circumstances in which systematic plans are neither possible nor even desirable, but the prevailing impression left by British policy in Ireland between 1918 and 1921 is one of decision-makers out of their depth. This is the more surprising, in that some of the most impressive talents in British politics and administration devoted some time, if rarely sustained thought, to the problem. The overall British performance provides an instructive case study in decision-making. The cabinet could not make up its mind on either a war policy or a peace policy. When it did 'sanction stern measures, such as the blanket ban on Sinn Féin or, later, martial law', it proceeded to sabotage its own decisions by denying the military the means to implement them.[184] It relied heavily on not merely mislead-ing, but uncomprehending, advice. In December 1920, for instance, it refused a truce on the terms it accepted in July 1921, apparently because Sir Hamer Greenwood, the Chief Secretary, believed the IRA to be on the verge of collapse and felt that Irish public opinion supported the British government![185]

There were 40000 soldiers in the country in 1921, but much of the fighting was borne by 7000 Black and Tans and 6000 Auxiliaries, ex-soldiers and ex-officers recruited for a 'police' operation, who began arriving in March and August 1920 respectively. The new recruits were too few to impose a real reign of terror, but numerous enough to commit sufficient atrocities to provoke nationalist opinion in Ireland and America, and to outrage British liberal opinion which felt that if Britain could not hold Ireland according to 'British' standards then she shouldn't hold Ireland at all. The British lost the propaganda war with a spectacular series of own goals. Civil resistance, especially by transport workers refusing to handle military material, further impeded the British effort.[186]

PARTITION

Lloyd George's legislative response to the Irish crisis was the Government of Ireland Act of December 1920, which proposed to establish parlia-ments in Dublin and Belfast with powers of local self-government. The Act partitioned Ireland along the six-county border, though retaining provision for the unification of Ireland if the two parliaments agreed. The degree of self-government conferred by the Act fell far short of Sinn Féin

---

[183] Fitzpatrick, *Politics*, p. 198.   [184] Townshend, *British campaign*, p. 32.
[185] Miller, *Church, state and nation*, pp. 474–5.
[186] C. Townshend, 'The Irish railway strike of 1920: industrial action and civil resistance in the struggle for independence', *IHS*, 21, 83 (1979), pp. 266–82.

demands. Control of defence, foreign policy and finance remained with Westminster. In addition, Westminster reserved the right to intervene at will in Irish affairs, insisting that 'the supreme authority of the parliament of the United Kingdom shall remain unaffected and undiminished over all persons, matters and things in Ireland, and every part thereof'. The Act reflected British more than Irish political realities in 1920. Lloyd George now relied mainly on the Conservatives, led by Bonar Law. The Act contained more concessions than any previous Tory administration had offered, but the Conservatives could not yet bring themselves to concede the essence of self-government. The difference between the terms of the Government of Ireland Act and the Treaty of 1921 – the difference between 'Stormont status' and effective sovereignty – measures the pedagogic influence of the intervening violence on the Conservative mind.

Sinn Féin's abstentionist policy allowed Lloyd George to push through his partition act with no real opposition in Westminster. John Redmond had fought tenaciously against the idea of partition, and had achieved some success on matters of detail. He had driven the Conservative Party to accept, for the first time, the idea of home rule in principle. He had whittled the unionist claim down from nine counties to six. Sinn Féin, consumed with its sacred egoism, failed to build on Redmond's work. Ironically for a movement prone to denounce the 'corruption' of Home Rule members by the Westminster atmosphere, Sinn Féin, for practical purposes, collaborated with the cabinet's partition policy in 1920.

The actual border imposed in the Government of Ireland Act represented a capitulation by the cabinet to Ulster Unionist pressure. The cabinet proposed a nine-county Ulster, though at least one member, Arthur Balfour, would have preferred local plebiscites to determine the boundary. It was the Ulster Unionists who insisted on six counties.[187] The Unionists did not flinch from breaking their own 'contract', the Covenant, and sacrificing the Protestants of Donegal, Cavan and Monaghan, with the same sacred egoism with which Sinn Féin sacrificed the Catholics of the six counties.

There were two differences, however, between Unionist and Sinn Féin behaviour. The first was that Unionists cherished a self-image of men whose word was their bond. They honoured their contracts.[188] The Sinn Féin self-image, while equally self-indulgent in general, was a shade more relaxed on this particular issue! It came now as cold comfort to the Protestants of the three abandoned Ulster counties that Carson had proclaimed the Covenant 'a contract between them as Ulster men, and

[187] N. Mansergh, 'The Government of Ireland Act, 1920: its origins and purposes. The working of the "official mind"', in J.G. Barry (ed.), *Historical Studies*, 9 (Belfast, 1974), pp. 44–6.
[188] Miller, *Queen's rebels*, p. 115.

that Ulstermen were not in the habit of breaking their contracts'.[189] The second difference was that if Ulster Protestants took their own protestations about Rome rule seriously, then they were consigning their fellow Protestants to a horrendous fate. If the Pope was indeed anti-Christ, if unionist fears of the persecution awaiting Protestants in a Home Rule, much less a Sinn Féin, state were valid, then the abandoned Protestants were being condemned to a hell on earth. In these circumstances, the desertion of the Protestants of Donegal, Monaghan and Cavan by their fellow Protestants counts as the basest of all 'betrayals' of the period.

The Government of Ireland Act formally established a six-county Northern Ireland. Partition had long existed in the mind. Now it existed on the map. But what a map! The geographical boundaries did not attempt to follow the mental boundaries. The Catholic majorities in Tyrone and Fermanagh were bigger than the Protestant majorities in Londonderry and Armagh! The inconsistencies became even more glaring at a constituency level. Unionists conceded the border constituency of North Monaghan, which had 33 per cent Protestants, but insisted on taking the border constituency of South Armagh, which had 32 per cent Protestants. Likewise, unionists conceded the border constituency of East Donegal with 40 per cent Protestants, but claimed the border constituency of South Fermanagh with 39 per cent Protestants.[190] 'Betrayed' unionists, cast into the outer darkness beyond the border, advanced these precise arguments in a desperate but unavailing attempt to escape their doom.[191]

It has been argued, on the premise that the border was devised to separate two peoples who could not live together in peace, that 'partition was the only possible democratic solution to the problem'.[192] The actual border seems difficult to reconcile, however, with 'democratic' principles, as commonly understood. The 'democratic' arguments advanced to justify the actual border might frequently be used more easily to justify the nationalist claim to either large areas of Northern Ireland, or even to a united Ireland. The border was not devised to keep two warring groups apart. The Catholic minority in Northern Ireland was proportionately larger than the unionist minority in Ireland as a whole. This brought the warring groups together more than it separated them. The border was chosen explicitly to provide unionists with as much territory as they could safely control. Its objective was not to separate unionists and nationalists in order to enable them to live peaceably apart. It was instead to ensure

[189] *Ibid.*, p. 97.
[190] Population percentages are derived from *Census of Ireland, 1911, General Report*, p. 220.
[191] Hepburn, *Conflict*, pp. 117–18.
[192] F.W. Boal and J.M.H. Douglas, 'Overview', in Boal and Douglas (eds.), *Integration and division: geographical perspectives on the Northern Ireland problem* (London, 1985), p. 336.

Protestant supremacy over Catholics even in predominantly Catholic areas.

The British government of 1920 bore no immediate responsibility for the racial and religious antagonisms in Ulster. It does bear responsibility for imposing a 'solution' to the Ulster question that contained within it the seeds of fresh struggle. It can be readily accepted that any 'solution' was likely to foster fresh resentments. A border justifiable only on the basis of racial supremacy was bound to do so. Winston Churchill, in a celebrated passage, sought to convey the impression of a benign government reacting helplessly to an insoluble problem:[193]

Then came the Great War. Every institution, almost, in the world was strained. Great empires had been overturned. The whole map of Europe has been changed. The position of countries has been violently altered. The modes of thought of men, the whole outlook on affairs, the grouping of parties, all have encountered violent and tremendous change in the deluge of the world, but as the deluge subsides and the waters fall short we see the dreary steeples of Fermanagh and Tyrone emerging once again. The integrity of their quarrel is one of the few institutions that have been unaltered in the cataclysm which has swept the world. That says a lot for the persistency with which Irishmen on the one side or on the other are able to pursue their controversies.

The sonorous Churchillian cadences can only too easily divert attention from the hollowness of the argument. There was nothing unique about Fermanagh and Tyrone. The integrity of similar quarrels in Europe was not altered by the First World War. All that happened was that borders were revised in central and eastern Europe in favour of smaller states. This was precisely what did not happen in Fermanagh and Tyrone. It is not the 'persistency' of Irishmen, but the inconsistency of Englishmen, in refusing to apply in the UK the 'solutions' they imposed on others, that is distinctive.

Redmond's 'one nation' theory left him with the worst of both worlds in trying to combat specific unionist territorial claims. Sinn Féin's abstentionism meant the nationalist voice was not heard at all when the border was being drawn. Unionists had a tenable claim, by normal nationalist criteria, to the exclusion of particular areas from home rule. They had no claim at all on some of the areas they eventually annexed. Nationalists did indeed seem to hope that they might achieve unity by some stratagem that would cajole or compel Ulster unionists into a nationalist parliament. It was as if they hoped that unity would come 'like a thief in the night' as Randolph Churchill warned of home rule in 1886.

If the Government of Ireland Act sacrificed Catholics in the North to the opportunism of Sinn Féin, it helped to consolidate Sinn Féin's control of

---

[193] W.S. Churchill, *Hansard*, 150, 16 February 1922, col. 1270.

the South. The 124 Sinn Féin candidates were returned unopposed in the general election under the Act in May 1921. Only the four unionists, representing Trinity College, made the futile attempt to convene as the parliament of Southern Ireland. Nevertheless, the opening of the Northern Ireland parliament in June provided Lloyd George with an opportunity, through the King's Speech, to suggest the possibility of negotiation with Sinn Féin.

THE TREATY

De Valera had returned in December 1920 from his financially successful, if politically controversial, tour of America, where he 'had been a magnificent publicist for Ireland'.[194] He found the military situation transformed during his eighteen-month absence. In 1920–21 the crown forces suffered 525 dead, and almost 1000 wounded. At least 707 civilians were to die between January and July 1921.[195] By Irish standards these were horrific figures. De Valera was humane enough to be disturbed. He also found Collins very much in the ascendant. He was human enough to be disturbed.[196] De Valera genuinely desired peace. He also realised that negotiations were inevitable, unless the IRA were crushed before Britain could be brought to the conference table.[197] It came as a relief when Lloyd George followed up the favourable response of British public opinion to the dramatic appeal for conciliation by George V on the opening of the Northern Irish parliament by proposing a truce, which came into effect on 11 July.[198]

Lloyd George succeeded in establishing, during a protracted bout of sparring with de Valera following the truce, that the achievement of a republic through negotiation was impossible. Nevertheless, de Valera eventually accepted Lloyd George's invitation to a conference in London 'where we can meet your delegates as spokesmen of the people whom you represent, with a view to ascertaining how the association of Ireland with the community of nations known as the British empire may be reconciled with Irish national aspirations'. So scholastic a scrutineer of texts as de Valera can hardly have overlooked the significance of 'how' rather than

---

[194] A.J. Ward, *Ireland and Anglo-American relations 1899–1921* (London, 1969), p. 235. On the significance of the tour, see D. McCartney, 'De Valera's mission to the United States, 1919–20', in A. Cosgrove and D. McCartney (eds.), *Studies in Irish history* (Dublin 1979), pp. 304–33.

[195] Kee, *Green flag*, p. 699. See also Fitzpatrick, *Politics*, pp. 10, 27.

[196] Miller, *Church, state and nation*, pp. 477–8; Earl of Longford and T.P. O'Neill, *Eamon de Valera* (Dublin, 1970), p. 148.

[197] Townshend, *British campaign*, pp. 179–96, discusses the balance of military strength in the early summer of 1921, as well as longer term prospects.

[198] *Ibid.*, p. 191.

'whether' in this formula, which already contained the seeds of compromise, as Collins correctly observed in the Treaty debate.[199]

Once the Sinn Féin cabinet accepted this invitation, it had to recommend the delegates to the Dáil. Ominous splits occurred immediately. The cabinet had seven members, de Valera, Collins, Griffith, Brugha, Austin Stack, Robert Barton and W.T. Cosgrave. Brugha and Stack refused to go to London at all. Neither one was regarded as serious negotiating material, however, and it is de Valera's refusal to go, decided by his own casting vote in the cabinet, that has aroused most controversy.

De Valera realised that the republic was unattainable in the short term. Compromise was inevitable. The crude realities of power politics made some form of association with the British empire unavoidable. He was already working on a constitutionally brilliant concept of 'external association'. According to this idea, Irish sovereignty in internal matters would be recognised, but Ireland would associate with the Commonwealth in external affairs and would guarantee her neutrality in wartime. Irish and British citizens would enjoy reciprocal, as distinct from common, citizenship. This would avoid the humiliations of the direct imperial link while simultaneously providing for British security, which de Valera acknowledged to be a legitimate concern of Westminster.[200] De Valera warned the Dáil in August 1921 as bluntly as was politically possible that compromise was inevitable. He stressed that he took office again as president only on condition that the Dáil recognised that

I have one allegiance only to the people of Ireland, and that is to do the best we can for the people of Ireland as we conceive it . . . I would not like, therefore, that anyone should propose me for election as president who would think I had my mind definitely made up on any situation that may arise. I keep myself free to consider each question as it arises – I never bind myself in any other way.[201]

This came as close as de Valera could safely go in implying that the oath to the Republic taken by members should be considered more a means to an end than an end in itself. This was the antithesis of the doctrinaire mentality, and de Valera rightly feared that doctrinaire republicans would reject any compromise.

No analysis of de Valera's motives can be definitive, for 'it was never quite clear what de Valera stood for; or with whom he stood, at least from December 1920 until June 1922.'[202] Nevertheless, there seems no reason to reject the claim of his authorised biographers that 'unity on his side was

---

[199] D.H. Akenson, *The United States and Ireland* (Cambridge, Mass., 1973), pp. 53ff; D.H. Akenson, 'Was de Valera a republican?', *Review of Politics*, 33, 2 (1971), pp. 244–7.

[200] Longford and O'Neill, *De Valera*, pp. 147–8.

[201] M. Moynihan (ed.), *Speeches and statements by Eamon de Valera 1917–73* (Dublin and New York, 1980), p. 70.

[202] S.M. Lawlor, *Britain and Ireland 1914–23* (Dublin, 1983), p. xi.

his over-riding objective'.[203] He had acted as the unifier of the Sinn Féin since 1916,[204] and continued to see himself in that role. His preoccupation with unity confirms that he realised the inevitability of compromise. Indeed, so intent was he on negotiation that between July and October 1921 he took care to provide Lloyd George with no excuse for calling off the truce.[205] Realising that bitter controversy was likely to arise over the terms of any possible agreement, he apparently hoped that if he were not involved in the negotiations himself, he could wean the doctrinaires into accepting 'external association' as an honourable solution. He argued, in addition, from a more procedural perspective, that by remaining at home he would provide the delegates with the tactical excuse that they had to refer proposals to him, which would gain them valuable respite from the immediate pressures of the negotiation table.[206]

For all the weight that should be attached to any de Valera calculation, or even rationalisation, it really did not make sense for 'the best player', as W.T. Cosgrave rightly called him, to remain a non-playing captain in the biggest match his team was ever likely to play. James Craig always tried to present Northern Ireland's case himself in negotiations with the British. Lloyd George, with a far busier schedule, and also presiding over a potentially awkward cabinet, made sure to lead his team. De Valera did sometimes advance the argument that he should not involve himself in negotiations because, as president, he was the symbol of the Republic, and symbols should not negotiate. This sounds suspiciously like an anti-Collins rationalisation. The one thing de Valera was, and that Collins was not, was president! And there would seem to have been little point remaining as symbol if there was a danger that one's absence might lead to the sacrifice of the symbol in the negotiations. De Valera would have gained a more acute appreciation of the negotiating possibilities in London, where he could also presumably have exerted greater influence on the Irish delegates.

De Valera seemed as determined that Collins should go to London as that he himself should not. Why Collins agreed to go when Brugha and Stack flatly refused, remains a mystery, unless one accepts his own explanation that a sense of duty overcame his reluctance. If Collins did not shirk negotiation, he advanced a good argument why he should remain at home. As he was regarded as the hard military man, the delegates could argue in London that any settlement would have to be acceptable to him.[207] But this argument implied that Collins, even Collins in cabinet, had power of veto. The President of the Republic would hardly enjoy

203 Longford and O'Neill, *De Valera*, p. 147.
204 T. Ryle Dwyer, *Eamon de Valera* (Dublin, 1980), p. 11.
205 S.M. Lawlor, 'Ireland from Truce to Treaty: war or peace? July–October 1921', *IHS*, 22, 85 (March, 1980), pp. 63–4.
206 Longford and O'Neill, *De Valera*, pp. 147–8.   207 Ó Broin, *Collins*, p. 88.

pleading to Lloyd George that a nominal subordinate exercised such authority.

Collins sensed a conspiracy against him by de Valera, Brugha and Stack. His suspicions reveal something of the atmosphere in the cabinet, but he was being perhaps hypersensitive. However diligently de Valera felt politicians should study Machiavelli,[208] his real blunder was less conspiracy than miscalculation. He staked everything on preserving unity through his 'external association' scheme. He achieved wonders in persuading Brugha and Stack to accept the idea. But he had little influence on more militarist republicans like Rory O'Connor and Liam Mellowes, with whom he had relatively little association, and who would prove the real stumbling blocks to the compromise he sought. They denounced external association as emphatically as did the British, equally unable to grasp so sophisticated a constitutional concept. And de Valera had no contingency plans. He does not seem to have pondered how the price of disunity could be minimised if unity proved impossible.

He also miscalculated the composition of the negotiating team from his own viewpoint. He seems to have assumed that the two senior members of the team, Griffith and Collins, were prepared to compromise on an oath to the crown.[209] He could nevertheless still anticipate a 5:2 cabinet majority against distasteful proposals. But by exposing the 'republican' Robert Barton, the only other cabinet member on the delegation, to the atmosphere of the negotiations in London, and to the powerful personality of Collins, even with his 'republican' relative, Erskine Childers, as secretary of the delegation to keep an eye on him, de Valera risked losing Barton's vote in the cabinet, as in the event happened. This would reduce his putative cabinet majority from 5:2 to 4:3 in the case of a split.

On 6 December, when faced after two month's negotiations with an ultimatum of 'war within three days'[210] by Lloyd George, the delegates signed articles of agreement, commonly called the Treaty. The Treaty conferred dominion status, formally equivalent to that of Canada, on the Irish Free State, but conceded certain naval facilities to Britain as well as the right to demand further military facilities in war time. Members of the Free State parliament must take an oath of allegiance to the king of England, but the negotiators had wrenched some final concessions on the wording of the oath. 'Instead of being, as in the other dominions, the straight-forward oath of allegiance to the king, the Irish oath prescribed allegiance first to the constitution of the Irish Free State, secondly to the crown in virtue of the common citizenship between the two countries and the association of Ireland with the Commonwealth of Nations.'[211] If the

---

[208] Longford and O'Neill, *De Valera*, p. 88.   [209] Ó Broin, *Collins*, p. 89.
[210] F. Pakenham, *Peace by ordeal* (London, 1935), p. 198.
[211] J.L. McCracken, *Representative government in Ireland* (London, 1958), p. 155.

parliament of Northern Ireland rejected inclusion in the Free State, a boundary commission would be established consisting of one representative each of the Northern and Southern governments, and a chairman appointed by the British government, to 'determine in accordance with the wishes of the inhabitants, so far as may be compatible with economic and geographic conditions, the boundaries between Northern Ireland and the rest of Ireland'.[212]

A torrent of recrimination immediately engulfed the signatories. Critics charged that the delegates had undertaken to sign no agreement without referring the terms to the cabinet in Dublin. Griffith had pledged as late as 3 December not to accept dominion status without referral back to the cabinet. Why had the delegates not even used the telephone to Dublin when faced with Lloyd George's ultimatum? Supporters of the Treaty taunted de Valera with moral cowardice for staying in Ireland, and asked what better terms could he have delivered.

The controversy about de Valera's decision to remain in Ireland rests on the assumption that his presence in London would have made a significant difference to the negotiations. This must mean either that he would have got better terms which would have avoided the subsequent civil war, or alternatively that, failing to achieve better terms, he would have engineered a breakdown of negotiations on the Ulster question, which would have allegedly kept Sinn Féin united, and strengthened its case in world opinion. Neither of these assumptions fully survives scrutiny.

Document no. 2, which de Valera produced in the Dáil debates on the Treaty, contained the best terms he himself dared contemplate. The main difference between it and the Treaty was that it embodied his external association concept, omitting the oath, and mentioning the king only in so far as 'for purposes of the Association [of Ireland with the states of the British Commonwealth,] Ireland shall recognise his Britannic majesty as head of the Association'. The shading here proved far too subtle for either doctrinaire Irish republicans or doctrinaire British royalists. The blood lust of Rory O'Connor, who would shout down even Cathal Brugha for being contaminated with politics – i.e. for daring to disagree with O'Connor – could not be slaked by means of what appeared to primitive political intelligences as mere semantic subtlety. Given the emotional immaturity of the British negotiators on the issue of the crown – the metaphysical republicanism of the anti-Treaty ultras was matched only by the metaphysical monarchism of the British[213] – it is difficult to see

---

212 Article 12 of the Treaty refers both to 'boundary' and 'boundaries' between North and South. Did the negotiators envisage the possibility of a geographically dispersed Northern Ireland? Or was this just casual drafting?

213 J. McColgan, 'Lionel Curtis and constitutional procedures', *IHS*, 20, 79 (March, 1977), p. 333, notes that 'both sides' in the Treaty negotiations, and not merely the impossible

how de Valera could have extracted anything further on the oath than the Treaty conceded. He showed curiously little grasp of Lloyd George's precarious political position as prime minister of a coalition dominated by Conservatives. De Valera thought that this coalition 'precluded the usual Tory opposition' whereas it severely limited Lloyd George's room for manoeuvre.[214]

If de Valera could not have improved the terms of the oath, could he have salvaged something by engineering a break on Ulster? Craig, now prime minister of Northern Ireland, confident of Conservative support, rejected attempts by Lloyd George to persuade him to budge on the border. Nevertheless, de Valera would have found it difficult to break on Ulster. He was known to be a relative moderate on the Ulster question. He had already courageously told the Dáil that he would not be a party to the coercion of Ulster, and was prepared to accept popular decisions to opt out on a county basis.[215] He could, of course, pretend to break on Ulster. But it was unlikely that Collins and Griffith, knowing his real views, would have long submitted to his will if they found the rest of the Treaty broadly acceptable.

And what did breaking on Ulster mean? It meant breaking on the Boundary Commission, which seemed to offer a possibility of revising the Government of Ireland Act after Sinn Féin had already sold the pass on partition. The Boundary Commission was the best that de Valera himself was hoping for at that particular state. He incorporated it verbatim into the first version of his Document no. 2.[216] The essentially subordinate role of partition in cabinet thinking emerges from the mainly tactical role allotted to 'Ulster' in the advice tendered to the delegation. If there was to be a break, they should try to arrange that it would appear to come on Ulster. But there should be no break on Ulster if other demands were conceded. The Treaty debate showed that the cabinet accurately reflected Dáil sentiment on this point. The boundary issue scarcely intruded into the debate, so obsessed were the members with the oath.[217] 'The break on Ulster' would almost certainly have required too much stylised acting to have long sustained fragile Sinn Féin unity.

Lloyd George could not, even if he wanted to, deliver unity in the face of resistance by Ulster unionists, supported by the Conservatives. It was part of Lloyd George's negotiating achievement to have bewitched Arthur Griffith into believing that he could, though Griffith merely reflected the

---

metaphysical Irish, were obsessed with symbols. See also G.W. Boyce, *Englishmen and Irish troubles* (London, 1972), p. 83.
[214] Boyce, *Englishmen*, pp. 182–4.   [215] Moynihan, *Speeches*, pp. 69, 72.
[216] His revised version of Document No. 2 did not adopt the Boundary Commission quite so explicitly as the first version, but his general approach remained unchanged.
[217] Maureen Wall, 'Partition: the Ulster question (1916–1926)', in T.D. Williams (ed.), *The Irish struggle*, p. 87.

immaturity of nationalist thinking about Ulster in allowing himself to be deluded.[218] De Valera, like Griffith and Collins, assumed that the Boundary Commission would so emasculate Northern Ireland that the rump would be forced into a united Ireland for economic self-preservation. All nationalists, whatever their position on the Treaty, insisted on misinterpreting the Ulster situation. They would predictably complain in due course when nobody came to rescue them for the consequences of their own proclivity for self-deception.

The main gain de Valera might have made in London was simply time. He would hardly have been so mesmerised by the brilliance of Lloyd George's performance as to accept the artificial deadline 'the Welsh wizard' succeeded in imposing. Lloyd George would certainly not wage war 'within three days' simply because de Valera insisted on more time, even if he convinced the susceptible delegates that he would.[219]

Even then, the consequences remain hypothetical. The assumption lurking behind the familiar question, why did the delegates sign before consulting the cabinet in Dublin, whether in person or by phone, is that the outcome would have been different. This silently assumes – it was an assumption de Valera himself liked to make – that the cabinet was in Dublin. In fact, only four members were in Dublin. Three were in London. A discussion could have altered little, unless de Valera could persuade Barton to change his mind once more. Once Barton had signed, and he would not renege on his signature, however reluctantly given, the pivotal position in the cabinet belonged to W.T. Cosgrave, the only uncommitted member. Collins, Griffith and Barton were for the Treaty, de Valera, Brugha and Stack against. It was not until 7 December that de Valera apparently suddenly realised that Cosgrave favoured acceptance.[220] De Valera, probably contrary to his calculations, found himself abruptly in a minority in the cabinet. It was now 4:3 against him, instead of the 5:2 for him that he could have anticipated in October.

If de Valera had gained time in London, what would time have gained? It is an illusion to assume that had the Treaty not been signed, everything could have continued simply as before, irrespective of the validity of Lloyd George's threat. De Valera might claim that he had seen politics for the first time in the manoeuvring after the arrival home of the signatories.[221] This was a disingenuous plea from a man 'who emerged from the American experience a hardened politician'.[222] Postures had now been struck, positions staked, animosities surfaced, insults hurled, that would neither be forgotten nor forgiven. Henceforth, whatever the immediate

---

[218] F.S.L. Lyons, 'Days of decision', in B. Farrell (ed.), *The Irish parliamentary tradition* (Dublin, 1973), p. 242.
[219] J.M. Curran, *The birth of the Irish Free State 1921–1923* (London, 1980), p. 129.
[220] Longford and O'Neill, *De Valera*, p. 168.   [221] *Ibid.*, p. 178.
[222] McCartney, 'De Valera's mission', p. 320.

outcome, there would be a bitter struggle between Collins and de Valera, both now fully alert to the incompatibility between their policies and personalities. Neither could reconcile himself for long to the role of second-in-command. Two ruthless men would inevitably be locked in a struggle for leadership, de Valera with the ruthlessness of righteousness, Collins with the ruthlessness of necessity.

Had Lloyd George implemented his threat of war – and it is possible that if he did not he would have been pushed aside by Bonar Law[223] – then the IRA would have had to face a formidably reinforced British army.[224] This weighed heavily with Collins, but his critics tended to pay scant attention to the military balance, maintaining that the principle involved in the oath could not be compromised, whatever the consequences. Anti-Treaty spokesmen paid equally scant attention to the wishes, however putative, of the mere Irish at this stage. De Valera found himself in a dilemma. His address to the electorate before the May 1921 election insisted that Sinn Féin stood not only for 'the legitimacy of the republic' but also 'for the right of the people of this nation to determine freely for themselves how they shall be governed and for the right of every citizen to an equal voice in the determination'.[225] De Valera acknowledged as early as 15 December that the majority would support the Treaty, though under duress.[226] Ever scrupulous, de Valera would extricate himself by formulating the principle that 'the people have never a right to do wrong'.[227]

It was ironic that those most critical of the delegates for failing to consult the cabinet were themselves so reluctant to consult the people. Many deputies, returned in an uncontested election, found themselves facing their constituents for virtually the first time during the Christmas recess. Public opinion seemed clearly in favour,[228] and the Dáil eventually accepted the Treaty on 7 January 1922 by 64 votes to 57. The debate exposed not only the intensity of the passions, and the occasional nobility of purpose, but the viciousness of personal animosities, and the mediocrity of mind of many deputies. The narrowness of the majority in favour of the Treaty hardly reflected public opinion at that stage. The majority in the country was already probably significantly larger than the majority in the Dáil.

Griffith was elected president of the Dáil by 60 votes to 58 for de Valera on 10 January. But real responsibility for launching the new state on a safe course lay with the Provisional Government, established under the Treaty, in obscure constitutional and administrative circumstances, for a

---

223 F.S.L. Lyons, 'The great debate', in Farrell, *Parliamentary tradition*, pp. 251–3. Longford and O'Neill, *De Valera*, p. 169, argue the contrary case.
224 Townshend, *British campaign*, p. 196.
225 D. Macardle, *The Irish Republic* (London, 1968 edn), p. 857.
226 Moynihan, *Speeches*, p. 86.   227 Ryle Dwyer, *De Valera*, p. 64.
228 Longford and O'Neill, *De Valera*, p. 175.

maximum period of one year with Collins as chairman.[229] The Irish had long been accustomed to hearing that they were incapable of self-government. It remained to be seen how they would cope with the responsibility.

[229] J. McColgan, *British policy and the Irish administration 1920–22* (London, 1983), pp. 91ff.

Chapter 2

CONSOLIDATION:
1922–1932

CIVIL WARS

Collins had no time to savour the satisfaction of taking over Dublin Castle, the centre of English administration in Ireland, on 16 January. The threat of civil war already hung ominously over the infant state. As early as 17 December 1921, Liam Mellowes repudiated the right of the Dáil, or indeed of anybody, to accept the Treaty. 'We who stand by the Republic still will I presume rebel against the new government that would be set up if this Treaty is passed.'[1] Relations became further strained as the debate proceeded. The anti-Treaty deputies, refusing to accept the verdict of the majority, boycotted the Dáil after losing the vote.

Both Treaty and anti-Treaty forces were internally divided between moderates and extremists. Griffith despaired of finding common ground with his critics. He was confident of public support, and impatient to embark on the historic task of state building. He therefore sought an early general election, urging confrontation with any elements that refused to abide by a majority verdict. Collins proved more reluctant to contemplate confrontation. He liked to imagine himself a bluff simple soldier, but he pursued both a more circuitous and a more conciliatory policy than the civilian Griffith. He hoped against hope that civil war could be avoided. If it could not, he wanted time to build up an army, for most of the active IRA units were probably anti-Treaty.[2] He therefore pursued a devious policy, intent on postponing confrontation as long as possible.

Both sides manoeuvred to get their men into key military positions. Pro-Treaty forces, finally deployed only at 4.00 a.m. the previous night, took possession of Beggars Bush Barracks in Dublin when it was evacuated by the British on 1 February, forestalling its seizure by the

[1] DD, private sessions, 1921–1922 (Dublin, n.d.), 17 December 1921, p. 243.
[2] J. O'Beirne-Ranelagh, 'The IRB from the Treaty to 1924', *IHS*, 20, 77 (March 1976), p. 33. On Collins and the police see C. Brady, *Guardians of the Peace* (Dublin, 1974), pp. 35–70, esp. 43, 48.

anti-Treaty section of the Dublin City Brigade.[3] During February and March the anti-Treaty forces infiltrated the new Regular army. They were apparently foiled from seizing, by an internal coup, Beggars Bush Barracks only half an hour before the designated time, on the eve of a Volunteer Convention of 26 March, which registered the formal split in the IRA. Over 200 delegates defied General Headquarters' instructions by assembling at the convention in Dublin. Collins probably still lacked the force, even if he had the will, to crush them. At the convention Rory O'Connor and Liam Mellowes repudiated the authority of the Dáil. They showed their respect for freedom of the press on 29 March by destroying the office of the pro-Treaty *Freeman's Journal*.[4] On 9 April this faction declared itself independent of civilian authority, assumed all responsibility for public order, and proposed to postpone elections 'while the threat of war with England exists'.[5] On 14 April, they seized the Four Courts, throwing down the gauntlet to the Provisional Government.

After the Volunteer Convention in March, Collins concentrated on winning the loyalty of as many Volunteers as possible. Gearóid Ó Sullivan and Seán MacMahon, his close colleagues on GHQ staff, sought to weed out anti-Treaty elements. 'From the time of the Irregular Convention up to the end of June it was a matter of both sides organising as swiftly as possible, and making every effort to sway both officers and men throughout the country.'[6]

Like Collins, de Valera groped for compromise. In moral and political stature he stood head and shoulders above everyone on the anti-Treaty side. Nevertheless, his performance in this period has been strongly criticised by some serious scholars.[7] It is true that he got his calculations wrong. Like Collins, he was the victim of his own capacity for grasping the complexity of situations, and trying to reconcile a range of considerations inconceivable to more primitive intelligences. He might indeed have been more successful had he been less sensitive to the delicacy of the situation. In the end, he fell between several stools. He could not safely appeal to public opinion, which he knew supported the Treaty. Neither could he appeal unequivocally to the anti-Treaty militarists. Mellowes and O'Connor detested his capacity for conciliation. From a practical military point of view they may have been right. Time was on the side of the Provisional Government. De Valera's agreement with Collins in February

---

[3] RM, P7/C/14, Army Inquiry Committee, Statement submitted by General Seán MacMahon, 5 May 1924, Section II, pp. 22ff.
[4] Curran, *Birth*, pp. 172–3.   [5] Macardle, *Republic*, p. 633.
[6] RM, P7/C/14, Army Inquiry Committee, Statement submitted by General Seán MacMahon, 5 May 1924, Section II, p. 6.
[7] T.D. Williams, 'From the Treaty to the Civil War', in Williams, *Irish struggle*, p. 124; O. MacDonagh, *Ireland* (Englewood Cliffs, 1968), p. 99. MacDonagh extends his criticism of de Valera's performance to include the whole 1918–23 period.

to postpone elections for three months may have helped erode the anti-Treaty military advantage. In trying to achieve some authority over the extreme military wing, de Valera made speeches which seemed to be inciting to civil war, though he himself maintained that he was simply warning against the danger in his own inimitable way.[8]

Collins and de Valera sought to blur the issues further by concluding an electoral pact in May. This provided that the two sections of Sinn Féin should be represented on a national Sinn Féin panel, in the election arranged for June, in proportion to their existing Dáil strength, and that 'after the election, a coalition cabinet would be formed, consisting of the President elected as formerly, the Minister of Defence representing the army, and nine other ministers, five from the majority party and four from the minority, each party to choose its own nominees'.[9] Other parties were graciously permitted to enter the contest. On the face of it, this pact was devised for a fantasy world. A Dáil and a cabinet constituted on these lines would simply restore the January situation, and would seem bound to result in recriminatory deadlock. The pact presumed to deny the Irish people much voice in the choice of Dáil or cabinet. However, it may not have been quite so straightforward, or so naive, as it seemed.

Collins entered the pact in defiance of the indignant expostulations of Churchill, now acting as watch-dog for British interests. Collins could be forgiven for feeling that Churchill's denunciations of the pact as 'an outrage of democratic principles' would have carried more conviction had it not come from one who had cheerfully denied democratic rights to the Irish for so long. Collins claimed to Churchill that the Dáil returned under the pact election would be a constituent assembly, not a parliament, and that its sole purpose would be the drafting of a constitution. He further claimed, probably more validly, that the pact was the only way of ensuring that an election could be held at all, given the anxiety of the anti-Treaty forces to prevent a popular verdict. Griffith happily contemplated relegating the four anti-Treaty ministers to 'extern' ministries, which would in effect leave the ministers members of the cabinet but not of the government! At an even more tactical level, the pact may have been intended by Collins and his advisers, as Kevin O'Higgins claimed, to split the anti-Treaty forces, by giving de Valera and his followers a face-saving way of dissociating themselves from the militarists. From de Valera's point of view, the pact had the attraction of continuing the political process, arresting the apparently inevitable slide towards war. De Valera could hope to retrieve something of his former authority only if politics remained the main medium of exchange.[10]

[8] Moynihan, *Speeches*, pp. 97–102.   [9] Longford and O'Neill, *De Valera*, p. 188.
[10] This paragraph is based on T. Towey, 'The reaction of the British government to the 1922 Collins–de Valera pact', *IHS*, 22, 85 (March 1980), pp. 65–76.

Two further considerations influenced Collins's procrastinating performance in 1922. He hoped, vainly, to circumvent the Treaty by devising a republican constitution acceptable to anti-Treaty opinion. British opposition, oblivious of the human cost to Ireland, and at least in some quarters relishing the prospect of civil war among the wretched natives, compelled him to modify the constitution in accordance with the Treaty. The constitution therefore contained the hated oath, and made provision for a governor-general. In a piece of sharp practice, Collins didn't publish the constitution until the morning of the election.[11] This deprived him of some of the credit of electoral victory by permitting anti-Treaty spokesmen to claim that the electorate did not have time to consider the constitution. However opportunistic this argument, Collins's behaviour did smack of the 'too clever by half' variety at this stage.

Collins therefore failed to achieve a constitution of conciliation. He was no more successful in his other area of major concern, Ulster. The events of 1920–1 further exacerbated ancestral animosities in Ulster. Sectarian riots in Derry and Belfast in the summer of 1920 claimed at least eighty-two victims. Soaring unemployment in the postwar slump, particularly severe in ship-building, put a premium on jobs. Protestant workers naturally expelled Catholics from the Belfast shipyards. Sinn Féin could think of no more imaginative response than a boycott of Belfast goods from September 1920, a striking application of 'one nation' theory![12] In the face of the deteriorating security situation, Protestants in border areas felt particularly vulnerable. From April 1920 Sir Basil Brooke organised paramilitary forces in Fermanagh and Tyrone to maintain the Protestant ascendancy. In October 1920 these groups were formalised, with British consent, as the Ulster Special Constabulary. The part-time B Specials, who soon acquired an unsavoury reputation among Catholics, were the key category here. Their propensity to *Herrenvolk* behaviour was controlled to an extent by enrolling them as Specials and subjecting them to some discipline, however inadequate this may have seemed to their victims.

When Sir Edward Carson, his hope of retaining a united Ireland within the United Kingdom blighted by the Government of Ireland Act, resigned as Ulster Unionist leader in February 1921, James Craig abandoned a promising political career in London to succeed him. The Ulster constituencies under the Government of Ireland Act were naturally arranged to maximise Unionist seats at the general election in May 1921. Unionists duly won 40 of the 52 seats, including 4 of 8 in Fermanagh and Tyrone

11 The revised draft of the constitution was not apparently ready until then, but Collins may not have been unduly disturbed at the delay.
12 D.S. Johnson, 'The Belfast boycott 1920–22', in J.M. Goldstrom and L.A. Clarkson (eds.), *Irish population, economy and society: essays in honour of the late K.H. Connell* (Oxford, 1981), pp. 287ff.

with 43 per cent of the vote. Craig showed his customary physical courage in travelling to meet de Valera in Dublin in May 1921, but de Valera's dialectic made little impression on his shrewd and rugged mind. He began immediately to consolidate his new regime, devotedly nursing the infant state through a convulsive first year. He proved, then as later, more than a match for all the negotiators he confronted, including such elusive customers as de Valera and Lloyd George. Craig could be neither cowed nor cajoled. He was willing to contemplate compromise, but only within the limits permitted by the temper of his Conservative allies in London and his own followers in the North. He took care to provide sufficient 'police' protection of Protestants to crush all Catholic threats. By mid-1922 there was one armed policeman to every two Catholic families in Northern Ireland. He dissolved the county councils of Fermanagh and Tyrone when they dared declare allegiance to the Dáil in late 1921. He sought to reassure Protestants in the border areas, panic stricken at the threat of the Boundary Commission, by interpreting Article XII of the Treaty in a manner that would restrict territorial changes to minimal local adjustments.[13]

The Treaty further embittered feelings in the North, which distinguished itself with atrocities that sound gruesome even in permissive retrospect. During the first six months of 1922, 171 Catholics and 93 Protestants were killed, often in the most revolting circumstances.[14] On a per capita basis, Protestants were scoring four kills to every one by Catholics. Craig introduced a Special Powers Act in April 1922, suspending the normal processes of law and empowering the Minister for Home Affairs with virtually dictatorial authority. He next introduced internment on 24 May, following particularly bloody clashes, and the military imposed a curfew from 1 June 1922.[15]

Collins wavered in his attitude towards the North at least until June. He had made his basic position clear during the Treaty negotiations:[16]

By force we could beat them perhaps, but perhaps not. I do not think we could beat them morally. If you kill all of us, every man and every male child, the difficulty will still be there. So in Ulster. That is why we do not want to coerce them, but . . . if we are not going to coerce the North East corner, the North East corner must not be allowed to coerce.

It was not incompatible with this basic viewpoint that Collins should react passionately to reports of Protestant pogroms in Belfast in spring 1922. It was more surprising that he should have made so little allowance for

[13] D.W. Harkness, *Northern Ireland since 1920* (Dublin, 1983), pp. 18–25; Buckland, *Northern Ireland*, pp. 31–54.
[14] See representative reports in *Irish Times*, 2, 19 June 1922.
[15] Harkness, *Northern Ireland*, pp. 29–30; Buckland, *Northern Ireland*, pp. 40–47.
[16] Jones, *Whitehall diary*, p. 131.

Craig's difficulties in trying to control his gunmen. Collins promised, in the course of three meetings with Craig in early 1922, to try to curb IRA attacks in the North, in return for a reorganisation of the Royal Ulster Constabulary to provide Catholics with some representation in, and protection from, the police.

Collins reacted furiously at what he took to be Craig's failure to fully implement his side of the bargain. But he himself allowed arms to be transferred via the anti-Treaty IRA to the Northern IRA, hoping to simultaneously protect vulnerable Northern Catholics and postpone a final rupture with the anti-Treaty forces.[17] While avowedly pursuing a peace policy towards the North, the Provisional Government rejected cooperation on a variety of minor matters in April 1922 because of 'the failure of the Belfast government to abide by the terms of the [Craig/Collins] agreement'.[18] This decision was taken in a fit of pique. It was contrary to all reason for a government intent on keeping the door to unity open. During this tantrum, the Provisional Government broke off a joint railway inquiry, and refused cooperation on questions of technical instruction. As late as 4 May, Collins went so far as to demand schemes from all ministers 'for non-cooperation in every possible way with the northern parliament. And, in addition, a scheme towards making it impossible for them to carry on.'[19] Only Agriculture, Education, and Finance responded actively to this injunction, and from early June onwards the government adopted a vacillating policy, insofar as it had a policy at all. On 19 August, following the appointment on 1 August of a Cabinet Committee to assess Northern policy, 'it was considered desirable that a peace policy should be adopted in regard to future dealings with North East Ulster'.[20]

How Collins would have responded to this suggestion – he only rarely attended meetings after 12 July, when he announced to the cabinet that he 'would not be able to act in his ministerial capacity until further notice', as he was taking over the duties of Commander-in-Chief, Cosgrave being appointed Acting Chairman and Acting Minister of Finance in his absence[21] – or how far he was kept fully aware of cabinet thinking on developments in this area, remains unclear. He may himself have been moving towards a more conciliatory position, whether out of conviction or expediency, torn by conflicting emotions though he doubtless remained. Even after his death, the cabinet, while groping for a way to disengage from Northern commitments, continued support for a Catholic

17 Lawlor, *Britain and Ireland*, pp. 184–5.
18 SPO, S1801A, Provisional Government Minutes, 21 April 1922.
19 *Ibid.*, 4 May 1922.
20 McColgan, *British policy*, pp. 111–12; Lawlor, *Britain and Ireland*, pp. 186ff; SPO, Provisional Government Minutes, 19 August 1922.
21 SPO, Provisional Government Minutes, 12 July 1922, morning.

teachers boycott of the Northern Ministry of Education until November.[22]

The Ulster question played relatively little role in the June general election, which revealed some intriguing voting patterns.[23] The bulk of anti-Treaty support appears to have come from poorer voters. But a substantial proportion of the poor, perhaps a majority, seems to have supported the Treaty. The Labour party, which was pro-Treaty, made unexpected gains, and Labour voters appear to have mainly transferred their later preferences, under proportional representation, to the pro-Treaty party.[24] The verdict of the people, whatever their mixture of motives, and whatever the constraints under which they voted, was clear. Even de Valera, never one to concede a case prematurely, privately admitted the anti-Treaty defeat.[25] The response of the militarist anti-Treaty forces remained to be seen.

Rory O'Connor and Liam Mellowes were as contemptuous as any Black and Tan of the opinion of the mere Irish as recorded in the election result. Having repudiated in April the legitimacy of any civil authority, they next repudiated, on 18 June, the authority of even the anti-Treaty IRA in general, and of its leader, Liam Lynch, in particular, when an Extraordinary Convention of the anti-Treaty IRA rejected their proposal to attack the remaining British soldiers in Dublin before they could withdraw from Ireland.[26] The assassination on 22 June of Sir Henry Wilson, military adviser to the Ulster government, probably on the orders of Collins,[27] who partly blamed him for the Belfast pogrom, provoked London into demanding immediate action against the Four Courts garrison, which it chose to hold responsible for the assassination. Collins reacted indignantly to the English communication, but he finally delivered an ultimatum on 28 June to vacate the Four Courts after the garrison had seized his deputy Chief of Staff in retaliation for the arrest of one of its own officers caught commandeering transport. When O'Connor refused, Collins attacked.[28]

It is not clear how clinically Collins had calculated the military odds. Dublin had declared by a majority of seven to one in favour of the Treaty.[29] But the military situation appears to have been finely balanced. Collins apparently had only about 8000 men altogether, only

[22] Harkness, *Northern Ireland*, p. 27.
[23] M. Gallagher, 'The pact general election of 1922', *IHS*, 21, 84 (September 1979), pp. 404–21.
[24] *Irish Times*, 19 June 1922.   [25] Ryle Dwyer, *De Valera*, p. 66.
[26] Macardle, *Republic*, p. 669.
[27] A sympathetic biographer of Collins leaves the issue open: Ó Broin, *Collins*, pp. 133–4.
[28] The decision-making process leading to the attack on the Four Courts remains a matter for debate. There is more than one plausible 'balance of probabilities'. Longford and O'Neill, *De Valera*, pp. 189–93, offer a reasoned presentation of the anti-Treaty viewpoint.
[29] *Irish Times*, 21 June 1922.

6000 of them armed, and only 3000 in Dublin.[30] His troops, who had little training, were exhausted after two days fighting 'and had to be urged to continue. It was the dash and courage of most of the officers who led the men . . . that brought us through and "cleaned up" the city.'[31]

Had O'Connor, Mellowes, Oscar Traynor and Cathal Brugha preserved their freedom of manoeuvre instead of cooping themselves up in the city centre they might have stood a better chance. The ineptness of their tactical dispositions on this crucial occasion might even prompt ungenerous reflections on the intelligence, as distinct from the courage, of their contributions to the independence struggle. The Four Courts surrendered on 30 June. The remaining anti-Treaty groups were driven back on the south within a week. In another six weeks the apparently strong initial position[32] of the anti-Treaty 'Irregulars' crumbled, as the Free State troops drove them out of the towns. A key struggle occurred around Limerick, a link between the Irregular forces in the south and west, from which they were driven between 15 and 23 July.[33] In July the government intensified recruitment, calling for 20 000 men immediately. The military outcome of the war was now only a matter of time, particularly as the recruitment drive swelled the size of the government forces to 55 000 in the next nine months. But the political situation was transformed when Griffith died suddenly on 10 August in Dublin and Collins was killed on 22 August in an ambush at Béalnabláth in his native Cork.

Though Griffith's judgement was clear and firm in early 1922, he seems to have been already in rapid physical decline before August.[34] His death probably did not seriously influence the course of subsequent events. The death of Collins, however, was the great public tragedy – indeed the only *public* tragedy – of the civil war. There were many private tragedies, apart from Griffith's death, like the killing of Harry Boland, the execution of Erskine Childers, the assassination of Seán Hales, the death in action of Cathal Brugha and Liam Lynch. But no other senior casualty, however tragic his death, however noble his character, however worthy his contribution to the struggle for independence, possessed pre-eminent abilities to distinguish him from the survivors. There may have been among the more obscure victims major potential contributors to the building of a new state.[35] If Seán Lemass, a junior member of the Four Courts garrison, had been killed, he would have counted as simply one more faceless casualty. Of the senior victims, however, none except

30 RM, P7/C/14, Statement submitted by General Seán MacMahon to Army Inquiry Committee, 5 May 1924, Section II, p. 13.
31 *Ibid.*   32 Lyons, *Ireland* (1973 edn), pp. 462–3.
33 RM, P7/C/14, Statement submitted by General Seán MacMahon to Army Inquiry Committee, 5 May 1924, Section II, p. 16.
34 Ó'Broin, *Collins*, p. 140.
35 Lyons, *Ireland* (1973 edn), p. 467, suggests up to 4000 may have died. This seems high.

Collins was irreplaceable. Only Collins might, just possibly, have significantly influenced the course of history. He dominated, insofar as any one man could dominate a guerrilla campaign, the military effort between 1919 and 1921. He grew rapidly in political stature after the Truce. He showed perception during the Treaty negotiations in anticipating the evolution of the Commonwealth more accurately than de Valera, or perhaps even Lloyd George.[36] In signing the Treaty he showed a moral courage rarely found in men of bravado disposition. It may be that as Chairman of the Provisional Government 'he tried to do too much'[37] to avert civil war, but then he needed time. Though buffeted by many contrary winds, and failing to reconcile the irreconcilable, his performance as a political tactician was at least as able as de Valera's in this traumatic period, and de Valera himself could hardly rival the popular electoral appeal of 'the finest of crowd psychologists . . . laying hands on the mood of the people'.[38]

Collins's final speeches, however garbed in generalities, however swayed by electoral calculations, suggest an ambition, unique among his colleagues in the Provisional Government, to create not only a new state but a new society. He professed to seek a country distinguished by social justice, economic efficiency, cultural achievement and political tolerance. 'We must not have', he warned, 'the destitution of poverty at one end, and at the other an excess of riches in possession of a few individuals.'[39] He scoffed at de Valera's belief that the people must be kept poor to nurture their idealism. He retorted that, on the contrary, 'In the ancient days of Gaelic civilisation the people were prosperous and they were not materialists. They were one of the most spiritual and intellectual peoples in Europe . . . We want such widely diffused prosperity that the Irish people will not be cursed by destitution into living practically "the lives of the beasts".'[40] He wanted to expand educational opportunity, to expropriate ranchers and urban land speculators, to embark on massive housing schemes to abolish the hideous urban slums, to harness the Shannon for electricity, to industrialise rapidly, to implement worker participation in management, and to generally foster a flourishing economy in the hope that 'a prosperous Ireland will mean a united Ireland'.[41]

Collins's vision was, no doubt, unhistorical and perhaps naive. And there is many a slip between public platforms and departmental desk. It would be unwise to hypothesise on the course Collins would have pursued

---

36 D.W. Harkness, *The restless dominion* (London, 1969), pp. 16–17; D.W. Harkness, 'Patrick McGilligan: man of commonwealth', *Journal of Imperial and Commonwealth History*, 5, 1 (October 1979), 121.
37 Williams, 'From the Treaty to the Civil War', p. 124.
38 *Irish Times*, 17 June 1922.
39 M. Collins, *The path to freedom* (Cork, 1968), p. 108.   40 *Ibid.*, p. 106.
41 *Ibid.*, pp. 106–17.

in an independent Ireland. He clearly had the convenient knack of leaving different people with congenial but conflicting impressions of his real policy. He was still a very young man at the time of his death, still learning, still developing. Which of his possibly inconsistent legacies he himself would have chosen must remain a matter of speculation. Circumstances would make many strange bedfellows in later years. Evidence could be found, on the basis of his performance as Chairman of the Provisional Government and as Minister for Finance, to support almost any assumption about his probable future policies. He was instrumental in having Joseph Brennan, who was to prove an arch-conservative, appointed to a senior position in the Department of Finance. He was determined that Finance should secure control, in best Treasury fashion, over the whole civil service.[42] He approved the loan of British Treasury officials in March and April 1922 to help organise the new Department. This may suggest that he was a willing slave to orthodoxy. And one could quote evidence to suggest that he would have become an even sterner advocate of the conventional economic wisdom than did his successors. But cases can also be cited where he brushed aside the conventional Treasury wisdom as he felt circumstances required.[43] He appears to have at least envisaged the possibility of significant innovations in departmental policies once the electorate gave a mandate for a new government.[44]

On a key question, the role of the Treasury, it may not be altogether fanciful to see in the handling of a relatively minor matter an indication of the gap that would open between the spirit of Collins and the approach of his successors. Collins suggested shortly before his death that a commission should be established to adjudicate on army pay, dependants' allowances and pensions for the wounded. He envisaged this commission as consisting of a chairman appointed by the government, one representative each from the government, the Treasury and the army authorities, and 'a representative who would be in touch with, and sympathetic to, the rank and file'.[45] Richard Mulcahy, his successor as Commander in Chief, advised against the appointment of any representative of the rank and file.[46] The commission as finally constituted consisted of a chairman representing the government, two representatives of the Treasury (Department of Finance), and two representatives of the army authorities.[47] The 'Treasury' had won a stronger position than intended by Collins. It may be that circumstances would also have compelled him to concede 'Treasury' primacy in the formulation of social and economic

[42] R. Fanning, *The Irish Department of Finance* (Dublin, 1978), p. 39.
[43] J. McColgan, 'Partition and the Irish administration 1920–22', *Administration*, 28, 2 (1980), p. 170.
[44] Fanning, *Finance*, p. 57.
[45] SPO, S1302, Mulcahy to Chairman, Provisional Government, 7 September 1922.
[46] *Ibid.*   [47] *Ibid.*, containing Provisional Government Minute, 12 September 1922.

policy in general, but that his successors could have adopted this different emphasis within a month of his death does suggest instinctive differences of approach between him and them.

Collins was capable not only of boisterous but of immature behaviour.
He could be histrionic and maudlin. In his final fateful days he seems to
have behaved like a caricature of his own glamorised image. If he really
believed that 'no one is going to shoot me in my own county', as he is
reputed to have said,[48] he showed a suicidal lapse of judgement. On the
day he died he had no need to stop to fight at the ambush site, but he
dismissed advice to drive on, behaving more like a cowboy than a head
of government. Yet, it is difficult to remember he was only thirty-one at
the time of his death, so pervasive had his presence become. He had
shown a striking capacity to grow into his earlier responsibilities, and it
is not unreasonable to assume that he would have continued to learn, as
would de Valera, from experience. It would certainly be presumptuous
to assert that one who accomplished so much so quickly could not have
risen to further challenges. It can at least be surmised that if he couldn't
have left his mark, then no one could. His unrivalled combination of
ability, energy, vision and magnanimity meant that his survival might,
just conceivably, have made a difference to the performance of the new
state.

The 42-year-old W.T. Cosgrave, the senior surviving civilian member
of the cabinet, was preferred by his colleagues to Mulcahy, more closely
identified with the army, for the succession. Collins's death removed the
main conciliating influence in the cabinet and inevitably hardened the
resolve of the survivors.[49]

After abortive peace moves in September, the government, reinforced
by episcopal denunciation of the Irregulars in October,[50] was granted
special powers by the Dáil to impose the death penalty for a variety of
offences after the expiry of an amnesty offer. Seventy-seven anti-Treaty
prisoners were executed between November 1922 and May 1923. The
execution of Erskine Childers in November provoked Liam Lynch, the
anti-Treaty leader, into adopting a retaliatory policy of assassination
against prominent Free State supporters. The consequent assassination
of one Dáil deputy, Seán Hales, and the wounding of a second deputy,
Pádraig Ó Máille, on 7 December, in turn provoked the government into
the summary reprisal execution of four senior anti-Treaty prisoners,
including Rory O'Connor and Liam Mellowes, on 8 December. Government resolve had so hardened at this stage that Cosgrave resisted a desperate attempt by his personal friend, the Archbishop of Dublin, Edward

[48] Ó'Broin, *Collins*, p. 141.   [49] Lawlor, *Britain and Ireland*, p. 201.
[50] D.F. Keogh, *The Vatican, the bishops and Irish politics 1919–39* (Cambridge, 1986),
pp. 95–6.

Byrne, to have the decision reconsidered.[51] Opinions differ on whether the executions shortened the war, and thus saved innocent lives, or prolonged it by reinforcing the resolve of the anti-Treaty forces.[52] There were no more assassinations of Dáil deputies. But relatives of leading Treaty supporters, including an uncle of Cosgrave and the father of Kevin O'Higgins, Minister for Home Affairs, were murdered.[53] This sordid struggle brought out most of the worst and little of the best in the belligerents. The 'terrible beauty' had become far more terrible than beautiful.[54] After the obdurate Liam Lynch was killed in April, the anti-Treaty forces dumped their arms on the orders of Frank Aiken, the first Irregular military leader over whom the hapless de Valera recovered some influence.[55]

The civil war was fought ostensibly over the Treaty, and particularly the oath.[56] But the Treaty was merely the occasion, not the cause, of the war. The cause was the basic conflict in nationalist doctrine between majority right and divine right. The issue was whether the Irish people had the right to choose their own government at any time according to their judgement of the existing circumstances. The clash might have been evaded but for the Treaty, but once the issue surfaced the choice lay between democracy and dictatorship. It did not necessarily follow that all Free Staters were instinctive democrats, and all Irregulars instinctive autocrats. Most of the leaders on both sides were, after all, veterans of the Easter Rising. The 'democratic' justification of the Rising was that the majority of the Irish people had reputedly opposed it only on tactical grounds, not in principle. The anti-Treaty forces might maintain, and some did maintain, that the majority of the Irish people supported the Treaty only on tactical grounds, and not in principle. If it could be shown that resistance was not impractical, then the anti-Treaty forces, like the 1916 rebels, might be legitimised by posterity. Some Free Staters, like Eoin O'Duffy and Ernest Blythe, who would later display distinctly autocratic tendencies, found their views now chancing to coincide with majority opinion. Some of the vanquished would in different circumstances come to embrace democracy and abide by adverse majority verdicts. 'There were many who took sides against the Treaty who had their spiritual home on the constitutional side and there were those who followed

---

[51] *Ibid.*, pp. 97–8.   [52] *Ibid.*, pp. 99–100.

[53] Ryle Dwyer, *De Valera*, p. 69; T. de Vere White, *Kevin O'Higgins* (Tralee, 1966), pp. 148–50.

[54] Frank O'Connor, *An only child* (London, 1964), pp. 240–4, conveys the fetid atmosphere. For details see C. Younger, *Ireland's Civil War* (London, 1970 edn), pp. 458–9, 501; Brady, *Guardians*, pp. 81, 91.

[55] Longford and O'Neill, *De Valera*, pp. 219ff.

[56] It was the late Maureen Wall who impressed on historical consciousness that it was the oath, not partition, that dominated the Treaty debate. See Wall, 'Partition', in Williams (ed.), *Irish struggle*, pp. 79–94.

Collins who would have been equally happy on the hillsides.'[57] Indeed, within only two years Kevin O'Higgins would be denouncing Richard Mulcahy as a bad democrat.[58] Probably only a minority of the anti-Treaty forces held that their will should be mandatory on the natives in all circumstances. Collins himself behaved more like a democrat than would many a man of his temperament in the circumstances, but it is not inconceivable that situations would have subsequently arisen in which he would have found the idea of at least a plebiscitary presidency not uncongenial. How long could he have preserved patience with the incompetence, and perhaps with the conservatism, of lesser men about him, and resisted the temptation to veer towards a version of Bonapartism?

In the event the aspiring military dictators were crushed. The mere Irish were not to exchange one jackboot for another. If the civil war illustrated with a vengeance the potential for autocracy lurking in Irish political culture, it illustrated even more emphatically the potential for democracy. Contrary to a comforting Irish illusion, civil wars were not normal events in the new states of the time. For all their internal instability, only two of the new east European states, Finland and Hungary, managed to mount civil wars after independence: and even they found substantive social issues on which to fight. India's civil conflict ran along ethnic and religious lines. It approximated more a Catholic–Protestant conflict in Ireland than a civil war of hibernian vintage. The Irish civil war must be attributed more to native genius than to the inescapable logic of universal historical circumstances.

The war occupies so pivotal a place in modern Irish history, and bequeathed so poisonous a legacy, that one must wonder if Collins and de Valera ought not to have made even greater efforts to avert it. Nevertheless, obdurate questions remain for more probing future investigation. The fragile coalition of Sinn Féin had already torn itself apart. The civil war was the consequence, not the cause, of the split. Of course it intensified the bitterness. But it was already certain that the body politic would be disfigured by vicious personal animosities for the foreseeable future. Nor did the fact of war in itself preordain the subsequent use that would be made of it in party politics. The impact of civil wars depends to some extent on the nature of the political cultures in which they occur. There could be quite different reactions among the participants themselves, ranging from an anxiety to never-let-it-happen-again to a lust for revenge. Some survivors suppressed their feelings in the interest of the national good. Others would miss no opportunity to lacerate the wounds.

Foul deeds were done during the civil war. It was natural that memories should be bitter. But it is necessary to keep the scale of the conflict, and

[57] De Vere White, *O'Higgins*, p. 169.   [58] *Ibid.*, p. 167.

even its viciousness, in perspective. The most apposite analogy appears to be with the Finnish civil war cf 1918. This took place in a newly independent country with the same population as the Free State. But it claimed far more victims. Even if the probably exaggerated estimate of 4000 Irish casualties be accepted, this still falls far below the 25 000 Finnish fatalities. It may be, however, that the manner of death leaves a more searing psychological scar than the number of dead. Did not the notorious 77 executions turn the heart to stone? But the 77 falls short of the 8300 executions in Finland, to say nothing of 1500 private enterprise murders, or the 9000 who died in prison camps.[59] It was natural that civil war memories should fester in Finland. But it does not seem as if the atmosphere of Finnish politics was more polluted than that of Irish politics. Steps towards conciliation began to be taken earlier in Finland, with former enemies prepared to serve together in government after 1937.[60] If the legacy of the more modest inheritance lasted longer in Ireland, this lay more in a retrospective need for bitterness than in the nature of civil war itself. Indeed, as other distinguishing features between the main parties become more difficult to discern, only memory continued to divide them. It may be that the image of the civil war had to be burnished and polished, and the fires of hatred stoked, to foster the illusion that fundamental differences remained between the parties. However, a definitive verdict must await detailed analysis of the various ways in which the survivors used the memory of the civil war to further their purposes.

THE FREE STATE INHERITANCE

Despite the potential for instability exposed by the civil war, the rulers of the Free State entered on the task of state building with many advantages. Ireland was already a relatively modernised society.[61] Although comparisons of per capita income are notoriously difficult, Ireland's standard of living seems to have been about average for western Europe. It was, of

[59] D.G. Kirby, *Finland in the twentieth century* (London, 1979), p. 64; D.G. Kirby, 'Rank and file attitudes in the Finnish Social Democratic Party 1905–1918', *Past and Present*, 111 (May 1986), p. 160; E. Jutikkala, *A history of Finland* (London, 1962), pp. 257–9; R. Alapuro and E. Allardt, 'The Lapua movement. The threat of Rightist takeover in Finland 1930–32', in Juan J. Linz and A. Stepan, *The breakdown of democratic regimes: Europe* (London, 1978), p. 125.

[60] Kirby, *Finland*, pp. 95ff; Jutikkala, *Finland*, pp. 264, 273; M. Klinge, *A brief history of Finland* (Helsinki, 1981), pp. 106–7.

[61] B. Chubb, 'Ireland', in S. Henig (ed.), *Political parties in the European Community* (London, 1979), pp. 118–19; B. Farrell, 'The new state and Irish political culture', *Administration*, 16 (Autumn 1968), pp. 238–46, substantially reprinted as the 'Introduction' in B. Farrell, *The founding of Dáil Éireann. Parliament and nation building* (Dublin, 1971); Lee, *Modernisation, passim*; McDonagh, *Ireland*, pp. 120–1; J. Prager, *Building Democracy in Ireland* (Cambridge, 1986), pp. 31–3.

Table 2. *Birth, marriage and death rates, 1922 (selected countries)*

	Births	Deaths	Marriages
Bulgaria	40.5	23.6	10.6
Romania	37.2	22.8	10.3
Poland	35.3	19.9	11.4
Yugoslavia	34.4	20.8	10.8
Hungary	30.8	21.4	10.8
Czechoslovakia	28.2	17.4	10.3
Northern Ireland	23.3	15.4	6.3
Irish Free State	19.5	14.7	5.0

Source: B.R. Mitchell, *European historical statistics 1750–1970* (London, 1975), pp. 114–20.

course, only about two-thirds that of Britain. But the rest of western Europe averaged only about two-thirds that of Britain also.[62] The manner in which Ireland achieved this average was unique, however, and potentially debilitating. For the rise in per capita income since the famine depended on falling population as well as on growing national product. For our present purposes, however, the level matters more than the trajectory.

The Free State occupational structure, while relatively simple by western European standards, was more diversified and complex than that of the eastern European states. Only about 50 per cent of the population was engaged in agriculture, compared with more than 60 per cent in Poland, Latvia, and Estonia, and more than 70 per cent in Lithuania, Romania, Bulgaria, Yugoslavia and Albania.[63] Among eastern European states, only Czechoslovakia, with 40 per cent, had a lower proportion of its active population in agriculture than the Free State in 1921.[64] And agriculture, with at least two-thirds of gross output sold off the farm in 1926–7,[65] was already predominantly market-oriented, however determined visiting anthropologists might be to excavate communities reputedly frozen in time.[66] There were of course internal gradations, with

[62] L.M. Cullen and T.C. Smout, 'Economic growth in Scotland and Ireland', in L.M. Cullen and T.C. Smout (eds.), *Comparative aspects of Scottish and Irish economic and social history 1600–1900* (Edinburgh, n.d.), p. 14; A.S. Milward and S.B. Saul, *The development of the economies of continental Europe* (London, 1977), p. 515. See below, pp. 513.

[63] J. Rothschild, *East Central Europe between the two world wars* (London, 1974), pp. 39, 285, 327, 359, 369.

[64] *Ibid.*, p. 91.

[65] D. Hannan, *Displacement and development: class, kinship and social change in Irish rural communities* (Dublin, 1979), p. 32; estimates by John Leydon, PM, P35/A/22.

[66] C. Arensberg, *The Irish countryman* (New York, 1937); C. Arensberg and S. Kimball, *Family and community in Ireland* (Harvard, 1940).

the west generally less commercialised than the east. In comparative perspective, however, the similarities are politically more significant than the differences. Even small farmers, as producers and consumers, were generally sensitive to market movements and accustomed to calculate by market criteria.

Nor was agriculture subjected to the pressure of the surging population growth that plagued the eastern European states, where it accelerated sub-division of holdings in a manner reminiscent of pre-Famine Ireland. Indeed, the Irish population problem, virtual stagnation, probably contributed to political stabilisation. North and south, Catholic and Protestant, had already generally perfected birth control through restricted and delayed marriage. Table 2 points the sharp contrast between Irish and eastern European demographic experience.

Comparison with post-1945 new states would expose even more glaring contrasts in Ireland's favour. A callously efficient socialisation process postponed marriage and effectively denied the right to a family to a higher proportion of the population than in any other European state, by the simple device of parents disinheriting a high proportion of potential grooms and brides among their children. The dispossessed were reconciled to their fate by emigration, which continued to channel the potential resentment of the disinherited out of the country in a manner largely denied to eastern European states after the imposition of American immigration controls in the 1920s.[67]

Rural Ireland not only controlled numbers in a clinical manner, but also effectively controlled the social structure. There was no longer a viable landlord system. Most Irish farmers became the effective owners of their holdings before 1921. The 1923 Land Act permitted the remaining tenants to purchase their holdings quickly, but the major changes in land ownership occurred before independence, contrary to frequent eastern European experience. The government was not therefore exposed to the temptation to manipulate land reform extensively for political purposes, which might have spawned massive corruption and provoked widespread grievance. Such limited land re-distribution as occurred continued to be channelled through the safer conduits of the Land Commission. Communities were not generally rent asunder by rival claims to land. At the other end of the scale, the proportion of agricultural labourers had fallen 'from over half the occupied male population in 1841 to less than one-third in 1911', and the decline was continuing.[68] Attempts by agricultural labour-

---

[67] P. Taylor, *The distant magnet: European emigration to the USA* (Harper Torchbook edn, New York, 1972), pp. 254–5. For a catalogue of the economic handicaps suffered by eastern Europe see D. Aldcroft, *The European economy 1914–1970* (London, 1978), pp. 47–9.

[68] D. Fitzpatrick, 'The disappearance of the Irish agricultural labourer, 1841–1912', *IESH*, 7 (1980), p. 84; Hannan, *Displacement*, p. 35.

ers to acquire a stake in the country were brusquely rebuffed by both farmers and government.[69] There were inevitably tensions between bigger and smaller farmers, but they shared an overriding interest in the security of property against the men of no property. And as these different farmer groups tended to be clustered in different areas, so ihe tensions between them tended to be expressed more in regional voting patterns than in direct confrontation. Nor was there a cultural chasm between town and country. Both were so inextricably linked in the fine mesh of commercial transactions, often linked too by kinship contacts, that the town–country contrast had far less analytical validity in Ireland than in many other societies.[70] Towns were not oases of literacy in deserts of rural ignorance. The petty town–country tensions that inevitably existed were trivial in the comparative context. Post-Famine Ireland had a land question. It had no peasant question.

This may help explain the otherwise puzzling failure of a major agrarian party to emerge. Farmers were under-represented occupationally in the first and second Dáils, accounting for only 10 per cent of the deputies in 1921.[71] This proportion rose to 22 per cent in 1923 and 34 per cent in 1937.[72] But these farmer deputies did not mainly belong to farmers' parties. A farmers' party did win a handful of seats in 1922, but failed to consolidate this modest achievement, and faded away within a decade. In the late 1930s another farmers' party, Clann na Talmhan, emerged in the west, but fizzled out two decades later. This absence of an influential agrarian party, in contrast to the experience of the eastern European states,[73] testifies to the relative political maturity of rural Ireland. The nuclear family had long been the dominant form in the agricultural community. Memories of Irish equivalents of the Mir or the Zadruga were, to say the least, hazy. Nor did a market oriented agriculture offer much incentive to invent ideologies irreconcilably hostile to an allegedly alien urban culture. The fact that there was little significant difference between urban and rural mentalities precluded peasant backlash. Most parties, North and South, articulated some agricultural interests, and made ritualistic reference to traditional rural virtues. There were streaks of peasantism in all major parties, but resentment at exclusion from the charmed circle of power, privilege and education never penetrated peasant consciousness sufficiently to form the effective basis of

[69] E. O'Connor, 'Agrarian unrest and the labour movement in Co. Waterford, 1917–1923', *Saothar*, 6 (1980), pp. 40–58.
[70] Lee, *Modernisation*, pp. 97–9.
[71] McCracken, *Representative government*, pp. 32–3.
[72] *Ibid.*, Table C, p. 98.
[73] For surveys of the eastern European situation see G.D. Jackson, Jr, 'Peasant political movements in eastern Europe', in H.A. Landsberger (ed.), *Rural protest: peasant movements and social change* (New York, 1973), pp. 261–315, and D.W. Urwin, *From ploughshare to ballotbox* (Oslo, 1980), *passim*.

a national peasant party, simply because there was relatively little exclusion.[74]

'Populism', a once honourable concept, has suffered much indecent assault in recent literature, and has come to be so promiscuously applied, that one despairs of retrieving its virtue from the verbal molesters. Suffice it to say that although elements of populism can be detected, and occasionally became obtrusive, in both Fianna Fáil and in the Unionist Party, neither ever became primarily populist parties. 'Indeed that Ireland did not produce a full fledged populism – as distinct from populistic themes that continued through de Valera to the present – is a paradox of European history.'[75] No serious radical right-wing peasant movements emerged. 'Back to the land' sentiments, Antaeus-like tributes to the renewing powers of the soil, were primarily the preserve of the clerisy. They did not generate much popular interest. The Dublin correspondent of the *Times* may have felt that 'the Farmers Union has many analogies with the Bulgarian Agrarians',[76] but there would be few pickings for an Irish Stamboliski.

The disproportionate influence of the urban milieu that has been detected in many new states[77] did not prevail in Ireland, for the simple fact that rural Ireland was already a highly politicised society. It accordingly contributed substantially to the leadership cadres and to the mass composition of all national political movements since at least the 1880s. The Home Rule Party, Sinn Féin, Cumann na nGaedheal and Fianna Fáil were all national parties, with regional variations in the extent of their support, certainly, but all drawing that support from across the country.[78]

A mechanistic, but useful, roll-call of the geographical origins of the Home Rule, 1916, Sinn Féin and Cumann na nGaedheal elites suffices to establish that they came from widely dispersed geographical backgrounds, from city, town and country. Of the four main Home Rule leaders in the early twentieth century, John Redmond came from Wexford, John Dillon from the borders of Roscommon and Mayo, William O'Brien from north Cork and Tim Healy from west Cork. Of the men executed in 1916, Ceannt came from Galway, Colbert and Daly from Limerick, MacDonagh from Tipperary, MacDermott from Leitrim, Mac-

---

74 The history of Clann na Talmhan does not invalidate this conclusion.
75 D. MacRae, 'Populism as an ideology', in G. Ionescu and E. Gellner (eds.), *Populism: its meanings and national characteristics* (London, 1969), p. 162. See also H.J. Puhle, 'Was ist Populismus?', *Politik und Kultur*, 10, 1 (1983), pp. 22–43.
76 *The Times*, 11 August 1923.
77 L.W. Pyle, 'The non-western political process', as discussed in H. Daalder, 'Government and opposition in the new states', *Government and Opposition*, 1, 2 (January 1966), pp. 218–19.
78 E. Rumpf and A.C. Hepburn, *Nationalism and socialism in twentieth-century Ireland* (Liverpool, 1977) surveys the electoral geography of the various parties. See also R.K. Carty, *Party and parish pump: electoral politics in Ireland* (Waterloo, 1981), p. 97.

Bride from Mayo, O'Hanrahan from Wexford, and Kent from Cork.[79]
Of the three outstanding Sinn Féin leaders, Griffith was a Dubliner, but
Collins and de Valera both hailed from intensely rural Munster back-
grounds. Cosgrave was a Dubliner, but his cabinet came from around
the country, O'Higgins from Offaly, Blythe from Armagh, MacNeill
from Antrim, McGilligan from the borders of Antrim and Derry,
Hogan from Galway, Mulcahy from Tipperary, Walsh from west
Cork.

The origins of politicians may be attributed, in part, to chance. This
may be less so with the administrative elite, even if their early promotion
may not be unconnected with their political contacts. The geographical
origins of the Irish civil service have not been systematically documented.
But even a cursory glance at some leading civil servants in the Free State
reveals the wide scatter of their origins, and, if any thing, the predominance of small town and rural Ireland in their backgrounds. Joseph
Brennan, secretary of the Department of Finance, 1923–7 hailed from
Bandon in west Cork. His successor from 1927 until 1953, the redoubta-
ble J.J. McElligott, came from Tralee, Co. Kerry. The secretary of the
Executive Council from 1922 until 1932, Diarmuid O'Hegarty, was a
Corkman. So was P.S. O'Hegarty, secretary of Posts and Telegraphs,
1922–44, who hailed from Carrignavar in west Cork. So was Daniel
Twomey, secretary of the Department of Agriculture from 1934 until
1946, who came from outside Macroom. Joe Walshe, secretary of the
Department of External Affairs from 1922 until 1946, came from
Killenaule in Tipperary. Maurice Moynihan, secretary to the Department
of the Taoiseach from 1937 until 1960, and his brother Seán, long
Establishments Officer in Finance, came from Tralee. John Leydon,
secretary of Industry and Commerce from 1932 until 1955, was the son of
a small farmer/coalminer from Arigna, Co. Leitrim. Whatever may be
thought of the specific policies with which these public servants would
become associated, they were not found wanting in the face of responsibility.

The point of this litany is a simple one. Its significance is that of the dog
that did not bark. It has been so taken for granted that few have lingered
to ponder the implications. The dispersed geographical origins of politicians and civil servants point to the relative homogeneity of urban and
rural society, of 'centre' and 'periphery'. Analytically important distinctions can, of course, be drawn from the intensity of regional and class
commitments to nationalist movements. For our current purposes,

---

[79] Another interesting feature of the 1916 leaders, including the Dublin-born ones, was their
exceptional geographical mobility. That would reinforce our present argument.

however, all that we are concerned to establish is the existence of an integrated, national polity.[80]

The political elite was characterised not only by a diversity of geographical origins. The events of 1916–22 also served to reveal the remarkable depth of the reservoir of leadership talent in the society. One could claim that four political elites disappeared in a decade. The Anglo-Irish elite was largely lost to the new state, at least in politics. The role that circumstances would permit the Anglo-Irish to play was problematical in any case. But Anglo-Ireland suffered its worst haemorrhage of talent in the First World War. The Trinity College, Dublin casualties were broadly in line with those of British universities.[81] It is possible to exaggerate the potential loss here. The elimination of a traditional elite may permit the rise of a more talented cadre deprived of opportunity by the existing power structure. Nevertheless, some of the Anglo-Irish were to achieve distinction abroad after 1922. On balance, it seems likely that they must have constituted some loss to Ireland, if only they could have been adequately integrated into public life. The Home Rule elite was swept aside by Sinn Féin in 1918. That Sinn Féin elite was itself only the second fifteen, following the decimation of the Easter Rising elite in 1916. The 1918 leadership was then itself decimated or temporarily eclipsed by 1922. None of the big three, de Valera, Collins and Griffith, was in government during the formative years of the state. Of the seven-man Sinn Féin cabinet in December 1921, only W.T. Cosgrave was still in office a year later. The manner in which the Cosgrave team performed was quite remarkable. Apparently a fourth or fifth team, they played as resolutely, as far as state-building was concerned, as a first team. Previous Irish generations had failed, at least until the late nineteenth century, to produce sustained systematic leadership of this sort, except perhaps in the Catholic Church. O'Connell's movement collapsed with himself. Leadership qualities failed to emerge in the eighteen fifties and sixties. If Parnell himself was never adequately replaced, his was the first movement to produce lieutenants of considerable leadership quality. The reserves of leadership on which Sinn Féin proved able to draw were unprecedented. For practical purposes, yet another new team, if led by an old captain, would take the field in 1932, and prove themselves no mean performers. This was no ordinary 'new nation'.

---

[80] Cork and Kerry appear even more 'integrated' than the rest! That may not surprise those familiar with the qualities of Corkmen and Kerrymen! For a more structured interpretation of the prominence of the south-west see Tom Garvin, 'The anatomy of a nationalist revolution: Ireland 1858–1928', *Comparative Studies in Society and History*, 28 (1986) pp. 468–501. Garvin explores in detail the origins of 304 members of the Sinn Féin elite, pp. 482ff. The focus of his concern is different from ours, but his evidence confirms the wide geographical distribution, rural and urban, of the political elite.

[81] Winter, 'Lost generation', p. 462.

This strength in depth partly reflected educational levels. Educational attainment was generally higher, and more widely dispersed, geographically and socially, than in the new eastern European states. Irish literacy levels, verging on 100 per cent, compared favourably with literacy rates of 70 per cent in Bulgaria and Poland, 60 per cent in Romania, 50 per cent in Yugoslavia, and 20 per cent in Albania.[82] Too much weight should not be laid on the proportion of university students in various countries because of the notorious problems affecting the comparability of the data. But the best available figures for 1922, for what they may be worth, suggest that Ireland, while having only about two-thirds the Swedish ratio, and perhaps three-quarters the Swiss and the Danish, had only slightly less than the British, French or Belgian ratios, and actually had a little higher than the Dutch, the Norwegian and the Finnish.[83] The precise figures may require revision, but unless the orders of magnitude are completely misleading, it seems that Ireland belonged to a western European pattern of access to higher education. In 1926 the Free State had more than 14 000 clergymen and nuns, more than 16 000 primary and secondary school teachers, more than 2000 doctors and 5000 nurses.[84] The educational system not only sufficed to supply domestic demand, but produced high export quotas of clergy and doctors.

Education, even higher education, was already so relatively widespread that the definition of 'intellectual' that Edward Shils employed in his seminal study of intellectuals in new states, 'all persons of advanced modern education',[85] has to be discarded as too permissive for Ireland at independence, precisely because Ireland was not a new state in the Third World sense.[86] However restricted by later standards, education was also sufficiently widespread to ensure that university students and soi-disant intellectuals did not constitute a political caste.[87] The level of literacy, and the sophistication of the educational infrastructure, militated against army rule rationalised on functional grounds. There was less objective justification for army officers to feel, like a Pilsudski, or later Third World

---

[82] Rothschild, *East Central Europe*, pp. 44, 276, 285, 332, 359. We have not included Greece in our eastern European comparisons because it was not a new state. But the Greek experience provides much to ponder for the student of Irish history. Greece was about 50 per cent illiterate in 1928 (George Th. Maurogordatos, *Stillborn republic: social coalitions and party strategies in Greece 1922–1936* (London, 1983), p. 293).

[83] B.R. Mitchell, *European historical statistics 1750–1970* (London, 1975), pp. 774–6.

[84] T. Brown, *Ireland: a social and cultural history 1922–79* (London, 1981), p. 91.

[85] E. Shils, 'Intellectuals in the political development of the new states', *World Politics*, 12, 3 (April, 1960), p. 332.

[86] Shils himself notes (*ibid.* p. 332, n. 5) that his definition was 'ceasing to be adequate' for Third World countries with expanding educational systems. See also E. Gellner, *Thought & Change* (London, 1965), pp. 169–70.

[87] *The National University Handbook 1908–1932* (Dublin, 1932), pp. 272–82 conveys a vivid sense of the triumphalist progress of Catholic secondary education in nineteenth-century Ireland.

generals, that 'only the army, with modern ideas of order, efficiency and probity in government' could modernise the society sufficiently to satisfy its self-respect.[88] The army was simply not 'the largest "modern" institution in a poor country' or 'a major arena for education and communications' or 'a likely instrument for collective tasks'.[89]

The Free State, then, inherited relatively strong economic, educational, social and political infrastructures. In addition, partition now saved the South from the most explosive internal problems subverting new states, race and religion, by the simple device of exporting them to the North. However objectively mongrel its genes, the Free State was subjectively virtually 100 per cent homogeneous, and that was all that politically mattered. In contrast, Romanians constituted – and knew they constituted – only 72 per cent of the population of Romania, Poles only 70 per cent of the population of Poland, Czechs only *c.* 50 per cent of the population of Czechoslovakia, Serbs only 43 per cent of the population of Yugoslavia.[90] However much partition embittered Southern politics, it did not subvert the state. The racial and religious issues may have proved less poisonous by incubating them in the North than they would have been in a united Ireland. However much sectarianism disfigured the Northern body politic, Craig may have coped with its disruptive potential more effectively than Cosgrave could have coped with Ulster Protestants in a united Ireland.

It is true that the 1922 Free State constitution had no sectarian bias. Nevertheless, the Catholic archbishop of Dublin insisted to Cosgrave that the Catholic Church had not merely the right, but the duty, to control Protestant consciences.[91] The existence of a tiny Protestant minority provoked small but virulent Catholic groups to preach militant anti-Protestantism in the South in the 1920s. These Catholic activists might have been stimulated to adopt a higher profile if there was a 25 per cent rather than a 5 per cent minority of 'heretics' whom they could depict as a cancer gnawing at the undefiled body of holy Catholic Ireland. But the 25 per cent was unlikely to have taken the attack on their freedom of conscience as supinely as did the 5 per cent. It is possible, of course, that the Catholic Church, guided by a politically pragmatic hierarchy, would have invoked the doctrine of the lesser evil to accommodate in practice what some bishops denounced in principle. A *modus vivendi* may have been found to permit freedom of conscience to Protestants if they proved

88 Shils, 'Intellectuals', p. 365, n. 25.
89 C. Tilly, 'Reflections on the history of European state-making', in C. Tilly (ed.), *The formation of national states in Western Europe* (Princeton, 1975), p. 75.
90 Rothschild, *East Central Europe*, pp. 36, 88–9, 192, 202, 284; Urwin, *Ploughshare to ballotbox*, p. 193.
91 SPO, S4127, E.J. Byrne to W.T. Cosgrave, 'Catholic teaching on marriage', 4 March 1923; E.S. Dugain to W.T. Cosgrave, 20 March 1923.

determined to create sufficient civil disturbance in defence of their religious rights. That however would hardly have been a situation conducive to the stability of the new state. It is difficult to say how church–state relations would have developed in a united Ireland, or to pronounce on the balance of probabilities in the response of the Catholic hierarchy to the new situation. There are several plausible scenarios, malign or benign according to taste.

The Free State was spared another racial virus that infected the body politic of the new states of eastern Europe. Despite considerable potential for anti-semitism, Ireland had no Jewish question. The Catholic Irish shared the Ulster Scot proclivity for conspiracy theory, their conspiratorial appetites whetted by the intensity of childhood indoctrination about Satan's works and pomps. The pathetic willingness of some Catholics to attribute to Freemasons an image of diabolical influence, the pathetic proclivity of allegedly hard-headed Ulster Scots to depict the Pope of Rome as anti-Christ, suggests that the Irish, North and South, were far from immune to conspiracy fantasies. The Limerick anti-semitic boycott, from 1904 to 1906, points to the potential for popular viciousness in propitious circumstances.[92] The IRA in the 1920s engaged in some violent actions against 'moneylenders', which could be construed as anti-semitic.[93] Miniscule though the Jewish population was, Cumann na nGaedheal tried to tap what it hoped was the latent anti-semitism of the Gaeltacht (Irish-speaking areas) by an attack on 'Mac Giolla Briscoe . . . agus na giollai iasachta eile' in a 1927 election.[94] The occasional clergyman, the best known being Fr Denis Fahey, would seek spiritual solace in anti-semitic diatribes in the congenial climate of the 1930s and early 1940s, as would a renowned local political broker, Oliver Flanagan, clawing his way up the greasy pole in Leix–Offaly politics during the Second World War.[95] This attitude became unfashionable, for obvious reasons, after 1945. Some Irish in New York found anti-semitism a palatable emotional diet in the depression of the 1930s.[96] The Irish patently enjoyed no special immunity against this particular virus. It was circumstances, not character, that prevented the latent anti-semitism from finding a more active outlet in Ireland.

The Free State enjoyed yet a further advantage. It was not the potential victim of irredentist or imperialist ambitions. The eastern European

---

[92] L. Hyman, *The Jews of Ireland* (Shannon, 1972), pp. 212–17.
[93] T.P. Coogan, *The IRA* (London, 1980 edn), p. 71.
[94] *Irish Independent*, 13 September 1927. Robert Briscoe, a Jew, was a well-known Fianna Fáil politician. The disparaging phrase may be translated as 'Briscoe . . . and the other alien ruffians.'
[95] J.T. Carroll, *Ireland in the war years 1939–1945* (Dublin, 1975), pp. 136–8.
[96] R.H. Bayor, *Neighbors in conflict: the Irish, Germans, Jews, and Italians of New York City, 1929–1942* (London, 1978), pp. 96–9.

states, nursing numerous claims against each other, and sandwiched between Germany and Russia, felt obliged to maintain large armies, which strained public finances and proved potential threats to internal constitutional stability. The lurking shadows of Stalin and Hitler were to exert a sinister influence on the internal stability of eastern European countries. It was the Free State's good fortune to have only England, now in growing, if not yet complete, control of her predatory passions, for a neighbour. Contrary to de Valera's prognostications during the Treaty debate, England proved to have no further territorial ambitions on the Free State. Southern Ireland had no Banat, no Bessarabia, no Bukovina, no Dobruja, no Macedonia, no Salonica, no Silesia, no Slovakia, no Teschen, no Thrace, no Transylvania. Northern Ireland was of course the object of irredentist nationalist claims. Ulster unionists did cherish a siege mentality,. But the psychological requirements of the *Herrenvolk* were such that if those claims had not existed they would have had to invent them to justify the degree of institutionalised discrimination against Catholics.

'Objective' advantages can be squandered through inadequate institutional response. Political systems, politics, and politicians matter.[97] It would have been difficult before the Treaty to have predicted the likely course of party politics. Sinn Féin had succeeded the Home Rule Party as a 'one big issue' party, an umbrella organisation subsuming a wide spectrum of views on a range of issues, subordinated by common consent to the main priority. The Free State did not therefore inherit a host of factions posturing as parties. Nevertheless, factionalisation remained a possible future development. But how, when and why? The most realistic analogy may be the experience of the Home Rule Party, when the 'one big issue' receded into the background until the party recovered the balance of parliamentary power in 1910. Splinter groups might break off, much as William O'Brien and Tim Healy broke from Redmond and Dillon at that time. Party politics might have degenerated into the type associated with Italian *trasformismo* following the fall of Minghetti.[98] The civil war may have helped polarise and stabilise animosities, but even after the civil war the *Irish Times* felt able to predict that 'as time progresses all the old party shibboleths and catchcries will disappear from Irish politics. The clear-cut issues of the past will be replaced by overlapping interests, and the Dáil of the future probably will assume the nature of the old German Reichstag . . .'.[99] The first 1927 election, when the two main parties won only 53 per cent of the vote between them, suggested a drift in that direction. Yet

---

[97] Though his interpretative emphases often differ from those advanced here, this is the convincing central theme of Carty's *Party and parish pump*.
[98] D. Mack Smith, *A history of Italy* (Madison, 1969), pp. 110–13.
[99] *Irish Times*, 1 September 1923.

in September 1927 the two main parties won 72 percent of the vote, and the *Irish Times* prediction failed to materialise.

Even in June 1927 nothing approaching the eastern European experience, where no fewer than 14 parties won seats in the 1920 election in Czechoslovakia, 16 in the Yugoslav election of 1920, 31 in the Polish election of 1926, prevailed in Ireland.[100] Where no party won more than 30 per cent of the votes between the wars, as in Czechoslovakia, or where the biggest party won only 20 per cent of the votes, like the Serbian Democrats in Yugoslavia in 1920,[101] multi-party coalition governments became unavoidable, with all the inevitable horse trading and the consequent disillusion of electorates disenchanted by the blatantly manipulative nature of party politics. Partition again simplified the party political structure in the Free State. The inclusion of the Unionist Party would have been conducive to fragmentation of some sort. Indeed unionists, if they themselves did not factionalise, might have held the balance of power between various nationalist groupings, or even won the biggest proportion of the votes in a fragmented party system, much as Henlein's Nazis did in Czechoslovakia in 1935.[102]

The political culture contained numerous ingredients conducive to the politics of faction. That was inevitable in a society where there were still few opportunities for occupational mobility outside the church, politics and public administration, and which relied heavily on the 'favours' network for getting things done. Kinship obligations were taken seriously. And localism became, if anything, more politically pronounced after independence than immediately before, if only because the Sinn Féin leaders were often young men thrust into the national limelight before they had time to sink deep local political roots. They secured their local bases in the first instance through their national prominence, rather than *vice versa*. But local preoccupations, however greased by the 'three Fs', family, favours and faction, did not prove incompatible with national politics. 'Fomorian fierceness of family and local feud'[103] did not preclude an organisational capacity or ideological commitment transcending purely local loyalties. Several organisations already flourished at a national level. The Catholic Church proved an efficient organisation of national mobilisation, marshalled by clergy with many of the instincts of political bosses, and providing bonds that forged a sense of wider identity. The success of the Gaelic Athletic Association (GAA), based on the co-option of intense local loyalties into a wider sense of national identity, reflected a capacity for organisation and a sense of communal coherence

---

100 Rothschild, *East Central Europe*, pp. 31, 102, 214.   101 *Ibid.*, p. 215.
102 *Ibid.*, p. 126. This is *not* meant to imply that the Unionist party was a Nazi party, but simply to point to the opportunities for a solid bloc in a multi-party situation.
103 Montague, *The rough field*, p. 17.

more developed than that in much of Mediterranean and eastern Europe. The GAA served not only as a recruiting ground for republican activists, but as an apprenticeship for national organisers. The prevailing political culture proved able to relate local loyalties to national issues. It simply was not the case, in contrast to the situation in many new states, that conflict could arise because 'a relatively modernised state structure is superimposed on a congery of disparate social groupings, that "have little sense of identity with one another, or with the national whole"'.[104] The Free State cannot be pressed into the factional model, however many familiar echoes that model may rouse in connoisseurs of Irish political culture.[105]

Ireland was no longer so grindingly poor that it had neither time nor stomach for mass participation in politics. Little approaching the 'amoral familism' of Montegrano vintage flourished in Ireland, however impressed myopic observers prone to lump all 'conservative peasant societies' into a holdall category may have been by Irish tendencies in this direction.[106] In the comparative context, the striking feature of Irish 'localism' was less its proneness to faction than the effectiveness with which it could transcend, without abandoning, its roots. The ability of the Irish, at home and abroad, to punch their weight in politics was at least partly due to this quality. Compared with other hyphenated Americans, for instance, they would prove remarkably successful in politics, because however strong the temptation might be to pull apart, they could also pull together. If the product of Irish peasant society fitted hand in glove into American political culture, if indeed he played some part in designing the glove, it was because the gap between rural Ireland and urban America was by no means as wide as the standard model, which mechanistically equates 'peasant' with 'traditional' or 'pre-modern', axiomatically assumes. It was quite consonant with this level of political culture that while brokers would flourish in Irish politics, patrons generally would

---

104 Daalder, 'Government and opposition', p. 206.
105 N.K. Nicholson, 'The factional model and the study of politics', *Comparative Political Studies*, 5, 3 (October 1972), pp. 291–314, provides a helpful introduction to the subject.
106 E. Banfield, *The moral basis of a backward society* (New York, 1958) is the *locus classicus*. Note, for instance (pp. 164ff.) the difficulties in sustaining even very modest sporting organisations in really backward societies. Banfield's work has been criticised in some respects (e.g. S.F. Silverman, 'Agricultural organisation, social structure, and values in Italy: amoral familism reconsidered', *American Anthropologist*, 70 (February 1968), pp. 1–20; '"Exploitation" in rural central Italy: structure and ideology', *Comparative Studies in Society and History*, 12 (1970), pp. 327–39; J. Davis, 'Morals and backwardness', *Comparative Studies in Society and History*, 12 (1970), pp. 340–53; E. Cohen, 'Who stole the rabbits?', *Anthropological Quarterly*, 45 (1972), pp. 1–14). The criticisms do not affect my argument. See also K.J. Arrow, *The limits of organisation* (New York, 1974), p. 26.

not.[107] One reason why Fianna Fáil would overtake Cumann na nGaed-heal was precisely because it realised the limited ability of local 'notables' to deliver the vote, and put its faith instead in far more elaborate national organisation. A Blaney may have been cock of the Donegal walk, but he was no Bratianu.[108]

It is true that

in the traditional . . . conception, a deputy is primarily a local representative, the spokesman for local grievances and the source of local patronage . . . in contrast with the clear British demarcation between local and national politics, the two were intimately related . . . Both local and national office must be held concurrently if the politician is to play his role as privileged mediator between the mass public and the political or administrative executive.[109]

But it is possible to acquire a distorted perspective on the Irish situation if it is seen solely through Westminster lenses. The quotation just cited refers to the France of the Fifth Republic, not to Ireland. The institutional arrangements of French politics are premised on an intense localism. Yet France has performed more effectively as an economy, and probably as a society, than Britain since the Second World War. Indeed, the more closely the political structures of western European societies are scrutinised, the more exceptional does England appear in this respect.

That local aspirations were channelled effectively into national politics reflects the underlying resilience of the national identity, particularly as the electoral system, proportional representation with the single transferable vote in multi-member constituencies, fertilised the roots of localism.[110] Proportional representation (PR) was incorporated into the Free State constitution as part of the understanding with England that the Protestant minority would be protected. The system encouraged parties to run candidates from different parts of constituencies to tap parochial patriotism, and permitted independents to flourish on the strength of lovingly manured local roots. The committee of advisers on the Free State constitution expected PR to spawn a plethora of parties, and result in unstable coalition governments. So convinced were they, despite the split on the Treaty, that the electoral system would prevent stable party government from taking root, that they adopted as an objective the virtual elimination of party politics from the Dáil and rule by non-party experts.[111] A decade later the leading commentator on the constitution,

[107] M. Bax, 'Patronage Irish style: Irish politicians as brokers', *Sociologische Gids*, 17 (1970), pp. 179–91; D. Schmitt, *The irony of Irish democracy* (Lexington, 1973), p. 60; Carty, *Parish pump*, p. 133.

[108] For a study of the Blaney political machine in Donegal see P.M. Sacks, *Donegal mafia: an Irish political machine* (London, 1976).

[109] J. Hayward, *The one and indivisible French Republic* (London, 1973), p. 71.

[110] B. Chubb, *The government and politics of Ireland* (London, 1970), pp. 348–52, explains the working of the PR system.

[111] McCracken, *Representative government*, pp. 161ff.

Dr Kohn, still accepted the diagnosis.[112] So did a senior politician, Ernest Blythe, Minister for Finance and vice-president of the Executive Council, who argued as late as 1931 that

The assassination of Kevin O'Higgins and the events which followed it have, so far, prevented the development in the Dáil of the French group system and it may be anticipated that the next general election will not give us the same number of small parties as were given by the election of June, 1927. I feel certain, however, that if we retain the present system of PR (proportional representation), the general election after next will see the end of government based on a stable parliamentary majority.[113]

Such scepticism proved unwarranted.

The increase in the number of deputies reinforced the factionalising tendencies inherent in PR. The growth in the size of the electorate, which more than doubled through extension of the franchise in 1918 and 1923, would have increased the ratio of Dáil deputies to voters, and hence restricted the potential of the face-to-face 'favours' system. But the Government of Ireland Act nearly doubled the number of deputies. Article 26 of the Free State constitution allowed the Dáil considerable latitude in deciding the number of deputies, simply specifying that the total number 'shall not be fixed at less than one member for each 30000 of the population, or at more than one member for each 20000 of the population'. The Dáil opted for 147. When the 6 university deputies permitted by Article 27 of the constitution were added, the 153 representatives touched on the permitted maximum, far above the required minimum of 105.[114]

It is difficult to assess the impact of PR on the politics of state-building. Devised originally to safeguard minority unionists, the first major minority it protected was anti-Treaty Sinn Féin, presumably saved by PR from land-slide defeat in the early Free State elections. Without PR, it might have been more difficult for de Valera to persuade his followers to take the parliamentary road, for their prospects might have looked hopeless. It would be unwise to speculate unduly on the probable consequences of a straight vote system at that stage. Other things would hardly have remained equal in such a situation. Nevertheless, PR probably contributed, however inadvertently, to the stability of nationalist Ireland, though imposed with unionist sensitivities in mind! The Labour Party too

---

[112] L. Kohn, *The constitution of the Irish Free State* (London, 1932), p. 186.

[113] SPO, S3766. Blythe first circulated his memorandum to the cabinet, 'Suggested new system of representation', on 12 January 1927. He re-circulated it, with the covering note contained in the text, on 4 February 1931.

[114] It is curious that the important decision concerning the size of the Dáil has received such little attention. It must have interesting implications for students of political culture and of political tactics.

would have been vulnerable, and presumably would have either vanished or been forced to find an alternative platform.[115]

PR intensifies the competitive element between members of the same party. This places a premium on local representatives being seen to deliver the goods to their constituents. It thrusts TDs (parliamentary deputies) into a 'messenger boy' role as brokers of public patronage, mediating between the bureaucracy and their constituents.[116] It has probably intensified the 'family business' nature of political representation, for the widows/children of the 'messenger boys' naturally come to learn the rounds with their beloveds. It may be that the pressure of constituency work, and the triviality of the tasks on which TDs are compelled to concentrate, has deprived the Dáil of some significant debating contributions.[117] But it may be asked if the proper function of the majority of public representatives in Irish circumstances should not be to act as 'messenger boys', linking the locals with the bureaucracy, an indispensable task which they perform devoutly. Their job is to get for their constituents everything they are entitled to, and as much as possible of what they are not entitled to.

Where TDs were expected by their constituents to act as mediators, a role which would develop further with the growing socio-economic activity of the state, PR may have accentuated, but hardly created, the pressure on TDs to fulfil these expectations. In Northern Ireland, James Craig abolished PR in favour of the straight vote in 1929. The change made little obvious difference to the 'favours' nature, or to the 'localism', of northern politics, to the standards of parliamentary debate, or to the quality of representatives. And their messenger boy role helps provide TDs with an insight into the actual impact of legislation at grassroots level. It may even provide a potentially useful check on the autocratic tendencies inherent in a centralised bureaucracy and in the monopoly power enjoyed by semi-state bodies. The frequent shallowness of the work ethic in public employment in Ireland is an everyday experience. A badgering TD is one of the few ways in which the public can pressurise monopolies into doing their job, if not properly, than at least improperly. If TDs inevitably attempt to foster the belief that justice can only be

---

115 John A. Murphy, 'The Irish party system', in K.B. Nowlan and T.D. Williams (eds.), *Ireland in the war years and after* (Dublin, 1969), p. 154.
116 B. Chubb, '"Going around persecuting civil servants": the role of the Irish parliamentary representative', *Political Studies*, 11, 3 (1963), pp. 272–86.
117 For a pained description of the 'degradation' of the messenger boy/voting fodder system see Joseph Connolly, *How does she stand? An appeal to Young Ireland* (Dublin, 1953), pp. 32–8. Connolly was a Fianna Fáil minister, 1932–6 and chairman of the Board of Public Works, 1936–50. *The Leader* (Christmas number, 1953), has interesting comments on the implications of PR for the quality of deputies and for Dáil standards. D. Thornley, 'Ireland. The end of an era?', *Studies* (Spring 1964), pp. 14–15, has an eloquent denunciation of the messenger boy system.

secured through them, when many of their constituents are legally entitled to the benefits they seek through 'influence', they are simply adapting to the level of ignorance, or of morality, or of realism, of their constituents.

PR may have damaged the quality of some Dáil candidates, by eliminating the 'safe' seat, and thus discouraging candidates whose talents would lie more in government than in electioneering.[118] But the charge must remain, on the whole, 'not proved'. The first Sinn Féin Dáil, elected on a straight vote system, or the Home Rule Party, or the Unionist party since 1929, hardly contained a plethora of people who would have graced the post-1922 Dáil. Nor has there been any obvious correlation between brokerage capacity and legislative ability. Brokerage takes time, but some of the outstanding brokerage politicians have also counted among the most creative contributors to policy formation. As a strong central bureaucracy was initially indispensable in Ireland, not least to counter the pervasive corruption of localism, it was useful that it should have a human face. The TD is that human face. His – and occasionally hers – may sometimes be a rubbery, leering, cynical face. But it is recognisably human. Calculating machines the TDs may be. Desiccated they are not. That the system prevents many TDs from devoting themselves 'to the careful examination and study of proposed legislation', as critics lament, may not be the least of its saving graces. It protects many TDs from the temptation to think for themselves, with the potentially lethal implications for national welfare. The Irish system has broadly produced strong, if not necessarily gifted, front benches, capable of generating policy or at least of promoting civil service policy, which the lobby fodder behind them has loyally supported. And that was probably the most that could be realistically hoped for until recently.

Proportional representation must be judged by its impact not only on the quality and role of the representative, but on the party system in general, and on the degree to which it satisfies voter requirements. It is arguable that in both respects it has proved more a stabilising than a destabilising influence hitherto. If it obliges TDs to compete with party colleagues,[119] nevertheless by preventing large majorities it has probably forced parties to close ranks more firmly than would have been the case with the straight vote.[120] Big majorities may have been more conducive to factionalisation within parties, and to possible splits, than the discipline of a narrow majority. In addition, by enabling voters to plump for a party list it reinforced their sense of party identity. By simultaneously allowing

---

[118] As argued by Mary Robinson, 'The role of the Irish parliament', *Administration*, 21 (1974), pp. 3–25.

[119] This is a matter of common observation, but for a vivid exposition see M. Bax, *Harp strings and confessions: machine style politics in the Irish Republic* (Assen, 1976).

[120] T. Gallagher, 'The dimensions of Fianna Fáil rule in Ireland', *West European Politics*, 4, 1 (January, 1981), p. 58.

them to choose their order of preference among their party candidates, it enabled them to satisfy local loyalties, thus proving a 'catch all' electoral system which nicely reconciled conflicting claims on the voter's conscience.[121]

The party loyalty of Irish voters, as reflected in the consistency with which they cling to the party slate, despite the counter-attractions, has been well documented.[122] It testifies not only to the consistency of the political outlook of the voter, but to his commitment to the idea of party. Concentration on the other ingredients in the cake of political culture diverts attention from the resilience of the party system, and even from the power of the idea of party, as independent variables in their own right. A crucial factor here is that Ireland was politicised at a remarkably early stage, and within the framework of party politics. Mass politicisation long preceded mass enfranchisement, substantially completed only in 1918 and 1923. The Lipset–Rokkan model cannot be applied to Ireland without taking into account that 'enfranchisement' and 'mobilisation' were far from concurrent developments, and are by no means interchangeable concepts.[123]

Daniel O'Connell's crusades for Catholic emancipation and for repeal of the Union politicised in large measure the farmers of the south and east. The Fenians, the Land League and the Home Rule Party mobilised and politicised the west. Ireland was one of the most advanced societies in Europe in terms of mass political mobilisation by the end of the nineteenth century. There was some truth, even as early as 1881, in the claim that 'If ever a country passed through a parliamentary apprenticeship of the fullest term, Ireland is that country.'[124] Insofar as the commonsense observation that 'to maintain a democratic system democratic norms have to be learned by experience'[125] carries conviction, Ireland, in contrast not

---

[121] Carty, *Parish pump*, pp. 117, 134. See below, pp. 546–7.

[122] M. Gallagher, 'Party solidarity, exclusivity and inter-party relationships in Ireland, 1922–1977: the evidence of transfers', *ESR*, 10, 1 (1978), 1–22; M. Gallagher, 'The impact of lower preference votes on Irish parliamentary elections, 1922–1977', *ESR*, 11, 1 (1979), pp. 19–32; Carty, *Parish pump*, pp. 63–9.

[123] For an approach along these lines see E.E. Davis and R. Sinnott, 'Political mobilisation, political institutionalisation and the maintenance of ethnic conflict', *Ethnic and Racial Studies*, 4, 4 (October, 1981), pp. 398–414. Rokkan's pioneering studies of the development of mass politics in western Europe repay careful scrutiny by historians. But his attempt to incorporate Ireland into a version of his model was not an entirely happy one. See S. Rokkan, 'The growth and structuring of mass politics in Western Europe: reflections on possible models of explanation', *Scandinavian Political Studies*, 5 (1970), pp. 68–83.

[124] *Freeman's Journal*, 17 September 1881.

[125] H. van Amersfoort and H. van der Wusten, 'Democratic stability and ethnic parties', *Ethnic and Racial Studies*, 4, 4 (October, 1981), p. 482. Daalder subscribes to the same viewpoint, 'Government and opposition', p. 220.

only to eastern Europe but, for instance, to India,[126] had acquired that experience by 1921. That did not guarantee the establishment of a party system after independence. Within Sinn Féin, and among the dafters of the Free State constitution, there was considerable suspicion of the idea of party either because party allegedly prostituted the national to the sectional, or because the techniques of compromise inherent in party politics proved repulsive to a particular type of temperament.[127] The hostility may to some extent be taken as a tribute to the roots which the idea of party had already sunk in popular political culture. That did not preclude the possibility of factionalism, or of dictatorship. There is nothing necessarily linear about political development. Most political cultures contain the seeds of a wide range of growths within them. It is usually a question of preponderant, not of exclusive, values. Circumstances can change the weightings attached to different values. Nevertheless, the momentum already acquired by the idea of party in Ireland did strengthen the likelihood that, *ceteris paribus*, party would maintain itself as a key institution for the articulation of political aspirations.

This concept of the nature and role of party was primarily due to one further legacy that distinguished the Free State from many other new states. That was the British legacy. Compared with the Habsburg, Tsarist and Hohenzollern legacies in eastern Europe, it appears to have made for political stability.

As Ireland had existed within the British sphere of influence for centuries, it would be inconceivable that she should not bear some marks of the relationship. But major conceptual problems arise in assessing the transmission of influences from one polity to another.[128] Many influences which an insular perspective might deem 'British' in the Irish context

126 J. Hennessy, 'British education for an elite in India, 1780–1947', in R. Wilkinson (ed.), *Governing elites: studies in training and selection* (London, 1969), p. 189 argues that 'Education for the public services and for business began sufficiently far back to penetrate and *to consolidate itself over several generations*; education for political life was, by contrast, too recent and spread over too few numbers.'
127 R. Fanning, 'Leadership and transition from the politics of revolution to the politics of party: the example of Ireland 1914–1939', XIV International Congress of Historical Sciences, San Francisco, 1975, pp. 11–13; B. Chubb, 'Cabinet government in Ireland', *Political Studies*, 3, 3 (1975), pp. 257–8.
128 H.A. Pochmann, 'The migration of ideas', in H.S. Commager (ed.), *Immigration in American history* (Minneapolis, 1961), pp. 107–14, comments on the difficulty of sorting out the extent and direction of influence in the transmission of ideas. For an instructive approach towards the evaluation of imperial influence, see A.A. Mazrui, 'Borrowed theory and original practice in African politics', in H.J. Spiro (ed.), *Patterns of African development* (New Jersey, 1967). For an illuminating case study, which suggests direct parallels with the Irish experience, see D. Smiley, 'Must Canadian political science be a miniature replica?', *Journal of Canadian Studies*, 9, 1 (February, 1974).

reflected developments in the wider field of 'western' culture.[129] An adequate analysis would have to distinguish uniquely British influences from originally non-British influences mediated through Britain.

Perhaps the safest surmise at our present primitive level of understanding is that there was no single monolithic 'British legacy.' There was instead a variety of British influences, whose nature must be carefully sifted before confident generalisation can be hazarded. Equally importantly, there was a variety of Irish responses. As Daniel Lerner has put it in a universal context, 'the initial intrusion comes, it is true, from the outside. But its impact depends upon the reaction of the indigenous people.'[130] Which influences were absorbed, which rejected, and which modified may reveal much about Irish political culture. Why did the Irish choose to domesticate certain British influences more than others? And how conscious was their choice?

Some simple, not to say simplistic, examples illustrate the difficulties in arriving at a balanced conclusion. In the first instance, influence on institutional structures must be distinguished, as far as possible, from influence on mentalities. The Royal Irish Constabulary was an armed paramilitary police force. British police were unarmed. The Royal Ulster Constabulary was an armed paramilitary force. The Gárda Síochána, the Free State police force after 1922, was unarmed. Which owed more to the British legacy? The British imposed proportional representation as the electoral system in Ireland, North and South, in place of the British system. Was it therefore part of the British legacy? Or a repudiation of the British legacy? Did Northern Ireland become less British by using PR between 1921 and 1929, and then become more British by abolishing PR in 1929? Was Mr de Valera being 'un-British' in trying to persuade the Irish people to send PR 'back where it came from' in 1959, and to replace it by the existing British system? Was it 'un-British' of the Free State to enfranchise all adult women in 1923, five years before Britain and Northern Ireland adopted a similar measure? Was Stormont an example of British influence? As far as parliamentary procedures, formalities and ritual were concerned, it was modelled closely on Westminster. But if 'the British parliamentary system in any comprehensive sense' consists of 'the intricate body of attitudes and understandings, including . . . respect for minority rights',[131] then some might question whether Stormont did conform to the Westminster model.

[129] C.J. Friedrich, 'Some reflections on constitutionalism for emergent political "orders"', in H.J. Spiro (ed.) *Patterns of African development* (New Jersey, 1967), pp. 9, 16.

[130] D. Lerner, 'The transformation of institutions', in W.B. Hamilton (ed.), *The transfer of institutions* (London, 1964), p. 9.

[131] A. Brady, 'Canada and the model of Westminster', in Hamilton, *Transfer*, p. 57; P. Alter, 'Nordirland zwischen Bürgerkrieg und Reformen', *Aus Politik und Zeitgeschichte*, B.35–36 (1970), p. 11.

Brian Farrell distinguishes between the liberal and conservative versions of the British constitution, and finds Ulster unionism leaning more towards the conservative version, with Irish nationalism leaning more towards the liberal version.[132] This is a useful refinement. But it does raise the question of how helpful the concept 'British influence' may be in its own right. The peculiar genius of the British constitution, it could be argued, was that it encompassed both the liberal and the conservative versions. The British aspect lay not in one or the other, but precisely in the balance between them. Once that balance was lost then, arguably, the individual variants ceased to be examples of 'British' influence and the idea of 'British influence' became vacuous. If both Northern Ireland and the Free State were primarily products of 'British influence', then 'British influence' would appear too elastic a concept to be analytically useful. If specific similarities with Britain, and specific differences from Britain, can both be attributed to 'British influence', then every feature of Irish life can by definition be attributed to the British legacy.

In the economic sphere, the Free State inherited at least two specifically British institutions that would, in their differing ways, affect economic growth. One was the banking system. This was modelled on the British joint stock banking rather than the European investment banking system. Opinions differ on the relative appropriateness of the two systems to the growth requirements of the Irish economy. The Free State would expend much time and ingenuity in trying to devise substitutes for investment banks.[133] The other institutional inheritance that would in time come to exert an influence was the structure of Irish trade unionism. This was based closely on the British model. It may be wondered how well it served either Ireland, or the Irish working class.[134]

In the public sphere, the main British institutional legacy was the civil service. Irish public administration closely and consciously imitated the English model.[135] The fact that 'Ireland at independence had the advantage of having a particularly large percentage of high level positions already filled by Irish men'[136] helped ensure administrative continuity and stability. The insinuation lurking behind much of the discussion about

---

132 B. Farrell, 'The first Dáil and after', in Farrell, *Parliamentary tradition*, pp. 212–14.
133 M.E. Daly, 'Government finance for industry in the Irish Free State: the Trade Loans (Guarantee) Acts', *IESH*, 11 (1984), pp. 73, 93.
134 J. Lee, 'Worker and society in modern Ireland', in D. Nevin (ed.), *Trade unions and change in Irish society* (Dublin and Cork, 1980), pp. 18, 23–5.
135 B. Chubb, 'Fifty years of Irish administration', in Edwards and Pyle, *Easter Rising*, pp. 182–90, summarises the main features of Irish administration between 1922 and 1966. More extended discussions include T.J. Barrington, *The Irish administrative system* (Dublin, 1980); Chubb, *Government and politics*, pp. 218–45; P. Pyne, 'The bureaucracy in the Irish Republic: its political role and the factors influencing it', *Political Studies*, 22, 1 (March, 1974), pp. 15–30.
136 Schmitt, *Irish democracy*, p. 26.

administrative continuity, however, is that the natives would have been incapable of achieving administrative stability after 1922 but for the good fortune of their apprenticeship in the British model. This assumes that the Irish were incapable of designing an appropriate administrative system of their own, and that the British model was the most suitable one for Irish circumstances. If the only alternative to continuity was administrative anarchy, this would be a compelling assumption. But was anarchy the likely alternative?

The fact that Ireland was a relatively modernised society in 1922 has direct implications for this question. It was not civil service experience *per se* that was important. That was no doubt helpful for establishing smooth procedures, and for activating useful contacts in Whitehall. But procedures, and even contacts, though not irrelevant, are not the key to good administration. What was important was that the civil servants who were inherited, or reinstated, had already acquired the education to achieve entry into the civil service through competitive examination. Their subsequent records confirmed rather than created their capacity. When Michael Hayes, the Speaker of the Dáil, sought bright young men for the civil service in 1922, he asked the president of University College Dublin to nominate five promising candidates for him.[137] They were to proceed to distinguished careers. Ireland already had an educational system more than able to produce recruits adequate for the Free State's administrative requirements. Long before independence, applications for civil service posts from candidates who satisfied the educational requirements vastly exceeded the number of openings. Many of the unsuccessful candidates may not have had the required administrative talents. But many others would probably have done more or less as good a job as most of their successful examination rivals. Comparison with later British administrative legacies confirms just how unusual was the Irish case, unusual not because the administrative system itself was unique, but because the nature of the wider society at the time of independence was exceptional.[138]

Education does not necessarily confer administrative ability. But one need only turn to the Catholic Church for evidence of the administrative abilities widely present among the Irish in the nineteenth and early twentieth centuries. The organisation of the American and Australian Catholic Churches counts among the major administrative achievements of modern history. Those achievements were in disproportionate measure

---

137 RM, P7/D/57, Notes by Michael Hayes, 3 June 1963, p. 7.
138 For comparative purposes see R. Braibanti (ed.). *Asian bureaucratic systems emergent from the British imperial tradition* (Durham, NC, 1966) and R. Symonds, *The British and their successors: a study in the development of the government services in the new states* (London, 1966).

Irish achievements.[139] Nor did the Irish, as the natural rulers of the American church, hesitate to adopt an imperial tone towards other Catholic immigrants, like the 'hot-tempered' Poles.[140] The Catholic Churches that reared their formidable edifices across the English speaking world in the nineteenth century bore testimony not only to the triumphalist imperialism of Roman Catholicism but to the administrative abilities of Irish Catholics. At home, the church had shown a capacity for organising not only strictly religious ceremonies, but for running an educational system, a hospital system, and a rudimentary welfare system, which testified to a capacity for administrative self-government that few emerging states could rival.[141] When Winston Churchill, in one of his frequent moments of exasperation with the impossible Hibernians, snorted 'the Irish have a genius for conspiracy rather than government',[142] he revealed his innocence of achievements that would endure long after the empire that claimed his own loyalty would have retired into the history books. The Irish, in short, had already shown an aptitude for government as administration, at home and abroad, that augured well for their potential in this sphere after independence.

There is little evidence that previous experience in the British civil service was a prerequisite for satisfactory administrative performance. The best-known Department inherited in 1922 was Agriculture and Technical Instruction, then thought to be functioning so effectively that its admirers claimed it would be a mistake to dismember it. Yet this Department had only been set up in 1900, and was distinguished at its foundation by 'the extent to which it was staffed by men who had not been brought up in the traditions of the British civil service'.[143] Another Department, which by definition could not enjoy administrative continuity, was External Affairs. Though very short staffed[144] it performed, despite the odd curious episode, with some distinction.[145] It is not

---

139 P.J. Corish (ed.), *A history of Irish catholicism*, contains surveys on Australia by J.J. McGovern and P.J. O'Farrell and on the USA by T.T. McAvoy and T.N. Brown. See also P.K. Egan, *The influence of the Irish on the Catholic Church in America in the nineteenth century* (Dublin, 1968).

140 C. Golab, *Immigrant destinations* (Philadelphia, 1977), p. 131.

141 E. Larkin, 'Economic growth, capital investment, and the Roman Catholic Church in nineteenth-century Ireland', *AHR*, 72 (1966–7), pp. 852–84; 'The devotional revolution in Ireland, 1850–75', *AHR*, 77 (1972), pp. 625–52; 'Church, state and nation in modern Ireland', *AHR*, 80 (1975), pp. 1244–75.

142 Quoted in Towey, 'Collins–de Valera Pact', p. 66.

143 D. Hoctor, *The Department's story: a history of the Department of Agriculture* (Dublin, 1971), p. 130.

144 EB, P24/562, P. McGilligan to E. Blythe, 3 December 1928. As late as 1930, the senior staff of External Affairs consisted of a Secretary and Assistant Secretary, a Principal Officer, two junior Administrative Officers, a Legal Adviser and an Assistant Legal Adviser – seven people! (*Thom's Directory*).

145 Harkness, *Restless dominion*, p. 244; Harkness, 'Patrick McGilligan', p. 123; P. Keatinge, *The formulation of Irish foreign policy* (Dublin, 1973), pp. 140–1; D.F.

self-evident that the continuity of administration in other Departments must have been indispensable for administrative efficiency in the new state, even by so modest a definition of efficiency as getting the files into correct order. Merrion Square was no oasis of administrative talent in a desert of aboriginal backwardness.

At a purely administrative level, the performance of the senior administrators in the early Free State years, whatever their background, was probably superior to that of the latter-day British administration in Ireland. That administrataion was not, it is true, regarded by demanding critics as the brightest jewel in his majesty's crown. The formidable Warren Fisher dismissed with disdain the calibre of Dublin Castle administrators in 1920. That Fisher had a different political viewpoint from most of them[146] does not necessarily invalidate his verdict on their professionalism.[147]

Nor must the relatively light nature of the administrative demands imposed on the early Free State civil service be overlooked in assessing the nature of the administrative achievement. The challenge cannot be compared with that confronting more recent new states. Most third world governments were committed to the view that the state should adopt a developmental role within their societies. The first Free State government was not. It broadly took the view that the state should do as little as possible. However formidable the contemporary challenge may have seemed to the Irish civil service, it was asked to do far less by its political masters than the civil services of later new states. This is not to underrate the importance of the decisions, some of them quite fundamental, that had to be taken. But there was nothing like the ceaseless flow of decisions that confronted later arrivals obliged to devise and implement more active programmes. It would seem unduly pessimistic to conclude that only British tutelage enabled Irish society to meet the limited demand for administrative talent at this stage. The concept of continuity in this area must be carefully probed lest it acquire a mechanistic meaning stifling critical reflection.

The price paid by the Free State for its fidelity to British administrative models is difficult to determine. Adherence to the model dominated mentalities as well as institutional structures. At one level, it contributed significantly to establishing standards of personal integrity among senior

Keogh, 'The Department of Foreign Affairs', in Z. Steiner (ed.), *The Times survey of Foreign Offices of the world* (London, 1982), pp. 278–9, 283; D.F. Keogh, 'The origins of the Irish foreign service in Europe (1919–1922)', *Etudes Irlandaises*, 7 (1982), pp. 160–1; Keogh, *Vatican*, pp. 126, 273, n. 6. That other departments regarded External Affairs with some initial disdain may reflect more on them than on it (P. Keatinge, *Formulation*, p. 107).

146 McColgan, 'Partition', pp. 150–2.
147 The intellectual quality of the memoirs of a senior Castle official at the time, Headlam, *Reminiscences*, provides independent support for Fisher's judgement.

civil servants that did not self-evidently derive from the values of Irish society. At another level, it enshrined the cult of the amateur in administraion. Britain managed to survive this cult, partly because the industrial revolution gave her an economic headstart over the rest of the world and enabled her to batten on the inheritance until the price of amateurism finally caught up with her. She also survived because she had the common sense to jettison the cult in wartime, when mere 'experts' were imported into government to help win the wars. The first decade of independence for any state might reasonably be regarded as a testing time requiring a virtual war effort, but the intellectual inheritance predisposed the Free State regime to conduct it mainly as a holding operation. Ireland was in no position to afford the intellectual style of the amateur, but she insisted on living beyond her means in this respect, in striking contrast to her parsimony in other directions.

It was difficult not to be impressed with the British model at the time. Britain appeared to be the greatest power in the world, still the biggest empire, recent victor in a clash of titans. Was it not great good fortune that circumstances permitted one to model oneself on not only the most familiar, but the most successful, example? Why bother searching out models in difficult foreign languages? Why look at the administrative structures of the smaller states of western and northern Europe? Why rise to the intellectual effort involved in asking whether Britain did offer the most relevant model, particularly when the desire to impress Britain, both on psychological and more narrowly tactical grounds, was itself a motive in government decision-making?

Many other factors should be taken into account in drawing up a comprehensive balance of the legacy inherited by the Free State. Enough has been said to suggest that the Free State began with immense advantages compared with most other new states in the twentieth century. Partition, in particular, saved the Free State from many of the problems of new nations. The creation for the first time in history of a united independent Ireland would indeed have meant the creation of a new nation. Nation-building would have occurred only had the state embraced all Ireland. That problem did not arise at the time. It has baffled all Irish politicians who have since contemplated it. D'Azeglio's cryptic comment 'We have made Italy. All that remains is to make Italians,' did not have to be applied to Ireland. No new nation had to be created in 1922, only a new state.

The Free State, then, inherited most of the pre-conditions of political stability. But human ingenuity has often thwarted objective opportunity, even in Ireland. England was responsible for bequeathing a situation in which civil war was a possibility. But the civil war was a product of native genius. Ultimate responsibility for reconciling security with liberty, and stability with progress, still rested on the politicians, above all on the first government of the Free State. It remained to be seen how Cosgrave and his colleagues would measure up to the challenge.

STATE-BUILDING

The 1922 election left several possibilities open for the longer term. If opinion tended to polarise around the Treaty issue, one-third of the electorate had nonetheless pronounced a plague on both Sinn Féin houses. The constitution, which the Dáil adopted in December 1922, required elections to be held within one year. Cosgrave, who became President of the Executive Council when the Free State came into formal existence on 6 December 1922, called a snap election for August 1923, probably to give the anti-Treaty forces as little time as possible to regroup politically.[148] He got a rude electoral shock. Some commentators expected his new party, Cumann na nGaedheal, which he launched in March 1923, to take up to 80 seats.[149] It actually won 63, a gain of only 5, in a Dáil enlarged from 128 to 153 seats. The constitution had extended the franchise to all women over the age of twenty-one, with the result that the electorate increased from 1.37 million in 1918 to 1.72 million. Cumann na nGaedheal did increase its popular vote from 245 000 to 409 000, but this just sufficed to hold its proportion of the valid poll at 39 per cent. In so far as part of the pro-Treaty vote in 1922 was a personal vote for Collins, some relative loss might have been anticipated. Probably more important was the economic depression that became widespread in 1923, and which inevitably provoked reaction against the government. Farmers suffered doubly as agricultural prices fell, and bad weather reduced output. The resultant slump affected the whole economy.[150]

Sinn Féin increased its popular vote from 135 000 to 290 000, and its share of the valid poll from 21.5 per cent to 27.6 per cent. Predicted to win about 30 seats,[151] this 'unexpected success'[152] enabled it to take 44 seats. The rise in its popular vote was, like Cumann na nGaedheal's, partly deceptive. It now included returns from the seven uncontested western constituencies of 1922. Nevertheless, Sinn Féin enjoyed a resounding political success. It faced the election in difficult circumstances. Most of its leaders, including de Valera, as well as over 10 000 potential activists, were in jail. It had only rudimentary organisation, and no coherent publicity machine. It lacked most of the resources normally

---

[148] *Statist*, 25 August 1923.   [149] *Ibid.*
[150] L.M. Cullen, *An economic history of Ireland since 1660* (London, 1972), p. 172; D. Gwynn, *The Irish Free State, 1922–7* (London, 1928), p. 288.
[151] *Statist*, 25 August 1923.   [152] *Irish Times*, 31 August 1923.

considered necessary for the successful conduct of elections. The result gave de Valera a chance to escape from the grip of the gunmen.

Labour returned only 15 of 45 candidates, compared with 17 out of 18 in 1922.[153] Despite the enlarged electorate, its popular vote actually fell, reducing its share of the poll from 21 per cent to only 12 per cent. Nor was this the result of a general rally to the two major parties. Other small parties, together with Independents, increased their vote from 115 000 to 222 000, or from 18 per cent to 21 per cent of the poll. Labour was the only big loser. It had performed quite respectably at the municipal elections in 1920.[154] Following the general election of 1922 the *Irish Times* announced 'The emergence of Labour as a definite political force . . . Labour has "arrived" as an important and highly organised factor in national affairs.'[155] Labour, not for the last time, snatched failure from potential success. The bitter internal wrangles within the trade union movement following the disruptive impact of Jim Larkin's return from America, and the rash of industrial disputes which resulted in the official loss of 1.2 million working days in 1923, provoked popular disillusion.[156]

The 1923 election was the first remotely normal one held since 1910. It went a considerable distance towards clarifying the party political structure of the new state. Sinn Féin remained a potentially important political force. Labour's decline proved a more accurate pointer to its longer term prospects than the initial success in 1922.[157]

Though Cosgrave had suffered a serious rebuff, Sinn Féin's abstentionist policy assured him of a comfortable Dáil majority, with 63 seats out of 109. Even had Sinn Féin entered the Dáil, Cosgrave could probably have secured the support of the smaller parties, and of a motley crowd of Independents, to command a comfortable coalition majority. Nevertheless, pressures on the government were obviously fewer when policy did not have to be constantly constrained by merely tactical considerations. In addition, the refusal of Sinn Féin deputies to take their seats may have given the Dáil a chance to establish decent standards of behaviour. The fierce passions of 1923, scarcely amenable to control by the dignified de Valera, whose hand still lay only lightly on many of his nominal followers, might have induced behaviour far from conducive to the reputation of parliament, even if it were not to descend to actual assassination on the

153 *Ibid.*, 27 August 1923, 5 September 1923.   154 Fitzpatrick, *Politics*, pp. 158–60.
155 *Irish Times*, 19, 20 June 1922.
156 Larkin, *James Larkin*, pp. 244–5; A. Mitchell, *Labour in Irish politics 1890–1930* (Dublin, 1974), pp. 189–91; C. McCarthy, *Trade unions in Ireland 1894–1960* (Dublin, 1977), pp. 64–5. *The Times*, 7 August 1923, reports Larkinite mobs attacking delegates to the annual Labour Party Conference.
157 Peter Mair rightly stressed this point in 'Labour and the Irish party system revisited: party competition in the 1920s', *ESR*, 9 (1977), pp. 57–70. See also M. Laffan, '"Labour must wait": Ireland's conservative revolution', in P.J. Corish (ed.), *Radicals, rebels and establishments*, Historical Studies 15 (Belfast, 1985), p. 218.

floor of the House, as occurred in the Yugoslav Assembly. In the
circumstances, Sinn Féin's best presence was its absence.

The most potentially dangerous threat to Cosgrave after the civil war
came not from Sinn Féin but from a Free State army swollen in size to
55 000 men and 3300 officers by the end of hostilities. On 6 March 1924,
General Liam Tobin and Col. C.F. Dalton presented an ultimatum to
Cosgrave, on behalf of the 'IRA Organisation'. This demanded 'the
removal of the Army Council' which consisted of Mulcahy, MacMahon,
O'Sullivan and Ó Muirthuile. It further demanded 'the immediate suspension of army demobilisations and reorganisation' as a prelude to a
conference 'with representatives of your government to discuss our
interpretation of the Treaty', which they had accepted 'only . . . as a
means of achieving . . . a republican form of government in this country'.

The cabinet reacted in a curious manner. It duly denounced the
ultimatum and ordered the arrest of Tobin and Dalton. But it also
appointed Eoin O'Duffy, the Chief of Police, to supreme command of the
army, over the heads of its own Commander-in-Chief and Minister for
Defence, Mulcahy. Joseph McGrath, Minister for Industry and Commerce, who had been close to the 'IRAO', resigned on 7 March in alleged
protest at the 'absolute muddling, mishandling and incompetency' of the
Department of Defence. Following intense discussion within the party,
Cosgrave authorised the departing McGrath to assure the mutineers that
an inquiry would be held into army administration, with the clear
implication that the Army Council would be dissolved. The mutineers
should surrender by 20 March, but there would be no victimisation, and
they would be immediately released on parole. Having apparently
achieved their 'conditions' as far as material grievances were concerned,
Tobin and Dalton withdrew their ultimatum before it expired on
12 March. On 18 March, however, the mutineers gathered at a public
house in central Dublin, apparently with hostile intent towards the Army
Council. The Adjutant General, Geároid O'Sullivan, having consulted
Mulcahy as Minister for Defence, but not O'Duffy, ordered their arrest.
With Cosgrave in hospital, Kevin O'Higgins, his vice-president,
responded the following day by persuading the cabinet to recommend to
Cosgrave that he demand the resignation not only of O'Sullivan, but of
the rest of the Army Council, and of Mulcahy as Minister for Defence.
Cosgrave acted accordingly. Mulcahy pre-empted the demand in his own
case by resigning in protest against the demand for the resignation of the
council, on the grounds that the mutineers should have been arrested and
not offered terms. Thus ended, at least as O'Higgins purported to see the
situation, a militaristic threat to civilian rule.[158]

[158] M.G. Valiulis, *Almost a rebellion: the Irish army mutiny of 1924* (Cork, 1985); L. Ó
Broin, *Revolutionary underground: the story of the Irish Republican Brotherhood*

In the background to the mutiny, problems of policy, principle and personality were, as usual, intimately interwoven. Michael Collins had necessarily included in his entourage a wide variety of personality types. His 'apostles', who included intelligence agents and assassins, were less than fully tutored for the civilian existence that threatened to emerge after the Treaty. They clustered around Liam Tobin. Even before the death of Collins, they were becoming restive at the declining demand for their specialised services. Already in the first half of 1922, 'the seeds of the recent mutiny were taking root', but the 'apostles' were placated by the characteristic Collins assurance that 'you will be alright'.[159] Tobin and his colleagues continued to enjoy high rank after the death of Collins. But they were increasingly isolated by, and estranged from, two other groups, one clustered around Mulcahy, who succeeded Collins both as Commander-in-Chief and Minister for Defence, the other around Kevin O'Higgins, Minister for Home Affairs.

Mulcahy's group had stood as close to Collins as Tobin's. It included MacMahon, O'Sullivan and Ó Muirthuille. But their Collins was Collins the administrator. They had been the organisers on the general headquarters staff. As administrators, they were contemptuous of Tobin and the 'apostles'. They had not fought to make Ireland safe for spies and assassins. But they too, like the 'apostles', sought to preserve the legacy of 'their' Collins.

The third group, which would eventually come to comprise most of the government, clustered around Kevin O'Higgins, the most formidable personality, apart from Collins himself, thrown up on the Free State side. O'Higgins supported Mulcahy instead of Cosgrave for the presidency of the Executive Council in August 1922, in the belief that he would prosecute the war more vigorously.[160] By January 1923, however, O'Higgins was turning against Mulcahy on the grounds that he was failing to take sufficiently energetic measures not only against the Irregulars, but against 'agrarian anarchy and other serious abuses'.[161] O'Higgins, strongly supported by Patrick Hogan, Minister for Agriculture, and Ernest Blythe, Minister for Finance, represented vigorous social reaction. All three came from comfortable rural backgrounds. For O'Higgins, son of a doctor who also happened to hold a hundred acres, 'the land had ... always had almost emotional significance'.[162] To him, the civil war was

---

1858–1924 (Dublin, 1976), pp. 207–20. de Vere White, *O'Higgins*, pp. 157–69. On the broader issues see T.D. Williams, 'The summing up', in Williams, *Irish struggle*, pp. 186–9.

159 RM, P7/C/20, Col. C. Russell, supplementary statement to Committee of Inquiry into army mutiny, 10 May 1924.

160 RM, P7/B/57, 'Notes by Michael Hayes . . .', 3 June 1963, p. 7.

161 RM, P7/C/21, K. O'Higgins to Chairman of Committee of Inquiry into army mutiny, 12 May 1924, containing O'Higgins memo, 11 January 1923.

162 de Vere White, *O'Higgins*, pp. 1, 3.

more a social war than a national war. He felt that 'only a very small proportion' of Irregular activity arose from genuine anti-Treaty motives. Most of it, he claimed, sprang from a feeling that anybody who had helped in any way against the British 'is entitled to a parasitical millennium. Leavened in with some small amount of idealism and fanaticism, there is a good deal of greed and envy and lust and drunkenness and irresponsibility.'[163] Not only must the Irregulars be crushed, but illegal holding of land, refusal to pay debts, not to mention poteen making, must be stamped out immediately. 'The problem is psychological rather than physical, we have to vindicate the *idea* of law and order to government, as against anarchy.'[164] He held that 'as a first sign of crumbling civilization, it may be pointed out that the bailiff, as a factor in the situation, has failed . . . There are large numbers of decrees (county court and high court) unexecuted in every county.'[165] Mulcahy himself could scarcely be counted a social revolutionary. But he realised that making Ireland safe for the bailiff had not featured among the more seductive slogans of the struggle for independence.

O'Higgins further argued that executions in Dublin made little local impact. Therefore, 'there should be executions in every county' because 'local executions would tend considerably to shorten the struggle'.[166] The murder of his father in February 1923 can only have reinforced this impatience, which surfaced when he pushed through the establishment of the Supreme Council of Defence in April 1923, consisting of Cosgrave, Mulcahy, Joseph MacGrath, and himself. Mulcahy, regarding this as a vote of no confidence in his conduct of the war,[167] felt indignant that the Supreme Council should take credit for ending a war which he claimed was effectively won before the council was appointed.[168] O'Higgins responded that while the formal war against the Irregular forces may have been won, the war against anarchy was still raging. Mulcahy further felt that it was the creation of this supreme council that encouraged factions in the army to go behind his back, Tobin to McGrath, and others to O'Higgins.[169]

Mulcahy found himself in a most awkward situation. He inherited a web, partly woven by the revered Collins, of intrigue and suspicion. He tried to finesse, in the manner of his dead mentor. Between August 1922 and March 1924 he faced several daunting, and inter-connected, prob-

[163] RM, P7/C/21, K. O'Higgins to chairman of Committee of Inquiry into army mutiny, 12 May 1924, containing O'Higgins memo, 11 January 1923.
[164] *Ibid.*   [165] *Ibid.*; Lyons, *Ireland since the Famine*, p. 482.
[166] RM, P7/C/21, K. O'Higgins to chairman of Committee of Inquiry into army mutiny, 12 May 1924, containing O'Higgins memo, 11 January 1923.
[167] RM, P7/C/35, R. Mulcahy, statement to Committee of Inquiry into army mutiny, 19 May 1924.
[168] *Ibid.*   [169] *Ibid.*

lems. Firstly, it fell mainly to him, and to his colleagues on the Army Council, to mobilise the heterogeneous collection that quadrupled army size to nearly 60 000 between the autumn of 1922 and April 1923. That was a major administrative feat, inevitably complicated by tensions about promotion that erupted from the outset.[170] The problem of mobilisation paled compared with the problem of demobilisation which proved 'nearly as difficult as breaking the Irregular opposition'.[171] Despite the difficulties, 'other ranks' were reduced to 32 821 men by 17 November 1923, and to 13 306 by 31 March 1924. By December 1923, 1000 officers were demobilised.[172] The climax came with the final stage of officer demobilisation in March 1924. The names of another 1000 officers selected for demobilisation, and many others who were to be reduced in rank, were to be posted on 7 March. How were they to be chosen?

Mulcahy's declared ideal was

An efficient army – bearing in mind the material from which the present army has grown, and the necessity and the possibility of utilising the older roots of the army, but it is no part of my conception of my policy to keep in the army men who are unfitted for it, who, when they had the opportunity of doing any work, did not do it, or did it badly, and who have not the proper attitude with regard to discipline. My general attitude too is that these men must be weaned away from the idea and the use of arms . . .[173]

During the rapid build up of the national army, Mulcahy had naturally turned to the main reservoir of military experience in the country, ex-British soldiers and officers. These men were often more amenable to the discipline of normal army life than many who had flourished in the less disciplined ranks of the IRA. Those who felt their positions threatened by this influx naturally invoked nationalist criteria. The Tobin faction, earlier demanding 'not so much rank as influence in the army'[174] became decidedly concerned with rank as demobilisation proceeded. They demanded increasingly stridently, in the name of Michael Collins, that the 'British' influence in the army be curbed, that their own position be safeguarded, and that 'Mick's' policy on the Treaty be implemented. Vigorously supported by Joe McGrath, closely involved with Intelligence, and enjoying the sympathy of a substantial section of the Cumann na nGaedheal party,[175] they posed a genuine problem for Mulcahy, who, in

170 RM, P7/B/194, E. O'Duffy to R. Mulcahy, undated.
171 RM, P7/C/14, Seán MacMahon, statement submitted to Committee of Inquiry into army mutiny, 5 May 1924.
172 EB, P24/222, E. O'Duffy to President and members of the Executive Council, 7 April 1924. In addition, soldiers' wages were reduced by 40 per cent.
173 RM, P7/C/12, R. Mulcahy to W.T. Cosgrave, 11 January 1924. See also RM, P7/C/12, G. Ó Suilleabháin, statement submitted to Committee of Inquiry into army mutiny, 6 May 1924.
174 RM, P7/B/195, Mulcahy memo, 7 July 1923.
175 RM, P7/C/24, Committee of Inquiry into army mutiny, Ev. P. Hogan, 24 April 1924.

his search for an efficient force, 'could not accept the position that because a man was an ex-British officer he should not be in the army'.[176]

In the course of 1923, Mulcahy increasingly succumbed to the temptation to use a revitalised Irish Republican Brotherhood against the 'old IRA' as Tobin and his supporters styled themselves. Collins had unavailingly tried to use the IRB to prevent the post-Treaty split. When Liam Lynch sought to reorganise the IRB in November 1922 for anti-Treaty purposes, Mulcahy and Ó Muirthuile, who had succeeded Collins as head of the organisation, responded by revitalising the Brotherhood, under their own control.[177] Mulcahy sought to use it for two purposes. He hoped that it would form the nucleus of an efficient army, by excluding Tobin and other undesirables from it. The 'new IRB' should act as an organisational counterweight to the 'old IRA'. Secondly, Mulcahy was prepared to use the IRB in June 1923 to allow Tom Barry and other Irregulars to destroy their arms, disband the anti-Treaty IRA, and form 'a national organisation into which the best "elements" of both sides could come and cooperate. A political organisation and also a secret organisation'.[178]

All this was anathema to Kevin O'Higgins. Like Arthur Griffith, on the one hand, and Rory O'Connor, on the other, O'Higgins saw right and wrong at this stage in terms of black and white. Unlike Mulcahy, still clinging to the Collins – and de Valera – hopes of early 1922 that some common ground could be found, still desperately groping for something to salvage from the civil war, O'Higgins saw total victory as the only solution. He not only felt 'that IRB policy demanded that the Irregular snake be scotched rather than killed'[179] but he dismissed the IRB itself as 'a Tammany, politically irresponsible, to which members of the Dáil would become the merest puppets'.[180] Whether Mulcahy was wise to revive the IRB, even as the instrument of the Army Council, to achieve his objective of a disciplined and efficient army, is doubtful. There was force in the arguments advanced by O'Higgins. Nevertheless, they failed to take account of the difficulties that would confront any Commander-in-Chief in the circumstances.

Mulcahy finessed on demobilisation partly because, like Tobin, he believed, much more than O'Higgins, in using the Treaty as a stepping stone, and partly because he realised the dangers of direct confrontation. With his ear closer to the army ground than O'Higgins, Mulcahy knew

176 RM, P7/B/195, Mulcahy memo, 7 July 1923.
177 O'Beirne-Ranelagh, 'The IRB', *IHS*, 20, 77 (March 1976), pp. 34–6.
178 RM, P7/C/10, R. Mulcahy, statement submitted to Committee of Inquiry into army mutiny, 29 April 1924.
179 RM, P7/C/21, K. O'Higgins, statement to chairman, Committee of Inquiry into Army mutiny, 12 May 1924.
180 RM, P7/C/22, Committee of Inquiry into army mutiny, Ev. K. O'Higgins, 16 May 1924.

that the Tobin position enjoyed widespread sympathy. The demand that the still vibrant memory of Collins, indeed of an increasingly idealised Collins, should not be dishonoured, nor his flag furled, roused a visceral response in men who craved assurance that history would vindicate their sacrifice in drinking the bitter dregs from the cup of compromise. Many officers, like Tobin, had accepted the Treaty 'in exactly the same spirit which we know the late commander-in-chief accepted it, namely, as we would have regarded the successful ambush of the enemy, prior to July 1921'.[181] Tobin, 'very hard and bitter', accused Mulcahy to his face of treachery to Collins at a meeting attended by Cosgrave in June 1923.[182] No other charge could have hurt Mulcahy so much. Mulcahy received frequent reports of the widespread dissatisfaction (some of which he shared himself) at the manner in which the government appeared to be reconciled to the Free State as the ultimate objective, and not merely as a staging post. Séamus Ó hAodha, referring as early as July 1923 to a 'mutiny' against the replacement of IRA officers by ex-Britishers, declared himself 'convinced that a complete administrative case can be made for the changes that have been made in the army, and therefore give you my moral support everywhere, but my sympathies are with the mutineers'.[183] Michael Brennan, the noted Clare guerrilla leader, warned in May 1923 from his important Limerick command that

We all here have been very worried for some time past at the prospect of finding that the Free State was the end for which we fought, and not the means to that end ... The whole Command Staff ... were absolutely unanimous ... that not a single one of them would have lifted a finger for the Free State if they hadn't felt sure that it was the best means of attaining the end for which they fought the British and for which their comrades died.[184]

In these circumstances, Mulcahy would have been irresponsible had he not sought to tread warily. Given the complexity of the situation, the charge levelled by Patrick Hogan that 'reviving the IRB was mutiny. Anything that weakens the allegiance the soldier bears to the government is mutiny, and all the more serious if done officially,'[185] may seem a trifle precious, however compelling in the abstract. It assumes that the allegiance of the soldier was unquestioningly to the government. Mulcahy knew how uncertain that was. He was trying to bring allegiance around in that direction by his circuitous route. For that, it was his fate to be bitterly

181 RM, P7/B/195, L. Tobin to W.T. Cosgrave, 6 June 1923.
182 RM, P7/B/195, Mulcahy memo, 25 June 1923.
183 RM, P7/B/195, S. Ó hAodha to R. Mulcahy, 7 July 1923.
184 RM, P7/C/10, M. Brennan to R. Mulcahy, 15 May 1923. The Army Council had to pay close attention to the views of powerful GOCs during the civil war. RM, P7/C/20, C. Russell, supplementary statement to Committee of Inquiry into army mutiny, 10 May 1924. In this case, Brennan's sentiments would certainly have been shared by all members of the Army Council.
185 RM, P7/C/24, Committee of Inquiry into army mutiny, Ev. P. Hogan, 24 April 1924.

assailed by Tobin, as a traitor to Collins, by McGrath, as a bungler, and by O'Higgins, as a traitor to democracy. None of the charges can be unreservedly accepted.

The charge that Mulcahy as Minister for Defence, and the Army Council, botched demobilisation is certainly grossly exaggerated, if not entirely false. Mulcahy, who had most to lose from the reduction in the size of the army, were he an ambitious man, nonetheless reduced its size effectively. Demobilisation was virtually complete at the time of his dismissal. Even as hostile a witness as Eoin O'Duffy had to acknowledge, as had the hostile Commission of Inquiry, that 'discipline and morale' in the army were 'generally good'.[186] It is difficult to prove conclusively that 'Mulcahy and others involved in the IRB reorganisation were not promoting members of the IRB in the National Army at the expense of others.'[187] But this contention does derive support from the fact that so few of his appointments were rescinded by the new military administration. McGrath's complaint about incompetence can be translated as a gripe that his cronies were not getting jobs, and as a response to Mulcahy's charge that McGrath, as Minister for Labour, was failing to provide employment for dismissed officers.[188] It may be, also, that McGrath felt personally aggrieved by Mulcahy's insistence that 'When there is interference with regard to persons who shall be demobilised or who shall not be demobilised, on the part of any outside minister, or the Executive Council, that case be made one of principle, which can be stated in memorandum form.'[189] O'Higgins, it is true, charged that Mulcahy failed to impose 'stern impersonal discipline' in the army.[190] He based the accusation mainly on the indiscipline of some IRB members in the Kenmare area. The situation was obviously unsavoury. But it was not only Mulcahy who trod cautiously on the matter. The Attorney General advised against prosecuting in the case. Ironically, within months, and again with respect to incidents in Kerry, O'Higgins himself advised against prosecution in some cases of agrarian crime, on the grounds that more evil than good would result – the quintessential Mulcahy argument throughout the contorted demobilisation process.[191]

O'Higgins, who was reported as behaving with less dignity than Mulcahy during the Dáil debates on the mutiny,[192] could not bring himself to admit that Mulcahy was as committed as himself to civilian

---

[186] EB, P24/222, E. O'Duffy to the President and members of the Executive Council, 7 April 1924.

[187] O'Beirne-Ranelagh, 'The IRB', p. 38.

[188] RM, P7/B/195, R. Mulcahy to W.T. Cosgrave, 11 January 1924.

[189] *Ibid.*

[190] RM, P7/C/23, Committee of Inquiry into army mutiny, Ev. K. O'Higgins, B6.

[191] EB, P24/194, K. O'Higgins to each member of the Executive Council, 6 October 1924.

[192] *Sunday Times*, 23 March 1924.

government. Mulcahy had already espoused the ideal of an efficient and politically impartial army 'that would be absolutely responsible to even a de Valera government, if such a government were returned'.[193] It was mainly on tactics that Mulcahy and O'Higgins differed. O'Higgins's achievement was to succeed in turning into an issue of principle, in the light of their growing personal antipathy, what to Mulcahy remained an issue of tactics.

The manner in which O'Higgins challenged Mulcahy, and outmanoeuvred him, in March 1924, would have been criminally reckless but for the fact that, contrary to the unworthy accusations levelled against him, Mulcahy was as devoted a democrat as O'Higgins himself. It was Mulcahy's restrained response to his dismissal that was crucial to the infant state.[194] Though far from universally popular among the rank and file, precisely because of his demobilisation measures, Mulcahy was the one man who might have roused sufficient military support to pose a real threat to the government. Had he been the type of character depicted by O'Higgins, he could have created a genuine crisis. It was precisely because O'Higgins's judgement of Mulcahy was mistaken that the recklessness of his own behaviour was concealed. The real significance of 1924 was the mutiny that never was. There were those close to Mulcahy who wanted to face down O'Higgins. Seán MacMahon refused the cabinet request for his resignation unless told the reason for it, and demanded instead that O'Duffy 'be withdrawn from the army'.[195] It was probably only Mulcahy's decision – the sign not of a weak man, but of a committed democrat – to accept his humiliation, that forestalled a really serious crisis, though the Army Council as a whole refrained from inciting unrest among other officers.[196]

If Mulcahy had tried to finesse over the previous eighteen months, so had Cosgrave. Next to Mulcahy and McGrath, he was the main loser in the struggle of March 1924. Cosgrave, who was kept reasonably well informed by Mulcahy of demobilisation problems, of the Tobin threat, and of his own IRB tactics, characteristically and sensibly tried to temporise between the strongest men in his cabinet, both of whom had much right on their side. He seems to have wanted a more conciliatory line towards Mulcahy in March, but was hospitalised during the decisive period of the O'Higgins–Mulcahy conflict.[197] The only member of the government to support Cosgrave was Hugh Kennedy, the Attorney

193 RM, P7/B/195, Mulcahy memo of meeting with Cosgrave and McGrath, 26 January 1924.
194 Valiulis, *Almost a rebellion*, pp. 83–4.
195 RM, P7/B/196, S. MacMahon to R. Mulcahy, 20 March 1924. The cabinet offered MacMahon appointment with the rank of Major General on 22 March (SPO CAB 2/73).
196 Valiulis, *Almost a rebellion*, p. 76.
197 It is not clear how 'diplomatic' Cosgrave's illness was.

General.[198] Ernest Blythe, often torn between Cosgrave and O'Higgins on other matters, 'was brutally with O'Higgins' on this occasion.[199]

O'Higgins, then, emerged as the real winner from the whole débâcle. He used the 'mutiny' not only to vindicate civilian government – if more in rhetoric than in reality – but also to isolate Mulcahy. He exploited the mutineers' demand for the abolition of the Army Council. He managed to eliminate two rivals from the cabinet, McGrath and Mulcahy. He had McGrath replaced by his own protégé, Patrick McGilligan.[200] He had his own devout admirer, Eoin O'Duffy, appointed to supreme control of the army.[201] The terms of reference of the Committee of Inquiry into the mutiny were adroitly phrased to divert attention from the opportunistic behaviour of the executive council.[202] It was also naturally packed with safe men, who gave O'Higgins an easy passage when his more impetuous charges against Mulcahy and the Army Council could not be sustained.[203] It was symptomatic of the behaviour of the participants over the previous year that even when the members of the Army Council had their request for a public inquiry rejected, they still agreed to appear in private before a hostile inquisition, in contrast to McGrath, who simply refused to give evidence.[204]

A cabinet that had failed to crush the real mutiny, and then postured in public as defenders of democracy by dismissing those who did take decisive action against the mutineers, and who posed no threat to democracy, showed that it had little to learn about the art of political manoeuvring at this level. O'Higgins by skilful rhetoric managed to project himself as the saviour of civilian rule from the danger lurking in a militarist Army Council. Mulcahy was denounced for contemplating compromise with the Old IRA, in the much more difficult earlier circumstances, by the very people who now chose to compromise with, rather than confront, the real mutineers in March 1924. The legend of a resolute executive council vindicating civilian authority despite a vacillating Mulcahy distorts historical reality. But Mulcahy 'ignored the importance of process, counting on end results to vindicate his position'.[205] While Mulcahy may have made errors of judgement in his handling of the whole demobilisation process, it is difficult to avoid the suspicion that reactions to the ultimatum of 6 March, and to the events of 18 March, owed more to cabinet faction fighting than to exalted concepts of the

198 RM, P7/D/115, unsigned note, 26 April 1965   199 *Ibid.*
200 O'Higgins had earlier offered McGilligan an assistant secretaryship in his own department (J. McColgan, 'Introduction to papers of P. McGilligan', PM, P35/B/1). McGilligan acted as Secretary to O'Higgins in 1922.
201 de Vere White, *O'Higgins*, p. 231.   202 Valiulis, *Almost a rebellion*, p. 85.
203 RM, P7/C/23. For a sample of cases where O'Higgins was either protected by, or not pressed by, the committee, see Committee of Inquiry into army mutiny, pp. B10, B14, E14, E16, F10–12.
204 Valiulis, *Almost a rebellion*, pp. 82, 86.   205 *Ibid.*, p. 120.

nature of democracy. The 'army mutiny' was an unedifying episode as much for the opportunist cynicism it exposed among the civilian politicians as for the militarist threat to civilian government.

Cosgrave salvaged what he could by frustrating, from his hospital bed, the ambition of O'Higgins to become Acting Minister for Defence, by assuming the office himself.[206] Cosgrave held Defence for eight months before appointing the relatively safe Patrick Hughes as his successor. He managed within a year to dismiss O'Duffy, who seemed to be more intent on exacting loyalty to himself than to the government, and confined him solely to his former police responsibilities.[207] Finally, Cosgrave recovered sufficient ground to bring Mulcahy back into the cabinet, as Minister for Local Government, following the general election of June 1927, and thus provide himself with some balance once more against O'Higgins. Cosgrave thus intimated that he gave little credence to the wild charges of O'Higgins against Mulcahy's commitment to the parliamentary process.

If the mutiny exposed rivalries within the Cosgrave government, economic and social policy generally provided, despite occasional differences of emphasis, a unifying bond. The regime publicly rejoiced in its commitment to the conservative conventional wisdom. 'We were,' boasted Kevin O'Higgins, 'probably the most conservative minded revolutionaries that ever put through a successful revolution.'[208]

This attitude was grist to the mill of the civil servants who masterminded the Ministers and Secretaries Act of 1924. Existing departments and boards were combined on an essentially *ad hoc* basis, showing little creative concept of the role of the civil service in a newly independent small state. Indeed the main criticism voiced by senior civil servants of the inherited system was that it deviated too far from English normalcy. Their objective was to substitute for the inherited structure of English government in Ireland, which made a hesitant attempt to cater for Irish circumstances, a more faithful imitation of English government in England. Such originality accurately reflected the calibre of their creativity.

The influence of C.J. Gregg, an Irishman loaned from the Board of Inland Revenue, London, and a personal friend of Cosgrave,[209] who 'more than any other single man, was responsible for the organisation of the . . . new civil service',[210] ensured that the service would bear the stamp 'made in England'. Gregg dominated the committee that formulated the final recommendations for the reorganisation of government, duly incor-

206 SPO, CAB 2/69, 19 March 1924, 2/72, 21 March 1924.
207 SPO, S3677, Memo by Attorney General, 6 February 1925; O'Duffy to Cosgrave, 9 February 1925.
208 Quoted in Laffan, 'Labour must wait', p. 219.
209 Information from Leon Ó Broin.
210 Fanning, *Finance*, p. 43.

porated into the Ministers and Secretaries Act. Gregg, devout guardian of
the conventional wisdom, even favoured retaining the title 'The Treasury'
for the Department of Finance, on the grounds that this 'will impress on
people that one particular minister and one state unit under him holds the
purse strings and is very difficult to get anything out of the purse'.[211] So
much for Pearse's plaintive cry that the treasury ruled Ireland!

Ernest Blythe was the only ministerial member of the Committee on
Government Organisation, which was established on Gregg's initiative,
and dominated by civil service thinking. Gregg considered the committee
a rubber stamp to formalise his arrangements. He reassured his minister
that 'the review itself is not a difficult problem and will not necessitate
very much time or enquiry'.[212] There can hardly be a blander commentary
on the administrative implications of the Irish 'revolution'. The Act
enshrined the principle of 'ministerial responsibility', establishing the
minister as the 'corporation sole', exclusively responsible for everything
done by his department. It is just possible that some departments were
determined to have so little to do in 1924 that a diligent minister could
actually keep himself abreast of everything done in his name, but the real
effect of the fiction was to provide a façade for civil service, and
particularly Finance, influence over government.

Gregg returned to the Inland Revenue in London in 1924.[213] The other
most influential civil servants were probably Joseph Brennan, J.J. McElligott, H.P. Boland and Arthur Codling.[214] Brennan, son of a comfortable
shopkeeper in the small west Cork town of Bandon, served in the Chief
Secretary's office in Dublin Castle from 1912 to 1922, from where he
provided Collins with useful information for the Treaty negotiations. He
became Comptroller and Auditor General of the Provisional Government
in 1922, and was appointed Secretary to the Department of Finance in
1923, at the age of thirty-six, with J.J. McElligott as his Assistant
Secretary. As Secretary, Brennan continued to focus an auditor general's
grudging eye on expenditure. His insistence on rigorous accountability
came as a culture shock to many of the heroes of the revolution. The
omens were hardly propitious for painstaking bookkeeping. The local
councils established under the 1898 Local Government Act soon acquired
a reputation for indifference to petty financial detail. And the other main
outlet for the administrative genius of the Irish laity – the great cities of the
United States – did not enjoy a universal reputation for rigorous financial
procedures. Brennan had few doubts that Ireland was swarming with men
eager to emulate George Washington Plunkitt who 'seen his opportunities

211 SPO, S1932, C.J. Gregg to E. Blythe, 17 July 1923.
212 SPO, S1932, C.J. Gregg to Minister for Finance, 12 January 1923.
213 Fanning, *Finance*, pp. 77–80.
214 The role of D. O'Hegarty, who had been close to Collins, and became Secretary of the
     Executive Council, would repay investigation.

and took 'em'. His image of the politician appears to have been that of a pig with his snout permanently stuck in the trough. Brennan, on the other hand, indulged an austere ideal of the civil servant perched above the public morass, immune from vulgar self-interest, holding the scales of public justice between conflicting selfish private interests. There was a certain cold grandeur about his cherished image of the public service, a body of incorruptible state servants valiantly resisting the rush of the Gadarene swine to the flesh pots of public money.

Perhaps the major achievement of the early years, and it remains one of the most remarkable achievements in the history of the state, was the creation of a Civil Service Commission, consisting of the Ceann Comhairle (Speaker), and two civil servants, to preside over the public appointments process.[215] The new government was naturally deluged with importunities for jobs. The scope for casualness in the appointments process was considerable. The Civil Service Commission did the state great service in setting ethical standards. Given the scope for corruption permitted by the feeble sense of public morality, the imposition of a high degree of integrity in appointments to the central administration verged on the miraculous. The same considerations did not apply to promotion within the civil service, where the criterion of seniority soon took precedence over that of merit even among men themselves originally appointed on grounds of merit.[216] Nevertheless, this was at the time a relatively venial transgression of the code of strict personal integrity which would be rightly regarded as one of the glories of the civil service.

Finance officials did, it is true, suffer the occasional reverse in attempting to widen their prerogatives in the early years. Gregg, for instance, remained so suspicious of the political process that he tried to overrule the Executive Council itself and to establish the authority of Finance on the Civil Service Commission against that of both the cabinet and the Speaker. Michael Hayes, the Speaker, was provoked to retort that 'as chairman of the Civil Service Commission I feel no responsibility whatever to the Finance Department, nor to the Minister as such. The appointment is made by the Executive Council.'[217] But this was a rare rebuff for Finance. Finance officials found it even easier than they might have anticipated to impose their views on their ministers in the very early years. The first two ministers, Collins and Cosgrave, were otherwise engaged for much of the time.

After the August 1923 election Cosgrave appointed the 34-year-old Ernest Blythe as Minister for Finance. This made little difference to civil service control in general. It was not that Blythe was a weak man. Far from it. He was that more dangerous type, so frequently found in senior

---

[215] Fanning, *Finance*, pp. 63ff.   [216] *Ibid.*, pp. 544–8.
[217] SPO, S1856A, M. Hayes to Minister for Finance, 22 May 1924.

posts in Ireland, a strong personality of narrow perspective, a Christian Brothers' boy par excellence – except that he was an Ulster Protestant! He and Brennan soon developed a powerful mutual antipathy. They were both healthy haters. Brennan was effectively dismissed in 1927 by being appointed chairman of the new Currency Commission. His relations with Blythe had by now reached breaking point, and his bitter criticism of aspects of the Shannon scheme alienated the cabinet.[218] But his dismissal owed little to cabinet reappraisal of administrative policy. Blythe largely shared Brennan's complacency with the existing structure of both the civil service itself and of Irish society. He had little interest in administrative innovation.[219] Blythe recommended as Brennan's successor the 37-year-old Assistant Secretary, J.J. McElligott, a somewhat less abrasive version of his friend Brennan, whose image of the public servant he fully shared.

Brennan and McElligott not only clung to existing economic orthodoxy. They also nurtured, logically enough, an aversion to the working class in general, and to organised labour in particular. They loathed the concept of Whitley Councils, which provided arbitration machinery for wage claims within the English civil service.[220] They were bent on economy, on reducing wages and salaries, which would have been much more difficult if the Whitley procedures were in force. They succeeded to the extent that the civil service cost only £3.9 million for the year ending 1 January 1932, compared with £4.2 million for the year ending 1 April 1922, despite an increase in numbers from 21 000 in 1925 to 23 396.[221]

Brennan and McElligott received strong support in their retrenchment crusade from H.P. Boland, who succeeded Gregg as establishment officer in Finance in 1924, and from Arthur Codling, who took charge of the supply division in Finance in 1923.[222] They rendered sterling service. But their minds were cast in an English mould. Leon Ó Broin recollected from his time as a young administrative officer in Finance in the twenties, that Boland conveyed the impression that 'he wanted all of us to become civil servants on the English model'.[223] And Codling was actually an Englishman, 'a Gladstonian liberal', who 'brought to his work a certain religious zeal'.[224]

The combination of Cosgrave, Blythe, Brennan and McElligott ensured that the new state would concentrate on rigorous retrenchment. Blythe reduced government expenditure from £42 million in 1923–4 to

[218] L. Ó Broin, 'Joseph Brennan: civil servant extraordinary', *Studies*, 66, 261 (Spring 1977), pp. 34–5. For other differences with Blythe, see Daly, 'Government finance', p. 82. On Brennan generally, see L. Ó Broin, *No man's man* (Dublin, 1982).

[219] N. Ó Gadhra, 'Earnán de Blaghd', *Eire–Ireland*, 11, 3 (1976), pp. 93–105, contains a character study of Blythe.

[220] *Commission of Inquiry into the civil service*, 2, p. 19, para. 87 (Dublin, n.d. [1935]).

[221] *Ibid.*, p. 2, paras 3–4.   [222] Fanning, *Finance*, pp. 72, 63.

[223] L. Ó Broin, *Just like yesterday* (Dublin, 1986), p. 81.

[224] *Ibid.*, p. 83.

£32 million in 1924–5 and £24 million in 1926–7. He thus found himself in the happy position of proving Irish fitness for self-government by reducing income tax from 5 shillings in 1924 to only 3 shillings in 1926, 6d less than in England, a historic triumph over the old enemy. Fiscal responsibility, and low taxation, were supposed to impress English doubters of the Irish capacity for self-discipline. A budget balanced at the lowest possible level of expenditure was a conventional mark of a self-reliant national personality. Economic and social orthodoxy, defined by English pundits, would contribute to the political stability coveted by Cosgrave. It would reassure sceptical English, and Anglo-Irish, observers of the adult attitude of the infant government. Low income tax was further presumed to offer a bait to the Anglo-Irish to keep their money in the country. In practice, this largely meant keeping it out of the country, in London.[225]

It was likewise presumed that low income tax would attract owners of capital to Ireland where they would provide more employment by industrial investment.[226] Unfortunately for this line of reasoning, the Southern economy had a surfeit, not a shortage, of capital. It enjoyed a powerful creditor position after the First World War,[227] and enjoyed a fair volume of savings after 1923. Bank deposits in Ireland did fall by nearly 20 per cent between 1922 and 1927, before levelling out. Though this was higher than the 10 per cent decline in England,[228] the difference cannot be attributed to a sense of insecurity. The sharper fall in agricultural than in manufacturing prices affected Ireland more seriously than England. Total bank deposits in the Free State amounted to about £110 million in 1927, compared with advances of only £60 million.[229] The Revenue Commissioners calculated that no less than £195 million was invested abroad by Free State residents as of 1926–7, compared with only £73 million invested in the Free State by non-residents.[230] It was not necessary to import capital for Irish industry. There was adequate capital in the country. The problem was, as it had long been, how to mobilise it.[231] Low income tax tended to attract rentier rather than risk capital, and

---

225 For a sympathetic account of Blythe's policy see T.K. Daniel, 'Griffith on his noble head', *IESH*, 3 (1976), pp. 57–60.
226 Gwynn, *Irish Free State*, p. 260.
227 L.M. Cullen, *An economic history of Ireland since 1660* (London, 1972), p. 172.
228 There are difficulties in distinguishing Free State bank deposits from those in Northern Ireland, but see *Statistical Abstract*, 1931, T. 170, p. 142, and B.R. Mitchell and P. Deane, *Abstract of British historical statistics* (Cambridge, 1962), p. 447.
229 PM, P35/A/19, memorandum prepared by the Revenue Commissioners: (1) Estimate of Free State capital invested . . ., 11 January 1929.
230 *Ibid*. The Revenue Commissioners emphasised the tentative status of some of the components in their calculations, but the orders of magnitude are unlikely to require extensive revision.
231 Daly, 'Government finance', pp. 73ff; Cullen, *Economic history*, p. 169; J. Lee, 'Capital in the Irish economy', in L.M. Cullen (ed.), *The formation of the Irish economy* (Cork, 1969), pp. 53–63.

it was risk capital and entrepreneurship that Ireland lacked. Rentiers didn't know what to do with their money in the country, except to export it. This was a rational decision for the individual rentier, but a largely unproductive one, even allowing for the contribution of the interest to the balance of payments, for the national economy. Patrick McGilligan, as Minister for Industry and Commerce, conceded the vacuity of the crude 'lack of capital' argument when he admitted that the poor response to the Trade Loans Act of 1924, which provided some capital for industrial investment, indicated that lack of capital in the absolute sense did not pose a major obstacle to economic development, thus demolishing an alleged premise for much of the government's taxation policy.[232]

Until 1926 Blythe could plead that uncertainty regarding the national debt precluded dangerous fiscal experiments. The Treaty specified that the liability of the Free State for the United Kingdom national debt and for British war pensions would be settled by agreement or arbitration. Following further negotiations in 1922 and 1923 the Free State consented to pay land annuities of £3.13 million per annum to the British government, and to pay a proportion of RIC pensions. The British in turn agreed to guarantee further land purchase bonds raised in the Free State. Cosgrave took pains to disguise the nature of this arrangement from the Dáil.[233] In 1926 London agreed to relieve the Free State from liability for the British national debt, but the Irish accepted continuing liability 'for civil pensions payable in respect of services in Ireland', and also for the land annuities.

From 1926 then, following this 'damned good bargain', as Cosgrave called it,[234] Blythe would appear to have had more room for manoeuvre. It made little apparent difference to his policy. This reflected a visceral as well as an intellectual response to economic conditions. Son of an Antrim strong farmer, he had shown himself unsympathetic to working-class demands during the Dublin lockout of 1913,[235] and spared little sympathy for social expenditure. It was unnecessary to insist on paying so high a proportion of 'abnormal' expenditure, incurred mainly as a result of the civil war, out of current revenue – about 60 per cent of £39 million between 1922 and 1931 – thus reducing the amount potentially available for either productive economic investment or for social expenditure. The Free State not only followed England back on to the gold standard, guarantor of fiscal responsibility according to the conventional wisdom, in 1925, but followed it at the existing parity with sterling. The policy may have been correct in the circumstances, but this served only

[232] Gwynn, *Irish Free State*, p. 283.   [233] Mitchell, *Irish politics*, p. 214.
[234] E. MacNeill, 'Ten years of the Irish Free State', *Foreign Affairs*, 10 (1932), p. 238.
[235] Mitchell, *Irish politics*, p. 58.

to emphasise that economic sovereignty did not come automatically with political sovereignty.[236]

One or two Free State politicians liked to refer, however vaguely, to the Danish model of government. A comparison of income and expenditure in the two states may prove instructive. Danish taxation per capita was 30 per cent higher than Irish in 1927. The Danes financed their national debt by fresh borrowing, and devoted more than double the Irish proportion of their public expenditure to welfare services and education.[237] The Danes even spent double the Free State proportion on the promotion of trade and industry. Yet Denmark somehow survived such irresponsible, not to say immoral, behaviour, and unsportingly prospered compared with Ireland.

Blythe's financial policy made sense in the context of the prevailing conventional wisdom. It also made party political sense. Income tax accounted for only about 20 per cent of government income. The rest was derived from custom and excise duties, and from incidental indirect taxes, which were probably disproportionately borne by the poorer strata. A low level of income tax was therefore electorally as well as financially congenial to Cosgrave's supporters. So was the de-rating of agricultural land in 1926 and in 1931, a sop to the strong farmer vote which Cumann na nGaedheal was assiduously cultivating, and pushed through in the face of the facts accumulated by the secretary of the de-rating commission, the young John Leydon, who scarcely bothered to conceal his contempt for the exercise.[238]

Government financial policy, which amounted to virtual abdication in favour of established financial interests, consolidated support for the regime in the financial community. Industry and Commerce had reservations about this approach. When the Bank of Ireland sought power 'to take or concur in taking all or any steps which appear to the directors to be necessary or desirable for . . . avoiding or helping to avoid disturbances prejudicial or which might be prejudicial to the financial interests of the community', Thomas Barrington observed that

I have seen nothing in the remote or recent history of the Bank of Ireland to inspire the hope that its directorate possess either the capacity or the outlook to exercise such powers wisely or even intelligently . . . the government are the proper custodians of the financial interests of the community and it would be a sorry day

236 T.K. Whitaker, 'An ceangal le sterling – ar cheart é bhriseadh?', *Administration*, 24, 1 (Spring 1976), 14.

237 MacNeill, 'Ten years', pp. 239–40.

238 PM, P35/A/22, supplementary memorandum by Mr Leydon, 31 July 1930 (the original memorandum, entitled, 'Are agriculturalists overtaxed?', was dated 28 July 1930.) While Leydon disavows any policy recommendations, the tenor of his report is unmistakeable. For his contempt for the 'politics' of the commission, see D. Roche, 'John Leydon', *Administration*, 27, 3 (Autumn 1979), p. 250.

for the country when they surrender expressedly or by implication their obligations in the matter to any body of bankers however reputable.[239]

The official departmental version transmitted to Finance expressed its disquiet a good deal more discreetly.[240] It made no difference. McElligott brushed the reservations aside.[241]

Blythe had a financial policy. He had virtually no economic policy, beyond the act of faith that prosperity would follow from fiscal rectitude. Although less instinctively hostile to proposals for expenditure than Brennan, as shown in the cases of the Shannon scheme and the Trade Loans Act, he broadly shared Brennan's belief that if Finance looked after the book-keeping the economy would look after itself. His attitude corresponded with general government economic policy. This relied heavily on agriculture as the engine of economic growth. It revolved around the vigorous efforts of Patrick Hogan, Minister for Agriculture, who believed that 'national development in Ireland, for our generation at least, is practically synonymous with agricultural development'.[242]

George O'Brien's classic obituary of Hogan, who was tragically killed in a car accident in 1936, distilled the essence of Hogan's policy, itself influenced by O'Brien, the gifted young professor at University College Dublin who would grace many Free State committees of economic enquiry.[243]

Hogan started from the assumption that agriculture was, and would remain, by far the most important industry in the Free State, and that the touchstone by which every economic measure must be judged was its effect on the prosperity of the farmers. He believed that economic policy should be directed to maximise farmers' income, because, the farmers being the most important section of the population, everything that raised their income raised the national income of the country.

Prosperity among farmers would provide the purchasing power necessary to sustain demand for non-agricultural goods and services, and it was useless to encourage secondary industries unless the primary industry was in a position to purchase their products. The principal aim of agricultural policy in the Free State should therefore be the maximisation of the farmers' income . . . Here, therefore, were the *data* of the problem with which Hogan was confronted: (1) agricultural policy must be directed towards the maximisation of the farmers' profit; (2) the farmers' profit is the difference between what they put into the land and what they take out of it, i.e. the difference between costs of production and selling prices; (3) selling prices were, in most cases, outside the control of the Free State government.

---

239 PM, P35/A/27, Bank of Ireland Bill 1929, T.J. Barrington memo, 2 December 1928.
240 PM, P35/A/27, Bank of Ireland Bill 1929, G. Campbell to Secretary, Department of Finance, 23 January 1929.
241 PM, P35/A/27, Bank of Ireland Bill 1929, J.J. McElligott to Secretary, Department of Industry and Commerce, 17 May 1929.
242 SPO S3557, P. Hogan memo, 'An analysis of the economic aspect of agriculture in the Irish Free State', 25 January 1924.
243 James Meenan has painted a memorable portrait in *George O'Brien: a memoir* (Dublin, 1980).

When the problem was stated in this way it becomes obvious that the only thing the government could do to help the farmer was to assist him to reduce his costs of production.[244]

Far-reaching conclusions for economic and social policy followed from this reasoning. The emphasis on paring farmers' costs to the bone precluded a general tariff policy, which might benefit industry, but which would inevitably, it was assumed, increase farmers' production costs by raising the price of imports, and might provoke retaliation against Irish agricultural exports. Taxation should be reduced as low as possible to help reduce agricultural production costs. In view of the government commitment to a balanced budget, this inevitably restricted expenditure on social services or industrial development.

The calculation was that if land, labour, capital and skill were applied in the first place to the further development of those forms of production which had proved to be most suitable wealth would be increased all the more quickly. Then, but not until then, would circumstances allow a diversion of resources to other objectives. Irish industries, which would presumably depend heavily on the domestic market, would best prosper when that market was prosperous. The money for social services must come out of revenue: the country had to increase its wealth before revenue was available.[245]

Hogan himself was far too vibrant a personality to subscribe to undiluted do-nothing dogma. He derided 'those who held one fixed dogma in politics and economics, and that is *laissez-faire*. How anyone can adopt that attitude after the experience of the last ten years simply baffles me.'[246] He pushed through the 1923 Land Act transferring the still unpurchased holdings from landlord to tenant. He pursued a vigorous, and far from universally popular, interventionist policy to improve breeding and marketing standards. The reputation of Irish agricultural produce had suffered in the First World War, when farmers took advantage of the boom conditions on the British market to deluge consumers with substandard produce. Hogan's insistence on improved standards of cleanliness, packaging, marking and honest description of the quality of produce caused culture shock to many farmers weaned on more relaxed ethical standards.[247]

But Hogan's policy, despite the coherence of its conception, and the clarity of its exposition, enjoyed only limited success. His insistence on improving standards did help raise the prices of first quality Irish butter and eggs on the British market. But little change occurred in the structure or in the volume of output, or of exports, during the Hogan years. The

244 G. O'Brien, 'Patrick Hogan', *Studies*, 25 (September 1936), p. 358.
245 J. Meenan, *The Irish economy since 1922* (Liverpool, 1970), p. 305. Meenan's section on Hogan, pp. 303–14, contains a cogent exposition and defence of his policy.
246 DD, 7, 19 June 1924, 2697.
247 Gwynn, *Irish Free State*, p. 291; Meenan, *Irish economy*, pp. 92–5.

policy was dynamic. The response was not. Not growth, but stagnation, characterised Irish agriculture in the twenties. Irish butter, it is true, did secure relatively high prices on the English market by 1929. But butter prices were generally sluggish. The value of butter exports rose only slowly from £4 million to £4.6 million between 1924 and 1929, before dropping to £3.3 million as slump spread in 1930.[248] Despite the emphasis on butter production, the volume of butter exports, having reached 92 per cent of their 1911–13 level in 1922, did not subsequently exceed 90 per cent of that level.[249] And the number of cows actually fell slightly between 1924 and 1930, with pig numbers rising only marginally.[250] Total cattle numbers fell from 4.38 to 4.04 million between 1922 and 1930, more than offsetting in livestock equivalents a rise in sheep numbers from 2.8 to 3.5 million.[251] Poultry numbers did increase, but no more rapidly on trend than immediately before the First World War, and the value of exports remained stable between 1924 and 1929.[252]

The total value of exports reached a peak as early as 1924, at £51.6 million. It then fell to £42 million in 1926, before recovering to £47.8 million in 1929.[253] That figure would not be exceeded again until 1948. But too much weight should not be laid on this. Several other countries, including Britain, France, Holland, Belgium, Switzerland, Austria, and Denmark failed to surpass their 1929 export levels until after the Second World War.[254] That does not necessarily prove that their economic policies during the 1920s were exceptionally enlightened, or their subsequent policies exceptionally obtuse.

Despite the disappointing results, it would be wrong to dismiss Hogan's policy as much ado about nothing. That so much commitment should have made such little impact does, nevertheless, raise the question of whether the policy was correctly conceived. The crucial influence on Irish agricultural output appears to have been the relative price relationship between the different products.[255] Hogan's assumption that he had little control over prices therefore automatically deprived him of the one major policy weapon that might have helped him achieve his objectives. Dairy

---

[248] *Statistical Abstract*, 1931, t 85(a), p. 87.

[249] *Irish Trade Journal*, February 1928, p. 43; November 1930, pp. 3, 5; February 1931, pp. 43–5.

[250] *Statistical Abstract*, 1931, t. 50, pp. 38–9.   [251] *Ibid.*

[252] *Ibid.*, p. 39. This table does record, it is true, an apparently impressive increase from 17.2 million in 1922 to 22.9 million in 1930 in 'total poultry'. But this increase is mainly accounted for by a jump from 17.3 million to 21.4 million between 1925 and 1926. This is probably largely due to more careful enumeration of individual categories and reflects a *de facto* statistical revision more than real growth. See also R. O'Connor and C. Guiomard, 'Agricultural output in the Irish Free State area before and after Independence', *IESH*, 12 (1985), p. 96.

[253] *Ibid.*, t. 81, p. 62.   [254] Mitchell, *European historical statistics*, pp. 493–7.

[255] For an analogous argument see R. Crotty, *Irish agricultural production: its volume and structure* (Cork, 1966), ch. 5.

and poultry output failed to increase mainly because price movements continued to favour meat producers.[256] The relative returns on meat, dairy and poultry produce would have had to shift much more dramatically to achieve major changes in the volume and structure of agricultural output. Only a policy of selective subsidisation of the products whose output it was desired to increase could have achieved satisfactory results, if even then. Hogan's policy combined vigorous interventionism at a sectoral level within agriculture with a pervasive fatalism at a general level. The assumption that government could do little to influence prices exposed the rest of his policy to every whim of the external economic climate. In the event the degree of change experienced during the 1920s had often been exceeded in previous decades, without benefit of a native agricultural policy.

The main criticism that can be made of Hogan's policy, however, is that even had it succeeded it could not have fulfilled the hopes it inspired. Even had international agricultural price movements proved more favourable, it seems highly unlikely that the longer term objective of sustained economic growth could have been achieved by this policy. Many of Hogan's assumptions were either illusory or, at the very least, debatable, even within his own terms of reference. Hogan axiomatically equated the welfare of the farmer with the welfare of 'the agricultural community'. But about 20 per cent of the workforce in agriculture consisted of labourers, not farmers.[257] Their interests were, at least in the short term, directly opposed to those of farmers. Reducing farmers' costs meant reducing labourers' wages. Relations between farmers and labourers were tense after the First World War. Labourers flocked to join the Transport Union in 1919,[258] and waged fierce if futile struggles against farmers as late as 1923.[259] Their wages fell by at least 10 per cent between 1922 and 1926, and by more than 10 per cent again between 1926 and 1931.[260]

Even among farmers, a reduction in labourers' wages would benefit only a small minority. The interests of small and big farmers were in some respects as different as those of labourers and farmers. The main cost to the grazier was the price of his young stock. But this cost was the income of the small farmer who had reared the stock. The graziers' cost was the small farmers' income. Hogan, the lawyer son of a senior Land Commission official, instinctively equated 'the ordinary farmer' with the 200 acre man, when only 8000 out of 382 000 holdings belonged to this category in 1930.[261]

256 *Statistical Abstract*, 1931, pp. 162–5.
257 *Ibid.*, T. 45, p. 35; Lyons, *Ireland*, p. 593.
258 Mitchell, *Irish politics*, p. 137; Fitzpatrick, *Politics*, pp. 156, 273.
259 Mitchell, *Irish politics*, p. 186; E. O'Connor, 'Agrarian unrest', pp. 40–58.
260 *Irish Trade Journal*, December 1932, p. 187.
261 Gwynn, *Irish Free State*, p. 371; *Statistical Abstract*, 1931, t. 48, p. 36.

The differences of interest within agriculture cast doubt on the argument advanced against state intervention on the grounds that 'in a country like Ireland, which is mainly agricultural, the cost of such assistance will be paid, for the most part, by the agricultural community itself by passing money from one pocket to another with the added expenses due to the cost of administrative services'.[262] 'The agricultural community' was a convenient cosmetic concept used to foster the illusion that what was good for the strong farmer was good for the country. A prime purpose of state intervention was, after all, precisely to pass money from one pocket to another if this was considered to be in the national interest. The pretence that 'the agricultural community' constituted one big happy family automatically assumed that the 1914 income distribution in agriculture maximised both economic and social welfare. Hogan shared this convenient assumption.[263] No serious attempt was made to analyse it. George O'Brien again offered the basic defence of Hogan's policy:

If Hogan's policy be regarded in relation to the situation in the Free State for the first ten years after the treaty, it can be defended on the following grounds. In the first place, it utilised to the maximum the physical and geographical resources of the country; secondly, it developed those branches of production which are particularly suitable for the average Irish farm; thirdly, it did not involve any breach of continuity in the tradition of Irish farming or in the constructive programme of the Department of Agriculture; fourthly, it promised to provide abundant rural employment, as the agricultural statistics prove that mixed farming with dairying as its principal feature gives more employment to labour than almost any other type of agricultural activity; fifthly, food production would be stimulated and the population of the Free State could never be reduced to famine in war time. The alternative objectives of agricultural policy, namely employment and food production, would thus be incidentally secured. The final justification of the policy is that it ensured that any public money spent on agriculture would be employed productively by being devoted to the building up of the efficiency of the industry rather than to deflecting production from one line to another.[264]

These are admirable sentiments. But too much weight should not be attached to some of them. 'Utilised to the maximum the physical and geographical resources' is little better than the vacuous rhetoric of the political platform. That the Free State should avoid famine in war-time was an uncontestable aspiration. But it is difficult to see how even the Irish, now that they had reduced their numbers (in the Free State) to only 3 million, could actually achieve another famine. They had just survived the First World War without undue discomfiture, and it wasn't clear why they should, at this juncture, be unduly concerned about their ability to feed

262 *Report of commission on agriculture* (Dublin, 1924), p. 32, para. 21.
263 SPO, S3557, P. Hogan, 'An analysis of the economic aspects of agriculture in the Irish Free State', 25 January 1924.
264 Quoted in Meenan, *Irish economy*, p. 305.

themselves next time. Hogan's policy did not envisage any great increase in wheat production, to which the self-sufficiency of the state in the Second World War is sometimes attributed, however erroneously. That the policy 'did not involve any breach of continuity' implies satisfaction with the inherited 'tradition of Irish farming', and with the economic performance of agriculture, a debatable contention rather than a self-evident truth.

Hogan's policy was not necessarily wrong. But it was, for the most part, based on assumptions rather than analysis, however apparently logical its reasoning. And Hogan's assumptions probably exaggerated the potential impact of farmer prosperity on economic development. 'Agriculture' employed 51 per cent of the gainfully occupied population in 1926, but contributed only 32 per cent of gross domestic product at current factor prices.[265] No doubt part of the prosperity of the services sector, and of industry, depended on agriculture. But agriculture was not the most important consumer sector of the economy. 'Prosperity among farmers' would not automatically 'provide the purchasing power necessary to sustain the demand for non-agricultural goods and services'. And if protection were to be rejected, in deference to the presumed interests of farmers as producers, it was difficult to see why farmers as consumers should have favoured home products against presumably more attractive imports. The bulk of farmers' imports were not producer goods but consumer goods. Apart from agricultural machinery, fertilisers were the only significant producer goods imported by farmers.[266] Total agricultural expenditure on investment goods in 1926–7 probably amounted to less than one-third of total agricultural expenditure. Dogmatic free traders cleverly succeeded in confusing all farmers' purchases with farming 'costs'. There was no immediate reason why protection on consumer goods should have directly and sharply increased farmers' costs of production, as distinct from cost of living. The convenient confusion between farmers' consumer purchases and producer purchases was a shrewd propagandistic non-sequitur. It still remains unclear, in view of their presumed propensity to import, how prosperity among farmers would spread throughout the economy at a rate sufficient to stimulate sustained economic growth. Even George O'Brien found himself compelled to concede that 'it would appear that the market provided by the agricultural population of the free state is abnormally small . . . '.[267]

Lack of adequate information permitted even intelligent policy-makers, like Hogan, and the Secretary of the Department of Agriculture, F.J.

[265] K. Kennedy, *Productivity and industrial growth: the Irish experience* (Oxford, 1971), t. 1.8, p. 10.
[266] *Statistical Abstract*, 1931, t. 78, p. 60; PM, P35/A/22, pp. 10–11.
[267] G. O'Brien, 'Agriculture and employment in the Free State', *Studies*, 19 (1930), p. 177.

Meyrick, to indulge their illusions throughout the twenties. Assumptions about the size of the agricultural market for industrial products, assumptions about patterns of saving and investment, assumptions about the propensity to import, were built into policy decisions. Nevertheless, they remained no more than assumptions. Kevin O'Higgins countered the criticism that Cumann na nGaedheal jettisoned the protectionist doctrines of Arthur Griffith with the argument that 'the propagandist political writings of any man cannot be accepted simply as revealed truth requiring no further investigation, something that must be accepted for ever beyond question, beyond doubt, beyond the needs of examination'.[268] This reply was as illusory as it was courageous. No adequate 'further investigation' occurred. The government did not reject Griffith's doctrines following a searching examination of the facts. It simply substituted for one set of unproven assumptions, based at least on some attempt, however perfunctory, to wrestle with the evidence of economic history, an alternative set of unproven assumptions based on no historical evidence at all.

Paddy Hogan did not do his sums during the twenties. Nor did Finance. It was left, as late as 1930, to John Leydon, a young Finance official, in his capacity as secretary to the De-rating Committee, to present relevant data. Leydon, noting that 'no reasoned estimate of the national income of the *Saorstát* has been published' stressed that his memorandum 'is not to be regarded as being in any sense an official document. For the picture it presents, and for any comparisons made or conclusions suggested, I am personally and solely responsible.'[269] So much for the eagerness of the more senior official mind to explore its own assumptions. Leydon's calculations concerning the place of agriculture in the economy cast serious doubt on some basic premises of Hogan's policy.

At first sight, the Fiscal Inquiry Committee of 1923 amounted to a major investigation of industrial policy. Cosgrave contended that it was appointed 'to secure a disinterested, balanced and exhaustive analysis of a complex problem', concentrating on 'fact and not policy', presenting 'impartial consideration of the issue of protection versus free trade'.[270] Critics, on the other hand, denounced the report as

probably the most disheartening document that has been published in Ireland since the inauguration of the *Saorstát*. To many who were hopeful that the ushering in of the new state meant a giving to the people of powers not only to determine the political trend of their national life but also the course of its economic

[268] Quoted in Meenan, *Irish economy*, p. 319.
[269] PM, P35/A/22, Memo by Mr Leydon on the agricultural communities contribution to taxation and its share of public expenditure, 28 July 1930, pp. 12–13.
[270] DD, 3, 15 June 1923, 2024.

development, the findings of the committee sounded almost like the death knell of such hope of a progressive future for the *Saorstát*.[271]

But ought not one to dismiss the bitter accusations of a partisan like Seán Milroy that the committee 'by special pleading, by suggestion and innuendo, by palpably false inference and by lopsided inferences from inadequate premises' presented a blatant piece of propaganda in the guise of an impartial report?[272] Unfortunately, study of the evidence makes it clear that the committee was arranged to secure a safe majority for the views of dogmatic free traders. It examined witnesses from several industries, subjecting demands for protection to rigorous scrutiny, while allowing arguments for free trade, even when sloppily presented, to pass without serious cross-examination. The committee duly felt entitled to report that the proportion of industry demanding some protection was 'small compared with that which desires no change in the existing system'.[273] George O'Brien, a free trade member of the committee, retrospectively conceded that 'there was a widespread desire not only among business-men who would have duly profited, but among the public generally for some attempt to revive Irish industry'.[274] The evidence reveals that twenty-three out of forty-one industries sought protection of some sort.[275] Some big industries did not give evidence to the committee at all, and could be considered to favour the existing arrangements. But it still requires an elastic use of language to describe twenty-three out of forty-one as 'a small proportion'. Little semantic subterfuges of this sort were all part of the game, which the conservative cohorts played with exquisite skill. So much for the 'further investigation' of O'Higgins's imagination. However partisan its provenance, and however unscholarly its language, Milroy's critique scarcely exaggerated the reality. This is not to suggest dogmatically that protection would necessarily have been in the national interest at that stage. It is to suggest that, behind the façade of 'scientific' investigation, the case was never considered on its merits.

The government relegated industry to second place behind agriculture. Convinced that industrialisation could not be 'forced', it took few initiatives to foster immediate development. Despite the protectionist rhetoric of Sinn Féin, the government contained only a small protectionist wing, identified with J.J. Walsh, Minister for Posts and Telegraphs, who was to abandon the party in 1927 because of its free trade orientation. Ernest Blythe would claim in 1924, when introducing some small 'experimental' tariffs, that he was no doctrinaire free trader.[276] His actions belied

[271] S. Milroy, 'Foreword' to *Protection for Irish industries: the Report of the Fiscal Inquiry Committee, an analysis and a reply* (Dublin, 1924).
[272] *Ibid.*, p. 5.   [273] *Report of Fiscal Inquiry Committee*, para. 66.
[274] Meenan, *George O'Brien*, p. 129.
[275] Calculated from the evidence presented before the Fiscal Inquiry Committee.
[276] Fanning, *Finance*, p. 204.

his words. The experimental tariffs proved relatively successful, in so far as the protected sectors seem to have accounted for most of the modest increase recorded in the size of the industrial labour force from 105 000 to 111 000 between 1926 and 1931.[277] In 1927 the government appointed a tariff commission to scrutinise applications for protection. But this was a mere cosmetic measure, designed to deprive the protectionist Fianna Fáil party, lately arrived in the Dáil, of easy propaganda. The commission was duly packed with three safe civil servants, including McElligott. Its pace of procedure was deliberate, its approach cautious, the quality of its thinking dubious. It was not until 1930, under pressure of changing international circumstances, that the government bothered to appoint the commission on a permanent basis.[278] Major government initiatives were confined to the Shannon scheme for the generation of electricity, and the establishment of the first sugar beet factory at Carlow, both ventures depending heavily on imported expertise.

It might have been expected that the Department of Industry and Commerce would champion industrialisation. This was not the case at first. Industry and Commerce showed little initial resentment at the Finance and Agriculture formula. But there may have already been some internal friction about the future role of the Department. Joseph McGrath, the first minister, dismissed Diarmaid Fawsitt, chief administrative officer of the Ministry of Economic Affairs of the Provisional Government, in favour of Gordon Campbell, later Lord Glenavy, who came from the Ministry of Labour in London in September 1922. Fawsitt, declining appointment as an assistant secretary in a dignified if despondent letter, claimed that his demotion 'denoted, to my mind, a change of policy on the part of the government'.[279] The situation remains obscure, for McGrath was not as instinctive a conservative as most of his colleagues. He actually established a 'Commission on reconstruction and development' in 1922, with ambitious terms of reference, even if it appears to have expired after presenting one interim report in May 1923.[280] J.J. Walsh tried to suggest that government structures be adapted to the putative needs of an underdeveloped economy by strengthening Industry and Commerce against Finance.[281] But Cosgrave was as conservative on administrative as on most other matters. His marginalia on proposals like the draft bill of the Ministers and Secretaries Act confined themselves to trivia. Whatever the motives behind the choice of Campbell

---

[277] H.D. Butler, *The Irish Free State: an economic survey* (Department of Commerce, Washington, 1928), pp. 31ff., contains a useful survey of employment in various industries. See below, pp. 193–4.

[278] Fanning, *Finance*, p. 205.

[279] RM, P7/B/250, D. Fawsitt to W.T. Cosgrave, 26 September 1922.

[280] SPO, S3185, Commission on reconstruction and development, 1923.

[281] SPO, S1932, J.J. Walsh to W.T. Cosgrave, 30 January 1923.

– the cabinet may have felt that the appointment of a unionist would reassure the mercantile community – it helped ensure a low profile for Industry and Commerce in the early years of the state.

Campbell's initial instinct was to reject responsibility for development policies. He pleaded, for instance, that the Congested Districts Board should be removed from his department's area of responsibility. It was no function of Industry and Commerce to relieve congestion and 'if we begin to subsidise one industry out of public funds we shall ... set an undesirable precedent.'[282] The Congested Districts Board had many weaknesses. But its very existence at least acknowledged that special problems required special solutions. One of the first administrative initiatives of the new government was to abolish the Board, as if it would thereby solve the problems.

Despite these instincts, Campbell soon showed greater receptivity than Brennan or McElligott to suggestions for change. He may have been partly responding to pressure from more activist officials, including E.J. Riordan, 'passionately interested in the possibilities of economic regeneration',[283] and T.J. Barrington, a vigorous critic of conventional wisdom, who differed so strongly from the conservative Fiscal Inquiry Committee, of which he was Secretary, that by the end of the inquiry he 'had come to sit in a separate room'.[284]

Campbell responded to a departmental recommendation in 1924 that Industry and Commerce should itself establish an industrial bank with the observation that 'this function is essential to development here but would not recommend the government undertake it in preference to private enterprise with, if necessary, government assistance'.[285] He was already wavering in his simple faith of the previous year. Soon he came to ask himself, what private enterprise? The calibre of Irish businessmen might condemn one to wait virtually indefinitely for exhibitions of productive enterprise. That same year, Campbell committed his department, with the approval of Patrick McGilligan (who succeeded McGrath as minister following the army mutiny), to preparing the ground work for the Shannon scheme. Brennan at Finance bitterly opposed this when he came to hear about it, after having apparently been kept in the dark, presumably with the connivance of Industry and Commerce, until it was too late for him to frustrate it.[286]

As Campbell became more convinced of the case for state intervention, he scoured the world to find experts in the economic and technological

282 SPO, S1932, G. Campbell to Secretary, Executive Council, 16 July 1923.
283 Meenan, *George O'Brien*, p. 95.
284 *Ibid.*, p. 129. Barrington wrote the classic paper 'A review of Irish agricultural prices', *JSSISI*, XV (October, 1927), pp. 249–80.
285 PM, P35/B/4, Campbell minute, 19 November 1924.
286 Fanning, *Finance*, pp. 178ff.

spheres, especially Irishmen with 'experience in other modernised countries'.[287] It may be that if he could have found them he would have contemplated more vigorous policies, for by 1927 he had become disenchanted with the Finance approach. He argued that because exports were essential to permit sustained industrialisation on the basis of efficiently sized factories, and because Ireland had so little industrial tradition, 'industrial development within any short period depends largely on attracting foreign enterprise, training and, for the present at least, capital'.[288] Government stimulus was therefore necessary. He didn't flinch from the short-term price to be paid, 'whether in the form of a tariff, subsidy, bounty, special credit or other fiscal adjustment'. He anticipated the reflex Finance argument that as this had not been done in Britain it could not possibly be done in Ireland. The contiguity of Ireland to Britain, he observed, should not obscure the fact that in smaller countries, 'it has been, since the war, a recognised necessity for government to take a gradually increased share of responsibility in measures for the direct promotion of industry'.[289]

Campbell hoped to entice foreign industrialists to Ireland by placing 'sufficient funds at the disposal and *under the full control of the Department of Industry and Commerce*' (my emphasis) to permit his officials 'to visit other countries and negotiate with industrialists who would consider opening works in Ireland', to enable the Department establish closer contact with Irish industries, to 'amend the Tariff Commission Act to enable the Department of Industry and Commerce to take the initiative in proposing tariffs' and 'set up a standing committee of the Executive Council not merely to consider proposals put before it but to call itself for proposals and see that it gets them'.[290] The Department realised that reliance on foreign investment might cause problems. Barrington warned against the danger of 'economic penetration' by foreign firms who set up behind a tariff barrier. 'This problem of economic penetration by outside concerns is no new one: of course the more backward the country economically the more acute is the problem as a whole.'[291] Foreign firms might provide useful models for domestic imitators, but they might also be reluctant to train domestic management. Despite the risk, Barrington broadly advocated some protection, on the grounds that 'the development of the country by outside firms represents a more satisfactory condition of things than no industrial development at all, but . . . industrial development by domestic firms is the ideal to strive for'.[292]

Campbell even revised his earlier thinking on the role of government in

[287] PM, P35/B/5, G. Campbell to J.G. Smith, 2 June 1925.
[288] PM, P35/B/10, G. Campbell memo, 'Industrial development', 19 July 1927.
[289] *Ibid.*   [290] *Ibid.*
[291] PM, P35/B/14, T. Barrington to E.J. O'Riordan, 18 October 1928.
[292] *Ibid.*

the Gaeltacht. 'Nothing but intensive organisation by persons of real experience and a mature conception of what is possible and what is not will improve a situation like this. *Departmental efforts within the narrow vision of the Department of Finance are useless*' (my emphasis).[293] He actually wanted a fund established which every relevant Department could use without having to submit every item of expenditure for sanction by Finance.

Campbell also came to resist Hogan's fascination with agriculture-led growth. He noted that agriculture was bound to be unstable, and cattle production for export particularly unstable, because of its vulnerability to weather conditions, to disease, and above all, to the changing circumstances of the importing country. He sought ideally a better balance between agriculture and industry, on cultural no less than on economic grounds.

The country that is mainly dependent on agriculture, while ultimately sure of the necessities of life, is the most poorly endowed in respect of its refinements. If a nation is to depend on agriculture it must produce mainly a population of farmers: men of patience, endurance, thrift and modest intellectual aspirations. If it produces other types it must export them at an early age if it is not to risk the continual ferment of disappointed and distorted minds denied by circumstances their exercise.[294]

His scepticism extended not only to the priority accorded to agriculture, but to Hogan's preference for mixed farming. He wondered if 'intensive farming' might not have to be seriously considered instead of mixed farming 'which supports a low proportion of persons, which produces a relatively small volume of wealth, and which is very sensitive to conditions in other countries on which it is necessarily dependent'.[295]

Industry and Commerce appears to have made little impression against entrenched social, economic and political interests. Departmental representatives found themselves generally isolated. The first Banking Commission established by the Free State took the Finance line, rejecting the evidence of R.C. Ferguson and of Barrington on behalf of Industry and Commerce on the inadequacy of existing Irish financial institutions. No wonder that Industry and Commerce felt that the complacent report of the Commission showed 'a failure of vision and energy'.[296] Campbell identified the fundamental problem. It was pointless, he warned McGilligan, for officials to devise proposals unless the political will existed to

293 PM, P35/B/12, Campbell memo, 30 September 1927.
294 PM, P35/B/10, Campbell, 'Industrial development', 19 July 1927.
295 PM, P35/B/9, Campbell to Minister for Industry and Commerce, 18 January 1927, commenting on a typical Hogan submission, 5 January 1927, entitled 'Memorandum on the dairying industry'.
296 PM, P35/A/26, T.J. Barrington to G. Campbell, 18 January 1928.

depart from British economic orthodoxy.[297] That will did not generally exist. McGilligan remained broadly sceptical of the merits of an interventionist policy, and after 1927 was probably more attracted by his role as Minister for External Affairs. Cosgrave's cabinet pursued a particular economic policy from choice and from conviction, not from ignorance of possible alternatives. Industry and Commerce would continue to beat its wings in vain until a new regime would display a different political will.

The cabinet pursued a clear social as well as economic policy. It took the view that the poor were responsible for their poverty. They should pay for their lack of moral fibre. The existing distribution of income, and of opportunities, largely satisfied the demands of social justice. Kevin O'Higgins had pleaded during the Treaty debate that 'the welfare and happiness of the men and women and the little children of this nation must, after all, take precedence over political creeds and theories'.[298] It was ironic that those who appealed for a chance to build up a new Ireland, who denounced servitude to 'political' creeds and theories, should so soon prove themselves prisoners of 'social' creeds and theories. O'Higgins impatiently dismissed the Democratic Programme, which had the temerity to echo the social aspirations, however vague, of the Proclamation of the Republic, as 'largely poetry', and he denounced the section dealing with natural resources, which purported to retain them for the nation, as 'communistic doctrine'.[299] The age of poetry was indeed dead. But there are many prose styles. Cosgrave's cabinet chose the iron style. The cabinet waged a coherent campaign against the weaker elements in the community. The poor, the aged, and the unemployed must all feel the lash of the liberators.

The government introduced Poor Law legislation in 1923 which substituted for what the Democratic Programme called 'the present odious, degrading and foreign poor law system', an odious, degrading and native system.[300] The government failed to act on the recommendations of the Commission on the Relief of the Sick and Destitute Poor in 1927, which drew unavailing attention to the plight of widows dependent on Poor Law relief. Cumann na nGaedheal promised to take the housing problem seriously. There was indeed a problem. It was a simple one. Housing was too dear for the poor. Infant and even child mortality in the worst housed districts of Dublin still reached frightening levels. One hundred and twenty out of every thousand babies under the age of one in urban Ireland died in their first year in 1926.[301] The cabinet had other

---

297 PM, P35/B/10, G. Campbell, 'Industrial development', 19 July 1927.
298 De Vere White, *O'Higgins*, p. 76.
299 Mitchell, *Irish Politics*, pp. 110, 177.
300 S. Ó Cinnéide, *A law for the poor* (Dublin, 1970), p. 2.
301 *Statistical Abstract*, 1931, t. 11, p. 7; Brown, *Ireland*, p. 16.

priorities. Only 14 000 houses were built from public subsidy between 1922 and 1929.[302]

Ernest Blythe launched an attack on the old and blind in his 1924 budget.

The pre-1924 scheme aimed at giving the pensioner, as a rule, an income of twenty shillings a week – where the means were ten shillings a week, the rate of pension was ten shillings . . . The scheme in operation at present aims at giving the pensioner, as a rule . . . an income of sixteen shillings per week . . . where the means are seven shillings a week the rate of pension is nine shillings . . . [303]

This economy drive reduced the total cost of old and and blind pensions from £3.18 million in 1924 to £2.54 million in 1927.[304] Despite an increase in 1928, which partly restored the cuts, in response to strong opposition pressure, total costs in 1932 still remained below the level of 1924.

The political consequences of the campaign against the aged are difficult to quantify. The procedures for processing pension claims certainly provoked resentment. In December 1924 the government appointed an old age pension committee of inquiry to expedite matters.[305] Blythe's legislation created a classic conflict between central and local authorities. The procedure for examining pension claims under the new Act involved in the first instance an old age pensions officer (in practice, a customs and excise officer) making a recommendation to the old age pensions sub-committees of the local authorities. These committees, inevitably, adopted a more lenient attitude than the officers, regularly 'allowing claims on insufficient evidence'.[306] The officers then usually appealed the matter to the minister, who tended to support them. In the year ending 31 March 1925, for instance, the officers recommended that only 5422 appeals by applicants be allowed. The committees allowed 16 224. The officers duly appealed 6773 of the extra claims allowed, and won 73 per cent of their appeal cases.[307]

Most pensioners' appeals were rejected on grounds of falsification of age, which was difficult to determine because a national system of registration of births had not begun until 1864. Nevertheless, despite the committee's distaste for the behaviour of the locals, it did concede that 'speaking generally claimants for old age pensions are very helpless people. They are no doubt anxious to secure the pension, but they are extremely ignorant of their exact legal rights, as to the kind of evidence they are expected to produce, and as to the steps they should take to

[302] *Statistical Abstract*, 1931, t. 87, p. 94.
[303] EB, P22/328, W.D. Carey to D.P. Shanagher, 30 January 1928.
[304] *Statistical Abstract*, 1931, t. 99, p. 102.
[305] *Report of Old Age Pension Committee of Inquiry* (Dublin, 1926).
[306] *Ibid.*, para. 17.   [307] *Ibid.*, paras 25–6.

procure it.'[308] This carried the comforting corollary that they were also unlikely to punch their electoral weight. Of the 114 000 pensioners in 1927, 67 000 were females,[309] a further reason for suspecting that they might not vote. But there may have been an indirect indignation vote. Blythe's policy may have helped reduce potential western support for the government. If old age pensioners themselves constituted less than 4 per cent of the total electorate, about one family in every four west of the Shannon had a pensioner. There were nearly 11 000 pensioners in Mayo's population of 173 000, 8000 in Galway's 169 000, 7000 in Kerry's 149 000.[310] The pension for the blind was also reduced, and the definition of blindness tightened. The blind vote was presumably limited, though some of those whose pensions had been stopped or reduced might not have been too blind to decipher a ballot paper![311] Cumulative resentment at the treatment of pensioners presumably played a part in rousing the west for de Valera. Fianna Fáil certainly sensed electoral potential in this issue in 1932.

Unemployment began to rise rapidly from 1920, despite resumed emigration, as the postwar boom turned into slump. The official unemployment figures do, it is true, record a fall in the rate from 8.9 per cent in 1922 to 4.2 per cent in 1929, before a fresh rise began in 1930. Much controversy, however, surrounds these figures. They were based on limited coverage, and may have fallen far short of recording total unemployment. The 1926 census reported 78 000 unemployed, a rate of 11.9 per cent, compared with the 6 per cent official unemployment rate. Among those who came under the Unemployment Insurance Acts, which excluded agriculture and domestic service, the census rate of unemployment was 17 per cent. John Hooper, the government's chief statistical adviser, remained adamant that the official figures were more accurate.[312] Hooper, however, contemplated unemployment with something less than outrage. He did not take the 1926 census figure seriously, because it included 'unemployables'.[313] The government's rejection of the recommendations of the Committee of Inquiry into Workmen's Compensation in 1925 for the creation of a compulsory state insurance scheme conveniently postponed the collection of adequate unemployment statistics.

Cosgrave institutionalised the neglect of labour by demoting the

---

[308] *Ibid.*, para. 37.   [309] *Statistical Abstract*, 1931, t. 99, p. 102.
[310] *Ibid.*, t. 100, p. 102.
[311] For anecdotal evidence, see J.B. Keane, *Man of the triple name* (Dingle, 1984), pp. 56–7. The writings of J.B. Keane are a fund of wisdom as well as wit on the mentalities and moralities of rural and small town Ireland.
[312] PM, P35/A/28, J. Hooper, Memo on unemployment – international comparisons, September 1930. Compare the official unemployment figures, DD, xvii, 18 November 1926, 379 with the figures in *Census of Ireland, 1926*, x, pp. 119–20.
[313] PM, P35/A/28, J. Hooper, Memo on unemployment – September 1930.

Department of Labour, established by the first Dáil, to a mere section of the Department of Industry and Commerce. When Patrick McGilligan, the lawyer son of a comfortable Ulster businessman, succeeded Joe McGrath, the only economics minister who might be suspected of labour sympathies, as minister in 1924, he made no secret of his sentiments. 'People may have to die in this country and may have to die from starvation'[314] he told the Dáil. He himself did not actually desire this,[315] but he would not be budged from the position that 'If it is said that the government has failed to adopt effective means to find useful work for willing workers, I can only answer that it is no function of government to provide work for anybody. They can try and develop tendencies, and can try and set the pace a bit, but it is not the function of the government to provide work.'[316] Even less could it be its function to provide work for unwilling workers.

The sentiment was widespread that unemployment was due primarily either to the laziness of the unemployed or the restrictive practices of trade unions. Philip Monahan, then commissioner for Cork city, assured McGilligan that trade union restrictive practices were primarily responsible for the prevailing high unemployment. In addition, 'I have never been a philanthropist and am inclined to be very sceptical of the social value of unemployment grants etc.' He was gratified, if surprised, 'to find now that my views are at present shared by many who have laboured in the different charitable organisations of the city'.[317] Trade union restrictive practices were indeed as little concerned with the public good as the restrictive practices of the professional classes. But the fact that unemployment fluctuated sharply while restrictive practices remained constant might have suggested that trade union restrictions were more often a symptom than a cause of unemployment.

Social resentments ran high, moreover, following the bitter labour unrest of 1923. A fleeting recurrence of workers 'Soviets' in a dozen Munster factories alarmed conservative opinion.[318] The first 'Soviet' takeover in 1920 had occurred, some might feel not wholly inappropriately, in a lunatic asylum. Timid rentier opinion took appropriate fright once more in 1923. Labour's spirit appears to have been broken by apparently worsening unemployment – whatever the official statistics recorded – until by 1928 the number of working days lost by strikes was a mere 5 per cent of the 1923 level. Workers were being duly put in their place.

Newly independent peoples tend to be suspicious of the inherited legal system. The Democratic Programme said singularly little about the matter. Sinn Féin set up its own courts during the war of independence. Some of

[314] DD, 9, 30 October 1924, 562.   [315] *Ibid.*   [316] *Ibid.*, 563.
[317] PM, P35/A/30, P. Monahan to E.T. McCarron, 28 June 1927.
[318] Mitchell, *Irish politics*, pp. 139ff.

them functioned. But the law they administered remained English law.[319]
Cosgrave's Attorney General, Hugh Kennedy, who had a capacious and
lively mind, was anxious to transform the legal system. When the
ever-vigilant C.J. Gregg expressed alarm about the possible expense of the
contemplated changes, Kennedy disdainfully replied that 'The committee
is preparing a new, quite new, scheme of judiciary for the *Saorstát*. It is not
merely tinkering at the existing judiciary.'[320] Gregg remained unimpressed, invoking the authority of his favourite economist, Juvenal, to
remind Kennedy of the first principle of economic theory:

Do not hanker after a mullet if you have only the price of a gudgeon in your
pocket.[321]

Kennedy completed the selection of personnel for his Judiciary Committee
in January 1923.[322] The circular he composed, over Cosgrave's signature,
seemed to breathe revolutionary fire:

The body of laws and the system of judicature so imposed upon this Nation were
English (not even British) in their seed, English in their growth, English in their
vitality . . . Thus it comes about that there is nothing more prized among our
newly won liberties than the liberty to construct a system of judiciary and an
administration of law and justice according to the dictates of our own needs and
after a pattern of our own designing.[323]

Yet the changes were very limited. Some minor improvements were
made in the direction of reducing litigation costs by abolishing the courts
of petty session, usually presided over by local notables, and correspondingly increasing the authority of the district courts, while also introducing
the circuit court on the Sinn Féin model. But 'the essentials of the previous
judicial system were maintained'.[324] Recourse to law remained limited to
those who could afford to go to law in the first instance.

It is not quite clear how satisfied Kennedy was with the work of the
commission. His choice of members, and particularly of Lord Glenavy as
chairman, militated against the recommendation of the sweeping changes
he himself appeared to envisage.[325] From Cosgrave's viewpoint, the
invitation to Glenavy killed several birds with one stone. It seemed to be,
as indeed it was, a magnanimous gesture towards a former political
enemy, an eminent Southern unionist. But it also ensured safe recommen-

---

[319] On the modest role of the republican courts, see Fitzpatrick, *Politics*, pp. 174–83.
[320] SPO, S1739, 'Observations by the Attorney General on Mr Gregg's notes, 7/5/23'.
[321] SPO, S1739, 'Further memo by Mr Gregg, Department of Finance, 15/5/1923'.
[322] SPO, S1739, H. Kennedy to W.T. Cosgrave, 23 January 1923.
[323] SPO, S1739, W.T. Cosgrave, Circular to members of the Judiciary Committee,
29 January 1923.
[324] T.D. Williams, 'Summing up', p. 183.
[325] Kennedy's foreword to L. Kohn, *The Constitution of the Irish Free State* (London,
1932), still seethes with a desire to make Irish law less intellectually dependent on
English.

dations. Cosgrave would show continuing political courage in replacing the bulk of the judges who retired under the Treaty by successors appointed as far as possible on legal merit. But this inevitably included a disproportionate representation of former unionists, not the least of whose qualifications may have been their social conservatism.[326] Kennedy himself abandoned politics in 1924 when resigning as Attorney General to become Chief Justice. The institutional changes in the legal system made little practical difference to the actual role of law in the country.

Education was one area where the omens seemed propitious for the new regime to leave a great name. It was less than a decade since Patrick Pearse had proclaimed that the first task of a free Ireland would be to reform the educational system root and branch. Eoin MacNeill, Cosgrave's first Minister for Education, a distinguished Celtic scholar, believed that the early Christian period, when 'the Irish were the schoolmasters of Europe', was the greatest in Irish history. He told the Dáil in 1923 that Ireland's destiny was to be a teaching nation, setting an example to the rest of the world with 'our ancient ideals, faith, learning, generous enthusiasm, self-sacrifice – the things best calculated to purge out the meanness of the modern world'.[327] It remained to be seen how close he would come to translating this vision into reality.

The Cumann na nGaedheal programme purported to envisage movement towards equality of opportunity in education. Clauses tending in this direction even crept into the draft constitution until that vigilant liberal conservative, George O'Brien, a consultant on the constitution, exposed so subversive a threat to the existing social order.[328] This was one field where reality was too important to make concessions to rhetoric. Cosgrave avoided establishing a committee of inquiry into education similar to the Lynn Committee in Northern Ireland, or to the Hadow Committee in England.[329]

A flurry of administrative activity served to conceal the essential continuity in the educational sphere. The eleven existing boards of education were incorporated into a single Department of Education. The Department, however, enjoyed little control over the management of national or secondary schools, which remained generally vested in the clergy of various denominations, the state merely paying the salaries of national school teachers, and offering building grants for secondary schools. The managers appointed the teachers. The Department exerted

---

326 Gwynn, *Irish Free State*, pp. 165–9, gives a sympathetic account of Cosgrave's policy in the legal sphere.
327 Quoted in B. Farrell, 'MacNeill and politics', in F.X. Martin and F.J. Byrne (eds.), *The scholar revolutionary* (Dublin, 1973), p. 194.
328 Meenan, *George O'Brien*, p. 124.
329 D.H. Akenson, *A mirror to Kathleen's face: education in independent Ireland 1922–1960* (London, 1975), pp. 33–6.

influence mainly through control of the curriculum, and through operating an inspection system to maintain minimum teaching standards. In
addition, the Department pursued the policy of reducing the number of
small, one-teacher schools. The cost of primary education to the state was
60 per cent higher per child in Ireland than in England and Wales in 1917.
But facilities for the children, far from being superior in Ireland, were
often grossly inferior. The extra expense was mainly incurred by the high
number of principal teachers as a result of the proliferation of small
schools – 7600 of the 13 400 teachers in 1917 drew the salaries of
principals.[330]

The Department felt growing unease at the quality of teaching in the
national schools. It instituted in 1929 a voluntary primary certificate
examination in an attempt to impose some control on standards. Only a
small minority of pupils were entered for the examination until it became
compulsory in 1943.[331]

The Department initially attempted to foster some individual initiative
on the part of secondary teachers. It abandoned the results system, by
which schools were subsidised according to their public examination
results, in favour of a capitation grant for each pupil. It also compelled the
clerical managers of the secondary schools to give the teachers security
and to pay a minimum wage, the state undertaking to pay a proportion of
the teachers' salaries. The Department further insisted on minimum
academic qualifications for recognised teachers in the shape of the Higher
Diploma in Education, conferred by universities. It even went so far as to
implement, consciously or unconsciously, a favourite injunction of
Pearse's, by abolishing the rigid reading programmes imposed by the
old Intermediate Education Board, and permitting schools general
freedom to choose their own courses and texts. It further relaxed the
examination grind by substituting two examinations, the Intermediate
and Leaving Certificates, for the previous three examinations in secondary
schools.[332]

The Department still insisted, however, on setting standardised
national examinations, and then publishing the results, which was hardly
in the spirit of Pearse's plan, right or wrong. The fruits of departmental
reliance on individual initiative among teachers proved disappointing.
The combination of flexible courses with the centralised examination
system did not work well, and the teachers successfully agitated for a
return to set texts.[333]

On balance, the Department of Education seems to have done a

---

[330] R.J. Lawrence, *The government of Northern Ireland* (Oxford, 1965), p. 106.
[331] S. Ó Catháin, 'Education in the new Ireland', in F. MacManus (ed.), *The years of the great test, 1926–39* (Cork, 1967), pp. 110–11.
[332] Lyons, *Ireland*, p. 639.   [333] Ó Catháin, 'Education', p. 107.

reasonably adequate job in the secondary sphere between the wars. With the material available it probably achieved as much as could reasonably be expected. The main criticism that might be made concerns the curriculum, particularly the neglect of science and the even more extraordinary neglect of modern languages. The Department did not require any scientific subject for secondary school examinations. As late as 1962–3 only 30 per cent of boys and 14 per cent of girls took a science subject in the Leaving Certificate. On the language side, the combination of compulsory Irish and virtually compulsory Latin – 88 per cent took Latin in 1962–3 – meant that few other languages were taught. A mere 21 per cent, almost all girls, took French, and only a handful of pupils took any other European language.[334] England thus remained the repository of the only living intellectual culture to which most Irish had access.

The universities responded to public demand by continuing to produce heavily for the professions. Of 4300 students registered in the universities and in Maynooth in 1929–30, about 800 were clerical, another 800 medical, and 200 legal. There were only 400 commerce students, 200 engineering, and 100 agriculture and dairy science. Most of the rest were arts students, who would usually become teachers. The universities thus catered for the prevalent effective demand. There was relatively little demand for business education, or for scientific or technological education. No attempt was made to establish a major polytechnic on continental lines. It would have been a meaningless initiative unless the government had been prepared to take a more active role in the economy to create the demand for polytechnic graduates. The real criticism that can be made of universities is not that they disproportionately favoured 'academic' subjects, but that within their chosen area of concentration, they achieved only moderate distinction. They did labour under immense handicaps, not all of their own making. Higher education was frugally financed. Libraries, except in Trinity College, and laboratory facilities everywhere, were grossly inadequate.

Only meagre measures were taken to implement the ideal of equality of educational opportunity. The government's main gesture in this direction was to pass a School Attendance Act in 1926 making attendance at primary level compulsory. Even this braved the indignation of strong farmers, to judge by the amendments tabled, though not in the event moved, by Michael Heffernan, a prominent farmer deputy, who wanted more relaxed requirements to apply to the children of agricultural labourers, so that elementary education for poor children should not interfere with the higher priority of cheap labour for strong farmers.[335]

334 Lyons, *Ireland*, p. 640.
335 SPO, S4606. See the checklist of amendments tabled, dated 3 February 1926, for School Attendance Act.

The Vocational Education Act of 1930, introduced by J.M. O'Sullivan, MacNeill's successor as Minister for Education, established thirty-eight vocational educational committees throughout the country to provide continuation and technical education. This did give some opportunity to poorer children to acquire a technically orientated education. The schools were, however, deliberately deprived, partly at clerical insistence, of the opportunity to prepare students for the Leaving Certificate, the then status symbol of a completed secondary education.[336] They were thus stamped from the outset as second rate by a public opinion weaned on the primacy of the more remunerative traditional education.

The existing educational system was devoted to the defence of the social structure. Secondary schools and universities charged fees which placed them beyond the pockets of most citizens. Entry was effectively restricted to the socially comfortable classes. The Christian Brothers salvaged some bright children from the poorer classes, and gave them a chance to climb the social ladder by providing cheap education. The state did little for the children of the poor. As late as 1932, 93 per cent of children did not proceed beyond primary education. The Local Government Act in 1923 did authorise local authorities 'to levy a rate not exceeding a penny in the pound' to finance secondary school scholarships. As the local authorities were elected on a restricted rate-payer franchise down to 1934, it could hardly be expected that they would show much interest in this option. The proportion of scholarships relative to entrants awarded from public funds for proceeding to secondary schools hovered between 2 per cent and 4 per cent during the inter-war years.[337] As late as 1960–1, only about 600 public scholarships, in addition to the small number offered privately by the schools themselves, were available for competition among the roughly 70–80 000 pupils completing their primary education annually. There was little danger of mere merit making a vulgar spectacle of itself in these circumstances.

The Department of Education found itself with relatively little time to think about education. It was entrusted, or burdened, with the task of reviving the Irish language.[338] Cosgrave asked 'How are you going to reconstruct this nation? Upon what basis is the super-structure to be built? Must we not look to the Minister for Education to mark the gaelicisation . . . of our whole culture . . . to make our nation separate and distinct and something to be thought of?'[339] The Minister for Education, MacNeill, held a different view. He had a horror of state intervention. 'The use of

336 J.H. Whyte, *Church and state in modern Ireland 1923–1970* (Dublin, 1971), p. 38.
337 *Statistical Abstract*, 1931, T. 120, p. 111; 1939, T. 148, pp. 136–7.
338 On the impulses behind Gaelicisation see M. O'Callaghan, 'Language, nationality and cultural identity in the Irish Free State, 1922–7: the *Irish Statesman* and the *Catholic Bulletin* reappraised', *IHS*, 24, 94 (November 1984), pp. 228–30.
339 DD, 5, 20 September 1923, 49.

Irish by public servants', he maintained 'was and would be mainly conditioned by the public attitude on the matter and . . . a purely bureaucratic and official favouring of Irish, in the absence of a strongly favourable public attitude, would lead to no desirable result, nothing more than a barren conformity.'[340] MacNeill couldn't even achieve barren conformity. And he had nothing to offer as an alternative. He apparently felt that 'you might as well be putting wooden legs on hens as trying to restore Irish through the school system'.[341] The challenge of the language revival was indeed a formidable one. But if neither the public service, nor the educational system, were to make a significant contribution towards it, then it was lost before it began. MacNeill's attitude seems prematurely defeatist. He did not even establish a research unit in his Department, as Pearse had urged, to keep the country abreast of educational thought abroad.

A vigorous Education memorandum claimed that 'Irish is dying because the people of the Gaeltacht think that Irish and poverty, Irish and social inferiority are inextricably connected. They will continue to think so until the government proved conclusively . . . *that Irish pays.*'[342] It argued that government officials were actually spreading English in the Gaeltacht: 'agricultural and fishery instructors and inspectors and land commission officials are at present some of the most powerful agents of anglicisation'.[343] It stressed that 'the Ministry of Education can and will gaelicise the young people up to 18 . . . but all their efforts will be wasted if the other departments do not cooperate in keeping them gaelicised when they leave the schools'.[344] The robust commonsense of much of this memorandum, which sought to create a Gaelic Ireland through manuring the roots of material self-interest, clashed brutally with MacNeill's own image of the island of saints and scholars. But if it stripped away that particular veil of illusion, it indulged its own extraordinary illusion that 'the young people up to 18' came under the influence of the educational system, when in fact the vast majority left school by the age of fourteen.

The Department identified two main problems. First, the teachers knew little Irish. Second, the people knew even less. Progress was made with the teachers. As early as February 1922 the Provisional Government began to intensify the use of Irish in the primary schools,[345] and crash courses were quickly introduced to familiarise the teachers with the rudiments of the language. Special preparatory colleges were opened in 1926 and in 1927 to train primary school teachers specially in Irish. By 1939 most primary

340 SPO, S3717, E. MacNeill to W.T. Cosgrave, 22 October 1924.
341 Ó Broin, *Yesterday*, pp. 66–7.
342 SPO, S3717, 'The Gaelicising of Ireland', undated (probably April 1924, see covering note, 15 April 1924, to M. MacDunphy).
343 *Ibid.*   344 *Ibid.*   345 Gwynn, *Irish Free State*, p. 30.

and secondary teachers were officially recorded as competent to teach through Irish.

The Cosgrave government decided that all instruction in the first two years in the national schools (children generally aged under seven) should be through Irish. This policy was implemented gradually until 1931, and then more rapidly. In addition, to accommodate the teaching of Irish as a language, the teaching of other subjects was curtailed. In 1934 the Fianna Fáil Minister for Education, Tomás Derrig, despite having been himself trained as a teacher, directed that the standard of the other subjects should be reduced to permit even greater emphasis on Irish.[346]

The intellectual rationale for teaching infants exclusively through Irish was provided by Fr T.J. Corcoran, SJ, professor of Education in UCD from 1909 until 1942.[347] Corcoran's qualifications for pronouncing on the subject were debatable, but he was good enough for enthusiasts seeking 'expert' support. As successive governments cowered from a scientific investigation of the problem, the Irish National Teachers' Organisation initiated its own inquiry into the educational efficiency of teaching through Irish. This revealed an overwhelming consensus among teachers by 1941 that in all subjects except singing and needlework the result was the relative retardation of the child.[348]

The emphasis on teaching infants in the national schools exclusively through Irish may have accounted in some measure for the educational retardation of Irish children compared with English children up to university level. The policy did not, of course, sacrifice all the children of the nation equally. Children from more affluent homes, whose parents could repair some of the damage done in the schools, naturally enjoyed an advantage over poorer children whose parents would not or could not take a comparable interest in their education. Teaching infants through Irish provided one further bulwark for the existing social structure in that it inevitably discriminated against already deprived children, and ensured that when they were despatched from the country as emigrants they would be equipped to serve their new masters only as hewers of wood and drawers of water. It was an eloquent commentary on MacNeill's vision of the Irish as 'the schoolmasters of Europe'.

While the language was being 'revived' in the schools, the existing Irish-speaking areas contracted relentlessly in size. The number of native Irish speakers fell from about 200 000 in 1922 to 100 000 in 1939 and 50 000 in 1964. The Cosgrave government duly appointed a Gaeltacht Commission and duly sabotaged its report. Finance, though presided over by a language enthusiast in Blythe, took panic at the proposals. It had

---

[346] Akenson, *Mirror*, pp. 35–62, describes the attempt to foster the language revival through the schools.
[347] *Ibid.*, p. 46.   [348] *Ibid.*, pp. 57–8.

good reason to. The commission actually recommended free secondary school education in the Gaeltacht! The government rejected this heretical suggestion on the disingenuous grounds that parents were too poor to avail of free secondary education because they had to send their children out to work at the age of twelve! Therefore free secondary education 'would not produce results commensurate with the cost'.[349] It rejected on the same specious grounds a recommendation to increase scholarships among Gaeltacht children, though if the scholarships were not availed of, it is difficult to see how they would increase costs![350] It may be surmised that the real reason for the alarm among the mandarins of Finance was that it would be difficult to confine these policies to the Gaeltacht. Political pressure might compel their extension to the rest of the country. An approach towards equality of educational opportunity was too high a price to pay for the gaelicisation of Ireland.

Education was right to insist that the revival could not succeed unless it was seen that Irish pays. The early spontaneous enthusiasm of vintage Gaelic League days failed to survive the influx of political republicans in 1918, as Sean O'Casey sardonically observed.[351] The government only tinkered with devising means to make Irish pay. It offered pupils inducements like extra marks for answering subjects through Irish in examinations, and penalised schools by withholding subsidies for teachers lacking qualifications in Irish, irrespective of their quality in their own subjects. This approach did little to elevate Irish, but much to demean education. A knowledge of Irish was made compulsory for certain state posts, but no genuine attempt was made to gaelicise either politics or the civil service, prerequisites for the success of the revival. The results of all this fertilising was a luxuriant crop of weeds, and a pervasive stench that offended all but the coarsest nostrils. The essential hypocrisy occurred less in the area of compulsory Irish in the schools than in the failure to provide opportunity, or obligation, for the regular use of Irish subsequently. The refusal of all governments since the foundation of the state to practise what they preached alerted an observant populace to the fact that the revival was a sham.

What might have been a noble chapter in the history of the new state became instead a sordid one. None of the instinctive ritualistic excuses could explain this away. The British could not be blamed. Partition could not be blamed. The civil war could not be blamed – though of course it was. A wicked world could not be blamed. Freemasons could not be blamed. The devil prowling about the shores of Ireland could not be

[349] Statement of government policy on recommendations of the Commission on the Gaeltacht, 1927, p. 9.
[350] *Ibid.*, p. 10.
[351] S. O'Casey, 'Down with the Gaedhilge', *Irish Opinion*, 9 March 1918, reprinted in Hogan, *Feathers from the green crow*, p. 35.

blamed. The responsibility for the failure of policy lay with the formulators of policy. When the heroes of the revolution failed their Irish test, the blame could not be shifted to the nation's children.[352]

NORTHERN IRELAND

If the Free State educational authorities faced a major cultural challenge, they did not at least have to suffer the sectarian spite that baffled their Belfast counterparts. James Craig genuinely wished to improve educational standards and opportunities. He had shown in his earlier career a serious interest in educational issues.[353] His choice of Lord Londonderry as his first Minister of Education was significant, in that Londonderry was the least sectarian and least provincial member of his cabinet.

As in the Free State, the institutional arrangements for education were revised, with the plethora of existing boards of education being incorporated into a single department. In glaring contrast to MacNeill, however, Londonderry quickly appointed a departmental committee of investigation, under R.J. Lynn, into the state of education. This included representatives from all interested bodies except the Catholic Church, which refused either to nominate members to the committee or to give evidence. The committee found a disturbing situation, particularly in Belfast, where the churches had so failed to provide schools that there were no places for about 12 000 children.[354]

The Londonderry Education Act of 1923 tried to reconstruct Ulster primary education, and to make greater provision for post-primary education. It counts among the most ambitious legislative measures ever undertaken in Irish education.[355] But it largely failed to achieve its objectives. It proceeded on the illusion that Catholic and Protestant clergies were more concerned with education than with power. It tried to increase parental control over education by entrusting local authorities with the responsibility for elementary education. This sent a thrill of terror through all clergies. The Act further alienated clergies by proposing that schools should be open to all children, irrespective of religious denomination, for secular education, that religious instruction should not be given during hours of compulsory attendance, and that religious tests should not be imposed on teachers. The state would pay all teachers'

---

[352] G. Ó Tuathaigh, 'The state and the language since 1922', *Irish Times*, 19 April 1977; O. MacDonagh, *States of Mind* (London, 1983), pp. 117–23. See below, pp. 670–2.

[353] Buckland, *James Craig* (Dublin, 1980), pp. 12–13.

[354] Lawrence, *The government of Northern Ireland*, p. 110.

[355] This section on educational policy in Ulster is based mainly on D.H. Akenson, *Education and enmity: the control of schooling in Northern Ireland 1920–50* (Newton Abbot, 1973); Lawrence, *Northern Ireland*, pp. 105–26; P. Buckland, *The factory of grievances: devolved government in Northern Ireland 1921–39* (Dublin, 1979), pp. 247–65.

salaries, but managers (i.e. clergy) who refused to accept a school management committee consisting of four members appointed by themselves and two approved by the local education authorities would receive only half the cost of maintenance and repairs.

The Catholic bishops rejected the principle of the 'four and two committees', which would control religious instruction and teachers' appointments. They held that the local authorities were in the process of being gerrymandered, and that they would be overwhelmingly Protestant even in many predominantly Catholic areas. The Department of Education would be a mainly Protestant department, which could easily 'cut off the supply' of Catholic teachers by denying certificates to otherwise qualified applicants.[356]

The refusal of the Catholic hierarchy to participate in the proposed structures made it simpler for the Protestant churches to capture the system and mould it to their taste. This suited the Catholic clergy, who might have had to manufacture further complaints if they weren't so generously supplied by their Protestant brethren. Londonderry, unable to shrivel his mind yet further to accommodate local standards, resigned as minister in 1925. A series of Acts between 1925 and 1930 conferred effective control over local authority school management committees on Protestant clergymen. In response to massive pressure from Protestant clergy, and the clergy-ridden Protestant public, Craig, against his better judgement, authorised legislation in 1930 imposing 'non-denominational' bible instruction when even a minority of parents requested it. This contravened the provisions in the Government of Ireland Act concerning religious discrimination, but the measure was not declared unconstitutional until 1945.[357]

The ecclesiastical authorities, North and South, Catholic, Protestant and Dissenter, fought tenaciously to consolidate their grip on the management of the educational system. Nevertheless, it would be misleading to imply that the churches were responsible for the stagnation of Irish education. Indeed, individual clergymen were disproportionately responsible for the few enlightened innovations that infiltrated into Irish educational thought or practice before 1960. The churches have endured much criticism for their insistence on segregated education, particularly in the North. Segregation had however been achieved in practice long before 1920. No major change occurred afterwards. Speculation concerning the consequences of integrated education must remain largely academic. Segregated educational systems exist in several societies without reaping the harvest of hatred that has distinguished Northern Ireland. It may be less the segregation of education than the values inculcated within

[356] Lawrence, *Northern Ireland*, p. 112, n. 4.
[357] Akenson, *Education*, pp. 86–118; Buckland, *Grievances*, pp. 256–65.

segregated sectors that transmit the ancestral hatreds of Ulster society. The optimistic image of integrated education as a device for building up resistance against the virus of sectarian hatred probably exaggerates the potential of education in this sphere as long as the homes remain carriers of the virus. 'Non-sectarian' teachers – if sufficient could be found – could offer only a weak antidote to parental poison unless attitudes in the wider society were themselves changing under pressure of other circumstances.[358]

The conflict over education was symptomatic of a general problem confronting Craig. He himself was no bigot. He could at times show physical and even moral courage well above the ordinary. He genuinely wished to reconcile Catholic and Protestant in Northern Ireland. He was even prepared to contemplate the possibility of a united Ireland in his own lifetime.[359] But he found himself confronted at every turn by his own extremists and by the Catholic opposition.

Unionism was united on little except the union. Otherwise it embraced a variety of factions, very much like the Home Rule Party or Sinn Féin. It was divided on a host of social, economic and personal issues. Craig's first object, and increasingly almost his sole object, was to maintain the unity of the party. And as a party leader he gave a virtuoso performance, fending off threats from both right and left.

The civil war in the South helped consolidate Craig's control in the North. By concentrating IRA activity in the South it probably reduced pressure on Craig to adopt more repressive anti-Catholic measures. Northern Catholics might have been the first victims of a colonel's regime in the Free State. Collins now recommended the northern IRA to engage only in passive resistance and in defensive action.[360] The IRA conceded an element of moderation to Craig, recognising his attempt to control the more enthusiastic terrorists among the B Specials, led by District Inspector Nixon, who threatened to form a break-away parliamentary faction.[361] Craig subsequently succeeded in having Nixon dismissed from the RUC.[362] Craig made a number of genuine if limited attempts to persuade Catholics to cooperate in the new administration. He reserved one-third of the places in the police force for them, and invited them to participate on the Lynn committee of inquiry into education. When they failed to respond, he seems to have decided that future initiatives for conciliation must come from them.

---

[358] On this contentious issue see D. Murray, 'Educational segregation: "rite" or wrong?', in P. Clancy, S. Drudy, K. Lynch and L. O'Dowd (eds.), *Ireland: a sociological profile* (Dublin, 1986), pp. 244–64.

[359] Buckland, *Grievances*, p. 16.

[360] SPO, S1801A, S. Woods (Officer commanding the third northern division of the IRA) to C. in C., 29 September 1922.

[361] *Ibid.*   [362] Buckland, *Grievances*, p. 31; Buckland, *Craig*, p. 96.

Craig appointed Dawson Bates as Minister for Home Affairs to protect his own right flank. As secretary of the Ulster Unionist Association since 1905, Bates had acquired an intimate knowledge of local unionist politics, and Craig relied heavily on him to relay grassroots feeling.[363] If he was a useful buffer for Craig against the barbs of the right, however, Craig in return had to allow him a virtually free hand in the area of security. And Bates, aided and abetted by his permanent secretary, Samuel Watt, as well as by other officials, was a confirmed sectarian. He refused to appoint Catholics to his ministry. His Offences Against the State Act in 1924 invested the government with extensive powers of arrest and detention. It was renewed annually until 1931, when it became a permanent adornment of Ulster Unionist political architecture.[364]

Though himself an honest man, Craig turned a blind eye to local corruption in Ulster Unionist politics in the interests of party unity. Where Cosgrave felt obliged to suspend Dublin and Cork corporations at various stages, Craig refused to sanction comparable action in the case of Belfast corporation, despite compelling evidence of widespread corruption.[365] Exposure of Unionist corruption would conform poorly to the self-image of honesty, serving neither psychic nor political purpose.

Craig had as little love as Cosgrave for labour. But he was cannier than Cosgrave. He took care to humour the Ulster Labour Unionist Association, which Carson had founded in 1918 as a barrier against the red tide threatening to inundate Europe. Craig, in contrast to Cosgrave, did establish a Ministry of Labour, instead of submerging it in Commerce, as less imaginative advisers suggested.[366] Craig found the postwar boom already turning to slump when he became prime minister. The two staple industries of the North, ship-building and linen, proved particularly vulnerable to international economic depression, and unemployment would remain an intractable problem until World War Two. It leaped to 20 per cent in 1921, and averaged 19 per cent of the insured work force between 1923 and 1930, and no less than 27 per cent between 1931 and 1939.[367] Potential labour unrest remained a recurring threat throughout Craig's career. In the 1925 general election radical unionists caused problems for him on the left. It is a tribute to his skill in handling a potentially awkward problem that the unrest generally remained potential. He was always sufficiently alert to the importance of main-

---

363 Buckland, *Craig*, p. 39.   364 Buckland, *Grievances*, pp. 204–20.
365 Budge and O'Leary, *Belfast*, pp. 146–7, 153–4.
366 Buckland, *Grievances*, p. 10.
367 D.S. Johnson, 'The Northern Ireland economy, 1914–39', in L. Kennedy and P. Ollerenshaw (eds.), *An economic history of Ulster 1820–1939* (Manchester, 1985), pp. 190–1.

taining a united unionist front to be prepared to make limited concessions to Protestant workers to keep them in line.[368]

Craig's Finance Minister, the septuagenarian flour importer, H.M. Pollock, was as wedded as Ernest Blythe to the principle of financial respectability. But Craig, unlike Cosgrave, never buttoned himself into the Treasury pocket. The financial arrangements of the Government of Ireland Act were complicated, and not very favourable to Northern Ireland. The government could raise certain taxes locally, called the 'transferred taxes', but these amounted to only about 20 per cent of its income compared with the 80 per cent or more deriving from taxes reserved for Westminster, including income tax and customs and excise. Northern Irish expenditure, on the other hand, was largely a matter for the Northern parliament, which had authority over most of the spending services.[369] But Craig decided early that Ulster would have the same social services as Britain, whatever the cost, and that Westminster would have to pay the difference between Ulster income and expenditure. Craig's disdain for the restrictive financial arrangements shocked the doctrinaires at the Treasury. His motto might have been 'live Ulster, perish financial orthodoxy'. He played a skilful hand in dealing with Whitehall and Westminster, leaving a trail of apoplectic officials to grapple with the consequences of his cavalier attitude towards milking the Treasury's sacred cows.[370] It was in the 1920s that Ulster welfare services began to draw ahead of those in the South, where they were sacrificed on the altar of fiscal responsibility by the Ulster Protestant, Ernest Blythe. The Northern Irish Labour Party would in vain warn Blythe that his attack on the old-age pensioners in 1924 might hinder unification, because Ulstermen could hardly be expected to submit to this brand of degradation once they had tasted something better.[371] There is a certain irony in the fact that the axiomatically irresponsible Southern Irish clung to austere fiscal rectitude at a moment when their axiomatically hard-headed, thrifty, Scottish brethren in the North did not flinch from following the primrose path of profligacy!

THE BOUNDARY COMMISSION

Brooding over the early years of the Northern state, relegating every other issue to secondary importance, was the uncertain future of the state itself. How would the Boundary Commission, to be established under Article 12

---

[368] P. Bew, P. Gibbon, and H. Patterson, *The state in Northern Ireland 1921–72* (Manchester, 1979), p. 90.
[369] For a clear explanation of a complicated arrangement, see Buckland, *Northern Ireland*, pp. 22–3.
[370] Bew, *et al.*, *The state*, pp. 78–82; Buckland, *Grievances*, pp. 86ff.
[371] Mitchell, *Irish politics*, p. 220.

of the Treaty, determine the frontiers of Northern Ireland? Article 12 was loosely drafted. It merely stipulated that the 'boundaries' would be drawn 'in accordance with the wishes of the inhabitants, so far as may be compatible with economic and geographic conditions'. It did not identify the 'inhabitants', whose 'wishes' were to be taken into account. The commission, not the 'inhabitants', would apparently decide how 'compatible' was 'compatible'. It didn't even specify when the commission was to meet. The casualness of the drafting faithfully reflected the casualness of Sinn Féin thinking on the Ulster question.

Sinn Féin had already reneged on Ulster nationalists by its abstentionist policy. It could not be pleaded that the implications of abstentionism had not been foreseen. The Irish Nation League, sponsored by Bishop McHugh of Derry, had opposed abstention in 1917 precisely on the grounds that it ignored the Ulster issue.[372] Neither the Provisional Government, nor anti-Treaty Sinn Féin, devised an effective Northern policy.

Article 12 posed a serious problem for Craig. He held almost all the cards, however, and he played them well. That steadfast man wanted no change. He took his stand on the territorial status quo, conceding 'not an inch'. That was Britain's simplest option too, at least in the short term. Article 12 raised more complex issues for Dublin. The Provisional Government now had to submit to the purgative process of actually devising a Northern policy. The fraudulent evasions of Sinn Féin would no longer suffice.

The exchanges between Dublin and Belfast reflected the limits imposed by circumstances on the freedom of manoeuvre of the principals. On 21 January 1922 Craig agreed to appoint a Boundary Commissioner. On 3 February he qualified this by claiming that he had understood the Commission would involve merely local rectifications, whereas Southern spokesmen were purporting to anticipate large transfers of territory.[373] The Provisional Government had declared its willingness, on 30 January, to fight for 'what they considered the proper boundary'.[374] Collins merely confirmed that Article 12 was highly ambiguous by insisting that there was 'nothing ambiguous about it', and then immediately proceeding to illustrate the ambiguity by completely ignoring the crucial clause 'so far as may be compatible with economic and geographical conditions'.[375] The Provisional Government appointed Ernest Blythe, an Ulster Protestant, as 'the most suitable person . . . to take charge of all correspondence etc. relative to the North East' in April. Blythe's advocacy in August of a

372 Miller, *Church*, p. 351.   373 *Irish Independent*, 4 February 1922.
374 SPO, S1801A, Provisional Government Minutes, 30 January 1922.
375 *Irish Independent*, 4 February 1922.

consistent policy of conciliation logically implied the abandonment of any territorial claims on the North.[376]

Cosgrave therefore succeeded Collins with no particular policy on Article XII. He appointed Blythe Minister for Local Government in his new cabinet, replacing him with Kevin O'Shiel, the assistant legal advisor, as director of the Free State North Eastern Boundary Bureau with responsibility for reporting regularly to the government 'in connection with the forthcoming Boundary Commission'.[377] The rationale for the shift in Blythe's responsibilities remains unclear.

O'Shiel, after some initial difficulty in finding suitable staff,[378] prepared a detailed case. He never tired of insisting that he tried to follow the thinking of Collins, whose legal advisor he had been, and with whose mind he was probably more familiar than many of the relatively new men in the cabinet. He claimed that

the late general never made any secret of his distrust in the Boundary Commission as a means of settlement per se. He used frequently to remark that 'the Boundary Commission will settle nothing'. He realised that even after the Boundary Commission had sat and made its decisions, and even if those decisions conceded to us our ultimate claim there would still be an 'Hibernia irredenta' to disturb the peace of future generations. Not only that, but there would be an increased feeling of intense hatred amongst the Northern secessionist populations against the rest of Ireland. Though the territory of Saor Stát might be broadened, the gulf between Saor Stát and those populations would also be broadened. So fully aware of all this was the late General that on a number of occasions he went out of his way to establish contact with the Belfast authorities in the hope that such contact would lead to a better and more enduring settlement between Irish men.[379]

O'Shiel's Bureau closely studied European precedents, with particular reference to the plebiscites in Silesia, Schleswig-Holstein and Hungary. It accumulated extensive information on local circumstances in Ulster. In January 1923 O'Shiel submitted two alternative revised boundary lines, a minimum, and a maximum, to the government.[380] The minimum demand would transfer all of Fermanagh, two-thirds of Tyrone, one-third of Londonderry, one-third of Armagh, and a quarter of Down to the Free State, resulting in a boundary of 124 miles (compared with the existing 280 miles), and still leaving 266 000 Catholics as a 27 per cent minority in the new Northern state. The maximum claim would transfer further sections to the Free State. This would reflect the wishes of the inhabitants of the areas concerned, but might not, O'Shiel felt, be as compatible with economic and geographical conditions.

[376] Fanning, *Ireland*, pp. 34–6; McColgan, *British policy*, pp. 121–2.
[377] SPO, Provisional Government Minutes, 2 October 1922.
[378] RM, P7/B/288, O'Shiel to Minister for Defence, 16 October 1922.
[379] RM, P7/B/288, O'Shiel memo, 29 May 1923.
[380] EB, P24/171, 'Report on possible boundary lines' by B.C. Waller (undated, apparently 9 January 1923).

O'Shiel was an ardent advocate of a united Ireland. His first major memorandum for the government defined 'our object' as

not the setting up of a Boundary Commission with the intention of wresting as much territory as possible from Craig, but a much more lasting thing than any temporary arrangement of purely arbitrary and utterly absurd boundaries, viz. *National Union . . .* because it is natural and efficient, because it is convenient and economic, and most of all because it is enduring and makes directly for peace, contentment and prosperity.[381]

He felt that 'unless and until Irish union is achieved there will be no perfect peace and therefore no absolute security in this country'.[382] He would concede the Protestant case for cast iron guarantees of their civil liberties, even if he considered their fears largely imaginary:

It is my belief that unless something very wonderful occurs national union must first take a federal form. We cannot expect Belfast to relinquish altogether its government (of which it is so proud) and become merged in us. Besides, there is sufficient differences [sic] to justify an autonomous parliament in that corner of Ireland. There will have to be mutual concessions on the minorities point, and probably, if it is urged, on *educational* point.[383]

Provided a settlement were 'based on national union', he contemplated England possibly acting 'as a Guaranteeing Power in order to soothe the North Eastern susceptibilities'.[384]

His basic pessimism concerning the likely outcome of the Boundary Commission moved O'Shiel to counsel postponement. He already noted in his December 1922 memorandum that Article 12 imposed no time limit for an agreement, specified no procedure for appointing the commission, nor indicated the consequences of one party refusing to appoint a commissioner.[385] In a major submission in February 1923 he urged the postponement of the commission until the end of the civil war because 'we must be in a position to maintain public order and to *guarantee the protection of the lives and property of possibly future citizens*'.[386] The commission was likely to attract international media attention to Ireland, which would be cast in a lurid light if the civil war had not ended. The fall of Lloyd George in July 1922, to be succeeded by none other than Andrew Bonar Law, had brought a hostile Tory government to power in Britain, able to gleefully point to the civil war as yet a further example of the axiomatic truth that the Irish 'do not belong to that type of population which is ripe for self-government', in striking contrast to 'loyal Ulster', where conditions were now 'peaceful'.[387] From an internal political

---

[381] EB, P24/171, O'Shiel memo (undated, early December 1922).   [382] *Ibid.*
[383] RM, P7/B/288, O'Shiel memo, 29 May 1923.
[384] *Ibid.*
[385] EB, P24/171, O'Shiel memo (undated, early December 1922).
[386] RM, P7/B/288, O'Shiel memo, 10 February 1923.
[387] *Ibid.*

viewpoint, an adverse decision by the commission while the civil war was still in progress would be the worst possible result, because it would 'give a new lease of life to irregularism . . . and will also stir up strife within the six counties as some of the irregular leaders (e.g. Frank Aiken) are not touching the North now until *after* the findings of the Commission'.[388] O'Shiel concluded:

If . . . we are certain that impartial justice will be done we should press the Boundary Commission for all we are worth; but if, on the other hand, we are certain that the result will be against us, or even if we have any uncertainty about the result, then we should undoubtedly work for an adjournment. As the matter stands at present with a strong Conservative government in power in Great Britain, it is very likely that the result will not be favourable to us.[389]

O'Shiel harboured few illusions about the likely outcome at that stage. As late as April 1923, he continued to advise delay, at least until the Free State could become a member of the League of Nations, which would give the government an opportunity to bring an unfavourable recommendation 'for review' before that body. Even if Craig merely refused to nominate a representative, and Britain took no action, 'we will be given a valid reason for bringing the whole matter up before the League of Nations or the Imperial Conference'.[390] Once peace was restored in the South, 'and the reign of law solidly established . . . we will puncture *ab initio* much of Craig's strongest argumentations'.[391]

It was only with the end of the civil war that the Free State government could hope for any sympathy in London or the slightest hint of conciliation from Belfast, or even find the time to turn their minds properly to the Ulster problem. The fact that a general election had to be held within a year of the constitution coming into effect, i.e. before December 1923, also helped concentrate cabinet minds on the electoral implications of Article 12. With public opinion beginning to become restive, the cabinet agreed 'that certain progress must have been made in the matter of the Boundary Commission before the coming general election'.[392] The official request to the British government on 19 July to activate Article 12, and the nomination of Eoin MacNeill as the Irish representative, may also have been partly influenced by O'Shiel's more optimistic tone following his June visit to England when he claimed to find, in contrast to previous reactions, 'a conviction (for the first time perhaps) that we are possessed of some at least of those qualities of purpose, tenacity and moral courage which English people have been largely brought up to

---

[388] EB, P24/171, O'Shiel memo (undated, early December 1922).   [389] *Ibid.*
[390] EB, P24/171, O'Shiel memo, 21 April 1923.
[391] *Ibid.*
[392] RM, P7/B/288, M. MacDunphy, memo, 11 July 1923, summarising cabinet discussion of 10 July.

believe are the particular and exclusive monopolies of the Anglo-Saxon race'.[393]

The story of the Boundary Commission is well known.[394] Following Craig's refusal to appoint a representative, the British government nominated J.R. Fisher, editor of the *Northern Whig* and well read in history,[395] as the Northern Ireland representative, and selected as chairman Mr Justice Feetham, an English-born judge of the South African Supreme Court. MacNeill quickly found himself in a minority when Feetham decided that essentially 'economic and geographical conditions' must overrule 'the wishes of the inhabitants'.[396] In contrast to Fisher, who apparently kept Craig well informed of developments, MacNeill interpreted the terms of reference of the commission to preclude his communicating with Cosgrave on the proceedings of the commission. In November 1925 the *Morning Post* disclosed that the commission would recommend a transfer of South Armagh to the Free State and of part of East Donegal to Northern Ireland, resulting in a net gain of 25 000 Catholics for the South, and 2000 Protestants for the North. The Cosgrave cabinet preferred no change to the loss of East Donegal (it would probably be too unkind to say, to the gain of South Armagh!). Cosgrave hurried to London, where he quickly agreed with Craig and Baldwin to suppress the report, and to accept the status quo. His one gain was to secure the waiving of Free State liability for part of the British (national) debt, which it had incurred under Article 5 of the Treaty. MacNeill felt that he could also probably have secured the remission of the land annuities had he pushed hard enough for them, and thus deprived de Valera of a lethal electoral weapon in later years.[397]

Controversy concerning the Boundary Commission has concentrated on the cabinet's handling of the issue, and on the choice of MacNeill as Free State representative. Professor Mansergh has observed that

a more agile, if need be less principled, Irish member would at least have ensured that . . . the break came earlier, when he had perceived the inevitable consequence for the Irish Free State of the chairman's reading of the terms of reference, and he would have made it at the moment favourable to the government whose representative he was. But in a sense all this is secondary for, given the chairman's legal interpretation of the terms of reference, break there was bound to be. That being so, the degree of foresight shown by the Cosgrave administration comes sharply into question.

393 RM, P7/B/288, O'Shiel memo, 17 July 1923.
394 Murphy, *Ireland*, has an incisive summary, pp. 62–3.
395 See Fisher's contribution in Rosenbaum, *Against Home Rule*, pp. 47–77.
396 G.J. Hand (ed.), *Report of the Irish Boundary Commission 1925* (Shannon, 1969), pp. xiv–xv.
397 N. Mansergh, 'Eoin MacNeill – a reappraisal', *Studies*, 73 (Summer 1974), p. 140; G.J. Hand, 'MacNeill and the Boundary Commission', in Martin and Byrne (eds.), *Scholar Revolutionary*, p. 272.

Desmond Williams gently wondered 'was it prudent of the Free State government to appoint such an ambassador?'[398]

Cosgrave's choice of MacNeill raises intriguing questions concerning his political judgement, as well as his own and his colleagues' expectations. They clearly did not envisage unification, or even revision, by force. Otherwise they would hardly have demobilised the army so quickly. Nor did they apparently envisage unification by attraction. Otherwise they would hardly have reduced old-age pensions in 1924, or prohibited divorce in 1925, while the commission was still sitting. Did they expect to secure by guile something that they could not, or would not, by stick or by carrot?

Cosgrave justified MacNeill's appointment on the grounds that he was a Catholic, a Northerner, and a minister. He did not explain why these qualities were necessary. Kevin O'Shiel had given the matter some thought. He described his ideal commissioner:

a man of great weight and sagacity, and one of irreproachable name. It matters not from what part of the country he hails, or even if he should come from outside our shores, as long as he has the requisite qualities. He should be a man without prejudice on the Northern question, and yet one who has a thorough mastery of the situation and with sufficient backbone to fight his corner hard and well, if necessary. Above all, he should be a person who is prepared to act on the government's slightest suggestion – to go hard when the government tells him to go hard, and to soften when the government tells him to soften. This is particularly important in view of the possibility of negotiations for a settlement proceeding outside the Commission while the Commission is actually functioning.[399]

O'Shiel recommended, ironically enough, not Eoin MacNeill, but his brother, James, who had enjoyed a distinguished career in the Indian civil service, was a lawyer, and was then Irish High Commissioner in London. The recommendation of James MacNeill must have amounted to a conscious rejection of Eoin MacNeill as the appropriate choice.

It is understandable, if only from a propaganda viewpoint, that a Northerner would have attractions, as O'Shiel's recommendation of James MacNeill itself implied. But there were other eligible Northerners. The brilliant young Patrick McGilligan was one. McGilligan in addition was a lawyer, a distinct advantage in Eoin MacNeill's own opinion.[400] A Northern Protestant might be considered better propaganda value than a Northern Catholic. Ernest Blythe satisfied the requirements. But why select a minister at all? A minister who remained departmentally active would only be a part-time commissioner. Neither Feetham nor Fisher were ministers. If Cosgrave did not make an error of judgement in

398 Mansergh, 'MacNeill', p. 140; Williams, 'Summing up', p. 190.
399 EB, P24/171, O'Shiel memo, 21 April 1923.
400 RM, P7/B/288, MacNeill marginalia on a letter from O'Shiel, 9 December 1922.

choosing MacNeill as the best man for the job, it must be asked for which job was he thought to be the best man.

Membership of the Boundary Commission threatened the political future of any Free State commissioner. Dublin realised already that partition was a *fait accompli*. What was needed was not so much an effective negotiator as a suitable scapegoat. Different qualities are sought in a sacrificial victim than in a negotiator. A senior man is necessary, a venerable name, whose sacrifice should satisfy the multitude. He must also be sufficiently selfless to accept his fate. MacNeill satisfied these requirements. He recognised, as did other possible candidates, that nomination to the commission meant the end of a political career.[401] He accepted nomination 'because no one else could be found to act instead of me'.[402] The cryptic reminiscent comment that 'MacNeill was thrown to destruction in the Boundary Commission' captures the mood of a colleague even across forty years.[403] On this reading, MacNeill was not selected because he was a Catholic, a Northerner, and a minister. Rather, a Catholic, a Northerner and a minister was selected because that was what Eoin MacNeill was.[404]

The puzzle does not end with MacNeill's appointment. Even if he resigned himself to the role of the sacrificial victim, he could have made life more difficult for his executioners. A more attractive personality than many of his colleagues, he seems to have combined integrity with incompetence.[405] A well-informed Northern priest, correctly anticipating the tenor of the commission's recommendations, noted in September 1925 that 'everything taking place and likely to take place, is in the Unionist camp. Fisher keeps them well informed. We can get no news. Of course if the Northern nationalists are going to be betrayed, the longer it is kept from us, all the better, I suppose.' He provided a crisp account of the procedure he felt MacNeill ought to have adopted:[406]

MacNeill should have determined and settled before any evidence was taken that (1) Free State territory did not come under the jurisdiction of the Boundary Commission and (2) a unit of territory should have been agreed upon by Feetham

---

401 Williams, 'Summing up', p. 189.
402 Hand, 'MacNeill and the Boundary Commission', p. 269; M. Tierney, *Eoin MacNeill, scholar and man of action, 1867–1945* (Oxford, 1980), p. 342.
403 RM, P7/D/115, unsigned note, 26 April 1965.
404 A mischievous historian might allow his mind to wander idly to one other possible choice – Mr de Valera. He had, it is true, no fixed address in July 1923, but that was hardly an insuperable difficulty. Had he refused, he could have been taunted that he had not once, but twice, shown moral cowardice in refusing the poisoned chalice. Had he accepted, he would presumably have been as baffled as he was to always remain by partition. Had he succeeded to any extent, the government would, as true patriots, have no doubt been delirious with joy!
405 Hand, 'MacNeill and the Boundary Commission', pp. 211–13.
406 EB, P24/498, Rev. E. Coyle to E. Blythe, undated (late September 1925). See also Hand, *Boundary Commission*, p. xii, n. 18.

and the Commission, in which the wishes of the people were to be determined . . .
If Feetham in the beginning had not decided these two essential points, MacNeill
should have withdrawn; declared the Treaty broken unless a guarantee were given
that the wishes of the people were to be made predominant.[407]

Opinion might vary on the precise tactics MacNeill should have
adopted. But it does seem curious that he did not pursue some course
along these lines, even given his sacrificial role. Not only did he accept
Feetham's highly unfavourable interpretation of Article 12, but he seems
to have offered little effective resistance to the chairman's analysis of local
detail. Feetham was thus able to adopt a static concept of economic
circumstances.[408] Of course, Dublin may not have wanted to know.

The nationalist position of Article 12 had involved a degree of self-
deception from the outset. Collins's tactics revolved around securing such
substantial territorial transfers that the rump Northern state could not
prove economically viable. The view was widely shared, or at least
expressed.[409] Repartition would therefore be merely a prelude to
inevitable unification. This assumption indulged two serious illusions.
Firstly, the Protestant heartland – Belfast, north Down, north Armagh,
south Antrim – didn't need the periphery to survive economically. On the
contrary, the periphery was probably an economic burden on the prosperity of the primarily Protestant east.[410] Secondly, however loosely
drafted, Article 12 clearly assumed the survival of a viable Northern
Ireland state. Otherwise there was no point inserting the qualifying clause
'so far as may be compatible with economic and geographic conditions'.
The widespread nationalist anticipation of substantial territorial transfers
under Article 12 could be correct only if the nationalist assumption about
the economic consequences for Northern Ireland of those transfers was
wrong. It probably was, but the assumption was shared by unionists as
well as by nationalists, and not least by Feetham, who accepted the
conventional wisdom that Northern Ireland could not survive serious
territorial amputation. In the light of that assumption, he was in honour
no less than in intellect bound to interpret Article 12 to the effect that only
minor rectification of the boundary, depending on immediate local
circumstances, could be contemplated. The nationalist abuse so copiously
vented on Feetham pays eloquent tribute to his refusal to connive at
nationalist self-deception.[411]

[407] EB, P24/498, Coyle to Blythe, undated (late September 1925).
[408] Hand, *Boundary Commission*, pp. 122ff, for the Newry question.
[409] EB, P24/621, Ernest Blythe's election address in August 1923; J.J. Walsh, *Recollections
       of a rebel* (Tralee, 1924), p. 69; Laffan, *Partition*, pp. 85, 87.
[410] It remains a common illusion to the present day to confuse size with economic viability.
[411] Hand's masterly 'Introduction' to *Boundary Commission*, pp. vii–xxii, retrieves the
       reputation of Irish scholarship in its dispassionate assessment of Feetham, 'a conscien-
       tious lawyer with a keen analytical mind'.

The danger for national aspirations was scented by the members of O'Shiel's Bureau, but too late to disabuse public opinion. O'Shiel's advisers, Joseph Johnston (a Trinity College economics don, who advised on regional economics), George Ruth, and E.M. Stephens, sought to refute the argument that their suggested revised boundary would leave Northern Ireland economically unviable with the contention that 'There are states in America and Australia and provinces in Canada which, with a population very considerably less than the population to which Northern Ireland would be reduced by the proposed line nevertheless maintained provincial governments with powers at least as great as those of the government of Northern Ireland.'[412] This was a hazardous line of reasoning. There were numerous cities with bigger populations than the rump Northern state, but this did not necessarily leave them economically viable, at least in public perception. The public mind conceived of viability more in terms of territory than of population. Had Feetham been privy to the Bureau's deliberations, he could only have been confirmed in his interpretation of Article 12.

O'Shiel concluded his major memorandum on the Free State demands with the observation that:

We have made our claim for two lots of territory – a maximum demand which we can argue well from the wishes of the inhabitants' point of view, but not so well from the economic and geographic point of view, and a minimum demand which will give us all Fermanagh and the greater part of Tyrone, west and south Derry, south Armagh and south and east Down, and which is supported with unanswerable statistical, economic and geographic arguments.[413]

O'Shiel was wrong. His arguments were 'answerable', if not in their own terms, then through the barrel of a gun. The border was begat by violence. It would beget violence. It would be held by violence.

There were sundry sequels to the commission. Northern nationalists responded relatively mutely. They were largely immobilised by the split between Belfast and border Catholics. Belfast Catholics were anxious to retain as many Catholics as possible in Northern Ireland. If there had to be partition, they preferred a six-county North to a four-county North.[414] Cosgrave probably lost some support in the South. The resignation of MacNeill from the cabinet presumably propitiated the unrest reported within Cumann na nGaedheal.[415] Kevin O'Higgins, who was intimately

---

[412] EB, P24/171, addendum to Mr Waller's 'Report on Possible Boundary Lines', 9 January 1923.
[413] EB, P24/171, O'Shiel memo, 21 April 1923.
[414] RM, P7/B/288, O'Shiel memo, 29 May 1923.
[415] Walsh, *Recollections*, p. 70. Walsh was Minister for Posts and Telegraphs in the Cosgrave government. He resigned in 1927. His *Recollections* must be treated with caution, but they cannot be ignored.

associated with cabinet policy on the Boundary Commission,[416] may have lost some standing in the party. The government sought to throw responsibility for the fiasco on to the anti-Treaty forces, O'Higgins fallaciously claiming that 'in 1922 the whole trend of thought in the North was to accept the situation created by the Treaty and come in, but the civil war disillusioned their Northern brethren'.[417] Perhaps the most important sequel of the commission was that it gave de Valera an opportunity of rationalising his return to constitutional politics.

FIANNA FÁIL

De Valera was imprisoned when he came out of hiding to contest the 1923 general election. His year in prison – probably the safest repose for him at that time – gave him the opportunity to reflect on the lessons of seven turbulent years, and particularly on the period since the Treaty. The civil war had given him his first real taste of the mentality of the gunman. Before 1916 he had been largely associated with thinkers, or at least with cultural nationalists. During the War of Independence he moved mostly in political circles. It was not until he enrolled as a private in the anti-Treaty forces that he finally came face to face with the authentic militarist mentality. He drew the lesson. Never again would he serve in another man's army. Never again would he, the most subtle Irish political intelligence of his generation, be kept waiting outside while those he deemed political illiterates pondered whether to even admit him to their primitive counsels, as happened as late as March 1923.[418] Never again would he remain a mere figurehead, 'powerless to intervene effectively', as he conceded himself.[419]

Despite his humiliation by the gunmen, de Valera would prove the real reaper of the harvest of death in the civil war. His two main potential rivals, Griffith and, above all, Collins, were dead. Equally importantly, his main 'allies' were dead. Cathal Brugha was dead; Liam Mellowes was dead; Liam Lynch was dead; Rory O'Connor was dead. They all now safely belonged to the ages. He was no longer as trapped as in June 1922. He would still have to manoeuvre carefully to reimpose his authority over a bitter, fragmented and demoralised anti-Treaty movement. But at least he now had room for manoeuvre. He moved with what would henceforth remain habitual caution on his release from prison in July 1924. He may have hoped initially that a reversal in public opinion would win him an electoral majority through which he could set up his own government

---

[416] *Ibid.*, pp. 68–9.
[417] Kevin O'Higgins, *Irish Independent*, 9 March 1925; for similar sentiments see W.T. Cosgrave, *Irish Independent*, 10 September 1927.
[418] Longford and O'Neill, *De Valera*, p. 217.   [419] Ryle Dwyer, *De Valera*, p. 70.

without taking the despised oath. But events soon conspired to subtly modify his perspective. The first test came in March 1925, when nine by-elections were held simultaneously following the resignation of Joe McGrath's 'National group' from the Dáil. The high hopes with which de Valera entered the election fray were quickly disappointed. Cumann na nGaedheal took seven of the nine seats. Compared with the general election of August 1923 it converted a loss of 1000 in South Dublin into a majority of 10 000, and a loss of 1000 in North Mayo into a majority of 5000.[420] De Valera wrestled with the implications in his inimitable way.

Recently an opportunity was given in the elections to the people to declare their will. They did not declare that will as we know it to be their will . . . It is a shame that it should be so . . . So far as he could see, it was really because of the teaching of the last three years. He would be sorry to think it was cowardice. There was no use in looking to one or other small body of men. It was only by the people that the people could be righted and it remained for the people to right the wrong they had done a couple of years ago, and apparently had been doing since.[421]

The Boundary Commission fiasco finally gave de Valera the escape route he sought into constitutional politics. He could now argue that only the absence of a 'republican' presence in the Dáil had allowed Cosgrave to push through his London agreement with Craig and Baldwin. De Valera had a second reason for interpreting the fiasco as an argument in favour of abandoning abstentionism. The IRA, tiring of the tedium of politics, abandoned in November 1925 yet again the pretence of deriving its authority from the Irish people, and vested all authority once more in the army council.[422] To de Valera, the spectre of June 1922 threatened to loom again. He had already decided that the partition card was the one to play,[423] and he came increasingly to interpret his stance on the Treaty as a protest against partition.[424]

Using the Boundary Commission as his excuse, de Valera seized the opportunity at the Sinn Féin Árd Fheis in March 1926 to propose that, provided the oath was abolished, Sinn Féin should regard entry into the Dáil as a matter of tactics rather than principle. When he narrowly failed to persuade the delegates, he seceded from Sinn Féin, and in May launched Fianna Fáil: the Republican party. For one who had declared himself sick of politics in 1921, de Valera had made a miraculous recovery. He would suffer no relapses. But what medicine would he prescribe for the electorate?

The *Irish Independent* shrewdly noted during the Sinn Féin by-election campaign in March 1925 that 'Mr de Valera and his followers have nothing to offer to the public. When the unemployed asked their plans for

---

[420] *Irish Independent*, 13 March 1925.   [421] *Irish Independent*, 18 March 1925.
[422] Longford and O'Neill, *De Valera*, p. 240.   [423] Ryle Dwyer, *De Valera*, p. 73.
[424] J.J. Lee and Gearóid Ó Tuathaigh, *The age of de Valera* (Dublin, 1982), pp. 96–9.

providing work, or the dwellers in slums asked their plans for building houses, Mr de Valera and his party can only reply "Wait until the Republic is recognised" . . . He would be doing some service to the country if he spoke less about war and more about work.'[425] Though this exaggerated the sterility of Sinn Féin's social thinking, de Valera duly drew the lesson that the apparent absence of a specific short-term programme was a recipe for political oblivion. His speech to the Sinn Féin Árd Fheis in March 1926 included proposals anticipating the basic social and economic aims of Fianna Fáil.[426] Fianna Fáil in turn presented the most specific social programme, for all its vagueness, offered by a republican party.[427] It was clear from the outset that Fianna Fáil was intent not only on guarding the republican faith, but on winning elections.

A short, sharp struggle took place between Fianna Fáil and Sinn Féin for the loyalties of the Sinn Féin deputies, of the party organisation, and of the voters.[428] A Fianna Fáil victory did not appear a foregone conclusion to all contemporaries. The Sinn Féin deputies actually opposed de Valera, if only by a small majority.[429] But the superior organisational ability of Gerry Boland and Seán Lemass, de Valera's main administrative assistants, as well as of de Valera himself, combined with Fianna Fáil's more realistic programme, and more effective leadership, crushed Sinn Féin as a political party within a year. De Valera seduced Sinn Féin supporters by appeals to their hearts, their heads and their pockets. So devastating was the Fianna Fáil onslaught, and so inadequate the Sinn Féin response, that in the June 1927 general election Sinn Féin managed to nominate only 15 candidates compared with Fianna Fáil's 87. Only five of the Sinn Féin candidates were returned, compared with 44 for Fianna Fáil. Cumann na nGaedheal suffered a severe setback, winning only 47 seats, a loss of 16, fewer than Fianna Fáil and Sinn Féin combined. Sensing his chance to topple the government, if only he could get into the Dáil without loss of face, de Valera decided to exploit the constitution he had so often denounced. The constitution obliged the government to hold a referendum on any issue on the presentation of a petition from at least 75 000 voters. Fianna Fáil began to collect signatures on 1 July 1927 for a referendum to have the oath of allegiance abolished. The result of such a referendum, which would be a foregone conclusion, would create a highly awkward situation for Cosgrave.

The assassination of Kevin O'Higgins on 10 July upset all calculations. O'Higgins, 'the most accomplished speaker' in the Dáil, was popularly

---

[425] *Irish Independent*, 2 March 1925.   [426] Moynihan, *De Valera*, p. 128.
[427] *Ibid.*, p. 131.
[428] P. Pyne, 'The new Irish state and the decline of the Republican Sinn Féin Party, 1923–1926', *Eire–Ireland*, 11, 3 (1976), pp. 33–65.
[429] T.P. O'Neill, 'In search of a political path: Irish republicanism, 1922–1927', in G.A. Hayes-McCoy (ed.), *Historical Studies*, 10 (Dublin, 1976), p. 170.

considered the strong man of the government. He certainly behaved as such during the army mutiny. His position weakened somewhat between 1924 and 1927, partly due to the Boundary Commission, and partly due to his Intoxicating Liquor Bill, which he introduced in February 1927, attempting to restrict opportunities for drunkenness. O'Higgins had been more alarmed than his colleagues to find '15 000 publicans' licences in the *Saorstát*, say one for every 200 persons, men, women and children' compared with one for every 400 in England and for every 700 in Scotland.[430] He appointed a commission of 'neutral public spirited persons who will think in a practical way in terms of national welfare and will not be handicapped by the partisanship of the publican or the prohibitionist'. The report of such a commission could scarcely be expected to gratify the relevant vested interests. The drink trade mobilised a storm of righteous public indignation at the proposed limitations on drinking hours. His cabinet colleagues maintained a loquacious silence. O'Higgins had the mortification of seeing his bill drastically amended.[431]

Despite this reversal, O'Higgins nevertheless symbolised the style of the Cosgrave government. He claimed to be a disciple of Collins.[432] But it is difficult to think of two more potentially incompatible personalities. They had little in common except for their age, and their physical and moral courage. Had Collins lived, a clash between them would have been even more likely than the clash between O'Higgins and the most dutiful disciple of Collins, Mulcahy. O'Higgins's view of human nature in general, and of Irish nature in particular, was profoundly pessimistic.[433] He had something of the character of the idealised Roman consul, or perhaps of the better sort of colonial governor. Able, energetic, fearless, stern, dedicated to his concept of the public good, he refused to be cowed, even by the murder of his father, from his duty to inculcate a sense of public responsibility into the reluctant natives. Few men in Irish public life have cherished so exalted a sense of the mission of the statesman to reform public morality, and improve the quality of the civic culture. He was the iron surgeon, cauterising the multiple malignancies of a diseased body politic, waging war on 'greed and envy and lust and drunkenness and irresponsibility'.[434] He 'won much respect, much hatred, and little popularity'.[435] 'A strong and extremely able man, but one who had no toleration for consultation much less for advice,'[436] he sought to cram the task of a century or more, forging a national character cleansed from the

430 SPO, S4251A, O'Higgins memo, 24 January 1925.
431 W. Moss, *Political parties in the Irish Free State* (New York, 1933), p. 142.
432 de Vere White, *O'Higgins*, p. 106.
433 R. Fanning, *The four-leaved shamrock* (Dublin, 1983), p. 6.
434 RM, P7/C/21, O'Higgins, to Army Inquiry Committee, 12 May 1924.
435 Walsh, *Recollections*, p. 68.   436 *Connaught Telegraph*, 20 February 1932.

mark of the serf, into a few years. He naturally roused fierce resentment among the intended beneficiaries.

Dedicated to rooting out militarism, and to stamping a civilian imprint on Irish culture, he pursued a policy of replacing the 7000 armed RIC men with only 5250 unarmed guards.[437] Himself brave to the point of foolhardiness, he rejected demands by Eoin O'Duffy to arm the gárdaí after the murder of two guards only months before his own death. It is as difficult to predict his probable subsequent role as it is that of Collins. He might have been happier on the wider world stage – he performed impressively at the Imperial Conference in 1926[438] – than in the turbulent defiles of Irish politics. His murder removed the main rival to Cosgrave within Cumann na nGaedheal, for it is not inconceivable that he would have contested Cosgrave's faltering leadership in the 1930s.

The death of O'Higgins was a long-term loss for his party. In the short term, it was more a setback for Fianna Fáil. De Valera hastened to denounce the killing, carried out apparently by a dissident IRA faction. Cosgrave reacted with considerable tactical skill. A Public Safety Act empowering the government to institute military courts against suspects was the instinctive response of men who had seen murder stalking the new state and a colleague callously slaughtered. In addition, however, Cosgrave introduced an Electoral Amendment Act requiring parliamentary candidates to pledge to take the oath. This would have made parliamentary republicanism impossible, because republican candidates could not even stand in a general election. De Valera's authority would thus have been undermined within the republican movement. The measure incidentally eliminated Sinn Féin from parliamentary contention and this may have conferred a bonus of a few seats on Fianna Fáil. Cosgrave proposed to forestall the Fianna Fáil attempt to amend the constitution by referendum by amending it pre-emptively in parliament – as he was constitutionally entitled to do for eight years after the passing of the constitution – to remove the permissive article. He thus closed de Valera's options for taking the oath without loss of face. Cosgrave might hope to split Fianna Fáil through these devices. Even if de Valera did swallow the bitter pill, or even if he should devise a technique for merely swirling it around in his mouth and spitting it out again – he would himself maintain that it had never touched his lips – it was reasonable to assume that he would bring a weakened party with him, his stature damaged by his capitulation.[439]

As Cosgrave backed de Valera into a corner, that sinuously scholastic

---

[437] Gwynn, *Irish Free State*, p. 172. On the police policy pursued by O'Higgins between 1922 and 1927 see Brady, *Guardians*, pp. 70–149.

[438] Harkness, *Restless dominion*, p. 122.

[439] See the bitter Fianna Fáil statement on Cosgrave's proposals, *Irish Independent*, 11 August 1927.

mind at last saw the logic of the 'empty political formula' approach to the oath. He devised a ceremony for duly reassuring his conscience that inscribing his name in the book containing the oath, which the clerk of the Dáil kept in his office, while placing the bible in the furthest corner of the room, face downwards, and covering the words of the oath while he was signing his name, insisting all the time that he was taking no oath, did not, indeed, amount to taking an oath. It didn't even amount to 'external relationship' with the oath! Thus, seeing no oath, hearing no oath, speaking no oath, signing no oath, the Soldiers of Destiny shuffled into Dáil Eireann in August 1927.[440]

De Valera's mental gymnastics on the oath inspired the Cork-born Archbishop Mannix in Australia to make his major contribution to theology – proudly displayed in Fianna Fáil advertisements – when he pronounced that the Fianna Fáil TDs who took (didn't take?) the oath 'no more told a falsehood than I would if I sent down word to an unfortunate visitor that I was not at home'.[441]

Fianna Fáil's entry transformed the political arithmetic in the Dáil. Cosgrave's social conservatism increasingly alienated Labour. He survived a vote of confidence in August only on the casting vote of the Speaker when Labour and Fianna Fáil combined against him. Had the five abstentionist Sinn Féin candidates taken their seats the government would have fallen. When Cumann na nGaedheal romped to two by-election victories later in August, Cosgrave called an immediate general election. It seemed a master stroke. Two elections in four months should weaken Labour, which had gained 8 seats in June, and would now be caught with depleted coffers. The humiliation of Fianna Fáil in taking/not taking the oath might alienate some of its grassroot republican support. Cosgrave's strong law and order platform following the assassination of O'Higgins should rally decent-minded people hitherto prone to vote independent. In addition, Cumann na nGaedheal entered into a pact with the Farmers' party, which had won 11 seats in June.

Some of the calculations worked. Labour duly lost 9 seats. Cumann na nGaedheal did increase its representation, from 47 to 62 seats. But the rest of the play departed from the script. Cumann na nGaedheal gains were made mainly at the expense of its potential allies, Farmers, Independents, and William Redmond's National League. Fianna Fáil won 57 seats, reinforcing its claim to be taken seriously as an alternative government. Cosgrave once again formed an administration. But he retreated psychologically into opposition as Fianna Fáil now stalked Cumann na nGaedheal and hunter became hunted.

[440] Longford and O'Neill, *De Valera*, pp. 246–58, chronicle de Valera's relationship with the oath.
[441] *Irish Independent*, 10 September 1927.

In striving to dampen the rising Fianna Fáil tide, Cosgrave was unfortunate in that the great slump, which affected Ireland increasingly from 1930, brought added economic difficulties. The slump was bad luck. But his response was ineffectual. He had no ideas, apart from clinging more desperately to the status quo, on social or economic policy. Blythe and McElligott, following the conventional economic wisdom, continued to insist on ruthless retrenchment to balance the budget.[442] Cosgrave compounded his difficulties by curious cabinet management. After the September election in 1927 he not only re-appointed Blythe as Minister for Finance, but also appointed him as Minister for Posts and Telegraphs and Vice-President of the Executive Council. He retained McGilligan as Minister for Industry and Commerce, but also appointed him to External Affairs. Even as the slump worsened, he kept them in their dual roles. However light their departmental responsibilities, it reflects a quaint sense of both electoral and economic responsibility that Cosgrave obliged his Ministers for Finance and for Industry and Commerce to bear dual burdens during the worst depression since 1879.

The government did achieve considerable success in international affairs. The Irish delegation of Desmond FitzGerald, O'Higgins and McGilligan played a prominent role at the Westminster conference in 1926, which declared the Dominions to be 'equal in status' to Britain in the Commonwealth. Dublin appointed its first Ambassador to Washington in 1928 and in 1930 won a seat on the Council of the League of Nations, which it had joined in 1923. McGilligan proved an impressive advocate of Irish constitutional claims at the 1931 Commonwealth Conference.[443] But if the international performance was diplomatically skilful, it proved electorally futile. The public laid little weight on the small change of international diplomacy, while the government's solicitude for ex-Unionist votes deterred it from emphasising the extent to which it was surreptitiously loosening the British connection. McGilligan's activities in External Affairs may conceivably have reduced his effectiveness in the more electorally significant Department of Industry and Commerce, and certainly offered his formidable shadow, Seán Lemass, an opportunity to accuse him of neglect.

Cosgrave failed to adapt to changing political circumstances. He tinkered with proposals for constitutional changes. He wondered if by-elections should not be abolished and the vacancies filled automatically by the bereaved party.[444] Blythe proposed the abolition of proportional representation.[445] Cumann na nGaedheal began to use 'red scare' tactics against Fianna Fáil as 'men who received dictation from Moscow'

[442] Fanning, *Finance*, pp. 192ff.   [443] Harkness, *Restless dominion*, pp. 224–8.
[444] *Round Table*, 84 (September 1931), p. 854.
[445] *Round Table*, 83 (June 1931), pp. 621–2.

– a sure sign of conceptual bankruptcy.[446] Blythe's proposal to de-rate agricultural land by £750 000 in the 1931 budget was a direct electoral sop to bigger farmers. And for all his public denunciations of de Valera's assault on the oath, Cosgrave himself secretly but unavailingly sought to persuade the British government to abolish it.[447]

The two main props on which Cosgrave relied to buttress his platform were law and order, and the defence of religion. Recruitment to the IRA increased in 1930 and 1931 when the American slump damned up emigration. The IRA notched up two more murders, including one of a garda superintendent, in the summer of 1931. Cosgrave responded by re-enacting the Jurors Protection Act to protect jurors against intimidation, and by amending the constitution to establish a military tribunal to try political crimes. His Public Safety Act of October 1931 was probably more drastic than the situation required, but it sufficed to provide a law and order platform for the imminent general election.[448]

CHURCH AND STATE

Cosgrave continued to court the Catholic Church throughout his tenure of office.[449] But he fell potentially foul of the church on a number of questions. Divorce, for instance, was permitted through private parliamentary bill under English law as inherited by the Free State. It was anathema to Catholic doctrine and soon became a lively issue.[450] Cosgrave was genuinely anxious to reconcile Protestants to the new state, and perhaps even to guarantee freedom of conscience in principle. On the other hand, he was himself a conventional Catholic and disliked divorce in principle. His idea of freedom of conscience did not extend as far as that of his Attorney General, Hugh Kennedy, who thought that 'we should make provision for divorce bills for those who approve of that sort of thing'.[451] Cosgrave came, probably not wholly reluctantly, under massive episcopal pressure on the issue. Archbishop Byrne of Dublin insisted that the Catholic Church had a right to decree marriage laws for Protestants no less than for Catholics because 'all members who had been baptised are members of the Church and under its jurisdiction'.[452] Byrne did not claim formal jurisdiction over unbaptised persons, but stressed that it would be contrary to Natural Law to permit dissolution of their marriages.[453] And

[446] *Irish Independent*, 14 March 1929.   [447] Keogh, *Vatican*, pp. 177ff.
[448] D.F. Keogh, 'The Catholic Church and the "red scare", 1931–1932', in J.P. O'Carroll and J.A. Murphy (eds.), *De Valera and his times* (Cork, 1983), pp. 134–59.
[449] Keogh, *Vatican*, chs. 4–6.   [450] Fanning, *Ireland*, pp. 54–6.
[451] SPO S4127, H. Kennedy to E.J. Duggan, 12 March 1923.
[452] SPO S4127, E.J. Duggan to Cosgrave, 'Catholic teaching on marriage', 4 March 1923; E.J. Duggan to Cosgrave, 20 March 1923.
[453] SPO S4127, E.J. Duggan to Cosgrave, 'Catholic teaching on marriage', 4 March 1923.

only the church could, of course, decide what was natural law. Dr Downey, Coadjutor Bishop of Ossory, threatened Cosgrave indirectly with the loss of the Catholic vote in his own constituency unless he complied with episcopal directions on the matter.[454] Cosgrave brought in legislation prohibiting divorce through private bills, indifferent to the fears of Northern Protestants who felt the legislation confirmed that freedom of conscience would not be permitted in the Free State.[455]

Cosgrave further accommodated this mentality by the Censorship of Publications Act in 1929. This empowered a censorship board to prohibit any work it considered 'indecent or obscene', as well as all literature advocating birth control. Legislation was actually rather less stringent than some critics feared;[456] but it was used to censor not only genuine pornography, but also serious work by major writers, including Joyce, O'Casey, O'Flaherty and Clarke, whose perspective cut too close to the purse for the comfort of the flint-minded men and women whose grandparents had done well out of the Famine and who intended to do even better themselves out of the Free State. The censorship legislation served the materialistic values of the propertied classes by fostering the illusion that Ireland was a haven of virtue surrounded by a sea of vice. It provided a convenient façade behind which a fabricated but reassuring self-image of moral probity could flourish. It helped to rivet the remunerative impression that immorality stopped with sex.

There was nothing uniquely Irish about this thought process. Societies with highly developed self-images of their own virtue find the ideal impossible to sustain in practice (why some societies require such self-images more than others raises issues which cannot detain us here). One device to reconcile the image with reality, without suffering the trauma of confessing the truth, is to shrivel the domain of 'real' morality to those teachings which happen to conveniently coincide with the objective material requirements of the dominant groups in society. Both Irish Catholics and Ulster Protestants hit on this happy technique. But they were by no means the only ones. New England Puritans – those Wasps who would be singularly reluctant to be reminded of any possible Hibernian analogies – struck on the same solution to their little local moral difficulties, when 'the identification of purity with private life and with morals seems to have permitted on almost free reign of tacticality in the public world of work, politics and man'.[457]

If the rhetoric of morality in the Free State was not wholly confined to, it nevertheless concentrated heavily on, the soft sexual option. A morbid

---

[454] SPO S4127, Dr Downey to Cosgrave, 17 September 1925; Cosgrave's apologetic reply, 21 September 1925.
[455] *Belfast Telegraph*, 12 February 1925.   [456] Brown, *Ireland*, pp. 74–5.
[457] J. Higham, 'Integrating America: the problem of assimilation in the nineteenth century', *Journal of American Ethnic History*, 1, 1 (Autumn 1981), p. 18.

preoccupation with occasions of sin in dance halls would dominate pastoral pronouncements throughout the twenties and thirties. This amounted in practice to issuing a moral blank cheque to other types of behaviour that wouldn't be found out, in a country where, South no less than North, papist no less than presbyter, as Heaney has put it, 'people think money and talk weather'. The Censorship Act confined itself to 'sexual immorality'. It did not ban 'immorality'. This would have raised the delicate question of defining immorality, and thus risk disturbing permissive assumptions about the observance of less relevant command-ments than the sixth. The obsession with sex permitted a blind eye to be turned towards the social scars that disfigured the face of Ireland. The number of agricultural labourers fell from 300 000 in 1911 to 150 000 in 1936. A whole class was vanishing off the face of the land, the statistics bearing a mute witness to the process. There was no room at the Irish inn for those who showed their deplorable lack of breeding by being born in a labourer's cottage. Censorship purported to protect the family, but no measures were taken to prevent the continuing dispersal of families ravaged by the cancer of emigration. Ireland continued to be characterised by a high incidence of mental disease, by hideous family living conditions in its urban slums, and by a demoralised casual working class, urban as well as rural. Few voices were raised in protest. The clergy, strong farmers in cassocks, largely voiced the concern of their most influential consti-tuents, whose values they instinctively shared and universalised as 'Chris-tian'. The sanctity of property, the unflinching materialism of farmer calculations, the defence of professional status, depended on continuing high emigration and high celibacy. The church did not invent these values. But it did baptise them. Rarely has the Catholic Church as an institution flourished, by materialistic criteria, as in the Free State. And rarely has it contributed so little, as an institution, to the finer qualities of the Christian spirit. Censorship, Irish style, suitably symbolised the impoverishment of spirit and the barrenness of mind of the risen bourgeoisie, touting for respectability.[458]

Censorship may have concelebrated the intellectual poverty of the period. But it did not cause it. Patrick Kavanagh, himself insulted by the censors, held that 'the censorship does not concern the creative writer'.[459] 'The big tragedy for the poet' Kavanagh believed, was 'poverty'.[460] Northern Ireland did not invoke censorship of the Free State vintage. But its intellectual history in this period was at least as undistinguished as that of the South. The sterility of the Ulster Protestant mind can scarcely be attributed to the malign influence of Free State censorship. It has been

---

[458] I am grateful to M.G. Valiulis for discussion on this issue.
[459] Patrick Kavanagh, *By night unstarred* (Curragh, Kildare, 1977), p. 195.
[460] Patrick Kavanagh, *Collected poems* (London, 1968), author's note, p. xiii.

thoughtfully argued that 'the harmful effect of censorship lay not so much in the absurdities of what was forbidden as in its stifling of adult discussion and the harm it did to serious Irish writers'.[461] There may be some validity in this, at least as far as creative writing is concerned. But it was not censorship that obliged the university to make so modest a contribution to the quality of social, economic or political thought in the Free State.[462]

Cosgrave further sought to consolidate relations with the church, at least in an electoral sense, by establishing diplomatic relations with the Vatican in 1930. He considered this something of a diplomatic coup, and would invoke the achievement as a virtual papal blessing on the Cosgrave government during the 1932 election campaign. Not all the Irish bishops were amused. They were not anxious to have a papal representative reporting directly to Rome on their performance. They most certainly did not want Home Rule to mean Rome Rule! But Cosgrave was prepared to risk private episcopal displeasure – their lordships could hardly protest in public against this gracious gesture, this undeserved honour – in the hope of making an electoral killing.[463]

If Cosgrave had to consolidate relations with the church, de Valera had to restore them. He faced widespread clerical hostility after 1922. The clergy strongly supported Cumann na nGaedheal in the March 1925 by-elections, when some clergy clearly considered the gospel injunction to turn the other cheek to be a clerical error.[464]

The bulk of the clergy, even of the lower clergy, were still drawn from social classes suspicious of Fianna Fáil's appeal to the men of no property and even the men of small property. Clerical hostility in the March 1925 by-elections incensed the young Seán Lemass to declare

The question of the political influence of the Catholic clergy, an influence that throughout our history has been used with uncanny consistency to defeat the aspiration of Irish nationality had to be faced sooner or later . . . Whenever the Irish people came within sight of achieving their national independence the full political power of the Church was flung against them, and forced them back. That

461 R. Fallis, *The Irish Renaissance* (Dublin 1978), p. 172. For other views on this controversial issue, see Brown, *Ireland*, pp. 76–8, and S. O'Faolain, 'Ireland after Yeats', *The Bell*, 18, no. 11 (Summer 1953). Two standard surveys are M. Adams, *Censorship: the Irish experience* (Dublin, 1968) and K. Woodman, *Media Control in Ireland 1923–1983* (Galway 1986).
462 See below, pp. 000.   463 Keogh, *Vatican*, pp. 138ff.
464 *Irish Independent*, 2 March 1925, reports election speeches containing violent attacks on de Valera by clergy. Moss, *Political parties*, pp. 170–1, reports active clerical intervention against Fianna Fáil in the September 1927 election. Keogh, *Vatican*, reveals a more complex attitude at the level of high ecclesiastical politics. De Valera had an influential admirer in Mgr. John Hagan, strategically situated as rector of the Irish College in Rome. Even at grassroots level, there were doubtless a number of younger clergy, in particular, who preferred de Valera to Cosgrave. They would emerge vociferously later. But the climate was not conducive to their adopting a high profile in the 1920s.

political power must be destroyed if our national victory is ever to be won . . . We are opening the campaign now against the political influence of the Church. If we succeed in destroying that influence we will have done good work for Ireland and, I believe, for the Catholic religion in Ireland.[465]

Some might detect there the authentic Fenian voice. But cleverer councils were to prevail. Fianna Fáil would not destroy the political power of the church. Fianna Fáil would capture the political power of the church. De Valera told the Dáil in 1922 that 'I hope when I die I will get a Fenian grave.'[466] But on church–state relations, de Valera was no Fenian. He was come not to fulfil the Fenian law but to bury it. He therefore set out to show that anything that Cosgrave could do in the spiritual line, he could do better. Fianna Fáil condemned Cumann na nGaedheal's alleged indulgence of 'immoral publications', demanded even more rigorous censorship, and fumed against the immorality of the rest of mankind whom a misguided God had been so careless as to create beyond the holy ground.[467]

The Dunbar-Harrison case provided a providential opportunity to outmanoeuvre Cosgrave and in the process help reconcile Catholicism with republicanism.

The full story of the Dunbar-Harrison episode remains shrouded in the murky depths of local Mayo politics. But the contours can be sketched. A vacancy occurred in the post of county librarian for Mayo in 1930 for the homely, if not exclusively Christian, reason that the county secretary and the librarian couldn't stand the sight of each other.[468] The Local Appointments Commission nominated Letitia Dunbar-Harrison for the vacancy. The Library Committee of Mayo County Council, which was legally required to recommend the appointment to the County Council itself, refused to endorse the nomination, on the grounds that Miss Dunbar-Harrison's knowledge of Irish was inadequate. The County Council duly refused to sanction the nomination. The government dissolved the County Council, appointing a Commissioner in its place. The other committees of the County Council, including particularly the Old Age Pension Committee, refused to obey his instructions. In December 1931, the government capitulated by transferring Miss Dunbar-Harrison from Castlebar to the library of the Department of Defence in Dublin.

This may superficially sound like a simple tale of country folk. But the case was more complex than emerges from this stark account. It reveals much about the nature of political culture in the Free State.

The county councils instituted under the Local Government Act of 1898 soon became a by-word for corruption in their appointments.

[465] *Irish Independent*, 14 March 1925.   [466] Moynihan, *De Valera*, p. 93.
[467] *Irish Independent*, 12 September 1927.
[468] SPO S2547A, H.P. Boland to D. O'Hegarty, 20 January 1931.

Arthur Griffith once said that it would be a much more difficult task to put an end to favouritism and family influence in appointments under local bodies in Ireland than to drive the British army from the country. What happened under the old regime was that in each rural district every position worth having went to the members of two or three families . . . A candidate no matter how highly qualified or widely experienced, had little prospect of securing an appointment if he or she were not related by birth or by marriage to one or other of the big three or four or five who ruled the Corporation, Council, Union, or Asylum committee.[469]

The Local Appointments Commission established by Cosgrave was therefore something of a wonder in Irish political culture. It naturally caused shock waves among the natives. The idea that assessors boards might evaluate candidates on their professional merits, rather than on their foresight in being born with the right connections, or at least in cultivating the right connections, imposed intolerable strains on many an imagination. It deeply offended the most devout convictions of local dignitaries, not excluding ecclesiastical dignitaries, who could previously count on their views commanding due influence. Natives would not have been natives had many not felt deep resentment. The local clergy, with Fr Geoffrey Prendergast of Castlebar and Dean E.A. D'Alton of Tuam particularly prominent, seized the opportunity to strike a mighty blow for the honour of the little village.[470] The plot thickened with the discovery of another woman in the case. Dean D'Alton sang the praises of an unsuccessful candidate, one Ellen Burke.[471] Critics accused the Local Appointments Commission of corruption in failing to appoint the estimable Miss Burke. Charges of jobbery flew thick and fast.[472] The corruption charges were so widespread in Mayo, and found so plausible by the Archbishop of Tuam, Dr Gilmartin, that Cosgrave felt obliged to despatch an emissary, Sir Joseph Glynn, to repudiate the charges.[473] So intensely were the accusations pressed that, contrary to previous practice, where the Local Appointments Commission 'had declined to allow any of the ministers to see the papers in connection with any appointment', 'in the present case, acting on the advice of the Attorney General, the President obtained all the papers and had examined the matters for himself'.[474]

It transpired from Cosgrave's perusal of the Local Appointments Commission file that the worthy Miss Burke had been rejected not by one but by two completely different boards, having, *inter alia*, neglected to take the elementary precaution of passing her Irish test – her knowledge of

469 *Connaught Telegraph*, 10 January 1931.
470 SPO, S2547B, undated, unsigned note on Prendergast.
471 *Irish Independent*, 31 December 1930.   472 DD, 36, 11 December 1930, 1341.
473 SPO, S2547A, Report by Sir Joseph Glynn on a visit to His Grace, the Archbishop of Tuam, on 8 February 1931. The disproportionate attention devoted to Miss Burke in this memorandum suggests that there must have been a hard clerical push for her in Tuam.
474 *Ibid.*

Irish was one of Dean D'Alton's explicit reasons for parading her around the paddock! She scaled the dizzy peak of 250 out of 700 marks from one board, and 230 out of 700 from another.[475] Nor did all members of the hierarchy share the suspicions of their Connaught colleagues concerning the integrity of the Local Appointments Commission. They knew the name of the game. Dr Harty, Archbishop of Cashel, advised the government to 'stick to the Local Appointments Commissioners', drawing on his own knowledge of bribery in the appointment of doctors in the South Tipperary area before the Commissioners were instituted.[476] Dr Harty went so far as to tell the government to rely on the commission even in the case of medical appointments, which were ethically more complex than librarian appointments.[477]

Even local resentment at what was perceived as metropolitan intrusion was not the core of the problem. It was rather that Miss Dunbar-Harrison suffered from the dual stigma of being a Protestant and a graduate of Trinity College Dublin. While no mere summary can do justice to the quality of the County Council debates on this or other matters, a few extracts may convey something of the rich flavour of indigenous political thought. J.T. Morahan was

opposed to the appointment of a product of Trinity to the position of Librarian in this County. Trinity culture is not the culture of the Gael; rather is it poison gas to the kindly Celtic people . . . At the command of the bigotted and Freemason press, Catholic rights are ignored . . . We are the connecting link between the past generations of our great Catholic dead and the generations yet unborn. We are the spearhead of the far-flung empire of Erin's exiled sons and daughters . . . Tolerance is synonymous with slavishness.[478]

Great exception was taken to the insinuation that some of the commotion was caused by supporters of a Castlebar candidate. The chairman indignantly challenged 'any man to say that corruption was ever practiced in Castlebar'.[479] When the miscreant allegation was repeated, Mr Morahan 'replied heatedly: "If you mention Castlebar again I will throw you outside the door." '[480] At the end of the exchange of pleasantries 'the Chairman commended the members of that Council, and during all that time he had never heard a finer display of eloquence and patriotism mixed

---

[475] SPO, S2547A, copy of statement by the Local Appointments Commissioners for the information of the President in connection with the appointment of Miss Dunbar Harrison as County Librarian, County Mayo, and given by the President to Sir Joseph Glynn for transmission to His Grace, the Archbishop of Tuam.

[476] SPO, S2547A, Minister's note for President: interview with the Archbishop of Cashel, 11 February 1931.

[477] *Ibid.* Carson had expressed his contempt long before for the moral standard of the appointments system to the poor law medical services. See Carson in Rosenbaum, *Against Home Rule*, p. 38. Keogh, *Vatican*, pp. 169ff explores the issue of medical appointments.

[478] *Connaught Telegraph*, 3 January 1931.   [479] *Ibid.*   [480] *Ibid.*

with decorum, and he was satisfied that it could compare favourably with any other discussion carried on by anybody within the four shores of Ireland'.[481]

It must not be supposed, however, that the Dunbar-Harrison case inspired an exceptional performance from Mayo County Council. Charges of 'political corruption' were commonplace in the chamber.[482] At the meeting where a successor to Miss Dunbar-Harrison was appointed – on the recommendation of the Local Appointment's Commission – the ritual charge of corruption now limped along behind even more contentious issues in an atmosphere marked by

some very highly explosive language . . . when members freely flung epithets at one another, and there were loud proclamations of corruption, slander, wind baggery and jobbery. The proceedings from beginning to end were of a most animated character, a fact which caused much rejoicing in the gallery, where a good crowd of unemployed was packed . . . [483]

The annuities question that would raise rural temperature in 1932 once again stimulated the County Council to offer a model for Ireland, when the proceedings were dignified by 'an exhibition of rowdyism in the gallery, a state of tumult amongst the members, heated verbal interjections and cat-calls from the audience, and plenty of cross-talk between the councillors'.[484]

Nor was the political philosophy of the council as rigid as might appear from a cursory survey of the Dunbar-Harrison proceedings. The indignation expressed about the appointment of a non-Irish speaker as librarian for Mayo would prove no bar to Mr Morahan successfully proposing a candidate for a post as teacher, despite her lack of Irish, on the grounds that she 'comes of very respectable stock, and her people have been tried when Irish hearts and parents had to bear a good deal'.[485] Nor was Dean D'Alton an uncritical admirer of contemporary Irish literature. He persuaded the Library Committee to ban the books of Pádraig Ó Conaire, a renowned writer in Irish, whose work was 'prescribed for use in the primary school' by the Department of Education.[486]

Mayo was an electorally marginal county. Fianna Fáil and Cumann na nGaedheal each held 4 seats, with the 9th held by Labour. In the September 1927 election, Fianna Fáil polled 15 597 first preferences in South Mayo, compared with Cumann na nGaedheal's 14 957 – and there were over 8000 others. In North Mayo, Fianna Fáil had 14 351 first preferences compared with Cumann na nGaedheal's 15 664.[487] This was

481 *Ibid.*   482 *Ibid.* 6 August 1932, 3 December 1932.
483 *Ibid.*, 5 November 1932, 3 December 1932.
484 *Ibid.*, 6 August 1932.   485 *Ibid.*, 24 September 1932.
486 *Ibid.*, 1 October 1932.
487 *Ibid.*, 30 January, 20, 27 February 1932.

a finely poised county, with both main parties strong, and seats to be won and lost. The situation was so delicate that the chairman of Mayo County Council, a Cumann na nGaedheal TD, felt obliged to censure his own party in the Dáil for dissolving the Council.[488]

Fianna Fáil handled the matter astutely. Whatever the party representatives on Mayo County Council might say, the party ideologists reiterated pure republican doctrine:

The Irish people are made up of men and women of different religious beliefs and for the majority to insist upon appointments for men and women of their faith only is unjust and anti-national. There must be only one test for the public service, ability to perform the work, and that can only be discovered and recognised through competitive examination or some similar method by which the best wins. In Miss Dunbar's case there was the obvious and fatal flaw that for a Gaeltacht appointment she had no knowledge of Irish . . . Therefore we believe she is not qualified to fill the position. But to declare her unfitted by religion or by the fact that she holds a Trinity Degree is to recreate under the cloak of Catholicism the spirit of ascendancy which cursed this nation for three hundred bitter years.[489]

The issue was inviting enough for de Valera himself to translate the party position into the realities of Mayo politics. He displayed his now mature mastery of the subjunctive in 'clarifying' his position in a speech in Irishtown.[490] Firstly, he took care to appeal to local sentiment by denouncing the excessive centralisation of the appointment system. Then he kept the religious issue to the fore, if in a suitably non-sectarian style:

The whole question hinged on the duties of a librarian . . . If the functions were simply the functions of an attendant in the Library, who handed out books asked for, having behind her a Committee responsible for the selection of those books, then the religious views of the Librarian would not matter very much. On the other hand, if the whole idea behind the scheme was that the Librarian should go into the homes of the people, and into the schools, and push the Scheme, if instead of her duties being passive they were active, the position was an entirely different one. They held that every person in the country, no matter what his religious belief, is entitled to a fair share of the public appointments. If in this case it was made a denominational post, in all justice they must provide similar facilities for those who do not agree with them. This had not been done in the Six Counties, but they did not propose to follow in their footsteps and ignore the rights of minorities here.

Cosgrave's reaction to de Valera's speech was politically naive:

That man is a type of arrested mental development – or perhaps a new type of administrator – who is prepared to spend public money to meet every contingency that may arise – republican police, republican Attorney General – republican Judge to try republicans – Labour ditto for Labour prisoners and so on.[491]

---

[488] DD, 39, 17 June 1931, 420. See also col. 545.
[489] *The Nation*, 13 December 1930.
[490] *Irish Independent*, 7 January 1931.
[491] SPO, S2547A, Cosgrave to D. O'Hegarty, 10 January 1931.

This flight into false analogy may have been provoked by his growing realisation that he had little choice but to capitulate, for capitulate he did. Behind the façade of his sternly righteous reply to Dr Gilmartin of Tuam, 'as I explained to Your Grace at our interview, to discriminate against any citizen – or exercise a preference for a citizen – on account of religious belief would be to conflict with some of the fundamental principles on which this state is founded',[492] he desperately searched for an escape route. He deplored Fianna Fáil glee at the closing of Mayo County Library:

The sad spectacle of Deputies Ruttledge and Walsh gloating over the demise of a Library – one may be pardoned the thought after the contributions made to the debate by County Mayo members that few Counties want greater educational facilities – less talk and more and deeper reading . . . [493]

But he had already conceded the case to Gilmartin, agreeing in April that Miss Dunbar-Harrison would be transferred 'within a certain time' and 'the new County Council, elected at the usual time, be allowed to function.[494] To save the government's face, the agreement was kept confidential.[495] The *Irish Press*, with its unerring instinct for the priorities, noted that 'on the eve of a General Election the transfer elsewhere of Miss Harrison might sway opinion in favour of the Cumann na nGaedheal party, there being clear indications that only a very few of the Mayo priests will on this occasion support the government nominees'.[496] Miss Dunbar-Harrison was reported as dismissing rumours of her impending move, on the grounds that 'I like the work; I love the people who have shown me every kindness, and I am not likely to resign my position because some people think I should go elsewhere.'[497]

Cosgrave's correspondence reveals just how agitated he could become about clerical criticism, and how concerned he was to avoid ecclesiastical censure of his policy.[498] It illustrates the somewhat distant relationship between government and hierarchy that the cabinet felt that

In general we suggest that the bishops make representations to the government directly when they have any cause of complaint or any suggestions to offer. It is embarrassing for the government to learn the bishops' views for the first time through a condemnatory pastoral letter, or a chance conversation between a bishop and a minister. The government feels it has a grievance here.[499]

---

492 SPO, S2547B, Cosgrave to Gilmartin, 11 March 1931.
493 SPO, S2547B, President's notes on Local Government Bill.
494 SPO, S2547B, Report of meeting between Cosgrave, J.M. O'Sullivan and Dr Gilmartin, 15 April 1931.
495 *Ibid.*   496 *Irish Press*, 2 January 1932.   497 *Ibid.*
498 SPO, S2547B, Cosgrave to the Bishop of Limerick, 19 February 1931; SPO, S2547B, Cosgrave to Cardinal MacRory, 28 March 1931. Keogh, *Vatican*, pp. 168–77, discusses the matter in probing detail.
499 SPO, S2547B, memo, undated, unsigned, 'returned by Professor O'Sullivan, 24/3/31'.

Cosgrave allowed himself to be upset not only by the prospect of episcopal condemnation, but by the effusions of the Catholic press, especially the *Catholic Bulletin*. The *Catholic Mind* tended, if anything, to be even less genteel than the *Bulletin*, but it managed to remonstrate with de Valera for not being Catholic enough! Clarifying its policies for any unenlightened reader, it declaimed that 'we do not mind good, honest slaughter. Gore-grimed tomahawks do not disturb us. In fact . . . we delight in the profusion of scalps which adorns our wigwam![500] And it launched an assault on de Valera as 'a traitor' who 'will strike a bargain . . . with the enemies of the people's faith'.[501] As the *Bulletin*, vigorously symptomatic of 'the sense of cultural inferiority that disoriented and confused many Irish men'[502] directed similar sentiments in Cosgrave's direction, he allowed his equanimity to be disturbed despite Archbishop Harty's brisk observation that 'we ought to know enough about politics not to mind them'.[503]

The normally more sedate *Standard* suggested that Catholic Ireland will 'make short work' of those Protestants who 'resent the desire of Catholics to live the full Catholic faith'. Under the banner headline, 'Will the Catholics of Mayo be overruled?', it carried a blistering condemnation of handing Mayo over to the Commissioner who would be no less than 'a dictator'. It saw no incongruity between this and its other front page story, singing a hymn of praise for that noted defender of democracy, Mussolini, under the heading 'Eight Years of Fascism reviewed: revival of religion and prosperity of the nation.'[504] Dictatorship is in the eye of the beholder!

In the event, Fianna Fáil did win that extra seat in Mayo, though ironically at the expense of Labour rather than Cumann na nGaedheal.

If de Valera played a skilful hand, aided by sympathisers among the clergy, and by the shrewd diplomacy of Seán T. O'Kelly, his virtual minister for ecclesiastical affairs, in retrieving relations with the church which had condemned him so severely in 1922, he still had other difficulties to surmount. He had to maintain the momentum achieved in 1927 by converting more moderate, or more apathetic, voters without alienating republican sentiments. Fianna Fáil party activists included a disproportionate number of IRA sympathisers. Several Fianna Fáil deputies were merely tactical constitutionalists. Seán Lemass would go so far as to describe the party, as late as 1928, in a famous phrase, as 'slightly constitutional'. The front bench had to wear Janus masks, reassuring some restive backbenchers, as well as grass roots republicans, of their

---

[500] *Catholic Mind*, February 1931, p. 28.   [501] *Ibid.*
[502] O'Callaghan, 'Language', p. 235. See also Meenan, *George O'Brien*, pp. 134–6, for a character sketch of the *Bulletin*.
[503] SPO, S2547A, Minister's note for President: interview with the Archbishop of Cashel, 11 February 1931.
[504] *Standard*, 13 December 1930.

undiluted doctrinal purity while simultaneously appealing to a potentially moderate constituency. Cosgrave's law and order policy, and particularly his Public Safety Act, played into their hands. De Valera skilfully seized the opportunity, steering his party delicately through the electoral rapids. He manoeuvred his way towards a repudiation of IRA military authority, while continuing to project a vigorous republican image. Although he condemned the murder of Kevin O'Higgins, the IRA murders of 1930 did not deter Fianna Fáil from attempting to stage a joint demonstration with the IRA to Wolfe Tone's grave at Bodenstown in June 1931.

In his post mortem on the débâcle of the 1925 by-elections, Seán Lemass linked the hostility of the press with the hostility of the church as a major obstacle to Fianna Fáil.[505] After a weekly, the *Nation*, was established in 1927, the break-through with a daily paper occurred in 1931, with the founding of the *Irish Press*. The *Press* quickly proved itself a brilliant journalistic venture, comparable in its immediate impact to William O'Brien's *United Ireland* of 1882. Indeed, the *Press* recalled much of the style and substance of the early William O'Brien. Its ebullient free-wheeling polemical style outraged genteel spirits, but for a stridently popular paper, it descended to the gutter level remarkably rarely. Cosgrave augmented the appeal of the *Press* by insensitively prosecuting the editor on the eve of the 1932 election. The *Press* played an important part in the Fianna Fáil election victories, not only by confirming the convictions of the faithful, but also by converting previous non-voters or even unbelievers. The increase in turnout, from 69 per cent in the September 1927 election to 77 per cent in 1932, before rising once more to a record 81.3 per cent in 1933, probably owed a good deal to the popular enthusiasm generated by the *Press*.

THE FALL OF COSGRAVE

Cosgrave called a general election for February 1932. He might have been wiser to have waited until after the Eucharistic Congress in June, where he could have been photographed incessantly with the papal nuncio for the edification of the plain people of the Free State. But the cabinet was at its wits end in financial matters. It reduced teachers' and policemen's salaries in 1931, and Blythe could see no alternative to an austere Budget.[506] With the situation threatening to deteriorate further, the cabinet presumably shared McGilligan's view that the prospects were too horrible to contemplate in an election year, and that it should go to the country sooner rather than later.[507]

The programmes of the two parties offered a clear choice to the

[505] *Irish Independent*, 14 March 1925.   [506] Fanning, *Finance*, pp. 211ff.
[507] Quoted in Fanning, *Shamrock*, p. 10.

electorate. Cumann na nGaedheal devoted one grudging paragraph out of fourteen to social and economic policy.[508] It based its platform squarely on law, order, religion and the 'red scare'. It tried to co-opt the Catholic Church as an honorary party agent. 'No other nation', it assured the electors, 'has such a tradition of suffering and sacrifice in the cause of Religion as our nation . . . Therein lies our strongest reason for pride in our past and our strongest hope for the future greatness of our people.' No wonder, therefore, that 'we intend to shelter our national heritage from doctrines which are subversive of religion, home and country'. The chaos inevitably consequent on a Fianna Fáil victory would bring irreligion in its wake, transforming Ireland 'into a field for the cultivation of those doctrines of materialism and Communism which can so effectively poison the wells of religion and national traditions'. A terrible denouement would follow:

Our place in the community of nations, the recognition we have received from the Holy Father and the principle powers of the world through the establishment of legations in our capital, will disappear with the destruction of the state.

The emphasis on religion and stability was designed to permit Cumann na nGaedheal to evade economic issues and to dismiss Fianna Fáil's programme in a single sentence on the grounds that 'no facade of pretended economic policies can obscure the fact that it is inherently impossible to attend to the economic interests of the people during the intense political agitation and unrest' that would inevitably follow a Fianna Fáil victory.[509]

This claim to be a revitalised version of the Pope's Brass Band in Ireland tended to be spiced with less than wholly charitable reflections on the moral character and social status of the opposition, inimitably expressed by Paddy Hogan:

If he had his way the Fianna Fáil party would be in jail long ago . . . They were the real culprits for shielding the gunmen. But their party was incapable of governing as, after all, you must have breeding to govern.[510]

Fianna Fáil gave pride of place in its statement to abolishing the oath of allegiance. But as the Cumann na nGaedheal attack made clear, the bulk of its programme was devoted to social and economic policy, encouraging an American observer to hail them as 'the youthful champions of the New Deal and the Irish five year plan'.[511] In the campaign itself, Lemass emphasised that unemployment was the main electoral issue.[512] Seán T. O'Kelly stressed that 'Fianna Fáil believes it is the duty of the state to

[508] *Irish Independent*, 7 February 1932, cited in Moss, *Political parties*, Appendix II.
[509] *Ibid.*
[510] *Irish Press*, 15 February 1932.   [511] Moss, *Political parties*, p. 194.
[512] *Irish Press*, 3 February 1932.

provide work, Cumann na nGaedheal do not.'[513] Fianna Fáil promised to launch a housing programme, and to increase expenditure on social services, while simultaneously whittling government expenditure by the happy device of reducing the highest paid public salaries, while maintaining the lower ones.[514] Fianna Fáil explicitly appropriated Griffith's economic policy, spiced with de Valera's own social policy, which he presented as the essence of 1916 social doctrine.

But Fianna Fáil too played the Catholic card astutely, whether on the platform or in the press. Seán T. O'Kelly commended the policy of work creation with quotations from encyclicals and with the reassurance that 'the Fianna Fáil policy was the policy of Pope Pius XI'.[515] When the Angelus bell in Tulla tolled out, 'Mr de Valera immediately ceased speaking, blessed himself and silently said the Angelus prayer, the crowd reverently followed his example'.[516] Who could doubt the Catholic credentials of a speaker capable of transforming an election crowd into a congregation? The *Irish Press* even envisaged the prospect of the conversion of the Anglo-Irish. The difference between the Irish and the Anglo-Irish, it claimed, 'is a difference, not of race, but of allegiance . . . If the Anglo-Irish continued to reject the national allegiance, they infallibly will die out of the land . . . Their every motion towards the nation ought to be encouraged, both for the sake of souls and for that of the country . . . the future is with the older race, the older faith: These inevitably will recover Ireland.'[517] It was perhaps just as well that *Irish Press* circulation on the Shankill was limited. But then, a providential dispensation had ensured that the Shankill would have no votes in Free State elections.

The electorate was therefore offered a clear choice between a party campaigning in defence of the status quo, and a party proposing sweeping constitutional, economic, and social changes. The verdict was also clear, if not electorally decisive. Fianna Fáil increased its popular vote from 412 000 to 566 000, or from 35.2 to 44.5 per cent of the valid poll. It gained 15 seats, returning 72 deputies compared with 57 in September 1927. Cumann na nGaedheal's popular vote fell from 453 000 to 450 000, or from 38.7 to 35.3 per cent of the ballot poll. It lost 5 seats, returning 57 deputies compared with 62 in 1927. Fianna Fáil was now the biggest party by 15 seats, but it still fell short by 5 seats of an absolute majority. With the Farmers' Party and the independents supporting Cumann na nGaedheal, Labour held the balance. Labour's popular vote had fallen from 111 000 to 98 000, and it returned only 7 deputies compared with 13 in September 1927. It had, however, broadly opted for Fianna Fáil in preference to Cumann na nGaedheal during the campaign.

[513] *Irish Press*, 15 February 1932.   [514] *Irish Times*, 4 February 1932.
[515] *Irish Independent*, 11 February 1932.
[516] *Irish Times*, 4 February 1932.   [517] *Irish Press*, 3 February 1932.

Labour transfers went heavily to Fianna Fáil. In voting for de Valera as Taoiseach, Labour undoubtedly opted in accordance with its mandate.

Cosgrave was in large measure the author of his own electoral misfortunes. His basic strategic error was the shift to the right. He should have consolidated the centre ground. In particular, he should have striven to retain Labour support. Labour supported the Treaty in 1922. Labour's vote nearly put him out of office in 1927, kept him in office as late as 1930, and finally put him out of office in 1932. Instead of conciliating Labour, he chose to conciliate the right. His anti-working-class policies alienated grass roots Labour sentiment. His pact with the Farmers' Party before the 1927 September election was probably unnecessary. In a straight fight between Cumann na nGaedheal and Fianna Fáil the bigger farmers represented by the Farmers' Party had nowhere else to go. Labour, on the other hand, needed to be wooed.[518] Cosgrave didn't even bother to woo. Labour could take him or leave him. They left him.

Cosgrave compounded this basic strategic error through a poor sense of electoral timing. In contrast to Craig and de Valera, he had a knack for picking the wrong moment to go to the country. Agricultural prices, having risen in 1924–5, began to fall again in 1926. Cosgrave called an election for June 1927, when the index stood at 132.9, its lowest level since independence. Prices recovered somewhat in 1928 and 1929, before beginning a long slide from early 1930. When he went to the country in February 1932 the agricultural price index stood at 108.7, nearly its lowest level yet.[519]

It was not that Cosgrave was 'above politics', as his more disingenuous admirers liked to plead. It was not that his government, with an elevated sense of public duty, refused to stoop to amiable political subterfuge. It was simply that Cosgrave was an inept subterfugist.

Cosgrave's place in history, however, does not ultimately depend on his performance as a vote-getter, but on his performance as a state builder. It is more than usually difficult for the historian to reach a balanced judgement on this issue. In doing so he must inevitably pronounce his verdict on a whole political culture, assessing Cosgrave's achievement in the context of the possibilities and limitations of the legacy he inherited.

That legacy was in many respects a promising one. But the civil war bequeathed a heritage of brooding bitterness that might otherwise have been less recriminatory. It also conferred, more concretely, continued respectability on the gun as a legitimate mode of political discourse. Cosgrave's success in curbing the level of post-civil war violence should not disguise the fact that violence lurked very close to the surface and that all his decision-making occurred under the strain created by the

---

[518] J.A. Gaughan, *Thomas Johnson, 1872–1963* (Dublin, 1980), pp. 294–5.
[519] *Irish Trade Journal*, December 1931, p. 187, June 1932, p. 75.

imminence of that violence. A.E. (George Russell) had written to Lady Gregory in 1901: 'if the stupefying influence of foreign control is removed, if we had charge of our own national affairs it would mean the starting up into sudden life of a thousand dormant energies, spiritual, intellectual, artistic, social, economic and human'. It didn't. The mere existence of the Dáil fostered the illusion that a new society was being shaped. Tom Johnson, respectable and respected Englishman, who led the Labour Party until 1927, and whose personal integrity and political ineffectuality did much to consolidate the Free State as a conservative regime, wondered in April 1927 if

perhaps the people who were writing history will look back upon this period and say 'what a great time it was to have lived'. The truth is that we are living in a history making period – one might say at the beginning of a new epoch. It is of the most tremendous significance that the law and government of the people of the country are being fashioned by an elected assembly . . . [520]

Johnson, ironically enough for the leader of a radical party, was celebrating not what the Dáil was doing, but the fact that the Dáil was doing it. Major Bryan Cooper, a respected ex-Unionist – respected not least for his formidable capacity for alcohol – told the Dáil in 1927 that 'they had in those four years done more than lay the foundations of a new state. They had put up the scaffolding and designed the architectural plan on which the edifice was to be built.'[521]

But what was the plan? What was the architect's inspiration? What materials went into the building? How was it furnished? The number of residents who continued to leave suggested that not everyone found the building satisfactory. 'Ah, the house is hardly worth livin' in . . . the insides in a shockin' state.'[522] If there were a few fine rooms, there were also too many servants' quarters. And much of the furniture was second-hand. A coat of paint was in danger of being mistaken for fundamental structural alterations.

The civil war accentuated the psychological need felt by Cosgrave and his colleagues to impress the world, which meant Britain, with their capacity for self-government. This inferiority complex *vis-à-vis* the old imperial masters was quite unjustified.[523] In a man-for-man comparison, Cosgrave's cabinets compared well with any contemporary British cabinet. His government was one of the youngest, and in terms of personal intelligence, one of the ablest, in post-Versailles Europe.[524] Even new rulers anxious for the plaudits of their erstwhile masters might have

[520] Gwynn, *Irish Free State*, p. 195.   [521] *Ibid.*, p. 196.
[522] Sean O'Casey, *Cathleen listens in* (performed in the Abbey in October 1923).
[523] For an instructive reference to 'the inferiority complex', see G. Fitzgerald, 'The significance of 1916', *Studies*, 55 (Spring 1966), p. 34.
[524] Verdicts tending in this direction include Williams, 'The summing up', pp. 184–5, and O. MacDonagh, *Ireland since the Union* (London, 1979), p. 100.

winced at the tribute paid them by the *Times* in 1923, 'that a people untrained, by the accidents of history, in self-government, and congenitally disposed towards political instability, should complete a critical election without bloodshed or even social disturbance is indeed proof that its present governors are men of understanding'.[525] 'Accidents of history' ranks as a delicious journalistic euphemism for centuries of occupation, revealing the effortless English capacity for self-exoneration, positively Hibernian in its imaginative scope. The condescending tone of the well-intentioned *Times* obituary on the Cosgrave government that 'their greatest service to Ireland lies in the proof they gave to an at first incredulous world that Irishmen could govern their own country and govern it well',[526] was objectively an impertinence, confusing as it still did an incredulous Britain for an incredulous world, and overlooking the record of sustained mediocrity of the Britain of Baldwin and MacDonald. It revealed more about the requirements of the British psyche than of Irish reality. But Cosgrave and his colleagues may have actually felt complimented. It is as much a psychological characteristic of the *arriviste petit bourgeoisie* of a colonial society to cherish the approval of their erstwhile masters as it is for them to despise the less materially successful sections of their own community.

Cosgrave did not fail in comparison with his international contemporaries. But he did fail in the context of historical expectations. That is a cruel, but not an unhistorical, criterion. He had, it is true, to contend with the inevitably deflating experience of the reality of self-government. That deflation did not follow mainly from the civil war, as more self-indulgent commentators like to aver. It is a normal reaction to independence, because of 'the dawning realisation that things are more complicated than they look, that social, economic and political problems, once thought to be mere reflexes of colonial rule, to disappear when it disappeared, have less superficial roots'.[527] Most European governments lost office during the great slump. But few fell while still enjoying so sound a financial position, and with such unused assets at their disposal, as Cosgrave's.

Nevertheless, the achievement of the Cosgrave government remains a historic one. It inherited a ship of state which, however firmly built, was buffeted by hostile winds, manned by a partly mutinous crew and with many disaffected passengers. Richard Mulcahy, standing at the graveside of Michael Collins, conveyed the sense of uncertainty and fragility that the young survivors felt as they gazed at the coffin of their dead leader:

[525] *The Times*, 3 September 1923.   [526] Quoted in *Irish Times*, 22 February 1932.
[527] C. Geertz, 'After the Revolution: the fate of nationalism in new states', in *The interpretation of cultures* (London, 1975), p. 235.

We are all mariners on the deep, bound for a port still seen only through storm and spray, sailing on a sea full of dangers and hardships and bitter toil.

Cosgrave, supported in their conflicting but symbiotic ways by Mulcahy and O'Higgins, steered the ship into quieter waters, and navigated a safe subsequent course. The ship may have been becalmed in 1932. It was no longer in immediate danger of foundering. Too many passengers were travelling in needlessly wretched quarters, but few were in danger of drowning. Some of Cosgrave's ministers had strong authoritarian streaks, but he resisted any temptation to constitute his regime into a one-party dictatorship. His government of young men had responsibility thrust upon them before they had a chance to mellow or to learn the arts of political manoeuvre. They did not enjoy de Valera's advantage of a ten-year apprenticeship in opposition to broaden their political perspective. They lacked the imagination to respond to changing conditions after 1927, when their performance anticipated their relative ineffectuality in opposition after 1932. Nevertheless, the retrospective admission by both Gerry Boland and Seán Lemass that Fianna Fáil were scarcely ready for government in 1927 was a handsome, if oblique, tribute to the calibre of the men who had proved themselves ready in even more trying circumstances.[528]

Cosgrave had responsibility thrust upon him in frightening circumstances, which would reinforce his natural caution. His vision was limited, and his instincts conservative. He had neither a capacious intellect nor a commanding personality. What he did have was a basic decency, a sense of public service, and sound judgement on matters of state. He was essentially a moderate, who had to learn, and did learn, however reluctantly, the fundamental lesson on which the survival of civilised public life depends, that moderates must be prepared, in the last resort, to kill in defence of moderation. It was due in large measure to him that things did not fall apart, that the centre did hold, that not so many but so few of the rough beasts slouching through the Ireland of the twenties would reach their blood-soaked Bethlehems. And Cosgrave would do the ship of state one final service, by the manner in which he quietly left the bridge and handed over the wheel to the rival captain. Bitter though it was in party terms – indeed precisely because it was so bitter in party terms – it was his finest hour.

[528] Gerry Boland's story, *Irish Times*, 10 October 1968; Seán Lemass looks back, *Irish Press*, 24 January 1969.

Chapter 3

EXPERIMENT: 1932–1945

THE IMPACT OF DE VALERA

Nothing so became Cosgrave in office as his manner of leaving it. There were widespread fears that the government, or the army, would attempt a preemptive coup to forestall the feared revenge of their civil war enemies. Saner counsels prevailed. For a government that based its legitimacy on majority rights to have rejected a majority verdict would have confirmed the charge of Irish incapacity for democratic self-government that Cosgrave was determined to refute. His regime was the victim of its own success. A coup would now involve an assault on an established tradition of stability. It could not be excused as the alternative to anarchy of the type that tempted Pilsudski to seize power in Poland in 1926, or King Alexander to suspend the Vidovdan constitution in Yugoslavia in 1929.

If Cosgrave ever contemplated a coup, he had taken peculiar preparatory steps. He succeeded to a remarkable degree in taking the army out of politics. After completing the first demobilisation drive in March 1924, he further reduced the size of the army from 13 000 in 1924 to only 6000 in 1931, and reduced the number of colonels from 28 in 1926 to 11 in 1931.[1] Michael Brennan, the new Chief of Staff, promoted after a protracted cabinet meeting in October 1931,[2] was probably the most conciliatory possible appointment. Richard Mulcahy, a key figure in any projected coup, had firmly demonstrated his commitment to democracy. Some ministers and officers may have been less committed than Cosgrave and Mulcahy to the primacy of the ballot box. Neither Ernest Blythe nor Eoin O'Duffy, the Gárda commissioner, were doctrinaire democrats. Both were rumoured to want an army coup. But calculation reinforced conviction. The army might split. An unsuccessful coup might provide

---

[1] *Statistical Abstract*, 1931, t. 151, p. 125.
[2] SPO, CAB G2/8, 9 October 1931; Brady, *Guardians*, p. 168.

the IRA and extreme Fianna Fáil elements with just the pretext they needed to wreck the feared revenge.[3]

De Valera too did much to facilitate a smooth transfer of power. He was fortunate that he had not been in a position to form a government in 1927. The temptation to certain elements in Cumann na nGaedheal to stage a coup would have been far stronger in the immediate aftermath of the murder of Kevin O'Higgins. Fianna Fáil in the meantime had learned something of the parliamentary ethic from their period of apprenticeship, as 'we were a pretty raw lot and the extra five years in opposition did us a lot of good'.[4] De Valera fought the election with dignity. Aware that his enemies considered his coming to power 'a seismic event'[5] he gave assurances that there would be no victimisation of Treaty supporters. In the event, only two senior civil servants seem to have been transferred to less politically sensitive offices.[6] He was to treat with circumspection applications for reinstatement on political grounds in the gárdaí.[7] He appointed J. Geoghegan, a former Cumann na nGaedheal supporter, as Minister for Justice. His nomination of Frank Aiken to the equally sensitive post of Defence proved an inspired choice. Aiken had been the last military commander of the anti-Treaty forces in 1923, but his heart was not in the civil war and he had no blood lust. He was probably more acceptable to the Free State officers than any other possible appointment. He soon reconciled the army to the new regime. Michael Brennan cooperated loyally with the government, which dispensed with his military services only in 1940, when he had served their purpose.[8] De Valera himself took the External Affairs portfolio, which enabled him to present himself as the embodiment of the nation, defending its interests against the usurping Saxon[9] and guarding against being outflanked by a zealot.

De Valera lacked an absolute majority. He could rule only with Labour support. That too may have contributed to his relative restraint. He would seek a clearer mandate at the first opportunity, and must therefore satisfy his supporters without alienating potential converts. He continued to play a shrewd electoral game. Lemass thanked the IRA for their support

[3] Munger, *Legitimacy, passim.*

[4] 'Seán Lemass looks back: an interview with Michael Mills', *Irish Press*, 24 January 1969; 'Gerry Boland's story', *Irish Times*, 10 October 1968.

[5] G. Fitzgerald, 'De Valera and contemporary Ireland', *Etudes Irlandaises*, 9 (1984), p. 235.

[6] O'Hegarty, Secretary to the government, who had been very close to Collins, moved to the Board of Works after the election but before Cosgrave went out of office (*Irish Press*, 24 February 1932). Henry O'Friel, Secretary of the Department of Justice, who was held partly responsible for an unsympathetic attitude to republicans during the 1920s, was transferred to the Tariff Commission, in 1933, much to his disgruntlement (SPO, S2469).

[7] SPO, S6442, CAB 7/51, 7 July 1933.

[8] SPO, S11607, M. Brennan to E. de Valera, 15 January 1940.

[9] J.P. O'Carroll, 'Eamon de Valera, charisma and political development', in O'Carroll and Murphy (eds.), *De Valera*, p. 29.

during the campaign.[10] In March the republican vote was further nursed by the release of all ninety-seven IRA prisoners, and the suspension of the detested Public Safety Act. In May, the Dáil abolished the abhorred oath and dismissed James MacNeill as governor general, replacing him with Dónal Ó Buachalla, a loyal acolyte of de Valera, who cooperated in demeaning the office.[11]

The Fianna Fáil campaign to capture the church continued after the election. Even as the results were declared, Seán MacEntee gloated that Fianna Fáil had won the Catholic vote.[12] MacEntee may have been reproved for so gross a sectarian appeal, for he hastened within a day to reassure unionists that they too were entitled to civil rights.[13] De Valera would square the religious circle in the most electorally remunerative manner. In June, the Eucharistic Congress provided him with a timely opportunity to baptize his synthesis of republicanism and Catholicism,[14] reminding the papal legate, in his feline way, that he was a loyal son of Rome.[15] The *Irish Press* played the Catholic card with a vengeance as it went from strength to polemical strength, increasing its average circulation from 78 000 copies in the first quarter of 1932 to 91 000 in the final quarter, before soaring to 115 000 in the election month of January 1933.[16] The *Press* continued to bestow vicarious papal benediction on Fianna Fáil's economic programme, urging the decentralisation of industry, as was allegedly the case in France and Italy, rather than its concentration, as allegedly in Germany or Britain, both of which had succumbed to the great slump. 'It happens that France and Italy are Catholic nations, while Germany and Britain are not. In Catholic countries man has not yet lost his importance in the scheme of things. He remains of more concern to the rulers than the machine.'[17]

New voters would be won, and transfers from Labour consolidated, mainly through social and economic measures. De Valera established an economic committee of the cabinet. The fact that it excluded the Minister for Finance[18] implied that it was to be a spending committee. Seán Lemass, Minister for Industry and Commerce, quickly extended protectionist measures, while Jim Ryan, Minister for Agriculture, launched a tillage campaign. Seán T. O'Kelly, Minister for Local Government, embarked on a housing programme much more extensive than that of Ernest Blythe. Seán MacEntee, Minister for Finance, quickly improved

[10] 'Con Lehane', *Hibernia*, 12 April 1979.
[11] The Cosgrave cabinet was already intent on keeping the Governor General in his place. It dealt firmly with the inflated assumptions of the first Governor General, T.M. Healy, concerning his prerogatives. SPO, S3229, T.M. Healy to W.T. Cosgrave, 18 July 1924, and Cosgrave's reply, 19 July 1924.
[12] *Irish Independent*, 22 February 1932.   [13] *Irish Independent*, 23 February 1932.
[14] Keogh, *Bishops*, p. 192.   [15] Moynihan, *Speeches*, pp. 218–19.
[16] *Irish Press*, 23 January 1933, 8 March 1933.
[17] *Irish Press*, 2 May 1932.   [18] Fanning, *Finance*, pp. 218–19.

improved old-age pensions. Not all these policies would achieve their economic and social objectives. Some were arguably counter-productive, even within their own terms of reference. But in 1932 they achieved the political objective of conveying an impression of unprecedented activity along a broad socio-economic front.

The annuities controversy provided the focal point of Anglo-Irish conflict in 1932. This issue fused emotional and economic appeal in an optimum electoral manner for de Valera. In June, he withheld the annuities hitherto paid to the British government. He offered to submit the issue to arbitration, but, remembering the Boundary commission, insisted that the arbitrators must come from outside the Commonwealth. The British government refused. It imposed in retaliation 20 per cent *ad valorem* duties on Irish exports of livestock and livestock products from July. De Valera in turn imposed duties on British coal. The retaliatory spiral continued until 1934, with British duties retrieving about two-thirds of the value of the annuities.[19] Ireland would suffer increasingly from the consequences. But in 1932 the burden was still only dimly perceived, whereas the benefits to the smaller farmers were immediate. The annuities, amounting to well over £3 000 000 a year, were a fixed burden, which pressed hard during a deflationary period, generally depriving smaller farmers of about 10 per cent of their net income. De Valera did not intend to actually abolish the annuities, but rather to halve them and acquire the other half for the Irish government. But this complication was not unduly stressed from Fianna Fáil platforms at this stage.

De Valera's vigorous policy provoked all opposition elements to negotiate for unification in a single party in late 1932.[20] Contrary to fond opposition illusions, Fianna Fáil was proving quite capable of ruling. The government was not going to collapse under the weight of its own incompetence. However, its reliance of Labour left it vulnerable to Dáil defeat, particularly as Labour began to become restive about the cabinet's apparent determination to impose wage cuts on some public sector workers. Public disorder was increasing with clashes between the IRA and the Army Comrades Association (ACA), founded in February 1932 to protect Cumann na nGaedheal supporters from IRA harassment. In August 1932 T.F. O'Higgins, brother of Kevin O'Higgins, and himself a Cumann na nGaedheal TD, assumed the leadership of the ACA. De Valera could not tolerate the disturbances indefinitely. But the behaviour of the ACA gave him a chance to wring the last inch of electoral mileage out of his republican sympathies before turning, if necessary, against the IRA. He startled the country, and perhaps his cabinet, by calling an

---

[19] Lyons, *Ireland*, p. 601.   [20] Moss, *Political parties*, pp. 191–2.

election for January 1933.[21] The result handsomely vindicated his gamble. Fianna Fáil swept to an absolute majority, winning 77 of the 153 seats, a gain of 5. Its share of the vote rose from 44.5 per cent to 49.7 per cent. In the crescendo of political excitement generated by energetic government, turn-out rose from 77 per cent to a record 81.3 per cent. The informal electoral alliance with Labour continued. Labour transfers went heavily to Fianna Fáil, 2 of whose 5 gains came in Dublin.[22]

De Valera, reinforced by the mandate, began to deal with the private armies, by force with the ACA, by stealth with the IRA. In February, he dismissed Eoin O'Duffy as gárda commissioner.[23] In March, the ACA adopted the blue shirt, by which it would become known to history.[24] In May, it began to take the sinister straight-arm salute.[25] In July, O'Duffy assumed the leadership of the ACA, which now rechristened itself the National Guard and adopted a constitution with a vague corporatist commitment to form 'coordinated national organisations of employers and employed, which, with the aid of judicial tribunals, will effectively prevent strikes and lockouts and harmoniously compose industrial differences'.[26] O'Duffy next proclaimed his intention to lead the National Guard in a parade past the Dáil in August. De Valera moved to crush the movement, before it had a chance to gather further strength, by banning not only the march but the National Guard itself. He reconstituted Cosgrave's excoriated military tribunal[27] and reinforced the special detective branch with hastily recruited Fianna Fáil reliables to guard against subversion.[28] O'Duffy's nerve failed in the face of de Valera's direct challenge. He cancelled the march.[29]

In September, the Blueshirts, the new Centre Party – essentially the old Farmers' Party – and Cumann na nGaedheal joined to form the United Ireland party, soon better known as Fine Gael, with O'Duffy as leader and Cosgrave as parliamentary leader. Cosgrave can hardly have been ecstatic about this arrangement. But two electoral defeats had weakened his authority. He may have felt that if he bided his time the erratic O'Duffy was likely to commit blunders which would help him re-establish his control.

Violence between the Blueshirts and the IRA escalated in late 1933, as agricultural circumstances worsened. The economic war, with its adverse impact on cattle prices, provoked many strong farmers into withholding their rates. But when Fianna Fáil won the local elections in July 1934, despite their being fought on the old ratepayer franchise which was

21 Gerry Boland's story, *Irish Times*, 11 October 1968.
22 Deduced from election results, *Irish Press*, 27 January, 30 January 1933.
23 M. Manning, *The Blueshirts* (Dublin, 1970), p. 65.   24 *Ibid.*, p. 55.
25 *Ibid.*, pp. 58–9.
26 *Ibid.*, pp. 55–9, 74.   27 *Ibid.*, pp. 89–90.   28 Brady, *Guardians*, pp. 197–9.
29 Manning *Blueshirts* p. 86.

assumed to favour Fine Gael, it became clear that O'Duffy was not the rich man's de Valera. O'Duffy's proposal in August 1934 that farmers should withhold the annuities, still being collected at the new reduced level, crystallised opposition to his unconstitutional attitudes amongst his Fine Gael critics. In September 1934 O'Duffy resigned abruptly as leader of Fine Gael, irritated by his colleagues' attempts to discipline his impetuous anti-parliamentary remarks.[30] The inept manner in which he handled his resignation, making no apparent attempt to alert his bewildered followers, confirmed his colleagues' reservations about his political capacity. A 'rumbustious child' in politics,[31] whatever his administrative talents, he found himself outmanoeuvred by Cosgrave who was duly confirmed as leader of Fine Gael in 1935. The alacrity with which the party executive accepted O'Duffy's resignation, and translated him into the past political tense, made it clear that only a bitter leadership battle could restore him. The executive immediately appointed another 'hard man' of civil war vintage, Ned Cronin, to succeed O'Duffy as Blueshirt leader.[32] Disputes duly broke out between the two old comrades. With the Blueshirts in disarray, the government struck hard at rate resisters.[33]

De Valera effectively crushed the Blueshirts by 1934. He moved more warily against the IRA. In the spring of 1933 he established an Army Volunteer Reserve to divert recruitment from the IRA. Pensions for anti-Treaty veterans served a similar purpose. The guards gradually began to seize IRA as well as Blueshirt propaganda, and the military tribunal began to be used against the IRA, if still relatively circumspectly. In 1934, it convicted 102 IRA members compared with 349 Blueshirts.[34] De Valera long hesitated, however, to declare the IRA illegal, until two particularly callous IRA murders, of a woman and an old man, gave him the opportunity to ban the organisation in June 1936.[35]

The Blueshirt episode permitted Fianna Fáil to pose as, and even to become, constitutionalists, defenders of law, order and majority rule against a militaristic threat. It thus enabled Fianna Fáil to unobtrusively make the difficult subjective transition from rule by divine right to rule by majority right. The Uniforms Bill banning the Blueshirts in February 1934 was a Fianna Fáil vote of confidence in the Irish people. Seán Lemass now felt that 'there has been a tendency in many countries towards a militarisation of politics, which it is very necessary to arrest if democratic institutions are going to be preserved'.[36] That was a new tune for the 'slightly constitutional' Lemass of only six years before to be playing. It

[30] *Ibid.*, pp. 146–63.
[31] T.D. Williams, 'De Valera in power', in F. MacManus (ed.), *The years of the great test*, 1926–39 (Cork, 1967), p. 36.
[32] Manning, *Blueshirts*, pp. 152, 163.   [33] *Ibid.*, p. 175.   [34] *Ibid.*, p. 136.
[35] Murphy, *Ireland*, p. 84.   [36] Manning, *Blueshirts*, p. 123.

was the spread of this mentality within Fianna Fáil that provided de Valera with an opportunity to move against the IRA as well as the Blueshirts, and allowed him to use the guards in a way that would otherwise have posed problems for even so resourceful a party manager.

The Blueshirts are frequently described as fascists. They were not. Fascism was far too intellectually demanding for the bulk of the Blueshirts. Blueshirts were simply traditional conservatives, decked out in fashionable but ideologically ill-fitting continental garb. They belonged to the same ideological vintage as the militant elements in the Irish Farmers' Union who had dreamt in 1919 and 1920 of forming a 'White Army' to crush the 'Red Guards' of the agricultural labourers.[37] The Blueshirts deviated widely from the standard fascist model. The shirt and the salute marked the summit of their ideological achievement. The Blueshirt goal was essentially restoration of the status quo ante, not the radical revolution of real fascism. Many Blueshirts, perhaps most, saw themselves as essentially moderate, founded to defend constitutional freedoms against the IRA threat,[38] though the toughs among them happily contemplated a dictatorship.[39] They were not pervasively anti-democratic in principle, but they allowed themselves to be manoeuvred into a position where Fianna Fáil were able to pose as hereditary democrats and denounce the Blueshirts as potential dictators. They were less adept than Fianna Fáil in exploiting the fascistic rhetoric of nationalism. They had little theoretical commitment to the purifying power of violence. The 'Hero' did not feature prominently in their pantheon of Blueshirt man. Indeed, they had no pantheon for Him to feature in. Their specific economic policies – thwarting the drive to autarchy by ending the economic war and restoring traditional trading connections with England – owed more to liberalism than to fascism, even if most of all to self-interest. They preached no agrarian utopia, nor did they lace their rhetoric with sustained anti-urban diatribes. They had no vision of a fascist society. Their corporatism, vague enough in itself, owed more to papal than to fascist inspiration. They were not generally anti-semitic, considerable though we have seen the potential for anti-semitism to have been among a people nurtured on stereotypes of satanic conspiracy against their version of the true faith. Their intense anti-communism, widely shared by Fianna Fáil supporters, did not derive from the same sources as Mussolini's or Hitler's. Most Irish people rejected communism as atheistic. They did not trouble themselves unduly about the dialectic. The crusade against communism was more religious war than class war. Anti-communist hysteria of this vintage stimulated devout Dublin mobs to assault suspected people and places in 1933.[40] De

[37] FitzPatrick, *Politics*, p. 273; *Connaught Telegraph*, 27 August 1932.
[38] Manning, *Blueshirts*, p. 29.
[39] *Ibid.*, p. 138.   [40] *Ibid.*, p. 61; Brady, *Guardians*, pp. 192–3.

Valera, with his essential sense of decency, kept his head and condemned the 'anti-communist' craze.[41] But it would be a travesty of the history of ideas to dignify those mobs, who in any case favoured eclectic sartorial styles, as fascist. The Blueshirts, in short, possessed few of the essential characteristics of fascist movements, as distinct from a small number of largely incidental similarities.

Certain pre-conditions normally conducive to successful fascist movements did indeed exist in the Free State. There was heavy urban unemployment and serious agricultural slump. Intense political excitement resulted in rising turn-out in the elections of 1932 and 1933. This increase appears to have been disproportionately concentrated, ominously by continental criteria, in economically backward areas and among the politically inarticulate. Previous non-voters, whether in age, class or area terms, provided a reservoir of fascist support on the continent. Foreign observers drew attention to the obvious and, by continental standards, disturbing participation of youth in politics.[42] In electoral terms, therefore, Ireland seemed to promise a potentially fruitful harvest for fascism.

Ironically, it was Fianna Fáil that most effectively harnessed this potential. Circumstances conspired to align forces, frequently sympathetic to fascism elsewhere, on the side of the party that came to be considered, because of the apparent Blueshirt association with fascism, peculiarly anti-fascist. Some isolated resemblances can certainly be detected between fascist and Fianna Fáil rhetoric. The more strident versions of integral nationalism favoured on some Fianna Fáil platforms could veer close to the fascist variant. Aspects of Fianna Fáil's autarkic economic policy were reminiscent of fascist panaceas. Some Fianna Fáil spokesmen clung to the ideas of an agrarian utopia as insistently as any fascist rhetorician. And Fianna Fáil certainly possessed the type of charismatic leader cherished by fascist ideologists.

Despite the trappings, however, Fianna Fáil was no more fascist than the Blueshirts. It was not even a populist party, although certain themes in its rhetoric roused echoes of populist propaganda elsewhere. If it preached the virtues of bucolic simplicity, it was essentially committed to industrialisation, whatever de Valera's private views, even if it did not necessarily equate industrialisation with 'decadent' urbanisation. In electoral terms, Fianna Fáil transcended the class bases of typical fascist support. It mobilised not only many lower-middle-class voters, but urban workers, small farmers and agricultural labourers. Labour was its natural electoral ally, not its enemy. It managed to be simultaneously sympathetic to trade unionism and to state capitalism. Franklin Roosevelt's Democratic coalition probably offers the best analogy of the range of interests, often

---

[41] Manning, *Blueshirts*, pp. 61–2.   [42] Moss, *Political parties*, pp. 194–5.

potentially conflicting, that Fianna Fáil subsumed within its expansive electoral embrace.

Fianna Fáil succeeded in capturing the market for the emotional resentment of the excluded underdog, who felt that the political 'system' was fixed against him. The vacuous corporatist rhetoric of O'Duffy made little impression at a time when the government itself appeared to be creating a new order. Fianna Fáil could hardly be denounced as decadent in 1933. And Fianna Fáil satisfied the demand for pageantry, and for vicarious participation, among the politically emotive. A charismatic leader, torch-light parades, blazing tar barrels, provoked a satisfying sense of fulfilment of the type craved by those seeking emotional reassurance by sinking their individuality in a communal identity. Continental fascists generally proved more adept than their enemies at mobilising the past. Fianna Fáil extended its emotional sway over past as well as present, establishing a virtual monopoly on the historical mythology market. O'Duffy did invoke the 'Old Irish system' in an attempt to strike a responsive chord in his denunciations of political parties and of parlia-ment.[43] But he was an amateur compared with so professional a manipu-lator of the past as de Valera, who felt sufficiently confident of his position to denounce the Blueshirts as lacking, in contrast to the IRA, roots in Irish history.[44] It was precisely this Blueshirt failure to summon ancestral ghosts from the national pantheon that moved John A. Costello, a future Fine Gael Taoiseach, to his extravagant boast that 'the Blueshirts will be victorious in the Irish Free State' just as 'the Blackshirts were victorious in Italy' and 'the Hitlershirts' were victorious in Germany.[45] Costello was forced to fashion for the Blushirts a pedigree by contemporary association which, precisely because de Valera had preempted the strategic ideo-logical ground of the past, they patently lacked by breeding.

Irish social structure was inimical to fascism. The conflicting interests within Irish agriculture, exacerbated by the economic war, precluded the danger of an agrarian movement, with its usual concomitant of a primitivist ideology, making a major impact. The fact that bigger farmers broadly opposed, while smaller farmers broadly supported, Fianna Fáil, prevented ideological divisions from congealing along agrarian lines. There was no widespread anti-capitalist feeling. Most Irish capitalists were small. The lower-middle classes and the artisanate admired more than they resented successful capitalists. Big financiers were no more conspicuous than big business men. Purging society through a purified monetary system did not feature prominently in the conventional popular wisdom. Oliver Flanagan, that accomplished vote-getter, would, it is true, combine during the Second World War coy hints of anti-semitism with

[43] Manning, *Blueshirts*, p. 215.   [44] *Ibid.*, p. 81.
[45] DD, 50, 2 February 1934, 2237.

demands for 'monetary reform'. The occasional small farmer spokesman, and the occasional cleric, would wax indignant against bankers.[46] But they roused only muted popular response. Nor was it possible to sustain the fixation with an imminent communist threat, devotedly though some laboured to imagine one. A young professor of history at University College, Cork, James Hogan, Patrick Hogan's brother, had already as O'Duffy's Director of Intelligence during the civil war managed to detect that the communists were one of the four 'forces in motion' in the Free State, along with the constitutionalists, the Irregulars, and the militarists.[47] Strenuously though Hogan subsequently strove to sustain this insight, his famous Blueshirt pamphlet, *Could Ireland become Communist?*[48] was destined to remain a monument to Sisyphean endeavour.

It would nevertheless be unhistorical to dismiss completely the potential for fascism in the Free State, despite the difficulties posed by the stage of economic development, by history, and by the accidents of circumstance. Fianna Fáil and the Blueshirts between them had woven a number of fascistoid threads into the traditional fabric of Irish politics. But the fascistic themes were so effectively domesticated that they lost much of their sinister comparative import. 'The coshes and knuckle-dusters, the programmes and slogans, the posturing of O'Duffy, the gang warfare between the Blueshirts and the IRA, these were not the death-agonies of a Gaelic Weimar, they were rather the last convulsive spasm of the fever that had been wasting the land since 1922 – they were the nemesis of civil war.'[49]

Had Fianna Fáil lost the 1932 election, however, it is not inconceivable that some of its constituent elements might have been tempted to lurch in a fascist direction. So might some elements in Fine Gael had de Valera acted with less restraint. Above all, sustained economic depression might have brought forth ugly political progeny. It was therefore important that Fianna Fáil's economic policy should produce results, quickly.

Fianna Fáil was ideologically committed to as much self-sufficiency as possible, which it hoped to achieve through 'balanced' growth based on protection for industry and a shift from livestock to tillage in agriculture. De Valera, believing that a tillage policy would bind a bold peasantry to the soil, introduced subsidies to encourage the production of wheat and beet. This tillage policy rested on a double illusion. As George O'Brien pointed out in a symposium in which Jim Ryan, shortly to become Fianna

[46] E. Cahill, SJ, *Capitalism and its alternatives* (Dublin, 1936), p. 26.
[47] RM, P7/C/6, report by James Hogan, Director of Intelligence of the Army, 7 August 1923. Apart from the revealing obsession with communism, the report as a whole confirms the precocious brilliance of the then 23-year-old Hogan, who was resigning to become a professor of history at University College Cork.
[48] J. Hogan, *Could Ireland become Communist?* (Dublin, 1933).
[49] Lyons, *Ireland*, p. 531.

Fáil Minister for Agriculture, also participated, wheat and sugar beet were mainly grown by big farmers on good soil in the south and south east.[50] Ryan, who represented Wexford, may have recovered rapidly from this revelation. The area under wheat rose from 24 000 acres in 1932 to 254 000 acres in 1936. But 147 000 of these acres were in Leinster and only 18 000 in Connaught.[51] Wheat and beet, the crops de Valera found growing when he looked into his own heart, were of little help to small western farmers. The classic crops of the west, oats and potatoes, were not subsidised.[52] And if wheat acreage expanded, total tillage did not. The strong farmer switched from barley and oats into more lucrative wheat. The total area under grain changed little, but the cost of grain products to the consumer rose. There was little economic justification for the increase in subsidised wheat acreage. The best that can be said for the policy is that it may have been accidentally justified in retrospect by the requirements of agricultural self-sufficiency during World War Two. Even this argument requires qualification. Wheat acreage actually fell slightly from 254 000 in 1936 to 235 000 in 1939, before bounding up to 662 000 in 1945. The growth during the war, far exceeding the pre-war expansion, owed more to compulsory tillage orders, and price controls, than to the pre-war increase. And self-sufficiency did not depend on wheat. The potato acreage could, if necessary, have been greatly expanded, as was generally the case throughout Europe.[53] Indeed, potato acreage in Northern Ireland rose by two-thirds between 1939 and 1944, compared with an increase of only one-third in the South.[54] The wartime wheat policy was more an electoral necessity than an economic one.

Total tillage acreage hovered around the 1.9 m mark between 1932 and 1939. Even if the shift from pasture had been more pronounced, it seems unlikely that it could have increased employment and reduced emigration. De Valera deployed historical illusion in place of Patrick Hogan's theoretical illusion. Like many others, de Valera managed to convince himself that the increase in livestock since the famine was an English conspiracy to depopulate Ireland. He axiomatically assumed that more tillage meant more employment. Agricultural employment had not, however, been closely related to tillage acreage since at least 1881.[55] In the 1930s, male agricultural employment fell fastest in Leinster, which

---

[50] George O'Brien, 'Agriculture and employment', *Studies*, 19 (1930), pp. 181–2.
[51] *Irish Trade Journal*, December 1936, 251.
[52] A point not lost on future Clann na Talmhan leaders; NLI, MS 931, CVO, 18 April 1941; q. 19,995.
[53] A.S. Milward, *War, economy and society 1939–1945* (Berkeley, 1979), ch. 8, esp. pp. 265ff.; Mitchell, *European historical statistics*, pp. 217–19. See below, pp. 233–4.
[54] Mitchell, *European historical statistics*, p. 217.
[55] Department of Industry and Commerce, *Agricultural statistics 1847–1926* (Dublin, 1928), lx–lxi; G. O'Brien, 'Agriculture', 181; Crotty, *Agricultural production*, p. 145, and app., n. 5.

recorded the biggest increase in tillage, and slowest in Connaught, where tillage acreage actually fell.[56]

The economic war seriously disrupted the already vulnerable cattle trade. The government introduced bounties on cattle exports, and also subsidised exports of butter and bacon by roughly the amount of the British retaliatory duties. The bounties and subsidies were paid by the Irish consumer through higher taxation and higher domestic prices. These were desperate defensive measures to prevent exports collapsing. State expenditure on agriculture leaped from 1.6 per cent of the value of agricultural output in 1930 to 15.7 per cent in 1935.[57] As the expenditure largely occurred in the form of subsidies for the prices forfeited in the British market, however, it provided little net benefit to agriculture.

The main consequences of Fianna Fáil's agricultural policy were to raise prices for consumers, coarsen the quality of product, reduce exports, and damage especially the small farm economy. Bacon curers, flour millers and perhaps sugar beet factories extorted monopoly profits from their Irish customers.[58] The vagaries of subsidy policy accentuated the notorious seasonal fluctuations in Irish butter and bacon exports, further depressing their price on the English market.[59] Egg production was more or less maintained, but only accidentally, because the ratio of the cost of feed to the price of eggs remained relatively favourable. The compulsory mixture of home barley with imported maize raised feed prices for the small farmer's pigs. Between 1933 and 1936 about half the aid to dairy farmers was apparently passed on, through lower calf prices, to graziers.[60] De Valera's policy probably sacrificed the small farmer to whose welfare he was genuinely dedicated, to salvage the economic interests of stronger farmers.[61]

The small farmer did gain some alleviation. The extension of unemployment assistance in 1933 to under-employed smallholders, the reduction in the land annuities, possibly coupled with a certain delicacy in pressing for rapidly rising annuity arrears, did help poorer farmers. But the small farmer owed less to Fianna Fáil economic policy than to compensation for that policy. He became less self-reliant, at however frugal a level, and more dependent on that type of public charity that had no place in de Valera's idealised image of a bold peasantry. It was one of the innumerable ironies implicit in the pursuit of 'self-sufficiency' that among de Valera's attractions for the people of the west, not least of the Gaeltacht, was the increase in state handouts from the apostle of frugal self-sufficiency.

Comparison of the structure of agricultural exports at the beginning

---

56 Crotty, *Agricultural production*, pp. 146–7.   57 *Ibid.*, p. 120.
58 *Ibid.*, pp. 148, 153.
59 *Ibid.*, p. 154.   60 *Ibid.*, p. 152.   61 *Ibid.*, pp. 147, 187–8.

and at the end of the 1930s reveals the futility of Fianna Fáil agricultural policy in the face of economic reality. Live animals still accounted for 50 per cent of total domestic exports in 1938, compared with 52 per cent in 1931. Not only did livestock remain the main agricultural export, but agricultural exports in general became even more crucial for the economy as a whole. And in 1937, despite the economic war, Ireland still depended on Britain to take 91 per cent of her exports.[62]

De Valera seems to have assumed that industrialisation would bring self-sufficiency. It meant instead growing reliance on raw material imports. As industry did not prove sufficiently competitive to export, these raw material imports had to be paid for by agricultural exports. Fianna Fáil found that 'balanced' growth did indeed involve inextricable linkages between industry and agriculture, but not in quite the same manner so blithely anticipated in 1932.

The emigration statistics recorded the failure of the tillage policy. There were apparently 7000 immigrants into Ireland in 1932, returning from the depressed British and American economies. But recorded emigration rapidly recovered to reach 26 000 in 1937.[63] De Valera yearned for a self-sufficient, bucolic, Gaelic utopia. He detested contaminating economic contact with a certain neighbouring island race, who, through some unfortunate oversight in divine regional policy, had been located within smelling distance of the chosen people. But his prime aim of frugal self-sufficiency, bucolic bliss and growing population were logically incompatible. The Irish people, for better or for worse, were not prepared to accept the level of frugality that a primarily agricultural society imposed on them. The result was sustained emigration. De Valera, to confuse the issue further, had a genuine, if paternalistic, compassion for the poor. He committed Fianna Fáil to social welfare policies that appeared extravagant in the eyes of Cumann na nGaedheal and the Department of Finance. Emigration would presumably have risen even faster but for the relative success of the industrialisation drive under Seán Lemass. It was Lemass, as Minister for Industry and Commerce, who drew a more or less straight line through the coils of de Valera's thought to actually bring some semblance of coherence to Fianna Fáil's socio-economic policy.[64]

Lemass was only thirty-two when he took office. He had already proved an outstanding party organiser and director of elections. He spearheaded Fianna Fáil's assault on Cosgrave's economic policy. Though he claimed to have immersed himself in economic literature, including Arthur Grif-

[62] *Ibid.*, p. 155; K. Kennedy, *Productivity and industrial growth*, p. 34.
[63] *Statistical Abstract*, t. 24, p. 24.
[64] For a classic expression of de Valera's approach towards economic policy, see his speech in Dáil Éireann, 12 July 1928, reprinted in Moynihan, *Speeches*, pp. 153–62.

fith's writings, in prison after the civil war, the sources of his policy
inspiration remain to be fully clarified.[65] If in 1928 he claimed to believe
'that Ireland can be made a self-contained unit providing all the necessities
of living in adequate quantity for the people residing in the island at the
moment, or probably, a very much larger number',[66] by 1932 protection
was for him already more a means to an end than an end in itself. He
denied that he was 'bound to the economic theory of protection'. Instead,
he declared himself a pragmatic protectionist. 'Protection is given unless
facts coerce us to modify them [sic] in some particular way.'[67] He would
not sacrifice the welfare of the Irish people, as he conceived it, on the altar
of any doctrine. He repeatedly proclaimed his scepticism about theories
that did not work. Starting from his concept of Irish reality, and not from
English axioms of Victorian vintage, he urged Patrick McGilligan – what
a combination they might have made if only they could have worked in
harness! – to 'try to judge these matters in the light of our experience and
not in the light of some theory which he had dug up from the textbooks of
English economists'.[68] His policy suggests that he subscribed to the view
of John Busteed, Professor of Economics at University College Cork, one
of the few professional economists to detect some merit in Fianna Fáil's
programme, that

a nation condemned to peasant specialisation in farming is doomed to be a nation
of hewers of wood and drawers of water, no matter what improvement may be
effected in production and market efficiency by the farmers. Ireland's hope then
rests in making the greatest possible effort and in carrying the heaviest possible
burden to promote industrialisation.[69]

The effort was indeed stupendous. But Lemass got things done. He
quickly restored the morale of a department where expansion, and
therefore promotion, depended on a policy of industrialisation. He was
perhaps fortunate that Gordon Campbell's resignation, to enable him
succeed his brother as Lord Glenavy, allowed him to appoint John Leydon,
a young recruit from Finance, as Secretary for Industry and Commerce.
The circumstances of the appointment, the most important ever made by
Lemass, did credit to both young men. Cosgrave offered the post to
Leydon during the interval between the 1932 general election and the

---

65 Lemass claimed to have read deeply in economic literature while in prison after the civil
    war, 'Seán Lemass looks back', *Irish Press*, 3 February 1969. It is not very clear what
    there would have been to read.
66 Quoted in J. Meenan, 'From free trade to self-sufficiency', in MacManus (ed.), *Great test*,
    p. 74.
67 DD, 42, 8 June 1932, 886. During the election campaign he even criticised the
    government because it 'in some cases . . . wrongly applied tariffs, so as to discredit in
    men's minds a protectionist policy' (*Irish Press*, 1 February 1932).
68 *Ibid.*
69 J. Busteed, 'Agriculture and employment in the Free State 1926–30', *Studies*, 19 (1930),
    p. 188.

government going out of office. Leydon was thirty-seven. No comparable opening was likely to arise, given the age structure of the senior civil service, for many years. His promotion prospects in Finance itself were limited, given that McElligott was still only forty-two. Nevertheless, Leydon rejected Cosgrave's offer on the grounds that it was impolitic, if not indeed improper. McElligott was presumably hastening to try to batten down the hatches against the proclaimed interventionist principles of the incoming government, anathema to his *laissez-faire* self. Leydon at this stage was a powerful critic of state intervention.[70] He did not hesitate to risk his promotion prospects by expressing his reservations about some of the proposed policies of the incoming minister. Lemass, replying that there was nothing sacrosanct about his specific policies if better ones could be devised, and insisting that 'the last thing I want is a yes man', renewed the invitation.[71] It would appear that Lemass and Leydon educated each other – or at least influenced each other – to a remarkable degree, though the precise progress of their relationship remains to be clarified. In any case, Leydon was soon asserting the independence of his new department against the assumptions and presumptions of his old one.

Lemass was fortunate too in that the paralysing hand of Finance weighed politically as well as administratively a little less heavily on development after 1932. The new Minister for Finance, Seán MacEntee, was a formidable figure. His tastes were far more philosophical, more intellectual, than those of Lemass. Although educated as an engineer, he had published poetry, and was a lover of art and literature – he gave his fellow prisoner, Frank O'Connor, a copy of Heine after the civil war![72] He had 'an insatiable thirst for information, an extraordinary inquisitiveness about things', but he was also 'woefully longwinded'.[73] Able, persistent and opinionated, he no doubt soon came to regard the attempt to downgrade Finance as a personal slight, and became a doughty defender of departmental interests. This inevitably brought him into conflict with Lemass, with whom he had little enough temperamentally in common in any case. But Lemass's idealism, energy, toughness and self-discipline gave him a powerful place in cabinet, even if he by no means won all his battles with Finance. He handled not only his civil servants but de Valera adroitly, as indeed de Valera must have handled his ablest, but also his most independent minded and most impatient (indeed his only impatient) minister.[74]

---

[70] PM, P35/8/18, Leydon's memo dated 31 August 1929.
[71] Fanning, *Finance*, p. 258; D. Roche, 'John Leydon', p. 235.
[72] O'Connor, *An only child*, p. 259.   [73] Ó Broin, *Yesterday*, p. 99.
[74] See Longford and O'Neill, *De Valera*, p. 329, for a carefully worded description of the most remarkable personal relationship in Irish political life. D. McMahon, *Republicans and imperialists: Anglo-Irish relations in the 1930s* (London, 1984), pp. 17–21, discusses the personalities of Lemass, MacEntee, Ryan, O'Kelly and Aiken.

The Fianna Fáil election manifesto had adopted a coyly cautious tone on protection. Though it advocated tariffs, it also noted that

the people of Britain and ourself are much the other's best customer. Our geographical position, and other factors, make it unlikely that this close trade relationship will rapidly change. Machinery and other capital equipment for our industries will have to be purchased from abroad. We can in these purchases accord a preference to Britain in return for a preference in her markets for our agricultural produce.[75]

Within a few months Fianna Fáil and Britain were engaged not in an exchange of preferences but in economic war, as hostilities escalated following de Valera's withholding of the land annuities. Lemass had conceded in the election campaign that protection should not be granted indiscriminately.[76] The changed circumstances now compelled and permitted him to encourage more widespread protection than he originally envisaged. The Control of Manufactures Acts, 1932–4, tried to ensure, in an increasingly pragmatic way,[77] that the companies established behind the soaring tariff barriers, supplemented by a maze of quota and licensing restrictions, would remain under Irish control by requiring that more than half the equity of new firms should be Irish owned. The Industrial Credit Corporation, whose capital issues would exceed £6 million by 1937,[78] was established in 1933 to provide financial support for industry. Where private enterprise demonstrably lacked enterprise, Lemass sponsored more state bodies, including the Irish Sugar Company, Aer Rianta and Bord na Móna. He faced formidable problems, not all self-inflicted.

The excesses of the economic war have tended to divert attention from the serious deterioration in the fortunes of the Irish economy in 1930 and 1931. The value of exports fell nearly 25 per cent in those two years. Invisible income also fell sharply, with the decline in dividends from investment abroad, and in emigrants' remittances.[79] Unemployment and under-employment rose with the steep fall in emigration due to contracting opportunities overseas. Industrialisation would have to occur in the context of an already shrinking home market. This market then suffered further decline due to the economic war. Industrialisation would have been no easy matter even in a period of booming world trade. A drive to industrialisation at a moment of severe disruption of normal trading patterns seemed singularly ill-timed. There was too a lack of detailed forward planning. Despite the vociferous commitment of Fianna Fáil to

---

[75] Moss, *Political parties*, p. 207.   [76] *Irish Press*, 1 February 1932.
[77] M.E. Daly, 'An Irish-Ireland for business?: the Control of Manufactures Acts, 1932 and 1934', *IHS*, 24, 94 (November 1984), p. 267.
[78] Lyons, *Ireland*, p. 604.
[79] SPO, S6157A, memo by Seán Moynihan, Secretary to the Executive Council, 20 May 1932. See also SPO, S6157B, for the statement submitted by the Irish delegation to the Ottawa conference.

protection since 1926, the actual policy pursued after 1932 gives an impression of spontaneity. The English reaction to de Valera's annuities policy appears to have caught him by surprise. He did not have many contingency plans. Lemass found himself engaged in a series of activities to which little prior thought had been devoted. While de Valera liked to dwell on the idea of a 'balanced' economy, Lemass pursued a policy that was neither balanced nor unbalanced, but simply improvised. Industry and Commerce scanned the import lists and sought to encourage domestic production of any remotely acceptable substitutes.

If the effort was indeed enormous, Busteed's 'burden' was borne mainly by the consumer. Lack of competition on the protected home market inevitably led to profiteering. Critics claimed that pricing policies in many firms amounted to a conspiracy between employers and workers to exploit consumers. This compelled Lemass to intervene with measures to influence prices and wages. When raw materials were of Irish origin, Lemass was sucked into controversies between suppliers and manufacturers about costs. Little of this appears to have been anticipated. The writings of Arthur Griffith provided singularly sparse guidance on the actual mechanics of industrialisation behind the tariff barriers. Controversy between protectionists and free traders had tended to concentrate more on principles than on techniques.[80]

Lemass was further handicapped by a dearth of relevant information. He would himself recall that 'we proceeded to take policy decisions largely by guess work and not by statistical fact' because 'there was very little detailed knowledge about the country'.[81] The regularity with which academic economists lavished praise on Irish statistics reflected their detachment from actual decision-making. The complacency in the earlier years of independence testifies more to the restricted vision of the commentators and policy-makers than to the superior quality of the statistics, whose inadequacies became glaringly apparent once government actually tried to do something.

Even within Industry and Commerce some remained wedded to a passive policy. Stanley Lyon, director of the Statistics Branch, could imagine as late as 1939 no conceivable use for some of his statistics.[82] Ireland did actually collect an unusual amount of information for an economy at her stage of development. However, curiously little of the data conscientiously accumulated by the statisticians was to prove operationally relevant for the policy-makers. Lyon could think of no reason, except precedent, for collecting occupational returns in the

---

[80] For examples of the problems of implementation see Daly, 'Irish-Ireland', pp. 246–72 and J.P. Press, 'Protectionism and the Irish footwear industry', *IESH*, 13 (1986), pp. 74–89.
[81] 'Seán Lemass looks back', *Irish Press*, 1, 4 February 1969. See below, pp. 000.
[82] NLI, MS 922, CVO, 23 November 1939, ev. S. Lyon, q. 1332, 1336.

census.[83] His attitude towards unemployment exposes something of the complacency confronting Lemass even in some circles in his own department. 'Of the 503 000 male employees in the country in April 1936, only 175 000 or 35 per cent experienced any unemployment in the twelve months April 1935 – April 1936.'[84] There can be no more revealing 'only' in the public comments of senior civil servants of that generation.

Those public servants who did not worship at the shrine of *laissez-faire* tended to feel intellectually isolated. They received little consolation from outside experts. Few academic economists knew much about industry, and they devoted peculiarly little attention to the nuts and bolts of industrialisation policy after 1932. Most economists found it difficult to share fully in the ecstasy of de Valera's searing vision of frugal self-sufficiency. They found it all the more difficult in that most of them belonged to the political opposition. Fianna Fáil policy had to be pushed through in the teeth of the public derision of the professional economists and the somewhat more discreet distaste of many civil servants. As one of the more sensitive of the senior officials, R.C. Ferguson, Acting Secretary of Industry and Commerce during the Second World War, complained, 'this country suffers very definitely as compared with other countries from a lack of authoritative reports relating to economic matters'. Whatever the quality of the available statistics, they were merely 'the bone of the animal; but, the flesh and the blood, and the actual working of them, no, that you have not got'.[85]

Automatic imitation of the British model, Ireland's traditional substitute for thought, did not suffice in these circumstances. There were no really helpful models available in 1932. Lemass and his officials were thrown back on themselves. They had no guidelines, beyond rough rules of thumb, to help them appraise linkages between different sectors. They had no criteria for the location of industry, beyond a vague commitment to decentralisation, which could lead to economically curious decisions, at least from a short-term perspective.[86] A policy of economic self-reliance found itself obliged to depend more heavily than anticipated on intellectual self-reliance. Lemass would later claim that 'if we had available to us in the 1920s and 1930s the type of assistance that is available to new states today, we would have been able to do a great deal more.'[87]

The Fianna Fáil approach was all the more striking in that it did not seek to accelerate industrial investment by sacrificing the welfare of the

83 *Ibid.*
84 S. Lyon, 'Unemployment: the statistical background', *JSSISI*, 17 (1942–3), p. 121.
85 NLI, MS 929, CVO, 26 September 1940, ev. R.C. Ferguson, q. 14976.
86 Daly, 'Irish-Ireland', p. 261. The 'curiosity' applies as much to decisions between different 'decentralised' locations as to the decentralisation itself. Presumably political considerations ought not to be excluded!
87 'Seán Lemass looks back', *Irish Press*, 21 January 1969.

weak, as has often occurred in 'forced' industrialisation drives. Busteed's 'burden' was not borne disproportionately by the poor. On the contrary, not only did the government increase unemployment benefits and old-age pensions, but Seán T. O'Kelly, Minister for Local Government, launched an ambitious housing programme. An average of 12 000 houses a year were built with state aid between 1932 and 1942 compared with fewer than 2000 a year between 1923 and 1931. The building boom created employment, consolidated working-class support for the government and helped alleviate a social scandal. By 1946, despite the cessation of building during the war, appreciable improvement had occurred. The proportion of persons in families living in 'homes' of one or two rooms between 1926 and 1946 fell from 28 per cent to 21 per cent in Cork city, from 39 per cent to 23 per cent in Limerick city, and from 50 per cent to 25 per cent in Dublin.[88]

This housing programme naturally proved grist to the pockets of the contractors. Fortunes were made in this field more easily than in manufacturing. The building industry soon came to be widely regarded as an extension of the Fianna Fáil patronage system. Whatever the political implications, the new dwellings were a marked improvement on the foul slums that had for so long disgraced Dublin and other cities.

In all the circumstances, Fianna Fáil's industrial policy appeared to achieve substantial success. Gross industrial output rose from £55 000 000 in 1931 to £90 000 000 in 1938. Industrial employment (including building) rose from 162 000 to 217 000 over the same period. Or did it? These figures have provoked serious doubts. Much of the recorded increase, it has been suggested, merely reflected more accurate coverage through improved enumeration procedures. The real increase may have been very much less. The earlier censuses of industrial production, beginning in 1926, omitted the self-employed and many small enterprises. Discrepancies between the figures derived from the population censuses of 1926 and 1936, and the more uncertain figures recorded in the censuses of industrial production, have reinforced the reservations. As coverage of smaller firms increased in successive industrial censuses, and as a number of workers transferred from smaller into bigger firms, they may have become 'statistics' for the first time, thus conveying an exaggerated impression of the real growth in employment.

It is clear that further work is necessary to clarify the differences in the data recorded within and between the censuses of population and the censuses of industrial production. In the meantime, generalisation must be tentative. The 1936 census of production reported an increase of 42 000 since 1926, from 157 000 to 199 000, in the numbers at work in manufacturing industry (including building). The census officials were

---

[88] *Statistical Abstract*, 1931, t. 90, p. 96; *Statistical Abstract*, 1960, t. 155, p. 201.

aware of the discrepancies between the industrial and population returns. Their attempt to reconcile the figures suggested that about two-thirds of the increase since 1926 was genuine. Their revision excluded certain categories, however, and their handling of the discrepancies does not always command complete confidence. Nevertheless, it is not clear that more refined revision will dramatically affect the results.

Further complications arise if one seeks to 'correct' distortions that may arise from using the 1931 census of production rather than that of 1926 as a base. The 1931 figures are obviously more relevant for an assessment of Fianna Fáil policy than those of 1926. They have not yet been subjected to adequate examination. The Census Commissioners assumed that the figures for the first three censuses of industrial production, in 1926, 1929 and 1931, were comparable. Nevertheless, nearly 10 per cent more forms were issued in 1931 than in 1929. The published reports are not clear on the comparative rate of response. Recorded gross industrial output actually fell about 15 per cent between 1929 and 1931. The 1931 census records a modest increase in industrial employment since 1926. If coverage were increasing over this period, however, it may be that this figure conceals a real decline rather than an increase.

Where the evidence is so suspect, confident conclusions are premature. A reasonable interim verdict would seem to be that while the growth in recorded employment in the industrial sector overrates the real increase, nevertheless substantial real increase did occur between 1931 and 1938. An adequate investigation will have to recalculate not only the number of jobs created, but the number of jobs saved by the interventionist policy in general, and by protection in particular. A comparison between the censuses of industrial production in 1929 and 1931, for what the figures are worth, suggests virtual stagnation in employment in those sectors that were to grow particularly rapidly after 1932. It seems reasonable to assume that without the change in policy existing Irish industry would have suffered severely from intensified British competition, in view of the depressed state of international trade. It is by no means unlikely that output and employment would have actually fallen but for the vigorous implementation of the new policies. The new approach therefore probably did make a significant impact, at least in the short term, particularly in the light of the adverse prevailing circumstances, both internationally and on the domestic agricultural front.[89]

89 This summary of a complex and obscure situation is based on the following sources: M.E. Daly, *Social and economic history of Ireland* (Dublin, 1981), p. 150; D. Johnson, *The interwar economy in Ireland* (Dundalk, 1985), pp. 29–30; G. Fitzgerald, 'Mr Whitaker and industry', *Studies*, 48 (Summer, 1959), pp. 146–7; B. Girvin, 'Protectionism and economic development in independent Ireland 1922–1960' (PhD Thesis, University College, Cork, 1986), pp. 141–5; *Census of population*, 1936, 8 (Dublin, 1940), v–vi, p. 1; 9 (Dublin, 1942), pp. 28–30; *Census of population*, 1926, pp. 7, 8; *Census of industrial*

Though Fianna Fáil's economic policy helped increase employment outside agriculture, unemployment continued to remain a chronic problem. The Unemployment Assistance Act of 1933 provided unemployment benefits even for those uninsured against unemployment. For the first time many smallholders, unemployed in all but name, and unemployed agricultural labourers, enjoyed some relief. Other attempts were also made to extend a minimum of protection to the more vulnerable groups in society. The National Health Insurance Act of 1933 created a single insurance society on which all members could draw, irrespective of the size of their own contributions. This significantly improved, much to the chagrin of the more affluent societies, who tried to resist the change, the facilities available to the poorer members, who had previously been confined to the meagre resources of their own societies.[90] Pensions for widows and orphans were introduced by 1935. The Conditions of Employment Act of 1936 was designed to improve working conditions not least of juvenile labour.

Fianna Fáil's social and economic achievement between 1932 and 1936 was, in the circumstances, impressive. It halted, despite the partly self-inflicted wounds of the economic war, the slide into the economic abyss that appeared to threaten in 1931, and thus blunted the potential appeal of political extremism. In assessing the impact of policy in these years, it is necessary to keep in mind the probable alternative. McElligott was busy during 1931 devising a series of hair-shirt measures for the poor. Things must get worse before they got better. He had no solution to the slump beyond parroting the text-book truths of his youth ever more stridently. Cosgrave's government resisted most of these in the pre-election situation of 1931. It confined itself to introducing a supplementary budget increasing income tax by sixpence, and promising further austere measures.[91] McElligott indulged in prophecy, masquerading as fact, with the warning that 'if the budget is not balanced or even if a serious budget deficit is to be feared then the credit of the state will be seriously damaged and there will be a material set-back to trade and industry'.[92] He continued to denounce industrialisation as 'uneconomic' as late as 1937.[93] As McElligott offered no alternative that could have improved matters in the short run – whatever views may be held of the prospects of long-term economic redemption by continued adherence to the tenets of his economic faith – his prescription threatened to provoke

production, 1931 (Dublin, 1934), p. vii–viii; *Census of industrial production*, 1936 (Dublin, 1938), v–x; *Census of industrial production*, 1938 (Dublin, 1940), v–vii; *Irish Trade Journal*, 7 (September 1932), p. 101; 8 (December 1933), pp. 127–31; 9 (December 1934), pp. 170–5; 10 (March 1935), pp. 26–7; 12 (September 1937), pp. 145–7.
90 NLI, MS 927, CVO, 14 June 1940, q. 11, 412.   91 Fanning, *Finance*, p. 214.
92 *Ibid.*, p. 213.   93 *Ibid.*, p. 269.

bitter social unrest in the prevailing circumstances. It may be reasonably surmised that the change of government in 1932 significantly shifted the social distribution of sacrifice between 1932 and 1935.

Fianna Fáil brought to their 1932 election campaign a genuine commitment to social reform. Power soon subtly modified perspectives. In particular, as MacEntee began to be increasingly influenced by McElligott, he took a more charitable view of the status quo. The Fianna Fáil manifesto included a provision to investigate the civil service. MacEntee appointed a commission in June 1932 'to inquire into and report on the organisation of the Civil Service, with special reference to the arrangements for ensuring efficiency in working'.[94] The membership of the commission, however, suggests that MacEntee had already been nobbled, if that was necessary, by McElligott. The chairman was none other than Joseph Brennan, sometime Secretary of Finance, who was now invited to pronounce on his own earlier handiwork. His role guaranteed the satisfactory report, from McElligott's viewpoint, that duly emerged in 1935.

The report was, predictably, a highly conservative document. The lumping together in the terms of reference of 'efficiency in working' with wages, age of retirement, and the perennial problem of arbitration, ensured that serious substantive issues about the wider role of the civil service could be conveniently buried beneath the mountains of detail refuting specific complaints about working conditions. Brennan seized the opportunity to launch a vigorous attack, under the guise of a condemnation of the Congested Districts Board, abolished in 1923, on the whole idea of state sponsored bodies:

This board was engaged in administering an extensive public service in a semi-independent fashion . . . Instead of being financed by the ordinary machinery of votes and being subjected to the limitations which such a procedure would entail, the Board had funds allotted to it from special sources by statute and enjoyed a large discretion in the application of them. The Board appointed its own officers and it is important to observe that these officers were in general not civil servants. It will be seen that the arrangement as a whole was an uneasy compromise between the regular method of administration of the Civil Service under full ministerial responsibility and a method of independent control by a body not answerable to parliament.[95]

Brennan could perceive no excuse for the existence of either state sponsored bodies or for regional planning. Given his contempt for politicians, 'answerable to parliament' was naturally a euphemism for 'answerable to Finance'.

94 Commission of Inquiry into the Civil Service 1932–1935, *Interim and Final Report*, vol. 1 (Dublin, n.d., but final reports presented in November and December 1935), p. 3, para 1. On the report in general see T.J. Barrington, 'Public Administration, 1927–36', in MacManus, *Great test*, pp. 82–5.
95 Commission of Inquiry into the Civil Service 1932–1935, *Interim and Final Report*, vol. 1, p. 64, para. 14.

It was ironic that the one major note of dissent within the commission was sounded by a Labour figure, Luke Duffy, and that it was a representative of a political movement particularly concerned with wages and conditions who should have risen above the myopic vision of his colleagues to protest that

It is not the function of the Commission of Inquiry to ascertain merely whether the machine is an effective one in the civil service sense, but that on the contrary, it is the duty of somebody in this country to design for the state a form of organisation which harmonises with the traditions and responds to the aspirations of the Irish people. I entertained the hope that the present Commission which included clergymen, businessmen and educationalists would sketch the outlines of an organisation suitable to the needs of this country and regret that they should have based their conclusions on the existence of an organisation designed to serve other purposes.[96]

Duffy tried to conceive of the civil service as 'the spearhead of the nation's fight for political liberty and economic freedom. Upon its efficiency depended the success of the nation's efforts to organise its economic life in an orderly fashion.'[97] Sharply criticising the failure of the existing civil service to achieve this purpose, he thought it natural in the context that the commission should enquire into the relationship between the educational system and the civil service. He emphasised that

It is not realised sufficiently the extent to which the requirements of the civil service examinations mould the character of our educational system. There is no other country in which the character of the education demanded by the State services colours the school curriculum as with us. Injury is thereby inflicted on the service and no less on education. This defect is not new; it has persisted for many years but strangely enough the new order has riveted rather than relaxed it. As P.H. Pearse remarked in 1913, the specialists still 'grind' our young boys and girls for the Civil service . . . [98]

Duffy had a point. In the civil service entry examinations in 1931 and 1932, for example, there were fifteen applications for every vacant post as writing assistant (seventh standard, national school), nineteen applications for every clerical grade post (Intermediate Certificate level), fifteen applications for every junior executive post (Leaving Certificate level), and twenty-two applications for every post at junior administrative level (university degree).[99] Civil service entry requirements powerfully influenced the educational system at all levels, for better or for worse. McElligott remained unperturbed. He would later claim that the civil service 'attracts the best classes of students' from all levels of education, but then lamely conceded that whether the educational system produced the right kind of recruit for the civil service 'is a very big question. I am

[96] *Ibid.*, p. 205, para. 5.   [97] *Ibid.*, p. 203, para. 2.   [98] *Ibid.*, p. 210, para. 14.
[99] *Ibid.*, vol. 11, memo furnished by Department of Finance on the civil service, p. 17.

afraid I am not competent to answer it'.[100] One might wonder who was, if not the *de facto* head of the civil service!

The real point, however, is not whether Duffy's specific criticism of the commission's approach was justified in detail. It is rather that the banality of the commission's report cannot be explained on the grounds that it had no opportunity of proceeding along different lines. It was, it is true, an eloquent commentary on the absence of serious thought in the country at large about the role of the civil service that nobody outside the service responded to the invitation to present evidence.[101] It was highly unlikely, in the light of the short shrift it gave to Duffy's plea that it reconsider its assumptions, and in the light of the record of inquiries instituted by the Free State, that this commission would have responded enthusiastically to uncongenial outside views. But assessment of the government's record in the 1930s, and particularly of the performance of any minister trying to get something done, must make some allowance for the intellectual inertia of the surrounding society.

The commission's views on state-sponsored bodies had little effect on government policy. But the cabinet did not dissent from the general conclusion of the report that the civil service was functioning so satisfactorily that no serious changes need be contemplated. It was presumably conducive to the stability of the state that Fianna Fáil did not engage in a purge of civil servants in 1932. But continuity extended to structures as well as personnel. De Valera basically shared Cosgrave's 'British' view of the role and organisation of the civil service. The 'administrative reform' that Fianna Fáil promised before coming into office only envisaged reduced expenditure, not revised roles.

Quite significant changes in personnel did occur in the 1932–7 period. Gordon Campbell succeeded his brother as Lord Glenavy in 1931 and John Leydon's appointment as Secretary to an Industry and Commerce notorious for strained personal relations and for poor morale had a rapid impact.[102] F.J. Meyrick, Secretary for Agriculture since 1922, had been seeking early retirement from 1931, and left as soon as he reached the age of sixty in 1934.[103] His successor, Daniel Twomey, was less unsympathetic to Fianna Fáil policy. Two of the three main economic departments thus changed Secretaries in the early years of Fianna Fáil. In combination with their Ministers, Lemass and Ryan, the new Secretaries helped to restrict, if by no means eliminate, the influence of Finance. At the Department of Local Government, poor personal relations between Seán T. O'Kelly, the Minister, and E.T. McCarron, the Secretary, led to the

100 NLI, MS 928, CVO, 12 September 1940, ev. J.J. McElligott, q. 13573.
101 Commission of Inquiry into the Civil Service, *Interim and Final Report*, vol. 1.
102 'Seán Lemass looks back', *Irish Press*, 24 January 1969; Roche, 'John Leydon', p. 235.
103 RM, P7/C/88, 13 June 1931; D. Hoctor, *The Department's story, a history of the Department of Agriculture* (Dublin, 1971), p. 172.

latter's dismissal in 1935 in circumstances whose clarification might cast further light on the nature of the prevailing political culture.

The secretaryship of the president's own department was a more obviously political choice than was the case in most other departments. Seán Moynihan, who belonged to an anti-Treaty Tralee family, replaced Diarmuid O'Hegarty on de Valera's accession. When Moynihan became Assistant Secretary in Finance in 1937, as Establishment Officer, he was succeeded as Secretary by his brother Maurice, already serving since 1932 as Private Secretary to de Valera. Maurice Moynihan, who would remain Secretary of the Department of the Taoiseach until 1960, came closer than anyone to understanding the mind of de Valera, with whom he established an extraordinary rapport, based on deep mutual respect and affection. Moynihan shared the technical ability of his contemporaries as a drafter of lucid and incisive memoranda. That alone would not, however, have qualified him to become Secretary of the most politically sensitive of departments. It was his devotion to de Valera, a devotion which never lost its utility by descending to obsequiousness, his integrity, his unswerving dedication to the public interest, his balanced and humane judgement, his total discretion, and his modesty, that must have commended him to de Valera and that indubitably entitled him to be considered a truly great public servant.[104] But Moynihan, for all his outstanding qualities, was too much a product, like Leydon, of the thought processes of the Finance of the twenties, which he had entered as one of a remarkable band of administrative officers in 1925, to conceive of alternative administrative structures, as distinct from alternative policies within existing structures. And it is certainly arguable that in the prevailing political circumstances, no alternative structure would have served the state as well as the inherited one.

The increasingly conservative reality behind the still radical rhetoric gradually became clearer. The Banking Commission, appointed by MacEntee in November 1934, reported in 1938 in favour of the status quo ante. The majority report in effect reaffirmed the correctness of Cosgrave's economic and social policy. It criticised the increase in the national debt, demanded a policy of debt redemption that would have required the abandonment of the housing programme, and found that the commercial banking system adequately served the needs of the country. A report along these lines was wholly predictable given the composition of the commission. Joseph Brennan once again acted as chairman. The members included McElligott and several safe bank directors, three economics professors, at least two of whom, George Duncan of Trinity College Dublin, and George O'Brien, were safe. Two foreign authorities, Professor T.S. Gregory of the London School of Economics, and Per

[104] Moynihan's career details from his interview on RTE, 3 August 1982.

Jacobsson, of the Bank of International Settlements, were distinguished traditionalists, who served to lend a spurious veneer of international impartiality to the work of the commission.[105] Jacobsson's diary casts instructive light on the proceedings, even if 'part of the charm the Irish had for Per Jacobsson was that he never really understood them'.[106] Sound though Jacobsson was, he was only McElligott's second choice behind the venerable and even more conservative Gustav Cassel.[107] No wonder the composition of the commission satisfied the Currency Commission.[108]

In the event, the report had only a muted impact. It was presented in the spring of 1938, but not published until August, after a general election which returned Fianna Fáil with a clear majority. De Valera must have infuriated McElligott, who had sought to discredit the third minority report, submitted by P.J. O'Loghlen, by smearing it as 'Labour' policy,[109] when he declared that 'as far as our social aims are concerned, we are at one with the Labour party', and even went on to picking out 'the social objectives' of the third minority report for particular praise.[110] By this stage, however, de Valera's radicalism consisted of little more than resisting reaction.

MacEntee's conservatism extended to social as well as financial and administrative affairs. His budget statement in 1936 that 'within a short period there have been provided in this little State social services adopted to our political needs, which for liberality, comprehensiveness and practical utility are not surpassed by any in Europe' displayed an impressive range of comparative innocence. His argument that 'they have been built up on a sound foundation of private enterprise and individual thrift – sources which for thousands of years have furnished our material progress',[111] displayed a correspondingly encyclopaedic innocence of Irish economic history. It was precisely the absence of 'a sound foundation of private enterprise' that had left Ireland in that state of 'material progress' which required the Fianna Fáil industrialisation drive. MacEntee insisted that a sound budget must be the base for all social reform.

105 For Gregory's ultra-conservative position see D. Winch, *Economics and polities* (London, 1972), p. 159. Jacobsson was to enjoy an influential career in international finance as an able advocate of sound money. Many of his warnings were sorely needed in the changed circumstances of the postwar world.

106 E.E. Jacobsson, *A life for sound money: Per Jacobsson's biography* (Oxford, 1979), p. 131. Under the name E.E. Jucker-Fleetwood, Jacobsson's daughter contributed a longer account, 'The Irish Banking Commission 1934–1938, as seen by Per Jacobsson', *Central Bank of Ireland Quarterly Bulletin* (Winter 1972), pp. 69–89.

107 Fanning, *Finance*, pp. 373–4 contains a list of 'outside experts' considered as possible members of the Banking Commission. Except for Keynes, they were all safe.

108 M. Moynihan, *Currency and central banking in Ireland 1922–1960* (Dublin, 1975), pp. 180–1. Moynihan contains discreet biographical sketches of the members, Appendix III, pp. 500–2.

109 Fanning, *Finance*, p. 363.

110 Moynihan, *Speeches*, p. 405.

111 DD, 62, 12 May 1936, 30–1.

'There has been no recourse to inflation and no tampering with the currency. We have not resorted to the nostrums and panaceas which are held out so often as easy ways to encompass a most difficult thing: the provision of a frugal sufficiency for everyone's need.'[112] The 22 000 emigrants who left that year were not included in 'everyone'! MacEntee possibly believed his own rhetoric. But the presentation may have also contained an element of electioneering. And electioneering was becoming necessary again, for signs had begun to multiply that the electorate, after the euphoria of 1932 and 1933, was growing disenchanted with 'frugal sufficiency'. Despite the objective achievement of Fianna Fáil policy between 1932 and 1936, it involved losses as well as gains, and failed to fulfil the expectations roused in 1932. As late as August 1933 de Valera committed himself reasonably cheerfully to the oft-quoted view that 'so far as I can see the British market is gone forever'. His economic sight would soon improve. He described the coal–cattle pact of January 1935, which increased the British quota on cattle imports from Ireland by one-third, in return for a comparable increase in Irish coal imports from Britain, and which would be renewed annually until superseded by the Anglo-Irish Trade Agreement of 1938, as 'a business transaction based on the mutual interests of the two countries'.[113] The Irish made the first move, with J.W. Dulanty, Irish High Commissioner in London, playing a key role.[114] The British proved receptive, thanks partly to the fear that Irish furnaces might be converted to German coal, which could deprive the depressed British coal industry of Irish markets.[115] The pact marked a recognition by de Valera that historical illusion must sometimes succumb to economic reality. Nevertheless, 1935 was to be a bad year for the economy. Agriculture remained depressed, despite the maze of subsidies. Unemployment rose to nearly 100 000, where it would hover for the rest of the decade. It became clear that in the next election, probably in 1937, Fianna Fáil could not rely for victory on its socio-economic achievements. The platform needed another strong plank.

THE 1937 CONSTITUTION

De Valera was pondering the potential of a new constitution as early as 1935.[116] Like Cosgrave before him, but with different motives, he kept

---

[112] *Ibid.*, 39. [113] Manning, *Blueshirts*, p. 182.
[114] D.S. Johnson, 'Northern Ireland as a problem in the economic war 1932–38', *IHS*, 22, 86 (September 1980), pp. 145–6; McMahon, *Republicans*, p. 150.
[115] Johnson, 'Northern Ireland', pp. 145–6; McMahon, *Republicans*, p. 151; D.W. Harkness, 'England's Irish question', in G. Peele and C. Cook (eds.), *The politics of reappraisal 1918–39* (London, 1975), p. 55.
[116] Longford and O'Neill, *De Valera*, p. 290, record that he instructed the legal adviser to the Department for External Affairs to begin drafting the heads of a new constitution in April and May 1935.

chipping away piecemeal at the existing constitution.[117] His ambition to replace it with his own was a natural one in the circumstances. It is not clear when the happy thought struck him of holding the referendum on the new constitution on the same day as the next general election. He appears to have chosen his election date, 1 July, early in March 1937. The cabinet authorised on 9 March the introduction of the draft constitution to the Dáil 'with a view to the second reading being taken when the final text would be available'.[118] Such unseemly haste was presumably not unrelated to the decision that the referendum would be held 'at the same time and in the same manner as the forthcoming general election'.[119]

Much remains to be uncovered about the planning and the drafting of the constitution, including not least the roles of John Hearne, the legal adviser to External Affairs, and of Maurice Moynihan.[120] The cabinet minutes in early 1937 are nothing if not discreet, even by their normal standards of reticence. Any verdict on the genesis, content, or consequences of the constitution must be even more provisional and subjective than normal historical judgements.[121]

Articles 2 and 3 claimed the constitutional right of the Dublin government to exercise jurisdiction over the whole of Ireland, though confining the exercise in practice to the twenty-six counties, 'pending the reintegration of the national territory'. But the constitution did not, curiously, then proceed to declare Ireland a republic, allegedly in deference to Ulster sensitivities.[122] Immediately on Edward VII's abdication in December 1936, de Valera had seized the opportunity offered by the domestic difficulties of the royal family to eliminate reference to the king and the governor general from the Free State constitution.[123] The king was retained in the new constitution, indirectly and anonymously, only insofar as

for the purpose of the exercise of any executive function of the State or in connection with its external relations, the Government may to such extent and subject to such conditions, if any, as may be determined by law, avail of or adopt any organ, instrument, or method of procedure used or adopted for the like purpose by the members of any group or league of Nations with which the State is or becomes associated for the purpose of international cooperation in matters of common concern.[124]

---

117 For a succinct survey of how the 1922 Constitution 'proved to be completely at the mercy of the legislature', see J.M. Kelly, *Fundamental rights in the Irish law and constitution* (Dublin, 1967, 2nd edn), pp. 2–7.
118 SPO, CAB 7/398, 9 March 1937.   119 SPO, CAB, 7/399, 12 March 1937.
120 Keogh, *Vatican*, pp. 207–20, marks a breakthrough on the religious clauses. Hearne is mentioned in Longford and O'Neill, *De Valera*, p. 290.
121 See, nevertheless, the arresting analysis in Murphy, *Ireland*, pp. 88–92.
122 Lyons, *Ireland*, pp. 534–5.
123 Longford and O'Neill, *De Valera*, p. 293.
124 *Bunreacht na hÉireann*, Article 29.2.

De Valera's declared solicitude for Ulster sentiment on the issue of the Republic seems curious in view of the fact that the constitution contained numerous clauses bound to be repugnant to any self-respecting Protestant. If de Valera's avowed aim 'was to produce a constitution which would not require any fundamental change when the unity of Ireland was accomplished',[125] then he had a strange sense either of Protestant principles or of 'fundamental change'. Article 44, which would be expunged in 1972, roused much resentment for recognising the 'special position' of the Catholic Church 'as the guardian of the Faith professed by the great majority of the citizens'. But the resentment was more retrospective than contemporary. The Article also took care to recognise the other churches existing in Ireland at the time, including explicitly 'the Jewish congregations', a gesture not without dignity in the Europe of 1937. De Valera's text constituted an ingenious squaring of the formal circle, circumventing Catholic clericalist demands for more triumphalist recognition, and residual republican resistance to any recognition at all, while satisfying the other churches.[126] It was an astute and not ignoble formulation of the principle of religious liberty in a predominantly Catholic country.

Non-Catholics could find much more substantive cause for concern in other features. Article 41 forbade divorce or the remarriage of persons divorced elsewhere. The divorce provisions would not in practice have affected many people, North or South, at that time. But non-Catholics could feel that in principle they restricted liberty of conscience. When considered in conjunction with section 17 of the Criminal Law Amendment Act 1935, which prohibited the importation and the sale of contraceptives,[127] it was difficult to avoid the impression that the state considered it a duty to impose specifically Catholic doctrine on all citizens, irrespective of their personal convictions. Critics might be excused for dismissing as hypocrisy, in these circumstances, the apparently comprehensive guarantee in Article 44.3 that 'the state shall not impose any disabilities or make any discrimination on the ground of religious profession, belief or status'.

Other provisions could also be construed as potentially sectarian, however innocent the intent behind them. Article 40 forbade 'the publication or utterance of blasphemous, seditious or indecent matter', all of which would, in practice, be defined, if they were defined at all, by primarily Catholic courts.[128] The same article conferred freedom of speech and freedom of assembly, except where these might be used 'to

---

125 Longford and O'Neill, *De Valera*, p. 296; J. Bowman, *De Valera and the Ulster question 1917–73* (Oxford, 1982), pp. 151, 153.
126 Longford and O'Neill, *De Valera*, p. 297; Keogh, *Vatican*, pp. 213, 217, 220.
127 Whyte, *Church and state*, p. 49.
128 Kelly, *Fundamental rights*, pp. 131–2, notes a singular dearth of issues of this sort in Irish courts. But that is within an almost homogeneous Southern society.

undermine public order or morality' or 'to cause a breach of the peace or to be a danger or nuisance to the general public'. Might not these powers be conveniently invoked against Protestant preaching or Protestant parades?

Article 8 specified that provision could be made 'for the exclusive use' of either Irish or English 'for any one or more official purposes, either throughout the State or in any part thereof'. This was presumably intended to reassure anxious Northerners (the cynic might add, no less than anxious Southerners!) that they would not be compulsorily gaeli-cised. It is doubtful, however, if this clause did much to reassure Protestants alarmed at the manner in which 'compulsory Irish' require-ments for entry to the public service militated against their prospects. They could read accounts, in the very month of the referendum, of the Galway Harbour Commissioners deliberately discriminating against a Trinity College graduate, and in favour of a National University of Ireland graduate, when appointing a resident engineer, on the grounds that the NUI man could both read and write Irish, while the Trinity man could only read it![129] The responsibilities of the post had little requirement for either qualification. The practice of some Irish nationalists clearly bore only tenuous relationship to the principles of the Proclamation of the Republic!

Many of these possible difficulties might have been circumvented by the application of Article 15, which permitted the 'creation or recognition of subordinate legislatures'. The constitution thus made provision for the possible 'recognition' of Stormont in the event of unification. De Valera genuinely felt that in a united Ireland the North should keep its own parliament 'in which it would continue to look after its own affairs'.[130] There was here an echo of John Redmond's idea of home rule within home rule. But the proposal raised even more difficulties in the context of the constitution of 1937 than in Redmond's day. Redmond envisaged a non-sectarian constitution for Ireland. There would be no clauses inimical to the religious or cultural convictions of non-Catholics. Would a 'subordinate legislature' at Stormont have to implement the 1937 consti-tution? How could the Stormont majority in that case be expected to feel loyalty to a constitution containing not only unacceptable clauses, but introduced by the preamble 'We, the people of Éire, humbly acknowledg-ing all our obligations to our Divine Lord, Jesus Christ, Who sustained our fathers through centuries of trial'? Would this not instantly beg the question, as Professor Whyte has asked, 'Whose fathers?'[131] 'Our fathers' who sustained their trials at Derry, Enniskillen, Aughrim and the Boyne?

129 *Irish Press*, 10 June 1937.
130 PRO, CAB, 24/271, CP 228/37, memo by Malcolm MacDonald, 6 October 1937.
131 Whyte, *Church and state*, p. 48.

Was this the same God that Protestant people celebrated as 'Our help in ages past'? 'Gratefully remembering their heroic and unremitting struggle to regain the rightful independence of our nation' immediately eliminated the vast majority of the Protestant people as an integral part of 'our nation'. If there was only one Irish people, must the Protestant people jettison their heritage and deny their own fathers before they could become truly part of 'the people of Éire'?

The very structure of the constitution betrays the difficulties of the de Valera dialectic on the crucial question of identity. Articles 1–3 deal with 'The Nation'. Articles 4–11 deal with 'The State'. But de Valera makes no attempt to define 'the Nation'. The definition contained in Article 2 is not of the nation, only of the national territory. That so scholastic a thinker, so punctilious a draftsman, as de Valera, who would consult a dictionary to define 'republic', should avoid the fundamental issue of definition, in a constitution laden with definitions, suggests that even he could find no definition that could not be turned by the Protestant people into a definition of their own 'nation'.

The distinction drawn between nation and state in the constitution was, at least potentially, no mere semantic quibble. Article 9 claimed that 'fidelity to the Nation and loyalty to the State are fundamental political duties of all citizens'. Mere loyalty to the state, if Ulster Protestants ever entered the state, would not apparently fulfil their constitutional obligation. They would also have to acknowledge 'fidelity' to an apparently undefinable 'nation', few of whose distinguishing characteristics, however elusive, they shared. This potentially sinister clause gave any self-appointed group – including, ironically, within their own terms of reference, Ulster Protestants – a right to deny the legitimacy of majority decisions. If it has not hitherto attracted much attention, some of the lethal implications lurking in its phraseology have already been identified by a former cabinet minister, when he claimed that in the event of the Irish people repealing Articles 2 and 3 of the Constitution, citizens would then have to choose between 'fidelity to the nation' and 'loyalty to the state'.[132]

The constitution, which read straightforwardly enough to citizens of the Free State, contained several clauses of highly ambiguous portent, when applied to the 'national territory' as defined in Articles 2 and 3. But the electorate to which de Valera would submit the constitution was not, of course, the electorate of the 'national territory'. 'We are going back to the sovereign authority, to the Irish people, or that section of the Irish people whom we can consult on the matter.'[133] The qualification was

---

132 See letter by C. Ó Beoláin (Kevin Boland), *Irish Times*, 30 October 1981. Although Boland had severed his connections with the party, he belonged, as Gerry Boland's son, to a distinguished Fianna Fáil family.
133 Longford and O'Neill, *De Valera*, p. 299.

crucial. It did not wholly escape contemporaries. Eamon Donnelly, a Fianna Fáil TD, an Ulsterman himself, moved a Dáil amendment that the constitution be deferred until partition was solved 'so that, if and when a solution of the problem is found, Bunreacht na hÉireann can be submitted to the whole people of Ireland for ratification or otherwise'. Donnelly's contributions might not be universally regarded as having elevated the average level of Dáil discourse. But his amendment contained a shrewd comment on the legitimacy of a constitution which claimed jurisdiction over the whole of Ireland, but was not submitted 'to the whole people of Ireland'. Nor was there any provision for re-submission to 'the whole people' in the event of unification. Who then was to decide that it 'would not require any fundamental change when the unity of Ireland was accomplished'? The pragmatist would no doubt respond that these were matters of distant detail (though for platform purposes unification was always just around the corner!), to be regulated in due course according to changing circumstances. Others might feel that a constitution was meant to be a solemn statement of political principle, not a mere exercise in electoral expediency.

The composition of the electorate inevitably left its mark on de Valera's thinking about the constitutionally possible, as distinct from desirable. An appeal aimed at a 93 per cent Catholic electorate could afford to, indeed could not afford not to, adopt a different emphasis from one aimed at the people of the whole island. Republican rhetoric had to be reconciled with Catholic reality. Hence the otherwise puzzling incongruity of the platform claims of intelligent and not insincere men. De Valera declared himself convinced that his constitution would simultaneously allow Ireland to give a lead to the world 'as a Catholic nation' and yet form 'a secure basis' for unification.[134] Seán T. O'Kelly could likewise display an enviable command of the dialectic in claiming that 'the constitution was worthy of a Catholic nation and brought nearer the promised land of a united republic'.[135]

The social clauses of the constitution blended prevailing Catholic concepts with popular attitudes rooted in the social structure. De Valera devoted particular attention to the role of the Irish woman. Article 41 emphasised her place 'within the home'. De Valera was clear that this was the only proper place for her. He rejected an amendment substituting woman's work 'for the home', for the phrase 'life within the home' as worthy of constitutional solicitude.[136] The injunction that 'the State shall . . . endeavour to ensure that mothers shall not be obliged by economic necessity to engage in labour to the neglect of their duties in the home' was

[134] Longford and O'Neill, *De Valera*, pp. 298, 300.
[135] *Irish Press*, 24 June 1937. I owe this reference to Kathleen Doyle.
[136] DD, 67/8, 9 June 1937, 221–2.

to be honoured more in the breach than in the observance. Some Catholic writers emphasised that the most Christian deterrent against mother and child labour was a decent wage for husbands.[137] Needless to say, male wages were not raised to relieve mothers of poor families from the necessity of eking out their husbands' miserable pittances. The illusion fostered by the constitution that Irish society placed special value on motherhood diverted attention from the fact that social values prevented a higher proportion of women from becoming mothers than in any other European country. The marriage rate was 40 per cent higher even in excoriated Northern Ireland at the time, low though the Northern Irish rate remained compared to the European average.[138]

De Valera clung to an ideal-type image of the Irish family as a loving haven of selfless accord. It was as if he were subconsciously striving to obliterate the memory of his own childhood. He had lost his father when he was a baby, and his mother had sent him back to her family in Ireland while she went out to work in New York. However happily he was reared by his relatives, he would hardly have been human had the experience not left its mark throughout his life. He appears to have made strangely little allowance for his mother's plight, and for that of thousands like her. It was as if the constitution tried to blot out the memory of the experience by denying that it could really happen. He made little attempt to ensure that women who found themselves in his mother's position would enjoy a decent chance of rearing their own children in any sort of comfort, even his habitual 'frugal comfort'. The ideal of the family projected in the constitution ignored the realism, however reluctant, with which Irish parents sacrificed their children to the emigrant ship.

De Valera's image of woman was widely cherished in Ireland, not least by women themselves. Helena Moloney, a doughty defender of women's 'rights', would claim that 'We all believe that woman's place is in the home provided she has a home.'[139] However, a few educated women did repudiate the kitchen sink role allotted them in the constitution. Criticism by the National University Women Graduates' Association disturbed de Valera and the *Irish Press* sufficiently for them to devote considerable space to refuting it. The *Press* sneered at the 'learned ladies whose zeal in the national cause had in many cases been conspicuous by its absence'. This attempt to suffocate the women in the Green Flag had to be quickly abandoned in the face of Kathleen Lynn's indignant response, listing ladies of impeccable republican credentials who now rejected their confinement to the kitchen. The *Press* thought discretion the better part of

---

[137] C. Lucey, 'The problem of the woman worker', *Irish Ecclesiastical Record*, 48 (1936), pp. 449–67; *The Standard*, 14 May 1937. I owe these references to Patricia McCaffrey.
[138] Mitchell, *European historical statistics*, p. 117.
[139] NLI, MS 925, CVO, 19 April 1940, ev. H. Moloney, q. 8327.

polemical valour in evading the charge that the constitution denied women the equal rights and equal opportunities guaranteed to all citizens by the Proclamation of the Republic.[140]

There seems to have been more popular sympathy, including female sympathy, for de Valera's view than for that of the women graduates. However, he won less support for another social principle 'that in what pertains to the control of credit the constant and predominant aim shall be the welfare of the people as a whole'. Article 45, 'Directive principles of social policy', was carefully contrived to appeal to instinct without damaging interests. Having enunciated radical sentiments about the primacy of the public good over private gain, it then explicitly declared that 'the application of those principles . . . shall not be cognisable by any Court under any of the provisions of this Constitution'. The practical import of the piece of mummified flatulence concerning the control of credit in the interest of 'the welfare of the people as a whole' can be deduced from Lord Glenavy's cryptic comment on behalf of the banks three years later: 'it is not a document I am very familiar with.'[141]

Apart from the concern expressed by the women graduates, controversy concentrated on the clauses relating to the presidency. Fine Gael feared that de Valera aspired after a presidential dictatorship. But the role of the president was confined mainly to ceremonial affairs, though he acquired some residual authority that might prove important in constitutional crises. The president's potential authority depended partly on the interpretation of the constitution by the judiciary whose role was greatly, if perhaps not fully intentionally, enhanced. The constitution gave the judiciary authority potentially comparable to that of American rather than British courts. Once judges became alert to this potential 'they began to take more seriously their role as the final interpreters of the constitution and defenders of the citizen's constitutional rights'.[142] Citizens would also become more alert to the potential of the constitution in cases of civil rights. The number of decisions reported on constitutional law cases increased from ten between 1918 and 1938 to thirty-one between 1939 and 1958, and then to forty-four between 1959 and 1970.[143]

The constitution, for all the reservations that may be expressed from various viewpoints about particular clauses, and despite internal logical

---

[140] The exchanges can be followed in the *Irish Press*, 22, 25, 26, 28 June and 1 July 1937. See also Mary Hayden's charges concerning discrimination against women in Irish society, *Cork Examiner*, 29 June 1937.

[141] NLI, MS 926, CVO, 3 May 1940, ev. Lord Glenavy, q. 9033.

[142] D. Barrington, 'The Council of Ireland and the constitutional context', *Administration*, 20, 4 (1972), p. 40.

[143] See B.M.E. McMahon, 'Developments in the Irish legal system since 1945', in J.J. Lee (ed.), *Ireland 1945–70* (Dublin, 1979), pp. 83–95.

contradictions,[144] was a remarkable document. Its importance lay not only in what it changed, but in what it retained, from the constitution of 1922, and indeed from British constitutional practice.[145] In procedural terms, it tidied up the increasingly confused constitutional situation arising from Cosgrave's and de Valera's piecemeal revisions. It was, not least, a significant achievement in a party political sense. The 'slightly constitutional' party of a decade before now closed ranks behind its very own constitution. De Valera's constitution broadly codified the subjective transition to parliamentary democracy made by Fianna Fáil during the intervening period.[146]

Fianna Fáil fought a frenetic electoral campaign in 1937. It mounted once again an elaborate demonstration at Bodenstown, where Seán MacEntee assured the mourners that 'from Tone . . . we have inherited a precious testament, a philosophy and code of practical statecraft, which we have but to apply in order inevitably to triumph'.[147] Fianna Fáil certainly gave an impressive display of 'practical statecraft' in the campaign. Seán T. O'Kelly had already piloted the first revision of the constituency boundaries through the Dáil in 1935. Article 26 of the Free State constitution specified that the Oireachtas should periodically revise the constituencies 'with due regard to changes in distribution of the population'. There is an engaging *naïveté* about the early memoranda of the Department of Local Government, strenuously trying to operate this provision as a matter of administrative routine.[148] By 1930, however, a hint of political realism had begun to break in, with Fianna Fáil now breathing down Cumann na nGaedheal's neck. The executive council postponed the final decision on revising constituencies 'pending further examination of the relevant figures' before finally deciding to let matters lie.[149]

Fianna Fáil were no sooner in office than the cabinet asked the Minister for Local Government to examine the matter. With perhaps a lingering hint of the *naïveté* of the administrative approach to the subject, Seán Moynihan penned an appropriate few lines which ended with the hope that 'this note will serve to prevent the matter being overlooked'[150] – as if

---

[144] D.M. Clarke, 'Emergency legislation, fundamental rights and Article 28.3.3 of the Irish Constitution', *The Irish Jurist* (1977), pp. 217–35, and 'The concept of the common good in Irish constitutional law', *Northern Ireland Legal Quarterly*, 30, 4 (Winter 1979), 319–42.

[145] J.F. O'Connor, 'Article 50 of Bunreacht na hÉireann and the unwritten English constitution of Ireland', in O'Carroll and Murphy (eds.), *De Valera and his times*, pp. 173–81.

[146] A. Fitzgerald, 'Eamon de Valera', *Studies*, 64 (Autumn 1975), p. 210.

[147] *Irish Press*, 14 June 1937.

[148] SPO, S1817A, memoranda dated 13 October 1922 and 7 October 1926.

[149] *Ibid.*, S. Moynihan to Private Secretary, Minister for Local Government, 1 August 1930; cabinet special meeting, 21 January 1931.

[150] SPO, S1817B, CAB 6/28, 20–21 May 1932; S. Moynihan to Private Secretary, Minister for Local Government, 24 May 1932.

there was any danger that a Fianna Fáil Minister for Local Government would 'overlook' such a 'matter'. After the 1933 election a cabinet committee, consisting of de Valera, O'Kelly, Lemass and Ryan, pored over the possibilities.[151] Their perusal lasted a year until the cabinet approved the proposed redistribution of seats.[152]

The committee performed the operation with surgical skill. The revision reduced the number of seats from 153 to 138, abolishing *inter alia* the six university seats, four of them tactlessly held by Fine Gael. In 1933 Fianna Fáil won only two more seats than entitled to on strict proportionality, whereas Cumann na nGaedheal won three. In 1937, Fine Gael won no 'extra' seat, but Fianna Fáil won six. In 1938 Fine Gael gained one seat less than their exact proportionate share. In 1943 they gained their exact share. In 1944 they won two seats more than their share. Fianna Fáil won four seats more in 1938, nine more in 1943 and seven more in 1944.[153] The deliberations of the cabinet committee of 1933 contributed powerfully to the electoral stability of the following decade! Even with this boost, Fianna Fáil still suffered a sharp setback in 1937. Its popular vote fell from 689 000 to 599 000, the first decline in five elections. Its share of the vote fell from 49.7 per cent to 45.3 per cent. It lost its absolute majority in the Dáil, winning just half of the 138 seats. Turn-out, useful indicator of enthusiasm, fell from 81.3 per cent (in a January election) to 76.2 per cent (in a July poll).[154] The fall in the west was particularly sharp, from 79.8 per cent to 70.9 per cent. Independents increased their vote in agricultural constituencies from 2 per cent to 10 per cent, mainly at the expense of Fianna Fáil,[155] while Labour's share of the vote rose from 5.7 per cent in 1933 to 10.3 per cent in 1937, its first increase in four elections.

Fianna Fáil suffered this reverse despite holding the election on the same day as the referendum on the constitution. De Valera could reasonably have hoped that the constitution, appealing so strongly to the Catholic vote, might increase Fianna Fáil support. The party presumably did gain something from the referendum spin-off. But the plebiscite vote appears to have been heavily influenced by party political loyalties. The constitution was approved by 685 000 voters, and rejected by 527 000. The bulk of Labour voters probably did support the constitution, but the combined Fianna Fáil and Labour vote exceeded the 'yes' vote by 50 000. Insofar as one can judge from the constituency returns, it seems that the

151 SPO, CAB 6/113, 31 January 1933.   152 SPO, CAB, 7/101, 5 January 1934.
153 C. O'Leary, *Irish elections 1918–1977* (Dublin, 1979), pp. 102–3.
154 As with all other electoral statistics, unless otherwise stated, these figures are taken from Chubb, *Government and politics*, p. 332.
155 M. Gallagher, *Electoral support for Irish political parties 1927–1973* (London, 1976), p. 22.

overwhelming majority of Protestants voted heavily against the constitution.[156]

De Valera explained the disappointing response of the people of God to God's constitution – only 56 per cent responded to the will of God – with the charming contention that 'a written constitution, to be completely understood, required to be explained to the people over a long period. They were pressed for time, as the general election was due.'[157] The only reason the general election was due, of course, was because de Valera chose it to be due. He need not have gone to the country for another six months. Nor need he have linked the referendum with the election.

TRIUMPH

Fianna Fáil once more formed a government. But it had to rely on Labour support. The election result made it too dangerous to risk turning the choice of the first President under the constitution into a party political contest. Dr Douglas Hyde emerged as a suitable 'non-party' candidate. An Irish language enthusiast, a former president of the Gaelic League, a professor and a Protestant, he satisfied sundry national self-images and, at the age of seventy-seven, seemed unlikely to be unduly assertive.

In the sobering aftermath of the 1937 election, de Valera discerned distinct merit in the viewpoint that Britain and Ireland shared certain economic interests. The coal–cattle pacts already hinted at his willingness to make ideological concessions in return for economic advantage. He now sought *rapprochement* more urgently. The timing was propitious on several counts. Changing circumstances in Ireland, Britain and Europe reinforced the case for conciliation on the British as well as on the Irish side.[158]

---

[156] Even the *Irish Press* (7 July 1937) conceded that the exceptional proportion of spoiled votes, nearly 10 per cent, or 117 000 out of a total poll of 1 240 000, largely reflected hostility to the Constitution. See also PA, Hempel-AA, England–Irland, 1 (A 183), 20 December 1937.

[157] Moynihan, *Speeches*, p. 333.

[158] Recent work has clarified the course of Anglo-Irish relations between the civil war and the Second World War, not least the circumstances surrounding the Anglo-Irish Agreement of 1938. Differences of emphasis among the specialists about the motives and the achievements of de Valera serve as a reminder of the extent to which historians must still, even after sifting the documents, form their verdicts on his performance on the basis of their overall assessment of the way his mind worked. The present text takes particular cognisance of the following accounts: Longford and O'Neill, *De Valera*, pp. 311–26; Fanning, *Finance*, pp. 296–307; Bowman, *De Valera*, *passim*; D.W. Harkness, 'Mr de Valera's dominion. Irish relations with Britain and the Commonwealth 1932–1938', *Journal of Commonwealth Political Studies* 8, 3 (1970), pp. 206–8; Harkness, 'England's Irish question', pp. 39–63; Ged Martin, 'The Irish Free State and the evolution of the Commonwealth, 1921–49', in R. Hyam and G. Martin (eds.), *Reappraisals in British imperial history* (London, 1975), pp. 201–24; D. McMahon, '"A transient apparition": British policy towards the de Valera government,

De Valera was frightened by the imminence of European war, with the danger of Ireland becoming embroiled as long as Britain held the Treaty ports of Berehaven, Cobh and Lough Swilly. The internal political implications of Britain exercising her legal rights under the Treaty were disturbing. With the constitution safely rewritten, negotiations could not now be threatened by the British obsession with the symbolism of the Crown. De Valera perceived the economic situation to be deteriorating.[159] He might not be able to rely on Labour support in the event of his failing to resist McElligott's remorseless pressure for retrenchment.

Finance was mounting a vigorous assault on housing policy on the grounds that 'there is no parallel in any other country to the assistance afforded by the government of the *Saorstát* in the matter of housing. The Department of Finance strongly maintains that the time has arrived when the burden on the Exchequer should be eased . . . '[160] De Valera would not wish to have to go to the country again in those circumstances.

On the British side, Neville Chamberlain was also consumed with anxiety about the danger of imminent conflict. He was determined to secure a friendly Ireland at his back. The Dominions Secretary, Malcolm MacDonald, who succeeded J.H. Thomas in late 1935, was anxious for an Irish settlement on grounds of general equity. De Valera established excellent personal relations with both, despite the occasional exasperation he caused Chamberlain. Indeed, the two prime ministers had much in common, with their headmasterish temperaments, their genuine search for justice in international relations, their conscious sense of integrity, and their intimations of personal infallibility. De Valera would always remember Chamberlain with a respect verging on affection, hoping that he would 'find the honoured place in British history which is due to him, as certainly he will find it in any fair record of the relations between Britain and ourselves'.[161]

De Valera's bargaining stance in his exploratory discussions with MacDonald in autumn 1937 raises intriguing issues. The question remains to what extent MacDonald may have been 'psyched' by de Valera at this stage. MacDonald was young, eager, impressionable. De Valera was not. He probably exaggerated his undoubted difficulties at home to extract greater concessions from the English. Nevertheless, many of MacDonald's reports of de Valera's views are internally consistent both

1932–5', *IHS*, 22, 88 (September 1981), pp. 331–61; McMahon, *Republicans*; P. Canning, *British policy towards Ireland 1921–1941* (Oxford, 1985), pp. 176–220; R.J. Raymond, 'The Anglo-Irish talks 1938: a reappraisal' (paper presented at the Duquesne History Forum, Pittsburgh, 14 October 1981. I am grateful to Dr Raymond for providing me with a copy of his paper).

159 PRO, CAB 24, 271, CP 236 (37), Malcolm MacDonald, memo, 12 October 1937.
160 SPO, S10341, Finance memo, 11 November 1937.
161 Moynihan, *Speeches*, p. 475. De Valera made this point in his reply to Churchill in 1945, when it was distinctly unfashionable.

with each other and with what we know, or can reasonably surmise, about the cast of de Valera's mind. MacDonald concluded that 'I am convinced that he is really genuine in desiring wholehearted friendship and cooperation between the Irish Free State and Great Britain, but would rather like to get that friendship on his own terms.'[162] When MacDonald reported to the cabinet that de Valera 'often spoke of his political difficulties; I hoped that, *as a realist* [my emphasis] he would recognise ours',[163] he himself took a major step towards British reappraisal of de Valera. The little phrase, 'as a realist', spoke volumes. A man who only a few years earlier had been dismissed as some sort of freak[164] was now coming to be recognised, at least in adult British quarters, as a practical politician of uncommon capacity. His astute handling of Irish affairs since 1932, and his measured performance at the League of Nations, to whose deliberations he made several impressive contributions, may have helped some British (and indeed, some Irish) observers to appreciate the 'pragmatic and pacific side'[165] of his policy, and enabled them to revise their earlier superficial judgements.

According to MacDonald, de Valera acknowledged that

Ireland's freedom was bound up with the freedom of Great Britain; if the latter were threatened the former was also threatened and no responsible person in the Free State could escape that fact . . . Cooperation was essential . . . If he were to order military aeroplanes, he would wish to order types like our own, and the same applied to raw material generally. The plan should be worked out so that the Irish Free State and the United Kingdom forces could cooperate. Of course, if the United Kingdom became involved in war there would be those in Ireland who would say 'Britain's difficulty is Ireland's opportunity' but he did not hold that view at all; he would guarantee that in any case the Irish Free State would not be used to embarrass us in war. The wish of his countrymen in any war would be to remain neutral . . . But he thought it very likely that the Irish Free State would be drawn in on our side . . . [166]

De Valera went on to ruminate that

there was a time when he was in favour of Ireland breaking her connection with the Empire . . . that time had gone by. Later, he had been in favour of the Irish declaring a Republic, and so breaking with the Empire, but afterwards coming back into association with it. He had thought that process necessary in order to establish Ireland's independence.

But the constitutional changes in the relationship between Britain and the Commonwealth as a result of the Imperial Conference of 1926 and the Statute of Westminster 'had brought changes into the situation. He no longer thought it necessary for Ireland to break away from the Commonwealth in order to establish her freedom. Her freedom was already

[162] PRO, CAB 24, 271, CP, 128 (37), MacDonald memo, 6 October 1937.   [163] *Ibid.*
[164] Bowman, *De Valera*, pp. 110–11.   [165] *Ibid.*, p. 118.
[166] PRO, CAB 24, 271, CP, 128 (37), MacDonald memo, 6 October 1937.

established' – though if partition were to continue indefinitely, it might still be necessary to sever links.[167]

De Valera led the Irish negotiating team in London himself, no doubt recollecting the débâcle of 1921, and even the unreliability of O'Kelly, Lemass and Ryan at Ottawa in 1932, when, contrary to their expressed instructions, they actually dared to sign some – admittedly trivial – agreements.[168] His approach to the conference that began in January 1938 was to imply that he was the most credible guarantor of political stability in Ireland. He used his electoral reverse in 1937, as well as the destabilising threat of possible IRA activity, as ploys to plead his domestic difficulties. He even sketched a scenario in which he might find himself, on the outbreak of a war, as vulnerable as John Redmond turned out to have been in 1914.[169]

The agreement eventually reached in April 1938 represented in domestic politics, no less than in international relations, a deserved triumph for de Valera. He failed, it is true, to make any progress on partition, about which he had few real, as distinct from rhetorical, illusions.[170] But he achieved his other objectives, and more handsomely than he could have hoped. The agreement terminated the economic war, granting some preferential treatment to British industrial exports to Ireland in return for the elimination of the special restrictions on Irish agricultural imports to Britain. The English waived their remaining claims on the annuities and other payments, nearly £100 000 000, in return for a lump sum payment of only £10 000 000. Above all, Britian returned the ports. De Valera owed this good fortune to an assessment by the British chiefs of staff that the ports would be more trouble than they were worth in wartime. Nevertheless, whatever the causes of his success, success it undoubtedly was, and sufficient to overcome alleged reservations within his own cabinet from the 'republican' Ruttledge, reputedly resentful of any agreement that did not 'solve' partition.[171] The British gain was largely psychological. London was now satisfied that Ireland would not be used as a base, insofar as de Valera could ensure that, for hostile operations against the United Kingdom in the event of war. As de Valera had never any intention of allowing such a situation to develop, this involved no real concession on his part.

The agreement marked the culmination of a remarkably successful guerrilla diplomatic campaign to revise the Treaty out of existence. De Valera had conducted that campaign with tenacity and skill since coming

167 *Ibid.*; see also Bowman, *De Valera*, p. 144 and PA AA, Hempel – AA, 20 December 1937, A183, England–Irland, 1.
168 SPO, S6157A, and CAB 6/59, 30 August 1932; McMahon, *Republicans*, pp. 74–9.
169 PRO, CAB 27/642, IN (38), 17 January 1938.   170 Bowman, *De Valera*, p. 161.
171 B. Quinn, 'Dev's last ditch stand on partition', *Sunday Independent*, 4 March 1979, McMahon, *Republicans*, p. 247.

to power. It was, in diplomatic and party terms, a masterly performance. It was, however, one of the innumerable ironies in his career that his moment of greatest diplomatic triumph also marked the effective end of his isolationist ideal. His dreams of self-sufficiency could not survive the reality of Anglo-Irish economic relations. But he salvaged political victory from ideological retreat. He called a snap general election after the agreement and handsomely recovered his overall majority in June 1938. Fianna Fáil won over 50 per cent of the vote for the only time in his career, its share rising from 45.2 per cent to 51.9 per cent.[172] When the *Irish Times* had predicted in the immediate aftermath of the 1937 returns that 'another general election at an early date would provide no solution. The results would differ very little, if at all, from those in the elections that have just been completed . . . ',[173] it failed to allow for the resourcefulness of a more perceptive reader of the electoral entrails.

The 1938 election marks something of a watershed in the history of Fianna Fáil. The triumphant party now differed in some important respects from that of 1932. From being a hungry fighter on the outside, it had moved to capture the middle ground, and to become increasingly an umbrella party of the centre.[174] It had established itself as the natural governing party, with a concomitant obligation to satisfy a wide range of vested interests. It recovered the ground lost to independents in 1937 in rural areas.[175] It also attracted the first significant influx of previous Fine Gael and ex-unionist voters.[176] The Labour Party manifesto expressed rather radical intentions concerning higher social benefits, which may have frightened conservative voters worried that de Valera might remain dependent on Labour support. The *Irish Times* took the opportunity to discreetly abandon Fine Gael. Already in 1937 the *Irish Times* wavered: 'We are glad to admit that in many ways President de Valera's government had confounded its former critics including ourselves; that it has acted fairly and uprightly towards political and religious minorities, and that its Ministers, on the whole, have done their job conscientiously and well.' It reserved particular praise for MacEntee's responsible financial policy, which 'since his party came into power had much to recommend it. Mr MacEntee is a valuable member of the Oireachtas and we should be sorry if he should be defeated.' Nevertheless, it still counselled support for Cosgrave in 1937 because 'the major issue' remained the Commonwealth link.[177] Within a year, it found the results of the 1938 election 'eminently satisfactory', concluding, in words inconceivable only five years before, 'We are glad that he [Mr de Valera] has been returned to power.'[178] De

[172] O'Leary, *Elections*, p. 102.   [173] *Irish Times*, 9 July 1937.
[174] T. Garvin, *The evolution of Irish nationalist politics* (Dublin, 1981), p. 167.
[175] Gallagher, *Electoral support*, pp. 22–3.   [176] *Irish Press*, 1 July 1938.
[177] *Irish Times*, 30 June 1937.
[178] *Irish Times*, 21 June 1938.

Valera had established himself as the guarantor of social and political stability. A quiet election allowed voters to reflect on the calm haven into which the Taoiseach, whom many had distrusted as an erratic helmsman intent on churning up the waters, now seemed to have safely steered the ship of state.[179]

De Valera was wise to seize on the opportunity offered by the Anglo-Irish agreement to snatch his election triumph. The deteriorating financial and economic situation was reflected in the severe budget of May 1939. MacEntee introduced his eighth budget 'in a speech of inspissated gloom', making no attempt to 'minimise the gravity of the situation'. Imposing heavier duties on tobacco and petrol, and raising the standard rate of income tax from 4/6 to 5/6, 'the change of tone from his earlier budget speeches was very remarkable'.[180] Fianna Fáil lost badly in the next by-election. With turnout down to a mere 40 per cent, its vote in South Dublin City fell from 30 768 in June 1938 to only 20 059 in June 1939, while the opposition vote held virtually stable, at 15 877 compared with 16 083. 'The reasons for this apathy are not hard to find. Growing unemployment, the rise in the cost of living, the slowing down of the housing programme and the increased taxation imposed by the budget, have all helped to alienate support from the government . . . '.[181] Incipient signs of the postwar malaise could already be detected. The *Economist* concluded that 'the country badly needs a new party competent to frame a realistic economic programme and to implement it courageously'.[182]

Fianna Fáil was already coming close to constituting at least two parties in matters of economic policy, as the internal contradictions that had been submerged in the surging wave of the early years now began to surface. MacEntee was reputed to have driven his Budget through the cabinet in the face of strong resistance. Financial commentators expressed relief at MacEntee's orthodoxy 'and it would be still more comforting if one could be sure that his orthodoxy was fully shared by all his colleagues'.[183] As the industrialisation drive slowed down, Lemass began to grope for an alternative to the protectionist policy. By 1938 the home market was virtually saturated with Irish goods.[184] The scope for further industrialisation on the basis of domestic demand was very limited, and certainly not sufficient to generate full employment. The only possibility of creating adequate employment lay in developing an export trade. The problem was that the industries built up behind the protectionist barriers had neither

---

179 *Round Table*, 112 (September 1938), pp. 740–7.   180 *Economist*, 20 May 1939.
181 *Ibid.*, 10 June 1939. See PA AA, Hempel-AA, 5 May 1939, no. 790, StSekr., Irland I, on the general decline in Fianna Fáil standing.
182 *Economist*, 10 June 1939, p. 595.   183 *Ibid.*, 20 May 1939, p. 432.
184 For a case study see Press, 'Protectionism', 83.

the ability, nor in many cases the will, to compete internationally. The Lemass rhetoric of industrialisation shifted accordingly.

The Trade Agreement with Britain raised the possibility of more intensive British industrial competition on the Irish market. It aroused considerable misgivings among Irish industrialists. Unkindly described by an *Irish Independent* reporter at the talks as 'that section of racketeers which is making money on tariffs',[185] they complained bitterly that Industry and Commerce had not consulted them.[186] A decade earlier, Lemass had been prepared to hope that a flourishing domestic agriculture could provide sufficient demand for industrial output and that as 'the goal of our efforts should be to keep the Irish people in Ireland and provide prosperity for them here' then 'everything else, even cheap living or accepted notions about efficiency, must be sacrificed to that end'.[187] Now he was convinced that, at least in principle, efficiency was a pre-requisite for sustained growth. The emphasis in his public pronouncements shifted increasingly from self-sufficiency to efficiency. 'It was never conceived as possible', he now claimed, 'that the state could be made completely independent of foreign trade or locked in a water-tight compartment cut off from the current of international life.'[188] He told the audience at the opening of the Galway hat factory that 'now their industries had passed beyond the infancy stage and were capable of facing comparison with industries in other countries, and they would have to be prepared to face that comparison'.[189] The *Irish Press* took up the theme with a vigour that must have distressed business readers, arguing that Irish industry could now 'be reasonably expected to stand on its own feet . . . the era of spoon feeding is over'.[190] The *Press* pronounced with a reluctantly acquired authority on the subject of efficiency.

BEHIND THE HEADLINES

The *Irish Press* had already endured a chastening experience. Launched in 1931 in anticipation of a circulation of 'almost 100 000', compared with less than 50 000 for the *Irish Times* and the *Cork Examiner*,[191] the *Press* quickly achieved this target.[192] Written with rumbustious flair, it became a brilliant journalistic success under the founding editorship of Frank

185 Bowman, *De Valera*, p. 181.
186 NLI, MS 924, CVO, 14 March 1940, ev. Erskine Childers, TD, Secretary to the Federation of Irish Manufacturers, q. 6357ff; MS 929, 26 September 1940, ev. R.C. Ferguson, Acting Secretary, Industry and Commerce, q. 14952ff.
187 NLI, MS 18339, FG, undated memo by Seán Lemass (probably June 1929), p. 11.
188 *Irish Press*, 22 April 1938. 189 *Irish Press*, 19 July 1938.
190 *Irish Press*, 20 July 1938.
191 NLI, MS 18361 (1), FG, undated prepublication circular, 'An Irish daily newspaper'.
192 *Irish Press*, 23 January 1933; NLI, MS 18361 (4), FG, Circulation of the *Irish Press*, 1931–6.

Gallagher. The directions to sub-editors conveyed the cast of the editor's mind:

1 'Always give Irish angle in the headlines.
2 Do not use agency headlines: the other papers will have these.
3 Be on your guard against the habits of British and foreign news agencies who look at the world mainly through imperialist eyes. For instance:
   (i) Do not pass the word 'bandits' as a description of South American revolutionaries.
   (ii) Pirates and robbers in China are not necessarily communists and therefore should not be described as such.
   (iii) Tammany is an American institution disliked by British agencies. Be careful of one-sided accounts of its activities.
   (iv) These agency stories show ignorance of Catholic practices and things: Check all doubtful references in such copies.
   (v) Propagandist attacks on Russia and other countries should not be served up as news.[193]

More general instructions urged staff to find angles to stories of interest to women, and warned them 'Do not make the *Irish Press* a Dublin paper: There are O'Connell Streets in other cities also.' A residual Fianna Fáil aversion to the forces of law may be detected behind the injunction that 'It is not necessary to report every word of praise spoken to policemen' or to report judges' jokes 'unless they are real jokes'![194]

Despite the rapid achievement of the circulation target, the financial circumstances of the paper were unsatisfactory. An American efficiency expert was hired to retrieve the situation. Conflicts between editorial and commercial criteria quickly flared up. Strenuously resisting 'economies' Gallagher claimed that the *Press* 'was created by me out of the most mixed elements, trained, partly trained and untrained . . . men who for the most part were schooled in a journalism wholly foreign to the democratic and republican outlook which is the essential mark of this newspaper and on which its appeal to the people is based'.[195] Relations continued to deteriorate. Gallagher offered his resignation in September 1933.[196] Though prevailed upon to reconsider, he again offered his resignation a year later[197] and, after consulting de Valera, the Board finally accepted after a six months delay.[198]

Gallagher was no longer prepared to work in conditions in which 'if matters of major policy have to be written of by editor, editorial is written

---

[193] NLI, MS 18361(3), FG, undated.   [194] *Ibid.*
[195] NLI, MS 18361(5), FG, Gallagher to General Manager, 8 July 1933. See also MS 18361(6), Gallagher to de Valera, 17 July 1933.
[196] NLI, MS 18361(5), FG, Gallagher to Chairman and Board of Directors of *Irish Press*, 3 September 1933.
[197] NLI, MS 18361(5), FG, Gallagher to Secretary of Board of Directors of *Irish Press*, 29 October 1934.
[198] NLI, MS 18361(5), Gallagher to J.C. Dowdall, 5 April 1935; F.A. Ridgeway to Gallagher, 29 April 1935.

in gaps between ordinary work or if time allows at the tea-break or later at the supper hour'.[199] The atmosphere in the *Press* was obviously distasteful. Even the Holy Name was no longer sacred. 'I can't and won't forgive de Valera', Gallagher's secretary wrote to him, 'he let you down badly, and as for Vivion, he is despicable – all that underhand, furtive dealing and never to say a word.'[200] M.J. MacManus, who assumed some of Gallagher's duties, quickly found himself 'endeavouring to write leaders on subjects I had never thought about'[201] in this place 'of desolation, doom, suspicion and intrigue'.[202]

The early years of the *Press* offer a cautionary tale, anticipating in cameo the fate of Fianna Fáil itself, with the exultant promise of the dawn soon fading before the grey light of common day. There would be no question, however, of the equivalent of editorial resignation there! Instead, much expertise was devoted to the lighting effects to persuade the audience that the stage remained as brightly lit as before.

FIANNA FÁIL VERSUS THE IRA

After the Blueshirt/IRA disturbances of the earlier years of Fianna Fáil government, illegal political agitation was already declining before the ban on the IRA in 1936 reduced it further. The number convicted under the Public Safety Act of 1931 declined from a peak of 451 in 1934 to 138 in 1936 and to only 18 in the first nine months of 1937.[203] However, the impending lapse of Cosgrave's much criticised measure, 'the most rigorous public safety statute which Ireland had known in a long history of coercion,'[204] prompted anxious consideration in the Department of Justice and in the cabinet in the winter of 1937. Divisions within the government were reflected in the failure of the cabinet sub-committee on the issue to reach agreement.[205] The Minister for Justice, P.J. Ruttledge, in particular, known for his IRA sympathies, resisted as premature the introduction in the spring of 1938 of legislation granting the government sweeping coercive powers.[206]

By late 1938, as renewed IRA activity appeared imminent, de Valera's patience was exhausted. He demanded from Justice as a matter of urgency and 'subject to the consideration of certain amendments which this Department had in mind' a response to the cabinet decision of

---

199 *Ibid.*, MS 18361(1), FG, Gallagher to General Manager, 20 November 1933.
200 *Ibid.*, MS 18361(7), FG, Maureen Kennedy to Gallagher, 2 July 1935.
201 *Ibid.*, MS 18341, M.J. MacManus to Gallagher, 28 August 1935.
202 *Ibid.*, MS 18361(7), M.J. MacManus to Gallagher, 4 July 1935.
203 SPO, S10209, Defence memo, 6 October 1937.
204 Longford and O'Neill, *De Valera*, p. 274.
205 SPO, S10454A, Department of Taoiseach memo, 16 February 1938.
206 SPO, S10454A, Justice memo, 6 May 1938.

18 November instructing Justice to prepare permanent legislation dealing with Special Criminal Courts, treason and treasonable offences, and unlawful associations.[207]

The response of Stephen Roche, Secretary of Justice, reveals something of the official mind at that stage. Roche noted that 'the marked tendency in this state has been to follow the English practice in these matters'.[208] 'Admirable in its scrupulous respect for the liberty of the citizen and its dislike of "extraordinary courts",' the English system gave the suspect more rights than he would have enjoyed in most European states. But it depended for its success on 'a long tradition of internal security and of cooperation between the public and the police, a tradition which does not exist here.' If the government failed to take extensive powers, Roche warned that it might find itself forced to seek more authority later, and in the event of government pusillanimity the police 'will either stand idly by in the face of crime, or, if sufficiently goaded, will retaliate by counter crime . . . '. Despite these considerations, Roche recommended against the immediate introduction of internment 'although the government may be forced to use it at a later stage if events take an unfavourable course'. While recognising that 'one of the weakest points in our legal system . . . is that we have neither as in England, a general willingness to help the police nor, as on the Continent, a machinery capable of dealing with people who obstruct or simply refuse to help the officers of the law', he also recommended against conferring the special powers of interrogation on the police that they had used extensively under the Public Safety Act.

While the cabinet may have paid close attention to so cogent a memorandum, it nevertheless conceded the police demand for powers of interrogation, 'the most valuable and most effective means' at their disposal under the Public Safety Act, and whose absence from the proposed Bill the guards felt would cripple them.[209]

In January 1939, when the IRA began a bombing campaign in Britain that was to claim at least 7 dead and nearly 200 wounded during the year, de Valera certainly took to heart Roche's shrewd point that at a time of international friction 'a small country cannot afford to invite attacks from without by a seeming inability to keep order within its own territory. The danger in this case becomes acute when the unlawful organisations extend their activities into other states, while using this country as a base.'[210] De Valera kept a close eye on the preparation of the legislation. Anxious to avoid accusations that he was simply returning to Cosgrave-type

[207] SPO S10454A, M. Moynihan to Private Secretary, Minister for Justice, 20 November 1938, and M. Moynihan to S. Roche, 20 November 1938.
[208] SPO S10454A. Justice memo, December 1938. A slightly revised version, submitted in January 1939, is contained in S10454B.
[209] SPO, GC 2/47, 10 February 1939.
[210] SPO S10454B. Justice memo, January 1939.

measures, he resorted to a typical ploy to divert criticism. Roche was authorised to include as many of the Cosgrave provisions as he felt necessary. But he should adopt the device of actually repealing the relevant Cosgrave legislation, and only then should he re-enact the substance of it, as far as required, while taking care to change the phraseology as far as possible.[211] De Valera himself acted as arbitrator on disputed points in the drafting of the legislation.[212] He faced some party resistance, but cabinet changes in the draft mainly concerned amendments concerning the liability of the press for the reporting of relevant matters, following representations by newspaper interests, though the concessions fell short of the papers' requests.[213]

The Offences against the State Act became law on 14 June 1939. The government suppressed the IRA Bodenstown commemoration scheduled for 25 June.[214] When war broke out, de Valera had no doubt that neutrality was the only feasible policy. The Dáil unanimously declared Ireland neutral, on 2 September 1939, when authorising the government to proclaim a state of emergency at its discretion. It was simple common-sense to seek to avoid the horrors of war. In addition, de Valera believed that public opinion would be too divided on any other policy. Only one TD, James Dillon, in 1942, publicly opposed neutrality.[215] Public opinion, like all Dáil parties, seems to have been overwhelmingly in favour. There was therefore little dissent on the policy. How to implement it most effectively was another matter. The real question was whether it could be sustained in the light of circumstances largely beyond Irish control. Threats might come from several quarters. The fortunes of war itself would be ultimately decisive. If Hitler conquered Britain, Ireland would be at his mercy. How he chose to treat it would be for him to decide, not for the Irish. In the event of a protracted war, the economy might stagger to the brink of collapse if the British chose to cut off Irish imports, or refused to take Irish exports, animal or human. This was highly unlikely. It was in Britain's interest to maintain the supply of cheap Irish food and cheap Irish labour. Nevertheless, the decision once more lay outside Irish control. More immediately, any apparent division within the country, and especially possible IRA support for the Nazis, might encourage German designs on Ireland or provoke a pre-emptive British strike. This was one area over which the government could exert control.

---

211 SPO, S10454B, M. Moynihan to S. Roche, 25 January 1939.
212 SPO, S10454B, note. For instance, 'Decision of the Taoiseach in regard to unlawful organisations', 10 February 1939. See also PA AA, Hempel-AA, 5 May 1939, no 790, England–Irland, 2.
213 SPO, GC 2/66, 25 April 1939.
214 SPO, S11318, Unlawful Organisations (Suppression) Order, 23 June 1939.
215 R. Fisk, *In time of war: Ireland, Ulster and the price of neutrality 1939–45* (London, 1983), p. 145.

Immediately following the outbreak of the war, on 8 September, de Valera transferred Ruttledge to Local Government, replacing him in Justice by Gerry Boland, loyal, tough, and with an equally impeccable IRA record. The Committee on Internal Security established by the cabinet on 16 September included Ruttledge, but with de Valera himself as chairman, O'Kelly as Tánaiste, Boland, Aiken, newly appointed Minister for Coordination of Defensive Measures, and Oscar Traynor, the new Minister for Defence.[216]

When IRA men began to be detained under the new legislation, they created problems with a series of hunger strikes. The most harrowing early case concerned Patrick McGrath, a partly disabled veteran with a distinguished record during the war of independence. His case elicited a moving response from his brother, J.J. McGrath, himself confined to a sanatorium.[217] The genuineness of their idealism could not be doubted. De Valera relented, much to his subsequent regret. He would learn that leniency earned only contempt. The released McGrath would be duly convicted and executed for his part in the murder of two detectives in August 1940.[218]

De Valera found too that intransigence feeds on concession. When more prisoners went on hunger strike in Mountjoy Jail in the spring of 1940, he came under intense pressure. The usual arguments were on this occasion leavened by the sense of outrage of the risen petty bourgeoisie among the female of the species. Craving Victorian respectability, they waxed indignant at the slur on their status involved in confining their relatives in Mountjoy, 'where sexual degenerates are also imprisoned', as Josephine Mary Plunkett, mother of one of the prisoners on strike, John Plunkett, brother of the executed 1916 leader, Joseph Mary Plunkett, indignantly expostulated.[219] She stressed to Cardinal MacRory, whose intervention she sought, that 'if the sentenced men were transferred to non-*criminal* jails, the hunger strike could cease and sentences for offences could be endured'.[220] When the Cardinal passed this on to de Valera, he replied that as the IRA prisoners were kept segregated from the others in Mountjoy, there was no danger of 'depravity'.[221]

In deference, no doubt, to the status conferred on Mrs Plunkett by her son's role in 1916, de Valera went to great lengths to justify his policy. 'The government did not want the hunger strikers to die', he explained patiently. 'They had made up their mind, however, that they could not yield to the demands which prisoners sought to enforce by means of the hunger strike. Prisoners would not be allowed to dictate the conditions

[216] SPO, GC 2/99, 16 September 1939.
[217] SPO, S11515, J.J. McGrath to E. de Valera, 12 November 1939.
[218] Longford and O'Neill, *De Valera*, p. 357.
[219] SPO, S11515, Josephine Mary Plunkett to Cardinal MacRory, 14 March 1940.
[220] *Ibid.*   [221] SPO, S11515, E. de Valera to Cardinal MacRory, 20 March 1940.

under which they would be kept in detention.'[222] When the Lord Mayor of Dublin, Mrs Tom Clarke, widow of another executed 1916 leader, remonstrated with de Valera that only 'petty technicalities' were preventing the government 'from acting humanely',[223] de Valera was not amused. 'The demand of the prisoners', he replied,

was not for any vague status such as 'political treatment' or any concessions with regard to the conditions under which they should be detained. It was that men belonging to their organisation sentenced for any offence whatsoever should 'serve their sentence in military custody', and thus be treated as though they were members of a military force engaged in legitimate warfare and entitled to be treated as such.[224]

The essential issue was the legitimacy of the state. De Valera was regularly taunted with reneging on his own earlier persona, as when William Norton, leader of the Labour Party, enquired, 'am I to understand that hunger strikes or thirst strikes of this nature which were right in 1922 and 1923 are wrong in 1939?' De Valera equally regularly replied that the constitution of 1937 had invested the state with a new legitimacy and 'there were no longer any obstacles in the way of any section to utilising constitutional means'.[225]

If de Valera's resolve needed stiffening in the face of hunger strikes, then Gerry Boland supplied whatever steel was necessary. Boland, who would recall that de Valera could be sometimes 'indecisive',[226] obviously regretted the concession to McGrath.[227] He did not bother to justify the government's position in de Valera's terms. For him, the duty of a government was to govern, and he did not conceal his contempt for the insidious opportunism of the likes of Norton.[228] But the final decision rested with de Valera. Less than a year after his appointment as minister, Boland was to claim that 'Mr de Valera would not try to force me to do anything.'[229] Nevertheless, it is clear that he could not proceed on his own, but 'had to wait for the Taoiseach'.[230] In its resolve to defend the state, the cabinet had six IRA men executed during the war for the murder of servants of the state whose legitimacy they denied, allowed three others to die on hunger strike, had more than 500 interned without trial, and had another 600 committed under the Offences against the State Act.

There was an elementary irony informing the whole situation. Stephen

---

[222] SPO, S11515, E. de Valera to Mrs Dillon, 2 April 1940.
[223] SPO, S11515, Caitlín Bean Uí Chléirigh to E. de Valera, 18 April 1940.
[224] SPO, S11515, E. de Valera to Mrs Clarke, 20 April 1940.
[225] DD, 77, 19 November 1939, 831. See also R. Fanning, '"The rule of order": Eamon de Valera and the IRA, 1923–1940', in O'Carroll and Murphy, *De Valera*, p. 167; Moynihan, *Speeches*, p. 424.
[226] 'Gerry Boland's story', *Irish Times*, 19 October 1968.   [227] Coogan, *IRA*, p. 186.
[228] DD, 77, 19 November 1939, 831.
[229] SPO, S11515, inquest on John McNeela, 24 April 1940.
[230] *Ibid.*

Roche had no high opinion of the motives of 'professional' IRA men. The main objective of the special powers legislation was 'to prevent a small group of older people, who make a hobby of violent political agitation from leading the younger generation into folly and crime in order to gratify their own vanity and drive for leadership'.[231] Nowhere, however, for all his obvious quality of mind, does he ask how could the young be misled in this manner unless they were already predisposed in this direction. He did not query, for instance, the quality of the history taught in Irish schools, or the official glorification of the tradition of violence. The cabinet committee on internal security was blissfully oblivious to the incongruity. The prisoners might, for instance, choose to be instructed in 'such educational subjects as may be approved, i.e. Irish language, Irish history and geography, etc.'.[232] One wonders what 'Irish history' the internees were to be taught that might divert them from their purpose? The 'fairytale text books on history'[233] flourishing under the patronage of the Department of Education could only confirm the prisoners in the correctness, indeed in the nobility, of their cause. It is difficult not to feel some sympathy for many of the twenty-six IRA men who went to their eternal reward between April 1939 and May 1946, by one route or another, for they could not unreasonably claim to be the logical products of the official political culture which now sought to suppress them.[234]

WAR ECONOMICS

Repression was only one weapon, however indispensable, in the struggle for security. Equally important was the effort to prevent circumstances arising which would enhance the appeal of the IRA. Hence, in part, de Valera's concern with maintaining economic stability. As he explained to bankers in 1940, in soliciting their support for government measures, urban unemployment would be 'a danger in our midst', particularly if the young men on the dole 'might be given money from another quarter'.[235]

How was economic stability to be best achieved? De Valera steered a careful course between the conservative instincts of McElligott and the expansionist impulses of Lemass. Finance saw in the war a golden opportunity to achieve the cherished objective of reducing 'extravagance' in state expenditure. From January 1939 McElligott was manoeuvring to take advantage of the prospect of 'suspension or curtailment of non-

---

231 SPO, S10454A, Justice memo, December 1938.
232 SPO, S11438A, Cabinet Committee on Internal Security, 16 September 1939.
233 S. O'Faolain, 'The plain people of Ireland', *The Bell*, 7, 1 (October 1943), 6; T.D. Williams, 'Conclusion' in MacManus (ed.), *Great test*, p. 183.
234 Lyons, *Ireland*, p. 550.
235 SPO, S11466, Meeting between government representatives and representatives of the banks, 4 June 1940.

essential services in time of emergency' to try to impose his own concept of 'essential' on the country.[236] At Finance behest, a Civil Service Economy Committee was established on the outbreak of the war.[237] But the committee failed to fulfil Finance hopes. The chairman, Hugo Flinn, Parliamentary Secretary for the Board of Works, was a Cork TD with a sharp mind. He was no uncritical admirer of Finance. His committee approved various economies, but the final report rejected or deflected several Finance recommendations for retrenchment, including yet another attempt to reduce old age pensions.[238] Some trivial concessions were made to McElligott's distaste for the language revival, including the suspension 'of a scheme for a series of gramophone records in Irish which would have cost £200 in 1940–41'.[239] The report concluded on a sardonic note calculated to irk McElligott, implying that a penchant for misplaced economies was depriving the civil service of personnel adequately qualified to make worthwhile recommendations on economies![240]

If Finance failed to convert the Economy Committee to its gospel, neither did the committee offer much support for the Lemass line. Like McElligott, Lemass sought to use the new circumstances to promote his policies.'The government', he remonstrated in November 1939 'has not yet attempted to consider the economic position as a whole or to formulate a programme to see us through the war with the least possible damage.'[241] Proposing that 'the reduction of unemployment' should be 'the central aim', he recommended that public building should be increased and loans provided to encourage more private building, that additional powers should be granted to the Industrial Credit Corporation to finance industrial development, that more loans should be provided for farmers, and that the privately owned railway companies be enabled to undertake badly needed capital expenditure. In addition, he envisaged harbour improvement schemes, construction of airports, turf production schemes, etc. On the question of finance he was disingenuous, certainly politically and probably economically. 'If the provision of capital is the main difficulty . . . we can get over it by the control of investment by the public.' If investment in the transport system was considered risky, 'the state can protect itself against ultimate loss, at the expense of the shareholders in these concerns, if it is considered a good policy to do so'.[242] It was a typically impatient Lemass effort. Grants and loans were to be lavished on anybody, whether in the public or the private sectors, who would undertake to do anything.

While de Valera would have been attracted by the prospect of increased

[236] SPO, S10913A, Finance memo, 6 January 1939.   [237] *Ibid.*, 9 September 1939.
[238] SPO, S10913A, Economy Committee, Final Report, 23 November 1939, p. 2.
[239] *Ibid.*, p. 11.
[240] *Ibid.*, p. 24.   [241] SPO, S11466, S. Lemass to E. de Valera, 7 November 1939.
[242] *Ibid.*

employment, he would have pondered the electoral implications of Lemass's cavalier attitude towards private interests. Nevertheless, Lemass was not as isolated as he usually found himself in sketching his expansionist scenarios. Professor Smiddy, de Valera's private economic adviser, took much the same view, if in more restrained terms. Smiddy was generally orthodox on monetary matters, but he refused to blanch before the heretical idea of an unbalanced budget. 'It is better economics and more prudent statesmanship to maintain as far as possible our present economic activities, even at the expense of unbalancing the budget. Otherwise it might be more seriously unbalanced at a later date.'[243]

The outcome of the conflicting pressures was more or less stalemate. Few new programmes of the type envisaged by Lemass were undertaken. But relatively few cutbacks occurred in existing commitments. Total government expenditure rose gradually from £48 000 000 in 1939 to £64 000 000 in 1945. But this represented an actual fall in public expenditure as a proportion of gross domestic product, a truly remarkable record.[244]

One explanation for the unusual Irish record was emigration. This got rid of more than 100 000 excess bodies, mostly male, to Britain, thus enabling recorded unemployment to fall from 15 per cent to about 10 per cent, thanks to this providential dispersal of an otherwise expensive and potentially dangerous labour surplus.[245]

But the exodus contained its own threat. Or so at least Lemass sought to argue as he tried once more to convert de Valera to an expansionist policy in 1942. The immediate origins of a Lemass memorandum on 'Labour policy' require further research. It may have been influenced by the thinking of F.H. Boland, Assistant Secretary of External Affairs. Boland, who would enjoy a distinguished career in Ireland and later at the United Nations, combined an expansionist instinct in matters of economic policy with an urbane, capacious mind that enabled him to locate economic concerns intelligently in a wider context. When Industry and Commerce proposed restricting the exodus of key workers to Britain in 1942, Boland widened the discussion. He warned against the potential diplomatic consequences of imposing serious restrictions because the British were 'very anxious to get these workers'.[246] They might therefore retaliate by reducing 'the supply to us of raw materials, which tend to keep up the level

---

[243] *Ibid.*, memo by Professor Smiddy, 'Some observations on the effect of the war on Irish economy', 25 September 1939.

[244] M. O'Donoghue and A.A. Tait, 'The growth of public revenue and expenditure in Ireland', in J.A. Bristow and A.A. Tait (eds.), *Economic policy in Ireland* (Dublin, 1968), p. 288.

[245] Mitchell, *European historical statistics*, p. 178.

[246] SPO, S11582A, J.P. Walshe to de Valera, 18 May 1942, transmitting Boland's memorandum (all further quotations from this memo come from this source).

of employment and thereby to restrict the amount of labour available for emigration to Britain in the urban areas'. Boland did not, however, share the *laissez-faire* Finance approach:

In a recent conversation, Mr McElligott mentioned to me some of the arguments which are, no doubt, being urged very strongly in favour of allowing the traffic to continue. He claims that it provides a safety valve against revolution, that the resulting inflow of ready money – he put it as high as £100,000 or £150,000 a week – did a great deal to relieve distress and maintain economic activity, and that it would be contrary to sound social ethics and inequitable to prevent the poor man from marketing his most valuable asset – that is to say his labour – in the best market. No doubt, a further argument, which Mr McElligott was not so indelicate as to mention is the saving in unemployment assistance which results to the exchequer!

Rejecting this approach as cavalier, Boland then offered the suggestion that seems to be the genesis of the subsequent Lemass proposals.

The best method for dealing with the whole problem, to my mind, however, would be to get away from general arguments entirely and to aim at an efficient central organisation which, with the help of the local employment exchanges, would ensure that: (a) new demands for manpower in agriculture, turf production and other essential services were promptly met, (b) a manpower reserve would be maintained in the country – with increased unemployment benefits if necessary – which would be adequate to meet all the requirements, and (c) that any balance of unemployed labour remaining over would be free to go to Britain if they liked.

Boland raised the discussion to a new level with his sombre reflections on likely postwar developments:

Whatever the danger of social revolution in this country may be, it is certain to be at its maximum during the last year of the war and during the next year or two after it. Now, if there is one thing more certain than another, it is that immediately the 'ceasefire' order is given, the whole aim and purpose of the British authorities will be to rush all these workers back to this country as quickly as they can . . . Therefore, no problem that we are likely to have to face during the war is likely to be so serious as the problem we will have when up to as many as a hundred thousand or more unemployed men (who will, no doubt, have imbibed a good deal of 'leftism' in Britain) are dumped back here within the course of a few weeks . . . To have piled on top of them, in the course of a short time afterwards all the Irish citizens demobilised from the British armed forces.

It seems reasonable to assume that this memorandum of May 1942 prompted Lemass to propose his own more elaborate, and characteristically more drastic, solution to the problem. The undated Lemass memorandum did not go through the usual departmental channels. Nor was it circulated to other departments in advance of cabinet for their views, though it would affect them all. Rather was it, as a disapproving official hand noted, 'understood to have been furnished to the Taoiseach by Mr S. Lemass . . . June 1942'.[247] It appeared immediately on the cabinet

[247] SPO, S12882A, Lemass memo on Labour policy (all further quotations from this memo come from this source).

agenda, having evaded the gauntlet of departmental obstructionism, presumably reflecting the success of Lemass in persuading de Valera, normally punctilious about procedural propriety, of the urgency of the matter.

While Lemass claimed that 'the outline of a possible policy . . . is for illustration purposes only', he recommended a distinctly *dirigiste* approach. He began by defining labour policy to mean

an aim and a plan for the control and direction of the nation's resources of labour so as (a) to serve the requirements of essential production during the Emergency; (b) to reduce and if possible to eliminate hardships resulting from unemployment; (c) the preservation for the country in the post-war situation of the skill and experience acquired by workers in essential industrial occupations now temporarily suspended; and (d) the training of workers in the light of post-war needs. The term also covers such matters as industrial relations and wage control.

Briskly observing that present labour policy was 'unrelated to any general predetermined aim' he then proposed the establishment of a Ministry of Labour as a labour planning agency for the introduction 'either directly or through the appropriate departments or organisations of plans for constructional works and other desirable development schemes . . . '. The Department 'should have independent contacts with such organisations as the Tourist Board, the Minerals Development Company, etc. to ensure that their planning was kept in conformity with the ministry's general programme'. He envisaged possible large-scale restrictions on freedom of movement, adding almost casually that 'the successful operation of his system would necessitate either the active cooperation of the trade union movement or, alternatively, a prohibition of trade union interference with it'. Nor was Lemass contemplating these measures as a temporary response only. 'The general scheme of control of labour, introduced to cope with the circumstances of the Emergency, should be retained after the Emergency has passed and become a permanent feature of the state's labour organisation.' In addition, 'the idea of amalgamating the social services in one Ministry might be implemented after the Emergency through the Ministry of Labour'. And 'the Ministry of Labour should advise the government on problems relating to army demobilisation'.

This 'outline' obviously had wide-ranging implications for social and economic policy, for the role of individual departments in government, and for the role of government in society. Lemass clearly envisaged a high redundancy rate among other departments – and other ministers! There could be little doubt who the Supremo of the new Super Ministry would be! The cabinet was sufficiently alarmed, whether at the dangers depicted by Lemass, or at the threat to departmental positions, or both, to record an unprecedented declaration of intent concerning economic policy on 30 June, and to authorise de Valera to seek proposals for expenditure plans from all Departments. De Valera's draft of 6 July for Finance contained the startling observation that 'so far as the general question of finance is concerned financial considerations will need to be subordinated to the imperative necessity of getting the work under way'.[248] Recovery was rapid. The final draft for Finance, dispatched on 8 July, dispensed with this subversive sentiment.[249] De Valera now felt able to reassure Departments that

we all agreed that whilst an extensive reorganisation of our whole economic and social life might ultimately prove necessary and this possibility needs always to be kept in sight, we should plan at once some such use and development of our resources and potentialities as seemed reasonably practical without a revolutionary change in the foundations.[250]

The wilder yearnings of Lemass clearly found little support among his colleagues.

It soon became clear that de Valera himself most definitely did not share the Lemass approach. He crushed the suggestion from John Leydon that the Secretaries of Industry and Commerce, Finance and Agriculture should be seconded from their normal departmental responsibilities to devote 'the greater part of [their] time to planning problems'.[251] Leydon's suggestion can hardly have been made except on the authorisation of Lemass, if not at his instigation. De Valera preferred to keep the 'planning' in political hands. So potentially sensitive a subject would not escape his own control. Instead of the committee of senior civil servants, the cabinet established a Committee on Economic Planning, consisting of de Valera, Lemass and the Minister for Finance, Seán T. O'Kelly. The history of that committee provides an instructive example of de Valera's techniques of man management, and furnishes further evidence of the primacy of the political in his mind.

The committee met almost sixty times in the two and a half years after December 1942. But Lemass could make little headway. With general elections imminent – there were two between December 1942 and June 1944 – the committee found itself pondering such weighty matters as 'surfacing the embankment between the Great Northern Railway and Dollymount Pier at Clontarf', 'South Wall Reclamation Scheme,' and 'Dunlaoghaire refuse dump', noting en route that 'the Department of Defence were not interested in the growing of fruit trees from the defence

---

[248] *Ibid.*, De Valera's draft for Finance, 6 July 1942.
[249] *Ibid.*, De Valera to Minister for Finance, 8 July 1942.
[250] *Ibid.*, De Valera's revised draft, 7–9 July 1942.
[251] *Ibid.*, J. Leydon to M. Moynihan, 22 September 1942, with Moynihan's note of de Valera's decision, 28 September 1942.

viewpoint', and even lingering over 'policy in regard to Irish' (which had not loomed large in the Lemass memorandum on 'Labour policy'!).[252]

The propoals submitted by Departments relating to postwar reconstruction would have involved an expenditure of about £86m.[253] Industry and Commerce responded quickly and ambitiously. But the committee proved unresponsive. Further proposals from Lemass after the 1943 election for an expanded building programme ran foul of Finance. De Valera sided with O'Kelly, feeling that the building proposals 'should be somewhat more restricted' than Lemass recommended.[254] In March 1944 Industry and Commerce was told that its 'planning' projects were to be deferred unless they could be shown to be 'urgently necessary'.[255] Lemass was fighting a more and more futile rearguard action as the committee increasingly acted as a watchdog to curb rather than encourage expenditure. The sense of alarm generated by the impending return of a mass body of emigrants no longer prepared to tolerate Irish conditions evaporated once it became clear that Britain herself was committed to a programme of domestic reconstruction.[256] Although the committee still accepted the view of Lemass in December 1944 that 'an immediate *temporary* employment policy must be devised' to cater for the return of emigrants, nothing happened.[257]

Lemass became further embroiled with Finance on the issue of the relevance of the British White Paper on Full Employment, published in May 1944, for Ireland. Finance dismissed the White Paper as either irrelevant or wrong-headed, concluding that Ireland must revert to the policy of the 1920s as soon as possible.[258] Lemass promptly responded with a long memorandum that challenged not only the Finance mind, but the de Valera mind, across a wide spectrum of social and economic thought.[259] Lemass sought to slaughter so many sacred cows in this document that it is difficult to believe he can seriously have expected to convert his colleagues.[260] If he did, his political judgement was seriously at fault. Not only did he inject a potent dose of Keynes and Beveridge, but

252 SPO, S13026A, Cabinet Committee on Economic Planning, 3 March 1943.
253 SPO, S12882A, Dept. of Taoiseach memo, 10 January 1944.
254 SPO, S13026A, Cabinet Committee on Economic Planning, 15 November 1943.
255 *Ibid.*, 20 March 1944.
256 This was beginning to become accepted in 1943. See J. Meenan, 'Irish industry and postwar problems', *Studies*, 32 (1943), pp. 361–8.
257 SPO, S13026B, Cabinet Committee on Economic Planning, 6 December 1944.
258 SPO, S13101A, Finance memo, 31 October 1944.
259 R.J. Raymond, 'De Valera, Lemass and Irish economic development: 1933–1948', in O'Carroll and Murphy, *De Valera*, pp. 125–29, summarises the Lemass memorandum. See also P. Bew and H. Patterson, *Sean Lemass and the making of modern Ireland* (Dublin 1982), pp. 25ff.
260 SPO, S13101A, Lemass memo on Full Employment Policy, 21 November 1944.

he foolishly combined this with an attack on Fianna Fáil small farm ideology. He had already clashed with de Valera on the general question of agricultural policy. In July 1944, with the election safely out of the way, the Committee on Economic Planning had agreed that it 'should aim at avoiding the consideration of matters of detail',[261] presumably a rebuff for de Valera. The discussion on the general principles of land and agricultural policy exposed the fundamental incompatibility between Lemass and the Taoiseach. In September, at a meeting attended by Jim Ryan,

stress was laid on (a) the need to promote economic agricultural production, (b) the importance of the export market from the point of view of the maintenance and improvement of the standard of living and (c) the importance, from the national and social point of view, of the maintenance on the land in economic security of as many families as might be practicable.[262]

This rather suggests that the last point, de Valera's favourite nostrum, limped along in third place behind the first two points, which were subversive of the assumptions underlying traditional Fianna Fáil policy.

The tension can be gleaned from a draft minute inadvertently included in the file containing the cryptic official minutes. The meeting, called to discuss land policy, was attended by Seán Moylan, Minister for Lands. A straight conflict of opinion between Lemass (and probably Moylan) on the one side, and de Valera on the other, can be detected.[263] Lemass pressed Moylan to explain precisely the criteria of the Department of Lands in connection with land allocation, stressing the importance of efficiency as a criterion. De Valera's view that 'on the question of the size of farms . . . there was more real work and thrift on small farms' went distinctly against the drift of the discussion.

Given that Fianna Fáil had just won a comfortable overall majority in the June 1944 election, and that the emigrants were now expected to stay safely away, Finance would probably have prevailed anyway at this stage against the Lemass penchant for more expenditure. But the impetuous manner in which Lemass chose to launch so direct an assault on the cherished party pieties, instead of embarking on the type of flanking and infiltrating movement of which de Valera was master, must have buttressed McElligott's position. The terms in which Lemass couched his demand for an efficient agriculture alienated colleagues, who were not only ideologically committed to preaching peasant virtue, but depended heavily on the votes of precisely the people whom Lemass proposed to banish to the dustbin of history. Some may have felt, 'give us efficiency, but not yet'. Others may have detected no need for even a deferred dose of

[261] SPO S13026B, 13 July 1944.   [262] *Ibid.*, 5 September 1944.
[263] *Ibid.* 22 November 1944; E. Magner, 'Sean Moylan: some aspects of his parliamentary career 1937–1948' (MA thesis, UCC, 1982, ch. 3).

the distasteful medicine. Jim Ryan, with whom Lemass normally worked well, might have been flexible on Keynes. But he was bound to react sharply, as he duly did, and in terms designed to appeal to de Valera, against the attack on inefficient farmers.[264] It is unlikely that many cabinet members fully grasped the technicalities of the Lemass–McElligott exchanges on full employment. But they were left in little doubt of the Lemass attitude towards small farmers, and were likely to have resented his whole approach for this alone. McElligott of course shared the Lemass disdain for the bold peasantry. They differed less on their image of the ideal farmer, than on the role of agriculture in the economy. However, McElligott was shrewd enough to focus his assault on the Keynesian heresy.

Lemass could still count on getting the better of the discussion as long as the argument was confined to the Committee on Economic Planning. Neither de Valera nor O'Kelly were likely to relish direct confrontation with Lemass on his chosen ground. De Valera was not one to allow himself to be pinned down in this manner. In April 1945 the committee became a committee of the whole cabinet.[265] Lemass was swamped. Discussion of his proposals was regularly deferred, and when a verdict was pronounced in June, it registered clear defeat for Lemass. To add insult to injury, the main decision to emerge was that Finance should submit a memorandum 'on the subject of the law and practice in relation to transactions in stocks and shares'.[266] So much for a full employment policy! Finance hadn't even bothered to respond a year later.[267]

However sceptical de Valera remained of Lemass's grand designs for the future, he relied heavily on him to carry the country, and the party, through the Emergency. For the war taught the prophets of self-sufficiency a painful lesson in elementary economics. In 1928 de Valera lamented that 'We will, unfortunately, not be able to cut ourselves completely off' from the world economy. He dreamed of the arcadia that would flourish 'if the country was surrounded by a wall'. 'If by any chance we were cut off', he prophesied, 'I am satisfied that we could now, in this country, maintain a population two or three times the size of our present population.'[268]

The dream came true in 1940. Ireland was cut off. The dream now became a nightmare. Ireland, one of the most sparsely populated countries in western Europe, couldn't maintain its paltry population, much less a bigger one. By making the country more dependent on imported raw materials, industrialisation had reduced rather than increased self-sufficiency, as Smiddy sought to impress on de Valera.[269] Industrial

---

[264] Bew and Patterson, *Lemass*, p. 27.
[265] SPO S13026B, Cabinet Committee on Economic Planning, memo, 13 September 1946.
[266] *Ibid.*   [267] *Ibid.*   [268] Moynihan, *Speeches*, pp. 158–9.
[269] SPO, S11466, Smiddy memo, 25 September 1939.

production fell about 25 per cent during the war, and the government got a good deal more self sufficiency than it bargained for. Circumstances would probably have deteriorated even further but for the vigorous performance of the Department of Supplies, which de Valera established under Lemass on the outbreak of the war. The energy and ingenuity of Lemass in his new post, partnered again by Leydon as Secretary, and reinforced by the recruitment of several promising young civil servants, consolidated his reputation as an effective minister. The task was daunting, because Ireland was 'very largely at the mercy of other countries, and particularly of the United Kingdom, in respect of our external trade'.[270] Ireland had virtually no merchant marine, relying for 95 per cent of its trade in 1938 on foreign owned vessels.[271] Lemass was obliged to establish Irish Shipping in 1941, to maintain contact with a once excoriated outside world, now granted at least temporary remission for its sins in the new economic theology.

Circumstances were more difficult than in the First World War. The supply situation was then nowhere as critical as it became during the Second World War. Nor was it the case in Ireland, for obvious reasons, that 'the First World War had left massive files of invaluable administrative experience on the shelves of government, which in 1939 had only to be reached for and dusted . . . '.[272] Hence, in part, the air of fumbling improvisation of so much of the initial Irish response.

Irish farmers did well out of inflated British food prices in the First World War. Now Britain kept food prices under closer control. Irish agriculture therefore did not reap such easy rewards again. The one major unearned gain for the country was the accumulation, however involuntarily, of substantial sterling surpluses because of the decline in imports. The difficult situation obliged the government to impose not only rationing, but price and wage controls. A wages standstill order came into effect in May 1941. By April 1942 Emergency decrees had frozen virtually all incomes, except for speculative and black market profits.

Nevertheless, Ireland had a relatively cosy war. Not only the belligerents, but some other neutrals, faced far more daunting economic problems. Compulsory tillage orders more than doubled wheat output between 1939 and 1944. The furore over wheat revealed the Irish concept of hardship – how white would the bread be? Ireland was able to indulge the luxury of expanding wheat acreage by far more than the European average. Other countries relied relatively more on increasing the output of potatoes, which supplied more nutrition from less ground. True, Irish per capita potato consumption was still high by European standards in 1939. However, it had been falling steadily. By 1944 Irish potato acreage had

270 *Ibid.*   271 Fisk, *In time of war*, p. 84.
272 Milward, *War, economy and society*, p. 17.

just recovered the level of 1922, for the same population.[273] In calculating precise per capita consumption levels, some adjustment would be required to allow for the implications of the smaller pig population. But the general point stands. That the war should have obliged the Irish to revert to 1922 levels of potato consumption can scarcely be deemed a disaster. Ample scope remained for increasing potato production further if a real food shortage threatened. Ireland had the good fortune to be, for practical purposes, self-sufficient in food. She faced nothing like the problem confronting Switzerland, only 52 per cent self-sufficient before the war.[274] That Ireland could afford to fret over the colour of bread and the rationing of tea 'which is so extraordinarily important for the Irish' reflected the relative comfort of her situation.[275]

The main reason Ireland came through the war relatively comfortably, however, was a simple one. She economised on defence. This was the secret of her astonishing achievement in reducing public expenditure as a proportion of gross domestic product between 1939 and 1945. Having risen from 22.5 per cent to 28 per cent in 1939, the proportion fell steadily to 22.8 per cent in 1945. It began to rise again only with the end of the war![276] This performance can be placed in perspective by comparing it with that of the other successful democratic neutral states, Sweden and Switzerland. Irish government expenditure rose about 33 per cent during the war. Between 1938 and 1944 Swiss government expenditure increased about 120 per cent, and Swedish about 150 per cent.[277] As a proportion of gross domestic product, Swedish public expenditure rose by more than 40 per cent, and Swiss by almost 50 per cent. Irish *fell* by about 20 per cent![278]

Ireland was wholly unprepared for war in 1939.[279] The Munich crisis had exposed her utter lack of preparation.[280] Despite some increased provision for expenditure, defence continued to take second place to finance, until the fall of France in June 1940.[281] Not until then did the danger of actual invasion prompt the government to increase the nominal size of the army from 19 000 to 42 000.[282] In addition, a Local Security Force, 'a form of paramilitary police based on the gárdaí which could, if

273 Mitchell, *European historical statistics*, pp. 217–19.
274 H.E. Volkmann, 'Landwirtschaft und Ernährung in Hitler's Europa, 1939–45', *Militär-geschichtliche Mitteilungen*, 1 (1984), p. 57.
275 BA-MA, Wi/1a.2/II, Deutsche Reichsbank, Volkswirtschaftsliche Abteilung, 4 November 1941, Irland.
276 O'Donoghue and Tait, 'The growth of public revenue', p. 288.
277 P. Flora *et al.*, *State, economy and society in Western Europe 1815–1975* (London, 1983), vol. 1, pp. 395, 426, 433. A comparison of 1938 and 1944 shows an even smaller rise in the Irish case, but this was due to special factors.
278 *Ibid.*, pp. 394, 428, 433.   279 Fisk, *In time of war*, p. 66.
280 O'Sullivan, *The Irish Free State and its Senate* (London, 1940, Arno reprint, 1972), p. 584.
281 Fisk, *In time of war*, p. 66.   282 *Ibid.*, pp. 136–7.

necessary, be used against the IRA', began to be organised after a German agent parachuted into Ireland in May 1940. It reached a strength, or at least a membership, of 148 000 by August.[283]

These Irish figures may be compared with those of Sweden and Switzerland. Dissatisfied though Swedish military authorities would remain with her preparations, she nevertheless mobilised in April 1940, following the German invasion of Denmark and Norway, her regular forces of 95 000 men, and more than 200 000 extra effectives.[284] She stretched herself on later crisis occasions, by drawing on all her reserve forces, to mobilise 600 000 men and 110 000 women out of a population of 6.4 million.[285] The total of effective front-line fighters ran at about half this figure.[286] Switzerland, with a population of 4.2 million, mobilised up to 400 000 effectives at moments of crisis. When auxiliary services and the home guard were counted, Switzerland brought her mobilisation potential to 850 000![287]

Numbers were less important than training and equipment. However insistent their military authorities remained that scope for improvement continued to exist, both Sweden and Switzerland took reserve training seriously. Of the 12 000 reserves included in the nominal Irish army strength of 19 000 in 1939, 7000 were 'inadequately trained' by even euphemistic criteria.[288] This was not their fault. They could not have trained adequately had they tried. Their equipment was obsolete. Sweden and Switzerland strained to develop their defence industries. Ireland did not. Self-sufficiency did not extend to this most basic of all criteria for a sovereign state.

It is doubtful if anything significant could have been accomplished once the war began. Ireland lacked the intellectual, administrative, managerial and technological infrastructures, as well as many of the raw materials, necessary to build up an arms industry quickly. Although Sweden supplied 87 per cent of new equipment during the war from her own industry, it was not until the later stages that she was able to complete, despite her superior standards and resources, and her existing heavy

---

[283] *Ibid.*, p. 137.

[284] W.M. Carlgren, *Swedish foreign policy during the Second World War* (London, 1977), p. 60.

[285] F.D. Scott, *Sweden: the nation's history* (Minneapolis, 1977), p. 507.

[286] C.A. Wangel, 'Verteidigung gegen den Krieg', in R.L. Bindschedler, *et al.* (eds.), *Schwedische und schweizerische Neutralität im zweiten Weltkrieg* (Basel, 1985), p. 47. Another useful general survey is S. Ekman, 'La politique de défense de la Suède durant la seconde guerre mondiale', *Revue d'histoire de la deuxième guerre mondiale*, 126 (April 1982), pp. 3–36.

[287] E. Bonjour, H.S. Offler, G.R. Potter, *A short history of Switzerland* (Oxford, 1952), p. 367.

[288] G.A. Hayes-McCoy, 'Irish defence policy, 1938–51', in Nowlan and Williams (eds.), *War years and after*, p. 40.

industry, the bulk of the 600 planes and 720 tanks that she built herself.[289]

For practical purposes, Ireland had neither an air force nor a navy. She had almost no anti-aircraft artillery, which served as both an excuse and a justification for negative responses to American pressure to cede the ports to Britain in 1940.[290] Attempts to procure arms from Britain and America yielded meagre results.[291] Even had the Irish demands been met, she would still have remained seriously under-equipped. In the event of invasion, the Irish forces would have paid the price for a policy of long-term neglect of national security, diligently though they strove, under the driving discipline of General Dan McKenna, the wartime Chief of Staff, to compensate for their inherited inadequacies.[292] Ireland was not therefore a neutral of Swedish or Swiss vintage. They both pursued a policy of armed neutrality. Ireland pursued, at most, a policy of half-armed neutrality.

It was thanks mainly to the failure to mount a defence effort remotely comparable to that of the other successful democratic neutrals that the public finances could remain so relatively unscathed by the war. Not only did total public expenditure rise much less than in Sweden or Switzerland. Defence as a proportion of public expenditure accounted for little more than 20 per cent in Ireland, compared with more than 40 per cent in both those countries.[293]

WAR POLITICS

The happy corollary, from a party political viewpoint, of the relatively modest level of defence expenditure, was that taxes did not have to rise to the punitive levels that a more intensive defence effort would have required. The tax payer, doubtless, did not see it quite like that. Income tax payers would have been more conscious of an increase in the standard tax rate from 5/6d to 7/6d between 1939 and 1942. Total direct taxes duly rose from £10.3 million in 1939 to £13.3 million in 1945. However, only a small proportion of the population paid income tax. Revenue from indirect taxation fell, partly because tariffs could no longer so effectively fulfil their function as revenue earners.[294]

[289] U. Olsson, *The creation of a modern arms industry: Sweden, 1939–1974* (Gothenburg, 1977), pp. 77, 111, 128.

[290] FRUS, 1940, III, S. Welles memo, 9 November 1940, pp. 166–7; Gray to Secretary of State, 10 November 1940, pp. 168–9.

[291] Fisk, *In time of war*, pp. 264ff.; T. Ryle Dwyer, *Irish neutrality and the USA 1939–47* (Dublin, 1977), pp. 53, 57, 81ff; J.L. Rosenberg, 'The 1941 mission of Frank Aiken to the United States: an American perspective', *IHS*, 22, 86 (September 1980), pp. 162–77; J.T. Carroll, *Ireland in the war years*, pp. 102–4; FRUS, 1940, III, pp. 161–6.

[292] J.P. Duggan, *Neutral Ireland and the Third Reich* (Dublin, 1985), p. 195.

[293] Flora, *State, economy and society*, pp. 399, 430.

[294] O'Donoghue and Tait, 'The growth of public revenue', p. 291.

It need not be suspected that taxation decisions were governed solely, or perhaps even mainly, by party political considerations. But party thinking continued to flourish during the war. In contrast to Sweden, where Per Albin Hansson brought the Conservative opposition into his Socialist dominated government – and where taxes trebled[295] – 'de Valera dismissed opposition demands for an emergency coalition government'.[296] Fine Gael and Labour, despite their staunch parliamentary support for neutrality, were treated as virtual pariahs. De Valera would only go so far as to give them seats in a National Defence Conference, a purely advisory body. Insofar as he paid any attention to it, he appears to have regarded it as merely another pawn in the party political game.[297] Civil war memories remained bitter. Indeed, they probably had to become more bitter as other differences between the parties disappeared. Nothing could be allowed to violate the sacred egoism of party politics. Fianna Fáil would provide whatever national government was required.

The advantage of going it alone for de Valera was that he could pursue his personal policy, which did not always coincide with the impressions he intended the public to form of that policy, without danger of indiscretion, much less obstruction, from party political opponents. De Valera's own instincts were in many respects as anglophile as Fine Gael's. But it was just as important that Fine Gael should not suspect this any more than Fianna Fáil! The risk of going it alone, in party terms, was that Fianna Fáil would bear the full brunt of any public backlash that might occur. This alone precluded the possibility of imposing the financial burden that a massive defence effort would have required. Only a national government, with all parties equally implicated, could have conceivably inflicted the necessary burden.

A national government had no function in de Valera's concept of 'Emergency' leadership. But he moved vigorously to improve the ability of his cabinet to confront the new situation. Having made only a handful of changes since 1932, he engaged in an extensive reshuffle of portfolios in September 1939. The establishment of new Departments of Supplies and of the Cordination of Defensive Measures created the openings. When Lemass vacated Industry and Commerce for Supplies, de Valera transferred MacEntee from Finance to Industry and Commerce. On the face of it, this was a serious demotion for MacEntee. Industry and Commerce was likely to enjoy little scope for initiative during the war. It could be no more than a shadow of its old self, particularly with Leydon following Lemass

---

295 I. Nygren, 'The Swedish credit market and government borrowing for defence and interest rates stabilisation 1935–1945', in M. Fritz *et al.*, *The adaptable nation* (Stockholm, 1982), p. 93.

296 Fisk, *In time of war* p. 138.

297 H. Dickel, *Die deutsche Aussenpolitik und die Irische Frage von 1932 bis 1944* (Wiesbaden, 1983), p. 114.

to Supplies. De Valera then moved Seán T. O'Kelly from Local Government and Public Health to Finance. He may have been anxious to have a more pliable Minister for Finance than MacEntee during a war that might compel deviation from financial orthodoxy. Ruttledge, who had to be kept in the cabinet both as an old friend and as a 'republican', replaced O'Kelly when de Valera moved Gerry Boland from Lands to Justice. Tom Derrig was sent from Education to Lands. The filling of Education apparently posed problems. It would no doubt be facetious to suggest that Fianna Fáil had nobody capable of dealing with the subject! O'Kelly took it on, in addition to Finance, for three weeks. Then de Valera, himself already Taoiseach and Minister for External Affairs, which one might have thought would have given him enough to do on the outbreak of the war, took over Education for nine months. It was an intriguing decision, in that the assumption of a portfolio to which he could patently devote little time, however ardent his declared interest in the subject, suggests certain tensions among possible aspirants.[298] De Valera soon brought Derring back to Education, which he held with Lands until 1943.

This game of musical chairs arising from the original Lemass move to Supplies contrasts with the relative simplicity of the solution to the opening created in appointing Frank Aiken Minister for Coordination of Defensive Measures. De Valera transferred Oscar Traynor from Posts and Telegraphs to Aiken's former post at Defence. After a three-week hiatus, during which Tom Derrig held Posts and Telegraphs as well as Lands, P. J. Little succeeded Derrig at the Post Office. The only notable feature about Little's appointment was that he was the only new man brought into the cabinet in the whole reshuffle. De Valera would rock the party boat as little as possible.

But the reconstructed cabinet did not survive the war unscathed. Tensions appear to have become acute between Lemass and MacEntee. The resignation of Ruttledge on health grounds in August 1941 allowed de Valera to accede to pressure from Lemass – who told the Taoiseach he did not have enough to do![299] – by restoring Industry and Commerce to him, which he held jointly with Supplies for the rest of the war. MacEntee succeeded Ruttledge at Local Government. After the general election of 1943, Derrig ceded Lands to Seán Moylan, the second new face to enter the cabinet during the Emergency. Complete justice cannot be done to de Valera's managerial style until the precise calculations behind his cabinet reshuffles can be fully elucidated.

The final ministerial moves in the Emergency cabinet had longer-term

---

[298] De Valera did find time in Education to guide his controversial bill on the Institute for Advanced Studies through the Oireachtas. See D. McCartney, *The National University of Ireland and Eamon de Valera* (Dublin, 1983), p. 45.
[299] 'Seán Lemass looks back', *Irish Press*, 25 January 1969.

implications. When the presidency became vacant in 1945, de Valera, confident of a Fianna Fáil victory in the election, departed from the non-party principle involved in the choice of Douglas Hyde in 1938, and nominated his popular Tánaiste, Seán T. O'Kelly, as candidate. Aiken, no longer occupied in coordinating defensive measures, was deposited directly in Finance in place of O'Kelly. Aiken was probably the closest person in the cabinet to de Valera. However, he did not become Tánaiste. Instead, it was the man who was temperamentally furthest from himself, and from his colleagues, Seán Lemass, whom de Valera chose as his new Tánaiste. This was a key decision. It would be interesting for students of de Valera to know if one motive in nominating O'Kelly for the presidency was to permit the appointment of Lemass as Tánaiste. O'Kelly had been mentioned for the presidency in 1938. While it was unduly disparaging to dismiss him as 'the Nick Bottom of Irish politics',[300] for he could be capable of shrewd and independent judgement, nevertheless the succession could be considered open as long as O'Kelly remained Tánaiste. The same age as de Valera, Seán T., who 'liked company, particularly the company of women, and . . . could drink a glass or two or more of whiskey',[301] was not widely considered Taoiseach material. The 45-year-old Lemass was. Appointing the youngest member of the cabinet as Tánaiste meant jumping over the older heads of MacEntee, Ryan and Aiken, whose reactions may not have been benign. If it did not ensure the succession for Lemass, it did distinctly enhance his prospects, insofar as it seemed to lay the chief's hands upon him.

In 1945 succession to the party leadership seemed to guarantee succession as Taoiseach. Fianna Fáil had won a handsome election majority in 1944. That victory, however, followed a period of considerable electoral uncertainty.

Public opinion rallied to the government at outset of the war. It then gradually became disillusioned with Fianna Fáil's performance. The government was far more successful in curbing wages than in controlling prices. The decline in real incomes, aggravated by the irksome intrusions of bureaucracy, alienated support. Fianna Fáil was threatened from two directions. It failed to deliver the goods to the agricultural population. After the halcyon days of 1932 and 1933, the solid west showed signs of cracking in 1937. The recovery of 1938 proved short-lived. A new party, Clann na Talmhan (Family of the land) founded in 1938/9 as a sort of *Landvolk* movement, appealed to small and medium-sized farmers, denouncing Fianna Fáil's failure to fulfil its somewhat lavish promises. The other threat came from Labour, which stood to reap the harvest of urban discontent at wartime stringencies. The gravity of the situation could be deduced from the fact that de Valera postponed the general

[300] *Round Table*, 112 (September 1938), p. 743.   [301] Ó Broin, *Yesterday*, p. 158.

election, contrary to his normal habit, until June 1943, the last possible moment under existing constitutional conventions.

His fears proved well founded. Fianna Fáil's popular vote fell from 668 000 to 558 000, or from 51.9 per cent to 41.9 per cent of the valid poll. This resulted in a loss of 10 seats. Though it still won 9 seats more than it was entitled to on a strict proportionality basis, Fianna Fáil nevertheless lost its overall majority, with 67 seats out of 138. Its share of the vote in the most agricultural constituencies fell from 61 per cent to 41 per cent, with Clann na Talmhan winning 13 seats, mostly in the west. Labour, scenting prospects of success, ran 71 candidates compared with 30 in 1938. Its popular vote rose from 129 000 to 209 000, and its number of seats from 9 to 17. The main consolation for Fianna Fáil was that Fine Gael, lacking leadership and policy, also lost heavily, with its popular vote falling from 429 000 to 307 000. Fianna Fáil continued to rule after the election only because of the inability of the other parties to coalesce into an effective alternative. De Valera must have been quietly grateful that the modesty of defence expenditure enabled him to avoid increasing taxation to Swiss or Swedish levels, and to refrain from imposing Swiss-type special levies on wealth, which would presumably have diminished Fianna Fáil's electoral appeal even further.

The 1943 election saw Fianna Fáil's support spread remarkably evenly throughout the country.[302] The problem was that this achievement reflected a decline in the western vote rather than an increase in the eastern vote. It was not so much that Fianna Fáil became a national party, for it had long been that, as that it ceased to dominate the west, thanks to the electoral impact of Clann na Talmhan. De Valera was not amused. He set out to rectify the situation. A split in Labour gave him the chance to pounce.

Labour appeared poised to at last emerge as a major party after the 1943 election. With Fianna Fáil and Fine Gael losing 230 000 votes between them, the future seemed promising. Labour had nearly trebled its vote since the trough of 1933, when it trembled on the threshold of extinction. It stood to make further gains due to the continuing economic hardships of the war. It promptly rose to the challenge by tearing itself apart in an internecine struggle between the ancient adversaries, William O'Brien and 'Big Jim' Larkin. O'Brien, the powerful General Secretary of the Transport Union, was mainly responsible. Larkin, the stormy petrel of earlier years, was gradually making his peace with the party. O'Brien was determined to stop him. Failing to persuade Labour to withhold the hand of conciliation from Larkin, O'Brien did not hestitate 'to rip the party

302 T. Garvin, 'Change and the political system' in F. Litton, *Unequal achievement* (Dublin, 1982), t. 5, p. 35.

asunder at the point of its major opportunity'.[303] He formed a new National Labour Party from some of the Transport Union TDs, and then ran a 'red scare' campaign against Labour, gleefully abetted by Fianna Fáil, especially Seán MacEntee. O'Brien was a classic case of the successful apparatchik so frequently found in Irish organisations, combining fine administrative abilities with a domineering personality and a narrow mind. He was the type of man, only too common in Ireland, who prefers to wreck a movement rather than lose control of it. Having rendered sterling service to trade union organisation, he was now instrumental in dragging Labour down at a crucial moment.[304]

Fine Gael fell into even more disconsolate disarray after the 1943 election. Failing to profit from the unpopularity of Fianna Fáil, it seemed to be drifting into oblivion. W.T. Cosgrave, much more a man of government than of opposition, resigned the leadership. His successor, Richard Mulcahy, had actually lost his Dáil seat. With Labour split, and Fine Gael dispirited, de Valera predictably called a snap election in May 1944. He emerged yet again with an overall majority, with 76 seats out of 138 on 48.9 per cent of the valid poll. Fianna Fáil won some credit for de Valera's success in thwarting American demands for the expulsion of Axis diplomats early in 1944. In addition, it fought a somewhat more hard-headed campaign than the previous year. De Valera had launched the election campaign in 1943 in his famous St Patrick's Day broadcast in which he invited the public to share his 'dream' of, *inter alia* 'a land whose countryside would be bright with . . . the laughter of comely maidens'. The response to the dream was depressing. Urban workers wanted higher wages. Farmers wanted higher prices. The election result did not enhance the market value of comely maidens. Female favours filled no pockets. As the Fianna Fáil nag trotted up to the starting tape for the 1944 election, 'comely maiden' was unceremoniously dumped out of the saddle, and 'rural electrification' plonked in her place as a better bet to brighten up the countryside.[305]

Despite the more propitious circumstances, however, victory in 1944 reflected despair in the opposition more than confidence in the government. Turnout, down to 67.7 per cent, was the lowest since 1923. In absolute terms, Fianna Fáil recovered less than half the votes lost in 1943. Labour, of all denominations, lost 70 000 votes and 9 seats. William O'Brien succeeded in dissipating the gains of 1943 at a stroke. Fine Gael

[303] C. McCarthy, *Trade unions in Ireland 1894–1960* (Dublin, 1977), p. 259.
[304] *Ibid.*, ch. 6; Whyte, 'Church and state', pp. 85–6. On O'Brien's career, see A. Mitchell, 'William O'Brien, 1881–1968, and the Irish labour movement', *Studies*, 60, 239 (Winter 1971), pp. 311–31. For a more sympathetic view than mine, see *Leader* Profile, 'William O'Brien', 31 January 1953.
[305] M. Manning and M. MacDowell, *Electricity supply in Ireland: the history of the ESB* (Dublin, 1984), p. 127 discuss electrification policy.

nominated only 57 candidates, not even enough to win a majority. It got only 20.5 per cent of the valid poll, and 30 seats. Apart from Fianna Fáil, only Clann na Talmhan had some cause for satisfaction. It did not succumb to the one-two of quick elections, and retained 11 seats.

Fianna Fáil felt it could afford to shrug aside the circumstances of victory. It was victory that counted, whatever the style of it. With Fine Gael paralysed and Labour split, no alternative government appeared possible for the foreseeable future. De Valera seemed secure in office for as long as he wished. It was a gratifying outcome to a period of uncertainty in which both the existence of the state and the fortunes of the party had seemed at times to be threatened.

It needed no supreme act of statesmanship to declare neutrality. Most European countries, to say nothing of the United States, did so in 1939. If declarations of neutrality were the definition of statesmanship, the world never had so many statesmen as in September 1939. But declaring neutrality was one thing. Preserving it was another. Only five of the twenty countries that declared their neutrality in September 1939 succeeded in preserving it throughout the war.[306] In the five months from April to August 1940, Hitler and Mussolini occupied eight neutral countries, whose only crime was that they had the misfortune to lie in the path of the predators.

The Irish case was not so pressing. Germany seemed a long way away. Nor did neutrality require exceptional skill in purely domestic political terms. All Dáil parties supported the policy. When James Dillon, deputy leader of Fine Gael, broke ranks in 1942 to argue that Ireland should, on moral grounds, align herself with America, he found himself promptly expelled from the party. Neutrality was the line of least resistance for any Irish government. It was the policy that divided the nation least. It did not, for instance, require the political skills with which a MacKenzie King brought a potentially divided Canada into the war. All it required was the suppression of IRA subversion, a nuisance certainly, but no new imposition, even if it now had to be pursued with rather less indulgence for 'the lads', particularly after they were so unsporting as to make a laughing stock of the government by appropriating the army's main, if meagre, ammunition reserves in a raid in December 1939.[307]

Every belligerent behaved according to its own perceived self-interest. The two key variables that would determine the fate of Irish neutrality were exactly the same as applied in the case of all other neutrals. Firstly, did any belligerent consider the occupation of Ireland vital for its own

[306] A. Roberts, *Nations in arms: the theory and practice of territorial defence* (London, 1976), p. 38.
[307] M. Laffan, 'Violence and terror in twentieth-century Ireland: IRB and IRA', in W.J. Mommsen and G. Hirschfeld (eds.), *Social protest, violence and terror in twentieth-century Europe* (London, 1982), p. 203.

purposes? Secondly, would the cost of invasion be worth the effort? De Valera's task was to ensure that no major belligerent answered either question in the affirmative.

He faced a delicate problem. There was no way he could persuade any major power that the military occupation of Ireland would be a dangerous enterprise. His neglect of defence before the war, and the failure to equip the armed forces adequately during the war, meant that the defence effort contributed more to maintaining internal morale than to providing a serious deterrent. The British military had no high opinion of Irish ability to resist a German invasion, reckoning that little more than a division would suffice, assuming IRA collaboration, to capture the country.[308] This compared with the two and a half divisions Germany had launched against Denmark, or the six against Norway, or the maximum of twenty-one that the Germans considered necessary to reduce a resolute Switzerland.[309]

De Valera could properly reply to juvenile charges of the 'cowardice' of neutrality that 'Neutrality is not a cowardly policy if you really mean to defend yourself if attacked.'[310] But he realized what a wide gap existed between intention and capacity in a country, as he conceded in 1940, 'almost completely unprepared for war'.[311] Insofar as Britain, Germany or the United States took Irish defence seriously, it was probably mainly due to recollection of the tenacity displayed in the guerrilla struggle during the War of Independence.[312] How far even that consideration would have influenced the Germans, who had ways of dealing with recalcitrant populations that made the Black and Tans seem a boy scout brigade, must remain conjectural.

The country's state of permanent military unpreparedness imposed heavy demands on the statecraft of de Valera. He spoke from a position of exceptional military weakness, even by the standards of small states. Everything therefore hinged on his ability to persuade the belligerents that the occupation of Ireland was not vital to their interests. He had two crucial allies. The first was geography. The second was partition.

De Valera knew that there was little danger of a German invasion as long as England held out. He also knew there was no hope of effectively resisting German occupation if England fell. Some Germans may have toyed with ideas of invading Ireland from France in the summer of 1940.

---

[308] Canning, *British policy*, p. 282.

[309] H. Senn, 'Schweizerische Dissuasionstrategie im Zweiten Weltkrieg', in Bindschedler, *Neutralität*, p. 211.

[310] Duggan, *Neutral Ireland*, p. 123.

[311] PRO, DO 114–17: Neutrality of Éire (World War 1939–1945), M. MacDonald report to cabinet, 20 June 1940, p. 1; FRUS, 1940, III, Gray to Secretary of State, 18 May 1940, p. 160.

[312] PA AA, Hempel-AA, 18 September 1940, no. 571; 10 November 1940, no. 726; 29 November 1940, no. 774, StSekr. Irland, 1; Fisk, *In time of war*, p. 213.

Some low-level clandestine activity occurred. But there was no real threat.[313] In so far as Germany had a coherent Irish policy, it was largely directed at keeping Ireland neutral, as constantly urged by the perceptive Dr Hempel, German minister in Dublin since 1937. This was the best that German diplomacy could realistically hope for unless Britain collapsed. Until then a threat of German invasion would provoke an immediate British response.[314]

It was from Britain that the only serious invasion threat could come unless she herself fell. Had Britain's circumstances become so desperate that she considered Southern Irish bases crucial to her survival, she would have inevitably seized them, with unpredictable consequences for Irish domestic politics. It was therefore in de Valera's interest that Britain's case should not reach desperation point. He consequently played, as he had to play, a double game. He rigidly maintained the formality of Irish neutrality right to the end, even to the extent of raising a storm of indignant Allied protest when conveying his condolences to Hempel on the death of Hitler.[315] But he simultaneously took care to cooperate sufficiently with Britain, and later with the United States, to ensure that they did not feel provoked into aggressive action against Irish interests. He had to ensure that Britain could not acquire by conquest much more than she gained through cooperation. He could not, and did not, keep Ireland strictly neutral during the war. He kept Ireland benevolently neutral for Britain. Out of sheer self-interest, he maintained the supplies of men and food to Britain. He behaved, in other words, absolutely normally by the standards of other neutrals, including Sweden and Switzerland, during the war. If few neutrals had to perform the gymnastic heroics of Turkey, the neutral with the most awkward assignment of all, in that she was militarily vulnerable from all sides for much of the war, they were all neutral for the power that potentially threatened them most.[316]

De Valera obliged Britain not only on the economic front – the days of the economic war belonged to another age – but on the military and intelligence fronts also. The Irish army, while ready to resist a British invasion, also collaborated closely with the British military authorities north of the border, envisaging extensive cooperation in the event of a German invasion.[317] Irish intelligence performed impressively.[318] The

---

[313] Dickel, 'Deutsche Aussenpolitik', p. 127, n. 219.

[314] H. Dickel, 'Irland als Faktor der deutschen Aussenpolitik von 1933–1945', in M. Funke (ed.), *Hitler, Deutschland und die Mächte* (Düsseldorf, 1976), pp. 571ff.

[315] For speculation on de Valera's motives, see Carroll, *Ireland in the war years*, pp. 160–1; T. Ryle Dwyer, *Irish neutrality and the USA 1939–47* (Dublin, 1977), pp. 202–3.

[316] W. Hofer, 'Neutralität im totalen Krieg', in W. Hofer, *Mächte und Kräfte im 20. Jahrhundert* (Zurich, 1983), pp. 102–3.

[317] Fisk, *In time of war*, pp. 200ff.

[318] Duggan, *Neutral Ireland*, p. 196; C.J. Carter, *The shamrock and the swastika* (Palo Alto, 1977).

American intelligence services were so gratified at the solicitude of neutral Ireland for American interests that Irish officers were even recommended for American decorations![319] Cooperation with British intelligence seems to have been extensive from early in the war.[320]

Whether even this intense collaboration would have sufficed to preserve territorial integrity in the absence of partition may be doubted. Irish bases were important, perhaps vital, for Britain's security. They allowed her to provide crucial extra cover for the transatlantic convoys. Access to Southern ports would have saved British and American lives, but the precise location of Irish bases was more a matter of convenience than necessity.[321] Once she had Northern Irish bases Britain could route her supplies past the north coast. But she could hardly have survived, or at least taken the risk she would not survive, without some foothold in Ireland. Partition was therefore a prerequisite for successful neutrality.[322] At the same time it was a prime Irish justification, if not reason, for neutrality.[323]

The summer of 1940, when the fall of France turned the world upside down, casts revealing light on the mentalities of the actors on the Irish public stage. Much remains to be reconstructed concerning the response of Irish diplomacy to the new circumstances. But the contours can be discerned, however dimly, even from the fragmentary evidence currently available.

'A small state on the edge of Europe, reviewing its policy in the last week of May 1940, could not possibly avoid taking into consideration the German armies' overwhelming victories in the west and the prospect of an ultimate German victory.'[324] This comment by a leading historian of Swedish neutrality applies with equal force to Ireland. De Valera himself seems to have kept a cooler head than External Affairs officials during May and June.[325] When the sympathetic Malcolm MacDonald found de Valera depressed in mid-June, it is possible that even he may

---

[319] Fanning, *Ireland*, p. 124.

[320] *Ibid.*, pp. 123–4; Dickel, *Deutsche Aussenpolitik*, p. 112.

[321] Longford and O'Neill, *De Valera*, p. 503; S.W. Roskill, *Churchill and the admirals* (London, 1977), pp. 122–3.

[322] A point repeatedly emphasised by T.D. Williams. No study of neutrality policy should fail to acknowledge the seminal contribution of his work. See T.D. Williams, 'A study in neutrality', *Leader* (31 January–25 April 1953); 'Neutrality', *Irish Press*, 27 June–18 July 1953; 'Ireland and the war', in K.B. Nowlan and T.D. Williams (eds.), *Ireland in the war years and after, 1939–51* (Dublin, 1969), pp. 14–27.

[323] Murphy, 'De Valera', in O'Carroll and Murphy, *De Valera*, pp. 4–5.

[324] Carlgren, *Swedish foreign policy*, p. 65.

[325] DGFP, D, ix, Hempel-AA, 21 June 1940, no. 506; DGFP, D, x, Hempel-AA, 1 July 1940, no. 79. It seems likely that de Valera would have consulted closely not only with his External Affairs officials, but with Maurice Moynihan and General McKenna, the chief of staff, at this time. The documents currently available do not permit elucidation of their role.

have been momentarily gripped by the 'panic' that Hempel detected in Dublin following the stunning German victories and the discovery of a German agent in Ireland in late May.[326] But de Valera remained fundamentally anglophile, even if he too succumbed for a time to the belief that Britain was 'definitely losing the war . . . '.[327]

Emphatically a man of Munich, de Valera accepted Hitler's claim to the Sudetenland.[328] He would later claim that he had supported Hitler only until the invasion of Czechoslovakia, which obliged him to revise his views after March 1939.[329] Even after revelation was reputedly vouchsafed, however, Dublin still criticised England for taking a stronger line against further German expansion.[330] De Valera duly counselled the British to refrain from war over Danzig.[331] Opinion was widespread in Dublin before the war that Britain should make 'substantial concessions' to German colonial demands, not only on grounds of expediency, but on grounds of equity.[332] But it was probably more de Valera's anglophilia than any *schadenfreude* that induced him to suggest to MacDonald in June 1940 that England should agree to give Germany a free hand in Europe as the price for the preservation of her empire.[333]

De Valera had the decency to publicly denounce the German invasion of Belgium and the Netherlands in May 1940.[334] Although the Italian minister attributed the protest to clerical indignation at the violation of the neutrality of Belgium, with which the Catholic Church had close ties, and considered de Valera's phraseology mild, it was still an act of rare courage.[335] But External Affairs beat a rapid retreat in the face of German indignation, at least to the extent necessary to allow the Germans assume Dublin had apologised.[336] F.H. Boland explained to Hempel that the Department had not had an opportunity of vetting de Valera's speech![337] Even when the immediate panic of late May and early June 1940 subsided, Hempel noted that Boland and Joe Walshe, Secretary of External Affairs, were highly conscious 'of the great and decisive importance even to Ireland of the changed situation in world affairs and of the obvious

[326] DGFP, D, IX, Hempel-AA, 21 June 1940, no. 506.

[327] PRO, DO 114–117, MacDonald telegram, 26 June 1940, Annex II, p. 3.

[328] D. McMahon, 'Ireland, the Dominions and the Munich crisis', *Irish Studies in International Affairs*, 1 (1979), p. 31; De Valera interview with the *Evening Standard*, as reported in *Irish Times*, 18 October 1938; PRO, PREM, 1–242, 26 September 1938, MacDonald meeting with Dominion representatives; PA AA, Hempel-AA, 5 May 1939, England–Irland, 2, no. 790.

[329] PA AA, Hempel-AA, 5 May 1939, England–Irland, 2, no. 790.   [330] *Ibid.*

[331] PRO, FO 371-23966, W10518, Liesching report, 5 July 1939.

[332] *Ibid.*   [333] PRO, DO 114–117. MacDonald memo on meeting of 17 June.

[334] DGFP, D, IX, p. 401, n. 1.

[335] DDI, 9, IV, Berardis–Ciano, 25 May 1940, no. 572.

[336] DGFP, D. IX, Woermann memo, 21 May 1940, no. 291.

[337] PA AA, StSekr. Irland I, Hempel-AA, 14 May 1940, no. 239.

weakness of the democracies'.[338] When the normally judicious and anglophile Boland wavered to the extent of going surprising distances to find a vocabulary soothing to German susceptibilities, it could only be expected that Walshe, more excitable and anglophobe, should have given numerous verbal hostages to the New Order.

As early as 1937 Walshe not only expressed complete 'understanding' for German colonial claims in Africa and the Pacific, but also felt that the Sudeten question had to be resolved. Hempel was sufficiently impressed to consider Walshe friendly to Germany.[339] Walshe would have liked to use the German victories in 1940 to have Hitler deliver the North to Dublin.[340] Purporting to be more afraid of Britain than of Germany, he chose to see Nazi victories partly from the 'England's danger is Ireland's opportunity' perspective, hoping that Hitler's declaration that he had no intention of destroying the British empire 'did not mean the abandonment of Ireland'.[341] The problem was that if the Germans ever came to be in a position to destroy the empire, or to deliver the North, they would by definition be in a position to deal as they wished with Dublin. It took no great imagination to deduce who would use whom. But Walshe seemed curiously oblivious to the fate of small and neutral continental countries. In mid-June he went out of his way to express 'his great admiration for the German achievements'.[342] One may wonder if this tribute from the senior diplomat of a small neutral state to a country with so voracious an appetite for small neutral states may not have been carrying a shade far what Hempel had earlier described as the Irish custom 'to say agreeable things without meaning everything that is said'.[343]

Walshe was, no doubt, assuming the certainty of German victory at this stage. When the general view in anglophile Finance was that 'England was beaten',[344] and when de Valera himself subscribed to that view, however reluctantly,[345] it was natural that those who may have felt less disturbed by the prospect of Nazi victory should have reached the same conclusion. Five months later, despite the resilience already shown by Britain, Walshe still anticipated either a German victory or stalemate.[346] That was not, indeed, an improbable outcome at that stage. Nor was Walshe perturbed by the prospect of stalemate. 'No-one outside of Great Britain', he was confident, believed that 'Great Britain was fighting for something worthwhile.'[347] Yet it must have been crystal clear that the victims of Nazi

[338] DGFP, D, *De Valera*, IX, Hempel-AA, 21 June 1940, no. 506, p. 639.
[339] DGFP, D, I, Hempel-AA, 17 November 1937, no. 28, p. 51.
[340] DGFP, D, IX, Hempel-AA, 17 June 1940, no. 473, pp. 602–3; 21 June, no. 506, p. 639.
[341] DGFP, D, IX, Hempel-AA, 17 June 1940, no. 473, p. 602.   [342] *Ibid.*
[343] DGFP, D, I, Hempel-AA, 17 November 1937, no. 28, p. 51.
[344] Ó Broin, *Yesterday*, p. 136.
[345] PRO, DO 114–117, MacDonald telegram, 26 June, Annex II, p. 3.
[346] FRUS, 1940, III, Gray to Secretary of State, 18 November 1940, no. 102, pp. 170–1.
[347] *Ibid.*

aggression had no hope of regaining independence unless Britain held out. That Britain was not fighting for their independence, but for her own, did not presumably render their desire for liberation any less 'worthwhile'. The logic of circumstances linked their fate inextricably to that of Britain. However indifferent, or indeed sympathetic, an Irish observer might be to the nature of the Nazi regime, and Walshe was not renowned for any deep philosophical repugnance to national socialism,[348] it might be assumed that an Irish public servant would take cognisance of the fate of other small neutral states before concluding that one of the weakest of all could bend Berlin to its will.

Walshe's tenderness towards the new masters of the continent in 1940 also presumably found expression in the performance of the Chargé d'Affaires in Berlin, William Warnock, whose 'unquestionable' hostility to Britain could easily be interpreted as sympathy for National Socialism.[349] It remains unclear how far Warnock was acting under general instructions from Dublin, or letting his personal enthusiasm get the better of him, in publicly applauding Hitler's Reichstag speech on 19 July, and in vigorously propounding the view in diplomatic circles that 'Not only the Germans but also other nations could expect the achievement of international justice' following Germany's victories.[350] Warnock's confidence in Hitler's thirst for 'international justice' and in Nazi solicitude for the rights of small states can most charitably be considered a triumph of imagination – whether his own or Walshe's – over evidence.

By no means all the policy-making elite would have shared Walshe's apparent satisfaction at the presumed imminence of German victory in June 1940. De Valera himself probably feared more than he relished the implications. It will be already clear from the present tentative exploration that Dublin's policy at this juncture, when the rulers of independent Ireland suddenly experienced real cold fear of invasion, whether from Britain or from Germany, for the first time since the foundation of the state, requires much more research. It was a frenzied and febrile atmosphere, probably intensified by exaggerated British intelligence reports of an imminent German invasion of Ireland, into which London launched a bizarre proposal in June 1940, attempting to inveigle Ireland into the war in return for a promise to try to persuade Craig to accept unity. De Valera rightly rejected the offer, doubting if the British could deliver on the promise even if they tried, a response justified by the vehemence of Craig's reaction when he found out.[351] Craig's response may even have come as a

---

348 Meenan, *George O'Brien*, p. 147.
349 PA AA, StSekr. Irland 1, Woermann memo, 14 July 1940, Dienststelle Ribbentrop, *Vertrauliche Berichte*, Likus report, 1, vol. 4, 29 December 1940.
350 PA AA, Dienststelle Ribbentrop, *Vertrauliche Berichte*, Likus report, 1, vol. 3, 23 July 1940; Dickel, *Deutsche Aussenpolitik*, p. 123, n. 182.
351 Bowman, *De Valera*, pp. 235–9; Fisk, *In time of war*, pp. 177–82.

relief to de Valera. For the British proposal was potentially dangerous for three reasons.

Firstly, the 'offer' of Irish unity, however vague, threatened the unity of Fianna Fáil. When de Valera rejected the initial English approach at his meeting on 17 June with Malcolm MacDonald, entrusted with the thankless task of seducing Ireland into the war, he did concede that 'perhaps some of his colleagues would take a different view'. Even if he immediately added 'but he did not think they would', the threat of internal cabinet dissension lurked in the background.[352] At a later meeting with MacDonald, de Valera had Aiken and Lemass with him, probably representing opposite wings in the cabinet, Lemass relatively receptive to the British approach, Aiken resolutely hostile. De Valera was determined to preserve party unity at all costs. His frequent references to John Redmond's misjudgement in 1914 were not wholly rhetorical.

Secondly, the whole tone of the discussions was influenced by the Irish fear that 'it would be a mistake' to ally with a Britain who was 'going to lose the war'.[353] This was a sensible viewpoint. Unless the Irish contribution could make the difference between victory and defeat, then Irish support for Britain was pointless – and could only bring down upon Ireland, or at least on the existing Irish government, the wrath of the victorious Germans. And it was distinctly unlikely that Irish support could make the difference between British victory and defeat. However much de Valera might personally regret Britain's defeat, it would have been the height of irresponsibility for a leader in his position to wantonly sacrifice the interests of his country to a futile purpose.[354]

Thirdly, de Valera sensed the possible dangers of a conciliatory Craig response for his constitution. For the British were so unsporting as to suggest that 'a joint body including representatives of the government of Éire and the government of Northern Ireland . . . be set up at once to work out the constitutional and other practical details of the union of Ireland . . .'.[355] Ernest Bevin had gone so far as to urge the British cabinet to make 'a statement that we are willing to accept a new constitution on the basis of a united Ireland at the end of hostilities', proposing 'that the chairman of the constitution-making body should be selected by the President of the United States'.[356] As de Valera insisted that his 1937 constitution was devised for all Ireland, the prospect of it being subjected to critical scrutiny by Northern Ireland representatives did not amuse him.

352 PRO, DO 114–117, MacDonald memo.
353 *Ibid.*, MacDonald telegram, 27 June 1940, Annex III, p. 3.
354 If a prediction were to be hazarded, it would be that further research would enhance the reputation of de Valera's statecraft in the light of the multiple pressures upon him in the summer of 1940.
355 Canning, *British policy*, p. 284.
356 PRO, PREM 4-53/2, E. Bevin to W. Churchill, 18 June 1940.

His reply on the proposed constitutional conference exposed fundamental and enduring ambiguities in the whole nationalist position. He now asserted that 'our present constitution represents the limit to which we believe our people are prepared to go to meet the sentiments of the Northern unionists . . . '.[357] The veil of delusion concerning the North in which the South cocooned itself was briefly torn aside. The issue now was not unity versus neutrality. It was unity versus the constitution. However hypothetical the prospect of unionist acquiescence in a united Ireland – and it was wholly hypothetical – de Valera was here saying that 'our people' would not compromise the constitution for unity. *Realpolitik* ripped through the rhetorical veil for a fleeting moment to expose the bleak reality beneath. The ethos of the state could not be changed in any circumstances. And unionists had no right to have any say about that ethos.

Craig had no choice in his response. His followers would have stood for no other. Had he been in a position to reply more adroitly, he could have caused immense embarrassment in Dublin. He could have exposed the hollowness of the constitution's claims on Northern Ireland all the more effectively. It would have been an astute ploy to have placed the onus for partition more on the pretensions of Dublin to control Protestant consciences than on the supremacist yearning of Ulster unionists.

The British approach was vague, chimerical, histrionic – very Irish! The Irish response was cold, clinical, calculating – very English!

Ireland's fate depended on the outcome of the wider struggle. Cold clammy fear would never again reach the level of the summer of 1940. There was, however, enough diplomatic pressure, and just sufficient economic hardship, to sustain a useful sense of foreign threat. Churchill, in one of his grandiloquent empty gestures, provoked yet further misunderstanding about the possibility of unification following America's entry into the war in December 1941. De Valera was not to be codded by another 'wild' Churchillian gesture.[358] Anglo-Irish relations would be further ruffled on occasion. However, they generally proceeded smoothly enough in the circumstances, thanks not least to the skill with which Dulanty represented Irish interests in London.[359]

Dublin's subsequent diplomatic difficulties were more with the Americans than with the British. David Gray, the American minister in Dublin since March 1940, did not achieve as cordial personal relations with de Valera as did Maffey, the British representative to Ireland since September 1939. Gray tended to represent his country's interests some-

---

[357] PRO, DO 114–117: Neutrality of Éire (World War 1939–1945), Annex v, de Valera to Chamberlain, 4 July 1940, p. 4; Fisk, *In time of war*, pp. 182–3.
[358] Fisk, *In time of war*, pp. 447–8; J. Keegan, 'Foreword', pp. xxiii.
[359] Williams, 'Irish neutrality', *Irish Press*, 15 July 1953.

what insensitively. De Valera's adroit manipulation of Gray's hamfisted handling of the 'American note' of February 1944, demanding that Ireland break off diplomatic relations with the Axis forces, out of exaggerated American fears that German intelligence agents in Ireland would secure vital information about D-Day plans, helped set up the victory scenario for the snap general election in May.[360]

Gray, no career official but a cousin of Roosevelt, already seventy when he arrived, 'a gauche and assertive personality',[361] lacked the finesse associated with professional diplomats.[362] It was not that he was anti-Irish. He was, if anything, too full of good intentions towards his new charge. He sought to encourage rapport between Dublin and Belfast in 1940, which enabled him encounter unionist resistance at first hand.[363] The refusal of the Irish to take their own defence wholly seriously made it difficult for others, like Gray, to take it wholly seriously either, as when he derisorily dismissed an Irish demand for one destroyer, on the grounds that 'the Irish government has no more use for one destroyer than I have for a white elephant'.[364] But he vigorously, if unavailingly, championed some Irish supplications for arms to Washington in 1940.[365] This was naturally in pursuit of American rather than Irish interests.[366] He nevertheless acted in what he genuinely believed to be the best interests of Ireland also, given his feeling that 'Ireland, Britain and America all had an equal interest in the defeat of Hitler'.[367] This view, right or wrong, was no more untenable than the alternative Irish views – either that Ireland had no interest in the defeat of Hitler, or, if she had, then Britain and/or the United States would defeat him for her, as well as for themselves. But Gray's style militated against his purposes. 'Instead of seeking to persuade he sought to impose.'[368] He unwisely gave the impression that his good intentions included knowing how to conduct Irish affairs better than de Valera. This did not endear him to government circles, and when he chose to frolic too much with the opposition, particularly with James Dillon, he damaged his standing further. His persistence in seeking bases for American forces after United States entry to the war became a particular

360 Ryle Dwyer, *Irish neutrality*, pp. 179ff.; Williams, 'Irish neutrality', *Irish Press*, 2, 4, 16 July 1953.
361 Duggan, *Neutral Ireland*, p. xiv.
362 Carroll, *Ireland in the war years*, pp. 99ff.; Ryle Dwyer, *Irish neutrality*, *passim*.
363 Ryle Dwyer, *Irish neutrality*, pp. 52ff.; DDI, 9, IV, Berardis–Ciano, 27 May 1940, no. 603, p. 470.
364 Williams, 'Irish neutrality', *Irish Press*, 2 July 1953.
365 FRUS III, Gray to Secretary of State, 4 June 1940, no. 31, p. 161; Gray to Secretary of State, no. 168, 15 August 1940.
366 Ryle Dwyer, *Irish neutrality*, pp. 81–2.
367 R.J. Raymond, 'David Gray, the Aiken mission and Irish neutrality, 1940–41', *Diplomatic History*, 9, 1 (Winter 1985), pp. 55–71.
368 (T.D. Williams), 'A study in neutrality', *The Leader*, 28 February 1953.

irritant – not least because it reminded Dublin of its own earlier disposition to think in these terms!

De Valera intimated to MacDonald in 1940 that his ideal solution to the Irish question in the prevailing circumstances was a united neutral Ireland guaranteed by the United States and Great Britain. In that case 'American ships could enter the Irish ports, and perhaps American troops into Ireland, to effect this guarantee.'[369] Walshe envisaged a situation where Ireland would offer America extensive naval and air facilities, even on a permanent basis – in an effort to keep the British out at all costs![370] This was not strictly incompatible with de Valera's view at the same time. But the Taoiseach's more anglophile instincts emerged from his view that 'the probable setup of the world' would be 'a German controlled Europe with England and Ireland aligned with the Commonwealth of Nations and the Americas'.[371]

Dublin played the Irish-American card against both the British and the Germans, even while colluding with the Germans in the United States to use Irish–American influence against the American government in an effort to induce Roosevelt to put pressure on Britain to refrain from seizing the ports. Official circles in Dublin even allowed their preference for Wilkie in the 1940 presidential election to become known – which can hardly have endeared them to Gray, Roosevelt's relation, much less to Roosevelt.[372] The disdain Roosevelt displayed for Aiken during their tempestuous encounter in the White House in 1941 may not have been entirely unrelated to Dublin's miscalculation of electoral realities the previous year.[373]

It may have been partly to counter American pressure that Ireland support Britain that Dublin showed such apparent *naïveté* in 1940 in assiduously courting an assurance from Berlin that the Germans had no intention of invading Ireland.[374] Even Walshe can hardly have persuaded himself that a bit of paper would guarantee the purity of German intentions. But Dublin may still have felt it worthwhile to have the bit of paper to wave before British eyes casting an appraising glance at the sister isle – and at American eyes doing nothing to discourage that glance. Otherwise the Irish search for a Hitler promise to respect Irish interests belongs to the theatre of the absurd. And there was rarely anything absurd by this stage about the diplomacy of de Valera.

Where Dublin played the Irish-American card against Britain, and against Roosevelt, with more force than finesse, it played it rather more

369 PRO, DO 114–117; MacDonald memo, 20 June 1940, p. 1.
370 FRUS, 1940 III, Gray to Secretary of State, 10 November 1940, no. 99, pp. 168–9.
371 *Ibid.*, Gray to Secretary of State, 24 November 1940, no. 105, p. 172.
372 PA AA, StSekr. USA, III, Hempel-AA, 29 October 1940.
373 Carroll, *Ireland in the war years*, pp. 102–4.
374 DGFP, B, x, Hempel-AA, 1 July 1940, no. 79, pp. 89–90.

adroitly against Germany. Berlin remained sensitive during July 1940 to the danger of driving Dublin into British arms by applying undue pressure during the envisaged blockade of Britain.[375] Ireland would naturally have lain at Germany's military mercy once Britain was defeated. The reluctance to provoke hitherto friendly Irish–American circles may have counselled even a triumphant Hitler to refrain from the invasion of Ireland unless the United States entered the war.[376] There were other ways of instructing the natives in the house rules of the New Order apart from actual occupation. Berlin decided against offering Ireland a secret agreement to guarantee imports during the proposed blockade of Britain.[377] And the economic planners among the German military did not linger over nuances of geographical detail. Already in July 1940 they blithely designated Dublin as one of the six control centres from which they would organise the economy of a conquered 'England'.[378]

The German failure to vanquish Britain in 1940 stabilised Dublin perspectives. Nevertheless, Hempel's early impression that 'Great emphasis was placed on forestalling any unfavourable German attitude towards Irish neutrality' remained valid.[379] Dublin protests against German violations of Irish airspace and attacks on Irish ships or territory continued to be couched in a respectful tone.[380] Walshe and Boland undertook to ensure that the censorship played down the fatal consequences of the misdirected enthusiasm of German bombers over Ireland during the Battle of Britain.[381] Great uncertainty prevailed about the outcome of the war until well after the entry of the United States. Not until fortunes had changed decisively did the Irish tone towards Hempel begin to alter. By 1944, Walshe's earlier gratuitously ingratiating approach would be superseded by a 'brusque and rude' manner.[382] Boland, whom Hempel had once found so congenial, had now become 'unhelpful and evasive'.[383] By 1944, 1940 was a long long time ago.

'WE ARE KING'S MEN'

Partition was regularly advanced as the main reason for Irish neutrality. But the war would have driven North and South further apart, if that were

---

[375] Dickel, *Deutsche Aussenpolitik*, p. 128.   [376] *Ibid.*, pp. 131–2.

[377] BA-MA, Rw 5/v, 236, AA-AbdK, 8 June 1940; Dickel, *Deutsche Aussenpolitik*, p. 128.

[378] Dickel, *Deutsche Aussenpolitik*, pp. 127–8; W. Schumann and G. Hass (eds.), *Deutschland im Zweiten Weltkrieg* (East Berlin, 1974), p. 402.

[379] PA AA, StSekr. Irland, 1, Hempel-AA, 14 May 1940, no. 239.

[380] PA AA, StSekr. Irland, 1, Hempel-AA, 2 August 1940, no. 444; 24 October 1940, no. 669; Woermann memo, 5 August 1940, 21 October 1940.

[381] PA AA StSekr. Irland, 1, Hempel-AA, 26 August 1940, no. 508.

[382] Duggan, *Neutral Ireland*, p. 225.

[383] PA AA, StSekr. Irland, 1, Hempel-AA, 21 December 1940, no. 845; Duggan, *Neutral Ireland*, p. 221.

possible. The thirties were a dreadful decade for the plain people of Ulster, Protestant as well as Catholic. Depression in the staple industries, linen and shipbuilding, kept unemployment at horribly high levels. Having reached 25 per cent of the insured workforce in 1932, it climbed to 28 per cent in 1938.[384] Some unionists even sought selective tariffs for Ulster. These were not, needless to say, the vulgar Free State variety – 'there is no question of Sinn Féin here'. Rather were they a 'scientific' Ulster variety![385] At a somewhat less 'scientific' level, the situation became so desperate that some Protestant and Catholic workers actually combined to riot in momentary unison at the inadequacy of outdoor relief provisions in 1932. It seemed as if the very fabric of civilisation was about to be rent, with the plebs rioting with, rather than against, each other. But they safely reverted to type in the sectarian riots of 1935, when 11 were killed and nearly 600 wounded.[386] God was once more in his heaven and all was well with the world.

An Ulster Blackshirt movement awkwardly mouthing the motto 'Loyalty to king and empire and the building of the Greater Britain' tried to capitalise on the manifold discontents of the time. But unionist political culture proved as resilient as nationalist against the appeal of fascism. The Blackshirts could offer little to rival the attraction of the Orange Order. There were few Jews in Ulster. In any case, anti-semitism palled beside the proven pleasures of papist bashing. And fascist spectacle paled beside the traditional pageantry of Orangeism. But the Orange Order was not ideologically fascist, even if it incorporated certain fascistic traits. Catholic and Protestant leaders in Ulster effectively combined to guide the frustrations of their flocks into safe hereditary hatreds. Fascism was simply 'crowded out' by the more familiar brands of resentment, which comfortably retained their market share of human frailty.

The lack of sympathy between the two sides remained evident in the public prints of the thirties. Cardinal McRory had the knack of fuelling the fire of Protestant resentment at the imperialist pretensions, real and presumed, of Catholic ecclesiastics.[387] The *Belfast Telegraph* greeted de Valera's victory in 1933 with the observation that 'it has often been said that the Southern Irish are not normal in politics',[388] a delicious tribute from such connoisseurs of 'normalcy' as Ulster unionists! The *Telegraph* used de Valera's triumph to stress that unity was strength. Ulster unionism 'can only be assailed by the enemy with any hope of success when there is weakness and dissension in the garrison inside'.[389] The self-image was artlessly revealing. The *Irish Press*, on the other hand, ignored any

384 Buckland, *Grievances*, pp. 52–3; Johnson, 'Northern Ireland as a problem in the economic war 1932–38', *IHS*, 22, 86 (September, 1980), p. 159.
385 *Belfast News Letter*, 25 February 1932.   386 Lyons, *Ireland*, p. 716.
387 *Ibid.*, p. 715.
388 *Belfast Telegraph*, 26 January 1933.   389 *Ibid.*, 23 January 1933.

reference to the anniversary of the Somme, the tragic theme that dominated the *Telegraph*, on 1 July 1932, even though it was able to find space
for such urgent international issues as 'Yugoslav fears' – a topic that no
doubt dominated household discussion in Killorglin! Had Ulster Protestants chosen to follow the *Press* closely, they would hardly have been
reasssured by the crass obituary for Sir Edward Carson,[390] or by the
accusation that Northern Ireland contained 'many of the worst features of
Nazi rule'[391] or by the strident and mendacious insistence that the
Stormont state was on the verge of collapse.[392]

The one relatively bright spot on the Ulster economic front was
agriculture. Although cattle numbers fell from 173 000 in 1930–1 to
156 000 in 1938–9, sheep numbers rose in the same period from 261 000
to 397 000 and poultry numbers from 5.5 to 6.2 million. Most remarkably, the stabilisation of the market that followed the establishment of the
Pig Marketing Board stimulated a handsome increase in the number of
pigs from 250 000 to 844 000.[393] By 1936 pigs already accounted for
20 per cent of Ulster agricultural income, compared with only 9 per cent in
1931.[394]

Craig's health deteriorated as the decade advanced. But he lost little of
his craft as a party leader. When 'Progressive Unionists' were sniping at
his failure to tackle the terrible unemployment, and the wretched housing
conditions, Craig seized the chance proffered by de Valera's irredentist
constitution, and by the putative threat to partition posed by the Anglo-
Irish negotiations, to call an election in January 1938, in which he routed
his Unionist critics by diverting attention from internal problems to the
alleged external threat.[395]

Having used the threat of the negotiations to help consolidate his party,
Craig then used Chamberlain's concessions to de Valera to extract useful
compensation for Northern Ireland. London agreed to extend British
levels of agricultural subsidies to the North, whose pig industry might
otherwise have been affected by new subsidies introduced in Britain, to
increase the contribution to unemployment benefit, and to make up 'any
deficit that arose from maintaining . . . social services at the British
level'.[396] If the full value of these benefits would not be appreciated for
some time, the most important gain of all would become clear very
quickly. For the return of the ports to de Valera reinforced Craig's hand
on partition. With Northern Irish bases now far more important for

[390] *Irish Press*, 23 October 1935.   [391] *Ibid.*, 30 March 1939.
[392] *Ibid.*, 13 July 1937.
[393] Lyons, *Ireland* p. 696.
[394] *Irish Press*, 12 April 1938; D.A.E. Harkness, 'The evolution of agricultural policy in
      Northern Ireland', *Ulster Year Book* (1935), pp. xx–xxi.
[395] *Round Table*, 111 (June 1938), p. 532.
[396] Johnson, 'Northern Ireland as a problem in the economic war 1932–38', pp. 160–1.

British security, Westminster was deprived of whatever leverage credulous nationalists felt it should have been in a position to use to induce unionists to abandon their principles. It was yet another irony of Ango-Irish relations that de Valera's greatest negotiating triumph should have copper-fastened partition.

The war economy brought relative prosperity to the North. The hideous unemployment virtually vanished from 1941 as activity revived in the shipyards and in the aircraft industry. England's danger was Ulster's opportunity for a job. Catholics, enjoying nearly full employment, in striking contrast to the South, provided scant support for IRA activity during the war. The spread to Northern Ireland, as the direct result of the war, and of Labour's victory in the British general election of 1945, of the expanding English concept of the welfare state, brought about significant improvements in Northern welfare services, helping to widen appreciably the postwar gap in living standards between North and South. Whereas the South had made more social progress during the thirties, the situation began to be reversed during the war itself. Infant mortality, consistently higher in the North than in the South between the wars, fell below the Southern level for the first time in 1943, and would remain below it for more than twenty years.[397]

Craigavon died in November 1940 at the age of sixty-nine, after several years of poor health. He had succeeded Carson in difficult circumstances in 1920. A man of great physical courage, he proved an outstanding organiser of the Ulster Volunteers, an exceptionally successful negotiator at international level, an astute party leader, and a successful Prime Minister by the standards of his followers. He probably genuinely hoped initially to secure conciliation between the communities in Northern Ireland, and to establish cordial relations with Dublin. However, the reluctance of Catholics in the North to recognise the legitimacy of his government, and the viciousness of both Protestant and Catholic extremists, soon convinced him that he must seek consolidation of his own forces rather than conciliation with his enemies as his first priority.

Craig and de Valera had much in common. They shared the same ability to operate an effective political machine, the same opportunistic skill in making quick diplomatic kills, the same refined sense of electoral timing, the same reluctance to change their cabinets. The main difference in their approach to man-management was that Craig did more of the straight fixing himself. He was always conscious that the favours should be seen to come directly from him,[398] whereas de Valera liked to imagine himself uncontaminated by the pervasive vulgarities of the culture he personified.

[397] Mitchell, *European Historical Statistics*, pp. 129–30.
[398] P. Buckland, 'The unity of Ulster unionism, 1886–1939', *History*, 60, 199 (June 1975), pp. 316–19.

Craig was as personally honest as de Valera, however. He lost money in office.[399]

As political tacticians, both Craig and de Valera took good care to suffocate whatever threat there may have been from Labour, sublimating the social aspirations of their constituencies in the rhetoric of community solidarity. Craig was more 'the prisoner of his party' than de Valera, for if 'he was able to interpret and express the views of those whom he led . . . he lacked those greater gifts of constructive statesmanship which enable a leader to bend his followers to his will'.[400] But de Valera's followers were more malleable than Craig's. There are some followers who cannot be 'bent' in any but the most exceptional circumstances. Ulster unionists were among them.

Neither Craig nor de Valera had much idea how to cope with economic problems. Craig succeeded to a more difficult inheritance in this respect, with Ulster's industrial structure more vulnerable to adverse international circumstances. But his willingness to overrule his officials, much to their chagrin, helped put a human face on bureaucracy.[401] The political kingdom always came first for him. Few prime ministers anywhere have managed to remain as independent of their Finance officials.[402] Within their own terms of reference, no generation in modern Irish history has been more successfully led in their time than were the Protestant people of the North by James Craig, Ulsterman.[403]

Craig was succeeded by J.M. Andrews, his deputy. Though by no means a total nonentity, Andrews is best remembered for his remark that he had counted the number of Catholics among the porters at Stormont. The exercise did not require a command of higher mathematics. Andrews, already sixty-nine, failed to measure up to a job that became more exacting in wartime. He was duly jettisoned in 1943 in favour of the 54–year-old Sir Basil Brooke, Minister for Agriculture. Probably the ablest man as well as the shrewdest politician in the cabinet, Brooke would remain prime minister until 1963. Hailing from the border county of Fermanagh, where Catholics had the bad taste to be in the majority, Brooke was more fundamentally sectarian than Craig. There would be no danger of premature exercises in reconciliation, either with Dublin or with Northern Catholics, during his tenure of office. He was fortunate in the timing of his accession. While it may be a shade expansive to claim that without Northern Ireland 'defeat in the Battle of the Atlantic would have

---

[399] Buckland, *Craig*, p. 121.   [400] *Irish Times*, 25 November 1940.
[401] Buckland, *Craig*, p. 107.
[402] P. Bew, P. Gibbon and H. Patterson, *The state in Northern Ireland 1921–72. Political forces and social classes* (Manchester, 1979), *passim*.
[403] It is only fair to note that Dr Buckland, Craig's biographer, does not take so benign a view of his subject, and that Professor Harkness endorses Buckland's criticisms.

been practically certain',[404] Ulster bases certainly saved many Allied lives, including many Irish-American lives, during the war. Brooke would be able to draw on the credit for long afterwards, while Dublin was obliged to pay, to its uncomprehending chagrin, a delayed, if still modest, price for neutrality.

PLATO'S CAVE?

Verdicts on the implications of neutrality vary widely. The celebrated lament of the late F.S.L. Lyons has attracted particular attention:

The tensions – and the liberations – of war, the shared experience, the comradeship in suffering, the new thinking about the future, all these things had passed her by. It was as if an entire people had been condemned to live in Plato's cave, backs to the fire of life and deriving their only knowledge of what went on outside from the flickering shadows thrown on the wall before their eyes by the men and women who passed to and fro behind them. When after six years they emerged, dazzled, from the cave into the light of day, it was to a new and vastly different world.[405]

This passage would repay close textual exegesis. One might wonder, for instance, if 'backs to the fire of life' is an entirely appropriate evocation of a war in which so many fell victim to the fire of death as the bombs rained from the skies. One might wonder if 'dazzled' serves any historical as distinct from stylistic purpose. It will be more rewarding, however, to subject the assumptions behind the assertions to historical scrutiny, particularly by comparing the Irish experience with that of the other two European democracies who succeeded in preserving their neutrality during the war.

In neither Sweden nor Switzerland did neutrality inhibit effective subsequent performance. Both countries would become, in their very different ways, success stories of the postwar world. Whether one admired or deplored their styles, they both gave performances of some distinction.[406] Nor did participation, on the other hand, guarantee an impressive postwar performance. Britain could take considerable pride in her war effort, even if vested interests clung to much that was shoddy and second rate. Whether she drew the right lessons in her longer-term interest is more doubtful.

Closer yet to home, Northern Ireland showed just how little difference participation could make to mentalities determined to resist fundamental

---

404 C. Falls, 'Northern Ireland and the defence of the British Isles', in T. Wilson (ed.), *Ulster under Home Rule* (London, 1958), p. 87.

405 Lyons, *Ireland*, p. 551.

406 See, for instance, A. Lindbeck, *Swedish economic policy* (London, 1975); R. Ruffieux, 'Changements et innovation dans la Suisse de l'après-guerre: quelques hypothèses de recherche', in *Cinq siècles de relations Franco-Suisses* (Neuchatel, 1984).

change. Material improvement did occur after 1945, thanks largely to British largesse. No 'new and vastly different world', however, opened up for the North after the war. Ancestral animosities continued to flourish, oblivious to the changes occurring in the wider world. Northern Ireland may as well have been a neutral of Éire vintage for all the difference that 'tensions, liberations, shared experience, comradeship in suffering' made to her 'new thinking about the future'. Some new personal relationships were no doubt forged under the bond of common danger. But tradition would remain in safe custody in Basil Brooke's solicitous hands. One must not generalise too loosely from so unrepresentative a case. Yet it would be unwise to entirely neglect its experience in an Irish context.

The war had a significant impact on many countries. But it was more likely to be defeat and occupation, rather than participation as such, that forced reluctant societies to look more closely into their own hearts. It was humilitation, the sense of ignominious failure, that broke, or at least shook, the pre-war moulds as new leadership cadres displaced discredited older elites and, in many cases, extensively adapted inherited institutional structures.[407]

Neither neutrality nor belligerency, therefore, determined the impact of war. Neutrality was itself neutral in this respect. It was not neutrality, but the response of the political culture to neutrality, that mattered. How neutral states emerged from the war, how receptive they were to change in the postwar world, depended in large measure on the potential of the political culture with which they entered the war and on how effectively they performed during the war itself.

Ireland brought a highly unusual heritage into the Emergency. Like most heritages it had strengths and weaknesses, complexities and contradictions. But it left the country unusually ill-equipped to respond constructively to the economic and psychological impact of the war.

Economically, Ireland was badly placed on three counts. Firstly, the thirties, for all their turbulence, had not been as dreadful a decade for Ireland as for many other countries. Although unemployment stood at 15 per cent in 1939, and the economy was probably poised to plunge downwards, that was soon forgotten.[408] By Irish concepts of normalcy, the thirties were far from a disaster, except for strong farmers during the economic war. Public opinion did not therefore generally share in the

---

407 For the social impact of the war on Axis-dominated countries see W. Długoborski (ed.), *Zweiter Weltkrieg und sozialer Wandel* (Göttingen, 1981). For a discussion of the general issue of the impact of the Second World War on continuity see the contributions by C.S. Maier *et al.*, 'The two postwar Eras and the conditions for stability in twentieth-century western Europe', *AHR*, 86 (1981), pp. 327–67. For ways of assessing the impact of the Second World War see C. Thorne, 'Societies, sociology and the International', in W. Outhwaite and M. Mulkay (eds.), *Social theory and social criticism* (Oxford, 1987), pp. 145–52.
408 Mitchell, *European Historical Statistics*, p. 170.

almost universal postwar feeling that the thirties had been a failure. The new thinking that emerged from the war in many countries reflected prewar as well as wartime experience. Both the war and its aftermath were perceived in Ireland less as an opportunity for a new beginning than as a threat to an inherited achievement, economically as well as politically.

Secondly, the war offered Ireland, in its then economic condition, fewer opportunities than Sweden or Switzerland. Both these countries suffered serious slump during the thirties, even if they responded relatively intelligently to their problems. It was mainly military expenditure that enabled them to reduce their unemployment. Swiss unemployment fell from 13.2 per cent in 1936 to 1.6 per cent in 1945, and Swedish from 13.6 per cent to 4.5 per cent.[409] Both countries, it is true, suffered severe disruption of their international trade. In Sweden's case, imports and exports fell heavily.[410] Swiss imports fell sharply from the outset, though exports actually increased until 1944, when they fell abruptly.[411] Both economies, nevertheless, proved sufficiently resilient to adjust to the restrictions imposed by war. As Ireland lacked the engineering base for an armaments industry, it was in no position to profit from the economic consequences of an armament drive proportionate to the Swiss or Swedish efforts. Neutrality was not responsible for this. Even had Ireland joined the Allies, there would have been little economic rationale in trying to establish instant industries in a country so lacking the appropriate human resources.

Thirdly, intensified emigration, now disproportionately male, continued to relieve Ireland of the necessity to find ways of creating employment for her surplus population. The more or less undisturbed continuance of emigration permitted 'business as usual' perspectives to dominate government thinking. The fear that Lemass inspired in 1942 with his scenario of a postwar return of the emigrants soon disappeared as it came to be realised that the threat was imaginary. Few would seek to return to such bleak prospects. Britain would provide. It was not neutrality in itself that fostered this mentality, however subtly it reinforced it. The instinct was already deeply rooted in the national psyche.

The proposition that Ireland became more intellectually isolated during the war is difficult to test. Ireland had already intellectually isolated herself in large measure since independence. Her links with the outside world were mainly confined to Britain and the Vatican. She had some contact with the United States at personal level, but little at an intellectual

[409] *Ibid.*; M. Fritz, 'Wirtschaftliche Neutralität während des Zweiten Weltkrieges', in Bindschedler, *Neutralität*, p. 56.
[410] Fritz, 'Wirtschaftliche Neutralität', p. 51.
[411] D. Bourgeois, 'Les relations économiques Germano-Suisses 1939–1945', *Revue d'histoire de la deuxième guerre mondiale*, 126 (April 1982), p. 61, n. 74.

level. She might envy American consumption standards. She had no intention of trying to emulate American creative capacity. It seems doubtful if she became more intellectually isolated from England as a result of neutrality. The debates within the administration on social and economic policy were conducted largely in terms of recent English thought. Lemass tried to introduce his colleagues to Keynes and Beveridge fairly promptly, just as McElligott fought him off by invoking earlier versions of English economic verity. In this respect, neutrality brought no more isolation than had peacetime.

Neutrality offered as much opportunity for political and administrative innovation as did war. It was the combination of inherited animosities and clinical party political calculations that precluded the possibility of a national government in Ireland. This was one English precedent that neither Dublin nor Belfast – for more understandable reasons in the Belfast case – chose to emulate. Sweden showed that neutrality did not preclude national government. The Swiss already had something approximating to it, although it was not until 1943 that the Socialists were brought into the Federal Council. And if the Irish were fearful that a national government would deprive them of the pleasures of the electoral game, as in Britain for the duration, a national government did not prevent Sweden holding three general elections during the war.

Administratively too, the Emergency proceeded largely on a 'business as usual' basis. The Department of Supplies was perceived as coping with a once-for-all emergency. It was not deemed to have longer term implications. In contrast to Britain, and to most other independent countries, there was no sense that developments in wartime economic administration 'required the use of experts, whether administrators, businessmen or economists, to a far greater extent in government service'.[412] It could not be said of Ireland, as it has been said of many other states, that 'by 1945 a great wealth of administrative experience and of economic confidence had been gained', which would be 'firmly applied' after 1945 'to avoid the cyclical disasters which had followed the First World War', nor that the war 'brought the pressure of society to bear to change political will in the direction of constructing a more humane society'.[413] But participation was highly unlikely to have led to any of these results in the Irish case. One might ask, for instance, where the 'experts' of the requisite calibre were to be found in the Ireland of 1939. There were, no doubt, some bright young men (and women – but few thought of women as a reservoir of talent) in the universities. Their recruitment might have injected more independent thinking into public decision-making in due course. But there was no obvious immediate pool of talent to be tapped. The performance of such 'administrators, businessmen or economists' as there happened to be

[412] Milward, *War, economy and society*, p. 110.   [413] *Ibid.*, p. 100.

outside the civil service did not inspire unreserved confidence in their potential as public servants.

Neutrality offered an opportunity to accumulate administrative experience, learn useful lessons and collect valuable information. Finance resisted these possibilities. Given the inherited cast of mind of senior administrators, and of most politicians, participation in the war was unlikely to have undermined the conventional wisdom on the organisation and functions of the civil service. Nor was pressure for 'a more humane society' likely to have impressed the majority of the electorate, much less of administrators. Developments towards a welfare state after the war would owe more to English example than to indigenous impulse. Only devastating defeat, in short, was likely to have called into question the sacrosanctity of the structures and mentalities of Irish society, whether in the public or the private spheres.

The pedestrian quality of much Irish performance during the Emergency was widely at variance with the perception of that performance. In public perception Ireland gave an outstanding display. However glaring the gap in certain respects between objective and subjective reality, the rationale behind this gap was itself a historical fact of the first importance. Skilful propaganda convinced a people anxious to be convinced that the preservation of neutrality was the supreme national goal. Indeed, it soon came to be seen as a form of warfare in its own right, the supreme assertion of sovereignty.[414] Ireland, said Elizabeth Bowen, 'invested her self-respect in it'.[415] This prompts the question, how demanding were Irish standards of 'self-respect'? An even fuller assertion of sovereignty would have been to actually go to war against Britain – the route the Finns were foolish enough to embark on against Russia! The Irish were cannier. Their ideal war was phoney war. This they could win, on one crucial condition. They could safely enjoy the fruits of victory over Britain in their phantom war only if Britain won the real war. Thanks to British cooperation on this matter, the Irish could duly enjoy their psychological triumph.

To fully savour this triumph, however, it was necessary to go through a variety of mental contortions. 'Self-respect' was a demanding, not to say capricious, mistress. Neutrality was the essence of common sense. But Ireland was not prepared to adopt the attitude of Sweden, for whom 'neutrality had always been the art of the possible, frankly unheroic'.[416] Common sense was not enough for a people fed on fantasies of their unique moral stature. Neutrality therefore had to be crowned with a halo, and exalted to a level that would allow those who, very sensibly, looked in

---

[414] As rightly emphasised by Fisk. And see Robert Kee's review of Fisk's *In time of war* in *The Sunday Times*, 15 May 1983, 'Neutrality as a form of warfare'.
[415] Fisk, *In time of war*, p. 352.   [416] Scott, *Sweden*, p. 508.

the first instance to their own safety, like everyone else, to pose as paragons of virtue.

This craving for a feeling of moral superiority, oblivious to the contradictions in one's own position, emerged even in de Valera's condemnation of Hitler's invasion of Holland and Belgium. In one respect it was more notable that the protest should be made at all than that it should be presented in a form that left it vulnerable to charges of hypocrisy or that External Affairs should subsequently scuttle around searching for a route along which to backtrack in the face of German displeasure. Nevertheless, it was characteristic of an Irish cast of mind that de Valera was not satisfied to denounce the German invasion. He had to do so because 'it would be unworthy of the small Irish nation not to protest against the cruel wrong perpetrated on Holland and Belgium'.[417] If it was now 'unworthy' not to protest, how then explain the complete Irish silence the previous month on the German invasion of Denmark and Norway, with their even smaller populations? *Raison d'état* would naturally dictate more intense concern at the threat of war now coming in an Irish direction. But dressing up *raison d'état* in the sartorial robes of virtue was itself a character trait that more austere moralists might consider 'unworthy'.

It was this apparent need of the Irish mind to feel a sense of moral superiority that mainly explains Irish touchiness about neutrality. What was striking was not neutrality, but the emotions clustering around it. Even Sean O'Faolain found himself justifying it as 'our first practical claim to independence', as if the whole course of Anglo-Irish relations since 1922 had not been a striking assertion of independence. O'Faolain's indignant repudiation of British and American criticisms of the immorality of neutrality showed just how such criticisms rankled precisely because of the moral connotations with which 'self-respect' sought to invest neutrality. 'As long as the neutrality of Switzerland, Sweden or Spain is not attributed to ignorance or indifference one must be at a loss to know why Ireland should be held up among so many as the one country which is neutral for immoral reasons' complained O'Faolain.[418] This argument would have been valid in 1940. It was no longer valid when O'Faolain made it in 1944. There was one crucial difference between the situation of the other three states and that of Ireland. They would all have been vulnerable to immediate invasion if they were so crazy as to declare war on Germany. Ireland was now safe from Nazi invasion. It was still in the national interest, even at that stage, that she should remain neutral. But she now had a real choice, unlike the others.

It was this emotional dimension that accounted for the rapturous public

417 PA AA, StSekr. Irland, 1, Hempel-AA, 13 May 1940, no. 234.
418 S. O'Faolain, 'One world', *The Bell*, 7, 4 (January 1944), pp. 282–3.

reception of de Valera's reply to Churchill at the end of the war. Churchill's ungracious comment on Ireland's war role in his victory speech provided de Valera with a golden opening not only to divert attention from his recent condolences to Hempel on Hitler's death, but also from his anglophile neutrality. De Valera was always wise enough to cooperate sufficiently with the Allies to ensure that they did not feel provoked into decisive action against Irish interests, even while his rhetoric satisfied national psychic needs by insisting on Ireland's equal independence from all belligerents. This burnished image of sovereign neutrality could hardly be maintained if it emerged that Dublin was cooperating so closely with the ancient enemy. It was vital for the national psyche from an emotional viewpoint, no less than for de Valera from a party political viewpoint, that the extent of Irish cooperation should not receive indecent exposure. Churchill gave him his chance. He swooped to seize it. Though his reply evaded certain moral issues, it did so with dignity and restraint, and then brilliantly exploited the dignity and restraint not only to score several shrewd debating points, but to restate certain basic truths about a just international order, while simultaneously reasserting historic Irish claims. It was a magisterial performance, exquisitely tuned to the emotional needs of his flock.

The Irish could indulge their investment in 'self-respect' only because of the restraint displayed by Churchill and Roosevelt, as de Valera rightly recognised, a restraint assiduously fostered by his own policy. It is not to disparage the skill and nerve of de Valera to recollect that Ireland had a relatively easy neutrality. Neither Hitler nor Stalin had to be dealt with directly. British and American attempts to inveigle Ireland into the war could not be compared with the type of pressure that Hitler brought to bear on countries in his orbit. No crises comparable to those faced by Hansson, Guisan or even Franco confronted de Valera. There was no Engelbrecht Division, no Field of Rütli or Order of the Day of 1 August 1940, not even a Hendaye.[419] Nor did the danger of invasion again loom so large as in 1940. It reached its peak for Sweden in the winter of 1942, and for Switzerland in the spring of 1943.[420] In addition, Ireland's total economic dependence on Britain relieved her of the pressures involved in

---

[419] Carlgren, *Swedish foreign policy*, pp. 116ff.; H. Senn, 'Schweizerische Dissuasionsstrategie im Zweiten Weltkrieg', in Bindschedler, *Neutralität*, pp. 204–5; H.R. Kurz, 'Problèmes militaires', *Revue d'histoire de la deuxième guerre mondiale*, 121 (January 1981), pp. 22–3; Denis Smyth, *Diplomacy and strategy of survival. British policy and Franco's Spain, 1940–41* (Cambridge, 1986), pp. 100ff.

[420] R. Bindschedler, H.R. Kurz, W. Carlgren and S. Carlsson, 'Schlussbetrachtungen zu den Problemen der Kleinstaatneutralität im Grossmachtkrieg' in Bindschedler, *Neutralität*, p. 446.

balancing economically between the belligerents, in contrast to Sweden and Switzerland.[421]

Ireland was not the only country to attempt a cut-price neutrality. Norway tried much the same, choosing to equate moral posturing with an effective defence policy during the thirties. She learned her lesson in 1940. Yet Irish neglect of self-defence was even more comprehensive than Norwegian. Norway, with a population of just 3 million, placed orders, however belated, for 129 planes. She had a navy of 63 ships, even if 44 of them dated from before 1918.[422] Ireland had 2! Not only that. It didn't strike many people as at all odd that she should have only two. God would provide for his children, in this case through the Royal Navy, and the Royal Air Force, hitherto unlikely agents of the divine will, but now constrained to protect Ireland in Britain's self-interest!

The popular mind remained oblivious to these considerations. Ireland had objectively a lucky war, for reasons that had ultimately little to do with itself.[423] But the Irish found it necessary to persuade themselves they did it on their own. Censorship fulfilled a crucial purpose in this regard. At first sight, the severity of the censorship might be suspected of exerting a confining influence on Irish perspectives. Censorship was implemented more comprehensively than in either Switzerland or Sweden, despite the objectively greater danger of their position.[424] The contempt frequently expressed for Nazi behaviour in the Swiss and Swedish press provoked furious reactions in Berlin. Nothing comparable was permitted in Ireland, whose censorship regime made it inconceivable that the cabinet should find itself having to 'appeal' to journalists 'for a more subdued tone' as had the Swedish government as late as 1942.[425] Boland's observation to Hempel in May 1940 that Dublin was surprised at the anti-German sentiments sanctioned in the presses of countries bordering on the Reich – sentiments which, he assured Hempel, would not be permitted in the Irish papers –

---

[421] M. Fritz, 'The Swedish economy 1939–1945', in M. Fritz, *et al.* (eds.), *The adaptable nation* (Stockholm, 1984), p. 10; P. Marguerat, 'La Svizzera e la neutralità economica, 1940–1944', *Italia contemporaneo* (June 1984), pp. 71–80.

[422] M. Skodvin, 'Norwegian neutrality and the question of credibility', *Scandinavian Journal of History*, 2 (1977), pp. 128–9.

[423] So had Northern Ireland, apart from the dreadful suffering in Belfast due to the German air raids of 15–16 April and 5–6 March 1941, which left 900 dead, as graphically described in Fisk, *In time of war*, pp. 416–38.

[424] Scott, *Sweden*, p. 508; A. Thulstrup, 'Die schwedische Pressepolitik im Zweiten Weltkrieg', in Bindschedler, *Neutralität*, pp. 128–43; G. Kreis, 'Die Pressepolitik des neutralen Staates', in Bindschedler, *Neutralität*, pp. 352–76; C. Graf, 'Innen- und aussenpolitische Aspekte schweizerischer Zensur während des Zweiten Weltkrieges', in U. Altermatt and J. Garamvölgyi (eds.), *Innen- und Aussenpolitik* (Berne, 1980), pp. 553–69; E. Bonjour, *Erinnerungen* (Basel, 1983), pp. 118–29.

[425] Carlgren, *Swedish foreign policy*, pp. 85, 139. On the severity of the Irish censorship see Carroll, *Ireland in the war years*, pp. 35–6, 136–8, 161–2.

scarcely counts among the immortal Irish contributions to the defence of liberty of speech.[426]

There was, at the level of objective reality, no necessity for the severity of Irish censorship. At two other levels, there was. The censorship was wielded partly as a weapon in internal security. There would have been comments on the fortunes of war that one or other faction within the country would have chosen to find offensive. Censorship was justified in so far as it suppressed the potential internal divisiveness of partisan commentary. And if it was an important weapon in deceiving the enemy, it was an even more important weapon in deceiving oneself. No suspicion of the degree of cooperation with Britain could be allowed disturb the equanimity of the neutral mind.[427]

Censorship was also a prerequisite for maintaining the necessary sense of righteousness. It was unfortunate that the first war in which the Irish found an opportunity of investing their self-respect was also one in which the scales of bestiality would be so unevenly weighed. By the simple device of excluding all accounts of Nazi atrocities as propaganda, the censorship deprived the populace of much of this knowledge.[428] It is difficult to know how many did not want to know, insisting like the 'Pádraic' whom Heinrich Böll met in Mayo in 1954, that reports of Hitler's atrocities were inventions of English propaganda.[429] Some – how many? – would have had to reconstruct their world view once their simple faith in the uniqueness of British iniquity was shaken.

This thirst for ignorance extended into some journalistic circles. As late as the end of April 1945, the editor of the *Irish Press* refused to carry reports of alleged Japanese atrocities against American prisoners on the grounds that 'It was not the policy to publish atrocity stories against any of the belligerents' because 'They are usually entirely undependable, have no other value than to inflame passions and are quite impossible for us to verify.'[430] Such editorial scepticism was admirable in principle. In practice, it required by this stage a heroic determination to avert one's gaze from reality to imply that all atrocity stories were equally undependable. This was the self-same *Irish Press* whose reluctance to 'inflame passions' was such that only two years before it had revealed that 'There is no kind of oppression visited on any minority in Europe which the Six County nationalists have not also endured',[431] a revelation that would no doubt have helped the victims lining up for the Auschwitz gas chambers place

[426] PA AA, StSekr. Irland, 1, Hempel-AA, 21 May 1940, no. 254.
[427] See, for instance, PRO, DO 114–117: Neutrality of Éire (World War 1939–1945), 'Facilities obtained from the government of Éire during the war', nos 50, 51, pp. 37–8.
[428] Fisk, *In time of war*, p. 144.
[429] H. Böll, *Irisches Tagebuch* (Cologne, 1961), p. 47.
[430] NLI, MS 18334, FG, W. Sweetman to D. Gray, 24 April 1945.
[431] *Irish Press*, 1 April 1943.

their plight in consoling comparative perspective if only circumstances had permitted them to gratefully clutch their copies of 'The Truth in the News'.

Neutrality was justified on the simple grounds of *raison d'état*, irrespective of varieties of behaviour among the belligerents. It became more difficult to sustain the desired sense of moral superiority, however, if the belligerents turned out to have been unevenly matched in the savagery stakes. It was not even entirely inconceivable that some troublesome cleric of Karl Barth vintage might make a nuisance of himself by insisting that matters of conscience were involved in any conflict involving Nazism.[432] The return on the investment in 'self-respect' would be safer if one did not know what one did not wish to know. If Irish ignorance had not existed, it would have been necessary to invent it — if only for the sake of 'self-respect'.

Neutrality was the happiest state for any people, at least given the ultimate outcome of the war. It is only the desiccated historian, no doubt, who may be tempted to regret that circumstances precluded the testing of the hypothesis of an English MP that 'a dose of Nazi-ism will do Southern Ireland all the good in the world'.[433] The full rigours of a Nazi occupation (providentially brief, of course) would have provided a valuable comparative perspective on occupation policies for those obsessed with the British record in Ireland. It would have allowed experience to at last satisfy the insatiable appetite for grievance. And it would have told us so much more than we can now know about ourselves.

The Regional Commissioners whom Dublin envisaged conducting such administration as would be possible in the event of invasion 'felt that there would have to be some measure of collaboration in the interests of the people . . . '.[434] But who would have been the real collaborators? There was only a small Irish Jewish community. What would their fate have been? How many locals would have led the witch hunts? What would the attitude of the church have been? How many bishops were as resolutely opposed to Nazism as Michael Browne of Galway?[435] How far was Hempel justified in detecting a growing sympathy for Germany among a hitherto suspicious clergy in the autumn of 1940?[436] How susceptible was Cardinal MacRory to the appeal of 'possible German action for the return of Northern Ireland' as Hempel surmised in June 1940?[437] What conflict of viewpoints was concealed in the hierarchy's statement of 25 June, according to which:

[432] Graf, 'Aspekte', p. 565.   [433] Canning, *British policy*, p. 285.
[434] Ó Broin, *Yesterday*, p. 285.
[435] PA AA, StSekr. Irland, 1, Hempel-AA, 29 May 1940.
[436] *Ibid.*, 1 October 1940, no. 616.
[437] *Ibid.*, 21 June 1940, no. 506.

That portion of our country which is still unfortunately separated from the rest of the nation in its political status calls for special sympathy and consideration. We exhort our Catholic people in that area to face their difficulties with calm and patience in the confident hope that any just settlement must remove them from the disabilities under which they suffer and restore them to that union with their country which they so ardently desire.[438]

Who would have fancied their chances of supping with Hitler? Who would have allowed themselves be manipulated in the name of Christ or country? How many torturers and sadists, racy of the soil, as well as opportunists and careerists, would have seized their chance in the New Order? Would the full rigours of occupation have broken the old moulds, North or South? Would the 'integrity of their quarrel' have preserved normalcy among the church steeples of Fermanagh and Tyrone, and among the brooding memorial crosses of civil war victims? Could even Hitler have disturbed the complacent certainties of hereditary hatreds?

However frustrating for the historian, the citizen can only rejoice that such things did not happen. It is sometimes happier for a country, as for an individual, not to have to learn too much about itself. It is precisely because these things did not happen, as they could so easily have happened if the fortunes of war had shifted, that the citizen of a small state must be grateful, not so much for neutrality, which in itself could do little to prevent such horrors, but for the most important event in the history of Irish neutrality, Allied victory.[439]

Had a German invasion, or even a British one, occurred, government policy was likely to have got the worst of all possible worlds for the country. No small state could repel all-out attack from a great power. In some cases, like that of Denmark, it made little sense to offer more than token resistance. Circumstances were more favourable to Sweden and Switzerland. But they would have had to stand alone if Germany attacked. Nobody could help. In other cases, like those of Norway and Ireland, one could expect, perhaps mistakenly, but nevertheless reasonably, that resistance might win sufficient time to bring outside support. The strength of the defence forces could therefore still make a crucial difference to the country's fate. A small country in those circumstances could hope to mount a sufficiently sustained resistance to deter the prospective invader from taking a gamble. In the event, neither Germany nor Britain took that gamble with Ireland. But it is doubtful if respect for Irish defence capacity was a serious factor in their calculations. The Irish policy of resisting to

---

438 *Irish News*, 26 June 1940, clipping in PRO, PREM 4, 53/2.
439 The Irish prefer not to think about this subject. One of the few to face the issue has been H. Butler, 'The invader wore slippers', in *Escape from the ant hill* (Mullingar, 1986), pp. 103–13, originally published in 1950. For a cognate speculation, see C. Cruise O'Brien, 'Passion and Cunning: an essay on the politics of W.B. Yeats', in A.N. Jeffares and K.G.W. Crosse (eds.), *In excited reverie* (London, 1965), p. 273.

the last gasp, but failing to provide remotely adequate means to sustain resistance against a determined enemy, hardly deserved its good luck, however astutely de Valera played his diplomatic cards.

The government's instinct was to repose only limited confidence in a weak if willing army, while hoping for strong popular resistance in collaboration with that army.[440] Had invasion actually occurred, this was a policy likely to bring catastrophe on the civilian population. Most of the cabinet were veterans of the War of Independence. Popular support, or at least popular acquiescence, had been crucial for the degree of success achieved then. Some cabinet members may even have deluded themselves that they had 'won' the War of Independence in a military sense. Had Ireland suffered occupation from either side in 1940, the Black and Tans were likely to have acquired a much more benign retrospective reputation. If it could not be fully foreseen, ominous though the portents were for those who observed Nazi behaviour, how bestial German treatment of civilian populations could be, there was little excuse for assuming that popular resistance would be treated indulgently. Nor was British behaviour likely to have been fastidious. Britain was unlikely to invade unless she felt her own survival to be at stake. If that was the mood in which she did invade, she was hardly going to be in a frame of mind to adhere punctiliously to the doctrine of minimum force. Black and Tan atrocities had occurred when Britain did not have her back to the wall. The behaviour of forces who felt themselves to be the last line against national disaster was unlikely to be unduly solicitous of the sensitivities of obstructive civilians.

The successful prosecution of neutrality was a considerable achievement. It was not neutrality, but the manner in which the Irish chose to misinterpret the nature of the experience, that deprived it of much of its potential value for the education of a people in genuine self-reliance. Viewed from this perspective, the Emergency takes its place in the mainstream of Irish history, as yet one more half-squandered opportunity, one more experience from which the Irish would choose not to learn. The potential of neutrality, any more than the potential of sovereignty, should not be judged by Irish use of it. The 'success' of neutrality fed further the popular fantasy that Ireland achieved it merely by proclaiming it. Ireland would continue after the war to evade the responsibilities of sovereignty in the field of defence. It was an index of her good fortune that she had not to endure the agonising reassessment of defence policy forced on postwar Norway after the collapse of her 'hibernian' posture of the thirties.[441]

It was less an index of good fortune than of a still impressive capacity for self-deception that public opinion could persuade itself that neutrality

---

[440] PA AA, StSekr. Irland, 1, Hempel-AA, 10 May 1940, no. 230.
[441] H-D. Loock, 'Zeitgeschichte Norwegens', *Vjh. f. Zeitgesch.*, 13 (1965), pp. 86ff.

had no implications for partition. The most frequent official justification for neutrality was the border. Yet neutrality reinforced partition. Even Dorothy Macardle, hagiographer royal to the Republic, sadly conceded in 1944: 'I want to live to see the day when Emmet's epitaph may be written, and I fear that it is further off now than it was a little while ago.'[442] The main reflection that the popular mind allowed itself on partition was that de Valera had once again demonstrated Southern magnanimity by instantly despatching Dublin fire brigades to help fight the fires following the German bombing of Belfast in 1941. Gesture, however worthy in itself, was once more magnified out of all proportion, while process continued to be ignored.

The feeling that neutrality was a significant achievement helped sustain national morale during the war. There is a good deal of validity in the official portrait of a country united behind a popular policy, and experiencing a sense of satisfaction at sustaining that policy in the face of pressure, real and imaginary, from the old enemy. Nevertheless, it is difficult to know how to test claims about morale. The net loss of votes by Fianna Fáil between 1938 and 1944, the relatively low turn-out in 1944, the muted victory of Seán T. O'Kelly in the presidential election in 1945, to say nothing of the continued flow of emigration, hardly suggests a sense of national exhilaration. This line of reasoning should not be pushed too far. Morale does not necessarily translate into support for the government of the day. Nevertheless, if it does not translate into something, it is not clear where its longer term importance lies. And it certainly did not translate into postwar performance.

[442] NLI, MS 18340, FG, D. Macardle to F. Gallagher, 2 April 1944.

Chapter 4

MALAISE: 1945—1958

THE CONSERVATIVE RESISTANCE

It offers an apt commentary on the growing conservatism of Fianna Fáil in the late 1930s that the most potentially radical initiative at that time, the demand for a corporatist (or, in Irish parlance, vocationalist) reorganisation of society, was launched by circles closer to Cosgrave than to de Valera.[1] Irish corporatists derived their intellectual stimulus in large measure from Pius XI's 1931 encyclical, *Quadragesimo Anno*. The general ideological thrust of the encyclical, condemning materialistic capitalism as well as materialistic communism, contained much to appeal to de Valera. But the demand of Irish corporatists, however vaguely formulated during the 1930s, for a national vocational council, to either advise or supersede parliament, had one decisive disadvantage from de Valera's viewpoint. It would curb the power of political parties, which in practice meant the power of Fianna Fáil. As if to confirm his reservations, the opposition sought to exploit the papal pronouncement for their own purpose. The Blueshirts mouthed corporatist rhetoric, and Fine Gael, out of office, and devoid of any idea of how to return to it, coquetted with the vocabulary of vocationalism.[2]

De Valera handled the vocationalist threat with consummate skill. He adopted the classic Augustinian posture – give me corporatism, but not yet. He told the Fianna Fáil Árd Fheis in 1936 that

I would like, personally, to see such an organisation for our society developed, but I want it quite clearly understood that I would like to see it developed voluntarily. I don't believe in a state-inspired organisation of that kind; a regime may support them in its power, but once the regime breaks, they break, and there is nothing permanent about them because they are not natural.[3]

[1] J. Lee, 'Aspects of corporatist thought in Ireland: the Commission on Vocational Organisation, 1939–43', in Cosgrove and McCartney, *Studies in Irish history*, pp. 324–5. The present account draws heavily on this article, and on the sources cited therein.
[2] See the Fine Gael manifesto for the 1937 general election, *Irish Press*, 15 June 1937.
[3] SPO, S10949A, de Valera's speech, 3 November 1936.

This could be interpreted as a sagacious response to the farce of Mussolini's corporate state, an affirmation that an artificial and *dirigiste* approach would not be imposed on a democracy. But de Valera's subsequent behaviour suggests that he put little faith in vocationalism, natural, democratic or otherwise. He could hardly publicly denounce an ideology commended by the papacy. He would instead smother it in his embraces, by incorporating vocational representation into his new constitution. It would have been difficult for him to avoid this in any case. If Article 45 of the 1922 Free State constitution had remained a dead letter in practice, it did genuflect in a vocationalist direction. Eliminating all reference to the subject in the 1937 constitution, when so much else from the Free State constituion was retained, might have provoked awkward questions. The manner of its inclusion was typical de Valera. 'I hope', he told the 1936 Árd Fheis, 'to see developed gradually here, a functional organisation of our society by voluntary action and when that day comes the Senate which we are now proposing can very well develop into a Senate that will be representative of that organisation.'[4] De Valera then proceeded to take good care that the new Senate should wield no real power. Having abolished the Free State Senate in 1936, after it had sought to obstruct Dáil proposals, he had no intention of permitting his new upper house an effective mind of its own. Article 18 of the constitution created a Senate of sixty members. Eleven were to be nominated by the Taoiseach and six elected by the universities. No fewer than forty-three were to represent vocational interests. This might seem a major move in the direction of corporatism, however limited the real powers of the Senate. And Article 19 duly provided that the forty-three members might be elected 'by any functional or vocational group or association . . . ' – but only if the Oireachtas so decided. In the meantime, Article 18 provided for an alternative electoral procedure for the forty-three candidates, to be drawn from 'five panels' – election by TDs and county councillors! There could be no more effective way of subverting the whole vocational concept. 'Vocationalism' was left to the tender mercies of party politicians. The designated electorate took to its task with a will. Genuine vocational representatives were swamped beneath the avalanche of party loyalists.[5]

The blatant manipulation of the 'vocational' categories in the Senate elections provoked Seán MacEntee, after observing the first three elections under the 1937 constitution, to try to persuade de Valera to at least take the cultural category seriously. He urged that nomination to the cultural

---

[4] *Ibid.*
[5] On the results of the first election see O'Sullivan, *The Irish Free State*, pp. 571–3. For a wider survey of the implications of the electoral system see B. Chubb, 'Vocational representation and the Irish Senate', *Political Studies*, 2 (1954), pp. 97–111.

panel should be confined to genuinely cultural bodies.[6] MacEntee's point was that only those with authentic 'scientific or artistic interest' in culture ought to be eligible to become candidates. This would exclude those with a purely economic interest, such as impresarios, theatrical agents, and the like. Several other panels, he noted, provided for economic interests of that sort. The 'cultural' panel was vulnerable to predators with a purely mercenary interest in the 'vocation'. But de Valera resisted, insisting that the matter be referred to the Attorney General as a point of constitutional interpretation.[7] As the matter was seemingly dropped, de Valera presumably got the answer he wanted.

It was not only the manner in which Article 18 appeared to subvert genuine vocational interests – 'It would be farcical to describe the new Senate as a vocational body'[8] – that left a sour taste on more refined palates. The elections quickly become a byword for 'influence' even by prevailing standards. Allegations of bribery in the first elections under the new constitution were already made at the Conference of the Association of Municipal Authorities in September 1938. Subsequent experience suggests that there was probably substance to the charges, however blandly de Valera dismissed them in the Dáil.[9] The most compelling response the Secretary for the Department of Local Government could mobilise was that the charges were patently untenable because they impugned the integrity of TDs![10]

The Municipal Authorities again alleged bribery after the next Senate election in 1943.[11] Jim Ryan was sufficiently perturbed to approach de Valera with proposals for changing the electoral system which 'would have the merit of preventing corruption of that kind'. But he conceded that as his suggestion 'removes definitely and finally any pretence at a Vocational Seanad', it required further refinement.[12] De Valera had no intention of having the pretence removed. Ryan's proposal found no favour with the great spider at the centre of the electoral web!

The issue flared up again when a former chairman of Dublin County Council, John A. Corr, became so careless in the 1944 election that he had to be charged with bribery. Despite his 'Christian Front' connections, Corr was sentenced to three months imprisonment for what the District Justice called 'an unusually serious offence which in my opinion has been aggravated by perjury',[13] a sentence upheld on appeal.[14] De Valera

6 SPO, S10949A, S. MacEntee to de Valera, 13 October 1944.
7 *Ibid.*, T.J. Barrington to M. Moynihan, 17 October 1944.
8 *Irish Times*, 12 August 1944.   9 DD, 73, 26 October 1938.
10 SPO, S10949A, Secretary, Local Government, to M. Moynihan, 22 October 1938.
11 *Irish Times*, 16 July 1943.
12 SPO, S10949A, J. Ryan to E. de Valera, 27 October 1943.
13 *Irish Press*, 9 December 1944.
14 *Ibid.*, 14 February 1945. The case can be followed in the *Irish Press*, 22, 25 November, 5, 8, 9, 19, 29 December 1944; 24, 26, 27 January, 9, 10 February, 29 March 1945.

eventually came round to accepting that 'some senators have been elected through corrupt practices, through bribery'.[15] But as the time had safely passed for amendment of the constitution in the Dáil before this revelation was vouchsafed to him, any changes would now require popular approval in a referendum.

The returning officer for the Senate elections, who was responsible for defining the eligibility of candidates representing 'vocational' interests, put the whole charade in perspective. After presiding at two elections, he explained that 'I am at a great loss to know what anyone means by the word "vocation" . . . The word "vocation" frankly left me in the air!'[16] There could have been no more deserved tribute to the delicacy of de Valera's handling of a potentially troublesome issue.

The Senate offered little consolation to genuine vocationalists. After the 1938 election there seemed no political alternative to de Valera for the foreseeable future. It was in this situation that Michael Tierney and Frank MacDermot proposed in the new Senate in July 1938 that a small commission of inquiry into vocational organisation should be established. It was not in de Valera's style to refuse such a request. But he made one qualification. The commission should be a big one. He then packed a twenty-five person commission with strong-willed personalities, under the chairmanship of Dr Michael Browne, Bishop of Galway, well known for his Fianna Fáil sympathies and his far from eirenic temperament. The deliberations of the commission should not reach a hasty conclusion due to a propensity for premature compromise! De Valera's lack of enthusiasm can be further detected in his constipated conception of vocationalism as an organisation of society 'in which people who are engaged in similar callings or professions naturally gravitate together to promote the interests of those professions or callings'.[17] The implication that vocationalism was merely a device for promoting the selfish interests of sundry pressure groups repelled idealists who envisaged the vocational order as providing an alternative to the greed of capitalism and the tyranny of communism. The self-governing cooperations would indeed represent the interests of their various occupational groupings, but only according to the criterion of the common good, thus acting on the one hand as a solvent of class conflict and on the other as a bulwark of individual liberty against the intrusive pretentions of state bureaucracy. The commission proceeded to ignore de Valera's discreet injunction, feeling that 'the Taoiseach did not intend it as a comprehensive definition'.[18]

The commission managed to overcome its cumbersome composition,

[15] *Irish Independent*, 12 October 1945.
[16] NLI, MS922, CVO, 23 November 1939, q. 1524, ev. W. Brown.
[17] Commission on Vocational Organisation 1943: *Report* (P. No. 6743), p. 3, para. 4.
[18] *Ibid.*

and the difficulties of wartime travel, to present a report in November 1943. The massive document, written mainly by Fr E.J. Coyne, made a gallant effort to grapple with the issues. This involved nothing less than presenting a blueprint for a new structure of governance for Irish society. It addressed itself essentially to the quality of governmental decision-making. It considered the existing system to stand condemned by its results. It denounced in terms that would become familiar a generation later, the anonymity, irresponsibility, and incompetence of 'bureaucracy', by which it specifically meant the Irish civil service. The inherent 'rigidity' of the service led to a refusal 'to create a new precedent or to experiment', and fostered 'a lack of personal responsibility and of inducement to produce results'. 'Where remuneration is not dependent on results, either negatively or positively, there is a temptation to adopt the easiest or most convenient course rather than the best.'[19] It proposed instead an elaborate structure of elected vocational councils, beginning at a local level, and culminating in a National Vocational Council, which would be responsible for recommending economic and social policy to the Oireachtas.

There were numerous weaknesses in the report which made it vulnerable to eager critics. By failing to cost the proposals, the commission left itself a lamb to the slaughter of willing knives in Finance. By launching indiscriminate assaults on the civil service it presumably alienated even potentially sympathetic individual officials. By failing to explore the relationships between the proposed National Vocational Council and the Oireachtas, it left the implications of its proposals for party political activity disturbingly obscure. Despite its vigorous and genuine denial that its vocationalism owed any inspiration to fascistic models, and its insistence that the corporate society it desired was fundamentally inimical to the corporate state of totalitarian regimes, opportunist critics could impute guilt by semantic association.

Many legitimate criticisms could be made of the report.[20] Nevertheless, its political reception was quite unworthy of the importance of the issues involved. Fundamental questions about the efficiency of government, not in the sense of cheeseparing, but with reference to the quality of decision-making, of the type so sedulously avoided by the Brennan Commission on the Civil Service, began to force themselves on ministers during the war. Seán MacEntee, however opportunistically, opposed increased state intervention partly on the grounds that the civil service lacked the capacity to deal with new problems. 'There are not staffs available to study them adequately in order to find solutions and they are becoming so numerous and pressing that the attention which can be given to any one of them, either by the political or permanent personnel

[19] Quoted in Lee, 'Corporatist thought', p. 337.   [20] *Ibid.*, pp. 341ff.

of the department, is intermittent, uncertain, inconclusive and ineffective.'[21]

The report was published in August 1944. Fianna Fáil, having won a
handsome majority in the May 1944 general election, was in no mood to
be impressed by sweeping suggestions for restricting the role of political
parties. Nor were government Departments likely to take kindly to a
report which consigned them to a distinctly bleak future. But there was
ideological as well as purely selfish resistance. This had little to do with the
alleged fascist connotations. Instead, it revolved around the highly
interventionist ideology that informed the report. The commission envisaged sweeping social and economic changes that would require a degree
of activism – 'vocational' rather than 'state', but still activism – far
exceeding anything contemplated before the war, or implemented during
the war. The elaborate vocational structures envisaged by the commission
were not proposed for their own sake. They were based on the assumption
that only massive participation by the public in the decision-making
process would rouse popular commitment to the highly ambitious 'planning' that the commission intended the National Vocational Assembly
should undertake. Its scorn for 'bureaucracy' was only partly due to the
antidemocratic irresponsibility of bureaucracies. It was also due to its
contempt for the incapacity of bureaucracy to implement the changes it
had in mind.

It was this sense of urgency informing the report, the impatience to do
something, the disdain for what it felt to be the pervasive mediocrity of the
official mind, together with its commitment to the general ideal of
'planning', whatever the nature of the institutional model it proposed,
that might have been expected to appeal to the gut instincts of Seán
Lemass. For Lemass was locked in a futile struggle to inject a similar sense
of urgency into his colleagues, and had already expressed impatience at
the ineffectiveness of parliament as a decision-making forum on 'industrial and mercantile' matters. But Lemass was needlessly alienated by the
censorious tone of the report's references to Industry and Commerce.[22]

Lemass had little to fear from a vocational assembly of informed
people. He might himself presume to dominate it. But he would have had
to regard the scheme as a non-starter in party political terms. And he
would also have had to ask, how would vocational policy be implemented? Would not any new administrative system rapidly succumb to
bureaucracy also? The report failed to adequately confront this issue.
Despite his running battle with Finance, Lemass had little reason to share
the commission's view that the existing civil service was so sunk in sloth
and self-interest that it could not deliver the goods, provided it got the

---

[21] SPO, S11109A, S. MacEntee to E. de Valera, 28 September 1943.
[22] Lee, 'Corporatist thought', p. 331.

right political and administrative leadership. He took a deep pride in the performance of 'his' Industry and Commerce. The Department of Supplies, over which he still presided when the report appeared, had devised techniques for reducing red tape to a minimum.[23] Indeed, it discharged its responsibilities with vigour unrivalled by any of the private 'enterprise' critics of bureaucracy. It might, however, be wondered if the search for a vocational order was any more futile than the search for sustained political and administrative leadership of the requisite quality!

The efforts of the vocationalists, then, prodigious though they were in time, energy, ability and idealism, proved futile. The official mind did not so much confront as simply squash the challenge.

The failure of the vocationalists to exert any influence on government thinking about decision-making structures in state or society was partly due to the resentment of party politicians and bureaucratic politicians at the threat to their own power. Even when that power was not threatened, however, the general complacency of the official mind made it difficult for even a strong and vigorous minister, as we have seen in the case of the Committee on Economic Planning, to induce any great feeling of dissatisfaction with 'normalcy' among his cabinet colleagues, much less in the senior civil service. Another illuminating example, from a different perspective, is furnished by the case of children's allowances. This was one of the few battles that the forces of resistance lost. But the extent to which they were able to postpone a decision on an issue on which Lemass enjoyed the support of de Valera, provides eloquent corroborative testimony to the difficulty of actually getting anything done in the type of regime that had emerged after two decades of independence.

It was Fine Gael's James Dillon who first raised the question of family allowances as a political question in 1939.[24] With the widely read Catholic newspaper, *The Standard*, quickly taking up the matter,[25] de Valera initiated immediate discussion in his own entourage.[26] The momentum was maintained sufficiently for cabinet to request Local Government to examine the question in July.[27]

July 1939 was not the happiest of dates on which to embark on a new venture. But the delays that would dog policy formulation in this area were only partly due to war-time pressures. In November the cabinet established a committee on family allowances. It had a chequered career. No chairman was appointed, presumably on the assumption that the Minister for Local Government, whose department had been entrusted with fact-finding responsibility, would take charge. But the new minister,

[23] Farrell, *Lemass*, pp. 56–8.   [24] DD, 75, 30 March 1939, 403ff.
[25] *The Standard*, 12 May 1939.
[26] SPO, S11265A, T.A. Smiddy to E. de Valera, 26 May 1939.
[27] SPO, GC 2/83, 11 July 1939.

P.J. Ruttledge, was in poor health. His Private Secretary, on whom much of the administrative responsibility fell, was Brian O'Nolan, better known to history as Myles na gCopaleen/Flann O'Brien. Myles had entered the civil service as a junior administrative officer in 1935. With an MA in Irish poetry, and a travelling scholarship in German to his credit,[28] he was immediately posted, for reasons best known to civil service personnel planners, to Local Government, a field for which he may already have imbibed some of his father's disdain.[29]

It may be doubted if any ordinary person with the background and qualifications of Myles would have long survived the grinding boredom of Local Government mundanity. And Myles was no ordinary person. His marvellous letters began to appear in the *Irish Times* in the course of 1939. *The third policeman* was finished in January 1940. The first column of Cruiskeen Lán appeared in the *Irish Times* on 4 October, 1940. *An Béal Bocht* was published in 1941. It was the fate of the Committee on Family Allowances that it happened to coincide with the flowering of the creative genius of its secretary. The administrative arrangements of the committee themselves constitute a little saga.[30] They quickly roused the ire of one member of the committee whose reputation does not rest on his standing as a man of letters.

Seán Lemass was so infuriated with the manner of proceeding when the committee eventually met in April 1940 that he immediately dispatched a four-page memorandum to Maurice Moynihan, fairly bristling with contempt for those responsible for the charade.

I am sending you herewith a document containing an outline of proposals for the payment of allowances to children which is desired to have submitted to the government. I am asking you to arrange for its circulation as otherwise it is not clear whose responsibility it is. The document has been prepared by me. It has of course no relation to the functions of the Department of Supplies. It has been prepared as a result of the discussions at the Cabinet Committee on Family Allowances, of which the Minister for Local Government is chairman. It is in a sense the report of that Committee. At the same time it should be clear that it has not been prepared by the Committee but that they are recommending its consideration by the government and particularly the proposal in the final paragraph. I will be glad if you will arrange to have it circulated at an early date.[31]

It wasn't only the eccentric administrative arrangements for the committee that caused delay. The 'proposal in the final paragraph' was that an

---

28 A. Clissmann, *Flann O'Brien* (Dublin, 1975), p. 6.
29 Brian O'Nolan was the son of Michael O'Nolan, who as a revenue commissioner had expressed his contempt for the morality of local authorities in his 'Reservation' to the *Report of Old Age Pension Committee of Inquiry* (Dublin, 1926), p. 20.
30 The saga may be followed in SPO, S12117A, in correspondence between the Taoiseach's Office, John Hurson, Secretary to Local Government, Brian O'Nolan. See the exchanges of 3, 15 November 1939, 10 January, 5 February, 5, 21 March, 6, 12 April, 14 May, 3, 4, 13 June, 1, 2, 13, 22 July, 2, 12, 13, 27, 30 August, 5 September 1940.
31 SPO, S12117A, S. Lemass to M. Moynihan, 8 April 1940. I am grateful to Brian Farrell for drawing this memorandum to my attention. See also Farrell, *Lemass*, pp. 61–3.

inter-departmental committee should be established 'to prepare the heads
of the necessary legislation'.[32] Finance naturally resisted the idea that any
legislation was necessary. McElligott was still relying on the usual tactics
as late as October. Alarmed that the matter had been placed on the cabinet
agenda, he wanted the terms of reference to be 'the subject of careful
preliminary examination by all the Departments concerned'.[33] The
cabinet, however, ignored McElligott on this occasion. The committee,
with O.J. Redmond, a senior Finance official as chairman, and the young
T.K. Whitaker, already making his early mark in Finance, as Secretary,
took nearly two years to report, despite prodding from the Taoiseach's
office.[34] But delay was not procrastination in this case. The report, an
impressive document, outraged McElligott by recommending a combined
contributory and non-contributory system of children's allowances.

De Valera was determined that something should be done about
children's allowances. He also seems to have felt that the only way to get it
done was to get Lemass to do it. His confidence in de Valera's support
allowed Lemass to ride roughshod over the opposition. Not that the
resistance was numerically powerful at this stage. It consisted mainly of
McElligott and MacEntee. But they deluged the cabinet with passionate
memoranda, and only brusque behaviour by Lemass prevented them from
postponing action even further.

Within two months of the inter-departmental committee's report,
presented on 15 October 1942, the cabinet, on 4 December, requested
Lemass to 'submit to the government the principles of a scheme for the
provision of children's allowances by the method of compulsory contributory insurance'. Lemass had proposals circulated at the very next meeting,
only four days later, which broadly endorsed his proposals and authorised
him to prepare the heads of a bill.[35] The pace at this stage left Seán T.
O'Kelly somewhat dazed, or so at least it suited him to imply to
McElligott. Maurice Moynihan chose to deliver a deliciously unhelpful
reply when McElligott protested that 'the Tánaiste states that no decision,
in principle, in favour of family allowances is intended to be conveyed by
this decision but, of course, a direction for the preparation of heads of a
Bill would seem to imply such a decision. I wonder if it would be possible
to clear up the matter?'[36]

Lemass based his initial proposals on the report of the interdepartmental committee. His scheme, which he calculated would cost about

32 SPO, S12117A, S. Lemass to M. Moynihan, 8 April 1940.
33 *Ibid.*, J.J. McElligott to P. Ó Cinnéide, 8 October 1940.
34 SPO, S12117B. The reminders were dated 1 November 1941, 11 July 1942 and 5
    October 1942.
35 SPO, GC 2/395, 4 December 42; GC 2/397, 8 December 12.
36 SPO, S12117B, J.J. McElligott to M. Moynihan, 14 December 1942; M. Moynihan to J.J.
    McElligott, 21 December 1942.

£2 500 000 per annum, envisaged both contributory and non-contributory allowances, and also contemplated the abolition or reduction of other types of assistance, including food subsidies, and the state contribution to the relief of rates on agricultural land. He subsequently dropped the contributory section, allegedly on grounds of administrative convenience. When Lemass had hammered his proposals into shape, he specifically instructed that 'the other departments concerned' should *not* be notified.[37] De Valera duly directed, the following day, 10 February, that the item be taken at cabinet on 12 February, 'on condition that decision to be taken would be decision in principle only'.[38] This did not suffice to prevent a blistering complaint from MacEntee about the transgression of the procedural proprieties. The details still required a good deal of discussion. The Act did not finaly become law until 1944, when an allowance of 2s 6d (12½p) per week became payable on all children after the second (second children would become eligible in 1952, and all children in 1963). But the forces of resistance were in retreat from March 1943. Neither de Valera nor Lemass was in a mood to be frustrated by the mobilisation of institutional inertia. No doubt, the precarious electoral situation helped concentrate the cabinet's mind.

The children's allowance issue was not one of the highest intrinsic importance. But it reveals much about the temperaments and calculations of the personalities involved, and about the style of decision-making. The copious memoranda submitted by McElligott and MacEntee, two of the central personalities in governance for thirty years, tell us a good deal about the cast of their minds.

McElligott's response to the report of the inter-departmental committee is a particularly notable performance,[39] repudiating recommendations reached under the aegis of one of his own senior officials, and drafted by Whitaker. Irish workers, McElligott asserted, were already really quite well off, thanks to trade unions. For McElligott to find a positive way of referring to trade unions (if this was indeed a positive way) must have already caused raised eyebrows among discerning readers. Children's allowances had been taken up by the governments of states like Germany, France, and Belgium, 'only, be it noted, in places where the problems of inflation had been acute and where wage levels continued low', whereas, 'no such problems . . . exist in this country at present'. For McElligott to assert that inflation was not acute must have left those who had recovered from the allegation about trade unions gasping for breath. Even had it been true, it was completely out of character for McElligott to admit it. And by December 1942, it wasn't even true! In addition, McElligott

---

[37] SPO, S12117B, memo by R.C. Ferguson, 9 February 1943.
[38] SPO S12117B, additional N.B. by Ferguson.
[39] SPO, S12117B, Finance memo, 2 December 1942.

proceeded, 'Our population is mainly rural and as such the problem of sustenance is not at all of the same serious degree as in highly industrialised countries where conditions of acute poverty and squalor prevail in urban slums.' Apart from the glamorisation of rural poverty in Ireland, and the apparent underrating of the still significant rural populations in most western European countries, including France and Germany, a few of his readers, though a diminishing few, might have reflected that even in 1942, after the Fianna Fáil slum clearing drive of the 1930s, bitterly resisted by McElligott, he need have only walked a mile from his office to have learned something about 'urban slums' in Ireland. Heinrich Böll had no difficulty finding the Dublin slums more than a decade later.[40]

Having asserted that 'the problem of sustenance' in Ireland was 'not at all of the same serious degree' as in England, McElligott then had no hesitation in criticising the report for failing to discuss 'the precise degree or incidence of severe hardship in this country of which no survey has been made'. The absence of evidence was 'a serious defect' in the report, but no obstacle to his own blithe assertions! Even then, he could hardly conceal his consternation that the report had been so reckless as to recommend anything that had not already been adopted in Britain: 'the campaign for family allowances here was taken up from Great Britain but we are now in advance of that country in that we have a firm recommendation from an Inter-departmental Committee for their introduction'. Being 'in advance of' Britain was apparently unnatural.

Having disposed of the 'practical' arguments in favour of allowances, McElligott then reverted to first principles.

The principle has not been generally accepted that the state has responsibility for the relief of poverty in all its degrees – the principle underlying any social measures undertaken by the state in this country up to the present is that the state's responsibility is limited to the relief of *destitution* i.e. extreme cases where employment and the minimum necessities of existence are lacking.

He proceeded to argue that 'social schemes in this country up to the present have tended to develop on lines of too great reliance upon the state as a source of help and assistance towards a situation where below a given wage level the incentive to work will be totally destroyed'. He may have been right. He may have been wrong. He produced no evidence either way.

McElligott then shifted onto another tack. 'A system of family allowances would introduce a further degree of state interference in the domestic affairs of families and strengthen the tendency of what in modern times is critically termed "bureaucratic control".' This must have finally eliminated the already elevated eyebrows of discerning readers.

40 Böll, *Irisches Tagebuch*, Cologne, pp. 22–3.

This was the same McElligott whose insistence on the doctrine of ministerial responsibility – a facade, most of the time, amiable or sinister, according to taste – for bureaucratic control, 'was certainly more rigid' than even in Britain 'where that doctrine originated'.[41]

McElligott next asserted that the present tax level 'does not permit of an increase'. 'This latter is true even though the rates of taxation are much less than in the UK', because 'it must be remembered that taxation in the latter country is easily the heaviest in the world.' British tax rates were certainly heavy. But the sole evidence McElligott chose to produce in support of this contention was that American tax rates 'are only about half those in the UK', while Irish rates were 'three-fourths'. For comparative purposes, the 'world' had suddenly shrivelled to the USA!

McElligott finally turned to the question of timing. No risk should be taken in wartime, when postwar circumstances were so uncertain. 'It is not at all unlikely that after the war the maintenance of our existing social services even at their present level may be extremely difficult.' Having banished the spectre of inflation three pages previously, when it suited his purpose, he now conjured it up again: 'Inflation is, even at present, a very real danger and the release of a further large volume of purchasing power . . . against a dwindling supply of consumer goods would most certainly further intensify the inflationary tendencies already at work.'

Three months later, in March 1943, McElligott elaborated on his vision of the postwar world, whose contours he now sketched in lurid colours.[42] Continental countries would be far more competitive than Ireland, thanks to their lower wages, weaker trade unions, etc. 'Hence', he deduced, in a spectacular non-sequitur, 'These countries will after a relatively short time be pressing their agricultural exports on the British market.' This bore so little relation to either historical understanding or logical rigour that one can only presume that McElligott was driven to distraction by the prospect of defeat on the issue. He further sought to induce the cabinet to pull back from the brink by stressing that the extra taxation necessary for children's allowances would be 'a disastrous step in our present circumstances. Such a burden could not be undertaken with any degree of safety except in conditions of expanding production and full employment. There is no reason whatever to assume that these conditions will be fulfilled in this country for many years after the war.'

With the cabinet still intent on pursuing the path of perdition, McElligott, in a final despairing attempt to avert disaster, adopted an approach that considerably extended the range of professional advice tendered by civil servants.[43] He now chose to lay particular stress on 'aspects on which

41 Whyte, *Church and state*, p. 116.
42 SPO, S12117B, Finance memo, 1 March 1943.
43 *Ibid.*, Finance memo, 11 March 1943.

public statements have been made from time to time of late by prominent Catholic ecclesiastics'. He invoked Catholic teaching, with specific reference to the encyclicals *Casti Connubii* and *Quadragesimo Anno*. The warnings of E.J. Coyne, 'a well known Irish writer and economist' on the dangers of 'impersonal bureaucracy' were quoted in glowing terms – the same Fr Coyne who was then busily drafting the report of the Commission on Vocational Organisation, for whose labours McElligott had already shown such a 'freezing lack of sympathy'.[44] This was a delicious case of quoting Scripture for one's purpose. He then proceeded to pronounce 'the moral danger' that a state scheme would 'wither up the roots of all Christian charity of a voluntary kind'. That would be 'a major disaster', especially as 'already in this country there are numerous charitable institutions and organisations which through voluntary effort and subscription of money cater most efficiently for the poor and the sick'.

This style of argument came much more naturally to Seán MacEntee than to McElligott. MacEntee had been consistently critical of the proposal from the outset. Finding *The Standard* deplorably weak on the issue, he made the first of his voluminous contributions to the discussion by dispatching to de Valera an extract from the English Catholic paper, *The Tablet*, on 'The family and the future', which expressed grave reservations about the whole idea.[45] In a major memorandum in October 1939 MacEntee attacked with gusto the proposal 'to institute a state system of family allowances' with which Frank Aiken was closely associated.[46] MacEntee denounced allowances because they would 'induce the less fitted to marry at the expense of everyone else in the community'. Even worse would follow. By a process of logic which he found wholly convincing, MacEntee decided that 'in order to drive the unfit into matrimony we are to drive the strongest, the most enterprising, the best educated of our young earners out of the country'. He naturally could see no justification for a proposal with such self-evidently calamitous consequences:

This generation inherited a sound social organisation of immemorial ancestry, deeply rooted in the traditions of our race, based upon the patriarchical principle that honour, respect and obedience were due to the heads of the household, because these shouldered great responsibilities. We have relieved the parents of a large measure of their household responsibilities – rightfully so in many cases – but we have also shorn them of many of their public privileges. Today the married man and his wife carrying the whole burden of their families has no more voice in the direction of our public affairs than the flapper or whipper snapper of 21. It is not natural that this should be so, but we have carried the doctrine of political egalitarianism to such extreme lengths in regard to public affairs that it is the case

[44] Whyte, *Church and state*, p. 114.
[45] SPO, S11265A, S. MacEntee to E. de Valera, 14 August 1939.
[46] *Ibid.* Notes by the Minister for Industry and Commerce on the proposal to institute a state system of family allowances, 28 October 1939.

here – a state of affairs for which it would be difficult to find a parallel in any other predominantly Catholic country. If we do want to make the married state more attractive we must reinvest it with some of its former dignity and privilege. It may be that the Dáil must continue to be based upon adult suffrage merely, but if so, we ought to reserve the right of electing the local authorities, and indeed the Seanad, to those who as married men and women have family responsibilities.

The Unemployment Assistance Acts, MacEntee believed, had subverted parental authority, especially in rural areas, and 'without the firm exercise of such authority a peasant economy such as ours, based upon the patriarchical principle, cannot exist'. If such payments were necessary at all, they should therefore 'be made direct to the father of the family, where his general character from the point of view of industry and sobriety warrants such payments, or if he be unsatisfactory from this point of view, then to the mother'.

MacEntee detected a grim fate for those lured by the siren song of allowances:

If the state subsidises parents to have children, it will be but a step to regulate the number of children, then to lay down who shall be permitted to have children and who shall not, how the subsidised children are to be brought up, to what purposes they are to devote their lives, what physical and mental characteristics are to be encouraged by subsidised breeding, who shall be bred to labour and who to govern, etc. etc., until we shall have traversed the whole ground between the initiation of a state system of family allowances and the servile state.

If this were not sufficient, MacEntee was soon envisaging the horrors of 'Communism for wives and children' when circulating a forty-five page memorandum, summarising Alexander Gray's *Family endowment* to his cabinet colleagues, who were certainly finding their range of literary reference involuntarily broadened by MacEntee's valiant efforts.[47]

MacEntee, now Minister for Local Government, returned to the fray when Lemass formulated his proposals in December 1942. In a mode of presentation reminiscent of McElligott, he combined shrewd criticism of points of detail with cosmic denunciation of the principles.[48] The proposals were 'objectionable' not only because they transgressed the prerogatives of Local Government, which should be responsible for the implementation of any scheme, but because they 'are likely to be severely criticised by Catholic sociologists'. In addition, 'they are fundamentally inadmissable in as much as they appear to be based on the assumption that a man has an inherent right to make himself and his dependents a charge on society'. The Lemass circular 'challenges first principles if it implies, as it seems to do, that it is no longer necessary for man to earn bread for himself and his household by the sweat of his brow . . . '. MacEntee anticipated strong episcopal opposition:

[47] *Ibid.*, MacEntee memo on 'Family allowances', 7 November 1940, p. 45.
[48] SPO, S12117B, Local Government memo on children's allowances, 18 February 1943.

There is no doubt, for instance, that the spiritual authorities will want to know what rights the state claims over all children when it is prepared to accept this obligation in respect of each and everyone of them irrespective of the need to do so. The assumption of obligations implies, and invariably carries with it, an arrogation of rights. The claim of the state to control the whole spiritual and temporal development of the child has already been put forward and bitterly resisted by the church in those states where schemes of the kind now under review were first put into operation.

The scheme, MacEntee vouched from his knowledge of the views of 'many far-sighted persons', might 'ultimately be used to justify a drastic invasion of parental rights later'.

When MacEntee shifted from philosophical issues to economic ones, he supported McElligott's contention about the consequences of higher taxation. With his customary combination of total assurance and total lack of evidence, he announced that 'in every country high and ill considered taxation has had as its invariable concomitance mass poverty and mass unemployment'. He shared also McElligott's belief that the lower orders already generally received adequate incomes. As the 36s a week an agricultural labourer earned was sufficient 'to enable a man to provide for himself and his wife and one child', any earnings above that level simply showed how relatively well off the rest of the labour force was. His habit of arguing from doctrine rather than evidence tended to conceal the fact that some of his individual criticisms of the Lemass scheme were well taken. It comes as something of a surprise, given the manner in which he scaled the heights of hyperbole, to find that he was actually in favour of an alternative scheme in which allowances would be means tested and contributory.

When MacEntee intervened again, in March 1943, it was in explicit support of McElligott's memorandum of 11 March, which had warned of the threat of ecclesiastical censure, mobilising Pius XI against the bureaucratic centralism of Beveridge – and of Lemass.[49]

MacEntee's regular invocation of Catholic principles makes his bitter public dispute with Dr Dignan, bishop of Clonfert, in 1944–5, all the more curious. Dignan, known for his Fianna Fáil sympathies, and MacEntee's own nominee as chairman of the National Health Insurance Society, published in October 1944 a pamphlet, *Social security: outlines of a scheme of a national health insurance*. This 'attempt to work out in detail the application of Catholic social teaching to a particular sector of Irish life'[50] might have been expected to have appealed to MacEntee's declared principles which were precisely those mobilised by him in his criticism of the Lemass scheme. Dignan's plan implemented the principle

[49] *Ibid.*, Local Government memo, Children's allowances, 'Beveridgeism' and the Catholic Church, 16 March 1943.
[50] Whyte, *Church and state*, p. 101.

of subsidiarity, exalted the authority of the father in the family, and was contributory. It was, it is true, weak on the cost factor, and also failed to meet a basic problem of all contributory schemes, 'that, where social services are based on insurance, a social assistance service, operated with a means test, has also to be provided for those who fall through the insurance net'.[51] Nevertheless, Dignan's heart appeared to be very much in the right place. Yet MacEntee responded in a manner that even as restrained an authority as Professor Whyte has felt obliged to describe as 'almost virulent'.[52]

It may help to contrast the Lemass response to the Report of the Commission on Vocational Organisation with MacEntee's response to the Dignan plan. Lemass rejected the report more on pragmatic than on philosophical grounds. While his resentment at the criticism of Industry and Commerce injected a sharp tone into his response, there is nothing in his previous or subsequent record to suggest that he would have resisted the report in principle, if he felt it could have worked. MacEntee, on the other hand, now found himself hoist with his own philosophical petard. For Dr Dignan denounced as un-Christian the existing social services, which MacEntee was prone to praise as incorporating the Christian ideal of frugal sufficiency. 'The whole Poor Law legislation', declared Dr Dignan, 'the Medical Charities Act and similar legislation should be blotted out from our Statute Book and – from our memory. The system is tainted at its root and it reeks now, as it did when introduced, of destitution, pauperism and degradation.'[53]

It seems reasonable to surmise that it may have been a basic conflict of gut instincts that lay at the root of the MacEntee response to Dignan. What MacEntee had championed as Christianity, the bishop denounced as degradation. However different their sources of inspiration, Lemass and Dignan had more in common with each other than either had with MacEntee, whose instincts were closer to those expressed from Cumann na nGaedheal benches in the 1920s by his fellow Northern Catholic, Patrick McGilligan. MacEntee resented the affront to his cherished self-image as a Christian.

MacEntee used the power of the state, which he excoriated in principle, to refuse to reappoint Dignan as chairman of the National Health Insurance Society in 1945. He replaced him with a civil servant[54] – a representative of that state bureaucracy which MacEntee so passionately denounced in principle. There was no nonsense about subsidiarity now. But MacEntee could not answer Dr Dignan's question: 'The Scheme is built on Christian principles of social justice and charity. Does the Minister mean that a social and economic system based on these prin-

[51] *Ibid.*, p. 104.   [52] *Ibid.*, p. 109.   [53] *Ibid.*, p. 102.   [54] *Ibid.*, p. 112.

ciples is impracticable in Ireland?'[55] Cabinet colleagues who had endured MacEntee's sermons on Christian principles may have allowed themselves a bleak smile at the spectacle of the biter bit.

When de Valera and Lemass found themselves obliged to resort to procedural subterfuges to expedite decisions on policies resisted by McElligott, an individual Minister for Finance who chose to 'take on' his own Department faced an impossible task unless he could match his officials not only in determination, but in technical competence and in staying power. Frank Aiken, for whom a job had to be found when his responsibility as Coordinator of Defensive Measures ended in 1945, asked de Valera for Finance when Seán T. O'Kelly became President.[56] Aiken had the requisite will-power; and he still had some fire in his belly. But the flames spluttered in various directions. He derived his theoretical inspiration from Major Douglas, of Alberta fame, with his penchant for credit creation as a solvent of economic problems.[57] McElligott was naturally alarmed at the prospect of a time bomb ticking away in the ministerial office. T.K. Whitaker was specially assigned to deal with the situation. Whitaker's efficient bomb disposal techniques soon left the new arrival safely defused. But there was a brief period when officials were exposed to an unaccustomed tone of voice. The theoretical and temperamental differences between the minister and his officials emerged most clearly over banking policy.

The government was experiencing some financial pressure during 1945, and wanted to arrange a loan from the banks to tide it over the final quarter of the financial year. This was a regular enough occurrence, and posed no insuperable problem. An issue of Exchequer Bills normally coped with such temporary stringency.[58] But Aiken flew into a rage at the refusal of the banks to take up the Exchequer Bills at a rate of interest identical with that paid for Treasury Bills in London. The banks' case was that their deposit rates were higher than English deposit rates and that they would therefore lose by lending at the English rate. After abortive discussions, during which Aiken advanced a *mélange* of arguments, not all by any means equally weak, and including a thinly veiled threat of bank nationalisation,[59] Aiken told McElligott that 'I regard their turning down of the request . . . as an act of undeclared war upon our people.'[60] He now proposed that the Central Bank, established in 1942, should impose penal

55 *Ibid.*, p. 199. 56 Fanning, *Finance*, p. 392.
57 *Ibid.*; P. Lynch, 'The Irish economy since the war, 1946–51', in Nowlan and Williams, *Ireland* p. 187.
58 SPO, S13749A, S. Hegan to J.J. McElligott, 13 December 1945.
59 *Ibid.*, memo on meeting between Minister for Finance and banking representatives, 17 December 1945.
60 *Ibid.*, F. Aiken to J.J. McElligott, 21 December 1945.

measures by obliging the banks to lodge non-interest-bearing deposits with itself.[61]

Aiken found no support for this proposal, either in Finance or at the Central Bank. Joseph Brennan, governor of the bank, had as little sympathy as McElligott, or as the banks themselves, with the expansionist credit policy sought by Aiken.[62]

Finding himself confronting not only the banks, but Finance and the Central Bank, Aiken turned to the constitution for support. When he triumphantly asserted that the constitution directed the Oireachtas 'to ensure that, in what pertains to the control of credit, the constant and predominant aim shall be the welfare of the people as a whole', he found to his consternation that while Article 45 did indeed use this form of words, they were merely 'for the general guidance' of the Oireachtas, which was in no way 'directed' by them. De Valera's constitutional formula was a purely political manoeuvre. It meant nothing in the real world of Finance. McElligott had already criticised the directive on social policy and especially the reference to credit because it would provide agitators with 'a weapon of attack'.[63] The 'agitator' was now his own minister. But McElligott, not Aiken, held the whip hand. Aiken had no constitutional ground on which to stand, and McElligott took additional pains to stress that it was the Central Bank, and not the government, that had the legal right to determine what measures, if any, should be taken against the banks.[64] Aiken was cornered.

Far from pursuing the expansionist policy of his credit creation dreams, Aiken found himself presiding over an austerity regime as Ireland recovered only haltingly from the 'Emergency'. True, industrial growth rates seemed reasonably satisfactory. Industrial employment recovered to the level of 1938 in 1946, and increased nearly 10 per cent by 1948. But the level of recorded unemployment scarcely changed, standing at 9.3 per cent in 1947, when savings amounted to only 4½ per cent of GNP and fixed investment came to only 9 per cent of GNP.[65] Unemployment remained stubbornly high despite rising emigration, with an average outflow of nearly 30 000 a year between 1945 and 1947. The hard winter of 1946–7 caused serious fuel shortages, and bread rationing was imposed in January 1947. In the autumn, Aiken had to introduce a severe supplementary

61 *Ibid.*, F. Aiken to J.J. McElligott, 28 December 1945.
62 *Ibid.*, Finance memo, 29 November 1945; 'Short statement of consideration urged by the Minister for Finance . . .' to Banks Standing Committee, 20 December 1945; S. Hegan to J.J. McElligott, 21 December 1945.
63 Fanning, *Finance*, p. 268.
64 SPO, S13749A. See the exchanges between Aiken and McElligott, 28 December 1945, 1 January 1946. For the Central Bank's response to Aiken's initiative see Moynihan, *Central banking*, pp. 324–32.
65 K. Kennedy and B.R. Dowling, *Economic growth in Ireland: the experience since 1947* (Dublin, 1975), p. 200.

budget.[66] Many could not, or would not, understand why hardship should continue after the war. Had they not made heroic sacrifices? Were they now to receive no reward? Wage demands were pursued with growing impatience in 1946, most conspicuously by the national teachers, whose union went on strike from March to October.[67] The workers' case after the war was a simple one. Prices had risen twice as sharply as wages since 1939. Wage earners now sought compensation. That income could ultimately come only out of production was a matter of indifference to them. In the teachers' case, status considerations helped further blur the issue of who would pay, or what 'the country' could afford. Government denunciations of strikes on the grounds that they were against the national interest made little impression on the strikers. The government held firm against the teachers. But it was clear from the manner in which the dispute was conducted that the collective interest was an elusive concept, self-interest a concrete one.

If excessive wage demands still played only a subordinate role in damaging national economic prospects, the signs had been accumulating for some time that poor labour relations could become an increasingly serious obstacle to sustained growth. While Aiken had to cope with the budgetary implications of increased wage demands in the public sector, it was Lemass whose Department was responsible for devising a framework within which labour relations could be conducted in a manner compatible with the national interest.

Lemass, who relied heavily on working-class votes in his Dublin constituency, regularly projected himself as a friend of labour. And his record confirms that, while he had no ambition to subvert existing property relations, he believed that workers should enjoy their 'fair share' of the gains from economic growth. This general sympathy for the trade union position did not blind him to the necessity for rationalising trade union structures in a small country where the workforce was fragmented into more than a hundred unions, many of them English based, or prevent him from advocating stern measures against what he perceived to be abuses of bargaining power. In May 1947 he persuaded the cabinet to extend the Special Powers Act to prohibit strikes or lock-outs in order to counter a threatened strike in the flour mills.[68] In the event, this did not prove necessary. De Valera himself met the trade union representatives on 'one of the first occasions – if not the first – on which the Taoiseach had intervened in an industrial dispute'.[69] De Valera's intervention, stressing that 'however reluctantly, the Government would take whatever steps it

[66] Lyons, *Ireland* (1971 edn), p. 553.
[67] T.J. O'Connell, *History of the INTO 1868–1968* (Dublin, n.d.), pp. 209–40, presents the INTO version of the strike.
[68] SPO, S11750B, GC 4/259, 19 May 1947.   [69] *Irish Times*, 23 May 1947.

felt necessary to protect bread supply', together with an improved offer from the employers, sufficed to prevent the strike.[70]

Where the Lemass line was generally conciliatory, MacEntee usually advocated firm anti-union measures. He had genuine sympathy for unemployed white-collar workers who strove to maintain their customary standard of living. 'The real problem' was 'to find a way to help those who are in this unfortunate position', in contrast to the condition of the normal unemployed, many of whom were either useless or malingerers.[71] As Minister for Industry and Commerce in 1940, MacEntee wanted to severely restrict the right to strike, but he was frustrated by opposition from the cabinet and, for once, from Finance.[72]

Lemass sought to restore better relations with the unions, or at least with the bigger Irish ones, on resuming his old office in June 1941. The Trade Union Act of September 1941 tried to introduce some coherence into trade union organisation by providing for the establishment of a tribunal, nominated by the Minister for Industry and Commerce, with authority to ensure that the biggest union in any specified industry should enjoy sole negotiating rights for all workers in that industry, and incidentally gratified nationalist instincts by confining negotiating rights to Irish-based unions.[73] Labour relations would be complicated by the Larkin/O'Brien split. In 1945 the Irish Transport and General Workers Union, together with a number of smaller Irish unions, seceded from the Irish Congress of Trade Unions to establish their own Congress of Irish Unions, a split that would not be formally healed until 1959. The Supreme Court further complicated matters in 1946 by declaring the restriction of union negotiating rights contained in the 1941 Act repugnant to the constitution. The decision was arguably contrary to any enlightened longer term concept of the national interest; but Lemass had to adapt to it. In August 1946 the Labour Court was established under the Industrial Relations Act, with equal employer and labour representation, under a chairman appointed by the Minister for Industry and Commerce. The court had strictly limited authority. Its recommendations were not binding. But it is generally believed to have helped to smooth industrial relations.[74]

Unless growth could be accelerated, even the most effective industrial relations system could make little difference to national performance. Lemass struck out in two directions to try to foster growth. Anxious to encourage exports, he proposed the establishment of a Foreign Trade

---

70 *Irish Press*, 17 June 1947.
71 SPO, S11916A. S. MacEntee to E. de Valera, 8 December 1943.
72 SPO, S11750A, MacEntee memos, 8 March, 2 April 1940; J.J. McElligott to R.C. Ferguson, 12 April 1940; GC 2/172, 28 May 1940.
73 MacCarthy, *Unions*, p. 202.
74 Lyons, *Ireland* (rev. edn, London, 1973), pp. 680–1; MacCarthy, *Unions*, pp. 374ff.

Corporation in March 1946, envisaging the establishment of an export-ers' insurance scheme, the provision of state grants to export industries, including grants for the training of workers.[75] However, Lemass himself did not proceed with the matter in 1946, apparently considering inter-national circumstances unpropitious. Not until October 1947 did he submit a new scheme to the cabinet. This proposed a Trade Advisory Council to assist exporters, and to advise the minister on grants of financial assistance, including 50 per cent of the cost of sites and/or factory buildings for export firms, as well as grants for training workers. Lemass was still locked in conflict with Finance on the proposals when the government fell.

The second string to the Lemass bow was the Industrial Efficiency Bill. The background to this is instructive, if only because the initial proposals had not the slightest prospect of receiving cabinet sanction. They were either a softening up process for the more moderate amended proposals, or else reflected a sense of desperation on the part of Lemass.

Efficiency was a prerequisite for exporting. But how was Irish industry to be made efficient? The Lemass response was distinctly *dirigiste*, displaying little confidence in the capacity of private enterprise to serve the national interest except under compulsion. Arguing in February 1946 that 'existing legislation does not provide sufficient powers to ensure that reasonable standards of efficiency have been, *or will be* [my emphasis] reached by industries, especially by protected ones', he proposed the establishment of an Industrial Efficiency Bureau to exercise continuous supervision of manufacturing firms. The bureau would 'ordinarily act as a friendly advisor', supplying if necessary 'expert consultants' to firms. However, 'should these methods fail', Lemass sought sweeping powers of intervention, including ultimate powers of compulsory acquisition of firms by the state.[76]

Finance naturally resisted the proposal. As unprotected industries were allegedly efficient, they should be automatically excluded. And the proposals would still be 'too drastic' for protected industries. When Lemass coyly spoke of 'business transferred' to the state, Finance sardoni-cally referred to 'the commandeered industry'.[77] The Finance response was in fact a shade more muted than might have been expected were MacEntee still minister. Little chance though the proposals had of securing cabinet assent, Lemass seemed reluctant to modify them. He retorted, for instance, that unprotected industries should be supervised because they 'may provide raw materials and essential supplies for

[75] PM, P35B/15. This paragraph is based on the summary of the Lemass proposals contained in this file.
[76] SPO, S13184A, Industry and Commerce memo, 26 February 1946.
[77] *Ibid.*, Finance memo, 4 March 1946.

protected industries and such products may be a vital consideration in the efficient production and cost of a protected commodity. That may be a vital consideration.' He also rejected the suggestion of Finance that any legislation should be implemented under the auspices of the Prices Commission rather than an Industrial Efficiency Bureau. 'The emphasis', Lemass insisted 'will be laid on efficiency rather than price control.'[78] His arguments made no difference. Finance won the battle on virtually call the disputed points. What was perhaps surprising was that the proposed legislation was not simply dropped. Instead, Lemass was authorised to proceed with a much modified version of the original.[79]

The revised proposal showed some interesting additions. It now included provision for the establishment of development councils in industry, consisting of representatives of manufacturers and workers, together with outside parties. The councils would be financed by levies on the relevant industry. Their functions would include
(a) Promotion of scientific and market research;
(b) The study of methods of production and the management and use of labour;
(c) The extension of facilities for technical training of workers;
(d) Improvements of design and standardisation of products;
(e) Encouragement of cooperative buying and selling organisations within the industry;
(f) Improvement of factory designs and conditions[80]
This approach would inflict a cultural revolution on Irish management. Another year's work was required before the much revised Bill was introduced on 3 July 1947. It reached a second reading on 8 October, before lapsing with the dissolution of the Dáil.

Abortive though the industrial efficiency proposals proved, the whole episode repays close scrutiny. It exposes the depth of Lemass's disillusion with the performance of Irish industry, protected and unprotected, whatever his public protestations to the contrary. It reveals yet again his disdain for doctrinal consistency. In a matter of months he swung from a scheme verging on ministerial dictatorship, potential if not actual, the epitome of bureaucratic centralism, to 'development councils' that came close in function, if not in inspiration, to vocationalist thinking. If this was a good example of his fabled pragmatism, it also serves to remind us that pragmatism should not be confused with practicality. For the initial proposals were far from practical not only in political, but in economic, terms. It was highly unlikely, for instance, that the public service, any more than the private sector, could supply 'efficiency inspectors' of the requisite type. The 'consultants' would have to be imported, and there

78 *Ibid.*   79 *Ibid.*, GC 4/145, 8 March 1946.
80 *Ibid.*, Industry and Commerce memo, 28 June 1946.

were few available at that time, however familiar they would later become.

'Industrial efficiency' contained the embryo of several initiatives that would come to fruition in more propitious circumstances in a later generation, as well as some that failed to resurface. The public reception at the time, to judge by newspaper comment, showed only sporadic grasp of the requirements for economic development.[81] Few, in cabinet or country, shared the Lemass sense of either necessity or opportunity. For the cabinet, political considerations had to be paramount, given the evidence of Fianna Fáil's growing postwar unpopularity, which naturally obliged the government to keep electoral considerations even more firmly in its sight than usual.

THE ELECTORAL GAME

After de Valera's electoral triumph in 1944, with Fine Gael moribund, and Labour split, the future beckoned with the promise of perpetual office for Fianna Fáil, and all the attendant rewards that flowed for the party faithful. There seemed little reason to drastically revise the constituency boundaries that yielded such happy results, beyond taking cognizance of the review mandatory under the constitution at a maximum of twelve-yearly intervals, which would be due by 1947. The temptation to revise boundaries had arisen in 1942, with Fianna Fáil fortunes waning during the war. The cabinet remained unimpressed by the main point made by Local Government, the Department responsible for revision, that Dublin was under-represented, with 1 member for every 25 000 population, compared with the average of 20 700 for the rest of the country.[82] There was little danger of Fianna Fáil increasing Dublin representation, with Labour poised to profit from working-class resentment at wages and prices policy. The cabinet duly decided to postpone the matter for twelve months,[83] which meant until after the next election. The 1943 election results confirmed the danger of increasing Dublin representation. Nothing was done. After the 1944 election, only the hurdle of the mandatory revision remained to be crossed. MacEntee, as Minister for Local Government, was anxious that the revision should occur 'before the electoral register is compiled in November 1945'.[84] The general scheme prepared by the committee established by the cabinet was approved, after modification, in March 1945.[85] The matter was proceeding smoothly.

[81] *Irish Independent*, 1 October 1947; *Irish Press*, 2 October 1947; *Irish Times*, 1, 2, 4, 20 October 1947.
[82] SPO, S12980A, Local Government memo, 14 October 1942.
[83] *Ibid.*, GC 2/386, 27 October 1942.
[84] *Ibid.*
[85] *Ibid.*, GC 4/24, 31 October 1944; GC 4/39, 19 December 1944; GC 4/60, 6 March 1945.

Then came the shock of the presidential election in June. Although Seán T. O'Kelly was elected, not only did he fail to win an overall majority, but the transfer situation made chilling reading for Fianna Fáil; 118 000 transfers from McCartan, a Republican candidate, went to Fine Gael's Seán MacEoin, compared with only 27 000 to O'Kelly.[86] Constituency revision had to be looked at again.

MacEntee duly submitted new proposals in November, carefully charting the consequences of his recommendations for Fianna Fáil. He was already disposed to take the combined vote of MacEoin and McCartan as a guide to the probable general election result in a difficult constituency like West Cork, 'as representing the strength of an anti-Fianna Fáil coalition of Fine Gael with Farmer, Labour and Independent'.[87]

News of the discussion must have leaked. Within days, MacEntee had to reply with a brazenly evasive reassurance to Norton's Dáil demand for an all-party committee on constituency revision to prevent what he inelegantly called 'hoofling'.[88] So sensitive had the issue become that MacEntee recalled his earlier memorandum, launching a full-scale hunt to trace all copies.[89] This was to be characteristic of the furtiveness of his subsequent procedures. Later memoranda 'were issued from the Minister's office direct – in view of the extremely confidential nature of the matter, they considered it preferable not to follow the usual Cabinet procedure' of circulation through the Taoiseach's office.[90] Paranoia reached the stage where, on one sensitive occasion, no papers were to be made available at all.[91] Suspicions were so intense that even MacEntee's private secretary was kept in the dark.[92]

MacEntee's scheme of November 1945 was superseded in January 1946. The new proposal showed a distinct advance on earlier thinking. Back in October 1942, Local Government took the view that

in considering a revision of constituencies the possibility of adhering to the county boundary should be considered. These boundaries are clearly defined and known. They have their individual significance whether from the standpoint of local administration or historical or sporting association, and there is generally an accepted community of interest within a county.[93]

By January 1946, following the revelation vouchsafed by the presidential election, the Department had discovered that counties were 'units which

86 *Irish Press*, 19 June 1945.
87 SPO, S12980A, Local Government memo, 2 November 1945.
88 DD, 98, 8 November 1945, 891–2.
89 SPO, S11980A, P. Ó Cinnéide to Private Secretary, Minister for Local Government, 5 December 1945.
90 SPO, S12980B, Taoiseach's Office memo, R. Ó Foghludha to N.S. Ó Nualláin, 11 April 1947.
91 *Ibid.*, N. Ó Nualláin to Private Secretary, Minister for Local Government.
92 *Ibid.*, N. Ó Nualláin directive, 11 June 1947.
93 SPO, S12980A, Local Government memo, 14 October 1942.

are anomalous and, in many instances, having no very great historical tradition behind them'.[94]

By April, counties were suddenly restored to grace. Their boundaries once more became paramount, and, in addition, constituencies should have odd numbers of members, either three or five.[95] The cause for the sudden shift was obviously the imminent formation of a new party, Clann na Poblachta, which would be launched in July 1946, and which threatened the 'republican' constituency within Fianna Fáil. The target was therefore no longer Fine Gael, but a putatively smaller party, whose prospects could be more effectively frustrated, under the PR system, in constituencies with odd rather than even numbers of TDs.

The uncertainty of the situation confronting Fianna Fáil is reflected in numerous succeeding memoranda, revisions, postponements in cabinet, etc. Constituencies that appeared particularly vulnerable to Clann na Poblachta blandishments attracted especially close scrutiny. Fianna Fáil's local election losses in June 1947, especially to Clann na Poblachta, caused new soul searching.[96] The saga eventually came to an end in October 1947 when the cabinet approved the text of the Electoral (Amendment) Bill. The contents clearly reflect the concern with the rise of Clann na Poblachta. The *Irish Independent* was sufficiently unsporting to point out that the 1935 Electoral Act had reduced the number of members from 152 to 138. Now, despite a fall in population, the number was raised to 147, the highest permitted under the constitution. The increase in the number of three-member constituencies from 15 to 22, 'inevitably loads the electoral dice in favour of the big party'.[97] Local Government's justification of the changes asserted unblushingly that they followed principles 'derived from considerations of commonsense and equity'. The sceptic might wonder why it had taken so protracted a process for 'commonsense and equity' to emerge. Local Government justified the rise from 138 to 147 members on the imaginative grounds 'that the consider-able amount of temporary emigration which took place between 1939 and 1946 is reflected in the Census returns. This temporary phenomenon, *which should be offset by a reverse trend in the next few years* [my emphasis] has been taken into account in the fixing of the future membership of Dáil Éireann'![98] This scenario – providing for anticipated (!) migration trends – opened innumerable possibilities for fertile minds. Given that emigration was on a rising trend, and that the government was grappling with a disastrous economic situation, it must qualify as one of

[94] SPO, S12980B, Local Government memo, 12 January 1946.
[95] *Ibid.*, Local Government memo, 12 April 1946.
[96] *Irish Times*, 19 June 1947.   [97] *Irish Independent*, 9 October 1947.
[98] SPO, S12980B, Local Government memo, 'Electoral (Amendment) Bill, 1947, explana-tory memorandum', October 1947.

the most delicious pieces of fiction ever devised by even a harassed electoral cartographer to frustrate the will of the people.

Fianna Fáil was entitled to be worried by the threat from Clann na Poblachta. The Clann, founded under the leadership of Seán MacBride on the basis of committees formed to help Republican prisoners during the war, 'had an appeal similar to that of Fianna Fáil in 1932 – an attractive blend of radical republicanism and of social and economic reform'.[99] MacBride, son of Major John MacBride, executed in 1916, and of Maud Gonne, of Yeats fame, himself a former IRA Chief of Staff, worked hard at cultivating the image of a man of destiny. More than twenty years younger than de Valera, with energy to match his boundless ambition, a highly developed self-righteousness, a somewhat exotic accent, as befitted his French education, immense debating skill, as befitted an accomplished barrister, he seemed the most exciting new arrival onto the political stage since independence. He entered the Dáil when Clann na Poblachta achieved two startling by-election victories in October 1947. His leadership appeal provided the unifying bond around which an otherwise motley group could coalesce. But it was no more motley than the Fianna Fáil of twenty years before, and seemed poised to capitalise on the growing disillusion with the pedestrian performance of a stale government, which was provoking backbench complaints in Fianna Fáil itself that 'the cabinet through long office have lost their moorings'.[100]

De Valera took fright at the threat posed to the ideological heartland of Fianna Fáil by the new party. Despite his handsome Dáil majority, he decided to go to the country early to deprive Clann na Poblachta of the chance of consolidating its organisation during a period of continuing austerity.

The election wasn't held until 4 February 1948, but campaigning was well under way in December. Apart from proposing sweeping social reform, Clann na Poblachta also played the 'new political morality' card that they had claimed to represent from their foundation.[101] The issue had a high public profile as a judicial tribunal was taking evidence on accusations of bribery and corruption levelled by the young Oliver Flanagan, TD for Laois–Offaly, at de Valera, Lemass, Gerry Boland, and de Valera's son, a respected medical doctor. The charges involved the proposed sale of Locke's Distillery in Kilbeggan to foreigners, in alleged contravention of the law. The Tribunal of High Court judges questioned witnesses on oath. They reported unanimously on 18 December that

we found it quite impossible to follow or appreciate Deputy Flanagan's evershifting evidence as to the meaning to be attached to the allegation that a minister of

[99] J.A. Murphy, 'Party system,' p. 160.
[100] NLI, FG, MS 18336, J. Kennedy to F. Gallagher, 18 December 1946.
[101] *Irish Times*, 8 July 1946.

state had a keen personal interest in the sale of the distillery. There is not a scintilla of evidence that any minister had a particle of such interest. The charge is an extremely grave one. We are satisfied that it is wholly untrue, that it is entirely without foundation and that it was made with a degree of recklessness amounting to complete irresponsibility.[102]

They expressed disquiet at Flanagan's concept of truth:

We found it necessary to exercise extreme caution in dealing with the evidence of Deputy Flanagan. We found him very uncandid and much disposed to answer questions unthinkingly and as if he were directing his replies elsewhere than to the Tribunal. On several occasions he contradicted himself and was disposed to shift his ground, when he found that answers already given would lead him where he did not wish to go. He was, on other occasions, in conflict with testimony which we believe to be true. In respect of two matters we are satisfied that he told us what he knew to be untrue.[103]

The report, published in a highly charged political atmosphere, did not command universal assent.[104] It did no damage to Flanagan's standing in his constituency. After his phenomenal success in winning 14 369 first preferences, double that of the next highest candidate, he dispatched a triumphant telegram to de Valera, gloating that 'Laois/Offaly's answer to Locke Tribunal leaves no doubt as to belief in existence of corruption. Eagerly awaiting assembly Dáil Éireann to reopen this and other similar public scandals.'[105]

While Flanagan flourished, it seems likely that the report of the tribunal provided Fianna Fáil with badly needed breathing space and helped halt a drift from them.[106] In addition, Clann na Poblachta damaged its own prospects by nominating 93 candidates, more than any other party except Fianna Fáil. Based on grossly exaggerated expectations, this overstretched its organisation, and dissipated support.[107] MacEntee's constituency revision achieved its purpose. The Clann would have won 19 seats instead of 10 had it secured representation proportional to its vote.

The result created an intriguing situation. Fianna Fáil remained much the largest party, but it lost 8 seats compared with 1944, and with only 68 members in a Dáil of 147, it could be clearly out-voted. However improbable it appeared initially that the other parties could coalesce, Clann na Poblachta's performance had paved the way for a change of

---

102 *Report of the Tribunal appointed by the Taoiseach on the 7th day of November, 1947, pursuant to resolution passed by ... Dáil Éireann and ... by Seanad Éireann,* (Stationery Office, P No. 8576), para. 54, pp. 17–18.

103 *Ibid.,* para. 49, p. 15.   104 Connolly, *How does she stand?,* p. 24.

105 SPO, S14153B, O. Flanagan to E. de Valera, 6 February 1948. Brian Inglis (*West Briton* (London, 1962), p. 116) felt that 'Oliver Flanagan's impudence entranced the Leix–Offaly electorate.' See also B. Ó h-Eithir, *The begrudger's guide to Irish politics* (Dublin, 1986), pp. 112–18.

106 I am grateful to P.D. O'Keeffe for discussing this question with me. See also his MA thesis (UCC, 1981), 'The origins and development of Clann na Poblachta'.

107 Murphy, 'Party system', p. 160.

government. Firstly, the Clann had borne the brunt of the Fianna Fáil assault. This obsession with the Clann rebounded in favour of Fine Gael. True, its popular vote rose only 13 000, and it gained only one extra seat. But had Fianna Fáil concentrated in the constituency revision on driving further nails into Fine Gael's coffin, it might have succeeded in reducing its number of seats below a credible minimum. Whereas Clann na Poblachta's 175 000 votes yielded only 10 seats, Fine Gael garnered 31 seats from 262 000 votes. Its index of proportionality – the ratio of seats to votes – reached 107, almost as high as Fianna Fáil's 110, compared with Clann na Poblachta's 52.[108]

Secondly, if the disciplined anti-Fianna Fáil transfers on the scale achieved in subsequent elections did not yet exist, the tradition that Labour transfers went mainly to Fianna Fáil clearly began to crumble. In Carlow and Kilkenny, more 'Official Labour' transfers went directly to Fine Gael than to Fianna Fáil. In other constituencies, like Cavan and South Tipperary, Clann na Poblachta provided the conduit through which Labour or Clann na Talmhan voters could transfer allegiance without going directly over to the traditional enemy.[109]

Thirdly, Clann na Poblachta's 10 seats, however anti-climactic, did deprive Fianna Fáil of its majority. Nevertheless, on the morrow of the election, Fianna Fáil had reason not to be displeased with the result. In all the circumstances, it had done well to contain the Clann threat. 1947 was a dreadful year for the economy, and Fianna Fáil went into the election burdened with blame for the condition of the country. This was in one sense unfair. There was no simple short-term solution to the immediate postwar problems, which mainly reflected longer term difficulties. The cabinet had, admittedly, little idea how to respond to the situation. But the legitimate criticism that can be made of its performance between 1945 and 1947 is not that it failed to cope with the short-term difficulties, which might have baffled any government, but that it had no vision of the future. The bulk of the electorate was profoundly uninterested in such distinctions. Its mental horizons were at least as blinkered as the cabinet's. It passed its verdict on present performance, not on future prospects. In addition, Fianna Fáil fought a jaded campaign. Apart from a few obeisances towards the current Lemass doctrine, by no means guaranteed to win votes, that 'Fianna Fáil wants efficient industries . . . It will not support projects based on antiquated plants or methods of operation,'[110] it relied on little more than 'Up Dev' to rally the faithful, beyond continuing the same abortive 'red scare' tactics against Labour and Clann

108 C. O'Leary, *Irish elections 1918–1977* (Dublin, 1979), p. 103.
109 *Irish Press*, 6, 7 February 1948; Carty, *Parish pump*, p. 69.
110 NLI, FG, MS 18376(6). This folio contains cuttings from the election literature.

na Poblachta that Seán MacEntee had so enthusiastically pursued in the October by-elections.[111]

THE FIRST INTER-PARTY GOVERNMENT

De Valera still expected to form a government after the election, counting on the support of the five National Labour deputies and one or two of the dozen Independents. The situation would not have been different from 1932, when Fianna Fáil ruled as a minority government with Labour support. His optimism was understandable. It did seem unlikely that parties covering the whole ideological range, even within the admittedly narrow spectrum of Irish doctrinal discourse, could sufficiently reconcile their differences to form a government. On one side stood Fine Gael, widely regarded as the Commonwealth, conservative, strong farmer party. On the other side stood the radical/republican Clann na Poblachta, the small farmer Clann na Talmhan, the two squabbling Labour parties, and a motley collection of Independents. Problems of personality compounded problems of policy. The obvious alternative nominee for Taoiseach was Richard Mulcahy, leader of Fine Gael; but MacBride could not stomach the commander of the Free State forces in the civil war. Mulcahy did play a decisive role in the negotiations leading to the inter-party government by inviting the other party leaders to discuss the possibility of such a government after the election, and then by agreeing to stand aside in favour of John A. Costello, a former Attorney General in the Cosgrave government, but untainted by civil war memories, and acceptable to MacBride, his fellow barrister.[112] De Valera had not allowed adequately for the resentment he inspired outside Fianna Fáil. A common enemy covers a multitude of differences.

The new government made a dramatic impact in the diplomatic and constitutional fields. An unexpected international repercussion of the election occurred in far away Australia, where it was reported that 'Archbishop Mannix didn't speak at all for two days after the results.'[113] Weightier consequences were soon to follow. MacBride, who exerted considerable influence on the composition of the cabinet,[114] himself took External Affairs. He proved a highly active minister, both in terms of expanding his Department and in adopting policy initiatives.[115] But it was Costello who made the biggest impact by declaring in September 1948, at a press conference in Ottawa, the government's intention to declare

[111] *Irish Press*, 13 October 1947.
[112] B. Farrell, *Chairman or chief? the role of Taoiseach in Irish government* (Dublin, 1971), p. 43; Fanning, *Ireland*, p. 164.
[113] NLI, FG, MS 18337, T.J. Kiernan to F. Gallagher, 20 April 1948.
[114] Fanning, *Ireland*, pp. 165–6.
[115] Keatinge, *Formulation*, pp. 80–1.

Ireland a republic. There has been some controversy on whether the cabinet was aware of the impending announcement.[116] It had at least the merit of diverting attention from Costello's reassurance to the bemused Canadians of 'Ireland's readiness to come to the assistance of Canada in the event of war with a Communist power,' a provocation in the face of which, to their credit, the Canadians kept their sense of humour.[117]

There may have been a number of motives for Costello's decision. He himself disliked the characteristic ambiguity of de Valera's External Relations Act of 1936, which left Ireland effectively a republic in her internal affairs, while retaining the king as a symbolic sleeping partner in external relations. But a passion for logical consistency rarely suffices to explain political decisions, even by a part-time politician like Costello. The 'Republic' could serve several purposes for Fine Gael. It stole Fianna Fáil's Sunday suit of constitutional clothes. Who were the real republicans now? By behaving in a manner so out of character with the performance of the party for more than a decade, it helped retrieve Fine Gael's fading image as a serious party concerned with the real business of politics, power. The declaration by Costello pre-empted the possible embarrassment of a threatened private 'Republic' bill by an independent TD, Peadar Cowan, and, reinforced by Costello's subsequent decision to introduce the relevant bill himself rather than leave it to his Minister for External Affairs, also had the advantage of stealing MacBride's thunder.[118] Costello himself justified the decision on the grounds that it would take the gun out of politics.

Ireland not only became a republic in 1949; it also left the Commonwealth, in contrast to India, which became a republic that same year. Some would regret that Ireland abandoned the possibility of playing a peacock role in the new Commonwealth, strutting on the stage in the guise of an elder statesman and providing a firm grip for the feeble fingers of the 'black babies'. Although Irish diplomats might have made worthy contributions, it seems doubtful on the whole if Irish absence made much difference to either Ireland or the Commonwealth. Canada, Australia and New Zealand retained benign links with Ireland.[119] Britain continued to treat Irish immigrants as Commonwealth citizens, and to offer a special relationship to the Irish economy.

Westminster also responded to the Republic with the Ireland Act in June 1949, affirming that 'in no event will Northern Ireland or any part thereof cease to be part . . . of the United Kingdom without the consent of the Parliament of Northern Ireland'. Although the Dublin government

---

[116] Fanning, *Ireland*, pp. 172ff.; N. Browne, *Against the tide* (Dublin, 1986), pp. 129ff.
[117] F.J. McEvoy, 'Canada, Ireland and the Commonwealth: the declaration of the Irish Republic, 1948–9', *IHS*, 24, 96 (November 1985), p. 511.
[118] Browne, *Tide*, p. 133.   [119] Harkness, 'Patrick McGilligan', pp. 129–31.

responded agitatedly to this copper fastening of partition, it made no difference to the *realpolitik* of the situation, beyond adding insult to injury.[120] The Republic naturally proved grist to the Ulster Unionist mill. Sir Basil Brooke showed himself an apt pupil of Craig by calling a snap election to rally dissident unionists to him and to squelch the Northern Irish Labour Party. He naturally won a resounding victory.

Whatever the merits of proclaiming a republic at that stage, the whole performance of the government, from Costello's Ottawa announcement to the inaugural Easter Sunday parade, seems to have been a shambles from start to finish, perhaps the most inept diplomatic exhibition in the history of the state. De Valera might or might not have chosen to declare a republic. But old hands in External Affairs and in the Department of the Taoiseach must have sighed for a touch of his professionalism as his successors lurched through the legislative process.[121]

De Valera had reservations about the declaration of a republic, on the grounds that it consolidated partition.[122] Remaining in the Commonwealth, or retaining the External Relations Act, despised by unionists,[123] would not, however, have advanced unification by one day. If the Protestant people had not been prepared to contemplate unification to persuade Dublin to enter the war, they were unlikely to do so just because Dublin chose to remain in the Commonwealth. Fianna Fáil's garrulous anti-partition campaign in opposition reinforced unionist resistance even further. De Valera embarked on a tour of the USA, Australia, New Zealand and India immediately after the election. It was necessary to pre-empt the danger of MacBride purloining the partition issue for himself and despoiling Fianna Fáil of such winnings as it had made on the partition stakes.

MacBride duly banged the anti-partition drum. The government refused to join NATO on the grounds that 'the continuance of partition precludes us from taking our rightful place in the affairs of Europe'.[124] MacBride himself would soon come to enjoy a degree of international esteem, not least through his work on the Council of Europe, of which Ireland became a founder member in 1949. But Irish insistence on making partition a European issue found little sympathy among continentals who regarded Britain as their liberator from real tyranny.

The Americans showed equally little concern. They were not unduly disturbed by the Irish refusal to join NATO, at least as long as they could

120 For a detailed account of UK responses see R. Fanning, 'London and Belfast's response to the Declaration of the Republic of Ireland, 1948–49', *International Affairs*, 58, 1 (1981–2), pp. 95–114.
121 Fanning, *Ireland*, pp. 173–5.   122 Bowman, *De Valera*, pp. 273–4.
123 *Ibid.*, p. 268.
124 Quoted in N. Mansergh, 'Irish foreign policy 1945–51', in Nowlan and Williams, *War years and after*, p. 137.

count on access to bases in Northern Ireland. Truman himself, irritated by Dublin's wartime attitude, may have preferred it that way. When MacBride, at that stage strongly pro-American, and conscious of Ireland's utter defencelessness, contemplated a bilateral defence treaty with the United States in 1950, Washington did not reciprocate. The manner in which the State Department neutered Francis P. Matthews, the Secretary of the Navy, who advocated achieving world peace through world war, by dispatching him as ambassador to Ireland in 1951, suggests no searing vision by the Potomac of Dublin's world historical role. For the Truman administration, Irish affairs remained more a matter for London than for Washington.[125]

Neither Britain nor Ireland allowed 'The Republic' to interfere with trading arrangements. The Anglo-Irish Trade Agreement of 1948 partly integrated the two livestock economies, though to a lesser degree than Dublin wanted, providing for Irish farmers some share in the benefits of British subsidisation by linking the prices of store cattle and sheep to British guaranteed prices for fat stock. This inevitably involved renewed emphasis on the role of store cattle in the Irish economy. The implications were unpromising for other sectors of agriculture. But James Dillon, the new minister, camouflaged the consequences by resurrecting Patrick Hogan's slogan, 'One more cow, one more sow, and one more acre under the plough.' Dillon's eneregetic and articulate promotion of his policies may have helped distract attention from the rather moderate results actually recorded during his tenure of office. The number of cows rose by a mere 16 000, from 1 166 000 to 1 182 000 between 1947 and 1951. The number of sows rose from 40 000 on 1 January 1948 to 59 000 on 1 January 1951. This still compared poorly with 103 000 sows who had graced the land on 1 January 1940. The number of acres under the plough (excluding flax) fell from 724 000 on 1 June 1948 to 620 000 on 1 June 1951. Poultry numbers fell about 10 per cent over the same period. Only the cattle and sheep sectors recorded significant expansion under the Dillon regime, reflecting market realities rather than ministerial injunctions. The number of sheep rose from 1 626 000 on 1 January 1948 to 2 400 000 on 1 January 1952, while the number of cattle (excluding milch cows) rose from 2 405 000 to 2 711 000. Judged

---

[125] FRUS, 1950, III, Relations of the United States with Ireland, pp. 1468–81; R. Fanning, 'The United States and Irish participation in NATO: the debate of 1950', *Irish Studies in International Affairs*, 1 (1979), pp. 38–48; Fanning, *Ireland*, pp. 176–8; R.J. Raymond, 'The Marshall Plan and Ireland, 1947–52', in P.J. Drudy (ed.), *The Irish in America: emigration, assimilation and impact*, Irish Studies 4 (Cambridge, 1985), pp. 309, 319–20; TL Transcript, T.K. Whitaker Oral History Interview, in R.J. Raymond, 'Ireland in the European recovery programme: 1947–1953' (1978), unpaginated; TL, Eben Ayers Diary, 1 November 1947; TL, speech, F.P. Matthews, reported in *Times-Herald*, 29 August 1950, Matthews Papers, box 60.

by the pedantic criterion of his declared ambitions, Dillon's policy failed.[126]

If his economic legacy remains dubious, the histrionic Dillon proved a resounding political success, the star electoral act of the inter-party government. Behind the facade of onomatopoeia, Dillon reversed Patrick Hogan's priorities by launching an ambitious Land Rehabilitation Project to reclaim more than a million acres, mainly in the poorer west, at a cost of £10 an acre. Critics contended that the money might have been more productively spent by improving efficiency on better land than in helping marginal farmers eke out a living for one more generation before inevitably succumbing.[127] Dillon may have helped the fathers at the expense of the sons and daughters. But it made sound political sense, whatever the economic merits. The children wending their way to the emigration boat would have no votes. Dillon, an orthodox theologian, was shocked at the theological levity of Patrick Hogan in consigning inefficient uneconomic farmers 'to the devil'. He determined to reclaim the lost souls. The Rehabilitation Project was a spiritual venture. Why go to the devil when Fine Gael was waiting? The project helped to reclaim at least some of the territory lost, indeed virtually handed, to Fianna Fáil in the 1920s, and which Clann na Talmhan had since shown could still yield a rich harvest if carefully fertilised.

The money for the Land Rehabilitation Project came from Marshall Aid. Finance was highly reluctant to accept Marshall Aid at all, essentially on the grounds that the politicians would squander the money on unproductive and inflationary expenditure. Unless it was received as a grant rather than as a loan needing repayment it would impose yet another burden on an already harassed taxpayer.[128] As Finance itself had no ideas on how to spend the money productively, apart from reducing the national debt, it was indeed likely that the politicians would devise their own schemes. It was above all likely that MacBride would produce proposals. And MacBride was the minister most directly involved, for Marshall Aid fell within the brief of External Affairs. What might have happened under a Fianna Fáil administration is a matter of surmise. External Affairs was already handling the matter departmentally, with F.H. Boland playing a central role. But it was Lemass who led the Irish delegation to Paris in July 1947 and it must be presumed that he would have been particularly active in cabinet on this issue. One of the first decisions of the new government was that MacBride would handle OEEC

126 *Agricultural Statistics 1934–1956*, pp. 9, 67–8.
127 Lynch, 'The Irish economy since the war, 1946–51', in Nowlan and Williams, *War years and after*, p. 192.
128 Fanning, *Finance*, pp. 411–23, 434–42, traces the Finance attitude. See also R.J. Raymond, 'The Marshall Plan', pp. 295–328.

affairs.[129] MacBride was less successful with the Americans, eventually extracting only £36 000 000, seven-eighths of it on loan, compared with the £120 000 000 grant with which he had hoped 'to transform our country'.[130]

MacBride found himself with little room for manoeuvre when he visited Washington in May 1948 to plead Ireland's case for a grant. Ireland's anti-communist credentials were impeccable. In fact, they were too good. The document submitted to Washington by MacBride began with the stirring proclamation that 'Ireland's approach to political economy problems is not based on materialism . . . Ireland believes in a policy based on idealism rather than on materialism.'[131] The Americans unsportingly took Dublin at its word, sardonically commenting that the Irish case 'suffered from the absence of a communist movement in Ireland . . . '[132] When MacBride urged Ireland's reluctance to accept a loan because she might be unable to repay it, the Marshall Aid officials blandly replied that Ireland would have no difficulty meeting the repayments out of the increased output which the delegation confidently predicted would result from Marshall Aid!

Intensive lobbying of reputedly sympathetic American politicians seems to have brought little immediate change in Washington's attitude.[133] MacBride could think of nothing more effective than to bang the partition drum again

The feeling in Ireland was that, in comparison with other European countries, Ireland did not get a square deal. This feeling was increased by the fact that Britain received vast sums by way of grant, portion of which sums was used to strengthen and develop the economy of the six north eastern counties of Ireland, which are under British rule. The Irish government has been at great pains to minimise the political effect of the disparity of treatment . . . [134]

The Americans were unlikely to be amused by this truculent display of ingratiating insolence. Memories of Northern Ireland's contribution to the American war effort were still lively, and the North was likely to play a significant role in western defence for the foreseeable future. MacBride's memo smacked too much of the beggar trying to intimidate his benefactor.

129 SPO, S14106A, GC 5/4, 2 March 1948.
130 SPO, S114106B. MacBride memo, 9 May 1948; TL, Truman Papers, Official File, box 823, folder 218, T. Tannenwald Jr memo for Charles Murphy, 25 February 1952.
131 *Ibid.*, External Affairs memo, 2 June 1948 (copy of document presented to ECA in Washington).
132 Fanning, *Finance*, pp. 420–1.
133 SPO, S14106C, MacBride memo, 8 June 1948; S. Nunan to F.H. Boland, 1 July 1948; R. Brennan to F.H. Boland, 1 July 1948; TL, Truman Papers, Official File, box 823, folder 218, J. Howard McGrath to M. Connolly, 6 August 1948.
134 SPO, S14160E, S. MacBride to J.E. Carrigan, 29 January 1949.

Though the size of Marshall Aid fell far short of MacBride's hopes, it nevertheless came as a bonanza to the government, accounting for about 50 per cent of total state investment during the inter-party administration. But the bonanza also brutally exposed the continuing inability of Irish governments to devise a coherent long-term programme of public expenditure. It was a formal condition of getting the money in the first place that a 'plan' had to be presented to the OEEC. External Affairs duly cobbled together a document which it dignified with the title *Long-Term Recovery Programme*, completed in October 1948 and published in January 1949. To describe the contents as a 'programme' would be a singularly elastic use of language. It blithely assumed a doubling of exports by 1952–3, a prediction unjustifiable in historical or any other terms. As the Anglo-Irish Trade Agreement of June 1948 had linked Irish store cattle prices with English fat cattle prices, the determination of the key agricultural price which would influence farmer responses to market incentives remained effectively out of Irish hands. The value of egg exports was assumed to quintuple between 1947 and 1949/50. Even the amiable device of taking 1947, with its notorious climatic difficulties, as a base year, simply underlined the opportunism of the exercise. All the programmes submitted by OEEC members were liberally laced with imaginative projections. Even an indulgent OEEC, however, felt obliged to request further information 'in respect of investment policy, about which we had given little information' and about 'internal consumption levels: the memo did not say much on this matter . . . '.[135]

The *Long-Term Programme* was, it is true, an *ad hoc* effort flung together for the prime purpose of submitting a claim, 'an exercise that had to be undertaken to persuade the Americans to give us Marshall Aid'.[136] But the quality of the 'exercise' reflected only too faithfully the continuing vagueness of the official mind about development possibilities. The bulk of Marshall Aid was spent on long-term – very long-term – projects, including in addition to Dillon's land rehabilitation, investment in electricity, telephones and afforestation, this latter a particular concern of MacBride, on which his instincts were right, though bitterly opposed by Finance and also by Lands. But it was spent on these projects, on which there could be little immediate return, only because the official mind could think of nothing more productive on which to spend it in the shorter term. MacBride himself sought to persuade the cabinet that some Marshall Aid should be used 'for the execution and fitting out of new factories which could then be leased out on hire purchase terms to private manufacturing

---

135 SPO, S14106D, External Affairs memo, 23 November 1948.
136 T.K. Whitaker, quoted in Fanning, *Finance*, p. 406; TL Typescript, F.H. Boland and Tom Murray, Oral History Interviews, in R.J. Raymond, 'Ireland in the European recovery programme: 1947–53' (1978), unpaginated.

concerns'. He wanted the government 'to determine the industries which are required and which should be set up', to decide on their location, and to decide on how the factories should be built and equipped.[137] His proposals proved as abortive as the earlier Lemass efforts in a similar direction.

MacBride enjoyed only modest success in achieving his economic policy objectives. His standing in the government steadily declined until he seems to have become little more than a pawn in Costello's calculations. A number of factors contributed to the decline in his influence.

MacBride entered government with an enormous reputation. He had the highest public profile of any cabinet member. His early memoranda are reputed to have reduced his colleagues to reverential silence when read out at length to the cabinet by Costello.[138] Clann na Poblachta still seemed to have a bright future, however modest its number of seats. It was so recent a creation that it had been obliged to devise some semblance of policies, behind which lay some genuine conviction. The procedural casualness characteristic of the government at the outset offered ample opportunity for an energetic prowler like MacBride to launch forays in numerous directions. The vagueness was understandable at the political level. An inter-party government was unprecedented. Relations between the Taoiseach and the other party leaders would have to develop gradually, particularly as Costello, for all his professional repute, had no commanding presence. His authority would develop only gradually.

The procedural laxity arising from the uncertain political relationships was compounded by a new uncertainty at the administrative level. This was mainly due to the exclusion of Maurice Moynihan from cabinet meetings, on the insistence of MacBride, who appears to have indulged an inordinate suspicion of civil servants as tools of British interest. There may have been valid reasons for doubting the quality of the official mind in some areas. Conscious subservience to foreign interests was not one of them. Senior civil servants served their country faithfully according to their lights. None had the national interest more genuinely at heart than Maurice Moynihan. His exclusion from cabinet meetings – even if the suspicion in his case involved party more than national loyalty – reflected scant credit on the politicians.[139]

As the rigid procedural conventions of the Fianna Fáil regime loosened rapidly, James Dillon was provoked into suggesting that

If the government would assign to each department its sphere of activity and require a department to satisfy the Taoiseach at stated intervals in regard to its procedure, it would greatly simplify and expedite public business ... Under

137 SPO, S14106D, External Affairs memo, 30 December 1948.
138 Browne, *Tide*, p. 128.
139 B. Farrell, 'Coalitions and political institutions: Ireland', in V. Bogdanor (ed.), *Coalition government in Western Europe* (London, 1983), p. 261, n. 13.

existing conditions it is frequently impossible to know who is ultimately responsible for anything, with the result that much time is lost circulating memoranda in the vague hope of attracting the attention of some minister who has an unknown interest in the matter in hand. Furthermore, the question of where the ultimate responsibility for final decision rests not infrequently gives rise to undesirable misunderstanding between departments which feel themselves unnecessarily hampered by the necessity for endless consultation where it appears that it should be for the department itself to decide and execute the matter. The volume of departmental work is at present overwhelming, and when to this is added the necessity for providing inter-departmental senior personnel for consultations and conferences in addition to the endless demand for similar personnel to attend international meetings (the number of which appears to grow daily) it is impossible efficiently to do the essential work . . . [140]

This state of affairs could not continue indefinitely. It was inevitable that MacBride's wings would be clipped as other departments sought to reassert their primacy in their traditional areas, with Finance in the forefront; and that the Taoiseach himself, if only out of self-respect, would seek to impose some institutional order, particularly as his working relationship with Moynihan became closer.

There were therefore good reasons to assume that MacBride's early dominance of the cabinet could not continue indefinitely. Yet his decline need not have been so precipitate. It was his ineptness as a party leader that undermined his influence. Some would compare him to de Valera. There were certain superficial similarities. Both suffered the early loss of a father, both indulged the same will to power, both cultivated a degree of exotic distance designed to entrance the indigenous peasantry, rural and urban. But the differences were more striking. If MacBride had something of de Valera's personality, he had little enough of his character. He had the self-righteousness without the emotional self-discipline. He lacked de Valera's ability to mould an effective working team around him. In his own party, he broke with Noel Hartnett, his main advisor, even before the spectacular final rift with Noel Browne, the only other Clann na Poblachta minister, in 1951. While much remains to be revealed of the working atmosphere in External Affairs at this time, it would seem that MacBride also failed to establish an effective working relationship with his Department, or at least with F.H. Boland, the secretary. On the face of it, this was surprising. Boland was expansionist minded. Before Mac-Bride's appointment he was already seeking to enhance his Department's influence, demanding that other departments, not excluding Finance, which cultivated close links with the Treasury, should in future conduct their negotiations through External Affairs.[141] It is not clear, however, that MacBride succeeded in fully mobilising the considerable talent of

---

[140] SPO, S14299, Dillon memo, 28 April 1948.   [141] Fanning, *Finance*, p. 408.

Boland, who became Ambassador to London in 1950, after only four years as secretary.

Rated by the CIA as 'definitely of Prime Ministerial caliber ... charming, affable and intelligent, an excellent diplomat', MacBride, out of the country much of the time, promenading on the world stage, presenting ambitious proposals for the reform of the OEEC, revelling in the 'Dear Ernie' and 'My Dear Seán' of his correspondence with Ernest Bevin, expounding to Dean Acheson on the moral basis of the universal struggle against communism, must have felt culture shock on returning to the provincial mundanities of Dublin.[142] Whatever the reasons, his influence in cabinet gradually waned.

Yet it is salutary to ponder the probable performance of the first inter-party government without MacBride. Finance was gleefully sharpening its knives with the departure of Lemass. As a famous profile of McElligott recalled

old hands in the Department of Finance, once more alert, aggressive, successful, looked back on the sad sixteen years just ended ... A period for Finance of constant retreat and guerilla delaying actions, with never an offensive except for a short burst when the war broke out, reduced to the beggarly expedient ... of Fabian warfare. Though the prospect seemed so hopeful what resulted was no victory. Fabius had to retire to far winter mountains, fighting rearguard actions all the way.[143]

It was no thanks to the new Minister for Industry and Commerce, 'the hapless Dan Morrissey', who carried little weight in cabinet, that Finance failed to fully retrieve its authority.[144]

Finance scored an early success in forcing cutbacks on Aer Lingus, of which Leydon was chairman much to the chagrin of J.F. Dempsey, the young general manager, who complained bitterly of 'the high degree of absenteeism, resignations and ... desertions' resulting from the consequent low morale.[145] Finance also largely succeeded in frustrating proposals for tourist development under state auspices. Some of the proposals emanating from interested parties were so clearly aimed at empire building that Finance had no difficulty exposing their dubious motives. But the main objection remained ideological. The state would be interfering with private enterprise.[146] The Finance objective, however, of

[142] TL, Truman Papers, President's Secretary's File, box 209, CIA, Ireland SR-48, 1 April 1949, p. 38; Milward, *Reconstruction*, pp. 183–4, 191–3; TL, Acheson Papers, box 66, Acheson memo, 13 March 1951.

[143] 'Silhouette', 'J.J. McElligott', *Administration*, 1, 1 (1953), pp. 69–70.

[144] Browne, *Tide*, p. 125.

[145] SPO, S13090C/1, J.F. Dempsey to J. Leydon, 14 May 1948. The arguments may be followed in Industry and Commerce memo, 25 June 1949 and Finance memo, 27 June, 1949, Leydon to M. Moynihan, 12 July 1948.

[146] SPO, S13087B, Industry and Commerce memo, 13 May 1949; Finance memo, 16 February 1950.

a full-scale assault on the state-sponsored sector through a detailed examination of the accounts of state-sponsored bodies in order 'to bring to light – if they exist – instances of waste or extravagance or, in the wider field, any course of action which appears to be either contrary to public policy as laid down by Parliament or to require explanation as being prima facie inconsistent with reasonable standards of prudence and economical management'[147] failed to convince the cabinet of the need for action in this direction.

Finance further failed in its bid to slow down the housing drive begun by the Minister for Local Government, T.J. Murphy, a modest but idealistic and committed Labour minister, whose initiative was sustained by M.J. Keyes when Murphy died suddenly in 1949.[148] Murphy inherited a sad backlog. The Fianna Fáil housing drive, having reached a peak with 17016 houses built in 1938/9, slowed down sharply under wartime pressure with only 2480 houses built in 1943/4.[149] There would be no postwar surge. MacEntee as Minister for Local Government had no crusading commitment to public building. Only 1108 new houses were completed with state aid in 1947.[150] The Department took its cue from the minister. Its submission to the Committee on Economic Planning in 1943, estimating that about 38 000 new houses were required in urban areas, drew severe criticism for its vagueness.[151] Local Government duly revised the estimate upwards to 'about 53 000' the following year.[152] With the continued building slump after the war, it was estimated that about 110 000 new dwellings were required in 1948.[153] Following Murphy's initiative, supported by Costello, who pressed the reluctant banks strongly for capital for the building programme on the grounds that the housing situation endangered social stability, with McElligott and Whitaker, despite their departmental reservations, providing Costello with formidable negotiating support, building activity increased sharply.[154] In 1951, 11 305 houses were completed with state aid, a ten-fold increase on 1947.[155]

The foundation of the Industrial Development Authority (IDA) in 1949 provoked a particularly instructive contretemps, with the new Authority

---

147 SPO, S13840B/1, Finance memo, 6 June 1950 (recapitulating a memo of 28 February 1948); Finance memo, 5 April 1951.
148 Browne, *Tide*, pp. 200–1.
149 SPO, S13059A, S. MacEntee to E. de Valera, 13 May 1944.
150 SA, 1955, p. 167.
151 SPO, S13059A, Local Government memo, 18 February 1943; Department of Taoiseach memo, 23 March, 1943.
152 *Ibid.*, Local Government memo, June 1944.   153 Lynch, 'Irish economy', p. 192.
154 SPO, 13059C, memos by P.K. Lynch and T.K. Whitaker on meeting between government and bank representatives, 18 November 1949.
155 G. Quinn, 'The changing pattern of Irish society, 1938–51', in Nowlan and Williams, *War years and after*, p. 132.

being launched in a welter of departmental and personal recrimination. The origins were inauspicious. Relations between Daniel Morrissey and his officials at Industry and Commerce were not the smoothest. Apart from de Valera himself, no minister had evoked such loyalty from his team as Lemass. The transition would have required tact on both sides, in any case. The problems were compounded when Morrissey's limited calibre contrasted so cruelly with the standards to which his officials had become accustomed. Some would therefore see the establishment of the IDA as a ploy by the minister to deprive his Department of some of its central functions.[156]

The IDA's brief was 'to investigate the effects of protective measures', 'to initiate proposals and schemes for the creation and development of Irish industry', and 'to advise on steps necessary for the expansion and modernisation of existing industries'. It was to some extent the inter-party alternative to the Industrial Efficiency Bill.

Gratified though Finance might feel at any reduction in the authority of Industry and Commerce, it could hardly be expected to welcome the creation of yet another new body, particularly as MacBride was actively supporting the idea. It launched a vigorous assault on the proposal

In view of the facilities already available, there must be a strong presumption that any industrial project offering a satisfactory propect of profit . . . will not be stillborn for lack of private enterprise to promote it. The government is likely to be left with the 'duds' of which it had enough already.[157]

Finance spared no feelings. If the Authority were created, it ought 'to supplement and assist but *not* . . . supplant private enterprise'. It should have no opportunity to initiate measures without government approval, because the scope for corruption would be so great. Nor were ministers themselves exempted from suspicion of either incompetence or impropriety. Mere ministerial approval should not suffice. Proposals should go to cabinet (which meant indirectly of course to Finance) 'insofar as cabinet is protection against foolish or corrupt ministers'.[158] And Finance was clear that the Authority should be so constituted as to acquire the confidence of the business community who 'must feel from the start that they will get a fair crack of the whip and that the Board is not a gang of crackpot socialist planners'.[159] It is not quite clear from the general intellectual calibre of this performance whether the emphasis here should be on 'crackpot', or 'socialist', or 'planners', or perhaps even 'gang', if not on all four together.

Finance was, as usual, very clear on what the proposed Authority should not do.

[156] B. Farrell, Seán *Lemass* (Dublin, 1983), pp. 82–3.
[157] PM, P35B/75, Finance memo, 31 December 1948.
[158] *Ibid.*   [159] *Ibid.*

The Board should not be envisaged as a Board of mastermind planners – to direct and plan the industrial development of the country, but rather as a Board of fact-finders and advisers to the community and to the government on the activities of private enterprise. They are there to search out possibilities of industrial development, to collect facts and statistics and to bring them to the notice of entrepreneurs in some fair and suitable manner. It should definitely *not* be within their scope or function to themselves . . . plan industry or any branch thereof. They should be purely an industrial development Advisory Board and it might be as well to title them as such.[160]

Despite the vigour of this statement, it represented a retreat from the earlier assumption that all profit prospects were already exhausted by private enterprise. It appears to concede that the legendary dynamos of the private sector might just conceivably have overlooked some relevant 'facts and statistics' or even some 'possibilities of industrial development'.

If Finance failed to prevent the establishment of the IDA, it succeeded in inducing a persecution complex in the new body, which felt itself crippled from the outset by inadequate resources, a feeling presumably exacerbated by Finance's vigorous objections to the proposed pension arrangements for the chairman, Dr J.P. Beddy,[161] an experienced and distinguished public servant, whose 'quiet genius . . . brought from infancy to strength the financial and promotional institutions on which our industrial progress has been based'.[162] MacBride wanted external assets to be repatriated to enable the IDA build advance factories. But his suggestions were frustrated on procedural grounds by Finance and Industry and Commerce, inspired to act in unwonted unison for the most human of reasons, a common enemy.[163]

The IDA compounded its initial problems by failing to consult other interested parties. Leydon was irritated that

it has not been the practice of the Authority to inform this department of the nature of the investigations it has in hand' [despite the fact that] 'the staff serving the Authority is composed of the officers who were previously engaged on similar duties in this department; and it appears to be the fact that in general these officers continue official action on files opened in this department before the Authority was established; in cases in which such files are in existence'[164]

Leydon would not be suspected of a benign view of the new Authority. But less partisan observers shared his sentiments. Within the Taoiseach's own department, Patrick Lynch also criticised the IDA's initial procedures, noting that 'the kind of proposals for foreign trade development that the Industrial Development Authority are considering are not new.

160 *Ibid.*   161 SPO, S14474A, Industry and Commerce memo, 31 October 1949.
162 T.K. Whitaker, *Interests* (Dublin, 1983), p. 291.
163 SPO, S14474A, MacBride memo, 9 November 1950; Department of the Taoiseach internal memo, 11 November 1950. See also Finance memo, 17 October 1949.
164 *Ibid.*, Leydon to M. Moynihan, 26 January 1950.

Somewhat similar ones were submitted to the former government by the former Minister for Industry and Commerce.'[165]

The IDA had a difficult birth. Public attention focused on the vigorous criticism of the proposal by Lemass in the Dáil, probably partly provoked by a sense of loyalty to 'his' officials, whose performance seemed to be slighted by the avowed purpose of the Bill. But the criticisms from within the administration were more dangerous. The Authority, however, though it made only a modest initial impact, survived the troubled early years to become later a virtually independent republic in the formulation of industrial policy.

If MacBride was McElligott's particular *bête noire*, Finance faced unexpected problems in two directions. The first arose from Costello's transferring a young Finance official, Patrick Lynch, to the Department of the Taoiseach to act as his personal economic advisor. In one sense, Lynch was to Costello what Smiddy was to de Valera. But Lynch's role went far beyond Smiddy's. A gifted and idealistic economist, who would move into academic life after the fall of the inter-party government and play a prominent role in the world of scholarship, policy studies and business, Lynch was already a ranking civil servant. Whereas Smiddy had made the occasional *ad hoc* response on specific issues at de Valera's request, Lynch was virtually a permanent presence in the Costello administration. With wide and catholic reading tastes, and an enviable command of Keynesian theory, Lynch could meet his former Finance colleagues on their own terms. He exerted influence not only on Costello, but also on the new Minister for Finance, McGilligan. He probably helped both men to take MacBride's measure, though to some extent only by taking MacBride's ground. McGilligan was a surprise convert to expansionist thinking. The scourge of mere humanitarians twenty-five years before seemed to have changed little during 1948 as he still denounced Fianna Fáil's excessive expenditure. But his views had begun to change even before returning to office, and he became an intellectual as well as a political convert to the potential of a moderate Keynesianism in Irish circumstances. He presided over the introduction of the first formal capital budget in 1950, repudiating his youthful discretion by insisting that 'one of the primary responsibilities of a government is to promote, by an enlightened budget and investment policy, the continuous and efficient use of national resources of men and materials'.[166]

McGilligan's change of attitude must have come as a sad shock to McElligott. For McGilligan was no Aiken. The first Finance Minister who was McElligott's intellectual superior, a formidable exponent of whatever

[165] *Ibid.*, P. Lynch to Costello, 11 November 1949.
[166] Moynihan, *Central banking*, p. 363; Lynch, 'Irish economy', p. 187; Meenan, *Irish economy*, pp. 259–61.

viewpoint he chose to represent, McGilligan could not be straightened by traditional Finance techniques.[167] While he could still subject spending proposals from other Departments to withering scrutiny in cabinet,[168] his general shift of direction left his reluctant officials badly exposed in 1949–51. The conflict in perspective was neatly summarised, perhaps by McGilligan himself, in response to objections to the 1950 budget by 'Treasury officials', who

measured the value of expenditure by its production of future revenue or files . . . We value the production of expenditure in terms of (1) social stability (2) expanding national income (3) efficient operation of government services, in that order of importance. Between such radically different systems of valuation, there never can be perfect understanding.[169]

No wonder that 'for the old Finance hands . . . their thumbs were through their gloves' by 1951.[170] Aiken denounced the allegedly inflationary impact of the 1950 budget, calling it 'treacherous' because it would discredit genuine Keynesian thinking by failing to increase taxation in an inflationary situation.[171] Lemass likewise conceded the principle of borrowing for capital investment, but simply argued that the amount was excessive in the circumstances. He also rejected in principle borrowing for 'unprofitable' investment, like the Land Rehabilitation Project, without deigning to specify the correct criteria of profitability.[172]

The main public opposition to McGilligan's policy came from the Central Bank. Brennan had already criticised the inflationary potential of policy in his 1950 report.[173] But it was his violent assault on the whole direction of policy in the 1951 report that caught the headlines, and provoked a political furore.[174] The report was not published until October 1951, when the government had lost office. Had it appeared with McGilligan still at Finance, the consequences would have been interesting.

But the furore over the Central Bank Report in late 1951 paled into insignificance compared with the controversy concerning the Mother and Child Scheme of Noel Browne, which animated the political scene earlier in the year, and has remained one of the great *cause célèbres* of Irish politics. The background was, as usual, confused. No government took much interest in health until the Second World War. The legislation of 1923, which officially abolished the Poor Law, was a cosmetic device. The dispensary service provided free medical treatment for about one-third of the population, but did not in practice offer choice of doctor.[175] The School Medical Service aimed to inspect children only once every three

167 See the *Leader* profile of McGilligan, 28 February 1953.
168 Browne, *Tide*, p. 199.
169 PM P35B/111, unsigned, undated memo.   170 'Silhouette', J.J. McElligott, p. 70.
171 DD, 120, 3 May 1950, 1064–66.   172 DD, 120, 4 May 1950, 790–1.
173 Annual Report of Central Bank for 1950, pp. 12–13.
174 Moynihan, *Central banking*, pp. 374–85.   175 Whyte, *Church and state*, p. 123.

years.[176] The war exposed something of the suffering among the poorer classes. Rising infant mortality disturbed some observers. Rising mortality from TB revealed even further the ravages of that scourge.[177] Inflation brought some articulate people within the nexus of the existing health services, whose inadequacy abruptly impinged on their consciousness. Moreover, the disparity between the treatment of the sick in Ireland and in Britain was brought increasingly home to the Irish by their emigrant relatives. In 1944 Dr F.C. Ward, a vigorous, amibitous politician, was given specific responsibility for public health matters within the Department of Local Government and Public Health.[178] In 1944 also, Dr James Deeny, a scholar of repute, who practised in Lurgan, and thus had experience of the Northern Ireland health service, was appointed Chief Medical Advisor by the Dublin government. 'Dr Deeny felt deeply the benefits which a vigorous public health policy could bring. It seems to have been he, more than any other individual, who was responsible for the shape which health legislation took in Ireland.'[179]

In January 1946 de Valera announced his intention to establish two new departments, Health and Social Welfare. This followed a protracted discussion on administrative reform in the general area of the social services stretching back to 1939.[180] Ward's Public Health Bill had to be postponed when he himself, apparently poised to become first Minister for Health, was obliged to resign office in 1946 due to irregularities in his income tax returns. De Valera indicated the importance he attached to the question by appointing the respected and canny Dr Jim Ryan as first Minister for Health and Social Welfare, with Pádraig Ó Cinnéide as first Secretary of the two Departments. Both appointments meant that Health would carry weight in the cabinet. They also suggest that de Valera realised health reform might require a delicate political touch.[181] Ryan was noted for his political astuteness, and Ó Cinnéide could not have worked closely with Moynihan and de Valera himself, as Assistant Secretary in the Department of the Taoiseach, without becoming alert to the nuances of politics. De Valera may not have fully anticipated at this stage a serious clash with the Catholic hierarchy. But he would have realised the immense influence wielded by the medical profession.

Ryan retained much of Ward's Bill, which sought to improve medical inspection in the schools, limit dangers from infectious diseases, provide a

176 *Ibid.*, p. 124.   177 *Ibid.*, p. 125.   178 *Ibid.*, p. 128.   179 *Ibid.*, p. 129.
180 SPO, S11109A, GC 2/42, 31 January 1939; GC 2/158, 21 March 1940; GC 3/13, 21 September 1943; MacEntee to de Valera, 28 September 1943; J. Ryan to de Valera, 10 January 1944; SPO, S11109B, GC 4/56, 20 February 1945; MacEntee memo, 26 February 1945; GC 4/58, 27 February 1945; Report of Interdepartmental Committee, 2 July 1945; Finance memo, 13 July 1945; GC 4/118, 13 November 1945; *Irish Times*, 13 February 1946.
181 Whyte, *Church and state*, pp. 133ff.

free medical service for mothers, and for children up to the age of sixteen, without a means test.[182] Some doctors were suspicious of the financial implications of the legislation, which might deprive them of lucrative private patients.[183] James Dillon sought a declaration on whether certain sections of the act were repugnant to the constitution.[184] Most ominously, the Catholic hierarchy protested privately to de Valera in September 1947 that

for the State, under the Act, to empower the public authority to provide for the health of all children, and to treat their ailments, and to educate women in regard to health, and to provide them with gynaecological services, was directly and entirely contrary to Catholic social teaching, the rights of the family, the rights of the Church in education, and the rights of the medical profession, and of voluntary institutions.[185]

The fall of the government enabled de Valera to evade the issue. It fell to the new government to implement Ryan's Health Act.

The health portfolio was allocated to Clann na Poblachta, which had stood on a platform of social radicalism, and had campaigned vigorously against TB. MacBride nominated the 32-year-old Noel Browne, himself a doctor, who thus became a minister on his first day in the Dáil.[186]

Browne brought a crusading zeal to the campaign against TB. Three of his family had died from it.[187] He achieved conspicuous success in the campaign, aided by the preparatory work already initiated, the timely appearance of the BCG vaccine and a dedicated team at Health. He was able to draw on an independent source of funding, from the Hospital Sweep Stakes, which he used imaginatively, and which enabled him to largely escape Finance control. The crusading style of his campaign against the disease left him with little opportunity in his first two years of office to acquire the qualities needed to deal with more resourceful enemies.

Browne decided in 1950 to activate the section of Ryan's Health Act proposing free (voluntary) ante- and post-natal care for mothers, as well as free medical care for all children under sixteen, without a means test.[188] Some doctors continued to feel that they stood to lose heavily. But many of those who worshipped at the altar of Croesus, while demurely draped in the robes of Hippocrates, were shrewd enough to oppose the scheme as 'socialised medicine'. Some unkind observers suspected that their real opposition was less to 'state medicine' than to 'cheap medicine'. Had 'socialised medicine' been considered likely to increase professional

182 *Ibid.*, p. 141.   183 *Ibid.*, pp. 140ff.   184 *Ibid.*, pp. 153–4.
185 Lyons, *Ireland* (1973 edn), p. 576.
186 On MacBride's reasons for nominating Browne, see Fanning, *Independent Ireland*, p. 166.
187 Browne, *Tide*, contains a harrowing account of his family background.
188 Whyte, *Church and state*, pp. 200–4, summarises the scheme.

incomes, its ideological horrors might have been more stoically endured. But there was a fundamental, long-term issue of principle also involved. If Browne's scheme succeeded, the strong likelihood was that private practice would gradually be superseded by a salaried state service. However hysterical and opportunistic the fears expressed in some medical circles, suspicion of the longer term *potential* autocracy of the state was by no means unwarranted.

Bishops were concerned that Catholic mothers might be exposed to instruction on gynaecological hygiene, infant care, etc. from non-Catholic doctors. However, it was essentially on the absence of a means test that the bishops chose to take their stand. Had Browne not been so obdurate about this, a compromise might have been arranged. Critics alleged that the ecclesiastical attitude lacked consistency. One commentator advanced the very argument with which Seán MacEntee had sought to frustrate the proposal for family allowances:

The objection made to Dr Browne's scheme was that it provided free medical service for *all* mothers and *all* children up to six [sic] years of age. It is therefore difficult to understand why the same exception has not been taken to the children's allowance, also instituted by Mr de Valera's government, which is paid to *all* parents regardless of their means. The only difference between the two forms of benefit would seem to be that while Dr Browne's scheme affected the income of the medical profession the children's allowance did not.[189]

This over-simplified the position of some bishops, passionate protagonists of a 'professional' ethos. Archbishop McQuaid of Dublin, a key figure in the affair, was a doctor's son,[190] with an exalted sense of the dignity of the professions. In 1946 he had expressed 'full sympathy' for striking teachers as representing a 'profession'. Dr Browne of Galway, another vigorous critic of the scheme, had shown a reverential attitude towards his idealised image of the professions in general, and of medical doctors in particular, during his chairmanship of the Commission on Vocational Organisation.[191]

Browne neglected to secure cabinet approval for the details of his proposal before embarking on his scheme, and thus left himself in an exposed position when the cabinet subsequently disavowed his approach. The complications arising from his lack of political instinct were further exacerbated through conflicting interpretations of what transpired at a meeting between himself and three bishops, including McQuaid and Browne, in October 1950. 'Through a series of misunderstandings that would have been farcical were not the consequences so tragic, Dr Browne believed he had satisfied the hierarchy when in fact he had done nothing of

189 *Round Table*, 43 (December 1952), p. 73.
190 J. Feeney, *John Charles McQuaid* (Dublin, 1974), p. 1; O'Connell, *INTO*, pp. 218, 233.
191 Lee, 'Corporatist thought', pp. 340–1.

the sort.'[192] While Browne's meetings with the bishops may have been a dialogue of the deaf, it was more the cabinet's handling of the affair than the bishops' attitude that determined the outcome.

Once Browne moved publicly to implement the scheme in March 1951 without explicit cabinet authorisation, and despite a strong protest from McQuaid to himself and Costello, the Taoiseach, who had previously played a shadowly conciliatory role, adopted a tougher attitude towards his minister. When Browne's naïvely undertook to abide by a decision of the hierarchy on the compatibility of his scheme with Catholic morality, he found himself immediately out-manoeuvred. At their meeting of 4 April, the bishops evaded the demand to pronounce on the morality of Browne's scheme, but denounced it on the ground that it conflicted with Catholic social teaching. That was good enough for the cabinet, by now probably thoroughly tired of Browne even where they may have had an open mind on the scheme, which many had not. Lemass later surmised that Costello and MacBride greeted the affair as a God-given – or at least bishop-given – opportunity to dispense with Browne,[193] whose temperament left even sympathetic observers 'with no illusions about the difficulties . . . colleagues must have faced in their dealings with him'.[194]

Costello and MacBride compelled Browne's resignation on 11 April.[195] As party politicians, however, their performances rated quite differently. Costello played an adroit hand. MacBride did not. The affair took an unexpected twist when Browne published correspondence between the bishops, Costello, MacBride and himself. Costello chose to position himself behind the episcopal robes, rushing to proclaim himself a good Catholic. He had as fluent a command of exalted rhetoric as de Valera. He had proclaimed in 1948 'the need of the world for spiritual fortification when the dark forces of materialism are threatening the foundations on which the great Christian nations of the earth endeavoured to build for their peoples'.[196] Now he insisted on proclaiming in the Dáil that he accepted 'without qualification in all respects the social teaching of the Church as interpreted by the Roman Catholic hierarchy of Ireland'.[197] The strength of Costello's position was that while his piety was absolutely genuine, it also happened to coincide with the material advantage of the interests he represented. Only the unsporting would descend to wondering how professional fees came to be in the front line of 'spiritual fortification' against 'materialism'.

If it made sense for Costello to consolidate the conservative Fine Gael vote in this manner, it made no sense for MacBride to jettison the radical

[192] Lyons, *Ireland*, p. 577.
[193] 'Seán Lemass looks back', *Irish Press*, 17 January 1969.
[194] Inglis, *West Briton*, p. 165.   [195] Whyte, *Church and state*, pp. 231–2.
[196] Quoted in Fanning, *The four-leaved shamrock*, pp. 16–17.
[197] Quoted in J.A. Murphy, 'Put them out', p. 14, n. 6.

Clann na Poblachta vote. MacBride's ineptness as party leader ruined whatever chance existed of an opening to the left in postwar Ireland. More a posturer and a conspirer than a leader, MacBride failed to provide his movement with the responsible leadership required to translate it from a party of protest into a credible party of government. Racked by internal tensions, Clann na Poblachta was already drifting into anarchy before the spectacular rift, made all the more public by Browne's publication of the correspondence. However anxious MacBride may have been to rid himself of his awkward colleague, it was more in his interest, if he wished not only to retain the leadership of a party, but to retain a party to lead, to have brought down the government on the issue. This was the only way he might have retrieved his waning radical reputation. Instead, he chose to split his party's support-base instead of splitting the government.[198]

Browne was probably his own worst enemy, despite the competition from Costello, MacBride and McQuaid. His career must count among the personal tragedies of recent Irish politics. He brought idealism, energy and ability to his task. He could often be difficult on detail, and sometimes passionately wrongheaded on principle. But his vision was generous. If he sometimes lent credulous support to doubtful causes, his instincts were decent. Yet his talents were largely squandered as the rest of his public career was to be passed in growing frustration and rancorous recrimination. He was out-smarted by slicker players of the political game, protecting their privileges, their pockets and their power. Yet Clio is a mistress of irony. Browne would exact sweet, if belated, retribution. Nearly forty years later, in 1986, he became the first Irish minister to publish detailed memoirs, embellished by portraits of his colleagues. Many of the portraits are etched in vitriol. But they will survive, because there is sufficient independent evidence to sustain their plausibility. No one can ever look at the first Costello cabinet again without seeing it at least partly through Browne's jaundiced but piercing eyes.

Nevertheless, the sardonic brilliance of Browne's portraiture should not disguise the fact that it is an over-simplification to present the Mother and Child Scheme, which can still evoke passionate controversy, as a straight conflict between church and state. It is difficult to dispute the judicious verdict of Desmond Williams, who maintained that it was an improbable series of coincidences that turned the matter into a crisis:

The conditions of coalition government, the tactics of the most successful trade union of all, the Irish Medical Association, Dr Browne's own misinterpretation of episcopal negotiation, the minister's own peculiar relationship with the leader of his party, Seán MacBride, and the special phraseology of Archbishop MacQuaid

---

[198] For a profile of MacBride, see *The Leader*, 2 August 1952.

– all these gave this particular political crisis a character which it would have lacked under different circumstances and with different personalities involved.[199]

MacBride was to pay a high price for his miscalculation in the general election that shortly followed Browne's resignation. That election did not, however, arise directly from the Browne affair. The government fell not over the Mother and Child Scheme, but over the price of milk – cows', not mothers' – which lost the vote of three rural deputies.[200] The June election results proved intriguing. The fortunes of the coalition parties varied widely.

The ostensible winner was Fianna Fáil, whose vote rose from 554 000 to 616 000. But this increase of 61 000 votes gained only one extra seat, leaving Fianna Fáil with 69 seats, still short of an overall majority in a 147 seat Dáil. In 1944 an increase of 45 000 votes had sufficed to gain 9 extra seats. Fianna Fáil would suffer, as Fine Gael would benefit, from the growing solidarity of the inter-party electorate in distributing their transfers in concerted anti-Fianna Fáil fashion.[201] Fine Gael thus won 9 extra seats from a rise of 81 000, from 262 000 to 343 000, in its vote. The Fine Gael gain in first preferences partly reflected the political impact of James Dillon.[202] The party vote rose by 8.7 per cent in the more agricultural constituencies, compared with an overall rise of 5.9 per cent.[203] Fianna Fáil's net gain of one seat was composed of 7 gains and 6 losses, with 5 of the losses coming in the west. Of the 6 constituencies in which it actually lost votes, 5 were in the west.[204] The solid west had not been solid for De Valera since the rise of Clann na Talmhan. Now, more ominously, its main rival began making inroads into the heartland.

The significance of the Fine Gael recovery emerges clearly when placed in the context of its long decline since 1932. The nadir was reached when it failed to nominate sufficient candidates in the general election of 1944 to win an overall majority, and did not contest four of five by-elections in 1945.[205] Fine Gael had largely forfeited credibility as a serious party by this stage, and it failed to improve its position in 1948. By 1951, however, it had re-established itself as the main repository of resentment against Fianna Fáil.

Clann na Talmhan won 6 seats, a loss of only 1, despite the lack of charisma of its leader, Joe Blowick, 'who under stress of extreme excitement sounded like a tape recorder played backwards'.[206] Labour just held its share of the vote, at 11.5 per cent compared with 11.3 per cent in 1948. It lost 3 seats, however, falling from 19 to 16, despite having

199 T.D. Williams, 'Conclusion', in Nowlan and Williams, *War years and after*, p. 211.
200 Whyte, *Church and state* p. 266.   201 *Irish Times*, 2 June 1951.
202 *Ibid.*, 2, 16 June 1951.
203 M.P. Gallagher, *Electoral support*, p. 37.   204 *Irish Press*, 1 June 1951.
205 Whyte, *Church and state*, pp. 112–13.
206 Inglis, *West Briton*, p. 175.

re-united in 1950, 'National' Labour having crawled under, into, and out of the bed to ensure that there were no red hussies defiling the ideological purity of their 'Official' Labour colleagues.

The big loser was Clann na Poblachta, which lost 8 of its 10 seats, its share of the vote crumbling from 13 per cent to 4 per cent. The Mother and Child Scheme was only incidental to the campaign, but insofar as the electorate was in a position to express a verdict, it plumped for Browne, who himself polled handsomely as an Independent. MacBride, in contrast, lost two-thirds of his vote, ignominiously scraping into his seat on the final count where he had headed the poll three years before, and enduring the mortification of winning only half the first preference vote of Dr Ffrench O'Carroll, a Browne supporter standing as an Independent, who challenged MacBride directly on the *débâcle*.[207] Other Browne supporters, Peadar Cowan and Jack McQuillan, were also elected. The support of Browne, Ffrench O'Carroll and Cowan helped Fianna Fáil return to office as a minority government.

Some observers have discerned a decisive 'acceleration in the pace of change' in the years 1948–51.[208] However, it is difficult to detect any coherent direction to such change as occurred. There seemed to be more activity than during the final dreary years of Fianna Fáil; but much of it was of the *bombinans in vacuo* variety. No sustained shift in policies or attitudes occurred. The verdict of Brian Inglis on the early fifties, 'it was not only the politics that were stagnant ... culturally, Ireland was moribund' seems the sounder judgement.[209] The most important achievement of the first inter-party government was simply its existence. It showed that there was a viable alternative to Fianna Fáil. Its second most important achievement was its defeat. It did not succeed in relegating Fianna Fáil into long-term opposition. The fact that it fell in the wake of an internecine squabble appeared to confirm de Valera's propaganda line that coalitions could not govern. Fianna Fáil, like all parties, was of course itself a coalition, however exquisitely orchestrated. But it presented a monolithic public image, and presumably continued to derive some support from the assumed coherence of its policy. Several economic variables, employment, savings and investment, all improved somewhat between 1948 and 1951, but apparently at the expense of a serious balance of payments deficit, which the reflexes of Brennan and McElligott automatically translated into a crisis. The reaction of the Fianna Fáil government to this 'crisis' in the 1952 budget helped rivet stagnation on the country. The verdict on the Costello government could be clearer had it remained in office a year longer. The handling of the balance of payments problem would have provided the litmus test of its calibre. A

[207] *Irish Press*, 1 June 1951.   [208] D. Thornley, 'Ireland', pp. 8–9.
[209] Inglis, *West Briton*, p. 210.

generous assessment of its performance would stress that a breathing space had been gained in which more appropriate policies might have been devised to create the basis for sustained economic growth, if the policy-makers were capable of conceiving them.

MORASS

De Valera played a waiting game of masterly inactivity during the Mother and Child controversy. He indicated his intention of continuing along the same general lines of reform by re-appointing Jim Ryan as Minister for Health and Social Welfare. Browne had been operating, after all, within the general framework of Ryan's 1947 Act. Ryan's new Health Act of 1953 significantly improved health services, raising the proportion of patients entitled to receive either free hospital treatment, or treatment at reduced rates, from 30 per cent to 85 per cent. Ryan originally intended to have no means test at all, but the episcopal critics of 'state' medicine took strong exception to the scheme once more. However, they now confronted cannier operators than Noel Browne. De Valera was, it is true, determined to avoid a public confrontation with the hierarchy, probably on grounds of both principle and calculation. But he also rejected the Costello doctrine that the Taoiseach disposes as the Hierarchy proposes. By making various concessions, largely tactical, including the introduction of a modest means test, Ryan detached the bishops, however reluctantly, from the Irish Medical Association, which eventually conceded the case even more grudgingly.[210]

Apart however from the delicate handling of this contentious issue, the cabinet of 1951–4 has strong claims to be considered the worst de Valera government. Opposition had not rejuvenated the party. Neither new men nor new ideas emerged. De Valera in opposition confined himself largely to the partition issue. Lemass, it is true, gave a vigorous performance. In addition to taking charge of party reorganisation, and becoming managing director of the *Irish Press*, he dominated the opposition front bench in the Dáil, and seemed at times to amount to a one-man party. Other former ministers generally preferred to keep a low profile, parroting the de Valera line that coalitions, according to some obscure but infallible decree, could not last. The exception was Seán

---

210 Browne regards the Health Act of 1953 as a capitulation to the bishops. Others may be impressed with what the government salvaged as well as with what it conceded. The various viewpoints can be followed in Browne, *Tide*, pp. 212–19; Whyte, *Church and state*, pp. 278–302; R. Fanning, 'Fianna Fáil and the bishops', *Irish Times*, 13–14 February 1985. Ruth Barrington, *Health, medicine and politics in Ireland 1900–1970* (Dublin, 1987) came to hand too late to be fully used. It does not oblige substantive revision of our conclusion, but the reader seeking a fuller perspective should consult Barrington's admirable study.

MacEntee who won party plaudits for the manner in which he baited Clann na Poblachta.[211]

An important consequence followed from de Valera's own weakening health. He no longer retained External Affairs. He appointed Frank Aiken to his vacated post. This was a bold move. Aiken's previous venture into international relations, his trip to the USA in 1941, had not been an unqualified success. But he would now prove a minister of distinction. De Valera did neglect at this juncture one conspicuous possible source of talent. His son Vivion possessed much of that rigidity in principle and flexibility in practice that made his father so accomplished a ringmaster of the diplomatic circus. He would have made an interesting Minister for External Affairs and might have relieved Aiken to resume as Minister for Finance. Instead, he took over the *Irish Press* when Lemass returned to office in 1951, and confined himself to a backbench career in the Dáil. Aiken's appointment to External Affairs opened the way for MacEntee's reappointment to Finance despite opposition from Lemass.[212]

Twenty years before, McElligott awaited MacEntee's entry with apprehension. Now he must have welcomed him back with relief. No longer would he have to contend with the intellectual audacity of McGilligan. MacEntee duly pursued a deflationary policy. His 1952 Budget, raising income tax by a shilling in the pound, and imposing price increases on bread and butter, tea and sugar, drink and petrol, came as a 'bombshell'.[213] The *Leader* observed in its budget preview that 'Mr Lemass is capable of explaining government policy with a clarity, authority, and breath of vision far beyond the reach of any of his colleagues. When Mr MacEntee presents a statement of the same policy, it seems to have become incoherent, distorted and attenuated.'[214] But the 1952 Budget represented a clear victory for MacEntee over Lemass. It raised a host of still unanswered, and perhaps unanswerable questions, from both political and economic viewpoints.

The Finance justification for the budget lay in the balance of payments situation.[215] The deficits of £35 000 000 in 1950 and £62 000 000 in 1951 had to be eliminated if confidence in the currency were to be maintained, and if the deficit with the dollar area were to be reduced. Sceptics might note that the reserves still sufficed to cover a much higher ratio of imports than the European average. But the immediate question at issue is whether the balance of payments was already adjusting itself before the imposition of the deflationary measures. The deficits in 1950 and 1951 could be attributed mainly to the rise in raw material import prices caused by the

211 *Irish Times*, 10 January 1984.   212 Farrell, *Lemass*, p. 95.
213 *Leader*, 12 April 1952.
214 *Ibid.*, 29 March 1952.
215 For the Finance viewpoint, see Fanning, *Finance*, pp. 468–84.

devaluation of the Irish pound to maintain parity with the devalued sterling of 1949, and by stockpiling due to the Korean War in 1950.[216] These were of a once-for-all nature. MacEntee argued, in the crucial analytical passage in the Budget, that

there is, unfortunately, no reason to think . . . that the balance of payments will right itself spontaneously. The opening months of this year showed virtually no improvement . . . and it seems clear that, without an improvement in personal savings and a reduction in inflationary government finance, the deficit in the balance of payments will remain excessive.[217]

He concluded that in the absence of corrective measures, a balance of payments deficit of £50 000 000 could be anticipated in 1952.[218]

MacEntee's confidence about the impending deficit could be disputed even on the basis of his own evidence. He recognised elsewhere in his speech that 'the tide had now turned' in raw material imports.[219] The world economy was notoriously passing through a phase of great uncertainty, to which MacEntee himself actually referred, and it was difficult to discern developing trends.[220] There might therefore have seemed to be a case for a relatively neutral budget, to be followed if necessary by a supplementary budget when trends became clearer. Instead, Finance seemed anxious to rush the budget through. It was introduced on 2 April, the earliest budget in the history of the state. Evidence was available that unemployment and emigration were already sharply increasing, and that industrial output was falling.[221] The incipient recession should itself help reduce the deficit, without inflicting more punishment on the economy. It seems likely, moreover, that Finance underrated the improvement in the external balance in late 1951 and early 1952. The White Paper, *The trend of external trade*, published in October 1951, not only sounded conventional panic warnings, but itself exaggerated the size of the deficit in 1951 by about 15 per cent. Forecasts of external trade patterns are notoriously hazardous. But to get the figure so wrong so late in the year was unfortunate. The most disturbing criticism of the White Paper was that it failed to foresee the rise of cattle exports in 1952, not because of the vagaries of the cattle trade, but because it did not know how to interpret the statistics.[222]

As late as 30 January 1952, MacEntee described the finances as 'difficult almost to the verge of desperation'.[223] Finance did not have monthly balance of payments figures later than February at the time of the Budget. The March figures, like those for January and February, recorded

---

[216] *Annual Report of the Central Bank*, 1950, pp. 10–11.
[217] DD, 130 2 April 1952, 1123.
[218] *Ibid.*, 1124.   [219] *Ibid.*, 1115.   [220] *Ibid.*, 1128.
[221] *Ibid.*, 1116; Kennedy and Dowling, *Economic growth*, p. 214.
[222] *Leader*, 27 September 1952.   [223] *Round Table*, 42 (June 1952), pp. 251.

a modest improvement on those of 1951. The April figure was particularly important. It showed a sharp increase in 1951. If it were now to record a significant fall, much of the 'uncertainty' would dissolve. The April figure indeed showed a dramatic improvement. This continued through the second quarter, owing little to budgetary policy, which could not begin to exert a significant impact until later in the year. Even the Central Bank conceded that 'the factors chiefly responsible for change were a marked increase in the export of beef in various forms and a recession in the stockpiling which was particularly active from the first half of 1951'.[224] Neither of these developments could be attributed primarily to the budget.

The timing of the budget is more likely to have been influenced by essentially political considerations, whether party political or administrative political, than by clinical economic exegesis. From McElligott's point of view, the opportunity offered by the balance of payments crisis to drive the economy back onto the straight and narrow path of deflationary virtue, was too good to be missed. McElligott needed a crisis to purge the economy of inter-party promiscuity. From a party political point of view, it is conceivable that if the cabinet were convined that a punitive Budget must be introduced, then the earlier the better. The Costello government could be blamed for the inherited mess. Independents, on whom Fianna Fáil relied for support, might swallow unpalatable medicine at this early stage, due to their reluctance to go to the country so soon again, that they would not stomach later.

A disturbing feature of the budget debate was the failure of the opposition to expose the basic weakness in MacEntee's assumptions about the balance of payments, although some evidence was already available in the *Quarterly Bulletins* of the Central Bank.[225] The opposition instead generally contented itself with vituperative but futile references to the malign influence of Brennan.[226] The budget might have been used to embarrass the government by dwelling on the differences between the MacEntee approach and the Lemass policy of increasing production and resisting deflation, which he had vigorously advocated in the Dáil as recently as November 1951.[227] Dillon, with a contribution verging on the irresponsible, allowed the government to escape, and permitted Lemass to buckle down to apparent support for the budget. Similarly, some careless personal jibes by Seán MacBride allowed de

---

[224] *Report of the Central Bank for the year ending 31 March 1952*, p. 8; *ibid.* for 1953, p. 10; *Quarterly Statistical Bulletin of the Central Bank*, July 1952; Kennedy and Dowling, *Economic growth*, pp. 215–16.

[225] *Quarterly Statistical Bulletin of the Central Bank* July 1951, October 1951, January 1952, p. 12, t. xiv in all cases.

[226] See the contributions of McGilligan, Norton and MacBride in DD, 130, 2 April 1952, 1160, 1161, 1170, and of Costello, *ibid.*, 3 April, 1988.

[227] Moynihan, *Central banking*, p. 381. For continuing differences between Lemass and MacEntee in 1953, see Moynihan, pp. 408–10.

Valera to speak 'for two hours without notes ... in first class fighting
form' with a marvellously diversionary effort, showing the old fox at his
cleverest in translating the divisive and obscure policy issues into a more
congenial personality conflict with MacBride.[228]

The mid-fifties were likely to have been a troubled time for the economy
in any case, due to deteriorating terms of trade. But the 1952 budget
probably contributed significantly to both the reality and the atmosphere
of depression. Even conservative commentators felt that MacEntee had
blundered and that domestic industry would suffer seriously from his
deflationary drive.[229] The relentless pursuit of deflation even when the
balance of payments deficit virtually vanished, and while the external
reserves were actually rising in 1953 and 1954, further accentuated the
slump.[230] The deflationary crusade appears to have discouraged investment in manufacturing industry and to have inhibited export developments. Brennan and McElligott assumed that exports would increase if
domestic demand were curtailed. But the most authoritative examination
of the issue has concluded that,

the stagnation in home demand in the 1950s does not seem to have assisted
exports. The postwar period does not provide any evidence to show that export
growth was greater when domestic demand pressures were restrained. It is more
likely that the stagnation of the whole economy was unfavourable to exports in
that it adversely affected manufacturing investment, company profits, savings and
possibly the capital inflow. Moreover, a more rapid growth of manufacturing
output might have been accompanied by a more rapid growth of productivity and
an improvement in competitiveness. Furthermore, the lack of confidence in the
economy, associated with falling employment and population, created an atmosphere unfavourable to the enterprise required for successful entry into export
markets.[231]

Nor is this the wisdom of hindsight. 'An economy with such a history of
defeat as ours', observed the *Leader*, in 1952, 'needs the stimulus for
enterprise of material progress, and private capital investment suffers if
this is not given while measures adopted to reduce the standard of living
incidentally tend to frighten away external capital'.[232]

MacEntee's deflationary impulses owed little to political sympathy with
Brennan, no friend of Fianna Fáil. By 1953, Brennan was a friend of
virtually nobody. He was subjected to frequent criticism, some of it
unfair, by politicians of all parties. The government accepted his resignation in March 1953, appointing the more elastic, if equally doughty,
McElligott to succeed him.[233] The 62-year-old Owen Redmond, who 'had

[228] *Round Table*, 42 (September 1952), p. 356; DD, 131, 23 April 1952, 205ff.
[229] *Round Table*, 42 (June 1952), p. 256.
[230] Kennedy and Dowling, *Economic growth*, p. 216.   [231] *Ibid.*, p. 218.
[232] *Leader*, 2 August 1952.
[233] Moynihan, *Central Banking*, pp. 388–400.

come up from the ranks and was notoriously meticulous. He changed the format of letters so often that his assistants found it quite impossible to give him one that he would not tamper with without affecting its substance' succeeded McElligott.[234]

McEntee's policy was honest and courageous. It was also misguided, in personal, party and national terms. His identification with austerity helped to condemn the government to premature demise, when Independent deputies withdrew their support in May 1954. The election result ruined MacEntee's succession prospects, for he took most of the blame for Fianna Fáil's poor performance. It lost 4 seats, falling to 65, the smallest number since 1927. Its popular vote fell from 616 000 to 579 000, or from 46.3 per cent to 43.4 per cent. The discrediting of MacEntee's approach allowed Lemass to recover lost ground and, insofar as his claims on the leadership had been weakened, to re-establish himself as the clear heir apparent.[235] Fianna Fáil's discomfiture was all the greater in that Fine Gael made striking gains, increasing its popular vote from 343 000 to 427 000, its share of the poll from 25.7 percent to 32 per cent, and its number of seats from 40 to 50, the highest since 1932. And it achieved this by the simple device of doing nothing in opposition. Fianna Fáil was entirely the architect of its own defeat. Just as MacEntee had been more responsible than any other individual for alienating Labour transfers from Fianna Fáil by his 'red scare' tactics during the war, his economic policy was now mainly responsible for consolidating the Fine Gael recovery of 1951.

John A. Costello once more formed an inter-party government. The cabinet now contained three parties, Fine Gael, Labour and Clann na Talmhan. Clann na Poblachta, while giving general supuport to the government, did not join it. The most significant appointment, however, was the one that was not made. McGilligan, now sixty-five and in doubtful health, preferred to become Attorney General rather than take Finance again. The alternative was Gerard Sweetman, a vigorous conservative. Despite broadly continuing MacEntee's policy, a balance of payments deficit of £35 000 000 emerged in 1955, thanks partly to a consumer boom arising from a wage round, but more fundamentally to the falling volume of agricultural exports.[236] The problem was exacerbated by a capital outflow, which increased the decline in external reserves to £47 000 000,[237] probably largely incurred because of lack of confidence due to the stagnation in manufacturing industry and the absence of opportunity for investment.

[234] Ó Broin, *Yesterday*, p. 101.   [235] Bew and Patterson, *Lemass*, pp. 74–6.
[236] Kennedy and Dowling, *Economic growth*, pp. 219–20.
[237] B.M. Walsh, 'Economic Growth and Development 1945–70', p. 29.

Once more, as in 1951–2, Finance did too much too late. Sweetman imposed special import levies and additional taxes in March 1956, intensified them in May and yet again in July, although there were by then some signs that the balance of payments was already improving.[238]

MacBride forced a general election in March 1957 by withdrawing Clann na Poblachta's support from the government, partly because of Sweetman's policy, partly because of Costello's hostility to the IRA campaign against Northern Ireland that broke out in 1956. The campaign aroused latent republican sympathies. Sinn Féin won 4 seats, though this appears to have partly reflected its apparent commitment to a radical social policy in a period of economic crisis as well as support for the border campaign. Ironically, Clann na Poblachta's share of the vote fell from 4.0 per cent to 1.7 per cent, and it lost 2 of its 3 seats, including MacBride's. Ten years earlier, Clann na Poblachta seemed poised to rejuvenate Irish politics. Under MacBride's leadership it fizzled out within a decade.

Fianna Fáil won a handsome overall majority, with 77 seats in a Dáil of 147. The 74-year-old de Valera enjoyed his greatest electoral triumph. But the result bore certain resemblances to 1944. It was more a vote of no confidence in the other parties than of confidence in Fianna Fáil, whose popular vote rose only marginally, from 578 000 to 593 000. Labour lost 7 seats, its traditional supporters reacting against its association with Sweetman's austerity measures, while Fine Gael lost 10 seats, falling from 50 to 40, with its popular vote down from 427 000 to 327 000.

Despite the losses, Fine Gael had some cause for consolation. Thanks to its recovery since 1951, it still held 40 seats, far above its nadir. If it retained this level of support in so gloomy an economic situation, it could hardly fare worse in the future. It lost much more in Dublin and the east than in the west.[239] Nevertheless, coalition voting discipline held to the extent that Labour transfers did not generally revert to Fianna Fáil. They tended to go to Fine Gael only as a last resort, preferring Clann na Poblachta or Independent. But in all the Dublin constituencies, except South Central, more appear to have gone to Fine Gael than to Fianna Fáil.[240]

Nevertheless, the few genuinely professional politicians in Fine Gael had cause to be bitterly disappointed at the blighting of the bright hopes of 1954. Fine Gael had then pulled to within 15 seats of Fianna Fáil. Now it lagged 38 seats behind. In contrast to the first period of inter-party government, from which Fine Gael emerged, even in the general election

---

[238] Kennedy and Dowling, *Economic growth*, pp. 220–1.

[239] B. Chubb, 'Ireland in 1957', in D.E. Butler (ed.), *Elections abroad* (London, 1959), pp. 215–16.

[240] *Irish Press*, 7 March 1957, for the transfers of M. Mullen, R. Connolly, J. Colgan, M. O'Carroll and J. Fitzgerald.

defeat of 1951, a clear winner in party terms, it now lost. The 1957 defeat was self-inflicted. Until Sweetman imposed his squeeze, there had been few signs of a Fianna Fáil recovery. By-election results in June 1955 showed no swing back to Fianna Fáil.[241] Had Fine Gael been cleverer, or luckier, the implications for Fianna Fáil could have been unsettling. The party political situation in the mid-fifties was probably the most fluid since the mid 1920s. Whether through misjudgement or through misfortune, Fine Gael forfeited the chance to overtake Fianna Fáil.

It remained to be seen how Fianna Fáil would respond to their reprieve. Could they improve on their lacklustre performance between 1951 and 1954 and between 1944 and 1948?

[241] *Leader*, 9 July 1955.

Chapter 5

EXPANSION: 1958–1969

DE VALERA DEPARTS

De Valera's last cabinet had some new faces. Death, disability and calculation were at last beginning to take their toll of the old faithfuls. Tom Derrig died in 1956. Seán Moylan lost his seat. De Valera immediately nominated him to the Senate, and appointed him Minister for Agriculture, but he died in November 1957. De Valera eased Gerry Boland out, perhaps under pressure from Lemass, by the characteristic ploy of appointing his son Kevin as Minister for Defence on his first day in the Dáil.[1] The new Department of the Gaeltacht, established by the Costello government in 1956, was first held, jointly with Education, by Jack Lynch, but was then tranferred to Micheál Ó Mórain within a few months. Another new face was Neil Blaney, first at Posts and Telegraphs, then at Local Government after the reshuffle following Moylan's death. In a move that 'created surprise'[2] de Valera signalled a crucial change of direction by switching Jim Ryan and Seán MacEntee, Ryan going to Finance and MacEntee to Health and Social Welfare. This suggested, as events confirmed, that Lemass had at long last established his ascendancy. He had always found Ryan easier to work with than MacEntee. But de Valera might have made the change even without the presumed pressure from Lemass. He would have wanted no repeat of the electoral consequences of a MacEntee performance of 1951–4 vintage.

The connoisseur of political conscience may regret that the 1957 election produced so decisive a Fianna Fáil majority. It would have been instructive to have watched de Valera's reaction in a situation where Sinn Féin TDs, with the wit to take their seats, held the balance of power. Inhibited by no such constraint, de Valera re-introduced internment in July 1957 and cooperated with Stormont to snuff out IRA border raids.

But the IRA was not de Valera's main problem. He had taken its

---

[1] Farrell, *Chairman or chief?*, p. 39.   [2] *Irish Review and Annual*, 1957, p. 7.

measure twenty years before. His prime preoccupation was his own impending retirement. Or was it impending? Now seventy-five, and almost blind, could even he contemplate leading Fianna Fáil into the next general election? He brooded increasingly on the implications. So did the cabinet. There are various accounts of whether he volunteered to leave, or was gently guided towards the exit.[3] The uncharacteristically petulant manner in which he responded to rumours of his resignation at the Árd Fheis in November 1957 suggests that he resented what he perceived as pressure. He told the assembled stalwarts that 'So long as this organisation wants me (if they do not want me, they can get rid of me very easily) and as long as Dáil Éireann thinks I am doing my work and can do my work, then I stay.'[4] But it seems that a consensus emerged among senior cabinet members in 1958 that Árus an Uachtaráin, due to become vacant when Seán T. O'Kelly completed his second term as president in 1959, would provide the ideal paddock for the old warhorse.

Many felt that Fianna Fáil could not flourish without 'The Chief'. The party was so intimately identified with him that his departure might herald its electoral eclipse. Speculation about the sad fate in store for the orphaned party had long been rife. As early as 1952 the *Leader* suggested that Fine Gael would already be the biggest party 'if it were not for the intangible element of Mr de Valera'.[5] In 1954 the *Leader* again felt that 'the future of Fianna Fáil is perhaps the most debated question in contemporary Irish politics', with only 'the unique personality and exceptional vigour of Mr de Valera' sustaining its otherwise suspect strength.[6] De Valera shared the fears.[7] There was one obvious solution. Under proportional representation, Fianna Fáil had to rest content with a number of seats only slightly bigger than its share of the vote. Could anything be more unfair?

De Valera's mind had frequently flirted, when Fianna Fáil's fortunes had momentarily faltered, with revising the electoral system.[8] However, 1959 was the first time he proposed to change the system after a handsome election victory. The party now required re-insurance against his departure. Though commentators continued to insist on the fabled conservatism of the Irish voter, de Valera knew well that the public had long displayed, from a party strategist's perspective, an irritating unreliability. He determined to make one final bid to guard against the consequences of fickle popular opinion. In the 'first past-the-post', straight vote English system,

[3] *Ibid.*, 40–1; Longford and O'Neill, *De Valera*, pp. 446–7; Profile of T. Desmond Williams, 'The course of an Irish historian', *Irish Times*, 26 May 1984.
[4] Moynihan, *Speeches*, p. 581, n. 1.   [5] *Leader*, 9 February 1952.
[6] *Ibid.*, 5 June 1954. See also 'Caon Todhchai Fhianna Fáil' (What future for Fianna Fáil?), *Leader*, 9 July 1955.
[7] Longford and O'Neill, *De Valera*, p. 445; *Irish Times*, 22 November 1958.
[8] *Irish Times*, 17 June 1938; *Irish Press*, 10 May 1943, 30 September 1943.

Fianna Fáil would be assured, as the largest single party, of massive parliamentary majorities, even with much less than half the vote. De Valera accordingly proposed to replace proportional representation by the straight vote.

He repeated the tactic of 1937, holding the referendum on the same day as the presidential election, 17 June 1959. In 1937 the referendum had been intended to pull the election in its wake. Now the election was intended to pull the referendum in its train. The tactic almost worked. But not quite. The public, who elected him president by 538 000 to 418 000 for Seán MacEoin, simultaneously rejected the proposal to abolish proportional representation by 487 000 to 453 000 votes. Slender though the margin was, the electorate's ability to detect a distinction between the two issues lent some credence to a leader writer's comment that 'Irish democracy has come of age; its political maturity is no longer in doubt.'[9] It is not recorded whether de Valera, who had already resigned as Taoiseach on the day of the election, before the announcement of the results, derived consolation from that reflection.

It may safely be predicted that the paradoxes of de Valera will intrigue historians for generations to come. Exploration of the recesses of that cavernous mind reveals ever more complex, ever more fascinating, formations. Born to an emigrant mother in America who sent him back to Ireland at the age of two when she lost her husband, he would bear the scars of maternal rejection throughout his life. As John Montague, poignantly recalling a later Brooklyn birth, would put it,

> All roads wind backwards to it.
> An unwanted child, a primal hurt.[10]

But de Valera would show little compassion for his mother's plight, enshrining in his constitution an image of womanhood that simultaneously exalted and confined woman to the condition of a mother living happily ever after. Reared in an agricultural labourer's cottage, by an uncle with labourer loyalties,[11] he sublimated the bitter social resentments of rural Limerick in a bland arcadian image of an ideal Ireland.[12] His life's journey could be entitled 'from labourer's cottage to presidential residence'. But he refused to invest this with ideological significance, despite his genuine sympathy for the poor.

A teacher by training, he virtually ignored education throughout his

9 *Irish Times*, 20 June 1959.
10 John Montague, *The dead kingdom* (Mountrath, 1984), p. 90.
11 T.P. Ó Néill agus P. Ó Fiannachta, *De Valera* (Dublin, 1968), p. 5.
12 On farmer–labourer tensions, see D.G. Bradley, 'The organisation of agricultural labourers in Ireland 1900–1976' (MA thesis, University College, Cork, 1984); E. O'Connor, 'Agrarian unrest', pp. 40–58; Limerick Rural Survey, *Third Interim Report, Social Structure* (Tipperary, 1962), chs. 3 and 4; NLI, MS 8342, Schrier collection, J.F. Costello to his parents, 11 January 1883.

political career, for all his firm personal views on pedagogic techniques, and on the proper role of education in society.[13] Chancellor of the National University of Ireland for fifty years, father of three professors in that university, the inadequacy of the resources his government devoted to higher education helped sabotage the pursuit of that intellectual excellence which would seem to be a prerequisite for fostering the cultivation of the mind that he was so fond of proclaiming as Ireland's mission in the modern world. Nevertheless, while neglecting all universities, he insisted that Trinity College should not be disproportionately neglected, in contrast to the meaner thinking of Costello and McGilligan during the first inter-party government.[14] His 1937 constitution allocated a prominent place to a 'cultural panel' in the Senate elections – and then he would insist on adopting so elastic a definition of culture as to demean the very concept!

The man who urged the Supreme Council of Sinn Féin in 1917 to 'smother every petty or selfish interest' and to 'taboo the chicanery, the intrigues and the cliques which are the characteristics of modern party machined politics',[15] came in due course to preside over the most professional machine Irish politics had yet seen, its multiple 'mafias' flourishing under the benignly blind gaze of the Incorruptible. Correctly resisting pressure to dismiss pro-Treaty civil servants and army officers when he came to power in 1932, he encouraged the gradual growth of an insidious, if initially discreet, spoils system in the army, the police, the judiciary, and the state sponsored bodies. He devised an electoral system for the Senate that invited corruption, and responded to pleas for reform by delicately holding his nostrils. Like his countrymen in general, he combined a rigid concept of private morality with a more selective one of public morality. He could never be flexible on a moral issue. Therefore, any issue on which he found it necessary to be flexible could not, by definition, be a moral issue. Protected from the contagion of evidence by the metallic carapace of his self-righteousness, he had the invaluable capacity of assuming that what he did not wish to see did not exist. Incapable of hypocrisy, he had a highly refined capacity for self-deception.

De Valera's authorised biographers tell us that he advised Dick Mulcahy in 1919 'that if he entered politics he should study Machiavelli and read economics'.[16] He cannot himself have devoted much time to economics. But neither can he be classified as a Machiavellian, instinctively familiar with the distinction between *virtù* and virtue though he

---

[13] J. Coolahan, 'De Valera's impact on education', *Irish Times*, 1 November 1982; Moynihan, *Speeches*, pp. 425–9; O'Connell, *INTO*, p. 206.
[14] R.B. MacDowell and D.A. Webb, *Trinity College Dublin 1592–1952* (Cambridge, 1982), p. 479; McCartney, *De Valera*, pp. 38–40.
[15] Moynihan, *Speeches*, p. 12.   [16] Longford and O'Neill, *De Valera*, p. 88.

would show himself to be.[17] An adroit tactician, a master of international and interpersonal relations, he swooped with exquisitely sensitive 'antennae of instinct' when opportunity offered for quick electoral or diplomatic kills, as in the snap elections of 1933, 1938 and 1944, and in the abdication crisis of 1936. Tactical skill and a sense of timing were the main prerequisites for mastery of the electoral and diplomatic games. When he confronted more stubborn issues, like partition, or the revival of the language, that could not be solved by guile, he floundered. When he found opponents as crafty and as committed as himself in James Craig and Basil Brooke, he had no answer.

He had no more idea of how to revive the language than of how to achieve unification. In 1939 he could assert that the people were wholly behind the revival policy, and 'all that we require is a suitable scheme'. Alas, 'no such scheme has come to my notice'.[18] Nor would it. A decade later he had to tell the Dáil that 'The restoration of the language depends more upon the attitude of the people outside than upon the attitude of the public representatives . . . it was not one of those things which the government can do by a wave of the wand.'[19] But 'the public representatives' did have some influence on 'the people outside'. The fact that his own party ignored the language closest to their chief's heart was not lost on the plain people. It is possible that de Valera's commitment postponed the apparently terminal decline of the language.[20] One is nevertheless confronted with the inability of the man who dominated the policy-making process, and whose personal devotion cannot be doubted, to carry the cause dearest to his own heart, even within his own party. He could not induce even his own cabinet to speak the language regularly. It is not clear how hard he tried.[21] The language could not be revived by constitutional formulae. Restoration required the application of sustained intelligence and relentless willpower. Incantation was no substitute for intelligence. His revealing metaphor, 'a wave of the wand', invoked a technique that he applied astutely in diplomatic and electoral matters. When the revival could not be achieved through this brand of magic, he had no solution.

It was only through mastering the economic problems of emigration and unemployment that de Valera could hope to build a viable society, Gaelic or otherwise. One reason for his failure to achieve so many of his political, cultural and social ideals lay in his truly profound ignorance of economics. Economic expertise provides no guarantee of policy success.

---

17 For a subtle disquisition dismissing the charge of Machiavellianism against de Valera, see 'Tact and foreign policy', *Leader*, 27 September 1952.
18 *Irish Press*, 1 April 1939.   19 Quoted in Farrell, *Chairman or chief?*, p. 29.
20 T.P. Ó'Néill, 'Eamon de Valera agus an teanga', *Feasta*, 35, 10 (October 1922), p. 26.
21 Further research is required into the extent of de Valera's effort to gaelicise the Fianna Fáil leadership.

In modern circumstances, however, economic ignorance condemns policy to almost certain failure. This ignorance suffused his famous 'dream' broadcast of St Patrick's Day 1943:

The Ireland which we have dreamed of would be the home of a people who valued material wealth only as a basis of right living, of a people who were satisfied with frugal comfort and devoted their leisure to things of the spirit; a land whose countryside would be bright with cosy homesteads, whose fields and villages would be joyous with the sounds of industry, with the romping of sturdy children, the contests of athletic youths, the laughter of comely maidens; whose firesides would be forums for the wisdom of serene old age. It would, in a word, be the home of a people living the life that God desires that men should live.[22]

De Valera regularly professed to know, not only what the people wanted, but what God himself wanted. God's ideal social order frequently surfaced in his thinking, especially when Fianna Fáil was locked in a close election race. The invocation of divine authority on this occasion serves to disguise the fact that much of the broadcast was an election speech masquerading in the guise of a festival homily. A general election had to be held within three months. The party conventions were already selecting candidates. The auguries for Fianna Fáil were unpropitious. The public mind had to be diverted from the discontents of wartime austerity, and particularly from the agrarian blandishments of the new party, Clann na Talmhan, which threatened to seduce small farmers from Fianna Fáil. A classic combination of the spiritually sublime and the electorally mercenary, the address nevertheless distilled the essence of de Valera's social ideals. His vision was heavily influenced by the aspirations of the agricultural labourer class from which he sprang, and which envied as a veritable utopia the apparent security of the small farmer.

De Valera's 'dream' has sometimes been derisively dismissed as impossibly 'naïve'. But there was nothing necessarily wrong about it. It is a matter of taste as to how his ideal society compares with rival visions. De Valera realised well enough that the dream deviated widely from existing reality.[23] The legitimate criticism of the 'dream' was not that it was naïve, but that de Valera not only had no idea how to move the existing reality in the direction of his ideal, but that many of his policies directly subverted it.

De Valera's 'dream' Ireland had never existed. The Irish people would come increasingly to enjoy the fruits of 'the wisdom of serene old age' as de Valera himself aged. Those fruits would wither on the tree. There would be fewer and fewer 'sturdy children' to romp in a wasting society. There would indeed be 'contests of athletic youths' – on the building sites of Britain, where 'McAlpine's God was a well-filled hod'. Not only would

22 Moynihan, *Speeches*, p. 466.
23 See his speech of 7 July 1939 on the Report of the Banking Commission, in Moynihan, *Speeches*, pp. 401–4, for a frequently accurate description of rural reality.

emigration soon reach levels unprecedented in the twentieth century, but Ireland would boast the highest rate of female emigration of any European country between 1945 and 1960. If the comely maidens would laugh, it would be the bitter sweet laugh of liberation through emigration from a sterile society where the Bridies left behind would be glad to settle, their girlhood dreams dashed, for the Bowser Egans.

In the bright dawn of 1934 de Valera had envisaged the day when the nation's children would no longer be reared for export. But that was what more and more of them would be brought up for as his regime tottered to its close. Himself reared in a family decimated by emigration,[24] he had no idea what to do. His monument was now to be found not in the cosy homesteads, but in the deserted homesteads, of the Irish countryside.

The disillusioned, and there were many, had grounds for claiming by 1959 that one need only apply to de Valera the acid test, 'if you seek my monument, look around you'. And there is a temptation to remark of de Valera, as the *Irish Times* remarked of Sir Edward Carson, that his career was 'crammed with great achievements, and yet strangely barren of great results'.[25] That temptation should be resisted. It fails to place his record in true historical perspective.

Political civilisation is a fragile plant. It needs constant tending in every generation. Even the blinkers of self-righteousness which de Valera habitually wore could not blind him to the potential for bestiality in the war of independence and the civil war. He was determined to integrate as far as possible under the civilising mantle of Fianna Fáil the potential perpetrators of what he now considered to be mindless violence. He sought to limit further futile violence after 1926 through a combination of emotional and material incentives, dispensed through the largesse of Fianna Fáil. He largely succeeded for his generation and for some time beyond.

As the focal point of public emotions through his ability to inspire love and hate, de Valera contributed to the stability of the new state after 1924.[26] The polarisation of politics around de Valera has been deplored, it is true, on the grounds that it led to the fossilisation of political life for nearly two generations. The implicit assumption that only the congealing of politics into their civil war mould prevented a 'natural' left—right division emerging, and then, through some mysterious osmosis by which the right disappears, the creation of an enlightened liberal (or is it socialist?) state, is a highly dubious one. It is more plausible to argue, given the nature of the political culture, that the alternative would have

[24] Ó Néill agus Ó Fiannachta, *De Valera*, pp. 1–3.   [25] *Irish Times*, 23 October 1935.
[26] For his 'bonding power' on the opposition, see Mary Ann Valiulis, '"The man they could never forgive": the view of the opposition: Eamon de Valera and the civil war', in O'Carroll and Murphy, *De Valera*, pp. 92–100.

been a more conservative, not to say reactionary, regime, founded on factionalism, as was indeed sometimes the case at the more primitive levels of local government. And the rise of Fianna Fáil may well have prevented the fragmentation of the party system into mere factionalism. In the election of June 1927, immediately prior to Fianna Fáil's entry to the Dáil, the two main parties secured only 53.6 per cent of the valid poll. The drift towards factionalism was immediately reversed once Fianna Fáil entered the Dáil. In the September 1927 election, the two main parties won 73.9 per cent of the vote.

A great party, any great party, irrespective of its policies, of its follies, or perhaps even of its crimes – as long as these are incidental to, and not inherent in, its philosophy – has an essential integrating role to play in society, however distasteful the fastidious observer may find the techniques of integration. It was the success of Fianna Fáil in becoming a dominant party that ensured the viability of the system. Stability depended in large measure on the effectiveness of the originally anti-system party. It is not the least of the ironies of the history of Fianna Fáil that a party dedicated to the destruction of the constitution of the Free State should by its very success have contributed to legitimising the broader political order of the new state.

De Valera led the party he founded with superb tactical judgement. 'The unity of the party' was not a central value of the political culture. The Home Rule party split. The Irish Volunteers split. Sinn Féin split. The IRA split. The Transport Union split. Clann na Poblachta split. De Valera was himself at the centre of the two great Sinn Féin splits, the Treaty split in 1921, and the Oath split in 1926. As leader of Fianna Fáil he was determined that no one should ever do a de Valera on him. His ability to bond together the coalition of disparate elements that he moulded into a single movement after 1926 was quite remarkable. Fianna Fáil became a beautifully nubile instrument of state integration, becoming a constructive, stabilising element in Irish politics, imposing a collective self-discipline on its members that few would have dreamed of imposing individually on themselves. That its unity should so soon be taken for granted is the supreme tribute to the integrating power of the personality, and the policy, of its leader.

De Valera's style as leader revealed something of his concept of politics. He usually nominated his ministers without consulting his colleagues.[27] But there was a curious contrast between his style of appointment and his style of government. Once he selected his ministers, he strove to secure unanimity in cabinet decisions. He spent an enormous amount of cabinet time simply wearing down opposition, even minority opposition, rather

---

[27]	Farrell, *Chairman or chief?*, pp. 27–8, 35–6.

than taking a vote after due discussion, as Lemass later preferred to do.[28] It was more the politics than the merits of decisions that preoccupied him. Or rather, haunted by fear of faction, he tended to equate the two. Some of the same considerations affected his choice of cabinet colleagues. Not only did he cling to the same ministers year after year, long after the necessity of establishing Fianna Fáil as a stable government had passed. It is doubtful if he would have made significant changes at all but for the outbreak of the Second World War. Only twenty-two men held minister-ial office in his governments between 1932 and 1954. Five of his changes were forced on him by death or illness.

Like many lonely men, de Valera craved the reassurance of familiar faces. It was therefore unfortunate that his judgement was sometimes uncertain, even if Lemass was only partly right in contending that de Valera 'was not the best of judges of the capacity of individuals to do particular categories of work'.[29] For de Valera's touch was often superb in making appointments to posts that demanded essentially qualities of personality and character, like Aiken to Defence in 1932, Boland to Justice in 1939, Ryan to Health in 1951, Aiken to External Affairs in 1951, and above all, Maurice Moynihan to the Secretaryship of his Department in 1937. But his touch was less sure in appointments to posts in which qualities of intellect were as necessary as those of character. The choice of Lemass for Industry and Commerce may be contrasted with that of Derrig for Education in 1932 – though Derrig was admittedly only second choice[30] – or MacEntee for Finance in 1951.

Possessed of a penetrating but narrow intelligence, de Valera showed little understanding of the technical links between various aspects of policy, failing to see the implications of policies (as distinct from politics) in one field for policies in others. The most serious criticism of de Valera is not that he failed to achieve so many of his goals. Rather it is that the means he adopted often sabotaged his own most cherished ideals. He never related his social vision of an arcadian utopia or his cultural vision of a Gaelic Ireland to his political vision of a united Ireland. His dream of the frugal fare of the small farm held no place for the Shankill or even for the Falls.

De Valera naturally remained to an extent the prisoner of the coalition of elements that he welded together to form Fianna Fáil. A generous and perceptive obituary by a political opponent even suggests that criticism of de Valera from the perspective of the present 'missed the point . . . as to the limitations imposed by the material in which the *Statesman* has to work. He can only do what is possible for him with his kind of party, and,

---

[28] *Ibid.*, p. 30; Longford and O'Neill, *De Valera*, pp. 331–2; Seán MacEntee's obituary of de Valera, *Irish Press*, 30 August 1975.
[29] Farrell, *Chairman or chief?*, p. 28.   [30] O'Connell, *INTO*. pp. 208–9.

perhaps, the quite different strains of support he enjoys at the time he does it.'[31] There is truth in this. But it does raise the question of how far de Valera can avoid responsibility for the nature of the 'material' with which he worked. Master of the ageless aboriginal arts of politics, he seems to have taken his raw material as given, and to have assumed that it was impervious to improvement. It could not be educated. It could only be manipulated.

He was a marvellous manipulator of private and public minds, of individual and collective mentalities. He manipulated the past, as he fashioned his version of a folk ideology as a powerful political weapon.[32] He manipulated the future to redress the balance of the present through successive revelations of his political visions. Above all, he manipulated words. The modifications made by him, or under his direction, to the text of the 1922 constitution when devising his revised version provide numerous examples of his feline feel for words. Article after article was revised, though usually only marginally. But marginal differences mattered enormously to de Valera. The stamp of a mind that could insist that the differences between Document No. 2 and the Treaty justified a civil war marked his approach towards every statement of principle. One example must suffice here. Article 9 of the 1922 constitution granted citizens 'the right of free expression of opinion'. The 1937 constitution revised this provision, in Article 40, to guarantee 'the right of citizens to express freely their convictions and opinions'. As a connoisseur of the culture of malleable misrepresentation, de Valera would have been sensitive to the distinction between conviction and opinion in a culture that invested so much effort in refining the arts of verbal circumlocution. The difference was sufficiently important to deserve constitutional safeguard!

It seems somehow sad that so much managerial skill, so much imaginative use of symbolism,[33] such choreographical control of the political dance, so much insight into human nature – into its strengths as well as into its weaknesses – should have been extended in no better cause than mere survival. But then de Valera could well have equated survival with success, calculating that survival, with its attendant stability, would itself silently shift political perspectives. If we were to adopt the Mackenzie King dictum that 'In politics, it is not what you do but what you prevent that counts,' then de Valera would rank very high indeed. But King, of course, was speaking in a country enjoying a powerful natural developmental and expansionist surge.

[31] Alexis Fitzgerald, 'De Valera', *Studies*, 64 (Autumn 1975), p. 210.
[32] G. Ó Crualaoich, 'The primacy of form: a "folk ideology", in de Valera's politics', in O'Carroll and Murphy, *De Valera*, pp. 47–61.
[33] O'Carroll, 'Eamon de Valera', pp. 17–34.

A supreme pragmatist in many respects, de Valera succeeded in shrouding his pragmatism in a cloak of immaculate idealism. A mathematician for whom the shortest distance between any two points on the political map was a semi-circle, he nonetheless conveyed the impression that he, and only he, clung undeviatingly to the straight line. The 'secular sermons' of the 'sacerdotal heron'[34] fulfilled so fully the psychological needs of so many of the party faithful, that his image flourished almost independently of his words, careful a craftsman though he was in the medium of language. He insisted as early as 1921 that he was no doctrinaire.[35] He interpreted politics as 'the art of the possible', to the extent of sprinkling the basic documents of his career, including the founding charter of Fianna Fáil, and the constitution of 1937, with the phrases 'as far as possible' or 'as far as is practicable' (in the Irish version, *an oiread is féidir*).

By the 1930s de Valera's behaviour was entirely consonant with the conviction that

> Civilisation is hooped together, brought
> Under a rule, under the semblance of peace,
> By manifold illusion.[36]

His concept of politics now seemed to conform to the classic Oakeshottian description:

In political activity, then, men sail a boundless and bottomless sea; there is neither harbour for shelter nor floor for anchorage, neither starting place nor appointed destination. The enterprise is to keep afloat on an even keel; the sea is both friend and enemy; and the seamanship consists in using the resources of a traditional manner of behaviour in order to make a friend of every hostile occasion.[37]

Yet, so extraordinary was his capacity for projecting a transcendental image that he long contrived to convince crew and passengers alike that the promised land lay just beyond the horizon.

Sean O'Faolain, in his passionate disillusion with the de Valera of the 1940s, hesitated to call him a great man. He was, said O'Faolain, merely a great Irishman, and there was a world of difference between permissive Irish criteria and universal standards of greatness.[38] Malcolm MacDonald too, while considering him 'the most consistent and honest statesman in his adherence to policies and principles whom I have known in any part of the world', insisted that 'he is not an international giant, only a national one'.[39] And it is true that his political intelligence was neither as wide nor

---

34 John A. Murphy, 'The achievement of Eamon de Valera', in O'Carroll and Murphy, *De Valera*, p. 7; Montague, 'A change of management', in Montague, *Death of a chieftain and other essays* (Dublin, 1978 edn), p. 97.
35 Moynihan, *Speeches*, p. 70.
36 W.B. Yeats, *Collected Poems* (London, 1971 edn), p. 333.
37 M. Oakeshott, *Rationalism in politics* (London, 1962), p. 127.
38 S. O'Faolain, 'Eamon de Valera', *The Bell*, 10, 1 (1945), p. 8.
39 M. MacDonald, *Titans and others* (London, 1972), p. 86.

as profound – only as sharp – as that of de Gaulle or of Gladstone, with whom he is sometimes misguidedly compared. We can only speculate what he might have encompassed had he but had the opportunity of sitting with the young Gladstone at the feet of Mr Biscoe in the room next to the great staircase in Christ Church, or even of matching the young de Gaulle stride for stride in St Cyr. But greatness cannot be an absolute concept. A man's stature has to be assessed in relation to the standards of his own society, and the calibre of the culture in which he operates. O'Faolain's criticism is less a reflection on de Valera than on Ireland. De Valera is entitled to be judged by the only standards with which he could reasonably be expected to be familiar. By those standards he has an indubitable claim to greatness.

Whatever the comparative criteria, de Valera did not abuse his trust as leader throughout his long public life. He revelled in the cult of 'The Chief'. But he used it primarily for party and national purposes. He never chose to invest it with the sinister contemporary connotations of Führer, or even the downmarket version of Duce. In few countries has so powerful a personality cult proved so relatively harmless as in de Valera's Ireland. That owed much to the personality of the leader himself. He showed courage in adversity, fortitude in defeat, correctness in victory, and at all times an adamantine strength of will. He bore his blindness with stoical resignation. He could rise to moments of real dignity, as in his rebuke to the hymn-singing 'anti-communist' hooligans in Dublin in 1934, in his reply to Churchill in 1945, in his dismissal of the Fethard-on-Sea boycott of Protestants in 1957,[40] and in rising from his own sickbed at the age of eighty-three to pay homage to Roger Casement, his comrade of fifty years before, on his internment in Irish soil in 1966. He died, we are assured on unimpeachable authority, as indeed he had lived, with 'a certain grandeur'.[41]

De Valera was, in a sense, greater than the sum of his parts. Behind the ceaseless political calculation and the labyrinthine deviousness, there reposed a character of rare nobility. His qualities would have made him a leader beyond compare in the pre-industrial world. It was in one sense his misfortune that his career should coincide with an age of accelerated economic change whose causes and consequences largely baffled him. But there are times in history when the stature of public men depends on what they are no less than on what they do. That was arguably the case in Ireland for at least the first generation of independence. No modern state in Irish circumstances could flourish under a succession of de Valeras. But a small nation that 'could never be got to accept defeat and has never surrendered her soul',[42] words that still held meaning when he spoke them

[40] DD, 163, 4 July 1957, 731.   [41] James Kavanagh, 'Social policy', p. 325.
[42] Moynihan, *Speeches*, p. 476.

in 1945, indeed held meaning largely because it was he who spoke them, should speak his name with pride.[43]

Seán Lemass succeeded de Valera without a leadership struggle. His succession was finally assured when his main potential rival, MacEntee, was discredited by his association with the unsuccessful policies of the previous Fianna Fáil administration. If the succession was smooth, the inheritance was not. The crisis confronted by the new government in 1957 was so severe that any measures it could take were unlikely to make a significant impact before the next election. Fianna Fáil was therefore virtually certain to lose seats even had de Valera remained. And there was no guarantee that Fianna Fáil could now succeed where all parties, including itself, had already conspicuously failed.

But circumstances were also in some respects more promising, at least from a Lemass perspective. 'Only a severe jolt is likely to alter "the politics of Irish economics"', a prescient observer predicted in 1953.[44] The 'severe jolt' soon came. The mood of deepening despair that spread during the mid-fifties gave Lemass more opportunity to slaughter sacred cows, including some of his own breeding, than had been the case a few years before. He now found a more receptive attitude towards change in key sectors of the public service. Younger officers in the service established the Association of Higher Civil Servants in 1952. The following year they launched the periodical *Administration* to provide, for the first time, some perspective on their own work. In 1953 too, Patrick Lynch's seminal paper, 'The economist and public policy'[45] raised key issues and focused attention inescapably on a crucial factor, the quality of the official mind. This was a subversive and lethal assault on the quality of existing thought, but presented with sufficient diplomatic finesse to make it difficult for the immediate targets to express public indignation. The Institute of Public Administration, for which Lynch called in 1952, was established in 1957, with Tom Barrington as director, to provide a forum for sustained

[43] In addition to the sources cited, this appraisal of de Valera takes cognizance of C.S. Andrews, *Man of no property* (Dublin, 1982), pp. 230–7; Anthony Cronin, 'Dev contra mundum', *Irish Times*, 5 September 1975; Garret FitzGerald, 'De Valera', 229–48; F.S.L. Lyons, 'Symbol of the era he bestrode', in *Irish Times* publication, *Eamon de Valera 1882–1975* (Dublin, 1976), pp. 93–8; Patrick O'Donovan, 'De Valera, the Irish de Gaulle', *Observer*, 31 August 1975; J. Bowman, 'Eamon de Valera: seven lives', in O'Carroll and Murphy, *De Valera*, pp. 182–94. I have learnt much from Owen Dudley Edwards, *Éamon de Valera* (Cardiff 1987) which the author kindly made available to me in manuscript.

[44] T.D. Williams, quoted in Bew and Patterson, *Lemass*, p. 77.

[45] P. Lynch, 'The economist and public policy', *Studies*, 42 (Autumn 1953), pp. 241–60. Lynch was presumably the author of an anonymous contribution with much the same message. 'The civil service and its critics', *Leader*, 27 September 1952.

self-appraisal. In personality terms, the change within the service was crystallised in the rise of T.K. Whitaker.

Whitaker combined exceptional ability with exceptional dedication. He belonged to the second generation of civil servants who entered in the 1930s rather than in the halcyon promotion years of the early 1920s. Indecently rapid though his progress appeared to more senior colleagues, he still had to proceed more slowly than the first generation, who found the plums dropping into their laps through happy circumstances. Whitaker had sufficient initiative to take an external degree from London University and sufficient imagination to take that degree in economics.[46] Whitaker has of course become identified with the transformation of economic policy in the late 1950s. It is far from clear, however, that Gerard Sweetman, who recommended Whitaker's promotion over the head of G.P.S. Hogan, the next in line when Owen Redmond retired after his three years as Secretary of Finance in 1956, intended the consequences. Nothing testifies more to the 'severe jolt' than the fact that career prospects in the public service should actually be jeopardised as a result! Whatever the role of Patrick McGilligan in the appointment,[47] it seems likely that Sweetman, a vigorous conservative, recommended Whitaker on the assumption that he would pursue a policy of 'thorough'. And Whitaker did precisely this during his first year in office, with the sharply restrictive July measures of 1956, and the far from reflationary budget of May 1957.

Whitaker at this stage appeared outstanding more for his energy and intellectual power than for imagination. He brought, however, in addition to a patriotism as dedicated as McElligott's, two further important qualities to his task, a feel for administrative politics, and a striking ability to learn. Above all, he possessed 'the intellectual capacity to respond to ideas', which Patrick Lynch had rightly emphasised as a crucial quality of the great public servant.[48] Where Brennan and McElligott lacked the calibre of mind to adapt to changing circumstances, Whitaker's willingness to adapt his views in the light of new evidence was one characteristic he shared to the full with Lemass. Already on the eve of his appointment, his paper to the Statistical Society, 'Capital formation, saving and economic progress', reflected a more ambitious concept of the responsibility of a Finance official for economic development than the incantation of eternal verities.[49] The introductory admonition in *Economic Development*, the 1958 report with which his name would be indelibly associated, that 'the greatest fault lies in pursuing a policy after it has proved to be

---

46 For Whitaker's departmental career see Fanning, *Finance*, p. 504.   47 *Ibid.*
48 Lynch, 'The economist', as reprinted in B. Chubb and P. Lynch (eds.), *Economic development and planning* (Dublin, 1969), p. 24.
49 Fanning, *Finance*, pp. 502–3.

unsuitable or ineffective',[50] could be read as a discreet rebuke not only to McElligott and Lemass, if for different reasons, but perhaps even to the younger Whitaker.

The growing ascendancy of Lemass after 1957 posed two problems for Whitaker, one departmental, one intellectual. Whitaker had spent much of his career criticising Industry and Commerce proposals. He knew how sternly the departmental struggle had been waged. Lemass, long frustrated with Finance, might well attempt to make Industry and Commerce, or the Department of the Taoiseach, or a new department entirely – he might still hanker after his wartime dream of a super ministry of labour – central to the formulation of economic policy. Whitaker had not become Secretary of Finance to preside over the decline of the premier Department. It was therefore necessary in terms of administrative politics to seize the initiative for Finance with a positive approach. The Capital Investment Advisory Committee, established in late 1956, came, it would appear, as a nasty surprise for Finance. This seems to have been established by the cabinet, and to have had the bulk of its membership nominated without reference to Finance.[51] Neither the chairman, John Leydon, who had resigned as Secretary of Industry and Commerce in 1956, nor the two young economists on the committee, Patrick Lynch and Louden Ryan, were likely to display an excessive reverence for the traditional Finance approach. Already in May 1957, Whitaker was urging his Assistant Secretaries that it was desirable 'that this Department should do some independent thinking and not simply wait for Industry and Commerce or the IDA to produce ideas'.[52] The same sentiment recurs in his minute of 12 December 1957 to Jim Ryan, requesting authorisation 'to work out an integrated programme of national development for the next five or ten years'.[53] 'The central position of the Department of Finance gives us a special responsibility for studying how economic progress can be promoted', he assured his minister, not an observation hitherto associated with Finance.[54] Little wonder that Garret FitzGerald interpreted *Economic Development*, when it appeared the following year, as 'the snatching by the Department of Finance of the initiative in planning'.[55]

If Whitaker felt it necessary to cover his institutional flanks, he may also have sought – the evidence here is necessarily more inferential – to head off a Lemass who might still have sufficient of the gambler in him to launch what Whitaker would regard as half-baked initiatives. Several conclusions in *Economic Development* can be read as an implicit rejection of the familiar Lemass approach. 'It would have been quite unreal to

[50] *Economic Development* (Dublin, 1958), pp. 5–6.   [51] Fanning, *Finance*, p. 507.
[52] *Ibid.*, p. 509.   [53] *Economic Development*, p. 227.   [54] *Ibid.*, p. 228.
[55] 'Analyst', *Irish Times*, 25 November 1958.

approach the question of development from the aspect of employment, that is by setting out the number of jobs required and then attempting to plan how these might be created', Whitaker insisted. 'There would be nothing to be gained by setting up fanciful employment targets; failure to reach such targets would only produce disillusionment'.[56] As this was a standard Lemass approach – his 1955 Clerys speech, ominously reprinted in the *Sunday Press* in January 1957, insisted that at least 15 000 jobs a year must be created[57] – it may be surmised that Whitaker felt concern at the prospect of an unbridled Lemass lashing out in desperation if the civil service could not supply him with the weapons he would demand.

In addition, it was only natural for the 40-year-old Whitaker to want to 'justify' his promotion 'over the head' of longer serving colleagues. While the 'successor-in-waiting', Sarsfield Hogan, 'accepted Whitaker's promotion with a gentlemanly generosity',[58] the fact that this was regarded as worthy of note is itself indicative of the prevailing civil service ethos, and the widespread assumption of senior officials that they enjoyed 'property rights' in promotion prospects. It would be surprising if there were no mutterings, not only in Finance, but in other departments. Whitaker can have entertained little private doubt about his clear superiority to the vast majority of his colleagues, whether in Finance or elsewhere. 'A great deed' would not silence his detractors. But it would help expose their pettiness and win for him more secure authority. It is clear from his 'Capital formation' paper that his mind was already moving in the direction of *Economic Development*. But the timing and the philosophy of the 'Grey Book', as it came to be called, were partly in the nature of a pre-emptive strike against critics of his Department, his policy, and himself.

Economic Development, completed in May 1958, became the basis for the White Paper published on 12 November 1958, *Programme for economic expansion*. The *Programme*, now usually referred to as the *First programme*, was rather more orientated towards industry than *Economic Development*, and there are sufficient differences in detail and in emphasis to titillate the connoisseur of the policy process until the archives are opened. Nevertheless, the *Programme* owed its inspiration to *Economic Development*, which was itself published on 22 November.

Four features make *Economic Development* and the *First programme* historic documents. Firstly, the content, signalling a shift from protection towards free trade, and from discouragement to encouragement of foreign investment in Ireland, involved a dramatic reversal of the rhetoric, and to a large extent of the practice, of all policy, but especially Fianna Fáil policy, since 1932. The IDA, it is true, was supposed to foster the import

[56] *Economic Development*. pp. 206–7.　　　[57] *Sunday Press*, 18 January 1957.
[58] Quoted in Fanning, *Finance* p. 504.

of foreign enterprise. The Control of Manufacturers' Acts were still in force, however, and the IDA was rather left floundering in the general economic morass of the decade. *Economic Development* also signalled a virtual return to Paddy Hogan's policy, with its emphasis on the primacy of an export-oriented agriculture.[59] The *First programme* was more inconsistent in this respect, presumably in obeisance to the sensitivities of de Valera and the scepticism of Lemass.[60]

Not only do sections of *Economic Development* sound reminiscent of Hogan. The basic Whitaker proposal, broadly endorsed by the *First programme*, to shift public expenditure from 'social' to 'productive' investment, initially by reducing expenditure on housing, seemed at first sight undiluted McElligott. And there was much of McElligott in it. The difference lay partly in the psychology of the presentation, and partly in the specification of a five-year investment programme. By substituting the specific target of a 2 per cent annual growth rate, over a five-year period, in place of familiar Finance exhortations for the country to wrap the hair shirt tightly around it – or rather for the poor to wrap their hair shirts more tightly around them – Whitaker and Lemass managed to present a rather bleak prospect as a glimpse of the promised land. The *Programme for economic expansion*, as its very title indicated, was presented to the public as a calculated wager on growth, not as a purgative exercise which might, at some uncertain distant date, be followed by recuperation. The problem with the traditional Finance approach was not primarily its obsession with fiscal rectitude. Even the budgets of MacEntee and Sweetman could probably be justified in the short term, although the 1952 budget almost certainly erred on the side of excessive and damaging severity. The real problem was that Finance had no idea what to do with fiscal rectitude. It assumed that if it looked after the finances, the economy would look after itself. It wouldn't, and it didn't.

The Finance perspective was even more myopic than that of the politicians, who at least often looked as far ahead as the next election. Finance gave the impression that it rarely looked beyond the next budget. *Economic Development* contained a good deal of traditional Finance thinking. But its angle of approach transcended the conventional wisdom of the official mind. Whitaker's minute of 12 December 1957 contained the secret:

What is urgently necessary is *not* to know that more resources should be devoted to productive rather than non-productive purposes but rather to know what are the productive purposes to which resources should be applied and what unproductive, or relatively unproductive, activities can, with the minimum social disadvantage, be curtailed to set free resources for productive development.[61]

59 *Economic Development*, p. 20.
60 Compare, for instance, paras 13 and 49 of *Programme for economic expansion*.
61 *Economic Development*, p. 227.

This one impatient sentence marked the transition of Finance from the age of faith to the age of reason.

In the event, reason received a powerful boost from additional injections of investment as the policy unfolded. The projected public investment for 1959–64 came to £220 million. The actual investment amounted to £297 million, an increase of 35 per cent.[62] But the general balance between 'social' and 'economic' expenditure was not revised. If anything, the additional 'economic' expenditure proportionately exceeded the additional 'social' investment.

The full story of the *First programme* cannot be told until we know much more about the manner in which the original investment intentions were modified, and modified in a quite expansionist direction, after 1959. The modifications presumably partly reflect its own psychological impact, which succeeded in substituting hope for despair, not least among the policy-makers themselves. Where the *First programme* insisted that 'any tendency for consumer spending to cause an external payment deficit . . . will be checked',[63] even its most severe critics acknowledge that after 1959 the government showed 'a much bolder approach to demand management and a greater willingness to take risks with the balance of payments in the determination to maintain a higher rate of growth of aggregate output'.[64] Already in 1959 the authorities indicated to the OEEC their determination to meet the next balance of payments crisis through depletion of the reserves rather than through deflationary measures.[65] Policy formulation at last smashed the strait-jacket of the balance of payments.

The publication of *Economic Development* was an essential part of the psychological campaign waged by the government. Whitaker had protested in 1953 that the real quality of the Finance mind was to be found in 'the minutes and oral discussions' rather than in 'White Papers or other means of commending policy decisions to the public.'[66] He had in the meantime come to endorse Patrick Lynch's perceptive observation that

There can be no doubt that public confidence in the administrative machinery of the state and in the capacity and judgement of its personnel would be immeasurably strengthened if the facts and conditions on which policy decisions are based were frankly and fully disclosed to the public by means of an extended system of departmental White Papers or otherwise.[67]

62 Meenan, *Irish economy*, pp. 260–1.
63 *Programme for economic expansion*, para. 10.
64 Kennedy and Dowling, *Economic growth*, pp. 232.
65 OEEC, *Ireland*, 1960 (Paris, 1960), p. 26.
66 T.K. Whitaker, 'The Finance attitude', *Administration*, 2, 3 (1953), reprinted in Chubb and Lynch, *Development*, p. 43.
67 Lynch, 'Public policy', in Chubb and Lynch, *Development*, p. 22.

Marginalia were not enough. The publication of *Economic Development* did reinforce confidence in the *Programme*. The *Irish Independent*, the biggest mass circulation daily, thought the *Programme* too ambitious, but greeted the 'masterly' *Economic Development* in glowing terms.[68] Whitaker's success encouraged him to take the public more into his confidence, during his thirteen-year tenure as Secretary of Finance, than any of his predecessors, or indeed any of his successors. A series of talks and papers on a variety of topics enabled the educated public to repose confidence in the sheer intellectual calibre of the man at the helm of the premier department of state.

The *First programme* has been criticised for methodological inadequacies.[69] And it is true that the *Programme* and *Economic Development* lack the technical sophistication of some later studies. But methodology must not be confined to technique. It includes consideration of all the variables relevant to economic growth. The combination of high intelligence, including the intelligence to revise initial projections in the light of changing circumstances, commonsense, and resolute leadership still remains the most sophisticated, and most elusive, methodology of all. Important innovations can often be very simple. Whatever reservations may be expressed about particular emphases within either *Economic Development*, or the *First programme*, they bear throughout the stamp of a first-class mind. Their sheer quality comes through more luminously with the passage of time, shining brightly through the murk of more recent effusions.

However conservative in retrospect the *First programme* appears to be, it was a radical initiative at the time. It is unhistorical to criticise it for conservatism. Its significance can be grasped more easily by comparing it with the Central Bank reports of the time, composed by McElligott, and with the commentaries in the *Irish Banking Review*.

The presentation of the annual Central Bank reports greatly improved when McElligott succeeded Brennan. The 1954 report, the first for which McElligott was directly responsible, went so far as to introduce an analytically coherent list of contents in place of Brennan's jumble. But the message remained the same. Reduced taxation would help increase exports, the bulk of which would come from agriculture. As agriculture was not directly subject to taxation, this was a decidedly long-term prospect. There was no perceived shortage of enterprise in the country. In 1955, it was 'scarcely tenable that the negligible proportion which risk capital occupies in new capital issues is due entirely or even mainly to any antipathy, traditional or otherwise, on the part of the investing public'.[70]

68 *Irish Independent*, 15, 26 November 1958.
69 Kennedy and Dowling, *Economic growth*, pp. 231–2.
70 *Central Bank Report, 1955*, p. 29.

In 1958, 'To suggest that we will be unable to find productive ways of expending whatever capital may be available would be truly a council of despair.'[71] McElligott now described the economy as recording 'in recent years . . . a period of more balanced growth' which 'resulted in some lowering of real earnings'.[72] This still counts among the more original definitions of 'balanced growth' in economic literature! Then came *Economic Development*. In his report for the year ending March 1959, McElligott performed some heroic gymnastics, as he made room for the bank to accommodate the new developments. He duly repeated the familiar (and in itself, correct) injunction that 'close attention to the growth of consumption is necessary to make sure that it does not advance so rapidly in relation to production as to endanger the availability of capital for economic development'.[73] Within two paragraphs, however, McElligott vaulted the analytical rubicon, jettisoning the pieties of a generation of Finance memoranda: 'The reason for the low rate of capital formation in Ireland has been lack of recognised outlets for productive investment and not lack of capital resources.'[74] He suddenly adopted the previously heretical view, expounded in *Economic Development*, that 'The nerve centre of the whole forward movement may lie, not in finance, but in entrepreneurial capacity.'[75] The fact, however, that he could still manage to detect that 'In recent years there has been evidence of a more favourable trend in this country's economic affairs'[76] reveals just how stuck in the balance of payments rut his mind still was. The mental habits of a lifetime could not be abandoned so abruptly. The coherence and clarity of *Economic Development* brings welcome relief from the confusion of the alternative official mind.

It also compares favourably with the alternative unofficial mind, as expressed in the *Irish Banking Review*. The *Review* began publication in November 1957 in order to encourage 'the provision of accurate information and the stimulation of informed economic comment'.[77] The first issue was introduced by a sermon entitled 'Ireland in the age of inflation'. However appropriate the warnings about the ravages of inflation in the long run, this simply reasserted the traditional Finance priorities. The following year, the *Review* criticised the excessive scale of state expenditure 'balanced at too high a level in the sense that the fraction of the national income spent by the government is unduly large'.[78] In December

---

71 *Central Bank Report, 1958*, p. 31.   72 *Ibid.*, p. 29.
73 *Central Bank Report, 1959*, p. 27.
74 *Ibid.*, p. 28.
75 The quotation comes from Alec Cairncross, 'Economic development and the west', *The Three Banks Review* (December 1957), quoted in *Economic Development*, p. 7.
76 *Central Bank Report, 1959*, p. 26.
77 H.W. Kennedy, 'Foreword', *IBR* (November 1957).
78 'The budget and the national economy', *IBR* (June 1958), p. 13.

1958 it determined to look on the bright side, deploring 'the mood of pessimism in recent years', with 'expressions of despair about the future of the country being heard on all sides'.[79] It found this inexplicable, reminding its readers that 'the country has largely recovered' from the crisis of 1955 – this in a year in which real national income fell, total employment fell, savings fell, and investment stagnated! What it meant was not that 'the country' had recovered but that 'the balance of payments' had recovered.

Despite this putative national recovery, the *Review* itself had come around the following year to expressing the heresy that 'an expansionist budget was necessary'.[80] It proceeded to list the advantages Ireland already enjoyed for economic development. In addition to a highly developed infrastructure, it had the inestimable advantage of the Irish people, who 'are generally admitted to being intelligent above the average. They are, on the whole, industrious, ambitious and moral . . .'.[81] In addition, 'Education is compulsory and universal. Illiteracy is unknown . . . The civil service is carefully recruited. Venality and bribery do not exist . . . Labour relations are reasonably good by modern standards.'[82] ('Modern standards' meant, of course, British standards.) The banking system was, needless to say, excellent. The unenlightened reader might have begun to wonder how a country so endowed could still have managed so unimpressive a record. Not at all. The record was actually highly impressive. The Irish enjoyed a significantly improved standard of living – compared with the Great Famine of 1845–50!

If the conditions were so propitious, why was the mood so pessimistic? Did perhaps the fabled energies of private enterprise leave something to be desired? The author almost, but not quite, brought himself to this heretical conclusion. 'To the extent that the country suffers at present from lack of enterprise or an undue craving for security, these conditions partly reflect the prevailing lack of confidence in the future.'[83] It was lack of confidence that damaged enterprise, rather than lack of enterprise damaging confidence. This lack of confidence was in turn largely due to emigration. 'It is arguable that the prolonged decrease in population is the most deep-seated cause of the prevailing pessimism.'[84] But this cast no reflection on private enterprise. Rather did it reflect the unfortunate tendency of the natives to measure their condition by British standards, and therefore to unrealistically inflate their expectations. Confidence would be restored at a stroke if only the Irish would count their blessings compared with the under-developed countries of Africa, Asia and the Mediterranean, and be satisfied with lower standards.[85] The author then

---

[79] 'Favourable aspects of the Irish economy', *IBR* (December 1958), p. 3.
[80] *IBR* (June 1959), p. 8.
[81] *Ibid.*, p. 6.　　[82] *Ibid.*　　[83] *Ibid.*, p. 8.　　[84] *Ibid.*, p. 4.　　[85] *Ibid.*, p. 5.

actually called for a plan, while insisting that all that a plan could do would be to create an atmosphere in which private enterprise could flourish.[86]

The *Review* responded constructively to *Economic Development* and to the *First programme*. It discreetly refrained from drawing attention to the implications of the *Programme* statement that 'In our present circumstances, we must be prepared to take risks under all headings – social, commercial and financial – if we are to succeed in the drive for expansion.'[87] Nevertheless, it still sought to impress its own imprint on the *Programme*, in terms highly reminiscent of the George O'Brien of the 1920s.[88] The White Paper, it stressed, recognised the pre-eminent position of agriculture in the economy. A prosperous and expanding agricultural sector must form the basis of any plan of economic resurgence. Although planning for further industrial development would be geared towards export markets, it was inevitable that 'The great majority of industries must continue to depend mainly on the home market for a long time to come . . .'[89] and 'It seems unlikely that development on the industrial side will be able to absorb more than a portion of those leaving the land. Until the flow from agricultural employment can be arrested, there can be little hope of any substantial improvement in this situation.'[90] The *Review*'s analysis did not misrepresent the letter of the White Paper; but it failed to fully capture its spirit. The emphasis on industrial development in the *Programme* was more emphatic than the *Review* allowed.[91]

By June 1959, then, the *Review* had come to accept as non-heretical the proposition that 'The emphasis in Irish economic discussion should shift from the economics of equilibrium to the economics of growth. The mere attainment of balance in external payments and the budget, however desirable in themselves, is not enough to generate the dynamism necessary for progress.'[92] It seemed a long way back to 1957, and even 1958. The change in perspective must be primarily attributed to the change in atmosphere generated by the publications of November 1958.

The determination of the *Review* to align the *Programme* with agricultural-led growth hints at one significant difference between Lemass and Whitaker at that stage. Lemass, despite occasional opportunistic obeisances to the importance of agriculture, had no basic confidence in the ability of agriculture to generate the rate of economic growth he deemed necessary. This marked him off from the emphasis in *Economic Development*, in the Central Bank reports, with their continuing insistence on the

---

[86] *Ibid.*, pp. 8–9.   [87] *Programme for economic expansion*, p. 36.
[88] Hardly surprisingly, in that it was probably the George O'Brien of the 1950s who wrote the piece!
[89] Programme for economic expansion', *IBR* (March 1959), p. 6.   [90] *Ibid.*, p. 10.
[91] *Programme for economic expansion* p. 49.
[92] 'Irish agriculture – problems of development', *IBR* (June 1959), p. 13.

primacy of agriculture, in the *Irish Banking Review*, in the abortive inter-party proposals of October 1956, which undertook 'to favour investment in agriculture over all other forms of investment',[93] and in the conclusions of a committee of departmental Secretaries in January 1957, which saw closer integration of the Irish economy with the British agricultural economy as the main hope for the foreseeable future.[94]

If Lemass was in a minority among policy-makers at this stage in his commitment to industry – though Whitaker was more balanced on the matter than McElligott – not all outside opinion shared the prevailing official faith in agriculture. Alfred Kuehn, a German economist, expressed scepticism that agriculture could provide a basis for sustained growth in Irish circumstances. After surveying Irish economic performance in a well-informed article, Kuehn concluded that, while agricultural output could be increased through more intensive methods, this offered no foreseeable prospect of creating the necessary employment to curb emigration. Only industrial development could cope with the pressing problems, and this implied substantial state participation in view of the proven incapacity of private enterprise.[95]

Whatever hopes were reposed in agriculture by others, Lemass devoted his attention mainly to industry. The full party-political story of the transition from protection to competition, from tariffs to free trade, remains to be told.[96] Lemass was building on measures towards which all governments since the war had been groping. These assumed more concrete shape in the grants and tax-free period introduced by the inter-party government in October 1956, to encourage exports, and already expanded in Ryan's first budget in May 1957.[97] But the political and ideological implications of the change were more serious for Fianna Fáil than for the other parties. It would be only natural for businessmen who prospered under protection to have considered their contributions to party funds an insurance against the threat of competition. Lemass took specious pains to deny 'the reversal of policy' with which the opposition taunted him, stressing the success of his pre-war policy, and simply claiming that new problems demanded new solutions. The tactical twists and turns of Lemass in opposition between 1954 and 1957 may have reflected genuine doubt in his own mind about the most appropriate

93 Fanning, *Finance*, p. 506.
94 Girvin, 'Protectionism and economic development', pp. 301–2.
95 A. Kuehn, 'Die Wirtschaft Irlands', *Vierteljahrshefte zur Wirtschaftsforschung* (1956), p. 258.
96 On the administrative experience, see T.K. Whitaker, 'From protection to free trade – the Irish experience', *Administration*, 21, 4 (Winter, 1973), reprinted in Whitaker, *Interests*, pp. 55–80. See also J. Lee, 'Lemass and his two partnerships', *Irish Times Supplement*, 19 May 1976.
97 Cullen, *Economic history*, p. 183.

initiatives, but also involved a pedagogic process, both for himself and for his party.[98]

Lemass struck on an astute compromise, politically and economically, after his return to office. 'War will rage over the government's Five Year Plan . . . when it comes before Dáil Éireann', warned the *Irish Times*.[99] It never did come before the Dáil. The reasons remain to be fully explored. It may be surmised that Lemass had little ambition to inflict on his backbenchers, or on de Valera, the enlightenment that would be willingly proffered from the opposition benches about the manner in which Fianna Fáil had at last seen the light, and was now reneging on its earlier self. Nor would any astute politician wish to sacrifice the advantage accruing to his party from a 'plan' ostensibly based on the work of a non-party civil servant.[100] The de-politicisation of 'planning' was too useful an asset to be wantonly surrendered to the capricious vagaries of Dáil debate.

In practice, Lemass squared the circle between the interests of party friends and the national interest by fostering conditions which would entice foreign firms to Ireland but only on condition that they produced primarily for export. They would therefore enhance the country's export capacity without competing directly with protected firms producing mainly for the home market. The hope was that in due course the models of managerial efficiency presumed to be provided by foreign firms would inspire imitation in the protected sectors.

Economic Development and the *First programme* were both keenly conscious of the changing nature of European economic relations. The formation of the EEC and of EFTA might offer opportunities, or pose threats. The scant sympathy shown by members of EFTA towards Irish demands for 'special treatment' carried the warning that a supplicant posture was unlikely to win concessions. Lemass held that once Britain applied for membership of the EEC, Ireland's dependency left her with little option but to follow suit, whether she liked it or not. There was some difference of public opinion as to whether Ireland should seek full or associate membership. Lemass himself, though as ignorant of European cultures as the majority of his countrymen, came to increasingly convey the impression that he relished the prospect of EEC membership. Ireland applied for full membership along with Britain in 1961, but her application lapsed, with that of Britain, following de Gaulle's veto in January 1963.[101]

---

[98] Bew and Patterson, *Lemass*, pp. 86ff; B. Girvin 'The dominance of Fianna Fáil and the nature of political adaptability in Ireland', *Political Studies*, 32 (1984), p. 466.

[99] *Irish Times*, 12 November 1958.

[100] S. Baker, 'Nationalist ideology and the industrial policy of Fianna Fáil', *Irish Political Studies*, 1 (1986), pp. 57–66.

[101] Miriam Hederman, *The road to Europe: Irish attitudes 1948–61* (Dublin, 1983), pp. 53–74.

To assist Irish firms to respond to the imminent challenge of free trade, the government established the Committee on Industrial Organisation in 1961 to recommend 'positive measures for adjustment and adaptation' of Irish industry. The CIO, which carried out detailed analyses of the efficiency of various industrial sectors, recommended a variety of aids and incentives for Irish firms.[102] Quickly sensing that the carrot of subsidies might not suffice to encourage sufficient Irish manufacturers to stir themselves to compete internationally – why abandon now the habits of a lifetime? – the government announced unilateral tariff cuts in 1962, and insisted on implementing them in 1963 despite the suspension of the Irish application for entry to the EEC. Tariff levels remained high by international standards. But even the more reluctant manufacturers could now grasp the earnestness of government intent. The success of the *Programme* helped steel the government's nerve to this manner of proceeding. It would have been more difficult to implement changes of this type had depression continued. Growing prosperity permitted policy ventures that stagnation would have rendered much more unpalatable to the industrial sector.

The Anglo-Irish Free Trade Agreement of 1965 was a bigger step in the same direction. The AIFTA gave Irish industry immediate tariff-free access to the British market. It also gave a guaranteed market for store cattle, and a higher quota for butter. In return, Ireland undertook to reduce by 10 per cent annually the tariffs against British imports, which would result in full free trade between the two countries by 1975. 'We needed the discipline of the challenge to our competitiveness' recalled Jack Lynch, Minister for Industry and Commerce at the time, 'if we could compete successfully against sophisticated British industrial imports we could become competitive in Europe.'[103] If this was a somewhat generous assessment of the competitiveness of British exports on world markets, the thrust of the thinking was nevertheless clear. The AIFTA was less an end in itself than a further step in the direction of fostering Irish competitiveness for the beckoning opportunities.

The 1958 *Programme* was followed by more technically sophisticated, but also more vulnerable, *Second* and *Third programmes*. The *Second programme*, scheduled to run from 1964 to 1970, was jettisoned in 1967. It was mainly notable for the final recognition of the limited ability of agriculture to act as the engine of growth. The *Third programme* was quietly shelved in 1971. The Irish economy proved exceptionally difficult to guide. There was relatively limited scope for policy, in a strictly technical sense, to influence developments. The exiguous tax base reduced the range of weapons at the disposal of government, at least until the

---

[102] G. FitzGerald, *Planning in Ireland* (Dublin, 1968), pp. 56–67. C. Brock, 'The CIO industrial survey', *JSSISI*, 21 (1963–4), pp. 176–86.
[103] Jack Lynch, 'Why Ireland joined', *Community Report*, 3, 1 (January 1983), p. 5.

introduction of Pay As You Earn and turnover taxes by the mid-1960s.[104]
The Central Bank's lack of effective control over interest rates and money
supply restricted the scope of monetary policy. Consumers in an open
economy with a high marginal propensity to import are likely to behave in
unforeseeable ways, much to the chagrin of the planners.

The largest sector of the economy, agriculture, was peculiarly difficult
to plan. It made little contribution to expansion during the 1960s, when
its annual growth rate averaged only 1 per cent. This naturally affected the
general level of performance. But there was probably relatively little that
could be done about it. The inadequacy of indigenous industrial management could be partly circumvented by importing managers. And a
relatively small number of first-class businessmen could energise whole
sections of industry. But farmers could not be imported. A small number
of first-class ones could make little impact. Thousands of decision-makers
had to be influenced to adopt new approaches if the sector as a whole was
to achieve higher growth rates. Improved education, combined with the
inexorable drift from the land, might effect significant long-term change.
But plans could make little short-term impact in this area. In all the
circumstances, and despite criticism of the *Programmes*[105] it was less
remarkable that they should have been shelved than that they should have
had any impact at all.

But did the programmes, even the *First programme*, have any impact?
May the upward thrust not have been mainly the result of impersonal
forces with which those responsible for the programmes chanced to
coincide, thus earning undeserved reputations that should really be
attributed to mere luck? This proposition naturally appeals to those, and
there are many, who seek to disparage achievement and success among
their countrymen. But the argument may be based on more than spite. For
even if it be conceded that Lemass and Whitaker were indeed outstanding
compared with possible alternatives, yet only a subordinate importance
might still be attached to their role, on the grounds that policy, however
correctly or courageously conceived, did not really much matter in any
case. Would not the economy have run just as well on auto-pilot? (If not,
indeed, better – though that would imply that policy made a difference, if
only a negative one.) May not the surge in growth rates, from a 1 per cent
annual average between 1950 and 1958 to a 4 per cent annual average
between 1959 and 1973, have simply resulted from the international
boom sucking Ireland onto the growth path?

Alternatively, one may argue, like Kennedy and Dowling, that policy did

[104] D. Norton, 'Estimation of the short-run effects of fiscal policy in Ireland, 1960–1970',
    ESR, 5 (1974–5), p. 385.
[105] B.M. Walsh, 'Economic growth', pp. 34–6; J.P. Neary, 'The failure of economic
    nationalism', *Crane Bag*, 8, 1 (1984), pp. 70–2.

indeed matter, but that the *First programme* was too conservatively conceived, and that only the good luck of improved terms of trade in 1958 and 1959, combined with fine weather in 1959 and 1960, which stimulated agricultural output, enabled the economy to register so rapid an advance at that stage.[106]

These propositions deserve serious consideration. The broader economic history of the 1950s remains to be written. It may not be possible to provide convincing answers until we know much more about the business history of the period, and about decision-making at the level of the firm. But some provisional responses may be hazarded.

The terms of trade gyrated during the decade.[107] They played a significant role both in depression and in growth. But the precise nature of that role still defies full comprehension. At first glance, the exceptional deterioration in the terms of trade, from 100 in 1953 to 87.2 in 1957, might seem in itself to largely account, irrespective of budgetary policy, for the malaise of the mid-fifties. And the sharp recovery, from 87.2 in 1957 to 93.5 in 1958 and 99.4 in 1959 seems to vindicate the Kennedy and Dowling argument. Further examination, however, points to a more complex situation.

In 1955 the balance of payments threatened to career out of control again, with imports rising from £180 million to £204 million, while domestic exports actually fell from £112 million to £107 million.[108] It was in response to this deterioration that Sweetman introduced his punitive measures in March 1956. But the balance of payments crisis of 1955 cannot be attributed mainly to a worsening in the terms of trade. They stood at 97.4 in that year, only a modest decline since 1953. It was in 1956 that they plunged to 90.4. The main deterioration followed, rather than caused, the external payments crisis and the restrictive measures. Indeed, the measures may themselves have contributed to the deterioration.

The nadir in the terms of trade was reached with the 87.2 of 1957. But 1957 recorded the first significant increase in exports since 1953. Terms of trade then improved markedly in 1958 and 1959. But exports actually fell slightly in both years! Having hovered at £127 million for each of the three years 1957, 1958 and 1959, exports then surged upwards to £148 million in 1960 and £175 million in 1961. The breakthrough on the export front had at last occurred. But the terms of trade deteriorated from 99.4 in 1959 to 95.9 in 1960 and 93.8 in 1961. The terms of trade for the five years 1959–63 were only marginally better, at just over 95, than for

---

106 Kennedy and Dowling, *Economic growth*, pp. 231–2.
107 Term of trade figures are based on the relevant tables in *Statistical Abstract*, 1953, 1957, 1962.
108 External trade figures in this section are based on the relevant tables in *Statistical Abstract*, 1953, 1957, 1962.

the five years 1954–8. The shift in export gear cannot be mainly attributed to a significant improvement in this respect.

The terms of trade were an important ingredient in the confused economic mix of the period. They are as important for what did not happen as for what did. It would be intriguing to speculate, for instance, on how Lemass and Whitaker would have responded to the highly probable payments crisis of 1958 and 1959 if the terms of trade had not improved. Imports continued to rise steadily in both years. Indeed, the rise in imports between 1957 and 1959 exceeded that between 1954 and 1955. The already stagnating domestic exports would have fallen discouragingly but for the improved terms of trade. Would the authorities have been forced into yet further restrictive measures? Would there have been a Ryan Budget to compare with Sweetman's and MacEntee's? Would Lemass have lashed out, and demanded expansion at all costs, following the philosophy of his Clerys speech, when he insisted that the country had to take a chance on the future? If so, would relations between Lemass and Whitaker, or indeed between Lemass and the cabinet, have become strained? The possibilities are intriguing, and there is no doubt that Lemass was lucky at this stage. But this is a quite different scenario from 'terms of trade-led growth'. The improved terms of trade did not, as we have seen, lead to export growth. They merely prevented decline. In this respect, the crucial year on the foreign front was 1960. However the pass might have been held in 1958 and 1959, the further increase in imports in 1960 would inevitably have led to a balance of payments crisis but for the sharp increase in exports.

Justified concern with the terms of trade must not divert attention from the important changes occurring in the commodity composition of exports in the late fifties. The growth in exports from £104 million in 1956 to £127 million in 1957 was impressive. But 1956 was a depressed base, the value of exports having fallen from £112 million in 1954. There was therefore a substantial 'recovery' component in the 1957 performance. And the increase was largely the result of a rise of £9 million in exports of live animals, and of £8 million in foodstuffs of animal origin. Only relatively small increases occurred in other areas. This was still very much the traditional export profile. Exports of foodstuffs of animal origin rose by £5 million in 1958. But exports of live animals fell by £7 million. Manufacturing exports continued to stagnate. It was not until 1959 that the first really significant signs of change occurred. The overall stagnation in exports in that year concealed important shifts in composition. Exports of live animals fell a further £8 million, while foodstuffs of animal origin fell back by £3 million. But manufacturing exports, apart from food, drink and tobacco, jumped from £25.1 million to £35.6 million. This almost equalled, in one year, the rise from £13 million in 1952 to £25 million in 1958. The export break-through of 1960 occurred because improvements occurred simultaneously in agricultural and industrial performance. Exports of live animals increased by £5.5 million, of foodstuffs of animal origin by more than £6 million, and of non-food manufactures by more than £8 million. Although agricultural exports remained important, the record exports of live animals in 1961 only just exceeded the previous record of 1957. Foodstuffs of animal origin only recovered their 1954 peak in 1960. But manufacturing exports in 1959 at £35 million, and in 1960 at £44 million, surged ahead of the previous record of £26 million in 1957. They were three times as high in 1960 as in 1953. This was no mere 'recovery', but a shift onto a new trajectory. Within manufacturing exports, it is true, the traditional sectors of textiles, clothing and footwear accounted for £6 million of the £19 million increase between 1958 and 1960. But relatively new sectors, including ores and metals, cutlery, hardware, implements and machinery, oils, fertilisers, and chemicals accounted for £9 million of the increase.

It would be unhistorical to overlook the 'recovery' elements in the performance of the economy from 1959. But it would also be unhistorical to overlook the significant changes occurring from 1959 itself in both the scale and composition of manufacturing exports. In that one year, 1959, these exports rose as much as between 1951 and 1958. In the two years 1959 and 1960 they rose almost as much as between 1946 and 1958. On the crucial export front, therefore, the key changes can already be detected in the course of 1959, before acquiring a firmer profile in 1960.

These changes cannot be wholly attributed to the *First programme*. How far they involved a response to the incentives introduced in October 1956, and extended in May 1957 requires further investigation. Lemass was already claiming, a month after Ryan's first budget, that a flood of proposals for new industrial projects had come in.[109] The precise impact of policy on the performance of individual sectors and firms remains to be analysed by business historians. But it seems reasonable to assume that the policy pursued in the late 1950s, including 'renewed expansion of the public capital programme and a large increase in the borrowing requirement in 1959 and 1960' was at least partly responsible for the sharp rise in domestic demand which, together with increased manufacturing exports, stimulated hectic restocking activity in 1959,[110] itself a pointer to the resurgence of morale perceptible in 1959 and 1960.[111]

Policy played some role in the recovery, even if it is difficult to quantify how much. It probably played a more significant role, perhaps a prepon-

109 *Sunday Press*, 16 June 1957.
110 Kennedy and Dowling, *Economic growth*, pp. 231–2.
111 T.K. Whitaker, 'Staid na tíre' [The state of the country], *Administration*, 8, 3 (Autumn 1960), p. 173.

derant role, in turning the recovery into the sustained growth of the sixties. It seems reasonable to suppose that the changes in fiscal policy and in industrial policy intimated in the documents of the late fifties affected performance in the sixties. It has been estimated that about half the increased growth of the sixties can be attributed to the direct impact of the more expanionist fiscal policy.[112] Such estimates are always fraught with uncertainty. But the refusal of the authorities to respond with restrictive measures of 1950s vintage to threats to the balance of payments, apart form some deflationary moves in 1965,[113] presumably reinforced business confidence that the market would continue to expand. Export policies clearly exerted influence on the direction of development. Foreign investment increased substantially following the amendment in 1958, and then the abolition in 1964, of the Control of Manufactures' Acts. By 1973 new grant-aided foreign firms accounted for at least 56 per cent of total industrial exports.[114] In the absence of such policy measures, it is difficult to envisage the index of production of transportable goods, which inched upwards from 91.4 in 1950 to 106.5 in 1958 (1953 = 100), jumping to anything like 180.4 in 1966, or 252.5 in 1971.[115]

Ireland did benefit to an extent from the rapid international economic growth of the sixties. Currency convertibility from 1959 made it much easier to attract trans-national companies, and the growth of the Euro-dollar market in the sixties facilitated borrowing.[116] Outward looking policies could hardly have enjoyed a similar degree of success earlier, unless Irish companies had responded more positively than they were to do in the sixties, if only because there were far fewer foreign firms in a position to avail of the incentives. To that extent, the policy-makers were lucky in that the new departure coincided with favourable international circumstances.

But one must be careful to delineate the precise nature of the impact of international developments on Ireland. The country failed dismally to benefit from rapid international economic growth in the fifties. International trends could offer opportunities for Ireland. They could not determine the quality of Irish response. The terms of trade, for instance, while outside the influence of a small open economy in the short term, cannot be treated as a wholly accidental variable. They did not descend from heaven. That Ireland was so vulnerable to adverse changes in the terms of trade in the 1950s was largely due to her heavy reliance on a narrow range of exports to a single market. A country's vulnerability can

---

[112] Norton, 'Fiscal policy', p. 385.
[113] Kennedy and Dowling, *Economic growth*, pp. 233ff.
[114] S.P. Nolan, 'Economic growth', in J.W. O'Hagan (ed.), *The economy of Ireland: policy and performance* (Dublin, 3rd edn 1981), p. 172.
[115] *Statistical Abstract*, 1970–1, p. 20.
[116] T.K. Whitaker, 'Financial turning points', in Whitaker, *Interests* (Dublin, 1983), p. 89.

be reduced, though not of course eliminated, by policies of diversification of products and of markets. Ireland had failed to pursue such policies since independence. More generally, Ireland was so closely locked into the British economy that many international trends affected her only as mediated through Britain. And Britain was, sadly, the great economic failure of the postwar world. She trundled along at about half the growth rate of western Europe during both the fifties and the sixties. Ireland grew at only half the British rate during the fifties, or only about a quarter the western European rate. There was no reason to expect any marked change in trend unless some new factor intervened. Ireland could not expect to be wafted upwards with the international tide in the 1960s any more than she had been in the 1950s unless she took some initiatives of her own. The international boom would remain as academic for Ireland in the sixties as in the fifties, assuming continued British retardation, unless Ireland could either win a larger share of the British market or diversify her exports into more rapidly growing markets. There was no reason why the Irish boat should rise on the international tide, any more than the British boat did, unless the Irish themselves changed their navigation tactics.

Nor was the change in the trajectory of growth during the Lemass years achieved either through irresponsible government borrowing, as would become the case later, or through repression of living standards, as prescribed in the penitentials of Brennan and McElligott. Current government expenditure as a percentage of GNP rose only modestly, from 21.0 per cent to 24.4 per cent between 1958–9 and 1965–6.[117] Foreign borrowing was minimal.[118] Servicing the public debt cost 5.09 per cent of the national income in 1963–7, a moderate increase compared with 4.06 per cent in 1953–7.[119] The deficit on the balance of payments as a proportion of national income ran at 2.38 per cent for 1963–7 compared with a virtually identical 2.35 per cent for 1953–7.[120] Lemass was an instinctive expansionist. But he was no ne'er-do-well squander-maniac, except by Brennan's standards. His example cannot be invoked to justify later borrowing binges.

SOCIAL CHANGE

The 'success or failure' of the *Programme for economic expansion*, predicted the *Irish Times*, 'will be measured by the emigration figures'.[121] Average net emigration fell from 43 000 per annum between 1956 and 1961 to 16 000 between 1961 and 1966, and to 11 000 between 1966

117 Meenan, *Irish economy*, p. 251.   118 *Ibid.*, p. 256.
119 R. Crotty, *Ireland in crisis: a study in capitalist colonial underdevelopment* (Dingle, 1986), p. 3.
120 *Ibid.*, p. 157.   121 *Irish Times*, 12 November 1958.

Table 3. *Total number of persons at work in 1961, 1966, 1971 (000)*[124]

	1961	1966	1971
Agriculture	379	334	273
Industry	257	293	323
Services	415	438	459
Total	1052	1065	1055

and 1971, or from an annual rate of 14.8 to 3.7.[122] Total population, which fell from 2.96 to 2.82 million between 1951 and 1961, then rose to 2.98 million by 1971. Lemass prated little about the sanctity of 'the family'. But 4 per cent economic growth and a rise of about 50 per cent in material living standards during the 1960s[123] at last made it feasible for the number of families to increase. The number of 'families', as recorded by the census, rose by 48 000 between 1961 and 1971, compared with a rise of only 11 000 in the preceding fifteen years. The number of marriages rose from a trough of 14 700 in 1957 to 16 800 in 1966 and 22 000 in 1971. Translated into marriage rates, this showed a rise from 5.1 to 5.8 between 1957 and 1966. The rate then rose, for the first time in the history of the state, above 6 in 1967. In 1970, it rose above 7 for the first time since records began in 1864. Mean age at marriage for men fell from 30.6 to 27.2 years, and for women from 26.9 to 24.8 years, between 1961 and 1973. Nor were the changes confined to the most advanced regions. Almost all counties lost population between 1956 and 1961. Between 1961 and 1966 the gains and losses were fairly evenly divided. Most counties then gained population between 1966 and 1971, several for the first time in the century. The changes were not spectacular in absolute terms. But they assumed historical significance in that they reversed the trend of more than a century.

'The vanishing Irish' were no longer vanishing. But the battle had to be unceasing. The advance on the employment front was painfully slow. Numbers employed increased only marginally, from 1.052 million in 1961 to 1.055 million in 1971. The relative growth in the industrial and service sectors barely compensated, as Table 3 shows, for the continuing decline in agriculture.

As the decline in agricultural employment was inevitable, only the growth

---

122 *Statistical Abstract*, 1970–71, p. 4. All further figures in this paragraph are drawn from the relevant *Statistical Abstracts*.
123 Walsh, 'Economic growth', p. 33. NESC, *Towards a social report*, t. 3, 4.
124 *Statistical Abstract*, 1970–71, p. 4.

of the other sectors prevented a further sharp fall in total employment. Unemployment still continued to hover discouragingly around the 6–7 per cent level, well above the OECD average.

The route sketched out in *Economic Development* pointed in the direction of efficiency, competitiveness, and quality – quality of administration, quality of management, quality of labour. Few of these goals could be achieved without a transformation of the quality and quantity of education. This in turn had fundamental implications for the nature of society. Lemass subsequently claimed that as late as 1956, when the government reduced the secondary school per capita grant by 10 per cent without serious public protest, 'There was no realisation of the importance of education in the modern world and there was certainly no evidence of this outburst of enthusiasm for education which is so characteristic now.'[125] Lemass appointed three of his best ministers, Patrick Hillery, George Colley and Donogh O'Malley, to Education. All were young, and anxious to make their mark by injecting some life into a traditionally moribund department.

Primary education experienced growing pressure on resources as numbers enrolled rose from 496 000 in 1960 to 544 000 in 1973. Teacher/pupil ratios nevertheless improved, if only slightly. The main advances came through reducing the sizes of appallingly large classes. The proportion of children in classes of more than forty-five pupils fell from 45 per cent in 1963 to 13.5 per cent in 1973. Facilities also improved as more than 1000 small one- and two-teacher schools were closed. The proportion of schools with piped drinking water, for instance, rose from 47 per cent to 76 per cent between 1963 and 1974, and the proportion with flush toilets from 46 per cent to 93 per cent. Free school transport services helped compensate after 1967/8 for the closures.[126]

The situation was particularly serious at second level. The key contribution here came from *Investment in education*, the report of an OECD survey team under the chairmanship of Patrick Lynch.[127] The report collected important statistical data for the first time, intended to indicate the resources available, and the efficiency with which they were used. It provided striking evidence of the lack of opportunity for poorer children to proceed to secondary and higher education. After its exposure of the waste of talent fostered by an educational system based on low intellectual and relatively high financial entry requirements to advanced levels, it was no longer possible to sustain fond illusions about the wonderful educational performance.

125 'Seán Lemass looks back', *Irish Press*, 4 February 1969.
126 NESC, *Educational expenditure in Ireland* (Dublin, 1975) summarises the main developments between 1963 and 1974.
127 *Investment in education. Report of a survey team appointed by the Minister for Education in conjunction with the OECD* (2 vols., Dublin, 1965, 1966).

Hillery announced in May 1963 that comprehensive schools would be established, under the control of the Department of Education, to provide a broader range of subjects than hitherto available and to improve the regional distribution of educational opportunities. He also announced that regional technical colleges would be established. Building grants for secondary schools were introduced in 1964. Policies initiated by Hillery, and continued by his successor, George Colley, laid much of the ground work for improving access to education. They also began to shift the balance of power in the administration of education between the traditionally hegemonic Catholic Church and the state. But it was during the tenure of the rumbustious Donogh O'Malley from 1965 to 1967 that education achieved a breakthrough in public consciousness.

O'Malley was to die suddenly at the age of forty-seven in 1968, at a moment when he had caught the public imagination to an exceptional degree. Many of his schemes were destined to remain stillborn, or to be buried beneath the crushing weight of vested interest (some of which may have chanced to coincide with the public interest). His best known initiative was the introduction of free secondary education. The 1923 Local Government Act had authorised local authorities to provide scholarships, financed from the rates, for secondary school pupils. The authorities, largely representing rate payer interests, naturally did relatively little under this provision for poor but able children. The amounts awarded were small, and as late as 1961 only 621 scholarships of this type were offered. An Amendment Act then proposed that the state should meet at least half the costs of these scholarships, and the number nearly trebled to 1775 in 1963.[128] But this still represented less than 2 per cent of the student body.

When O'Malley announced his free education scheme, reputedly with the prior approval of Lemass but without having consulted the cabinet or Finance, the government was swept along on the tide of public enthusiasm. The thinking of O'Malley and Lemass ran ahead of that even of the supportive Secretary of Education, Seán O'Connor.[129] Between 1966 and 1969 the number of secondary school pupils rose from 104 000 to 144 000, or as much as in the previous ten years. Recognising the extra pressure that would be placed on schools, the state now began to provide support for capital expenditure in this area. Free secondary education opened up many doors that were previously shut to children born into the wrong families. Seán O'Connor's judgement, however, is that the initiative was not followed up with adequate resources for the schools, and that the impetus went out of the commitment to education with the resignation

[128] Lyons, *Ireland*, p. 635.
[129] Seán O'Connor's interview with Christina Murphy, 'How O'Malley launched free scheme', *Irish Times*, 10 September 1986.

of Lemass and the death of O'Malley.[130] It does seem to be the case that 'once the displacement of fees by public expenditure is allowed for' there was little increase in real expenditure on secondary education between 1965 and 1975.[131] The main institutional initiative after O'Malley's death was the introduction of the idea of community schools in 1970. These were to be either new foundations in areas of rapidly growing population, or to be established by agreement between existing second level schools in the same locality.

The universities too began to shake themselves into contemplation of the twentieth century. A Commission on Higher Education, the first since the foundation of the state, was appointed in 1960. Its report in 1967 did not stimulate immediate dramatic change. But the need to give evidence before the Commission helped focus the minds of some university people more explicitly on their responsibilities. The government established the Higher Education Authority in 1969 to help guide expenditure in the third level sector. Donogh O'Malley's proposal to 'merge' University College Dublin and Trinity College Dublin was, however, successfully resisted by the two institutions. Polytechnic-type initiatives began to be promoted to cater for aspects of education felt to be relatively neglected by the universities. A National Institute for Higher Education was established in Limerick in 1970, to be followed by a second in Dublin in 1976.

The lack of scholarships at university level had traditionally helped confine opportunity for higher education to the more comfortable classes. In 1967 only 2 per cent of students came from lower income groups.[132] A more ambitious scholarship scheme increased the total number of grants from 1119 in 1968 to 6168 in 1975. Nevertheless, this still left only 26 per cent of university students in receipt of state support at that stage. Though in absolute terms 'Working class and marginal farming categories did record gains over those years in their educational participation rates,' the increased access to higher education was inevitably availed of much more by the middle than by the lower classes.[133]

It would be a generation before the full impact of the numerous changes worked their way through the higher educational system. Many of them promised to turn out for the better; but the quality of thinking behind them was distinctly uneven. The initiatives, often admirable in themselves, gave little evidence of systematic thought about the relationships between educational, economic and social change. This was one area in which the policy-makers could not be directly faulted. They obviously wanted to do something. But they were faced by the almost total dearth of serious

130 *Ibid.*   131 NESC, *Educational expenditure*, p. 27.
132 M. Nevin, 'A study of the social background of students in Irish universities', *JSSISI*, 21, 6 (1967–8).
133 D. Rottman, *et al.*, *The distribution of income in the Republic of Ireland* (ESRI, no. 109, 1982), p. 3.

thinking about higher education among higher educationalists. If the policy-makers are to be criticised it should be for failing to employ some first-class minds to think systematically about the role of higher education in society.

The two biggest social blots on the early Lemass years were health and housing. The Minister for Health and Social Welfare, Seán MacEntee, boasted in 1965 that the Irish health service was the best in the world, on the simple grounds that it was not state controlled.[134] Sickness and insurance benefits were much lower than in western Europe in general. Social assistance had to play a correspondingly more important role. The patronising attitude towards the sick poor enshrined in the legislative principles of the nineteenth century still prevailed into the 1960s. Lemass dispensed with MacEntee in 1965, appointing Donogh O'Malley to succeed him in order to make up for lost time. O'Malley duly sponsored numerous initiatives, intended to improve the quality of service and access to treatment.

Housing bore the main brunt of the curbs on social expenditure imposed in the deflationary drive following the balance of payments crisis in 1955. Between 1955 and 1959 the number of dwellings completed with state aid fell from 10 490 to 4894.[135] The *Programme for economic expansion* envisaged continuing restrictions in this direction. Although the curbs were later somewhat relaxed, the recovery was slow. The number of new houses built with state aid did not surpass the 1954 figure until 1968.[136] The relative stagnation on the housing front meant that the number of over-crowded households, defined as 'two or more persons per room', fell only slowly, from 63 000 in 1961 to 59 000 in 1966 and 54 000 in 1971.[137]

The quality of the civil service remained a matter of continuing public concern after the failures of the fifties. The changes in Finance were not always comprehended, much less emulated, elsewhere. In the hope of improving the quality of decision-making, the government appointed a commission of inquiry into the public service, under the chairmanship of Liam St John Devlin, in September 1966. The report, completed in 1969, recommended sweeping changes in decision-making structures. Its implementation would provoke a running bureaucratic battle into the 1980s, if not indeed into the twenty-first century. However controversial the recommendations of the Devlin Commission, the tone of the report provides an instructive contrast with the complacency of the Brennan report of 1935.[138]

[134] R. Kaim Caudle, *Social policy in the Irish Republic* (London, 1967), p. 30.
[135] *Statistical Abstract*, 1960, p. 2.
[136] *Ibid.*, 1970–71, p. 4.   [137] NESC, *Towards a social report*, p. 111.
[138] Fanning, *Finance*, p. 603; see below, pp. 547–53.

As well as attempting to reform the civil service internally, Lemass presided over the creation of an organisational infrastructure that would provide some alternative sources of advice for policy-makers. He did not visualise these other bodies as rivals to the civil service, but as reinforcements. The Economic Research Institute established in 1960, and An Foras Forbartha, established in 1964, were perhaps the most prominent additions to the IPA, AFT and the IMI, established in the course of the 1950s. The National Industrial and Economic Council, representing employers' organisations, trade unions and the government, was set up in 1963. It would be superseded in 1973 by a more broadly based body, now including agricultural interests, the National Economic and Social Council. The quality of many of the reports issued by these bodies improved the flow of information and intelligence available to such decision-makers as choose to take cognisance of them.[139]

POLITICAL CHANGE

Lemass succeeded to an insecure political inheritance. The election triumph of 1957 was deceptive. It was one of the lowest peacetime turnouts since 1927, 71.3 per cent. The referendum verdict in 1959 was a severe rebuff for Fianna Fáil. If even de Valera could not deliver a referendum victory in propitious circumstances, were not the electoral prospects under Lemass, wholly lacking the Chief's charisma, bleak? Many were predicting the decay of Fianna Fáil with the departure of its founder. The more closely Lemass identified himself with new economic policies the more his own leadership would be at risk in the event of electoral defeat. Nor did his accession arouse public enthusiasm. If the *Irish Press* dutifully asserted that 'it is clear to all that the man and the hour are well matched', the *Irish Times* and the *Irish Independent* gave no more than guarded welcomes.[140]

No policy could turn the economy around quickly enough to immediately satisfy the disillusioned. Emigration remained at high levels throughout 1959 and 1960, before falling to 27 000 in 1961 from 43 000 the previous year. In the event, the inevitable loss of seats in the October 1961 election did not prove as serious as feared. Fianna Fáil representation did fall from 78 to 70 in a Dáil reduced in size from 147 to 144 seats. The loss was comparable to that between 1933 and 1937, or between 1938 and 1943, the only two previous occasions on which Fianna Fáil had gone to the country after serving at least four years in

[139] M. Morrissey, 'The politics of economic management in Ireland 1956–70', *Irish Political Studies*, 1 (1986), pp. 79–95.
[140] *Irish Press*, 28 June 1959; *Irish Independent*, 22 June 1959; *Irish Times*, 24 June 1959.

office.[141] It can hardly be attributed without qualification to the departure of de Valera. Lemass was lucky in that Labour remained so demoralised after the experience of the previous inter-party government that it failed to fight the 1961 election on a coalition platform. Its transfers consequently proved less useful to Fine Gael than in 1954, or even 1957.

Nevertheless, the result was a setback. Lemass had to operate with a minority government from 1961 until 1965. Independents held the balance of power. There were moments of crisis, and of apparently imminent Dáil defeat. But Lemass steered a skilful parliamentary course, keeping his nerve when crisis threatened. He quickly dared the independents do their worst when rejecting a Fine Gael motion to bail out wheat farmers who had lost heavily from bad weather during the harvest, on the grounds that it would put the government at the mercy of every subsequent pressure group demand for special consideration.[142] He weathered a threatening storm over the introduction of PAYE income tax in 1963, and by-election successes in 1964 reassured any waverers in his own party unsettled by the pace of change. He felt sufficiently confident of a general election victory to threaten to go to the country if Fianna Fáil lost a Cork by-election in early 1965. When it did, he duly called a general election in April. The result consolidated his party political achievement. The number of Fianna Fáil seats rose by only two, from 70 to 72. But this sufficed to give him an absolute Dáil majority. David Thornley, a gifted young political scientist, had predicted the previous year that no party was likely to regularly win 550 000 votes in general elections over the next decade.[143] Lemass began to prove him wrong when the Fianna Fáil vote rose from 512 000 to 597 000 in 1965, higher than in 1957. Fianna Fáil would continue to comfortably pass the 550 000 mark for the rest of Thornley's decade, with the politicians once again proving cannier than even a brilliant pundit.

The 1965 result was notable in other respects. It was the first election in the history of Fianna Fáil where the party actually increased its vote after a 'normal' period of office. Mr de Valera's electoral triumphs in government, in 1933, 1938 and 1944, all partook of the nature of electoral coups, snap elections called to exploit an instant opportunity. The 1965 victory was the first time an incumbent Fianna Fáil government gained votes and seats in a 'normal' situation. It was also the first time since 1933 that any government improved its popular vote on an increased turnout.[144] Even before the election, Thornley acknowledged the achievement of Lemass as a party leader. 'Since 1959 Mr Lemass has worked

[141] C. O'Leary, *Irish elections 1918–1977* (Dublin, 1979), pp. 102–4.
[142] F. Tobin, *The best of decades* (Dublin, 1984), pp. 51–3.
[143] Thornley, 'Ireland', p. 17.
[144] A qualification may need to be made for 1938, where uncontested seats distorted turnout totals.

wonders' with a Fianna Fáil party that owed himself, in contrast to de Valera, no sense of instinctive loyalty. He had rejuvenated an ageing party, injecting it with renewed vigour, and 'over the whole apparatus hangs the supremely successful image of the leader – not a charismatic figure in the Dev mould, but a superbly gifted political tactician lurking behind the projection of an avuncular, pipe-smoking Mr Plain'.[145]

The success of Lemass as a party leader surprised observers who felt that his perspective, based on experience of only one department of state over nineteen years, was bound to be so narrow that he would have great difficulty making the transition from specialist to generalist. A brilliant *Leader* profile of Lemass in 1954 noted that

It is sometimes said that great administrators do not make good politicians: and there is no point in claiming that the Tánaiste could, in any way, be compared with the Taoiseach in the handling of complicated diplomatic or party political problems.

That was a valid observation. But the writer went on to remark that

As in industrial matters, he has shown unusual capacity of learning and of changing, so also in the political field his grasp of over-all pattern has widely extended itself.[146]

Lemass still had much to learn. But learn he did. He may have been happier in Industry and Commerce, but, as Taoiseach, he handled party political problems with aplomb. He defused the potential difficulty posed by the resignation of Paddy Smith as Minister for Agriculture in 1964, in protest against the receptivity of Lemass to trade union demands, by instantly appointing C.J. Haughey, his distinctly urban son-in-law, to Agriculture, thus distracting media attention from the substantive issue involved.[147]

Lemass could count on dominating economic policy within the cabinet on the basis of his existing reputation. He may have had to tread more carefully on Northern policy. He could of course have taken the easy way out, and had no Northern policy at all, standing four square in the tradition of all his predecessors. Instead, he sought to shift public and party attitudes, however circumspectly. Immediately on coming into office, he sought closer trade relations with Northern Ireland, but was repulsed by Brookeborough. His speech to the Oxford Union in 1960, and his Tralee statement on Northern Ireland in July 1963, simply recognising that the Northern state existed through the free will of the majority of its people, and above all his symbolic meetings with Terence O'Neill, the

---

[145] D. Thornley, 'The Fianna Fáil party', *Irish Times*, 1 April 1965.
[146] Profile: Mr Seán Lemass, TD, *Leader*, 13 March 1954.
[147] Farrell, *Chairman or chief?*, p. 104.

Northern prime minister, in January and February 1965, gave a new tone to Dublin's Northern policy.

De Valera's Northern policy was to have no Northern policy. But he had 'hard' and 'soft' lines in his rhetoric on the North. The latter predominated in his final years. He warned in 1954 that unification through coercion would lead to rule of the North 'by police methods'.[148] Sixteen years earlier, in an election speech, admittedly in Dun Laoghaire, not renowned as a hot-bed of irredentism, de Valera assured his audience that not only would 'we . . . get the six counties' but

We are going to get them in the right way. We want not the physical territory so much as the hearts of the people . . . We cannot afford in this country to lose a single Irishman, and we are going to get the unity of Ireland without the loss of a single Irishman. It is the greatest of our objectives. If we govern ourselves properly, take advantage of our resources, and improve the general standard of our people, then there will be something for the other people to join with.[149]

Lemass could not have expressed his own attitude more emphatically. The difference was that he set out more energetically to create a society that might conceivably prove attractive to others, both by improving economic and social opportunity, and by promoting a policy of 'detente' towards Stormont.

Imaginary though he held the fears of Protestants to be, he explicitly acknowledged in his Oxford speech that the 1937 constitution would require revision as a condition of unification, and that unionists could not be expected to rely merely on Catholic good will.[150]

We recognise, however, that the fears of Northern Ireland Protestants still exist and that it is unlikely that they could be removed by assurances of good intentions alone, no matter how sincere or how authoritatively expressed. An arrangement which would give them effective power to protect themselves, very especially in regard to educational and religious matters, must clearly be an essential part of any ultimate agreement.

Shortly before his resignation, he established, presumably to hasten the day when such 'an arrangement' might be possible, an all-party Committee on the Constitution, on which he himself served, and which recommended changes in 1967 that would have considerably modified the Catholic and irredentist ethos of de Valera's document. The committee unanimously recommended the deletion of the sections referring to the special position of the Catholic Church, and that divorce be permitted for members of those religions that accepted divorce.[151] They also recommended that Dublin's territorial claim on the North should be replaced by

---

[148] Bowman, *De Valera*, p. 289.   [149] *Irish Times*, 15 June 1938.
[150] Seán Lemass, *One nation* (address to the Oxford Union, 15 October 1959), pp. 8–9.
[151] *Report of the Committee on the Constitution* (Stationery Office, Pr 9817, 1967), pp. 44, 48.

the declaration that 'The Irish nation hereby proclaims its firm will that its territory be reunited in harmony and brotherly affection between all Irishmen.'[152]

This was an explosive legacy to leave to a successor. Jack Lynch moved quickly to defuse it. How Lemass himself would have acted if he were still Taoiseach must remain a matter for speculation. It is clear that he did not change his basic view in retirement. 'If we are ever going to have unity in Ireland', he told Michael Mills, 'We are going to have to bring all the people of the country into it and cherish them all equally. You cannot admit only to membership of the Irish Republic those who are in agreement with our political philosophy.'[153] The phraseology here may be a trifle disingenuous. After all, those who were not in agreement with 'our political philosophy' were hardly clamouring for admission to membership! Nevertheless, the sentiment is clear. And while in office, Lemass had tried to create not only an economy that might earn some respect, but to foster conciliation between different traditions in the South itself. He went out of his way during the celebrations of the fiftieth anniversary of the Easter Rising in 1966 to salute the memory of the Irishmen who volunteered in the First World War:

In later years it was common – and I also was guilty in this respect – to question the motives of those men who joined the new British armies formed at the outbreak of the war, but it must in their honour and in fairness to their memory be said that they were motivated by the highest purpose.[154]

With more cause for bitterness than most survivors of the civil war – his brother, Noel, had been gruesomely murdered, and he himself badly beaten up, he showed more magnanimity than most. His handsome Dáil tribute on the death of W.T. Cosgrave in November 1965 was both more generous and more historically valid than the correct but cold comment of President de Valera.

Lemass retained Frank Aiken as Minister for External Affairs. Ireland had already begun to play a relatively prominent role in United Nations diplomacy once she was admitted to membership in 1955. The timing of Ireland's entry enabled her to play an active part in guiding the general decolonisation direction of United Nations policy.[155] Outstanding officials in External Affairs, including Con Cremin, F.H. Boland, who would be elected President of the General Assembly in 1960, and Conor Cruise O'Brien, provided Aiken with cerebral support. O'Brien, in particular, sought to model Ireland's international role on that of

152 *Ibid.*, p. 5.   153 *Irish Press*, 28 January 1969.
154 *Sunday Press*, 19 February 1966. I am most grateful to Brian Farrell for supplying me with this reference.
155 T.D. Williams, 'Irish foreign policy', in Lee, *Ireland*, pp. 137–44; C.C. O'Brien, 'Ireland in international affairs', in O.D. Edwards (ed.), *Conor Cruise O'Brien introduces Ireland* (London, 1969), pp. 127ff.

Sweden.[156] Skilful public relations by Irish officials contributed to a national and international perception of the distinctiveness and importance of their contribution, particularly in the areas of anti-colonialism, disarmament, and peace-keeping. The most spectacular case was the Congo operation from 1961 to 1964. This was partly because it was 'the first major involvement which required a change in domestic legislation to allow Irish army contingents to serve abroad',[157] partly because General Seán MacEoin (not to be confused with the war of independence veteran!) served as Commander-in-Chief of the United Nations forces for a period, partly because Conor Cruise O'Brien, whom not even his most severe critics could accuse of unremitting self-effacement, served as the United Nations representative in Katanga for a short but exciting period, and partly because ten Irish soldiers were killed in an ambush at Niemba in 1960, causing a wave of sadness, mingled with pride, to sweep the country. The tragedy did not deter further Irish involvement in United Nations responsibilities. Ireland participated in seven of the twelve peace-keeping missions up to 1970, a ratio exceeded only by Sweden, Canada and Denmark.[158]

Though Lemass seems to have insisted on sending Irish troops to the Congo, despite Finance's inevitable (and proper) concern about costs, MacEntee's inevitable suspicion of communist conspiracy, and even Aiken's own rumoured reservations about the ability of Irish troops to stand the heat,[159] his main foreign policy concern increasingly revolved around the emerging economic blocs in Europe. As the EEC was defined as an economic rather than a political issue, Lemass himself took effective control of decision-making in that area.[160] The departmental distribution of responsibilities relegated External Affairs to a more peripheral role than it would play later, and 'It seems as if Mr Aiken made a tacit agreement with his colleagues not to intervene on the question of Ireland's entry into the EEC.'[161]

Lemass was widely considered a pragmatic 'European' in contrast to the allegedly more idealistic 'United Nations' Aiken. The issue, if issue it was, of where Ireland's priorities should lie in the event of a clash between 'European' and 'United Nations' loyalties, however those elusive concepts might be defined, did not in practice arise once de Gaulle rebuffed the British application in January 1963. Changing circumstances in the United Nations itself reduced Ireland's role as the decade advanced, but

---

[156] C.C. O'Brien, *To Katanga and back* (London, 1962), pp. 14–15.
[157] P. Keatinge, *A place among the nations: issues of Irish foreign policy* (Dublin, 1978), p. 159.
[158] *Ibid.*, p. 158.   [159] Farrell, *Chairman or chief?*, p. 118.
[160] P. Keatinge, 'Ireland and the world 1957–82', in F. Litton (ed.), *Unequal achievement* (Dublin, 1982), p. 229.
[161] Keatinge, *Formulation*, p. 87.

the Irish contribution remained positive. Aiken, the former guerrilla leader, brought a lively sense of anti-colonialism to his task. Here was one area where reverence for the English example was muted. There was, inevitably, a certain amount of familiar posturing for good and against evil. But there was also much solid work.

LEMASS

Lemass resigned as Taoiseach in November 1966, at the age of sixty-seven. The heart trouble from which he was to die in 1971 had already appeared. He not only had maintained Fianna Fáil in power, after the departure of de Valera, but confounded the doubters by handing on a rejuvenated party (perhaps too rejuvenated!) to his successor. But the reputation of Lemass does not finally rest on either his electoral record or on his record as party leader. It was neither his manner of gaining power, nor his manner of holding it, that distinguished him uniquely among Irish prime ministers. It was his manner of using it.

To succeed a leader of the stature of de Valera was a daunting challenge. Neither O'Connell nor Parnell had been followed by a successor of dominant stature. Carson was followed, it is true, by the even more effective Craig. But Craig was the *de facto* leader of his people in day-to-day affairs long before Carson's resignation. He did not have to live out the best years of his life in Carson's permanent presence. A more appropriate Northern analogy would be the succession of the unfortunate John Andrews, who lasted only three years as prime minister after twenty years in Craig's shadow. Few have proved successful as premier anywhere after spending a long period in the atmosphere generated by an outstanding predecessor. Anthony Eden and Ludwig Erhard are obvious examples. Across the Atlantic, St Laurent may appear an exception. However, he had spent only seven years in the entourage of Mackenzie King. If there were superficial similarities between the de Gaulle/Pompidou succession and the de Valera/Lemass one, the contrasts were even more striking. Pompidou, despite a long Gaullist connection, had not spent his life in the shadow of Le Grand Charles. When appointed Prime Minister in 1962 he had never been a member of parliament, nor even of the Gaullist party. And he and de Gaulle would break bitterly in 1968, before Pompidou fashioned his own succession as president. The extent to which Lemass succeeded as Taoiseach testifies in the first instance to his self-discipline in controlling his impatience as lieutenant for so long. John Healy, an astute political commentator, rightly called him 'The most professional politician of his time. He survived under de Valera and time and again swallowed the bile when the Chief had other priorities and insisted on them.'[162]

[162] John Healy, 'Death of a realist', *Irish Times*, 15 May 1971.

Why de Valera choose Lemass as Tánaiste in 1945, and thus gave him a
headstart in the race for the succession, however long-distance that race
would prove to be, remains uncertain. Probably no member of the cabinet
was less sympathetic to the Chief's prime preoccupations, or less en-
amoured of his style. There can be no doubting, however, the genuine
mutual respect between de Valera and Lemass, protracted though Lemass
must have found the fifties. One may also surmise a more utilitarian
assessment on both sides. Lemass needed de Valera to deliver the votes. De
Valera needed Lemass to deliver the goods. In many respects, in his
combination of functional ruthlessness with ideological magnanimity, in
his energy, efficiency, even impetuosity, Lemass was less the heir of de
Valera than of Michael Collins. There was one vital difference, of course.
He was absolutely loyal to Dev.

He was not necessarily the closest to his leader's heart and intentions; he was
among the most resolute and unswerving of his supporters. He never favoured
'cults' . . . but his loyalty to the Chief was unbounded: it was also sincere . . . he
was never a sycophant and refused to advocate policies such as might have
accorded more closely to the desires of his leader.[163]

De Valera, aware of predictions that Fianna Fáil might collapse into
factions following his own departure, recognised the importance of the
quality. In his brief inaugural address as president on 25 June 1959 it was
this he chose to stress in greeting his successor: 'I pray that you will receive
from others the same loyalty and devotion which you yourself have
always given.'[164]

No one could replace de Valera. His star charted a unique course
through the political firmament. Lemass made no attempt – it would have
been futile – to rival the charismatic image of de Valera. If anything, he
seemed to cultivate a style intended to take charisma out of politics. De
Valera, a brilliant short-term operator, nursed a searing long-term vision;
but he had little idea how to get from one to the other. Lemass could not
compare with de Valera as a short-term tactician. Nor did he regularly
return to any long-term vision of his ideal society. He preached little about
eternal verities, preferring to limit his exhortations to the present generation. It was at this middle range that he was at his best. Here he
introduced a new dimension into Irish governance. No longer could the
immediate word be taken for the eternal deed. Results were required. In
1959, on the eve of his election as Taoiseach, he described the challenge
facing him:

The historical task of this generation, as I see it, is to consolidate the economic
foundations of our political independence. These foundations are not by any
means firm enough to be certain of their permanency. The task of consolidating

163 'Profile: Mr Seán Lemass', *Leader*, 13 March 1954.
164 Moynihan, *Speeches*, p. 597.

and extending them cannot be postponed. It has got to be done now or in the years immediately ahead of us. This, I believe, is the crucial period in our attempt to build up an Irish state which will be capable of maintaining permanent independence. If we fail, everything else goes with it and all the hopes of the past will have been falsified. But if we succeed, then every other national problem including particularly the problem of partition, will become a great deal easier of solution.[165]

This was no new emphasis for Lemass. In 1939 he responded to the publication of the dispiriting 1936 census results in similar vein. The failure to solve social and economic problems, he then asserted, has 'created a situation in which the very disappearance of the race was a possibility that could not be ignored'. Therefore the next five to ten years 'will be the most critical in the history of Ireland' because 'in that period we will repair the ravages of the past and build up firm foundations of future prosperity, or we will fail, and our failure will mean the ultimate disappearance of our nation. We must not, and we will not, fail.' Employment should be expanded in agriculture if possible, he conceded, but as this was highly unlikely because modern methods increased output without leading to corresponding increases in employment, the only real solution was further industrialisation.[166]

In 1951 Lemass was again warning that 'The efforts we have made firmly to establish freedom here will be unavailing if we cannot secure our financial freedom as well.'[167] The year 1957 found him proclaiming that 'It is the survival of the nation that is involved now.'[168] Few wanted to listen until the final moment. The *Leader*, while regarding his claim on the succession as secure, observed in 1954 that 'It is not evident that he has the political authority in the party to sway his colleagues to effective action.'[169]

The authority of Lemass may have grown somewhat in the succeeding years. But it was the crisis of 1955–7, culminating in the shock administered by the 1956 census figures, conveying a sense of ignominious defeat, that convinced some key figures, notably in Finance, of the necessity for a fundamental change of direction. It was the closest Irish equivalent to the shame of surrender and occupation for continental countries in the Second World War, or of the English sense of 'backs to the wall'. If the Beveridge Report was the equivalent of an English resistance charter,[170] then *Economic Development* had something of the same character. There had been in all occupied countries, the faint hearted, not to mention collaborators, or those who, while not actively collaborating,

---

[165] DD, 175, 3 June 1959, 938.   [166] *Irish Press*, 28 March 1939.
[167] DD, 127, 7 November 1951, 307.
[168] *Sunday Press*, 16 June 1957.
[169] 'Profile: Mr Seán Lemass', *Leader*, 13 March 1954, p. 23.
[170] D. Thompson, *Twentieth-century England* (Harmondsworth, 1965), p. 211.

nevertheless resigned themselves without undue remorse to the changed circumstances. Many in Ireland had long persuaded themselves that emigration was normal, and adjusted without undue discomfort to the emigrant wave of the fifties. The *Leader* observed that many politicians were privately more relieved than disturbed by the postwar emigration because 'If emigration were to be stopped tomorrow conditions favourable to social revolution might easily arise.'[171]

Many felt that much of the emigration was irrational anyway. James Dillon, who would become leader of Fine Gael only four months later, had the courage to express bluntly views normally voiced more discreetly. The day before Lemass defined 'the historical task of this generation', Dillon contended 'that a great deal of this talk about emigration is fraud, a great deal of this talk is dishonest, a great deal of the suggestion that emigrants are driven from this country by economic want is untrue.'[172] The essence of Dillon's argument was that much emigration could not be attributed directly to 'economic want', but to the desire of people, some of whom had the temerity to be already above the poverty line, to improve their own condition and even that of their children. Dillon here struck a note sounded frequently in official commentaries on the causes of emigration. He equated 'economic want' with an unchanging level of physical subsistence, counting anyone who abandoned a patrimony above that level as a 'voluntary' emigrant. The blame accordingly lay with the emigrants themselves, not with the society they left.

Dillon was drawing on thought processes and reflexes deeply rooted among the more secure farming, business, bureaucratic and professional classes. The response arose from the need felt by many in those classes to explain emigration in a manner that exonerated them from responsibility. Emigration was not unique to Ireland. But the type of emigration, the scale of emigration, and the impact of emigration were. In no other European country was emigration so essential a prerequisite for the preservation of the nature of the society. The interests of the possessing classes came to pivot crucially around emigration. But as the spread of emigration during the nineteenth century chanced to coincide with the growth of national political consciousness, with emphasis on the family as the source of social virtue in society, and with the decline of population, it came to be felt as a shaming indictment. But indictment of what? British malevolence, or landlord tyranny, could be conveniently, and to some extent correctly, blamed for the dispersion of families in the immediate aftermath of the famine. But that explanation began to lose force after 1880 once the land legislation put the axe to the root of landlordism. And it became wholly untenable after independence. Not even the eager

171 X, 'The nature of Irish politics', *Leader*, Christmas 1953.
172 DD, 175, 2 June 1959, 777.

hibernian imagination was prepared to adopt so robustly simple an interpretation as that of the TD who felt able to assert 'without fear of contradiction' that 'The main cause of that emigration, of all the poverty, and of anything else that is wrong politically, nationally and economically with the country is due to the partition of Ireland.'[173] No other society found itself obliged to rationalise so remorselessly the subversion of the national and family ideals inherent in the emigration 'solution' to the problem of social structure.

The psychic impact of emigration on those who stayed, the price paid by the society for the subterfuges to which it had to resort to preserve its self-respect while scattering its children, has only begun to be explored.[174] But it may be surmised that the imprint left by emigration will feature prominently as the archaeology of the modern Irish mind comes to be excavated.[175] It would be unnatural if it were otherwise. It would be equally unnatural for any society enduring the traumas of nineteenth-century Ireland, including not only colonisation, but famine, depopulation, language loss and religious revival, not to have developed protective layers of ambiguity. Yet paradoxically this was simultaneously a society that had apparently come close to social and economic equilibrium by 1900, however precariously poised that equilibrium might be. The complacent bourgeoisie – *haute, moyenne, petit* or *lumpen* according to social and semantic taste – that emerged as the ultimate beneficiary of the post-famine settlement, had no urge to linger unduly on the implications of emigration. It naturally turned to the manufacture of ideologies of communal solidarity that shifted the onus of responsibility from itself to somebody – anybody – else. When the British government and the landlords had largely served their purpose in this regard, preachers, publicans and journalists began purporting to find the anxiety of emigrants, and especially of girls, to leave Ireland, increasingly incomprehensible. By the early twentieth century they had all but completed their communal self-portrait of a simple, natural, warm, homogeneous society, a veritable miracle of human and Christian harmony.

The *Freeman's Journal*, the organ of the corpulant Home Rule party, coyly captured this conventional wisdom when asserting in 1908 that most emigrants

will bitterly rue in dismal loneliness and homesickness and physical misery at the strange places, the day when they left their own land and their own folk . . . Irish

---

173 DD, 67–68, 11 May 1937, 117.
174 K.A. Miller, *Emigrants and exiles: Ireland and the Irish exodus to North America* (Oxford, 1985), pp. 102–30, 427–92; K.A. Miller, 'Emigration, ideology and identity in post-Famine Ireland', *Studies*, 75 (Winter, 1986).
175 See J. Lee, 'Reflections on the study of Irish values', in M. Fogarty, L. Ryan, J. Lee, *Irish values and attitudes* (Dublin, 1984), pp. 112–19, much of which is incorporated into the following analysis.

girls, beguiled by hopes of fantastic wages abroad, give up more than they know, when instead of the simple neighbourly village life or the friendly relations still existing in good Irish households, they choose at a distance the tawdry, uncertain splendours of a despised servant class, and take on themselves the terrible risk of utter failure far away from all home help. It is surely true that scarcely one Irish girl abroad is ever happy again at heart.[176]

Emigrants must obviously be deluded, if not depraved, to desert God's own island. Far from the society bearing responsibility, the fickleness of the female personality now sufficed to explain an otherwise baffling indictment of an axiomatically innocent society, basking contentedly in its own smug sense of moral superiority.

The concern with female emigration reflected the fact that Irish emigration was, to an extent unusual in Europe, female emigration. Whereas European emigration as a whole was predominantly male, with a roughly 2:1 male preponderance, Irish emigration hovered around the 50:50 mark, with female emigration often preponderant at particular periods. The solicitude for female virtue enabled the propagandists to conveniently divert attention from the causes of continuing male emigration by attributing an otherwise inexplicable display of irrational ingratitude to female flightiness. The cinema came as grist to this particular mental mill. It filled the minds of foolish maidens with fanciful views of the splendours awaiting them. It could not be the fault of either the possessing classes or the policy-makers if featherheaded females succumbed to the glossy image of foreign lands portrayed by the advertisers, despite the dutiful warnings of those who had their true welfare at heart. The cinema was regularly invoked to explain the flight of the girls from the small farms, which gathered irresistible momentum from the 1930s,[177] at the height of the official benediction of traditional values. The girls, refugees from the social desolation of the 'simple, neighbourly village life' of the *Freeman*'s fond imagination, were flying from the fate staring at them in the wizened faces of their own mothers and unmarried aunts. But those who invoked the cinema to explain the female 'surplus' emigration of the 1930s had to remain discreetly silent about the female surplus of the first decade of the century, innocent of cinema blandishments. They refused to take cognisance of AE's description of the situation in 1912. Honestly confronting the reality of the back-breaking toil and small thanks that was the frequent lot of women in rural Ireland, he was moved to reflect that 'Many a young Irish girl must have looked on the wrinkled face and bent back and rheumatic limbs of her mother, and grown maddened in a sudden passion that her own fresh young life might end just like this . . .'.[178]

---

[176] *Freeman's Journal*, 24 February 1908.   [177] Hannan, *Displacement*, p. 54.
[178] A.E. (G.W. Russell), *Cooperation and nationality* (Dublin, 1912; 1982 edn), p. 66. For a later period see E. Viney, 'Women in rural Ireland', *Christus Rex*, 22 (1968)

Concern for the threat, real and imagined, to the sexual morality of female emigrants resurfaced with the huge increase in the number of girls leaving after the Second World War, now that wartime restrictions on their freedom of movement no longer applied. Of every 100 girls in Connaught aged 15–19 in 1946, 42 had left by 1951.[179] James Dillon wanted restrictions to be imposed unless the emigrants could prove 'that they were proceeding to relatives'.[180] External Affairs felt, however, that 'nothing effective can be done to protect the moral and social interests of girls going to domestic service once they have left the country'. The thinking of External Affairs was in many respects enlightened and perceptive. It is therefore all the more instructive to find that it too felt that 'The present high volume of emigration is due at least to some extent to causes other than economic necessity'[181] and could even insist that the main explanation must be sought in 'those obscure, traditional, psychological factors in which it has its principal roots'.[182] External Affairs was driven to this conclusion by its belief that the 'abnormal emigration of young girls' was 'larger than the availability of employment openings in reasonable conditions in this country would seem to call for'.[183] But who should decide what constituted 'reasonable conditions'? External Affairs conceded that despite the alleged ample employment opportunities for domestic servants in Ireland 'money wages and working and living conditions are generally less attractive than in Britain'.[184] The more attractive British conditions included better living quarters, shorter working hours and more personal freedom.

When even External Affairs had not entirely shaken off deeply rooted inherited assumptions about what ought to be good enough for the mere Irish at home, it was only to be expected that Finance would stoutly deny that Irish population decline was due mainly to economic factors.[185] And R.C. Geary, not only Director of the Central Statistics Office, but a statistician of international repute, insisted that 'It is a gross over-simplification to suggest that emigration is due solely, or even principally, to lack of economic development in Ireland.'[186]

When this view was so widespread at the most elevated levels, it comes as no surprise to find the *Irish Press*, desperately defending Fianna Fáil's record during its sixteen-year hegemony from 1932 to 1948, casting

---

179 Meenan, *Irish economy*, p. 207.
180 SPO, S11582B, External Affairs memo, 30 August 1947.
181 *Ibid.*
182 SPO, S11582B, External Affairs memo, December 1947, 'Given to the Taoiseach 31/12/47'.
183 *Ibid.*, External Affairs memo, 30 August 1947.   184 *Ibid.*
185 SPO, S10612, Finance memo, 17 April 1939, p. 45.
186 R.C. Geary, 'Irish economic development since the Treaty', *Studies*, 40 (December 1951), p. 402. The evidence Geary actually adduced (pp. 409–10) came close to subverting his own proposition.

doubts on the economic rationality of the emigrants. The outflow during the war arose 'from various motives, amongst which economic pressure was not usually the most compelling'. On their arrival in Britain they discovered that, while they might have increased their money earnings, 'they had certainly lowered their standard of living'.[187] This was a panic article, marked by audacious statistical gymnastics, but it must be assumed that it invoked arguments which it felt would appeal to many of its readers.

The *Irish Banking Review* would never descend to the journalistic licence of the *Irish Press*. But in extolling emigration as 'a useful safety valve' in 1958, it displayed an impressive degree of complacency. The *Review* accepted that economic factors were fundamental. Emigration began when 'the supply of labour' exceeded the capacity to 'absorb [it] . . . locally'. But it did not succumb to any irresistible sense of urgency about the situation. Rather, 'when all that can be done is being done' to provide work in Ireland, then 'It is better to allow the unemployed surplus to move to areas of rising demand than to condemn it to chronic unemployment.'[188] The *Review* apparently assumed that at any time 'all that can be done is being done', and that therefore 'chronic unemployment' was somehow destined to be always part of the Irish way of life.

There was one escape route. If only the Irish were not so conscious of English and American material progress, and 'If they realised that these two neighbours are the richest countries in the world, they might be content to pursue their own way of life that would conform closer to the patterns and standards of other European countries.'[189] This revealed a remarkable innocence of the progress made by 'other European countries'. Many of them were already poised to overtake Britain, and to rival the United States, in terms of 'material progress'. In cultural terms, 'the patterns and standards' of most of them could comfortably stand comparison with that of Ireland's 'two neighbours'. Simply by sustaining the existing economic trend, the 'neighbour to the east' would soon be relegated to second division status within Europe.[190] Rarely has the assumption of inherent British superiority, instinctive in a particular cast of Irish mind, been so graphically illustrated.

In suggesting that the Irish could solve emigration by lowering their expectations, because they could never hope to reach English standards, the *Review* offered a permanent recipe for mediocrity. It also condemned the vast majority of the emigrants, agricultural labourers' and small farmers' children, to a life of under-employed futility and stunted emotional development. The *Review* assumed that the Irish must always

---

[187] *Irish Press*, 2 January 1948.
[188] 'Favourable aspects of the Irish economy', *IBR* (December 1958), p. 8.
[189] *Ibid.*, p. 9.   [190] E.F. Denison, *Why growth rates differ* (Washington, 1967), p. 22.

languish in a lower division. This complex affected many observers. McElligott at the Central Bank was busy that same year of 1958 chronicling the reasons why Ireland could never hope to emulate living standards 'elsewhere'.[191] Some still clung, as to an article of faith, to the assumption that Southern Ireland, or at least the Southern Irish, simply could not industrialise. Industrialisation required sterner qualities of character than Paddy, charming a chap though he could be in his sober interludes, could possibly muster. It was somewhat cruel to impose the strain of trying on the poor fellow. This view, reflected in the gloating of the unreconstructed, if benevolent, imperialist, Maurice Headlam,[192] was not, for obvious reasons, explicitly endorsed within the country. But the conclusions came to the same thing. An intelligent article in the *Leader* dismissed the possibility of serious industrial development, brushing aside agencies like Córas Tráchtala and An Foras Tionscail as extravagant exercises in futility.[193] A contributor to *Christus Rex*, the only sociological journal in the country, doubted in 1955 'whether the predominantly agricultural economy of the country will permit of urban absorption of an overflowing of rural population even in the next fifty years.'[194] Even those of more robust nationalist persuasion, like Seán de Fréine, who published a notable study of the impact of emigration in 1960, could see little hope of a rapid solution.[195]

De Valera's rhetoric remained suffused with hope. On closer inspection, it reinforces the view that neither he nor Ireland had anything left to offer. In the trough of the slump, he pronounced himself, it is true, 'far from being pessimistic about the situation of today'.[196] His prescription for 'the difficulties that beset us at the present time', turned out to be that infallible recipe, 'grit'.[197] After returning to office he was 'in no way despondent about the future of our country. I believe our sun is but risen, when others are setting.'[198] Four out of every five children born in Ireland between 1931 and 1941 emigrated in the 1950s,[199] 57 000 of them in the twelve months prior to de Valera's astronomical observations, no doubt flying, their suitcases packed with 'grit', from the brightness of the rising sun.

De Valera himself exhibited no symptom of servility. But some of his thought processes came surprisingly close to those of the *Irish Banking Review*, which probably stood at the opposite end of the party political spectrum. Thirty years earlier, de Valera had compared Ireland before independence to 'a servant in a big mansion'. If the servant wanted his

191 *Central Bank Report* (1958), p. 34.   192 Headlam, *Reminiscences*, p. 234.
193 'E', 'State intervention in economic affairs', *Leader*, 20 June 1953.
194 H.J. Grey, 'Catering for our emigrants', *Christus Rex*, 9, 1 (January 1955), p. 11.
195 S. de Fréine, *Saoirse gan Só* (Dublin, 1960), p. 11.
196 Moynihan, *Speeches*, p. 577.   197 *Ibid.*   198 *Ibid.*, p. 588.
199 Tobin, *The best of decades*, p. 156.

freedom he must 'give up the luxuries of a certain kind which were available to him by being in that mansion . . . If he goes into the cottage he has to make up his mind to put up with the frugal fare of that cottage.'[200] That implies the inevitable inferiority of the material standards of the cottage to those of the mansion, or of small countries to big countries (or is it of republics to empires, America presumably excepted?). England at the time still enjoyed the highest standard of living in Europe, though familiarity with the economic history of the preceding half century would have revealed that the gap between Britain and many smaller continental countries was closing. Thirty years later, England enjoyed no such decisive primacy.

The injunction may have been good enough for the sometime servants. It was no longer good enough for their children. 'The luxuries of a certain kind' for which those children yearned in 1957 included the 'luxury' of a family of their own, the 'luxury' of a job where they need not constantly touch the forelock, the 'luxury' of decent medical treatment. Some even dared contemplate the obscene 'luxury' of the opportunity, denied them in the morality of the cottage, of providing a decent education for their own children. An affluent society might be a squalid society. It did not have to be. That was a matter of choice. A frugal society had little choice. Choice was the biggest 'luxury' of all that it lacked. And 'the frugal fare' of de Valera's Ireland, however genuinely he himself would have wished it otherwise, was distinctly more frugal for some than for others.

Particularly revealing expression was given, by Alexis Fitzgerald in 1954, to views probably held quite widely among the possessing classes. Fitzgerald enjoyed an extensive and remunerative legal practice. He served as adviser to two Taoisigh, his father-in-law, John A. Costello, and later Garret Fitzgerald, the cabinet meetings of whose first administration in 1981 he attended.[201] He lectured brilliantly on political philosophy in UCD.[202] He served on the Commission on Emigration from 1948 to 1954, and his short but remarkable Reservation to the majority report deserves careful consideration from students of the mentality of the professional classes.

Fitzgerald contemplated emigration with reluctant but resigned equanimity:

I cannot accept either the view that a high rate of emigration is necessarily a sign of national decline or that policy should be over-anxiously framed to reduce it. It is clear that in the history of the Church, the role of Irish emigrants has been significant. If the historical operation of emigration has been providential, Providence may in the future have a similar vocation for the nation. In the order of

200 DD, 25, 12 July 1928, 474.
201 R. Fanning, 'The Life and Times of Alexis Fitzgerald', *Magill*, 8, 18 (September 1985), pp. 34–49.
202 Personal recollection. I had the pleasure of attending Fitzgerald's lectures.

values, it seems more important to preserve and improve the quality of Irish life and thereby the purity of that message which our people have communicated to the world than it is to reduce the numbers of Irish emigrants. While there is a danger of complacency I believe that there should be a more realistic appreciation of the advantages of emigration. High emigration, granted a population excess, releases social tensions which would otherwise explode and makes possible a stability of manners and customs which would otherwise be the subject of radical change. It is a national advantage that it is easy for emigrants to establish their lives in other parts of the world not merely from the point of view of the Irish society they leave behind but from the point of view of the individuals concerned whose horizon of opportunity is widened.

The weakness in our demographic experience is less the high emigration than the low marriage rate. High emigration might in circumstances be a sign of our vitality. Instead, while it is partly due to a failure of the community to order its affairs with sufficient intelligence, taken in conjunction with a prevailing mediocrity, it suggests that continued high emigration has had some deleterious consequences. Policies should be followed directed to removing the evil of a low marriage rate even if there were made inevitable by such policies a higher rate of emigration. While we should so cultivate our resources that as many Irishmen as possible can live their lives in Ireland this should not be done in a manner or to the extent of imperilling the imponderable values and liberties of our traditional society. I cannot look forward as to an improved state of society to an Ireland where a greatly increased population can be supported only at the expense of a reduced standard of living.[203]

The number of silent assumptions, untested empirically, about socio-economic realities, and about values, informing this perspective, deserves careful consideration. The key judgement is that 'high emigration, *granted a population excess*' (my emphasis) is desirable. That may well be true. But who grants 'a population excess'? In 1841 Ireland was one of the most densely populated countries in Europe. The argument may have made sense then. In 1954, Ireland was among the most sparsely populated inhabitable countries in Europe. By no comparative criterion could it be considered over-populated. Nor was the rate of natural increase surging out of control. Hovering between eight and nine per annum during the 1950s, it was lower than that of Northern Ireland, which incidentally had double the population density, lower than that of most Mediterranean and eastern European countries, and lower than that of the Netherlands, Norway and Finland. It was only a shade higher than that of Denmark or Switzerland.[204] The problem with this type of approach is that, given the absence of any rigorous demographic analysis, it defines 'population excess' by reference to emigration, rather than emigration by reference to 'population excess'. Emigration becomes, by definition, the criterion of 'population excess', dispensing with the necessity for any further investigation. It is an intellectually self-indulgent criterion.

203 A. Fitzgerald, 'Reservation No. 2', *Reports of the Commission on Emigration and other problems* (Dublin, 1956), p. 222.
204 Mitchell, *European historical statistics*, pp. 121–4. See below, pp. 511–2.

Fitzgerald's concern for the marriage rate rather than the emigration rate may be quite justified as a value judgement. It is unsustainable as an intellectual judgement. For high emigration and low marriage rate are historically intimately connected. They are products of the same processes. Marriage rate and emigration rate are inversely related, not directly related, in Irish experience. Policies that would remove 'the evil of a low marriage rate' would, by the logic of inescapable circumstances, also contribute to a low emigration rate. Emigrants essentially left for the chance of a job that would in turn give them a better chance of marriage than at home. By failing to recognise the connection, Fitzgerald was allowing society to escape responsibility for the creation of circumstances that led ineluctably to low marriage rates as well as high emigration rates. When marriage rates rose sharply in the sixties and seventies, emigration predictably fell rapidly. In the early eighties, emigration rates would rise as marriage rates fell once more.

Many would share the view that 'a greatly increased population' should not be sought 'at the expense of a reduced standard of living'. But this was once more to beg the question. Only in the pre-industrial world did rapidly rising population often occur at the expense of living standards. Virtually all western European countries 'greatly increased' their populations in the twentieth century. Ireland was the glaring exception.[205] And almost all these countries had increased their standard of living faster than Ireland. The question that had to be confronted was why Ireland, and Ireland alone, could support 'a greatly increased population' only 'at the expense of a reduced standard of living'. Instead, the assumption was taken as the answer.

When one turns to the actual experience of emigration, as distinct from the implications of emigration for social stability or demographic development, the assumption seems to be that the choice of staying or going was somehow a random one. There is no hint here that emigration was intimately related to the wealth, power and privilege structure of the society, to the accident of birth according to class and geographical location. One might be tempted to wonder about the 'imponderable values' of a society which could apparently preserve its quality only by expelling so high a proportion of its people. Indeed, if those values were so wonderful, one might wonder if it were not a duty to try to ensure that as high a number of citizens as possible could benefit from them. Here we begin to verge on the limits of historical analysis, and we pass quite beyond the boundaries of the historian's territory when we come to ponder Fitzgerald's analysis of the intentions of providence.

Some might think the casual co-option of 'Providence' in support of a particular social analysis rather questionable. But the thought process

[205] *Ibid.*, pp. 19–24. See below, pp. 511–5.

involved enjoys a respectable ancestry in what historically passed for social thought in Ireland. The problem is that 'Providence' was confidently co-opted in support of incompatible interpretations. The scope for interpreting the intentions of 'Providence' is literally infinite. Clergymen of an earlier generation, who yielded nothing to Fitzgerald in their worship at the altar of hibernian values, urged the emigrants to save their souls in Holy Ireland rather than to hazard them for the world's goods among American heretics.[206] The gentle Fr Guinan, deeply disturbed at the fate worse than death that awaited the unsuspecting country girl in America, implicitly wondered if 'Providence' had not let the side down.

How happy, in comparison, and how blessed would have been the lot of an Irish girl, the poor betrayed victim of hellish agencies of vice, had she remained at home and passed her days in the poverty, aye and wretchedness, of a mud wall cabin – a wife and mother, mayhap – her path in life smoothened by the blessed influences of religion and domestic peace until it ended at a green old age in the calm, peaceful repose of God's just.[207]

Once one abandons the normal standards of scholarly discussion, and enters into the logic of 'Providence', the possibilities for quantification open up new dimensions for cliometrics. It would now appear that the descendants of Irish Catholics, leaving aside entirely the vexed question of 'leakage' among the emigrants themselves, have lapsed on a mass scale, with only 7.5 million of the 44 million Americans who acknowledged at least partial Irish descent in 1979, claiming to be Catholics.[208] This may not be quite as devastating as it seems at first sight, though it is striking enough. It now appears that a significant proportion of Irish emigrants to America, who would duly increase and multiply in congenial circumstances, were Protestants. And it surely cannot have been part of the providential plan to populate America with Protestants! Or should one conclude that the falling away of the Irish from the faith in America is really a sign of divine displeasure at the presumption of the Irish in abandoning the country that 'Providence' designed for them? It is perhaps best to call a halt to such speculations. The historian can only confess his discomfiture at the lack of evidence, thanks to the unenlightened policy of the Elysian bureaucracy in imposing such unreasonable conditions of access to its archives.

Fitzgerald was the voice of cerebral and civilised conservatism. There can be no doubting the genuineness of his own convictions. But he was in practice rationalising a viewpoint that was widespread among a defeatist

---

[206] Miller, 'Emigration', p. 519.
[207] J. Guinan, *Priest and people in Doon* (Dublin, 1903: 6th edn 1925), as quoted in Lee, 'Women and the church', p. 43.
[208] D.N. Doyle, 'Contemporary Irish identity: a Roman Catholic's reflections', *Crane Bag*, 9, 2 (1985), p. 156, n. 38.

political and professional elite, spiritual collaborators in the mass eviction process that drove more than half a million out between 1945 and 1960.

The instinct among the more vulnerable classes was different. Largely uncomprehending though they were, and many sharing the stultifying belief that they were part of a morally superior society, which presumably made the pain of leaving all the more wrenching, yet they indulged few illusions about those 'obscure' reasons for their departure. They were driven overwhelmingly by economic necessity. And not by the necessity of exaggerated expectations either. No doubt many Irish expectations were exaggerated, especially among the urban working and lower-middle classes, who derived their concepts of income, if not of output, largely from Britain. But the emigrants were not drawn predominantly from these classes. They were mainly the children of the poorer sections of the rural population, labourers and small farmers.

'The Irish-speaking masses of boys and girls that sailed together in the forties', the 'suitcase brigade' who took with them 'the soul of west Kerry' and 'left a gap never again to be filled' were not flying from 'reasonable' Irish prospects.[209] They were flying from nothing. And whatevever about the streets of London or New York being paved with gold in the popular imagination of an earlier generation, there were few such illusions on the boat to Holyhead. The Connemara man whom Dónal Mac Amhlaoibh glimpsed at the customs in Holyhead, his suitcase empty to the world except for a solitary pair of wellingtons, harboured few fancies about the grandeur of his future estate.[210]

It is to the writers the historian must turn, as usual, for the larger truth. It is they, some themselves emigrants, who best convey the fetid atmosphere of the forties and fifties, the sense of pervasive, brooding hopelessness at home, the emptiness, the uncomprehending remorse, the heartbreak and heroism of many caught in the web of the 'experience of abandonment'[211] as families were sundered and communities withered.[212]

The mandarins, the bankers and the gombeen men may as well have lived in a different country from their victims. However blandly they might rationalise the experience that relieved the pressure on themselves to improve their performance, however opportunistically they might

---

[209] C. Ó Cinnéide, 'A west Kerry chronicle' in Denis P. Kelleher (ed.), *Kerryman, 1881–1981* (New York, 1981), p. 73.

[210] D. Mac Amhlaoibh, *Dialann Deorai* (Dublin, 1960), p. 5.

[211] John G. Driscoll, 'Upon first going home again' in Kelleher, *Kerryman*, p. 144.

[212] In addition to Mac Amhlaoibh's account, see John Healy, *Nineteen acres* (Galway, 1978), and *Death of an Irish town* (Cork, 1968); D. Foley, 'Oíche na hImirce' (The night of emigration), *Scríobh* 3 (1978), pp. 127–31. M. Ó hOdhráin, 'Dúchas', in *Sléibhte Mhaigh Eó* ('Breeding' in *The mountains of Mayo*) (Dublin, 1964), pp. 183–203, though strictly speaking about internal migration, can be read at several harrowing levels.

blame the victims for their plight, however frequently the emigrants might return as travel conditions improved, indeed however individually liberating emigration may in fact have proven (in itself, a sad reflection on the 'imponderable values and liberties of our traditional society'), the emigration figures for the forties and fifties stand as a permanent commentary on the collective calibre of the possessing classes. In one respect only did they display true talent. So effectively did they master the techniques of indoctrination that many of the victims would continue to cherish the values responsible for their own plight. But not all. Just occasionally the arrow winged to its mark. Seán Ó Riordáin, writing in 1949 on the eve of his sister's emigration to England, would caustically comment 'At home today. "The child" going to England tomorrow. The poor girl. And the bishops and the doctors and the professors and the motor car salesmen staying at home. "A thousand thousand slimy things . . ."'[213]

The writers counted for little with the policy-makers. The politicians, however, had to take cognisance of more popular expressions of public disquiet. Platform rhetoric naturally pandered to popular instincts by ritualistically denouncing the 'evil' of emigration, while equally naturally failing to contribute any solution. Even within the possessing classes, however, there were tensions between conflicting impulses. Not all found it possible to painlessly reconcile their perceived pocket interests with their sense of patriotism. The tension would become acute if emigration soared to 'unacceptable' levels. When this finally happened in the mid-fifties, the ensuing sense of crisis was largely responsible for giving Lemass his chance at last. Where he had failed for twenty years to elicit the response he sought, now his concept of 'crisis' prevailed. Obstructionism was muted, at least for a period.[214] *Economic Development* was pivotal in this respect too. Whitaker argued, like Dillon, that 'even employed persons are leaving their jobs for more highly paid employment in Britain'.[215] He did not, however, blame this on some character defect in the emigrants. He accepted that the basic causes of emigration were economic, candidly acknowledging that 'the common talk amongst parents in the towns, as in rural Ireland, is of their children having to emigrate as soon as their education is completed, in order to be sure of a reasonable livelihood'.[216] Instead of castigating them for this, he accepted their assessment of what constituted 'reasonable' in the circumstances. He did not attribute emigration to 'obscure' psychological factors, thus exonerating the policy-maker from any responsibility for solving it. The

---

[213] S. Ó Coileáin, *Seán Ó Riordáin* (Dublin, 1982), p. 269. My translation.
[214] It remains to be seen how revealing the archives will be on resistance to Lemass at this juncture.
[215] *Economic Development*, p. 12.   [216] *Ibid.*, p. 5.

rationalisations and excuses, refined or crude, aristotelian or gombeen, were stripped bare. The buck had stopped at last.

Lemass rejected the two fundamental assumptions of the escapist school of policy-makers. He had told his colleagues thirty years before that 'the emigration habit which has arisen in some areas can be traced to the initial operation of economic factors' and 'being contrary to the most fundamental human traits will be easily broken following a revival of prosperity'.[217] A decade later, he dismissed the 'cinema' explanation with the curt observation that 'the problem is primarily one of employment'.[218] The blunt statement in the *Programme for economic expansion*, instructively placed in the section on 'industry', that 'the persistence, decade after decade, in war and in peace, of a high level of emigration is at once the greatest challenge facing Ireland and the greatest obstacle to be overcome in the context of industrial expansion' summarised a Lemass view of thirty years standing.[219]

Lemass also rejected the assumption that the Irish should lower their expectations. Perhaps he wished they would. But he refused to make this the basis of policy. The key sentence in his Clerys speech was that 'Our standards must approximate to British standards, or our people will go.'[220] He did not share de Valera's instinct that the Irish should give up their 'luxuries'. He seemed to take it for granted that there was no reason the Irish could not achieve anything they wanted to, if only they had the determination. Here he was less careful than Whitaker, who took the view that 'Realism . . . demands an awareness that, at present, and for a long time ahead, the material reward for work here may be less than that obtainable elsewhere . . .'.[221] But that was a far cry from demanding that the Irish be satisfied with their lot, or from implying that through the workings of some obscure but immutable law the Irish could never hope to emulate more advanced standards.

Lemass had already displayed enormous stamina over thirty-five years, many of them years of frustration, in public life. No national leader, or prime minister, North or South, before or since, has spent so long as an elected representative before assuming the highest office. But stamina to what purpose? What drove him on? His memoranda provide little help for biographers searching for the springs of his motivation. They rarely contained, to the chagrin of his critics, statements of first principles. They tended to proceed on silent assumptions about the self-evident validity of the objective, and normally confined themselves to the means of achieving the goal. The truth was probably very simple. Lemass lacked imagination. He took nationalist rhetoric seriously.

[217] NLI, MS 18039, FG. undated memo by Seán Lemass (probably June 1929).
[218] *Irish Press*, 28 March 1939.
[219] *Programme for economic expansion*, p. 35.	[220] *Irish Press*, 18 January 1957.
[221] *Economic Development*, p. 5.

Irish nationalists had generally expressed 'a strong belief in the creative possibilities of political sovereignty'.[222] After independence, however, they either could not, or would not, exploit those presumed possibilities. De Valera, it is true, never lost his ability to rise to generalisations of cosmic vacuity about a glorious future. But Gearóid Ó Tuathaigh has noted a rare unguarded admission from him in November 1951, concluding rather wearily that 'in the long run, the amount you can do is not very much'.[223] Lemass would never admit that 'the amount you can do is not very much'. A rare statement of his political philosophy, intended for his colleagues in the early days of Fianna Fáil, asserted

We are not prepared to watch calmly the de-population and impoverishment of our country. We desire political and economic freedom so that we can take action to protect our vital nationality interests. Unless we are prepared to see the scattering of our people over the face of the world and the destruction of our nation, we must take steps to preserve and develop here the industries which mean employment for our people in their own country.[224]

One must therefore agree with Brian Farrell, the biographer of Lemass, that 'The starting point was a fervent nationalism, rarely expressed, masked by the image of the calculating man of affairs, but always central . . .'.[225] Seán MacEntee, in a handsome obituary of his long-time colleague and rival, which revealed much of MacEntee's own stature, insisted that

The authentic personality of Seán Lemass centred upon one, fixed nucleus; an abiding, restless, ever-active urge to make his country and her people, not only prosperous and peaceful, but of some account in the world as well. Those who did not recognise that this was the source of his abounding, venturous ambition and energy could never understand Seán Lemass.[226]

But did it really matter what motivated Lemass, or what he believed? However relevant these questions may be to a biographer of Lemass, are we not in danger of exaggerating his importance by lingering over them in a general history? For may he not simply have chanced to coincide with changes that would have occurred anyway as a natural result of the generation change taking place just when he became Taoiseach? There had, after all, been abrupt changes of political style on earlier occasions. Parnell had raised the pace of the political game when he became Home Rule leader in 1880. So had de Valera when he superseded Redmond and Dillon in 1918. On the venerable grounds that twice makes a precedent, might one not anticipate a similar change in the later fifties?

It might be remarked that while generation change was pronounced in

[222] M.A.G. Ó Tuathaigh, 'De Valera and sovereignty: a note on the pedigree of a political idea', in O'Carroll and Murphy, *De Valera*, p. 67.
[223] *Ibid.*, p. 71.   [224] NLI, MS 18339, FG. Lemass memo, p. 4.
[225] Farrell, *Lemass*, p. 113.
[226] *Ibid.*, p. 124.

1880 and 1918, this does not usually lead historians to the conclusion that Parnell and de Valera merely chanced to coincide with change. The change of 1959 was not, of course, a generation change in the 1880 or 1918 sense. Lemass was almost sixty when he became Taoiseach. If this left him seventeen years younger than de Valera, he belonged to no vibrant young generation, but to an already ageing one, far removed from the thirty-four years of Parnell in 1880, or the thirty-six of de Valera, much less the twenty-eight of Collins, in 1918.

Nor was Lemass surrounded initially by a Cabinet of thrusting young Turks.[227] He was in no position in party political terms to make immediate sweeping changes. The first, and crucial, Lemass cabinet belonged to the same generation as the preceding Costello cabinet. Lemass himself was only eight years younger than Costello. Costello's Ministers for Defence and for Posts and Telegraphs were, it is true, distinctly older than their Fianna Fáil successors. On the other hand, MacEntee was twenty-nine years older than Brendan Corish in Social Welfare and twenty-five years older than Tom O'Higgins in Health. The only potentially serious policy-making departments where the Lemass ministers were younger than their inter-party predecessors were Education, to which Lemass appointed Paddy Hillery as his first new blood, thirty-six years younger than Dick Mulcahy, and Industry and Commerce, to which Lemass transferred Jack Lynch, eighteen years younger than Norton. In the most important department of all, Whitaker did sense a change of generation – when Sweetman, with whom he felt he enjoyed a generational rapport, became minister in Costello's government in 1954![228] His Fianna Fáil successor, Jim Ryan, was seventeen years older than Sweetman!

If Lemass left a much younger cabinet when he resigned, it is easily forgotten, so active was his premiership, that some of the main changes did not occur until quite late. Paddy Smith did not resign from Agriculture until 1964, Ryan and MacEntee remained until 1965. Aiken survived Lemass in office. The sense of immediate all-change testified more to the dynamic impression conveyed by Lemass himself than to the mass disappearance of familiar faces. Indeed, as soon as Lemass left, his own third and youngest cabinet began to lose something of its momentum. The change in the style of cabinet meetings symbolised the winding down of the pace, as Jack Lynch reverted to de Valera's more deliberate manner of conducting business: 'I liked to engage everyone around the table the way Dev did', whereas 'Lemass was more direct in handling government meetings. Under Dev government meetings went on very long . . .'[229]

Nor did Lemass belong to a younger generation than the new oppo-

[227] *Ibid.*, p. 103.   [228] Fanning, *Finance*, p. 504.
[229] Jack Lynch, 'My life and times', *Magill*, 3, 2 (November 1979), p. 40.

sition leaders. Dillon, who succeeded Mulcahy as parliamentary leader of Fine Gael in 1959, was three years younger than Lemass, Liam Cosgrave, who succeeded Dillon in 1965, was twenty years younger, and Brendan Corish, who succeeded Norton as leader of Labour in 1960, was nineteen years younger. James Dillon had courage, but was not widely regarded as a successful party leader. Cosgrave had his father's craggy character. But he did not want to do anything in particular. He was at his best in defence. Whatever the qualities of Dillon, Cosgrave and Corish, few have ventured to claim that they conveyed a more intense sense of change, or brought a greater urgency to the conduct of affairs, than Lemass.

A second major difference between the accession of Lemass, and the rise of Parnell and of de Valera, was that change was not now directly associated with the emergence of a new political party. Parnell did nominally inherit Butt's Home Rule Party. But that was itself a very loose constellation that had emerged only a few years previously, and was still in a highly malleable condition. Sinn Féin was for practical purposes a new party in 1918. Lemass did not enjoy the relative freedom of manoeuvre of a leader sweeping into office at the head of a movement intimately identified with his prestige. Instead he faced the task, more daunting in many respects, of transmuting an old party. Contemporaries were acutely aware of the generational difficulties of the challenge.

Mr Lemass's principle, and most difficult, political task will be to rejuvenate the membership and re-orientate the policy of the Fianna Fáil party. If he can accomplish this almost impossible task without friction and disunion he will probably go far; but his time for doing so is short, for a new generation is waiting to take over.[230]

The party that should have emerged triumphantly, on both the new generation and the new movement premises, was Clann na Poblachta in 1948. There was a generation gap between the Clann's leadership and that of both Fianna Fáil and Fine Gael. Clann na Poblachta was the generation change that never was. Its experience warns of the danger of imputing almost deterministic influence to generational factors. In so far as an age discontinuity occurred in Fianna Fáil, and in Irish politics in general, it came more between Lemass and his successors than between Lemass and his predecessors. Only the activist Lemass style has disguised this. But his successor as Taoiseach rightly referred to it when remarking that 'It is little appreciated with what ease and tranquillity Seán Lemass effected the transfer of power from his generation to another.'[231]

A third, and crucial, difference between the Lemass years and the

---

[230] *Round Table*, 196 (September 1959), p. 364.   [231] Lynch, 'Life and times', p. 42.

Parnell decade or the age of de Valera lies in the nature and consequences of the changes involved, which again restrict the validity of the
generational analogy, even were it correct in purely physical terms. The
rise of Parnell was, it is true, linked with the social issue of the land war.
But that had begun independently of him, skilfully though he exploited
it, and he worked to dampen it as soon as it had served his political
purposes. Parnell could have no impact on the course of emigration,
even if he wanted to. He was not in office. Emigration actually increased
during the 1880s. The victory of Sinn Féin brought no significant change
in social trends or in social attitudes. Home Rulers, Sinn Féiners,
Cumann na nGaedheal and Fianna Fáil all shared the same fundamental
value system. The Cosgrave regime fostered a vigorous social continuity.
If the early Fianna Fáil articulated a more radical rhetoric, the pleasures
of office, as has often been noted, soon reconciled it to the inherited
social realities. Emigration remained as central to both the viability and
value system of de Valera's Ireland as of Cosgrave's or Redmond's. Few
of Lemass's contemporaries fully shared his concern about emigration.
His older cabinet colleagues stoically endured his obsession with doing
something about it. Nor was there much evidence that the younger
generation had more fire in their bellies than the young, or even the old,
Lemass. At a more refined level, Alexis Fitzgerald was twenty years
Lemass's junior. But there would be no dash for the future from that
perspective. The turning of the tide during the Lemass years did not
therefore simply mark one more turn of the generational wheel. Instead,
it represented a reversal of the dominant ethos not just of a generation,
but of a century. The essence of the Lemass approach can be defined as
the attempt to substitute the performance principle for the possessor
principle in Irish life. To fully grasp the magnitude of the challenge
confronting him, we must delineate the nature of the inherited ethos. For
the primacy of the possessor principle owed its power not to the whims
of individuals, but to attitudes deeply rooted in social structure and
historical experience.

The origins of the collective mentality of 'traditional' Ireland must be
sought far back in history. Here we can deal with its manifestations only
since the nineteenth century. The arbitrariness of relations between
landlord and farmer, and between farmer and labourer, fortified in the
Irish the craving for security natural and normal in an uncertain world.
This expressed itself most obviously in an obsessive attachment to land.
But this attachment was not fundamentally to land for its own sake,
though land could come to inspire an intense emotional identification
through acquired family associations. Land was equated with security.
The idea of property rights in employment, no less than in land, the
individual's right to fixity of occupational tenure, was also firmly rooted

in public consciousness before the Famine.[232] The concern with property rights was wholly natural in the light of the alternatives facing the holders of land or jobs. The price of failure was frighteningly high. It involved, for the vast majority of the victims, far more than mere temporary unemployment, a brief interlude until an adequate alternative source of income could be found. In a society characterised by intense population pressure in relation to available employment opportunities, loss of one's holding, whether in land or in a job, normally brought with it not only the economic but the social ruin of the family. Economic loss involved psychic humiliation. The husband had failed his wife, the father his children. Few would risk so bitter a price. It was entirely rational in those circumstances for the individual to prize security above all, and to abhor risk taking when the price of failure was catastrophe.[233]

Security was further coveted because so little discernible relationship existed between effort and reward. Inheritance within farming was generally confined to one son, and marriage to one daughter. Children's prospects remained largely unaffected by their own performance. The labourer, however well he worked, could not normally hope to become a farmer. Sluggish growth denied to most 'surplus' farmers' children, no less than labourers, the opportunity of non-agricultural employment.

The two biggest gains made by Irish farmers during the nineteenth century came from the Great Famine and from the Land War. The famine of 1845–50 allowed the survivors to tack on the cleared or vacated holdings to their own farms. They owed this windfall to no obvious merit of their own, beyond their capacity for survival. The gains that accrued from the Land War of 1879–82 were due to effort. But the effort was political rather than economic. The lesson for the farmer was that gain came more from collective political power than from individual economic performance.

The nature of farming itself fostered scepticism about the relation between effort and reward. The return on cattle or sheep, or even on butter and eggs, seemed to depend less on sustained forward planning or on unremitting effort, than on the 'luck' of British prices, and on the haggling skills of vendor, or vendeuse, at fair or market. The farmer became increasingly a speculator in livestock or livestock produce. The climate itself conspired to induce a certain complacency. Capricious in the short run, and indulgent in the long run, it neither permitted nor required the hand to be kept constantly to the plough, literally or metaphorically.

232 J.J. Lee, 'Patterns of rural unrest in nineteenth-century Ireland' in L.M. Cullen and F. Furet (eds.), *Ireland and France, 17th–20th centuries: towards a comparative study of rural history* (Paris, 1980), p. 229.
233 These paragraphs incorporate sections from J. Lee, 'Motivation: an historian's point of view', in An Foras Forbartha, *Ireland in the year 2000: towards a national strategy* (Dublin, 1983), esp. pp. 38ff.

Climate does not determine character. But it can influence the development of traits deriving from other influences.

Experience fostered other rational responses scarcely conducive to the performance principle. The time horizon of possession was eternity. The time horizon of pastoral agriculture was very short term, dispensing even with the perspective imposed by the rotational requirements of tillage. The structure of the Irish cattle industry, with animals passing through several hands in quick succession, made for short-term calculations. The time horizon of the farmer therefore tended to oscillate between the very long term, symbolised by the hoarded savings for the daughter's distant dowry, reposing undisturbed at minimal interest rates in the bank, irrespective of the fluctuating fortunes of the farm, and the very short term, reflected in the mentality of the fair day and the 'bargain'. There was relatively little scope to develop a sense of the medium term, or of the idea of goals to be achieved through accumulated regular effort. Reward came more from 'strokes' than from sustained labour.

The consequence of a rational preoccupation with security, and a not irrational distrust of effort, meant that performance broadly took second place to possession as a criterion of status. The two principles were not necessarily mutually exclusive. Possession was, after all, a pre-requisite for performance! 'I survived' might suffice for some as a genuine record of personal, no less than national, achievement. But the engrained attitude could not be easily changed, as Michael Davitt discovered when his proposals for a monitoring of the efficiency of farmers' performance, and for the imposition of a land tax, which would operate as a performance tax, fell on predictably barren ground in 1882. Davitt's concern for the quality of economic performance in the national interest could make little impression on this mentality. The primacy of the possessor principle would survive until at least the second half of the twentieth century. 'The prestige and social rank of the family as a whole depends on the ownership and *not* on the use of the property. Size of farm, not productivity, determines one's place on the class ladder.'[234]

The slow pace of industrialisation in post-Famine Ireland allowed these agricultural attitudes to continue to infiltrate the non-agricultural sector, which in any case had its own inherited share of them. The structure of the economy, with the partial, but only partial, exception of Belfast (for Catholic and Protestant had far more in common in this respect than either would care to concede) reinforced the mentality nurtured at the farmer's fireside.

Not industry, but trade and the professions, dominated the non-agricultural sector. They developed protective devices to shield themselves from the impersonal insensitivity of market forces. Like the farmers, they

234 Limerick Rural Survey, *Third Interim Report. Social Structure* (Tipperary, 1962), p. 53.

triumphantly maintained their claim to be considered more a way of life than an occupation. Here too possession criteria took precedence over performance. Growth might depend to some extent on providing a superior service. Survival generally did not. Clienteles often consisted of a web of 'favours' rather than 'efficiency'. And even the industrial sector did not foster widely different mentalities. Family firms predominated. They were not incompatible with performance criteria. Some did achieve impressive records. But they were quite compatible with fairly comfortable stagnation. Inheritance within the family may have partly depended on the apparent performance potential of the children. Even here, the ablest son was often guided towards the professions, and the commercial inheritance left to less talented siblings. It was next to impossible for an outsider, irrespective of his ability, to break into the family circle, except through marriage. And marriage prospects were more likely to be determined by the family status of the suitor than by his performance potential. Not until the state sponsored bodies began to develop did some openings arise for managers who had lacked the foresight to be born into the right families. As an eminent exponent of state enterprise observed 'The family-owned firm was dominant and the crown prince blocked promotion to the top posts.'[235] The family firm had much the same ethos as the family farm.

The industrialisation drive after 1932, which might at first sight have seemed conducive to the spread of the performance principle, did little in practice to inculcate a new ethic. Protection guaranteed possession of the home market to the new firms within very relaxed performance criteria. The disicpline of the market was generally kept at a discreet distance. 'For more than thirty years our many state and private enterprises have produced managers by accident rather than managers by design' complained *Irish Management* in 1957, adding that it was futile to speak of scientific management 'if such factors as family ties, friendship, religion, or national record are allowed to outweigh more significant qualifications.'[236]

Occupational expansion in post-Famine Ireland occurred mainly in the public service, in teaching, nursing and the Catholic Church. Their distinguishing feature was that they did require some qualifications for entry. Educational requirements therefore introduced some performance criteria. But the education remained primarily functional in its purpose as a means to the end, not of knowledge, but of security. 'Relevance' was the prime determinant of curricula. A type of education that has now come to be retrospectively condemned as 'academic' by the contemporary advertising agencies for 'relevance' was essentially motivated by the same

[235] C.S. Andrews, 'Comment', in Chubb and Lynch, *Economic development*, p. 198.
[236] *Irish Management*, 4, 5 (September/October 1957), p. 150.

instincts. What has happened is that the concept of 'relevance' has changed, not that 'relevance' has come to supersede an alternative traditional criterion. 'Traditional' society had difficulty grasping any concept of education except the provision of security for the educated. Agricultural education, therefore, appeared incomprehensible to most farmers. As education was for security, and as security on the land was not a consequence of education, the idea of agricultural education was almost tautologous for the vast majority of farmers.

Education had an ambiguous influence on the performer ethic. The post-famine educational system has been criticised for allegedly inculcating rigidity of perspective, lack of imagination, lack of entrepreneurial initiative. Perase's memorable criticism of the system in 'The murder machine' made many telling points. More recently, Ivor Kenny has noted that 'conservatism, authoritarianism – are lessons learned young . . . children are encouraged to think about what they want to be, not what they want to do.'[237] Yet, and despite the validity of specific criticisms, 'traditional' education conferred significant benefits not only on a number of deprived but able individuals, but also on society. The teacher training colleges, which attracted the academically brighter children of the medium and smaller-sized farms in the south and west, were in many ways, and far more than the universities, seminaries of a new work ethic. Many teachers would, no doubt, settle for the quiet life, but a substantial number sought to instil in their pupils the conviction that performance could lift them out of the ancestral rut. When the history of the Irish people finally comes to be written, the saga – for saga it was – of those teachers who struggled to inspire their pupils with a sense of their own potential will deserve belated homage.

Much of this performance ethic was directed to the goal of security. There was nothing either ignoble, or unusual, in that. The search for security has motivated many peoples who have suffered discrimination, or worse. Circumstances largely dictate in which direction the search will be pursued. It has inspired Jews and Quakers, for instance, into outstanding entrepreneurial feats in the field of industry.[238] The objective in Ireland was the security of 'permanent and pensionable' employment. Performer and possessor criteria therefore jostled together. Institutions that imposed some entry requirements frequently failed to maintain performance criteria once the entry threshold had been crossed. Entry to the civil service continued to be based on competitive examination. But many of the same civil servants who owed their preference in the first instance to performance, as measured by examinations, then hastened to

237 Kenny, *Government and enterprise*, p. 73.
238 W.J. Reader, 'Businessmen and their motives', in D.C. Coleman and P. Mathias (eds.), *Enterprise and history* (Cambridge, 1984), p. 44.

embrace the possession principle of seniority for promotion purposes.[239] Indeed, H.P. Boland, the first chief personnel officer for the civil service, sought to exclude women from entry to the senior civil service, as if the state were so inundated with talent that it could ignore the potential of half its population.[240] This did *not* mean that no senior civil servant felt obliged to exert himself, or to live laborious days. Such a conclusion would be patent nonsense. Many senior civil servants were among the most dedicated workers in the state. Some performed prodigies. But it did mean that their motives owed more to their own ethical sense, to internal impulses, than to any institutional imperative.

Much the same applied to the universities. The National University of Ireland, instituted under an Act of 1908, though nominally non-denominational, was the custodian of the highest educational values of Catholic Ireland. It devised an appointment system that dispensed with the vulgarity of professional assessment, and reposed complete confidence in the consequences of the canvassing capacity of the candidate. It was to take sixty years before it would even contemplate a role for a professional assessment system, and even then in so casual a manner that it created as many problems as it solved. Until then, appointment procedures offered only limited incentive for effort, because preferment bore no self-evident relationship to performance. That did not mean that the best people were not frequently appointed. They were. But they were not appointed necessarily because they were the best people.

As the university, faithfully mirroring the values of the dominant elements in the society it served, also refused to contemplate punitive action for so venial a transgression as inadequate performance, there was little to discourage those tempted to limit the intensity of their scholarly activity once they had crossed the appointments hurdle. Academics who failed to cultivate their subjects stood in no more danger of eviction than farmers who failed to cultivate their farms. Again, as in the civil service, a remarkable number of academics in the cirumstances did perform. As with civil servants, however, their performance derived from their individual sense of morality, not from the ethos of their institutions.

The most rapidly expanding major institution in the country in the century after the famine was the Catholic Church. The number of priests sextupled, the number of nuns rose even faster. And that was only at home. By 1950 the number of priests on the missions equalled the number on the home front. This expanding, confident, indeed triumphalist institution, attracted some of the finest performer talent in the country. Its administrative and managerial achievement, at home and abroad, in education, in health, in welfare, as well as in religion, owing much to

---

[239] See Fanning, *Finance*, pp. 587ff. for an absorbing example of conflicting moralities.
[240] *Ibid.*, p. 77.

women as well as men, deserves the highest recognition. The achievement at home has often been taken for granted, or even slighted, because of the over-politicisation of the perspective from which the role of the Catholic clergy has tended to be assessed in conventional historiography, and because of the superficiality of much public comment on the church in society. The missionary achievement abroad, despite the crudity of some of the cultural constructs it imposed on native peoples, was among the more remarkable conquests of the age of imperialsim. This was not the record of men, or women, who reclined comfortably on the platform of possession.[241]

The church could boast a galaxy of performers, and it was expanding sufficiently fast, unlike the country at large, to give many of them their heads. Indeed, the opportunity for performance probably called forth latent aspirations among the clergy. It provides evidence that performance criteria were not alien to Irish culture, that the primacy of the possessor principle was not the result of immutable qualities inherent in the Irish personality, but was shaped by a specific historical conjuncture – and can therefore be changed, if change be desired, by social engineers able to understand the lessons of history. This too was the lesson of the Irish emigrant performance, as many have observed.[242] The Irish respond rationally, by the criteria of western civilisation, to objective circumstances. Petty's pungent comment applies as much in the twentieth as in the seventeenth century: 'Their lazing seems to me to proceed rather from want of Imployment and Encouragement to work than from the natural abundance of Flegm in their bowels and blood.'[243]

'Imployment and Encouragement' remained as elusive in the mid twentieth century as in Petty's time. The generational concept does not provide the key to understanding the nature of social change or of the civic culture. There are 'plus men', 'neutral men', and 'minus men' in every generation in every society.[244] In Irish circumstances the conflict resolved itself largely into a struggle between the possessor ethic and the performer ethic. The possessor ethic had dominated the collective mentality for generations, but it was not universal. Indeed, the extent to which performer criteria infiltrated in so unpromising an environment is quite striking. But performer principles were undoubtedly subordinate to possessor principles in the Ireland of the fifties. Lemass was determined to shift the balance. It was a herculean, not to say a sisyphean endeavour.

---

[241] P.J. Corish, *The Irish Catholic experience: a historical survey* (Dublin, 1985), chs. 6–8 convey the spirit of the performance.

[242] P. Mathias, 'Leisure and wages in theory and practice', in *The transformation of England* (New York, 1979), pp. 164–5.

[243] Cited in *ibid.*, p. 164.

[244] T. Barrington, 'Systems', in H. Bohan (ed.), *Roots in a changing society* (Shannon, 1982), p. 49.

That he should embark on it at all helps place in clearer perspective the fabled pragmatism of Lemass.

Pragmatism there certainly was, in the sense of changing, or even reversing, the techniques of policy. Having argued in 1929 that as 'the goal of our efforts should be to keep the Irish people in Ireland and provide prosperity for them here', it was imperative that 'Everything else, even . . . accepted notions about efficiency, must be sacrificed to that end',[245] he would gradually revise that view until he was writing by the 1950s that 'efficiency . . . is the only basis on which Irish industry can expand'.[246] In 1929 protection was 'identical with the struggle for the preservation of our nationality'.[247] Thirty years later he would preside over the jettisoning of protection as free trade now became the favoured means for industrial development. He spelled out in 1929 the dangers of reliance on foreign investment:

The extent to which foreign capital had acquired control of Irish industry . . . is most undesirable for several reasons . . . Those who control industry can exercise a considerable influence on the determination of national policy. If such persons are foreigners, to any large extent, their only interest in the country is the profit they can make out of it and they will undoubtedly render it difficult to adopt measures designed to protect national interests when those interests are in conflict with their own. Secondly, industries which are only branches of foreign concerns are strictly limited in their development. Such concerns seldom develop an export trade. It is usual also for the higher executives in such firms to be filled by employees promoted from the parent branch.[248]

These criticisms were valid at the time. Some are still valid. But circumstances were different thirty years later. The development of multinational enterprise was tranforming the potential of foreign investment as an agent of *export* development. It was now precisely to 'develop an export trade' that he solicited foreign capital. The dangers he identified earlier were still there. But those dangers had to be risked rather than resign oneself to defeat in the proven knowledge that Irish management did not measure up to the task. There can be little doubt that Lemass would in turn have abandoned this technique once he felt it no longer served its purpose – and if he could have found an alternative.

If Lemass was flexible with respect to techniques, he remained as consistent as it is possible to be in public life in promoting performance criteria. He accepted, for instance, the necessity of compromising on the performer principle if the best were the enemy of the good, as in the allocation of cabinet portfolios, on the grounds that 'it is far more important to maintain good will and harmony than seek a more effective

[245] NLI, MS18339, FG, undated Lemass memo.
[246] *Irish Management*, 4, 5 (September/October 1957), p. 157.
[247] NLI, MS18339, FG, undated Lemass memo (probably June 1929).   [248] *Ibid.*

distribution of responsibility'.[249] He moved cautiously in making cabinet changes at first but he did make a number from 1961 and, with the qualification just mentioned, 'would have kept on making changes time and again, if for no other reason than to make it quite clear to any new man that if he showed he had ability the road to promotion was fairly open to him'.[250] When he explained in retrospect his decision to resign on the grounds that old people hung on too long – hastening with suspicious speed to exclude de Valera from this generalisation – he was once again invoking performance criteria.[251]

He could be caustic enough in debate, but it was always a matter for surprise when he descended to personal abuse. He tended to criticise opponents more for their performance than for their principles. The contrast between himself and MacEntee, for instance, is nicely caught in the normal style of their response to the Labour Party. Whereas MacEntee regularly professed alarm about the ideological threat allegedly posed by Labour, Lemass preferred to dismiss Labour on performance grounds. MacEntee had lost none of his polemical enthusiasm against 'reds' as late as the sixties. In 1963 he denounced the Labour Party for admitting Noel Browne to membership in such extravagant terms that the newspapers refused to publish parts of his speech on legal advice.[252] Lemass, on the other hand, dismissed Labour in 1966 on the grounds that 'Far from the Labour Party going "Red", they are not going anywhere . . . The Labour Party are a nice, respectable, docile, harmless body of men – as harmless a body as ever graced any parliament.'[253] The scurrility of MacEntee rankled because it was so patently unjust. The condescension of Lemass rankled even more because it was so patently just.

But pragmatism and performance to what purpose? There is an element of the sphinx about Lemass, though whether he is a sphinx without a riddle must await further investigation. Precisely because he so rarely articulated a vision of his ideal society, in distinct and perhaps conscious contrast to de Valera, his ideals must be inferred from his performance – a test one would hesitate to impose on many political leaders. The *Leader* profile noted that

It has always been a mistake shared by members of the Fianna Fáil party, as well as by the opposition, to assume that he is not interested in ideals . . . the difference is that he has always been interested in the results and cannot devote too much time to ideals which have no likelihood of being ever achieved. He is quite prepared, if necessary, to espouse losing causes; he would never tolerate a lost one.[254]

[249] Farrell, *Chairman or chief?*, p. 101.   [250] *Ibid.*, p. 102.
[251] 'Seán Lemass looks back', *Irish Press*, 31 January 1969.
[252] M. Gallagher, *Labour*, p. 53.   [253] *Ibid.*, p. 70.
[254] Lemass profile, *Leader*, 13 March 1954.

He occasionally sought to legitimise the drive to economic growth by rather speciously suggesting it would lead to a more Christian and more Gaelic society.[255] But that was only when he was driven to desperation. What is more striking is how relatively rarely he descended, or ascended, according to the reader's taste, to invocation of Ireland's 'Christian' mission in the manner that formed a stock-in-trade of de Valera, Costello, Cosgrave, Dillon, MacBride, and others. His relative silence spoke volumes about his disdain for the rhetoric that portrayed the Irish as a spiritually superior people. His own campaign rhetoric would vary according to electoral circumstances, sometimes espousing the virtues of private enterprise, sometimes of state enterprise – but always of enterprise. 'He does not disbelieve in private enterprise, nor does he not believe in state socialism.'[256] Always we return to his nationalism. He was basically neither capitalist nor socialist, but nationalist. Capitalism and socialism, like so much else, were but means to the end of 'the survival of the Irish nation as a strong prosperous self-reliant political unit'.[257]

By 1959 'self-reliance' had come to mean for Lemass not self-sufficiency, his once favoured slogan, but an economy sufficiently viable to enable all the Irish to live in their own country.[258] How did he propose to mobilise the sceptical or obstructive adherents of the possessor principle, including many businessmen, trade unionists, professional people, civil servants, not to mention farmers – in pursuit of that apparently impossible dream? It is here that the limitations of the 'pragmatist' interpretation of Lemass begin to appear. It is usual to contrast the murky pragmatism of Lemass with the unsullied idealism of de Valera. The semantic confusion involved in this contrast itself reflects certain values in the political culture. Strictly speaking, the converse of pragmatist is not idealist, it is dogmatist. Nor is idealist the converse of realist, a term also often applied to Lemass. The converse of realist is illusionist. The philosophical converse of idealist is materialist. The political converse is not realist, but cynic or sceptic. In one profound sense, it was de Valera who was the realist, Lemass the illusionist. Where de Valera, by and large, fatalistically accepted the national character with which he had to work, and then proceeded to brilliantly manipulate it, Lemass tried to fashion a new national character. Where de Valera picked out certain notes, often self-indulgent, in the national psyche, on which he played a reassuring and beguiling tune, Lemass tried to change the tune. In this he had something in common with that other impossibilist, Kevin O'Higgins, though the Lemass tune was as different from that of O'Higgins as from that of de Valera.

255 Baker, 'Nationalist ideology', *passim*.
256 Lemass profile, *Leader*, 13 March 1954, p. 23.
257 NLI, MS18339, FG, undated Lemass memo (probably June 1929).
258 See Girvin, 'Protectionism and economic development', pp. 308ff.

The struggle of Lemass to use the air of crisis in the late fifties to instil a new sense of national direction, to elevate the performer principle at the expense of the possessor principle, was striking in its audacity and little short of utopian in its ambition. In this respect, Lemass was a pragmatist but not a realist. The sense of crisis did, it is true, give him somewhat more scope for manoeuvre in the short term. But a society pervaded by the possessor principle normally responded more with apathy than anger to economic crisis, unless its possession of its property was directly threatened, as in 1879. Lemass did not inherit either a party or a country panting at the leash, waiting only the signal to surge forward. There was no excited response to his definition of 'the historical task of this generation', which 'received surprisingly little notice from the newspapers'.[259] He could not expect tumultuous applause when he dared blur the national self-image of injured innocence by implying that the natives were responsible for their own fate. The principle that 'the economic survival of this country depends entirely on our own efforts' or 'the world does not owe us a livelihood on our terms' roused resentment among those abruptly threatened with redundancy in 'the world owes us a living' industry.[260] How dare he imply that the Irish had no inalienable right to their sense of grievance. Was it not part of what they were? The performer ethic was not one to set every heart leaping with great joy.

Lemass predicted in 1962 that the inefficient industrial producer, the traditional farmer, the trade union leader rooted in Victorian assumptions, 'all these by 1970 will have become anachronistic relics of a dead past'.[261] He was a shade optimistic! He was doubtless trying to 'talk up' the performer principle. But the time-scale was singularly ambitious. He cannot have been unaware of the resilience of the forces of inertia. Why should those who enjoyed security on the basis of the possessor principle suddenly slough off the mentalities that had served them well. Sustained economic growth for a generation might create conditions propitious to the more extensive spread of the performer principle. But that would be over the dead bodies of those who had been socialised into the possessor ethic, and who would carry it with them to the grave. Even in the potentially dynamic state sponsored sector, it was not only the ESB which, partly under pressure from an earlier Lemass, was 'influenced by the compelling national need to maximise employment', which inevitably 'led in turn to a general emphasis on job creation and job retention which gradually became an integral feature of industrial organisation and trade union expectations in Ireland'.[262]

259 *Irish Review and Annual*, 1959, p. 8.
260 *Sunday Press*, 18 January 1957 (reprint of his Clery's speech, October 1955).
261 Tobin, *Best of decades*, p. 71.
262 Manning and McDowell, *Electricity supply in Ireland*, p. 240.

Lemass tried to use national consciousness as the weapon to undermine the possessor principle. In 1929 the young Lemass had attributed exceptional powers of mass motivation to patriotism:

The spirit of nationality is one of the most potent forces affecting the thoughts and actions of men and races and cannot be ignored. Its effects have sometimes proved destructive and even disastrous but, on the whole, they have been beneficial to humanity. It has brought us out of feudalism to democracy and it is, and will be, for a long time, the driving force of history. Pride in their country and a desire for its advancement can secure combined effort for the common good from men who would not be influenced by other considerations . . . The need for patriotism did not disappear with the handing over of Dublin Castle. In our efforts to bring prosperity to the country we will find that the spirit of Irish nationality – the determination of our people to survive as a separate nation – will be our greatest asset, and our surest guarantee of success.[263]

He would not always be so confident. His far from infrequent lurches in the direction of a *dirigiste* economic order – his demand for a putatively temporary economic dictatorship to meet the 'crisis' of 1933, his envisaged powers for a super ministry of Labour in 1942, his industrial efficiency proposals in 1946 – all reveal singularly limited confidence in the capacity of 'patriotism' to achieve economic objectives. Nevertheless he had in practice moved in the direction of working closely with trade unions. Disappointed by the parochialism of their sectoral perspective, he tried in 1945 to persuade them towards a more capacious concept of their role, suggesting to the Irish Trade Union Congress that

In a democratic state, the trade union movement must play an increasingly important part in the national life, not merely as a guardian of the workers' interests, but as an essential part of the machinery of industrial organisation, accepting the responsibilities which relate to its real power, and proceeding from the stage of negotiating particular agreements with private employers to the stage of formulating and carrying into effect a general policy for the furtherance of the long term interests of the workers as a class.[264]

The suggestion fell on barren ground. But he resumed the effort after 1959, inviting the trade unions to participate in the work of a number of national bodies concerned with 'planning', the Irish National Productivity Committee in 1959, the Employer–Labour Conference and the Committees on Industrial Organisation in 1961, the National Industrial and Economic Council in 1963.[265]

He was simultaneously trying to inculcate a sense of public responsibility into business. 'Nobody nowadays', he optimistically asserted in 1957

[263] NLI, MS18339, FG, undated Lemass memo (probably June 1929).
[264] McCarthy, *Unions*, pp. 265–6.
[265] *Ibid.*, pp. 572ff.

regards the operation of an important industrial undertaking as being the exclusive private concern of its owners. Rather is each such undertaking looked upon as a national asset contributing to the country's economic and social advancement, and entitled to bring its problems when they arise to the government and to expect help in coping with them. The social consequences of fluctuations in the level of business activity are matters of public debate. The contribution which a progressive and efficient industrial concern can make to national welfare, or to the prosperity of a particular locality, are widely understood. The industrial manager has unavoidable responsibilities, wider than those placed on him by his employer. He should be regarded and regard himself, as a public servant in the finest meaning of that term.[266]

This expressed an almost Japanese (or alleged Japanese) sense of the social responsibility of business. It bore no relation to Irish practice.

Neither businessmen nor trade union leaders had any less commitment to the national interest than representatives of other pressure groups. They were as likely to be conscious of their nationality as anybody else. They were also just as good Catholics (or occasionally, in the case of businessmen, Protestants). But they had long since perfected the principle of keeping patriotism, like religion, isolated from daily life. They were loyalties that were genuine enough, but were to be dusted down for ritual occasions, and then put into storage again. Patriotism provided no protection against the predator instinct. Lemass enjoyed only mixed success in striving to secure a policy on national wage agreements after 1959 that would serve the longer term national interest. Negotiators were keener on the immediate gains than on the longer term implications, even for their own members.[267] In 1964 Lemass yielded to trade union pressure to grant wage concessions larger than could be justified on any national grounds. Although less than they seemed at first sight, and relatively minor compared to later flights from reality, they nevertheless provided an ominous indication of emerging tendencies.

Developments in labour relations exposed the Achilles heel in the Lemass strategy of searching for a neo-corporatist national consensus on economic policy. Unless the possessor principle could be superseded by the performer principle, then the creation of powerful institutional bases for interest groups would enable them to defend the possessor principle even more emphatically than before. The consensus that Lemass sought would then become a consensus of predators which would threaten to subvert rather than sustain economic growth. The Lemass strategy could probably operate effectively only in an Ireland of little Lemasses. That was a distinctly unlikely eventuality. De Valera, more realistic than Lemass, had always been sceptical of institutionalising power outside the political

---

[266] *Irish Management*, 4, 5 (September/October 1957), p. 155.
[267] For details see J.F. O'Brien, *A study of national wage agreements in Ireland* (Dublin, 1981).

system. He resisted arbitration for civil servants, and particularly distrusted public sector trade unions, as reflected in his unyielding attitude towards the teachers' strike in 1946.[268]

De Valera may have been right in principle. But trade union membership surged in postwar Ireland. Greatly extended organisation of sectoral interests became a fact of political life. The choice for government lay between conflict or consensus. Either course posed difficulties. Neither could guarantee the successful defence of the national interest. Whatever about the circumstances of any specific issue, consensus was the only way forward for a small, vulnerable state. But consensus did ultimately depend, in large measure, on a sense of patriotism. The problem for Lemass was that the patriotism inherited from 'traditional' Ireland was so hollow that it could not bear even the weight he tried to place on it. It might suffice to motivate a small number of individuals to live laborious days, and to subordinate their private interest to the public interest. Even a small number could make a political revolution with the passive support of the masses. But more than passive support was required to make an economic revolution. Patriotism in Ireland had to be redefined to carry that responsibility. It would take a long, slow remoulding of the character and ethos of the society before it would be achieved, if ever. Lemass took up the challenge with extraordinary energy for a man whose stamina ought to have been sapped by the long years of obstruction and frustration. But there could be no quick victory, and indeed no final victory. For the struggle between the possessor ethic and the performer ethic would have to be unceasing in every generation. The performer ethic made striking gains in a short period as those who actually wanted to *do* something were now given their head to a greater extent than ever before. It remained to be seen whether the pace could be sustained.

There was significant achievement in a short period. Yet there were also distinct limitations to the legacy of Lemass, even in his chosen socio-economic field. Industrialisation had advanced gradually. But Lemass did not solve the problem that had baffled him since 1932 – how to create a viable *Irish* industry. By the mid-sixties, the continuing failure of Irish-owned industry on the export front, despite all the incentives, was becoming grimly clear. Only the success of foreign investment was now energising the export drive. The hope that foreign example would inspire native emulation was proving vain. Lemass, curbing the *dirigiste* impulses of 'industrial efficiency' vintage, had come to rely on subsidies, as dispensed on the basis of CIO reports, on education, partly through the IMI, which he strongly supported, and on emerging institutional structures tending in a neo-corporatist direction, as the main stimulants to

[268] O'Connell, *INTO*, pp. 221–2.

efficiency.[269] The subsidies seem to have been largely squandered. At least they did not achieve the objective of making *Irish* industry competitive. The bulk of Irish businessmen showed little interest in management education. Apart from the fact that Irish trade union, employer and civil service structures were based on English models not conducive to a corporatist approach requiring the subordination of short-term sectoral interests to longer term national interests, the legitimisation of the possessor ethic habituated a high proportion of the actors in every area to demand payment more for what they were than for what they did. There was a touch of desperation about the Anglo-Irish Free Trade Agreement of 1965. If all else failed, maybe fear would force the possessors to perform!

Despite these emerging problems, Lemass bequeathed a far more promising legacy than the one he inherited. The forces of resistance remained powerful. But they were coming under challenge for the first time since independence. They were now on the defensive, if by no means in retreat. The generation that came to manhood and womanhood in the 1960s was the first in more than a century to have a realistic chance of making a decent living in their own country. Only time would tell what they would make of it.

Assessment of Lemass raises elementary but fundamental questions about the link between longevity and stature in leaders. The four leaders accorded heroic stature by their own generation in the history of nationalist Ireland, O'Connell, Parnell, Collins and de Valera, all began relatively young, all were involved early in the movements that earned them 'heroic' stature. That is only rarely the case in more stable circumstances, where leaders normally emerge from existing parties at a fairly mature age. This in turn means they will hold the highest office for shorter periods. Unless dramatic events, preferably sanguinary, punctuate those periods, historians will not be able to invoke their traditional criteria for assessing their stature. There are naturally variations in the pattern. Collins died young. But his short life was sufficiently packed with drama for the aura of the 'lost leader' to linger. Of the leaders of unionist Ireland to enjoy exceptional stature in the eyes of their people, Carson, Craig, Brookeborough and Paisley, only Carson held centre stage for less than a

---

[269] *Irish Management*, 1, 1 (January/February 1954), p. 8. On the variety of corporatist impulses and models in Europe see C.S. Maier, 'Preconditions for corporatism', in J.H. Goldthorpe (ed.), *Order and conflict in contemporary capitalism* (Oxford, 1984), pp. 39–59. On the promise and pitfalls of a corporatist approach to Irish policy-making see S. Lalor, 'Corporatism in Ireland', *Administration*, 30, 4 (1982), pp. 74–97 and N. Hardiman and S. Lalor, 'Corporatism in Ireland: an exchange of views', *Administration*, 32, 1 (1984), pp. 76–88. For the defence of vested interests within the National Economic and Social Council in the 1970s see N..J. Gibson's review of J.J. Lee (ed.), *Ireland 1945–70*, *IESH*, 7 (1980), p. 124.

decade. Longevity itself tends to confer a certain stature even if the beneficiary, like Brookeborough, may not be otherwise remarkable.

Lemass is the historiographical litmus test in this as in many other respects. It is inevitably his fate to be always judged in comparison with de Valera, and frequently his fate to have the reality of his Ireland compared not with the reality, but with the ideal, of de Valera's Ireland. He was Taoiseach for only seven years. Many, impressed by his performance, lamented the period was not longer. 'One of the great tragedies of modern Ireland', it has been said, 'is that Lemass did not become Taoiseach immediately after the war.'[270] The *Irish Times* pungently commented that 'He came to power too late, he left power too early.'[271] But he may have been lucky.

Lemass, as we have seen, was thinking in 'crisis' terms from 1939. His countrymen were not. So habituated had they become to emigration, and to mediocrity of performance in general, that they had internalised these as normalcy, not as crisis. Lemass would have faced bitter internal resistance from many of his cabinet, who distrusted his policies and were irritated by his impatient manner. Some of his colleagues are reputed to have registered their annoyance at his appointment as Tánaiste to de Valera himself.[272] He needed time to educate not only his party but himself to postwar possibilities.[273] The war may have rescued Lemass, no less than de Valera, from a dilemma. It was not only de Valera who was given a new opportunity to display his talents at just the appropriate moment. Lemass, it will be recalled, had diagnosed the economic challenge in 1939. But it is far from clear that he had a solution.

Lemass, then, was fortunate in many respects in the timing of his accession. He was fortunate in the prevailing sense of crisis. He was fortunate that McElligott was gone, however much the connoisseur of conflict might relish the sight of Lemass and McElligott shaping up to each other for one final round. He was doubly fortunate in the rise of Whitaker. The coming of Irish television in 1961, too, widened the opportunity to adopt a more searching attitude towards the serene wisdom of old age. Television programmes took viewers on voyages of discovery of Irish society. Many did not like what they saw. But they now had to exert themselves to even more heroic self-deception to pretend it did not exist.[274] Frustrating then though the long wait must have been, it may be that in the end it was fortunate for his reputation that the precise constellation of political circumstances after the Second World War, or

270 Lemass profile, *Nusight*, December 1969. The following paragraphs draw freely on J. Lee, 'Seán Lemass', in Lee, *Ireland*, pp. 16–26.
271 *Irish Times*, 12 May 1971.   272 Lemass profile, *Nusight* p. 88.
273 Bew and Patterson, *Lemass*, *passim*.
274 D. Gageby, 'The media 1945–70', in Lee, *Ireland*, pp. 132–3; Murphy, 'Put them out!' in *ibid*., p. 10; J.H. Whyte, 'Church, state and society, 1950–70', in *ibid*., p. 79.

even in 1952, when there was a possibility that de Valera might become president.

Lemass may not therefore have been so unlucky in having had to wait. But this is another way of saying that he was unlucky in being born into the wrong society at the wrong time. Ireland was too small for Lemass. One can envisage de Valera in his element as a village head man, presiding sagely over a council of elders resolving petty disputes with the wisdom of the ages. De Valera's ideal world was timeless. Nothing would ever change. But Lemass needed space. Ireland was suffocating. It was both too advanced and not advanced enough. It did not offer the green field of an under-developed society, where old moulds could be pulverised, nor yet did it throb with the dynamic impulse of an advanced industrial society where the performer ethic was in the ascendant.

Lemass was no Hero. He wholly lacked de Valera's mystic rapport with the adoring faithful, and even the easy familiarity with the populace of his successor, Jack Lynch. But it may reflect less on Lemass than on the Irish political tradition that there is no place in Irish political culture for greatness outside the 'heroic' model. Greatness is defined in terms of defiance of the external enemy. De Valera's greatness ends abruptly in 1945, after which even fevered imaginations have difficulty detecting an external threat. If he were to be judged solely on his record from 1945 to 1959, he could not qualify for the Pantheon. But he was still de Valera. The example warns of the problems associated with the inherited criteria. When the standards deemed appropriate for a pre-independent country are carried over, without refinement, into the history of an independent state, we are in danger of belittling, by definition, the stature of all those who come after. By the criterion of defying the external enemy, Lemass by definition fell short of greatness, as did the later de Valera. For the only enemy Lemass engaged with as Taoiseach was the enemy within, the possessor ethic. And there were no glamorous roles in that conflict.

It was as if Lemass sought to demystify the very concept of leadership itself in Irish culture, to imply that a mature people had no need of charisma in their leaders, however indispensable it may have been at a more adolescent stage of national development. 'It is time I passed on. I don't want to become a national monument around the place', he was reported to have said in 1966.[275] He had an impeccable 'national' record himself. But it is striking how little he hawked it around, as if asking to be judged more on what he did than on who he was. Perhaps he felt, subconsciously or otherwise, that distinguished though his record in the struggle for independence had been for his age – how many others had been in the Post Office and the Four Courts by the age of twenty-two? – he

---

[275] *Irish Times*, 12 May 1971. See also M. Mills, Seán Lemass: a profile', *Irish Press*, 18 January 1969.

could have got where he was on merit alone, whereas many of the pensioners on the public purse who battened on the memory of the struggle had no other claim to public gratitude and were therefore reduced to permanent psychological dependence on their distant moment of gory glory.

As an adept professional politician, Lemass by no means scorned 'strokes' when opportunity offered. But his style was not built on strokes. It was built on the long haul. He presumed to rule not by right of tribal succession, but by the test of results. He was the Boss, not the Chief. He made no claim to close communion with God, nor did he try to project an aura of infallibility. He sought to shift the inherited obsession with aspirations to a comparable obsession with results. Aspirations were the appropriate criteria by which a subject people should judge its leaders. A frank appraisal of results better befitted a free people. The Irish had to learn how to emerge from the mentality moulded through centuries not only of poverty, but of 'tarcuisne', as the eighteenth-century poet put it, in this case the disdain of the conquering settler for the native, and to assume the more self-assured personality of the free man. None of this had the stuff of the Hero in it. Much of it had the stuff of greatness in it.

An adequately documented judgement on Lemass must be deferred until the records of his years as Taoiseach are opened. They will presumably reveal a less single-minded pursuit of change than appears from the public record. There are invariably in the career of any leader hesitations, doubts, compromises, tactical manoevures more or less edifying, that blur the clearer page of the public performance. It will be surprising if there are not revisions in detail in that direction even in the case of Lemass. But that is not the central issue. Other aspects carry us far beyond the immediate issue of Lemass, though he is the obvious test case. Differences in values among Irish historians have generally revolved around their attitude to the 'national' question and to Anglo-Irish relations. We have not had to work out the implications for our historical interpretations of independent Ireland of our concepts of Ireland as a normal country.

Much of the legislation of the Cosgrave–de Valera–Costello era can be attributed, like the constitution itself, to the prevailing social ethos. The official mind set of 'traditional' Ireland was monolithic. Intellectual dissenters either emigrated or were marginalised. The student of individual pieces of legislation, or individual legal judgements affecting matters of public policy, has to concern himself more with an ethos than with the impact of individuals. It probably did not matter greatly, for instance, who was appointed to the Supreme Court. The incisiveness of the judgement, but rarely its direction, might depend upon the appointment. All the possible candidates were likely to share the same basic assumptions about the nature of society. That monolith crumbled with remarkable rapidity during the Lemass years. He himself was always less *dirigiste* on social issues than the bulk of his contemporaries. Where the political tradition was broadly non-interventionist in economic matters, it was highly interventionist in the whole area of social morality. His perspective tended to be the contrary. His state might make windows into men's pockets, but not into their minds or souls. He, broadly, took the view that people should be entitled to do what they wanted as long as they did not bother their neighbours. His government appointed Cearbhall Ó Dálaigh Chief Justice in 1962, and nominated Brian Walsh, a personal friend of Lemass, and widely regarded as the outstanding reforming legal mind of his generation, to the Supreme Court.[276] And when Lemass appointed his son-in-law, the young Charles Haughey, as Minister for Justice, it can only have been in anticipation of significant change in a traditionally conservative department.[277]

These appointments, in contrast to earlier ones, did make a significant difference to the nature of the legislation introduced and of the decisions handed down. The historian's judgement must therefore take into account the impact of individual personality, of both politician and judge, to a far greater extent than in earlier decades. And his judgement will inevitably be influenced by his view of the desirability of the direction – the generally liberalising direction for more than a decade – followed in this area. Precisely because there were possible alternatives, as there were not previously, the responsibility laid on the historian's judgement is considerably greater. Of course, this is a normal part of the historiography of countries with less chequered histories than Ireland, an aspect of the shift towards 'normalcy' in general Irish experience.

Not until these issues, and doubtless others, have been addressed, and readdressed, by another generation of scholars, is a historically satisfying assessment of Lemass likely to emerge. Until then judgement has to be even more provisional than usual. A final verdict on Lemass lies far in the future. In the meantime this historian can do no better than concur with Gerry Boland's perplexed comment. 'Lemass', said Boland, 'is different somehow to the rest of us.'[278]

---

[276] B.M.E. McMahon, 'Developments', in Lee, *Ireland*, pp. 83–95, surveys the main changes over the period.

[277] Haughey did enjoy the support of an enthusiastic Assistant Secretary, Roger Hayes, for his law reform programme. Profile of Charles J. Haughey, *Irish Times*, 10 June 1969.

[278] 'Gerry Boland's story', *Irish Times*, 19 October 1968.

THE LYNCH SUCCESSION

The winner in the succession stakes, Jack Lynch, had become Minister for Finance the previous year when Jim Ryan retired. He was, strangely enough, not mentioned at first as a likely candidate.[279] But he emerged as an irresistible compromise choice between the two more thrusting candidates, Haughey and Colley, with Blaney struggling to appear a serious contender. Haughey withdrew in the light of Lynch's emergence, but Colley, not for the last time, showed no head for figures and insisted on going down to a 51:19 defeat. So complete was the acceptance of the Lemass line that none of the rivals for the succession thought of repudiating it. Their personalities and political styles differed considerably. Their policy profiles did not. But Lynch did not feel the same compulsion as Lemass to get things done. The manner of his victory in the succession race epitomised his style. He came quietly through on the rails, giving the impression that he was merely out for a canter, while his frothing rivals churned up the ground in the centre.

Lynch was instinctively a temporiser. Having no strong views himself on most things, he preferred to lead from behind, and to let policy 'emerge'. It was not that he could not act when his back was to the wall. He would show that he could, to the discomfiture of the doubters. But he was not a natural pacemaker. He preferred to move from a consensus position. Whether Haughey, the most temperamentally innovative of the candidates, would have made a significant difference is now impossible to say, though his potential performance in the circumstances of 1966 should not be inferred from his actual performance as Taoiseach in the very different circumstances of 1979–82.

The new generation got its chance from 1966. The pace of change soon began to wind down. Three major inquiries were still in progress when Lemass resigned. The Committee on the Constitution, and the Commission on Higher Education reported in 1967, and the Devlin Commission on the Public Service in 1969. Apart from appointing a Higher Education Authority of a type more or less recommended by the Commission on Higher Education, Lynch effectively ignored the reports of all three. Already, by the early seventies, it was observed that with the retirement of Lemass 'The vigour and drive seemed to go out of government.'[280]

Lynch's position was initially much weaker than that of Lemass. He presided over a cabinet in which several members felt themselves entitled to his job. He had to consolidate his party position. Electoral defeat might cost him the leadership. The prospects for the next election did not appear too promising. Although Fianna Fáil won two by-elections shortly after

279 *Irish Times*, 1 November 1966.
280 C. McCarthy, *The decade of upheaval* (Dublin, 1973), p. 22.

Lynch's succession, it lost heavily in a referendum, in October 1968, designed once more to abolish proportional representation.

But Lynch confounded his critics and frustrated his rivals within the party by winning a handsome general election victory in June 1969. He got the timing right and the result right, to the bewilderment of observers who expected Labour in particular to improve its position. Fianna Fáil's share of the popular vote actually fell, from 47.7 to 45.7 per cent. But the refusal of Fine Gael and Labour to make common electoral cause ensured that their transfers did not work systematically against Fianna Fáil. This, together with a surgical constituency 'revision' by Kevin Boland – 9 seats hinged on 6000 votes[281] – gave Lynch an overall majority with 75 seats, a gain of 3. Fine Gael, fighting its first general election under Liam Cosgrave, won 50 seats, also a gain of 3, while Labour fell to 18, a loss of 4. Labour fought the election on a more radical policy, actually veering towards socialism, and had acquired a prominent profile with the adhesion of well-known intellectuals and/or television personalities like Conor Cruise O'Brien, David Thornley and Justin Keating. Labour duly improved its position in Dublin. But it lost heavily in the country, where Lynch seized the opportunity offered by Labour's careless socialist rhetoric to play a 'red scare' hand with a velvet touch that Seán MacEntee must have envied. Not for the last time, the professionals silenced the pundits. 'Backbencher' did not think Fianna Fáil would get as many as 70 seats.[282] *Hibernia*, relishing the alleged ineptness of the Fianna Fáil campaign, had the grace to concede that the result 'came as a surprise'.[283]

In party terms, the 1969 results consolidated the status quo. In personality terms, however, they enhanced Lynch's standing in the country and in the party. Lynch at last appeared set for a comfortable tenure of office. The tone of politics in early July 1969 was delicately caught in media analysis preoccupied with which jobs for which boys in Lynch's cabinet.[284] Northern Ireland is not mentioned. It had intruded little into the election itself. But Lynch would have little time to savour his victory. A new 'Ulster crisis' was about to erupt.

[281] *Irish Times*, 28 June 1969.   [282] *Irish Times*, 14 June 1969.
[283] *Hibernia*, 6–26 June 1969, 27 June – 17 July 1969.
[284] *Irish Times*, 5, 12 July 1969.

Chapter 6

NORTH: 1945–1985

REFORM AND REACTION

When Seán Lemass reputedly told Terence O'Neill at their meeting in Stormont in January 1965 that he would get into trouble in Dublin over his visit, O'Neill retorted that he himself would get into much worse trouble. Events proved him right. He already had grounds for his premonition, for he had embarked on one of the most perilous enterprises in statesmanship, to persuade a triumphalist ascendancy to begin treating its hereditary inferiors as its contemporary equals. O'Neill's policy of integrating Catholics, however gradually, into the Stormont state, required not only a change in political behaviour, but the virtual assumption of a new political personality, by unionists.

The state that O'Neill inherited from the ailing Brookeborough in March 1963 was, in material respects, a vast improvement on the state Brookeborough himself had commandeered from John Andrews in 1943. That was due less to specific Stormont measures, though the number of these would increase, than to the stimulus of the war economy, and the expansion of the British welfare state after the war. The Unionist cabinet contemplated with distaste the election of a Labour government in Britain in June 1945. After reviewing the alternatives open to it, however, including dominion status and integration, it decided it had no option but to adhere to the existing constitutional arrangement and do its best to modify the more repellant features of Labour's welfare legislation.[1] The combination of war and welfare helped raise income per capita in the North, which had lagged at between 55–57 per cent of the United Kingdom level in 1937–8, to about 68 percent by 1950.[2] Subsequently, the continuing expansion of welfare expenditure, together with economic

---

[1] Harkness, *Northern Ireland*, pp. 106–8; D.W. Harkness, 'The difficulties of devolution: the post-war debate at Stormont', *Irish Jurist*, 12, (1977), pp. 176–86.
[2] Johnson, 'The Northern Ireland economy', p. 202; K.S. Isles and N. Cuthbert, *An economic survey of Northern Ireland* (Belfast, 1957), p. 457.

measures adopted by the government, extending the provisions of an Industrial Development Act of 1945, which sought to induce industry, by promises of land, advance factories, loans and grants, helped further raise the ratio to about 84 per cent by 1967–8.[3]

The social legislation arising from Westminster initiatives, heavily subsidised by Britain on the parity principle, brought a marked refinement in the quality of life. Particularly notable was the improvement in health services under an Act of 1948, including the conquest of tuberculosis, greatly accelerated by the work of the Tuberculosis Authority between 1947 and 1959.[4] Much better access to second level and higher education was facilitated by increased financial provision under the 1947 Education Act. About 113 000 houses were built between 1945 and 1963, which helped clear part of the backlog left by the mediocre inter-war performance, further exacerbated by the sharp decline in house building during the war.[5]

Health, education and housing were particularly sensitive political subjects. The Health Act gave rise to recriminations when the government refused to follow British practice in supporting voluntary hospitals under the National Health scheme and excluded the Catholic Mater Hospital from the service because it refused to accept complete government control. The treatment of the Mater would long remain a running sore for Catholics, and also diverted attention from the fact that the health services available to Catholics in the North were superior to those in the South. The Education Act, which contained improved provision for Catholic schools, drew bitter criticism from Protestant clergy and Orange representatives. The essence of the legislation survived the vituperative personal attacks, but the Minister, Col. Hall Thompson, 'no intellectual heavyweight but a fair-minded man',[6] one of the very few senior Unionist politicians not to have taken the precaution of becoming an Orangeman,[7] was forced out of office in 1949 by the clerical vendetta against him.[8] Much of the new housing was allocated by local authorities, providing further opportunity both for discrimination, and for accusations of discrimination.

The biggest blot on the postwar social record was unemployment. Although well below the hideous pre-war levels, it ran well above British rates between 1945 and 1963, hovering between 5 and 10 per cent, higher even than in Scotland and Wales, which had shared the level of Ulster

3 J. Othick, 'An economic history of Ulster: a perspective', in Kennedy and Ollerenshaw (eds.), *Economic history*, p. 239.
4 Harkness, *Northern Ireland*, p. 110.
5 *Ibid.*, p. 137; Johnson, 'The Northern Ireland economy', pp. 209–10; Oliver, *Working at Stormont*, p. 78.
6 Shea, *Voices*, p. 160.   7 *Ibid.*, p. 161.
8 *Ibid.*, p. 162; Harkness, *Northern Ireland*, pp. 115–16.

Table 4. *Net emigration rates from northern Ireland, 1937–71 (rate per 1000 per annum)*

	Total	Catholics	Non-Catholics
1937–51	3.7	6.5	2.3
1951–61	6.7	10.8	4.6
1961–71	4.3	6.8	2.8

Source: J. Simpson, 'Economic development: cause or effect in the Northern Ireland conflict', in J. Darby (ed.), *Northern Ireland: the background to the conflict* (Belfast, 1983), p. 102.

misery between the wars.[9] Differential unemployment between Catholics and Protestants actually increased compared with the pre-war period. When the Protestant east had been so depressed before the war, the Catholic west could take consolidation from equality of immiseration. Now the prosperity flowed in unevenly, with the east prospering far more than the west. As late as 1971, male unemployment among Catholics was 17.3 per cent compared with 6.6 per cent among Protestants.[10] This differential existed despite much higher Catholic emigration, as Table 4 records.

Even Protestant workers were becoming impatient. Some turned to the Northern Ireland Labour party, which won 4 seats in the 1958 general election. It improved its popular vote, but not the number of seats, in 1962.[11] This came as a disappointment to the party, in view of the heavy unemployment in the declining shipping and linen sectors. Shipbuilding continued to flourish in the first postwar decade. Once Germany and Japan returned to shipbuilding, however, Belfast could not match their superior efficiency. The industry, together with marine engineering, lost 11 000 jobs between 1960 and 1964. Linen likewise retreated before competition from cotton and from man-made fibres, losing 27 000 jobs between 1948 and 1964.[12] What was surprising in the circumstances was not how many, but how few, votes the Unionst Party lost to Labour. But the leadership was disturbed, and the losses were a contributory factor to Brookeborough's departure in March 1963. His resignation was heralded in February, when he categorically denied any intention of resigning: 'I

[9] J. Simpson, 'Economic development: cause or effect in the Northern Ireland conflict', in J. Darby (ed.), *Northern Ireland* (Belfast, 1983), p. 82.
[10] *Ibid.*, p. 101; R. Cooper and T. O'Shea, 'Northern Ireland: survey of social trends', *New Society*, 7 June 1973, 522ff.
[11] Harkness, *Northern Ireland*, p. 133.
[12] J. Bradley and B. Dowling, *Industrial Development in Northern Ireland and the Republic of Ireland* (Dublin, 1983), pp. 29–30.

want to say perfectly frankly and straightly that I have no intention whatever of resigning as your prime minister.'[13] He perfectly frankly and straightly resigned the following month, much to his disgruntlement, for he was still only seventy-five. His successor, Terence O'Neill, later wrote a caustic comment on his predecessor:

As I see it the tragedy of his premiership was that he did not use his tremendous charm, and his deep Orange roots to try and persuade his devoted followers to accept some reforms . . . His last act of political courage . . . had been in 1946.[14]

Brookeborough might have retorted equally caustically that his followers would not have allowed him, and that if he tried he would have, as O'Neill himself was soon to discover, become their former leader.

Despite Brookeborough's distaste for change, the 48-year-old O'Neill inherited a province trembling on the threshold of transition, though transition to what remained unclear. Not only were elements of the Protestant working class becoming restive, however unionist they remained. There were even stirrings of change among Catholics. The welfare state in general, and the Education Act in particular, made a rod for Stormont's back. A generation of Catholics weaned on the welfare state, educated to a higher level than ever before, began to emerge from the late fifties. The number of Catholic students at Queen's University rose from 200 to 700 between 1955 and 1959.[15] A Catholic graduate organisation, National Unity, founded in 1959, heralded the first alternative to the existing petit-bourgeois ethos of the Nationalist Party.[16] Something approaching an independent-minded Catholic middle class was beginning to emerge for the first time. Soon, Ulster nationalist politics would no longer be the preserve either of gunmen on the one hand, or of the 'pubocracy' and 'shopocracy', topped up by the clergy, drawn from broadly the same background, on the other. Relatively well-educated Catholics felt increasingly bitter at what they perceived as discrimination.

The wider world was changing too. With an 'Irish' Catholic in the White House rather conspicuously failing to conform to the stereotype requirement of the Orange psyche, with a Taoiseach in Dublin apparently seeking conciliation, with a Pope in the Vatican acknowledging the humanity of communists, much less Protestants, problems further compounded when Harold Macmillan resigned in October 1963, raising the spectre of an imminent Labour government in Britain, any Northern premier would have had to take increasing cognisance of life beyond Ulster, however he chose to interpret it.

O'Neill adopted a two-pronged strategy. He pursued, on the one hand, economic development, on the other, conciliation between the two

13 *Irish Independent*, 18 February 1963.
14 T. O'Neill, *Ulster at the crossroads* (London, 1969), p. 47.
15 Tobin, *Best of decades*, p. 30.   16 Buckland, *Northern Ireland*, p. 109.

communities.[17] He sought to blunt the threat from Labour by accelerating the rate of economic growth, and thus providing the disgruntled Protestant unemployed with jobs again, while incidentally benefiting Catholics, who suffered so heavily from unemployment. It was an uphill struggle. The economy had begun to stutter once the wartime and postwar surges petered out. There were no obvious alternatives to the ailing ship-building and linen industries. The Isles report of 1957, and the Hall report of 1962, permitted themselves to be so overwhelmed by the natural obstacles to Ulster economic development that they could see little hope of adequate progress. The administration was psychologically 'on the defensive', partly due to the animosities revived or accentuated by the IRA campaign of 1956–62. Even so staunch a champion of the regime as John Oliver noticed increasingly during the fifties that 'appointments to senior positions in the civil service were timid, mediocre men were being encouraged, grey figures were beginning to predominate'.[18]

O'Neill, a former finance minister, impressed by the Whitaker report, and apparently finding no Whitaker in the Stormont civil service, resolved to cut through the prevailing pessimism of the official mind by commissioning a new survey from Thomas Wilson, a distinguished Ulsterman who was Adam Smith Professor of Political Economy at the University of Glasgow, and whom he appointed economic consultant to the government in October 1963. Wilson's *Economic development in Northern Ireland*, completed in December 1964 and published in February 1965, set more ambitious targets than the earlier reports. Wilson's strategy was broadly similar to Whitaker's. He sought to compensate for the inadequacy of the performance of indigenous industry by importing more successful firms through improved incentives. Tax allowances and investment grants, supplemented by employment premiums, did stimulate industrial investment. Between 35 000 and 40 000 new jobs were created in the 1960s. However, as the staple industries continued to decline, the net gain was far less, somewhere between 10 000 and 15 000 jobs, of which only 5000 were in manufacturing.[19] Unemployment remained obstinately high, in the 6–8 per cent range. Nevertheless, the performance of the economy between 1965 and 1973, with GDP rising by more than 4 per cent per annum, distinctly higher than in the United Kindgom as a whole, was not unimpressive, though much would depend on whether it laid secure foundations for further growth.

[17] For less sympathetic interpretations see Edwards, *The sins of our fathers*, pp. 22–37, and Bew, Gibbon & Patterson, *The state*, pp. 152ff.
[18] Oliver, *Stormont*, p. 78.
[19] Buckland, *Northern Ireland*, p. 113; B. Moore, J. Rhodes and R. Carling, 'Industrial policy and economic development: the experience of Northern Ireland and the Republic of Ireland', *Cambridge Journal of Economics*, 2 (1978), pp. 101, 104; Bradley and Dowling, *Industrial development*, p. 31.

Economic and social planning was felt to require a rationalisation of administrative structures, as well as the cooperation of the 'social partners'. O'Neill established a new Ministry for Development, as well as a new Ministry for Health and Social Services, in 1965. He had already reversed Brookeborough's policy by recognising, in 1964, the Northern Ireland Committee of the Irish Congress of Trade Unions, against bitter cabinet opposition, in order to encourage trade union participation in his new Advisory Economic Council and in labour training programmes.[20]

O'Neill sought to reconcile Catholics to the regime by improving their status through a variety of symbolic gestures, like visits to Catholic schools, intended to imply their equality rather than inferiority within the state. His most courageous, not to say foolhardy, initiative was the invitation to Lemass to come to Stormont in January 1965, followed by his own return visit to Dublin in February, and a meeting with Jack Lynch in Stormont in December 1967. The furore caused among more exciteable Protestants by such simple gestures testified to the depths of distrust still prevailing.

Nevertheless, the general election of November 1965 seemed to vindicate O'Neill's bold policy. The Northern Ireland Labour Party lost two of its four seats, and the three Unionist gains were widely interpreted as indicating broad public support for O'Neill's initiatives. He further disoriented traditional unionists when declaring the Ulster Volunteer Force, an extremist organisation, illegal under the Special Powers Act in June 1966, simply because it had just bagged its first two Catholic kills. When he only narrowly survived two attempts by traditionalists to depose him, however, he hastened more slowly.[21] He had brought in a code of conduct in an attempt to oblige his cabinet 'to keep up to British ministerial standards of conduct'.[22] Even this not unduly demanding criterion posed problems. In April 1967 O'Neill dismissed Harry West, his recalcitrant Minister for Agriculture, who 'had been ill-advised' in a land deal, as Brian Faulkner coyly put it.[23] West was part of the Fermanagh political culture, which was non-sectarian on 'land deals'. Despite the rumblings within the Unionist Party, there appeared to be continued widespread public support for O'Neill's general approach, as reflected in the first reasonably reliable public opinion poll taken in Northern Ireland, and published by the *Belfast Telegraph* in 1967.[24] As

20 O'Neill, *Crossroads*, p. 63.
21 C. O'Leary, 'Northern Ireland, 1945–72', in Lee, *Ireland*, pp. 160–1.
22 O'Neill, *Crossroads*, p. 93.
23 B. Faulkner, *Memoirs of a statesman* (London, 1978), p. 80.
24 J.F. Harbinson, *The Ulster Unionist party 1882–1973: its development and organisation* (Belfast, 1973), p. 149.

well as still retaining substantial Protestant support, O'Neill enjoyed much goodwill among middle-class Catholics at this stage.[25]

But the goodwill of a small middle-aged middle class was no longer enough. It was overtaken by the impatience of a younger generation at the gradualness or, as some saw it, the hollowness, of the O'Neill reforms. Three decisions in particular served as focal points for articulate Catholic resentment. The first was the announcement in 1965 of the intention to locate a new city, following restrictions rightly imposed upon the growth of Belfast, not in the depressed west, but only thirty miles from Belfast – and then, adding insult to assumed injury, to baptise it Craigavon.[26] The resultant furore deprived the government of much of the credit it deserved for an innovative approach towards physical planning in the province.[27]

The second provocation, also in 1965, was the government's acceptance of the recommendation of the Lockwood committee, which was established in 1963 without a single Catholic member, that a second university, in addition to Queen's, should be established – and located in Protestant Coleraine, much to the chagrin of champions of the expansion of Magee College in Derry.[28]

Catholics could not be convinced that Craigavan and Coleraine were anything but sectarian decisions, designed to deprive the disproportionately Catholic west from ever catching up with the predominantly Protestant east. Consciousness of allegedly differential treatment became more acute as the rhetoric (and even to some extent the reality) of material improvement became more emphatic. Complaints of discrimination in general were particularly rife west of the Bann. Catholic sensitivities were sharpened by the more blatant discriminatory practices stretching back to the founding of the state, and beyond, that Protestants deemed necesssary to protect at local level their vulnerable majorities, and even more frequently, their vulnerable minorities.[29] Precisely because improvement now began to seem a possibility for the first time, Catholics became more conscious of levels of occupational discrimination in general, and particularly of discrimination in the civil service. Popular Catholic perceptions of discrimination were no doubt exaggerated. But the reality was bad enough.[30] Even in the civil service, about 95 per cent of senior officials remained Protestant in 1972, as they had been in 1959

25 C. O'Leary, 'Northern Ireland 1945–72', p. 161, and C. O'Leary, 'The Northern Ireland crisis and its observers', *Political Quarterly*, 42 (1971), pp. 264–5.
26 Harkness, *Northern Ireland*, p. 142.   27 Oliver, *Stormont*, pp. 83ff.
28 Harkness, *Northern Ireland*, p. 142.
29 J.H. Whyte, 'How much discrimination was there under the Unionist regime, 1921–68?', *Contemporary Irish Studies* (Manchester, 1983), p. 31.
30 E.A. Aunger, 'Religion and occupational class in Northern Ireland', *Economic and Social Review*, 7, 1 (1975), pp. 1–18; E. Moxon-Browne, *Nation, class and creed – Northern Ireland* (Aldershot, 1982), pp. 131–3.

and in 1927.[31] The only Catholic to have achieved the office of Secretary of a Department through promotion from the junior ranks, anxious though he is to testify to the fairness of his civil service superiors, was nevertheless obliged to note that while his colleagues invariably treated him correctly, and could in no way be accused of overt racism, many nevertheless accepted the discrimination against him as simply a way of life.[32]

The responses to Catholic contentions of discrimination were instructive. In 1955, Professor Thomas Wilson, of the Wilson report, dismissed complaints that Catholics did not have an appropriate ratio of administrative and academic posts, with the argument that 'ability and inclination, together with the competition of people from outside Ulster altogether, may dictate differently', adding for good measure that 'as for business life, Presbyterians and Jews are probably endowed with more business acumen than Irish Catholics'. He loftily dismissed Catholic grievances on the grounds that 'they have less to complain about than the US Negroes, and their lot is a very pleasant one as compared with the nationalists in, say, the Ukraine'. 'For generations', Wilson observed, 'they were the underdogs, the despised "croppies", the adherents of a persecuted religion, who were kept out of public affairs by their Protestant conquerors. They were made to feel inferior, and to make matters worse they often *were* inferior, if *only* in those personal qualities that make for success in competitive economic life'[33] (emphasis in original).

If Catholics were designated inferior in the academic, administrative and business fields, there were not too many occupational opportunities remaining for them! Perhaps they would flourish in the professions? But then William Craig, O'Neill's Minister for Home Affairs, 'defended the government against a charge of discriminating against Catholic lawyers in judicial appointments on the moral premise that they were educationally and socially inferior . . . '. That he 'was obliged to apologise immediately' presumably did not suffice to change his views.[34]

Wilson was, of course, no street corner orator, no pulpit demagogue, but one of the most eminent living Ulster scholars, with an international standing in his subject, a subject moreover that reputedly exorcised mere emotion from its 'scientific' endeavours. Nor was Wilson in any sense a

31 D. Donnison, 'The Northern Ireland civil service', *New Society*, 5 July 1973; Whyte, 'How much discrimination?', p. 9; R. Miller, 'Fair employment in the civil service: report of an investigation into the non-industrial Northern Ireland civil service', *Ireland, Politics and Society*, 1, 1 (Winter 1985), pp. 99–125. On discrimination in local government employment see *Disturbances in Northern Ireland* (Cameron Report) (Belfast, 1969), p. 60.
32 Shea, *Voices*, pp. 141–3, 177–80, 198.
33 T. Wilson, 'Devolution and partition', in T. Wilson (ed.), *Ulster under Home Rule* (Belfast, 1955), pp. 208–9.
34 K. Heskin, *Northern Ireland: a psychological analysis* (Dublin, 1980), p. 107.

rabid racist. He had earlier expressed numerous criticisms of the Unionist treatment of Catholics.[35] He still candidly acknowledged the historical injustices. What is striking is that not only did he not feel obliged to produce a scintilla of evidence in support of his assumption of pervasive Catholic inferiority, but that he failed to enquire if there might be any connection between the assumed inferiority and the admitted earlier discrimination. The rigour of the reasoning would scarcely pass muster with Wilson on any other subject. An exceptionally sensitive study of unionist mentalities holds that 'only a minority, mainly middle class, are racist in the sense of seeing Catholics as inherently inferior'.[36] Nevertheless, when a scholar of Wilson's stature could entertain such views, it seems reasonable to assume that he expressed instincts more widely shared among his less articulate countrymen. And it certainly gives a useful indication of the sort of psychic background against which O'Neill's approach has to be assessed.

John Oliver, an accomplished public servant, who became Second Secretary in O'Neill's new Ministry of Development in 1964, before becoming Permanent Secretary in 1971, stoutly resisted allegations of discrimination against the west. The real problem was 'that there was usually much less local initiative there. In the richer, more populous and more go-ahead eastern parts there was always far more locally-generated drive, private and commercial as well as municipal.'[37] Oliver presents this as a fact of nature. Even assuming it to be true, he does not ask why. Was it because of a higher proportion of Catholics? Or was there an objective lack of opportunity? Did the west stand in relation to the east as the east in turn stood in relation to England in general and the home counties in particular? Even the 'more go-ahead eastern parts' of Northern Ireland were rarely counted, rightly or wrongly, among the dynamic centres of European development in the twentieth century. It can be readily conceded that 'fairness' in the regional distribution of public resources is a subject charged both with objective difficulty and subjective emotion. Southern critics of Northern neglect of the west can be promptly reminded of the failure of the Dublin government to grapple effectively with the regional issue. Nevertheless, Oliver's dismissal of the matter is too bland by half.

[35] T. Wilson, 'Ulster and Éire', *Political Quarterly* (1939), reprinted in W.A. Robson (ed.), *The Political Quarterly in the 1930s* (London, 1971), pp. 214–27.

[36] S. Nelson, *Ulster's uncertain defenders* (Belfast, 1984), p. 13. For the disdain of a Catholic who would, it seems not ungenerous to say, become even more internationally renowned than Wilson in his own subject, at the denial of opportunity to someone of his background in Ulster, see Denis Donoghue's review of O'Shea's *Voices and the sound of drums*, 'Castle Catholic', *TLS*, 31 July 1981, reprinted in D. Donoghue, *We Irish* (Brighton, 1986), pp. 165–8. For another evocative account of a Catholic childhood, see G.J. Watson, 'Cultural identity: An Irish View', *Yale Review* (Summer 1986), pp. 503–16.

[37] Oliver, *Stormont*, p. 182.

It was not entirely inappropriate that it was in this area, so lacking 'local initiative', that the initiative was launched on the third issue to rouse Catholic resentment, the housing question, with particular reference to discrimination by local authorities. The Campaign for Social Justice was founded in Dungannon in January 1964. In February 1967 the new Northern Ireland Civil Rights Association (NICRA), learning from the experience of the Campaign for Social Justice, formulated a programme which included one man, one vote, in local elections; no gerrymandering of constituency boundaries, fair distribution of local council houses, the repeal of the Special Powers Act, the disbanding of the B Specials, and a formal complaints procedure against local authorities.[38]

The Campaign for Social Justice and the NICRA coalesced in the organisation of a civil rights march from Coalisland to Dungannon organised by Austin Currie, a new nationalist MP, to protest against specific cases of housing discrimination. The march achieved wide publicity thanks at least partly to the last-minute re-routing by the police when a counter-demonstration was organised by Protestant groups to prevent the civil rights march reaching Dungannon market square, which was 'Protestant territory'.[39] The idea of a public square being private territory may seem a trifle odd. But it is perfectly normal in a zero-sum tribal society, where one tribe's gain can only be, by definition, another tribe's loss. Parades in Ulster are therefore not like parades in more normal societies. Because of the territorial imperative, they are contests in machismo, expressions of tribal virility, taunts to the manliness and muscle-power of the tribal enemy. They were not therefore simple symbols of protest, bearing silent, or even raucous, witness to some grievance, real or imagined. They were directed against the self-respect of the other tribe. Right or wrong were irrelevant issues. The only real point at issue was us or them.

The success of the Dungannon affair in August encouraged local activists in Derry, with NICRA support, to propose a march for 5 October in Derry city along a 'non-sectarian route'. This meant, by definition, a dual sectarian route, given Derry's dearth of major atheist settlements. Derry was the most vulgarly gerrymandered constituency, where discrimination against Catholics, two-thirds of the population, was particularly blatant.[40] The Protestant Apprentice Boys sustained a particularly vigor-

---

38 Harkness, *Northern Ireland*, p. 145; *Sunday Times* Insight Team, *Ulster* (Harmondsworth, 1972), p. 49.

39 Harkness, *Northern Ireland*, p. 151.

40 The evidence on gerrymandering and on housing discrimination is so conclusive that there is little point reciting it in detail in the text. There are succinct descriptions in *Sunday Times* Insight Team, *Ulster*, pp. 34–8, T.W. Moody, *The Ulster question, 1603–1973* (Dublin, 1974), pp. 26–34; Budge and O'Leary, *Belfast*, pp. 94–5. C. Hewitt has argued that there was no systematic gerrymandering bias against Catholics ('Catholic grievances, Catholic nationalism and violence in Northern Ireland during the civil rights period',

ous master race mentality through their parading propensities in Derry. Outraged at the insufferable insult to Protestant ascendancy posed by the subversive claim of equality of opportunity, the Apprentice Boys threatened a rival march. This allowed William Craig, as Minister for Home Affairs, to prohibit all marches. The inevitable result was to increase support for the civil rights march. This does not appear to have been Craig's intention, though he may have been hoping that a delicately arranged confrontation would discredit O'Neill's 'softness' on Catholics, and permit himself to capture the premiership as 'the hard man'. Rioting broke out when the RUC, *de jure* the state police, but completely Protestant at senior level, and with 99 per cent Protestant membership, a *de facto* Protestant paramilitary organisation, enthusiastically implemented the minister's order. When the organisers defied it and sought to enter Protestant areas, the RUC took them on with a will.[41] But it calculated on this occasion without the nefarious influence of television. Their performance of *taigue*-bashing was suddenly exposed to an incredulous audience, much to RUC indignation at this intrusion on their privacy. As Brian Faulkner would delicately put it, 'the tactics used by the RUC in enforcing the ban left something to be desired',[42] – particularly when they found the game was on television!

The police performance on 5 October provoked widespread indignation, inside and outside Northern Ireland. Following further civil rights demonstrations, and pressure from Harold Wilson, O'Neill announced, on 22 November, sweeping reforms of local government to include a points system for the allocation of public authority housing, the appointment of an ombudsman, the abolition of the company vote, a development commission to replace the rigged Derry corporation, and the eventual withdrawal of some of the Special Powers.[43] 'One man, one vote' in local government elections still remained conspicuously absent from the reform programme.[44]

British Journal of Sociology, 32, 3, September 1981, p. 365). Hewitt draws no distinction, however, between constituencies where majorities were so overwhelming that gerrymandering could make no difference, and marginal constituencies. His analysis thus diverts attention from the fact that in eleven marginal constituencies, where the Catholic percentage of the adult population averaged 49 per cent, the proportion of Catholic councillors averaged only 36 per cent, thanks to the solicitous arrangement of the boundaries. A debate followed Hewitt's article, culminating in a three-way exchange in the *British Journal of Sociology*, 38, 1 (March 1987) between K.A. Kovalcheck, 'Catholic grievances in Northern Ireland: appraisal and judgment', pp. 77–87, C. Hewitt, 'Explaining violence in Northern Ireland', pp. 88–93, and D. O'Hearn, 'Catholic grievances: comments', pp. 94–100.
41 Heskin, *Northern Ireland*, pp. 107–8.
42 Faulkner, *Memoirs*, p. 48. On growing up in Catholic Derry see E. McCann, *War and an Irish town* (London, 1980, 2nd edn), ch. 1; T. Ó Canainn, *Home to Derry* (Belfast, 1986).
43 Harkness, *Northern Ireland*, p. 153.   44 Faulkner, *Memoirs*, p. 49.

The sudden revelation that British citizenship might have its duties as well as its rights infuriated Craig. The flaunted boast, 'Ulster is British', suddenly became a double-edged weapon, insofar as the wider implications were comprehensible at all. A later Grand Chaplain of the Orange Order presumably spoke for many at the time when he interpreted the British system of government to mean 'if you are strong enough you do as you like'.[45] By that undiluted criterion, Ulster was already more British than the British themselves! Craig's judgement was notoriously erratic.[46] The struggle for the leadership of the Unionist Party erupted into the open. Craig launched an immediate campaign against O'Neill, partly on the intriguing grounds that he was making the concessions under pressure from Britain. O'Neill's television address on 9 December, appealing to moderate opinion, brought him such massive public support that he felt strong enough to dismiss Craig on 11 December, and duly won a clear vote of confidence from the Unionist parliamentary party.

The next month may have proffered one of the few possible turning points in the sordid story that was about to unfold. The Derry Citizens Action Committee was established immediately after the march of 5 October by John Hume and Ivan Cooper. Hume was a young former clerical student who took his MA degree with an excellent thesis on the history of the port of Derry in Maynooth, and Cooper was a young Protestant graduate of Queen's. The committee announced a month's moratorium on demonstrations in response to O'Neill's initiative. Had a breathing space developed it is just conceivable, if still highly unlikely, that a modicum of civilised change might have proved possible. O'Neill needed time to consolidate the apparently emerging centre. But another new group, the People's Democracy (PD), its very name proclaiming that it was neither popular nor democratic, and composed partly of Queen's University students and graduates, with Bernadette Devlin and Michael Farrell particularly prominent, determined to deny O'Neill time.[47] People's Democracy, more a sect than a party, drew on both nationalist and socialist impulses. It insisted on marching through traditionally Protestant territory, en route from Belfast to Derry. Some of the participants imagined they were engaged on an Ulster version of the Selma to Montgomery march. The marchers were duly assaulted at Burntollet, a heavily Protestant area, with the complicity of the police, and apparently the participation of individual policemen. When the march, following its well-publicised suffering, reached Derry on 4 January, it sparked off

[45] J.F. Gallagher and G.C. DeGregory, *Violence in Northern Ireland: understanding Protestant perspectives* (Dublin, 1985), p. 139.

[46] *Sunday Times* Insight Team, *Ulster*, pp. 42–51.

[47] The standard work is P. Arthur, *The people's democracy* (Belfast, 1974). '"People's democracy": a discussion on strategy', *New Left Review*, 55 (May/June 1969), conveys the flavour of the PD mentality.

serious rioting and inevitable police brutality.[48] It was successful, from the organiser's viewpoint, insofar as it increased tension. This ensured bloodshed sooner rather than later.

People's Democracy succeeded in denying O'Neill his breathing space. In doing so, they would soon make themselves redundant also, for events would lurch beyond their control as well as beyond O'Neill's. On 15 January 1969 he announced a commission of inquiry into the Derry disturbances, an unprecedented step for the Stormont regime. Brian Faulkner, the Deputy Prime Minister, O'Neill's ablest rival, snatched the opportunity to resign from the cabinet in protest. Faulkner's position was, however, far from simple. It marks the distance already travelled that he did not make a point of resigning from opposition in principle to O'Neill's policy. On the contrary, he implied that he would concede 'one man, one vote' in local elections. He confined his criticism to tactics rather than principles, arguing that an inquiry, whatever its findings, could only exacerbate already excited emotions.[49]

O'Neill's position was now so shaken that he had little hope of survival unless he could mobilise massive public support to restore his crumbling authority. When twelve MPs demanded his resignation, he called a general election in February. This exposed the bitter divisions in the Unionist camp, with pro-O'Neill and anti-O'Neill factions fighting each other in several constituencies. The popular vote did appear to indicate widespread support for, or at least acquiescence in, O'Neill's policy; 230 000 voters supported O'Neill candidates, while 120 000 rejected them. In a presidential system, O'Neill would have cruised to victory. In the parliamentary system, however, public support did not translate into a crushing majority of seats. A dozen intransigent anti-O'Neillites were returned. Probably eight of the remaining twenty-three Unionist deputies, nominally O'Neillites, were of wavering stock. The anti-O'Neill candidates won strong support in Fermanagh and Tyrone, and in Belfast working-class constituencies. Their appeal was to those whose sense of identity and self-esteem revolved around protection of petty privilege, and to those who felt more threatened, whether geographically or psychologically, by Catholic upstarts.

In addition, O'Neill's personal position was jeopardised by the narrowness of his victory in his own constituency, where the People's Democracy struck again. When Ian Paisley, a Protestant fundamentalist, announced that he would oppose O'Neill in his Bannside constituency, Michael Farrell, who had no chance of winning this overwhelmingly Protestant constituency, stood specifically to damage O'Neill. Farrell's intervention,

[48] M. Farrell, *The Orange state* (London, 1980), pp. 249–52, for an account by an organiser.
[49] Faulkner, *Memoirs*, pp. 50–3.

by drawing off 2300 Catholic votes, many of which might have otherwise opted for O'Neill, reduced the prime minister's margin of victory to a mere 1400 votes, by 7745 to Paisley's 6331. The pattern of the next decade, or decades, was already set. The middle would be squeezed out through the tacit collusion of the two extremes. It is probable that little at this stage could have prevailed against a resurgence of sectarian sentiment and the virtually total polarisation of the two ethnic groups in Northern Ireland. But the tactics of the People's Democracy helped to consolidate the sectarianism their rhetoric denounced.[50] Bernadette Devlin became a media star on her election as a 'unity' candidate to Westminster from Mid-Ulster on 17 April. She proved an accomplished public performer, and her high media profile rubbed further salt into unionist wounds. Needless to say, her victory was despite, rather than because of, her socialism. But this was poor consolation for unionists!

Protestant extremists caused a series of explosions at electricity and water installations in March and April. Designed to discredit O'Neill's softness on Catholics, these achieved their objective insofar as they were naturally attributed to the IRA. On 23 April the Unionist parliamentary party voted by only 28 to 22 to implement universal adult suffrage at the next local government elections. Major James Chichester Clarke, Minister for Agriculture, immediately resigned, on the grounds that while universal adult suffrage might be tolerable in principle, it was an idea whose time had patently not yet come. The concern with 'timing' at this juncture – only thirty-four years after the axiomatically retarded Republic had adopted the principle – was deeply touching! The attempt to discredit demands for what was accepted as normalcy elsewhere in Britain and Ireland by arguing that they presented a threat to the state itself implicitly conceded that the state was some distance from 'normalcy'. But the furore was revealing. 'One man, one vote' could not endanger the Protestant majority in the state. That was a demographic fact for the foreseeable future. In itself it was harmless, unless the existence of the state was to secure not Protestant freedom, but Protestant supremacy. What the concession would endanger was not Protestant security, but the psychic satisfaction of Protestant superiority. Chichester Clarke's resignation may have been arranged in collusion with O'Neill, his cousin, who expected to be defeated soon within the parliamentary party anyway, and who resigned on 28 April. Chichester Clarke immediately emerged as a candidate for the succession, which he won by a single vote against Faulkner.[51]

Scion of an ancient family, educated at Eton, O'Neill's aloof manner alienated potential supporters. He was almost a caricature of a typical

[50] C.C. O'Brien, *States of Ireland* (London, 1972), p. 173, is convincing on this point.
[51] Harkness, *Northern Ireland*, p. 156.

English Tory. But Ulster was not England, even in caricature. While Unionist leaders had never been plebeian, 'the conspicuous nature of O'Neill's patrician manner and his Englishness . . . struck an offensive note'.[52] Faulkner paid him the unintended tribute of doubting if 'he ever felt really at home in Ulster politics'.[53] The most considered judgement is that 'O'Neill was the wrong man with the right ideas.'[54]

If the ideas were right, however, it must remain an open question if even leadership of genius could have secured acceptance for them. For the ideas had disturbing implications for most of the group actors on the Ulster stage when 'nearly all the reassuring old certainties were turned upside down'.[55] Virtually overnight, 'compromise and tolerance changed from vices to virtues'.[56] This was bound to be unsettling.

It now seemed that 'material values were put above the non-material. O'Neill was suggesting Catholics could be reconciled by worldly benefits . . .'.[57] This was doubly unsettling. For the Northern concept of materialism was as rich in potential for psychic exploration as the Southern one. 'Traditionalists' were not 'materialists'. The periodic expulsions of such Catholics as wormed their way into the shipyards, much less their initial large-scale exclusion, was not materialism. Sweating generations of girls in the linen sheds was not materialism. Rackrenting slum landlordism, in Belfast any more than in Dublin, was not materialism. Harry West's 'ill-advised' land deal was not materialism. Terence O'Neill's new industry was materialism. It was doubly so if the new managers hired workers without having the decency to ask their religion. Materialism was historically as close to the heart of the Northern as to the Southern way of life. But immense effort was devoted to disguising this. Now O'Neill, and to some extent Lemass, insensitively ripped aside the veil. Many felt a sense of almost personal violation – particularly the materially promiscuous who had persuaded themselves all along, by a supreme act of imagination, of their austere chastity.

'The zero-sum game was declared obsolete. O'Neill implied that everyone could share the new prosperity, that Catholics could also work for the Unionist party and not just for "their own".'[58] This too was unsettling in the extreme. There is a wonderful reassurance about the zero-sum game when you are always on the winning side. The winnings may not amount to much materially or objectively. That is not the point. The feeling of winning is itself the most important of the winnings. If Protestants were to be deprived of this pleasure, could an increase in their per capita income really compensate for the consequent decline in their quality of life?

[52] Nelson, *Defenders*, p. 51. [53] Faulkner, *Memoirs*, p. 53.
[54] Harkness, *Northern Ireland*, p. 139. For an analysis of O'Neill's dilemma, see Harkness, pp. 156–7 and T.E. Utley, *Lessons of Ulster* (London, 1975), pp. 39–44.
[55] Nelson, *Defenders*, p. 49. [56] *Ibid.*, p. 50. [57] *Ibid.* [58] *Ibid.*

Shortly after resigning, O'Neill gave a memorable exhibition of the gentle art of alienating people.

The basic fear of Protestants in Northern Ireland is that they will be outbred by Roman Catholics. It is as simple as that. It is frightfully hard to explain to a Protestant that if you give Roman Catholics a good house they will live like Protestants, because they will see their neighbours with cars and television sets.

They will refuse to have eighteen children, but if the Roman Catholic is jobless and lives in a most ghastly hovel, he will rear eighteen children on national assistance.

It is impossible to explain this to a militant Protestant, because he is so keen to deny civil rights to his Roman Catholic neighbours. He cannot understand, in fact, that if you treat Roman Catholics with due consideration and kindness they will live like Protestants, in spite of the authoritative nature of their church.[59]

As can be imagined, this well-intentioned observation provoked indignant spluttering. The problem was that O'Neill's observation was, in essence, true. The reference to 'eighteen children' was, of course, loose arithmetic for a sometime Minister for Finance. It was exaggeration. But it was not substantive error. What it meant was that Catholics were not inherently inferior. Catholics would respond in the same way as Protestants to similar circumstances. Nurture, not nature, explained Catholic behaviour. Protestants suddenly had nothing left to feel superior about. O'Neill was right. But he would learn that truth was no excuse. The substance of his remarks outraged Protestants. The style outraged Catholics. Where self-images were so sensitive, truth was a form of psychic emasculation, so intimately dependent on deception, self and other, was the sense of identity of the two peoples.

O'Neill defied so many household deities that the wonder is not that he failed, but that he lasted so long. His unforgiveable sin was that 'he refused to be paranoid'.[60] That was not an accusation that could be lightly levelled at his successor as member of parliament for Bannside. The winner of the by-election following O'Neill's resignation from Stormont, was the redoubtable Reverend Ian Paisley who, 'in the scope and depth of his endeavours, had developed religio-political paranoia beyond the wildest dreams of his unionist contemporaries'.[61] Born the son of a Baptist preacher in 1926, voracious for status and power, a gifted orator, far more intelligent than the vast majority of the unionist establishment, which he detested, and with an agile polemical mind, he founded his Free Presbyterian Church of Ulster in 1951. An enterprising ecclesiastical entrepreneur, he polished his advertising talents on the fundamentalist fund-raising circuit of the American South, a society he found, for obvious reasons, particularly congenial. He carved out a growing niche for himself and his Free Presbyterian product in the extensive Ulster market for

[59] Heskin, *Northern Ireland*, pp. 105–6.   [60] *Ibid.*, p. 106.   [61] *Ibid.*

bigotry and hate. He founded as his main advertising agency the *Protestant Telegraph* in 1966, a vitriolic anti-Catholic paper, which would make the fulminations of even the *Catholic Bulletin* and *Catholic Mind* of inter-war Free State vintage seem almost Christian. He began to achieve the publicity he craved by protesting against O'Neill's expression of condolence on the death of Pope John XXIII in 1963, and against a visit by O'Neill to a Catholic school in 1964. Raucous nationalist celebrations of the fiftieth anniversary of the Easter Rising offered Paisley further opportunity for high-profile protests. He would duly denounce the murders of two Catholics in sectarian killings in Malvern Street by the resuscitated UVF in 1966, but there is evidence that some of the perpetrators drew inspiration from Paisley's preaching. In 1966 too he formed the Protestant Unionist Party (PUP), which, graduating into the Democratic Unionist Party (DUP) in 1971, would provide him with a party base which he would extend and dominate for many years.[62]

Paisley preached a rabid anti-Catholicism. But he was much more than a rabid anti-Catholic, even at this relatively early stage. As an intelligent and perceptive man, he would doubtless learn from the range of experience on a wider stage that he now began to accumulate. Paisley drew a sharp distinction in his preaching between Catholics as harmless individuals, and Catholicism as a sinister and malignant creed. The distinction is an interesting one for the student of Paisley. It is largely irrelevant for the student of Paisleyism. For the compulsive image of the Catholic Church as the embodiment of conspiratorial evil is so powerful, so engulfing, that minds more subtle than those of Paisley's congregation might have difficulty sustaining the validity of the distinction in daily life. It makes no more sense to approach the history of Paisleyism from this perspective than it does to interpret the history of the Orange Order in Ulster in terms of the injunction that every member should be 'ever abstaining from all uncharitable words, actions or sentiments towards his Roman Catholic brethern'. For Paisley is merely the spokesman, however volcanic and commanding a spokesman, for Paisleyism, which is not only fundamentalist anti-Catholicism, but fundamentally anti-Catholic. There would be a Paisleyism without Paisley, though hardly so sharply profiled. But there could not be a Paisley without Paisleyism. To remain on top for so long in so potentially fissiparous a political constituency and so fetid an atmosphere requires talents far beyond the ordinary.

If Paisley is a supreme showman, he is also a shrewd one. But the shrewdness consists, not least, in knowing when to abandon any intiative that fails to find support among his followers. For Paisley knows that he is

---

[62] Heskin, *Northern Ireland*, pp. 111–25; O.D. Edwards, *The sins of our fathers*, pp. 39–59; Buckland, *Northern Ireland*, pp. 119–27; Moxon-Browne, *Nation, class and creed*, pp. 95–8.

as much the prisoner as the master of the sectarian demon, and he has had to fall quickly back into line whenever he has dared voice deviationist sentiments.[63] It would be interesting to see his performance if only he could capture the undisputed leadership of unionism in general and could balance over a wider range of factions.

In 1969 Paisley's greatest triumphs still lay in the future. Chichester Clarke was the man of the hour. If not quite as incapable as suggested by 'his habitual air of shambling bewilderment',[64] Clarke inherited a virtually hopeless situation. It was not so much a torch as a time bomb that O'Neill had handed on, and one on a very short fuse. It is arguable that Clarke's victory prevented Brian Faulkner, the only Unionist with a chance of implementing a reform policy without alienating grass roots unionism, from attempting to pull off such a coup while this approach still had some prospect of success, however remote. A solution, if there was a solution by this stage, demanded a flair that Clarke patently lacked. Drifting in the hope that something would turn up, Clarke continued O'Neill's reform policy, while managing to convey the impression that he 'really stood for nothing'.[65] He proved equally unable to cope with his own followers. Once the Orange marching season, with its ritualistic invocation of triumphalist tribalism, opened in earnest in July, the resources of the RUC were stretched beyond breaking point.

Every government was an annual prisoner of the marching tradition. Until this, with its guarantee of trouble, could be broken, the scope for governmental manoeuvre was severely restricted. In 1969 Stormont lacked the will and/or the ability to ban the primitive exhibitions. The RUC was therefore in danger of becoming involved as participants rather than arbiters, conscious as some members were that the reforms were inflicting a form of sensory deprivation on the Protestant people. On 15 July Clarke mobilised the B Specials, provoking further Catholic resentment. The Apprentice Boys held their usual march in Derry on 12 August, under RUC protection, and were at last themselves seriously attacked. The police reacted to a pelting with stones from the Bogside, responding to the usual Apprentice Boy taunts, by attacking the locals. The RUC had some difficulty distinguishing between the measures necessary to protect the parade, and actions that could only be construed as displaying a desire for revenge on the Catholic majority in Derry for its

---

[63] P. O'Malley, *Uncivil Wars* (Belfast, 1983), p. 193; E. Moloney, 'Paisley', *Crane Bag*, 4, 2 (1980), pp. 23–7; J.B. Bell, 'The chroniclers of violence in Northern Ireland revisited: The analysis of tragedy', *Review of Politics*, 36 (1974), p. 531. See also the portrait by T. Paulin, 'Paisley's progress', *London Review of Books*, 4, 6 (1–14 April 1982), reprinted in T. Paulin, *Ireland and the English crisis* (Newcastle-upon-Tyne, 1984), pp. 155–73.

[64] Lyons, *Ireland*, p. 765.

[65] P. Johnson, *Ireland: land of troubles* (London, 1980), p. 189.

temerity during the previous year, which had stretched RUC patience to the limit.[66]

The primitive police response, once again captured on television, provoked Jack Lynch into declaring on 13 August that 'we will not stand by'. The actual practical measures announced by Lynch included the moving of Irish army units to the border and the opening of field hospitals to deal with refugees from the North. Lynch was signalling to the politically literate that he would do nothing. But the audience included the politically illiterate, Catholic and Protestant, who failed to decipher the code of Lynchspeak. Lynch's declaration provoked further Protestant rioting in Belfast.[67] Belfast Catholics in turn attacked the RUC station in the Falls Road to relieve the police pressure on Derry. Communal violence erupted as unionist crowds invaded the Falls. The RUC lost their heads, the Minister of Home Affairs sent in the B Specials, and the situation deteriorated drastically.[68] At least 7 people were killed and about 100 wounded in this exhibition of unionist muscle; 3500 families, 3000 of them Catholic, were driven from their homes in Belfast in August and September. At least as many Catholics again would be driven from their homes over the next four years, in the most vicious exhibition of the 'territorial imperative' seen in Western Europe since the end of the Second World War. Protestants in their turn would be driven out of their enclaves in Catholic areas. The principle was the same. It just so happened that more Catholics were at risk.[69] Exultant unionists celebrated the burning of Bombay street:

On 14 August we took a little trip,
up along Bombay Street and burned out all the shit,
we took a little petrol and we took a little gun
and we fought the bloody Fenians . . .
till we had them on the run.[70]

It was in these circumstances of apparently incipient pogroms that 10 000 British troops were despatched to the North, arriving in Derry on 14 August, and in Belfast on 15 August.[71] The balance of expectations could be deduced from the relieved reception given the troops in Catholic areas, and the sullen reaction among Protestants cheated of their prey.

British intervention stabilised the physical force situation, and frus-

---

[66] O'Brien, *States of Ireland*, pp. 178–80. [67] Coogan, *The IRA*, p. 424.
[68] Harkness, *Northern Ireland*, p. 159.
[69] J. Darby, *Conflict in Northern Ireland* (Dublin, 1976), pp. 43–5.
[70] Ulster Defence Association, *Detainee songbook 1974*, quoted in G. Bell, *The Protestants of Ulster* (London, 1976), p. 52. For interesting Protestant myths about the burning of Bombay Street, which do credit to their hearts if not their heads, see Nelson, 'Protestant "ideology" considered', p. 164.
[71] Technical military issues, though of high interest and importance, cannot be dealt with in detail in the text. On the deployment of the troops see R. Evelegh, *Peace-keeping in a democratic society: the lessons of Northern Ireland* (London, 1978), pp. 6–7.

trated what were coming to look dangerously like the genocidal impulses of the Shankhill and the Specials. Despite Lynch's mutterings, the South could not intervene even if it wanted to. Lynch's gesture had presumably been primarily to encourage British intervention. The South, having taken no serious steps to be in a position to defend itself since independence, was in even less of a position to defend Belfast Catholics. Both London and Dublin had played Pontius Pilate on the North for fifty years. They now had to find new instant roles. But the pressure on Britain was even greater, for she was in possession. The political implications of the intervention had not been fully thought through, understandably enough in the pressure of immediate events if not in longer term perspective. The troops could gain a breathing space for the politicians. But they could not themselves impose a solution because they had none to impose.

British policy now proceeded on the assumption that the struggle was essentially about civil rights, not about political power, and that the two could be separated. Several quick initiatives did deal directly with civil rights. The Downing Street Declaration of 19 August 1969 committed Stormont to the implementation of British standards of justice. This included immediate action on the reorganisation of the RUC, the creation of a new Ministry of Community Relations, and an independent Community Relations Commission, the establishment of a Commission of Complaints, reform of the local government franchise, and measures to prevent sectarian discrimination in the distribution of public posts, as well as the allocation of local authority housing on a points system. In addition, Stormont had to accept an inquiry by Sir John Hunt into security. As evidence of Westminster's determination to control matters, two senior civil servants, including Oliver Wright, a former Private Secretary to the prime minister, were transferred to Ulster to provide direct information to Whitehall on local realities.

James Callaghan, the Home Secretary, made two regal visitations to the province. The second was timed to coincide with the publication in October 1969 of the Hunt Report, which recommended the disarming of the RUC, bringing them into line with standard British and Irish practice, and the disbandment of the B Specials, who would be replaced by an Ulster Defence Regiment under the control of the British army. The predictable Protestant riots in Belfast on news of the fate of the Specials, who had acquired a mythical status as symbols of security/supremacy, were suppressed by the army. The UDR duly came into existence on 1 April 1970.

British initiatives were based on the assumption that administrative justice would reconcile the Catholic community to the existing political structure. The speed of the concessions left Catholics as well as Protestants somewhat breathless. So vacuous was political life in the province that professional politicians, Catholic or Protestant, had little to suggest after Westminster intervention. The civil rights leaders, seeing their programme officially adopted, had no further specific plans for political activity.[72] The government, assuming that once British standards of justice were seen to be implemented, life could continue on a new level of normalcy, lost its initial sense of urgency.[73] The crisis had been managed.

It was important that the political vacuum should be filled, because it would inevitably be some time before any concrete consequences of the reform programme, even assuming no resistance, could be felt at grass roots level. The Alliance Party was founded in April 1970 under Oliver Napier to try to bridge the sectarian divide. But it could hardly hope for more than 10 per cent electoral support in view of the inherited animosities. It was not until August 1970 that six MPs of nationalist disposition could finally agree to come together under the loose direction of Gerry Fitt, Republican Labour MP at Westminster for West Belfast since 1966, to form the Social Democratic and Labour Party. This would soon provide some coherent political thrust for the Catholic community, and develop into a far more effective constitutional movement than the old Nationalist party. The SDLP differed both in composition and programme from previous nationalist movements. It was much more cerebral. Eight of its representatives in the 1973 Assembly were teachers, and only two were publicans, compared with four publicans and no teachers among Nationalist representatives in Stormont between 1945 and 1969. In policy terms, it accepted that there could be no united Ireland without the consent of a majority within Northern Ireland. It propounded a set of social and economic policies which left it somewhere left of centre in the conventional ideological spectrum, in contrast to the conservative social tendencies of the Nationalist Party. And it established an organisation, in contrast to the Nationalist Party which was merely a coalition of individuals controlling their personal fiefdoms.[74]

Much happened to damage the prospects of constitutional development in the year between the arrival of the troops and the formation of the SDLP. The political vacuum following the concession of the civil rights programme abandoned political initiative to extremists of various hues. The vacuum opened at the very moment when the IRA began to return to the public stage. The invasion of August 1969 exposed the vulnerability of the Falls to sectarian assault. IRA became a synonym in the Catholic mind for 'I ran away.' Even Brian Faulkner conceded the IRA was in no position to take effective action at that time.[75] The commanding officer of a British

---

[72] G. FitzGerald, *Towards a new Ireland* (Dublin, 1972), pp. 124–5.
[73] Bell, 'The chroniclers of violence', p. 526; J. Darby, *Conflict in Northern Ireland*, p. 191.
[74] I. McAllister and S. Nelson, 'Modern developments in the Northern Ireland party system', *Parliamentary Affairs*, 32 (1979), p. 301.
[75] Faulkner, *Memoirs*, p. 63.

battalion that served in the Falls in 1972 and in 1973 recollected that the memory of the invasion burned itself into the Catholic mind,

when, in their eyes, the Catholics were left by the forces of the British state that were supposed to protect them, to be attacked by the Protestants unhindered, to have their families terrorised and their houses burnt by a mob of their traditional enemies, was a powerful influence. 'Remember Bombay Street' was the most persistent and emotive single rallying cry for the Catholics there, as I and anyone else who has operated in the Falls Road area can testify. The 'burning of Bombay Street' was the oft repeated and most regarded underlying justification for the IRA's claim to be needed as the only defence force that the Catholics of Belfast could rely on in dire emergency to protect their lives and homes. The bulk of the Catholic population accepted this claim, and justification of the IRA, and although many of them thoroughly dislike the bombing and murdering by the IRA, they were not prepared to cooperate with the forces of the Crown to destroy the IRA, just in case another 'Bombay Street' situation might arise, with no one but the IRA to keep the murdering Protestant mob away from them.[76]

After the failure of the 1956–62 border campaign, the IRA had turned toward social policy, and even contemplated participation in parliamentary politics. Individual members of this new-style IRA were involved in the civil rights association, but the organisation was virtually useless in situations of communal struggle. In the aftermath of its helplessness in August 1969, the Belfast IRA purged its social reformers in September and reverted to straight militarism.[77] Under the growing pressure of events in Ulster, the IRA formally split in January 1970. A group styling itself the Provisionals rejected the socialism, the gradualism, and the incipient parliamentarianism of the Official IRA.[78] Enjoying several advantages over the Officials, the Provisionals quickly built up their support, particularly in Belfast in early 1970.[79] The Provisionals were simply more realistic than the Officials in their analysis of the aspirations of the constituency whose support they sought. Their conservative social instincts reassured the Catholic lower-middle classes and aspirant lower-middle classes. That they were mainly green Orangemen commended them to some sympathetic Southern politicians. Above all, they proved more effective than the Officials at getting guns quickly. From February 1970 contacts in the Dublin government promised money once they separated themselves from the 'socialist' Dublin IRA and concentrated on socially harmless traditional republicanism. Up to £80 000 may have been slipped to the Provisionals for arms.[80]

[76] Evelegh, *Peace-keeping*, p. 5.
[77] S. Cronin, *Irish nationalism* (Dublin, 1980), pp. 184–91.
[78] *Ibid.*, p. 196.
[79] On the growth of the Provisionals, see J. Bowyer Bell, *The secret army: a history of the IRA, 1916–1979* (Dublin, 1980), pp. 373ff.; Coogan, *The IRA*, p. 464; S. MacStiofáin, *Memoirs of a revolutionary* (London, 1975), pp. 120ff.; Farrell, *Northern Ireland*, pp. 267–76.
[80] Cronin, *Irish nationalism*, pp. 197–9; Lyons, *Ireland*, pp. 769–71.

The Provos disposed of a more acceptable ideology, and a more effective weaponry. In Seán MacStiofáin they had a energetic organiser, with an aptitude for guerrilla warfare superior to that of his Official rivals. MacStiofáin's ambition and effectiveness were partly responsible for the rapid growth of the Provos during 1970, and for the increasing level of technical sophistication they began to acquire in urban conflict. That the Provisionals achieved widespread support among Belfast Catholics, however, was due more to the British army than to themselves. For the army made rapid progress in translating the initial Catholic welcome firstly into suspicion and then into hate.

The army found itself in a more complex situation than it was trained to contemplate. It was the victim of Stormont's failure to create impartial security forces of its own. It therefore had to be kept in the North to prevent civil war. But its presence provided those determined to destroy the state with an ideal target. If the army did nothing but wait, the IRA might gradually acquire the resources to mount an aggressive campaign against it. If it seized the initiative through 'arms searches' it would inevitably foster IRA recruitment among outraged Catholics whose homes it had vandalised. The army may have behaved with relative restraint by comparative military standards. But the victims of the 17 262 house searches in 1971 were not in a position to ponder army behaviour against a hypothetical average.[81] Evelegh has explained the inevitably counter-productive nature of the 'arms search' approach:

Without inside information as to the exact whereabouts of terrorist weapons and documents, the security forces have little option but to search on the vaguest suspicions – than which nothing is more certain to alienate the population. To search a house thoroughly, it is necessary to pull up floorboards, push in wooden panels, prise out fireplaces, sift through debris in the roof, read private letters, look through cupboards and chests of drawers containing such things as women's underclothes, and search children's beds. All this usually has to be done between midnight and 6 a.m. to give the searching troops the cover of darkness, as they become too vulnerable to snipers if they stay around one house for two or three hours in daylight . . . A mother who has had soldiers breaking up her home and incidentally terrifying her children at 3 a.m. is unlikely to wish to help the government.[82]

The 'arms searches' came as a godsend to the IRA.[83] And they yielded derisory results to the army. Only 47 of the 1183 houses 'searched' between 30 November 1971 and 90 January 1972 produced any arms.[84] Nevertheless, the army was eighteen months in Northern Ireland before

[81] P. Hillyard, 'Law and order', in J. Darby (ed.), *Northern Ireland: the background to the conflict* (Belfast, 1983), p. 41.
[82] Evelegh, *Peace-keeping*, p. 70. See Buckland, *Northern Ireland*, p. 162 for a description of what it was like to be at the receiving end of army 'intelligence' activity in 1972–3.
[83] O'Brien, *States of Ireland*, pp. 246–7.   [84] Arthur, *Northern Ireland*, p. 128.

suffering its first fatality in February 1971. The RUC had to be rearmed after two if its men were shot in Belfast in February. The breathing space won in August 1969 was frittered away with what, in retrospect, seems remarkable casualness. When the IRA provoked a riot in Ballymurphy, a Catholic enclave, in April 1970, the army made more enemies by using CS gas against the rioters, thus achieving the Provo objective.[85] The Tory victory in the British general election of June 1970 caused triumphalist rejoicing among Protestants, who now assumed they would have a free hand to squash Catholic upstarts.[86] If there was a decisive turning point in Catholic attitudes to the army, and one hesitates to suggest there was, because of the feeling that if it was not one thing, it would have been another, it was probably the thirty-four-hour curfew imposed on the Falls in July 1970 to facilitate 'arms searches'. The searches were implemented with even more crudity than usual and yielded predictably few arms, though claiming five lives. 'In political terms it was a disaster', and Provisional influence increased enormously.[87] The IRA was left in a monopoly position as potential protector of the Catholic community in a doomsday situation, with the army, not unreasonably, now assumed to be on the unionist side. Provo membership mushroomed from about 100 to about 800 in the second half of 1970.[88] A silly Criminal Justice Act in July 1970 made a six-month prison sentence mandatory for riotous behaviour, including illegal marches. Marches, legal or illegal, would indeed have to be dealt with if Ulster were ever to approach sanity. But this Act left the RUC as prosecutors, and was therefore naturally interpreted by Catholics as sectarian.[89]

Unionist gloating at the Tory victory was premature. The new prime minister, Edward Heath, had no intention of placing Britain in moral bondage to Ulster unionism. But his energies were absorbed by more pressing priorities in the vital short term. The new Home Secretary, Reginald Maudling, was probably an unfortunate choice from a Northern Ireland point of view. He combined intelligence with indifference at a time when time was all-important. His reputed comment on the plane back to London after his first visit to the North, 'what a bloody awful country', testified more to his intelligence than to a sense of responsibility.[90] The 'bloody awful country' was, after all, Britain's creation, and Britain's responsibility. It is difficult to see how any Home Secretary, or civil servant, could have coped with the challenge without a proper appreciation of historical forces, or grasped how little time they had before events

[85] For the army viewpoint see D. Hamill, *Pig in the middle: the army in Northern Ireland 1969–1984* (London, 1985), pp. 31ff.
[86] *Sunday Times* Insight Team, *Ulster*, pp. 205ff.   [87] Hamill, *The army*, p. 39.
[88] Lyons, *Ireland*, p. 773.
[89] Buckland, *Northern Ireland*, p. 141.
[90] *Sunday Times* Insight Team, *Ulster*, p. 213.

would hurtle out of control. It should be ruefully admitted that it is also difficult to see how a proper appreciation of the historical forces would have enabled them to cope much better with the grim realities of the 'bloody awful country'.

THE FALL OF STORMONT

Chichester Clarke's solution to the worsening relations between the army and the Catholics was to demand more troops. When Heath refused, the hapless Clarke finally brought his somnambulatory premiership to a close by resigning in March 1971. Brian Faulkner defeated William Craig for the doubtful delights of the succession by twenty-six votes to four.

Faulkner, born in 1921, had enjoyed a highly successful career. As Minister for Home Affairs from 1959 to 1963 he had taken the credit for defeating the IRA campaign. He was an active Minister for Commerce from 1963 until 1969, and for Development from 1971. His memoirs, however self-indulgent, convey something of the briskness of the man. Had he succeeded Terence O'Neill directly in 1969, he might just possibly have managed to change the course of subsequent events. But he now succeeded to an even more poisoned legacy than had Clarke. O'Neill was brought down by a party revolt, before the IRA and the army appeared on the scene. Clarke was essentially a victim of army–IRA relations on the one hand, and of constant harassment by the Paisley wing of unionism on the other. The IRA would inevitably intensify the campaign against the Unionist Party's last hope. And Faulkner had certain handicaps. Although 'widely respected as the most able of Unionist politicians',[91] he had acquired a reputation of being too clever by half, having been 'conspicuous at every end of the unionist spectrum'.[92]

It was difficult for a man of Faulkner's ability and energy to avoid acquiring a reputation for excessive cleverness, given the calibre of the company he had to keep. But the fact that he was 'probably the man in the Unionist hierarchy . . . most heartily detested by Catholics'[93] would make it particularly difficult for him to have genuinely conciliatory proposals taken at face value. The Catholic population was now far more sympathetic to the IRA campaign, or at least hostile to the anti-IRA campaign, than in 1956–62. Catholics in the Belfast ghettos now saw the IRA as primarily defensive, whereas in 1956–62 it had pursued an offensive policy in border areas.

Faulkner hoped to incorporate Catholics into a new governmental

---

[91] O'Leary, 'The Northern Ireland crisis', 263. See also P. Bew and H. Patterson, *The British state and the Ulster crisis* (London, 1985), p. 34.

[92] Edwards, *Sins of our fathers*, p. 38.

[93] E. McCann, *War and an Irish town* (London, 1980, 2nd edn), p. 89.

structure, which would give them a veto on sectarian legislation. But he could not appear to do this too openly without forfeiting his own support, subject as he was to constant sniping from Paisley. He selected a cabinet covering a wide range of opinion, running from David Bleakley, a liberal member of the Northern Ireland Labour party, to Harry West, on the extreme Unionist right.[94] The appointment of ministers holding such incompatible ideological viewpoints tended to alienate those who detested the inclusion of their enemies more than they were gratified by the inclusion of their friends. In June 1971 Faulkner made his bid for SDLP support, by offering places on parliamentary committess to the opposition, and thus allowing it, for the first time in the history of Stormont, potentially to influence legislation. These committees had, it is true, no final authority. Some dismissed them as merely a public relations exercise, 'in reality meaningless forms'.[95] But this effort to get members of traditionally hostile political persuasions to recognise that horns didn't grow out of each other's heads might have sown some seeds of conciliation. Time would quickly tell how 'meaningless' the reforms were.

But Faulkner was denied time. Like all parliamentarians who did not control their own military, he was the prisoner of the streets. In particular, he was the prisoner of the army's genius for infuriating Catholic opinion at politically delicate moments. During riots in Derry in the traditional rioting month of July, the army killed two local men, Seamus Cusack and Desmond Beattie, whom the locals vehemently claimed were unarmed. While 'local eyewitnesses' are no more notorious for unwavering commitment to inconvenient truth than official sources, it does seem as if the local version may have coincided with the truth on this occasion. That was certainly the impression conveyed from the combination of lies, bluster and contradictions that constituted the army public relations effort over the incident. John Hume, the SDLP MP for Derry, had no option but to call for a public inquiry. When this was refused – the army not even paying its own version the compliment of pretending it could sustain it – the SDLP had little alternative but to withdraw from Stormont on 16 July.[96]

Faulkner sought to justify the rejection of a public inquiry in his memoirs. If his proposed committee system was as important as Faulkner claims, however, then his explanation of the refusal to countenance the inquiry demanded by Hume on the grounds that 'they could not . . . hold an inquiry every time someone died' is suspiciously facile.[97] If it was not, then Faulkner's claims for the importance of his initiative are exaggerated,

[94] Faulkner, *Memoirs*, pp. 83–7.   [95] Harbinson, *Ulster Unionist party*, p. 162.
[96] Farrell, *Orange state*, p. 280; I. McAllister, *The Northern Ireland Social Democratic and Labour Party: political opposition in a divided society* (London, 1977), pp. 92–3; McCann, *An Irish town*, pp. 88–91.
[97] Faulkner, *Memoirs*, p. 109.

if not fraudulent. The most likely explanation is that the army blundered, realised it would be exposed in an inquiry, and that Faulkner fell victim to the military priority of cover-up.

Faulkner, and the army, now vastly aggravated their problems by introducing internment in August 1971. Faulkner himself claims to have grasped at the straw more in hope than in confidence. He had used the tactic successfully against the IRA border campaign a decade before, but he claims to have appreciated that circumstances were now different.[98] The army was apparently opposed to the idea.[99] If the reported reluctance among both political and military decision-makers is in fact true, the decision to go ahead must count as a particularly bizarre case study in decision-making. Faulkner felt himself prisoner of the tribal imperative. The marching season was in full spate again. The tom-toms were booming their message of triumphalist tribalism across the Ulster political jungle. Faulkner had tried to persuade the Orange Order to reduce the number of marches.[100] He wanted to ban the Apprentice Boys march scheduled for 12 August. He did not dare take the risk unless he could offer an irresistable palliative. His solution was internment, which allowed him to ban the march without rousing a vicious reaction in the prevailing jubilation.

The price to be paid, by Ulster and by Faulkner, for his failure to find a more effective treatment for the marching fever, was to be high. Internment proved a colossal blunder. In fairness to Faulkner, it should be stressed that the alternatives available to him were bleak unless he could saturate the province with soldiers. Whatever he did was likely to be wrong at this stage. Internment merely offered a high profile set-piece issue for which he could be denounced. Faulkner's dilemma would have baffled anyone in the circumstances. But Faulkner aggravated it by making the wrong decisions. Even doing nothing, however frustrating, would probably have been wiser. Few though Faulkner's options were, he chose the worst one. Internment massively increased support and sympathy for the IRA in the South. The Lynch government now found it far more difficult to take steps to impede such assistance as the IRA was receiving from the South. Lynch himself felt obliged to demand the abolition of Stormont and its replacement by a power-sharing regime. Internment also increased IRA support abroad, particularly among Irish-Americans, thus augmenting Provo financial resources. Not only internment itself, but the political illiteracy of the army in implementing it, brought a hitherto inconceivable surge of recruitment to the IRA.[101]

[98] *Ibid.*, pp. 117–19.
[99] Bew, Gibbon and Patterson, *The state*, p. 183; R. Clutterbuck, 'Comment', in D. Watt (ed.), *The constitution of Northern Ireland* (London, 1981), p. 143.
[100] Faulkner, *Memoirs*, p. 106.   [101] Mac Stiofáin, *Memoirs*, p. 192.

The political illiteracy of the army existed at two levels. Firstly, the actual technique of implementation roused immense and enduring resentment. Operation Internment began in the middle of the night, at 4 a.m. on 9 August.

> The terrifying circumstances of that morning were never to be forgotten. Whole areas were sealed off. Paratroopers smashing down doors and literally dragging men from their homes in front of hysterical wives and terrified children, the brutal knock in the middle of the night reeking of totalitarianism about its dirty work. The random brutality, the abuse of rights, the uncertainty, the spread of rumours and counter-rumours, the callous indifference of the army to inquiries as to the whereabouts or the fates of internees, and the holding of a small number at secret locations for interrogation in depth transformed the psychology of the conflict.[102]

It was no flight into the irrational that left Catholic communities like the Bogside 'hysterical with hatred' after internment, or caused recruitment to the IRA to soar.[103]

Some of this was, no doubt, inherent in the exercise. But little attempt seems to have been made to minimise the inevitable repercussions.

Even all the negative consequences might have been justified, at least from a purely technical point of view, as the inevitable price that has to be paid for a successful coup against urban guerrillas in Ulster circumstances. But the coup was spectacularly unsuccessful.

Whatever about the wisdom of the policy, the sheer ineptitude of the security forces wrecked any chance of success. Not only did the army telegraph its intentions a week in advance, but its intelligence was so poor that it captured relatively few senior Provos while detaining several innocent, or at least useless, prisoners.[104] The army relied on defective RUC intelligence. The RUC had information on the IRA old guard. But it was largely a new guard that had taken the initiative since September 1969. In a curious piece of timing, General Farrar-Hockley, commander of land forces, was replaced on 1 August by General Robert Ford, who had little time to familiarise himself with the situation before plunging into action.[105] Even Faulkner conceded that many of the most wanted escaped the net, while many unwanted fell into it. He actually refused to issue detention orders for 97 of the first 337 suspects hauled in.[106] Of the 2357 people arrested during the first six months of interment, 1600 would be released after interrogation.[107] Not many of them, it may be presumed, would have become friends of the army for life.

The army compounded its failure by engaging in selective torture in a manner that ensured it would lose the propaganda battle even more

---

[102] O'Malley, *Uncivil wars*, p. 208.   [103] McCann, *An Irish town*, p. 92.
[104] MacStiofáin, *Memoirs*, pp. 176ff.
[105] For the army perspective see Hamill, *The army*, pp. 54–65.
[106] Faulkner, *Memoirs*, pp. 122–3.
[107] P. Hillyard, 'Law and order', in Darby, *Northern Ireland*, p. 37.

decisively. Army methods simply steeled IRA resolve, and fostered further sympathy for them at home and abroad. Torture proved an inadequate substitute for intelligence. It was also probably counter-productive in general political terms, though this did not prevent the army, and the RUC, from persisting with it until William Whitelaw succeeded in reducing it after the institution of direct rule in 1972.[108] It is true that an inquiry under Sir Edmund Compton sought refuge in the sophistry that army treatment of prisoners, while amounting to 'physical ill-treatment', could not be described as 'torture', only as 'brutality'. Such semantic refinements damaged the standing of England, which still had a reputation to lose. The European Court gave a sort of twisted support to Compton when choosing to distinguish between 'inhuman and degrading treatment', which it considered had occurred, and torture, which it decided had not, in a case brought by the Irish government against Britain.[109] The judgement did little to enhance the reputation of either European law or European morality. Once again, as with internment in general, and whatever about the morality of the matter, 'physical ill-treatment' was yet another political own goal.

Far from snatching a lightning victory, and scotching the snake before it could mature to its full serpentine length, internment ensured that if there was to be victory for the army at all, it would come only after a long hard slog, and with the virtual certainty, in the absence of political development, that 'victory' would only be an interlude before the next instalment of 'one more round'. Casualties soared in the wake of internment. Compared with 30 deaths from 1 January to 9 August, there were a further 143 from then until the end of the year.[110] Instead of delivering a crushing blow to the IRA, the sympathy fostered by internment allowed them to operate more extensively than before. Faulkner vigorously defended his decision, on the grounds that after the peak of casualties in August, there was a gradual but steady decline in terrorist violence. If the security measures had only been 'consistently and firmly applied', he felt, the IRA would have been defeated by the end of 1972.[111] But his argument, based on doubtful manipulation of the data, remains unconvincing. Sympathy for the dilemma of anyone in his position should not cloud judgement about the consequences of a misguided decision.

The SDLP was even less likely to respond to his proposal for an embryonic version of power-sharing after internment. Nevertheless, his Green Paper of October 1971 floated the idea once more, and also contemplated the introduction of proportional representation. But his

---

[108] *Sunday Times* Insight Team, *Ulster*, pp. 292ff.' *New Statesman*, 13 July 1973, pp. 44–6.
[109] Hillyard, 'Law and order', p. 41.   [110] Harkness, *Northern Ireland*, p. 170.
[111] Faulkner, *Memoirs*, p. 137.

continuing initiatives towards political conciliation, however hesitant, were buried completely by Bloody Sunday, 30 January 1972, when paratroopers killed thirteen men, following a march in Derry.[112] The paras won the military match comfortably.

PARAS THIRTEEN, the walls said,
BOGSIDE NIL.[113]

But they shot straight to the bottom of the political league table. The subsequent Widgery inquiry failed to establish that any of the victims were armed. The government made out-of-court settlements with next of kin. The circumstances would remain a matter for dispute long after the Widgery report. Whatever the circumstances, the para performance was unprofessional in the extreme. The background was simple enough. It was yet another illegal march, like all marches since 9 August. But several had already occurred, including five under Civil Rights Association auspices in January.[114] However salutary, and probably ultimately essential, in civilising the political culture of the province an effective ban on marches would have been, enforcing such a ban would have required the political will and the military ability to impose sterner measures than anyone cared contemplate. Neither the will nor the capacity were present. Nor did the paratroopers prevent the Derry march taking place. The march was dispersing when the troops sought to arrest marchers retrospectively, so to speak, as they withdrew into the Bogside. In the circumstances, arrest was a pointless exercise. The troops maintained that at this juncture they came under fire, which they returned, claiming thirteen victims in the process. While it was certainly not beyond the bounds of possibility that troops would come under fire in these prevailing conditions, the circumstantial evidence overwhelmingly supports on this occasion the accounts of the residents. The professionals gave an amateur performance.

It may be, as John Whale argued a little later, that in the immediate aftermath of Bloody Sunday many Protestants would have responded to a quick political initiative by the British government for a new Northern Ireland.[115] As the government had apparently no contingency plans prepared for any such eventuality, the opportunity, if it existed, was missed. And it is unclear what the initiative could have been, given the reluctance of the government to impose a military settlement on either or both communities. In the event, unionist opinion shifted evermore to the right. William Craig, sensing Faulkner's crumbling authority, formed the Vanguard movement on 12 February 1972 to reassert unionist ascendancy. The Ulster Defence Association, which would incorporate

---

[112] A fourteenth victim died later. O'Malley, *Uncivil wars*, p. 209.
[113] S. Heaney, 'Casualty', in *Field Work* (London, 1979), p. 22.
[114] McCann, *An Irish town*, p. 100.   [115] *Sunday Times*, 19 March 1972.

several, though not all, Protestant private enterprise vigilante groups and sectarian killer gangs, under the general direction of Andy Tyrie, formally emerged to give Protestants the reassurance of a private paramilitary organisation of their own, now that the RUC were no longer in complete control of security.[116]

Faulkner, moving to guard his right flank from Craig, demanded from Edward Heath in March authority to fully rearm the RUC and to re-establish the B Specials, in return for some compromise on internment.[117] Heath insisted instead on complete British control of security, including the RUC. In addition, Whitehall would assume full responsibility for law and order, justice, and appointments to the bench. When Faulkner and his cabinet refused to accept these conditions, Heath prorogued Stormont for a year from 30 March and introduced direct rule from 1 April, with William Whitelaw as Secretary of State for Northern Ireland. It would have been much more difficult for a Labour government to take this step, faced as they probably would have been with Conservative opposition in parliament![118] At the end of the proroguement period, the Northern Ireland Constitution Act duly abolished Stormont itself as well as the office of governor, replacing them by a Northern Ireland assembly and executive.

THE SEARCH FOR A SOLUTION

The Provos achieved considerable success through the more technically proficient use of explosives in 1971. This allowed them to mount a car bomb and land mine campaign at little expense to themselves during 1972.[119] The number of innocent victims inevitably increased. Of the 474 deaths from violence in 1972, 242 were civilian victims.[120] The Provos correctly calculated that however uneasy individual Catholics might feel at particular atrocities, this would have little effect on basic allegiances. The Provos problem was that their talents lay almost solely in destruction. They were by no means all political illiterates. On the contrary, their appraisal of the parameters of the politically possible was often relatively realistic. But it is arguable that they lost their best opportunity of acquiring a political profile at that time by failing to announce a ceasefire immediately on the introduction of direct rule, and publicising realistic conditions for a cessation of hostilities. That they did not do so pre-

---

[116] B. White, 'From conflict to violence: the reemergence of the IRA and the Loyalist response', in Darby, *Northern Ireland*, pp. 187–8.
[117] Harbinson, *Ulster Unionist party*, p. 164.
[118] M. Rees, *Northern Ireland: a personal perspective* (London, 1985), p. 16.
[119] Mac Stiofáin, *Memoirs*, pp. 220–1, 242.
[120] P. Brennan, 'La Violence politique des republicains', *Ireland, Politics and Society*, 1, 1 (Winter 1985), p. 46.

sumably indicates how close to forcing British withdrawal they thought themselves to be. And they may, of course, have been racked by internal dissension on the matter. The safest way to avoid dissension was to insist on total victory.

Whitelaw's shrewdness, and his relative success at public relations, as he conveyed an impression of amiable good intentions to all communities, forced the IRA to think again. After he amnestied those imprisoned for illegal marches, and released over 500 internees, more than half the total, a truce was arranged in June 1972, and Whitelaw discussed possible peace terms with the Provos in July. But the IRA pitched its demands unrealistically high, and the more militaristic elements quickly resumed hostilities with a bombing spree on 21 July, 'Bloody Friday', in which they scored 11 kills and wounded another 130, many maimed for life.

Whitelaw countered with a dual approach. On 31 July, in 'Operation Motorman', the army reoccupied the 'no go' areas from which the representatives of state law had been excluded by Provo control. Having cleared the military decks in this manner, he pressed ahead with measures to establish that the majority wished to remain in the United Kingdom, and at the same time to provide representative institutions in place of Stormont. A referendum held on 8 March 1973 duly reaffirmed the desire of the majority to remain citizens of the United Kingdom. The SDLP and the IRA recommended their supporters to abstain. Forty-one per cent abstained, only 1 per cent voted against, while 58 per cent voted for continuing union with Britain. The recommendation to abstain was an obvious political ploy, insofar as normal non-voters, including some unionists, would now be counted as positive abstentionists. Even making no allowance for this, the vote did represent a clear repudiation of a united Ireland by the Northern Ireland electorate, not that any doubts could have been entertained on that score.

Northern Ireland Constitutional Proposals, a White Paper published by Whitelaw on 20 March 1973, rejected the idea of an Executive representing 'only one section of a divided community'. This accorded official recognition to the idea of consociational democracy in preference to majoritarian democracy in the Northern Ireland ethnic situation.[121] This White Paper built on a Green Paper, *The Future of Northern Ireland*, published in October 1972, which offered an impressive survey of the alternative possibilities being canvassed by various interested parties at that stage. The first election to the new Northern Ireland Assembly, held on 28 June 1973, reflected the fragmentation of viewpoints at the grass

---

[121] The views of A. Lijphart, a leading academic analyst of the concept of consociational democracy, are conveniently summarised in his paper 'Consociation: the model and its application in divided societies', in D. Rea (ed.), *Political cooperation in divided societies* (Dublin, 1982), pp. 166–86.

roots. Faulkner's supporters, with 26.5 per cent of the votes, won 23 of the 78 seats. But a variety of other Unionist representatives, including Paisley's DUP, Craig's VUPP (Vanguard Unionists Progressive Party), and some Official Unionists who had refused to pledge themselves to Faulkner, won 35 per cent of the vote, and 27 seats. The non-sectarian Alliance Party won 9 per cent of the vote and 8 seats, while the SDLP, with 22 per cent of the vote, won 19 seats.[122]

This may have been once more a critical moment in determining the fate of the North, insofar as there were any critical moments. Had all nominally constitutional parties chosen to cooperate, the lines would have been clearly drawn between constitutionalism and violence. By refusing to cooperate with Catholics in the Executive, Paisley and Craig pandered to the supremecist instincts of their grass roots, and effectively sabotaged whatever possibility there may have been of peaceful evolution. They might have responded that their supporters would not permit them. But if the unionist grass roots was not prepared to contemplate powersharing with a Catholic party to try to make the state work, then it was difficult to see what future there could be for Northern Ireland as a state.

Faulkner had arguably adopted excessively cautious tactics at the June election. He chose to compete with the Alliance, which he feared might attract support from his own left, instead of trying to protect his right wing from the blandishments of Paisley and Craig. Faulkner was far more likely to lose votes in this direction than in the Alliance direction. And even if he had lost some support to Alliance, he could still form an Executive with them within the terms of Whitelaw's White Paper, because their support could be interpreted as coming from both communities. On the other hand, he could not form an Executive, on Whitelaw's conditions, with the Unionist right.[123] But it probably did not make much difference in the end. The size of Faulkner's 'left' was decidedly finite.

The Assembly did not enjoy the most auspicious of starts. The wranglings of Paisley, Craig and their followers made the exchanges of the Dáil seem positively cerebral. But they were still mild compared with the performance of Paisley later in the session.[124] After protracted discussions, in which he showed impressive negotiating skill, Whitelaw was able to appoint, on 22 November, an Executive consisting of six Official Unionists, one Alliance and four SDLP members, with Faulkner as Chief Executive and Gerry Fitt as his Deputy. Heath then transferred Whitelaw back to Britain, appointing Francis Pym to succeed him as Secretary of State on 3 December.

---

[122] R.D. Osborne, 'Voting behaviour in Northern Ireland, 1921–1977', in F.W. Boal and J.N.H. Douglas (eds.), *Integration and division: geographical perspectives on the Northern Ireland problem* (London, 1982), p. 156.
[123] Utley, *Lessons*, pp. 103ff.   [124] Faulkner, *Memoirs*, pp. 200–2, 227, 248.

Even before assuming office in January 1974, the Executive had lost the confidence of the majority of the Ulster people, insofar as it had ever really enjoyed it. In the Sunningdale Agreement of 9 December 1973, following a meeting between the British and Irish prime ministers, and representatives of the Executive parties, Faulkner agreed to the establishment of a Council of Ireland. To Faulkner, this was purely a 'token' concession in order to secure that the Irish government 'fully accepted and solemnly declared that there could be no change in the status of Northern Ireland until the majority of the people of Northern Ireland desired a change in that status'.[125] The participants also agreed to try to improve security, particularly in the pursuit and conviction of those accused of murder in Northern Ireland who took refuge in the South. But the legal and constitutional situation was complex, and the best Sunningdale could achieve was for the two sovereign governments to 'jointly set up a commission to consider all the proposals put forward at the conference'.

The proposed Council of Ireland had a somewhat elaborate structure, but it was unlikely to wield any real power for the foreseeable future. Nevertheless, Faulkner was immediately repudiated by the Ulster Unionist Council, and forced to resign as leader in January 1974, to be succeeded by Harry West. Nineteen of the remaining twenty-one Official Unionist MPs continued to support him, however, and he remained chief of the Executive, though with greatly diminished moral authority. The unionist furore over Sunningdale, and particularly over the Council of Ireland, may seem to have been exaggerated. The council was largely symbolic, and likely to remain so. But the Protestant ascendancy was as much about symbols as about substance. Or rather, symbol was part of substance, for the psychology of ascendancy revolves as much around symbols as around substance. Symbol is no decorative embellishment of substance, but integral to it.

It quickly became brutally clear that the Executive had no mandate. When Heath called a snap general election in February 1974, Faulkner supporters were routed at the polls, winning only 94 000 votes compared with 367 000 for the United Ulster Unionist Council (UUUC) representing all other shades of unionist opinion. All eleven Unionist MPs returned to Westminster were anti-Sunningdale. Liam Cosgrave, who had succeeded Jack Lynch as Taoiseach the previous year, added to Faulkner's embarrassment by choosing to defend a challenge in the Irish courts by Kevin Boland on the constitutionality of the Sunningdale Agreement by asserting that it was not in conflict with the territorial claim of the Republic on the North, even while stressing that 'the factual position of Northern Ireland is that it is within the United Kingdom and my government accepts this as a fact'.[126] Few unionists were in a mood, naturally enough, to accept the

[125] *Ibid.*, pp. 235–8.   [126] *Ibid.*, p. 247.

prosaic distinction between a constitutional claim and 'a fact'. Both the IRA and the UUUC intensified their assaults in order to destroy the Executive. Faulkner had forfeited representative authority, but continued with his artificial majority until the Assembly defeated a motion condemning Sunningdale on 14 May. This provoked the Ulster Workers' Council, representing Protestant workers in key installations, to call a general strike.

The new British government, under Harold Wilson, with Merlyn Rees as Secretary of State, refused to move against the strikers, who succeeded in becoming the *de facto* government in many areas until the Executive resigned on 28 May, obliging London to resume direct rule. Although intimidation, massive or modest, depending on one's standards on these matters, may have been necessary to produce the desired response in the first instance,[127] there was little political hostility to the strikers among middle-class Protestants.[128] When the crunch came, they all belonged to the same community.

Sunningdale arguably represents one of those tantalising 'lost opportunities' for a new start. The British government, and especially Wilson and Rees, were subjected to much abuse by nationalists, North and South, for failing to crush the strike by military force. There would have been a certain irony in a Labour government moving against an authentic expression of mass proletarian power. It may be that they had already resigned themselves, reluctantly or otherwise, to the imminent collapse of the Executive.[129] How far Rees may have been influenced by a certain distaste for the SDLP and for the Dublin government is problematical.[130] The decisive factor, however, was probably less the personal predilections of Wilson and Rees than army advice – or army pressure.

The army was anxious to avoid conflict with the strikers.[131] Whether more resolute civilian leadership would have permitted the army to indulge its anxiety – or how far its reluctance would have surfaced had it anticipated more resolute civilian leadership – must remain conjectural. Rees, 'who just seemed to have gone into a flap', effectively abdicated responsibility.[132] The army, on the other hand, had a definite view of its role, supported by the Ministry of Defence in London. While it might be able to crush the strike militarily, it could not operate the essential services, especially the power services, on which daily life depended.[133] It feared sabotage in the power stations, and painted a horrifying scenario of the consequences, one version culminating in an outbreak of cholera.[134]

[127] *Ibid.*, pp. 261–2.
[128] Shea, *Voices*, p. 200; R. Fisk, *The point of no return* (London, 1975), p. 161.
[129] J. Downey, *Them and us* (Dublin, 1983), p. 134.   [130] *Ibid.*, p. 142.
[131] Faulkner, *Memoirs*, p. 263; Hamill, *The army*, pp. 144–5.
[132] Faulkner, *Memoirs*, p. 263.   [133] Rees, *Northern Ireland*, p. 80.
[134] *Irish Times*, 15 May 1985.

The army drew a line, convenient for itself, between 'terrorism' and the strike. The strike was 'political', and it was none of its responsibility to deal with it unless it became 'terrorism'.[135] But this was a political judgement, involving the army in a usurpation of civilian authority – assuming there was a civilian authority to usurp. It remains unclear what role the civil servants, especially Frank Cooper, the powerful Permanent Under Secretary, who had a Ministry of Defence background himself, played at this juncture.

Turning from the interesting constitutional issues raised by the governmental decision-making process during the strike, how valid was the army's judgement of the likely consequences of moving quickly and firmly against the strikers? This must of course remain conjectural. Rees has argued that 'despite what armchair theorists said at the time, permanently to remove the road blocks that had been erected all over the province was impossible'.[136] This avoids the real question, which is whether an immediate move by the authorities to restore normalcy would not have eliminated the need for 'permanently' removing roadblocks. Confrontations of this type turn at least as much on perceptions of the nerve and will power of the other side as they do on objective assessment of the balance of military power. Some observers, and not only nationalist ones, continue to hold the view that an immediate move against the strike would have broken its potential, which depended initially partly on intimidation.[137]

Cosgrave urged Rees to crush the strike.[138] Dublin's position was at least consistent with traditional Irish policy. When it came to military matters, it was somebody else's business, in this case the British army's, to do the necessary. When confronted with a massive affirmation of the indomitable resolve of the plain protestant people of Ulster, Dublin, however willing to wound, was afraid to strike. It refused to have a credible army of its own, even in relation to its paltry population. It had little defensive, much less offensive, capacity. That made for a civilised society in some ways. But it meant that Dublin habitually relied on others to bear the brunt of any measures involving serious military action. It would not be in a position to play any military role in Ulster even if it wanted to. Whether it should have wanted to is an entirely different matter. It may well be that it was in the best long-term interests of Ireland, North and South, that Dublin politicians should not have been in in a position to exercise real power, depending on one's opinion of their likely performance if they actually

---

[135] *Ibid.*   [136] Rees, *Northern Ireland*, p. 70.
[137] J. Cole, 'Security constraints', in D. Watt, *The constitution of Northern Ireland* (London, 1981), pp. 133–4; Fisk, *No return*, p. 163.
[138] Rees, *Northern Ireland*, p. 73.

had real power to exercise. But it was certainly no business of the British army to respond to Dublin's behest. It was its business to respond to London's behest – if there was a London behest.

Wilson's refusal to take resolute measures against the strikers won him few unionist plaudits. Instead, they remembered his speech depicting them as 'spongers on British democracy'. Wilson's futile and self-indulgent sneer provoked both fury and incomprehension among unionists. It was of course objectively true that they enjoyed their standard of living less through the sweat of their manly brows than because of transfers from English tax revenue. But as citizens of the United Kingdom, they were perfectly entitled to it. 'Sponging' is not a helpful analytical concept when discussing intra-state transfers. Ulster Unionists may have been as much the victims of their location in the United Kingdom as were those, at a more local level, misguided enough to remain in residence west of the Bann, or for that matter west of the Shannon. And the bulk of the recipients among Protestants would have been presumably working class, despite the tendency of the welfare state to benefit the middle class! The Ulster Workers' Council could claim to genuinely represent many Protestant working-class interests.[139] But it was not along such scholarly lines of disquisition that popular Protestant opinion responded to Wilson. Their self-image was being mocked. How could they, the salt of the earth, God's anointed, be spongers? Catholics sponged. Protestants did not. Their self-image depended to no small degree on the contrast between their own sturdy Protestant toil and Catholic layabout propensities. 'I am not a beggar with a begging bowl going to an English politician and asking for a mess of pottage', said Paisley. 'If anything, the British government owes to Northern Ireland more than we ever owed to them.'[140] Paisley's attitude was widely shared. Some felt they were 'even more loyal than most Britons, because they accepted far lower wages than mainlanders'.[141] Did not Britain owe her freedom to Ulster from the Boyne to the Somme, and to the dark days of the Battle of the Atlantic? When Protestants sported sponges in their lapels, or on their cars, it was in derision at so juvenile a jibe.

A key question arising out of the whole imbroglio is whether Sunningdale could have survived but for the misguided Council of Ireland clause. Some respected observers felt that unionist opinion was prepared to accept power-sharing, however reluctantly. But the omens for power-sharing, even in the absence of a Council of Ireland, do not seem to me to have been particularly promising. More than half the popular unionist vote in June supported parties opposed to power-sharing in principle.

[139] G. Eley, 'The left, the nationalists and the Protestants: some recent books on Ireland', *Michigan Quarterly Review*, 22, 1 (Winter 1983), p. 125.
[140] O'Malley, *Uncivil wars*, p. 185.   [141] Nelson, *Defenders*, p. 114

Even within his own party, Faulkner won only narrow majorities for power-sharing at meetings in October and November, before Sunningdale. It may be doubted if Faulkner would have won a solitary extra seat in February 1974 had the Council of Ireland never been broached at Sunningdale. It made good tactical sense for the opponents of power-sharing to concentrate on the Council of Ireland. There may have been some slender unionist support for, or at least resignation to, power-sharing. There was virtually none for a Council of Ireland. Once the Council of Ireland vanished from the agenda after 1974, unionist opinion remained resolutely opposed to the principle of power-sharing. It may be claimed that the second loyalist strike in May 1977 failed because there was no Council of Ireland issue involved. But there was no power-sharing issue involved either. The strike was called against direct rule, not against an Executive type arrangement. And there were many other variables affecting the outcome in 1977, not least the resolute attitude adopted by the government from the outset.

Following the collapse of the Assembly, the Northern Ireland Act, 17 July 1974, made the Secretary of State and his ministers directly responsible once more to Westminster for the government of Northern Ireland. Rees published a new White Paper in July, *The Northern Ireland Constitution*, proposing the election of a constitutional convention, which would permit representatives of the Ulster people to frame their own proposals for the constitution of the province. The White Paper set three conditions: power-sharing of some type, a governmental structure acceptable to the people of the United Kingdom as a whole, and the recognition of a special relationship between the North and the Republic.[142]

Faulkner suffered a resounding defeat in the elections to the Convention in May 1975 as unionist voters turned massively to his enemies. His Unionist Party of Northern Ireland took only 51 000 votes and 5 seats, compared with the 356 000 first preferences and 46 seats for the UUUC. Faulkner himself retired from politics the following year, and was killed in a hunting accident in 1977. The Convention elections retrospectively endorsed the strike. And who are nationalists, or at least republicans, to quibble about retrospective legitimisation?

The Protestant vote appeared to drift steadily to the right between 1969 and 1975. In reality, it probably shifted rather little.[143] What seems to have happened is that as the implications of their votes became clearer to the electorate, they plumped for the more obviously hard-line parties. The once-great Unionist Party disintegrated under the impact of genuine

---

[142] M. Wallace, *British government in Northern Ireland* (Newton Abbot, 1982), pp. 99–100.
[143] R. Rose, *Northern Ireland* (London, 1976), pp. 99–100.

British government. But it remained true to form even in its disintegration. For it did not split fundamentally according to materially objective socio-economic groupings. Harry West's Official Unionists, and the handful who followed Brian Faulkner into his new Unionist Party, may have been a shade more middle class than the DUP followers of Ian Paisley or the VUPP followers of William Craig. But that was scarcely the fundamental reason for the form their regrouping assumed. The primacy of the identity question was reflected in the fact that the divisions between the new factions reflected more closely differences in attitude towards constitutional/ideological issues than towards social or economic policy.

Faulkner's political misfortune, and possibly Ulster's and even Ireland's, was that he came to power too late. When he did, he showed a capacity for compromise, and a willingness to experiment, that might have stood his country in good stead a decade earlier. He might not, of course, have shown comparable capacity but for the lessons of the intervening decade. But at least he seemed able to learn some lesson. There was probably no internal political solution for Northern Ireland, at least in the short term, by the time he came to office. Concessions to Catholics would inevitably isolate him among Unionists, unless he could rise to the level of a Macmillan or a de Gaulle and disguise from his followers the true nature of his policy. And even a Macmillan or a de Gaulle would have found the scope for verbal manoeuvre limited in the Ulster context. And if Faulkner's followers would not perceive the true thrust of his policy, it was equally unlikely that Catholics would perceive it. They would therefore be alienated by his apparent intransigence. His reputation as an opportunist proved a handicap in winning confidence. He was also the prisoner of the gunmen in the sense that they were able to sabotage conciliatory initiatives by provoking incidents guaranteed to rouse communal bitterness. In addition, he probably compounded his own difficulties by faulty tactics. He relied too much on the British government, and had no fall-back positions prepared – if indeed any could be prepared. He set his face against integration with Britain, which might just possibly, if Heath and Whitelaw had been prepared to back it, have made some unionists more receptive to his policies.[144] Whether this was a realistic option at the time may, however, be doubted. Faulkner was trapped between unionists who insisted on majority rule in Northern Ireland, on the model of Westminster, in order to frustrate the creation of a Westminster-type ethos, and the SDLP, which forfeited whatever chance it might have had of securing popular unionist acceptance of the idea of power-sharing by consistently linking this, to protect itself from the IRA, with the demand for institutional advances, especially the Council of Ireland, towards Irish unity. This insistence, however cosmetic the institu-

[144] Utley, *Lessons*, p. 89.

tions, inevitably aroused unionist suspicions of the real motives underlying SDLP commitment to power-sharing – and left Faulkner stranded.

Relations between the UUUC and the SDLP in the Convention were
complicated by the struggle for power within the UUUC, fanned by the
rival ambitions of Paisley, Craig and West. When agreement actually
threatened between the UUUC and the SDLP on a form of power-sharing
in the intended new Executive, it was promptly denounced by Paisley and
West, partly because Craig seemed likely to be the main beneficiary, as he
had been most intimately involved in the negotiations. Craig himself was
in any case immediately repudiated by his VUPP MPs when he broached
the possibility of some form of power-sharing for an emergency period of
up to five years. He was duly expelled from the UUUC in October. Craig's
fate, like that of Faulkner, illustrated once more the elementary truth later
enunciated by Jim Molyneux, Official Unionist leader in Westminster,
that 'the lesson of Northern Ireland politics is that it is not the slightest use
any leader getting so far ahead that his troops are not following. This
should be a consideration uppermost in the mind of all party leaders.'[145]
The Convention collapsed in November 1975 with the rejection by the
UUUC of any form of power-sharing, and the refusal of Rees to recognise
an Executive representing one community only.

The profile of terrorist activity changed during 1975. The troubles
claimed 252 dead in 1973, 221 in 1974, and 244 in 1975. In 1975,
however, loyalist paramilitary groups scored far more kills than republican ones, and the security forces claimed only seven victims. This partly
reflects a quasi-IRA ceasefire that lasted from the beginning of the year
until October. Rees sought to reconcile republicans by phasing out
internment by the end of 1975, when all 2000 suspects, 95 per cent of
them Catholic, had been released.[146] General Sir Frank King, GOC in
Northern Ireland, registered his disquiet at this approach in a semi-public
statement on 12 April, asserting that the army was on the verge of
defeating the IRA. Even allowing for the fact that the army was always on
the verge of defeating the IRA, this signalled professional military
resentment at the attempt by Rees to buy Provo cooperation.[147] Rees also
initiated a policy of 'Ulsterisation' of the conflict. The size of the army was
gradually reduced from 21 000 in 1973 to 12 000 by 1980, while the total
of the various police forces rose from 14 500 to 19 500.[148] When the
conciliatory policy failed to pay the desired dividends, Rees reversed his
approach by ending 'special category' status in prisons, under which

[145] *Sunday Times*, 27 March 1977.
[146] Rose, *Northern Ireland*, pp. 24, 28; K. Boyle, T. Hadden and P. Hillyard, *Ten years on in Northern Ireland* (London, 1980), p. 24.
[147] Farrell, *The Orange state*, p. 323. For the Rees version, see Rees, *Northern Ireland*, pp. 225–6.
[148] Boyle, Hadden and Hillyard, *Ten years on*, pp. 24–5.

prisoners claiming political motivation for their offences were permitted to live in largely civilian fashion, wearing their own clothes, and residing in compounds rather than cells. Henceforth, those convicted of terrorist offences after March 1976 would be treated as ordinary criminals, having been tried in the courts.[149] The partiality of those same courts would provide a regular bone of contention for years to come.

Roy Mason, who succeeded Rees, blessedly released from his penance by a grateful Jim Callaghan who transferred him to the Home Office in September 1976 after he had managed Callaghan's campaign for the premiership, adopted a more robust approach. Rees's elevation, incidentally, illustrates the changed impact of involvement in the Irish question on British political careers. Nineteenth-century Ireland was held to be the graveyard of political prospects. It is almost impossible for a British politician not to retire from Ulster with honour, and with improved prospects, unless of course he has been sent there in the first place, as James Prior would be sent, to bury his political career. But Whitelaw, Rees, Mason, and Hurd all vaulted through service in Northern Ireland into the higher ranks on their return to the 'mainland'. Even Humphrey Atkins, not widely regarded as the most glittering jewel in Stormont Castle's crown, did no worse on his release than had he never been incarcerated. It did not even seem to greatly matter how well or poorly the victims performed. It was assumed their task was hopeless anyway, and that, except in cases of ineffable ineptitude, their failure was due to the intractable nature of the problem and the irrationality of the impossible indigenes.

Mason vigorously pursued the policy of Ulsterisation – which might be a euphemism for Protestantisation – with the rejuvenated and modernised RUC assuming prime responsibility for security, and the army relegated to a supporting role. The statistics of the number of civilians killed suggest considerable success, at least in the short term, for the security forces at this stage. 'Only' 31 civilians were murdered in both 1978 and 1979, compared with 55 in 1977 and 221 in 1976. And not all civilians would have been 'innocent'.

Two factors contributed to this improvement. The Provos were increasingly penetrated by intelligence, and suffered severe losses to the security forces in 1976. But a reorganisation, based on the introduction of the small cell strategy in 1978, restored their internal cohesion, and increased the likelihood of a rising death toll.[150] On the other side, the failure of the second loyalist strike in May 1977 weakened the Protestant paramilitaries. The strike, called in a confused sort of way to achieve greater self-government for the North, foundered on the rock of Roy Mason. Mason was in many respects a quintessential Ulsterman *manqué*.

[149] *Ibid.*, p. 24.   [150] Coogan, *IRA*, pp. 474–5.

Brusque, impatient, self-righteous, devoid of subtlety, it would not be every literary gathering he would grace. But there are circumstances in which robust qualities of character serve a more useful purpose than more refined ones. Ulster worker strikes certainly count among them. Mason faced down the strikers. The situation was not as objectively threatening as in 1974, but it might have become far more awkward had Mason proved as vacillating as Rees. He didn't. It was the strikers who backed down, much to the discomfiture of Paisley, who had made one of his few tactical errors by associating himself prematurely with the strike. Mason's handling of the strike challenge, his refusal to deal with the IRA, his simultaneous insistence, which now began to be believed, that there would be no British withdrawal, to some extent reassured both Catholics and Protestants, and sapped the credibility of the IRA as a possible alternative government, a hope, or fear, which Rees's policy had fostered. The implication that *de facto* integration with Britain was becoming a reality also served to reassure many Protestants without provoking the majority of Catholics. Direct rule was becoming the system that least divided Ulstermen.

Direct rule had particularly unfortunate implications for the SDLP. The party was condemned to a derisory minority role within the United Kingdom as a whole. It was therefore understandable that it should become rather frantic in the search for 'devolved government' in Ulster. It was also understandable, in view of the resolute refusal of the vast majority of Unionist politicians to participate in power-sharing, that the SDLP should abandon its tentative commitment to the Northern Ireland state, feeling that it had no alternative but to assert the failure of Northern Ireland as a political entity and demand the withdrawal of British troops. In line with this thinking, it refused to respond to an invitation from Humphrey Atkins, who succeeded Mason as Secretary of State following the Conservative victory in the 1979 British general election, to participate in talks confined to the search for a purely internal solution.[151]

The most notable grass roots development of 1976–7 was the peace movement. This developed when Mairéad Corrigan, a relative of three children killed in the troubles, founded, with Betty Williams, the Women's Peace Movement in 1976 in an attempt to shame the politicians and the paramilitaries into a solution. It seemed a long way from societies whose codes of honour required kinsfolk to themselves directly avenge the death of kinsmen by hunting down the perpetrators, although the logic of the Ulster situation has more of that in it than of peace. The women won more sympathy abroad than at home, where paramilitaries and many politicians, sensing a threat to their own interests, reacted against them. The

---

151 Girvin, 'National identity', pp. 125–6; J.H. Whyte, 'Why is the Northern Ireland problem so intractable'?, *Parliamentary Affairs*, 34 (1981), p. 423.

movement soon lost momentum, plagued by internal problems, and unable to harness the genuine but undisciplined idealism tapped by the momentary revulsion against particular outrages. It served to illustrate in a particularly graphic way that good intentions were not enough. 'Blood and iron', or at least guile, callousness and cynicism, remained more relevant recipes.

After the failure of the loyalist strike in 1977, Paisley recovered some ground in the Westminster elections in May 1979, when his party won three seats. An even bigger moment of electoral triumph came the following month in the European elections. He himself had opposed EEC membership. The European community was self-evidently a papal conspiracy, being based, after all, on the Treaty of *Rome*! He now topped the Ulster poll with 170 000 votes, far ahead of John Taylor, who took the third seat for the Official Unionists, with 69 000 votes, while Harry West, Unionist Party leader since Faulkner's departure in January 1974, was humiliatingly eliminated. West would quickly surrender the leadership to Jim Molyneux, whose public appeal was not irresistable, but who was an adroit operator. He needed to be. John Hume took the second seat, enjoying a personal triumph comparable to that of Paisley. In fact, he took a bigger percentage of the Catholic vote than did Paisley of the Protestant vote, with 140 000 first preferences, despite the hostility of the Provos and of sundry Republican Clubs, whose candidate, Bernadette MacAliskey (the former Bernadette Devlin) won 21 000 votes. By the end of the year Hume was to become leader of the SDLP when Gerry Fitt resigned on the grounds that the party was becoming too nationalist.

Humphrey Atkins functioned until September 1981, when he 'departed as he arrived . . . bewildered and bemused'.[152] Atkins found himself dropped into the job intended for Airey Neave, Thatcher's adviser on the North, who was assassinated in March 1979 by the INLA, a splinter group who refused to abide by the 'Official' IRA ceasefire of 1972. Neave would have been an interesting appointment. Atkins has generally been derogatorily dismissed. Molyneux compared him to 'a blank piece of paper – you could write on him what you liked'.[153] As it transpired, Molyneux could not. It was apparently only Foreign Office officials, who, ever eager to betray loyal Ulster into the vulpine paws of the Republic in the Unionist conspiracy scenario, elaborated most eloquently by Enoch Powell, had reached the requisite literacy levels. Powell, for whom the Unionists found a constituency in Down, was commonly considered the Unionist brain, not that Molyneux himself was incapable of entertaining exotic racial notions.[154]

152 Arthur, *Northern Ireland* (London, 1984 edn).
153 O'Malley, *Uncivil wars*, p. 162.
154 J. Molyneux, 'Northern Ireland', *Right Ahead*, October 1985.

Whatever about his personal ability, Atkins had rank bad luck. He had the misfortune to find himself dealing with H-block hunger strikes. When Rees withdrew the'special category' status for convicted terrorists after 1 March 1976, new prisoners reacted by refusing to wear prison uniform, confining themselves to a blanket only. The action escalated into a general blanket protest which acquired even more malodorous connotations as the prisoners chose to remain confined to their cells, and live in the resultant filth, when they were refused permission to leave the cells without wearing prison uniform. When this failed to achieve the restoration of 'special category' status, seven prisoners began a hunger strike on 7 October 1980. The prisoners called off the strike on 18 December, partly because one of them was on the verge of death, and partly because agreement appeared to have been reached on the sartorial issue. However, the accord broke down when the authorities refused to permit the prisoners to wear clothing brought in by their relatives before donning prison clothing. The prisoner's understanding was that they would proceed to prison clothing from normal clothing, rather than *vice versa*, on which the government insisted. Following predictable recriminations, the hunger strike resumed. On this occasion, however, it was not to be a group strike, lest the collective resolve of the members be weakened by one of them succumbing prematurely. Instead, individuals were to go on hunger strike at intervals. Ten prisoners would die, beginning with Bobby Sands on 5 May, before the strike ended on 3 October 1981, when the relatives of prisoners on strike, or scheduled to go on strike, finally refused to allow them to be exploited any longer, and when government made some minimal concessions on the clothes issue.[155]

The British handling of the whole H-block situation was inept to the point of criminality. It threatened to endanger the political stability not only of Northern Ireland, but of the Republic, where emotions ran high. In the North, 'the hunger strike and the authorities' response did more to unite Catholic opinion than any other single event since internment in 1971 or Bloody Sunday in 1972'.[156]

The IRA gained massive publicity triumphs, not only in the Republic but in the United States, by making effective use of the hunger strike drama. When Frank Maguire, MP for Fermanagh/Tyrone, died suddenly in April 1981, the Provos outwitted the SDLP into withdrawing their candidate on the assumption that an agreed independent candidate, Maguire's brother, would stand. They then forced the brother's withdrawal a few minutes before the handing-in of nominations. This left the dying Bobby Sands with a clear run, and he would sweep to victory over

---

[155] Arthur, *Northern Ireland* (1984 edn), p. 127.
[156] Hillyard, *Law and order*, p. 57.

Harry West in the contest for Westminster. This attracted unprecedented publicity for the hunger strikers.

Despite protracted negotiations, and desperate attempts at mediation by intermediaries who could in no way be considered IRA stooges, the drama did not end until October. A combination of the sacrificial capacity of the prisoners and the exquisitely manipulative publicity talents of the Provos, assisted by a host of sympathisers in the national and inter-national media, kept emotion at fever pitch. It was the more politically minded Sinn Féin strategists, like Gerry Adams and Danny Morrison, rather than the IRA militarists, insofar as a distinction can be drawn, who profited most from the public sympathy and from the organisational experience accumulated during the H-block campaigns.[157] This newly demonstrated organisational talent, together with popular sympathy for the strikers, would soon be reflected in an unprecedented level of Sinn Féin electoral success.

In the October 1982 elections to the Northern Ireland Assembly, which both parties were committed to boycott, Sinn Féin won 10.1 per cent of the vote compared with 18.8 per cent for the SDLP. In the Westminster elections of 1983, Sinn Féin won 13.4 per cent compared 17.9 per cent. It also overtook the SDLP in Belfast, where Gerry Adams won the nation-alist seat. It was a measure of Sinn Féin's progress that its failure to come closer to John Hume in the European parliament elections of 1984, when it won 'only' 13.3 percent of the vote compared with Hume's 22.1 percent, was considered a setback. It was one of the multiple ironies of the Northern situation that in a province without a government of its own, elections nonetheless occurred annually at this time. And every election was a virtual plebiscite, not only between the communities, but now within them as well.

The hunger strike was central to the upsurge in support for Sinn Féin, which also acquired a higher profile through spectacular assassinations, like that of Lord Mountbatten in August 1979 and attempted assassi-nations, like that of Mrs Thatcher and the British cabinet during the Conservative Party conference in Brighton in 1984. It was not so much that Sinn Féin secured the allegiance of previous SDLP voters, but that it mobilised previous non-voters and first-time younger voters, who saw no prospect of any sort of fulfilling life within the Northern Ireland they knew. The SDLP vote held up quite well in the circumstances, increasing from 119 000 in 1982 to 151 000 in 1984.[158] The pattern of vote transfers showed that the cleavage between Sinn Féin and the SDLP was

157 White, 'From conflict to violence', p. 182.
158 Girvin, 'National identity', pp. 28–9; W.H. Cox, 'The 1983 general election in Northern Ireland: anatomy and consequences', *Parliamentary Affairs*, 37, 1 (Winter 1984), p. 48.

much sharper than that between the OUP and the DUP, who transferred more regularly to each other than did the two nationalist parties to one another.[159] While it suited unionist propaganda to suggest there was no real difference between the SDLP and Sinn Féin, this does not seem to have been the view taken by the supporters of the two nationalist parties.

The SDLP naturally came under intense pressure in the aggravated atmosphere arising from the hunger strike. The initiatives for devolved government launched by Atkins, and by his successor, Jim Prior, foundered on the familiar intransigences, with the SDLP particularly reluctant to be put in a position where Sinn Féin could accuse it of appeasement. Hume's response to the Sinn Féin electoral threat was to seek to mobilise Southern support by persuading the main parties in the Republic to establish the New Ireland Forum in 1983. He hoped that this would, for the first time, oblige nationalists to face the reality of unionist fears of a united Ireland, and stimulate them to indicate their willingness to contemplate a new type of Irish society in which unionists would have nothing to fear. The Forum lasted a year, touching on many issues, confronting some and evading others, before publishing a report in May 1984. The report, when compared with standard nationalist rhetoric, marked a significant advance on previous official thinking in recognising the legitimacy of unionist identity, and acknowledging the need for a new agreed constitution in the event of Irish unity. But it was subjected to withering scorn by Unionists.

The negativity of the Unionist reaction made it inevitable that if Dublin could persuade London to respond to any extent to the Forum's analysis, the consequences would have to be worked out in direct discussion between them without consultation with the Unionists. Total negativity is not a negotiating position. The SDLP, on the other hand, strongly influenced the Irish government's approach. Correspondingly hysterical was Unionist response to the Hillsborough Agreement of 15 November 1985, signed by Mrs Thatcher and Dr FitzGerald. While falling far short of the Forum aspirations, this nevertheless gave the Republic a voice in Northern Ireland affairs by establishing an Intergovernmental Conference 'concerned with Northern Ireland and with relations between the two parts of Ireland, to deal on a regular basis with political matters, security and related matters, legal matters, including the administration

159 L.E. Dutter, 'Perceptions of group identity and recent political behaviour in Northern Ireland', *Political Psychology*, vi (1985), p. 58; E. Moloney, 'SDLP expressed changed nationalist psyche', *Irish Times*, 21 August 1985.
160 A. Kenny, *The road to Hillsborough* (London, 1986), pp. 37–56; J.J. Lee, 'Forging a new reality?', *Administration*, 32, 2 (1984), pp. 115–21; M. Laver, 'Actors, words and images', *ibid.*, pp. 122–7. The wider implications of the report are discussed below, pp. 675–80.

of justice, and the promotion of cross-border co-operation'.[161] This marked, in principle, a deeper recognition than ever before by the British government of the legitimacy of the Republic's concern with Northern Ireland, and of its potential contribution to the resolution of the Ulster question. To that extent it was a modest, but not insignificant, concession to reality.[162]

[161] Kenny, *Hillsborough*, p. 98.   [162] See below, pp. 680–7.

Chapter 7

❊

DRIFT: 1969–?

THE LYNCH GOVERNMENT

The Northern virus inevitably infected the Southern body politic. The wonder is that it infected it so little for so long. This was partly due to the quarantine measures adopted by Jack Lynch. His own instinct was against involvement. But he had to tread carefully. 'Re-unification' held ritualistic pride of place not only on the agenda of 'national aims' but in Fianna Fáil rhetoric. Public opinion, as far as one can tell in the absence of specific surveys, had subscribed overwhelmingly to the aspiration of a united Ireland since partition, at least as long as nothing need be done about it. In 1969 the majority seemed to be mainly concerned to prevent the problem spilling over into the South, while at the same time being anxious to protect Catholics in the North from feared Protestant pogroms.

Lynch thus found himself confronting a confused popular instinct, searching for a way to do nothing while persuading itself of its anxiety to do something. How to disengage from the implications of the rhetoric without affronting self-respect required a sustained mastery of shuffle techniques. The challenge became even more demanding when the issue got ensnared in the tangled coils of a struggle for the leadership of Fianna Fáil. The scale of Lynch's victory in the 1969 election left his rivals restless. He could no longer be dismissed as an interim party leader, a mere stop-gap while the heirs apparent, and semi-apparent, fought out the real battle between themselves. They could now anticipate long years of thwarted ambition. George Colley, Lynch's most persistent rival in 1966, had since settled, it is true, for a lieutenant role, prepared to bide his time for the succession. Three of the other hopefuls, however, Haughey, Blaney and Boland, were less resigned to their failure. His frustrated rivals still wielded immense influence in Lynch's cabinet. He in turn was manoeuvring to isolate and demote them.[1]

---

[1] Farrell, *Chairman or chief?*, pp. 78–9.

The Northern crisis provided his rivals with the ideal issue on which to mobilise the party rank and file against a leader who could be portrayed as renegeing on the founding aims of the party. But Lynch skilfully mobilised the issues of party unity, and of loyalty to the leader, to outmanoeuvre not only the vociferous Blaney and Boland, but the craftier Haughey, who emerged as the most dangerous threat of all.[2]

When the crisis broke, Blaney and Boland immediately adopted a hawkish line. Blaney, representing a Donegal constituency, and coming, like Boland, from a 'republican' background, urged that the army should occupy Derry city. Blaney's attitude was in character. What was unexpected was the involvement of Haughey, whom Lynch had appointed to succeed himself as Minister for Finance in 1966, and who had not hitherto been popularly associated with the 'republican' wing, in a plan to import arms to be used by the IRA in the North 'for defensive purposes'.

Following a series of murky manoeuvres, Lynch dismissed Haughey and Blaney on 6 May 1970, on the grounds that they failed to fully subscribe to government policy on the North. Micheál Ó Moráin, Minister for Justice, who was in hospital at the time, had already resigned on health grounds at Lynch's request.[3] Boland resigned in sympathy with the dismissed ministers. On 28 May, Haughey and Blaney were arrested and charged with conspiring to import arms and ammunition.[4]

Lynch seems to have been pushed into action by a threat from Cosgrave to publicly reveal information he had received that ministers were involved in supplying arms out of public funds to the IRA. Lynch might have brazened this out, or even insisted that it was his government's duty to assist Catholics in the North by any means at his disposal, and defied Cosgrave to do his 'Free Stater' worst. To have adopted this attitude, however, would have been to open a pandora's box in terms of Anglo-Irish relations, and would have reversed his own policy, which was to convey a feeling of deep concern while resisting pressure for any action – the traditional policy of speaking loudly and carrying a small stick. But circumstances now exposed the hollowness of the rhetoric more cruelly than in balmier political weather, when Northern Catholics could be relied on to behave in a manner that would not unsportingly expose the contradictions in the posture of platform republicans. It would also have delivered himself into the hands of Blaney and Haughey, who might outbid him for the soul of Fianna Fáil. Haughey had begun playing an adventurous game, though how far he had it thrust on him by Lynch remains unclear. Unable to resign himself to a subordinate role to his

---

[2] *Ibid.*, pp. 80–1.   [3] V. Browne, 'Arms crisis 1970', *Magill*, 3, 8 (May 1980), p. 56.
[4] Various viewpoints may be sampled in B. Arnold, *What kind of country?* (London, 1984), pp. 16–91, K. Boland, *We won't stand (idly) by* (Dublin, 1972), and Walsh, *Inside Fianna Fáil*, pp. 101ff.

despised leader, the Northern crisis faced him with a dilemma. Once Blaney began to make a bid for the leadership of the republican camp, Haughey had either to outbid him or else mutely follow the Lynch line, thus abandoning his own leadership ambitions for the foreseeable future. While he was more careful than Blaney with his rhetoric, always insisting that he acted only on the authority of the cabinet and of Lynch himself, thus simply implementing policy rather than engaging in a subversive private venture, he found himself in a situation which made it difficult for him not to position himself in such a way that he could appear to embody authentic republican aspirations.

The evolution of Haughey's position in 1968–9 requires further research. But his contempt for Lynch may have misled him into underrating the Taoiseach's toughness and guile as a tactician, and thus into overreaching himself. Lynch's diffident style would continue to mislead many observers into under-estimating his determination to maintain his position. He fought a wily campaign to hold his ground as the moderate leader of a rhetorically extremist party. In the circumstances, survival was success.

Lynch suffered setbacks, particularly when Blaney was acquitted in July on the charge of conspiracy, on the grounds that there was no case to answer, and Haughey was found not guilty by a jury in October. Haughey immediately demanded Lynch's resignation. Lynch retorted by demanding and winning a vote of confidence. Haughey voted for him, swallowing short-term defeat to secure the basis for longer term victory, convinced that outside the party there was no redemption. Both Lynch and Haughey showed professionalism and poise under pressure. Lynch continued to cling grimly to office, playing a canny political hand to maintain his authority. The passions roused were reflected in turbulent scenes at the 1970 Árd Fheis, where proceedings were enlivened by distinctly robust exchanges.

The dissident ministers went their different ways. Ó Moráin retired from politics. Boland resigned from Fianna Fáil in June 1970, after losing the whip, and formed his own party, Aontacht Éireann, in a futile attempt to mobilise support on the unification issue. Blaney, expelled from Fianna Fáil in 1972, established his own Independent Fianna Fáil, but used it only to consolidate his local position. He would long remain a power in Donegal politics, but even his spectacular success in the Connacht–Ulster constituency in the European elections of 1979 would not tempt him to challenge Fianna Fáil nationally. Haughey, much the ablest and most complex, climbed slowly, painfully and grittily back onto the front bench over five long years, and would eventually gain revenge by succeeding Lynch as leader in 1979. The irony was that he would probably have succeeded him more or less at that stage anyway without any of the intervening trauma if he had not misjudged prospects in 1970.

As the Northern situation deteriorated, and the violence became more vicious, a heavy responsibility fell on the new 31-year-old Minister of Justice, Desmond O'Malley, whom Lynch appointed to succeed Ó Moráin. The IRA tended to mobilise Southern public opinion at moments of high emotional drama, like the Bloody Sunday killings in Derry, which provoked the burning of the British Embassy in Dublin by an angry crowd on 2 February 1972, or the hunger strike of Seán MacStiofáin, in December 1972 and January 1973. The circumstances called for qualities of decision not required since Gerry Boland's days at Justice during the Second World War. Lynch and O'Malley reacted much as de Valera and Boland reacted, by introducing severe measures against subversives, in particular by reactivating sections of the Offences against the State Act, which had lain dormant since 1945 except for a brief period in 1957 when de Valera had used them against the more innocuous IRA of that time.

Policy also developed under the pressure of events from the purely instinctive reaction of 1969, when Lynch made noises, most obviously in a television speech on 13 August, to the effect that the government 'can no longer stand by', an exquisite choice of phrase which excluded no interpretation that the variety of viewers wished to impute to it, and the doomed demand for a United Nations peace-keeping force presented by Dr Hillery, to a more realistic appraisal of possibilities. In the course of 1971 and 1972 the government came to adopt a new approach based on a recognition that Ulster Protestants had a separate identity, and that a united Ireland would require a revision of existing structures of governance, including a new constitution, and not merely the incorporation of the North into the existing Southern state. Until this became practical politics, Lynch demanded in February 1972 a power-sharing arrangement in the North.[5] A British White Paper on Northern Ireland in October 1972 recognised an 'Irish dimension' to the problem, thus apparently conceding Dublin's demand for negotiating rights on the issue.

Despite the brooding presence of the Ulster question, it was largely 'business as usual' in the daily life of the Republic. The government's standing probably gained from the relatively attractive terms on which entry to the EEC was negotiated by Dr Hillery. Once President Pompidou relented on French objection to British entry in 1969, the Irish reactivated their dormant application. The Department of External Affairs (now rechristened Foreign Affairs) acquired control of negotiations, a major

---

[5] D. Herz, 'The Northern Ireland policy of the Irish Republic', in Girvin and Sturm (eds.), *Contemporary Ireland*, pp. 138–41. For a formal elaboration of the government's considered position see J.M. Lynch, 'The Anglo-Irish problem', *Foreign Affairs*, 50 (1972), pp. 601–19.

stroke in enhancing its own departmental standing. A White Paper of January 1972, *The Accession of Ireland to the European Communities*, presented the case for entry. It sought to counter the main fears expressed by critics, that increased competition from imports would cause unemployment, and that membership would pose a threat to Irish sovereignty and subvert the existing foreign policy based on neutrality.[6]

Confidently anticipating the sustained growth of the international economy, the White Paper felt that although some jobs would be at risk in 'traditional' sectors especially clothing, textiles and footwear, the extra employment created by the additional foreign investment attracted to Ireland by the prospect of access to the wider EEC market would more than compensate for any jobs lost. 'The overall trade effects were at worst expected to be neutral and at best strongly positive, in the sense that balance of payments equilibrium at a higher level of activity could be maintained at the existing exchange rate.'[7] It seems possible that the authors were being a shade disingenuous about the impact on 'traditional' jobs. They took care to make their forecast of 'no net redundancy in existing industry' conditional on 'full advantage' being 'taken by all those engaged in industry of the period of transition'. They drily warned that 'any long-term view of industrial development must be . . . speculative' because 'so much will depend on the response of all those engaged in industry to the new environment in which they must work'.[8] Membership would not, the White Paper predicted, 'add significantly to the competition which Irish industry will face in the home market', because by mid-1975 the Anglo-Irish Free Trade Agreement (AIFTA) of 1965 would have come into full efffect, exposing Irish industry generally to unrestricted British competition.[9]

The economic logic of EEC membership was a simple continuation of the logic of the AIFTA, except that the terms appeared to be far better for Ireland. As 'traditional' industry was already showing itself incapable of meeting British competition even before the full effect of AIFTA had been felt, though this may not have been appreciated at the time, it was almost certain that it would suffer severe job losses in EEC circumstances. As these industries were increasingly parasitic on the public, long-term national interest probably lay in sharply reducing their size, if not

---

6 The arguments advanced by the critics are summarised in A. Coughlan, 'Ireland', in D. Seers and C. Vaitsos (eds.), *Integration and unequal development* (London, 1980), pp. 123–4. The following paragraphs draw freely on J.J. Lee, *Reflections on Ireland in the EEC* (Dublin, 1984), pp. 1–3.

7 D. McAleese, 'Ireland and the European Community: the changing pattern of trade', in P.J. Drudy and D. McAleese (eds.), *Ireland and the European Community*, Irish Studies 3 (Cambridge, 1983), p. 151.

8 *The accession of Ireland to the European Communities: January 1972* (P 2064), pp. 36–39.

9 *Ibid.*, p. 35.

altogether eliminating them – provided alternatives could be found. Only time would tell where, in retrospect as distinct from in prospect, the balance of national interest would lie. But the White Paper's assumptions were reasonable at the time.

Whatever residual doubts might be detected in the careful phraseology of the White Paper about the capacity of 'traditional' industry to confront change, no such reservations can be read between the lines about the huge gains expected to accrue to agriculture from the higher prices paid under the Common Agricultural Policy of the EEC. An increase of no less than 150 percent in agricultural incomes between 1970 and 1978 was predicted. In addition, the authors based their dismissal of the argument for associate membership, which some of the critics of full membership would have preferred, on the grounds that no possible alternative form of association could possibly compensate for the losses that would arise from the exclusion of agriculture, which simply could not expect favourable access to EEC markets from associate membership, and might indeed lose its open access to the British market once the United Kingdom became a full member.

Critics who held that accession would amount to the sale of the national birthright for a mess of common agricultural pottage, and that the jewel of Irish sovereignty was a pearl of too great price to be bartered for the flesh pots of Brussels, were bluntly told that Ireland could not lose what it had not got. The White Paper, reflecting the calibre, the courage and the integrity of the Foreign Affairs officials responsible for the relevant section, contained a blunt, honest and incisive description of the reality of foreign policy in Irish circumstances. Defining sovereignty as 'the freedom to take autonomous decisions and actions in domestic and foreign affairs' the White Paper asserted that as 'a very small country independent but with little or no capacity to influence events abroad that significantly affect us', Ireland enjoyed very little effective economic sovereignty.[10] It drew a clear distinction between independence and sovereignty:

For most countries other than the major powers, the real freedom, as distinct from the nominal right, to take national action and pursue policies in the economic and trading sectors is circumscribed to a very great extent by the complex nature of international, economic and trading relationships . . . our vital interests may be affected by the policies and actions of other larger countries or groups of countries. This gravely restricts our capacity to exercise the right of freedom of action and thus represents a very real limitation on our national sovereignty.[11]

The national interest was the only valid criterion in policy formulation. Everything else, even sovereignty, which was merely a means towards serving the national interest, must be subordinated to that decisive consideration. The other member states of the EEC had already 'accepted

[10] *Ibid.*, pp. 58–9.   [11] *Ibid.*, p. 60.

the limitations involved on their own national freedom of action because they consider that their national interests are best being served by membership'.[12]

Whereas the superb section on sovereignty confronted the critics head-on, daring them to challenge its formulations, there was no comparable disquisition on the nature of neutrality. Rather than entering into a discussion on the realities of international relations in this sphere, the White Paper contented itself with the cryptic, and somewhat disingenuous reminder, that 'the Treaties of Rome and Paris do not entail any military or defence commitments and no such commitments are involved in Ireland's acceptance of these treaties'.[13]

The debate was pitched overwhelmingly at the material level. Some did hope that membership would lessen dependence on Britain, countering the anglicisation that had become even more pronounced since the advent of television. C.S. Andrews, a notable public servant, gave expression, at once robust and sensitive, to this viewpoint:

Since my schooldays, I had a deep emotional conviction that the only way by which Ireland could survive as an entity distinct from the Anglo-Saxon world which surrounded it was by identifying itself with the continent of Europe culturally, and if possible, commercially. I did not then foresee the establishment of the European Economic Community, but I felt very strongly that unless we absorbed something of the traditions and manners of Europe and acquainted ourselves with its art, architecture and literature we would inevitably degenerate to the level of a province of Britian, second-rate suppliants for small privileges.[14]

Some would hope that exposure to a wider range of major cultures would stimulate a sense of pride in a distinctive Gaelic culture, and encourage the revival of the language and of Irish literature.[15] Apart from a few ritualistic recitations, however, of the manner in which Irish monks had reputedly salvaged Europe from barbarism a thousand or more years before, whose immediate relevance to the situation pertaining in 1972 was not universally apparent, and which rarely enhanced the scholarly standing of the expositors, the cultural dimension was almost as extensively ignored in the rhetoric of platform and studio as it would be in the subsequent reality.

Entry required a constitutional amendment which involved potentially quite sweeping subordination of the constitution to the Treaty of Rome, and extensively affected administrative law.[16] However, as both Fianna

---

[12] *Ibid.*   [13] *Ibid.*, p. 57.   [14] Andrews, *Man of no property*, p. 197.

[15] T.K. Whitaker, 'Todhchaí eacnamaíoch agus shóisialta na hÉireann', *Central Bank of Ireland, Quarterly Bulletin* (Spring 1971), p. 108.

[16] B.M.E. McMahon, 'EEC membership and the Irish legal system', in Drudy and McAleese (eds.), *Ireland*, pp. 57–76; F. Murphy, 'The European Community and the Irish legal system', in D. Coombes (ed.), *Ireland and the European Communities: ten years of membership* (Dublin, 1983), pp. 29–42; D. Scott, 'Adapting the machinery of central government', in Coombes (ed.), *Ireland*, p. 72.

Fáil and Fine Gael supported entry, and as the dangers appeared distant, vague and abstract, while the gains appeared immediate, precise and concrete, 83 per cent of those who voted in the 71 per cent turnout in the referendum of May 1972 endorsed the terms negotiated by Dr Hillery and incorporated in the Treaty of Accession signed on 22 January 1972.[17]

If the decision to enter the EEC, with effect from 1 January 1973, makes 1972 a memorable date in Irish economic history, it was also a notable year for the history of the public finances. It was in the 1972 Budget that George Colley, appointed Minister for Finance by Lynch after the dismissal of Haughey in 1970, departed for the first time since the foundation of the state from the principle of balancing the current Budget. It is true that the line between current and capital expenditure was a notoriously hazy one in budgetary practice. It is also true that the actual deficit incurred turned out to be only 0.2 per cent of GNP, which was less than the actual deficit incurred in 1968 and 1970, when a balanced Budget had been projected. But Colley's envisaged deficit would have come to 1.3 per cent of GNP, which had more ominous implications for the cavalier manner in which the traditional discipline would be relaxed in future.[18] It exposed the bankruptcy not only of government, but of opposition economic policy, for Fine Gael enthusiastically endorsed the new principle.[19]

Colley's justification was that 'the economy is for the third year in succession running at well below capacity. Unemployment is high. We lack the economic buoyancy required to tackle quickly and effectively the adaptation which membership of the EEC will demand.'[20] There had been a deterioration in the general quality of economic performance since about 1968, partly masked from a short-term consumer perspective by improved terms of trade. The Public Capital Programme was cut back sharply in 1970 and 1971 after rapidly expanding in 1969, an election year. Nevertheless, the average balance of payments deficit on current account for 1969–72 was more than double that for 1961–8, and was covered not only by increasing capital inflows on private account, but by a sharp increase in the foreign borrowing of the public sector. This was still low, but about five times higher than the annual average from 1961–8.[21] There was scope for improved economic performance. But deficit budgeting was not the way to achieve it.

'Economic buoyancy' is a vague and elusive concept in itself. The relationship between it and the capacity for 'adaptation' to the EEC was singularly obscure. The reasoning in this regard provided no justification

[17] A detailed chronology of the accession negotiations is contained in D.J. Maher, *The tortuous path* (Dublin, 1986).

[18] Statistics of projected and actual current budget deficits from V. Browne, 'Who's to blame?', *Magill*, 10, 2 (November 1986), p. 8.

[19] *Ibid.*, 6.   [20] *Ibid.*   [21] Kennedy and Dowling, *Economic growth*, pp. 255ff.

for the policy. Inflation was already surging at an alarming pace. Much of this was imported. The international trend rate of inflation began to rise sharply in the later 1960s, with 'an underlying trend towards a deterioration in performance already occurring' in most European economies.[22] The Consumer Price Index rose by an annual average of 8.3 per cent from 1968 to 1972.[23] Growing trade union aggressiveness was reflected not only in intensified strike activity, but in national pay agreements which took scant account of economic reality and further fuelled inflation. The 1970 agreement allowed the average male worker an 18 per cent increase over an eighteen-month period, the 1972 agreement a 21 per cent increase over eighteen months.[24] The deliberate refusal on the part of both government and trade unions to think in terms of long-term national strategy, and to opt instead for the short-term fix, became an integral part of Irish policy-making in those years. There are, no doubt, longer and more complex continuities to be discerned. But the flight from reality, which would assume such gadarene proportions over the following decade, had already begun in earnest before 1973. The 1972 Budget can stand as a symbol of that breakdown in national discipline that Whitaker was lamenting in 1971, sensing that the fruits of fifteen years labour were beginning to be frittered away by a people who lacked the character and the intelligence to build on the foundations he had been instrumental in laying.[25]

Whitaker resigned as Secretary of Finance at the early age of fifty-three, to succeed Maurice Moynihan as Governor of the Central Bank in March 1969. This was a curious decision. While the Central Bank was growing in importance, and would acquire enhanced legal powers in 1971, it was not as crucial to policy-making as Finance. It would not be entirely surprising if Whitaker's decision were related to a lack of sympathy for the style of Haughey, his then minister. Haughey had flair and dash. His tenure of Finance is probably best remembered for his introduction of free travel for old-age pensioners and tax concessions to artists. But it is not inconceivable that his style may have grated on his less flamboyant Secretary. Whitaker reveals revealingly little of their relationship in his important survey of the financial history of the state. But a turn of phrase like 'the new Minister for Finance considered it justifiable . . . ' suggests a certain distaste on his part for Haughey's approach.[26]

Whitaker would continue to earn distinction as Governor of the Central Bank 1969–76, and subsequently in a variety of public roles, including

22 A. Boltho, 'Introduction', in A. Boltho (ed.), *The European economy: growth and crisis* (Oxford, 1982), p. 4.
23 Kennedy and Dowling, *Economic growth*, p. 263.
24 C. MacCarthy, 'A review of the objectives of the national pay agreements 1970–1977', *Administration*, (Spring 1977), p. 125.
25 Whitaker, *Todhchaí eacnamaíoch, passim*.   26 Whitaker, *Interests*, pp. 96–7.

Chairman of Bórd na Gaeilge, Chancellor of the National University, a member of the Senate, joint chairman of Anglo-Irish Encounter, and President of the Royal Irish Academy. A scholar can only rejoice that his release from official responsibilities gave him time to write and to lecture even more actively than before. Nevertheless, it is impossible not to feel that the state which he served with such distinction failed to make full use of his abilities. It is not as if that state were so liberally endowed with talent that it could afford to wantonly squander so valuable a resource.

Haughey's precipitate departure from office in May 1970 may have offered Finance an opportunity to regain control over its minister. However, it was Colley who transgressed the basic budgetary principle in 1972. Whitaker's departure probably weakened the authority of Finance, though his successor, C.H. Murray, long his close collaborator, could present an argument astutely. Colley embarked on his initiative against the strongest advice of Whitaker at the Central Bank, and doubtless of Murray.[27] Colley conceded the existence of strong and rising cost push inflation, as well as a weak balance of payments position. But nothing could deter him from plunging ahead on the grounds of rising unemployment, up from 6.7 per cent in 1968 to 8.1 per cent in 1972, and of the need for 'buoyancy'.

The most convincing explanation for Colley's initiative is political. A general election was likely within a year. The 'political business cycle' was no stranger to Irish political thought. Policy had been heavily electorally orientated before the 1969 election. A bastardised Keynesianism provided a convenient façade to give respectability to the most opportunistic impulses. The resolve that nothing would stand in the way of electoral victory became even clearer when the government accepted a 21 per cent national pay agreement in the summer of 1972, well above the level of inflation. Had this agreement been achieved in the face of bitter government resistance, Colley might have claimed that his Budget was based on the assumption of reasonable self-restraint in income policy. But his Budget speech specifically recognised that 'whatever our hopes, there is no certainty that the new national pay agreement will diminish the pace of cost inflation'.[28] This signalled to the unions that they need only push an open door. With a general election in the offing, they needed no second invitation.

The government might have been irresponsible in any case. Even the most ordinary of general elections makes contemplation of the post-electoral world a luxury that practical politicians are rarely able to enjoy. But the Northern crisis exerted a baneful influence on Fianna Fáil in this regard. Since the bitterness of the arms crisis the festering resentments within the party made it even more incumbent on Lynch to win elections,

[27] *Ibid.*, p. 100.   [28] *Ibid.*

or at least lose them only narrowly. He was now at risk to revenge seekers. A general election was even more of a battle than in 1969 for his own position against spiteful rivals. It placed an even higher premium on electoral calculation. The injection of unprecedented bitterness into personal relations made the grip on the party leadership of a defeated Taoiseach much more precarious than hitherto. The irresponsibility of the government in 1972 can be explained, if not justified, in terms of its consciousness of the price of defeat in purely internal party terms. The really disturbing aspect is that the possibility cannot be entirely ruled out that Colley may have actually believed in the validity, as well as in the expediency, of his policy.

Whatever the longer term implications of the cabinet's cavalier financial management, it seemed likely to ensure a Fianna Fáil victory in the election that Lynch called for February 1973, fifteen months before the expiry of his term. He had intended to go to the country in December 1972 when Fine Gael split on its attitude to a severe amendment of the Offences against the State Act, which proposed that IRA suspects could be convicted on the unsupported word of a senior gárda officer.[29] Fine Gael decided to oppose the bill, overruling Cosgrave, who was determined to support it.[30] A potential leadership crisis loomed. The explosion of bombs, whose provenance has never been satisfactorily explained, killing two people on 1 December in Dublin, forced his party back into Cosgrave's arms. There is a view that if Lynch had called the election immediately after the bombs, irrespective of Fine Gael's precarious unity, he could have won handsomely.[31] And a de Valera might have been scheming to have called an election for the same day as the referenda to reduce voting age from 21 to 18, and to eliminate the reference in the constitution to the special position of the Catholic Church. Both proposals were approved, though on a turnout of only 51 per cent, on 7 December. Of course, Lynch would have had to decide on that ploy at least a month in advance. And if a week is a long time in politics, a month is an eternity.

Lynch postponed the election until February. By then circumstances had changed dramatically. Fine Gael and Labour, who had been pursuing independent opposition policies since 1957, suddenly agreed on 6 February to an electoral pact, and fought the election as an alternative coalition government. It says much for Lynch's skill as a party manager that Fianna Fáil would almost certainly have won, despite all the traumas of the previous four years, but for the electoral pact, based on a fourteen point manifesto containing promises for virtually everyone. Fianna Fáil might have its Budget deficit, but the coalition was not going to be

---

[29] Lynch, 'My life and times', p. 46.   [30] Downey, *Them and us*, p. 101.
[31] B. Harvey, *Cosgrave's coalition* (Dublin, 1977), pp. 7–8.

outdone in the profligacy stakes. Nevertheless, Fianna Fáil actually increased its share of the popular vote from 45.7 per cent to 46.2 per cent. Fine Gael also increased its share, from 34.1 per cent to 35.1 per cent, while Labour fell from 17 per cent to 13.7 per cent. But the vagaries of PR, in a pact situation, with voters transferring in disciplined manner to their coalition partner, ensured not only a gain of 4 for Fine Gael, from 50 to 54 seats, but a gain of 1 for Labour, from 18 to 19 seats, while Fianna Fáil fell from 75 to 69 seats. Fianna Fáil held its share of seats in Dublin, where four-seater constituencies predominated. Here it could win 2 seats out of 4 with 40 per cent of the vote, compared with only 1 out of 3 for the same percentage in rural areas. And the increase in the number of rural three-seaters, which worked so well for Fianna Fáil in 1969, now had a backlash effect. Three-seaters were lethal against a divided opposition, but potentially suicidal against a united one. Three-seaters favoured the smallest party, once it reached the threshold level, where there were heavy transfers in its favour. Labour and Fine Gael transferred almost as solidly to each other as Fianna Fáil voters transferred internally. In some of the crucial three-seater marginals, Fianna Fáil required twice as many votes to elect candidates as did Labour.[32]

THE COSGRAVE GOVERNMENT

Largely untroubled by the type of inter-party wrangling that characterised previous coalitions, the 'National Coalition' under Liam Cosgrave as Taoiseach, with Brendan Corish as Tánaiste, proved a more formidable combination than its predecessors. It needed to. Not only did the dark shadow of Ulster continue to loom over Southern affairs, but the industrial world was about to suffer a serious shock with the quadrupling of oil prices from the end of 1973. Richie Ryan, Cosgrave's Minister for Finance, bore the brunt of the challenge. How far Ryan, with little experience in the area – he had been shadow spokesman on Foreign Affairs – dominated financial policy, how far other ministers, particularly Garret FitzGerald, influenced the cabinet, how far the presence of Labour imposed constraints on Ryan's room for manoeuvre, how far the advice of officials was followed, are questions that cannot yet be confidently answered. It is doubtful if Ryan enjoyed the authority of McGilligan or Sweetman in previous coalitions, and it may be that he was not directly responsible for some of the more misguided measures introduced under his aegis.

Ryan began badly. Far from reverting to one of the few familiar disciplines in a period of increasingly licentious economic behaviour, he

---

[32] P. Murray, 'Irish elections: a changing pattern', *Studies* (Autumn 1976), pp. 196–7, 203; Gallagher, *Labour party*, p. 193.

projected a deficit of about 1.5 per cent of GNP in his first Budget in 1973. This was not only higher than Colley's projected deficit. It was seven times higher than the actual deficit incurred in 1972. In the event, the actual deficit in 1973 would also fall below the projected deficit, at 0.4 per cent of GNP, thanks to a rapid rise in revenues from value added tax due to increasing inflation.[33] It is the projected deficit, however, that exposes the quality of government thinking. On the assumption that Finance was counselling caution, there must be interesting questions to be answered in connection with the process by which the cabinet immediately embarked on deficit spending. It is against this background that the response to the oil crisis that began to be felt in November must be assessed.

The crisis created unanticipated problems. But it also enabled Ryan to justify the soft option of mortgaging the future in the form of a massive increase in borrowing. The oil crisis merely exacerbated, however abruptly, the underlying inflationary trend. This arose partly from the shift in the balance of institutional power in full employment economies in favour of labour. Ireland was not a full employment economy. Unemployment hovered around 8 per cent in the early 1970s. But trade unions in general, and the public sector in particular, behaved as if it were. And for the public sector it was. Its members enjoyed effective security of tenure. Public sector trade unions could therefore behave as if their members belonged to a full employment economy, confident that it would be workers in the private sector who would suffer whatever unemployment might occur, in due course, as a result of their demands. Inflation was already rampant by historical standards. The rate was running at 11 per cent during 1973, *before* the oil crisis, up from 8.6 per cent in 1972.[34] Given the rising trend, the increase in oil prices cannot even be held responsible for the whole rise in inflation to 17 per cent in 1974 and 21 per cent in 1975.

The cabinet, ignoring Whitaker's advice, and presumably Murray's, choose to respond as if the crisis was of a once-for-all nature, whose consequences would soon vanish as a new surge of economic growth resolved the resultant problems. It was not the only government to respond in this manner.

Although OPEC had imposed a real impoverishment on the rest of the world, the social, economic and political system in most countries was unable – and in most cases also unwilling – to make the general public bear the burden of this impoverishment. Instead, all kinds of mechanisms were invented to shift this burden or to put it off to the future. An optimistic belief in growth was still deeply engrained and it was thought that all the problems would be simply solved by a new and long lasting expansion.[35]

[33] Browne, 'Who's to blame?', pp. 6, 8.   [34] Whitaker, *Interests*, p. 102.
[35] J. Stokx, 'Belgian economic reforms 1982', *IBR* (December 1982), p. 52.

Table 5. *Current exchequer deficit, 1973–77 (£ million)*

	Projected	As % of GNP	Actual	As % of GNP	Borrowing	
					Foreign	Total
1973–4	39.3	1.5	10.4	0.4	44	206
1974 (9 months)	76.2	2.3	92.3	3.1	147	310
1975	241.6	6.4	258.8	6.9	164	601
1976	327.0	7.1	201.4	4.4	324	506
1977	217.0	3.8	187.0	3.6	71	545

Source: T.K. Whitaker, *Interests* (Dublin, 1983), p. 106; V. Browne, 'Who's to blame', *Magill*, 10, 2 (November 1986), pp. 6, 8.

In the circumstances, there has to be some sympathy for an Irish government that inherited an unemployment rate more than double that of more successful countries. Indeed, despite the lavish expansion in public expenditure, the number of registered unemployed rose from 71 000 in March 1973 to 116 000 in March 1977, or from 7.9 per cent to 12.5 per cent of the insured labour force.[36]

Despite the dramatic change in domestic and international circumstances since the now distant sixties, government continued to behave as if nothing had changed. Inflation accelerated in all European states in 1974 and 1975, but the Irish rate far exceeded the average, with only the Italian and the United Kingdom rates coming close to the Irish. GDP fell not only in Ireland, but throughout most of western Europe, in 1975.[37] The Irish insisted on ignoring reality. The national pay agreement of 1974 awarded a staggering pay increase of 29.4 per cent, even if that of 1975 came down to a miserly 16.6 per cent.[38] Table 5 summarises the implications for public finances of government's general approach.[39] As the figures suggest, the coalition did adopt a less irresponsible, though still far from responsible, attitude in the course of 1976 and 1977.

Foreign borrowing, which reached unprecedented heights in 1976, fell sharply in 1977, though total borrowing remained very high. The 1977 Budget was an election one. It was not, however, the recklessly opportunistic effort an election year might be presumed to inspire,[40] though perhaps only because the cabinet, like most commentators, calculated that the coalition was already set fair for victory, and need pay no higher price for it. Ironically, the government began to veer in the direction of

[36] Gallagher, *Labour party*, p. 198.
[37] Boltho, 'Growth' in Boltho (ed.), *European economy*, p. 21.
[38] Whitaker, *Interests*, p. 102.　　[39] *Ibid.*, p. 106; Browne, 'Who's to blame?', pp. 6, 8.
[40] Whitaker, *Interests*, pp. 107–8.

Whitaker's advice only after he vacated office as Governor of the Central Bank in March 1976. He was succeeded by C.H. Murray, who in turn was succeeded in Finance by M. Murphy, who remained Secretary for little more than year before moving to an EEC post.

During Ryan's tenure of office, the exchequer foreign debt rose from £126 million in the year ending March 1973 to £1040 million at the end of 1976. The net foreign debt moved from a credit of £175 million – Ireland was actually still a creditor country in 1973, dim though the memory would be only a decade later – to a net foreign debt of £313 million by the end of 1976. Government expenditure as a proportion of GNP rose from 42.2 per cent in 1973–4 to 50 per cent in 1975, before falling to 48.5 per cent in 1977.[41]

One must have some sympathy for the government's dilemma. It was not unreasonable to hope initially that the crisis would pass quickly. A public already in rapid retreat from reality might turn very nasty if obliged to face the full truth. Ireland chose to treat itself as a closed economy for standard of living purposes, behaving as if no change had occurred in the world outside, insisting on borrowing to sustain increases in living standards that it could not earn for itself. The real criticism that can be made of borrowing policy was not that it was wrong to borrow, up to a point, to try to maintain employment levels. The problem was that much of the increased borrowing was not due to a gallant attempt to curb unemployment. Rather was it due to the determination to improve the standard of living of those already in employment. They insisted on enjoying a standard of living to which they believed they had a right to have become accustomed irrespective of their contribution to earning it. The combined weight of servicing the public debt and of providing pay and pensions in the public sector rose from 15.8 per cent to 21.6 per cent of GNP between 1973–4 and 1977.[42] In addition, gross expenditure on social welfare rose from 6.5 to 10.5 per cent of GNP during the coalition period.[43] However welcome in principle such an increase might be, at least when it went to deprived members of the community, of whom there were still many, this would inevitably lead to more unemployment in Irish circumstances in due course.

Ryan's policy sought to banish the spectre of reality. Whitaker would continue to argue, as he argued at the time, that in the changed circumstances only the discipline of living within one's means could provide a secure base for future development.[44] Whitaker was doubtless right in principle. But 'future development' was far from the thoughts of the instant spenders among the populace, and it must remain very

---

[41] 'Trends in the public finances', *IBR* (June 1982), p. 13.
[42] *Ibid.*; S. Nolan, 'Economic growth', p. 160.
[43] Gallagher, *Labour party*, p. 200.   [44] Whitaker, *Interests*, p. 106.

doubtful if a national consensus could have been secured at that time for the discipline involved. Ryan's argument that the plunge into debt was warranted to keep the economy from sinking into deeper slump has yet to be adequately analysed. Much depended on the expenditure patterns of the actual beneficiaries of the borrowing, who were by no means necessarily the most needy. Whether the borrowing policy could have been more judiciously managed, whether it was necessary to go so far and so unproductively into debt, remains to be examined. And there was of course always the hope that something would turn up – the favourite 'some thing' being an oil well and a Brussels bonanza.

Justin Keating, the Labour Minister for Industry and Commerce, presided over the first round of serious exploration for oil in Irish waters. Anxious to ensure the safeguarding of the national interest, and with the assistance of an able civil servant, J.C. Holloway, whose command of the subject earned him an impressive reputation, he devised licensing terms, announced in April 1975, that would secure 50 per cent as the state's share and oblige companies to use an Irish base of operations. Hopes for a find waxed and waned throughout the period, but always at the back of the mind lurked the idea that wet gold would be struck.

Industry and Commerce lost many of its central earlier functions as the IDA assumed increasing responsibility throughout the sixties for investment policy. The IDA played an even more prominent role in the 1970s, its authority enhanced by legislation in 1969, and a sympathetic public profile achieved under a dynamic young managing director, Michael Killeen. Government effectively abdicated to the IDA responsibility for industrial policy. There was much to be said for hiving off the implementation of industrial policy from central government, and entrusting it to a virtually autonomous agency. Given the pervasive involvement of the state in the area of industrial policy, politicians and civil servants came under enormous pressure to influence the location of industry according to electoral requirements. The IDA could not, inevitably, remain unaware of these pressures. But it was somewhat further removed from the immediate political process. Insofar as the industrial policy that seemed likely to deliver most immediate returns was a reliance on foreign investment, lured to Ireland through generous tax benefits and heavy subsidies, the country required negotiators of a different personality type from those associated with the civil service. There had to be a willingness to take risks, to make quick decisions, to engage in a style of negotiation alien to many (though not all) civil service temperaments.

The IDA opted, in its 1973 plan, to concentrate on the electronic and chemical sectors, two areas with high growth potential that were unlikely to be undercut by emerging third world countries. Both industries had to be virtually completely imported. The IDA took advantage of entry to the

EEC to persuade foreign firms, especially American ones, to establish branches in Ireland. It faced huge problems of job creation, not so much in gross as in net terms. Job losses mounted throughout the seventies, particularly in native firms that succumbed to competition, whether from the EEC, or from third world countries. This marked a continuation, and at times an accentuation, of inherited trends.[45] There appeared to be little that anybody could do to arrest the decline of Irish-owned business by this stage. It is not clear that the government grasped, or wanted to grasp, the extent of the problem, despite Killeen's clear recognition of the difficulties.[46]

If Richie Ryan was unfortunate in the timing of the oil crisis, Mark Clinton, the Fine Gael Minister for Agriculture, inherited the windfall of the Common Agricultural Policy (CAP). Not that adjustment to EEC membership was quite as immediately rewarding as farmers anticipated. A collapse of cattle prices in 1974 caused considerable unease, bringing an early portent of the difficulties that would emerge to plague the CAP from the end of the decade. In the meantime, however, farmers reaped a golden harvest. The official projections of output increases proved optimistic.[47] But here something did turn up. Irish farmers benefited from unforeseen but highly favourable price increases due to green pound movements, following the substantial devaluations of sterling against the 'snake'.[48] Taken in conjunction with other price increases, these enabled farmers to enjoy a prosperous period after 1975. By 1978 real incomes in agriculture had doubled compared with 1970.[49]

Clinton proved a quietly effective minister in the short-term context, winning lucrative concessions for Irish farmers in the regular Brussels haggling. But the gains were largely dissipated from a national point of view. It was not so much that consumers paid dearly for farmers' gains, although they did. On the calculation that Irish consumers paid about £30 in higher food prices by 1978 for every £100 extra received by farmers, the net national gain, in simple accounting terms, was only about three-fifths the gross gain to farmers.[50] The more serious criticism was that while the government had effective tactics for Brussels negotiations, it had no strategy for agriculture beyond making the biggest possible short-term killings. Ireland's fundamental interest was to secure as large a market share as possible. Given her presumed comparative advantage in many agricultural products, Ireland would probably have benefited in the medium term from a slower rise in the prices of many agricultural

[45] NESC, *An analysis of job losses in Irish manufacturing industry* (Dublin 1983).
[46] M. Killeen, *Industrial development and full employment* (Dublin, 1976). See below, pp. 530ff.
[47] S.J. Sheehy, 'The common agricultural policy and Ireland', in Drudy and McAleese, *Ireland*, p. 80–2.
[48] *Ibid.*   [49] *Ibid.*, pp. 85–6.   [50] *Ibid.*, p. 87.

commodities, which would have helped reduce her competitors' market share. Irish policy-makers helped keep in production marginal continental farmers, and stored up trouble for Irish agriculture, not only in the long term, but within a few years. Of course Irish representatives might have had little influence on the final outcome. Irish farmers were not the only ones mainly interested in short-term gains. But more advanced countries could afford to indulge their agriculture with less damage to the national interest.

The biggest beneficiary from EEC entry was the new Foreign Minister, Garret FitzGerald. The 46-year-old son of Desmond FitzGerald, first Minister for External Affairs in the Free State, a university lecturer in economics, a prolific speaker and writer, a prominent television performer, an open personality with a popular public image and a reputation for liberal instincts, FitzGerald was first elected to the Dáil in 1969, after serving in the Senate from 1965. He was the most active member of the Fine Gael front bench in opposition, sometimes seeming to constitute a one-man party. Shadow spokesman on finance, his triumph over George Colley in a television debate during the election campaign was widely felt to have influenced the result. Cosgrave suspected him of harbouring designs on the leadership, and had no sympathy with his generally liberal attitude towards social issues. Instead of nominating him to Finance, Cosgrave appointed him to Foreign Affairs, which Richie Ryan had been shadowing. That decision did much to determine the subsequent fortunes of the two ministers, and even the future of Fine Gael.

Irony piles up on irony. If Cosgrave may have regarded FitzGerald as unsound on finance, he himself was determined not to repeat the mistake he associated with Sweetman that brought down the second inter-party government, in which he had been Minister for External Affairs, and which led to a further sixteen years of Fianna Fáil rule. His coalition would not be identified with austerity. The irony for Richie Ryan was that despite presiding over the most generous, not to say promiscuous, expansion of public expenditure in the history of the state, he acquired such unenviable sobriquets as Richie Ruin, and even Red Richie, for a courageous but essentially abortive attempt, under Labour pressure, to impose some minimal taxation on wealth and on farmers. FitzGerald was likely to have been far more enthusiastic. But, safely ensconced in Foreign Affairs, he took none of the blame. His appointment smoothed his rise to the leadership and consigned Ryan in due course to a peripheral role. Cosgrave had scarcely intended such a denouement. It might not be too speculative to surmise that from Cosgrave's viewpoint, Foreign Affairs might do a Seán MacBride on FitzGerald. Cosgrave, as Parliamentary Secretary to John A. Costello, had an intimate knowledge of the working of the 1948–51 government. FitzGerald might lose touch with the party, as MacBride had lost touch which his party. At worst, Foreign Affairs should keep him out of harm's way. The more he was abroad, the less of a nuisance he could be at home. If this entered into Cosgrave's calculations (and it would be optimistic to expect documentary confirmation!), it rebounded with a vengeance.

Membership of the EEC transformed the role of Foreign Affairs.[51] FitzGerald quickly acquired a glowing reputation abroad, which gradually penetrated domestic consciousness. The expansion of the responsibility of the Department enabled him to make an effective case for increasing its size, thus enhancing his internal reputation. Expansion always means promotion in the short term, though it can stir up problems when expansion ends. But FitzGerald's reputation rested on much more than simple departmental expansion. His ability, affability, appetite for hard work, and genuine idealism, reinforced by his fluency in French, made a starling impact on European foreign ministers and officials, unaccustomed to Irish performers of this calibre. His presidency of the EEC Council of Ministers in 1975 enhanced Ireland's reputation.[52] As one of the few Irish politicians whose baggage was perceived to be carrying more than a begging bowl, he did much to contribute to a positive image of his country, countering the stereotype of Paddy the amiable pickpocket. He was fortunate too in that most of the news from the EEC in the early years of membership was found good. The messenger inevitably got some of the credit for the message.

The stormy petrel of the Cosgrave administration was Conor Cruise O'Brien. An intellectual, O'Brien had a distinguished international career as writer and diplomat. Returning to Ireland in the late 1960s, he won a seat for Labour in 1969, and held it in 1973. Too prominent and too dangerous a personality to be left frolic on the backbenches without a guide dog, he was safer in cabinet than out of it. But where could he be 'lost' in cabinet? The choice of a Department for O'Brien posed delicate problems.[53] He himself might have liked Foreign Affairs or Education. But his penchant for arguing his case from logic and the awkward conclusions that logic sometimes reached, created culture shock in conventional political circles. The party leaders could not risk so eccentric a choice for Education in view of the need to maintain harmonious relations with the Church. And they can have had no intention of putting

51 P. Keatinge, *A place among the nations* (Dublin, 1978), pp. 210ff.
52 D. Scott, 'Adapting the machinery of central government', in Coombes (ed.), *Ireland*, p. 77.
53 R. Ó Glaisne, *Conor Cruise O'Brien agus an liobrálachas* (Conor Cruise O'Brien and liberalism) (Dublin, 1974), p. 93 has sardonic, if speculative, reflections on the issue. Corish appointed the Labour ministers, having agreed the Departmental allocations with Cosgrave. But Corish can hardly have chosen the Departments without having his men in mind for them.

into Foreign Affairs someone capable of marching in an anti-Vietnam War demonstration.

The apppointment of O'Brien as Minister for Post and Telegraphs was a cute ploy in turning poacher into game-keeper, even if neither Cosgrave nor Corish may have quite anticipated how capaciously O'Brien would interpret his duties. O'Brien now became responsible not only for trying to introduce civilised industrial relations into a Department notorious for tension between civil servants and post office workers, but also for radio and television policy, which naturally had implications for the Northern question. This was a highly sensitive issue, which had already led Fianna Fáil to dismiss the RTE authority in 1972 because of an interview with an IRA man in breach of Section 31 of the Broadcasting Act. O'Brien introduced legislation in a Broadcasting Amendment Act in 1976 designed to curb IRA opportunities for propaganda, while nevertheless providing some safeguards for serious comment. O'Brien was naturally bitterly criticised from a variety of angles. His reply was to add insult to injury by developing a rationale for his approach which obliged his critics to elaborate their's. He went further. Not content with his ministerial role, he launched a one-man crusade to provoke Southern society into an agonising reappraisal of the implications of unity. Convinced that the IRA was so evil that the survival of civilised values depended on immunising the country against the virus of violence, he did not remain satisfied with the rather furtive shift in public opinion since the previous IRA border campaign. That shift he regarded as largely opportunistic, based on fear of the implications of spillage from Ulster for Southern comfort, rather than on a principled rejection of violence. He outraged traditional nationalist opinion by asserting that the Republic's claim on Northern Ireland was a variety of imperialism. This was patently unjust to some nationalists. It cut too close to the bone for others, and provoked predictable frothing at the mouth.[54]

Much of O'Brien's denunciation of nationalist self-delusion, posturing and hypocrisy was unanswerable. But he increasingly failed to assess the nationalist case in the context of the unionist case. He refrained from submitting unionism to the same clinical examination with which he dissected nationalism, though neither could be fully understood except in relation to the other. This lack of balance weakened his case, for he attempted to apply absolutes where the issue revolved around relativities. Ironically, he paid a curious compliment to Irish nationalists, the main target of his criticism, for he demanded from them a maturity of mind, an emotional discipline, and a generosity of spirit

---

[54] For a good example of the type of resentment he aroused see 'Seán Ó Riordáin ag caint le Seán Ó Mórdha', *Scríobh*, 3 (1978), pp. 179–81.

that he never demanded from either Ulster unionists or English nation-alists.[55]

Unbalanced though O'Brien's attacks on nationalism became, his moral courage in daring to defy the tribal gods had few precedents in Irish public life. His whole style threw down a gauntlet to a political culture that had brought ambivalence, evasion and illusion to such a pitch of refinement that many no longer could even recognise their existence. The antipathy he roused could not be explained solely in intellectual terms, though his style of discourse could goad intellectual as well as visceral resistance. The manner in which he mocked the popular pieties, and dared desecrate the temple of nationalism provoked outraged response from the votaries of the household gods. They could never forgive him. In a culture where 'notionalism' played so central a role, the courage to defy the notionalist consensus, and especially to defy it by reason rather than by an alternative variety of posturing, fostered deep psychological discomfort.[56] The implications for notionalism as well as for nationalism help explain the fury of the reaction. It was not merely a specific belief, but a whole technique of thinking, a cast of mind, a mental map, whose validity was challenged and affronted. No wonder that O'Brien provoked rabid hostility from his critics and profound silences from his colleagues. His actual policy, as distinct from the moral fervour with which he flagellated deviants, corresponded with that of the government. But 'he espoused it much more often than most Ministers thought necessary', and in such a style that 'O'Brien's support for almost any idea became enough to turn Fianna Fáil against it.'[57]

Despite the resentment roused by O'Brien's remorseless probing of the Irish psyche, his crusade probably did something to impress on his countrymen the reality as distinct from the mythology of unification. Opinion poll surveys, however fragile their own bases, suggest a sharp increase between 1968 and 1978 in the proportion of the Republic's electorate, from roughly 20 per cent to over 60 per cent, prepared to postpone unification until a majority of the electorate in Northern Ireland voted for it.[58] The public was, no doubt, responding to a variety of influences and perceptions. Some may have begun to reject the idea of unification entirely. More may have continued to desire unification, but were revolted at the thought of picking up a united Ireland out of a plastic bag. Others may have felt less squeamish about that aspect, but preferred unity in the longer than the shorter term. O'Brien may have converted few

55 Brown, *Ireland*, pp. 283–91.
56 On 'notionalism' in Irish culture see G. Daly, 'On formulating national goals', in *Ireland in the year 2000: towards a national strategy* (Dublin, 1983), pp. 30ff.
57 Gallagher, *Labour party*, p. 211.
58 K. Kyle, 'The panorama survey of Irish opinion', *Political Quarterly*, 50, 1 (January/March 1979), p. 29.

directly to his viewpoint. But his relentless campaign may have stimulated some to reconsider their position, even if they did not fully accept his. Any mature culture could take pride in its ability to produce a critic, despite his occasional eccentricities, of O'Brien's calibre and courage.

The new mood of questioning extended to the Constitution. Clauses that roused little interest when they applied to a 95 per cent Catholic majority in the Republic, where Protestants could like them or lump them, as far as the majority was concerned, acquired a different connotation when applied to the Protestants of the North. The South had always succeeded in eliminating these from consideration when it came to the conduct of everyday politics. But a society that was now obliged to formulate some policy on unification, apart from simple annexation, had to confront the question, however surreptitiously, why anybody should want unity with it. This new questioning attitude marks the biggest single change in the nationalist response to the Ulster question in the 1970s. Nationalist Ireland had hitherto steadfastly refused to contemplate the implications for Protestants of a Catholic parliament for a Catholic people. Some were now prepared to begin seriously considering the question.

Liam Cosgrave was not one of them. His vote on his own government's bill for the Control of the Importation, Sale and Manufacture of Contraceptives in July 1974 showed his metal. It need hardly be said that a Cosgrave government did not embark spontaneously on legislation in the area of contraception. Some semblance of an attempt at legislation was forced on it by a Supreme Court ruling in the McGee case in December 1973 which declared the ban on the importation of contraceptives under a 1935 Act to be unconstitutional. When the government introduced legislation in 1974 to license chemists to sell contraceptives to duly married couples, Cosgrave helped defeat the Bill by opposing it in a free vote without giving any prior warning to the cabinet over whose deliberations he had presided during the formulation of policy on the legislation.[59] His vote, however intriguing to connoisseurs of cabinet convention, was a nine days' wonder. But it did emphatically underline Cosgrave's personal distaste for the type of legislation that would appear to be necessary if a united Ireland were to emerge by agreement in the foreseeable future.

If Cosgrave seemed to care little about the North, he cared passionately for social and political stability in the South. His policy did not differ greatly from that of Lynch. His style did. Lynch managed to convey the impression that he moved reluctantly, if inexorably, against sometimes well-intentioned but misguided men. Cosgrave conveyed no such impression. A series of murders, robberies and kidnappings enabled him mobilise

[59] Gallagher, *Labour party*, p. 202.

a broad-based public opinion in favour of stronger measures against subversives. He handled the demands of the kidnappers of the Dutch industrialist, T. Herrema, in October 1975 with apparent firmness. The gárdaí eventually persuaded the kidnappers to surrender. He dealt sternly with the IRA attempt to exploit the funeral of Frank Stagg, an honorable republican of the old school, who died on hunger strike in Britain. He was not cowed by threats of assassination into conceding IRA demands for privileges for prisoners in Portlaoise jail.[60] Neither he nor his Minister for Justice, Patrick Cooney, showed public concern about allegations of gárda mistreatment of suspects. However exaggerated, cynical and opportunistic many of these allegations, some incidents left a nasty taste in the public mouth.

Despite episodic disquiet of this type, Cosgrave seemed to be playing the political game with rare professional skill. Even at the trough of the economic depression, the government enjoyed an impressive by-election record. Its victory in the West Mayo by-election in November 1975 appeared particularly ominous for Fianna Fáil. It was true that the Fine Gael winner, Enda Kenny, was the personable son of the popular dead deputy, and that the saga of the Herrema kidnapping had been brought to a triumphant conclusion with his rescue the previous day. But Fianna Fáil's failure in its heartland still sent a thrill of fear through the party. Or, at least, through the Lynch section of the party.

Lynch's position had inevitably weakened in the wake of the electoral defeat in 1973. His difficulties accumulated in opposition. He lost two of his most popular front bench spokesmen before going into opposition at all. His nomination of Patrick Hillery as the first Irish EEC Commissioner in Brussels deprived him of a reassuring colleague in January 1973. Hillery's successor as Minister for Foreign Affairs, Brian Lenihan, an amiable virtuoso of shadow language, lost his seat at the election, languishing in the Senate until 1977. Added to the losses of Donagh O'Malley in 1968 and of Haughey in 1970, these departures left gaping vacancies in Lynch's front bench. It quickly became obvious in opposition that several former ministers had survived their years in office only through the support of their departments. Lynch now established his own 'think tank', to provide some alternative to civil service thought. It served its purpose reasonably well, to the extent that it enabled shadow spokesmen to perform more professionally than some might have managed on their own.

Lynch still seemed the best electoral bet as Fianna Fáil leader, but he had to keep a wary eye on party matters, particularly as his position was further eroded as the coalition increasingly appeared likely to win the next election. In 1975 he felt obliged to accept a more hawkish line on the

60 *Ibid.*, p. 205.

North, attributed to Michael O'Kennedy, his spokesman on foreign affairs, calling for 'an ordered withdrawal' of Britain from Northern Ireland. More to the point, he also felt obliged to reappoint Haughey to Health and Social Welfare, where it was difficult to make a parliamentary killing. The minister Brendan Corish, enjoyed a genial public image. His Parliamentary Secretary, Frank Cluskey, was proving exceptionally active. Haughey had little scope to criticise improvements in this area, many long overdue. He tried to turn the tables on Lynch by engaging in a series of wide-ranging speeches throughout the country on issues far beyond his shadow portfolio. His campaign made little impression on his parliamentary colleagues at this stage, but broadened his support base among the grass roots.

Haughey's main potential rival for the succession, George Colley, was also redeeming himself. After his unfortunate television debate with Garret FitzGerald in 1973, he shaped up increasingly well in Dáil exchanges with Richie Ryan. Des O'Malley, too, as shadow spokesman on Industry and Commerce, proved a formidable critic of Justin Keating, particularly in relation to his handling of the Bula Mine affair, where O'Malley argued trenchantly that the state had secured poor terms in comparison with the private interests involved.

Sound parliamentary performances by individual Fianna Fáil spokesmen were not sufficient to undermine Cosgrave's position. He seemed to be doing sufficiently well throughout 1976 to make him a warm favourite to win the general election widely expected in 1977. And if the government's performance should not suffice to ensure victory, then commentators were convinced that the 'Tullymander' did. The Labour Minister for Local Government, Jim Tully, had responsibility for the latest constituency revision. A quintessential local politician, Tully was in his aesthetic element. The redrawing of the electoral boundaries gave his artistic instincts free rein. He laboured lovingly to reverse Kevin Boland's previous gerrymander. It was the sheer professionalism of his handiwork that earned his own arrangement the half-grudging description of Tullymander, threatening to consign the venerable Governor Gerry to semantic oblivion.

Tully naturally substituted three-seaters for four-seaters in Dublin, seeking to exploit Fianna Fáil's weakness in the capital. He equally naturally increased the number of four- and five-seaters in those rural areas where Fianna Fáil was traditionally strong.[61] Commentators agreed that he did a marvellous job for his side. But Tully's arrangement, though few detected this at the time, was as potentially counter-productive as Kevin Boland's proved in 1973. In the event of a minor swing against the government, it would certainly preclude proportionate Fianna Fáil gains.

[61] Murray, 'Irish elections', pp. 204–5.

And a minor swing was all that practising politicians considered within the realm of possibility. It was reasonable for coalition strategists to work on this assumption. But in the event of a massive swing against the government, it would provide disproportionate Fianna Fáil gains. That seemed so improbable at the time that few connoisseurs of electoral cartography spared it a thought.

Cosgrave began to behave with growing confidence, not to say arrogance, in the year before the election. The assassination on 23 July 1976 of the British Ambassador, Christopher Ewart-Biggs, by the Provisional IRA, led the government into over-playing a strong hand by declaring a state of emergency. The declaration was delayed, so that the immediate sense of public concern had faded by the time the Dáil made the declaration on 1 September. The President, Cearbhall Ó Dálaigh, a distinguished former Chief Justice, quite correctly referred the Emergency Powers Bill to the Supreme Court before signing it on 16 October once the court declared it constitutional. At a meeting of army officers, Cosgrave's Minister for Defence, and close colleage, Paddy Donegan, denounced the President, who was, under the constitution, Commander in Chief of the army, in language which was part of Ireland's glorious Anglo-Saxon heritage but had not yet acquired official parliamentary status, for his temerity in presuming to refer the Bill to the Supreme Court at all.[62] When Donegan offered to resign, on learning of his departure from the expected standards of constitutional propriety, Cosgrave refused to accept the resignation, indicating that a letter of apology was quite sufficient. Ó Dálaigh then resigned, on 22 October, 'to protect the dignity and independence of the presidency as an institution'. By agreement between Cosgrave and Lynch, Paddy Hillery, whose term of office as an EEC Commissioner was due to expire on 31 December, was returned unopposed as Ó Dálaigh's successor on 9 November.

At one level, the whole affair appeared a masterly Cosgrave move in the party political game. Donegan, a publican by trade, was not renowned for a fastidious sense of language. He may not have deliberately insulted the President to provoke the resignation of a man known for his fastidious sense of integrity. Whatever Donegan's motives, if any, Cosgrave handled the ensuing controversy as a purely partly political matter. Hillery appeared at that moment the most dangerous potential leader of Fianna Fáil from Cosgrave's viewpoint. In the event of the widely expected defeat of Fianna Fáil in the next election, Jack Lynch would come under intense pressure to resign. The party, given the personal animosities known to exist between leading contenders for the succession, might be expected to tear itself apart in a leadership struggle. Hillery was the obvious consensus successor. With him now safely isolated in the presidency, Cosgrave could

62 Ó hEithir, *The begrudgers*, p. 173.

gleefully anticipate Fianna Fáil ripping itself asunder in a vicious power struggle.

Ó Dálaigh had been a Fianna Fáil Attorney General from 1946 to 1948, and again from 1951 to 1954, having stood unsuccessfully as a Dáil candidate in 1948 and 1951. Cosgrave treated him from the outset more as a Fianna Fáil politician than as president.[63] But Ó Dálaigh was no party hack. He had been a notable Chief Justice from 1961 to 1973, and had served with distinction as a judge of the European Court between 1973 and his nomination as president in December 1974 on the sudden death of Erskine Childers. He was widely respected as a scholar and a gentleman. His resignation was the only proper course for a president, even had he not been a man of honour. If Cosgrave lost few votes directly over his handling of the affair, he hardly won any either. The main casualty was the proud name of his own family as defenders of constitutional propriety.

Cosgrave probably blundered further at the Fine Gael Árd Fheis in May 1977 when, through over-confidence, he fumed against 'blow-ins' – a jibe apparently aimed at Bruce Arnold, the English-born parliamentary reporter of the *Irish Independent* (imagine Irish indignation at comparable English sneers against prominent Irish personalities in the English media!) – and seemed to take deliberate pleasure in repression for its own sake rather than treating it, like Lynch, as disagreeable neccessity. Again, the performance probably lost him few votes, but it suggested a degree of emotional self-indulgence curiously at odds with the clinical professional game he had seemed to be playing as Taoiseach.

Cosgrave called the election for June 1977, nine months before the expiry of his term. Ministers were reputedly evenly divided on a June or October date, with Cosgrave deciding for June.[64] By-elections in Donegal Northeast and Dublin Southwest had continued to show strong support for the coalition as late as June 1976. The mildly indulgent January 1977 Budget was well received. Political commentators generally predicted that the coalition would sweep to victory, probably transforming Fianna Fáil into the natural party of opposition for the late twentieth century.

But Fianna Fáil fought much the most effective campaign of any party. Impressively organised by Seamus Brennan, who succeeded the veteran Tommy Mullins as General Secretary in 1973, they produced an enticing list of promises in a sleek manifesto, including the immediate abolition of rates and of motor taxation as well as lump sum subsidies for first time house purchasers. The campaign also revolved very much around the amiable image of Jack Lynch, contrasting so conspicuously with the constipated image of Cosgrave. Images were even more important than

---

[63] Downey, *Them and us*, pp. 157–9.
[64] Gallagher, *Labour party*, p. 216; S. O'Byrnes, *Hiding behind a face: Fine Gael under FitzGerald* (Dublin, 1986), pp. 1–2.

usual in view of the fact that the voting age was reduced to eighteen for the first time. Indeed, a quarter of the electorate was aged under twenty-six. Jack Lynch was a new man for many of these voters, and Fianna Fáil's emphasis on the issue of youth unemployment, which remained stubbornly resistant to the modest economic recovery, seems to have reaped rich dividends among this section of the electorate.

The North featured as little in the campaign as in 1973. It was only when Fianna Fáil drove him back on the defensive by the unexpected vigour of their assault on his economic and social policy that Cosgrave found himself forced to adopt Lynch's tactics of four years earlier by emphasising the law and order issue. Some observers seized on the defeats of Conor Cruise O'Brien and Patrick Cooney, who were associated in the public mind with repression of the IRA, to allege that the irredentist cancer was still knawing at the vitals of Irish society. But there was no consistent pattern in votes for ministers. O'Brien and Cooney probably lost their seats more through neglect of their constituencies than for ideological reasons. So did Justin Keating, whose views on the North hardly coincided with theirs. Jim Tully, who had refrained from philosophical speculation on the North, or on anything else, just scraped home. The only two ministers to increase their personal vote, Garret FitzGerald and Paddy Donegan, were certainly not associated in the public mind with indulgence for the IRA. They also belonged to opposite wings of Fine Gael. The Ulster question doubtless affected some votes, but it probably had as little to do with the overall result in 1977 as in 1973.

And the overall result was a sensation. Fianna Fáil won 50.6 per cent of the vote, compared with 46.2 per cent in 1973, and 84 seats out of 148, the biggest majority ever recorded. Even de Valera in 1938 had not enjoyed so spectacular a triumph. The Fine Gael vote fell from 35.1 per cent to 30.5 per cent, the lowest proportion since 1957, and the number of seats from 53 to 43. The Labour vote fell from 13.7 per cent to 11.6 per cent, leading to a loss of 3 seats, from 20 at the dissolution to 17.[65]

The consequences for the party political leaders were immediate and unprecedented. No defeated Taoiseach or Tánaiste had ever resigned immediately following election defeat. Now Liam Cosgrave, at the early age of fifty-six, after eleven years as leader of the party, and four years as a strong Taoiseach, abruptly resigned as leader. He may have feared lingering, as his father lingered for twelve futile years after 1932, as leader of the opposition. He may have feared even more that he would not linger that long, in view of the likelihood of imminent moves against him. Brendan Corish, still only fifty-eight, seventeen years leader of the Labour Party, also resigned immediately. It was presumably the manner rather

---

[65] For a detailed study of the election and its background, see H. Penniman (ed.), *Ireland at the polls: the Dáil elections of 1977* (Washington, 1978).

than the fact of defeat that led both men to their decisions. Both resignations were perhaps understandable in the circumstances. But they introduced yet further pressure on future party leaders in government, in creating a presumption, for the first time, that defeat would instantly threaten their position. This would make the premium on electoral victory, and hence the recklessness of pre-election promises, even higher.

Cosgrave's case was particularly striking. A month earlier, he could have reasonably anticipated at least one, if not two, further terms of office, while he relished the internecine strife in Fianna Fáil. Now he was no longer even party leader. There would be no age of Cosgrave. It must have seemed a poor reward for his four-year stewardship of the coalition cabinet, particularly when Garret FitzGerald was unanimously elected his successor as party leader. Unlike the Fine Gael Taoiseach of the two previous coalition governments, John A. Costello, Cosgrave was a full-time professional politician. He had always been a man of craggy principle by his lights – he was not his father's son for nothing. It was noted at an early stage in his career that 'he has always displayed independence and though his loyalty to the party has never been in doubt, he did not hesitate to speak his mind, even if he never publicly opposed cabinet or party colleagues'.[66] He continued to show the quality of independence in holding, contrary to the predominant view in his party, that proportional representation should be abolished.[67] In later years the independence did extend to publicly opposing cabinet and party colleagues, as in his willingness to risk his leadership on the Criminal Justice Bill in December 1972, or in his vote against the contraceptive legislation of his own cabinet in 1975.

But his prime purpose in office was, as a true professional, to win the next election. The cup of office had twice been snatched from his lips, in 1951 and again in 1957, by what it would not have been uncharitable for him to have considered the rank political amateurism of Costello. He was determined to avoid Costello's mistakes. The sixteen dreary years in the desert of opposition that followed his term as Minister for External Affairs left an indelible mark on his political thinking. His distaste for Fianna Fáil was reflected in his determination to defeat the enemy by bettering the instruction. A zealous constituency TD, his political tactics and style were indistinguishable from those that Fine Gael moralists liked to associate exclusively with Fianna Fáil. In office, he avoided his father's more transparent mistakes. He cooperated with Labour, and was for a time prepared to curb some of his own more conservative instincts as the price of power. He soon came to dominate his cabinet, and proved not only a strong chairman, but even in the eyes of Labour ministers, a fair

[66] 'Profile: Mr Liam Cosgrave', TD, *Leader*, 27 February 1954.
[67] *Irish Times*, 1 February 1968, as quoted in Gallagher, *Labour party*, p. 279, n. 37.

one.[68] His courage under fire stood the country in good stead. When he was not under fire, there was nothing in particular he wanted to do. He dreamed no dreams. The game was about possession, not performance. He was essentially a local politician operating at national level, and operating, by the standards of local politics, very effectively. He played the patronage game with unconcealed satisfaction, conveying the impression that it never entered his head that there could be any other game to play. He was, in other words, the model of a professional party politician by the standards of the prevailing political culture. It was peculiarly ironic in those circumstances that he so completely mishandled the election itself, approaching it more like a constituency TD than like a Taoiseach.[69]

In contrast to the situation in Fine Gael, there was no obvious successor to Corish in Labour. Keating and O'Brien were removed as possible contenders by their election defeats. Tully suddenly found himself in near disgrace after his apparently foolproof constituency revision had so unsportingly backfired. This left, among the outgoing ministers, only Michael O'Leary. But Frank Cluskey had been a *de facto* minister as parliamentary Secretary to Corish, and defeated O'Leary by one vote to enter into the dubious delights of the succession.

Keating, an exceptionally hardworking minister, had to feel bitterly disappointed at losing his seat. O'Brien, who had better things to do with his time, grandly thanked the electorate for giving him a mandate to continue with his writing. Tully felt a particular sense of bereavement. Had not commentators been virtually unanimous, until the actual moment of decision, in admiring his work as a masterpiece, worthy of inclusion in a hall of fame of electoral fixes? It was not his fault that the coalition could not collect the number of votes his scheme required. Nobody claimed that his performance as a minister affected the result. Had he not refrained from taking precipitate, or indeed any, action on the Kenny report of 1973 which sought to impose restrictions on speculation in building land, which would have threatened a powerful pressure group?[70]

Tully rendered one inadvertent service to electoral democracy. The Tullymander had been so blatant that Lynch could reckon that a boundary review commission was bound to suggest changes, however unintentionally, that would prevent comparable swings occurring in future. Fianna Fáil, now in a handsome majority, would be the first beneficiaries from an injection of fairness into the system – unless something else went disastrously wrong in the interim! He therefore set up a commission to take constituency revision out of the hands of politicians. The result would bring more fairness, but less stability.

[68] Gallagher, *Labour party* p. 219.   [69] O'Byrnes, *Hiding behind a face*, pp. 3–5.
[70] J. O'Malley, 'Labour's wigging weekend', *Sunday Independent*, 14 November 1976.

Lynch had surprised his critics by the resilience he had shown under intense internal pressure during his earlier years in office. But it could not be claimed that the had stamped his style on an epoch. It remained to be seen whether there would now be an age of Lynch.

THE CROCK OF GOLD

Lynch seemed benignly bemused by the scale of his victory. The measures he took in the months following his triumph would soon undermine the basis of his majority and his command of the party. Above all, he badly misjudged the economic situation. There was much to be said for a serious policy of sustained but disciplined expansion. After the trauma of the mid-seventies, the coalition cobbled together a Green Paper in 1976, which purported to form the basis of 'a plan for economic revival'. But this was more a pious cosmetic gesture to Labour's axiomatic belief in 'planning' than a serious attempt at any long-term thinking. With Lynch now safely in office, and the economy already recovering from the trough of 1975–6, there was no need for a short-term boost. There was a need for strategic thinking, to try to turn recovery into long-term improvement.

Lynch relied heavily on his principle economic adviser, Martin O'Donoghue, an economics professor at Trinity College Dublin, whom he appointed Minister of Economic Development and Planning on his first day in the Dáil. Lynch's first mistake was in creating a new department for O'Donoghue. If strategic thinking is to be given administrative weight, it must be undertaken under the aegis of Finance. This naturally creates tensions within Finance, where there will always be a cluster of negative instincts. But that may be no harm if personnel policy is also directed to encouraging some constructive temperaments. Virtually irrespective of the quality of the Finance mind at any given time, however, conflicts will automatically arise between Finance and any department specifically entrusted with developmental thinking, which it would be better to have fought out within Finance. The creation of a new department simply adds fresh administrative rivalries and exacerbates jealousies, particularly if officials in the new department enjoy what Finance men regard as excessive promotion opportunities.

A dose of Finance scepticism would, for once, have done no harm in the euphoria of 1977. But it is doubtful if any institutional arrangement could have brought government thinking closer to reality. O'Donoghue diagnosed accurately enough the challenge facing the economy. His instinct that the cyclical recovery already underway would not provide a basis for the rate of development necessary to achieve full employment in the 1980s was correct. Not only could there be no going back to the slump of the mid-1970s. There could be no going back to the 'normalcy' of 1969–73

Table 6. *Projected and actual economic indicators, 1981*

	1981 Projected	1981 Actual
Growth in GNP (%)	5	2.61
Inflation (%)	below 5	20.4
Unemployment	c. 50 000	147 000
Public expenditure (% GNP)	48.5	65.4

Source: *Programme for national development 1978–1981* (Dublin 1979), pp. 19, 111; *A strategy for development 1986–1990* (NESC 83, 1986), pp. 8, 10, 38.

either, because that 'normalcy' was itself a variety of failure. But O'Donoghue's prescription, which he acknowledged to be a gamble at the time, proved sadly misguided. The second oil crisis of 1979 gave it the *coup de grâce*. But it had already contracted terminal illness. The first O'Donoghue plan, published in January 1978, projected a 7 per cent annual increase in output from 1978 to 1980, with a 6 per cent annual rise in the standard of living, and the creation of 25 000 *net* new jobs a year.[71] A further Green Paper published in June 1978 envisaged full employment 'in the early 1980s'.[72]

Colley's budget in February 1978 supported this expansionist tactic by reversing Ryan's belated attempt to reduce deficit financing. It raised the projected current deficit from 3.8 per cent to 6.2 per cent, and increased the exchequer borrowing requirement to an extraordinary 13 per cent of GNP. The reasoning behind the gamble on growth was that a consumer boom would so stimulate the private sector that the economy would shift gears into a higher, and sustained, growth path. The share of public expenditure in GNP could then be reduced from 51 per cent in 1978 to 48.5 per cent in 1981, back down to the 1977 figure. Exchequer borrowing could then fall from 13 per cent of GNP to less than 8 per cent.[73] This reasoning still predominated as late as January 1979, when another White Paper insisted on projecting a glowing prospect of the economic scenario only three years hence. Rarely can the real world have deviated so sadly from the projected one, as Table 6 indicates.

Comment on Table 6 is almost superfluous. The second surge of oil prices in 1979 did, it is true, upset some assumptions on which the forecasts were based. The terms of trade deteriorated from 103.7 in 1978 to 89.7 in 1981. This does not suffice to explain the débâcle, however. The

[71] *National development 1977–1980* (Dublin, 1978), p. 20.
[72] *Development for full employment* (Dublin, 1978), p. 14.
[73] 'The economy – some EEC comparisons', *IBR* (March 1982), pp. 8–9.

Table 7. *Wage increases and inflation rates, 1978–81 (%)*

	Ireland		EEC (10)	
	Wages	Inflation	Wages	Inflation
1978	14.9	7.6	9.7	7.4
1979	16.6	13.2	10.2	9.6
1980	20.5	18.2	13.4	11.9
1981	18.4	20.4	11.6	11.6

Source: 'The economy – some EEC comparisons' *IBR* (March 1982), 8–9.

Table 8. *Balance of payments deficits, 1978–81 (% GDP)*[74]

	Ireland	EEC
1978	2.4	–
1979	10.1	0.5
1980	8.3	1.5
1981	12.5	1.5

Source: 'The economy – some EEC comparisons' *IBR* (March 1982), 8–9.

inflation rate was already rising in the first quarter of 1979, before unforeseen international influences had an impact. Much inflation was imported, but internal factors accentuated the inflationary pressures. The Irish continued to insist on paying themselves far more than they were earning. This caused further inflation, which in turn provoked further wage claims, as the dog chased after its own tail. Wage increases, and inflation, far exceeded the EEC averages between 1979 and 1981, as Table 7 indicates. With the wages boom fuelling a consumption boom in an economy with a high marginal propensity to import, and with declining export competitiveness, the balance of payments deficit inevitably worsened sharply, as can be seen in Table 8. These two tables tell a grim tale of financial irresponsibility as the Irish insisted on living in a dreamland. Reality could not be banished for long. Unemployment, the presumed beneficiary of policy, did decline from 106 000 to 90 000 between 1977 and 1979. Then it began to rise again, to more than 100 000 in 1980 and to 147 000 in April 1982. The price for the flight from reality would be paid by those whose jobs were at risk.

[74] *Ibid.*

The O'Donoghue strategy did not 'go wrong' as a consequence of unforeseeable accidents. It was seriously flawed from the outset by two fundamentally erroneous assumptions. The assumption that the private sector would respond with a surge of expansion to increased domestic demand ignored the lessons of history. Defenders of private businessmen would claim that inflation scared off investment, and that rapidly rising labour costs damaged the confidence the consumer boom was supposed to stimulate. But these are more excuses than explanations. There was no historical justification for reposing such confidence in Irish business, particularly when the high propensity to import meant that the consumer boom was sucking in competing goods. O'Donoghue reposed an enormous burden of hope on very fragile foundations.

The second assumption was equally optimistic. The lavish promises of the 1977 manifesto were conditional on a degree of cooperation from trade unions in observing wage restraint. This was highly unlikely, not necessarily because of malign design by trade union leaders, but because Fianna Fáil rhetoric so whetted public expectations that even responsible trade union officials could not have settled for the terms the government optimstically sought. A public not only cossetted from reality during the previous four years by heavy borrowing, but encouraged to envisage a glowing future, would not settle for the paltry 5 per cent that Colley proposed in his 1978 Budget.[75] The tactic of creating jobs in the public sector, where in the prevailing circumstances they would be largely unproductive, simply ensured further demands from workers who felt that whoever might pay for their gains, *they* wouldn't. A luxurious crop of 'special claims' naturally flourished in the hothouse atmosphere. Nurses, guards, postal workers, telephone operators, Aer Lingus workers and garbage collectors all found reasons for extra claims over and above the already extravagant national agreements.[76] Confident of their complete security of tenure, they derisively dismissed warnings that their claims would fuel further the ravages of inflation, or lead to widespread unemployment elsewhere in the economy. The operative term was 'elsewhere'.

But in 1978 all that was in the future – if not very far in the future; 1978 was a bonanza year. In the year to mid-August 1978, personal borrowing from the banks increased by an extraordinary 45 per cent.[77] It was the year of the big spenders. In addition to the injection of purchasing power through the budget deficit, farmers revelled in the largesse of the CAP. The Feoga guarantee jumped from £102.2 million in 1976 to £245.1 million in 1977, and to no less than £365.6 million in 1978. Land prices leaped to unprecedented heights. The banks were only too happy to accommodate

75 Whitaker, *Interests*, p. 108.   76 Browne, 'Who's to blame?', p. 8.
77 P. Tansey, 'The Central Bank rules Finance', *Magill*, 3, 3 (December 1979), p. 73.

the demands of a clientéle who could offer land as a security on the expectation of permanently rising prices. Many an improbable *hacienda* in rural Ireland dates from the year of the big spenders. Ireland recorded the fastest rate of growth in the OECD that year, at 7 per cent faster even than Japan, relegated into second place by the spectacular Irish performance.

The secret of the Hibernian miracle began to emerge in 1979. Nemesis overtook the agricultural sector somewhat more quickly than the public sector. The reduction in the rapid rate of increase in agricultural prices under the CAP, as the EEC finally took fright at the runaway over-production stimulated by prices far above the world average, ushered in a slump in agriculture in 1979. Feoga payments rose only slightly, from £365.6 million to £381.1 million. This was still a handsome figure. But it was much less than expected, as farmers and banks had habituated themselves to assuming an ever-swelling flood of subsidies from Brussels. No thought had been taken of the morrow, though it was clear that the goose could not continue to lay golden eggs indefinitely. Many farmers heavily in debt now found themselves caught on a falling market. As land prices first stabilised, and then fell from their inflated levels, borrowers and purchasers found their security worth much less than they and the banks had assumed. The banks did not intend to suffer. They began putting pressure on borrowers who could not meet repayments, having borrowed on the security of land whose value was falling instead of rising. Rural resentment festered during 1979.

Farmers were already affronted by the 1979 Budget. Public expenditure was outrunning public income at so glaring a rate that even the government felt that something had to be done. But the steps it took showed a strange lack of political sensitivity, either through the complacency engendered by the massive majority, or because Jack Lynch was simply losing interest in his job. As the cabinet scratched around for new sources of income, Colley proposed to introduce a 2 per cent levy on farmers' sales. He had a case. Income tax on farmers in 1978 accounted for only 1 per cent of their gross incomes, compared with 16 per cent – up from 9 per cent in 1970 – for the average industrial worker.[78] As the rise in land prices during the CAP windfall was common knowledge, and as a number of farmers chose to spend their winnings in normal *nouveau riche* fashion, the ostentatiousness with which they were enjoying their bonanza began to gall some PAYE taxpayers. The rights and wrongs of the relative incomes, work loads, work ethics, etc. between farmers and the PAYE sector could be argued, and were argued, *ad nauseum*. Perceptions of farmers reputedly reaping fortunes and then refusing to pay their taxes provoked intense anger among PAYE workers resentful of the tax burden

[78] Sheehy, 'Common Agricultural Policy', p. 87.

and doubly resentful at their lack of opportunity to evade it. If they could not escape, neither should others. But farmers' organisations reacted furiously to the Colley Budget, organising threatening anti-levy marches in February. This in turn infuriated PAYE taxpayers, who retaliated, under trade union guidance, with even more massive anti-tax and, by implication, anti-farmer protests in March. For the first time in Irish history, town/country tension flared up in a graphic manner. This was still not town/country conflict of the classic continental type. It remained more a conflict of pockets than of cultures. But the potential for bitter sectoral conflict was accumulating.

The government twisted and turned in a vain effort to conciliate the conflicting interests. It gave the impression of having been caught wholly unawares by the range and intensity of the resentment engendered, although some of this was due to its own rhetoric, for great was the indignation when it appeared that the public could not continue to enjoy something for nothing indefinitely. Critics rebuked it for rousing expectations it could not satisfy, and for fostering a never never mentality among a public who now irritatedly refused to pay the price of profligacy. In the event, Colley backed down on his levy, introducing substantial remissions for types of farmers generally considered Fianna Fáil voters, and discontinuing the levy subsequently, thus managing to get the worst of all worlds.

It may have been consciousness of the indecisive performance on farmer taxation, as well as a dawning realisation that its economic strategy was being undermined by excessive wage claims, that induced the government to stand firm on a postal worker strike that broke out in February 1979 and continued until June. The government's resolve probably eroded its support base further among a public still reluctant to recognise reality.

The decision in December 1978 to join the European Monetary System (EMS), which would come into operation in March 1979, despite Britain's refusal to enter, was impelled by the search for cheap money and cheap discipline. The cheap money aspect was straightforward. Lynch was offered grants and interest subsidies of £250 million, and loans of £1 250 million over a five-year period to cushion the Irish economy against the shock of exposure to a hard money area.[79] It was the hard money that was expected to provide the chief discipline. The key arguments for entry, at an intellectual level, were that association with the hard currency, the German mark, instead of the soft currency, sterling, would reduce inflation, now running at about 15 per cent in Britain and Ireland, compared with 5 per cent in Germany. A monetary policy similar to the German one should help impose the discipline on incomes that the government felt was needed but did not have the courage to impose

[79] A. Coughlan, 'Ireland', in D. Seers and C. Vaitsos (eds.), *Integration and unequal development* (London, 1980), p. 130.

directly.[80] There were the same basic contradictions in this attitude as there had been in the 1977 manifesto and in the O'Donoghue plan. Entry to the EMS made sense if the authorities were prepared to impose restraints on income and on public expenditure commensurate with membership of a hard money area. If they were not, then entry was another escapist lurch. Government sought in the same breath to escape from the permissive sterling link while demanding yet more grants and loans from the EEC. How it expected the public to accept self-discipline while it simultaneously boasted of more 'free' donations flowing into bottomless Irish pockets remained unexplained.

The economic advisers who recommended membership were therefore probably exaggerating the political possibilities at home.[81] Nevertheless, membership was a courageous and historically correct initiative.[82] It soon resulted in the break in parity with sterling for the first time since 1826. The Irish pound fell quickly to about 80p rather than appreciating considerably, as many observers had anticipated. Due to the unpredicted, and in fairness, unpredictable behaviour of sterling over the next few years, the consequences turned out to be largely benign for Irish exports to Britain, if only because the exchange rate moved in a direction contrary to that anticipated. While this should theoretically have assisted Irish exports, inelasticities on both the import and export sides meant that the benefit to the balance of payments was probably less than might have been expected.[83] Membership of the EMS had no impact on popular expectations, unless it was to raise them, on the assumption that more grants meant more domestic handouts. This mentality, inherent in Irish political culture, had been fostered even further by the image of the EEC as a welfare agency for Ireland, and by the O'Donoghue prescription.

That prescription was doomed to failure. It failed to take account either of national character or of its own implications for the balance of institutional power in the labour market. An unfortunate consequence of the failure of the O'Donoghue plan is that it not only discredited his prescription, but also discredited his diagnosis, which had considerable validity. His failure tends to be implicitly contrasted with a presumed satisfactory alternative. No such alternative was available. The recovery

---

[80] P.J. Drudy and D. McAleese, 'Editorial introduction' in Drudy and McAlese, *Ireland*, pp. 8–9.

[81] This section draws heavily on B.M. Walsh, 'Ireland in the European Monetary System: the effects of a change in exchange rate regime', in M. de Cecco (ed.), *International economic adjustment: small countries and the European Monetary System* (Cambridge, 1983), pp. 160–88 and 'Ireland's membership of the European Monetary System: expectations, outturn and prospects', in Drudy and McAleese, *Ireland* pp. 173–90.

[82] Whitaker, 'An ceangal le sterling', pp. 12–18; T.F. Ó Cofaigh, 'Slabhra scaoilte: smaointe ar neamhspleachas airgeadais' (The broken chain: thoughts on monetary independence), *Central Bank Quarterly Bulletin* (Winter 1985), pp. 56ff.

[83] Walsh, 'Ireland in the European Monetary System', pp. 182–3.

of 1976–7 would almost certainly have remained a modest one, unless measures could be taken to build more solidly on it than had been the case with growth before 1973. A responsible financial policy could not in itself generate the growth necessary to keep Irish unemployment levels down to average OECD levels, much less at the lower levels of the successful small OECD countries, including Switzerland, Austria, Finland, Sweden and Norway. Even the relatively unsuccessful small countries of the period, like Denmark, Belgium and the Netherlands kept their nominal unemployment rates below Irish levels, and their real unemployment rates probably even further below.

The alternative to O'Donoghue would not have been a full employment, or nearly full employment, growth economy. It would almost certainly have been an economy only a little less depressed by the mid-1980s than was actually the case. The trajectories of unemployment, inflation, and borrowing would have been somewhat less steep. But they would still have reflected/caused deep depression. O'Donoghue was right to perceive the extent of the looming problem. Even if everything had been done 'correctly' by the canons of the conventional wisdom, the eighties would still have been a deeply depressed decade. The conventional wisdom had no solutions to the challenge confronting the country after 1977. O'Donoghue serves a useful function as scapegoat in permitting more fundamental questions about the capacity of Irish decision-making processes to achieve a viable economy to be evaded.

If there can be sympathy for the O'Donoghue diagnosis, however little for the prescription, it is difficult to understand the political calculation in any terms. Jack Lynch must take responsibility for this. O'Donoghue was not a professional politician. Lynch was. If the objective was to win the next election, then it would have been usual to get the bad news out of the way in the first two years of office, to leave scope for more expansionist policies in the pre-election period. Gambling on a spending spree in the first two years, making an act of faith in the ability of private enterprise to respond to the incentive to carry the economy through the second half of the term of office, seems an extraordinary risk for an experienced politician to have taken. The only party political calculation that could have introduced an element of rationality into the affair would have been if Jack Lynch were already determined to resign half way through his term of office, and was determined to leave the economy so flourishing at that stage that Colley would succeed smoothly to the leadership, leaving no opportunity to Haughey, now at Health and Social Welfare, to snatch the leadership. If this was the calculation, it came badly unstuck. The manner in which the government attempted, however belatedly, to impose some discipline on popular attitudes by its resistance to the postal workers' strike in the course of 1979 seems to make even that an improbable hypothesis. But if Lynch was not thinking along some such lines, what on earth did he think he was doing?

Whatever was on his mind, it was his misfortune that the first European Parliament elections were held in June 1979, permitting an early electoral expression of taxpayer discontent following the Colley Budget performance, and of public resentment at the inconvenience caused by the postal strike, then in its fifth month. Fianna Fáil performed very badly, winning only 35 per cent of the vote. June 1977 might have belonged to a different century by June 1979. The public was truly a capricious mistress. Lynch himself treated the elections with a casualness so curious for so sensitive an electoral tactician that it becomes explicable only on the assumption that he had already decided definitely to retire in the near future and saw no reason to inflict one more gruelling campaign on himself. His standing in the party suffered a severe setback. Several marginal Fianna Fáil deputies now felt themselves at risk. The huge majority of 1977 became a millstone around Lynch's neck. If a farmers' leader, the non-party T.J. Maher, could romp home in Munster well ahead of Fianna Fáil stalwarts, many rural representatives naturally felt themselves threatened.

There was a further unsettling feature of the election. In Connaught–Ulster, the maverick, Neil Blaney, won a seat. Some strove to attribute this to sheep farmers who 'remembered that it was Neil T. who first introduced the two pound subsidy.'[84] The hawkish faction in Fianna Fáil preferred to interpret the Blaney vote as a verdict on Lynch's Northern policy rather than as a thank you vote from sheep breeders. They now found themselves with wider potential support within the parliamentary party than they might have anticipated only a short while before, on electoral if not on ideological grounds. Widespread dissatisfaction with the drift of general party policy, combined with a feeling that Lynch's grip was faltering, led to growing disquiet in the party throughout the summer of 1979.

Emboldened by the Blaney result, this restiveness was exploited by the hostile faction when Síle de Valera, a young Fianna Fáil TD, granddaughter of Eamon de Valera, chose the Liam Lynch annual commemoration ceremony in September to portray Lynch's increasing cooperation with the British government on cross-border surveillance, since the assassination of Lord Mountbatten by the IRA in August, as collaboration, thus revealing the depths of the smouldering resentments in the party.

The problems were compounded for Lynch in November, when Fianna Fáil lost two by-elections in Cork, one of them in his own constituency.

[84] The drover, 'Farmers can still make powerful impact at the polls', *Farming Independent*, 16 June 1979.

The results could be interpreted as popular repudiation of either his economic policy, or of his Northern policy, or both. Whatever the interpretation, the conclusion was the same. Jack Lynch had lost his electoral magic. His enemies in the party, whom he had been able to isolate as long as he looked the safest vote-getter, suddenly began to appear a more attractive prospect. Manoeuvres were initiated against him by Haughey supporters. Were Lynch still determined to fight, he could probably have repulsed the challenge. But he preferred not to fight. Though still only sixty-two, he had not disclaimed rumours of his likely resignation before the next election. He seemed increasingly bored by politics, deftly though he had played the party game when the humour was on him. It may even be that the sudden death at the age of fifty-eight in March 1979 of the legendary hurler Christy Ring, with whom Lynch had shared in many a memorable victory in the red jersey, and at whose funeral, the biggest in Munster since the burial of Terence MacSwiney, Lynch was visibly distraught, left its mark on him.[85] But Lynch had not fought so tenaciously to hold the leadership, in government and opposition, for more than a decade, simply to prepare the succession for Haughey. He was apparently assured by Colley's supporters that they had the votes to win. Seemingly confident that Colley would succeed him, Lynch chose to resign on 5 December.

It is peculiarly difficult to assess Jack Lynch's stature, if only because the alternative possibilities remain so debateable. He inherited an economy that had entered a period of sustained growth. It continued to broadly perform, at least on paper, at the inherited level during his first period of office, from 1966 until 1973. However, this can hardly be attributed to any distinctive initiative on his part. He had no long-term perspective, and little grasp of underlying trends. He presided over the wanton decision to unbalance the current budget in 1972, and it seems unlikely that he would have dealt any more effectively with the economic circumstances of the mid-seventies than did Cosgrave. When he returned triumphantly to office, he presided over an unfortunate escapade in the history of economic policy. In ordinary circumstances, Lynch would have been as ordinary a Taoiseach as Cosgrave.

But circumstances after 1969 were not ordinary. Opinions differ widely, according to ideological proclivity, on his handling of the Northern question. To unionists, he appeared an irredentist, to the IRA an appeaser. To his critics in Fianna Fáil, his Northern policy offered a softer target than his economic policy, to which they themselves in any case usually offered no alternative. It was his misfortune to find himself facing the logical consequences of a generation and more of official posturing on the North. His basic objective was clear, but circumstances obliged him to

[85] Val Dorgan, *Christy Ring* (Cork, 1980), pp. 229–38.

play a delicate party game, shuffling sideways rather than following a straight line. In leading an ambivalent public, and an even more ambivalent party, he brought the use of nuance to a pitch of refined perfection. 'It has always been characteristic of Mr Lynch as a politician than it has not been possible to tell for certain whether the air of misunderstanding that frequently surrounds his pronouncements on delicate subjects is accidental or intentional.'[86] It was not for nothing that Lynch had studied at the feet of the master, and could claim that 'I learned a lot of the need for precision in speech from Dev.'[87]

Once back in office in 1977 Lynch began to disengage from the more aggressive rhetorical line that he felt obliged to accommodate in opposition, which demanded a British commitment 'to implement an ordered withdrawal from her involvement in the Six Counties of Northern Ireland', in addition naturally to subsidies, subsidies, subsidies 'for a specified period to enable the transition to take place smoothly.'[88] After his election victory, Lynch defused the implications of this demand. Once the British government 'indicated in a general way they'd like to see the Irish people coming together', and would not continue to support the North financially, 'I believe that the people of the North could be realistic enough and hard-headed enough to know that there should be accommodation found between the minority and themselves in the first instance, and between them and us in the long run.'[89] This was a typical example of the elasticity of Lynch's use of language to dilute irredentist designs. Yet he took few initiatives that might have signalled an ambition to mould a society fit for a united rather than a partitioned Ireland, or indeed fit for a more vital society in the South irrespective of Northern responses. The removal of Article 44, concerning the 'special position' of the Catholic Church from the constitution, was as far as he would go. He could reply that the Ulster Protestant response to the revocation of Article 44 made such exercises pointless, contending that it was 'futile making any constitutional changes in advance of unity'.[90] Understandable though this may be in party terms, and correct though it be in terms of relations with unionists, it conveys no compelling vision of a better society for all citizens, Catholic as well as Protestant. John A. Murphy's comment, that Lynch stood 'for nothing in particular except a kind of affable consensus' captures his basic dynamic.[91]

Nevertheless, the country that this 'easy going and likeable man'[92] left behind in 1979 was not nearly as grim a place as it might have been. It is here that the verdict has to conjure with what did not happen. 'Affable

[86] K. Kyle, 'The panorama survey of Irish opinion', *Political Quarterly*, 40 (1970), p. 26.
[87] Lynch, 'My life and times', p. 40.   [88] Kyle, 'Irish opinion', p. 24.
[89] *Ibid.*, p. 25.
[90] Lynch, 'My life and times', p. 46.   [91] Murphy, 'Put them out!', p. 7.
[92] Gallagher, *Labour party*. p. 61.

consensus' can be a considerable achievement if the likely alternative is a breakdown of civilised discourse, or government by the elect instead of the elected. If Lynch lacked the charisma of de Valera, or the creative energy of Lemass, he had not only a basic decency, but qualities of shrewdness and tenacity that, in addition to his remarkable ability as a vote getter, made him a more formidable adversary than his critis imagined. His skill as a party manager appears all the more impressive with hindsight, in view of the difficulties his successor, himself no mean manager, would encounter. After 1969, Lynch's main objective was the preservation of peace in the Republic. He achieved that. If, as has always remained conceivable, the conflict in the North should spill over into the South, Lynch's defence of the decencies and his success in keeping the rough beast at bay in a highly charged atmosphere will appear all the more remarkable to posterity. And if more innocent blood is not shed, that may well be because Lynch's holding operation gave the populace time to reappraise the implications of the inherited posture.

The candidate of the anti-Lynch forces, Charles Haughey, won the succession against George Colley by 44 votes to 38 in an election conducted in a 'sulphurous' atmosphere.[93] Haughey's assiduous cultivation of the grass roots now bore fruit. Much of his support came from TDs 'with stronger links to local politics, to the activist organisation and, perhaps, to local opinion generally'.[94] Colley had meantime forfeited the credit he had gained by his performance in opposition through his inept handling of the tax proposals in his last Budget, and the growing doubts about the economy in general. The extent of his support, given that he can hardly have been regarded as an electoral saviour at that stage, and given that the Haughey camp waged much the more effective election campaign,[95] reflected bitter resistance to Haughey, who was opposed by almost all the cabinet. Colley's petulant performance in the immediate aftermath of defeat, acknowledging loyalty to Haughey as Taoiseach, but not as leader of the party, on the grounds that Haughey had intrigued against Lynch, reflected more credit on his human than on his political instincts.[96]

Haughey had been an active minister in Justice, Agriculture and Finance, between 1961 and 1970. On his appointment to Health and Social Welfare in 1977, he dealt deftly with the delicate contraceptive issue. The manner in which he massaged the Catholic hierarchy into accepting his 'Irish solution to an Irish problem', as he sardonically described his Family Planning Act of July 1979, which legalised the sale of

[93] T. Garvin, 'The growth of faction in the Fianna Fáil party, 1966–80', *Parliamentary Affairs*, 34, 1 (Winter 1981), p. 118.
[94] *Ibid.*, p. 119.
[95] *Ibid.*, p. 118; J. Joyce and P. Murtagh, *The Boss* (Dublin, 1983), p. 93.
[96] Garvin, 'Faction', p. 121.

contraceptives to married couples on a doctor's prescription, skilfully reconciling the consciences and pockets involved, as well as bringing the law into line with the constitution, testified to his continuing command of nubile political skills. Only time would tell whether, as a superior profile surmised, he 'lacks the political will to sustain the statesman's ambitions. So medium-term strategies exhaust his patience as he presses for evidence of more immediate political results'.[97]

This criticism was an oblique tribute to him. Few figures in public life could pass the test of conceiving, much less adhering to, medium-term strategies. Haughey was more harshly judged because of the expectations his abilities aroused. An accountant by profession, with a capacity to master a brief quickly, he had abundant flair and imagination, immense public self-control, an ability to cut through red tape with an incisiveness that infuriated those wedded to the corruption of bureaucratic mediocrity, and an energy capable of sustaining his insatiable appetite for power. He was patently Taoiseach material. Yet, widely admired for his talents, he was also widely distrusted for his use of those talents. He radiated an aura associated in the public mind with a Renaissance potentate – with his immense wealth (discreetly acquired after his entry to politics), his retinue of loyal retainers, his Florentine penchant for faction fighting, his patronage of the arts, his distinctive personality, at once crafty and conspiratorial, resilient and resourceful, imaginative but insecure. It remained to be seen if he was anything more, despite all his undoubted talents, than solely and simply a political animal in the state of nature.[98] What some felt to be unsavoury specimens in his entourage – unflatteringly described as his 'collection of overdressed bookies runners'[99] – duly provoked the *Irish Times* to wonder, after he had repelled yet one more challenge to his leadership in the frenetic party faction fighting, 'What a pity that he does not have around him people with courage to equal his own, but, even more, with intellect and an unqualified devotion to the welfare of the people of this state'.[100] His detractors would seize on the opportunity offered by the careless 'Duce' rhetoric of an ebullient spokesman to draw the analogy with Mussolini. But there was more to Haughey than to the Mediterranean mountebank. A more apposite analogy could be found closer to home. Haughey exercised much the same public fascination, and for much the same reasons, as another political virtuoso with whom he had temperamentally much in common, David Lloyd George.

It is difficult to assess Haughey's performance after December 1979, and certainly premature to pronounce a final verdict. He did not enjoy,

97 J. O'Malley, 'Can C.J. pass the credibility test?', *Sunday Independent*, 14 October 1984.
98 *Corriere della Sera*, 20 February 1987.   99 Ó hEithir, *The begrudgers*, p. 183.
100 *Irish Times*, 7 October 1982.

during his two tempestuous spells as Taoiseach, in 1979–81, and again in 1982, a clear majority of his own. It is impossible to predict which of his conflicting qualities would predominate in circumstances that enabled him, or obliged him, to take the longer term view. He inherited a bitterly divided party, and a resentful cabinet. It did not help that his own style was the source of much of the resentment.

No Taoiseach except de Valera was as obsessed with his place in history. Still only fifty-four, with a remarkable if chequered career behind him, living and breathing politics, Haughey could aspire to lead the country into the twenty-first century – if only he could win elections. But he might not get far into the 1980s if he lost his first one. Winning the election had to take precedence over everything else. He was not the first party leader to adopt that priority. In the circumstances of December 1979, he had more justification than many. Given the vulnerability of his position, he had to place priority on internal party considerations in shaping his own team, and could pay relatively little attention to actual ability to do the job. His cabinet reflected the pressures on him. Loyalty had to come before efficiency. Some of his appointments, notably Ray MacSharry in Agriculture, and Albert Reynolds in Posts and Telegraphs, performed impressively. Others did not. Some of his Ministers for State were indulgent appointments even by the relaxed standards of political indebtedness.[101]

'We've got what we needed, a strong man, able to handle the political and economic challenges now facing the country', exulted Síle de Valera following Haughey's election.[102] The challenges were certainly there, and even more formidably than Ms de Valera surmised. The fundamental economic problem, exacerbated by policy misjudgements from the beginning of the seventies, now hung like a millstone around the national purse. The year 1979 was truly bruising on the financial front. Net foreign debt jumped from £297 million at the end of 1978 to £1089 million a year later. The deficit in the balance of payments soared from 2.4 per cent of GNP in 1978 to 10.1 per cent in 1979.

If Haughey succeeded to a *damnosa hereditas* in the field of public finance, he was further unfortunate in that no agricultural boom now occurred to carry that sector safely through the difficulties exacerbated by the second oil crisis. On the contrary, agriculture suffered a severe setback. Family farm income is recorded as having actually fallen in money terms, much less in real terms, from £834.5 million in 1978 to £734.3 million in 1979. It would fall further to £673.7 million in 1980.[103]

---

[101] For considerations relevant to particular appointments, see J. O'Malley, *Sunday Independent*, 21 December 1980, and A.M. Duffy, *Sunday Press*, 21 December 1980.

[102] Arnold, *What kind of country?*, p. 141.

[103] New Ireland Forum, *A comparative description of the economic structure and situation, North and South* (Dublin, 1983), p. 61.

Membership of the EMS deprived farmers of windfall gains from green pound devaluations. The end of the five-year transition period to full EEC price levels, smaller price increases under the CAP, bad weather, as well as high and rising interest rates, which bore heavily on those who had borrowed in the expectation of continuing rapid price increases, combined to inflict on farmers a harrowing experience.[104] Net receipts from the EEC, having bounded up from £104 million in 1976 to £448 million in 1979, then levelled out at £457 million in 1980 before actually falling to £387 million in 1981.[105] The problem lay beyond Haughey's control. But the disgruntlement inevitably damaged the government of the day. Haughey could not rely on buoyancy in the agricultural sector, whether political or economic, to cushion severe measures that might be required in the wider economy. Haughey recognised the nature of the problem. It did not, in truth, take exceptional diagnostic powers to grasp that the country, and the government, were living well beyond their means. He spelled out the reality on 9 January 1980 in a television broadcast that would long haunt him.

As a community we are living away beyond our means . . . we are living at a rate which is simply not justified by the amount of goods and services we are producing. To make up the difference we are borrowing enormous amounts of money, borrowing at a rate which just cannot continue . . . we have got to cut down government spending. We will just have to reorganise government spending so that we undertake only the things that we can afford.[106]

What happened next remains one of the major questions to be answered when the definitive history of the period comes to be written. It would seem that the response to the address, presumably not least from deputies in marginal seats to whom he owed much of his support, must have convinced him that prudent financial management would bring political ruin. The question at issue was the character of the Irish people. Would they accept reality? The reaction to his diagnosis must have persuaded him that they would not. He might have quipped, with Tony O'Reilly – but it was a quip in deadly earnest – 'I have seen the enemy and the enemy is us.' The politician in him would have added the more venerable adage, 'if you can't beat them, join them'. He obviously recoiled from the electoral implications of financial responsibility, deciding that what had been sauce for the Lynch goose would remain sauce for the Haughey gander.

There could now be no question of controlling the inflationary impulses arising from deficit financing and permissive national pay agreements. In direct contrast to his television declaration. Haughey judged that the

104 Sheehy, 'Common Agricultural Policy', p. 99.
105 New Ireland Forum, *Comparative description*, p. 117.
106 Browne, 'Who's to blame?', pp. 9–10.

Table 9. *Current budget deficits. 1979–82 (£ million)*

1979	Projected	Actual	Excess of actual over projected
1979	289	522	233 (81%)
1980	347	547	200 (58%)
1981	515	802	287 (56%)
1982	679	988	309 (46%)

Source: T.K. Whitaker, *Interests* (Dublin, 1983), p. 112.

balance of electoral gain still lay in raising taxes rather than reducing 'free' services. Total taxes rose from 33 per cent of GNP in 1979 to 42 per cent in 1982, with indirect taxes accounting for more than half the total increase.[107] The resultant rise in prices naturally helped fuel continuing inflationary wage settlements, particularly in the public sector, protected from the threat of unemployment. The extravagant settlements, occurring at a time when many Irish firms were failing to compete effectively on the home market, much less abroad, virtually guaranteed severe balance of payments deficits, as the extra purchasing power chased after imported goods. Indigenous Irish industry, heavily dependent on the home market, thus became even more vulnerable to the imports sucked into an open uncompetitive economy. Haughey justified the wage settlements, in both the public and the private sectors, on the grounds that financial austerity could only create further unemployment in an already rapidly worsening situation. In the circumstances, this was a travesty of Keynesianism. The consequences of allowing the public finances fall into further disarray would aggravate unemployment in the very near future. But that future, though very near, would still be after the next election. And that was all that now mattered.

The January 1981 budget projected a deficit of £515 million. Haughey was to be severely criticised when the real deficit exceeded £800 million. It would probably have substantially exceeded even this but for the fact that Haughey lost office in June 1981. A corrective supplementary budget introduced by the new government in July helped reduce the size of the deficit. Table 9 summarises the weird budgetary situation.

Disturbing though the figures are, they suggest that Haughey simply continued an already established practice. The excess of actual over projected deficit was in fact proportionately smaller during his years of office than in Lynch's last year. It is true that the 1979 estimates were affected by the second oil crisis, and that the 1981 deficit was reduced

[107] Walsh, 'Ireland in the European Monetary System', p. 187.

Table 10. *Government expenditure, 1977–82 (% GNP)*

	1977	1978	1979	1980	1981	1982
Current	36.1	38.4	39.8	42.8	46.5	50.0
deficit	3.7	6.3	7.1	6.3	7.8	8.4
Capital	12.7	13.4	13.2	15.1	18.4	16.9
deficit	6.3	6.6	6.7	7.8	9.0	8.1
Exchequer borrowing requirement	10.0	12.9	13.8	14.1	16.8	16.5
Total (current plus capital)	48.8	51.8	54.0	57.9	64.9	66.9

Source: OECD Annual Survey, 1983: *Ireland*, p. 21.

through no fault of Haughey's. Nevertheless, if Haughey was a careless big spender, he belonged to what was now the mainstream of political convention on the matter. He just did it with more style, panache and sardonic contempt for the patriotism of the public than anyone else. Whitaker's stern judgement that 'the underestimation of current deficits, and consequently of the Exchequer borrowing requirement, has been so seriously disproportionate as to invalidate the whole budgetary exercise' is of course right.[108] But it was an obvious temptation for a harrassed politician to spend his way out of trouble to an even greater extent than he had initially planned. After all, if the political culture accepts the legitimacy of an unbalanced Budget, why not unbalance it just a bit more in the course of the year as circumstances warrant? Government expenditure naturally soared as a proportion of GNP in the escapist atmosphere of 1977–82. Table 10 records the salient detail.

It was a natural response to the situation he inherited, and to his own penchant for a presidential style, that Haughey should expand the Department of the Taoiseach. He did so partly by abolishing the Department of Economic Planning and Development, a prime target if only to enable him to dismiss O'Donoghue from the cabinet.[109] Many of the new officials in the Taoiseach's office, where the number of administrative grade officers rose from fifteen in 1979 to forty-four in 1981, came from Economic Planning.[110] Other officials in Economic Planning returned to Finance, where, as has been delicately said, 'work was eventually found for them'.[111] With its staff increased, the Department of the Taoiseach was now 'marking' several other departments with its own sections on economic and social, international, cultural and legal affairs.

[108] Whitaker, *Interests*, p. 112.
[109] It could be strongly argued that the Department ought not to have been created in the first place. (See Whitaker, *Interests*, pp. 169–75.) But nobody suspected Haughey of thinking in these terms in December 1979!
[110] Scott, 'Adapting the machinery', p. 79.   [111] *Ibid.*

Noel Whelan, the young Secretary of Economic Planning and Development, moved into the Department of the Taoiseach. An early initiative of
the Haughey–Whelan combination was to launch an inquiry, ultimately
to bear fruit in the Telesis report, into industrial policy. For all Haughey's
preoccupation with the short term, he could recognise the importance of
industrial strategy. This intiative would stimulate in due course the first
serious debate on industrial policy for more than twenty years.[112] But
industrial policy could have little impact on the next election.

The 'efficiency' constituency in the party, recalling Haughey's reputation as a dynamic departmental minister, nostalgically recalling the
golden sixties, expected instant economic miracles. Stubbornly oblivious
to economic reality, ignoring the deterioration in the public finances, and
the growth in the power of vested interests, that restricted his room for
manoeuvre, they expected him to somehow restore the situation without
having to prescribe painful treatment. Precisely because he himself clearly
understood the difficulties of fulfilling the extravagant hopes reposed in
him by this constituency, he felt obliged to appeal even more raucously to
the 'republican' element in the party.

Haughey played the green card with skill. It was no easy task. He had to
square the circle between keeping both his own republican wing, and Mrs
Thatcher, happy. He satisfied his own supporters through a nubile display
of political body language that once again underlined his sheer political
artistry on his home ground. His tactic was to deal directly with London,
and ignore Ulster unionists on the grounds that the North was a failed
political entity, as he declared at the Fianna Fáil Árd Fheis of February
1980. It could not be restored to 'normalcy' because it never had been
normal. There could therefore be no purely internal settlement. New
institutional arrangements, which would shade into new constitutional
arrangements, must be found. He succeeded in establishing relatively
cordial relations with Mrs Thatcher in December 1980, when she agreed
to the initiation of joint Anglo-Irish studies of particular areas of potential
cooperation, with a view to discussing at their next meeting in 1981 'the
totality of relationships within these islands'. It was a notable negotiating
achievement.

However, in an unfortunate lapse, forgetting that he was now playing
on a bigger stage than an Árd Fheis platform, Haughey undermined the
achievement by exaggerating its extent. He insisted on describing it as an
historic turning point in Anglo-Irish relations, when it was only a
potentially historic one. By flaunting the intention for the achievement, he
undermined its prospects.[113] Public restraint would have served the cause
better at this stage. His performance, together with the secrecy surround-

112 See below, pp. 531ff.   113 Downey, *Them and us*, pp. 192–3.

ing the talks, enabled Ian Paisley to portray the apparently emerging Anglo-Irish accord as a dagger pointed at the heart of Protestant Ulster.

Haughey constantly proclaimed his good intentions towards Ulster unionists. There was no objective reason to doubt his sincerity. But his style could provoke scepticism. At one stage he appeared to offer unionists a separate constitution if only they recognised Dublin sovereignty. But if the difference between North and South was so wide that separate constitutions were required, did this not confirm the legitimacy of the unionist demand for self-determination? On another occasion he assured Ulster Protestants they would be 'surprised' at the lengths to which he would go to meet their fears and satisfy their aspirations in a united Ireland. Again, there was no reason to doubt his commitment. If any politician could find a constitutional formula for squaring the circle between the claims of the Catholic Church and Protestant insistence on the primacy of individual conscience, it was Haughey. But he refrained from elaborating on the nature of the 'surprise'. This was understandable in terms of domestic Southern politics. Revelation of his potential flexibility could only have offended the susceptibilities of important vested interests. But he can hardly have expected his reluctance to reassure his putative Protestant audience.

Having handsomely won a Donegal by-election in November 1980, extracted gratifying publicity from his meeting with Mrs Thatcher, and introduced a permissive Budget in January, Haughey seemed poised to call an election in the spring of 1981. He knew that matters were likely to get worse before they got better (or worse again!) on the economic front, and that he could not stave off the day of reckoning for the licentiousness of the seventies much longer. The consumer price index, which rose 18.2 per cent in 1980, would rise by 20.4 per cent in 1981. Registered unemployment, having risen by 12 000 in 1980, would rise by 26 000 in 1981. A spring election would give him the breathing space he needed. But Haughey began to suffer an extraordinary run of bad luck just from this time. He was due to deliver his presidential speech to the Fianna Fáil Árd Fheis, almost certainly intended as an election Árd Fheis, on 15 February. The night before, St Valentine's night, a fire at the Stardust ballroom in his own constituency claimed 48 victims, and left more than 150 injured, many with hideous burns. He felt obliged to postpone, and eventually to cancel, the Árd Fheis. Then the second big IRA hunger strike, led by Bobby Sands, began in the Maze on 1 March. When Haughey called the general election for June, still a full year before the end of his term, but presumably the last date at which he felt circumstances might enable him to appear in command of the situation, he found the opposition concentrating on the economy, while he had to fight mainly on Ulster, the standard pattern for winner and loser in 1977 and 1973. His calculations were badly upset when 9 H-block candidates were nominated, thus siphoning off votes from precisely the republican constituency that Haughey had laboured so assiduously to cultivate.

In the election, Fianna Fáil's share of the vote fell from 50.6 per cent to 45.3 per cent, Fine Gael's jumped from 30.5 per cent to 36.5 per cent, and Labour's fell from 11.6 per cent to 9.9 per cent. In terms of seats, Fianna Fáil won 78 out of 166 compared with 84 out of 148 in 1977, Fine Gael 65 compared with 43, and Labour 15 instead of 17. Independents of various hues won 8 seats, including 2 by H-block candidates. Fianna Fáil would normally have expected to win these, which, allied to the support of Neil Blaney, might just have sufficed for Haughey to retain office. The result was clearly a major advance for Fine Gael, and a setback for Fianna Fáil, but the outcome left so finely-balanced a situation that a new election was likely fairly soon anyway.

AT THE END OF THE RAINBOW?

Following an agreement between Fine Gael and Labour, now under Michael O'Leary, who succeeded as leader when Frank Cluskey lost his seat in the election, Garret FitzGerald was elected Taoiseach on 30 June, with the support of several independent deputies. He brought to the office a remarkable combination of qualifications, having already enjoyed, by the age of fifty-four, an exceptional career. He had been lucky in the timing of his entry to the Dáil. He had spent only four years in opposition before the coalition's unexpected victory in 1973, and had not succumbed to the cynicism that longer periods in opposition can foster. He was lucky in being appointed to Foreign Affairs instead of Finance in 1973. He was lucky again in the extent of the government defeat in 1977, which opened the way to the leadership without a fight. But he had shown the talent to make the most of his luck. And since his election as party leader in 1977 he had, through the aegis of Peter Prendergast, a marketing executive whom he appointed to reorganise and sell the party, transformed Fine Gael from a collection of individuals of varying degrees of professionalism, into a tightly-knit organisation. Fine Gael took a leaf out of Fianna Fáil's book, and by 1981 was already an organisational match for the old enemy.[114] For a leader elected as a man of ideas rather than an organisation man, this was itself a striking achievement. Fine Gael's impressive gains in the general election partly reflected this improvement in organisation, as well as the personal appeal of FitzGerald, reinforced by disillusion with Fianna Fáil. But sustained success can breed carelessness, a lack of attention to political details. Only time would tell whether his luck would hold, and whether, on assuming office during 'a national mood of dithering des-

114 O'Byrnes, *Hiding behind a face*, p. 94.

pair',[115] circumstances and temperament would allow him to fulfil his potential.[116]

FitzGerald immediately gave evidence of an unsuspected toughness, and exposed internal tensions in Fine Gael whose depth had been kept concealed more skilfully than those in Fianna Fáil, when he refused to appoint to his cabinet, much to their disgruntlement, three former ministers, Richie Ryan, Dick Burke and Tom O'Donnell.[117] And he faced the two threats that dominated the previous decade, the financial and the Northern, with immediate firmness.

A protest march by supporters of H-block hunger strikers on 18 July left such a trail of destruction in the vicinity of the British Embassy in Dublin that the question of internal security loomed large once more in the public mind. The Minister for Justice, Jim Mitchell, showed a striking sureness of touch in handling an ugly situation, defusing the threat with a nicely judged combination of firmness and restraint.

The financial situation was even worse than FitzGerald had feared. Spending was already far exceeding the level of the substantial predicted deficit. FitzGerald's young Minister for Finance, John Bruton, brought in an emergency July Budget, sharply increasing taxation, and adopting a surprisingly austere approach for a government so reliant on independents. The speed with which the emergency budget was introduced suggested that Finance officials had been vainly pressing this on the previous government, and that somewhat similar proposals might have been introduced had Haughey himself been returned to office with a working majority.[118]

Haughey faced his own problems in opposition. He had failed either to reconcile or rout his enemies in the party. With his reputation for efficiency tarnished, he found himself increasingly obliged to rely on his guile, on his skill as an operator rather than on his ability as an achiever. In December 1981 one of his original supporters, Charlie McCreevey, attacked him in a newspaper interview.[119] But the resulting furore in Fianna Fáil was soon overshadowed by a cabinet own-goal. Fitzgerald fell when Bruton's January Budget was defeated. Independents on whose support the government had hitherto been able to rely voted against a politically inept imposition of value added tax on children's clothing and footwear on 27 January 1982.

In the ensuing February general election, Fianna Fáil increased its share of the vote from 45 per cent to 47.3 per cent, and its number of seats from

[115] V. Buckley, *Memory Ireland* (Harmondsworth, 1985), p. 199.
[116] For a sympathetic but discerning portrait, see P. Lynch, 'Garret Fitzgerald: a personal memoir', in J. Dooge (ed.), *Ireland in the contemporary world: essays in honour of Garret FitzGerald* (Dublin, 1986), pp. 28–36.
[117] O'Byrnes, *Hiding behind a face*, pp. 103–5.
[118] *Ibid.*, pp. 113–17.   [119] *Sunday Tribune*, 27 December 1981.

78 to 81. Fine Gael actually increased its share of the vote from 36.5 per cent to 37.3 per cent, but lost 2 seats, falling from 65 to 63. This was a remarkable performance in the circumstances, given that the government had preached and even practised austerity during its seven months in office, and had fallen on the first Budget in a decade that strove to face reality. Labour held 15 seats on a slightly reduced poll. There were 7 others, including 3 Workers' Party TDs. Haughey became Taoiseach once more, after foiling a bid by Desmond O'Malley for the party leadership,[120] and negotiating the 'Gregory deal' in which he outbid FitzGerald for the support of a new independent TD from the Dublin central constituency, Tony Gregory. Critics denounced the idea of a special deal as disgraceful, allegedly debasing the political coinage. What was disgraceful in this case was less the deal than the fact that it needed a deal to win some attention for one of the most deprived areas of the country, an inner city constituency ravaged by poverty and neglect, and their concomitants, unemployment, bad housing and a vicious drugs problem.

Haughey continued to show the stuff of which he was made by disappointing expectations in his own party of the coveted vacant Irish commissionership in Brussels, following Michael O'Kennedy's return to domestic politics. Haughey audaciously offered the post to Dick Burke, the previous Fine Gael commissioner, now representing a constituency that Fianna Fáil could reasonably hope to win, and in the person of Haughey's sister-in-law, Eileen Lemass, who had lost her seat in February. Great therefore was the consternation when Fine Gael actually won the by-election in May, despite a campaign by Fianna Fáil that displayed signal solicitude, even by by-election standards, for voter sensitivity.[121] Even a highly publicised attempt to co-opt General Galtieri as a Fianna Fáil election agent by performing somersaults on Irish policy on the Anglo-Argentinian war in an effort to seduce the anglophobe vote in the constituency, improbably rationalised by reference to higher ideals in international relations, failed to deliver the goods. It was a mortifying result.

Haughey's Finance Minister, Ray MacSharry, initially poured scorn on coalition purveyors of 'gloom and doom', promising instead 'boom and bloom'. However, the horrible realities of the situation impinged on him as the country continued to live beyond its means, with the net foreign debt rising from £3451 million at the end of 1981 to £5114 million a year later. MacSharry belatedly announced in July 1982 the postponement of a 5 per cent instalment in the pay rises for public servants negotiated under the latest national pay agreement, as well as a series of spending cuts. Government began to prepare a new plan, *The way forward* designed to

---

[120] Joyce and Murtagh, *Boss*, pp. 26–44.
[121] *Ibid.*, p. 173; O'Byrnes, *Hiding behind a face*, pp. 176–9.

adjust, at long last, economic policy, if not quite to the underlying realities, at least in their general direction, rather than pretending that the realities could be ignored indefinitely and the country live as if tomorrow would never come. It seemed that Haughey was finally determined to treat the disease he had diagnosed in January 1980, but whose spread he had since been instrumental in assisting.

The way forward, largely the work of Pádraig Ó hUigínn, Secretary of the Taoiseach's Department, was published in October, and committed the government to the phasing out of the huge deficit by 1986.[122] It seemed as if the profligate was at last donning the hairshirt – though simultaneously raising his eyes to the uplands in the distance if only the path of virtue were pursued, for the plan also assumed a 5 per cent growth rate until 1987! It has to be assumed that the more optimistic projections were more the handiwork of politicians than of civil servants.

Repentance had to be its own reward, however. *The way forward* had soon to double as an election manifesto. For luck again deserted Haughey. McCreevey ruptured the fragile unity of the party by introducing a motion of no confidence in Haughey as leader in September. Haughey won, after a lacerating debate on 6 October, by a 58 to 22 majority.[123] But the tension was hardly conducive to effective government. Haughey had no time to enjoy his victory. Bill Loughnane, TD for Clare, died suddenly. Jim Gibbons, TD for Carlow–Kilkenny, suffered a serious heart attack that kept him from the Dáil. Though Gibbons and Haughey were bitter enemies since the arms trial of 1970, when the judge had declared their evidence on oath to be irreconcilable – Gibbons was Minister for Defence at the time – Haughey desperately needed every vote in so tight a parliamentary situation. The Workers' Party chose this precise moment to withdraw its support from Haughey in protest at *The way forward*. When Fine Gael snatched the opportunity to win a motion of no confidence, Haughey was forced to seek a dissolution of the Dáil.

In the November general election, Haughey fought an anti-British campaign, in the hope of capturing seats in key marginals renowned for their less than ecumenical attitude towards the sister isle. Fine Gael, unable to seriously criticise *The way forward*, which adopted much of its own economic programme, concentrated on Haughey's credibility, presenting Garret FitzGerald as the more trustworthy leader. Haughey's credibility had indeed suffered during a summer distinguished by a series of such improbable events that Haughey himself was moved to describe one of them, the location of a murder suspect in the apartment of the unsuspecting Attorney General, as 'grotesque, unprecedented, bizarre and unbelievable'. Conor Cruise O'Brien, not renowned as an ardent admirer

[122] *The way forward: National economic plan 1983–1987* (Dublin, 1982), p. 18.
[123] Joyce and Murtagh, *Boss*, pp. 262–5.

of Haughey, instantly christened the government the Gubu government, its image tarnished by a variety of other and far more unsavoury episodes, or rumours of episodes, in which the Minister for Justice, Seán Doherty, featured prominently.[124]

Labour's main attraction appeared to be a new leader, the 32-year-old Dick Spring, catapulted into the leadership after Michael O'Leary decided to join Fine Gael a few weeks before the election, driven to desperation by the repudiation of his views on coalition by the party, and by a decision-making process which itself offered rich material for the student of the grotesque and the bizarre.

Haughey suffered a severe setback in the election. Fianna Fáil's share of the vote fell from 47.3 per cent to 45.2 per cent, Fine Gael's climbed from 37.3 per cent to 39.2 per cent, while Labour rose slightly from 9.1 per cent to 9.4 per cent. In terms of seats, Fianna Fáil lost 6, while Fine Gael gained 7 and Labour 1. When Fitzgerald and Spring cobbled together a joint programme for government after the election, FitzGerald became Taoiseach with a clear working majority. With Fine Gael's 70 seats and Labour's 16, the government had 86 seats out of 166. The country could anticipate its first period of stable government for some years. FitzGerald seemed to have got what both Haughey and he himself had hitherto been denied, a safe majority. It remained to be seen what he would make of it.

[124] O'Byrnes, *Hiding behind a face*, pp. 197ff.

Chapter 8

PERSPECTIVES

How well has independent Ireland performed? Opinions naturally differ on the quality of the cultural, intellectual and spiritual performance, where criteria of assessment are highly subjective. Opinions differ too on the quality of social and economic performance. But here it should be possible to focus the discussion on more impersonal issues. Two criteria for assessing a country's material performance are the number of citizens it can support, and the standard of living at which it can support them. Table 11 places the Irish population performance in western European perspective.

It is clear that population grew exceptionally slowly in both North and South. Both also had population densities well below the western European average of 175 in 1983/4. The implications of this exceptional experience can be addressed from a number of viewpoints. Had the South achieved the average western European growth rate of about 50 per cent since independence, she would now have a population of 4.5 million instead of 3.5 million. The North would now have nearly 1.9 million, compared with 1.6. However, Ireland was already a demographic oddity in the early twentieth century, with a population density far below the western European average. If Ireland approximated to that average, the South would now have a population of about 12 million, the North nearly 3 million.

There is nothing sacrosanct about average rates of growth or average densities. There may be many valid reasons for wide divergencies between countries recording broadly comparable general levels of socio-economic performance. But even by the most relaxed criteria, the actual population path followed by Ireland, especially by the South, was distinctive. The only countries with densities below the South, Finland, Sweden and Norway, have huge areas of uninhabitable land. Their real density is far higher than their recorded density. Sweden's density, for instance, is just ten times

Table 11. *Population, 1919–84 (selected countries)*

	1919[a]	1983/4[b]	Approximate increase %	Inhabitants per km² 1983/4[c]
Austria	6.4	7.6	19	90
Belgium	7.6	9.9	30	323
Denmark	3.0	5.1	55	119
England/Scotland/Wales	42.8	54.5 (1981)	28	c. 225
Finland	3.1	4.9	55	14
France	39.0	54.9	40	100
Germany (West)[d]	43.0	61.2	40	246
Greece	5.0	9.8	96	75
Italy	35.9	57.0	58	189
Netherlands	6.8	14.4	110	387
Norway	2.7	4.1	60	13
Portugal	6.4	10.1	58	110
Spain	21.0	38.2	75	76
Sweden	5.8	88.3	40	19
Switzerland	3.9	6.5	60	157
N. Ireland[e]	1.26	1.6	27	111
S. Ireland[f]	3.14	3.5	12	50

Notes:

[a] B.R. Mitchell, 'Statistical appendix', in C.M. Cipolla (ed.), *Fontana economic history of Europe*, 6 (2) (London, 1976), pp. 642–3.

[b] OECD, *Basic statistics: international comparisons*.

[c] Ibid.

[d] For 1939 rather than 1919. See Mitchell, *Historical statistics*, p. 20.

[e] Vaughan and Fitzpatrick, *Historical statistics*, pp. 10–13; *New Ireland Forum: a comparative description of the economic structure and situation, North and South* (Dublin, 1983), p. 8.

[f] Vaughan and Fitzpatrick, *Historical statistics*, pp. 11–16.

higher in relation to cultivated area than to total area.[1] Our calculations are not intended to provide retrospective justification for those nationalists who, in the early twentieth century, blithely claimed that Ireland could support four or five times its then population. Prolific nationalist conceivers of population rarely paused, in their more exotic flights of procreative fancy, to ponder the standard of living they envisaged for the increased population. A population of that size could not have been sustained at the then average standard of living without extensive industrialisation. The highest recorded Irish population, more than 8 000 000 in 1841, lived at a miserable level. But that was no longer the

[1] Swedish Institute, *The Swedish economy: Facts and figures 1986* (Stockholm, 1986), p. 4.

Table 12. *National product per capita, 1910 (selected countries) (at 1910 exchange rates)*

Belgium	75.6
Germany	70.3
France	69.6
Denmark	67.6
Ireland	62.0
Norway	60.4
Sweden	60.3
Italy	40.5
Finland	34.6

Sources: N.F.R. Crafts, 'Gross national product in Europe 1870–1910: some new estimates', *Explorations in economic history*, 20 (1983), p. 390; L.M. Cullen and T.C. Smout, 'Economic growth in Scotland and Ireland', in Cullen and Smout (eds.), *Comparative aspects of Scottish and Irish economic and social history 1600–1900* (Edinburgh, n.d.), p. 13. The Irish proportion is a ratio of the United Kingdom level in 1911.

issue by the twentieth century. Both population and living standards had risen together throughout the western world from the mid nineteenth century. What seemed fantasy in the fond musings of the ideologues does not seem so fantastic in comparative perspective, had Ireland followed a more representative western European course. The biggest demographic fantasy of all was the actual population experience of Ireland in the past century.

The rationale for controlling population through a combination of relatively few marriages, relatively late marriages, and emigration, was that it enabled an otherwise unattainable standard of living to be sustained. Did then the Irish route justify itself by achieving a rate of improvement in per capita income superior to that of countries whose populations grew so much more rapidly?

There are notorious difficulties in comparing the standard of living between countries at the same time, much less over a long period. The estimates are in a state of permanent transition. Much work remains to be done. For our present purposes, however, precise accuracy is not necessary. It will suffice if the orders of magnitude are broadly correct. All we need to establish is whether Ireland was peculiarly impoverished by western European standards on the eve of independence, and whether she has significantly improved her relative standing since then.

The simplest way to place the Irish position in the early twentieth century in perspective is to compare Ireland's standing relative to Britain with that of those continental countries for which relatively reliable estimates of per capita income exist. Table 12 summarises our current state of knowledge.

The point at issue here is not the precise ranking, or even the precise ratios. Other estimates give somewhat different rankings, and rather different ratios.[2] But all reinforce the impression conveyed by our table that Ireland was *not* impoverished by western European standards.

The Ireland involved here is the thirty-two counties. It may be held that per capita income in the twenty-six counties was significantly lower than in the six counties. Contrary to popular opinion, this does not appear to have been the case. In the immediate postwar period, per capita incomes seem to have been very similar in the two parts of the country.[3] The South did well out of the First World War. So did the North. Per capita income in the Free State appears to have risen relative to that of Britain after the war, reaching 67 per cent of the United Kingdom level in 1926.[4] A ratio of between three-fifths and two-thirds for the twenty-six counties does not therefore appear improbable for the early twentieth century. Whatever differences may have existed between North and South in 1910/11 would not have significantly altered the standing of the twenty-six counties relative to general western European incomes.

The picture looked very different by 1970. Ireland recorded the slowest growth of per capita income between 1910 and 1970 of any European country except the United Kingdom. Every country ranked above Ireland in the early twentieth century pulled much further ahead. Every country below Ireland either overtook her, or significantly narrowed the gap. The result was that Ireland slid from being a reasonably representative western European economy, in terms of income per head, at the time of independence, to a position far below the western European average in 1970.[5]

Income per capita is itself an indulgent criterion by which to assess Irish achievement. Precisely because of the unique Irish population performance, a wide gap opened between developments at the individual and the national levels. Not even such notoriously sluggish performers as Great Britain and Northern Ireland lagged as badly as Ireland in terms of national income. The Irish growth rate came at the bottom of the European table by a long way. No other European country, east or west, north or south, for which remotely reliable evidence exists, has recorded

---

[2] P. Bairoch, 'The main trends in national economic disparities since the Industrial Revolution', in P. Bairoch and M. Levy-Leboyer (eds.), *Disparities in economic development since the Industrial Revolution* (London, 1981), p. 10; P. Bairoch, 'L'Economie suisse dans le contexte européen: 1913–1939', *Schweizerische Zeitschrift für Geschichte*, 34, 4 (1984), p. 494; A. Milward and S.B. Saul, *The development of the economies of continental Europe 1850–1914* (London, 1977), p. 515; Cullen and Smout, *Economic growth*, p. 13.

[3] D. Johnson, *The inter-war economy in Ireland* (Dundalk, 1985), pp. 39, 43.

[4] Cullen and Smout, *Economic growth*, p. 14. It is possible that the ratio was even higher.

[5] Bairoch, 'Main trends', p. 10.

so slow a rate of growth of national income in the twentieth century.[6] By this criterion, the strategy of ruthless population control proved a resounding failure, however resourcefully the tactic itself had come to be used.

May it not be misleading, however, to lay so much weight on the figures for 1970? Had not Irish growth rates improved rapidly in the 1960s? Did not Irish rates, however adversely affected by the oil crisis, compare favourably with those of the OECD during the 1970s? Did not Ireland enjoy the highest growth rate of any OECD country in 1978? And did not population increase during the 1970s at a rapid rate, reversing the trend of a century and more? All that is true. But the figures flatter only to deceive. The growth rates recorded for the 1970s, and increasingly for the later seventies, are largely bogus. Insofar as they record real growth, this was achieved only by plunging into debt on a massive scale to sustain a standard of living that the Irish would not earn for themselves. Ireland was still a creditor country, as she had been since independence, in 1970. By 1975 a total state foreign debt of £688 000 000 had been incurred. The external reserves covered most of this, however. The net state foreign debt still came to only £12 000 000, or about £4 per head of population. By 1985, the net state foreign debt had soared to £8 092 000 000, or to £2269 per head of population.[7] Even allowing for inflation, the figures reflect a gadarene rush into debt, as the Irish chose to live in a ne'er do well fashion, frittering away the inherited savings of generations in little more than a decade. The price soon began to be paid. The slump of the eighties was in large measure the direct consequence of the nature of the 'boom' of the later seventies. The rate of population growth declined quickly in the early eighties, with marriage rate falling, birth rate falling, and emigration rising once more. The sixties now seemed a long time ago, a mere mirage.

The role of the population growth of the seventies in exacerbating, or even causing, unemployment was a matter of dispute. The relationship between demographic and economic variables is a highly complex one. The Southern rate of population growth surged far above the European average during the seventies, though it would fall quickly during the eighties. If population rose from 3 million to 3.5 million between 1966 and 1986, would not this alone largely explain (if not over-explain!) a rise of 200 000 in the number of recorded unemployed? Many politicians laboured to cultivate this impression. By mechanistically counting the rising number of new jobs required to provide employment for the growing population, the policy-makers could try to impress on the public the herculean scale of the challenge they confronted – and exonerate

6 P. Bairoch, 'Europe's gross national product, 1800–1975', *Journal of European Economic History*, 5, 2 (Fall 1976), p. 307.
7 P. Tansey, 'The foreign debt burden gets heavier', *Sunday Tribune*, 8 June 1986.

themselves in advance for responsibility for failure. How valid was this approach?

If population growth was a major contributory factor to high unemployment, this puts earlier Irish performance in an even more lurid comparative light. Ireland managed to achieve higher unemployment levels than most European countries during the preceding decades when their populations were rising much more rapidly than hers. Without lingering over that polemical but not irrelevant point, it is possible that population growth could have had adverse consequences, at least in the short term, by increasing the dependency ratio. But the dependency ratio was actually higher during the booming sixties than during the seventies and eighties.[8] The age composition of the dependents did, it is true, change. The proportion over sixty-five declined, while that under fifteen rose. If there was a direct relationship between population growth and unemployment one might therefore expect an exceptionally high level of youth unemployment as the younger generation came on the job market. But Irish youth unemployment was not exceptionally heavy by EEC or OECD standards.[9] This was probably due to the fact that much of the actual unemployment was caused by jobs lost in existing industry. The claim that 'over a hundred thousand new jobs' were created outside the public service in 1979, 1980 and 1981 exaggerates the level of the achievement.[10] By no means all these jobs would prove viable. Nevertheless, there was achievement. But the 40 000 new jobs created in manufacturing industry in 1980 and 1981 were more than offset by a loss of 54 000 existing jobs.[11] This was due at least partly to a loss of competitiveness on the home market, where export penetration 'increased from 29 per cent in 1977 to 37.5 per cent in 1980'.[12] This loss of jobs owed little to rising population, at least directly. In these circumstances, unemployment would have risen sharply even with a stagnant population. The workers who lost their jobs could not transfer easily into new sectors. They were often the wrong age, the wrong sex, with redundant skills, and with the wrong work ethic to satisfy employers in the new export sectors. Northern Ireland had a quite different demographic history from the Republic. It experienced none of the population growth of the seventies. Yet its unemployment levels also rose rapidly. The increase was exacerbated by the Troubles. But many of the same underlying causes existed as in the South, independently either of political factors or of population change.

8 Cooperation North, *Economic Indicators in Northern Ireland and the Republic of Ireland* (Dublin, 1983), p. 37.
9 T. Corcoran, 'Irish Youth Employment Policies in the 1980s', *Administration*, 33, 2 (1985), p. 259; B.M. Walsh, 'Youth unemployment; the economic background', *ibid.*, pp. 159–61.
10 *The way forward*, p. 10. 11 *Ibid.*, p. 33. 12 *Ibid.*, p. 44.

The rate of Irish population growth, even at its peak of 1.4 per cent per annum during the seventies, did not significantly exceed the 1.2 per cent per annum for Japan and Canada, or the 1.1 per cent per annum for the United States. Indeed, the rate of growth of the labour force was higher in the United States than in Ireland.[13] Yet American unemployment rates remained far below the Irish levels. And if the American analogy be inappropriate, the Irish rate of both population and labour force growth was equalled or exceeded in several lesser developed countries, where nevertheless 'employment in the traditional manufacturing, service and informal sectors has grown much more rapidly than would be required to absorb the growth of the Irish labour force'.[14] If population growth proved more a problem than an opportunity in Ireland, then it is to the internal arrangements for the conduct of Irish affrairs, including the rigidities reflected in the restrictive structures and mentalities fostered by the primacy of the possessor principle, that the explanation should be sought. There was no inevitable correlation between rising population and rising unemployment. Population growth, in short, was more an excuse than an explanation for soaring unemployment.

At first sight, the rates of growth of gross domestic product in the first half of the 1980s did not seem to justify the general mood of depression. True, they fell sharply from the annual average of 4.6 per cent from 1975 to 1980, to only 1.8 per cent from 1980 to 1985.[15] But 'only 1.8 per cent', however modest by the standards of the sixties, still exceeded the trend rate of growth from 1920 to 1960. And it did not fall too far below the OECD average. Unfortunately, gross domestic product was no longer a reasonably reliable indicator of national economic fortunes. Gross *domestic* product represents the value of national output. Gross *national* product represents the share of this output that a country is able to retain for itself. In the 1975–80 period, the rate of growth of GNP was already lagging behind that of GDP. Between 1980 and 1985, GNP not only lagged further behind GDP, but actually fell in absolute terms. In the jargon of the economists, Ireland achieved negative growth.

The divergence between GDP and GNP was no accident. It was the inevitable consequence of the policy choices made by successive governments. As borrowing spiralled upwards during the seventies, interest payments on the debt began to consume a growing proportion of national income. Total state debt, domestic and foreign, reached 128 per cent of GNP in 1984, the highest figure in the OECD. Public sector *foreign* debt amounted to about 70 per cent of GNP, and the country

---

[13] B.M. Walsh, 'Employment: a private sector strategy', *IBR* (June 1985), pp. 44–5.
[14] *Ibid.*, pp. 46–7.
[15] NESC, *A strategy for development 1986–1990* (Dublin, 1986), p. 8.

had reached the point where it was borrowing abroad to pay the interest on earlier borrowing.[16]

Debt repayment had now become the biggest single millstone around the national financial neck. It was not that the borrowing policy was necessarily wrong in itself. Borrowing for productive purposes can make sense. Interest can be paid out of the return on the initial investment in due course. But much Irish borrowing continued to be for consumption purposes, mainly by financing wage increases, particularly in the public sector. Even the proportion nominally directed to investment was at least partly squandered. The exceptionally high incremental capital–output ratio, 50 per cent higher than for most OECD countries, suggested that 'the return on much public investment has been low and sometimes even negative'.[17] Nor could the disappointing return on public capital investment in Ireland be attributed mainly to the type of objective factor in the structure of the economy that helps explain, for example, the traditionally high Norwegian capital–output ratio.[18] It would appear that the explanation has to be sought mainly in a combination of incompetence in conceptualisation, and profligacy in implementation.[19]

A second reason for the widening gap between GDP and GNP was the repatriation of profits earned by foreign investors in Ireland. This was the inevitable consequence of reliance on foreign investment as the main engine of industrial development. Repatriated profits, dividends and royalties rose five-fold from £258 million in 1980 to £1321 million in 1985.[20] This equalled 22 per cent of the value of manufactured exports. As no other western European economy relied on a strategy that left it owing so much to foreigners, whether through direct debt payments or through profit repatriation, the comparison of Irish performance with that of other European countries in terms of GDP exaggerates the quality of the Irish performance since the mid-seventies.

A third factor affecting the relationship between GDP and GNP raises a variety of other issues. Because tax concessions were a central feature of industrial policy, it was naturally in the interests of the multi-national companies with branches in Ireland to exaggerate the profits attributed to their Irish operations. This could be achieved by the delicately contrived device of transfer pricing, by which they understated the cost incurred by their Irish enterprises, and exaggerated their earnings. The result was that

---

[16] OECD, Economic surveys 1984–1985, *Ireland* (Paris, April 1985), p. 31.
[17] *Ibid.*, p. 30.
[18] *Ibid.*, p. 54, n. 20; p. 28.
[19] D. McAleese, 'Is there a want of capital in Ireland?', *Administration*, 31, 4 (1984), pp. 389–411.
[20] NESC, *Strategy*, p. 12.

exports, industrial production, and ultimately GDP may all have been exaggerated.[21]

The consequence of Irish spending and borrowing policies was a sharp rise in taxation from 38 per cent of national income in 1978 to 52 per cent in 1984. Between 1974 and 1984 taxes on personal incomes rose at more than double the rate of inflation.[22] The widespread feeling that real living standards were falling during the early eighties was no consumer illusion. Personal disposable income fell about 12 per cent between 1979 and 1982.[23]

The main excuse for the borrowing splurge was that it would reduce unemployment. Judging from the use made of the money, the main objective was to curry votes by granting unjustifiable wage increases, particularly in the sheltered sector, where employees not only continued to enjoy security, but rising wages and salaries as well, at the expense of those in the exposed sector. The bulk of the borrowing therefore amounted to a covert conspiracy between politicians and the more advantageously placed groups, intent on maintaining public office on the one hand, and rising incomes on the other, at the expense of more vulnerable sections in exposed sectors. In the circumstances, borrowing did not reduce unemployment except in the shortest of short terms. It probably exacerbated it in the medium term, much less the long term. By 1985, Ireland had the second highest recorded unemployment in the OECD. It probably had the highest real unemployment, if one were to take into account the renewed emigration, as well as the variety of 'make work' schemes devised to artificially deflate the unemployment statistics, to say nothing of the non-recording of a significant proportion of potential women workers. All comparisons must be treated circumspectly. Many countries engaged in dubious practices to finesse their unemployment figures. This may be one area, however, in which the Irish were no laggards.

Pundits regularly proclaimed that Ireland was only suffering from the same malaise that afflicted western economies in general. This claim cannot survive scrutiny. Several small countries including Switzerland, Austria, Finland, Sweden, and Norway reached only one-third the Irish unemployment rate. Even Denmark, which occasionally succumbed to inanities of Hibernian vintage, reached little more than half the Irish level of unemployment in 1985.[24]

21 J. O'Leary, 'Some implications of the revisions to the balance of payments and the national accounts', *IBR* (September 1984), p. 33.
22 P. Tansey, 'Money matters', *Sunday Tribune*, 2 June 1985.
23 Cooperation North, *Economic indicators*, p. 49.
24 L. Wrigley, 'Ireland in economic space', in J.J. Lee (ed.), *Ireland: towards a sense of place* (Cork, 1985), p. 79. I am grateful to Professor Wrigley for valuable discussion of several issues in this chapter.

Some achievements were recorded under the FitzGerald government. The consumer price index, which rose 20.4 per cent in 1981 rose 'only' 5.4 per cent in 1985. The balance of payments deficit fell from a staggering 14.7 per cent of GNP in 1981 to 3.6 per cent in 1985.[25] If the total public foreign debt continued to rise rapidly, nevertheless the rate of increase in foreign borrowing was reduced in 1984 and 1985. These were not insignificant achievements. But they were largely negative ones. They merely began to compensate for earlier excrescences. And even then they were facilitated by the continuing grants from the EEC, and by an improvement in the terms of trade.[26]

There may be a danger that a decade or more of wanton irresponsibility in the handling of the public finances will unduly influence our judgement on longer term national performance. Even if the sixties are included, however, the verdict on Irish economic achievements since 1945 has to be unenthusiastic. Relatively backward countries, such as Ireland had become by the postwar period, are normally expected to 'catch up' with more advanced economies, at least once they have acquired the growth habit. The theory is not very rigorous. The European experience, however, is clear. 'The thirty years of growth after World War Two were characterised by an even more rapid development of the poorest of the developed countries', which 'brought about a very sharp reduction in the disparities of income.'[27] Ireland features as the solitary exception. Even her unprecedently rapid average annual growth rate of GNP per capita between 1960 and 1974 still fell below the average for any of the three main trading blocks, the EEC, EFTA or COMECON. On this scale, Ireland ranked eighteenth of twenty-four European economies for which figures are available.[28]

Ireland did duly experience the main mechanism contributing to the 'catching up' process, the sectoral shift of labour from lower productivity agriculture to higher productivity industry and services. Finland, the northern European economy which had, next to Ireland, the highest proportion of its labour force in the primary sector in 1950, has had much of its impressive subsequent performance attributed to precisely this shift.[29] The impact of the shift on Irish growth proved disappointing.

One consequence of Ireland's sustained slippage in the comparative league table was that it became extremely difficult for her to close the gap with even the western European average, much less with the leaders. As the Telesis report pointed out in 1982, 'though Ireland has been improv-

---

[25] NESC, *Strategy*, pp. 10–11.   [26] *Ibid.*, p. 10.   [27] Bairoch, *Main trends*, p. 12.

[28] R. Stone, 'Discussion of M. Abramovitz, "Rapid growth potential and its realisation: the experience of capitalist economies in the postwar world"', in E. Malinvaud (ed.), *Economic growth and resources*: vol. 1: *The major issues* (London, 1979), pp. 36–7.

[29] P.S. Andersen and J. Åkerholm, 'Scandinavia', in A. Boltho (ed.), *The European economy* (Oxford, 1982), p. 618.

ing its living standards, the income gap between it and most other industrialised countries has seriously widened over the past twenty years'.[30] The base from which Ireland started in 1960 was so much lower than the average that similar percentage rates of growth meant smaller absolute additions to income, and left Ireland lagging cumulatively further behind. If she now aspires after western European levels of income, therefore, quite spectactular growth rates, far exceeding the average, are necessary.

Rankings at any given time do not necessarily offer a reliable guide to subsequent performance. If it could be reasonably claimed that Ireland seemed well positioned to take advantage of possible openings, and that policy had been designed to prepare her for a great leap forward, then the verdict on the recent record might be modified. Such a leap forward may still occur. History, even economic history, is nothing if not unpredictable. If such a transformation occurs, however, it will not have been the result of foresight. It will be sheer accident.

It is difficult to avoid the conclusion that Irish economic performance has been the least impressive in western Europe, perhaps in all Europe, in the twentieth century. It must count as one of the more striking records in modern European economic history. How has Ireland achieved and sustained this level of relative retardation? What can the explanation be?

POTENTIAL

Before embarking on the search for explanations, we must ponder the possibility that we may be asking the wrong questions, or adopting the wrong comparative criteria. To adapt Denison's warning, 'an appropriate evaluation would have to be based on a comparison of Irish achievements with Irish possibilities. It cannot be based on casual comparisons of the Irish growth rate with the rates of countries having quite different opportunities for growth.'[31] But how does one identify 'possibilities' and 'opportunities'? They are often discerned, for countries no less than for firms or for individuals, only because others demonstrate their existence by seizing them. Comparison must focus on like with like. Comparison between the Irish and the American economies, for instance, should not be pressed too hard for numerous reasons. But comparison with a number of European countries can help us achieve a deeper perspective on Irish performance. Ireland belonged to the same geographical zone, had access to the same markets, belonged to the same per capita income and life expectancy categories as western Europe in the early twentieth century. The differences in detail between European and Irish experience were

[30] NESC, *A review of industrial policy* (Dublin, 1986), p. 247.
[31] Denison, *Why growth rates differ*, p. 345.

often no greater than the differences between the individual European countries themselves.

Perhaps the Irish simply did not want economic growth?[32] Were not the Irish renowned for their dedication to things of the spirit, for their renunciation of the temptations of materialism, to which a decadent Europe, lacking Hibernian strength of character, sadly succumbed? It is an engaging thought, sedulously cultivated by some of the Irish themselves. Suffice it here to note that, despite impressive examples of individual self-denial, particularly among missionary and nursing orders, the image of Ireland as an island sublimely submerged in a sea of spirituality carries little conviction.

Few peoples anywhere have been so prepared to scatter their children around the world in order to preserve their own living standards. And the children themselves left the country to improve their material prospects. Their letters home are full of references to their material progress, preferably confirmed by the inclusion of notes and money orders. Those who remained at home further exhibited their own worship of the golden calf in their devotion to the primacy of the pocket in marriage arrangements calculated to the last avaricious farthing, in the milking of bovine TB eradication schemes, in the finessing of government grants, subsidies and loans, of medical certificates and insurance claims, in the scrounging for petty advantage among protected business men, in the opportunistic cynicism with which wage and salary claims, not to mention professional fees, were rapaciously pursued. The Irish may have been inefficient materialists. That was not due to any lack of concern with material gain. If their values be deemed spiritual, then spirituality must be defined as covetousness tempered only by sloth.

Even those inclined to attribute superior spirituality to the Irish must hesitate to explain the relative retardation of Northern Ireland in similar terms. The North was a striking economic failure by European standards, long before the 'troubles' aggravated the problem after 1969. But the Ulster Scots are renowned for their Calvinist capacity to discern in material gain a sign of divine pleasure. They must then have done something to cause distinct displeasure to the Deity, for He would frown severely on the efforts of His Chosen Race on the Lagan after partition. Indeed, He was so thoughtless as to leave His Elect standing shoulder to shoulder with Paddy in propping up the northern European league table as the twentieth century drew to a close!

If the Irish coveted material gain as eagerly as other western Europeans, is the explanation for their failure to be found in an objective lack of opportunity? Was the Irish supply of natural resources so inherently

32 B. Hutchinson, 'On the study of non-economic factors in Irish economic development', *ESR*, 1, 4 (July 1970), pp. 509–29.

inferior that she had little hope of emulating the performance of the thirteen other states in northern Europe. Ireland lacked the mineral resources on which much of the first phase of European industrialisation was based. So did most of Europe. Coal and iron imposed their own logic of location in the initial stages of industrialisation. But those stages were essentially completed in the nineteenth century.[33] Lack of mineral resources has been normal, not exceptional, for European countries. There is no correlation between mineral resources and standards of living in contemporary Europe. The classic centres of the first phase of European industrialisation have long ceased to be the most dynamic. Ireland cannot claim any unique disadvantage in this respect.

Timber was more widely spread than coal or iron. Finland and Sweden, in particular, would exploit their timber reserves intelligently to contribute to their economic development. In contrast to coal and iron, however, timber can be produced. Ireland has some good potential woodland, at least for certain types of timber. She failed to adequately exploit it. Civil servants, whether in Finance or in Lands, were slow to share the enthusiasm of 'wild men' like Alfred O'Rahilly and Seán MacBride for forestry development. The stark arboreal bleakness of the Irish landscape in the late twentieth century can no longer be attributed to the destructive frenzies of Tudor and Stuart. Nor is it solely the result of bureaucratic inadequacy. There were objective problems for the policy-makers, not least those posed by landholding patterns and peasant mentalities. But the source of the bleakness must still be sought more in the inertia of the indigenes than in the niggardliness of nature. Not until the 1980s would forestry policy, stimulated by a pungent NESC report, begin to be taken seriously.[34]

Irish soil, even if often growing 'just as little as it is physically possible for the land to grow under an Irish sky',[35] in the caustic phrase of a New Zealand consultant in 1949, counts among the more fertile soils of Europe. The climate to whose mercies the soil was exposed ranks among the more equable in the world. If relatively unfavourable for wheat production, it is indulgent towards most types of agricultural activity. Irish coastal waters appear to be sufficiently favoured by fish to make it worthwhile for foreign fishermen to come here. If Irish fishermen cannot compete with them, it is not because the fish have chosen to boycott them. Nature, it must be concluded, has not been conspicuously niggardly towards Ireland.

[33] The standard work interpreting the location of industrial activity in terms of the regional distribution of physical resources is S. Pollard, *Peaceful conquest. The industrialisation of Europe 1760–1970* (Oxford, 1981).

[34] NESC, *Irish forestry policy* (Dublin 1979); SPO, S11555B, Lands memo on MacBride's forestry proposals, 28 January 1949.

[35] Quoted in Meenan, *Irish Economy*, p. 89.

Did not nature, however, place Ireland in an unfortunate position? Did she not inflict a 'peripheral' location on this 'island behind an island'? The island she was behind was for two centuries the 'centre' of the world economy! Less fortunately located competitors, who lacked Ireland's ease of access to so enticing a market, envied Irish 'peripherality'. If Ireland failed to win a larger share of the British market, location could not be blamed. When the lead shifted from England to the continent after the mid twentieth century, Ireland became somewhat more peripheral, but only marginally so. A Córas Tráchtála inquiry into transport costs in the mid-eighties confirmed earlier conclusions that they were not a major problem for most Irish exporters.[36] There may be problems for specific products catering for specific markets arising from disadvantages of location. In general, however, Ireland can hardly claim to be victimised in this regard.

As a small open economy Ireland was particularly susceptible to sharp changes in the terms of trade. It could gain and lose substantially from international price movements largely beyond its control. The terms of trade, the ratio between export and import prices, therefore deserve close attention from students of Irish economic history. They are often crucial to the explanation of short-term fluctuations. But they do not suffice to explain longer term levels of income or trajectories of growth in small open economies. These depend more on the flexibility of the small states in responding to rapid external change. Far from absolving the indigenous decision-makers from responsibility for the outcome, smallness and openness place even greater onus on them to devise structures and mechanisms that take adequate cognizance of the implications of their size. If vast impersonal international forces determine the circumstances in which they operate, the adeptness of their response to these forces helps determine the long-term relative performance of their economies. However vulnerable small open economies may be to changes in terms of trade, they have shown themselves capable of achieving as high income levels as more self-contained economies. It is instructive in this respect to compare the Irish and Danish performances in the 1950s.

Denmark had a difficult fifties. Her growth rates fluctuated sharply, with her rate of growth of GNP plunging from 7.2 per cent in 1950 to 0.6 per cent in 1951, from 5.9 per cent in 1953 to 1.0 per cent in 1955, and from 5.0 per cent in 1957 to 2.2 per cent in 1958.[37] She faced much the

---

36 John R. Healy, 'Access transport – how is it serving the Irish exporter?', Address to the Annual Conference of the Chartered Institute of Transport in Ireland, 28 February 1986. I am grateful to Declan Lyons of Córas Trachtala for making this paper available to me. See also NESC, *The importance of infrastructure to industrial development in Ireland – roads, telecommunications and water supply* (Dublin, 1981), p. 27.

37 H.C. Johansen, *The Danish economy in the twentieth century* (London, 1987), p. 107; K. Laursen, 'A survey of the Danish economy after 1950', *Weltwirtschaftliches Archiv*, 98, 2 (1967), pp. 183–5.

same balance of payments constraints as Ireland, and experienced similar difficulties on the British food market. She suffered a drastic deterioration of more than 30 per cent in her terms of trade between 1949 and 1953, worse than the combined impact of the two oil crises of 1973 and 1979 on Ireland, and more than double the Irish deterioration between 1953 and 1957 that contributed so much to the gloom of the mid-fifties.[38] The immediate problems confronting Denmark were even more difficult in some respects. Not only did her agriculture, like Ireland's, suffer from international protectionism. In addition, her industry experienced rapid trade liberalisation under OEEC regulations that disproportionately affected Denmark from the early fifties – a threat that Irish industry would not confront for more than another decade. It was not the nature of the challenge that was particularly striking, however, about Denmark's case compared with Ireland's. It was the nature of the response.

In agriculture, Denmark found herself trapped by the same constraints on beef production as Ireland, with cattle numbers growing at very similar rates between 1949 and 1959. But the Danes seized their chance in food processing, where they developed canned meat production to compensate for the limited prospects for bacon sales in Britain. As a result, where Irish pig numbers rose modestly from 675 000 in 1949 to 852 000 in 1959, Danish numbers rose from 2.7 million to 6.1 million in the same period.[39] Danish industry had a mixed record. The rapid increase in imports of manufactured goods created problems for hitherto protected producers. Textiles and footwear suffered absolute falls in output between 1950 and 1958. Vigorous growth occurred, however, not only in food processing, but in the engineering sector, as Danish industrialists succeeded in responding to changing threats and opportunities far more effectively than did indigenous Irish industry in the relatively more favourable climate of the 1960s.[40]

The Danish experience suggests that if the terms of trade may indeed impose serious restraints on the options available to small open economies, even adverse movements need not induce paralysis. And by no means all movements are adverse. It is not as if Ireland has suffered from permanently deteriorating terms of trade since independence. Yet improvements in the terms of trade tend to attract less attention than deterioration. The eighteen point worsening in the terms of trade in the year after the oil crisis of 1973 has been regularly lamented. One is rarely reminded that the terms had improved eighteen points in the preceding two years![41]

[38] Johansen, *Danish economy*, p. 105; *Statistical Abstract*, 1961, p. 321; 1976, p. 925; 1982–1985, p. 360.

[39] Johansen, *Danish economy*, p. 115; Mitchell, *European historical statistics*, pp. 309, 312.

[40] Johansen, p. 115.   [41] *Statistical Abstract*, 1974 and 1975, p. 315.

Perhaps independent Ireland was just plain unlucky? Did it not endure a civil war, an economic war and an Emergency?[42] It may be wondered, however, if Ireland has not been, on the contrary, exceptionally lucky. If we confine the comparison to the new states of eastern Europe after the First World War, we find that the damage inflicted on Ireland between 1919 and 1923 came to only a fraction of the destruction inherited by the successor states. Sinn Féin Ireland had the great good fortune to find herself, however inadvertently, on the winning side in 1918. The Republic of Austria, on the other hand, found itself in 1920 with agricultural output at 50 per cent of its pre-war level, and industrial output at 33 per cent. Agricultural output in Hungary stood at 56 per cent of pre-war levels, industrial output at 35–40 per cent. Poland suffered extensive destruction, with 2 million cattle and 1 million horses killed, 5 million acres of forests ruined, more than 10 million acres of land lying fallow, and the railway system wrecked. Serbia lost most than a quarter of her total livestock. Even in Czechoslovakia, the least affected successor state, industrial output in 1920 had recovered to only 70 per cent of its pre-war level. The foreign trade of most of the new countries was decimated, amounting in 1921 to roughly half its pre-war level.[43]

Production problems in agriculture and industry were compounded by the cancer of inflation that swept through central Europe in the postwar years. Hungarian bank deposits were only worth 8 per cent of their pre-war value in 1921. Austrian bank deposits fell to 11 per cent of their pre-war value by 1925. Valiantly though Czechoslovakia tackled her budgetary problems, and resolutely though she resisted inflationary temptations, she still suffered drastic currency depreciation. The main reason for inflation in central Europe was not the irresponsibility of the politicians, but the simple fact of losing the war.[44] The war had to be paid for. Of course the inflation got out of control. Insofar as it became a destablising factor, however, it derived in large measure from the logic of circumstances. The Cosgrave government faced no remotely comparable financial problems.

Despite the depredations of the war, and the subsequent difficulties, the central European economies rallied in the mid-twenties. They had experienced rapid growth before 1914, and now seemed poised to resume the sharp upward trend. The great slump of 1929, aggravated by the financial crisis of 1931, devastated their economies. They were doubly vulnerable,

---

[42] See the exchange between S. Cromien, 'As good as any – a perspective from inside the civil service', *Seirbhís Phoiblí*, 6, 2 (1985), p. 8, and J.J. Lee, 'Letter to the Editor', *Seirbhís Phoiblí*, 7, 1 (1986), p. 30.

[43] I.T. Berend and G. Ranki, *Economic development in East Central Europe in the nineteenth and twentieth century* (New York, 1974), pp. 174–7.

[44] G.D. Feldman, C.L. Holtfrerich, G.A. Ritter and P.C. Witt (eds.), *The experience of inflation* (Berlin, 1984).

as exporters and as borrowers. The value of exports, taking 1929 as 100, fell in 1932 to 44 for Romania, 39 for Yugoslavia, 38 for Poland and 32 for Hungary. It was still 74 for Ireland in 1932, and even at the trough of the economic war in 1934 it did not fall below 65. With exports dwindling, and borrowing impossible, the twin props on which the economic recovery of central Europe had rested collapsed.[45] So pressing did the problems become that the League of Nations had to arrange moratoria on many foreign debts in 1931–2. Ireland, on the other hand, entered independence as a substantial capital exporter.[46] Inconvenient though international developments after 1929 happened to be, Ireland chanced to be far less vulnerable to these developments than the other new states of the time. No sooner had these states begun to recover from the impact of the slump than most of them were overrun, first by Hitler, then by Stalin, enduring some of the worst destruction, physical and human, of the Second World War – from which Ireland was spared largely by the luck of her location.

Or consider the case of Finland. With the same population as Ireland, she lost 25 000 dead in her civil war in 1918. In the Second World War, she lost nearly 100 000 dead out of a population of 3.5 million. After the war, she had to settle 400 000 Karelian refugees, flying from Soviet annexation, more than the number of emigrants whose threatened postwar return struck such fear into the Dublin government in 1942. In addition, she had to pay substantial reparations to Russia.[47] Yet Finland recorded one of the most impressive of all postwar European growth performances.[48]

It would be nice if Ireland disposed of vastly more mineral resources, basked in a sunnier climate, was located closer to the 'centre', enjoyed constantly improving terms of trade, or were just 'luckier'. But in none of these respects can Ireland claim to suffer from grave and consistent discrimination compared with the European average. Professor John Kelleher's pungent comment of 1957 remains valid thirty years later:

Ireland has no right to be sick. If she compares her resources with those of other small Western European countries, and its population with what those have to support, one can hardly avoid deciding that Irish ills are largely psychosomatic.

[45] Berend and Ranki, *East Central Europe*, pp. 243ff., 285ff.; M.C. Kaser, 'Introduction', in M.C. Kaser and E.A. Radice (eds.), *The economic history of eastern Europe 1919–1975*, 1 (Oxford, 1985), p. 5: E.A. Radice, 'General characteristics of the region between the wars' in Kaser and Radice, *Eastern Europe*, pp. 39, 49, 52.
[46] Cullen, *Economic history* p. 170.
[47] Jutikkala, *Finland*, pp. 284–5; M. Klinge, *A brief history of Finland* (Helsinki, 1981), pp. 109–11; M. Klinge, 'Aspects of the Nordic Self', *Daedalus*, 113, 2 (Spring 1984), p. 271.
[48] Andersen and Åkerholm, *Scandinavia*, p. 611; L. Jörberg and O. Krantz, 'Scandinavia 1914–1970', in C.M. Cipolla, *The Fontana economic history of Europe: contemporary economies*, part 2 (London, 1976), p. 379.

True, they can all be explained from history; but to explain is not always to excuse, the less so indeed since Irish history records so little energetic common sense and so much casual acceptance of accidental developments. Any conversation on Ireland in Ireland is almost bound to produce some defensive mention of the terrible troubles the Irish have survived and the hard time of it the nation has had generally. Alas, the truth is that Ireland has had an almost fatally easily time of it, at least in this century.[49]

To probe further the causes of Irish social and economic backwardness, we must turn from the supply of material resources to the use the Irish have chosen to make of their resources. For it is at the human level that the solution to the mystery of the mediocrity of Irish socio-economic performance seems likely to lie.

Economic policy since 1922 has revolved around the search for that elusive factor, enterprise. Paddy Hogan sought it in agriculture. Seán Lemass sought it in industry. Neither found enough of it. Lemass turned in desperation to importing it, if only to provide yet a further breathing space for an adequate native supply to emerge. It didn't.

There is no consensus on the reasons for the dearth of enterprise in Ireland. Some attribute it wholly to lack of objective opportunity. Others attribute it partly to this, but also partly to an absence of an adequate performance ethic in the society. For those, like myself, who take the latter view, the really interesting historical question is how a culture chooses to perceive 'opportunity', and why the performance ethic is so muted. We have suggested earlier that a blend of economic and psychological factors helps explain the primacy and the tenacity of the possessor rather than the performer ethos.[50] Here it is proper to stress further the lack of incentive provided by the peculiar nature of the home market. The Free State population in 1922 was identical to that of Denmark and Finland, bigger than Norway's, and only a little smaller than Switzerland's. In purchasing power it was rather smaller than Denmark's and Switzerland's, bigger than Finland's or Norway's. As their population and purchasing power grew faster than Ireland's, however, a gap emerged. The Irish market today, in contrast to the position earlier in the century, is even smaller than it looks in relative population terms, simply because per capita income has now fallen so far relative to the other economies of western Europe. Even in more favourable circumstances, however, the structure of Irish purchasing power offered relatively little incentive to Irish industry. The Irish marginal propensity to import was exceptionally high, due to the country's incorporation into the English sphere of economic and cultural influence. Above all, Irish agriculture provided only a meagre and sluggish market for Irish industry.

[49] John V. Kelleher, 'Ireland . . . and where does she stand?', *Foreign Affairs*, 35 (April 1957), pp. 491–2.
[50] See above, pp. 390–6.

Table 13. *Agricultural machinery (Denmark and Éire)*

Type	Denmark (1936)	Éire (1929)
Power machinery		
Tractors	6660	797
Steam engines	1268	580
Electric motors	73 511	177 (1928)
Oil, petrol and gas engines	34 822	2430
Windmills	15 514	74
Field machinery		
Seed-sowing machinery	112 237	13 134
corn drills	15 823	3372
broadcast sowers	126 539	106 472
Mowers and reapers	82 303	17 558
Self binders	7133	10 826
Potato diggers	19 954	n.a.
Beet lifters	11 965	
Manure distributors	5499	3343
Table and barn *machinery*		
Ordinary threshers	33 163	8473
Other threshers (including combined threshers and finishers and winnowers)	109 020	20 648
Straw balers (or compressors)	43 796	292
Crushers	86 089	6033
Chaff cutters	139 728	22 011
Liquid manure containers or pits	174 418	n.a.
Ensilage containers or pits	1218	n.a.

Source: J.P. Beddy, 'A Comparison of the principle economic features of Éire and Denmark', *JSSISI*, 17 (1943–4), p. 214.

Agricultural output increased exceptionally slowly in the century after 1850. And agriculture's demand structure provided only an exiguous market for industry. Danish engineering developed partly on the basis of the agricultural market for machinery, just as the Danish chemical industry developed partly on the basis of demand for artificial fertiliser.[51] No such stimulus existed for Irish industry. Beddy's comparison of the size of the market for agricultural machinery in the two countries between the wars tells its own tale.

The response of Irish farmers to market conditions was rational enough in the short term. It was, however, subversive of their own longer term

[51] I.T. Berend and G. Ranki, *The European periphery and industrialisation 1780–1914* (Cambridge, 1982), p. 147; D. Senghaas, *The European experience* (Coventry, 1986), p. 84.

interests, and that of their children, assuming they wanted to remain in the country. For it was all but impossible for an economy to expand rapidly on the basis of an agriculture that generated little increased output, that provided so limited a market for industrial products, and that operated in so seasonal a fashion that the bulk of its output was exported in a raw rather than a processed state. The standard growth pattern for European exporters of primary sector products has been to move from raw to processed commodities, and then to increasingly diversify both products and markets.

The Danish case again offers a useful example. In the years 1921–5, 81 per cent of her exports consisted of agricultural products. This fell to 72 per cent in the 1936–9 period, to 54 per cent by 1955–8, and to 23 per cent by 1967–70.[52] As her industrial exports grew, so her markets diversified, 62 per cent of her total exports went to Britain in 1921–5, 55 per cent in 1936–8, 29 per cent in 1955–8, and 21 per cent in 1968–9.[53] The point about the Danish analogy here is that, as we have seen, Denmark by no means enjoyed sustained economic success in the twentieth century. Danish growth rates fluctuated considerably. Germany, to which Denmark aspired to be a substantial exporter, was an uncertain trading partner. Danish businessmen, who relied on a protected home market, showed no instinctive enthusiasm for free trade. Denmark did not have 'opportunities' presented to her on a plate. Neither government nor private enterprise got the answers consistently right. Nevertheless they got the strategy sufficiently right to still give an impressive overall performance.

The failure of Irish agriculture to provide a spring-board for industrialisation exacerbated the problems facing policy-makers. If development of a major agri-business sector was at best a very long-term option, for reasons like seasonality of supply largely beyond the policy-makers' control, and if evidence were accumulating, as it was during the 1960s, that not only were Irish businessmen loath to export, but that they were failing to adequately defend the home market, then an even bigger wager on foreign investment remained the sole realistic alternative.[54] It was recognition of this challenge that led to a virtual second founding of the Industrial Development Authority in 1969 under Michael Killeen.

The new foreign firms during the 1960s had come mainly with 'technically mature, labour intensive products'. These could be located almost anywhere in the semi-industrial world 'because they have no great dependence on contact with specialised skills, knowledge, suppliers, and

52 Jörberg and Krantz, 'Scandinavia 1914–1970', p. 406.   53 *Ibid.*, p. 403.
54 E. O'Malley, 'The problem of late industrialisation and the experience of the Republic of Ireland', *Cambridge Journal of Economics*, 9 (1985), p. 145; *Irish Times*, 14 February 1984, 'Profile: Michael Killeen'.

services of advanced industrial centres'.[55] The IDA now sought to shift to 'more sophisticated products', especially electronics and pharmaceuticals 'where links on the product chain from research through production to marketing could be geographically separated'.[56]

This policy found a general acceptance. But there were critics, though not many, from the outset. The Cooper–Whelan report of 1973, co-authored by Noel Whelan, a rapidly rising civil servant, who became Secretary to the Department of the Taoiseach when Haughey succeeded Lynch in 1979, expressed intense scepticism of the likely longer term benefits of such heavy reliance of foreign investment.[57] By 1979 there were grounds for suspecting, despite the buoyant growth of electronics and chemicals, and the propaganda barrage from the IDA, that the apparently striking success of the foreign sector was not feeding back into the wider economy. Native industry was resolutely refusing to grow. It was in these circumstances that the NESC, under Whelan's chairmanship, commissioned the Telesis enquiry into industrial policy in July 1980. The Telesis report, when finally published in February 1982, provoked an instructive public debate that illuminated the quality of thinking and the *realpolitik* involved in the formulation of economic policy.

Claiming that no country had su:ceeded in achieving sustained economic growth except on the basis of native industry, Telesis queried the Irish emphasis on foreign investment, and advocated greater commitment towards developing an indigenous industrial base. However successful the foreign investment policy in the short term, Telesis insisted that it should still be revised. But Telesis also insisted that the policy was not remotely as successful as IDA propaganda implied. Telesis simply noted that the IDA tended to trumpet the number of jobs approved for new industry, diverting attention from the distinctly less publicised fact that only 30 per cent of these jobs were actually in existence in 1981.[58] As, in addition, job losses were already reaching serious levels, the apparently glittering performance in job creation during the 1970s lost a good deal of its shine. The foreign industry that did exist was a virtual enclave, creating few linkages with the rest of the economy, carrying out little of its basic research and development function in Ireland, and potentially repatriating profits.

In the light of this bleak diagnosis, Telesis prescribed a variety of treatments. Government should insist that foreign companies establish research and development activities here, and favour Irish sub-suppliers in

55 O'Malley, 'Late industrialisation', 149.
56 Wrigley, 'Ireland in economic space', p. 72.
57 C. Cooper and N. Whelan, *Science, technology and industry in Ireland* (Dublin, 1973). See also J. Teeling's contribution to 'A symposium on increasing employment in Ireland', *JSSISI*, 23, pt. 3 (1975–6), pp. 75–7.
58 NESC, *A review of industrial policy* (Dublin, 1982), p. 33.

order to expand backward linkages. More specifically, 'a goal of raising the proportion of funds allocated to indigenous export or skilled sub-supply firms from less than 40 per cent over the past 10 years to 50 per cent by 1985 and 75 per cent by 1990, should be made explicit'.[59] This still left it facing the fundamental problem that had foiled all previous policies – the absence of an internationally competitive Irish entrepreneurial cadre. Telesis did not shirk the challenge.

Its solution to the dilemma was that the government should pick out about fifty to seventy-five 'winners' among Irish companies, and support them to the hilt, building them up into world class firms, capable of competing against all comers on the international market. Distinguishing sharply between the 'exposed' and 'sheltered' sectors of the Irish economy, it felt that only firms in the 'exposed' sector deserved substantial support. The successful Irish firms, most of which seemed to operate in the 'sheltered' sector, protected from international competition by high transport costs, should be induced to re-deploy their management skills towards export-oriented activity by providing them with access to a 'development fund' within the IDA.[60] The specific object of this fund would be to aid firms whose managerial calibre had already stamped them as 'winners'. 'The development effort aimed toward new indigenous industry', Telesis recommended in a much quoted phrase 'must be reorganised to emphasise the building of structurally strong Irish companies rather than strong agencies to assist weak companies.'[61]

Finally, Telesis recommended that central government departments should reassume greater authority over the formulation and implementation of industrial policy.[62] Whereas the number of IDA staff had increased from 460 to 750 between 1975 and 1981, the number of staff in the industrial policy division of the Department of Industry had only increased from 27 to 30.

The report, as may be imagined, sent shock waves through the policy establishment. Publication was delayed for more than a year. Rumours of bruising encounters between government departments, the IDA, Córas Tráchtala and other interested parties began to circulate. Leaks and counter-leaks titillated public curiosity. The publication of the report in February 1982 was by no means the end of the institutional manoeuvring. A White Paper on Industrial Policy, the government response to Telesis, appeared only in July 1984, three-and-a-half years after completion of the report. No more eloquent tribute could be paid to the validity of the report's suspicions concerning the quality of decision-making on Irish industrial policy than the protracted delay in responding to it.

The reasons for the delay are not far to seek. They naturally have more

59 *Ibid.*, p. 231.   60 *Ibid.*, p. 232.   61 *Ibid.*   62 *Ibid.*, pp. 223, 242.

to do with administrative and party politics than with the economics of industrial policy.

Michael Killeen fashioned the IDA into a formidable organisation, respected by its rivals for its success in luring coveted firms to Ireland. He succeeded in creating a tight sense of 'corporate loyalty' within the organisation.[63] The IDA proved as skilful at promoting itself at home as abroad. Its tactical error was to exaggerate its success. Precisely because the propaganda had been so successful the reaction was all the more disillusioned when the public discovered that the figures it had swallowed uncritically did not convey the whole truth. The IDA thus left itself exposed to a Telesis-type critique when it transpired that the number of jobs created fell far short of those announced. If the emperor was not now entirely naked, he was certainly left in a state of sartorial disarray.

There were two major issues involved. From a national point of view, much the more important was the quality of industrial policy. From the point of view of the interests at stake, this became inextricably intertwined with personal and institutional prospects. Critics of the IDA, whether in central government departments, or in Córas Tráchtala, sought to use Telesis as a lever with which to prize some of what they felt to be its excessive power from it. The IDA naturally resisted. Its resentment was fuelled by the feeling that it was 'set-up' for a hatchet job. Killeen 'found it extraordinary' that Telesis 'should confine itself to just a ten-minute chat' with himself.[64] To him, clearly, Telesis was little better than a hired gun.

The IDA embarked on a skilful damage-limitation exercise in the wake of Telesis. It sought to discredit the report, while simultaneously insisting that it had already initiated many of the recommended changes! It tried to shift the criterion of success from job creation to wealth creation. Wealth creation, whatever its intrinsic merits, had the great attraction that, unlike job creation, it was an exquisitely elusive concept. The idea behind it was that wealth creation would generate nineteen new jobs in the service sector for every one new job in manufacturing.[65] Back in 1975, Michael Killeen had estimated that it took two new jobs in manufacturing to generate an extra job elsewhere in the economy.[66] Circumstances may have changed in the meantime. But they can hardly have changed to that extent. McAleese estimated in 1982 that every extra industrial job created one spin-off job elsewhere.[67]

The IDA disputed the Telesis claim that Irish inducement to foreign

[63] Des Crowley, 'How IDA wins war while losing battles', *Sunday Tribune*, 2 June 1985.
[64] *Irish Times*, 14 February 1984, 'Profile: Michael Killeen'.
[65] According to the IDA's leaked ten-year strategic plan, reported in Maev-Ann Wren, 'Dáil procrastinates while jobs evaporate', *Irish Times*, 5 March 1984.
[66] Killeen, *Industrial development*, p. 15.
[67] D. McAleese, 'The changing economic environment', in F.S.L. Lyons (ed.), *Bicentenery essays: Bank of Ireland 1783–1983* (Dublin, 1983), p. 154.

firms were excessive, on the simple grounds that it knew better from its own experience.[68] It responded indignantly to Telesis allegations of its excessive reliance on the electronics industry, the apple of its developmental eye. It had to concede that linkages with Irish firms, and the amount of research and development conducted in Ireland, were very limited. But it retorted that the electronics industry was a new one, that it had achieved remarkable success, and that prospects were good. It was itself already proceeding to the next logical step of creating locally-based ancillary functions.[69] It simply rejected the Telesis prediction that foreign-owned high technology firms were likely to retain research and development functions close to their headquarters instead of locating them in Ireland.

The whole electronics strategy was a high risk one. Only time would tell whether the pessimistic Telesis scenario, or the optimistic IDA one, would prove valid. There were three elements to the risk. Firstly, in a rapidly-changing industry, many firms would fail. If the IDA enticed the wrong ones to Ireland, it would have a high fatality rate on its hands. In general, its judgement on individual firms was good.

Even if it chose the right firms, however, the logic of the industry might dictate that Ireland would remain little more than an assembly line for the major firms. This was the main Telesis fear. As the 1980s progressed, 'the unskilled parts of some production processes . . . are increasingly being located outside the metropolitan economies entirely, either in European countries with low wages and 'flexible' labour such as Ireland, Spain, or Yugoslavia, or in the 'free production zone' of the Third World'.[70]

Even if the doubts about the wager on electronics prove to be misplaced the question must still remain whether a small open economy should concentrate so heavily on a single growth sector. It may have little choice, but if it chooses as volatile a sector as electronics, then it must expect to pay the consequences, including occasional severe setbacks.

Intensifying linkages between foreign firms and Irish suppliers is a protracted process, not least because supply standards frequently fail to meet specifications. Some improvement has occurred. In the whole non-food foreign investment sector, purchases of Irish raw materials rose from 16 per cent in 1976 to 26 per cent in 1983.[71] This still left scope for improvement.

The hope that foreign investment would provide a demonstration effect for native management was only partly realised. The demonstration effect

---

[68] NESC, *Industrial policy*, para. 9.   [69] *Ibid.*, para. 11.

[70] J.R. Lewis, 'Regional policy and planning: convergence and contradiction', in S. Bornstein, D. Held and J. Krieger (eds.), *The state in capitalist Europe* (London, 1984), p. 146.

[71] OECD, *Ireland 1984–85*, p. 47. IDA, *The Irish economy expenditures of the Irish manufacturing sector: a statistical profile* (Dublin, 1985), p. 8.

must inevitably remain limited where investment concentrates on low levels of skills, with little research and development, and with a market often created by the parent company. Not all foreign investment was of this type. But the opportunities to learn were often confined to production skills so specific that they could not be transferred between industries.[72] Promising Irish managers within these firms are likely to transfer to higher responsibilities within the company, which will often mean out of the country. The foreign sector may therefore actually serve as an agent for recruiting Irish managerial talent abroad rather than, or as well as, a source for fostering a native managerial cadre.

The Telesis debate did help expose the dearth of hard evidence available for assessing the contribution of foreign investment to national economic performance. The IDA, which had been relatively open-minded about explaining its thinking, at least by the familiar standard of furtiveness of the official mind, itself provided further information. Padraic White, appointed chief executive of the IDA when Michael Killeen became chairman of Irish Distillers in 1979, claimed that 'foreign industry, in particular, had suffered from much destructive comment based on lack of information'.[73] He pointed out that the cost effectiveness of industry could only 'be properly evaluated' with the type of information the IDA was not only making available but collecting, for the first time.

This carried the corollary that the IDA itself was only now in a position to evaluate the effectiveness of its policies! Some of its earlier confident claims must therefore be taken with a double grain of salt. Even if it had wanted to tell the truth, it could not. It did not know what it was. Nor would all readers necessarily find the figures as reassuring as did the IDA. In 1983, foreign firms exported goods to the value of £5000 million. In achieving this, they imported £1150 million worth of raw materials, and repatriated £550 million profits. They contributed about £2250 million to the Irish economy through wages and salaries, purchase of local raw materials and services.[74] While the net exports helped the balance of payments, this may not seem the most glittering of achievements in view of all the hopes reposed in the foreign investment policy. And these figures were themselves suspect. If transfer pricing were as extensively practised as some feared, the gain to the Irish economy would be less, perhaps significantly less.

Telesis and the IDA fundamentally agreed that native businessmen of the necessary quality simply were not, for whatever reason, available. Sixty years after independence, fifty years after blanket protection, twenty years after the Committee on Industrial Organisation, fifteen years after the Anglo-Irish Free Trade Agreement, eight years after entering the EEC,

---

[72] I owe this point to Paul Coughlan, MBA.   [73] IDA, *The Irish economy*, p. 1.
[74] OECD, *Ireland 1984–85*, p. 55, n. 34.

a native entrepreneurial cadre of the requisite quality had failed to emerge. Irish-owned industry could not compete internationally. It could not even compete on the home market. Neither carrot nor stick, neither free trade nor protection, had sufficed to create a competitive native industry.

The IDA, rather than selecting fifty to seventy-five strong Irish companies who should be built up, preferred to devise a two-stage strategy 'which seeks to identify and support stronger companies *after* initially increasing the population of business entrepreneurs'.[75] Telesis did not specify the mechanism by which 'winners' or 'vertically integrated Irish firms' would emerge. Even if the Telesis recommendation that successful 'sheltered' Irish firms should reorient their activities towards the 'exposed' sector were accepted – and it can be argued that managements are wiser to keep to areas they know most about – this still left open the question of which activities in the exposed sector offered most promise for long-term development. Should agencies try to identify them? Should it be assumed that the market itself would determine the answers? There was widespread scepticism about the capacity of the 'government' to pick even a solitary winner, much less seventy-five winners, both on grounds of its technical competence, and of likely corruption. Where then were the international class Irish industrialists to come from?

One response, associated with the Labour Party, was that a new agency, a National Development Corporation (NDC), should be established to supply the missing dynamic. With rapidly rising unemployment in the early 1980s, it might seem as if this ambitious proposal for job creation would arouse enthusiasm. But the public had so lost confidence in the capacity of any state organisation to serve any purpose except its own self-interest that the proposal generated more scepticism than enthusiasm. A series of poor returns on several enterprises, and the apparent casualness with which public sector trade unions resorted to the tactic of inflicting suffering on the public, the same public they claimed to serve in their more esoteric flights of rhetorical fancy, in order to intimidate government into concessions, left public opinion increasingly dubious about the likely results of direct state intervention. Some state companies continued to perform well. It was unfair that they should be tarred with the same brush in the public mind as the others. But that was inevitable, given the widespread view, expressed by the Minister for Finance, that 'state companies have not, on the whole, distinguished themselves commercially in recent times. They have been criticised for being over-staffed, over-paid and for offering poor service. Many of them are in a poor financial state.'[76] Ministers for Finance might be regarded as jaundiced

[75] NESC, *Industrial policy*, para. 8.
[76] Address by Alan Dukes to the Institute of Bankers in Ireland, 16 November 1984. I am grateful to the Minister's office for supplying me with a copy of this speech.

witnesses. But *Building on Reality 1985–1987*, the national plan of a
government that included Labour, acknowledged that the 'perception' of
'public employment . . . as a drain on the economy and a burden on the
tax payer . . . has become more widespread in recent years'.[77] The editor
of the *Irish Press* expressed the same sentiment in more homely style,
when advocating that attention should be given to fisheries and horticul-
ture on the grounds that 'the tide comes in and the tide goes out, as does
the sun rise and set without anyone needing a grant or a chance to set up a
semi-state company to make a bags of either phenomenon'.[78]

Ivor Kenny posed the basic questions to supporters of an expanded
state sector:

Where are the ideas for new state sponsored projects to come from? Fruitful ideas
and experienced managers cannot be summoned at will . . . There is no pumped
up reservoir of management initiative ready to go cascading into the economy
once the state takes action. There is little evidence of an immediate pool of
untapped entrepreneurial ability. The capacity to take risks, to anticipate opportunity, and sheer entrepreneurial flair, are essential in a competitive environment.
Second, there is the question of viability. If profits are not forthcoming, will the
projects concerned be closed down? If viability really is insisted upon, state
sponsored projects will meet exactly the same limit to their job creating capacity
that the private sector has to contend with.[79]

The White Paper on *Industrial policy* devoted a particularly dismissive
chapter to the idea of the NDC. Consumed with the fear that the NDC
would become yet another white elephant, it concentrated as much on
what it must not do as on what it should do. 'The corporation will not be a
grant-giving agency and will not engage in "rescue-type" operations.'[80]
To save it from being commandeered by vested interests, 'the NDC will
have a small and expert board of seven to nine people. It will not be
directly representative of specified interest groups.'[81] Insofar as it
intended to respond to the challenge of Telesis, 'a separate subsidiary of
the NDC will be established to undertake the tasks envisaged for the
corporation in relation to the development of structurally strong Irish
firms . . . '. But in case the disease of state paralysis should strike again
'the operation of this NDC subsidiary will be similar to the MIP equity
fund in the Netherlands set up jointly by the government and private
sector interests.'[82] 'Private sector interests' would apparently restrain the
NDC from the familiar excesses of a purely state operation. Successful
NDC operations were viewed as suspiciously as unsuccessful ones. 'The

77 *Building on reality*, (Dublin, 1984), p. 33. See also John Horgan, *Labour. The price of power* (Dublin, 1986), pp. 152–4.
78 Tim Pat Coogan, Saturday Column, *Irish Press*, 6 October 1984.
79 I. Kenny, *Government and enterprise in Ireland* (Dublin, 1984), p. 19. For further sceptical comment see R.S. Thompson, 'The national development corporation: prospects for a state investment company', *IBR* (September 1985), pp. 20–26.
80 *Industrial policy* (Dublin, 1984), p. 95.   81 *Ibid.*, p. 98.   82 *Ibid.*, p. 97.

NDC should aim to become self-financing in 6–8 years. It should therefore be able to sell off its investments profitably in order to replenish its capital.'[83] This latter provision went beyond mere scepticism concerning the efficacy of state activity, and soared into the realms of the ideological. Why should a profitable venture be sold to private enterprise which had, presumably, been unable to perceive the same opportunity, or to realise it – in effect, had been less enterprising? Perhaps it was assumed that no state enterprise could achieve sustained profit, even if by some alchemic quirk it made profit in the first place. It should therefore get out while the going was good.

Whatever their precise reasoning, the authors were on strong grounds in view of public disillusion with the performance of the semi-state sector. They could shrug off criticism, by the Irish Congress of Trade Unions, of the relegation of the NDC to a subordinate role, confident that public perception of trade union exploitation of the state sector had already deeply discredited the idea of an expanded public role. It was along the lines of this much muted version of the original proposal that the NDC was eventually established in 1986, to a deafening public silence.

And yet the basic issue remained. All governments since independence had put their faith in policies designed to foster a 'climate' of enterprise. Only modest success could be claimed. Unless the performance of private enterprise suddenly improved spectacularly, there was no prospect of coping with the economic problems of the late twentieth century. One need not accept all the assumptions of the barriers-to-entry argument, which claims that firms in countries industrialising late face insuperable barriers in breaking into competitive markets without direct state support, to recognise that Irish industry had failed by the acid test of competitiveness. Whatever the reasons, given the repeated failure of private enterprise to respond to either threat or opportunity, only the state, whether directly, or in partnership with the private sector, could supply the deficiency. The problem now was that the state itself had largely lost credibility. Apart from the impressive performance of a handful of companies, private and public, both sectors seemed to have failed.

Industrial policy contained several sensible individual recommendations. It suffered, however, from a narrowness of focus.[84] Industrial policy cannot be devised without analysis of the nature of the wider society in which it must operate. The White Paper was suffused with assumptions about the nature of that society, particularly about the relative levels of competence and corruption in the public and private

---

83 *Ibid.*, p. 95.
84 Frances Ruane, 'The White Paper on industrial policy', *IBR* (September 1984), pp. 35–45.

sectors. But nowhere did it analyse its own assumptions with any rigour. It is true that *Building on reality* purported to face the challenge of creating 'an economy and a society that provides justice and security for all of its people'.[85] But *Building on reality* contained relatively little on 'society'. No more than *Industrial policy* did it reflect the play of a superior controlling intelligence. Both documents involved the cobbling together of a variety of pet schemes of a number of vested interests within the public service. The cabinet, far from applying any grand design, simply traded off the claims of sundry importuners to achieve a modicum of harmony between the contending factions. Garret Fitzgerald unveiled the plan, in an astute piece of public relations, to divert attention from short-term difficulties for the government, during the week preceding the Fine Gael Árd Fheis in 1984. The 'national plan' had now joined the cavalcade of party politics. The smooth stage managing of the whole launch ensured a successful Árd Fheis, achieving the first, and for the party managers the main, objective of the plan, to see Fine Gael through the weekend. The medium was now the message.[86]

In the circumstances, it is hardly surprising that the document showed traces of hasty composition. Nevertheless, certain sections deserve attention. Some committed people worked on the plan, however cynically they may have been manipulated. Paragraph 1.9, for instance, set down fairly, indeed bravely, the assumptions about international developments on which many proposals depended. The plan recognised the gap between national potential and national performance. It dismissed the contention that the economy could not achieve full employment because 'such a defeatist attitude could be based only on the failures of the past and not on any *real* constraints facing the nation'.[87] It frankly acknowledged that it saw no alternative to the *Industrial policy* target of 200 000 unemployed by the end of 1987.[88] But it remained coy about one 'reality'. That was emigration. While discreetly noting that 'the size of the working age population' was 'affected by migration flows',[89] the labour force projections merely implied a 'significant' increase in emigration.[90] They did not linger on the issue.

By the mid eighties, then, policy makers in the social and economic spheres contemplated discouraging prospects. A variety of prescriptions for economic development since independence had yielded only modest results. Minds were once more turning to the escape hatch of emigration. The historian searching for the sources of long-term mediocrity must

85 *Building on reality*, p. 9.   86 O'Byrnes, *Hiding behind a face*, pp. 282–3.
87 *Building on reality* p. 33.
88 *Ibid.*, p. 26.   89 *Ibid.*, p.25.
90 D. McAleese, 'Building on reality 1985–1987: a commentary', *IBR* (December 1984), p. 25.

examine at least four factors influencing national performance, institutions, intellect, character, and identity.

INSTITUTIONS

Ireland appears to defy generalisations that assume a close relationship between political stability and the level of development of the wider society. 'In economic, social, even cultural, terms it seems at best to belong towards the bottom of any standard rank ordering of developed systems. Yet it has enjoyed a degree of internal political and governmental stability that places it among the small cluster of states at the top of that significant scale.'[91] Is there a paradox here?

Without lingering unduly over which of the many models posited by political scientists the Irish party system deviates least from, it may be claimed that the political parties have in many respects served the Southern state rather well. However close-run a thing it was, the manner in which the supremacy of parliament was achieved consolidated the democratic tradition in Irish nationalism.

The state that was moulded in the bitter crucible of the civil war proved highly creative in party political terms. Many observers felt that the Irish could not create a coherent party political order, particularly in the context of an electoral system based on the potentially destabilising principle of proportional representation with the single transferable vote in multi-member constituencies. That the nexus of ideals and interests out of which political movements are fashioned has hitherto sufficed to provide so striking a degree of governmental stability testifies to the professional skill with which the politicians responded to the challenge. The system might have been designed to maximise internal tension within parties, and to aggravate the difficulties of party leadership. But the leaders, with de Valera in a class of his own, displayed surpassing skill in manipulating the system to achieve stability.

They did so partly by fashioning solid blocs of party support. To achieve this, they had to appeal fundamentally to the socio-economic interests of the electorate. This requires explanation. Not only is there a good deal of opinion to the contrary. There is some evidence as well. The old-age pensioner in Clare who is reputed to have retorted to the jibe of a Fine Gael shopkeeper that de Valera's economic war obliged her to pay more for her food, 'I would vote for him if it meant having to starve,'[92] evokes the legend of the ethereal appeal of de Valera. And it is true that 'it

91 B. Farrell, 'Ireland: from friends and neighbours to clients and partisans: some dimensions of parliamentary representation under PR-STV', in V. Bogdanor (ed.), *Representatives of the people? Parliamentarians and constituents in western democracies* (London, 1985), p. 237.
92 Quoted in Ó hEithir, *The begrudger's guide*, p. 91.

was this capacity to inspire blind loyalty in people by appealing to their genuine patriotism, even when he was doing it all with mirrors, that makes de Valera such an uncomfortable figure in Irish politics'.[93] This blends nicely with the view that de Valera's *faculté maîtresse* was 'the ability to convey a fervent sense of justice' so that 'the depressed small farmers of the countryside, who had for generations been deprived of their rights on the land, debased, and humiliated . . . saw in de Valera an uncompromising champion of their rights, far more than they ever saw in him, or he ever was, a champion of their interests'.[94]

The evidence cannot, however, sustain this distinction between 'rights' and 'interests'. It is difficult to find compelling evidence that any substantial sector of the public voted against its perceived socio-economic interest. De Valera did give the deprived a sense of dignity. But this sense of dignity was by no means unrelated to their perception of their material interest. They might indeed have felt they would vote for him even if they starved. But they also believed that he would take good care to ensure that they would not starve. Like the poor of the Gaeltacht, the poor in general voted for de Valera because, '*É seo is mó a thug relief dos na daoine bochta*'[95] (he it was who gave most relief to the poor people). Fianna Fáil electoral propaganda achieved a masterly blend of the material with the ethereal. *The Irish Press* was quite clear on the main issues in the 1932 election. It did not neglect the constitutional dimension. But when insisting that 'along the whole range of political affairs there is an almost complete conflict of view between the two principal parties', it added 'nowhere is this more marked than in their social and economic policies'.[96] On election day itself it concluded that 'finding work for the workless . . . is a determining factor in that swing of public opinion which has been noted . . .'.[97] De Valera himself referred regularly to the material progress that Fianna Fáil would achieve. But it was part of his appeal that he appeared to transcend mere material mundanities by invoking a satisfying self-image of spiritual superiority ideally adapted to the psychic needs of his public. He had the gift of translating a greedy horde into a holy congregation. Thus Fianna Fáil emphasis on economics, however effectively it played on pocket principles, was not really 'materialism'. When the *Press* castigated the 'materialistic philosophy' of Cumann na nGaedheal, the unsuspecting might assume that the alternative would be a call to spirititual meditation. Far from it. The alternative was state intervention to create jobs, which was 'a Christian concept of society'.[98]

[93] *Ibid.* See also Walsh, *The Party*, p. 31.
[94] Rumpf and Hepburn, *Nationalism and socialism*, p. 100.
[95] S. Ó Riordáin, 'De Valera, de Gaulle agus Dia', in M. MacInerney (ed.), *Eamon de Valera, 1882–1975* (Dublin, 1976), p. 121.
[96] *Irish Press*, 15 February 1932.   [97] *Irish Press*, 16 February 1932.
[98] *Irish Press*, 30 January 1932.

The *Press* could claim that Fianna Fáil, after only nine months in office, 'has translated the sweetness of Christianity into social progress . . . bank deposits have risen, savings in the form of post office certificates have enormously increased, bank clearances have gone up . . . '.[99] Far from constituting a vulgar appeal to mean materialistic instincts, this simply demonstrated that Fianna Fáil's social policy was 'Christianity translated into economics', for 'there is not a social or economic change Fianna Fáil had proposed or brought about which has not its fullest justification in the encyclicals of either Leo XIII or the present Pontiff'.[100] There is ample evidence to support the conclusion that 'cheap food and better job prospects go a long way towards explaining the substantial working-class support won by Fianna Fáil during the 1930s . . . '.[101] Nevertheless the skill with which Fianna Fáil rhetoric enabled the beneficiaries to wrap their material gains in the demure drapery of moral uplift provides one clue to the emotional appeal of the party. A secret of de Valera's success was his uncanny ability to caress the feelings of his followers in so feline a way that they could, to crudely adapt Heaney, 'Talk Christ and think money.'

There was, of course, a hard anti-Treaty core to the Fianna Fáil vote. It would be more difficult to claim that there was a hard pro-Treaty core to the Fine Gael vote. Rather at its core was a hard anti-anti-Treaty vote. But that was based more on who the anti-Treaty people were, than on the fact that they were anti-Treaty. And that division was predominantly one of socio-economic perceptions of status and self-interest.

At a party organisation level, constitutional issues doubtless provided the prime motivation for many early party activists. The Treaty split in the Dáil 'had few socio-economic correlates'.[102] Yet the sources of popular support for pro- and anti-Treaty forces did reflect socio-economic differences. Economic interest groups, like Farmers and Labour, also attracted a striking degree of support even in the fetid atmosphere of the 1922 election. The conservative policies of Cumann na nGaedheal reinforced the initial social distinctions between pro-Treaty and anti-Treaty, and differences in the social bases of party support crystallised during the twenties.[103]

Is it possible to deduce some rough orders of magnitude of the degree of 'socio-economic' support for the two main parties, assuming that the vast

[99] *Irish Press*, 23 January 1933.   [100] *Irish Press*, 11 January 1933.
[101] J.P. Neary and C. Ó Gráda, *Protection, economic war and structural change: the 1930s in Ireland* (London, 1986), p. 9.
[102] T. Garvin, 'Decolonisation, nationalism, and electoral politics in Ireland 1832–1945', in O. Büsch (ed.), *Wählerbewegung in der Europäischen Geschichte* (Berlin, 1980), p. 272.
[103] M.A.G. Ó Tuathaigh, 'Party politics, political stability and social change in Ireland 1932–73: the case of Fianna Fáil', *XVe Congrès International des Sciences Historiques, Actes IV (2)* (Bucharest, 1982), p. 927.

bulk of support for other parties derived mainly from this source? Complications naturally arise from entries to and exits from, the electorate. The subject, however, is sufficiently interesting to excuse heroic assumptions. The 290 000 Sinn Féin voters in 1923 may be considered the ceiling of the undiluted anti-Treaty vote. Even that number surely contained many voters opposing the government mainly on social and economic grounds in the prevailing depression. Fianna Fáil's vote came to only 299 000 in June 1927, despite the discontent with Cumann na nGaedheal, whose share of the valid poll fell from 38.9 per cent to 27.5 per cent. If Fianna Fáil's abstention from the Dáil satisfied fundamentalist yearnings, it failed to attract new supporters. Between then and 1932, support for Fianna Fáil rose from 299 000 to 566 000 votes. Most of the extra 267 000 voters can be reasonably assumed to have been attracted mainly by its policy on social and economic issues, once it began to seriously formulate a programme in this area. The six extra seats it won in 1932 in the western small farmer constituencies, the two gains in Dublin working-class constituencies, the transfers from Labour that gained seats in Carlow/Kilkenny and in Meath, represented hopes roused more by a programme that promised solutions to urban unemployment and to rural poverty than to primeval hostility to the Treaty.

Nor was the 1932 election unique in this respect. The Treaty simply did not polarise the electorate to anything like the extent that party stalwarts would have wished. The shifts in popular support for Fianna Fáil after 1932/3 can continue to be attributed primarily to its social and economic policies. It lost 90 000 voters in 1937 as it failed to sustain the promise of four years before. The difference between the 1937 election returns and the vote on the referendum on the constitution, held on the same day, is particularly instructive. Only 527 000 voted against the constitution, while 725 000 voted against Fianna Fáil. In addition, the majority of those who opposed the constitution probably did so more on party grounds than on ideological grounds in a strict sense. If constitutional issues were paramount in the mind of the electorate it may be surmised that de Valera at this stage would have enjoyed the support of the vast majority of the public. This, no doubt, is to over-simplify the situation. But it is much less of an over-simplification than the axiomatic attribution of voting patterns to attitudes towards the Treaty.

Fianna Fáil lost 110 000 votes in 1943, during wartime austerity. Neutrality was at that stage allegedly conferring a new legitimacy on the state and on de Valera as national leader. It did not translate into votes. This was due to working class defections in Dublin, and to small farmer defections in Connaught. Clann na Talmhan won 137 000 votes at its first general election in 1943. The small farmers who supported the Clann were clear that Fianna Fáil was failing to promote their 'interests'. It is difficult to attribute these quite significant shifts in support for Fianna Fáil to changing attitudes towards the Treaty. Nor can the decline in the Fine Gael vote from 429 000 in 1938 to only 262 000 in 1948 reflect belated disillusion with its stance on the Treaty, any more than its recovery to 427 000 in 1954 implies further reflection by the electorate on the Treaty issue.

The geographical distribution of support for the main parties reflected socio-economic structures. Cumann na nGaedheal won disproportionate support in the more affluent east, and Sinn Féin/Fianna Fáil in the poorer west. But there were plenty of the relatively poor in the east, and a stratum of the relatively affluent in the west. These voted predominantly for Fianna Fáil and Cumann na nGaedheal respectively. Laver's finding, that within constituencies socio-economic differences affected party support, makes historical sense.[104] Cumann na nGaedheal won as much support as Fianna Fáil in the west until 1932. But this was more a function of turn-out than of loyalty. Once Fianna Fáil launched its land annuity and dole policies, it roused a massive response among previous non-voters. The 1930s was the great decade for Fianna Fáil in the west. The apparent 'evening out' of the geographical distribution of Fianna Fáil support in the 1943 election owed, as we have seen, less to gains in the east than to losses in the west, where it was now failing to deliver on its social promises.[105]

Dublin, emphatically Sinn Féin in 1918, strongly supported Cumann na nGaedheal in 1922. There was a significant 'peace' vote, and substantial Unionist and Labour votes. Dublin remained broadly Cumann na nGaedheal during the 1920s, but shifted significantly in 1932 and more particularly in 1933, when Fianna Fáil had implemented in its first year in office a sweeping range of social reforms. The Dublin working class, whether previously non-voters, or Labour voters, now rallied to the promise of a new social policy. Dublin's political loyalties changed mainly as a result of developments within Dublin itself. The rest of the east of Ireland did not show any marked change in party loyalties until social structures began to shift in the 1960s.

The party leaders had to reconcile popular instincts of post-colonial vintage with an objective socio-economic situation much closer to western European experience. Many features of alleged Irish deviance can be explained reasonably rationally in the light of this unusual combination. The techniques of party leaderships employed to establish the popular legitimacy of the new regime largely reflect the demands and pressures arising from these circumstances.

With the population drifting towards Dublin, and the standard of living

104 M. Laver, 'Party choice and social structure in Ireland', *Irish Political Studies*, 1 (1986), p. 49.
105 R. Sinnott, 'Interpretations of the Irish party system', *EJPR*, 12 (1984), p. 295.

rising in absolute terms, however relatively retarded Ireland became by western European standards, Fianna Fáil in particular faced problems of adjustment to the changing sources of its social and geographical support after the Second World War. The rejuvenation of Fianna Fáil after its uncertain performance in the postwar decade reflects the skill of the leadership in responding to the changes. That the readjustment was accomplished relatively smoothly testifies to the high quality of the leadership's party and electoral management in the Lemass years.[106] If Fine Gael was slower to take party and electoral management seriously, when it finally did so, under Garret FitzGerald, it too displayed a high degree of professionalism.[107]

For all the skill of the party leaders in achieving stability, they had to rely on *de facto* gerrymandering of constituency boundaries to reinforce their more orthodox talents. Only this enabled majority governments, or at least majority one-party governments, to emerge on minority popular votes. On strict proportionality, Fianna Fáil secured an absolute majority only in 1938 and 1977.[108] The restriction imposed on gerrymandering by the establishment of an independent commission on constituency boundaries by Jack Lynch after the 1977 election made it far more difficult for a single party to achieve an overall majority. Coalition governments and minority governments can rule well. Nevertheless, and despite the resolution displayed by the minority government of Lemass between 1961 and 1965, and the general ability of coalition cabinets to more or less stay the course,[109] it is doubtful if, other things remaining equal, strict proportionality of seats to votes would have led to a comparable degree of governmental stability.

The character of many politicians in the early days of independence was well adapted to achieving stability. But stability to what purpose? Stability must always be an end in itself in civilised society, but it cannot be the only end, or it degenerates into stagnation. Stability apart, the Irish have been nearly as sterile in government as they have been creative in politics. The party system has not adapted to the changing role of the state. The

106 Baker, 'Nationalist ideology', pp. 57–66; Girvin, 'The dominance of Fianna Fáil', pp. 466–9.
107 O'Byrnes, *Hiding behind a face, passim*; D.M. Farrell, 'The strategy to market Fine Gael in 1981', *Irish Political Studies*, 1 (1986), pp. 1–14. For wider reflections on issues discussed here, see M. Gallagher, 'Societal change and party adaptation in the Republic of Ireland, 1960–1981', *EJPR*, 9 (1981), pp. 268–85; M.A. Marsh, 'Ireland', in I. Crewe and D. Denver (eds.), *Electoral change in western democracies: patterns and sources of electoral volatility* (London, 1985), pp. 173–201; P. Mair, *The changing Irish party system* (London, 1987).
108 O'Leary, *Elections*, pp. 100ff.
109 B. Farrell, 'Coalitions and political institutions; the Irish experience', in V. Bogdanor (ed.), *Coalition government in Western Europe* (London, 1983), p. 259; A. Cohan, 'The open coalition in the closed society: the strange pattern of government formation in Ireland', *Comparative Politics*, 11, 3 (1979), pp. 336–8.

catch-all nature of the two main parties, now less ideologically distin-
guishable than in earlier decades, leaves both appealing to the total
electorate, and therefore slow to take a stand against any pressure group.
The party system has thus become inordinately exposed to extortionate
demands.

Interest groups play an indispensable role in modern society. Their
influence, however, has been increasingly exerted against the national
interest as the more muscular have sought to force others to pay for their
winnings. The failure of the political parties to resist their more avaricious
demands has damaged the country's competitiveness, intensified
unemployment in the exposed industrial sectors, blighted the prospects of
a younger generation, and fostered a cynicism that has further corroded
the sense of the public interest. Creating conditions in which the filching
fingers of pressure group leaders can be chopped requires political as well
as administrative reform. The electoral system, which served the country
well for the first half-century or so of independence, now exerts a paralytic
influence on many politicians. Efforts to change the multi-member
constituency system were rightly rejected by the public in 1959 and 1968
when they so patently served the interests of a single party. Circumstances
have changed since then. The precise party advantages of change are much
less certain, at least if the constituencies are determined by an independent
commission. It has become increasingly important to protect deputies
from themselves. For the present system obliges them to squander much
time in barren intra-party competition. It may be time to consider again
the 'Norton amendment' of 1968, which unavailingly proposed the
creation of single member constituencies with the single transferrable
vote.

Electoral reform alone will not protect the parties from the predatory
passions of the pressure group. It could, however, lighten the constituency
loads of TDs, and even give some of them time to think. The role of the TD
as a local representative looms almost as large in reality as in folklore. But
there is nothing particularly unusual about localism in Ireland. Localism is
the rule, not the exception, in European political cultures, including those
in economically-advanced countries. It is somewhat less pronounced in
England than elsewhere, for historical reasons, which helps explain why
those whose comparative perspective is confined to England tend to
regard Irish localism as quaint. But England is by no means representative
of Europe. Localism in Ireland does enjoy a higher profile in national
studies than tends to be the case in continental countries, however, for two
reasons.

Firstly, the Irish electoral system puts a premium on deputies of the
same party competing within constituencies to persuade the electors of the
quality of their service. Candidates in other electoral systems do not

hesitate to remind electors of their concern for the constituency. But they do not normally have to descend to such vulgar levels of ingratiation as their Hibernian colleagues. Secondly, Ireland has almost no serious local self-government, in marked contrast to many western European countries. 'Local issues decided locally' are relatively rare in Ireland. Local issues are largely decided nationally, insofar as they are decided at all. National decisions have fundamental implications for local welfare in areas like policing, education, health, and conservation, which often come under local control elsewhere. Local interests therefore have to be hawked prominently around the national political arena, instead of being decided at less obtrusive local levels. It is less the intensity of localism that is peculiar to Ireland than the mechanisms devised to elevate the local to the national. Indeed, localism has become even more pronounced, and inevitably so, as the role of central government has grown. The prominence of the local at national level is the reverse side of the coin of administrative centralisation.[110]

It may be, then, that the political system has failed to serve the country as well in recent as in earlier years. No doubt illogicalities, even inanities and absurdities, abounded from the outset. But they are part of the stuff of politics in any country. However bizarre the behaviour of individual politicians on occasion, there is no compelling evidence that the Irish political system has, on the whole, served the country worse, even from the point of view of socio-economic performance, much less of the achievement of a tolerably civilised polity, than the systems of other countries. There is a danger that the blatantly irresponsible behaviour of certain ministers, and even cabinets, since 1972 may disguise this fact, and allow others, whether civil servants, businessmen, trade unionists or academics, to exonerate themselves from their historical responsibilities by pointing the accusing finger at the politicians, as if they themselves were recording consistently first-class performances only to find the fruits of their husbandry squandered by a profligate political class. That, quite simply, has not hitherto been the case, if only because governments have been as much the prisoners as the masters of the political culture in general, and of the administrative culture in particular.

The senior civil service did not become unduly concerned with its own performance until the 1960s.[111] The general assumption in the early days was that as the British civil service came as close to perfection as the mind of man could devise, Ireland was fortunate in having a service so closely

---

110 R. Roche, 'The high cost of complaining Irish style: a preliminary examination of the Irish pattern of complaint behaviour and of its associated costs', *Irish Business and Administrative Research*, 4, 2 (1982), p. 102; Farrell, 'Friends and neighbours', pp. 254–6; L. Komito, 'Irish clientelism: a reappraisal', *ESR*, 15, 3 (April 1984), p. 188.

111 N. Whelan, 'The Irish public service: its reform', *Administration*, 25, 1 (Spring 1977), p. 3.

modelled on the ideal. Critics made little impression on the carapace of complacency until Patrick Lynch's *Studies* article in 1953. Whitaker would be the first Secretary of Finance to give sustained thought to the quality of civil service performance, as Lemass was the first Taoiseach to seriously ponder the subject. Both were cautious reformers. Both knew the strengths as well as the weaknesses of the existing service. They were instrumental in the establishment of the Public Service Organisation Review Group (PSORG), under the chairmanship of Liam St John Devlin, in 1966, to review the working of the public service. The Devlin Report, submitted in 1969, provoked extensive debate. Many civil servants and politicians devoutly wished to see Devlin buried. But the problems would not go away. Eventually, in 1985, a White Paper, *Managing the country better*, was to appear, addressing some of the issues raised by Devlin. Why was this parturition so protracted?

Devlin's diagnosis was simple. Decision-makers were 'so involved in the press of daily business that they have little time to participate in the formulation of overall policy'.[112] To extricate them from submersion in a morass of detail, Devlin recommended that policy formulation should be separated from policy implementation. A distinct policy-making group of senior officials in every department should, together with the minister, form the policy-making body (called the Aireacht), while the execution of policy would devolve upon executive offices. Everything else in Devlin revolved around this central recommendation.

Devlin was a major report. Its reception has become a saga in itself, unhappily confirming the Devlin diagnosis of the widespread 'built-in resistance to change' in the service.

Executive Offices accountable for their actions, and Aireacht's in which ministers would share responsibility for policy-making, would undermine the venerable doctrine of 'ministerial responsibility'. That was part of Devlin's purpose. The concept of 'ministerial responsibility', cherished in Britain, but dismissed as quaint in most advanced countries, provided a convenient façade behind which some civil servants could exercise power without responsibility, and others enjoy the rewards of a quiet life. Yet the whole organisation of public business, revolving around Dáil questions and assuming that ministers had to take responsibility for every decision in their departments, could ultimately be traced to what was by now, at best, a polite fiction. Not only many civil servants, but also many ministers, were reluctant to dispense with this fiction. Some feared they might not be able to claim credit for the 'favours' done by their department. Some, only too aware of the route by which they had reached office, might harbour reservations about the exposure of their mental

---

[112] Public Service Organisation Review Group Report (*Devlin Report*) (Dublin, 1969), p. 138.

processes to the full glare of the Aireachts. Was it for this the wild geese fled? Was it for this they had pushed, shoved, gouged their way to the state car? All those *bóithríns* traipsed, hands shook, backs slapped, convent tea manfully swallowed, funerals looked suitably forlorn at, sympathies sincerely extended, transfers of surpluses sweated through at interminable counts with the final references flying in all directions as ungrateful wretches forgot favours done them – and all for what? That they should land on their Aireachts up in the department? All that, and then to be expected to think too! Was there no respite for an honest soul in a vindictive world? It was not entirely a matter for surprise that observers, not excluding politicians themselves, should detect a certain lack of political will in the implementation of Devlin.[113]

Devlin's proposals for widening promotional possibilities, and its insistence that promotion should be on merit, roused resistance among those suspicious of 'policies for the transfer and promotion of staff across traditional barriers of grade and organisation . . .'.[114] Some would gain. But many feared they stood to lose if 'barriers between organisations and barriers of class and seniority within organisations' could no longer be relied on 'to impede the flow of the best talent where it is most needed'.[115] 'Failure to advertise . . .' was a useful weapon in the defense of promotion on a seniority basis.[116] If some 'people of ability' could not continue to be 'forced to spend their careers in isolated branches of the public service',[117] would they not threaten the security of people of less ability in not so isolated branches? The country and the service might gain. But what was that to the likely losers?

There could be no more compelling evidence of the need for Devlin than the reaction to Devlin. The most ingenious, and disingenuous, excuse advanced for resistance was that the civil service was too busy to implement it.[118] This reinforced the Devlin perception that alternative structures were urgently required to give the harrassed officials a chance to reflect on what they were doing.

Not every Devlin recommendation was necessarily justified. Devlin itself observed that it was the process of built-in change that was most important, noting that 'the remedies we describe today may, in some

---

[113] S. Calleary, 'Devlin – ten years on', *Administration*, 27, 4 (Winter 1979), p. 395; N. Whelan, 'Public service adaptation – its nature and requirements', *Administration*, 27, 1 (Spring 1979), p. 96; C. Ó Nualláin, 'Public service reform', *Administration*, 26, 3 (Autumn 1978), pp. 301–2.

[114] Calleary, 'Devlin', pp. 397–8; Whelan, 'Adaptation', p. 93. On some trade union and staff reluctance to participate in staff assessment, see R. Chapman, 'The Irish public service: change or reform?', *Administration*, 23, 2 (1975), p. 138 and Seán Dooney, '1969–1979: a decade of development?', *Seirbhís Phoiblí*, 1, 2 (1980), pp. 29, 32.

[115] *Devlin Report*, p. 141.   [116] *Ibid.*   [117] *Ibid.*

[118] Calleary, 'Devlin', p. 395.

respects, be outmoded in ten years time'.[119] 'In ten years time' it was impossible to say. The remedies had not been tried. The annual reports of the Public Service Advisory Council, established on a Devlin recommendation to monitor the implementation of the reforms, instead chronicle their non-implementation.[120] The Director of the Institute of Public Administration would refer discreetly to 'the formidable nature of the inertia and opposition to change within organisations and within the system' that frustrated the implementation of Devlin.[121] Reformers might come, and reformers might go. But after Devlin, as before, '"an executive redoubt", independent of the party machine, survived and even prospered, relying on its own indispensability and on its own very considerable sense of corporate responsibility and self interest.'[122] How far that 'self interest' coincided with the national interest remains to be seriously researched.

Balanced responses to Devlin suggested that the institutional structures recommended were too elaborate for many departments, and also expressed scepticism about whether policy-making and policy-executing functions could be so clearly separated in practice.[123] A further substantive criticism was that Devlin concentrated excessively on structures as distinct from individuals.[124] Noel Whelan, a persistent advocate of organisational reform, became so conscious of the potential for resistance over fifteen years sad experience after Devlin, that he came to accept that 'public service change is so tortuously slow' that less importance should be attached to 'changing institutions' than to changing 'the people in the institutions'.[125]

Was this criticism justified? Why did Devlin reach such a conclusion? Was it a commission of woolly-minded theorists, unfamiliar with the daily problems of running organisations? The composition of the commission left little scope for the familiar sneers on this score. Devlin himself was an experienced businessman. Of the other members, only three, Paddy Leahy, Professor of Mechanical Engineering at UCD, Tom Barrington, Director of the Institute of Public Administration, and Magnus Bratten,

119 *Devlin Report*, p. 137.
120 Ó Nualláin, 'Reform'; S. Dooney, 'Why do we need a Public Service Advisory Council?' *Seirbhís Phoiblí*, 3, 2 (1982). See the disillusioned comment of the first Chairman of the PSAC, Patrick Lynch, in M. Healy and J. Davis (eds.), *The control and management of technology in society* (Dublin, 1981), p. 93.
121 C. Ó Nualláin, 'Sharing the nation's resources: problems of administration in the public service', *Administration*, 27, 4 (Winter 1979), p. 454.
122 Garvin, *Irish Nationalist Politics*, p. 206.
123 P.T. O'Connell, 'The civil service in the modern state', *Studies* (Summer 1970), p. 167; R.W. Wilding, 'The civil service in the modern state', *ibid.*, pp. 174–5. The Dept. of Health duly transferred nearly 80 per cent of its staff into the Aireacht on these grounds: (NESC, *Service type employment and regional development* (Dublin, 1976), 4.4).
124 G. MacKechnie, 'Devlin revisited', *Administration*, 25, 1 (Spring 1977), p. 17.
125 *Irish Times*, 12 November 1984.

the Head of Education and Training in the Norwegian civil service, could be considered academically tainted. Sir Geoffrey Thompson was Managing Director of Guinness, Jerry Dempsey, General Manager of Aer Lingus, Thekla Beere, a former Secretary of the Department of Transport and Power, and Louis Fitzgerald, head of the establishment division of the Department of Finance. They could hardly be indicted for unfamiliarity with decision-making in large organisations, including the public service.

Devlin's terms of reference obliged the commission to concentrate on structures. Their brief was 'to examine and report on the organisation of the Departments of State at the higher levels, including the appropriate distribution of functions as between both departments themselves and departments and other bodies'.[126] These were strangely restrictive terms of reference. Strange, because Lemass and Whitaker both earlier expressed the view that a key to change lay in attitudes. As early as 1961 Lemass purported to detect a significant improvement in the recent performance of the civil service,

mainly I believe, because a change has taken place in the attitude of the Heads of the Civil Service to national development possibilities. In the administration of any government in any country, the mood and attitude of the Finance Department is felt throughout the whole administration . . . At this time, the public spirited and stimulating attitude of our Department of Finance is a very important factor in the building-up of the widely successful development effort which is now evident.[127]

If, in the same speech, he made his famous reference to the continuing tendency 'of some government departments . . . to wait for new ideas to walk in through the door',[128] he also insisted that 'the quality of our civil servants is very high'.[129] Whitaker had anticipated the organisation issue around which Devlin revolved: 'how Secretaries and other senior officers can organise their time and work to get away from their desks every day sufficiently to read, consider and consult with others in order to be able to give sound and comprehensive advice on future development policy'.[130] Yet he too emphasised attitudes, arguing that, 'reform from within is, from my view, more a matter of reorientation of outlook, of recognition and acceptance of wider personal responsibilities than a very big change in organisational structure'.[131]

In view of this emphasis on attitudes, it is surprising that Devlin's terms of reference concentrated almost exclusively on organisation. But Devlin

---

[126] *Devlin Report*, p. 3.
[127] S.F. Lemass, 'The organisation behind the economic programme', in B. Chubb and P. Lynch (eds.), *Economic development and planning* (Dublin, 1969), p. 206.
[128] *Ibid.*, p. 205.   [129] *Ibid.*
[130] T.K. Whitaker, 'The civil service and development', in Chubb and Lynch, *Development*, p. 18.
[131] *Ibid.*, p. 215.

was not unduly perturbed by this restriction. On the contrary, it concluded that,

our review of the present structure and organisation of the Public Service has led us to the conclusion that the faults are largely those of institutions. Where there has been a failure, it has been in the reluctance to recognise the need for action of the institution as a whole. If structural and organisational faults are corrected, it is possible that the personnel may still not measure up to the requirements but, in that event, a fresh look at the institutions may reveal that they are deficient in identifying and training the right people. For this reason, the continuous review of institutions is essential.[132]

This does seem to invest institutions with an autonomous decision-making capacity, independent of the calibre of the individuals involved in the decision-making process. After all, once 'structural and organisational faults are corrected', subsequent failure to identify and train the 'right people' can hardly be a failure of the institution, but of the individuals running the institution. Devlin then may have laid excessive emphasis on structures. But it was certainly right to draw attention to organisation. It is not of course necessarily a question of either/or. As Lemass put it, 'all experience teaches that the right kind of organisation can help in developing the right attitudes'.[133] Performance will still vary widely from person to person, according to attitude and aptitude, even within the best organised institutions. But structures are not neutral. They cannot, it is true, do much to improve the performance of totally negative personalities. But they can prevent the more parasitic, or the more selfish elements, of which there are always many, from dragging down the more productive or the more patriotic, of which there are often many, to their own level. Too many Irish institutional structures, whether in the public or in the private sector, have historically conferred a built-in advantage on the limpets, enabling them to thwart initiative behind a respectable façade of concern for the common good. Many Irish institutions seem to have devised structures that foster widespread frustration, bringing to a fine art the pernicious knack of demotivating people. It is doubtful if many of even the best people are achieving their full potential as they feel themselves trapped within 'the system'.[134]

Yet another ironic justification of Devlin's concern was provided when the first major institutional change attributable to Devlin was implemented in such a way as to subvert a main principle of the report. The Department of the Public Service (DPS) was established in 1973. It was a caricature of the department proposed by Devlin. Instead of being a primarily creative department, concerned with implementing Devlin, its

---

[132] *Devlin Report*, p. 142.   [133] Lemass, 'Organisation', p. 205.
[134] These paragraphs draw on J.J. Lee, 'Whither Ireland? The next twenty-five years', in K.A. Kennedy (ed.), *Ireland in transition* (Dublin, 1986), p. 158.

main responsibility was to control staff numbers and pay levels throughout the public service. Its role was little different from that of the establishment division of Finance, from which indeed it was mainly staffed. Dynamic organisational functions envisaged by Devlin remained stillborn. Private sector workers with experience in the civil service noted the tension between the DPS objective 'of reducing and controlling resources', and 'the more expansionist aspirations of individual departments'.[135] It would be several years before the department began to address the original purpose which Devlin envisaged for it.[136]

The biggest influence on working styles in the main departments during the 1970s derived less from Devlin than from entry to the EEC. Other significant institutional change likewise owed little to Devlin. By the late 1970s, public irritation at the quality of the telephone service and, to a lesser extent, of the postal service, became so intense – even among a people capable of tolerating almost any level of shoddiness of service – as to begin to create political embarrassment. A special inquiry, chaired by M.J. Dargan, who had wide experience in the private and public sectors, documented the inadequacies of the Department of Posts and Telegraphs so remorselessly that something had to be done.[137] The report hardly came as a revelation to ministers with experience of the department. P.J. Lalor, a former minister, recalled that 'work there was a matter of moving paper'.[138] Posts and Telegraphs could not be salvaged. Two new state boards, under the chairmanship of successful private businessmen, were established to replace departmental control of the two services.

Far from steps being taken to counter the fragmentation identified by Devlin, the civil service continued to grow in size and incoherence. Total numbers rose from 36 000 in 1970 to 60 000 in 1983.[139] More did not mean better. A growing number of serious commentators felt sufficiently incensed to record their disdain. Barrington's periodisation of the quality of public service performance counted ten years of high quality, from the late 1950s to the late 1960s, a five-year plateau, and then ten years of decline.[140] A distinguished group of businessmen and economists appointed by the government to review the economic situation noted that

---

135 T. Thurston, 'A meeting of Ireland's two greatest natural resources', *Seirbhís Phoiblí*, 5, 2 (1984), p. 34.
136 R. Roche, 'The role of the Department of the Public Service', *Administration*, 27, 4 (Winter 1979), pp. 411ff. It may be surmised that the more reformist the Department became, the more jaundiced the Finance eye cast in its direction. (The Department was duly abolished and reincorporated in Finance after Fianna Fáil returned to office in 1987.)
137 Posts and Telegraphs Review Group Report (*Dargan Report*) (Dublin, 1979).
138 *Irish Times*, 1 and 2 April 1983.
139 P.C. Humphreys, *Public service employment* (Dublin, 1983), pp. 50–2.
140 T. Barrington, 'Whatever happened to Irish government?', in F. Litton (ed.), *Unequal achievement* (Dublin, 1982), p. 90.

while many criticisms of the public service were 'of a kind which are made from time to time against any large-scale organisation, whether public or private, profit-making or voluntary', nevertheless the service itself 'has now a reputation of over-cautious conservatism . . . seen as over-manned, under-managed and consuming an inordinate share of resources for the services given'.[141] A cerebral businessman would refer to 'the deteriorating condition of the administrative sector'[142] while Ivor Kenny, a former Director of the IMI, condemned the public decision-making system as no longer viable.[143]

At a more specific level, Dermot McAleese, a distinguished economist and a director of the Central Bank, welcomed some features of *Building on Reality*. However, he found that its 'incongruities . . . combined to give an impression of hasty compilation and half-baked policy stances'.[144] Joe Durkan, a respected forecaster with the ESRI, dismissed *Industrial Policy* as fit only for quick burial. He identified 'the most disturbing aspect' of *Building on Reality* as 'the apparent failure of the public sector to respond intellectually to the problems of society'. Compared with the first three economic programmes it was 'a sorry document. If this is the best the public sector can come up with, then we have to start again.'[145] Paul Tansey, a leading economic journalist, dismissed a white paper on tourism as 'a sorry disappointment', finding its 'tone . . . evasive, its factual base poor and its social content negligible'.[146] There was a consensus among students of resource and environmental issues that 'there appears to be a systemic incapacity on the part of the political/administrative apparatus to produce and implement policy, in spite of the passage of a very extensive volume of legislation'.[147]

A closer look at the process through which the white paper *Industrial Policy* emerged reveals the deterioriation in the decision-making capacity of the system. *Industrial Policy* purported to be the first major re-evaluation of industrial policy for twenty-five years.[148] The contrast with *Economic Development* is instructive. The idea for *Economic Development* gestated in Whitaker's mind in the autumn of 1957. Preliminary work had been initiated when formal authorisation to proceed was

[141] *Proposals for a plan* (Dublin, 1984), pp. 330–1.
[142] D.S.A. Carroll, 'Foreword', in I. Kenny, *Government and enterprise* (Dublin, 1984), p. 7.
[143] I. Kenny, 'Planning and process', in *Ireland in the year 2000: towards a national strategy* (Dublin, 1983), pp. 22–3.
[144] McAleese, 'Building on reality', p. 28.
[145] J. Durkan, 'The National Plan', *IBR* (December 1984), p. 19.
[146] *Sunday Tribune*, 6 October 1985.
[147] F.J. Convery, 'Resources and environment 1983: synthesis', in J. Blackwell and F.J. Convery (eds.), *Promise and performance: Irish environmental policies analysed* (Dublin, 1983), p. 411.
[148] *Industrial Policy* (Dublin, 1984), p. 3.

received in December. *Economic Development* was completed in May 1958. It was published in November 1958, as was the White Paper based on it. The idea for Telesis, as already noted, gestated in the minds of Noel Whelan and Charles Haughey in December 1979/January 1980. The NESC approached Telesis in July 1980. The study was conducted between September 1980 and March 1981. Hitherto, the pace could compare with that of 1958–9. But Telesis was not published until February 1982. *Industrial Policy* then took another two-and-a-half years to emerge.

Some delay was due to cabinet wrangling, with Labour reputedly unhappy about the disdainful Telesis tone toward public enterprise.[149] Cabinet procrastination delayed publication by nearly a year, the White Paper having been ready in the autumn of 1983. But that was still two-and-a-half years after Telesis completed its enquiry. The delay might have been understandable if *Industrial Policy* did in fact represent a revolutionary change of policy. However, it represented nothing like so fundamental a revision of prevailing assumptions as did *Economic Development*. Indeed, it compares poorly with Whitaker's document not only in quality but in range, reflecting the fragmentation of economic policy formation which institutionalised the growing incapacity to take a total view.

Some departments had earlier performed impressively, given clear political and/or administrative leadership, like the Industry and Commerce of Lemass/Leydon, the Health of Noel Browne, the Finance of Whitaker.[150] It was now becoming increasingly difficult to create a similar sense of direction. The growth in the variety of vested interests, inside no less than outside the public sector, in the twenty-five years since *Economic Development* made it difficult for even determined and clear-sighted leaders, whether politicians or administrators, to slice their way through the intestinal intricacies of the institutional maze. Clear vision, and firm political leadership, may not suffice to attain national goals. Without them, however, paralysis prevails.

In view of the growing disdain, even among responsible citizens, for the performance of the public service, the challenge confronting John Boland, whom Garret FitzGerald appointed Minister for the Public Service in December 1982, the first time the Department had a separate minister, was a formidable one. 'A gritty performer with a dash of the street fighter in his make-up',[151] Boland needed all his willpower and astuteness to wear down or circumvent the forces of resistance.[152] He would first have to establish bridge-heads within the perimeters of Fortress Bureaucracy,

149 S. O'Byrnes, *Irish Independent*, 26 April 1984.
150 Browne, *Against the tide*, pp. 112–13, 121.
151 P. Tansey, *Sunday Tribune*, 21 July 1985.
152 Jim Dunne, 'Public sector: a hitch for Boland's reforms', *Business and Finance*, 12 July 1984, p. 28.

and then try to infiltrate deeper into the enemy camp. It would be a war of attrition. Appearances would often belie reality, for nominal acquiescence could be as lethal a defensive weapon as indignant resistance.

Boland succeeded in smashing through a major change in appointment procedures, with the creation of the Top Level Appointment Committee (TLAC) in January 1984. Devlin had briskly asserted that 'several essential matters can be attended to at once. First among these, we would put the reform of the present system of promotion.[153] 'At once' would take fifteen years! Some *ad hoc* progress was made in the direction of recognising the principle of merit in the intervening period. Several worthwhile appointments were made. But these were still seen as exceptions that proved the rule. The purpose of the TLAC was to change the rule. This committee was to recommend the best candidate available 'irrespective of department, background or specialty, thereby bringing to an end the dual structure – a system under which professionals and non-professionals have their own career structures'. In addition, Secretaries appointed under the new system would serve for not more than seven years and, except for a transitional arrangement, not beyond the age of sixty.[154] These may appear to be dreary administrative details. In fact, they cut to the core of civil service culture, not to say of national culture. The implications for the private interests of many officials were so ominous that Boland was apparently driven to the device of getting it through the cabinet without circulating the proposals to other interested departments (in effect, all departments, according to normal procedures). That would have guaranteed another fifteen years delay!

This was a valiant attempt, and a potentially revolutionary one, to resolve the difficulties that regularly arose from inappropriate appointments at senior level due to limited competition. It attempted to anticipate some of the personnel problems that would inevitably arise when the big number of talented younger people recruited during the 1970s would find themselves frustrated by the log jam of promotion if they had to 'wait their turn'. These did not always recognise their elders as self-evidently their betters. How to mobilise this massive reservoir of talent, how to harness its potential idealism, how to prevent it from vegetating, how to save it from the corrosive cynicism induced by the techniques perfected by the forces of resistance, presented a major managerial problem, of the utmost significance for the national interest. Boland's initiatives counted as a major innovation, and not only in civil service terms. All changes bring their own difficulties, of course. Fresh problems were bound to occur. Mistakes would be made. Genuine problems often arise in assessing merit in non-market situations. But, as Thursten wryly and rightly noted,

---

153 *Devlin Report*, p. 197.
154 'Top level appointments in the civil service', *Administration*, 31, 4 (1984), pp. 335–6.

'without a mechanism to remove dead wood, some form of performance appraisal is essential'.[155] The new system began retreieving the reputation for intellectual integrity of the civil service, by elevating the principle of the national interest, however imperfectly and however elusively, above that of individual interest.

Younger civil servants, socialised into the mores of a system that subtly discouraged innovation by insinuating that 'too much challenge of the status quo would at best be unwelcome and blocked by senior levels, and at worst result in the application of the label "trouble maker"',[156] could now venture on the occasional heresy without threat of relegation in the promotional stakes. But the shock of the change was traumatic for many older officials. There was a certain poignancy attaching to some of the response.[157] Many who had served the state loyally and well by their standards would now inevitably be 'passed over'. Those who had spent thirty or forty years edging their way up the ladder of preferment, never taking a risk, never putting a foot wrong, now found themselves suddenly told they were supposed to have displayed initiative over all those years. Personalities stunted in the ceaseless defence of convention now learned they were expected to have been innovative all the time. The shock was all the more unsettling in the case of those who had entered the service with potential for initiative, only to have it remorselessly ground out of them by the system – which had now suddenly betrayed them.

The techniques of resistance to change in the civil service, as in the wider society, have yet to be systematically probed. The manner in which many an eager young novice – not all novices of course were equally eager – was tamed, the manner in which an anxiety 'to do something' for the country could be gradually assuaged, while at the same time a collective veneer of self-justification could serve to hide from many the corrosion of their ideals, even while it drove the less malleable to apathy or despair, offers a major challenge for the student of the relationship between individual potential and collective performance.

The civil service had many men of high natural talent. It was true that too few of those recruited in the first generation of independence had enjoyed access to an education of the quality their minds deserved. It was also largely true that their subsequent experience too rarely provided them with the opportunity to develop their conceptual capacity, deepen their perspectives or broaden their horizons. They often remained inexperienced even after reaching senior level. Such mentalities had so little instinct for innovation that a disproportionate number of such new ideas as infiltrated Irish government for more than a generation after independence came from the politicians. Officials of their calibre and disposition

[155] Thurston, 'A meeting', p. 35.   [156] *Ibid.*
[157] T. Duggan, 'Juventus ad Astra', *Seirbhís Phoiblí*, 6, 2 (1985).

could nevertheless perform prodigies in particular circumstances. Where problems largely defined themselves, and where public servants received clear political leadership, they could rise splendidly to the occasion. But they were at their best on the defensive. They were generally much less equipped to take the initiative. Where problems were more diffuse, where issues were of a more long-term developmental character, and could not be grasped as immediate crises, the response tended to be uncomprehending. It was no accident that the public service generally responded well, and sometimes superbly, to the pressures of the Second World War. There, the problem was defined for them. It was equally no accident that only a handful learned anything from the experience.

Observers conscious of the difficulty of achieving change in any Irish institution can only marvel at the tenacity and idealism of those who sustained the Sisyphean struggle against the forces of resistance and inertia. In 1979 the DPS launched a small but lively journal, *Seirbhís Phoiblí*, that enhanced the public image of the service by providing a forum for vigorous discussion, not least among civil servants themselves. Kevin Murphy, a future Secretary of the DPS, committed himself to a courageous public statement on the possibilities for improved productivity in the civil service.[158] Few senior decision-makers in other institutions, whether in the public or private sector, would comment as candidly or as intelligently on the difficulties they faced.

The magnitude of the task undertaken by Boland can be gauged from the fact that Lemass himself half-conceded defeat in his effort to improve matters. Though he was no administrative revolutionary, some of the Lemass ideas certainly appeared subversive of the private interest of public servants, even if he sought to strike a balance between innovatory impulses and 'the accumulated experience of years'. Lemass confessed that the forces of resistance had baffled him:

At one time I put forward the idea of the interchangeability of senior officers between departments, and between the civil service and state boards. The idea never got off the ground. Even ministers who supported it in theory were reluctant to apply it in practice when it meant passing over 'the next in line' for promotion or involved the risk of discontent among their officers. I suppose I was really trying to change human nature, and that the idea is in practice unworkable. Nevertheless, I believe that the efficiency of the public service would be considerably improved if it could be made to operate even in limited degrees.[159]

That Boland got the idea 'off the ground' where Lemass failed must count as a notable achievement.

Boland's tactics on the TLAC could not be repeated in connection with

---

[158] K. Murphy, 'Raising productivity in the civil service', *Seirbhís Phoiblí*, 3, 1 (1982), pp. 2–14.
[159] *Léargas*, 12 (Jan.–Feb. 1968), p. 2.

a white paper. The various drafts of *Serving the Country Better* ran the gauntlet of internal criticism, causing repeated delays in publication. Originally promised for the autumn of 1984, it eventually appeared a year late, and then in bowdlerised form. Nevertheless, appear it did. The more ardent advocates of change were disappointed at the modesty of the achievement.[160] There were indeed notable lacunae. But its appearance at all was, in the circumstances, a major achievement, another marker on the rocky road to national competitiveness. Of course, the implementation of even the relatively modest aspirations may be frustrated. But for the chronicler of a country's fortunes, it provides a benchmark against which the genuineness of public service commitment to the national interest can be measured.[161]

The quality of the official mind is now probably exerting an even greater influence than heretofore on the quality of national life, if only because the role of the state has so greatly expanded since 1960. State expenditure as a proportion of GDP is exceptionally high in Ireland compared with the OECD average. It appears spectacularly high, double the average, when compared with the proportion in OECD states when they were at the 1983 Irish level of per capita income. In many cases that was fifteen or twenty years earlier. Even in Sweden, normally regarded as a highly interventionist welfare state, the state played a far more limited role when the country had the same level of income per head as Ireland has today.[162]

If public expenditure has become bloated, public administration has become centralised to an extreme degree by the standards of more economically advanced countries. The thrust of central government since independence has been to restrict the scope of local authorities, and to centralise control over financial resources. This was partly intended to curb expenditure, and partly to reduce opportunities for corruption. The congenial consequence of this blend of financial and moral rectitude was augmentation of the power and prestige of the central bureaucracy. As long as there was a strong ethical resistance to state expansion, this did not involve a marked growth of the role of central government, as distinct from centralisation of public expenditure. But the role of the state, and the size of the public sector, have increased at an unprecedented rate since 1970. While government was becoming bigger and more complex, it was also becoming increasingly centralised. Civil servants are disproportion-

---

160 T. Barrington, 'Serve you right?', *Administration* 33, 4 (1985), pp. 431–4.
161 For Boland's own defence of the White Paper, see J. Boland, 'Serving the country better: a debate', *Administration*, 34, 3 (1986), pp. 287–90. For an overview of the condition of the civil service immediately following the White Paper see K. Murphy, 'A changing civil service?', *ibid.*, pp. 338–63.
162 *CII Newsletter*, 44, 8 (24 December 1985), pp. 2–3. I am grateful to C. Fanning for drawing my attention to this newsletter, and for providing me with a copy of it.

ately located in Dublin, and the headquarters of virtually every state-sponsored body, including nearly fifty new ones established since 1960, are also located there.

The intense centralisation of government helped foster further the dependency syndrome throughout society. Citizens were expected to behave responsibly despite having little responsibility to exercise. Officials who genuinely deplored the intensity of public demands on the state, themselves helped reinforce those demands through their craving for centralised authority. Changes in mental attitudes were fundamental to improvement of national performance. But it was difficult to change attitudes as long as citizens were reduced to such a level of dependency on central government.[163]

The rhetoric of local self-help is, of course, woven into an idealised self-image of national character. The reality is very different. The only concrete regional planning during the 1970s was done by the IDA. The division of the country into nine planning regions by Michael Killeen obliged the IDA to produce results in all regions. And the IDA did achieve a degree of success in this approach, demonstrating that determination was a major contributory factor towards the relative success of policy.

At government level, a flurry of regional planning activity in the late 1960s, including a White Paper on Local Government in 1972, all came to nothing.[164] The whole thrust of policy, as distinct from rhetoric, continued to be towards centralisation. The NESC noted the palpable lack of measures to implement the proclaimed regional policy of 1972.[165] In 1977 Fianna Fáil, by abolishing rates, deprived local authorities of their main source of independent financing, reducing them to even further dependence on central government. Local government has never been adequately developed in Ireland, and the current local government system is patently incapable of providing adequate local government. This indisputable fact is then used by centralisers, who have progressively undermined even the rudimentary inherited system, as a clinching argument against devising a proper system of local government! A small number of civil servants were, it is true, 'decentralised' to offices in Castlebar and Athlone during the 1970s. The exercise verged on the farcical, however, seeming to be designed in such a way as to discredit the whole idea.

The case against the devolution of centralised power was rarely articulated. There was no debate. Bureaucratic centralists refrained from

---

163 W.J. Smyth, 'Explorations of place', in Lee, *Ireland: towards a sense of place*, pp. 12–13; T. Walsh, *Developing national potential in the new era* (Dublin, 1984), p. 6.
164 M.A.G. Ó Tuathaigh, 'The regional dimension', in K. Kennedy (ed.), *Ireland in transition* (Dublin, 1986); G. Walker, 'Previous plans: targets versus performance', *Ireland in the year 2000: towards a national strategy* (Dublin, 1983), pp. 10–11.
165 NESC, *Urbanisation and regional development in Ireland*, p. 51.

entering into discussion, relying on their entrenched authority to foil any serious threat. Their reasoning has therefore to be largely inferred. Their revulsion against the prospect of decentralisation coincided with their own self-interest. This could not be decently publicised, or perhaps even admitted to oneself. A convenient rationalisation, and perhaps even a genuine case, was probably the feeling that Ireland was too small for devolution, whether geographically or demographically, or both. Examples from other countries, even small ones, were silently dismissed as irrelevant to Irish circumstances.

The centralisers enjoyed one decisive advantage apart from their hold on power. All they had to do was to do nothing. For centralisation was itself inexorably leading to the growing concentration of population in the Greater Dublin area, with concomitant implications for the location of decision-making power, social, political, economic, ecclesiastical, cultural, and intellectual.

The growth of Dublin is a distinctive feature of contemporary Irish social and demographic experience. Most other European capitals expanded in the twentieth century. But none, except Athens, grew to Dublin's relative size. In 1926 Dublin city and county contained 17 per cent of the national population. In 1985 they contained about 35 per cent. Very few European metropolitan areas contain more than 20 per cent and that proportion has been generally stable for a generation or so, whereas Dublin's has been rising rapidly.

If the growth of Dublin were the result of fundamental economic forces, it might be argued, at least by those who worship at the altar of the market, that this simply reflected the dictates of presumed economic efficiency, and that policy should strive to reinforce rather than retard a development allegedly in the national economic interest. But the growth of Dublin since independence owes much to purely political and administrative forces.

Social expenditure per capita is highest in the poorest regions of the country, partly because social payments are closely related to dependency ratios, which are normally higher in out-migrant regions. But total state expenditure per capita is highest in Dublin, due to the size of the public wages bill.[166] The distribution of state expenditure therefore reinforces tendencies towards the concentration of population.

In economic terms, Dublin came to dominate the state as the state came to dominate the country, if only because the state was so disproportionately located in Dublin. The net flow of resources, financial and intellectual, was heavily Dublin orientated. Dublin's intellectual and cultural dominance, immensely reinforced by television, was even more emphatic

[166] M. Ross, 'Comprehensiveness in regional policy', in B.R. Dowling and J. Durkan (eds.), *Irish economic policy* (Dublin, 1978), pp. 317–21.

than its economic dominance. Whether dominance should be equated with superiority may remain a more open question! Centralisation places a high premium on intelligence. Centralised mistakes exert a more pervasive influence on national performance than decentralised ones. It is not clear that concentrated mediocrity would serve the national interest more effectively than diffused mediocrity. Of course, what is concentrated may not be mediocrity. Centralisation may offer superior performers wider scope for their talents. It may improve the quality of decision-making if the centralisers are clearly more intelligent, informed, dedicated, skilled and energetic than they, or anyone else, would be in alternative decision-making structures.

Judged by the acid test of its behaviour, the central bureaucracy clearly regards the Irish as unfit for effective local government. The central bureaucrats may be right in a static sense. A people socialised into so acute a sense of dependence on centralised largesse would be likely to make many mistakes initially if required to rely more heavily on themselves. It may indeed be that the Irish are as unfit for devolved self-government at the local level as their imperial masters once persuaded themselves that they were unfit for self-government at the national level. One cannot know until the experiment is tried. What one does know is the capacity of the Irish for centralised government as demonstrated by the results of sixty-five years. How satisfied one ought to be with those results is to some extent a subjective matter, depending largely on one's standards. This does not allow us to evade the challenge of judgement. For the standards individuals, or collectivities, find acceptable are themselves central to the quality of their performance. They are not an exogenous variable.

We have already noted the widespread contempt in cerebral circles for the quality of much Departmental decision-making in recent times. To what extent have decision-making cadres displayed the quality required to justify so intense a centralisation of authority? How capacious was their intelligence? How adequate was their information? Just how competitive were they in the market for ideas?

INTELLIGENCE

Little systematic investigation has been conducted into the size and structure of the market for ideas in Ireland. In exploring this crucial theme, a short but seminal observation by Basil Chubb provides a useful perspective on the period before 1960:

Few enquiries of any depth were made into social and economic problems, and even those were mostly of pedestrian quality or, like the *Report of the Commission on Vocational Organisation* (1943), by common consent were ignored. New social services and new legislation tended to follow *mutatis mutandis* the existing British pattern. Neither public servants (politician or professional) nor the universities provided new ideas, and there were few attempts to observe and adapt the experience of countries other than the United Kingdom.[167]

Why then was the market for ideas in independent Ireland so small? Why was it so stagnant? Was it due to lack of effective demand? Or of effective supply? How developed were the mechanisms for importing, assembling and distributing ideas on the Irish market? How efficient was the indigenous production process?

The market for ideas in the Department of Finance was probably the single most important influence, at least as far as policy was concerned, on long-term national socio-economic performance. Finance was intensely interested in ideas. Neither Brennan nor McElligott, nor many of their colleagues, could be considered anti-intellectual. Some of them were serious readers. Most could claim to be highly intellectual by the lights of the surrounding society. But their own light, however brightly it could shine, illuminated only a very narrow surface. Four examples must suffice to indicate the disdain with which the Finance of McElligott treated deviants.

Finance bitterly resisted the Agricultural Wage Regulation Bill of 1936 with a barrage of strident assertions. As agricultural wages, despite the fall from their postwar peak, 'are still better than the 1917 and 1918 level and about 9 shillings a week above the 1914 level' at 21s 3d compared with 12s, the labourers were not really that badly off.[168] And even if they were, 'the really important matter . . . is the ability of the farmers to pay and the consumers to bear the cost of better wages . . .'[169] Any significant rise in wages, Finance predicted, 'will tend to drive the farmer out of production'[170] The resulting fall in agricultural exports would pose a threat to the stability of the currency and induce capital flight.[171]

Finance refrained from producing a scintilla of evidence to support so hysterical a response. It required a soaring imagination to conceive of big farmers being driven out of production by any likely rise in labourers' wages. The memorandum did not calculate the number of big farmers driven out of production by the allegedly sharp rise in wages since 1914! Nor did it contain any analysis of the actual costs of production in agriculture, or of labour as a proportion of total costs, or of the relationship between wages and productivity, or indeed of any relationship in the real economic world. Neither was it, however, an argument from theory. It would be an insult to theory to dignify the intellectual posturing of the memorandum as theoretical. The arguments were drawn neither from theory nor from fact. They were drawn solely from ideology.

Finance had high hopes of the Banking Commission that sat from 1934

[167] B. Chubb, *The government and politics of Ireland* (2nd edn, London, 1982), p. 22.
[168] SPO, S8744, Finance memo, 21 March 1936.   [169] *Ibid.*   [170] *Ibid.*
[171] *Ibid.*

to 1938. Finance intended the commission to reassert the validity of eternal economic truths following threats of deviance in the early Fianna Fáil years. The majority report did not disappoint Finance expectations. Great umbrage was taken, however, in Merrion Street at those members of the commission so churlish as to pen minority reports. Finance was particularly incensed at the insensitivity of Alfred O'Rahilly, the main drafter of the first minority report. O'Rahilly, though not renowned as the easiest of colleagues either in University College Cork, or outside it, was on tolerable terms with de Valera. His arguments had to be taken more seriously than Finance felt their intrinsic value deserved. O'Rahilly roused Finance indignation by suggesting that consideration should be given to credit creation, to repatriation of sterling assets, and to a more interventionist financial policy in general. Finance went to the length of composing a 136 page memorandum offering robust refutation of O'Rahilly.

Sternly rebuking O'Rahilly and his co-signatories for their failure to approach the subject 'with judicial and scientific minds'[172] Finance proceeded to give a vintage exhibition of 'judicial and scientific' analysis. A selection of sentences and phrases reveals the depth of Finance indignation.

'The irrational instability of judgement and purpose which characterises every paragraph of Minority Report no. 1.'[173]

'They talk vaguely and at random, letting their pen nibs do their thinking for them, and ending where they began, in cloudy generalities.'[174]

'Carried by the pendulum-like action of their minds to the opposite extreme.'[175]

'Rubbish heap.'[176]

'The public overthrow of the seventh commandment.'[177]

'Flatfooted.'[178]

'Speciousness.'[179]

'Windy polemics.'[180]

'Blatant contradictions.'[181]

'It is a pity that the minority's fondness for the use of the cliché is not controlled by some consideration for truth and relevance.'[182]

'Details, like certain sins stigmatised by Saint Paul, were not even to be mentioned among us.'[183]

'An evil.'[184]

'A compact of fallacies.'[185]

---

[172] SPO, S10612, Finance memo, 17 April 1939, p. 24.   [173] *Ibid.*, p. 15.
[174] *Ibid.*, p. 27.
[175] *Ibid.*, p. 31.   [176] *Ibid.*, p. 36.   [177] *Ibid.*, p. 38.   [178] *Ibid.*, p. 46.
[179] *Ibid.*, p. 53   [180] *Ibid.*, p. 54   [181] *Ibid.*, p. 58   [182] *Ibid.*, p. 74.
[183] *Ibid.*, p. 109.
[184] *Ibid.*, p. 125.[185] *Ibid.*, p. 130.

'Puerility.'[186]
'We thus emerge early and inevitably into the totalitarian state.'[187]

Other features of the reply shed more light on the Finance concept of 'judicial and scientific' analysis. When it denounces the suggestion of devaluation, for instance, it is mainly on the grounds that it is 'a proposal to destroy blindly, and without advertance to justice, right, title or expediency, assets which are in the rightful ownership of large numbers, perhaps even the majority of our citizens'.[188] Devaluation was 'an expedient of so desperate a character that it ought not even to be considered as a possibility unless the need for it were inescapable and unless that need were demonstrated by incontrovertible argument based upon hard facts'.[189] It is indeed probable that devaluation made no sense in the Irish circumstances of 1938. However, as many countries, including Britain, had devalued during the 1930s without catastrophic consequences, this was but one more dogma masquerading as science. Devaluation was a desperate expedient – but emigration was not. Finance confined its concern about the emigration that had resumed a few years before to the alleged departure of the non-Catholic population, whose presence conferred such disproportionate benefits on the country.[190]

The Finance hero was Hjalmar Schacht. On Schacht's authority, Finance concluded that 'the work provision schemes' of the United States and France were 'unsuccessful'.[191] Schacht is quoted three times to the effect that credit creation is a bad thing. Finance denounced the New Deal on the grounds that 'the whole economic machine tends continually to run down to a standstill' in the United States, proving 'the utter uselessness of Roosevelt's policy'.[192] The New Deal was indeed far from being a resounding economic success. It was also far from being a resounding economic failure. To refer to the 'utter uselessness' of Roosevelt's policies without deigning to provide any evidence was to make the wish the father of the thought.

The quality of the Finance discussion of German economic policy in 1933 and 1934 further confirmed its immunity to inconvenient evidence. It pronounced, on the authority of Schacht, that the German public works programme 'failed to effect any sustained improvement in the employment position ... in 1933 and in 1934'.[193] Many criticisms can be advanced of the public works programme. But it did contribute significantly to improving the employment position. Nor was this an arcane secret. C.W. Guillebaud's major work, *The economic recovery of Germany from 1933 to the incorporation of Austria* was reviewed in the *Times Literary Supplement* on 4 March 1938, several weeks before

[186] *Ibid.*, p. 132.   [187] *Ibid.*, p. 136.   [188] *Ibid.*, p. 78.
[189] *Ibid.*, pp. 78–9.
[190] *Ibid.*, pp. 45–6.   [191] *Ibid.*, p. 101.   [192] *Ibid.*, pp. 66–7.   [193] *Ibid.*

submission of the Finance memorandum. If this be deemed too short a period for Finance to have taken cognizance of its findings, Grebler's survey was already available in English for a full year. Grebler was rightly critical of many aspects of the public works programme, but he was still far too balanced for Finance purposes.[194]

Veneration for Schacht was rivalled only by disdain for the Labour Party. Sedulously insinuating unworthy motives to the signatories of the Minority Report,[195] Finance sought to tarnish them further by exposing their partiality for 'the economic panaceas which formed the stock-in-trade of the Labour party here.'[196] McElligott regularly resorted to this tactic (arguably constitutionally improper), whether in denouncing another minority report of the Banking Commission,[197] or in making gratuitous reference to Labour Party proposals for raising agricultural labourers wages.[198]

O'Rahilly and his colleagues sought to reinforce their argument by invoking the authority of James Meade. Finance was as unimpressed by Meade as by the Labour Party. It had an instructive technique for dealing with uncongenial arguments. It cited some reservations about Meade's latest book expressed by Keynes in a review in the *Economic Journal* to deny that Meade's 'competence as an economist is admitted'[199] Finance cultivated an intense distaste for Keynes, whom McElligott would later describe as belonging to 'the escapist school' of economics.[200] It knew how to quote scripture for its purpose.

There was always a certain other-worldliness about Meade. He would be frequently chided by fellow economists for his lack of 'both historical and common sense'.[201] Even his ideological critics, however, would not deny his 'competence as an economist'. Harry Johnson concluded that 'James Meade has delivered a lifetime of high standard performance in economic theory, characterised *in spite of his socialist political views* [my emphasis] by an unusually high degree of objectivity and scientific detachment in the employment of theory in the clarification and solution of policy problems and theoretical problems arising in the context of policy'.[202]

The occasion for Johnson's assessment was the award of the Nobel prize in economics to Meade! However many years in the future that was in 1939, Meade's professional standing was already established. He had

[194] L. Grebler, 'Work creation policy in Germany 1932–35', *International Labour Review*, 35 (March 1937), pp. 329–51; (April 1937), pp. 505–27.
[195] SPO S10612, Finance memo, 17 April 1939, pp. 36–7, 60.   [196] *Ibid.*, p. 64.
[197] Fanning, *Finance*, pp. 359–64.   [198] SPO, S8744, Finance memo, 21 March 1936.
[199] SPO, S19612, Finance memo, 17 April 1939, p. 63.
[200] Raymond, 'De Valera, Lemass', p. 128.
[201] Harry Johnson, 'James Meade's contribution to economics', *Scandinavian Journal of Economics*, 80, 1 (1978), p. 66.
[202] *Ibid.*, pp. 79–80.

been a fellow of Hertford College, Oxford, and a lecturer in economics in the university from the age of twenty-two in 1930. His competence was already sufficiently 'admitted' for him to have been appointed economist to the League of Nations and editor of the League's *World Economic Survey*. He had published three books and several articles, including one in the *Economic Journal* (edited by Keynes, whose review Finance was so pathetically trying to use to professionally discredit Meade) and three in the *Review of Economic Studies*. Finance's inability to distinguish between specific criticisms of a scholar's work, which are normal in academic discourse, and assessment of his professional competence, reflected much more on itself than on Meade.

McElligott's technique of presenting a case imposed few demands on the supply of information. He saw little point in wasting time in presenting ministers with objective facts and inflicting on them the strain of making up their own minds. His 'facts' were naturally chosen to clinch his case. His handling of evidence in his renewed assault in 1946 on agricultural labourers, for whom he seems to have harboured a visceral animosity, reflects once more his manner of handling evidence.

Many farmers are abandoning lines of production which involved hired labour. No less serious perhaps than the wage question in regard to agricultural labour is the question of hours and of holidays for whole or half days. This does not fit in with what may be called the farm cycle, and its inappropriateness is particularly marked in the case of dairying. There is a tendency to get out of the dairying industry notwithstanding that the country is particularly suited to it, and the production of milk is declining.[203]

McElligott produced no evidence to substantiate this claim. No 'tendency to get out of the dairying industry' can be detected in the official statistics. Cow numbers and milk production were virtually identical in 1940 and 1945.[204] The number of cows did fall from 1 220 000 to 1 200 000 between 1945 and 1946, and total milk output from 483 000 to 463 000 gallons. But this sort of fluctuation had occurred frequently in earlier years, without initiating any trend. Production was to drop further in 1947, due to bad weather. Milk output exceeded that of 1946 once more in 1949, and the number of cows reached the 1946 figure in 1950. Milk production in the decade after 1946 comfortably exceeded output in the preceding decade.[205] It is difficult to detect the basis for McElligott's fears in the official data.

As Finance came under growing pressure in the early 1950s concerning the inferior employment performance of the Irish economy compared with that of western Europe in general, it snatched at any weapon to hand

[203] Fanning, *Finance*, p. 395.
[204] *Agricultural statistics, 1934–1956* (Dublin, 1960), p. 187.
[205] *Ibid.*

to strike back at its tormentors. In 1953, it felt sufficiently vindicated by alleged difficulties in two economies identified with Keynesian policies, Britain and Sweden, to go to the length of circulating the cabinet with a memorandum intended to devastate its critics. It was one of the few occasions on which ministers found themselves contemplating analysis of the economic performance of other countries.

Finance gloated that Britain was now suffering serious unemployment, and that Sweden soon would be, even if it was not sufficiently sporting to have already succumbed to the multiple defects of welfare policy. The type of data that Finance found good enough for the cabinet revealed a certain disdain for both evidence and ministers. The source for the British situation was an extract from the *Manchester Guardian* under the alarmist journalistic headline 'Where men run to find a job.' Finance commented primly on this exposure that:

When it is recollected that Great Britain has absorbed millions of workers into her defence forces and has millions more employed on rearmament work, that there is widespread unemployment in the British automobile industry and that there has been only partial recovery in the British textile industry, furniture trades and clothing trades, the unemployment among workers in the productive industries is relatively very much greater than here.[206]

This provided an unexpected perspective on the condition of the British labour market in 1953. It suggests that the thousands of Irish emigrants then flocking to Britain must have been living in a dreamland. Before succumbing to the Finance vision, however, its use of evidence deserves close examination. Had the cabinet time to read *The Manchester Guardian* it would have noted that it referred to the situation not in Britain, but only on Merseyside.[207] Even there, the unemployment rate was no more than 4.4 per cent. At the national level, recorded British unemployment rates fell from 2.0 per cent in 1952 to 1.6 per cent in 1953.[208] The recorded Irish rate was hovering around 9 per cent at that time.[209] In addition there was also massive unrecorded underemployment in Ireland.

Apart from the manner in which Finance snatched at this journalistic straw, the use of slovenly phrases like 'millions of workers' hardly reached the level of professional competence that might reasonably be expected in a memorandum for the government. The correct figures were 870 000 in the defence forces, and 850 000 to 900 000 in defence production.[210] The increase during the Korean war in the total numbers in the defence forces and defence production together amounted to no more than 500 000.[211] Motor car production did fall about 15 per cent between the peak of 1950

206 SPO, S13101B, Finance memo, 9 February 1953.   207 *Ibid.*, Appendix A.
208 Mitchell, *European historical statistics*, p. 171.
209 *Ibid.*, p. 170.   210 C.J. Bartlett, *The long retreat* (London, 1972), pp. 75, 80.
211 *Ibid.*, p. 80; T. Wilson, 'Manpower', in G.D. Worswick and P.H. Ady, *The British economy 1945–50* (Oxford, 1952), p. 228.

and 1952. This was, however, due mainly to shortages of raw materials connected with the Korean war. It still left output well above the 1949 level. In 1953, production surged forward to a new record. The immediate problems were more on the supply than on the demand side, and contemporaries could only see a continuing seller's market.[212] There were many potential weaknesses in the British performance. But the problems of 1952 were not those identified by Finance.

Finance took equal pleasure in its portrait of the Swedish situation. So important did it consider the revelations about the 'failure' of Swedish economic policy in the *Neue Zürcher Zeitung* of 19 December 1952 that it circulated copies to the cabinet on 6 January 1953. It also sought support in the *Stockholms Tidningen* of 4 September 1952, and in a *Financial Times* article of 7 January 1953, both of which referred to a deterioration in Swedish economic circumstances due to wage inflation and consequent declining export competitiveness. Finance concluded optimistically that 'this description of current conditions in Sweden suggests that the policy of "full employment" was not the universal panacea which the propagators of the theory have held it out to be'.[213] How well does the Finance use of evidence survive scrutiny?

The *Financial Times* listed several reasons for concern about Swedish export prospects. It did not conclude, however, that Swedish full employment policy had failed. The *Financial Times* may have had as little sympathy as Finance for Swedish socialism, but it expressed itself a good deal more guardedly:

All in all, 1953 looks like being a testing year for the Swedes. After years of plenty by Europe's war damaged standards, they are in for a spell of austerity. If they can weather it without strikes on the one hand or exploitation on the other, they can rightly claim that their small neutral corner of Europe is a political oasis.

The *Neue Zürcher* made several sensible points about general economic policy, particularly that 'the dilemma of the "over employed" economy consists mainly in the fact that it is not possible to ensure development of productivity *pari passu* with the development of wages and to avoid a continuous inflationary expansion of incomes'. The kernel of truth in that observation would become much clearer two decades later. It must have come as something of a surprise, however, to a cabinet wrestling, as it thought, with problems of chronic unemployment, to learn that the Minister for Finance 'considered that the conditions referred to in the particular case are those existing in this country at present'.[214] It would

---

212 Bartlett, *Retreat*, p. 65; S. Pollard, *The development of the British economy 1914–1967* (London, 2nd edn. 1973), p. 415. B.R. Mitchell, *European Historical Statistics*, p. 469; W. Lewchuk, 'The motor vehicle industry', in B. Elbaum and W. Lazonick (eds.), *The decline of the British economy* (Oxford, 1986), pp. 148–9.
213 SPO, S13101B, Finance memo, 9 February 1953.   214 *Ibid.*

have been interesting to have heard the cabinet's response to the revelation that Ireland was suffering from *over-employment* in 1953! If ministers had found time to peruse the memorandum more closely, their
suspicions might not have been completely allayed. It contains not a
solitary reference to the actual unemployment level in Sweden, or to
Swedish growth rates, either long term or short term. There was no hint of
a scholarly study of the Swedish performance, as distinct from an eager
snatching at convenient assertions.

The Swedish economy was indeed experiencing rapid inflation in 1951
and 1952, thanks partly to wage pressures, partly to the Korean war. The
government successfully adopted a more restrictive monetary stance in
1952–53 to cope with the inflationary pressures. Recorded Swedish
unemployment rates duly soared – from 1.8 per cent in 1951 to 2.3 per
cent in 1952 and to all of 2.8 per cent in 1953! They then fell once more,
unsportingly spoiling the Finance scenario.[215] The Swedish adjustment in
1952–3 occurred against a background of continuing full employment,
and in the context of a remarkable long-term performance. From being an
emigrant country in the late nineteenth century, Sweden was now able to
create jobs at high and rising wages for a population that more than
doubled between 1850 and 1950. Insofar as policy contributed to this
performance, it is possible to entertain the suspicion that Swedish
policy-makers may not have been irredeemably inferior to their Irish
counterparts.

Had those ministers sceptical about the severity of the Irish 'over-
employment' crisis been in a position to compare the Finance memorandum with the original article they might have sought further clarification.
The *Neue Zürcher* report (of 20 December incidentally, not 19 December)
was a rather superior one, as one would expect. Not all its diagnoses, it is
true, carried conviction, and few of its prognoses for either Sweden or
Denmark would be vindicated. Nonetheless, it deserved close exegesis. It
was less concerned with the theological rectitude of Keynes than with his
relevance to Swedish circumstances. Only when it had noted the virtually
full employment already prevailing in postwar Sweden, and the 'almost
unbounded entrepreneurial propensity to invest', did it conclude that his
prescriptions were irrelevant to the existing situation. These Swedish
circumstances were also quite different from those of post-1945 Ireland.
Keynes may not have been relevant to Irish circumstances either – but that
case had to be argued on its merits, and could not be deduced from the
Swedish analogy.

In the light of this survey, it does not seem unduly speculative to surmise
that Finance offered a rather limited market for new ideas in the first

215 Mitchell, *European historical statistics*, p. 171; Lindbeck, *Swedish economic policy*,
   pp. 12, 71ff., 112.

generation of independence. The range of ideas that found favour with Brennan and McElligott during their daily lunches – they dined regularly until 1953[216] – would seem to have been circumscribed. There would be little premature flirting with fresh thought there.

The Finance mind shared many of the assumptions of George O'Brien, who devoutly believed that he represented an 'intellectual' approach to Irish economic problems in contrast to the 'emotional' approach of his critics.

Ever since the Treaty, I have ranged myself with the economists who accepted Ireland as it was rather than those who wished it to be in some ways different. I accepted the facts of geography and history instead of attempting to charm them away. I was among the physicians who prescribed the hard diet for the Irish patient and the surgeons who were prepared to recommend a painful operation, not among the faith healers and the Christian scientists. This was the intellectual rather than the emotional approach to Irish economic problems.

O'Brien went on to claim that his approach

was based on my legal training which taught me to see facts as they were and not as I would have liked them to be. I have been taught at the Bar to discuss any case on its strict legal merits and to avoid considering the abstract rights and wrongs of the parties or the social consequences of judicial decisions . . . every country needs a corrective, an antidote against the hysterical outbursts of screaming fanatics. There must be a sane section in every society . . .[217]

This is as instructive for what it unconsciously, as for what it consciously, reveals. O'Brien was naturally correct to insist on the need for sanity. He himself, as well as Finance on occasion, stood courageously against irresponsible proposals. But his assumption that there was only one sanity, and that the only alternative was fanaticism, seemed to elevate economics to a scientific status independent of time and place. There was little hint here of Myrdal's penetrating critique of the unscientific assumptions lurking behind 'scientific' methodology. The analogy with law reinforces this impression. It implies a static rather than a developmental approach to economics, a reliance on eternally valid economic 'laws' rather than on a grasp of the potential for change in specific historical circumstances – despite O'Brien's three volumes on the economic history of Ireland. And O'Brien deluded himself if he believed he ignored 'the social consequences' of policy. Finance certainly did not. It had a highly partisan social perspective. Indeed, O'Brien's earlier analogy with physicians and surgeons exposes only too clearly the pervasive influence of a social perspective. It was hardly to be wondered at if those who were to be at the receiving end of the operation were less enthusiastic about the knife work than the wielders of the knives!

The point at issue is not whether Finance was right or wrong. Some of

---

[216] Ó Broin, *Yesterday*, p. 241.   [217] Meenan, *George O'Brien*, pp. 139–40.

the specific criticisms of O'Rahilly, for instance, were probably right by any criterion. It is partly that on broader economic issues the Finance touch was curiously uncertain. Not only do the comparisons with Sweden and Britain in 1953 display a disturbing lack of perspective, but the treatment of Irish population patterns in the tirade against O'Rahilly exposes a shallow understanding of Irish demographic history.[218] Even more noteworthy is the failure of Finance to discern the emotional basis of its own proclaimed rationality.

While the Finance use of evidence must raise eyebrows, it would be quite unhistorical to call Finance officials, with James Dillon in 1950, 'the "con men" par excellence of recent times'.[219] Precisely because Finance was a seething cauldron of emotion, Finance men were *not* conscious fakirs. They passionately believed in their mission to save Ireland from profligacy. Behind the façade of bureaucratic detachment surged massive waves of paranoia. The Finance approach was more doctrinal than intellectual, more visceral than cerebral. The Finance mind was a repository of revealed truth. One is constantly struck by the failure of Finance memoranda to appeal to either systematic historical or systematic comparative reasoning. The arguments instead tend to descend from dogma. Here were no 'scientific' physicians and surgeons. Here were crusaders for truth, valiantly defending the ramparts of rectitude against the assaults of the unholy and the unclean.

The early Finance men may have felt that they had little enough to learn from outsiders. From whom should they learn? There was only a handful of economists in Dublin anyway, with whom they were on easy terms of intellectual equality, and who shared their ideological instincts. Economics had not become, as yet, so specialised a subject that only those trained in it could presume to become votaries. Finance men were at least as capable of expressing themselves cogently as the academics, and more so than the occasional businessman, usually banker, whose existence they acknowledged. Dublin had no serious financial journalism. Trade unionists were still only fit for the tradesman's entrance. In addition, their confidence in the doctrinal validity of economic laws fostered a mentality suspicious of the idea that there was actually anything more to learn. In addition, Finance was technically competent. It would have been unthinkable in 1932, for instance, that External Affairs should have felt obliged to recruit an economics professor, as happened in the Canadian case, to prepare a memorandum on monetary policy for the Irish delegation attending the Ottawa conference because nobody in Finance could tackle

---

[218] SPO, S10612, Finance memo, 17 April 1939, pp. 39–47.
[219] Fanning, *Ireland*, p. 170.

the task.[220] Finance felt no need to seek out alternative sources for the supply of ideas. Without being anti-intellectual, it nevertheless offered a formidable barrier to the penetration of ideas.

Finance was probably broadly representative of the official mind in its attitude towards 'outsiders', whether 'outside' ideas or 'outside' people. In many countries, the Second World War and its immediate aftermath generated a sharply increased demand for new men and new measures. The Department of Supplies brought together several promising young men, but these were already in the civil service. Just as there was to be no wartime government of all the talents, neither was there to be an administration of all the talents. The existing civil service would supply any necessary thought. Irish administration was not therefore leavened by an influx of wartime recruits. The contrast with Canada could not be more glaring, where many of the special recruits during the war rapidly achieved high national and international administrative repute.[221] They may not have existed in Ireland. In any case, little effort was made to discover or develop them.

The failure to recruit fresh blood was particularly significant in that the normal recruitment process for future senior officials involved their direct admission at the age of eighteen from secondary school. Only a quarter of all Secretaries of government departments between 1923 and 1968 had university degrees. And in the late 1960s 'perhaps ninety per cent of the posts of assistant principal and above were filled by people recruited from secondary school, and four of the fifteen heads of departments had entered as clerical officers'.[222] This did not necessarily mean that any particular individual was unreceptive to thought. In general, however, this cadre was unlikely to provide an expanding market for ideas. The Irish secondary school system in the early decades of independence inculcated many worthy qualities. Neither intellectual independence nor intellectual originality were normally among them.

The Economy Committee, under the chairmanship of Hugo Flinn, after interviewing a number of senior civil servants at the outbreak of the war, could not forbear from observing, presumably to the chagrin of Finance, that senior officials obviously needed more time to concentrate on their most important tasks. Therefore, the committee recommended, more junior administrative posts should be established. But instead of recruiting to these from the internal pool of secondary school graduates, the service should look for young candidates,

---

[220] J.L. Granatstein, *The Ottawa men: the civil service mandarins 1939–1957* (Toronto, 1982), p. 44.
[221] *Ibid., passim*; D.A. Wolfe, 'The rise and demise of the Keynesian era in Canada: economic policy 1930–1982', in M.S. Cross and G.S. Kealey (eds.), *Modern Canada: 1930–1980s* (Toronto, 1984), pp. 53–5.
[222] Chubb, *Ireland* (2nd edn), p. 265.

possessing special initiative and ability, and with the widest and most cultivated view of public affairs and problems that it is possible to obtain. These officers, in close touch with department chiefs, should be entrusted with tasks of a high order requiring specialised investigation and initial planning for which adequate provision does not appear to exist in the existing organisation of departments.[223]

The cabinet duly approved this recommendation. Nothing appears to have happened.

Not only did Finance feel little need for external enlightenment. It felt equally little need for information. Early in the war, it demanded that the statistics section of Industry and Commerce, the main source of national economic statistics, be reduced in scale.[224] It was the politician, Hugo Flinn, as chairman of the Economy Committee, who was instrumental in rejecting the Finance demand on the grounds that 'in a time of crisis such as the present, statistics are so dynamic that to suspend their collection or to limit the ordinary activities of the statistics branch might leave the country without information which might be found extremely valuable later.'[225] It offers sufficient commentary on the Finance appetite for information that at a time when the government of virtually every advanced country was discovering the importance of statistical data, and accordingly augmenting its statistical service, it could detect so little relationship between information and decision-making that it could urge further restrictions on the role of the already meagrely-endowed statistics service.

Flinn explored the implications further just before his sudden death in 1943. Not only had the Economy Committee resisted the Finance demand, he reminded de Valera, but he felt that far from being curtailed, the role of the statistics branch should be enhanced. It should not only collect information but 'should reason from that information'! He acidly noted that 'as its reasoning may affect policy generally, the second function tends to be discouraged'. Flinn sought not only a reinforced statistical branch but recommended that 'a separate statistical expert should be attached to the office of the Taoiseach for purposes of consultation, through him, by the government'.[226] Thus was loosed a spectre that threatened to stalk the corridors of departments blissfully innocent of the informed use of statistical evidence.

It was a Finance official who would throw the next stone into the still stagnant statistical pond. Patrick Lynch seized the occasion of a discussion on unemployment in the Statistical Society in 1945 to lament the lack of adequate statistics for Irish economic analysis.[227] This seemed to set the

---

223 SPO, S10913B, Economy Committee Final Report, 23 November 1939, para. 68.
224 SPO, S10913B, Department of the Taoiseach, memo, 5 February 1940.
225 SPO, S10913B, Economy Committee Final Report, 23 November 1939, para. 48.
226 SPO, S14336A, H. Flinn to E. de Valera, 20 January 1943.
227 P. Lynch, 'Discussion on the problem of full employment', *JSSISI*, 17 (1944–45), p. 439.

familiar Finance view on its head. It was a far cry from the complacent croonings of economists, statisticians and officials hitherto. But the young Lynch was a very unusual official. An economics graduate of UCD, one of the earliest to respond to the intellectual excitement generated by Keynes, he stressed the importance of improved information for purposes of economic management. A subversive seed was being sown within the citadel itself!

Industry and Commerce might have been expected to have offered a bigger market for ideas than Finance. Gordon Campbell, the Secretary, expressed reservations about the narrowness of the Finance mind frequently enough during the Cosgrave years, and R.C. Ferguson, Leydon's deputy, lamented the lack of relevant economic analysis as the Department struggled to implement the policy of industrialisation.[228] It is, however, premature to pronounce on the general issue of the use of information by Industry and Commerce until further work clarifies the precise relationship between the statistics branch and policy-making in the Department.

After an 'epic bureaucratic brawl',[229] the Central Statistics Office was established in 1948 under the aegis of the Taoiseach's office, with Roy Geary, who enjoyed an international reputation as a statistician, as director, and Professor M.D. McCarthy, a Cork mathematician of genuine distinction, as deputy director. It was a formidable combination. Geary and McCarthy were both trojan workers, who scarcely concealed their disdain for either the ability or the work ethic of the economists. If Ferguson criticised the economists as non-producers of analyses, Geary and McCarthy criticised them as non-consumers of statistical material. They were not amused by the indifference of the economists to their data. 'Though the absence hitherto of any criticism whatsoever of this aspect of the work might be taken as a compliment to the works' compilers', McCarthy told the Statistical Society in 1952, 'it is far more likely to be due to lack of interest among those who have the duty and should have the ability to provide such criticism.'[230] As one rarely slow to detect the lack of moral fibre in others, Duncan took umbrage at this reference to his 'duty'. It was, he retorted, not 'lack of interest', but 'lack of staff and money' that prevented university economists from responding to the challenge thrown down by McCarthy. But he hastened to add that in any event university economists were entitled to follow their research interests as they wished, without reference to the applied aspects of the subject.[231]

This conflict between statisticians and economists in 1952 raised

[228] See above, p. 192.
[229] R. Fanning, 'Economists and governments: Ireland 1922–52', in A. Murphy (ed.), *Economists and the Irish economy from the eighteenth century to the present day* (Dublin, 1984), p. 150.
[230] *Ibid.*, p. 152.   [231] *Ibid.*

fundamental issues about the responsibilities of economists in a small and intellectually isolated society. There was no obvious instant answer, for there were strong arguments on both sides. But there was also an embryonic ideological conflict underlying the exchanges. Earlier statisticians, like John Hooper, first director of statistics in Industry and Commerce, and Stanley Lyon, his successor, felt no compelling urge to press their findings on others. Hooper, Busteed of UCC and Bastable, the venerable Professor of Economics in Trinity, who were appointed to a committee on statistics in 1924, agreed that there was no great urgency in building up 'a complete organisation'.[232] George O'Brien expressed his satisfaction at the quality of Irish statistics throughout the twenties, but made scant use of the copious Irish data in his 1929 book on agricultural economics. The small number of academic economists made only sporadic contributions to the detailed study of the Irish economy, as distinct from pronouncing on *a priori* grounds on policy issues. The first estimate of Irish national income was compiled by the young T.J. Kiernan, who was only briefly an academic economist in Cork before becoming a general practitioner in public affairs. Duncan compiled estimates of national income, but only as a by-product of his membership of the Banking Commission 1934–8. There was some point to Duncan's response to the statisticians in 1952. Geary brushed aside his defence, however, warning darkly that if the economists 'continued to sulk in their tents' then 'we must travel alone'.[233] The abrasiveness of the exchanges owed something to the personalities involved. It also derived from the fact that Geary and McCarthy, in contrast to Lyon and Hooper, were scholars, anxious to enhance the prestige of their subject. Likewise in contrast to their predecessors, and also to Duncan and O'Brien, they had some faith in the potential of policy. They wanted government to do things. A *mélange* of motives inspired the injection of this sterner tone into a normally club-like atmosphere.

Sentiment was beginning to shift a little even in Finance by this stage. The influence of Lynch was felt more directly once he transferred to the Department of the Taoiseach in 1948. But Whitaker was already impressing on McElligott the importance of statistical information.[234] This may still have been partly to ensure that the Finance finger could be kept ever more firmly in the dyke, now that the floods were beating against it. Whatever the motives, it heralded a changing perspective. The Finance market grew rapidly once Whitaker became Secretary in 1956. When the government established the Capital Investment Advisory Committee, it pointedly bypassed the senior economists in the Republic. The one

---

[232] SPO, S4766, Report of Committee . . . on economic statistics . . ., 19 January 1925, p. 16.
[233] Fanning, 'Economists', p. 154.   [234] Fanning, *Finance*, pp. 552–5.

professor of economics included was C.F. Carter from Belfast. The only professional economists from the Republic were Patrick Lynch, now a lecturer in UCD, and Louden Ryan. The introduction to *Economic Development* mentioned no Irish economist, but did cite Alec Cairncross, a respected advisor to the British government. The reference was revealing. Cairncross was no idealogue. Whitaker's minute to Jim Ryan of 12 December 1957 observed that 'at some point consideration might perhaps be given to inviting a wider range of views than those of departments only, but this is still some distance off'.[235] In one sense, this minute neatly captures the caste-like mentality of Finance – thirty-six years after independence, consideration of 'a wider range of views' was still 'some distance off'. It can scarcely be described as the language of promiscuous demand. But it did suggest a capacity for contemplating the inconceivable – there might actually be something to be learned from outside!

If the public sector provided only a limited demand for ideas, the private sector offered an even more exiguous market. Most Irish businessmen were simply not interested in ideas. Indigenous industry consisted overwhelmingly of small firms enjoying a captive domestic market and enduring few competitive pressures. They were not, in this respect, very different from government departments or university departments. They were small, sheltered, and rarely obliged to cope with the threat of competition. When the threat materialised in the 1960s, their instinctive response was to seek subsidisation and protection through the 'grants' economy, rather than face the challenge of the market. The voice might be the voice of the market, but the hands were the hands of politics.

The Irish Management Institute (IMI), strove to change this attitude after 1953. Supply ran well ahead of demand. A long-serving former director of the IMI, Ivor Kenny, could detect as late as 1984 'a suspicion of the intellectual process and the value of ideas' among businessmen.[236] Kenny attributes this primarily to the pervasive anti-intellectualism of Irish culture. Even this may be too generous. Much of the suspicion may be more sub-intellectual than anti-intellectual. Anti-intellectualism is too intellectually demanding. The IMI depended heavily on support from a handful of big businessmen in the private sector, with a more capacious perspective than the vast majority, and on the enthusiasm of the chief executives in the state sponsored sector. The bulk of Irish businessmen provided no market for business ideas, much less for ideas in general. A variety of factors have contributed to the poor performance of native Irish business, but sheer intellectual inadequacy counts among the basic weaknesses. A first-class business mind could be a joy to behold. There were too few of them in Ireland.

If the stereotypical image of the businessman is of somebody basically

[235] *Economic development*, p. 229.   [236] Kenny, *Government and enterprise*, p. 74.

hostile to thought anyway – though this, insofar as it is not a caricature, may hold rather less in more advanced economic cultures than in Britain or Ireland – the stereotype tends to portray 'the left' as an axiomatic progenitor of new ideas. The image bears little relation to Irish reality. The political left, insofar as it was represented by the Labour Party, had little interest in ideas, left wing or otherwise, 'the poverty of its ideas' counting among its more conspicuous features.[237] While trade unions liked to posture as left wing, the sheer conservatism of trade union thinking in Ireland, valiantly though a handful of individuals strove to leaven the lump, left most trade union officials most of the time at least as conservative as the small businessmen and small farmers whose mirror image so many of them were.

Farmers, the biggest occupational group in the country, likewise offered little market for ideas, even for agricultural ideas. The demand for agricultural education was strikingly limited in Ireland compared with Britain or the continent.[238] Farmers offered as exiguous a market for ideas as did businessmen themselves.[239]

This relative indifference to thought extended far beyond the economic sphere. Those responsible for the formulation of social policy had little contact with the supply of ideas in Ireland, much less in the wider world. Catholic thinking, or assumed Catholic thinking, or selected Catholic thinking, may have influenced some. However, what is striking about social policy in the first generation of independence is not the demand for Catholic principles among policy-makers, but the general indifference in policy formulation to any social thought, Catholic or otherwise. The furore over the Mother and Child Scheme, which appeared to reflect church dominance over the social policy of the state, served to conceal the relative lack of church influence on wider social policy. Government coldly ignored the report of the Commission on Vocational Organisation, although it was drafted by a priest and the commission chaired by a bishop. It brusquely dismissed the Bishop of Clonfert when he sought to explore the implications of Catholic teaching in a direction which the minister involved had no wish to follow. This was not because of any inherent hostility to the church. It was because of inherent hostility to alternative thought processes. It may even be that the government was right on both occasions. The manner in which it dismissed the recommendations, however, exposed a philistine streak in the official mind.

T.D. Williams would observe, in the aftermath of the Mother and Child

237 Gallagher, *Labour party*, p. 34; M.D. Higgins, 'Making sense of change', *Saothar*, 19 (1984), p. 74; B. Girvin, 'Industrialisation and the Irish working class since 1922', *Saothar*, 10 (1984), pp. 31–41.
238 J. Richard Orpen, 'Reservation No. 10', in *Report of the Commission on emigration and other population problems 1948–1954*, pp. 243–4.
239 Cooper and Whelan, *Science*, p. 17.

débâcle, that 'it is only recently in Ireland that Catholic sociology has been brought to bear, in public manner, upon "political" problems in which sociologists are interested'. Williams noted that it had seemed as if 'administrators and sociologists' had 'remained determined to avoid each other. One says: here are the principles and it is your business to discover the facts. The administrator takes the line: it is not my business to concern myself with the principles, but I alone know the facts to which they apply . . .'[240] Bishop Michael Browne of Galway had no illusions about the demand, outside the civil service no less than within it, for uncongenial church thinking on social issues. When he posed the question in the first issue of *Christus Rex*, the sociology journal founded in Maynooth in 1947, 'why Catholic priests should concern themselves with social and economic questions', he denounced not only socialists on the one hand, but the 'bank director and economist' on the other, who wanted to confine the Church to 'confessional, sacristy and armchair'.[241]

If demand was distinctly limited, did this reflect the nature of supply? Was supply itself limited by the size of the market? Or could it create its own demand? It may be hazarded as a general observation that during the first generation of independence slack demand was the main reason for market sluggishness. Thereafter, the market became livelier, with strengths and weaknesses being more evenly distributed between the supply and the demand sides. M.D. McCarthy was broadly justified in asserting in 1952 that economists had hitherto failed to make adequate use of the statistics. But it could also be the case that inquirers into particular problems found themselves floundering in an information vacuum. The protracted inquiry into Dublin housing between 1939 and 1943 observed that 'no records exist . . . from which even indirect conclusions can be drawn with any degree of certainty' about working-class incomes, or about 'how many persons in Dublin county borough are in receipt of incomes exceeding, say, £6 per week'.[242]

The views of the statisticians on what the users ought to want did not always coincide with the views of consumers on what they needed. It would not be until 1984 that the clause in the 1926 Statistics Act providing for a Statistical Council to advise on the appropriateness of statistical supply would be activated, despite at least one intervening attempt, by Alfred O'Rahilly, to press its establishment on de Valera.[243] Nevertheless, statistical supply in general, however defective in absolute

---

240 T.D. Williams, 'Review of Fr Thomas Gilby, *A philosophy and theology of the state*', *Administration*, 1, 2 (summer 1953), p. 101.

241 M. Browne, 'Why Catholic priests should concern themselves with social and economic questions', *Christus Rex*, 1 (1947), pp. 3–4.

242 *Report of Dublin Housing Inquiry 1939–43* (Dublin, 1943), para. 114.

243 *A new institutional structure for the Central Statistics Office* (Dublin, 1985), p. 4; NLI, MS 922, CVO, 23 November 1939, q. 1 408, ev. A. O'Rahilly.

terms, probably ran comfortably ahead of demand until the 1960s. It may then have fallen behind a rapidly growing demand, although this in turn may have been due in part to a failure to supply it with adequate resources, until by the early 1980s serious concern came to be expressed about the quality of available data.[244]

If economists made only sporadic use of statistics, it was partly because they were so small a group. Economists today enjoy so prominent a position in moulding the climate of opinion that it is difficult to grasp that in 1922 'economics had not . . . become a profession. There were very few graduates in the subject.'[245] There were only a handful of professional economists in the country. The key figures initially were O'Brien, who held a chair in UCD from 1926 to 1962, Duncan who held a TCD chair from 1932 to 1963, and Busteed, who held a UCC chair from 1923 to 1964. All feature occasionally in Finance calculations. O'Brien and Duncan broadly shared the ideological assumptions and policy perspectives of Brennan and McElligott. Busteed was somewhat less ideologically reliable. He had a sharp critical mind, and could be original. He actually joined with Alfred O'Rahilly in 1944 in conducting a survey of poverty in Cork on the Rowntree model.[246] Steering a somewhat erratic course in later life, however, and absorbed in College and local affairs, he did not provide a sustained alternative to the official mind.

The economists had some contact with Finance. They had almost none with Industry and Commerce or with Agriculture. There were some personal reasons for this. O'Brien and Duncan were both 'ferociously hostile to the economic policies of the Fianna Fáil government'.[247] The gifted young James Meenan in UCD found the philosophy of protectionism uncongenial, while Joseph Johnston, an acute but acerbic TCD economist, regularly flayed Fianna Fáil's agricultural policy. Even had the economists been more politically acceptable, it is unclear how professionally qualified they were to advise on the type of decision confronting Lemass and Leydon, or Ryan and Twomey. Highly prescriptive on policy issues, they were rarely descriptive in terms of industrial economics. Recitation of the catechism of classical economics was one thing. Once those principles were transgressed, the economists had few professional skills for advising on the location of firms, the selection of industrial sectors for support, the most effective subsidy levels for farmers, etc. The economists published little on decision-making of this type. Their denunciations of Fianna Fáil policy derived from general principles, whereas the policy-makers were concerned with nuts and bolts. Both demand and

[244] *A new institutional structure for the Central Statistics Office*, passim.
[245] Meenan, *George O'Brien*, p. 146.
[246] L. Ryan, 'Urban poverty', in S. Kennedy, *One million poor?* (Dublin, 1981), p. 38.
[247] Fanning, *Economists*, p. 141.

supply remained ineffective because they were largely operating in different markets.

Circumstances changed rather rapidly about 1960. The publication of *Economic Development* was a major contribution to the supply of organised economic intelligence. Whitaker would continue to publish regularly after 1958. For all McElligott's confidence in economic laws, for all his disdain for deviants, he refrained from unduly troubling the printers. McElligott was busy. So was Whitaker. That did not prevent him from contributing to both the supply of, and the demand for, ideas. Some other officials, in Finance and elsewhere, had the intellectual self-confidence to publish under their own names. *Administration* offered a convenient forum. The numbers were not large. They did not have to be. In a small country, a small number can make a big difference – in the civil service, as in academia or in business – if only they have the class.

The Economic Research Institute (ERI) enormously expanded the supply of applied economics after 1960. It was symptomatic, however, of the state of Irish economics that while George O'Brien duly became first chairman of the board, the first director was none other than Roy Geary, the earlier scourge of the economists. And Geary's successor was M.D. McCarthy. McCarthy's successor was Michael Fogarty, an authority on industrial relations. It was not until Fogarty's resignation that an Irish economist, Kieran Kennedy, became director in 1971. A trained economist and sometime civil servant, who had done his doctoral research on leave of absence from the enlightened Finance of Whitaker's day, he had worked under Simon Kuznets, who had a demanding concept of the scholar's duty to publish.

The academic scene changed quickly with the establishment of the ERI, the retirement in rapid succession of O'Brien and Duncan, and the death of Busteed. James Meenan, who had published a superior study of Italian corporatism, as well as penetrating papers on population, protection and finance, succeeded O'Brien. Patrick Lynch continued to play a prominent role in the application of informed economic thought to public affairs, and was to introduce generations of students to advanced theory. Louden Ryan, whose doctoral thesis studied the actual working of protection in Ireland, and who subsequently established an international reputation with his work on price theory, succeeded Duncan in Trinity. He played an active role as chairman of numerous official committees over the next thirty years. David O'Mahony, Busteed's successor in Cork, wrote scholarly papers on industrial relations, and published in 1964 the first textbook on the Irish economy by a professional economist.[248] This was followed six years later by Meenan's encyclopaedic study of the Irish

248 D. O'Mahony, *The Irish economy* (Cork, 1964).

economy since independence.[249] Students now had a much improved foundation on which to base their study of the economy.

This generation in turn would be followed by a cluster of brilliant UCD students, including Kieran Kennedy at the ESRI, Dermot McAleese, who succeeded Ryan in Trinity, Brendan Walsh and Peter Neary, who succeeded Meenan and Lynch at UCD, and Patrick Geary, foundation professor of economics at Maynooth. They constituted a formidable array of professorial talent. There were also several other able exponents, not only in the universities and the ESRI, but in the Central Bank, the Agricultural Research Institute, and in consultancies.

The growth in the number, status and influence of economists has been a striking feature of the intellectual market since about 1960. The economists deserve admiration for the manner in which they have come to occupy the high ground of intellectual discourse, not only by force of circumstances but by force of intellect. Yet it may be queried if this dominance of the policy studies market by economists is entirely healthy from a national viewpoint. Reservations can be expressed on three main grounds.

The standard criticism, that economists had little knowledge of the actual functioning of decision-making in business institutions, has been repeated recently in the light of empirical studies of decision-making in Irish business. Charles Carroll concludes that the facts of the real world 'largely confound the economists' model'.[250] Carroll regards even Telesis, which consciously tried 'to avoid the shortcomings of economics, by relying on extensive experience at the level of the firm'[251] as suffering from over-simplification, succumbing to the temptation to stereotype sectors in such categories as 'high growth', 'mature', 'high tech' or 'low tech', in a manner which can grossly distort their true promise.[252] While some of the criticisms may be exaggerated, there would seem to be a case for subjecting the assumptions of economists to the discipline of both boardroom and shopfloor perspectives.

The second familiar reservation concerns the appropriateness of the prevailing assumptions. Without fully subscribing to the vigour of Bressand's assault on the relevance of economic thought to the real world,[253] it is certainly true that Irish economists have devoted little time to pondering their own assumptions. If 'one of the most striking aspects of contemporary discussions of the health and well-being of Irish society is the extraordinary predominance of the economic perspective and of the

249 Meenan, *Irish economy.*
250 C. Carroll, *Building Ireland's business* (Dublin, 1985), p. 3.
251 *Ibid.*, p. 21.   252 *Ibid.*
253 A. Bressand, 'Mastering the "world economy"', *Foreign Affairs*, 61, 4 (Spring 1983), p. 748.

economic practitioner',[254] it is even more striking that 'economists can get away with playing the philosopher king because there is so little challenge to the dominant orthodoxy'.[255] This is by no means unique to Ireland in a subject where 'group conformity' may be particularly pronounced.[256] It is noteworthy, however, in a country which in economic no less than in social experience 'tends to defy classification'.[257] Most Irish economists have clung to neo-classical models with a diligence which largely precludes conceptual originality even while fostering technical virtuosity. There tends to be a certain metallic quality about the pronouncements of economists who, though professionally competent, are not in quite the first rank intellectually. If the professional perspective of the economists sharpens insight, it may blur vision. Only capacious intellects may be good enough to transcend the limitations imposed by the nature of the subject. The consequence is that while contemporary Irish economics can be impressive in accounting for short-term movements, it has contributed relatively little to understanding the long-term development of the Irish economy. There is little incentive for the economists to think otherwise. The demand structure that has developed with the growth of a variety of institutions like the NIEC, NESC, etc. tends to seek instant solutions to immediate problems. The premium is on tunnel thinking, blind to either long-term perspective or lateral linkage. In short, with the exception of a handful of superior intelligences, Irish economists are far more impressive as technicians than as thinkers.

The kernel of the problem is the desire to exclude 'non-economic' factors from 'economic' analysis. It is striking that a country with so distinctive a pattern of under-development has made so little contribution to development economics. Myrdal has explained some of the limitations of the neo-classical approach:

Naively we started out by applying to the under-developed countries the models, theories and concepts we had, with some success, been using in our study of growth, stagnation and instability in developed countries. We are by no means out of that phase yet. This implies playing down power relations, social and economic stratification, institutions generally, upheld by and themselves supporting, attitudes. These 'non-economic' factors in under-developed countries are systematically much stronger impediments to what we conceive of as development.[258]

Another Nobel Prize winner, of rather different ideological persuasion, equally emphasised the importance of 'non-economic' factors. 'Of course, one can always argue', said Kuznets:

[254] J. Pratschke, 'Economic philosophy and ideology in Ireland', *Studies*, 74 (Summer 1975), pp. 145–54.
[255] A. Matthews, 'Economics and ideology', *Crane Bag*, 9, 2 (1985), p. 59.
[256] G. Myrdal, 'Crises and cycles in the development of economics', *Political Quarterly*, 44 (1973), p. 9.
[257] M. Peillon, *Contemporary Irish society* (Dublin, 1982), p. 1.
[258] Myrdal, 'Crises', p. 17.

that economic analysis must deal with economic processes *per se* and leave the analysis of non-economic conditions to other disciplines. But this argument assumes an independence of the economic processes . . . although such independence may perhaps be assumed in the analysis of short-term changes and relations, it cannot be a premise in the analysis of the long-term changes involved in economic growth. In any case, awareness of the full range of factors – regardless of their classification in the rather uncertain nomenclature of the social sciences – should be useful in an analysis of problems of economic growth.[259]

Closer to home, Patrick Lynch, drawing on his own extensive experience, concluded that 'policy-making must draw from different disciplines, not merely from the economist, whose importance has often, perhaps, been exaggerated, but also from the sociologist, the social administrator, and the social historian . . .'[260]

It was, however, precisely at this nodal point of interaction between the various social studies that the major problem arose. Slowly though economics developed as a research discipline, it was exceptionally advanced compared with cognate subjects. Few lectureships, much less chairs, were established in sociology, political science, anthropology, international relations, law, geography, social psychology, or economic history, until long after economics had achieved a secure position as a standard university subject.

Maynooth did establish a chair of Catholic sociology in 1937, while UCC instituted an unpaid lectureship in sociology the same year.[261] Further chairs followed only after a long delay, beginning in 1966 in UCD and finally breaching the bulwarks of Trinity in 1974. Queen's and TCD established the first full lectureships in political science in the country in 1948, which they ventured to turn into chairs in 1960. UCG had a joint chair of politics and sociology from 1969. UCD separated a chair of politics from that of ethics in 1983. Neither UCC nor Maynooth made any appointments in politics at all. Queen's established the first chair of geography in 1945, followed by UCC in 1954, UCD in 1960, TCD in 1963, UCG in 1968, and Maynooth in 1978. Social anthropology developed gradually in the North after securing a toehold in Queen's in 1962, twenty years before a Southern university, Maynooth, made a

259 S. Kuznets, *Economic growth and structure* (London, 1965), p. 121.
260 P. Lynch, 'Whither science policy?', *Administration*, 27, 3 (Autumn 1979), p. 268.
261 This paragraph is compiled from the following sources: J.A. Gaughan, *Alfred O'Rahilly: academic* (Dublin, 1986), p. 92; T. Garvin, 'The teaching of politics in Ireland: (1) University College, Dublin', *Political Studies Association of Ireland Bulletin*, 3 (May 1986), pp. 5–6; C. O'Leary, 'The teaching of politics in Ireland: (2) Queens University, Belfast', *ibid.*, 4 (November 1986), pp. 4–5; C. Ward, 'The background of the Department of Social Science, UCD', *UCD News* (October 1984); G. Herries-Davies (ed.), *Irish geography: the Geographical Society of Ireland Golden Jubilee 1934–1984* (Dublin, 1984), p. 17; Barrington, *Administrative system*, p. 92; B.M.E. MacMahon, 'A sense of identity in the Irish Legal System', in Lee, *Ireland: towards a sense of place*, p. 35; information supplied directly by the relevant departments, to whom I am grateful.

formal appointment. After an abortive attempt to establish a chair of international relations in TCD in the 1940s, there is still no chair in that subject, North or South. Law as a serious academic subject developed mainly after 1960. Public administration is yet another late developer as a university subject. The first, and still the only chair of economic history was established in Queen's in 1967. Chairs of business management did not begin to emerge until the 1970s.

The creation of a chair was sometimes the final rather than the first step in the development of a subject. Estyn Evans, who acquired a world reputation, began teaching geography in Belfast in 1929.[262] Trinity had a diploma in geography from 1930, thirty-three years before it created a chair.[263] Geographers developed an early *esprit de corps*, reflected in, and encouraged by, the founding of the Geographical Association of Ireland in 1934, and regular periodical publication, culminating in *Irish Geography*, from 1944. Few other subject areas developed as systematically. Public administration was relatively well served in terms of publication outlets, thanks mainly to *Administration*. It was not until 1981, however, that a general analytical survey, Barrington's *Irish Administrative System*, was published. The first economic history of Ireland to satisfy modern standards, Louis Cullen's *Economic history of Ireland since 1660*, appeared in 1972. The journal, *Economic and Social History* was first published in 1974. The Irish Labour History Society, founded in 1974, launched its journal, *Saothar*, from 1976. The Sociological Association of Ireland, founded in 1975, brought out, somewhat precariously, annual conference reports from 1976. The first textbook on the sociology of Ireland, Peillon's *Contemporary Irish society*, appeared in 1982. The *Irish Business and Administrative Review* was first published in 1982. Law texts drawing on specifically Irish experience did not begin to emerge until the 1970s and 1980s. The Royal Irish Academy launched *Irish Studies in International Affairs* in 1979. The first issue of *Irish Political Studies* did not appear until 1986. The *Irish Journal of Education* was first published in 1975, and *Irish Educational Studies* in 1981. Growth there obviously was. But sporadic and uncoordinated growth, depending more on the institutional fortunes of individual disciplines than on a coherent response to perceived national problems. Little hint of a distinctive Irish approach towards social science emerged.

Economics would have remained central to the supply of policy analyses in contemporary Ireland irrespective of what happened in other social disciplines. But the economists held the high ground to some extent

262 H.J. Fleure, 'Emer Estyn Evans: a personal note', in R.H. Buchanan, E. Jones and D. MacCourt (eds.), *Man and his habitat: essays presented to Emer Estyn Evans* (New York, 1971), pp. 2–3.
263 McDowell and Webb, *Trinity*, p. 450.

by default, simply because most other subjects remained so relatively under-developed.

Why was the supply of social thought so limited? The reasons for the poverty of supply take us close to the heart of the Irish intellectual condition. The diagnosis is crucial to understanding the nature of Irish society, North and South. To place the Irish performance in proper perspective, however, we must first broaden our approach to cover two further areas of inquiry, education and history, whose experience may be instructive.

We have tended to assume that the grudging recognition accorded by universities to social studies retarded their development. The fate of the relatively early sociology appointments in Maynooth and Cork before the Second World War gives us cause to pause. Neither would make a systematic contribution to national thought for some decades. The experience of education obliges us to pause further. Education was an established subject in universities before independence. This was an area in which demand might be presumed to exist. The Department of Education regularly affirmed its dedication to the improvement of educational standards. But the quality of the official mind in the Department would long remain suspect, not least in the eyes of civil servants themselves.[264] The Department had direct responsibility for the teacher training colleges. It made no effort to encourage research among their staff. 'Lecturers were neither expected nor facilitated to engage in educational research other than lecture production' in these institutions, where 'the libraries were inadequate and little-used'.[265]

If the Department evinced little interest in closer relations between the training colleges and the university departments of education, neither did the universities apparently show much concern for closer relations. If anything, the two institutions 'grew apart from one another', despite the fact that they shared a common approach to the study of education, 'unimaginative, instrumental and intellectually shallow'.[266] University staff in education did little to encourage research on the role of education in society. 'No books which dealt with wider aspects of education' were published in Ireland between 1922 and 1962.[267] Dónal Mulcahy could introduce his seminal study, *Curriculum and policy in Irish post-primary education* in 1981 by noting that at no time since independence 'has any sustained assessment and critical analysis been undertaken in regard to the overall purposes and programmes of post-primary education'.[268] Small

264 Ó Broin, *Yesterday*, p. 66.
265 J. Coolahan, 'The fortunes of education as a subject of study and of research in Ireland', *Irish Educational Studies*, 4, 1 (1984), p. 15.
266 *Ibid.*, pp. 1, 15.   267 *Ibid.*, p. 18.
268 D. Mulcahy, *Curriculum and policy in Irish post-primary education* (Dublin, 1981), p. 1.

wonder that the Commission on Higher Education felt obliged to note the 'paucity' of research on educational problems.[269] It was symptomatic that at an unusually exciting period in Irish educational history, the chairs of education were left vacant, in UCD from 1950 to 1966, in UCC from 1962 to 1969, and in Maynooth from 1956 to 1966.[270] Thus, just when education suddenly became a subject of serious public and political concern, 'university education departments were in a weak position to contribute to, or indeed cope with, the situation'.[271] It may be doubted, of course, in view of their inertia when chairs had been filled, whether leaving them vacant made much difference, though one would need to know the calibre of potential appointees before reaching a final verdict. In any case, when a market for educational ideas abruptly opened up, thanks to the receptivity of some politicians and of new Secretaries of Education, Terry Raftery and Seán O'Connor, the initiative on the supply side was taken more by the economists, particularly Patrick Lynch, and the Education Research Centre established in St Patrick's Training College in Dublin, thanks largely to the initiative of Fr Donal Cregan, who was not only president of the college, but also a serious scholar.[272]

Yet the salutary example of history cautions us against the temptation to assume that the only sorrier fate for a subject than rejection by the university was acceptance by the university. The achievement of the generation of historians that emerged in the 1930s serves as a reminder of the standards that could be achieved even in grim circumstances, and of the way in which scholars of ability and integrity could improve the quantity and quality of supply in their chosen fields.

Compared with the subjects whose institutional fortunes we have just reviewed, history was highly-favoured in the early twentieth century. It had about a dozen chairs in the 1920s. Among the professors were some eminent scholars, like Eoin MacNeill in UCD and Edmund Curtis in TCD, intelligent thinkers like J.M. O'Sullivan in UCD and James Hogan in UCC, and dedicated teachers like J.E. Todd in Queens. Some good work got done. But activity, as in academia in general, occurred in fits and starts, with no overall sense of direction. W.F. Butler rejoiced in 1913 that as 'now with the establishment of the National University, provision has been made for the first time for the foundation in this country of a School of Historical Science, we may look at last for the adequate treatment of our own land'.[273] More than two decades were to pass, however, before

---

[269] Coolahan, 'Fortunes of education', p. 21.

[270] *Ibid.*, pp. 16–17; Commission on Higher Education, *Report of Commission on Higher Education*, 1967, p. 217.

[271] Coolahan, 'Fortunes of education', p. 17. [272] *Ibid.*, p. 22.

[273] W.F. Butler, 'Some untilled fields in Irish history', *Studies*, 2 (1913), p. 402. The following paragraphs draw on J. Lee, 'Some aspects of modern Irish historiography', in

Butler's hopes began to be systematically realised. UCC and UCG were too small, and enjoyed too little access to source material, to enable them develop flourishing schools at this stage. Responsibility therefore rested with UCD to provide the cutting edge. Circumstances decreed otherwise. Much of the energy of Eoin MacNeill and J.M. O'Sullivan was diverted into party politics. The choice of Mary Hayden in preference to Edmund Curtis as first professor of Irish history in 1909 does not seem to have been justified in the event, whatever the apparent merits of the candidates at the time.[274]

If the work of MacNeill and Curtis was central to the establishment of a worthy reputation for Irish scholarship in the fields of early and medieval history, serious contributions to modern Irish history by university scholars scarcely began before the 1930s. It was then, through a happy combination of intellectual ability, strength of character, and institutional chance, that two young historians, R.D. Edwards in UCD and T.W. Moody, first in Queen's, Belfast and then in TCD, supported by another young Irish scholar in Liverpool, D.B. Quinn, finally fulfilled the hopes expressed more than twenty years before, by creating a professional school of historical enquiry and establishing a sound international reputation for modern Irish history. The achievement was the more remarkable for encompassing North and South. Moody, a Belfast man, played a crucial role in this respect. The Ulster Historical Society and the Irish Historical Society were both founded in 1936. They jointly provided the institutional basis for the periodical, *Irish Historical Studies* (*IHS*), whose first number appeared in 1938, under the joint editorship of Edwards and Moody. IHS would serve as an indispensable outlet for the fruits of the research of the band of mainly young scholars, mostly in Dublin and Belfast, who sustained the momentum of the new development for a generation.

If IHS was a relative latecomer by European and North American standards, it quickly achieved striking vitality. Augmented from 1944 by a series of volumes entitled *Studies in Irish history*, edited by Edwards, Moody and Quinn, it contributed significantly to the diffusion of a more mature interpretation of Irish historical experience. Much historical writing hitherto had been not only polemical, but partisan. A widely-read textbook by Mary Hayden, and an account of Anglo-Irish relations between 1906 and 1923 by W.A. Phillips, Lecky Professor of History in

---

E. Schulin (ed.), *Gedenkschrift Martin Göhring: Studien zur Europäischen Geschichte* (Wiesbaden 1968), pp. 438ff.

[274] T.W. Moody, 'Edmund Curtis', *Hermathena*, lxiii (1944), p. 74, n. 10; D. Dickson 'Historical journals in Ireland: the last hundred years', in B. Hayley and E. McKay (eds.), *300 Years of Irish periodicals* (Mullingar, 1987), p. 88.

TCD from 1913 to 1939, were vintage cowboy and indian stuff.[275] With IHS 'history as the handmaiden of nationalism' (or imperialism) began to be 'replaced by history as an independent discipline'.[276] Rigorous scrutiny of source material, and scrupulous integrity in the use of evidence, characterised IHS from the outset, as it had already distinguished the major early works of the two editors, Edwards' *Church and state in Tudor Ireland* (1936) and Moody's *Londonderry Plantation* (1939). It is easy, almost trite, to say this. Perhaps only those who have waded through earlier writing on Irish history can fully appreciate the extent of the 'revolution' involved.[277] As history had been so incestuous a handmaiden of politics, Edwards and Moody, together with Quinn and other allies like G.A. Hayes McCoy, R.B. McDowell and J.C. Beckett, were not only challenging a venerable tradition, but throwing down the gauntlet to cherished nationalist and unionist self-images.

That this was not immediately apparent to a wider public was probably due to the self-denying ordinance adopted by the editors with regard to contemporary history. The rules of the journal excluded any reference to Irish politics after 1900.[278] This was slowly relaxed, though it was not until the late 1970s that IHS advanced as far as its own thirty-year rule.

Understandable, if regrettable, though the editorial instinct was, it probably helped discourage the development of systematic historical thinking about the twentieth century, thus in effect abandoning the contemporary terrain to thinkers versed in other disciplines, or in no discipline at all. It was no coincidence that a journalist, Tim Pat.Coogan, editor of the *Irish Press*, could validly claim that his *Ireland since the Rising*, published in 1966, was the first attempt at a general survey of contemporary Irish history. It was not until Oliver MacDonagh's brilliant, but brief, *Ireland* (1967), the detailed study by F.S.L. Lyons, *Ireland since the Famine* (1971) and the synoptic survey by John A. Murphy, *Ireland in the twentieth century* (1975), that university historians sought to provide a general interpretation of developments since independence. Lyons, though originally a Moody student, was then based in England. MacDonagh wrote from Australia, and his approach had in any event long transcended that of *IHS*. Murphy wrote from Cork, another faraway country of which *IHS* knew little. This reluctance to confront the contemporary provides some support for the view that the *IHS* school

275 M. Hayden and G.A. Moonan, *A short history of the Irish people. From the earliest times to 1920* (Dublin, 1921); W.A. Phillips, *The revolution in Ireland, 1906–23* (London, 1923).

276 J.A. Murphy, 'Comment' in D. Watt (ed.), *The Constitution of Northern Ireland* (London, 1981), p. 67.

277 N. Mansergh, *The Irish question 1840–1921* (London, 1965), p. 13.

278 R. Fanning, '"The great enchantment": uses and abuses of modern Irish history', in J. Dooge (ed.), *Ireland in the contemporary world: essays in honour of Garret FitzGerald* (Dublin, 1986), pp. 131–47.

achieved success partly through the very 'blandness' of its approach. 'The agreed truth was not a prophet's, but a bureaucrat's.'[279]

Whatever justification the delicacy about twentieth-century history may have had in 1938, it had none after 1945. The continuing refusal of *IHS* to encourage the study of contemporary history is all the more puzzling in view of the fact that Desmond Williams succeeded Edwards as joint editor, with Moody, in 1957. When the 28-year-old Williams, who had a world class mind, returned to the chair of modern history in UCD in 1949, the prospects for another powerful surge forward in historical studies seemed bright. Williams came with an already glittering international reputation, and with an exceptional range of English, American and European contacts. He had the good fortune too to enjoy the staunch support of Edwards who, far from resenting, as might a meaner man, the return of the prodigy trailing clouds of Cambridge glory, sought to smoothen the path in UCD for him.

Williams flung himself into Dublin intellectual life with demonic energy. He devoted immense effort to the fortnightly *Leader*, which he edited between 1951 and 1955. Contributions to the *Leader* were anonymous. But pieces that can be reasonably attributed to Williams, would come to at least 200,000 words over this period. He expanded his 30 000 word series on Irish neutrality in 1953 to about 50 000 words later that year. Though unannotated, these were clearly based on an extensive command of archival material. His probing 25 000 word study of the Anglo-Polish Agreement of 1939 appeared in 1956–7, prelude to his important analysis of the historiography of the causes of the Second World War, published in 1958. His short, brilliant introduction (written with R.D. Edwards) to *The Great Famine* had appeared in 1956.

Some of these publications are not without traces of hasty composition, as was inevitable in the circumstances. In their formidable knowledge of documentary material, however, and even more in their sureness of touch in decoding the meaning of that material, their sensitivity to the play of personality and to the pressure of process in decision-making, their subtlety in disentangling the threads in the thinking of figures as diverse as de Valera, Churchill, Hitler, Beck and Charles Trevelyan, their originality, their judiciousness, their extraordinary maturity for a scholar still in his early thirties dealing with issues of such emotive power as Famine and Appeasement, they bear the stamp of a major historical mind. In UCD, the range, authority and sheer intellectual power of his lectures on European and American history, and on international relations, would leave an indelible impression on many students, some of whom would themselves be enabled to pursue further study through his generosity in mobilising his

---

[279] L. de Paor, 'As we are', *Irish Times*, 4 July 1985.

international contacts to secure them the research support in England, Germany and America that Ireland denied them.[280]

When Williams became joint editor of *IHS* in 1957, it might be assumed that its receptivity to both contemporary history and to a comparative approach to Irish history, would increase. But there was little opportunity to reconsider the format or the approach before he himself, already affected by ill-health since youth, fell victim to debilitating life-long illness, which would see him given up for dead on more than one occasion, and which, seriously restricting his mobility, sapped his phenomenal energy of the fifties, and made it virtually impossible to conduct archival research. His initiatives would still contribute to the promotion of contemporary history, particularly through his editing of series of Thomas Davis radio lectures, sometimes in conjunction with supportive colleagues like Kevin Nowlan. And his own short but seminal essays would establish the framework within which subsequent study of topics like the civil war, de Valera, and neutrality would have to be conducted. The series of lapidary formulations in which he sketched the contours of contemporary Irish history continued to show that there was no substitute for sheer class. But he could no longer make the expected profound impact through his writings. And the fortitude with which he bore his affliction must make both the scholar and the citizen lament that he chose to devote so much of his remaining energies to the ephemera of university affairs, at a frightful cost for a mind of his quality.

One can understand, from an English perspective, the sentiment behind the sympathetic observation that, 'One wishes that he had written more . . . or does one? Fine historians abound; there was only one Desmond Williams.'[281] But from an Irish perspective, the supply of fine historians, however impressive in the cultural context, was far from bountiful. The sombre Irish proverb, *Maireann lorg an phinn, ach ni maireann an béal a chan* (tersely translated, 'Ink lasts, talk doesn't') seems, sadly, more apposite.

The verdict of the obituary in the London *Times* – 'Distinguished historian who wrote too little'[282] – has to be endorsed. It is a poignant tribute to Williams. And this, even after taking into account that he wrote far more than is usually recognised, or that the exceptionally high ratio of mind to matter in his writings ensures that his 'less' surpasses in value the 'more' of many a bulkier *oeuvre*. Confident of his class, he rarely bothered to 'place' his published work to ensure maximum professional exposure. Many of his profound perceptions lie buried in Thomas Davis lectures, sometimes dismissed by 'serious' scholars as inadequately austere to

[280] Personal knowledge.
[281] Peregrine Worsthorne, 'Desmond Williams', *The Spectator*, 24 January 1987.
[282] *The Times*, 21 January 1987.

qualify as 'real' history. His observations on the origins of the Second
World War in *Historical Studies* would attract wider attention only when
republished more than a decade later by Esmonde Robertson in his
collection of the crucial contributions to the subject.[283] He allowed his
study of the Anglo-Polish Agreement to languish in the relative international obscurity of *Irish Historical Studies*, while his reflections on the
Risorgimento appeared in the guise of an occasional publication of the
Italian Institute in Dublin.[284] When he rescued his study of Irish neutrality
from the anonymous files of the *Leader*, it was only to transfer the
expanded version to the *Irish Press*.

The Actonian analogy is irresistible. There is much of the same
erudition, of the same penetration, of the same capaciousness, of the same
concern with the relationship between morality and power – though on
the role of moral judgement Williams was firmly with Butterfield and
against Acton. There is also the Actonian touch of perfectionism that
might have, even had his health been spared, obliged the obituarist to
lament another Madonna of the Future.

Despite this suspicion, one still cannot help wondering what heights he
might have scaled if only he had never returned to Dublin. Neither can one
help wondering why a small, and in so many respects still embattled
country, has never sought to devise mechanisms for harnessing the
intelligence of minds of his quality so that they might be enabled to devote
more systematic thought to the national condition rather than have their
time frittered away in the enervating minutiae of Irish university life,
which may sustain routine thinkers adequately enough, but which provides little opportunity for creative minds to realise their full potential.
This was one more example of the country failing to make anything like
the most productive use of its scarcest resource – the time of the truly
first-class mind.

So little trace did a Williams-type perspective leave on *IHS* that it must
be concluded that his joint editorship was largely honorary long before his
name vanished silently from the cover of the March 1974 issue. Moody
continued to edit the journal alone until joined, again silently, by the
younger generation in the person of Ronan Fanning in March 1976.
When Moody finally retired after forty years devoted service, in 1978,
Fanning would be joined by another younger scholar, David Harkness. By
then, circumstances had changed so greatly since 1938, thanks partly to

---

283 T.D. Williams, 'The historiography of World War Two', in *Historical Studies*, 1 (1958),
pp. 33–49, reprinted in E.M. Robertson (ed.), *The origins of the Second World War*
(London, 1971), pp. 36–64.
284 T.D. Williams, 'Negotiations leading to the Anglo-Polish Agreement of 31 March 1939',
IHS, 10, nos 37 and 38 (March and September 1956), pp. 59–93, 156–92; 'The
Risorgimento in retrospect: an Irish historian's view', in R.W.D. Edwards (ed.), *Ireland
and the Italian Risorgimento* (Dublin, 1960), pp. 57–73.

the contribution of *IHS* itself, that no single journal could again play the crucial role of the early *IHS*. The role of *IHS* declined further as the productive schools of history that now emerged in Cork and Galway largely bypassed the *IHS* circle as they forged their own independent connections with centres of European and American scholarship.

Apart from the fear of faction, the failure of the generation of the thirties to respond to the challenge of the contemporary derived from at least two sources inherent in their approach to historical study. The concern of the founders of *IHS* with adequate documentation, a prerequisite for the establishment of satisfactory scholarly standards, involved a distaste for the study of more recent subjects on which sufficient source material was deemed not to be available. It would not be until the 1970s that Irish cabinet records became accessible. On that basis, there could be no argument on the matter. But there was more to it than that. The *IHS* concept of a 'source' was itself largely a product of a particular concept of history. History was essentially the study of institutions, mainly political and ecclesiastical, rather than of society or of mentalities. Sources were therefore narrowly defined. The type of source material already beginning to be widely used by some continental and American scholars, even in the study of political history, much less the types of sources used by social and economic historians, remained largely a closed book to this mentality.

Yet many distinctive features of modern Irish history involved society much more than the state. Anglo-Irish relations were, of course, of high importance. They could not be addressed without close attention to the nature of the state. Many other striking aspects of Irish experience, however, like the nature and role of population change, including the unique intensity of emigration, the changing language situation, the role of popular religion, the relatively slow industrialisation, could not be explained through the type of source analysis that Irish scholars brought back with them from their English sojourns. Many crucial features of Irish experience would therefore remain beyond the imagination of professional historians until well after the Second World War.

The techniques of enquiry nurtured by *IHS* could not illuminate vast tracts of Irish spiritual, intellectual, cultural and material experience. *IHS* even rivetted an unnecessarily narrow concept of politics on political history, its own forte. Fine work of the type pioneered by Nicholas Mansergh in *The government of Northern Ireland* and *The government of the Free State*, published in 1934 and 1936 respectively, lay largely beyond not only its chronology, but its concept, of history. So, for practical purposes, did the blend of the history of ideas and politics pioneered by Mansergh in *Ireland in the Age of Reform and Revolution*, published in 1940. Political history did not, for long, include electoral history. James Hogan's *Elections in Ireland*, published in 1944, found few immediate emulators among *IHS* historians, even for earlier periods. Hogan's work was continued by his student, Cornelius O'Leary, from the haven of a political science department in Belfast. Many potential sources on modern history in general, and on contemporary history in particular, remained unexploited simply because historians generally lacked the imagination to think of them as sources.

That the history of *mentalité* made such little impression on the *IHS* school may have owed something to its revulsion at the work of Daniel Corkery, Professor of English in UCC, and particularly at his *Hidden Ireland* (1927). Corkery's virulent political partisanship made him anathema to apostles of the new faith. But in rightly rejecting the bias, *IHS* devotees also neglected the potential of Corkery's concern with excavating the mental archaeology both of individuals and of collectivities, his fascination with society rather than with the state, and the European dimension of his thinking. Corkery's use of material has since stimulated lively discussion.[285] But that is not the main matter at issue. It may have been impossible to take adequate cognisance of the Corkery concept until the more blatant prejudices were exorcised from the writing of political history. In retrospect, historical studies might have developed more fruitfully if Corkery's critics could have appreciated the value of no less than the flaws in, his approach. It was left mainly to Sean O'Faolain, however critical of Corkery in detail he might be, to show how the potential could be fulfilled from a quite different political perspective.[286] O'Faolain's *The Irish*, first published in 1947, explicitly invoked Collingwood's dictum that 'History proper is the history of thought. There are no mere events in history.' It was not a sentiment that found much favour in the pages of *IHS*, which did not review *The Irish*.

Why *IHS* remained so wedded for so long to its original approach, long after that had secured its objective, remains unclear. That the revolutionaries of one generation, in intellectual no less than in political life, tend to become the conservatives of the next, is hardly an original observation. This description would, however, do less than justice to Edwards. His essay on the nationalism of Young Ireland, published in 1947, showed a striking sensitivity to the history of ideas.[287] Edwards' thinking could, on occasion, prove a shade too subtle for more pedestrian minds. In his later

---

285 L.M. Cullen, 'The hidden Ireland: reassessment of a concept', *Studia Hibernica*, 9 (1967), pp. 7–47; S. Ó Tuama, 'Dónall Ó Corcora', in S. Ó Mórdha (ed.), *Scríobh*, 4 (1979), pp. 100–8; B. Ó Buachalla, 'Ó Corcora agus an Hidden Ireland', *ibid.*, pp. 109–32; M.A. G. Ó Tuathaigh, 'Is do chuala croí cine soiléir', *ibid.*, pp. 75–83.

286 This paragraph, and my general approach, have been much influenced by unpublished lectures delivered in Cork in November 1985 by Gearóid Ó Tuathaigh on Corkery, and Liam Hourican on O'Faolain.

287 R.W. Dudley Edwards, 'The contribution of Young Ireland to the development of the national idea', in S. Pender (ed.), *Féilscríbhinn Tórna* (Cork, 1947), pp. 115–33.

writings he would strive to expand the conceptual range of Irish historians, as when seeking to interpret Irish history through the concept of
'community' rather than that of state.[288] Edwards would never feel so
proprietorial towards *IHS* that he failed to give full credit to older
scholars, in particular Eoin MacNeill, for their contribution to the
development of historical studies in Ireland.[289] And his resignation as
editor in 1957 suggests that he felt the time propitious for new developments. They were not to be.

The issues intimately identified with the *IHS* school in the areas of
constitutional and political history, and in the history of Anglo-Irish
relations, remain of enduring importance. The remorseless search for a
true historical past in the pages of *IHS* may have helped foster the
realisation among those capable of contemplating historical truth that the
Irish political experience was decidedly more complex than the traditional
one-dimensional popular version allowed. And even if Moody, in particular, tended to exaggerate the impact of 'scientific' history on popular
perceptions, more pessimistic recent pronouncements, while providing a
necessary corrective to uncritical assumptions, may underrate the influence of the *IHS* generation on later perspectives, at least in the
Republic.[290]

But the challenges confronting independent Ireland, despite the abiding
significance of the Anglo-Irish relationships, were in many respects
internal to Ireland itself. If political history were to be properly understood, it had to be integrated with administrative, economic, social and
intellectual history. If history were to realise its full potential as a linking
subject, and not merely become one more sectoral approach towards
understanding disconnected segments of Irish experience, then it had to
fundamentally reappraise its own approach. It was not that the growth of
economic, social, and cultural history led to the fragmentation of the
subject. There was no subject to fragment. It is true that political history in
particular sometimes masqueraded as history. That it was itself a fragment remained decently obscured until the emergence of new fragments
made the general fragmentation clearer. Historical studies had already
been established on a fragmented foundation. There came to be several
different rooms in the historical mansion. Some of them were quite well
furnished. But there was no overall design to the building, and little

---

[288] R.W. Dudley Edwards, *A new history of Ireland* (Dublin, 1970).
[289] R.W. Dudley Edwards, 'Professor MacNeill', in F.X. Martin and F.J. Byrne (eds.), *The scholar revolutionary* (Shannon, 1973), pp. 279, 295; 'An agenda for Irish history, 1978–2018', *IHS*, 21, 81 (March 1978), pp. 3–6. T.W. Moody also acknowledged the support of MacNeill ('Twenty years after', *IHS*, 11, 41 (March 1958), pp. 1–2.
[290] R.F. Foster, 'History and the Irish question', *TRHS*, 5th series, 33 (1983), p. 192; F.S.L. Lyons, 'The dilemma of the Irish contemporary historian', *Hermathena*, 115 (Summer 1983), p. 56.

connection between rooms. In short, history proved unable to encompass within its conventional categories the range of relationships crucial to understanding the functioning of contemporary Irish society. It was therefore inevitable that historians would be gradually marginalised as more immediately 'relevant' sectoral approaches, especially economics, exerted greater appeal for policy-makers and even for the public.

The denouement for the historians came with the New Ireland Forum in 1983–4. The Forum commissioned numerous studies. They were mainly from economists. A few historians were in turn fleetingly consulted by consultants, but only to acquire instant information as distinct from historical understanding. That was all. It may be that, from a longer term view, the assumptions of some of the participants in the Forum were influenced by the historical perspectives they had acquired over the years, in so far as they had acquired any at all. Nevertheless, the illusions of the historians about their centrality to the formation of the contemporary Irish mind were rudely dispelled. If the Forum was a 'gigantic academic session, a "teach-in" on the national question',[291] the historians were conspicuously ignored. And that was some fifteen years after Moody initiated *A new history of Ireland*, a mammoth multi-volume project, whose early volumes were hailed by some as a milestone, though admittedly dismissed by others as a mausoleum.[292]

It was fitting in another way that the historians should count for so little at this juncture. The Forum was designed essentially to devise ways to safeguard the nationalist population of the North against seduction by Sinn Féin. One result of the combined neglect of the contemporary and the social by Irish historians was that the history of the nationalist community in the North remained almost wholly unwritten. The Catholic people of Ulster were almost as much a non-people to the dominant school of Irish historians as they were to the hereditary *Herrenvolk* of the North. The detached observer might detect a certain poetic justice in the manner in which those who had ignored them were now themselves ignored.

It would nevertheless be unhistorical to conclude a survey of the

---

291 L. O'Dowd, 'Intellectuals in twentieth-century Ireland: and the case of George Russell (AE)', *Crane Bag*, 9, 1 (1985), p. 6.

292 J. Clark, 'A period of consolidation', *Times Higher Educational Supplement*, 27 June 1986; W. Davies and D. Tierney, 'Nouvelle Clio', *Peritia*, 3 (1984), pp. 558–66; A.T.Q. Stewart, 'History by committee?', *Irish Times*, 2 August 1986; N. Canny, 'Early modern Ireland: an appraisal appraised', *Irish Economic and Social History*, 4 (1977), pp. 56–65; D.F. Cregan, 'Early modern Ireland', *IHS*, 20, 79 (1977), pp. 272–85; A. Clarke, 'Recent works (1977–1982) on early modern British history: Ireland 1450–1750', in *Tijdschrift voor Geschiedenis*, 97 (1984), p. 518; A. Clarke, 'Ireland, 1534–1660', in J. Lee (ed.), *Irish Historiography, 1970–79* (Cork, 1981), pp. 34–6, 51. M.A.G. Ó Tuathaigh, 'Early modern Ireland, 1534–1691: a reassessment', in P.J. Drudy (ed.), *Irish Studies*, vol. 1 (Cambridge, 1980), pp. 153–60; N.P. Canny, 'The Power but not the Glory', *Times Literary Supplement*, 19 December 1986; T. Bartlett, 'A New History of Ireland', *Past and Present*, 116 (August 1987), pp. 216–19.

performance of the historians on a negative note. Nothing should detract from the achievement of the generation of Edwards and Moody, Quinn and Beckett. The decline in nationalistic history has been widespread in the west during the twentieth century.[293] Irish circumstances, however, were most unusual in 'the west'. More inhibitions had to be overcome in the search for truth than in many other countries. The *IHS* generation insisted on scholarly standards. It rose above partisan passions. It bore witness, both through the integrity of its perspective, and the integrity of its performance. It did its duty. It produced. If every succeeding generation contributed as much as that of Edwards and Moody, Clio could have few complaints about the devotion of her Irish acolytes. The performance of the founding generation of *IHS* established the benchmark by which not only later achievements in their own profession must be measured, but by which the performance of their contemporaries in other fields can be assessed.[294] If every other area of Irish life, academic and non-academic, had emulated the achievement of the generation of historians that began work in the thirties, Ireland would today be a prouder country by far. Of how many generations in any field of activity can that be said?

Before reaching even a tentative verdict on the overall functioning of the market for intelligence, it behoves us to keep the comparative perspective in mind to insure that our criteria are as fair as possible, and that we are not subjecting earlier generations to anachronistic measures of performance. Is there a danger that we may be demanding too much from a small country? What are reasonable criteria? Even a rapid reconnaissance of the situation in economics, sociology and political science in some small countries may provide guidelines towards a provisional judgement.

Sweden had a population of 5.9 million in 1920, and a per capita income more or less equal to that of the Irish Free State.[295] A gifted succession of scholars achieved world renown for Swedish economics from the late nineteenth century. Davidson, Wicksell, Cassel and Heckscher established a reputation that would be enhanced by Lindahl, Myrdal, Ohlin and many others. Political circumstances were conducive to their influence. With the impact of the great slump, the 'handful of young economists' who worked systematically on inquiries into the 'extent, character and causes of unemployment', found a responsive ear when Ernst Wigforss became Minister for Finance in the Social Demo-

---

293 P.M. Kennedy, 'The decline of nationalistic history in the west, 1900–1970', in W. Laqueur (ed.), *Historians in politics* (London, 1974), pp. 329–52.

294 For an affectionate portrait of Moody, see F.S.L. Lyons, 'T.W.M.', in F.S.L. Lyons and R. Hawkins (eds.), *Ireland under the Union* (Oxford, 1980), pp. 1–33. Obituary appreciations of Moody include F.X. Martin, 'Theodore William Moody', *Hermathena*, cxxxvi (Summer 1984), pp. 5–8 and H. Mulvey, 'Theodore William Moody (1907–84): an appreciation', *IHS*, 24, 94 (November 1984), pp. 121–30.

295 All statistics in this section, unless otherwise stated, are drawn from the sources cited in notes 2, 8 and 9 of this chapter.

cratic government in 1932. Though Wigforss's doctorate was in linguistics (savour that description of any Secretary of Finance, much less minister, in Ireland) he read widely in economic theory.[296] The Riksbank had already sought, and implemented, the advice of Cassel, Davidson and Heckscher on monetary policy in October 1931.[297] There were, not for the only time, differences among the economists themselves. But it seems to have been, if only partly, due to the contribution of the economists that Sweden coped with the challenge of the inter-war depression relatively successfully.[298]

Sociological research flourished in Sweden throughout the twentieth century, partly as a result of the conscious decision to respond to the challenge of emigration since the late nineteenth century, culminating in Sundbarg's inquiry of 1909. The first chair of sociology was not founded until 1947, but sociological research was actively pursued under other institutional arrangements previously.[299]

Modern political science in Sweden can be traced to the establishment of a chair in history and political science in Lund in 1889. A political science journal first appeared in 1897, two years before the *Swedish Journal of Economics*, and ninety-nine years before *Irish Political Studies*. But today, it has been said, Swedish political science 'constitutes a periphery in the international political science community. The subject receives its impulses in terms of the selection of objects of study, and research questions and methods, chosen mainly from political science research in other countries.'[300] The standards on which this judgement is based are clearly demanding. An Irish observer can only gaze in astonishment at the sheer professionalism of Swedish contributions to a whole variety of policy issues, ranging from the relationship between central and local government to media studies. He will also ruefully note that much of this research, even basic research, is directly sponsored and financed by the state, for 'there has always been a tendency in Swedish politics and administration to attempt to utilise social science and research findings'.[301]

May not Sweden be an exception to everybody's rule? Are the Swedes not renowned for a cerebral approach to policy? Have they not brought a reservoir of intellectuality to bear on their problems since the mid

[296] G.C. Uhr, 'Economists and policy-making 1930–1936: Sweden's experience', *History of Political Economy*, 9 (1976), p. 91, n. 4.
[297] L. Jonung, 'The depression in Sweden and the United States', in K. Brunner (ed.), *The Great Depression revisited* (Boston, 1981), p. 300.
[298] Myrdal, 'Crises and cycles', p. 14.
[299] G. Boalt and H. Martin, 'Sociology in Sweden, 1965–73', in R.P. Mohan and D. Martindale, *Handbook of contemporary developments in world sociology* (Westport, Conn., 1975), p. 91.
[300] O. Ruin, 'Political science in Sweden', *Politologen*, 15, 1 (1986), p. 3.
[301] *Ibid.*, p. 8.

nineteenth century?[302] Is it reasonable to expect others to display the same respect for organised intelligence? And are they not a depressingly earnest people anyway, notoriously joyless except when committing suicide?![303] The Norwegian experience may provide a more relevant pointer to the quality of Irish performance. Norway had a population of 2.65 million in 1920, with a per capita income lower than that of the Free State. She achieved full independence only in 1905. She may therefore offer a fairer criterion for comparison.

Ireland may have been meagrely supplied with only five chairs of economics in 1921. Norway had only two. Ragnar Frisch was appointed to one of them in 1932. Frisch, who would duly take a Nobel prize, combined charisma as a teacher with a wide range of contacts in public life.[304] Norway valued scholarship. 'The fact that early in his career Frisch became the first Norwegian economist with an international reputation added tremendously to his reputation in Norway as the indisputable leader of the economics profession.'[305] Although Frisch himself preserved a certain distance from policy-making, his influence and that of his students soon pervaded the civil service and even the political establishment. There were already twenty economists in the Norwegian civil service in 1938, and about a hundred by 1950, with several occupying 'leading administrative posts'.[306] Not only were deputy ministers frequently economists after the war, but so were 'a majority of the postwar ministers of Finance and Trade'.[307] It has even been claimed of Norwegian economists that,

more than any other profession, they have changed and expanded the role of civil servants. They have radically changed the process of economic policy-making. Their ambition was to increase 'rationality' in economic policy-making, and they have been successful in developing a new mode of thinking among policy-makers, whether in government, parliament, or the civil service . . .[308]

This type of claim is impossible to definitively prove. From our point of view what is interesting is that it could be made at all.

Norwegian political science and sociology achieved world renown through the contribution of Stein Rokkan, who took a leading role in the international development of both subjects in the postwar world, building

---

[302] L.G. Sandberg, 'The case of the impoverished sophisticate: human capital and Swedish economic growth before World War I', *Journal of Economic History*, 39 (1979), pp. 225–41.

[303] A favourite Irish image of Sweden, which flourished particularly in the 1950s, casting rich if lurid light on Ireland, though little on Sweden. No Yeatsian bounty there!

[304] L. Johansen, 'Ragnar Frisch's contribution to economics', *Swedish Journal of Economics*, lxxi, 4 (December 1969).

[305] T. Bergh, 'Norway, the powerful servants', *History of Political Economy*, 13, 3 (1981), p. 496.

[306] *Ibid.*, p. 472.   [307] *Ibid.*, p. 489.   [308] *Ibid.*, p. 508.

on the already firm foundation of social scientific inquiry in Norway itself.[309]

Perhaps Norway, though it be not 'suicidal' Sweden, may yet be too similar to Sweden to serve as an adequate alternative to it? And does Norway not have its notorious 'dry' areas, so inhospitable to the eager hibernian seeker after knowledge and truth? Finland may offer a better example. Is it not a country that consciously reacted against Swedish influence, and which, though retaining close contact with Sweden, and having its own Swedish-speaking minority, nevertheless cherishes a distinctive language and culture, and which is, moreover, notably more understanding towards the thirst problem of the weary traveller than Norway. In 1920 it had a population of 3.1 million, and a per capita income well below the Irish level. Finnish economists had a rather low international profile. There were, however, already fifteen full professors of economics by 1961.[310] They achieved a high level of professional competence, and exerted considerable influence on the formulation of economic policy in a country that has had a notably successful record of economic growth, despite intense fluctuations, in the twentieth century.

The Finnish international profile was higher in political science and sociology than in economics. Erik Allardt served as 'exemplar' of both disciplines, acting as a mediator and coordinator between Finnish and international developments.[311] It is true that Allardt himself refers without any sense of incongruity to 'the absence of a long intellectual history of significant social philosophy and macro-sociological speculation' as 'a conspicuous feature of the Scandinavian countries'.[312] But Allardt's standards are clearly not Irish standards. It transpires that 'sociology was already well established as an academic field in Finland' by 1960.[313] And Allardt can refer to 'an explosion of sociological information' on such a scale that 'it has become increasingly difficult to keep track of everything important published or mimeographed even in such a small country as Finland'.[314] That was not the most pressing of problems facing Irish sociologists. Even Allardt was prepared to concede that Finland was strong in applied sociology, especially in social policy and social administration.[315] His concept of normalcy can also be gauged

309 E. Allardt and H. Valen, 'Stein Rokkan: an intellectual profile', in P. Torsvik (ed.), *Mobilisation, centre-periphery structures and nation-building* (Bergen, 1981), pp. 12ff.
310 M. Leppo, 'Die wirtschaftswissenschaftliche Ausbildung in Finnland', *Weltwirtschaftliches Archiv*, 88, 1 (1962), p. 121.
311 V. Stolte-Heiskanen and I. Heiskanen, 'Intellectual styles and paradigmatic changes in Finnish sociology and political science', in R. Alapuro, M. Alestalo, E. Havio-Mannila and R. Väyrynen (eds.), *Small states in comparative perspective* (Oslo, 1985), pp. 185–6.
312 E. Allardt, 'Contemporary sociology in Finland', in Mohan and Martindale, *Handbook*, p. 107.
313 *Ibid.*, p. 110.   314 *Ibid.*, p. 121.   315 *Ibid.*, p. 112.

from his observation that Finnish research on criminology did not develop until the 1960s,[316] and that 'peace research started rather late in Finland', with the first Institute of Peace Research being established only in 1970.[317]

When we turn to countries further south, we find much the same pattern repeated. The Netherlands in 1920 had a population of 6.8 million, with an income per head slightly higher than that of Ireland. Jan Tinbergen, who shared the first Nobel prize in economics with Ragnar Frisch, exerted considerable influence on the development of economic thought and policy. He served as an official in the Netherlands Central Bureau of Statistics from 1929 to 1945, while also holding a chair at the Netherlands School of Economics in Rotterdam. After discovering the cobweb theorem in 1930, and acting as an economic adviser to the League of Nations from 1936 to 1938, he served as director of the newly-created Planning Bureau of the Netherlands from 1945 to 1955.[318]

Although other Dutch universities did not follow the initiative of Amsterdam in creating a chair in sociology in 1921 until after the Second World War, the inter-war sociography school of Steinmetz achieved distinction through the quality of its empirical research.[319] Sociology flourished after the war, with four specialised journals catering for its requirements.[320] Political science too would flourish in postwar Holland, with Hans Daalder and Arend Lijphart as particularly eminent representatives.

Austria had a population of about 6.5 million in 1921, and a per capita income somewhat below that of Ireland. Pre-war Vienna, an imperial capital, was a renowned centre of intellectual activity. Austria found the adjustment from empire to republic particularly gruelling. The sad political history of the inter-war period made it difficult to establish, or even imply, any connection between intellectual distinction and general socio-economic performance. The pre-1914 Austrian school of economics was world famous. It still boasted eminent economists in the twenties. But political and other tensions obliged a galaxy of talent, including Schumpeter, Hayek, Mises, Morgenstern, Haberler, Machlup, Rosenstein-Rodan, Gerschenkron and Hoselitz to emigrate between the wars.[321]

Austrian sociology too had a brilliant pre-1914 record. In the 1920s,

---

[316] *Ibid.*, p. 118.   [317] *Ibid.*, p. 115.

[318] B. Hansen, 'Jan Tinbergen: an appraisal of his contribution to economics', *Swedish Journal of Economics*, lxxi, 4 (December 1969), pp. 323–36.

[319] J.M.M. de Valk, 'Contemporary sociological theory in the Netherlands', in Mohan and Martindale, *Handbook*, p. 49.

[320] The first volume of *Acta Politica* in 1965 listed 303 books and articles published by Dutch authors on political science between 1945 and 1965 (pp. 262–75).

[321] F. Machlup, 'F.A. von Hayek', *Swedish Journal of Economics*, 76, 4 (1974), p. 499; E. Craver, 'The emigration of the Austrian economists', *History of Political Economy*, 18, 1 (1986), pp. 1–32.

Lazersfeld began opening new vistas for social research into the psychology of unemployment before he was obliged to emigrate. Post-1945 Austrian sociology was the heir of an extraordinarily rich, if broken, tradition of thought.[322] It did not lack critics who found it wanting by ancestral standards. The criteria of criticism, however, belonged to a different intellectual world from that of Ireland. A caustic commentator did casually note that the sociologists whom he criticised so vigorously managed to publish about a thousand articles between 1955 and 1975.[323]

Austrian political science after the Second World War was highly conscious of its dependence on Germany. Nevertheless, it produced from 1970 a distinguished quarterly periodical, the *Österreichische Zeitschrift für Politikwissenschaft*, and published impressively in the area of international relations, insisting on taking the intellectual implications of neutrality seriously. Through the Laxenburg papers, in particular, published by the Austrian Institute for International Affairs, it contributed to international as well as national thinking on world affairs.

The 3.9 million Swiss in 1920 enjoyed the highest standard of living in continental Europe. Economic thinking pervaded Swiss culture. The first annual Swiss economic bibliography, in 1937, came to eighty-two pages.[324] The National Bank introduced *monthly* reports as early as 1936. By 1958 the monthly reports, coming to nearly a hundred pages each, ranged over not only financial matters, national and international, but foreign trade, labour markets, etc. with copious information on international developments. It is an education to compare it with the publications of the Central Bank of Ireland at that time. Theory and practice were interwoven, with close connections existing between academics, businessmen, and officials from the federal, cantonal and municipal statistical offices. It was no accident that Switzerland promoted management studies from an early date, with the establishment of a chair of management at the University of Zurich from 1903.[325]

Swiss academic, official and business publications tend to blend the theoretical with the applied, and the economic with the non-economic, in a distinctive manner. Thus, when the National Bank celebrated its fiftieth anniversary, it prepared a handsome volume dealing not only with the history of the bank, but providing a detailed survey of the Swiss economy during the period.[326] When the *Association Suisse d'organisation scienti-*

322 R. Knoll, G. Majce, H. Weiss, G. Wieser, 'Der österreichische Beitrag zur Soziologie von der Jahrhundertwende bis 1938', in M. Rainer Lepsius (ed.), *Soziologie in Deutschland und Österreich 1938–1945* (Cologne, 1981), pp. 59–101.
323 J.H. Bunzel, 'Contemporary sociology in Austria', in Mohan and Martindale, *Handbook*, p. 87.
324 *Schweizerische Bibliographie für Statistik und Volkswirtschaft* (Berne, 1937).
325 E. Kilgus, E. Rühli, P. Weilenmann (eds.), *Betriebswirtschaftslehre an der Universität Zürich* (Zurich, 1978).
326 *Banque Nationale Suisse 1907–1957* (Zurich, 1957).

fique sought to predict the main economic developments for the 1970s, it not only mobilised a wealth of comparative data, and paid close attention to likely technological developments, but also pondered the future of 'men at work', and of the relations of 'state and society'.[327] A striking feature of Swiss economics in the twentieth century was a massive publication performance displaying a capacity for strategic thinking based on detailed knowledge not only of the local economy, but of the local society.

The University of Geneva pioneered courses in sociology from 1886. Nevertheless, Swiss sociologists were acutely conscious of their subordinate status, both intellectually and institutionally. Girod would lament in 1975 that Swiss sociology was only 'a fragment of west European sociology', and that 'the absolute number of sociologists remains modest'.[328] It quickly becomes apparent, however, that he derives his criteria from an intellectual universe alien to the Irish mind. The Swiss Sociological Association was founded in 1955, eighteen years before the Irish association. The difference in scale can be appreciated from the fact that at the annual Swiss congress of sociology in 1973, 65 papers were presented, and more than 200 sociologists attended, inconceivable figures in Irish circumstances.

Swiss political science developed rapidly after the Second World War, strongly supplementing Swiss activity in contemporary history, notably exemplified in the work of Hofer and Bonjour. It made distinctive contributions to the study of two themes central to the Swiss experience, the functioning of federalism, and the nature of neutrality.[329]

In venturing comparisons between the intensity of activity in the human sciences in other small European states and in Ireland we must make allowance for a variety of factors. Most of the other states, however small, still had bigger populations than Ireland (or at least the South) in 1920. Over time they became relatively more populous and relatively more prosperous. Nevertheless, at any given population level, and at any level of income per head, other small northern European countries, without exception, appear to have devoted significantly more resources to the effort to understand society in general, and their own society in particular. Our rapid review conveys nothing like the full extent of the difference in the intensity of the effort devoted to the search for self-knowledge between these countries and Ireland. In several other relevant fields, including social psychology, education, management, public administra-

---

327 *L'Entreprise suisse dans le monde de demain* (Zurich, 1969).
328 R. Girod, 'Contemporary sociology in Switzerland', in Mohan and Martindale, *Handbook*, p. 59.
329 See, for instance, U. Altermatt and J. Garamvölgyi (eds.), *Innen- und Aussenpolitik* (Berne, 1980); A. Riklin, H. Haug, H.C. Binswanger (eds.), *Handbuch der schweizerischen Aussenpolitik* (Berne, 1975); A. Riklin (ed.), *Handbuch Politisches System der Schweiz* (Berne, 1983); Bonjour, *Erinnerungen*.

tion, international relations, criminology, and anthropology, the smaller northern European states were disproportionately more active than Ireland. The difference in self-knowledge derived less from the role of any particular discipline than from the importance attached to the mind educated in social thought.

None of this implies that everything was done well, or necessarily better than in Ireland, in the small continental countries. They had no shortage of domestic commentators to severely criticise their performance. But it is also clear that these observers tended to apply more demanding standards than was customary with Irish critics of Irish performance. One further example must suffice. Danish economic historians were prone to lament the relative neglect of the subject in their country. A survey in 1974 did not fail to repeat this lament – before it proceeded to consider the work of *ninety-five* authors – after excluding periodical literature![330] Nor did self-criticism preclude self-confidence. The first issue of *Acta Sociologica* in 1965 proclaimed on one and the same page that sociology was late to develop in Scandinavia, and that Scandinavian sociologists felt they had something to contribute to the wider world.[331]

It might be unreasonable to expect so small a country as Ireland to make significant contributions to social thought over a wide field. But it is not unreasonable to expect it to make a contribution in some area. Nor is this based on *naïve* assumptions about the level of investment in thought a small country can afford. Not out of altruism, not out of self-respect, but out of sheer self-interest, should Ireland have been exploring the implications of many of the major issues that preoccupied thinkers in other small countries. Thought was not the hobby of esoteric coteries of leisured savants. It was directly relevant to the quality of national performance. Rokkan's work derived its initial impetus from his concern with the societal implications of Norwegian 'peripherality'. Ireland was as 'peripheral' in certain respects as Norway. Barth's basic work on ethnicity derived its inspiration from his perception of ethnic boundaries within Norway. These boundaries were certainly no more obtrusive than those on the island of Ireland. Many Irish, laity as well as clergy, devoted themselves unstintingly to helping poorer peoples. But Irish thought on under-development remained under-developed. No Irish equivalent to Norway's Ragnar Nurske emerged. No country in Europe offered so striking an experience of changing relationships between population and agricultural development over the past two centuries, but it was the Dane, Ester Boserup, who produced the seminal study on the subject. No

---

[330] O. Hornby and G. Viby Mogensen, 'The study of economic history in Denmark: recent trends and problems', *Scandinavian Journal of Economic History*, 22 (1974), pp. 60, 86.

[331] 'Editorial', *Acta Sociologica*, 1 (1965), p. 1.

country in Europe could draw on so striking an experience of language shift. Yet the Irish contribution to international discussion on the role of language in cultural identity and national performance was muted. Ireland has urbanised relatively rapidly in the past thirty years. Dublin has grown at a faster rate than any western European capital. Yet Irish social scientists have made few contributions to thinking about urbanisation. The work of a single centre in Zurich, the Institute of Local, Regional and National Planning at the Swiss Technical Institute, dwarfs the totality of Irish effort in this sphere.[332]

Nor was the Irish failure to develop a tradition of thought confined to matters of domestic policy. Few states have made so heavy an emotional investment in the rhetoric of neutrality. Yet, it has chosen to ignore the study of international relations, including the study of neutrality, to an extent unparalleled in any other small western European neutral. Were it not for the isolated efforts of a handful of individuals, the study of Irish foreign policy, not to mention wider issues of international affairs, would be wholly neglected.

None of this implies that the average level of natural intelligence among the scattered Irish labourers in the field of social comprehension was inferior to that of their counterparts in other countries. What was and is inferior is the mobilisation and organisation of that intelligence at national level. This is itself a symptom of the same syndrome that led to such neglect of sustained thinking about Irish conditions across the whole range of social life. A sound intellectual infrastructure did not guarantee an impressive level of national performance. The political culture and the administrative culture had to be receptive to high quality thinking. Nevertheless, no small European state has achieved significant socio-economic progress in the twentieth century without developing a firm intellectual infrastructure in the human sciences.

All the successful small states of Europe took care to construct an intellectual infrastructure. The Irish, in contrast, often gave the impression that they could not understand the concept.

Both the demand for, and the supply of, social thought were highly constricted in the first generation of independence. Earnest efforts to improve supply began to be initiated during the 1950s. Some ground was retrieved. Nevertheless, thirty years later, Ireland still lagged well behind the average level of European social thought.

Responsibility lay in the first instance with demand. Limited and fragmentary though supply was, it comfortably exceeded demand in most areas. The fate of *The Irish Statesman*, of *The Bell*, above all of *The Leader*, during the editorship of Desmond Williams, reflects the lack of

---

[332] ORLDOC – Literatur datenbank, Veröffentlichungen des ORL – Instituts der ETH 1946–1982/83 (Zurich, 1983).

public demand for superior analysis. On returning to Ireland from a foreign sojourn that included the co-editorship of the *Cambridge Journal*, Williams sought to leaven the sodden lump of Irish thought through *The Leader*. Together with a brilliant band of writers, including Denis Donoghue, Brian Inglis, Val Iremonger, Patrick Lynch, Conor Cruise O'Brien, and Tommy Woods, he ensured that *The Leader* reached an exceptional level of intellectual sophistication on both national and international affairs. Yet one may wonder if the effort was worth it. Seeds were presumably sown whose fruits would ripen in some minds in due course. But one is tempted to wonder if acute analyses of 'Franco-German relations', or of 'Dr Adenauer's difficulties', or of 'The case of Mr George Kennan' or of 'The aims of foreign policy' did not come depressingly close to casting pearls before Paudeens engrossed in their pitch and toss.[333]

There was little tradition of major scholars writing routinely for newspapers. The first regular economics column was not launched until 1957, and then by the still very junior Garret FitzGerald in the *Irish Times*. This may be contrasted with the Swedish tradition. The internationally eminent Eli Heckscher 'year in, year out ... wrote one, sometimes two articles a month' for *Dagens Nyheter*.[334] Nor did he fail to include many of these in his list of 1148 bibliographical items recorded for his seventieth birthday. Heckscher treated everything he wrote, from his massive tomes on mercantilism to his newspaper work, earnestly. He knew he always wrote seriously. He had none of the pathetic lack of self-confidence that induced so many Irish academics to dismiss articles in 'non-refereed' publications, irrespective of their quality, as ephemera, unworthy of the genuine scholar. There could be no more genuine scholar than Heckscher. He judged the value of work by the calibre of content, not by place of publication. 'From adolescence to old age' Heckscher's life 'was governed by a relentless sense of work to be done. But to work meant to serve and amassing knowledge meant communicating it to others.'[335] The austere Gustav Cassel also contributed regularly to newspapers, while Heckscher's successor at the Stockholm Business School, Ohlin, became economics editor of the *Stockholms Tidningen* in 1931, and published over 1100 articles in the press.[336] Ohlin, with one of the most beautiful theoretical minds to grace economics, did not shrink from the challenge of regular analysis of current issues. This frequent contribution by world class minds to public discussion seems to have been one reason

333 *Leader*, 3 July, 19 July, 25 October 1952; E. Sagarra, 'Dreissig Jahre Bundesrepublik – aus irischer Sicht', in J. Haas-Heye, *Im Urteil des Auslands* (Munich, 1979), p. 108.
334 A. Gerschenkron, 'Eli F. Heckscher' in E.F. Heckscher, *An economic history of Sweden* (Cambridge, Mass., 1954), p. xviii.
335 *Ibid.*, p. xiii.
336 Jonung, 'Depression', p. 310; R.E. Caves, 'Bertil Ohlin's contribution to economics', Scandinavian Journal of Economics, 80, 1 (1978), p. 98.

why the level of economic literacy was exceptionally high among Swedish policy-makers. The same attitude prevailed among leading Swiss scholars. The compilers of Eugen Böhler's bibliography, for instance, considered it natural to include his contributions to the *Neue Zürcher*, the *Aargauer Tagblatt*, the *Berner Tagblatt*, etc. among his numerous publications.[337]

Irish newspapers could not risk regular contributions of such rigor, even had they been available. When *The Leader* complained of the intellectual poverty of Irish journalism, it overlooked the fact that any newspaper that sought to run too far ahead of its readers would quickly become defunct.[338] The German Ambassador observed in 1954 that Irish newspapers lacked perspective on world affairs, mainly because of 'the inadequacy of Irish journalists, who are intellectually incapable of comprehending world events . . . '. He pondered the reasons:

If Ireland is a small country on the side lines of world political events, that is no excuse for the relatively poor quality of its press. The example of other small countries, such as the Scandinavian countries and Switzerland, shows that it is possible for a small country to have a good press . . . The Irish press in general only reaches the level of a provincial press . . . The papers have no foreign correspondents . . . The journalists are badly paid, so that they lack the incentive to improve their knowledge, and they have no resources to undertake foreign travel.[339]

These difficulties were gradually overcome as education and prosperity spread in the 1960s. The *Irish Times* became a paper of genuine quality, but only when the potential readership expanded, thanks to educational change. It had never, it is true, pandered to popular passions. But neither had it been a paper of penetrating social analysis. A number of notable newspaper columns, in English or Irish, subsequently emerged, like those of Desmond Fennell in the *Sunday Press*, Anthony Cronin, Liam de Paor, Seán Ó Riordáin, and Breandán Ó hEithir, as well as the 'Beocheist' column, in the *Irish Times*, or Conor Cruise O'Brien in the *Irish Times* and the *Irish Independent*, which sought to address issues of enduring importance.

All these developments had to await the emergence of a steady, if still modest, market. Desmond Williams was moved to note in 1953, when introducing his *Leader* study of Irish neutrality, that other small neutral countries had published extensively from their official archives on their war policies. In Ireland, on the contrary, 'our administrators have steadfastly refused to consider publication which would throw light on the execution of neutrality'. He felt obliged to ruefully add that this reticence

---

[337] Schweizerisches Gesellschaft für Konjunkturforschung (ed.), *Kultur und Wirtschaft* (Zurich, 1963), pp. 431–6.
[338] *Leader*, 25 October 1952.
[339] PA AA, 2, 205-00-33, Katzenberger-AA, 3 August 1954, 1999-54.

aroused no criticism, 'for public opinion on the subject simply does not exist'.[340]

It is understandable, in view of the frequent contradictions between actual policy and the public presentation of that policy during the war, that the official mind should have economised on its efforts to educate the public into the realities of foreign policy. But the specific reticence on this issue was merely a species of the wider genus of the furtiveness that often seemed to characterise the official mind in Ireland, where 'the general lack of openness in public administration' remains striking down to the present day.[341]

Radio and television offered a rather different type of platform. Leon Ó Broin, sometime Secretary of Posts and Telegraphs, took a distinctly unsentimental view of scholarly response to the medium of radio:

The university world generally, on which Kiernan [Director of Radio Éireann], would have liked to have been able to draw, kept its distance from Radio Éireann, and that remained the case until the Thomas Davis lectures at £30 in 1953 made it worthwhile for a scholar to produce an original script.[342]

This does rather imply that Radio Éireann had hitherto put little value on academic time. If so, it would not have been the only Irish institution to assume that a scholar's time ought to cost nothing. In any event, it was the more confident and productive of the historians, notably T.W. Moody, who were instrumental in launching the Thomas Davis lectures, which constitute one of the minor wonders of Irish intellectual life – indeed, not minor at all, given the morass through which a path has to be picked.[343] Moody too would play a key role in pioneering television lectures on Irish history, the first series being published as *The course of Irish history*, edited by Moody himself and F.X. Martin in 1967.[344] Numerous academics appear regularly on television, but usually as protagonists in debating atmospheres that compel severe over-simplification and reward speed rather than profundity of response. The television audience for lecture or seminar-type performances is distinctly finite. RTE has, in recent years, courageously braved the risk, or rather the certainty, of relatively small audiences by undertaking one 'university' type lecture series a year.[345]

The sporadic attempts made on the supply side to create, or anticipate,

340 T.D. Williams, 'A study in neutrality', *Leader*, 31 January 1953. On the more open Swiss style see E. Bonjour, *Erinnerungen*, pp. 230–47.
341 NESC, *Information for policy* (Dublin, 1985), p. 130.
342 Ó Broin, *Yesterday*, p. 169.
343 H. Mulvey, 'Moody', 136–7; F.X. Martin, 'The Thomas Davis lectures, 1953–67', *IHS*, 15, 59 (March 1967), pp. 276–302.
344 Mulvy, 'Moody', pp. 136–7.
345 RTE/UCD lectures, *Ireland: Dependence and independence*, *Crane Bag*, 8, 1 (1984); J. Lee (ed.) *Towards a sense of place* (Cork, 1985), G. Ó Tuathaigh (ed.), *Community, culture and conflict* (Galway, 1986).

demand have generally proved futile. But why should demand respond? Why should established interests voluntarily forfeit the consolations of a quiet life passed in no great discomfort – except out of fear? And they had little to fear since the end of the civil war, apart from a momentary flutter in the early years of Fianna Fáil rule. The removal of potential threats to social stability through emigration removed the main likely incentive for enhanced self-knowledge. In that sense, emigration provides a key not only to the political stability but to the intellectual derivativeness of independent Ireland. There was no major problem of rural unrest once the lingering aspirations of agricultural labourers were decisively crushed in the slump of the early twenties. Nor was there any major problem of urban unrest, which might have stimulated emulation of the *enquetes* of continental Europe on the condition of the working classes. There was no women's question. Few sought to emulate the work of a Maria Jahoda or a Käthe Leichter on the condition of working women in Austria, or of youth in Switzerland.[346] There was no decline in religious observance of a type to prompt the development of empirical religious sociology before the 1970s. It has been suggested that we are too close to our history of poverty 'to be able to analyse, conceptualise and synthesise' the lessons of the experience.[347] On the other hand, it may also be that we are not close enough to it, because we have 'solved' the problem by exporting it. Finland was a poorer country than Ireland at the time of independence. Indeed, its national anthem came close to celebrating a self-conscious cult of poverty. But this did not prevent Finland from setting about solving the problem, and with some success.[348]

There was therefore no gut craving, fuelled by fear, to learn more about the nature of Irish society. Inquiry and policy would have to derive from the impulses of patriotism, intellect or conscience rather than from an elemental instinct of self-preservation. Patriotism proved powerless, except in brief and specific conjunctures, against the instincts of the possessing classes. Intellect proved an even weaker reed on which to lean.

Conscience, as ever, is more problematical. The possessing classes in general, and many a prelate and parish priest recruited from comfortable circumstances, were receptive to the view that poverty existed to provide opportunities for the rich to save their souls by giving charity to the poor. If the rich forgot to do so, it is not quite clear what the poor were supposed to do, beyond presumably lamenting the lost souls of the rich. The theological possibilities of this perspective are endless. Rather than linger over them, one may note the painfully honest observation of the Bishop of

346 Knoll, *et al.*, 'Österreichische Soziologie', pp. 88–90.
347 M. Mernagh, 'Poverty and community work', in S. Kennedy (ed.), *One million poor?* (Dublin, 1981), p. 234.
348 M. Klinge, 'Aspects of the Nordic self', *Daedalus*, 113 (Spring 1984), pp. 259–60.

Ossory in 1981 that the Catholic Church had failed to provide 'a richly Christian body of thought on any social topic'.[349] To proceed from this, however, as many are inclined to do, and blame the church not only for failing to develop a serious body of social thought of its own, but for suffocating social enquiry in general and preventing the emergence of that critical capacity which is a prerequisite for the growth of self-knowledge, is simply unhistorical. Insofar as clerical hostility to independent thought was a factor it offers only a very partial explanation of Irish intellectual retardation, and even then it reflected, far more than it created, influences at play in the wider society.

The tone of some ecclesiastics, it is true, provided scant encouragement for sustained social inquiry. But ecclesiastics contributed disproportionately to such sociology as there was. The *Irish Ecclesiastical Record* contained much penetrating comment on social affairs, particularly in the 1930s. The first specifically sociology journal, *Christus Rex*, later rechristened *Social Studies*, was founded in Maynooth in 1947. The Jesuit journal, *Studies*, which began publication in 1912, had close connections with UCD. It long provided the main periodical outlet for Catholic social thought.[350] While it contained interesting articles at all periods, it played a notably constructive role between 1950 and 1967 under a 'brilliant and inspiring editor', Fr Roland Burke-Savage, who fostered wide-ranging discussion on the contemporary condition.[351] If in 1972 sociology could still be described as being 'in its infancy' in Ireland,[352] it seems likely that it would have been at the preconception stage were it not for the initiatives, however halting, of churchmen.

There were numerous obscurantist clerics. There were also numerous enlightened ones. Alleged Catholic anti-intellectualism or social conservatism could not account for the differential development of various subjects of inquiry. History was a delicate area for Catholic sensitivity. And if history had not developed, the church could conveniently be blamed for the failure. But history did develop. And if it be true that political history developed far ahead of social and economic history, that can scarcely be attributed to the pleasure of churchmen. Attribution of prime responsibility for the retardation of social thought to the Catholic Church diverts attention from the main issues, including that of why Ireland had her particular type of church.

The self-interest, or at least the perceived short-term self-interest, of the majority of those in a position to make the effort to understand the

349 P. Birch, 'Poverty and the church', in Kennedy, *One million poor?*, p. 165.
350 B.P. Kennedy, 'Seventy five years of *Studies*', *Studies*, 75 (Winter 1986); J. Meenan, 'Comment on Brian Kennedy's article', *ibid.*, pp. 374–7.
351 Lynch, 'Garret FitzGerald', p. 29.
352 Bill MacSweeney, 'The threat of sociology', *Social Studies*, 1, 6 (December 1972), p. 663.

functioning of Irish society, provided little incentive for the promotion of systematic inquiry. Keynes, in a famous dictum, contended that:

the ideas of economists and political philosophers, both when they are right and when they are wrong, are more powerful than is commonly understood. Indeed the world is ruled by little else. Practical men, who believe themselves to be quite exempt from any intellectual influences, are usually the slaves of some defunct economist. Madmen in authority, who hear voices in the air, are distilling their frenzy from some academic scribbler of a few years back. I am sure that the power of vested interests is vastly exaggerated, compared with the gradual encroachment of ideas.[353]

One may wonder if his confidence would have survived study of the Irish policy-making process (though of course his own statement was an 'interest' as well as an 'ideas' one!). The acid test would be to find the successful advocacy of ideas that were perceived to be contrary to the self-interest of the dominant power groups. Even strategically placed politicians or civil servants could drive their social and economic ideas through only when circumstances were propitious. Circumstances largely determined how far protectionists or free traders, interventionists or apostles of *laissez-faire*, could implement their views. That applied to Catholic social thinking as much as to any other. It was more vested interest than intellect that led to the disdainful bureaucratic and political dismissal of the thinking associated with the Commission on Vocational Organisation, however impeccably Catholic its lineage. The student of Irish performance since independence is obliged to share the scepticism of a Mill or a Hintze who held that 'ideas, unless outward circumstances conspire with them, have in general no very rapid or immediate efficacy in human affairs'.[354]

If ideas were to blossom anywhere in virginal purity, undefiled by the improper attentions of interests, it could only be in the universities. How far then did the universities promote, how far retard, the development of self-knowledge in Irish society? The first rueful observation must be that, however great their thirst for knowledge, it did not extend to knowledge about themselves. None of the colleges of the National University has been the subject of a sustained study. Queen's had the courage to commission Beckett and Moody to write a handsome two-volume centenary history. Basic though their work remains, it was conceived more as institutional than as intellectual history. Only Trinity has had the self-confidence and the class to venture 'an academic history' which assesses the quality of its performance as a centre of scholarship.

353 J.M. Keynes, *The general theory of employment, interest and money* (London 1961 edn), p. 383.
354 T.W. Hutchinson, 'Economic thought and policy: generalisations and ambiguities', *International Congress of Economic History* (Moscow, 1970), 6; F. Gilbert (ed.), *The historical essays of Otto Hintze* (New York, 1975), p. 24.

Until other institutions emulate Trinity's achievement in this respect, generalisations about the performance of Irish academia in general must rely heavily on the verdict of MacDowell and Webb. The ethos of Trinity was rather different from that of the National University. It is doubtful if any provost of Trinity could have hazarded the view about the past, whatever about the future, advanced by the president of UCD in 1973 that the 'main function of the National University of Ireland . . . has been and will be to build the Irish nation'.[355] The practice of the two universities was much more similar than the ethos, however. At least when they came to studying Irish society, it would be difficult to decide which of the two practised the more ambitious neglect in the first generation of independence.

Insofar as the causes of Irish retardation should be sought in a failure to mobilise the intellectual resources of the country properly, how far did the universities bear responsibility for this? Insofar as the performance of the universities fell short of their potential, how far were their administrators responsible for this? How much did their achievements owe to their adminstrators? A remarkably small number of men have held high office in Irish universities since independence. How many of them have left a great name? How many senior administrators were authentic university men? How many were ward bosses *manqué*, draped in the decorous but ill-fitting robes of academe? Were first-class scholars likely to make successful administrators? Were second-rate scholars? Did university administration serve as a circuitous but effective conduit for the transfer of active academics into administration? Or was administration an amiable form of indoor relief for failed academics, who would now become parasites on their institutions as they had earlier been parasites on their subjects? Could any trace of 'the deadening hand of the mediocre middleaged', which Edward Shils held 'responsible for the sterility of much of India's university life' be detected among administrators, as well as among academics, in Irish universities?[356]

Close examination of the performance of most presidents, provosts, registrars, finance officers and other relevant university officials has yet to be undertaken. University administrators have not been exposed to even the modest degree of scrutiny to which civil servants have been subjected. Until their qualifications, motivation and general performance have been adequately assessed, it is premature to offer firm answers to the question of how well administered, or how well managed, or how well led, were universities. So much depended, particularly in small institutions, on the performance of key individuals, that it is also dangerous to generalise

355 Jeremiah Hogan, 'Foreword', in Martin and Byrne (eds.), *The scholar revolutionary*.
356 E. Shils, 'Toward a modern intellectual community in the new states', in E. Shils, *The intellectuals and the powers and other essays* (London, 1972), p. 347.

from one institution to another, or even from one registrarship or presidency within an institution to that institution's longer term perform- ance. There are, however, a few straws in the wind. Deep dissatisfaction in Trinity at the performance of the old guard fostered an atmosphere conducive to the emergence of A.J. McConnell as provost in a 'palace revolution' in 1952.[357] James Meenan painted a devastatingly kind portrait of the performance of the UCD administration in the inter-war period, and F.X. Martin's description of the appointment of Michael Tierney to the presidency of UCD in 1947 as 'a second founding'[358] hardly counts as an immortal tribute to Tierney's immediate predecessors. Alfred O'Rahilly was hyper-active, first as registrar and then as president of UCC between 1920 and 1953.[359] Whether his judgement equalled his energy remains to be determined in the wider context of the history of higher education.

All universities had to cope with severely limited resources. Whether the resources were inadequate, however, depends on the use likely to have been made of extra funding. It seems improbable that more money would have helped promote deeper understanding of Irish society. The money would not have been applied to that purpose. Only a handful of the former academics among university administrators were familiar with social thought, not surprisingly given that so many of the relevant subjects were not even taught in the institutions. As late as 1965, a Danish consultant expressed his surprise at the scant support for the social sciences.[360] This raises prosaic but important issues. Resources for all research were undoubtedly meagre in all Irish universities by European standards. This was to some extent a matter of choice by the wider society. Ireland was not an exceptionally poor country at the time of independ- ence. It had the opportunity to invest comparable resources in studying itself to those invested in other countries at a comparable standard of living, if it so chose. The allocation of resources within institutions has yet to be studied. George Duncan, it will be recalled, responded to Roy Geary's criticisms of the non-productivity of the economists, with a plaintive reference to his inadequate resources. George O'Brien, for all his distinction, apparently found his department relatively neglected by the UCD authorities in the allocation of resources.[361] The impression one gets is that resources were invested within universities, not according to any

357 McDowell and Webb, *Trinity College*, pp. 480–97.
358 Meenan, *George O'Brien*, pp. 147–8; F.X. Martin, 'Michael Tierney, 1894–1975', in M. Tierney, *Eoin MacNeill, scholar and man of action 1867–1945*, ed. by F.X. Martin (Oxford, 1980), p. vii.
359 Gaughan, *O'Rahilly*, pp.77–161. I have also learned much from Brian Girvin's unpublished history of University College Cork.
360 H. Friis, *Development of social research in Ireland* (Dublin, 1965), pp. 30–1.
361 Meenan, *George O'Brien*, p. 154.

objective criteria (insofar as there can be objective criteria) of departmental need, or of scholarly distinction, or of national interest, but on more primitive criteria. Busteed complained bitterly of the paucity of provision in UCC for even the most elementary research requirements.[362] And if the economists felt neglected, the odds must be that more peripheral social subjects suffered disproportionately.

Only Trinity, which enjoyed copyright access to British publications, had a library of genuine university quality at the time of independence, although UCC had some surprising collections. Even Trinity took little cognisance of European scholarship. Independence, however, brought a real blight for Free State libraries. Provision shrank under 'Uhuru' to a fraction of that provided under tyranny! Whether this was the result of an objective lack of resources, or of indifference among the academics, or incomprehension among the administrators, remains to be investigated. The library of the Royal Dublin Society, more comprehensively stocked with the requisite publications than that of UCD, provided an opportunity for George O'Brien, who was almost promiscuously productive by the acceptable standards of his academic milieu, to read intensively.[363] There was truth in Duncan's lament about the lack of resources, about departments of one or two people obliged to engage so heavily in teaching that they had little time left for research, particularly after the time and effort normally required to gouge within their institutions for the limited resources available. Duncan's complaint could be made even more justifiably by his colleagues in UCD, and especially in UCC and UCG. Such members of the Cork and Galway staff as were disposed to engage in sustained thought had, unlike George O'Brien, no alternative libraries in which to immerse themselves.

The library situation deteriorated even further after the Second World War. With the explosion in publishing in the social sciences, the proportion of the main journals taken by Irish universities declined yet further, so that Irish scholars were in danger of falling more and more behind the moving frontier of international social thought. The libraries of the colleges of the National University beggared belief. Not until the 1970s were serious efforts made to close the gap. The history of librarians has scarcely been studied in Ireland. It is not clear what role they sought to play, or were permitted to play, within universities.

The absence of resources included absence of resources to travel. The National University, in an imaginative initiative, instituted travelling studentships from the outset to enable the brightest postgraduates to pursue research abroad. The number of awards was very small, but the

362 D. O'Mahony, 'Introduction', to K.A. Kennedy, *The unemployment crisis* (Cork, 1985), p. viii.
363 Meenan, *George O'Brien*, p. 93.

travelling studentship nevertheless played an important role in providing talented graduates with a rare opportunity to broaden their horizons. It had relatively little impact, however, in the social sciences. As most of the disciplines were not taught, or even if taught did not enjoy full departmental status, the students who might have benefited either did not exist or were not eligible. A striking difference between the career paths of leading continental economists and their Irish colleagues, for instance, lay in the fact that so many continentals went to the United States at an early age. There was no intellectual necessity for an Ohlin or a Hayek to visit the United States shortly after graduation.[364] The Stockholm and Vienna schools were more eminent than any American centre at that time. But travel broadened their general cultural experience, allowed them make important personal contacts, and inculcated the self-confidence that effective performance in a foreign language can bring. The leading young Canadian economists of their generation would remain largely within the English-speaking world. That world, however, embraced Oxford and Cambridge, Harvard and Chicago.[365] Sean O'Faolain, F.H. Boland and Alfred O'Rahilly went to the United States, but access to wider intellectual environments would not become normal among Irish graduates in the social sciences until well after the Second World War. Not until then could Irish students even begin to conceive the poverty of the library resources at home on which they had been expected to become internationally competitive. Irish life abounds, whether in the senior civil service, in university administrations, or among academics themselves, with people of high but narrow intelligence. It is impossible not to wonder how much more of their own potential they might have realised if only they had enjoyed early exposure to wider intellectual cultures.

If support within the universities was meagre, few alternative sources were available. Even in 1985, no research council existed in Ireland, in contrast to most western European countries, to support study of one's own society. Hennig Friis already felt this to be worthy of comment in the mid-sixties.[366] In the meantime, some state funding has become available for applied research, but virtually none for fundamental or even strategic research. Yet in the social sciences, above all, fundamental research cannot be imported, as it may be in some of the natural sciences, because so much of it is specific to the individual society.

Even were the resources available, however, it is possible to wonder if they would have made much difference to the basic quality of performance, either by university administrators or academics. McDowell and Webb dismissed the School of Commerce established in 1925 as 'a fairly

[364] See Craver, 'Austrian economists', for Vienna's American connection.
[365] Granatstein, *Ottawa*, pp. 31, 42, 46, 135–8, 140, 154.
[366] Friis, *Social research*, p. 31.

humdrum affair . . . [which] pottered along until 1962, when it was replaced by a School of Business Studies'.[367] A Diploma in Geography, established in 1930, was sustained mainly by the commitment of T.W. Freeman, 'who initially in the teeth of some ridicule eventually persuaded the College that a subject taken seriously at Manchester and Leeds should also be taken seriously in Dublin'.[368] Just before the First World War, Trinity, following public criticism of its reluctance to initiate an agricultural school 'rather hastily fudged up a course which was to lead to a Diploma as Cambridge and Reading had already started courses and Oxford was just about to do so'.[369] The National University in which 'the B.Comm. now came into its own'[370] proved somewhat more receptive to commerce and agriculture, but not to geography or to social thought, for which an immediate market could not be perceived.

The National University, despite its conscious ideological reaction against Trinity as a representative of alien values,[371] nevertheless imbibed many of the prevailing academic assumptions of the disparaged anti-national milieu. Research counted for relatively little in early twentieth-century Trinity, intent on mimicking fashionable English attitudes. It was still only in the German university system, and in systems based on it, that the function of the university was considered to embrace research as well as teaching.[372] Only two of the eighteen Fellows elected in Trinity between 1896 and 1915 'produced original work of any substance and distinction'.[373] The others 'left behind as their literary monuments only a few scattered articles, some high class hack work, or in several cases nothing at all'.[374] After an intense canvass of the various alternatives to research through which fellows might occupy their time, MacDowell and Webb conclude that 'pure recreation' must have accounted for nearly twenty weeks a year.[375] But they stress that 'neither in their own eyes nor those of their contemporaries was their failure to publish original work a serious charge . . . It was realised that if the College were to maintain its renown, it must continue to produce some first-class scholars; but it was not the business of anybody in particular to see to this . . . '.[376]

Trinity came under no immediate threat from the National University, product of the same intellectual infertility drug. When George O'Brien expressed the view that teaching rather than research was at the heart of the university[377] – though he himself would show admirably how the two

367 McDowell and Webb, *Trinity College*, p. 449.   368 *Ibid.*, p. 450.
369 *Ibid.*, p. 415.
370 H.F. Kearney, *Scholars and gentlemen* (London, 1970), pp. 181ff. contrasts Trinity and the NUI as far as Commerce is concerned.
371 Donoghue, *We Irish*, pp. 172–3.
372 R.R. Locke, 'Business education in Germany: past systems and current practice', *Business History Review*, 59 (Summer 1985), p. 233.
373 McDowell and Webb, *Trinity College*, p. 400.   374 *Ibid.*   375 *Ibid.*, p. 402.
376 *Ibid.*   377 Meenan, *George O'Brien*, p. 157.

could be combined – he was simply reiterating the predominant view that research was almost a hobby, a happy but incidental by-product of the duty to initiate the next generataion into the inherited decencies at a somewhat superior, but far from exhausting, level of intellectual alertness. Colm Ó hEocha, president of University College Galway, recalling in 'Beocheist' the attitude of the staff when he was a student in the late 1940s, captures the prevailing self-image even at so relatively recent a date

When I was a student in Galway, only a handful of the staff acknowledged that the university had any obligation beyond teaching. A few sought successfully to do research. Some others recognised that the college should be active in preserving the language and the gaeltacht on their doorstep. But it was preservation, rather than the development of the region, particularly economic development, that preoccupied that generation.[378]

It was wholly consonant with this ethos that, as *The Leader* recorded in 1952, 'much less than twenty years ago it was possible for the medical faculty of one college to cast an all but unanimous vote against a candidate upon the grounds (explicitly stated) that he had been guilty of the indiscretion of research work'.[379] The tone of the comment showed that attitudes were changing. Indeed, even in the case cited, the faculty was overruled by the university (though not necessarily on mere academic grounds)!

Teaching then, rather than research, was the *raison d'être* of the university. Until after 1920 in Trinity, 'it was held that if a man lectured well, looked after his pupils conscientiously and did his share of minor administrative jobs he was earning his salary'.[380] By definition, there could be little teaching about the nature of Irish society. So little systematic had been written that there was little to be taught. But if a man did not lecture well, what then? Nothing. He was in no danger of losing his job. The most that McDowell and Webb will claim for the Fellows before the First World War is that 'as regards teaching . . . at least half were reasonably competent'.[381] It would seem that professors remained exempt from the expectation of lecturing well for at least a further generation![382] Nor did the National University permit Trinity any monopoly in this regard. The teaching performance of most lecturers has gone unrecorded. There were, no doubt, as there always are, brilliant teachers. The present author can gladly testify that the teaching of both history and economics in University College Dublin during his undergraduate years from 1959 to 1962 was not only generally outstanding but, on a man-for-man basis, probably compared, in the light of the opportunities

[378] Colm Ó hEocha, 'Cad é ar domhan atá i ndán don Ollscoil?' (What on earth is in store for the University?), *Irish Times*, 8 November 1984 (my translation).
[379] 'Provincial medical schools', *Leader* (Christmas 1953), p. 25.
[380] McDowell and Webb, *Trinity College*, p. 402.
[381] *Ibid.*, p. 397.   [382] *Ibid.*, pp. 450–60.

available, with the quality in any university in the world. But much teaching, one fears, was (is?) to be more endured than enjoyed. Joseph Brennan was unimpressed by his teachers in UCD.[383] If UCD promoted commerce teaching in advance of Trinity, as distinguished an early graduate as C.S. Andrews long remembered the 'abysmally low' quality of the teaching.[384] Sean O'Faolain, in a rare portrait of a professor at the podium, paints a picture of the UCC professor of English, Stockley, immediately after the First World War. Stockley, with a mind like 'a lady's sewing basket after a kitten had been through it', scaled a peak of memorable ineffectuality, lecturing in a perpetual fog, but for one crucial saving grace – he could convey enormous enthusiasm for his subject, even if it was never quite clear what the subject was![385]

It may be wondered, in view of the relaxed research and teaching ethos in the universities, if extra resources would have resulted in significant contributions to the understanding of Irish society, at least before the 1950s. Even if the funds were correctly allocated within universities, there may have been too few scholars anxious to avail constructively of them. Attitudes changed gradually. Extra resources, if properly allocated, could have been reasonably effectively used from the sixties.

It may even be doubted if the legendary appointment system of the National University made any great difference until fairly recently. No doubt better appointments could sometimes have been made than those that emerged from a system where a large number of electors with no necessary qualifications for assessing the credentials of the candidates reached their verdict after intense canvassing. No one familiar with appointment systems in other academic cultures will indulge the illusion that scholarly standing is the sole criterion of appointment. There is no system of appointment in any walk of life that is not open to abuse. But few institutions have devised systems that appear to invite the intrusion of extraneous criteria as blatantly as that of the National University. The general academic ethos that prevailed until the sixties (or in certain cases, beyond) made it unlikely, however, that an alternative system would have resulted in superior appointments. Trinity's system disdained the more vulgar opportunism of the *arriviste* National University. It is by no means clear that it produced superior results. And some of the losers in the NUI stakes could console themselves later on their good fortune, sharing in O'Faolain's sigh of satisfaction at his good luck in failing in his memorable bid for the UCC chair of English in the early

383 *Leader* Profile, 'Joseph Brennan', 5 July 1952.
384 C.S. Andrews, quoted in M. Manning, 'The pride of Ballaghadereen', *Magill* (March 1986), p. 35.
385 S. O'Faolain, *Vive Moi! an autobiography* (London, 1965), pp. 129–31.

thrities, 'I can only believe that I would have been out of the place within three years, or else stayed on and gone to seed.'[386]

By the 1960s the disdain for the appointments system of the National University was such that representatives of the Dublin Institute of Advanced Studies felt able to respond to the threat of incorporation into the university by coyly wondering if 'the quality of research staff could be maintained' if the university appointment system were applied to itself.[387] It was not until well after the Second World War, when more was coming to be expected from senior academics, that mistakes could exert a blighting influence. The system had the consequence of encouraging the investment of an immense amount of the time and energy of intelligent people, many of whom might have had much to contribute to improving the quality of Irish life, if only their talents had been channelled in a more fruitful direction, into intestinal institutional politics. The appointments system offered no irresistable inducement to scholarly activity simply because success was not seen to bear self-evident relationship to performance.

It would take an array of anthropologists to do full justice to the role of the university in Irish culture, as no doubt in many others. Here we can barely scratch the surface.[388] Of the many hypotheses that might be ventured, we shall confine ourselves to three. McDowell and Webb conclude their search 'for an explanation of this paradox of talented and cultured men willing to hand on to posterity so little of their knowledge or insights' with the reflection that 'though we can condemn the generation, we can excuse the individuals', for they merely conformed to the spirit of the age.[389] Nevertheless, the abiding impression is that in scholarship, as in all else, character was crucial. There were, as ever, many jostling influences subsumed under the broad mantle of the spirit of the age. That spirit does not exist independently of the attitudes of individuals. It is their attitude that stamps the spirit on the age, however many in turn will be influenced by a dominant ethos.

Even within the resource limitations of Irish academia, dramatic differences existed between the contributions of individuals working in comparable circumstances and facing similar obstacles. These differences cannot be explained primarily in cultural or impersonal terms. They have to be sought in character, temperament and sense of morality. Cork and Galway were normally at a relative disadvantage in resource terms

---

[386] *Ibid.*, p. 261.

[387] Commission on Higher Education 1960–67: *Report*, vol. 1 (Dublin, 1967), p. 348.

[388] For positive features of recent developments see J. Lee, 'University, state and society in Ireland, 1983', *Crane Bag*, 7, 2 (1983), pp. 5–12. E. Shils, *The intellectuals and the powers and other essays: selected papers of Edward Shils*, 1 (London, 1972), offers much food for thought to students of the Irish case.

[389] McDowell and Webb, *Trinity College*, pp. 400–2.

compared with Dublin-based scholars, though that relative disadvantage has sharply increased since 1960, particularly in the social sciences, in view of the proliferation of research institutions and concentration of research resources in the Dublin area. Nevertheless, levels of individual activity did not necessarily reflect the relative advantages of location.

In small countries, even more than in big ones, almost everything hinges on the contribution of individuals. Solow's observation that 'an intellectual tradition, even a firmly rooted one like that of Norwegian economics, is always fragile in a small country' can be applied with sad vengeance to Ireland.[390] If Edwards and Moody had not chanced to come on the scene when they did, one may wonder how long delayed the development of Irish historiography would have been. The heavy teaching commitments of Estyn Evans in Belfast did not prevent him from achieving a prolific output. Evans was clearly exceptional by any standards, but small countries depend disproportionately on exceptional people. In Queen's too, J.E. Todd, appointed Professor of Modern History in 1919, 'almost single-handed, built up a flourishing school, which owed its very existence to his enthusiasm, energy, and power of inspiring others'.[391] There can be little quarrel with Mitchell's verdict on 'the Irish reluctance to publish',[392] but he himself pays tribute to the extensive publication of the archaeologists R.A.S. MacAllister, S.P. Ó Riordáin and M.J. O'Kelly.[393] In contrast to these there were, no doubt, many to emulate Pearse McGarrigle's head of department, Professor McCreedy, in the 'University College Limerick' of David Lodge's *A small world*, who believed 'in keeping a low profile' so that 'not many people know we exist'. Enough has been said to suggest that much further probing is required before the sources of scholarly productivity can be fully understood.

McDowell and Webb revealingly and rightly trace the failure of so many Trinity staff to trouble the printer mainly to internal institutional circumstances, and to the dominant ethic of the academic profession, rather than to the nature of the society outside. They do not feel it necessary to invoke the anti-intellectualism, real or imagined, of peasant Catholic Ireland to account for the relaxed approach of the Fellows to scholarly inquiry in general, and to understanding Irish society in particular. It would seem anachronistic to interpret the publication performance of this happy band as a precociously ecumenical gesture towards the

390 R.M. Solow, 'Leif Johansen (1930–1982): a memorial', *Scandinavian Journal of Economics*, 85, 4 (1983), p. 446.
391 T.W. Moody and J.C. Beckett, *Queen's Belfast: the history of a university*, vol. 2 (London, 1949), p. 511.
392 G.F. Mitchell, 'Antiquities', in T. Ó Raifeartaigh (ed.), *The RIA. A bicentennial history 1785–1985* (Dublin, 1985), p. 159.
393 *Ibid.*, pp. 152, 158.

Catholic ethic or to seek the sources of Trinity sloth in Catholic culture. If the nature of Irish Catholicism cannot be ignored in discussing any major question of social significance in modern Ireland, it is by no means the only factor requiring scrutiny.

Neither the government nor university administrations developed any particular concept in the first generation of independence of the role of the university in a small new state. The National University, like Trinity, and however vociferous its occasional protestations to the contrary, was steeped in the English university ethos. That ethos had great strengths, but it derived its assumptions from the culture of a country that could take its identity and its success for granted. The role of the university in Irish circumstances required serious thought. It was nobody's responsibility to think about it.

The same deficiencies that ensured so little thought about Irish society in the universities themselves ensured equally little thought about universities in that society. The government largely funded the National University. But government thinking about university finance, as about so much else, was more concerned with cheapness than with performance. The basic questions therefore, in this as in so many other areas, remained not only unanswered, but largely unasked, at least until the 1950s. Because those who then asked them had little experience of thinking systematically about them, the answers, though often courageous, were frequently amateurish. The result was the emergence of numerous new institutions, many doing good work within their terms of reference, but none contributing its full potential to either scholarship or development because of the lack of any overall design for the system as a whole. The higher education system is not in any real sense a system. It is bits and pieces of what might have been a system had the basic thinking been done in time, but now constitutes such a conglomeration of vested interests that it is itself an obstacle to the emergence of a system. Higher education has been one of the worst sufferers from the lack of the social research that is a prerequisite for the adequate design of a higher educational system.

Because nobody, in government or in the universities, considered it their responsibility to think about how knowledge of Irish society could be most effectively advanced, little disciplined thinking was devoted to the problem.[394] The Social Research Committee, an *ad hoc* body instituted by the IPA in 1963 under the chairmanship of Patrick Lynch, enjoyed very mixed success, if one is to judge by results, in persuading a frequently uncomprehending constituency of the necessity for systematic thought. In these circumstances it was left largely to the discretion of individual scholars to decide whether they had any particular obligation to think about Ireland. Appointment and promotion schemes in the universities,

[394] Friis, *Social research*, pp. 7, 34.

largely based on the conventions of the natural sciences, have not generally sought to provide incentives for work on Ireland. Career prospects can be jeopardised if scholars choose to publish in journals that will be accessible to Irish policy-makers rather than in international scholarly journals, however inadequately refereed on Irish matters these may be.

Devoting time to Irish affairs is often a waste of time for those Irish thinkers who can play in the first division internationally. There is no necessary conflict of interest in the case of natural scientists, whose subjects are not area specific, nor in the case of most humanity subjects, which are not primarily based on Irish material. In the social sciences, however, the question is crucial. The issue confronts decision-makers, almost by definition, in small countries. Skelton, the virtual founder of the professional civil service in Canada, responded directly both by publishing extensively on Canadian history himself before becoming Under-Secretary of State for External Affairs, and by urging Canadian scholars to study Canadian subjects.[395] Canada was very similarly positioned to Ireland in this respect, not only because of its small population, but because of the threat of American intellectual dominance and the attractions offered by the wider English-speaking world.

The briefs of research institutes, like the ESRI and AFT, naturally obliged them to concentrate on specifically Irish work. They often produce fine research. However, precisely because the main thrust of that research is 'applied', they should be able, in the correct organisation of resources, to draw on the fundamental thinking of university researchers about the nature of Irish society. When they cannot, they are obliged to base their empirical work largely on imported theoretical models. Even the very organisation of such social research as exists in Ireland is based mainly on standard British disciplinary distinctions, with no attempt being made to create an original 'development science', or even a development economics, that may be more appropriate to the circumstances of a country that can scarcely be considered to fully belong to north American or western European economic culture, from which virtually all the theories are imported.

The applied researchers constitute a new type of market, an intermediate market, being themselves both consumers and producers of research. Here demand has outrun domestic supply since about 1960. The obvious solution is to rely heavily on imports to fill the gap. Intellectual imports inevitably assume high importance for small countries, even countries with vibrant native traditions of social thought. As an English-speaking country, the Irish market for ideas has long been open to Anglo-American imports, whether in the form of ideas imported directly, or in the form of

395 Granatstein, *Ottawa men*, pp. 32–4. See also p. 155 for the views of W.A. MacIntosh.

imported personnel. It seems doubtful if any country in western Europe has relied so heavily on imports in the area of policy studies.

There were three main direct import routes. The first, more or less casual, came through the unsolicited individuals, mostly academics, who chose to publish on Ireland. They found themselves until at least the 1960s in much the same position as Irish scholars who tried unavailingly to create a market for their products. The standard works, and in many cases the only works, on Irish political parties, rural or urban anthropology, sociology, political science, many historical subjects, even constitutional law, were for long due to foreign scholars. Where demand did not exist, even high quality work found itself unappreciated. Promising inter-war initiatives, like Kohn on constitutional law, Moss on political parties, Clarkson on labour history, Arensberg and Kimball on social anthropology, remained isolated monuments which one now stumbles across, with a sense of wonder, in the bleakness of the intellectual landscape, sad glimpses of what might have been. Northern Ireland has had to rely just as heavily on contributions of this type, the intellectual terrain of the North being at least as barren as that of the South.

The other two routes were more purposive, if not necessarily always more fruitful, in that they were demand led. The first was through the import of consultants, normally short term, to advise on specific problems. The second was through the immigration, often permanent, of individual scholars. The manner in which the Irish chose to use these varieties of intellectual import may repay investigation.

The orthodox justification for the use of foreign consultants, that they bring a detached mind to bear on issues, naturally bears little relation to reality. Most consultants, whether as individuals or as representatives of companies, deploy a limited range of ideas and techniques to provide a predictable set of answers. They bring a standard bag of tricks with them. The tricks may be good ones, but the consultants are normally neither detached nor particularly open-minded. They may be detached in terms of the country. They are not detached in terms of their own ideological or technical commitments. Consultants are not normally hired to open the eyes of their clients to new perspectives. A client who did not know what to expect from his consultant could be legitimately indicted for carelessness. The approach of Telesis, for instance, would have been known in advance to anyone who had taken the trouble to familiarise themselves with the work of Ira Magaziner. No doubt its approach was known in advance. There is little difficulty in predicting what McKinseys will recommend in any particular case. They bring a largely pre-packaged programme. Only the details have to be filled in on the Irish application form. As Chandler has ruefully noted 'McKinsey and Company made a fortune reorganising European companies in the 1960s into an M-form structure. One European manager even reported that he advised his colleagues to save the $100 000 fee McKinsey charged by reading the edition of *Strategy and structure* which then sold for $2.95.'[396]

Consultants have become quite the fashion since the 1960s. There have been a few interesting reports. But foreign consultants, however intelligent, however committed, however intellectually excited by the Irish problem, cannot acquire a fundamental feel for the nature of the society during their inevitably fleeting sojourns. Consultancy work is, virtually by definition, applied work only. Foreign consultants automatically work on the basis of their chosen foreign models. Most of their contributions could probably be more cheaply replicated by indigenous consultants except for the requirements of diplomacy in the piranha pool of institutional vested interest. Where consultants come from international organisations, like the OECD or the United Nations, they can serve a useful function by lending a veneer of respectability, and perhaps some political muscle, to the relevant enquiries. Of course they bring their own biases with them, and there is usually little about their findings that should not be familiar to any properly read Irish official in advance. The sources on which they draw are not top secret. They are freely available to anybody who keeps himself abreast of international developments. If Irish officials cannot, for whatever reason, do that, then they will fail to derive full advantage from the often useful reports of this type of consultant whose recommendations cannot be divorced from their intellectual style. There is no cut-price route to sustained intelligence in policy formulation.

Brennan and McElligott, in their day, had no desire to learn from consultants. They simply sought confirmation of revealed truth. Thus, in selecting experts for commissions of inquiry, the Finance objective was to solicit ideological support from respectable names. The case of Per Jacobsson is particularly revealing.

Of all the Swedish economists who might have been selected for membership of the 1934–8 banking commission, Jacobsson was among the most conservative. Brennan and McElligott adopted a reverential approach towards him on the commission.[397] Jacobsson was certainly sympathetic to their perspective, but he posed some unexpected problems. He was a product of the Swedish intellectual ethos, which valued intelligence. His conservatism was cerebral as well as visceral. He had sufficient confidence in his conservatism to assume that his position could be sustained by evidence. However much his ideological stance coincided

[396] A.D. Chandler, Jr. 'Comparative business history', in P. Mathias and D.C. Coleman (eds.), *Enterprise and history* (Cambridge, 1984), p. 16.
[397] R. Fanning, 'Economists and governments: Ireland 1922–52', in A. Murphy (ed.), *Economists and the Irish economy* (Dublin, 1984), p. 150.

with that of Finance, he basically despised the Irish way of doing things. He had

found here in the *Saorstát* no co-ordinated annual review of the financial position of the country . . . Where so much is heard about planning, one ought at least obtain from the authorities the full facts regarding their own financial position, or the full estimate of the financial results of the various public activities. We know that there is in fact very little real public information about this matter, that there is no public feeling with regard to them, that there is no real co-ordination of policy . . . It should be somebody's position to review the whole situation . . . There must be some permanent organisation whose business it should be to continue the studies which have begun and see that government departments are acquainted with the main facts of the balance of payments, national income, etc.[398]

Brennan and McElligott wanted no such organisation. It smacked of subversion to suggest that revealed truth required the support of mere evidence. They responded in a very Irish manner. They deluged Jacobsson with praise, and ignored any of his recommendations they found distasteful. It would not be their fault if any 'permanent organisation' were established to improve the supply and analysis of information. Jacobsson's recommendation that the proposed Central Bank should conduct some actual research[399] did not feature among Brennan's priorities on assuming the governorship. What is striking is how little the official mind chose to learn from Jacobbson. That some of its conclusions chanced to coincide with his did not suffice to put it in his league.

Jacobsson could refer as a matter of course to the 'national income'. Since the 1920s Sweden had been probing its economic history, attempting to compile statistics as far back as 1860 that would give it some basis for assessing its performance.[400] Lindahl's famous pioneering survey appeared in 1934. The first official Irish estimate of national income emerged in 1946, but its retrospective estimates went back no further than 1938. Earlier estimates were due to the private enterprise of Kiernan and Duncan. Nor was the Swedish search for knowledge a bizarre socialist perversion of financial propriety. The Swiss generally pursued policies of impeccable conservative lineage, but they shared with the Swedes a high respect for informed intelligence. Isolated though they were in Axis Europe they published their first calculations of national income in 1941, with an estimate for 1924, and an annual series beginning in 1929.[401]

Among scholars who came to settle in Ireland, three types can be distinguished. One group virtually created their subjects in Ireland. The study of Irish geography owes an incalculable amount to the contributions

---

[398] *Ibid.*   [399] *Report of Banking Commission* (Dublin, 1938), 2, appendix 17, p. 522.
[400] Uhr, 'Sweden's experience', p. 92.
[401] Eidgenössisches Statistisches Amt, *Schweizerisches Volkseinkommen, 1924, 1929 bis 1938* (Berne, 1941) and *Schweizerisches Volkseinkommen, 1939–1942* (Berne, 1943).

of Evans in Queen's, Freeman in Trinity, and Jones Hughes in UCD. Yet another Welshman, Emrys Jones, succeeded Evans in Queen's, before moving to a chair at the LSE. Between 1957 and 1984, six of the Geographical Society of Ireland's presidents were immigrants.

To what extent can it be claimed of other subjects that 'the interaction of insider and outsider' has fructified them, as it has fructified geography?[402] The development of political science is inconceivable without the unique contribution of Basil Chubb in Trinity. Peillon has made his mark on sociology from Maynooth. The ESRI, having relied heavily on imported economists in its early years, found itself once again relying heavily on imported sociologists and social psychologists when it expanded its brief to embrace social research from the mid-sixties. As late as 1985, seven of the twenty-three sociologists in Southern universities, and fifteen of the twenty-two in the North, came from outside Ireland.[403]

There were two other categories of imported scholar. Some settled down to an agreeable but undemanding existence, more Irish than the Irish themselves. Then there were those who never settled down, like W.A. Phillips, Moody's predecessor in Trinity history from 1913 to 1939, who 'remained the undisguised and unashamed Englishman doing a job in a foreign land and spending in Dublin only the minimum period needed for his lectures and examinations'.[404] Queen's is a special case; 48 per cent of the professors in 1909, 63 per cent in 1949, came from Britain.[405] Some were distinguished scholars. Relatively few, however, seem to have regarded Ireland as an appropriate object of study, at least until the latest round of troubles attracted international attention to the province, when its status on the scale of scholarly concern soared. Tensions were not unknown between those, like the internationally renowned social historian, Kenneth Connell, who wished to concentrate more resources on the study of Ireland, and those who did not.[406]

The contribution of immigrant scholars has been, on balance, a major one, particularly in the area of social inquiry. If on occasion the best use has not been made of them, that is for much the same reason that the best use has not been made of native talent. There is no national design on how to optimise the returns on investment in the study of Irish society.

It would be an exaggeration to claim, as has been claimed in the case of Canada, that Irish higher education institutions have been victims of 'the

402 W. Nolan, 'Preface', in Herries-Davies, *Irish Geography*, p. 7 (Dublin, 1984).
403 L. O'Dowd, 'Sociological research in Ireland; an overview and a proposed strategy', Paper delivered to RIA conference on social science research in Ireland, October 1986.
404 McDowell and Webb, *Trinity College*, p. 113.
405 Moody and Beckett, *Queen's Belfast*, pp. 625, 627.
406 L.A. Clarkson, 'K.H. Connell and Economic and Social History at Queen's University, Belfast', in J.M. Goldstrom and L.A. Clarkson (eds.), *Irish population, economy and society* (Oxford, 1981), pp. 3–6.

politics of external domination' or that they constitute mere 'branch plants' of British institutions.[407] It would be no exaggeration, however, to claim that Irish thinking has been dominated by imports. The capacity of a country to learn, whether from its own experience, or from that of others, is a defining characteristic of its level of development. Small countries must pay particular attention to learning techniques. How they decide what they want to learn, who to learn from, how to learn, are important ingredients of their national performance. How effectively did the Irish learn from abroad? How discriminatingly did they select their acquisitions? Did they conceive of imported ideas as raw material, as intermediate goods, or as finished products?

Importing intellectual produce is a highly skilled activity. Ireland's experience is paradoxical in the extreme. It has imported much, but it has learned little. A people who imitate so extensively devote little time to thinking about the art of learning. There is a significant difference between an independent state choosing consciously to learn, accordingly to carefully conceived criteria, for specific national purposes, and the mentality of a dependent people engaged in permanent mimicking of their presumed betters. Many decision-makers in many countries, and by no means only small ones, from Petrine Russia to Meiji Japan, from Caroline England to Adenauer's Germany, set out consciously to learn, to adapt, and to domesticate, institutions, policies, and even attitudes from selected 'model' states. The history of the Scandinavian countries can be read, it has been suggested, as a systematic process of importing and then adapting ideas in the light of local circumstances.[408] Not merely did the Irish not do this. Apart from a fleeting flurry among the constitution makers in 1922, it seems to have occurred to few decision-makers that they ought to even think of doing it.

The incapacity of the Irish mind to think through the implications of independence for national development derived largely from, and was itself a symbol of, the dependency syndrome that had wormed its way into the Irish psyche during the long centuries of foreign dominance. The Irish mind was enveloped in, and to some extent suffocated by, an English mental embrace. This was quite natural. A small occupied country, with an alien ruling class, culturally penetrated by the language and many of the thought processes of the coloniser, was bound in large measure to imitate the example of the powerful and the prosperous. There is no need to impose an unhistorical retrospective romantic nationalism on every

[407] A.B. Anderson, P.A. Sinclair, S.B. Bolaria and S. Parvez Wakil, 'Sociology in Canada: a developmental overview', in Mohan and Martindale, *Handbook*, pp. 168–9.

[408] B. Hagtvet and E. Rudeng, 'Scandinavia: achievements, challenges', *Daedalus*, 113, 2 (Spring 1984), pp. 230–1. The issue is treated in a broader perspective in Shils, 'Intellectuals, public opinion and economic development', in Shils, *The intellectuals and the powers*, p. 440.

aspect of relations between England and Ireland over the centuries to recognise that the relationship with the dominant power contributed fundamentally to the making of the modern Irish mind. England was the only model the Irish were familiar with for several centuries. Native political success in claiming some voice in decision-making during the nineteenth century was won not by rejecting the rules of the English political game, but largely by mastering them, and playing effectively within English terms of reference.

Reliance on the English model allowed a seductive economy of intellectual effort in Ireland. Irish experience appears sufficiently similar to English to seem merely a deviation, sometimes substantial, more often quaint, but still only a deviation, from the English norm, and not a difference in kind. Ireland was not sufficiently backward at independence to seem to require any fundamental theoretical reorientation of familiar propositions in the social sciences, and particularly in economics. Applying the existing stock of ideas should suffice to improve performance, if only they were correctly and courageously applied. The conceptual challenge of *defining* the problem was unlikely to be confronted because it was unlikely to be perceived. The problems therefore tended to be defined, both by administrators and by academics, in conformity with imported assumptions or, to put it more paradoxically, the answers defined the questions. Analytical tools were rarely refined and honed to respond to the specific challenge of understanding the Irish situation. Imports substituted for the theoretical originality the situation required. Thought transfer, we have suggested, is much more difficult than technology transfer. Social thought cannot be imported into a society and applied as if that society were more or less identical with the one in which the concepts were originally formulated.[409]

Problems of scale blended with levels of development to confuse the issue. Seminal ideas were often conceived internationally with reference to big societies. Adapting them to smaller societies was not just a question of reducing them in scale. Their very applicability to societies of a different scale itself posed a formidable intellectual challenge and called for sustained theoretical work. Theory is not an alternative to practice in Irish policy analysis and policy implementation. It is normally a prerequisite. The practical man who disparages social theory is the most impractical of men. Precisely for this reason the lack of financial support 'for more

---

[409] See, for instance, R.D. Navarro, F.C. Alvariez and L. Karps, 'The teaching of political science in developing countries', *International Social Science Journal*, 31 (1978), pp. 167–70; L. Sterling, 'Introduction', *Social and Economic Studies*, 33, 1 (March 1984), p. 2.

fundamental and long-range research work' was particularly counter-productive in Irish circumstances.[410]

The difference in scale between an independent Ireland with a population of 3 million and Britain with a population of 50 million, making no allowance for differences in economic circumstances, and in historical experience, made much of the British example of doubtful relevance to Ireland. When the Irish thought about scale at all, it seemed to be mainly with a shrug of the shoulders, to assume that smaller meant worse, a second or third division version of the axiomatic British first division, at least in material matters. But smaller did not necessarily mean worse. It meant different. Jacobsson noted that 'the Irish economists and almost *all* other Irishmen only know London and England and something of the USA, i.e. all *big* countries . . . I had to try to teach the Irish to take Sweden or Switzerland as their models and not England.'[411] Jacobsson here was referring only to monetary matters, but his observation holds true for virtually all areas of Irish activity.

Absorption in the English model gravely limited Irish perspectives. When allied to the elusive but crucial psychological factors that inspired the instinct of inferiority, it shrivelled Irish perspectives on Irish potential.[412] Those who imitated so assiduously lacked the discipline to acquire the comparative perspective that would enable them to decide what they ought to learn. The absence of a language barrier lulled them into the belief that they could imitate without learning. The pity of it was that the Irish, finding they could imitate so easily, did not even learn how to learn from England, and therefore learned less than they might have from one of the world's most creative cultures.

Learning is hard work. It is slow. It is purgative. It is a process, not an event. O'Faolain stressed that:

The outstanding thing about the development of a national intellect is the amazing slowness, difficulty and complexity of what we once thought of as a simple process. The new Ireland is still learning this old lesson the hard way, like a brilliant but arrogant boy whose very brilliance acts as a dam against experience, so that he learns everything quickly – except experience . . . if, in the long view of history we Irish have thus far learned little, and that slowly, from our actions and our passions, we have at least begun to learn how to learn.[413]

O'Faolain added, for good measure, 'we will, painfully, learn more'. Since he wrote, the pain has been as prominent as the learning. Learning

---

[410] K. Kennedy, 'Social science research and public policy', *Administration*, 21, 3 (Autumn 1973), p. 309.

[411] Fanning, 'Economists', p. 150.

[412] For the implications of a cultural inferiority complex see M. MacGréil, 'Education and cultural development', *Social Studies*, 1, 6 (December 1972), p. 670. On implications of 'cultural cringe' elsewhere, see S. Graubard, 'Preface: Australia, terra incognita', *Daedalus*, 114 (Winter 1985), p. x.

[413] O'Faolain, *The Irish*, pp. 168–9.

requires a profound knowledge of other countries and of one's own. One cannot tear out single threads from the fabric of other cultures, on the assumption that they can be woven into the texture of one's own culture without reference to the overall pattern. That may be occasionally feasible at the level of technology transfer. It is impossible at the level of thought transfer. One cannot import foreign institutions or foreign attitudes under licence. Successful thought transfer requires a deep knowledge of the whole foreign culture, not just of some isolated features, even explicitly economic ones. This requires so intimate a familiarity with its history, the capacity to share its silent assumptions, that busy men of affairs cannot be expected to cope with the challenge. Equally demanding, it requires a knowledge of the totality of one's own society, a feeling for how the individual parts fit together. Societies have to be comprehended as organic wholes to understand their ethos, to grasp how one 'gets its act together' more effectively than another. Only then can thought transfer have a prospect of success.

But at least the importance of learning has begun to make some impact, even if the techniques of learning are still sadly inadequate. Charles Carroll of the IMI identifies the key to the learning process. It is about strategy, not about bits and pieces that can be soldered onto the body politic or economic in a patchwork sort of way. He warns that the price 'of a series of strategic mistakes at this time could be very high', and that therefore 'maybe it is right for a small country that hard thinking and planning should take precedence over precipitative action'.[414] The deduction that we should not blindly follow the wrong foreign experience – he is thinking particularly of the United States, whose circumstances were so different from Ireland's – suggests a healthy growth of scepticism about the danger of promiscuous imports. 'Great care needs to be taken about what experience to borrow and whose experience to follow.'[415] Devising a *strategy* of national development is a herculean task, particularly for a people who because of their own experience of imitating English example in an *ad hoc* sort of way have never learned the art of grasping the totality of the foreign experience from which one proposes to learn.

In addition to importing, one could learn from one's own experience. Two processes may be distinguished. One is the 'hands on' approach of policy-making, 'learning by doing'. This often serves as a euphemism for 'learning from mistakes'. It can be a useful process – provided the mistakes are indeed learned from. Kennedy and Dowling suggest that this learning process may have been one of the most valuable experiences acquired by the civil service between the Second World War and the early 1970s.[416] It is not clear that the lessons may not have been forgotten

---

[414] Carroll, *Building Ireland's business*, p. 193.   [415] *Ibid.*
[416] Kennedy and Dowling, *Economic growth*, pp. 251–2.

subsequently. 'Unlearning' is a little researched topic. Two events in 1975–6 provided the sceptics with grounds for concern. Richie Ryan dismissed the very idea of planning in his 1975 Budget with so vigorous a rhetorical flourish that it suggested Finance felt free at last to escape from the intellectual legacy of the Whitaker era: 'Of all tasks which could engage my attention the least realistic would be the publication of a medium or long-term economic plan based upon irrelevancies in the past, hunches as to the present and clairvoyance as to the future.'[417] Presumably his short-term plan, if his Budget could be deemed such, was based on the same mix of ingredients! The clear message was that the only lesson to be learned from experience was that no lesson could be learned from experience.

The scope for clairvoyance was considerably enhanced the following year when the government decided to cancel the scheduled census. Rarely can a census have been so urgently required. The size and structure of the population was known to be changing at a pace unprecedented in the twentieth century. No serious policy-making in relation to urban planning, educational provision, health services, employment patterns, etc. could be based on the existing out of date figures. Yet a government that was running the biggest budget deficit in the history of the state chose to cancel the census on the grounds of expense, paltry though the cost was in relation to the total deficit. The public could have received more value for the amount of money involved than from virtually any other expenditure of similar amount, assuming that the results would be effectively, or even half effectively, used. The explanation was so patently specious that sceptics were obliged to assume that it was necessary that no fresh census results should appear before the next election, for fear that Jim Tully's gerymander would have to be reviewed.

Small states must rely heavily on the quality of their strategic thinking to counter their vulnerability to international influences. Without superior strategic thinking, they will be buffeted rudderless, like a cork on a wave. It is virtually impossible for a small country to 'plan' in a rigorous sense. That is all the more reason for striving to devise a strategy that will help one respond coherently, rather than epileptically, to changing circumstances. There is little point in bewailing factors beyond one's control until one has taken the steps necessary to achieve the best results from those within one's control. That is the enduring validity of the original Sinn Féin insight, shorn of its more extravagant rhetorical excesses.

In addition to 'learning by doing', there is a second possible source of education lurking in indigenous experience. It is called learning from history. It may be that one reason the Irish have been so slow to learn from

417 Whitaker, *Interests*, p. 103.

abroad is that they have acquired so little experience in learning from their own history. Whether it be true or not that 'no European country understands or interrogates its past less than Ireland',[418] it is certainly true that the Irish have devoted extraordinarily little effort to wondering how to learn from their history, whether pre- or post-independence. It was ironic that the emphatic doctrinal declaration of Finance nihilism in 1975 should have been made at a time when it had commissioned 'the definitive history' of the Department from a professional historian in 1970, a decision which a historian may be permitted to consider among its most enlightened![419] Not only had 'no professional historian . . . previously been given access to the archives of an Irish government department' but Professor Fanning found that 'the absence of proper archival arrangements' made his task all the more difficult.[420] If that was the situation in Finance, it seems singularly unlikely that it was better anywhere else.

There was, apparently, no sense that lessons might be learned from professional perusal of the archives. Indeed, when Leon Ó Broin, then Secretary of Posts and Telegraphs, and a noted historian in his own right, 'wanted to publish a history of Irish communications, including, of course, those for which the post office had been responsible', and had secured an appropriate author, of considerable distinction, who had written the history of the British Post Office, and was willing to do this at no expense except the refunding of the cost 'of an occasional visit to Dublin in connection with his work', Finance refused to sanction this expenditure, 'and the project fell through'.[421]

While it may be readily conceded that Irish decision-makers learned little from history, the fault was not, in the first instance, theirs. It was in this respect that the historians, who were in a unique position to contribute deeper understanding, failed. A successful national strategy required recognition of the inter-relationship between the cultural, social, spiritual, intellectual, economic and political. The ability to perceive the inter-relationships is itself a key variable in developmental strategy. The historians might have offered the perception, but their concentration on political and diplomatic history, to the virtual exclusion of other areas, meant that they illuminated only a narrow segment of the totality. However important that segment in its own right, it could not be properly perceived in isolation. Because of their failure to explore the other aspects at anything like the same level of professionalism that they devoted to the political, the historians were unable to adequately illuminate the linkages. The decision-makers therefore, even when they were familiar with historical work, could only learn indirectly and coincidentally from it. Not

[418] S. Deane, 'Postscript', *Crane Bag*, 3, 2 (1979), p. 512.
[419] Fanning, *Finance*, p. xiii.
[420] *Ibid.*, pp. xiii–xiv.   [421] Ó Broin, *Yesterday*, pp. 171–2.

only was there no systematic contemporary history until very recently, there were few coherent studies even of the politics of the second half of the nineteenth century, much less of the social, cultural, economic or intellectual history of post-famine Ireland, much less again of the crucial linkages between the variables. Mansergh's work of the thirties might have been expanded upon. But Mansergh himself, while never losing interest in Ireland, made his major subsequent contributions to wider Commonwealth studies.

The one happy exception proves the rule. Desmond Williams exerted considerable influence on External Affairs, partly through his close relations with senior officials, partly through the recruitment of many of his brightest students, inevitably influenced by his perspective, for it was impossible for quality minds not to respond to so luminous an intelligence, into the Department. Even this learning from history, through Williams, occurred more indirectly and coincidentally than in some other Departments of Foreign Affairs, which did not share the Irish confidence in the adequacy of 'on the job' learning. Theodor Schieder, the 'pope' of German history, for instance, gave fifteen years service to training programmes in the postwar German Foreign Office.[422]

Even had the historical research existed, it might have been ignored if its lessons were uncongenial. Supply was not more likely to have created its own demand here than elsewhere. Nevertheless, if the supply achieved a certain momentum, a deliberate decision would have had to be taken to ignore it. Maybe the sceptics would have been provoked into suggesting alternative interpretations, and a learning dialogue might have commenced. Instead academics and policy-makers existed as virtually separate castes, small though the country was and cordial though relations could be at a personal level. Maybe there were no lessons to be learned from history. Establishing even that 'lesson' would have required substantial research!

It is curious how little investigation historians have conducted on the theme of learning from history. One such enquiry, ranging over the whole of Europe, does conclude, after a far from sentimental survey of the issue, that with respect to agricultural policy the evidence does indeed suggest that 'only from a long and unflinching look' in the mirror of national history 'was satisfactory guidance towards a correct strategy likely to be found'.[423] For good or ill, Ireland chose to ignore the potential of this approach. Irish policy-makers, it is true, seem to suffer an almost emotional block when confronted with European experience. They some-

---

[422] A. Hillgruber, *Vom Beruf des Historikers in einer Zeit beschleunigten Wandels: Gedenkschrift für Theodor Schieder* (Munich, 1985), p. 10.

[423] A.S. Milward, 'Strategies for development in agriculture: the nineteenth-century European experience', in T.C. Smout (ed.), *The search for wealth and stability* (London, 1979), p. 40.

times seem more partial towards the Japanese example. It may therefore be worth observing that 'economic and social history have traditionally occupied an important place in the curricula of universities' which, with a stunning lack of hibernian imagination, is considered 'quite natural' because 'Japan's goal until recently was to catch up with western countries'.[424] Likewise, 'business history has been treated as an important subject in the faculties of commerce or management in postwar Japan'![425]

Ireland desperately needed thinkers capable of synthesising varieties of experience. Unfortunately, her institutional structures forced most of her best minds to think sectorally. The demand for integrated thinking has scarcely existed. Government departments are, naturally, organised on the tunnel principle. It is nobody's responsibility to think in terms of linkages between the tunnels. Linkage in policy terms tends to be much more the outcome of collision between, rather than coordination of, the traffic emerging from the tunnel exits. When the third economic programme appeared as an 'economic and social plan' in 1969, it might have suggested to the unwary that a new era of intellectual integration was at last beginning. Not only, however, was there little cohesion between the social and the economic elements. There was little cohesion among the various social elements themselves. The social component of the third programme consisted of little more than 'assorted shopping lists' from various departments of the projects they would like to see implemented.[426] It reflected only too clearly the paucity of systematic thinking that not only the *ad hoc* Social Research Committee, but other observers, had regularly lamented.[427]

Small states have to work consciously at devising mechanisms and procedures to foster strategic thinking. This has not been attempted in Ireland. It is doubtful if it has even been comprehended. The ESRI has come closest to acting as a substitute for a centre of strategic thought. It has done immensely useful work. But the titles of publications in the earlier years suggest that the objective was to address a series of problems rather than to formulate a strategy. It has more recently moved closer to injecting a strategic dimension into Irish public discourse through a variety of wideranging publications and its first explicitly medium-term projections, launched in 1985 and intended for revision on a regular basis.

Ireland's small population already exposes her to many acute diseconomies of scale. She has further exacerbated the problem by devising a highly fragmented decision-making system. It is exceedingly difficult for strategic

[424] S. Yonekawa, 'Recent writing on Japanese economic and social history', *Economic History Review* n.s., 38, 1 (February 1985), p. 107.
[425] *Ibid.*, p. 108.   [426] Barrington, *Administrative system*, p. 130.
[427] In addition to previously cited examples, see P.R. Kaim Caudle, *Social security in Ireland and Western Europe* (Dublin, 1964), p. 19; A. Coughlan, 'Public affairs, 1916–66: the social scene', *Administration*, 14, 3 (Autumn 1966), p. 214.

thinking to emerge from the administrative structure. This organisational fragmentation, which has flourished with the growth of government, reflects as well as reinforces intellectual fragmentation, with a consequent dearth of strategic thinking. The rapid growth in the size of the civil service since 1970, and the proliferation of institutions in the semi-state sector, not least in the knowledge industry, run up without any sense of overall direction, have now congealed into a 'disorganised overcomplexity' of formidably obstructive vested interests that impedes effective decision-making.[428]

Government departments are fragmented within and between themselves. Des O'Malley, a vigorous Minister for Industry and Commerce, recalled that although the Department was 'only across the street from the Department of Agriculture in Dublin, they might as well be a thousand miles apart because of the very little coordination that goes on between them'.[429] Among the innumerable difficulties, many man-made, bedevilling forestry policy, was the lack of cooperation between the IDA and the relevant section of the civil service.[430] The consumer soon finds himself mesmerised by the maze of overlapping state agencies. In the modest but promising field of fish farming, for instance, the industry must liaise with no fewer than fifteen official bodies, presumably reflecting the 'massive duplication of effort . . . between the many state agencies in agriculture and food'.[431] Fragmentation in the semi-state sector has gone so far that proposed solutions have to realistically rely more on hope than on faith.[432] Fragmentation is endemic in all administrative structures,[433] but it is particularly subversive of the national interest in a small retarded country.

Fragmentation of mind is potentially even more damaging than fragmentation of function. Patrick Lynch rightly warned that 'segmented education without the ability to make the right connections between scientific, humanistic and socio-cultural concerns helps to create segmented and compartmentalised people where we desperately need generalists'.[434] Of course, only a handful of minds can ever rise to this level. The most that can be hoped for from the rest, including many who may be

428 Louden Ryan, 'Prospects for the '80s', in ESRI, *The economic and social state of the nation* (Dublin, 1982), p. 85.
429 D. O'Malley *Irish Times*, 10 March 1986.
430 F.J. Convery, 'Beocheist', *Irish Times*, 24 May 1984.
431 E. Gallagher, 'The development of marine resources', *Administration*, 33, 1 (1985), p. 12.
432 J. Zimmerman, 'Irish state sponsored bodies: the fractionalisation of authority and responsibility', *Seirbhís Phoiblí*, 7, 2 (1986), pp. 27–41.
433 See H. Machin, 'France', in F.F. Ridley, (ed.), *Government and Administration in Western Europe* (London, 1979), pp. 74–5, 92, 106; D. Southern, 'Germany' in *ibid.*, pp. 141ff.; J. Richardson, 'Convergent policy styles in Europe?', in J. Richardson (ed.), *Policy styles in Western Europe* (London, 1982), pp. 201ff.
434 Lynch, 'Whither science policy?', p. 280.

superb in their own field, is that they become good specialists. But the full potential of the work of good specialists cannot be realised without the contribution of the generalists. Because Ireland has failed to see that, it has reaped a far poorer return on its now heavy investment in specialised knowledge than it might have, had it been able to think through the implications of its investment patterns in education and research at an earlier stage. There is a certain irony in the reluctance of the knowledge industry to acquire knowledge of itself! The chairman of the National Board of Science and Technology (NBST) lamented in 1986 that lack of coordination in science and technology investment was leading to the frittering away of much of the actual investment.[435] Yet the NBST regarded 'lack of coordination' as a topic unworthy of research. It fell into the area of knowledge of the society, which the NBST had since 1983 dismissed as unfit for support. Indeed, it felt such disdain for the society's need for self-knowledge, however modest the funding necessary to promote research on that topic, compared with the insatiable demands of technology, that in effectively abolishing its support it felt obliged to resort to no more subtle subterfuge than a disengenuous presentation of the figures.[436]

The very idea of synthesis as the most demanding specialisation of all, seems to be alien to a certain type of Irish mind, whether literary, administrative, or technological. León Ó Broin would hear the poisoned whisper 'as to how the head of a department could also be a writer'.[437] The sceptic might suggest that there are clearly many, whether in the public service or in academia, who regard reading and writing as mutually exclusive specialisms. Sean O'Faolain still leaves many uncomfortable, it has been observed, because of the popular inability to conceive 'the imaginative writer who is also an intellectual, deeply concerned with both the life of the mind and life as it is lived in the street, in the market place, in the institutions of social and political power, and in the confrontation with this world through ideas'.[438] It may not even be too fanciful to detect in this a symptom of the serf mentality, a feeling that there is something suspicious about the person who does not know his appointed place in the hierarchy of specialisms, and seeks to transcend the boundaries of conventional specialisation, so reassuring to the dependent psyche.

The consequences of fragmentation have become glaringly evident in

435 *Irish Times*, 17 January 1986.
436 *Position paper of the Executive Committee of the Sociological Association of Ireland: the National Board for Science and Technology* (November 1983), reprinted in M. Daly, et al., *Draft report of the working group on funding, employment conditions and the Sociological Association of Ireland* (October 1986).
437 Ó Broin, *Yesterday*, p. 162.
438 T. Kilroy, 'The Irish writer: self and society, 1950–80', in P. Connolly (ed.), *Literature and the changing Ireland* (Gerrard's Cross, 1982), p. 176.

the area of urban development since about 1950. It was not that the official mind did not gradually perceive that economic growth would, by definition, imply increasing urbanisation.[439] An Foras Forbartha was duly established in 1964, but it became mainly concerned with the physical planning dimension of urbanisation. The social consequences were nobody's business in particular. Ireland, as a late urbaniser, had the opportunity of learning from the mistakes of earlier urbanisers. She failed to learn. If P.J. Little, the first 'cultivated' Minister for Posts and Telegraphs, was offended in the mid-forties by the 'dirty, run-down condition . . . of so many of our towns',[440] the engineers, architects, and builders of the new towns a generation later seemed largely oblivious to either the visual or social consequences of their behaviour as they stamped their imprint of ugliness on the face of the land. 'Our new towns are horrifying examples of how utterly oblivious to all aesthetic values those who create them are . . . '.[441] There is no need to romanticise the communal pleasures of earlier Dublin generations to appreciate that the capital suffered a sad decline in the quality of life, particularly for the poor and the aged, as population in the greater Dublin area roughly doubled from 600 000 in 1950 to well over a million in 1985. Crime, fear, loneliness, became much more widespread. If some of this was inevitable, there was no need for much of it. Those responsible could not be bothered to learn.[442] Long after cities like Frankfurt had come to lament their devotion to the motor car in the immediate postwar period, and their sacrificing of living conditions to the primacy of the car, Dublin's traffic engineers continued to press ahead with their primitive thinking. Well trained, but badly educated, they were themselves victims of a teaching process that left them socially illiterate, largely devoid of a concept of urbanity, and incapable of learning from the experience of others.

The apotheosis of the indifference to learning came with the Eastern Region Development Organisation (ERDO) report of 1985. The study team exuded good intentions and was technically competent. But its cast of mind essentially segregated the physical from the human. Despite the glaring evidence to the contrary in Dublin's own experience, much less in that of innumerable cities abroad, they still clung essentially to the principle, look after the roads and the sewers, and the people will look after themselves. The report was eventually buried in response to public outcry. But it was not superseded by any more coherent philosophy. It

439 B. Clarke, 'The environment, 1945–70', in Lee, *Ireland 1945–70*, pp. 96–110, surveys the early developments.
440 Ó Broin, *Yesterday*, p. 169.
441 A. Cronin, 'The artless philistines', *Irish Times* 16 September, 1986.
442 M.J. Bannon, 'Irish urbanisation: issues in the built environment' in An Foras Forbartha, *Ireland in the year 2000* (Dublin, 1985), p. 64; F. McDonald, *The destruction of Dublin* (Dublin, 1985), pp. 300ff.

remains an enduring monument to a particular type of mentality, arising from the fragility of the intellectual infrastructure, and the consequent fragmentation of perspective, in the Ireland of the 1980s.[443]

Small countries, unless they be exceptionally rich in natural resources, must rely heavily on the quality of their thinking to adapt to changing international circumstances. Difficult though it is to quantify these issues, and impressionistic though such judgements must inevitably remain, it may be argued that a main reason for the inferior performance of Ireland since independence has been the poverty of its thinking. The main difference between itself and the smaller European countries who have moved far ahead of it in the twentieth century is that, for all their mistakes, misjudgements and vulnerability to factors beyond their control, they have organised their main resource, their intelligence, far more effectively. The Irish have proven themselves talented as individuals in many areas of endeavour. But they have yet to develop the talent to effectively harness their individual talents for collective purposes.

Despite the plethora of reports by various public bodies and consultancy groups in recent years, few have sought to address this fundamental issue. Many of the reports reach high standards within their terms of reference. But their terms of reference almost invariably involve them in tunnel thinking, devoid of analysis of their own assumptions. Far from there being 'paralysis by analysis', as the fashionable phrase (itself imported out of context) goes, Ireland remains conspicuous for the striking dearth of fundamental analyses of its condition.[444]

The favourite tactic for evading the challenge posed by the necessity to organise intelligence efficiently was the gadarene rush towards 'high technology'. Historians have scarcely begun to grapple with the role of science and scientists, much less of technology and technologists, in Irish experience.[445] We sadly lack, in particular, sustained historical inquiry into the engineering professions. This does not necessarily reflect any fundamental hostility to technology. The history of most professions has been equally comprehensively ignored by Irish historians, however unrelated their activities to technology.

The first major modern technological innovation to be widely and rapidly diffused in Ireland, the railway, found the commercial promoters

---

[443] Eastern Region Development Organisation, *Eastern region settlement strategy 2011, Main Report* (Dublin, 1985).

[444] For variations of this argument see my essays, *Reflections on Ireland in the EEC*, pp. 10–20; 'Perspectives on Ireland in the EEC', pp. 57–8; 'Centralisation and community', pp. 91ff; 'Whither Ireland', pp. 161ff.

[445] For initial approaches to the subject see D. Outram, 'Negating the rational: or why historians deny Irish science', *Irish Review*, 1 (1986), pp. 45–9; R.W.H. Johnson, 'Science and technology in Irish national culture', *Crane Bag*, 7, 2 (1983), pp. 58–63; G.L. Herries Davies, 'Irish thought in science', in R. Kearney (ed.), *The Irish mind* (Dublin, 1985), pp. 294–310.

floundering in the face of the engineering dimension. 'As commercial people, we are so ignorant of these matters' lamented even the more successful railway entrepreneurs.[446] A certain similarity may be detected between the abrupt introduction of the railway into a technologically under-developed society and the abrupt introduction of high tech into a still technologically under-developed country more than a century later. Just as the railway failed to fully realise the ambitious hope that it would act as the engine to pull the economy in its train, so high tech has hitherto failed to fully realise the hopes of its champions. The analogy is not perfect. There are significant differences between the two epochs, but the comparison is close enough for our initial purposes here.

Irish society remained technologically under-developed in the century after 1850, despite the early, extensive and rapid diffusion of the railway, and despite the fact that daily life was shaped by technological develop-ments in numerous ways. These developments were experienced largely at individual consumer level, however, rather than at mass production level. Technology, from the coming of electric light to television, was something that happened from outside, and to which one contributed little beyond consuming its products. This attitude changed dramatically about 1970. A consensus emerged remarkably rapidly at official level that high technology held the key to the future of the economy. There were, it is true, preparatory probings in the sixties, particularly an OECD inquiry into the place of science and technology is the Irish economy, under the chairmanship of Patrick Lynch, which produced a substantial report.[447] But many a report, however substantial, has been born to vegetate on the official shelf, to fade from memory until resurrected by the historians. The rapid conversion of the official mind to the technological imperative owed, as usual, more to circumstances than conviction. An effective technology lobby was already emerging and was quick to learn the marketing strategems to persuade the official mind to buy its conceptual wares. Hard-pressed policy-makers, seeking instant solutions to the accumulating problems of the late sixties and early seventies, and with little experience of diagnosing national issues in historical depth, saw in technology an escape route from their dilemma. The economic strategy elaborated by the new IDA of Michael Killeen after 1969 reposed immense faith in the high tech future of the country. Much of this activity was desirable, or at least defensible. A keener awareness of the potential of technology for national development needed to be promoted, but the

---

[446] J. Lee, 'Merchants and enterprise: the case of early Irish railways 1830–1855', in L.M. Cullen and P. Butel (eds.), *Négoce et industrie en France et en Irlande aux xviiie et xixe Siècles* (Paris, 1980), p. 155.

[447] *Science and Irish economic development* (Dublin, 1966: 2 vols). See also C. Ó hEocha, 'The science budget', *JSSISI*, 23, pt. 2 (1969–70), pp. 120–39.

process by which the shift in official perspectives occurred deprived it of a good deal of its potential value.

The official mind embraced the ideology of high technology with little grasp of the criteria by which it might assess and control the performance of this new wonder drug. As late as 1984 *Industrial policy* virtually equated industrial policy with technological policy. Little had been learned, it appeared, from the preceding fifteen years. Despite the accumulated evidence that technology was as much part of the problem as of the answer, it was still projected as the open sesame to a prosperous future. It is difficult to blame the official mind. It received little assistance (though it also sought little assistance) from professional social thinkers. It therefore relied heavily on the technology lobby for both its perspectives and its arguments. Bureaucratic rivalries between and within departments sometimes curbed its effectiveness. But its relations with the lobby were as intimate, if not as direct, as those of the Department of Agriculture with the farm lobby. Both essentially represented sectoral interests skilfully masquerading as the national interest. Little cognisance was taken of the reflections of the doyen of international thinkers on science policy, Edward Shils, who identified a set of general but central concerns in the formulation of science policy which Irish policy-makers largely failed to address systematically.[448]

The tactics of the technology lobby were adroit and effective. Its problem was that technology was highly expensive. It was therefore necessary to paint its promise in glowing terms to extract financial support from government for both educational institutions and industrial interests.[449] The purpose of education, and particularly of higher education, had to be defined in a single slogan, 'relevance'. Education had to be 'relevant'. 'Relevant' to what? To a strategy of national development? That issue was delicately avoided. The technologists, as technologists, had themselves no qualifications for assessing national or social 'relevance'. Discussion of the fundamental assumptions underlying the demand for 'relevance' had therefore to be sedulously avoided. The general impression conveyed, though rarely articulated, was that a value-free technology predicated a value-free society. Consequently, the commanding heights of the educational system had to be captured, behind an appropriate rhetorical smoke screen, from those who myopically clung to a concept of education as something mainly concerned with the fostering of personality, character, imagination and intellect. Education had to be subordinated to training, to indoctrination in both the perspectives and the techniques of the immediately functional. And the immediately functional

---

[448] E. Shils, 'Scientific development in the new states', in Shils, *The intellectuals and the powers*, pp. 457–66.

[449] The following discussion incorporates material from Lee, 'Society and culture', pp. 5–7.

was largely conceived not even in terms of economic growth, of whose dynamics the technology lobby had little grasp, but of technology itself. The medium became the message. The perspective received official benediction from the Department of Education in the chapter on third level education in the 1983 White Paper, which grabbed at the technology option with all the commitment of a drunk grabbing at a lamp post, and failed to contain a solitary mention of the significance of thought, any thought, to the welfare of either society or the state. The transition to a new concept of the role of education in society was accomplished all the more easily insofar as the inherited educational system had frequently failed to achieve its declared objective. The answer, however, was to bring the performance closer to the ideal, not to jettison the ideal.

The virtual absence of discussion on the role of technology in society, as distinct from innumerable exhortations from representatives of technological interests within government and the higher educational system to embrace technology, offered its own sad commentary on the poverty of inherited intellectual perspective. Few countries needed such a debate, in view of the vulnerability not only of their economy, but of their society and identity, to the implications of technological change, as urgently as Ireland. The official mind wanted no debate. If doubt were cast on the new faith in high tech, what was there left? Every other economic option had failed.

The conviction that technology held the secret to all economic progress, that there was a crock of gold buried at the end of the technological rainbow, and that if one looked after the technology, the society would look after itself, had a seductive appeal to politicians and officials alike. It substituted so conveniently for thought that subjecting the assumption to serious debate would be unsporting. Yet, if 'the true locus of the problem' in economically-advanced societies is not in the technology *per se* but in the social system in which that technology is embedded' then serious social thought becomes all the more necessary.[450]

The response to Patrick Lynch's fundamental contribution, 'Whither science policy?' speaks volumes for the anxiety of the policy-makers to engage in discussion. This 1979 Kane lecture was as seminal as his 1953 *Studies* article on economists and public policy. Lynch played a central role in raising awareness of the importance of both scientific and technological change for Irish development. But he preserved a sense of perspective. Drawing on a wide-ranging knowledge of national and international decision-making, Lynch brought a rare breath of vision to discussion of the theme. He sought to ensure that thinking on technology would not evade the question of values by concentrating exclusively on

---

[450] D. Bell, 'Communication technology – for better or for worse', *Harvard Business Review* (May/June 1979), p. 36.

techniques. Nevertheless, the technology lobby felt sufficiently confident to simply ignore him. Indeed, the organisation of the state machine itself, whether deliberately or not, contributes to the neglect. It is nobody's responsibility in that machine to think about the implications.

It is important that a sense of balance be acquired on the potential contribution of technology to both the economy and the society. The technological enthusiasts did a service by alerting policy makers to the potential of technological change, even if they themselves became prisoners of their own enthusiasm. But the cult of technology threatens serious damage to the already frayed fabric of national identity. Three particular problems can be identified.

In purely economic terms, the fetish of technology has distorted perspectives on the dynamic of economic growth. At the level of the individual firm, the arguments for instantly embracing the latest high technology discoveries can be queried. Charles Carroll argues that:

One of the most powerful signals to emerge from the Pims data base research concerns heavy investment in modern plant technology. Far from being the salvation it is touted to be, it is, in many circumstances, the source of the most insidious profit drain identified by Pims – the *investment intensity trap* . . . Very many Irish companies, public and private sector alike, have fallen foul of this trap – seduced by a false model of 'cost competitiveness' and the siren voice of 'modern technology' . . . This is probably the most crucial issue facing Irish industry.[451]

Carroll suggests that 'while there will be exceptions, it is by no means obvious that Ireland should invest very heavily in 'high tech' industries. Technological sense is by no means always identical with business sense.'[452]

Circumstances naturally vary from sector to sector. But there is ample evidence that in many sectors the human factor remains as important a consideration as the technological factor. Liam Devlin takes the view that 'there is a greater need to exchange information and experience about the management of individuals than there is to exchange technological information'.[453] Yet the White Paper on *Industrial Policy* simply wiped its hands of the whole issue of attitudes as 'beyond the scope of this Paper'.[454] In the circumstances, the wager on 'hard' technology was the soft option for the policy-makers.

It is an irony of technological progress that it makes the quality of social thought more rather than less 'relevant'. Contrary to the shrivelling perspectives of technological determinists, the basic values of a society become even more important when technology enhances the range of choice open to that society. The moralities of most societies are strongly

---

[451] Carroll, *Building Ireland's business*, pp. 5–6.   [452] *Ibid.*, p. 8.
[453] L. St John Devlin, 'The management of change', *Seirbhís Phoiblí*, 5, 2 (1984), p. 19.
[454] *Industrial Policy* p. 18.

influenced, and severely constrained, by the limitations of choice imposed by natural scarcity. As those limits are pushed backwards, as societies advance ever further beyond the level of physical subsistence, the scope for free will becomes ever wider. Character becomes even more central to the conduct of human affairs.[455]

CHARACTER

However imaginatively the institutional and intellectual infrastructures of a society may be designed, and however firmly they may be constructed, they will be inadequate in themselves to sustain effective collective action unless they are supported on a firm moral foundation. De Valera insisted that

Underneath all other qualities, supporting them all, as the foundation supports a house, is the underlying character of the people. If that is sound and durable, the various builders of the superstructure will have a surety that if their efforts are worthy ones, a nation can be created here which will be one of the spiritual forces of the world. If, on the other hand, the basic foundation of character is weak, no amount of construction on that foundation can make up for the inherent weakness . . . The essential thing in any state is not the governmental framework but the standard of citizenship on which it rests.[456]

De Valera distinguished too sharply between 'the governmental framework' and 'the standard of citizenship'. If the framework rested on the values of the civic culture, the state in turn could exert influence on 'the standard of citizenship'. Nevertheless, de Valera's fundamental point contains a profound truth. Whitaker suggested in 1960 that Ireland's comparative advantage in the search for economic growth resided in the qualities intrinsic to the Irish people, patriotism, dedication, cooperativeness, skill.[457] One may have grave reservations about the optimism of this perception, even at the time, but the perception was itself important. Whitaker did warn that progress would depend on how committed the country was to these qualities, and stressed that the educational system had a key role to play in fostering national character.[458]

Did then a decisive shift in values, from collective solidarity to individual selfishness, occur during the sixties? Charles McCarthy, meditating on the changes of the time, sketched a classic contrast between two very different types of society. 'Traditional Ireland' he felt, still survived into the fifties, its pervasive sense of community giving people a feeling of belonging in a society where 'their roles were set and explicit', where 'there was a powerful sense of *gemeinschaft*', which allowed them sink

[455] I draw here on Lee, 'Whither Ireland?', pp. 164–5.
[456] Moynihan, *Speeches*, pp. 431–2.
[457] Whitaker, 'Staid na Tíre', p. 179.
[458] T.K. Whitaker, 'Todhchaí eacnamáioch agus shóisialta na hÉireann', p. 107.

'into the warmth of a vast kinship, powerfully supported by the great unshakable moral edifice of the Catholic church'. Then came the sixties, when:

The growing affluence, the new technologies, the great shift in personal relations which television produced, and above all the revolution in the Catholic church which made provisional much that appeared timeless and changeless – all this produced something of a state of *anomie*: that lonely anxious state where men no longer look to the warmth of fellowship, but seek all the time to acquire goods, to compete for success, to appear dominant since they had no other means of winning the regard of others and consequently of achieving self-regard; and because they must ruthlessly seek these things, they seem to be caught up by a greed that is never satisfied, and an envy that is so naked as to be disreputable.[459]

This contains an important truth. But much more research would be required to confirm the historical accuracy of the image.[460] Pending such detailed research, it may be provisionally concluded that McCarthy's portrait does not convey the whole reality. It accepts at face value the self-image of traditional society. We have earlier had occasion to suggest, in discussing the central role of emigration in 'traditional' Ireland, that this was a society that devoted much of its energy to skilfully socialising the emigrants into mute resignation to their fate.[461] The dispersal of the surplus children whose claims could not be allowed to interfere with the enjoyment by the possessor class of their enhanced status, offers the single most eloquent commentary on the values of the society. Parents may, as individuals, have sought to provide fairly between their children.[462] But they were essentially collaborators in the socio-economic system that decreed mass emigration and national population decline as prerequisites for the comfort of the survivors. When choices had to be made, there was no nonsense about 'the warmth of a vast kinship'. There were winners and losers, both within families and between classes. There is a danger, which McCarthy did not entirely avoid, of contrasting the reality of the present with an idealised image of the past.

The same cultural style that accommodated itself so malleably to emigration marked other features of Irish life. This was not surprising. Those who remained were obliged to respond to the same economic sluggishness that decreed that so many should leave, a sluggishness

---

[459] C. McCarthy, *The decade of upheaval* (Dublin, 1973), pp. 219–20.

[460] S. Ó Tuama, 'Stability and ambivalence: aspects of the sense of place and religion in Irish literature', in Lee (ed.), *Ireland: Towards a sense of place*, p. 29. Students of the Irish case have much to learn from H. Eckstein, *Division and cohesion in democracy* (Princeton, 1966), esp. chs. 5–10. See also L. Lönnroth 'The intellectual civil servant: the role of the writer and scholar in nordic culture', *Daedalus*, 113, 2 (Spring 1984), pp. 118ff.

[461] See above, pp. 374–85.

[462] D. Fitzpatrick, '"A share of the honeycomb": education, emigration and Irish women', *Continuity and Change*, 1, 2 (1986), pp. 217–34 discusses strategies of adaptation adopted by potential female emigrants.

reflected in turn in the high degree of internal immobility and the small scale of institutions. These in turn contributed to the powerful, if never exclusive, grip of the possessor principle.

A sluggish society clinging to the possessor principle inevitably places decisive emphasis on inheritance patterns. God and Mammon collaborated to produce a predictable structure of morality in the circumstances. The technique of birth control devised by post-famine Ireland, late and few marriages, required rigorous sexual self-control from the disinherited, and indeed from the inheritors until they belatedly came into their legacy. Exceptional emphasis was naturally laid on the perils of sex, whose uncontrolled consequences would threaten the whole edifice. The obsessive equation of sin with sex was much less pronounced in popular pre-famine Irish traditions. It was partly imported from Victorian England, where it flourished for somewhat different reasons. In Ireland, it proved useful in reconciling the disinherited to their involuntary celibacy if they failed to emigrate in time, and ensured that inheritance patterns would not be spoiled by untimely accidents occurring during the long wait for marriage. It therefore protected the property interests of the farmer, whose children dominated the clergies, Catholic and Protestant, which preached these necessary values.

The preoccupation with sex, the virtual equation of immorality with sexual immorality, conveniently diverted attention from less remunerative tenets of Christian doctrine. It was as if a rigorous sexual morality was felt to compensate for a more relaxed concept of other moralities. Irish society had difficulty grasping even the idea of public morality. Not until the 1970s did the idea take root, and then only precariously, that public morality could concern anything other than the sexual lives of public men. The morality of violence, the morality of perjury, the morality of deceit in commercial and legal transactions, all tended to be relegated in popular consciousness to reassuringly venial status in the hierarchy of moralities. Drunkenness was even translated into the weakness of 'the good man'. And there would be no shortage of 'good men', as many of the disinherited, or of the mercenarily married, sought spiritual solace through the quickest 'Exit' out of Ireland.[463]

It was inevitable in these circumstances that envy, jealousy and spite would become rampant. There was nothing unique to Ireland in that.[464] It was not on an Irish gallows that Brueghel perched his magpie. But these qualities are now perceived to be so central to the Irish way of life that the Irish have devised their own word to describe the resultant personality

---

[463] Pedants may wish to note that this 'Exit' route was not incompatible with considerable 'Voice'!

[464] F.G. Bailey (ed.), *Gifts and poison* (London, 1971), offers instructive comparisons for students of Irish circumstances. For a philosophical approach see P. Masterson, 'The concept of resentment', *Studies*, 68 (1979), pp. 157–72.

type, the begrudger. The Irish carry from their mother's womb not so much a fanatic heart as a begrudger one. The begrudger mentality did derive fairly rationally from a mercantilist concept of the size of the status cake. The size of that cake was more or less fixed in more or less stagnating communities and in small institutions. In a stunted society, one man's gain did tend to be another man's loss. Winners could flourish only at the expense of losers. Status depended not only on rising oneself, but on preventing others from rising. For many, keeping the other fellow down offered the surest defence of their own position.

It was difficult for an individual to rise rapidly in an agricultural society, particularly one with so sluggish a land market, except at his neighbour's expense. It was not only John Healy's mother in Mayo who was making 'an almost culturally-programmed response' when holding that 'her village was the best village, her family the best family, and you did honour to it by denigrating the families from villages which threatened both'.[465] Threats to the family could also come from within one's own village. The success of the neighbour's child in the United States was acceptable. That did not disturb the local pecking order. It could even be glossed as a tribute to the village as a whole. The success of the same neighbour's child at home would upset assumptions about the natural order of things. The reactions were correspondingly more resentful in the steeper valleys of the squinting windows when the rare individual dared to rise above his alloted place. Envy of the thrusting neighbour frequently lurked beneath the cloak of ridicule, 'a method of cutting others down to size, especially those who tried to shake off the local apathy and get ahead . . . '.[466]

This mentality transferred into behaviour within institutions. Where promotion followed iron rules of seniority, it had at least the consequence of dampening jealousy, on the assumption that one's own turn would come in due course, provided one displayed no unsettling degree of initiative. Where promotion, as in the dwarf departments of universities, came by a complicated election process on the relatively rare occasions when openings occurred, then it was glaringly obvious that winners won at the expense of losers. The loser was often a loser for life. The lack of lateral mobility meant there were no alternative openings elsewhere, even for men of high ability. Many in those circumstances lacked the strength of character to rise above their bitter disappointment. Many an intelligent man vegetated, many a once-vibrant personality rotted into putrescent decay, sporadically jerking into spiteful activity in splenetic surges of jealousy. Immense amounts of time and effort were devoted to spiting the

465 Healy, *Nineteen acres*, p. 437.
466 D. Dunne, 'Psychiatric problems in Co. Mayo', quoted in A.M. Greeley, *That most distressful nation* (Chicago, 1972), p. 107. This section incorporates material from Lee, 'Motivation', pp. 41–2.

other fellow. Nothing could sweeten the rancid pill of a rival's success. And, by a cosmic displacement of bilious resentment, any successful person tended to be translated into a rival.

The systematic study of the influence of begrudgery on behaviour poses certain problems. The documentation, for one thing, tends to be elusive! Yet the role of spite in individuals and institutions is a patent and potent fact of Irish life. If a Yeats could feel the baleful breath of 'the daily spite of this unmannerly town', the destructive impact on more vulnerable spirits can be imagined. Ireland offered a hot-house environment for the cultivation of the poisoned weed. The inter-related combination of economic, marital and mobility patterns meant that Ireland had more than her fair share of individuals suffering from thwarted ambition, disappointed dreams, frustrated hopes, shattered ideals. The society was too static for the begrudgers to be able to diffuse their resentments on a wide circle of targets. Day after day, year after year, a stunted society obliged them to focus obsessively on the same individuals as the sources of their failure. The Irish begrudgers must return again and again to the same obsessive resentment, like a circle of Invidias eternally gnawing at the same heart. The cancer of begrudgery probably drove many to drink, for spite and drink were often children of the same frustration.

If begrudgery is rampant in contemporary Ireland, it is a direct inheritance from, not a perversion of, traditional Ireland. There is no reason to posit that the present generation of Irishmen, by no means forgetting Irish women, is more naturally corroded by envy than any earlier generation. Circumstances have conspired, however, to achieve a high profile for more recent exhibitions of envy.

Traditional Ireland was consumed with envy. But the public opportunities for its display were relatively few. One might plot silently to damage a rival, one would rarely expose one's enmity in public. If one did, one made sure to drape it in acceptable garb. At least four developments since 1960 have contributed to making begrudgery more conspicuous, if not more intense. In 1961, before Irish television was launched, only 30 000 homes out of a total of nearly 700 000 were estimated to be receiving British television. Already by 1966, 380 000 homes were receiving RTE, by 1971 536 000. 'If you've got it – flaunt it', a line actually used in one motor car advertisement, nicely captured the general ethos of television advertising, as well as of many of the values transmitted in television programmes, especially American ones. Whatever the consequences of such a philosophy in a dynamic economy, they encouraged an inflation of aspirations, and of exhibitionism, in an economy which, though growing unprecedentally rapidly by its own standards, was still relatively poor by the standards of the societies whose values the advertisers transmitted.

With a wider range of goods now available to be flaunted, petty personal rivalries could flourish at every level over a variety of consumer goods, from clothes to cars, to other consumer durables, to foreign holidays. Begrudgery now had a wider range of grievances on which to fester. The number of small institutions grew, both in the public and the private sectors, reproducing the circumstances that fostered the spread of envy and jealousy among shrivelled personalities. The number and aggressiveness of vested interests, whether within the expanded state sector, or outside it, grew appreciably. Pressure groups became, if not more insidious, certainly more blatant, expressing their demands more stridently, more self-righteously, and more avariciously, as they launched demand after demand for 'our' money from a growing but ineffectual state.

Entry to the EEC in 1973 reinforced this tendency. The substantial net flow of grants and subsidies approved for Ireland was brushed aside with the simple demand, 'more'. At moments of particular horror, when there loomed a momentary danger that the Irish might actually have to pay their way, begrudgery achieved its masterpiece by demanding that the others to dragged down to Irish levels. Dutch and Danish farmers had no right to perform better than Irish farmers! Dastardly Dutch cows, unsportingly stuffed with 'artificial' food, were performing above their full potential, while the underprivileged Irish cow, fighting a gallant battle with only 'natural' grass as her weapon, had still to reach hers! The begrudger mode of discourse the pressure groups choose to cultivate in connection with the EEC scarcely elevated the level of public discussion in Ireland!

In other areas too, observers detected sharp declines in the standard of personal conduct in contemporary Ireland. What distinguishes contemporary from traditional society, however, it may be suggested, is not so much a higher level of corruption as a failure to construct a new symbolic universe that would provide a façade behind which the society could get on with its less edifying activities while continuing to savour a satisfying sense of its own moral superiority.[467]

The construction of the symbolic universe that constituted the dominant public myth of post-famine Ireland, and would only begin to dissolve in the 1960s, was a supreme imaginative achievement. We have already explained how the professional image-makers coped with the challenge posed by emigration to the self-image of the society.[468] The task was far from completed once the emigrants were dispatched. Even the scattering of so high a proportion of several young generations did not ensure domestic tranquillity. Irish society remained riven by the potential con-

---

[467] The following paragraphs draw on Lee, 'Continuity and change', pp. 167–9; 'Motivation', pp. 41–5; 'Irish values', pp. 114ff. I have found T.J. Jackson Lears, 'The concept of cultural hegemony: problems and possibilities', *AHR*, 90, 3 (June 1985), pp. 567–93, illuminating.

[468] See above, pp. 374–86.

flicts inherent in the multiple tensions between agricultural labourers and farmers, between urban workers and employers, between various types of property, between families pursuing ancestral feuds, and within families between the inheritors and the disinherited 'relatives assisting'.

Distributional conflict is no new product of present-day Ireland. It has been central to Irish life for centuries, and never more so than in traditional post-famine Ireland. The losers included the landlord class, and the agricultural labourer class. The children driven into emigration were often losers in the domestic distribution struggle, however successful abroad. The losers who remained at home, for whatever reason, became 'relatives assisting'. Their history has yet to be written. Some might eventually inherit property, but at too advanced an age to found a family of their own. In general, they lingered through life, half-indulged, half-despised, as the maiden aunt and uncle, a legion of stunted personalities, mute victims to the failure of the society to create sufficient work to provide for even a dwindling population and to give its members a decent chance of personal fulfilment. Montague has memorably captured the consequent brooding fate of 'creatures crazed with loneliness', for whom indeed 'the only true madness is loneliness', in *The Rough Field*. History would continue to happen to the losers in the Irish possession stakes, long after their country had begun to make its own history again. Kavanagh's 'Great Hunger' evokes the futility of traditional existence for Paddy Maguire, who 'will hardly remember that life happened to him' in the emptiness of his *gemeinschaft*, where,

> Like the after-birth of a cow stretched on a branch in the wind
> Life dried in the veins of these women and men:
> The grey and grief and unlove
> The bones in the backs of their hands,
> And the chapel pressing its low ceiling over them.

There could be no bleaker contrast with the 'warmth of a vast kinship' imagined in McCarthy's portrait.

Yet McCarthy contains a good deal of truth. The same chapel was both prison and escape tunnel, the 'low ceiling' both suffocating and supportive, the priest both gaolor and liberator. For religion served as the indispensable lightning conductor for the repressed psychic tensions of a society whose hegemonic bloc relied on the disinheritance of the majority, through whatever technique, to preserve its patrimony. If the chapel did not create, it did consecrate, the circumstances where Paddy Maguire

> Cried for his own loss one late night on the pillow,
> And yet thanked the God that had arranged these things.

Kavanagh may have never heard of Gramsci before the 'Great Hunger' was published in 1942, but he would have had no difficulty relating the central thrust of Gramsci's thinking to the society whose ethos he so poignantly evoked.

The 'God that had arranged these things' was a very special God. He was a God of stern judgement, on the one hand, Who in His infinite mercy would refrain from exercising that judgement if only the sinner repented. And sin was sculptured in a style appealing to the aesthetic interests of the possessing classes. The church was potentially a church of condemnation, if its commandments were disobeyed. But it was even more truly a church of consolation, officered and largely manned by the scions of the possessing classes offering a sanctuary of solace for the weak and the lonely. This is *not* to argue that religion in 'traditional' Ireland was merely a front behind which the material interests of its patrons could be more covetously pursued. If it was perhaps mainly that in some cases, it is the essence and the glory of authentic religious belief that it can never be reduced to mere expression of material interests. The precise manner in which the spiritual and the material interact, however, reveals much about the nature of a society. In the case of 'traditional' Ireland, it requires exploration of surgical delicacy.

The churches, not least the Catholic Church, gave ample evidence of partiality for the performer principle in their conduct of their own affairs. The doctrinal influence of the Catholic Church, however, lent a veneer of legitimacy to the possessor principle, or at least could be appropriated by the possessors for their own purposes. 'What does it profit a man if he gains the whole world and loses his immortal soul?' was not necessarily a reflection to ignite potential performers. The converse – that failing to gain the whole world by no means guaranteed eternal salvation – may have been too complex a construction for those congenitally disposed to the possessor principle to unduly ponder. It would be instructive to know how the parable of the 'talents' was interpreted from the pulpit. One may surmise that it had a mixed reception among Irish congregations. No church can be indicted for the manner in which its teaching is manipulated by the dominant elements in society to surround their own interests with a protective halo. If Catholic doctrine had as much protean potential as Protestant, it was naturally the possessors who most effectively determined the dominant interpretive direction in both cases.

The obvious, indeed instinctive response of the emerging post-famine hegemonic bloc, which constituted an increasing proportion of the population as total numbers rapidly fell, was to extol the claims of communal and spiritual solidarity. This had little to do with any genuine feeling of collective responsibility. The lack of a viable civic culture testifies to the slender hold of the idea of the public good. The communal ethic was devised to discourage disturbance of the natural order of things, as willed by God, particularly once the land war had 'restored' their property rights to the natural owners of the land to the discomfiture of the unnatural 'alien' predators. Nationalism served a useful function as a secular religion in this respect. Internal tensions could be sublimated in a demand for loyalty to a higher good against the threat of a common enemy, who had incidentally the happy double advantage of also being a heretic. Nationalism cannot, any more than religion, be reduced to the mere expression of material interests. It too could generate extraordinary spontaneous idealism on the part of a minority of activists. But it was quite compatible, however anti-materialistic the doctrines of individual nationalist preachers, with a solicitude for the material interests of the possessing classes.

The post-famine image makers set eagerly to work chiselling a face and a form for Caitlín Ní hUallacháin that would be virtually completed by the turn of the century and that would anticipate the main features lovingly unveiled a generation later by functionalist Harvard anthropologists. There was no conspiracy among the image makers. Many worked in isolation. But they all responded to the same compulsion of circumstances. They did their work so well that Arensberg and Kimball could add little except detail to the inherited portrait in *The Irish countryman* (1937) and *Family and community in Ireland* (1940). Their brilliantly articulated model of West Clare society in the 1930s portrays a community in equilibrium, having apparently acquired the secret of eternal stability. It would be difficult to glean from this account of the Irish countryman that 165 000 emigrants left Clare between 1851 and 1920, or that the population of the county had fallen from 212 000 in 1851 to 95 000 in 1926. Emigration scarcely intruded into this classic portrait of a serene society, at peace with itself and with the world, functioning like a beautifully balanced clockwork mechanism, a perfect *gemeinschaft*. By an ingenious slight of functionalist hand, the anthropological 'high priests of cultural stability' portrayed secular decline as timeless stability. A community that had undergone traumatic cultural, demographic and economic shock in the previous three generations, and which objectively was threatened with virtual extinction of its way of life within another generation or two, somehow appears, as viewed through the spectacles of its own hegemonic bloc, as suspended in time, outside history.

The image makers showed something approaching genius in the manner in which they composed so powerful a construct. The result was a highly selective social construction of reality. Our normal response to evidence of sharp contrast between proclaimed ideal and perceived practice is to suspect hypocrisy. The study of hypocrisy would doubtless yield instructive insights into the 'traditional' value system. Even irrefutable evidence of a 'traditional' Irish psyche swaddled in thick layers of hypocrisy, however, would not necessarily condemn the Irish, Catholic or

Protestant, on a charge of being more inherently pharasaical than others. Hypocrisy, like most collective characteristics, is partly a product of circumstances. It has played an indispensable mediating role in ritualising the compromises essential to civilised public discourse in many societies, including some that would be generally considered more sophisticated than Ireland.[469]

The self-image of 'traditional' Ireland, was, it may be suggested, characterised less by hypocrisy than by a capacity for self-deception on a heroic scale. It was this that gave it such enormous emotional power, and could achieve such resonance even among those who might objectively be regarded as the victims. When Paddy Maguire 'thanked the God that had arranged these things' he was accepting a role, unconsciously, as an accomplice, a collaborator, in a manner that turned him into a mere cipher in the grand design of the hegemonic bloc. The ultimate perfection of the design had been achieved when it could be conceived not only by its architects but also by its victims, for all their inner sense of deprivation, as a divine dispensation.

Only a heroic capacity for self-deception invested the traditional self-image with such extraordinary appeal and stamina. Collective self-deception by a society over several generations is a singularly elusive historical topic to pursue. But it may be central to understanding the Irish mind and the Irish character in the past century. That I can do no more than point to its potential significance here reflects my ignorance, not the irrelevance of the issue.[470]

The self-portrait of traditional Ireland was a work of art, a triumph of imagination, will power and technique over refractory raw material. If it be the case that 'It is the nature of myth to mediate contradictions',[471] it may not even be too fanciful to suggest that the emotional effort involved led to that exhaustion of the constructive imagination that prompted Roy Foster to observe that:

> The myths of the Irish are not used in the creative way defined by Levi-Strauss as 'evoking a suppressed past and applying it like a grid upon the present' to discover how the structural and historical aspects of man's reality coincide; their function is rather as a refuge in which to evade analysis.[472]

Traditional Ireland worshipped its authorised self-portrait with an idolatrous fervour. By the fifties, however, the features bore such tenuous relation to reality that a growing number, including key figures within the establishment, were no longer willing to sustain the required degree of

---

[469] T. Zeldin, *France 1848–1945*, 2 (Oxford, 1977), p. 1152.

[470] H. Fingarette, *Self-deception* (London, 1969). For difficulties associated with the use of 'self-deception' by historians see T.L. Haskell, 'Capitalism and the origins of the humanitarian sensibility, part I', *AHR*, 90, 2 (April 1985), pp. 348ff.

[471] Mary Douglas, *Implicit meanings: essays in anthropology* (London, 1975), p. 156.

[472] R. Foster, *Times Literary Supplement*, 4 June 1976, p. 673.

self-deception. The portrait faded away. But no alternative self-portrait would emerge to command comparable conviction. This was not surprising. It had taken at least a generation for the traditional self-portrait to achieve finished form. The post de Valera generation was a transitional one. Transitional to what was not quite clear. All peoples need their public myths. But all public myths are not equally mythical. Not all feel the same need to disguise so much of the truth as had the traditional Irish one. The more mature a people the less their need for a flattering self-portrait. It would be intriguing to think that the Irish have outgrown that phase. It remains to be seen, however, what will emerge from the debates of recent years. Garret FitzGerald sought to replace the crumbled hegemonic consensus, built around a *de facto* Catholic state, with a pluralist consensus embracing Catholic and Protestant religious traditions equally. However genuine his aspiration to greater religious tolerance, his pluralism was too anaemic, his vision of Ireland too devoid of any sense of a distinctive national identity, to rouse mass support. It was by no means too anaemic, however, to rouse bitter resistance among conservative Catholics, whose resentment at the direction of 'liberal' changes in Irish life crystalised in the 'abortion referendum' of 1983.

If the nominal issue involved were not so tragic a one, the referendum could best be treated as vulgar farce. About 4000 Irish girls were going to Britain every year for abortion. The referendum was not about them. It was not *de facto* about abortion at all. Abortion was already illegal. The vast majority of Irish Catholics were clearly and adamantly opposed to it. There was no likelihood of its introduction in the foreseeable future as a result of public demand. But it was not explicitly prohibited in the constitution. It was therefore possible to envisage that court decisions might effectively legalise it, even in the face of a hostile public opinion. However improbable this might appear, it sufficed to justify the formation of a pro-life amendment campaign (PLAC) following the visit of Pope John Paul II in 1979, which soon provided a rallying point for a variety of mentalities resentful at recent social changes.[473] The emergence of a small but strident Women's Right to Choose Group in 1980, advocating abortion as a female right, supplied PLAC with useful ammunition.

After a variety of manoeuvrings and posturings among the political parties, extensive discussions within the hierarchy, exchanges among the medical and legal professions, and a campaign profuse in those idiosyncracies that delight connoisseurs of Hibernian peculiarities, the electorate carried by a majority of two to one in September 1983 the amendment that 'the state acknowledges the right to life of the unborn and, with due regard to the equal right to life of the mother, guarantees in its laws to

---

[473] B. Girvin, 'Social change and moral politics: the Irish constitutional referendum 1983', *Political Studies*, 34 (1986), p. 68.

protect, and as far as practicable, by its laws, to defend and vindicate that right'.[474]

It is difficult to draw confident conclusions from the referendum result. On the surface, it represented a pyrrhic victory for the PLAC forces. The two most striking features of the referendum were that only 55 per cent of the electorate actually voted, and that a sharp cleavage emerged between voting patterns in Dublin and in the rest of the country. The turn-out was well below what might have been expected in view of the call by the Catholic bishops for a 'yes' vote – while acknowledging that Catholics had a right to freedom of conscience – shortly before the referendum. Party loyalties appear to have had some influence on the vote. Neither of the main parties campaigned officially, but Haughey supported the amendment, while FitzGerald eventually opposed it.[475] That the amendment was carried in Dublin with the slimmest of majorities seemed to bode ill for the future of traditional thought, at least if the Greater Dublin area continued to grow relative to the rest of the country, and if the assumption that national attitudes eventually followed Dublin attitudes was valid.

It is not clear what problem the result solved for the participants. The exercise was symbolically significant, despite or perhaps because of the fact that it would change little or nothing in practice. It was a cleansing ritual, of a type central to the traditional value system. That value system had now broken up, but substantial fragments still survived. The high profile accorded to an issue of sexual morality was itself a qualified victory for some of the PLAC persuasion. Many PLAC supporters were genuinely aghast at the thought of abortion ever polluting Irish life. In addition, there was, from the 'traditional' point of view, a dangerous drift during the seventies towards redefining morality to include issues of justice, jobbery, peace, etc. A bishop expressed the subversive view that morality was as relevant to the boardroom as the bedroom.[476] Nothing would be sacred if that tendency were allowed to continue. Morality was in danger of becoming a jack-in-the-box that might pop up anywhere, to the discomfiture of traditionalists. The beauty of traditional morality was that the area to which it applied was so conveniently circumscribed. Traditional Ireland had largely succeeded in excluding from the agenda of moral discourse doctrines potentially subversive of the material interests of the dominant social elements. It was now important for traditionalists

---

[474] *Ibid.*, pp. 68ff.; J.P. O'Carroll, 'The politics of the 1983 "abortion referendum debate" in the Republic of Ireland' (unpublished paper delivered at European Consortium of Political Research Conference, Salzburg, April 1984), pp. 14–15. I am grateful to Dr O'Carroll for providing me with a copy of this paper.

[475] Girvin, 'Social change', pp. 76–80.

[476] J.A. Murphy, 'The Church, morality and the law', in D. Clarke (ed.), *Morality and the law* (Dublin, 1982), p. 108.

to divert ecclesiastical concern away from the dangerous area of public morality, and confine itself once more to the safe tunnel of sexual morality. The referendum may not have fully succeeded in restoring the 'traditional' concept of morality, but it sufficed to divert attention from other issues for a time.

The most distinctive feature of the debate 'was that dialogue was never entered into at a conscious level'.[477] The opposing groups talked past each other, reflecting 'an almost total lack of a well-developed public sphere in Irish society'.[478] Public debate on issues of moral principle were so under-developed in the political culture that neither side was able to relate to the assumptions of the other. It was a dialogue of the deaf, though not of the mute! It exposed not only the continuing hollowness of the symbolic universe of traditional thought, but also the shallowness of much liberal thought, fashionable in the media, and reeking with conde-scension towards the 'peasantry', defined to include virtually anyone who dared query their assumptions. Too many Irish liberals were giving liberalism a bad name by equating liberalism with self-indulgence.

The most important result of the referendum was the implication for the Catholic hierarchy. The hierarchy found itself obliged in the sixties, in the wake of the internal social changes, and the external shock of the Vatican Council, to take conscious cognisance for the first time in a century of rapidly changing circumstances. Periods of change always pose particular problems for churches, which must cater for all their flock, not merely conservatives alone, or progressives alone. They have obligations to all generations among their members, not just to the younger ones pressing most urgently for change, sometimes with scant regard for the susceptibilities and frailties of their elders – to which they themselves may become prey in due course. The doctrinal emphases in Irish Catholicism were partly the product of a momentary conjunction of circumstances after the Great Famine. But they assumed an authority in the eyes of the faithful of later generations based on the belief that they stretched back to the dawn of Christianity. Some of them did, but it was the balance between the various teachings that constituted the essence of the church's message. That balance shifted significantly with the Vatican Council, inducing culture shock among many clergy and laity, even while it came as liberation to others. Catholics who equated ritual with religion suffered severe trauma. In the circumstances, the hierarchy navigated skilfully. The cautious, but not reactionary, course charted by the episcopal helmsmen, guided by shrewd judges and congenial consensus figures in Cardinals William Conway and Tomás Ó Fiaich, may have been an important factor in helping the wider society adjust to the pressures of change, indirectly in secular as well as directly in religious matters. The church continued to

477 O'Carroll, 'Politics', p. 20.   478 *Ibid.*, p. 10.

provide psychic moorings for many who might otherwise have suffered a good deal more emotional disturbance in the face of incomprehensible change.

The church faced a dilemma by the 1980s. The changes in sexual morality spread quickly in the seventies. _De facto_ marriage breakdown had doubtless occurred, perhaps frequently. But it was concealed by the cover-up techniques that came as second nature to a society that placed such value on inheritance and appearances. Birth control had been central to traditional values, but the techniques changed in the seventies, with contraception superseding celibacy. Now more and more husbands and wives apparently came to acknowledge the breakdown of their marriages, with a consequent rising clamour for divorce legislation. By 1980 traditional church teaching on contraception was ignored by a substantial proportion, perhaps by a majority, of the relevant age groups. Church teaching on the indissolubility of marriage in any circumstances had come to be rejected in principle by the majority of the population of the Republic by 1985, at least according to opinion polls. Divorce in practice could still be rejected if the terms of the proposed divorce legislation failed to inspire confidence. But it was only on abortion, of the trinity habitually linked by traditional preachers, that church teaching was still overwhelmingly accepted by Irish Catholics.

Some of the change in popular attitudes was probably due to genuine humanitarianism, but it seems clear that much of the general drift in terms of sexual morality was based on mere hedonism. No self-respecting church could compromise with this mentality. At a more mundane political level, given that Fine Gael and Labour were now broadly associated, despite much internal discord, with the liberalising direction, and Fianna Fáil with the more conservative ethos, a strong traditional line could be interpreted as an intrusion into party politics, an undesirable implication from the church's point of view in any but the shortest of short terms. And the more imperiously it pronounced on matters of sexual morality, the more it would reinforce the resolve of Protestants, not only in the North, but increasingly in the South, to resist what they saw as tyrannical tendencies to deprive them of liberty of conscience.

The Irish Bishops' Conference generally took a moderate stance on the issues, stressing the Catholic position, as was its duty, while insisting, as in the 'abortion referendum', that Catholics had the right to follow their own consciences. Some individual bishops, nevertheless, continued to publicly resist the concept of freedom of conscience. If the church relied on the informed Catholic conscience rather than on the laws of the state to oblige citizens to behave according to Catholic doctrine, it was possible that many Catholics, for whom religion may have been more a code than a conviction, might fail to grasp the role of conscience, as distinct from legislation, in determining their behaviour. Critics were not slow to suggest that the patent lack of confidence of many clergy in the laity exposed the hollowness of 'traditional' morality.

The church's dilemma, to which there is no easy answer, should deeply concern civic leaders. The church is a bulwark, perhaps now the main bulwark, of the civic culture. It is the very opportunism of the traditional value system that leaves religion as the main barrier between a reasonably civilised civil society and the untrammelled predatory instincts of individual and pressure-group selfishness, curbed only by the power of rival predators. Evidence of a sharp decline in formal religious observance among the younger urbanised generation has deeply disturbed some observers, who detect 'shallow' religious roots and a church suffering from 'spiritual malnutrition'. The more comforting conclusion that 'what the church is experiencing is less a crisis of faith than a crisis of culture' may be optimistic in a society where faith and culture are so intimately intertwined. It is precisely this close connection that leaves the civic culture so vulnerable to a rapid decline in the role of institutional religion. If religion were to no longer fulfil its historic civilising mission as a substitute for internalised values of civic responsibility, the consequences for the country no less than for the church could be lethal.[479]

This dilemma of the church should cause even more concern, to both church and political leaders, in view of the crisis of Irish nationalism. For nationalism acted, apart from religion, as the main bonding element in 'traditional' Ireland. Like religion, it could be manipulated to legitimise, beneath a cloak of communal solidarity, predatory private interests. It could also foster, again like religion, and however opportunistically it might be manipulated, a feeling of belonging, nurture a sense of psychological security, and inspire extraordinary idealism. The weakening of the twin pillars on which the identity of traditional Ireland rested confronted the succeeding generations with a fundamental challenge.[480]

---

[479] This section draws on Lee, 'Society and culture', pp. 11–13. See M.P. Gallagher, 'What hope for Irish faith?', *The Furrow*, 29, 10 (October 1978); Liam Ryan, 'Church and politics: the last twenty five years', *The Furrow*, 30, 1 (1979); P.R. Connolly, 'The Church in Ireland since Vatican II', *The Furrow*, 30, 12 (December 1979); Liam Ryan, 'The Church now', *The Furrow*, 32, 2 (February 1981); Corish, *Catholic experience*, p. 258; A. Falconer, E. McDonagh and S. MacReamoinn (eds.), *Freedom to hope? the Catholic Church in Ireland twenty years after Vatican II* (Dublin, 1985).

[480] For a wide ranging survey of the issues discussed here, see G. Ó Tuathaigh, 'Religion, nationality and a sense of community in modern Ireland', in Ó Tuathaigh (ed.), *Community, culture and conflict* (Galway, 1986), pp. 64–81. For sage reflections on the need for tradition, see E. Shils, *Tradition* (London, 1981).

IDENTITY

Liam de Paor concluded his notable series of meditations on twentieth-century Ireland in 1985 with the observation that,

The country is young, for the first time in many decades, and the young country takes its 'identity' and nationality for granted . . . It is . . . just possible to see that under the rapid and bewildering changes now occurring in Ireland, a completely new sense of national identity and destiny is taking shape . . . We are living now in a period of extraordinary energy and productivity. The arts, particularly the literary arts, flourish. People are going back to first principles in politics. Unionists talk to nationalists, nationalists to unionists, as never before . . . the shape of an independent Ireland emerges.[481]

This was a refreshingly buoyant note to strike in a period widely perceived as one of national malaise and of identity crisis. Indeed, an acute Australian observer concluded that 'when you come right down to it, there is almost no civic sense at all; that concept is too wide for people's life-experience . . . they have little sense of a nation, and none of a *polis*'.[482] De Paor did note that 'the shape of Ireland in the future, remains unpredictable, largely because 'the people who run our affairs have taken their ideas from the bankrupt stock of our large neighbours in Europe and America . . . '.[483] It may be suggested that the shape would remain unpredictable even if the ideas of the public decision-makers were not so derivative. It is difficult to prophesy which, if any, of the indigenous ideas jostling each other will acquire future dominance in the face of intense resistance from the entrenched establishment.[484]

As if to confirm de Paor's hopes and fears, the *Irish Independent* carried only two days later a stimulating article by Kevin O'Connor on Ireland as a 'nation caught in the middle of an identity crisis'.[485] For O'Connor, the crisis was 'about finding a way to cast off the protective skin of nationalism and still say "we are Irish" '. We no longer feel

the need to prove we're Irish by waving the three-leaved shamrock of race, language and Catholicism which were an imposition by nineteenth-century nationalists: valid for their time, distinguishing marks upon a dispossessed peasantry, patches of poverty and humiliation – aim marks in the shoot-out between Protestant landlord and Catholic peasant. A war not resolved until 1923. For us to bear now as distinguishing marks of a sovereign people, into the 1990s . . . ? You must be joking!

O'Connor's dismissal of the traditional trinity of identification tags derives in part from his revulsion at the brutality of the Provisional IRA, who have 'driven a wedge between North and South which will not be

481 L. de Paor, *Irish Times*, 18 July 1985.   482 Buckley, *Memory Ireland*, pp. 48–50.
483 De Paor, *Irish Times*, 18 July 1985.
484 D. Fennell, 'A state we don't know what to do with', *Irish Times*, 3 December 1986.
485 K.D. O'Connor 'Ireland – a nation caught in the middle of an identity crisis', *Irish Independent*, 20 July 1985.

bridged this century'. He finds both Irish Catholicism and the Irish language distasteful. Like the rest of us, he therefore sets to work to impose his own social construction of reality. Catholicism he declares, without regret, to be a declining force. 'All the figures show less attendance at religious practice.' His revulsion against Irish is graphically expressed

We don't want an imposed language at the price of being stopped in O'Connell Street by jackbooted gaelgeóirí and asked to spout Irish at the point of a gun. We know, deep down, that the real language of this country is the talk of the street. English as she is spoken with an Irish inflection. Which is to say one of the richest languages in the world, in its capacity to express colourfully, the myriad sensations of the human spirit.

There is, he believes, an alternative. Far from being a racial purist, O'Connor rejoices in belonging to 'the common mass of most mongrel Irishmen. A polyglot patchwork of races, cultures and religions which is all the stronger for being mixed.' He suffers 'from no ancestor worship, anymore than I suffer from ancestor inferiority'. He laments the anti-British neutrality of the Second World War, which 'designed as an expression of sovereignty, in fact left the Free State isolated from the postwar changes that swept Europe'. Authoritarianism therefore 'flourished in the Ireland of the late forties and fallow fifties', when 'a ferocity of imposed identity which was learned from the old Protestant ascendancy, passed on to a demoralised population . . . a passive people hobbled to it in the same old servile way'. But now, 'nationalism – the posture provoked by imperialism – is being replaced by pragmatism, now that nationalism has served its usefulness'.

Pragmatism can cover a multitude of postures. It is an even more elastic concept than nationalism itself. How does O'Connor portray his 'pragmatism'? It flourishes, apparently, as 'an organic attempt at redefinition'. By whom? 'Unwittingly among the crowds spilling out from U2 and rugby internationals, where a generation ago they came from Mass and Croke Park.' This vision of empty churches and a deserted Croke Park (the headquarters of the Gaelic Athletic Association) may be realised in the future. However, it bears no relation to 1985. The churches are not empty. And U2 is no substitute for religion. It is an alternative to the pop idols of a generation ago, not to Mass. The alternative to religion is not U2. The alternative to religion is nothing. Croke Park attendances at All-Ireland finals remain bigger by far than those at rugby internationals. There need be no incompatibility between enjoying gaelic games and rugby. But O'Connor writes, in the mirror image of the gaelic parochialism of a generation ago, which forbade members of the association to play 'foreign' games, as if a mutually exclusive choice must be made. The Irish apparently now aspire 'to British standards of living and leisure' and 'to emulate the culture of London more than bitter Belfast'. How does this differ from a generation ago? They then aspired equally emphatically to British standards 'of living and leisure'. The only difference is that British standards were then world standards. Now they have slipped sadly down the scale. If O'Connor is right, all that has happened is that the Irish have lowered their aspirations. What de Paor denounced as the derivativeness of the bankrupt mind, O'Connor welcomes as liberation. It duly transpires that despite his reference to 'postwar changes that swept Europe', his only real point of reference is London. He does, it is true, enquire 'who wants geometry through Irish inflicted on their children, when their future lies in Brussels or Strasbourg?' Despite his denial of any sense of 'ancestor inferiority', he appears here to share the assumption derived from an inferiority complex that the Irish are permanently incapable of providing a living for themselves in their own country, and must seek succour elsewhere. Indeed, he seems to envisage not just a trickle, but a flood of emigrants into the welcoming arms of the burghers of Brussels and Strasbourg. Presumably then it should be in French that geometry should be inflicted on Irish children, given the unsporting habit of the natives in those parts of continuing to speak their own tongue, despite the invasion of English as an EEC and tourist language.

Language clearly touches raw nerves in O'Connor's psyche. Despite his protestations of distaste for the authoritarianism of traditional Ireland, he wants the bilingualism of road signs reduced to monolingualism. Who, after all, bothers to read the road signs in Irish? Doubtless very few. But apparently they should not be entitled to have them even if they want them. They are an affront to the monoglot anglicised mind. Ironically, even his claim for 'English as she is spoken with an Irish inflection' as 'one of the richest languages in the world' already sounds anachronistic. The logic of his model, duly implemented by the apostles of uniformity, has left no scope for deviance from standard English. John A. Murphy has noted that while 'Hiberno-English, of an almost Syngeian quaintness, was the language . . . spoken in many parts of Ireland' in the 1940s 'the present generation speak conventional and idiomless English – the result of the culturally levelling influence of the media and more so, perhaps, of second level schooling. Hiberno-English which some optimists saw as a linguistic identity in its own right has proved to be purely a transitional phase.'[486] In so far as the distinctive quality of Hiberno-English derived from the transition to English of a Gaelic turn of phrase, it was doomed from the outset. 'The lore of the Irish' can no longer be applied to the bulk of Irish writing in English.[487]

---

[486] Murphy, 'Identity change', p. 148.
[487] H. Kenner, *A colder eye* (London, 1983), pp. 86–110, surveys, the transitional phase.

The description of Ireland as 'a polyglot patchwork of races, cultures and religions which is all the stronger for being mixed' amounts to heroic self-deception. The races in the Republic are Celt, Viking, Norman and English. Viking and Norman, however enriching their original historical contributions, are now amiable affectations. Only Celt and English are left for practical purposes. The religions are Catholic and Protestant. Few Protestants are left in the Republic. As O'Connor wishes to eliminate Irish, the 'polyglot patchwork of cultures', even if it existed, would soon be reduced to a monoglot.

The relentless pursuit of anglicisation inherent in O'Connor's 'organic attempt at redefinition' emerges from his presentation of his approach as a search for normalcy, as an escape route from the burden of a deviant history. For his 'three-leafed shamrock' of race, language and religion is not at all unique to the Irish concept of identity. It is the defining characteristic of normal European states and normal European peoples. The leaves combine, in varying degrees, depending on specific historical circumstances, to constitute the core of the individual identities of the European peoples. This is not to glorify them. They were very often abused in unworthy causes in various countries. The banners of nationalism, as of many another ideology, are bathed in innocent blood. But they cannot be cleansed by jettisoning one nationalism in favour of another. No sovereign European state has chosen to voluntarily shed its historic identity, forged out of these components, in the manner which O'Connor now advocates for Ireland. It is his image that is strikingly deviant, and positively hibernian in the presumption that this deviancy constitutes normalcy.

'Pragmatism' transpires, on closer scrutiny, to be nothing else than thoroughgoing anglicisation. It turns out to be that jaded alternative to an Irish identity, an English identity in Ireland. Or at least, the appearance of English identity. It is easy enough to transpose the English body to Ireland. It is far more difficult to transpose the soul, or the essence, of English identity. O'Connor's ideal therefore comes close to what Vincent Buckley considers Ireland already to be 'a nothing – a no-thing – an interesting nothing, to be sure, composed of colourful parts, a nothing-mosaic'.[488] The inhabitants of such a 'no-thing' are 'non-entities'. There is a good deal of truth, if not quite the whole truth, in Buckley's observation. O'Connor is entitled to indulge his ideal, which may indeed be shared by many. But he is not entitled to present it in so illusory a guise. For it is no more than a typical case of that 'sensitive provinciality' which 'produces a feeling of its inferiority to the metropolis; it feels the necessity and obligation to acknowledge the standards – moral, cultural, intellectual and political –

---

[488] Buckley, *Memory Ireland*, p. ix.

which are believed to obtain in the metropolis'.[489] The degree of self-deception involved makes the self-deception of traditional Ireland seem unimaginative by comparison.

O'Connor makes several shrewd individual points. It is precisely the blend of realism and fantasy in so intelligent an observer that excites curiosity and that points to the intensity of the crisis of identity. His attitude towards the language, in particular, exposes so visceral a resentment that the crucial role of the language in the Irish psyche must be explored further.

The relationship between language and national identity is notoriously complex.[490] Scholars, and not only in Ireland, are only now beginning to seriously grapple with the multiple implications of the historical role of language.[491] The historian must therefore tread warily, not alone because of the emotive nature of the subject, but because of his consciousness of the inadequacy of his analytical tools. But it is hardly going too far to say that but for the loss of the language, there would be little discussion about identity in the Republic. With language, little else seems to be required. Without language, only the most unusual historical circumstances suffice to develop a sense of identity. Those unusual circumstances existed in Ireland for perhaps two centuries. As that phase, broadly characterised by the reality, or the memory, of an obtrusive imperial presence, of a national revival, of a struggle for independence, draws to a close, the importance of the lost language as a distinguishing mark becomes more rather than less evident. As circumstances normalise, only the husk of identity is left without the language.

It is instructive to ponder the reasons advanced for the loss of the language in the eighteenth and nineteenth century. The most frequent argument is that the language had to be abandoned to ensure Irish participation in the economic progress of the modern world, because 'Irish doesn't sell the cow.' Only a knowledge of English could bring Ireland into the mainstream of material progress by facilitating inter-course with the more advanced British economy, and thus enabling the proverbial cow to be sold at a remunerative price. Strictly speaking, this argument would explain the acquisition of English, but not the loss of Irish, unless it be assumed that Irish brains were too small to accommo-

489 E. Shils, 'Metropolis and province in the intellectual community', in Shils, *The intellectuals and the powers*, p. 357.

490 I have found J. Edwards, *Language, society and identity* (Oxford, 1985) helpful, though I reach rather different conclusions on the Irish case, on which Edwards is an authority and to which he frequently refers.

491 W.J. Bouwsma, 'From the history of ideas to the history of meaning', *Journal of Interdisciplinary History*, 12, 2 (Autumn 1981), p. 290; J.G.A. Pocock, 'Languages and their implications', in Pocock, *Virtue*, p. 13.

date two languages, or that the Irish were simply too lazy, or too utilitarian, to be bothered with the less materially useful one.

We cannot know how the economy would have performed if the country had remained Irish speaking, but it seems not unreasonable to draw inferences from the economic performance of other small countries exporting to the English market. In one case, Ireland faced direct competition, almost literally in the 'cow' market, with such a country. Ireland enjoyed a cosy position on the English butter market until about 1870. Then Denmark began to enter the dairying industry seriously. Between 1870 and 1904, Irish exports rose from about 600 000 cwts per annum to just over 800 000.[492] Danish exports rose from 127 000 cwts to more than 1 500 000. The Danish performance easily eclipsed the Irish one. There were numerous reasons for the superior Danish achievement. Abandoning their obscure language in favour of English was not one of them. Knowledge of English was naturally indispensable for the marketing process. Yet the Danes did not jettison their own language to accommodate English. There were only 2 million Danes in 1880. Their superior economic performance has been widely linked to the national revival which fostered a growing sense of identity throughout the nineteenth century.[493] At the very least this loyalty to their language did not inhibit their performance.

This was the most spectacular case of direct competition between the linguistically progressive Irish and a more 'backward' culture that had not the wit to abandon its language. In more general terms, however, it can be seen that the burden of the small language did not suffice to prevent Sweden, or Norway, or the Netherlands, or Flanders, from exporting successfully to Britain, from growing more rapidly than Britain since the late nineteenth century, and from overtaking British living standards in the course of the twentieth century.

Finland offers a particularly instructive example. Here, if anywhere, was a poor, peasant, primitive, peripheral country, with a virtually impenetrable language. Fewer people spoke Finnish in 1870 than spoke Irish in 1850. Finnish living standards lagged well below Irish living standards in 1880, yet Finland achieved an exceptionally high rate of economic growth in the following century. Far from being associated with the abandonment of her language, her economic performance seems, if anything, to have derived a certain impetus from a highly self-conscious national revival, including considerable emphasis on the language as a

---

[492] C. Ó Grada, 'The beginnings of the Irish creamery system, 1880–1914', *EHR*, n.s., 30, 2 (May 1972), p. 286.

[493] A.S. Milward and S.B. Saul, *the economic development of continental Europe, 1780–1870* (London, 1973), pp. 502–3, 509–10.

bearer of national culture in defiance of imperial power.[494] Not only did Finnish children have to devote much of their time to learning their own obscure and internationally useless language. The second compulsory language in Finnish schools was for long Swedish, scarcely a language to provide the Finns with the cosmic perspective of a world tongue.

It is sometimes asserted that Irish lacked the vocabulary of the modern technological world, and was therefore an 'inefficient language'. The argument, even if true, is trivial. All languages have to regularly improvise new terms. All languages lacked an adequate vocabulary for the economic changes occurring since the mid eighteenth century. Vocabularies appropriate to industrial society had to be forged in all languages. They were. Obscure languages proved no barriers to industrialisation in nineteenth or twentieth-century Europe. The case closest to Ireland is Wales. To the extent to which the Welsh abandoned their language, and they clung to it far more tenaciously than the Irish, it was not because it could not cope with the linguistic demands of industrialisation. On the contrary, the industrialisation of South Wales proceeded in Welsh until it reached a point where an English-speaking immigrant labour force was enticed by the growth in job opportunities. Industrialisation brought anglicisation, not *vice versa*, and then only through direct occupation by English workers.[495]

The assumption that industrialisation was, through some mysterious mechanism, incompatible with minor languages, derives little support from the European record. Irish, incidentally, was spoken by as many, if not more, people in the early nineteenth century than Flemish, or Dutch (or Dutch and Flemish combined), or Danish, or Norwegian, or Swedish, or Finnish, or Basque, or Welsh. The rapid growth in the size of these peoples, combined with the rapid fall in Irish population since the famine, has led to a quite different population ratio today than that prevailing 150 years ago. Irish was not a particularly minor language by European criteria in the early nineteenth century.

As the Irish have recorded the slowest rate of growth of gross national product in the western world since the mid nineteenth century, it is difficult to believe that national economic performance could have been much more unsuccessful, at least by this measuring rod, had the country clung to the language. There may be no direct connection between the loss of the language and the economic performance. Abandoning the language as a master stroke in the struggle for material progress, however, scarcely seems to count among mankind's more inspired initiatives.

---

[494] W.A. Wilson, *Folklore and nationalism in modern Finland* (London, 1976), pp. 42ff.; Klinge, 'Aspects of the Nordic Self', p. 267.

[495] Glanmor Williams, 'Language, literacy and nationality in Wales', in Glanmor Williams, *Religion, language and nationality in Wales* (Cardiff, 1979), pp. 143ff.

If abandoning Irish was not a prerequisite for economic development, why did the Irish jettison their first language? The answer is to be sought mainly in their response to two other incentives which not only made acquisition of English attractive, but left Irish redundant for material purposes. Parents assumed, quite naturally, that their children would enjoy advantages as English-speaking rather than Irish-speaking emigrants. Once emigration became a virtual way of life after the famine, it made sense to compel the children to concentrate on the likely language of their adult lives. A certain paradox was involved here. English was allegedly embraced as the reputed language of economic growth. When adequate growth failed to materialise, emigration became an alternative. Once again English was embraced as the reputed language of effective emigration. Thus both economic growth, and lack of economic growth, apparently encouraged the drift to English. No other emigrant European people chose to abandon their language before emigrating. Germans, Swedes, Norwegians, Italians, Poles, Jews and others emigrated in substantial numbers to the United States. Only in America did they engage in language shift, and only relatively slowly did they abandon their own languages entirely, however rapidly and ardently they sought to embrace English.

It is difficult in the present state of evidence to decide whether the parental assumption that a knowledge of English would enhance the prospects of their emigrant children was in fact correct. The Irish made a spectacular mark in American public life – in politics, in municipal administration, in the police, in the fire services, as well as in trade unions and in the Catholic Church. Perhaps a natural disposition towards politics, inherited from their experience in Daniel O'Connell's various organisations, allied to their knowledge of English, predisposed the Irish to career paths in these particular directions. Yet Irish social mobility in the United States, respectable though it was, does not seem to have been decisively faster than that of any other white immigrant group, taking length of residence into account. There seems to be no definitive evidence, for instance, that a knowledge of English affected school performance in the United States.[496] When there are so many variables that cannot be held constant, and when regional experience varied so greatly, the safest conclusion at this stage seems to be that their knowledge of English affected more the manner than the degree of Irish mobility, more the route than the rate. If this be the case, then the natural but unproven assumption that a prior knowledge of English *must* have significantly improved their prospects in America may require modification.

The main reason why the Irish did not remain satisfied, as did other trading partners of England, with acquiring the modicum of English

[496] D. Ravitch, *The great school wars* (New York 1974), p. 178.

required for economic intercourse, while retaining their own language as the vernacular, was the nature of the state. As the role of the state expanded it became a major source of employment, of social mobility, and of favours. But the whole state apparatus was an agency of anglicisation. The more interventionist the state became, often in an effort to respond to nationalist 'grievances', the more pervasive became the pressure for anglicisation. When knowledge of English sufficed for all the transactions of public life, Irish became increasingly redundant. As literacy began to spread, it came to be equated almost solely with literacy in English, because it was needed mainly for contact with the state. The history of language shift in Ireland, therefore, is intimately bound up with political history. If Ireland had not come under English political control, even the closest economic contact need not have led to the loss of the language.

A unique language is not, in principle, a necessary source, or marker, of a distinctive identity. In practice, it usually is, at least in Europe, where it is not only in Poland that 'the language is the homeland'. Belgium and Switzerland, it is true, have no unique language of their own, but they have a unique language situation because of their mix of languages. Austria does not have a distinctive language. It is not, however, as if she had jettisoned her ancestral tongue. German is her historic language. The pull of language is so powerful that it took very unusual historical circumstances indeed for the Second Republic to opt for a more definite independence from Germany than the First Republic. Sensitivities about Austrian identity continue to affect historical controversy.[497]

It is therefore quite natural that the problem of identity should be acute in the South mainly because of the language situation. There might otherwise be much dissatisfaction with national performance, but there could be no anxiety about national identity. There is, in present circumstances, no substitute for the language. However exhilarating gaelic hurling and football may be at their best, however exuberant the beat of the *bodhrán*, however enriching 'the great resurgence of traditional music',[498] these are only details in the overall design of a distinctive culture. The language is now, for practical purposes, the design.

The importance, indeed the growing importance, of the role of language in Irish circumstances goes beyond the normal importance attaching to it more generally. Substituting English for Irish is not an 'ordinary' language shift. It powerfully reinforces the nature of the wider relationship between Ireland and Anglo-America. Ireland's historical and geographical circum-

---

[497] A lively controversy is summarised in R.G. Ardelt, 'Drei Staaten – zwei Nationen – ein Volk? oder die Frage' "Wie Deutsch ist Österreich"?', *Zeitgeschichte*, 13, 7 (April 1986), pp. 253–68.
[498] Murphy, 'Identity change', p. 149.

stances leave her exceptionally exposed to the influence of the two major English-speaking countries. When the language of those countries dominates international communications networks and global mass culture, then a tiny country, shorn of her own linguistic defences, is peculiarly vulnerable to inundation by the mass culture of the bigger countries. Given the exposure of Ireland to English mass media, the virtual domestication in Ireland of large areas of English and/or American music, sport, TV serials, etc., the language shift brings the incorporation into daily life of many features of English normalcy. Many of these may be harmless, or even desirable, in themselves. Some are extensively imported into other European countries. When they are communicated directly through English, however, rather than in translation, they assume a more pervasive role in the culture of the importing country. If some Scandinavian commentators can insist on the need for a 'cultural security policy' to ensure the 'national survival' of their own countries the vulnerability of Ireland appears all the more extreme.[499]

There are at least three other implications of the language shift. The universality of English offers Ireland an opportunity. It also poses a threat. It is convenient to have a vernacular command of a world language, but that language, by inducing a certain linguistic insularity, also erects a barrier between Ireland and the wider world. Knowledge of English has opened some doors for the Irish. It has, ironically, helped close many others. It has made the Irish bad linguists. They have been able to assume, in contrast to small countries who kept their languages, that once they had English as their vernacular, they need learn nothing else. The Irish have learned less effectively from the English-speaking world than have countries who retained their own languages. Precisely because their independence of language, and their knowledge of a wider range of languages, enabled them to preserve independence of mind, they were able to choose more discriminatingly among those features of English experience most appropriate to their own circumstances.

Ironically, Irish thinkers have contributed less to the thought of the English-speaking world than the leading thinkers in small European languages, much less in bigger ones. Ireland has, of course, contributed to world culture through outstanding writers in English, but few Irish contributions to the social thought of the English-speaking world can compare with those of Barth, or Rokkan, or Frisch, or Nurske, or Cassel, or Heckscher, or Ohlin, or Lindahl, or Myrdal, or Westermarck, or Allardt, or Tinbergen, or Daalder. This is not to imply that Ireland

[499] B. Hagtvet and E. Rudeng, 'Scandinavia, achievements, challenges', *Daedalus*, 113, 2 (Spring 1984), p. 249. For a synoptic survey of the Irish situation see G. Ó Tuathaigh, 'The media and Irish culture', in B. Farrell (ed.), *Communications and community in Ireland* (Dublin, 1984), pp. 97–110.

produced no thinkers of high quality in these fields, but their thought was often more provincial, even if they were reared in a world language, than that of thinkers from other small countries who learned English as a foreign tongue. Is it purely accidental that the sole European sovereign state in the twentieth century to have acquired the supreme gift of English as her vernacular in the nineteenth century should have made so insignificant a mark on international thought since independence? We conclude that it is provincialism of a pathetic kind to persuade ourselves that Ireland today would be necessarily a more incompetent or a more retarded society if she were Irish-speaking or bilingual rather than English-speaking.[500]

Something of the same syndrome may be found among Irish businessmen. There is little evidence of that widening of horizons, which knowledge of English reputedly brought, when the locomotive of European economic growth shifted from Britain to the mainland. Ireland then became somewhat more peripheral geographically. That was not the real problem. It became much more peripheral psychologically. The most rapidly-growing markets in the postwar world were located in different cultures, requiring command of different languages, familiarity with different consumption habits, different traditions of style and design, different mentalities. If Ireland failed to adjust to changing market opportunities, it was not because she clung to an obscure, petty, peasant patois. Ironically, her world language exerted a peripheralising influence on her perspectives. It erected a barrier between Ireland and both the language learning process and the wider learning process in general which was so crucial to her welfare.

Did language shift acquire particularly significant connotations in a culture where mastery of words long had to substitute for mastery of things, and where the power of the tongue was the only power the Irish were long in a position to exercise? Nuala Ní Dhómhnaill, a leading Irish language poet, recalls that in the Dingle Peninsula of her youth 'you were so poor that all you were left with was your tongue'.[501] It may be that there is an Irish emotional reality which is silenced in English. It may be too that many Irish no longer experience that emotional reality, that it has been parched out of them, that a particular stream of Irish consciousnes has dried up with the decay of the language. It may be also impossible to assess the psychic price of dispensing with a language that offered such potential for loquacious evasiveness, a language that has been described, with only a touch of Mylesian exaggeration, as one in which

---

[500] For sombre reflections on the derivativeness of Irish thought, see S. Ó Tuama, 'The Gaelic League idea in the future', in S. Ó Tuama (ed.), *The Gaelic League idea* (Cork, 1972), pp. 99–100.
[501] C. Carty, 'Translations', *Sunday Tribune*, 27 July 1986.

apart from words with endless shades of cognate meaning, there are many with so complete a spectrum of graduated ambiguity that each of them can be made to express two directly contrary meanings, as well as a plethora of intermediate concepts that have no bearing on either.[502]

Nevertheless, for all the fears of Stephen Dedalus, the Irish soul need not fret for ever in the shadow of English. It is not necessary to dramatise language loss for individuals in all circumstances as a traumatic experience. Gellner can rightly claim at one level that 'changing one's language is not the heartbreaking or soul destroying business which it is claimed to be in romantic nationalist literature. Highlanders in Glasgow became anglophone, Berbers in Marrakesh became arabophone, Czechs in Vienna, etc. etc.'[503] But these are mainly cases of individuals, or small groups, who move as internal migrants or as emigrants to embrace a new life in a community that already speaks another language, which they adopt. That is a quite different psychological experience than the collective abandonment of one's own language *in situ* in favour of the language of the conqueror, at just about the time when a growing sense of political estrangement from that conqueror is taking place, and when language is on the threshold of becoming both a symbol and a weapon in a conflict assuming a new intensity.

The issue is as elusive as it is important.[504] There seems sufficient evidence to indicate that the loss of the Irish language carries a host of psychological consequences, which do not necessarily apply in other situations of language shift, and which can only be tentatively addressed here. It would need the social psychologist or the cultural anthropologist to answer whether the loss of the language may not have affected the national personality by fostering further the inferiority complex that required as a reflex compensating mechanism an exaggerated anglophobia, leading, as Douglas Hyde sardonically observed, to the hibernian habit of denouncing England while imitating everything English. It may also have been a reason why the Irish have remained hyper-sensitive to English views of themselves, reflected recently in their indignation at the spate of Irish jokes on English television. Many Irish were incapable of seeing that these reflected much more on the condition of England than on that of Ireland (and that one or two of them were rather good jokes!).

The very assumption that not only acquiring the language of the conqueror but abandoning one's own was a prerequisite for material development was itself a culturally conditioned one, based on an

---

502 Flann O'Brien, *The best of Myles* (London, 1968), p. 278. For an instructive example see Corish, *Catholic experience*, p. 257.

503 Gellner, *Thought and change*, p. 165.

504 De Fréine, *Saoirse gan só*, surveys many of the issues. See also D.D. Laitin, 'Linguistic dissociation: a strategy for Africa', in J.G. Ruggie (ed.), *The antinomies of interdependence* (New York, 1983), pp. 317–68.

inferiority complex. It is natural for imperial powers to denigrate the cultures they destroy. The psychological requirement of the neo-imperialist mentality to still have a kaffir to kick intellectually, even if it be out of fashion physically, continues to lead to philistine observations on Irish by soi-disant cosmopolitans who, ignorant in the precise meaning of that term, confuse cosmopolitanism with their own particular provincialism.[505] The true cosmopolitan, it has been rightly observed, cherishes cultural diversity rather than uniformity, at least within broad parameters.[506]

The blind frenzy that can still be provoked by the defiant refusal of a conquered language to lie down and die exposes the destructive passions smouldering behind the façade of metropolitan rationality. It is more unusual for descendants of a destroyed culture to join in the disparagement of a lost language. It smacks of a parracidal impulse. The failure to revive the language has to be justified on the grounds that the discarded language wasn't worth reviving anyway. The values of the destroyer can thus be legitimised and internalised. Those Dublin children who taunted Leon Ó Broin's daughter at school in the 1930s because she spoke Irish[507] doubtless reflected the attitude of their parents, a servile breed craving social status through an ingratiating relationship with an axiomatically superior culture, consumed with loathing for a language 'associated with defeat, poverty or ignorance' that mocked the vanity of their social pretensions.[508] It would be nice to think that this dismissal of the language in certain 'respectable' quarters expressed the indignation of intrepid champions of higher intellectual values at finding their burning ambition to immerse themselves in other great cultures frustrated by the obligation imposed on their children to learn mere Irish. It would indeed be nice to think that.

Despite the festering resentment in some circles, the public attitude towards the language after 1922 was, as far as we can tell, broadly if inertly benign. All governments henceforth embraced the idea of revival, and promptly subcontracted the implementation of the policy to the Department of Education. The Department lacked the intellectual calibre to conceptualise the challenge correctly. In fairness to the Department, it was difficult for it to realise, in the then state of the intellectual infra-

---

505 See, for example, J. Vaizey, 'The mind of republicanism', in D. Watt (ed.), *The constitution of Northern Ireland* (London, 1981), pp. 57–8. See also the refutation by John A. Murphy, 'Comment', p. 69.

506 Hans Maier, 'Sprache, Nation, Kulturgemeinschaft', in *Möglichkeiten und Grenzen einer nationalen Geschichtsschreibung* (Madrid, 1984), p. 522.

507 Ó Broin, *Yesterday*, p. 105.

508 G. Ó Tuathaigh, Lecture in BBC Radio Ulster Series, 'People in Ireland', reported in *Irish Times*, 2 December 1986. See also M.I. Murphy, *Tyrone folk quest* (Belfast 1973), p. 67; M. Cruise O'Brien, 'The two languages', in O.D. Edwards (ed.), *Ireland*, p. 58 and *passim*.

structure, the magnitude of the endeavour on which it was embarking, and the extent of the cultural change involved in the effort to revive a language. The official mind was blinkered by the view that just as the schools had allegedly killed the language in the nineteenth century, so they could revive it in the twentieth. Apart from the fact that this grossly exaggerated the role of the educational system in the decline of the language, it failed to take cognizance of the fact that changed socio-economic circumstances would make it much more difficult to revive the language by the same route.[509] In any case, that officials should have considered a purely stylized literary command of the language, on an artificial series of restricted topics divorced from daily life, as adequate preparation for the real world, reflected the general quality of the Departmental mind at the time. Small wonder that the 1941 report of the Irish National Teachers Organisation, which dared dispel many illusions fostered by the pious litanies of progress in the Department's annual reports, roused the wrath of officialdom. No wonder either that the minister from 1932 until 1948, Tom Derrig (with the brief interlude of de Valera's tenure in 1939–40) bitterly and successfully resisted demands for an inquiry, even from the teachers themselves, into the effectiveness of the official approach. Sacred cows could not be submitted to the most cursory veterinary inspection. While it may be that 'the ferocious minister and his appartchiks' can be rightly described as 'merciless zealots, not to add unscrupulous bigots', the ultimate criticism has to be more of their intelligence than of their character.[510]

The failure, however, did not lie mainly in the schools. It was the blatant failure of the state itself to devise arrangements for the subsequent use of the language that largely discredited compulsory Irish. The children were given no incentive to master Irish as a living language, only as a dead one. The charade of Irish language tests for public employment, when everybody knew the language would hardly ever be used again, the whole fetid system of favouritism associated with language knowledge, as distinct from language use, inevitably left its mark, stamping the most idealistic and most important task undertaken by the new state as yet one more sleazy political racket. Genuine language lovers who 'loathed the way that the politicians, the pedagogues, the urbanised peasants had sucked the life and beauty from it'[511] were brushed aside. The characteristic combination of hypocrisy and incompetence precluded any possibility of increasing the number of Irish speakers, as distinct from increasing the nominal command of the language among a broadly benevolent but apathetic and sceptical populace. As a French observer has commented, the state 'fulfils

[509] Edwards, *Language*, p. 86.
[510] O. MacDonagh, 'The politics of Gaelic' in MacDonagh, *States of mind*, p. 124.
[511] H. Butler, '*The Bell*: an Anglo-Irish view' in Butler, *Escape from the anthill*, p. 149.

the letter of the project, the better to betray the spirit . . . it prefers to use Irish as a sort of symbol of nationality, more or less relegated to a ritualistic and ceremonial role'.[512]

Irish could only be revived from the top down. It wasn't. The cabinet, the Dáil, the political establishment in general, failed to give a lead. The refusal of the political, administrative, ecclesiastical, commercial and academic elites to be heard speaking Irish has hitherto doomed the revival. The challenge for the politicians and the administrators was not to compel children to learn to read or write Irish. It was to read and write it, and above all to speak it, themselves. Many senior civil servants in the first generation of independence had a genuine commitment to the revival. Others had not. Some were openly hostile. Finance tended to adopt an attitude of freezing disdain. Whitaker would be the first Secretary of Finance to be a language enthusiast. The Finance perspective was widely shared among 'practical men' throughout the country. Why waste time on so chimerical a cause when there were far more important matters calling for attention? Why retreat from a world language into a peasant 'patois' – and endure the attendant status loss for a lower middle class craving respectability?

The same thinking dominates the attitude of the technological determinists of the later twentieth century. It would be agreeably reassuring to feel that the economic failure of the state, taking one decade with another, could be attributed to the diversion of the time and energy of outstanding 'practical men' into a hopeless revival crusade. That is one excuse that even a people prolific in excuses have yet to dream up. Nor did the revival fail because 'practical men' were too busy creating a name for their country in other areas. The 'practical men' might even have been justified in their disdain for the revival – if only they had succeeded as 'practical men'. Despite occasional impressive individual performances, they did not. They simply had not got the class. The failure of the revival was more obtrusive than other failures, but it was cut from the same cloth.

The politicians naturally played the revival for its political potential. De Valera's own dedication cannot be doubted, but he failed to bring his senior party members with him, at least to the extent of getting them to speak Irish reasonably regularly.[513] The foot soldiers knew how to interpret the signals. The sprouting of voluntary organisations, good work though many performed, could not compensate for the effective indifference of the state.[514] 'As late as 1959 over one-third of the civil

---

[512] Peillon, *Irish society*, p. 189.

[513] Ó Néill, 'Eamon de Valera agus an Teanga', *Feasta*, 35 (1982).

[514] G. Ó Tuathaigh, 'Language, literature and culture in Ireland since the war', in Lee, *Ireland* p. 114. On voluntary work in the universities, see G. Ó Tuathaigh, 'Bunú an Chomhchaidrimh: Nóta ar an gCúlra', in S. Ó hAnnracháin (ed.), *An Comhchaidreamh: Crann a Chraobhaigh* (Dublin, 1985), pp. 9–16.

service had little or no Irish, while in gaeltacht areas, almost half the public servants were incompetent in Irish.'[515] Having resisted attempts to force it to think about the revival for a generation, the government largely ignored the recommendations of the commission on the revival of the language that reported in 1963. 'That the state showed little interest in harnessing the available expertise in linguistic planning in the late 1960s and early 1970s signalled the indifference of the authorities clearly enough.'[516] Irish was dropped as a compulsory subject for the Leaving Certificate and for civil service entry by the Cosgrave government in 1973. Only the fact that the National University has continued to insist on a pass in Irish in the Leaving Certificate for entry has prevented the total collapse of the language in schools. By the late 1970s, the population of the real Gaeltacht (as distinct from the political Gaeltacht, whose boundaries seem to have been drawn essentially to massage the flow of grants to political supporters) was calculated to be only 32 000, compared with more than ten times that number at the foundation of the state.[517]

Policy for about two decades has clearly been to let the language die by stealth. For once, the policy-makers are achieving success, although there has been a small but nonetheless striking efflorescence of voluntary education effort in some middle-class urban circles in the past decade. This may staunch the haemorrhage, but it can only revive the patient if it can capture some of the commanding political heights.

Not only the failure of the revival, but the ignominious manner of its failure, inflicted a further psychological burden on the indigenes. The shift from Irish to English was no purely neutral enterprise, with the cost-benefit ratio calmly and clinically calculated. It included a large element of psychological warfare. The conscious and explicit denigration of one language as inferior, and the conscious and explicit exaltation of another language as superior, were central to the psychology of the language shift. Irish, battered, bruised and humiliated, recovered some dignity through the revival efforts of the Gaelic League, and the idealism and intellect of many of the early enthusiasts. It then fell into bad company again with the founding of the state. The ethos of the official revival, despite the commitment of genuine revivalists, fostered precisely those qualities of national character that were accentuated by colonial experience, ambiguity, evasiveness, furtiveness, mendacity. The manner of the revival thus contributed more to reinforcing the inherited flaws in the national personality than to adapting, however gradually, the national character to the new dignity of independence.

The Welsh experience warns of the resentment that can be aroused

---

[515] *Ibid.*   [516] *Ibid.*, p. 117.
[517] *Ibid.*, p. 112; D. Fennell, 'The last years of the Gaeltacht', *Crane Bag*, 5, 2 (1981), pp. 839–42.

among determined monoglots by any attempt to extend bilingualism.[518] And yet, the Welsh experience is also an encouraging one. Despite the vicissitudes, and the still precarious condition of Welsh culture, bonded around the language, the Oxford History of Wales can claim that it 'had survived and had been triumphantly renewed, against all the odds' in the twentieth century.[519]

Reviving a language, if only to create a bilingual society, is a daunting challenge. The purpose of independence is, at least in part, to respond to daunting challenges. It would, no doubt, be an exaggeration to suggest that sovereignty was the final death blow for Irish! It need not have been. The historian exercising, however dangerously, his prophetic function, might declare that it still need not be. Despite all the mundane pressures to the contrary, despite the apparently imminent and inevitable victory of the big battalions, even cultural history may still have many futures.

The relationship between language shift and national performance is an elusive one. The connection between culture and material performance in general cannot be quantified. Many comfortable conventional assumptions about the contribution of language loss to material progress may not survive sustained scrutiny. In however complex and convoluted a way, it is quite possible that the manner in which the language was lost has damaged Irish potential for self-respect, with all the psychological consequences for behaviour patterns that flow from that, even in the purely material sphere. Material progress has itself come to be a component of identity, if only because it offers the most easily measurable criterion of national performance (even if measured wrongly!).[520] Identity cannot be divorced from the general level of national performance. The chances are that the international identity of a small country will depend disproportionately on its cultural contribution, defined in the widest sense, to the larger world. This does not amount to proclaiming a mission in the grandiloquent manner of nationalists of Mazzini vintage.[521] It does amount to winning respect through contributions of enduring quality to art and thought. Ireland's writers in English have brought her distinction, but there is no reason why a successful bilingual society could not foster a vibrant literary tradition, in English as well as in Irish, nor contribute significantly in thought as well as literature by drawing nurture from a distinctive rather than a derivative identity.

When identity posed so formidable a challenge for the relatively homogenous Republic, those trying to grapple with so sensitive an issue in an all-Ireland framework faced a peculiarly intractable problem, as the

[518] Gwyn Williams, *When was Wales?* (London, 1985), pp. 299–302.
[519] K. Morgan, *Wales: rebirth of a nation 1880–1980* (Oxford, 1982), p. 421.
[520] E. Gellner, *Contemporary thought and politics* (London, 1978), p. 156.
[521] Murphy, 'Identity change', pp. 143–6.

conveners of the New Ireland Forum soon discovered. The Forum was a remarkable occasion. It embarked on a conscious search for an Irish identity that would simultaneously embrace and transcend the conflicting identities of unionism and nationalism. It emerged out of fears for the future of constitutional nationalism in Northern Ireland, and ultimately in the Republic, generated by the effective Sinn Féin exploitation of public resentment at the inept British handling of the Maze hunger strikes in 1981. John Hume feared that unless Dublin could present an analysis of the Northern situation capable of convincing the British of their prime responsibility for the problem, and unless constitutional nationalists were able to agree on a set of proposals to which the British government would be obliged to respond, then his party might succumb to the Sinn Féin threat. The four main constitutional nationalist parties, Fianna Fáil, Fine Gael, Labour and the SDLP participated in the Forum, which amounted to a year-long public examination of conscience by constitutional nationalists, under the chairmanship of Colm Ó hEocha, President of University College Galway. Unionist parties refused to attend, but some individual unionists presented their viewpoints. The Forum initiated a range of studies concerning the economic and legal implications of unity, solicited submissions from the public, and 'invited oral presentations from thirty-one individuals and groups in order to allow for further elaboration and discussion of their submissions'.[522]

The twenty-seven members and fourteen alternate members of the Forum consisted solely of party politicians, who naturally found it impossible to completely shed their instinctive habits of thought. The drafting of the report called for high technical skill to blend the conflicting emphases of the party political actors.[523] This made their ability to agree on the actual text of the report, even if differences of interpretation instantly surfaced following publication, the more impressive. In its own eyes,

the establishment and work of the Forum have been of historic importance in bringing together, for the first time since the division of Ireland in 1920, elected nationalist representatives from North and South to deliberate on the shape of a new Ireland in which people of differing identities would live together in peace and harmony and in which all traditions would find an honoured place and have equal validity.[524]

The deliberations, if the opening statements of the four party leaders were to be taken at face value, were to be characterised above all by the determination 'to face reality'.[525] This amounted to little less than a

---

[522] New Ireland Forum, *Report* (Dublin, 1984), 1.6.
[523] Laver, 'Actors, words and images', pp. 122–7. This section also draws on J. Lee, 'Forging a new reality?', pp. 115–21 and B. White, *John Hume* (Belfast, 1984), pp. 261–7.
[524] New Ireland Forum, *Report*, 1.2.
[525] New Ireland Forum, *No. 1, Public Session*, 30 May 1983, pp. 2–3, 7, 19–20, 22.

challenge to forge a new political culture in Ireland, where reality had only fitfully intruded on illusion. To what extent did the results actually constitute a new stage in the evolution of Irish political identity?

The report can be read at many levels. In the context of the traditional vocabulary of European and English nationalism, not to mention Irish, it refers with quite exceptional generosity to the 'unionist identity and attitude'. It goes further than Irish nationalists had ever collectively gone before in publicly acknowledging the reality of a distinctive unionist identity, and in conceding the objective basis for unionist fears of a united Ireland. Indeed, the references to the unionist tradition are often so generous as to be patently unhistorical. The 'supremacy' dimension to the unionist reality only rarely intrudes.[526] More conceretely, the Forum's preferred solution of a 'unitary state'

would represent a constitutional change of such magnitude as to require a new constitution that would be non-denominational. This constitution could only be formulated at an all-round constitutional conference convened by the British and Irish Governments. Such a constitution would contain clauses which would guarantee civil and religious liberties to all the citizens of the state on a basis that would entail no alteration nor diminution of the provisions in respect of civil and religious liberties which apply at present to the citizens of Northern Ireland.[527]

This amounted to recognition, even by de Valera's own party, that the constitution of 1937 was unsuitable for the united Ireland whose *de jure* existence it proclaimed. It also managed to imply that a higher level of civil and religious liberties existed in Northern Ireland than in the South, in that the new constitution would have to bring the South's level up to that of the North rather than *vice versa*!

The report regularly referred to 'identity'. It devoted some attention to the nature of unionist identity.[528] Cursory though this was, it exceeded the specific attention devoted to the nature of Irish identity, whose essence has to be divined as a presumed polar opposite to unionist identity. The few references to the Irish language are either anodyne or disingenuous. In the 'unitary state' of blessed aspiration, 'the Irish language and culture would continue to be fostered by the state, and would be made more accessible to everyone in Ireland without any compulsion or imposition on any section'.[529] In the light of the facts, this was a euphemism for euthanasia. Earlier, the report apparently sought to make the language as big a bogey as religion for unionists, who are alleged to have historically feared 'forcible absorption . . . into an all-Ireland Republic, dominated as Unionists saw it by a Roman Catholic and a Gaelic ethos'.[530] Many

526 New Ireland Forum, *Report*, 3, *passim*; 4, esp. pp. 8–16. For a contrary view of the
      Forum see Bew and Patterson, *British State*, pp. 128–32 and Clare O'Halloran,
      Partition and the limits of Irish nationalism (Dublin, 1987), pp. 194–210.
527 New Ireland Forum, *Report*, 6.1.   528 *Ibid.*, 4.9.   529 *Ibid.*, 6.7.
530 *Ibid.*, 3.10.

unionists doubtless disliked the whole 'Gaelic' thing after 1922, but to suggest that they equated it in importance with the Catholic threat is simply unhistorical. The vehement unionist opposition to home rule existed long before national movements acquired any exotic Gaelic connotations. The gratuitous association of Gaelic with Catholic in the report would seem to have little to do with Northern Ireland, but rather to be a tactic adopted by some ardent anglicisers within the Forum to use the occasion to discredit the Gaelic dimension by associating it with Catholic as an obstacle to conciliation with unionists.[531]

A further striking feature of the report was its failure to confront the reality of Irish performance since independence. It evaded any analysis of the issue. No wonder that it took care to ensure that, of the thirty-one witnesses invited to present evidence, only one, David Harkness, was a practising professional contemporary historian. The report is suffused with the romantic but utterly unsubstantiated notion that:

Had the division not taken place, or had the nationalist and unionist traditions in Ireland been encouraged to bring it to an end by reaching a mutual accommodation, the people of the whole island would be in a much better position to benefit from its resources and to meet the common challenges that face Irish society, North and South, towards the end of the twentieth century.[532]

The two specific examples cited were hardly decisive. The report suggested that 'In the absence of co-ordinated long-term planning, capital investment in areas such as energy, education and health has entailed considerable duplication of expenditure'. Perhaps. But it is the quality of the expenditure that counts. Not a shred of evidence is advanced to suggest that the quality of 'planning' would have been superior in a united Ireland. Indeed, the denizens of the North indubitably enjoyed superior educational and health facilities since at least the Second World War. They probably gained from their insulation from the quality of Dublin thinking in these areas for much of that period. It cannot suffice to reply that Dublin thinking would have been improved by an influx of Northern civil servants. For the direction of development in the North was largely due to the pressure of the English connection. A big question mark hangs in any case over the appropriateness of highly centralised 'planning' in the fields of education and health. In many advanced countries, responsibility for both these activities lies, in varying degrees, with local and regional authorities. The report itself, when presenting its federal/confederal option, concluded that education and health 'might best be administered by the individual states'![533] Perhaps the most analytically incongruous allusions in the whole report, from the point of view of a correct

---

531 For a similar linking of Catholic and Gaelic see G. FitzGerald, 'Ireland's identity problems', *Etudes Irlandaises*, n.s., 1 (December 1976), pp. 138, 141.
532 New Ireland Forum, *Report*, 3.8.   533 *Ibid.*, 5.7.

perspective on Irish development, are the two references to the emigration
of Catholics from Northern Ireland since 1920, – in contrast to the total
lack of reference to emigration from the South![534]

The other example cited by the report of the damage inflicted by
partition was the 'particularly adverse . . . impact on areas contiguous to
the border'.[535] Not only were these areas 'detached from their trading
hinterlands, but the difficulties of their location were worsened by their
transformation into peripheral regions at the dividing line of two new
administrative units'. This argument may apply to the Northern side of
the border which, at least in nationalist grievance, and to some extent in
reality, was neglected by Stormont. The implication for the Dublin
administration was particularly damaging. If the border areas in the South
were treated as 'peripheral regions' it was only because Dublin took that
decision. The intense centralisation of the Dublin state did indeed
contribute to the fostering of 'peripheral regions'. The border areas were
among them. A 'unitary state', apparently to be at least as intensely
centralised as the existing Republic, would continue to have its peripheral
regions, unless a dramatic shift in mentality occurred among the central
administrators. There was little prospect of that.

The report rightly detected the gap between the potential and the
performance of the Dublin state since independence, however rapidly it
skated over the reality of the performance. It produced no compelling
evidence, however, to suggest that partition was a factor in the sloven-
liness of the national performance.

A year later the success of Bob Geldoff's Live Aid inspired Conor Brady
to reflect on the contrast between the constructive potential of the younger
generation and the sterility of the inherited performance. After reciting a
few recent personal reminiscences, which any reader could parallel from
their own experience, including the incompetence of the staff, and the filth
of the lavatories, on an Irish Continental ferry, the further filth of Coffin
Point, a picnic spot on the Shannon near Athlone, tastefully arrayed with
the latest designs in disposable nappies and plastic bottles by departed
picnickers, the sublime indifference of officials in permanent and pensionable employment in Dun Laoghaire Corporation to the inconvenience for
the mere citizenry caused by a burst water main, Brady saluted the success
of Geldoff's venture,

because something organised and run by an Irish person did not fall short of
expectations; because, although so many things characterise us as a slovenly,
careless people, Geldoff's marathon concert and Ireland's response to it showed
that we can still be inventive, thorough and generous . . . Geldoff is an unusual
and gifted individual, but not unique. There are hundreds of thousands of young
Irish people with a good deal in common with him. Somehow we have failed to tap

534 *Ibid.*, 3.9, 4.7.   535 *Ibid.*, 3.8.

their potential, to mobilise their capacities and their sense of idealism. What a terrible waste of energy and resources and enthusiasm, while so many small, but important, things remain to be done which could make this country a better place to live.[536]

Denis Brosnan expressed a similar sentiment: 'Irishness I define as the capacity of the Irish to accept and/or deliver standards which appal many of us . . . It is the antithesis of quality.'[537] The observations of Brady, the journalist, and Brosnan, the businessman, touch on a central theme of this book. That theme was wholly evaded in the Forum report. Are we to suppose that the despoilers of Coffin Point were deploying the nappies in protest against partition?

Ironically then, the report is singularly weak in confronting the reality of either Southern identity or Southern performance. It should not, however, be judged mainly on that score. It was, after all, more a party political and propaganda exercise in relation to Northern Ireland than a search for truth about the South. On those aspects of the South perceived to be most directly relevant to the North, particularly the nature of the constitution, it showed courage and imagination enough, at least at the rhetorical level. In addition, the participants struck on an astute compromise, from a party political viewpoint, between their preferred recommendation of 'a unitary state, achieved by agreement and consent, embracing the whole island of Ireland and providing irrevocable guarantees for the protection and preservation of both the unionist and nationalist identities'[538] – a proposal that had no chance whatever of immediate implementation – and the sketching of two alternative 'structural arrangements', a federal/confederal state, and joint authority, which left the door ajar, as did, more beckoningly, the simple invitation that 'the Parties in the Forum will also remain open to discuss other views which may contribute to political development'.[539]

It was on the basis of these proposals that Irish diplomats launched a publicity blitz in London, orchestrated by Noel Dorr, the accomplished ambassador, with John Hume adding his tireless advocacy to official Dublin efforts on the American and EEC circuits. After a summer during which the government raised Irish expectations to unrealistic heights,[540] Mrs Thatcher delivered her pungent 'out, out, out' dismissal of all three schemes mooted in the report in her Chequers news conference after a meeting with FitzGerald in November 1984. Her performance provoked a natural, if immature, public response of outraged indignation in Ireland. FitzGerald, despite the devastating humiliation, refused to indulge in the

[536] C. Brady, 'The lost potential of Geldoff's generation', *Irish Times*, 17 July 1985.
[537] *Irish Independent*, 29 November 1986.
[538] New Ireland Forum, *Report*, 5.7.   [539] *Ibid.*, 5.10.
[540] See *Irish Times*, 8 October 1984 for a report of Dr FitzGerald's address to the Fine Gael Árd Fheis, 6 October.

vindictive diatribe designed to appeal to the more primitive instincts of the indigenes. His dignity in duress rightly earned him immense credit. His reward would come just over a year later when, after patient and tenacious diplomacy, FitzGerald had the satisfaction of signing with Mrs Thatcher the Hillsborough Agreement of 15 November 1985.

Hillsborough emerged gradually out of intense dialogue between Dublin and London following the Forum Report. Despite occasional public hiccups in the exchanges, not to mention the Thatcherian belch, acute observers detected as early as the Westminster debate on the *Report* in July 1984 that:

There is now a consensus amongst the British parties that the government and parliament of the Irish Republic has a legitimate interest in the future governance of Northern Ireland. It is increasingly clear that Britain's future constitutional moves will endeavour to embody that interest in some form.[541]

Mrs Thatcher's press conference concealed the fact that the Chequers discussions marked a stage in the evolutionary process.

The Agreement intoned yet again – this time as an accord between the two sovereign governments registered at the United Nations as an international agreement – that no change could occur in the constitutional status of Northern Ireland without the consent of a majority of the province's population.[542] It then proceeded to establish an Inter-Governmental Conference designed to permit the Republic 'to put forward views and proposals' on specific topics, particularly on security and law and order, including 'the role and composition' of the Police Authority for Northern Ireland, and of the Police Complaints Board (art. 6). Dublin could also raise 'policy issues relating to prisons', including consideration of 'individual cases' (art. 7(d)).

Dublin had a right of consultation only, and no actual decision-making authority. Article 2(b), however, obliged both parties to make 'determined efforts' to resolve differences that might arise. Both also declared their desire for a measure of devolution within Northern Ireland on condition that the terms were acceptable to 'constitutional representatives of both traditions there' (art. 4(c)). The Agreement was to be formally reviewed by both governments within three years.

The influence of the Forum can be detected in the analysis of the situation underlying the Agreement. The essence of the Forum critique of British policy was that the unionist veto on territorial change had 'in practice . . . been extended into an effective unionist veto on any political change affecting the exercise of nationalist rights and on the form of government for Northern Ireland'.[543] Hillsborough in effect declared that

---

541 W.H. Cox, 'The politics of Irish unification in the Irish Republic', *Parliamentary Affairs*, 38 (1985), p. 453.
542 Anglo-Irish Agreement 1985, Art. 1(c).   543 New Ireland Forum, *Report*, 4.1.

Map 2 Catholics as proportion of the total population in the district council areas of Northern Ireland, 1981
Source: Kevin Boyle and Tom Hadden, *Ireland: a positive proposal* (Penguin Special, Harmondsworth, 1985), p. 36.

MOYLE 51%
BALLYMONEY 29%
BALLYMENA 19%
LARNE 24%
CARRICKFERGUS 8%
NEWTOWN-ABBEY 13%
NORTH-DOWN 9%
ARDS 13%
BELFAST 38%
CASTLE-REAGH 8%
ANTRIM 33%
LISBURN 21%
DOWN 59%
BANBRIDGE 28%
CRAIGAVON 41%
NEWRY and MOURNE 74%
COLERAINE 24%
MAGHERAFELT 57%
COOKSTOWN 53%
ARMAGH 45%
LIMAVADY 54%
DUNGANNON 53%
DERRY 68%
STRABANE 61%
OMAGH 64%
FERMANAGH 54%

30 km
20 miles

unionists 'have no veto on policy formulation within Northern Ireland'.[544] The Forum stressed that the problem had to be tackled from outside as well as from inside the North, 'because the problem itself transcends the context of Northern Ireland'.[545] As had earlier been observed:

one cannot ignore the British and Irish dimensions, if only because the problem would be quite different if Britain and Ireland did not exist. If the Protestant people of Ulster did not feel a particular affinity for Britain, and if the Catholic people of Ulster did not feel a particular affinity for the Republic of Ireland there might still be an Ulster problem, but it would be a quite different Ulster problem from the present one and the options open to the conflicting communities would be significantly different. The extreme Irish nationalist pretence that Britain should not be involved in any way, and the extreme British nationalist pretence that Ireland should not be involved in any way provide a recipe for continuing conflict, and postpone the possibility of any enduring solution.[546]

The Agreement could in no way be regarded as approximating the 'joint authority' possibility sketched by the Forum. 'An Inter-Governmental Conference, to the services of which the Republic contributes five or six civil servants', it has been noted, 'can only by a great stretch of the admittedly paranoid unionist imagination be regarded as joint sovereignty.'[547] Nevertheless, the thinking behind the 'joint authority' section of the Forum Report clearly influenced Hillsborough. Like 'joint authority', Hillsborough was 'an unprecedented approach to the unique realities that have evolved within Ireland and between Britain and Ireland'. Like 'joint authority', Hillsborough included an 'enabling provision for the exercise of major powers by a locally elected assembly and executive', if unionists agreed to accept a power-sharing arrangement. Like 'joint authority', the hope behind Hillsborough was that

structures would . . . be provided with which the nationalists in the North could identify, which might reverse their progressive alienation from existing structures. Security arrangements in which for the first time both nationalists and unionists could have confidence could be developed, thus providing a basis for peace and order.[548]

Some of the thinking behind the Agreement was, no doubt, opportunistically short term. Britain sought quick returns in the area of security through closer cooperation with the Republic. Dublin hoped to halt the rise of Sinn Féin by arresting the spread of alienation among Catholics. It

---

[544] B. O'Leary, 'The Anglo-Irish Agreement: folly or statecraft?' *Western European Politics*, 10, 1 (January 1987), p. 7. See also M. Connolly and J. Loughlin, 'Reflections on the Anglo-Irish Agreement', *Government and Opposition*, 21, 2 (Spring, 1986), p. 150.

[545] New Ireland Forum, *Report*, 4.2

[546] J.J. Lee, 'Sub-national regionalism', p. 117. See also Cathal B. Daly, 'Violence destroys the work of Justice', *The Furrow*, 31, 2 (February 1980), p. 84.

[547] Cox, 'An appraisal', p. 94.   [548] New Ireland Forum, *Report*, 8.2 and 8.7.

took the risk of appearing to become implicated in potentially sectarian actions – or actions that might be construed as sectarian – in the legal and security areas. In the short term, it might seem that the returns on the investment to both sides would fall far short of the costs involved, particularly if unionist and nationalist extremists intensified their destabilising activities. In the longer term, however, Hillsborough offered hope, as a foundation if not as a completed structure.

Hillsborough has been called 'a unique and imaginative attempt on the part of two sovereign states to bend their constitutions to a joint endeavour to manage a mutually troublesome frontier region, within the framework of existing boundaries and sovereignties'.[549] If there were 'no real parallels' to the arrangement in international law, that seemed singularly appropriate.[550] There were 'no real parallels' to Northern Ireland elsewhere either. It was precisely because Hillsborough was a unique arrangement that it offered some hope, however uncertain its initial prospects, that the beginning of the end of the Ulster tragedy was at last coming into sight. Northern Ireland was an abnormal regime. Trying to cope normally with abnormalcy was itself abnormal.

Hillsborough was the first attempt by the two sovereign governments to escape from the paralysis of zero-sum thinking in connection with the North, of an all or nothing conflict about sovereignty in which one side's gain could only be the other side's loss. This in itself involved a shift in the perspectives of both governments. In particular, London's acceptance of Dublin's right to make certain official representations implied a recognition that partition had not solved the Ulster Question. It conceded that the nationalist areas – amounting to over half the area of Northern Ireland – ought not to be ruled simply as occupied territory.

It was only to be expected that extremists on both sides would denounce the Agreement. Whereas Hillsborough was broadly welcomed by representatives of the majority of Northern nationalists, it was rejected by the overwhelming majority of unionists. It still seemed extraordinarily difficult for even moderate unionists to think in terms of nationalist equality within Northern Ireland, much less to contemplate any role for Dublin. A relatively restrained Official Unionist response to the Forum Report had observed that

the sight of Irish policemen on Northern Irish streets would inevitably produce a tremendous reaction. The direct involvement of Irish officials in governing Northern Ireland would be a source of great resentment. The tensions thus created would be readily exploited by terrorist organisations . . .[551]

549 W.H. Cox, 'Managing Northern Ireland inter-governmentally: an appraisal of the Anglo-Irish Agreement', *Parliamentary Affairs*, 40, 1 (January 1987), p. 80.
550 J.F. O'Connor, 'Agreement gives North new international status', *Irish Times*, 21 November 1985.
551 Quoted in Kenny, *Hillsborough*, p. 58.

This sounds reasonable enough. Yet the writer seemed oblivious to the fact that precisely this scenario had prevailed for more than half a century in an even more extreme reverse version in nationalist areas within Northern Ireland. In this case, however, the 'great resentment' and 'tremendous reaction' were denounced as unnatural. The instinctive assumption was that Catholics were not entitled to Protestant feelings. Until unionists went some distance towards self-examination of the type that nationalists, however haltingly, had begun, it would be impossible for them to escape from the paralysing shackles of supremacist thinking.

Hillsborough offered unionists the chance to finally escape from those shackles, little though they appreciated the opportunity in the immediate aftermath of the Agreement. An interesting aspect of Hillsborough-type thinking was that it could be applied to protect unionist identity in the face of a nationalist majority just as it could be initially applied to defend the identity of a nationalist minority.[552] If a nationalist majority was to emerge in the North, as seemed possible on some demographic projections – though population projections are notoriously fallible – the unionist use of the majoritarian democracy argument would presumably be undermined even among those who reject the contention that Northern Ireland is in any case an artificial political entity. The Ulster Question would not disappear, however, if Catholics were to constitute 51 per cent of the population of Northern Ireland. There would remain a unionist majority in the present Protestant heartland in the north-east of the north-east. Could the unionists of Antrim, north Down, north Armagh and east Londonderry be expected to meekly surrender their birthright and enter a united Ireland? If their fate under a Dublin regime were to be really as appalling as they now assert, could it be assumed that they would go quietly, or that they should go quietly? All the arguments unionists have found compelling for a six-country Northern Ireland could be advanced more credibly for a genuine Protestant redoubt in the north-east.

Fifty years ago the German Minister to Ireland anticipated the issue. Protestant contempt for 'inferior and incompetent' Catholics would, he believed, provoke armed unionist resistance even if a majority in the North should vote for unification.[553] The performance of the Dublin state in the past half century scarcely provides decisive evidence to persuade unionists of the capacity of Irish Catholics to rule themselves well, much less to rule Protestants.[554] It is in any case inconceivable that Britain could quietly withdraw, oblivious to the implications of massive unionist unrest, in the event of Dublin seeking to assume active sovereignty over the

---

[552] Kenny, *Hillsborough*, p. 55.
[553] PA AA, Hempel-AA, A 183, 20 December 1937, England–Irland I.
[554] The exaggerations and occasional distortions in R.L. McCartney, *Liberty and authority in Ireland* (Derry 1985), should not divert attention from the many valid points he shrewdly makes.

North. Stability in Ireland must remain a British interest. From a strategic point of view too, unconditional British withdrawal seems highly unlikely. Even if the British wished to depart – itself a distinctly doubtful assumption, despite lachrymose London rhetoric to the effect that Britain would gladly leave if only the impossible indigenes could be persuaded to dwell in peace with one another – they would presumably come under strong NATO pressure to acquire compensatory assurances from the Irish authorities. Though assumptions about the nature of a future war may have changed in the meantime, it seems reasonable to assume that 'the denial of Ireland to enemy forces', an objective 'already encompassed' in NATO strategy in 1950, and reconfirmed in 1960, remains 'an unavoidable principle of United States security'.[555] It also seems likely that it remains American as well as British policy that any settlement of the partition question 'should provide suitable guarantees for the strategic unity of the British Isles in time of war, so that the full cooperation of Ireland would be assured and bases and other necessary facilities would be made available'.[556]

Hillsborough raised the possibility that the relative roles of the British and Irish governments in the North might shift over time. Both London and Dublin are now engaged in a gradual learning process, as indeed are the two communities in the North. Sixty years is a short period in the history of Catholic/Protestant relations in Ulster. It is far shorter again in the history of Ireland. Irish statesmen, whatever about British, have a moral obligation to look to the longer-term implications of their Northern policy for North as well as South. An enduring solution is more important than a quick 'solution' for all the participants, including Dublin, where the regime might prove more vulnerable than the Protestant people of Ulster who, in the last analysis, can defend themselves, to the consequences of a precipitate British withdrawal.

There can be no permanent civilised solution to the Ulster Question within the terms of reference of either triumphalist unionism or triumphalist nationalism.[557] For a Catholic supremacy to simply supersede a Protestant supremacy in the North would be as massive a defeat for the founding principles of Irish republicanism, however dishonoured those principles have been in practice, as it would be for Ulster unionism. Pedestrian though the performance of unionist government may have been in Ulster, historically the unionist people are no petty people. If unionists are ever to enter into closer association with the Republic, then

---

555 FRUS, 1950, III, Relations of the United States with Ireland, p. 1477; (TL Truman Papers, President's Secretary File, Box 209) CIA Report, *Ireland*, SR-48, 1 April 1949; Fanning, 'The United States and Irish participation in NATO', pp. 41, 48.
556 FRUS, 1950, III, Relations of the United States with Ireland, p. 1470.
557 P. Alter, 'Wandel und Kontinuität des Nationalismus in Irland', in H.A. Winkler (ed.), *Nationalismus in der Welt von heute* (Göttingen, 1982), p. 50.

the higher they can legitimately hold their heads as that association develops, the better not only for Ulster, but for Ireland – and for Britain.

It is difficult to see such a relationship developing in a healthy manner as long as Protestants remain fearful about the threat to their identity. The safest way to provide some reassurance is to devise arrangements for a continued British role in Northern Ireland as long as a substantial number of unionists desire that, even after any putative transfer of sovereignty from London to Dublin in however distant a future. It is important for Ireland, no less than for Ulster, that 'the essential minimum conditions of the Protestant sense of identity (or way of life) be guaranteed and cherished', in any evolving triangular relationship between London, Dublin and Belfast.[558]

It is therefore desirable that unionists compose themselves. The nationalist temptation to indulge in *schadenfreude* at 'the disarray of Loyalist parties'[559] should be resisted. That would be to reduce a national issue to a tribal level once more. It is in the national interest that unionists should constitue a confident and coherent political community rather than a 'demoralised and divided' one.[560] Only when unionist self-confidence no longer needs to cling to the crutch of sectarian supremacy can the unonist people achieve their own full potential.

Only time can tell how far the hopes reposed in the Anglo-Irish Agreement, or the fears roused by it, were justified. The Agreement was vulnerable from many directions, unonist and nationalist, inside and outside Northern Ireland. It could collapse through a lack of will on the part of either the British or the Irish governments. The details of the Agreement mattered less than the spirit in which it would be implemented. Indeed, the phraseology left much to depend on British goodwill. The signatories, for instance, after some distinctly disingenuous references to the role of violence, declared they would introduce legislation to give effect to the wishes of a future putative Northern majority for unification only if 'a majority of the people of Northern Ireland clearly wish for and formally consent to the establishment of a united Ireland . . .' (Art. 1(c)). This clause was as potentially fertile in misunderstanding, confusion and recrimination as Art. XII of the Anglo-Irish Treaty of 1921. Who would define 'clearly'? What did 'formally' mean? Did 'a majority of the people' mean a majority of the 'people' or of the 'electorate'? (Due to different age structures, Protestants could be in a majority among the electorate, but in a minority among the 'people'.) These may be academic points for the foreseeable future. They may not always remain so. In a more short-term

---

558 C. Townshend, 'Fifteen years on', *Times Literary Supplement*, 1 November 1985, p. 1232.
559 P. Arthur, 'Northern Ireland: the "unfinished business" of Anglo-Irish relations', in P.J. Drudy (ed.), *Ireland and Britain since 1922*: Irish Studies 5 (Cambridge, 1986), p. 176.
560 *Ibid.*

perspective, the timing, procedures, and implications of the review process were left strikingly vague. It may be presumed that this apparent casualness on the part of experienced negotiators was deliberate. It presumably reflected a desire on both sides to avoid testing the implications of the Agreement through an untoward anxiety to achieve premature precision in defining what exactly they meant, in the hope that agreed interpretations would emerge as part of the process itself. That was a legitimate negotiating tactic. But it left a great deal dependent on London's continuing acceptance of the Forum analysis.

Yet, if the hope 'that two crazed peoples may make an end'[561] was ever to be realised, then it had to be along some such lines as those sketched in the Agreement, however many vicissitudes the process might suffer. The ultimate agreement, from an Irish perspective, had to be one between Dublin and Belfast. But agreement between Dublin and London was a practical prerequisite for that internal agreement, given Belfast's refusal to talk to Dublin as long as it felt completely covered by London's gun.

If Hillsborough was more than a mere tactic on the English side, the dawning of a recognition that the healing of the Ulster wound required long-term treatment, then it could come to be regarded as having launched a historic process of genuine conciliation between Britain and Ireland. Anglo-Irish relations remained affected long after Irish independence, and to some extent still remain so, by the characteristic English combination, in matters Irish, of ineptitude and condescension,[562] reciprocated by characteristic Irish sensitivity to English condescension – a sensitivity natural enough in the historical circumstances, for the colonial victim of an imperialist relationship rarely finds itself taken as seriously in a post-colonial era as pubescent self-esteem demands. Yet Dublin had, despite occasional opportunism and pusillanimity, taken at least as responsible an attitude as London towards the exceedingly difficult Ulster Question since 1968. Hillsborough may come to be recognised as a milestone on the way to open and genuine friendship, as distinct from the more familiar type of furtive accommodation, between Ireland and England, and as a necessary step on the tortuous path to an enduring settlement within Ireland – unless it turns out to be one more futile initiative in a long and gloomy chronicle.[563]

561 Montague, *The dead kingdom*, p. 51.
562 J. Peck, *Dublin from Downing Street* (Dublin, 1978), pp. 16–19; P. O'Farrell, *England and Ireland since 1800* (Oxford, 1975), pp. 105–9.
563 For a sombre assessment, see C.C. O'Brien, 'Ireland: the mirage of peace', *New York Review of Books*, 21 April 1986.

BIBLIOGRAPHY

This bibliography includes titles to which I had access before the summer of 1987, and which are cited in the notes. It does not purport to be an exhaustive compilation of work on twentieth-century Ireland, much less of work that has influenced my understanding of Irish history

Primary sources

Unpublished documents

Dublin
State Paper Office
Cabinet Minutes
Cabinet Secretariat files
National Library of Ireland
Frank Gallagher papers
Schrier collection
Vocational Organisation Commission: Minutes of evidence
University College Dublin Archives
Ernest Blythe papers
Patrick McGilligan papers
Richard Mulcahy papers

London
Public Record Office
Cabinet Office
CAB 24   Cabinet Papers (1937)
CAB 27   Irish Situation Papers (1937); Irish Negotiations (1938)
PREM 1   Commonwealth Attitudes towards Germany and Czechoslovakia (1938)
PREM 3   Mr Chamberlain's negotiations with Mr de Valera and Lord Craigavon (1940)
PREM 4   Danger of Invasion by Germany (1940)
Foreign Office
FO 371   Liesching Report (1939)

Dominions Office
DO 114–117   Neutrality of Éire in World War (1939–1945)

Bonn
Politisches Archiv des Auswärtigen Amtes
Büro Staatssekretär
Irland, 1 (1939–40)
USA, 3 (1940)
Politische Abteilung II
Politische Beziehungen zwischen England und Irland, 1, 2 (1936–1939)
Dienststelle Ribbentrop
Vertrauliche Berichte, Teil I: 3, 4 (1940)

Freiburg
Bundesarchiv-Militärarchiv
OKW/Amt Ausland-Abwehr: Kriegstagebuch der Abwehr II
OKW/Wehrwirtschafts-und Rüstungsamt: Irland (1938–1944)

Independence, Missouri
Harry S. Truman Library
Acheson Papers
Eben Ayers Diary
Francis P. Matthews Papers
Transcript, oral history interviews: T.K. Whitaker, F.H. Boland, Tom Murray, in
R.J. Raymond, 'Ireland in the European Recovery Programme: 1947–53'
(1978).
Truman Papers.

Official publications

Debates and reports
Minutes of evidence taken by the Committee on Irish Finance, with appendices.
H.C. 1913 (Cd. 6799), xxx
Report on recruiting in Ireland, H.C. 1914–16 (Cd. 8168), xxxix
Report of the proceedings of the Irish Convention. H.C. 1918 (Cd. 9019), x
Dáil Éireann. Official Report for the period 16–26 August 1921 and 28 February
to 8 June 1922 (1922)
Dáil Éireann. Parliamentary Debates: Official Report 1922–
Constitution of the Irish Free State (1922)
Report of Commission on Agriculture (1924)
Report of Fiscal Inquiry Committee (1924)
Report of Old Age Pension Committee of Inquiry (1926)
Commission of Inquiry into the civil service, 1932–1935: interim and final report
(n.d. 1935)
Bunreacht na hÉireann (Constitution of Ireland) (1937)
Report of the Commission of Inquiry into Banking, Currency and Credit. P. no.
2628 (1938)

Report of Dublin Housing Inquiry (1943)
Report of Commission on Vocational Organisation, 1943. P. 6743 (1944)
Report of the Tribunal appointed by the Taoiseach on the 7th day of November,
1947, pursuant to resolution passed on the 5th day of November, 1947, by
Dáil Éireann and on the 6th day of November, 1947, by Seanad Éireann.
P. 8576 (1948)
Long-term Recovery Programme. P. 9198 (1948)
Report of the Commission on Emigration and other population problems.
Pr. 2541 (1956)
Economic Development. Pr. 4808 (1958)
Programme for economic expansion. Pr. 4796 (1958)
Science and Irish economic development. Pr. 8975. 2 vols. (1966)
Investment in education. Report of a survey team appointed by the Minister for
Education in conjunction with the OECD. Pr. 8311. (2 vols.) (1967)
Report of Commission on Higher Education. 2 parts: Pr. 9326; Pr. 9588 (1967)
Report of the Committee on the Constitution. Pr. 9817 (1967)
Report of Public Services Organisation Review Group (Devlin Report). Prl. 792
(1969)
Disturbances in Northern Ireland (Cameron Report) (Cmd.) 532 (1969)
The accession of Ireland to the European Communities. Prl. 2064 (1972)
Posts and Telegraphs Review Group Report (Dargan Report), Prl. 7883 (1979)
National Development 1977–1980. Prl. 6836 (1980)
The Way Forward. Pl. 1061 (1982)
Proposals for a plan. Prl. 2309 (1984)
Industrial Policy. Pl. 2491 (1984)
Building on Reality. Prl. 2648 (1984)
Serving the country better: a White Paper on the Public Service. Pl. 3362 (1985)
A new institutional structure for the Central Statistics Office. Pl. 3483 (1985)

Statistical sources
Agricultural statistics 1847–1926. SO. I, 22 (1928)
Agricultural statistics 1934–56. Pr. 4335 (1960)
Census of Ireland
Census of Industrial production
Central Bank of Ireland: *Annual Reports* and *Quarterly Bulletins*
Irish Trade Journal
Statistical Abstract
Ulster Yearbook

National Economic and Social Council (NESC) Reports
12   *Educational expenditure in Ireland* (1975)
25   *Towards a social report* (1977)
28   *Service Type Employment and Regional Development* (1977)
46   *Irish Forestry Policy* (1979)
56   *Industrial policy and development: a survey of literature from the early*
1960s to the present (1981)
57   *Industrial Policy and the Regions* (1981)

59 *The importance of Infra-structure to industrial development in Ireland –*
   roads, telecommunications and water supply (1981)
64 *A review of industrial policy* (1982)
67 *An analysis of job losses in Irish manufacturing industry* (1983)
78 *Information for policy* (1985)
83 *A strategy for development, 1986–1990* (1986)

Diplomatic documents
DDI, Series 9, IV
DGFP, Series D, I, IX, X
FRUS, 1940, III; 1950, III

Newspapers and periodicals

The following have been cited extensively:
Irish Independent
Irish Press
Irish Times

The following have been cited on specific topics:
Belfast Evening Telegraph
Belfast Newsletter
Catholic Bulletin
Catholic Mind
Clare Champion
Confederation of Irish Industry Newsletter
Connacht Tribune
Connaught Telegraph
Cork Examiner
Corriere della Sera
Daily Express (Dublin)
Daily Telegraph
Economist
Financial Times
Freeman's Journal
Hibernia
Irish News
Kerryman
Kilkenny People
Leader
Leinster Leader
Limerick Leader
Nenagh Guardian
Neue Zürcher Zeitung
Observer (London)
OECD Economic Surveys: *Ireland*
Roscommon Herald
Round Table

Standard
Statist
Sunday Independent
Sunday Press
Sunday Tribune
Thom's Directory
Times
Tipperary Star
Wicklow People

Secondary sources

Books, articles and theses

Adams, M., *Censorship: the Irish experience* (Dublin, 1968).

A.E. (G.W. Russell), *Cooperation and nationality* (Dublin, 1912; 1982 edn).

Akenson, D.H., *Education and enmity: the control of schooling in Northern Ireland 1920–50* (Newton Abbot, 1973).

The United States and Ireland (Cambridge, Mass., 1973).

'Was de Valera a republican?', *Review of Politics*, 33, 2 (1971).

A mirror to Kathleen's face: education in independent Ireland 1922–1960 (London, 1975).

Alapuro, R. and Allardt, E., 'The Lapua Movement: The threat of Rightist takeover in Finland, 1930–32', in J.J. Linz and A. Stepan (eds.), *The breakdown of democratic régimes: Europe* (London, 1978).

Aldcroft, D., *The European economy 1914–1970* (London, 1978).

Allardt, E., 'Contemporary sociology in Finland' in R.P. Mohan and D. Martindale (eds.), *Handbook of contemporary developments in world sociology* (Westport, Connecticut, 1975).

Allardt, E. and Valen, H., 'Stein Rokkan: an intellectual profile', in P. Torsvik (ed.), *Mobilisation, centre-periphery structures and nation-building* (Bergen, 1981).

Alter, P., 'Nordirland zwischen Bürgerkrieg und Reformen', *Aus Politik und Zeitgeschichte*, B.35–36 (1970).

'Wandel und Kontinuität des Nationalismus in Irland', in H.A. Winkler (ed.), *Nationalismus in der Welt von heute*, (Göttingen, 1982).

Altermatt, U. and Garamvölgyi, J. (eds.), *Innen- und Aussenpolitik* (Berne, 1980).

Anderson, A.B., Sinclair, P.A., Bolaria, S.B., and Parvev Wakil, S., 'Sociology in Canada: a developmental overview', in R.P. Mohan and D. Martindale (eds.), *Handbook of contemporary developments in world sociology* (Westport, Conn., 1975).

Andersen, P.S., and Åkerholm, J., 'Scandinavia', in A. Boltho (ed.), *The European economy* (Oxford, 1982).

Andrews, C.S., 'Comment', in B. Chubb and P. Lynch (eds.), *Economic development and planning* (Dublin, 1969).

Man of no property (Dublin, 1982).

Ardelt, R.G., 'Drei Staaten – zwei Nationen – ein Volk?, oder die Frage: "Wie Deutsch ist Österreich"?' *Zeitgeschichte*, 13 (1986).

Arensberg, C., *The Irish countryman* (New York, 1937).

Arensberg, C. and Kimball, S., *Family and community in Ireland* (Harvard, 1940).

Arnold, B., *What kind of country?* (London, 1984).

Arrow, K.J., *The limits of organisation* (New York, 1974).

Arthur, P., *The people's democracy* (Belfast, 1974).

    Government and politics of Northern Ireland (London, 1980; 2nd edn 1984).

    'Northern Ireland: the "unfinished business" of Anglo-Irish relations', in P.J. Drudy (ed.), *Ireland and Britain since 1922*, Irish Studies V (Cambridge, 1986).

Aunger, E.A., 'Religion and occupational class in Northern Ireland', *ESR* 7 (1975).

Bailey, F.G., *Gifts and Poison* (London, 1971).

Bailyn, B., 'The challenge of modern historiography', *AHR*, 87 (1982).

Bairoch, P., 'Europe's gross national product, 1800–1975', *Journal of European Economic History*, 5 (1976).

    'L'Economie suisse dans le contexte européen: 1913–1939', *Schweizerische Zeitschrift für Geschichte*, 34 (1984).

    'The main trends in national economic disparities since the Industrial Revolution', in P. Bairoch and M. Levy-Leboyer (eds.), *Disparities in economic development since the Industrial Revolution* (London, 1981).

Baker, S., 'Nationalist ideology and the industrial policy of Fianna Fáil: the evidence of the *Irish Press*', *Irish Political Studies*, 1 (1986).

Baker, S.E., 'Orange and green', in H.J. Dyos and M. Wolff (eds.), *The Victorian city: image and reality* (London, 1973).

Banfield, E., *The moral basis of a backward society* (New York, 1958).

Bannon, M.J., 'Irish urbanisation: issues in the built environment'? in An Foras Forbartha, *Ireland in the year 2000* (Dublin, 1985).

Banque Nationale Suisse 1907–1957 (Zurich, 1957).

Barrington, D., 'The Council of Ireland and the constitutional context', *Administration*, 20 (1972).

Barrington, R., *Health, medicine and politics in Ireland 1900–1970* (Dublin, 1987).

Barrington, T., 'A review of Irish agricultural prices', *JSSISI*, 15 (1925–6).

Barrington, T.J., 'Public administration, 1927–36', in F. MacManus (eds.), *The years of the great test 1926–1939* (Dublin, 1967).

    The Irish administrative system (Dublin, 1980).

    'Whatever happened to Irish government', in F. Litton (ed.), *Unequal achievement* (Dublin, 1982).

    'Systems', in H. Bohan (ed.), *Roots in a changing society* (Shannon, 1982).

    'Serve you right?', *Administration*, 33 (1985).

Barrington, T.J. and Walsh, T., *Towards a New Democracy* (Dublin, 1983).

Bax, M., 'Patronage Irish style: Irish politicians as brokers', *Sociologische Gids*, 17 (1970).

Harp strings and confessions: machine style politics in the Irish Republic (Assen, 1976).

Bayor, R.H., *Neighbors in conflict: the Irish, Germans, Jews, and Italians in New York City, 1929–1941* (London, 1978).

Beckett, J.C., 'Carson – unionist and rebel', in F.X. Martin (ed.), *Leaders and men of the Easter Rising: Dublin 1916* (London, 1967).

'Northern Ireland', *Journal of Contemporary History*, 6 (1971).

The Anglo-Irish tradition (London, 1976).

Beddy, J.P., 'A comparison of the principal economic features of Éire and Denmark', *JSSISI*, 17 (1943–44).

Bell, D., 'Communication technology – for better or for worse', *Harvard Business Review* (May/June 1979).

Bender, T., 'Wholes and parts: the need for synthesis in American history', *JAH*, 73 (1986).

Berend, I.T., and Ranki, G., *Economic development in East Central Europe in the nineteenth and twentieth century* (New York, 1974).

The European periphery and industrialisation 1780–1914 (Cambridge, 1982).

Bergh, T., 'Norway: the powerful servants', *History of Political Economy*, 13 (1981).

Bew, P., Gibbon, P. and Patterson, H., *The state in Northern Ireland 1921–72. Political forces and social classes* (Manchester, 1979).

Bew, P. and Patterson, H., *Seán Lemass and the making of modern Ireland* (Dublin, 1982).

The British state and the Ulster crisis (London, 1985).

Bindschedler, R., Kurz, H.R., Carlgren, W. and Carlsson, S., 'Schlussbetrachtungen zu den Problemen der Kleinstaatneutralität im Grossmachtkrieg', in R. Bindschedler, H.R. Kurz, W. Carlgren and S. Carlsson (eds.), *Schwedische und Schweizerische Neutralität im Zweiten Weltkrieg* (Basel, 1985).

Birch, P., 'Poverty and the church', in S. Kennedy (ed.), *One million poor?* (Dublin, 1981).

Blackwell, J. and Convery, F.J. (eds.), *Promise and performance: Irish environmental policies analysed* (Dublin, 1983).

Boal, F.W. and Douglas, J.M.H., 'Overview', in F.W. Boal and J.M.H. Douglas (eds.), *Integration and division: geographical perspectives on the Northern Ireland problem* (London, 1985).

Boalt, G. and Martin, H., 'Sociology in Sweden, 1965–73', in R.P. Mohan and D. Martindale (eds.), *Handbook of contemporary developments in world sociology* (Westport, 1975).

Boland, J., 'Serving the country better: a debate', *Administration*, 34 (1986).

Boland, K., *We won't stand (idly) by* (Dublin, 1972).

Böll, H., *Irisches Tagebuch* (Cologne, 1961).

Boltho, A., 'Growth', in A. Boltho (ed.), *The European economy: growth and crisis* (Oxford, 1982).

'Introduction', in A. Boltho (ed.), *The European economy: growth and crisis* (Oxford, 1982).

Bonar Law, A., 'Preface', in S. Rosenbaum, *Against Home Rule* (London, 1912, Kennikat edn, 1970).

Bonjour, E., *Erinnerungen* (Basel, 1983).
Bonjour, E., Offler, H.S., and Potter, G.R., *A short history of Switzerland* (Oxford, 1952).
Bourgeois, D., 'Les Relations économiques Germano-Suisses 1939–1945', *Revue d'histoire de la deuxième guerre mondiale*, 126 (1982).
Bouwsma, W.J., 'From the history of ideas to the history of meaning', *Journal of Interdisciplinary History*, 12, (1981).
Bowman, J., 'De Valera on Ulster, 1919–1920: what he told America', *Irish Studies in International Affairs*, 1 (1979).
De Valera and the Ulster question 1917–73 (Oxford, 1982).
'Eamon de Valera: Seven Lives', in J.P. O'Carroll and J.A. Murphy (eds.), *De Valera and his times* (Cork, 1983).
Bowyer Bell, J., *The secret army: a history of the IRA, 1916–1979* (Dublin, 1980).
'The chroniclers of violence in Northern Ireland revisited: the analysis of tragedy', *Review of Politics*, 36 (1974).
Boyce, D.G., *Nationalism in Ireland* (London, 1982).
Englishmen and Irish troubles (London, 1972).
'"The marginal Britons": the Irish', in R. Colls and P. Dodd, *Englishness: culture and politics* (Beckenham, 1986).
Boyle, J.W., 'The Belfast Protestant Association and the Independent Orange Order', *IHS*, 13 (1962).
Boyle, K. and Hadden, T., *Ireland: a positive proposal* (London, 1985).
Boyle, K., Hadden, T. and Hillyard, P., *Ten years on in Northern Ireland* (London, 1980).
Bradley, D.G., 'The organisation of agricultural labourers in Ireland 1900–1976', MA thesis, University College, Cork, 1984.
Bradley, J. and Dowling, B., *Industrial development in Northern Ireland and the Republic of Ireland* (Belfast and Dublin, 1983).
Brady, A., 'Canada and the model of Westminster', in W.B. Hamilton (ed.), *The transfer of institutions* (London, 1964).
Brady, C., *Guardians of the Peace* (Dublin, 1974).
'The lost potential of Geldoff's generation', *Irish Times*, 17 July 1985.
Braibanti, R. (ed.), *Asian bureaucratic systems emergent from the British imperial tradition* (Durham, NC, 1966).
Brennan, P., 'La Violence politique des republicains', *Ireland: Politics and Society*, 1 (1985).
Bressand, A., 'Mastering the "world economy"' *Foreign Affairs*, 61 (1983).
Broad, R. *et al.*, *The Troubles* (London, 1980).
Broszat, M., 'Aufgaben und Probleme zeitgeschichtlicher Unterrichts', *Geschichte in Wissenschaft und Unterricht*, 9 (1957).
Brock, C., 'The CIO Industrial Survey', *JSSISI*, 21 (1963–4).
Brown, T., *Ireland: a social and cultural history 1922–79* (London, 1981, 2nd edn 1985).
Browne, M., 'Why Catholic priests should concern themselves with social and economic questions?', *Christus Rex*, 1 (1947).
Browne, N., *Against the tide* (Dublin, 1986).
Browne, V., 'Who's to blame?', *Magill*, 10 (1986).

'Arms Crisis 1970', *Magill*, 3 (1980).

Buckland, P., *Irish unionism: the Anglo-Irish and the new Ireland, 1855–1922* (Dublin, 1973).

'The unity of Ulster unionism, 1836–1939', *History*, 60 (1975).

The factory of grievances: devolved government in Northern Ireland 1921–39 (Dublin, 1979).

James Craig (Dublin, 1980).

A history of Northern Ireland (Dublin, 1981).

Buckley, V., *Memory Ireland* (Harmondsworth, 1985).

Budge, I. and O'Leary, C., *Belfast: approach to crisis* (London, 1973).

Bunzel, J.H., 'Contemporary sociology in Austria', in R.P. Mohan and Martindale, D. (eds.), *Handbook of contemporary developments in world sociology* (Westport, 1975).

Busteed, J., 'Agriculture and employment in the Free State 1926–30', *Studies* 19 (1930).

Butler, H., *Escape from the ant-hill* (Mullingar, 1986).

Butler, H.D., *The Irish Free State: an economic survey* (Washington, 1928).

Butler, W.F., 'Some untilled fields in Irish history', *Studies*, 2 (1913).

Cahill, E., *Capitalism and its alternatives* (Dublin, 1936).

Callaghan, J., *A house divided* (London, 1973).

Calleary, S., 'Devlin – ten years on', *Administration*, 27 (1979).

Canning, P., *British policy towards Ireland 1921–1941* (Oxford, 1985).

Canny, N., 'Early modern Ireland: an appraisal appraised', *Irish Economic and Social History*, 4 (1977).

'The power but not the gory', *The Times Literary Supplement*, 19 December 1986.

Carlgren, W.M., *Swedish foreign policy during the Second World War* (London, 1977).

Carroll, C., *Building Ireland's business: perspectives from PIMS* (Dublin, 1985).

Carroll, D.S.A., 'Foreword', in I. Kenny, *Government and enterprise* (Dublin, 1984).

Carroll, J.T., *Ireland in the war years 1939–1945* (Dublin, 1975).

Carson, E., 'Introduction', in S. Rosenbaum, *Against Home Rule* (London, 1912; Kennikat edn, 1970).

Carter, C.A., *The Shamrock and the Swastika* (Palo Alto, 1977).

Carty, C., 'Translations', *Sunday Tribune*, 27 July 1986.

Carty, R.K., *Party and parish pump: electoral politics in Ireland* (Waterloo, Ontario, 1981).

Caudle, P.R., *Social security in Ireland and Western Europe* (Dublin, 1964).

Caves, R.E., 'Bertil Ohlin's contribution to economics', *Scandinavian Journal of Economics*, 80 (1978).

Chandler, A.D., Jr, 'Comparative business history', in P. Mathias and D.C. Coleman (eds.), *Enterprise and history* (Cambridge, 1984).

Chapman, R. 'The Irish public service: change or reform?', *Administration*, 23 (1975).

Chubb, B., 'Vocational representation and the Irish Senate', *Political Studies*, 2 (1954).

'Cabinet government in Ireland', *Political Studies*, 3 (1955).

'Ireland in 1957', in D.E. Butler (ed.), *Elections abroad* (London, 1959).

'"Going around persecuting civil servants": the role of the Irish parliamentary representative', *Political Studies*, 11 (1963).

'Fifty years of Irish administration', in O.D. Edwards and F. Pyle (eds.), *1916: the Easter Rising* (London, 1968).

'Ireland', in S. Henig (ed.), *Political parties in the European Community* (London, 1979).

The government and politics of Ireland (London, 1970; 2nd edn 1982).

'Britain and Irish constitutional development', in P.J. Drudy (ed.), *Ireland and Britain since 1922*, Irish Studies, 5 (Cambridge, 1986).

Chubb, B. and Lynch, P. (eds.), *Economic development and planning* (Dublin, 1969).

Clark, J., 'A period of consolidation', *Times Higher Education Supplement*, 27 June 1986.

Clarke, A., 'Ireland, 1534–1660', in J.J. Lee (ed.), *Irish historiography 1970–79* (Cork, 1981).

'Recent works (1977–1982) on early modern British history: Ireland 1450–1750', *Tijdschrift voor Geschiedenis*, 97 (1984).

Clarke, B., 'The environment: 1945–70', in J. Lee (ed.), *Ireland 1945–70* (Dublin, 1979).

Clarke, D.M., 'Emergency legislation, fundamental rights and Article 28.3.3 of the Irish Constitution', *The Irish Jurist* (1977).

'The concept of the common good in Irish constitutional law', *Northern Ireland Legal Quarterly*, 30 (1979).

Clarkson, L.A., 'K.H. Connell and economic and social history at Queen's University, Belfast', in J.M. Goldstrom and L.A. Clarkson (eds.), *Irish population, economy and society* (Oxford, 1981).

Clissmann, A., *Flann O'Brien* (Dublin, 1975).

Clutterbuck, R., 'Comment', in D. Watt (ed.), *The Constitution of Northern Ireland* (London, 1981).

Coakley, J., 'Social Science Research in Ireland: Political Science', paper read to RIA Conference on Social Science Research in Ireland, 23 October 1986.

Cohan, A., 'The open coalition in the closed society. The strange pattern of government formation in Ireland', *Comparative Politics*, 11 (1979).

Cohen, E., 'Who stole the rabbits?', *Anthropological Quarterly*, 45 (1972).

Cole, J., 'Security constraints', in D. Watt, *The constitution of Northern Ireland* (London, 1981).

Collins, M., *The path to freedom* (Cork, 1968).

Connolly, J., *How does she stand? An appeal to Young Ireland* (Dublin, 1953).

Connolly, M. and Loughlin, J., 'Reflections on the Anglo-Irish Agreement', *Government and Opposition*, 21 (1986).

Connolly, P.R., 'The Church in Ireland since Vatican II', *The Furrow*, 30 (1979).

Convery, F.J., 'Beocheist', *Irish Times*, 24 May 1984.

'Resources and environment 1983: synthesis', in J. Blackwell and F.J. Convery (eds.), *Promise and performance: Irish environmental policies analysed* (Dublin, 1983).

Coogan, T.P., *The IRA* (London, 1980 edn).

Coolahan, J., 'De Valera's impact on education', *Irish Times*, 1 November 1982.
'The fortunes of education as a subject of study and of research in Ireland', *Irish Educational Studies*, 4 (1984).

Cooper, C. and Whelan, N., *Science, technology and industry in Ireland* (Dublin, 1973).

Cooper, R. and O'Shea, T., 'Northern Ireland: survey of social trends', *New Society*, 7 June 1973.

Cooperation North, *Economic indicators in Northern Ireland and the Republic of Ireland* (Dublin, 1983).

Corcoran, T., 'Irish youth employment policies in the 1980s', *Administration*, 33 (1985).

Corish, P.J., *The Irish Catholic experience: a historical survey* (Dublin, 1985).

Coughlan, A., 'Ireland', in D. Seers and C. Vaitsos (eds.), *Integration and unequal development* (London, 1980).
'Public affairs, 1916–66: the social scene', *Administration*, 14 (1966).

Cox, W.H., 'The 1983 general election in Northern Ireland: anatomy and consequences', *Parliamentary Affairs*, 37 (1984).
'The politics of Irish unification in the Irish Republic', *Parliamentary Affairs*, 38 (1985).
'Managing Northern Ireland intergovernmentally: an appraisal of the Anglo-Irish Agreement', *Parliamentary Affairs*, 40 (1987).

Crafts, N.F.R., 'Gross national product in Europe 1870–1910: some new estimates', *Explorations in Economic History*, 20 (1983).

Craver, E., 'The emigration of the Austrian economists', *History of Political Economy*, 18 (1986).

Cregan, D.F., 'Early modern Ireland', *IHS*, 20 (1977).

Cromien, S., 'As good as any – a perspective from inside the civil service', *Seirbhís Phoiblí*, 6 (1985).

Cronin, A., 'Dev contra mundum', *Irish Times*, 5 September 1975.
'The artless philistines', *Irish Times*, 16 September 1986.

Cronin, S., *Irish nationalism* (Dublin, 1980).

Crotty, R., *Ireland in crisis: a study in capitalist colonial underdevelopment* (Dingle, 1986).
Irish agricultural production: its volume and structure (Cork, 1966).

Crowley, D., 'How IDA wins war while losing battles', *Sunday Tribune*, 2 June 1985.

Cullen, L.M., *An economic history of Ireland since 1660* (London, 1972).
'The hidden Ireland: reassessment of a concept', *Studia Hibernica*, 9 (1969).

Cullen, L.M. and Smout, T.C., 'Economic growth in Scotland and Ireland', in L.M. Cullen and T.C. Smout (eds.), *Comparative aspects of Scottish and Irish economic and social history 1600–1900* (Edinburgh, n.d.).

Curran, J.M., *The birth of the Irish Free State 1921–1923* (London, 1980).

Daalder, H., 'Government and opposition in the new states', *Government and Opposition*, 1 (1966).

d'Alton, I., 'Southern Irish unionism: a study of Cork unionists, 1884–1914', *TRHS*, 5th series, 23 (1973).

'A contrast in crises: southern Irish Protestantism, 1830–43 and 1885–1910', in A.C. Hepburn (ed.), *Minorities in history* (London, 1978).

Daly, C.B., 'Violence destroys the work of justice', *The Furrow*, 31 (1980).

Daly, G., 'On formulating national goals', in An Foras Forbartha, *Ireland in the year 2000: towards a national strategy* (Dublin 1983).

Daly, M. *et al.*, *Draft report of the working group on funding, employment conditions and the Sociological Association of Ireland* (Dublin, 1986).

Daly, M.E., *Social and economic history of Ireland* (Dublin, 1981).

'Government finance for industry in the Irish Free State: the Trade Loans (Guarantee) Acts', *IESH*, 11 (1984).

'An Irish-Ireland for business: the Control of Manufacturers Acts, 1932 and 1934', *IHS*, 24 (1984).

Dangerfield, G., *The damnable question* (London, 1977).

Daniel, T.K., 'Griffith on his noble head', *IESH*, 3 (1976).

Darby, J., *Conflict in Northern Ireland: the development of a polarised community* (Dublin, 1976).

Northern Ireland: the background to the conflict (Belfast, 1983).

D'Arcy, C.F., 'The religious difficulty under home rule: the church view', in S. Rosenbaum, *Against Home Rule* (London, 1912; Kennikat edn, 1970).

Davies, N., *Heart of Europe*: A Short History of Poland (Oxford, 1986).

Davies, W., and Tierney, D., 'Nouvelle Clio', *Peritia*, 3 (1984).

Davis, E.E., and Sinnot, R., 'Political mobilisation, political institutionalisation and the maintenance of ethnic conflict', *Ethnic and Racial Studies*, 4 (1981).

Davis, J., 'Morals and backwardness', *Comparative Studies in Society and History*, 12 (1970).

Deane, S., 'Postscript', *Crane Bag*, 3 (1979).

Denison, E.F., *Why growth rates differ* (Washington, 1967).

de Paor, L., *Divided Ulster* (Harmondsworth, 1970).

'Ireland's identities', *Crane Bag*, 3 (1979).

'Gone with the wind', *Irish Times*, 4 July 1985.

'As we are', *Irish Times*, 18 July 1985.

Devlin, L. St John, 'The management of change', *Seirbhís Phoiblí*, 5 (1984).

de Valk, J.M.M., 'Contemporary sociological theory in the Netherlands', in R.P. Mohan and D. Martindale (eds.), *Handbook of contemporary developments in world sociology* (Westport, 1975).

de Vere White, T., *Kevin O'Higgins* (Tralee, 1966).

Dickel, H., *Die deutsche Aussenpolitik und die irische Frage von 1932 bis 1944* (Wiesbaden, 1983).

'Irland als Faktor der deutschen Aussenpolitik von 1933–1945', in M. Funke (ed.), *Hitler, Deutschland und die Mächte* (Düsseldorf, 1976).

Dickson, D., 'Historical journals in Ireland: the last hundred years', in B. Hayley and E. McKay (eds.), *300 years of Irish periodicals* (Mullingar, 1987).

Długoborski, W. (ed.), *Zweiter Weltkrieg und sozialer Wandel* (Göttingen, 1981).

Donoghue, D., *We Irish* (Brighton, 1986).

Donnison, D., 'The Northern Ireland civil service', *New Society*, 5 July 1973.

Dooney, S., '1969–1979: a decade of development?', *Seirbhís Phoiblí*, 1 (1980).

'Why do we need a Public Service Advisory Council?', *Seirbhís Phoiblí*, 3 (1982).

Dorgan, V., *Christy Ring* (Cork, 1980).

Douglas, M., *Implicit meanings: essays in anthropology* (London, 1975).

Downey, J., *Them and us: Britain, Ireland and the Northern Ireland question 1969–82* (Dublin, 1983).

Doyle, D.N., 'Contemporary Irish identity: a Roman Catholic's reflections', *Crane Bag*, 9 (1985).

Drake, K.M., 'Professor K.H. Connell', *IHS*, 19 (1974).

Driscoll, J.G., 'Upon first going home again', in D.P. Kelleher (ed.), *Kerryman, 1881–1981* (New York, 1981).

Drudy, P.J. and McAleese, D., 'Editorial introduction', in P.J. Drudy and D. McAleese (eds.), *Ireland and the European Community*, Irish Studies 4 (Cambridge, 1983).

Duggan, J.P., *Neutral Ireland and the Third Reich* (Dublin, 1985).

Duggan, T., 'Juventus ad Astra', *Seirbhís Phoiblí*, 6 (1985).

Dunne, J., 'Public sector: a hitch for Boland's reforms', *Business and Finance*, 12 July 1984.

Durkan, J., 'The national plan', *IBR* (1984).

Dutter, L.E., 'Perceptions of group identity and recent political behaviour in Northern Ireland', *Political Psychology*, 6 (1985).

Eastern Region Development Organisation, *Eastern region settlement strategy 2011, Main Report* (Dublin, 1985).

Eckstein, H., *Division and cohesion in democracy: a study of Norway* (Princeton, 1966).

'Editorial', *Acta Sociologica*, 1 (1965).

Edwards, J., *Language, society and identity* (Oxford, 1985).

Edwards, O.D., 'Press reaction to the Rising in general', in Edwards, O.D. and Pyle, F. (eds.), *1916: the Easter Rising* (London, 1968).
'*The Irish Times* on the Easter Rising', also in Edwards and Pyle.
The sins of our fathers (Dublin, 1970).

Edwards, R.W. Dudley, 'The contribution of Young Ireland to the development of the national idea', in Pender, S. (ed.), *Féilschribhinn Tórna* (Cork, 1947).
'The achievement of 1916', in Edwards, O.D. and Pyle, F. (eds.), *1916: the Easter Rising* (London, 1968).
A New History of Ireland (Dublin, 1970).
'Professor MacNeill', in Martin, F.X. and Byrne, F.J. (eds)., *The scholar revolutionary* (Shannon,, Ireland, 1973).
'An agenda for Irish history', *IHS*, 21 (1978).
'Resurrection of the spirit of independence', *Irish Press*, 16 April, 1979.

Edwards, R.W. Dudley and Williams, T.D. (eds.), *The Great Famine* (London, 1956).

Edwards, Ruth Dudley, *Patrick Pearse: the triumph of failure* (London, 1977).
James Connolly (Dublin, 1981).

Egan, P.K., *The influence of the Irish on the Catholic Church in America in the nineteenth century* (Dublin, 1968).

Eidgenössisches Statistisches Amt, *Schweizerisches Volkseinkommen, 1924, 1929 bis 1938* (Berne, 1941).

Ekman, S., 'La Politique de défense de la Suéde durant la second guerre mondiale', *Revue d'histoire de la de deuxième guerre mondiale*, 126 (1982).

Eley, G., 'The left, the nationalists and the Protestants: some recent books on Ireland', *Michigan Quarterly Review*, 22 (1983).

Ervine, St John, *Craigavon: Ulsterman* (London, 1949).

Ession-Udom, E.U., 'Tribalism and racism', in L. Kuper (ed.), *Race, science and society* (London, 1975).

Evelegh, R., *Peacekeeping in a democratic society: the lessons of Northern Ireland* (London 1978).

Falconer, A., McDonagh, E., and MacRéamoinn, S. (eds.), *Freedom to hope? the Catholic Church in Ireland twenty years after Vatican II* (Dublin, 1985).

Fallis, R., *The Irish Renaissance* (Dublin, 1978).

Falls, C., 'Northern Ireland and the defence of the British Isles', in T. Wilson (ed.), *Ulster under Home Rule* (London, 1958).

Fanning, R., 'Leadership and transition from the politics of revolution to the politics of party: the example of Ireland 1914–1939', XIV International Congress of Historical Sciences, San Francisco, 1975.

The Irish Department of Finance (Dublin, 1978).

'The Irish policy of Asquith's government and the cabinet crisis of 1910', in A. Cosgrove and D. McCartney (eds.), *Studies in Irish history presented to R. Dudley Edwards* (Dublin, 1979).

'The United States and Irish participation in NATO: the debate of 1950', *Irish Studies in International Affairs*, 1 (1979).

'London and Belfast's response to the Declaration of the Republic of Ireland, 1948–49', *International Affairs*, 58 (1981–2).

Independent Ireland (Dublin, 1983).

The four-leaved shamrock (Dublin, 1983).

'"Rats" versus "ditchers": the die-hard revolt and the Parliament Bill of 1911', in A. Cosgrove and J.I. McGuire (eds.), *Parliament and community (Historical Studies*, 14) (Belfast, 1983).

'"The rule of order": Eamon de Valera and the IRA 1923–1940', in J.P. O'Carroll and J.A. Murphy (eds.), *De Valera and his times* (Cork, 1983).

'Economists and governments: Ireland 1922–52', in A. Murphy (ed.), *Economists and the Irish economy from the eighteenth century to the present day* (Dublin, 1984).

'Fianna Fáil and the bishops, *Irish Times*, 13–14 February, 1985.

'The life and times of Alexis Fitzgerald', *Magill*, 8 (1985).

'The Anglo-American alliance and the Irish application for membership of the United Nations', *Irish Studies in International Affairs*, 2 (1986).

'"The great enchantment": uses and abuses of modern Irish history', in J. Dooge (ed.), *Ireland in the contemporary world: essays in honour of Garret FitzGerald* (Dublin, 1986).

Farrell, B., 'The new state and Irish political culture', *Administration*, 16 (1968).

'A note on the Dáil constitution 1919', *The Irish Jurist*, 4 (1969).

Chairman or chief? The role of Taoiseach in Irish government (Dublin, 1971).

The founding of Dáil Eireann. Parliament and nation-building (Dublin, 1971).

'The first Dáil and after', in B. Farrell (ed.), *The Irish parliamentary tradition* (Dublin, 1973).

'MacNeill and politics', in F.X. Martin and F.J. Byrne (eds.), *The scholar revolutionary* (Dublin, 1973).

Seán Lemass (Dublin, 1983).

'Coalitions and political institutions: the Irish experience', in V. Bogdanor (ed.), *Coalition government in Western Europe* (London, 1983).

'Ireland: from friends and neighbours to clients and partisans: some dimensions of parliamentary representation under PR-STV', in V. Bogdanor (ed.), *Representatives of the people? Parliamentarians and constituents in western democracies* (London, 1985).

Farrell, D.M., 'The strategy to market Fine Gael in 1981', *Irish Political Studies*, 1 (1986).

Farrell, M., *The Orange State* (London, 1980).

Faulkner, B., *Memoirs of a statesman* (London, 1978).

'Favourable aspects of the Irish economy', *IBR* (1958).

Feeney, J., *John Charles McQuaid* (Dublin, 1974).

Feldman, G.D., Holtfrerich, C.L., Ritter, G.A., and Witt, P.C. (eds.), *The experience of inflation* (Berlin, 1984).

Fennell, D., 'The last years of the Gaeltacht', *Crane Bag*, 5 (1981).

'A state we don't know what to do with', *Irish Times*, 3 December 1986.

Fingarette, H., *Self-deception* (London, 1969).

Fisk, R., *The point of no return* (London, 1975).

In time of war: Ireland, Ulster and the price of neutrality 1939–45 (London, 1983).

Fitzgerald, A., 'Reservation No. 2', *Report of the Commission on emigration and other population problems* (Pr 2451, 1956).

'Eamon de Valera', *Studies*, 64 (1975).

FitzGerald, G., 'Mr Whitaker and industry', *Studies*, 48 (1959).

'The significance of 1916', *Studies*, 55 (1966).

Towards a new Ireland (Dublin, 1972).

'Ireland's identity problems', *Etudes Irlandaises*, 1 (1976).

Reconciliation in a divided community (Pittsburgh, 1982).

'De Valera and contemporary Ireland', *Etudes irlandaises*, 9 (1984).

Fitzpatrick, D., *Politics and Irish life, 1913–21* (Dublin, 1977).

'The disappearance of the Irish agricultural labourer, 1841–1912', *IESH*, 7 (1980).

'"A share of the honeycomb": education, emigration and Irish women', *Continuity and Change*, 1 (1986).

Fleure, H.J., 'Emer Estyn Evans: a personal note: in R.H. Buchanan, E. Jones and D. MacCourt (eds.), *Man and his habitat: essays presented to Emer Estyn Evans* (New York, 1971).

Flora, P., *et al.*, *State, economy and society in western Europe 1815–1975* (London, 1983).

Foley, D., 'Oíche na himirce', *Scríobh*, 3 (Dublin, 1978).

Foster, R.F., 'The emerald image', *Times Literary Supplement*, 4 June 1976.

'History and the Irish question', *TRHS*, 5th series, 33 (1983).

Friedrich, C.J., 'Some reflections on constitutionalism for emergent political "orders"', in H.J. Spiro (ed.), *Patterns of African development* (New Jersey, 1967).

Friis, H., *Development of social research in Ireland* (Dublin, 1965).

Fritz, M., 'The Swedish economy 1939–1945', in M. Fritz, *et al.* (eds.), *The adaptable nation. Essays in Swedish economy during the Second World War* (Stockholm, 1984).

'Wirtschaftliche Neutralität während des Zweiten Weltkriegs', in R. Bindschedler, Kurz, H.R., Carlgren, W. and Carlsson, S. (eds.), *Schwedische und Schweizerische Neutralität im Zweiten Weltkrieges* (Basel, 1985).

Gageby, D., 'The media 1945–70', in Lee, J.J. (ed.), *Ireland 1945–70* (Dublin, 1979).

Gallagher, E., 'The development of marine resources', *Administration*, 33 (1985).

Gallagher, J.F. and DeGregory, G.C., *Violence in Northern Ireland: understanding Protestant perspectives* (Dublin, 1985).

Gallagher, M., *Electoral support for Irish political parties 1927–1973* (London, 1976).

Political parties in the Republic of Ireland (Dublin, 1985).

'Party solidarity, exclusivity and inter-party relationships in Ireland, 1922–1977: the evidence of transfers', *ESR*, 10 (1978).

'The impact of lower preference votes on Irish parliamentary elections, 1922–1977', *ESR*, 11 (1979).

'The pact General Election of 1922', *IHS*, 21 (1979).

'Societal change and party adaptation in the Republic of Ireland, 1960–81', *EJPR*, 9 (1981).

The Irish Labour party in transition 1957–82 (Manchester, 1982).

Gallagher, M.P., 'What hope for Irish faith?', *The Furrow*, 29 (1978).

Gallagher, T., 'The dimensions of Fianna Fáil rule in Ireland', *West European Politics*, 4 (1981).

Garvin, T., *The evolution of Irish nationalist politics* (Dublin, 1981).

'The destiny of the soldiers: tradition and modernity in the politics of de Valera's Ireland', *Political Studies*, 26 (1978).

'Decolonisation, nationalism and electoral politics in Ireland 1832–1945', in O. Büsch (ed.), *Wählerbewegung in der Europäischen Geschichte* (Berlin, 1980).

'The growth of faction in the Fianna Fáil party, 1966–80', *Parliamentary Affairs*, 34 (1981).

'Change and the political system', in Litton, F. (ed.), *Unequal achievement* (Dublin, 1982).

'The teaching of politics in Ireland:' (i) University College Dublin', *Political Studies Association of Ireland Bulletin*, 3 (1986).

'The anatomy of a nationalist revolution: Ireland 1858–1928', *Comparative Studies in Society and History*, 28 (1986).

Gaughan, J.A., *Alfred O'Rahilly: academic* (Dublin, 1986).

Thomas Johnson, 1872–1963 (Dublin, 1980).

Geary, R.C., 'Irish economic development since the Treaty', *Studies*, 40 (1951).

Geertz, C., 'After the Revolution: the fate of nationalism in new states', in *The interpretation of cultures* (London, 1975).

Gellner, E., *Thought and change* (London, 1965).
   Contemporary thought and politics (London, 1978).
'Gerry Boland's story,' *Irish Times*, 10 October 1968.
Gerschenkron, A., 'Eli F. Heckscher', in E.F. Heckscher, *An economic history of Sweden* (Cambridge, Mass., 1954).
Gibbon, P., *The origins of Ulster unionism* (Manchester, 1975).
Gibson, N.J., Review of J.J. Lee (ed.), *Ireland 1945–70*, *IESH*, 7 (1980).
Gilbert, F. (ed.), *The historical essays of Otto Hintze* (New York, 1975).
Girod, R., 'Contemporary sociology in Switzerland', in R.P. Mohan and D. Martindale (eds.), *Handbook of contemporary developments in world sociology* (Westport, 1975).
Girvin, B., 'Industrialisation and the Irish working class since 1922', *Saothar*, 10 (1984).
   'The dominance of Fianna Fáil and the nature of political adaptability in Ireland', *Political Studies*, 32 (1984).
   'National identity and conflict in Northern Ireland', in B. Girvin and R. Sturm (eds.), *Politics and society in contemporary Ireland* (Aldershot, 1986).
   'Protectionism and economic development in independent Ireland 1922–1960', PhD thesis University College, Cork, 1986.
   'Social change and moral politics: the Irish constitutional referendum 1983', *Political Studies*, 34 (1986).
   'Towards a history of University College, Cork', Ms., 1986.
Golab, C., *Immigrant destinations* (Philadelphia, 1977).
Goldring, M., *Faith of our fathers: the formation of Irish nationalist ideology 1890–1920* (Dublin, 1982).
Graf, C., 'Innen- und aussenpolitische Aspekte schweizerischer Zensur während des Zweiten Weltkrieges', in U. Altermatt and J. Garamvölgyi (eds.), *Innen- und aussenpolitik* (Berne, 1980).
Granatstein, J.L., *The Ottawa men: the civil service mandarins 1939–1957* (Toronto, 1982).
Graubard, S., 'Preface: Australia, terra incognita', *Daedalus*, 114 (1985).
Grebler, L., 'Work creation policy in Germany 1932–35', *International Labour Review*, 35 (1937).
Greeley, A.M., *That most distressful nation* (Chicago, 1972).
Greene, D., 'Language and nationalism', *Crane Bag*, 2 (1978).
Grey, H.J., 'Catering for our emigrants', *Christus Rex*, 9 (1955).
Gwynn, D., *The Irish Free State, 1922–7* (London, 1928).
   The life of John Redmond (London, 1932; 1971 edn, Freeport, New York).
Hagtvet, B., and Rudeng, E., 'Scandinavia: achievements, challenges', *Daedalus* 113 (1984).
Hamill, D., *Pig in the middle: the army in Northern Ireland 1969–1984* (London, 1985).
Hand, G.J. (ed.), *Report of the Irish Boundary Commission 1925* (Shannon, 1969).
   'MacNeill and the Boundary Commission', in F.X. Martin and F.J. Byrne (eds.), *The Scholar Revolutionary* (Shannon, Ireland, 1973).
Hannan, D. F., *Displacement and development: class, kinship and social change in Irish rural communities* (Dublin, 1979).

Hannan, D.F., and Katsiaouni, L., *Traditional families? From culturally prescribed to negotiated roles in farm families* (Dublin, 1977).

Hansen, B., 'Jan Tinbergen: an appraisal of his contribution to economics', *Swedish Journal of Economics*, 51 (1969).

Harbinson, J.F., *The Ulster Unionist Party 1882–1973: its development and organisation* (Belfast, 1973).

Hardiman, N. and Lalor, S., 'Corporatism in Ireland: an exchange of views', *Administration*, 32 (1984).

Harkness, D.A.E., 'The evolution of agricultural policy in Northern Ireland', *Ulster Year book* (1935).

Harkness, D.W., *The restless dominion* (London, 1969).

Northern Ireland since 1920 (Dublin, 1983).

'Mr de Valera's dominion. Irish relations with Britain and the Commonwealth 1932–1938', *Journal of Commonwealth Political Studies* 8 (1970).

'England's Irish question', in G. Peele and C. Cook (eds.), *The politics of reappraisal 1918–39* (London, 1975).

'The difficulties of devolution: the post-war debate at Stormont', *Irish Jurist*, 12 (1977).

'Patrick McGilligan: man of commonwealth', *Journal of Imperial and Commonwealth History*, 5 (1979).

Harris, Henry, 'The other half million', in O.D. Edwards and F. Pyle (eds.), *1916: the Easter Rising* (London, 1968).

Harvey, B., *Cosgrave's coalition* (London, 1977).

Haskell, T.L., 'Capitalism and the origins of the humanitarian sensibility, part 1', *AHR*, 90 (1985).

Hayden, M. and Moonan, G.A., *A short history of the Irish people: From the earliest times to 1920* (Dublin, 1921).

Hayes-McCoy, G.A., 'Irish defence policy, 1938–51', in K.B. Nowlan and T.D. Williams (eds.), *Ireland in the war years and after, 1939–51* (Dublin, 1969).

Hayward, J., *The one and indivisible French republic* (London, 1973).

Healy, M. and J. Davis (eds.), *The control and management of technology in society* (Dublin, 1981).

Headlam, M., *Irish reminiscences* (London, 1947).

Hederman, M., *The road to Europe: Irish attitudes 1948–61* (Dublin, 1983).

Healy, J., *Death of an Irish Town* (Cork, 1968).

Nineteen acres (Galway, 1978).

'Death of a realist', *Irish Times*, 15 May 1971.

Healy, J.R., 'Access, transport – how is it serving the Irish exporter?', Address to the Annual Conference of the Chartered Institute of Transport in Ireland, 28 February 1986.

Heaney, S., *Fieldwork* (London, 1979).

Hennessy, J., 'British education for an elite in India, 1780–1947', in R. Wilkinson (ed.), *Governing elites: studies in training and selection* (London, 1969).

Hepburn, A.C., 'Catholics in the North of Ireland, 1850–1921: the urbanisation of a minority', in A.C. Hepburn (ed.), *Minorities in history* (London, 1978).

The conflict of nationality in modern Ireland (London, 1980).

Herries-Davies, G.L., 'Irish thought in science', in R. Kearney (ed.), *The Irish mind* (Dublin, 1985).

(ed.), *Irish geography: the Geographical Society of Ireland Golden Jubilee 1934–1984* (Dublin, 1984).

Herz, D., 'The Northern Ireland policy of the Irish Republic', in B. Girvin and R. Sturm (eds.), *Politics and society in contemporary Ireland* (Aldershot, 1986).

Heskin, K., *Northern Ireland: a psychological analysis* (Dublin, 1980).

Hewitt, C., 'Catholic grievances, Catholic nationalism and violence in Northern Ireland during the civil rights period', *British Journal of Sociology*, 32 (1981). 'Explaining violence in Northern Ireland', *British Journal of Sociology*, 38 (1987).

Higgins, M.D., 'Making sense of change', *Saothar*, 10 (1984).

Higham, J., 'Integrating America: the problem of assimilation in the nineteenth century', *Journal of American Ethnic History*, 1 (1981).

Hillgruber, A., *Vom Beruf des Historikers in einer Zeit beschleunigten Wandels: Gedenkschrift für Theodor Schieder* (Munich, 1985).

Hillyard, P., 'Law and order', in J. Darby (ed.), *Northern Ireland: the background to the conflict* (Belfast 1983).

Hoctor, D., *The Department's story: a history of the Department of Agriculture* (Dublin, 1971).

Hofer, W., 'Neutralität im totalen Krieg', in W. Hofer, *Mächte und Kräfte im 20. Jahrhundert* (Zurich, 1983).

Hogan, J., 'Foreword', in F.X. Martin and F.J. Byrne (eds.), *The Scholar Revolutionary* (Shannon, Ireland, 1973).

Hogan, R. (ed.), *Feathers from the green crow: Sean O'Casey 1905–1925* (Columbia, Mo., 1962).

Horgan, J., *Labour. The price of power* (Dublin, 1986).

Hornby, O. and Viby-Morgensen, G., 'The study of economic history in Denmark: recent trends and problems', *Scandinavian Journal of Economic History*, 22 (1974).

Howard, M., 'Empire, race and war in pre-1914 Britain', in H. Lloyd-Jones, V. Pearl and B. Worden (eds.), *History and imagination: essays in honour of H.R. Trevor Roper* (London, 1981).

Hughes, H.S., *History as art and as science* (Chicago, 1964; 1975 reprint).

Humphreys, P.C., *Public service employment* (Dublin, 1983).

Hutchinson, B., 'On the study of non-economic factors in Irish economic development', *ESR*, 1 (1970).

Hutchinson, T.W., 'Economic thought and policy: generalisations and ambiguities', *International Congress of Economic History* (Moscow, 1970).

Hyman, L., *The Jews of Ireland* (Shannon, 1972).

IDA, *The Irish economy expenditures of the Irish manufacturing sector: a statistical profile* (Dublin, 1985).

Inglis, B., *West Briton* (London, 1961).

Isles, K.S., and Cuthbert, N., *An economic survey of Northern Ireland* (Belfast, 1957).

Jackson, G.D., Jr. 'Peasant political movements in eastern Europe', in H.A.

Landsberger (ed.), *Rural protest, peasant movements and social change* (New York, 1973).

Jacobsson, E.E., *A life for sound money: Per Jacobsson's biography* (Oxford, 1979).

Jalland, P., *The Liberals and Ireland. The Ulster question in British politics to 1914* (Brighton, 1980).

Johansen, H.C., *The Danish economy in the twentieth century* (London, 1987).

Johansen, L., 'Ragnar Frisch's contribution to economics', *Swedish Journal of Economics*, 71 (1969).

Johnson, D.S., *The inter-war economy in Ireland* (Dundalk, 1985).

'Northern Ireland as a problem in the economic war 1932–38', *IHS*, 22 (1980).

'The Belfast boycott 1920–22', in J.M. Goldstrom and L.A. Clarkson (eds.), *Irish population, economy and society: essays in honour of the late K.H. Connell* (Oxford, 1981).

'The Northern Ireland economy, 1914–39', in L. Kennedy and P. Ollerenshaw (eds.), *An economic history of Ulster 1820–1939* (Manchester, 1985).

Johnson, Harry, 'James Meade's contribution to economics', *Scandinavian Journal of Economics*, 80 (1978).

Johnson, P., *Ireland: land of troubles* (London, 1980).

Johnson, R.W.H., 'Science and technology in Irish national culture', *Crane Bag*, 7 (1983).

Jonung, L., 'The depression in Sweden and the United States', in K. Brunner (ed.), *The Great Depression revisited* (Boston, 1981).

Jörberg, L. and Krantz, O., 'Scandinavia 1914–1970', in C.M. Cipolla (ed.), *The Fontana economic history of Europe*, 6 (2) (London, 1976).

Joyce, J. and Murtagh, P., *The boss* (Dublin, 1983).

Jucker-Fleetwood, E.E., 'The Irish Banking Commission 1934–1938, as seen by Per Jacobsson', *Central Bank of Ireland Quarterly Bulletin* (1972).

Jutikkala, E., *A history of Finland* (London, 1962).

Kain, R., 'A diary of Easter Week: one Dubliner's experience', *Irish University Review*, 10 (1980).

Kaser, M.C. and Radice, E.A. (eds.), *The economic history of eastern Europe 1919–1975*, 1 (Oxford, 1985).

Kavanagh, J., 'Social policy in modern Ireland', *Administration*, 26 (1978).

Kavanagh, Patrick, *Collected poems* (London, 1968).

By night unstarred (Curragh, Kildare, Ireland, 1977), ed. by Peter Kavanagh.

Keane, J.B., *Man of the triple name* (Dingle, 1984).

Kearney, H.F., *Scholars and gentlemen: universities and society in pre-industrial Britain, 1500–1700* (London, 1970).

Keatinge, P., *The formulation of Irish foreign policy* (Dublin, 1973).

A place among the nations: issues of Irish foreign policy (Dublin, 1978).

'Ireland and the world 1957–82', in F. Litton (ed.), *Unequal achievement* (Dublin, 1982).

'Unequal sovereigns: the diplomatic dimension of Anglo-Irish relations', in P.J. Drudy (ed.), *Ireland and Britain since 1922*, Irish Studies, 5 (Cambridge, 1986).

Kee, R., 'Neutrality as a form of warfare', *Sunday Times*, 15 May 1983.

The green flag (London, 1972).

Keegan, J., 'Foreword', in J.P. Duggan, *Neutral Ireland and The Third Reich* (Dublin, 1985).

Kelleher, J.V., 'Ireland . . . and where does she stand?', *Foreign Affairs*, 35 (1957).

Kelly, J.M., *Fundamental rights in Irish law and constitution* (Dublin, 1967, 2nd edn).

Kennedy, B.P., 'Seventy-five years of *Studies*', *Studies*, 75 (1986).

Kennedy, K., *Productivity and industrial growth: the Irish experience* (Oxford, 1971).

'Social science research and public policy', *Administration*, 21 (1973).

Kennedy, K. and Dowling, B.R., *Economic growth in Ireland: the experience since 1947* (Dublin, 1975).

Kennedy, P.M., 'The decline of nationalistic history in the west, 1900–1970', in W. Laqueur (ed.), *Historians in politics* (London, 1974).

'The pre-war right in Britain and Germany', in P.M. Kennedy and W. Mock (eds.), *Nationalist and racialist movements in Britain and Germany before 1914* (London, 1981).

Kenner, H., *A colder eye* (London, 1983).

Kenny, A., *The road to Hillsborough* (London, 1986).

Kenny, I., *Government and enterprise in Ireland* (Dublin, 1984).

'Planning and process', in An Foras Forbartha, *Ireland in the year 2000: towards a national strategy* (Dublin, 1983).

Keogh, D.F., *The rise of the Irish working class* (Belfast, 1982).

The Vatican, the bishops and Irish politics 1919–39 (Cambridge, 1986).

'William Martin Murphy and the origins of the 1913 lockout', *Capuchin Annual* (1977).

'The origins of the Irish foreign service in Europe (1919–1922)', *Etudes Irlandaises*, 7 (1982).

'The Department of Foreign Affairs', in Z. Steiner (ed.), *The Times Survey of Foreign Offices of the world* (London, 1982).

'The Catholic Church and the "red scare", 1931–32', in J.P. O'Carroll and J.A. Murphy (eds.), *De Valera and his times* (Cork, 1983).

Keynes, J.M., *The general theory of employment, interest and money* (London, 1961 edn).

Kiberd, D., *Anglo-Irish Attitudes* (Derry, 1984).

'Inventing Ireland', *Crane Bag*, 8 (1984).

Kilgus, E., Rühli, E., Weilenmann, P., *Betriebswirtschaftslehre an der Universität Zürich* (Zurich, 1978).

Killeen, M., *Industrial development and full employment* (Dublin, 1976).

'Michael Killeen, profile', *Irish Times*, 14 February 1984.

Kilroy, T., 'The Irish writer: self and society, 1950–80', in P. Connolly (ed.), *Literature and the changing Ireland* (Colin Smythe, Gerrard's Cross, Bucks., 1982).

Komito, L., 'Irish clientelism: a re-appraisal', *ESR*, 15 (1984).

Kirby, D.G., *Finland in the twentieth century* (London, 1979).

'Rank and file attitudes in the Finnish Social Democratic Party 1905–1918', *Past and Present*, 111 (1986).

Klinge, M., *A brief history of Finland* (Helsinki, 1981).
'Aspects of the Nordic self', *Daedalus*, 115 (1984).
Knoll, R., Majce, G., Weiss, H., Wieser, G., 'Der österreichische Beitrag zur Soziologie von der Jahrhundertwende bis 1938' in M. Rainer Lepsius (ed.), *Soziologie in Deutschland und Österreich 1918–1945* (Cologne, 1981).
Kohn, L., *The constitution of the Irish Free State* (London, 1932).
Kovalcheck, K.A., 'Catholic grievances in Northern Ireland: appraisal and judgment', *British Journal of Sociology*, 38 (1987).
Kreis, G., 'Die Pressepolitik des neutralen Staates', in R. Bindschedler, H.R. Kurz, W. Carlgren and S. Carlsson (eds.), *Schwedische und Schweizerische Neutralität im Zweiten Weltkrieg* (Basel, 1985).
Kuehn, A., 'Die Wirtschaft Irlands', *Vierteljahrshefte für Wirtschaftsforschung* (1956).
Kuper, L., *Race, class and power* (London, 1974).
Kurz, H.R., 'Problèmes militaires', *Revue d'histoire de la deuxième guerre mondiale*, 121 (1981).
Kuznets, S., *Economic growth and structure* (London, 1965).
Kyle, K., 'The panorama survey of Irish opinion', *Political Quarterly*, 50 (1979).
Laffan, M., *The partition of Ireland 1911–1925* (Dundalk, 1983).
'The unification of Sinn Féin, 1917', *IHS*, 17 (1971).
'Violence and terror in twentieth-century Ireland: IRB and IRA', in W.J. Mommsen and G. Hirschfeld (eds.), *Social protest, violence and terror in twentieth-century Europe* (London, 1982).
'"Labour must wait": Ireland's conservative revolution', in P.J. Corish (ed.), *Radicals, rebels and establishments* (*Historical Studies* 15) (Belfast, 1985).
Laitin, D.D., 'Linguistic dissociation: a strategy for Africa', in J.G. Ruggie (ed.), *The antinomies of interdependence* (New York, 1983).
Lalor, S., 'Corporatism in Ireland', *Administration*, 30 (1982).
Larkin, E., *James Larkin: Irish Labour leader 1876–1947* (London, 1968 edn).
'Economic growth, capital investment and the Roman Catholic Church in nineteenth-century Ireland', *AHR*, 72 (1966–7).
'The devotional revolution in Ireland, 1850–75', *AHR*, 77 (1972).
'Church, state and nation in modern Ireland', *AHR*, 80 (1975).
Laursen, K., 'A Survey of the Danish Economy after 1950', *Weltwirtschaftliches Archiv*, 98 (1967).
Laver, M., 'Actors, words and images', *Administration*, 32 (1984).
'Party choice and social structure in Ireland', *Irish Political Studies*, 1 (1986).
Lawlor, S.M., *Britain and Ireland 1914–23* (Dublin, 1983).
'Ireland from Truce to Treaty: war or peace? July–October 1921', *IHS*, xxii (1980).
Lawrence, R.J., *The government of Northern Ireland: public finance and public services 1921–1964* (Oxford, 1965).
Lears, T.J. Jackson, 'The concept of cultural hegemony: problems and possibilities', *AHR*, 90 (1985).
Lee, J.J., 'Some aspects of modern Irish historiography', in E. Schulin (ed.), *Gedenkschrift Martin Göhring: Studien zur Europäischen Geschichte* (Wiesbaden, 1968).

'Capital in the Irish economy', in L.M. Cullen (ed.), *The formation of the Irish economy* (Cork, 1969).

'Irish agriculture 1815–1914', *Agricultural History Review*, xvii (1969).

The modernisation of Irish society 1848–1918 (Dublin, 1973).

'Lemass and his two partnerships', *Irish Times Supplement*, 19 May 1976.

'A Jabobin (sic) after his time', *Irish Press*, 21 April 1977.

'Women and the church since the Famine', in M. MacCurtain and D. Ó Corráin (eds.), *Women in Irish society* (Dublin, 1978).

'Sub-national regionalism or sub-state nationalism: the Irish case', in W. Link and W.J. Feld (eds.), *The new nationalism: implications for trans-Atlantic relations* (New York, 1979).

'Seán Lemass', in J.J. Lee (ed.), *Ireland 1945–70* (Dublin, 1979).

'Continuity and change in Ireland, 1945–70', in J.J. Lee (ed.), *Ireland 1945–70* (Dublin, 1979).

'Aspects of corporatist thought in Ireland: the Commission on Vocational Organisation, 1939–43', in A. Cosgrove and D. McCartney (eds.), *Studies in Irish history presented to R. Dudley Edwards* (Dublin, 1979).

'Worker and society in modern Ireland', in D. Nevin (ed.), *Trade unions and change in Irish society* (Dublin, 1980).

'Merchants and enterprise: the case of early Irish railways 1830–1855', in L.M. Cullen and P. Butel (eds.), *Nègoce et industrie en France et en Irlande aux xviii et xix siècles* (Paris, 1980).

'Irish nationalism and socialism: Rumpf reconsidered', *Saothar: Journal of the Irish Labour History Society* 6 (1980).

'Patterns of rural unrest in nineteenth-century Ireland: a preliminary survey', in L.M. Cullen and F. Furet (eds.), *Ireland and France, 17–20th centuries: towards a comparative study of rural history* (Paris, 1980).

'Irish economic history since 1500', in J.J. Lee (ed.), *Irish historiography 1970–79* (Cork, 1981).

'Society and culture', in F. Litton (ed.), *Unequal achievement: the Irish experience 1957–1982* (Dublin, 1982).

'Motivation: an historian's point of view', in An Foras Forbartha, *Ireland in the year 2000: towards a national strategy* (Dublin, 1983).

'University, state and society in Ireland, 1983', *Crane Bag*, 7 (1983).

Reflections on Ireland in the EEC (Dublin, 1984).

'Perspectives on Ireland in the EEC: a review essay', *ESR*, 16 (1984).

'Forging a new reality?' *Administration*, 32 (1984).

'Reflections on the study of Irish values', in M.P. Fogarty, L. Ryan and J.J. Lee, *Irish values and attitudes* (Dublin, 1984).

'Centralisation and community', in J.J. Lee (ed.), *Ireland: towards a sense of place* (Cork, 1985).

'A third division team?', *Seirbhís Phoiblí: Journal of the Department of the Public Service*, 6 (1985).

'Letter to the Editor', *Seirbhís Phoiblí: Journal of the Department of the Public Service*, 7 (1986).

'Aspects of Irish identity', in *Half the lies are true: Ireland/Britain; a microcosm of international misunderstanding* (Dublin, 1986).

'Whither Ireland? The next twenty five years', in K.A. Kennedy (ed.), *Ireland in transition: economic and social change since 1960* (Dublin, 1986).

Lee, J.J. and Ó Tuathaigh, M.A.G., *The age of de Valera* (Dublin, 1982).

Lee, R.M., 'Intermarriage, conflict and social control in Ireland: the Decree "Ne temere"', *ESR*, 17 (1985).

Lemass, S.F., *One Nation* (Dublin, 1959).

'The organisation behind the economic programme', in B. Chubb and P. Lynch (eds.), *Economic development and planning* (Dublin, 1969).

'Seán Lemass looks back' (interviews with Michael Mills), *Irish Press*, January–February 1969.

L'entreprise suisse dans le monde de demain (Zurich, 1969).

Leppo, M., 'Die wirtschaftswissenschaftliche Ausbildung in Finland', *Weltwirtschaftliches Archiv*, 88 (1962).

Lerner, D., 'The transformation of institutions', in W.B. Hamilton (ed.), *The transfer of institutions* (London, 1964).

Lewis, J.R., 'Regional policy and planning: convergence and contradiction', in S. Bornstein, D. Held and J. Krieger (eds.), *The state in capitalist Europe* (London, 1984).

Lijphart, A., 'Consociation: the model and its application in divided societies', in D. Rea (ed.), *Political cooperation in divided societies* (Dublin, 1982).

Limerick Rural Survey, *Third Interim Report: social structure* (Tipperary, 1962).

Lindbeck, A., *Swedish economic policy* (London, 1975).

Locke, R.R., 'Business education in Germany: past systems and current practice', *Business History Review*, 59 (1985).

Logan, B.M., 'From vanguard to base camp: new perspectives on Irish public administration', *Administration*, 32 (1984).

Lönnroth, L., 'The intellectual civil servant: the role of the writer and scholar in nordic culture', *Daedalus*, 113, (1984).

Loock, H-D., 'Zeitgeschichte Norwegens', *Vierteljahrshefte für Zeitgeschichte*, 13 (1965).

Lucey, C., 'The problem of the woman worker', *Irish Ecclesiastical Record*, 48 (1936).

Lynch, J.M., 'My life and times', *Magill*, 3 (1979).

'The Anglo-Irish problem', *Foreign Affairs*, 50 (1972).

'Why Ireland joined', *Community Report*, 3 (1983).

Lynch, P., 'Discussion on the causes of unemployment', *JSSISI*, 17 (1945).

'The economist and public policy', *Studies*, 42 (1953).

'The social revolution that never was', in T.D. Williams (ed.), *The Irish struggle 1916–1926* (London, 1966).

'The Irish economy since the war, 1946–51', in K.B. Nowlan and T.D. Williams, *Ireland in the war years and after, 1939–51* (Dublin, 1969).

'Whither science policy?', *Administration*, 27 (1979).

'Garret FitzGerald: a personal memoir', in J. Dooge (ed.), *Ireland in the contemporary world: essays in honour of Garret FitzGerald* (Dublin, 1986).

Lyon, S., 'Unemployment: the statistical background', *JSSISI*, 17 (1942–3).

Lyons, F.S.L., 'Dillon, Redmond and the Irish Home Rulers', in F.X. Martin (ed.), *Leaders and men of the Easter Rising: Dublin 1916* (London, 1967).

John Dillon (London, 1968).

Ireland since the Famine (London, 1971).

'Days of decision', in B. Farrell (ed.), *The Irish parliamentary tradition* (Dublin, 1973).

'The great debate', in B. Farrell (ed.), *The Irish parliamentary tradition* (Dublin, 1973).

'The meaning of Independence', in B. Farrell (ed.), *The Irish parliamentary tradition* (Dublin, 1973).

'The dilemma of the Irish contemporary historian', *Hermathena*, 115 (1973).

'Symbol of the era he bestrode', in *Irish Times, Eamon de Valera 1882–1975* (Dublin, 1976).

Culture and anarchy in Ireland, 1880–1939 (Oxford, 1980).

'T.W.M.', in F.S.L. Lyons and R. Hawkins (eds.), *Ireland under the Union* (Oxford, 1980).

McAleese, D., '*Building on reality 1985–1987*: a commentary', *IBR* (1984).

'Ireland and the European Community: the changing pattern of trade', in P.J. Drudy and D. McAleese (eds.), Irish Studies, 1 (Cambridge, 1983).

'The changing economic environment', in F.S.L. Lyons, *Bicentenary essays: Bank of Ireland 1783–1983* (Dublin, 1983).

'Is there a want of capital in Ireland'? *Administration*, 31 (1984).

McAllister, I., *The Northern Ireland Social Democratic and Labour Party: political opposition in a divided society* (London, 1977).

McAllister, I. and Nelson, S., 'Modern developments in the Northern Ireland party system', *Parliamentary Affairs*, 32 (1979).

Mac Amhlaoibh, D., *Dialann deorai* (Dublin, 1960).

McAvoy, T.T. and Brown, T.N., 'The United States of America', in P.J. Corish (ed.), *A history of Irish Catholicism* (Dublin, 1970).

McCann, E., *War and an Irish town* (London, 1980, 2nd edn).

Macardle, D., *The Irish Republic* (London, 1968 edn).

MacCarthy, C., 'A review of the objectives of the national pay agreements 1970–1977', *Administration*, 25 (1977).

The decade of upheaval (Dublin, 1973).

Trade unions in Ireland, 1894–1960 (Dublin, 1977).

McCartney, D., 'De Valera's mission to the United States, 1919–20', in A. Cosgrave and D. McCartney (eds.), *Studies in Irish history presented to R. Dudley Edwards* (Dublin, 1979).

The National University of Ireland and Eamon de Valera (Dublin, 1983).

McCartney, R.L., *Liberty and authority in Ireland* (Derry, 1985).

McColgan, J., *British policy and the Irish administration 1920–22* (London, 1983).

'Lionel Curtis and constitutional procedures', *IHS*, 20 (1977).

'Partition and the Irish administration 1920–22', *Administration*, 28 (1980).

McCracken, J.L., *Representative government in Ireland* (London, 1958).

MacDonagh, O., *Ireland since the Union* (Englewood Cliffs, 1968, 2nd edn, London, 1979).

States of mind (London, 1983).

McDonald, F., *The destruction of Dublin* (Dublin, 1985).

MacDonald, M., *Titans and others* (London, 1972).

McDowell, R.B., *The Irish Convention 1917–1918* (London, 1970).

McDowell, R.B. and Webb, D.A., *Trinity College Dublin 1592–1952: an academic history* (Cambridge, 1982).

MacEntee, S., 'Obituary of de Valera', *Irish Press*, 30 August 1975.

McEvoy, F.J., 'Canada, Ireland and the Commonwealth: the declaration of the Irish Republic 1948–9', *IHS*, 24 (1985).

McGovern, J.J. and O'Farrell, P.J., 'Australia', in P.J. Corish (ed.), *A history of Irish Catholicism* (Dublin, 1971).

MacGréil, M., 'Education and cultural development', *Social Studies*, 1 (1972).

MacKechnie, G., 'Devlin revisited', *Administration*, 25 (1977).

MacKnight, T., *Ulster as it is* (2 vols., London, 1896).

MacMahon, B.M.E., 'A sense of identity in the Irish legal system', in J.J. Lee (ed.), *Ireland: towards a sense of place* (Cork, 1985).

'Developments in the Irish legal system since 1945', in J.J. Lee (ed.), *Ireland 1945–70* (Dublin, 1979).

'EEC membership and the Irish legal system', in P.J. Drudy and D. McAleese (eds.), *Ireland and the European Community*, Irish Studies, 4 (Cambridge, 1983).

McMahon, D., 'Ireland, the Dominions and the Munich Crisis', *Irish Studies in International Affairs*, 1 (1979).

'"A transient apparition": British policy towards the de Valera government, 1932–5', *IHS*, 22 (1981).

Republicans and imperialists: Anglo-Irish relations in the 1930s (London, 1984).

MacNeill, E., *The Ulster difficulty* (Dublin, 1917).

'Ten years of the Irish Free State', *Foreign Affairs*, x (1932).

MacNeill, R., *Ulster's stand for union* (London, 1922).

MacRae, D., 'Populism as an ideology', in G. Ionescu and E. Gellner (eds.), *Populism: its meanings and national characteristics* (London, 1969).

MacSharry, R., 'The White Paper "Serving the Country Better" – a step in the right direction', *Seirbhís Phoiblí*, 7 (1986).

MacSweeney, B., 'The threat of sociology', *Social Studies*, 1 (1972).

MacStiofáin, S., *Memoirs of a revolutionary* (London, 1975).

Machlup, F., 'F.A. von Hayek', *Swedish Journal of Economics*, 76 (1974).

Machin, H., 'France', in F.F. Ridley (ed.), *Government and Administration in Western Europe* (London, 1979).

Mack Smith, D., *A history of Italy* (Madison, 1969).

Maddison, A., *Economic growth in the west* (London, 1964).

Magner, E., 'Sean Moylan: some aspects of his parliamentary career 1937–1948' (unpublished MA thesis, University College, Cork, 1982).

Maher, D.J., *The tortuous path* (Dublin, 1986).

Maier, C.S., *et al.*, 'The two postwar eras and the conditions for stability', *AHR*, 86 (1981).

'Preconditions for corporatism', in J.H. Goldthorpe (ed.), *Order and conflict in contemporary capitalism* (Oxford, 1984).

Maier, H., 'Sprache, Nation, Kulturgemeinshaft', *Möglichkeiten und Grenzen einer nationalen Geschichtschreibung* (Madrid, 1984).

Mair, P., *The changing Irish party system* (London, 1987).

'Labour and the Irish party system revisited: party competition in the 1920s', *ESR*, 9 (1977).

Manning, M., *The Blueshirts* (Dublin, 1970).

'The pride of Ballaghadereen', *Magill* (1986).

Manning, M. and MacDowell, M., *Electricity supply in Ireland: the history of the ESB* (Dublin, 1970).

Mansergh, N., *The Irish Free State: its government and politics* (London, 1934).

The government of Northern Ireland (London, 1936).

The Irish question 1840–1921 (London, 1965).

'Irish foreign policy 1945–51', in K.B. Nowlan and T.D. Williams (eds.), *Ireland in the war years and after: 1939–51* (Dublin, 1969).

'Eoin MacNeill – a reappraisal', *Studies*, 63 (1974).

'The Government of Ireland Act 1920: its origins and purposes. The working of the "official mind"', in J.G. Barry (ed.), *Historical Studies*, 9 (Belfast, 1974).

Marguerat, P., 'La Svizzera e la neutralità economica, 1940–1944', *Italia contemporaneo* (1984).

Marsh, M.A., 'Ireland', in I. Crewe and D. Denver (eds.), *Electoral change in western democracies: patterns and sources of electoral volatility* (London, 1985).

Martin, F.X., 'Eoin MacNeill on the 1916 Rising', *IHS*, 12 (1961).

'1916 – myth, fact and mystery', *Studia Hibernica*, 7 (1967).

'Michael Tierney, 1894–1975', in F.X. Martin (ed.), *Eoin MacNeill* (Oxford, 1980).

'Theodore William Moody', *Hermathena*, 136 (1984).

Martin, F.X. and Byrne, F.J. (eds.), *The Scholar Revolutionary* (Shannon, Ireland, 1973).

Martin, G., 'The Irish Free State and the evolution of the Commonwealth, 1921–49', in R. Hyam and G. Martin (eds.), *Reappraisals in British imperial history* (London, 1975).

Mason, D., 'Nationalism and the process of group mobilisation: the case of "loyalism" in Northern Ireland reconsidered', *Ethnic and Racial Studies*, 8 (1985).

Masterson, P., 'The concept of resentment', *Studies*, 68 (1979).

Mathias, P., 'Leisure and wages in theory and practice', in P. Mathias, *The transformation of England* (New York, 1979).

Matthews, A., 'Economics and ideology', *Crane Bag*, 9 (1985).

Maurogordatos, G.T., *Stillborn republic: social coalitions and party strategies in Greece 1922–1936* (London, 1983).

Mazrui, A.A., 'Borrowed theory and original practice in African politics', in H.J. Spiro (ed.), *Patterns of African development* (New Jersey, 1967).

Meenan, J., 'Irish industry and post-war problems', *Studies*, 32 (1943).

'From free trade to self-sufficiency', in F. MacManus (ed.), *The years of the great test 1926–39* (Cork, 1967).

The Irish economy since 1922 (Liverpool, 1970).

George O'Brien: a memoir (Dublin, 1980).

'Comment on Brian Kennedy's article', *Studies*, 75 (1986).

Megahey, A.J., 'The Irish Protestant churches and social and political issues 1870–1914' (PhD, Queen's University, Belfast, 1969).

Memoirs of Desmond FitzGerald 1913–1916 (Dublin, 1968).

Mernagh, M., 'Poverty and community work', in S. Kennedy (ed.),*One million poor?* (Dublin, 1981).

Miller, D.W., *Church, state and nation in Ireland, 1898–1921* (Pittsburgh, 1973).

Queen's rebels: Ulster loyalism in historical perspective (Dublin, 1980).

Miller, K.A., *Emigrants and exiles: Ireland and the Irish exodus to North America* (Oxford, 1985).

'Emigration, ideology and identity in post-Famine Ireland', *Studies*, 75 (1986).

Miller, R., 'Fair employment in the civil service: report of an investigation into the non-industrial Northern Ireland civil service', *Ireland: Politics and Society*, 1 (1985).

Milroy, S., 'Foreword', in *Protection for Irish industries: the Report of the Fiscal Inquiry Committee: an analysis and a reply* (Dublin, 1924).

Mills, M., 'Seán Lemass: a profile', *Irish Press*, 18 January 1969.

Milward, A.S., *War, economy and society 1939–1945* (Berkeley, 1979).

The reconstruction of Western Europe 1945–1951 (London, 1984).

'Strategies for development in agriculture: the nineteenth-century European experience', in T.C. Smout (ed.), *The search for wealth and stability* (London, 1979).

Milward, A.S. and Saul, S.B., *The economic development of continental Europe 1780–1870* (London, 1973).

The development of the economies of continental Europe 1850–1914 (London, 1977).

Mitchell, A., *Labour in Irish politics 1890–1930* (Dublin, 1974).

'William O'Brien 1881–1968 and the Irish Labour movement', *Studies*, 60 (1971).

Mitchell, B.R., *European historical statistics 1750–1970* (London, 1975).

'Statistical appendix', in C.M. Cipolla (ed.), *Fontana economic history of Europe*, 6 (2) (London, 1976).

Mitchell, B.R. and Deane, P., *Abstract of British historical statistics* (Cambridge, 1962).

Mitchell, G.F., 'Antiquities', in T.Ó Raifeartaigh (ed.), *The RIA. A bicentennial history 1785–1985* (Dublin, 1985).

Moloney, E., 'SDLP expressed changed nationalist psyche', *Irish Times*, 21 August 1985.

'Paisley', *Crane Bag*, 4 (1980).

Molyneaux, J., 'Northern Ireland' in *Right ahead* (1985).

Mommsen, W.J., 'Die Geschichtswissenschaft in der modernen Industriegesellschaft', *Vierteljahrshefte für Zeitgeschichte*, 22 (1974).

Montague, J., *Death of a chieftain and other essays* (Dublin, 1978 edn).

The rough field (Dublin, 1979, 3rd edn).

The dead kingdom (Mountrath, 1984).

Moody, T.W., *The Ulster question, 1603–1973* (Dublin, 1974).

'Edmund Curtis', *Hermathena*, 64 (1944).

'Twenty years after', *IHS*, 11 (1958).

Moody, T.W. and Beckett, J.C., *Queen's Belfast: the history of a university*, vol. 2 (London, 1959).

Moore, D., Rhodes, J. and Tarling, R., 'Industrial policy and economic development: the experience of Northern Ireland and the Republic of Ireland', *Cambridge Journal of Economics*, 2 (1978).

Morgan, K.O., *Wales: rebirth of a nation 1880–1980* (Oxford, 1982).

Morrissey, M., 'The politics of economic management in Ireland 1956–70', *Irish Political Studies*, 1 (1986).

Moss, W., *Political parties in the Irish Free State* (New York, 1933.

Moynihan, M., *Currency and Central Banking in Ireland 1922–1960* (Dublin, 1975).

Speeches and statements by Eamon de Valera 1917–73 (Dublin and New York, 1980).

Moxon-Browne, E., *Nation, class and creed – Northern Ireland* (Aldershot, 1982).

Mulcahy, D., *Curriculum and policy in Irish post-primary education* (Dublin, 1981).

Mulvey, H., 'Theodore William Moody (1907–84): an appreciation', *IHS*, 24 (1984).

Munger, F., *The legitimacy of opposition: the change of government in Ireland in 1932* (Beverley Hills, Cal., 1975).

Murphy, F., 'The European Community and the Irish legal system', in D. Coombes (ed.), *Ireland and the European Communities: ten years of membership* (Dublin, 1983).

Murphy, J.A., *Ireland in the twentieth century* (Dublin, 1975).

'The Irish party system 1938–51', in K.B. Nowlan and T.D. Williams (eds.), *Ireland in the war years and after* (Dublin, 1969).

'Irish identity', in *Etudes Irlandaises*, 1 (1976).

'Further reflections on Irish nationalism', *The Crane Bag*, 2 (1978).

'Put them out! Parties and elections, 1948–69', in J.J. Lee (ed.), *Ireland 1945–70* (Dublin, 1979).

'Comment', in D. Watt (ed.), *The Constitution of Northern Ireland* (London, 1981).

'The Church, morality and the law', in D.M. Clarke (ed.), *Morality and the law* (Dublin, 1982).

'The achievement of Eamon de Valera', in J.P. O'Carroll and J.A. Murphy (eds), *De Valera and his times* (Cork, 1983).

Murphy, K., 'A changing civil service?', *Administration*, 34 (1986).

'Raising productivity in the civil service', *Seirbhís Phoiblí*, 3 (1982).

Murphy, M.J., *Tyrone folk quest* (Belfast, 1973).

Murray, D., 'Educational segregation: "rite" or wrong?', in O. Clancy, S. Drudy, K. Lynch and L. O'Dowd (eds.), *Ireland: a sociological profile* (Dublin, 1986).

Murray, P., 'Irish elections: a changing pattern', *Studies*, 65 (1976).

Myrdal, G., 'Crises and cycles in the development of economics', *Political Quarterly*, 44 (1973).

National University Handbook 1908–1932 (Dublin, 1932).

Navarro, R.D., Alvariez, F.C. and Karps, L., 'The teaching of political science in developing countries', *International Social Science Journal*, 31 (1978).

Neary, J.P., 'The failure of economic nationalism', *The Crane Bag*, 8 (1984).

Neary, J.P. and Ó Gráda, C., *Protection, economic war and structural change: the 1930s in Ireland* (London, 1986).

Nelson, S., 'Protestant "ideology" considered: a case of discrimination'", in I. Crewe (ed.), *British Political Sociology Yearbook*, 2 (London, 1975).
  Ulster's uncertain defenders (Belfast, 1984).

Nevin, M., 'A study of the social background of students in Irish universities', *JSSISI*, 21 (1967–8).

New Ireland Forum, *A comparative description of the economic structure and situation, North and South* (Dublin, 1983).

New Ireland Forum, No. 1, *Public Session*, 30 May 1983 (Dublin, 1983).

New Ireland Forum, *The cost of violence* (Dublin, 1984).

New Ireland Forum, *Report* (Dublin, 1984).

Nicholson, N.K., 'The factional model and the study of politics', *Comparative Political Studies*, 5 (1972).

Nolan, S., 'Economic growth', in J.W. O'Hagan (ed.), *The economy of Ireland: policy and performance* (Dublin, 1981, 3rd edn).

Nolan, W., 'Preface', in G.L. Herries-Davies (ed.), *Irish geography: the Geographical Society of Ireland Golden Jubilee 1934–1984* (Dublin, 1984).

Norstedt, J.A., *Thomas MacDonagh* (Charlottesville, North Carolina, 1980).

Norton, D., 'Estimation of the short run effects of fiscal policy in Ireland, 1960–1970', *ESR*, 5 (1974–5).
  'Problems in economic planning and policy formation in Ireland, 1958–74', *ESRI Broadsheet*, No. 12 (1975).

Nygren, I., 'The Swedish credit market and government borrowing for defence and interest-rate stabilisation 1935–1945', in M. Fritz, *et al.*, *The adaptable nation. Essays in Swedish economy during the Second World War* (Stockholm, 1984).

Oakeshott, M., *Rationalism in politics* (London, 1962).

O'Beirne-Ranelagh, J., 'The IRB from the Treaty to 1924', *IHS*, 20 (1976).

O'Brien, C. Cruise, *To Katanga and back* (London, 1962).
  States of Ireland (London, 1972).
  'Passion and cunning: an essay on the politics of W.B. Yeats', in A.N. Jeffares and K.G.W. Crosse (eds.), *In excited reverie* (London, 1965).
  'The embers of Easter, 1916–1966', in O.D. Edwards and F. Pyle (eds.), *1916: the Easter Rising* (London, 1968).
  Ireland in international affairs', in O.D. Edwards (ed.), *Conor Cruise O'Brien introduces Ireland* (London, 1969).
  'Northern Ireland: its past and its future: the future', *Race*, 14 (1972).
  'Nationalism and the reconquest of Ireland', *Crane Bag*, 1 (1977).
  'Ireland: the mirage of peace', *New York Review of books*, 21 April 1986.

O'Brien, F., *The Best of Myles* (London, 1968).

O'Brien, G., 'Agriculture and employment in the Free State', *Studies*, 19 (1930).
  'Patrick Hogan', *Studies*, 25 (1936).

O'Brien, J.F., *A study of national wage agreements in Ireland* (Dublin, 1981).

O'Brien, M.C., 'The two languages', in O.D. Edwards (ed.), *Conor Cruise O'Brien introduces Ireland* (London, 1964).

Ó Broin, L., *Revolutionary underground: the story of the Irish Republican Brotherhood 1858–1924* (Dublin, 1976).

Michael Collins (Dublin, 1980).

No man's man (Dublin, 1982).

Just like yesterday (Dublin, 1985).

'Joseph Brennan: civil servant extraordinary', *Studies*, 66 (1977).

Ó Buachalla, B., 'Ó Corcora agus an Hidden Ireland', *Scríobh*, 4 (1979).

Ó Buachalla, S., *A significant Irish educationalist* (Dublin and Cork, 1980).

'An Piarsach mar Oideachasóir', *Feasta*, 29 (1976).

O'Byrnes, S., *Hiding behind a face: Fine Gael under FitzGerald* (Dublin, 1980).

O'Callaghan, M., 'Language, nationality and cultural identity in the Irish Free State, 1922–7: the *Irish Statesman* and the *Catholic Bulletin* reappraised', *IHS*, 94 (1984).

O'Carroll, J.P., 'Eamon de Valera, charisma and political development', in J.P. O'Carroll and J.A. Murphy (eds.), *De Valera and his times* (Cork, 1983).

'The politics of the 1983 "abortion referendum debate" in the Republic of Ireland', unpublished paper delivered at European Consortium of Political Research Conference, Salzburg, April 1984.

O'Casey, S., *Drums under the window* (Pan edn, London, 1980).

Ó Catháin, S., 'Secondary education in Ireland', *Studies*, 44 (1955).

'Education in the new Ireland', in F. MacManus (ed.), *The years of the great test, 1926–39* (Cork, 1967).

Ó Cinnéide, C., 'A west Kerry chronicle', in D.B. Kelleher (ed.), *Kerryman, 1881–1981* (New York, 1981).

Ó Cinnéide, S., *A law for the poor* (Dublin, 1970).

Ó Cofaigh, T.F., 'Slabhra scaoilte: smaointe ar neamhspleachas airgeadais', *Central Bank Quarterly Bulletin* (1985).

Ó Coileáin, S., *Seán Ó Riordáin* (Dublin, 1982).

O'Connell, P.T., 'The civil service in the modern state', *Studies* (1970).

O'Connell, T.J., *History of the INTO 1868–1968* (Dublin, n.d.).

O'Connor, E., 'Agrarian unrest and the labour movement in Co. Waterford, 1917–1923', *Saothar*, 6 (1980).

O'Connor, F., *An only child* (London, 1964).

O'Connor, J.F., 'Agreement gives North new international status', *Irish Times*, 21 November 1985.

'Article 50 of Bunreacht na hÉireann and the unwritten English Constitution of Ireland', in J.P. O'Carroll and J.A. Murphy (eds.), *De Valera and his times* (Cork, 1983).

O'Connor, K.D., 'Ireland – a nation caught in the middle of an identity crisis', *Irish Independent*, 20 July 1985.

O'Connor, R. and Guiomard, C., 'Agricultural output in the Irish Free State area before and after independence', *IESH*, 12 (1985).

O'Connor, S., 'How O'Malley launched free scheme', *Irish Times*, 10 September 1986 (interview with Christina Murphy).

Ó Crualaoich, G., 'The primacy of form: a "folk ideology" in de Valera's politics', in J.P. O'Carroll and J.A. Murphy (eds.), *De Valera and his times* (Cork, 1983).

Ó Direáin, M., *Feamainn Bhealtaine* (Dublin, 1961).

O'Doherty, J.F., 'The Catholic Church in 1937', *Irish Ecclesiastical Record*, 5th series, li (1938).

O'Donoghue, F., 'Ceannt, Devoy, O'Rahilly and the military plan', in F.X. Martin (ed.), *Leaders and men of the Easter Rising: Dublin 1916* (London, 1967).

O'Donoghue, M., and Tait, A.A., 'The growth of public revenue and expenditure in Ireland', in J.A. Bristow and A.A. Tait (eds.), *Economic policy in Ireland* (Dublin, 1968).

O'Donovan, P., 'De Valera, the Irish de Gaulle', *The Observer*, 31 August 1975.

O'Dowd, L., 'Intellectuals in twentieth-century Ireland: and the case of George Russell (AE)', *Crane Bag*, 9 (1985).

'Sociological research in Ireland: an overview and a proposed strategy', Paper to RIA conference on social science research in Ireland, 23 October 1986.

Ó hEithir, B., *The begrudger's guide to Irish politics* (Dublin, 1986).

Ó hEocha, C., 'The science budget', *JSSISI*, 23 (1969–70).

'Cad é ar domhan atá i ndán don Ollscoil?', *Irish Times*, 8 November 1984.

O'Faolain, S., *The Irish* (Harmondsworth, 1962 edn).

Vive Moi! (London, 1965).

'The plain people of Ireland', *The Bell*, 7 (1943–44).

'One world', *The Bell*, 7 (1943–44).

'De Valera', *The Bell*, 10 (1945).

'Ireland after Yeats', *The Bell*, 18 (1953).

O'Farrell, P., *Ireland's English question* (London, 1971).

England and Ireland since 1800 (Oxford, 1975).

Ó Gadhra, N., 'Earnán de Blaghd', *Éire-Ireland*, 11 (1976).

Ó Glaisne, R., *Conor Cruise O'Brien agus an liobrálachas* (Dublin, 1974).

Ó Gráda, C., 'The beginnings of the Irish creamery system 1880–1914', *Economic History Review*, n.s., 30 (1977).

O'Halloran, C., *Partition and the limits of Irish nationalism* (Dublin, 1987).

O'Hearn, D., 'Catholic grievances: comments', *British Journal of Sociology* 38 (1987).

O'Keeffe, P.D., 'The origins and development of Clann na Poblachta', MA thesis, University College, Cork, 1981.

'Transition from the politics of war to the politics of peace: General Richard Mulcahy, the army and the cabinet, 1919–24', PhD thesis, University College, Cork, 1987.

O'Leary, B., 'The Anglo-Irish Agreement: folly or statecraft?', *Western European Politics*, 10 (1987).

O'Leary, C., *Irish elections 1918–1977* (Dublin, 1979).

'The Northern Ireland crisis and its observers', *Political Quarterly*, 42 (1971).

'Northern Ireland, 1945–72', in J.J. Lee (ed.), *Ireland 1945–70* (Dublin, 1979).

'The teaching of politics in Ireland: (iii) Queen's University, Belfast', Political Studies Association of Ireland Bulletin, 4 (1986).

O'Leary, J., 'Some implications of the revisions to the balance of payments and the national accounts', *IBR* (1984).

Oliver, J.A., *Working at Stormont* (Dublin, 1978).

Olsson, U., *The creation of a modern arms industry: Sweden, 1939–1974* (Gothenburg, 1977).

O'Mahony, D., *The Irish economy* (Cork, 1964).

'Introduction', in K.A. Kennedy, *The unemployment crisis* (Cork, 1985).

O'Malley, E., 'The problem of late industrialisation and the experience of the Republic of Ireland', *Cambridge Journal of Economics*, 9 (1985).

O'Malley, J., 'Can C.J. pass the credibility test?', *Sunday Independent*, 14 October 1984.

'Labour's wigging weekend', *Sunday Independent*, 14 November 1976.

O'Malley, P., *Uncivil wars* (Belfast, 1983).

O'Neill, T., *Ulster at the crossroads* (London, 1969).

O'Neill, T.P., 'In search of a political path: Irish republicanism, 1922–1927', in G.A. Hayes-McCoy (ed.), *Historical Studies*, 10 (Dublin, 1976).

'Eamon de Valera agus an teanga', *Feasta*, 35 (1982).

O'Neill, T.P., and Lord Longford, *Eamon de Valera* (Dublin, 1970).

Ó'Neill, T.P. and Ó Fiannachta, P., *De Valera*, 1 (Dublin, 1968).

Ó Nualláin, C., 'Public service reform', *Administration*, 26 (1978).

'Sharing the nation's resources: problems of administration in the public service', *Administration*, 27 (1979).

Ó hOdhráin, M., 'Dúchas', in *Sléibhte Mhaigh Eó* (Dublin, 1964).

'Seán Ó Riordáin ag caint le Seán Ó Mórdha', *Scríobh*, 3 (Dublin, 1978).

Ó Riordáin, S., 'De Valera, de Gaulle agus Dia', in M. MacInerney (ed.), *Eamon de Valera 1822–1975* (Dublin, 1976).

ORLDOC, *Literatur datenbank. Veröffentlichungen des ORL-Instituts der ETH 1946–1982/83* (Zurich, 1983).

Orpen, R.J., 'Reservation No. 10', in *Report of the commission on emigration and other population problems 1948–1954* (Dublin, 1956).

Osborne, R.D., 'Voting behaviour in Northern Ireland 1921–1977', in F.W. Boal and J.N.H. Douglas (eds.), *Integration and division: geographical perspectives on the Northern Ireland problem* (London, 1982).

O'Sullivan, D., *The Irish Free State and its Senate* (London, 1940, Arno reprint, 1972).

Othick, J., 'An economic history of Ulster: a perspective', in L. Kennedy and P. Ollerenshaw (eds.), *An economic history of Ulster 1820–1939* (Manchester, 1985).

Ó Tuama, S., 'The Gaelic League idea in the future', in S. Ó Tuama (ed.), *The Gaelic League idea* (Cork, 1972).

'Stability and ambivalence: aspects of the sense of place and religion in Irish literature', in J.J. Lee (ed.), *Ireland: towards a sense of place* (Cork, 1983).

Ó Tuathaigh, M.A.G., 'The state and the language since 1922', *Irish Times*, 19 April 1977.

'Is do chuala croi cine soiléir', *Scríobh*, 4 (1979).

'Language, literature and culture in Ireland since the war', in J.J. Lee (ed.), *Ireland 1945–70* (Dublin, 1979).

'Early Modern Ireland, 1534–1691: a reassessment', in P.J. Drudy (ed.), *Irish Studies*, 1 (Cambridge, 1980).

'The land question, politics and Irish society, 1922–1960s,' in P.J. Drudy (ed.), *Ireland: land, politics and society*, Irish Studies, 2 (Cambridge, 1982).

'Party politics, political stability and social change in Ireland 1932–73: the case of Fianna Fáil', *XVe Congres International des Sciences Historiques*, Actes 4 (2) (Bucharest, 1982).

'De Valera and sovereignty: a note on the pedigree of a political idea', in J.P. O'Carroll and J.A. Murphy (eds.), *De Valera and his times* (Cork, 1983).

'The media and Irish culture', in B. Farrell (ed.), *Communications and community in Ireland* (Dublin, 1984).

'Bunú an Chomchaidrimh: Nóta ar an gCúlra', in S. Ó hAnnracháin (ed.), *An Comhchaidreamh. Crann a Chraobhaigh* (Dublin, 1985).

'The regional dimension', in K. Kennedy (ed.), *Ireland in transition* (Dublin, 1986).

'Religion, nationality and a sense of community in modern Ireland', in M.A.G. Ó Tuathaigh (ed.), *Community, culture and conflict* (Galway, 1986).

'Ireland and Britain under the Union, 1800–1921: an overview', in P.J. Drudy (ed.), *Ireland and Britain since 1922*, Irish Studies, 5 (Cambridge, 1986).

'People in Ireland', *Irish Times*, 2 December 1986.

Ó Tuathaigh, M.A.G., and Lee, J.J., *The age of de Valera* (Dublin, 1982).

Outram, D., 'Negating the rational: or why historians deny Irish science', *Irish Review*, 1 (1986).

Pakenham, F., *Peace by ordeal* (London, 1935).

Patterson, H., *Class conflict and sectarianism: the Protestant working class and the Belfast labour movement 1868–1920* (Belfast, 1980).

Paulin, T., *Ireland and the English crisis* (Newcastle-upon-Tyne, 1984).

Pearse, P., *Political writings and speeches* (Dublin, 1966 edn).

Peck, J., *Dublin from Downing Street* (Dublin, 1978).

Peillon, M., *Contemporary Irish society: an introduction* (Dublin, 1982).

Penniman, H. (ed.), *Ireland at the polls: the Dáil elections of 1977* (Washington, 1978).

'"People's democracy": a discussion on strategy', *New Left Review*, 55 (1969).

Phelps Brown, E.H. and Browne, M.H., *A century of pay* (London, 1968).

Phillips, A.W., *The revolution in Ireland, 1906–23* (London, 1923).

Pochmann, H.A., 'The migration of ideas', in H.S. Commager (ed.), *Immigration in American history* (Minneapolis, 1961).

Pocock, J.G.A., *Virtue, commerce and history* (Cambridge, 1985).

Pollard, S., *The development of the British economy 1914–1967* (London, 2nd edn, 1973).

Peaceful conquest. The industrialization of Europe 1760–1970 (Oxford, 1981).

Prager, J., *Building democracy in Ireland: political order and cultural integration in a newly independent nation* (Cambridge, 1986).

Pratschke, J., 'Economic philosophy and ideology in Ireland', *Studies*, 74 (1985).

Prenter, S., 'The religious difficulty under Home Rule: the non-conformist view', in S. Rosenbaum, *Against Home Rule* (1912: Kennikat edn, London, 1970).

Press, J.P., 'Protectionism and the Irish footwear industry', *IESH*, 13 (1986).

'Programme for economic expansion', *IBR* (1959).

Puhle, H.J., 'Was ist Populismus?', *Politik und Kultur*, 10 (1983).

Pyne, P., 'The bureaucracy in the Irish Republic: its political role and the factors influencing it', *Political Studies*, 22 (1974).

'The new Irish state and the decline of the Republican Sinn Féin party, 1923–1926', *Éire–Ireland*, 11 (1976).

Quinn, B., 'Dev's last-ditch stand on partition', *Sunday Independent*, 4 March 1979.

Quinn, G., 'The changing pattern of Irish society, 1938–51', in K.B. Nowlan and T.D. Williams (eds.), *Ireland in the war years and after* (Dublin, 1969).

Radice, E.A., 'General characteristics of the region between the wars', in M.C. Kaser and E.A. Radice (eds.), *The economic history of eastern Europe 1919–1975*, 1 (Oxford, 1985).

RTE/UCD Lectures, 'Ireland: dependence and independence', *Crane Bag*, 8 (1984).

Rafroidi, P., 'Change and the Irish imagination', in P. Connolly (ed.), *Literature and the changing Ireland* (Colin Smythe, Gerrard's Cross, Bucks., 1982).

Ravitch, D., *The great school wars* (New York, 1974).

Raymond, R.J., 'The Anglo-Irish talks 1938: a re-appraisal', paper presented at the Duquesne History Forum, Pittsburgh, 14 October 1981.

'De Valera, Lemass and Irish economic development: 1933–1948', in J.P. O'Carroll and J.A. Murphy (eds.), *De Valera and his times* (Cork, 1983).

'David Gray, the Aiken mission and Irish neutrality, 1940–41', *Diplomatic History*, 9 (1985).

'The Marshall Plan and Ireland, 1947–52', in P.J. Drudy (ed.), *The Irish in America: emigration, assimilation and impact*, Irish Studies, 4 (Cambridge, 1985).

Rees, M., *Northern Ireland: a personal perspective* (London, 1985).

Reader, W.J., 'Businessmen and their motives', in D.C. Coleman and P. Mathias (eds.), *Enterprise and history* (Cambridge, 1984).

Richardson, J., 'Convergent policy styles in Europe', in J. Richardson (ed.), *Policy styles in Western Europe* (London, 1982).

Riklin, A., Haug, H., Binswanger, H.C. (eds.), *Handbuch der schweizerischen Aussenpolitik* (Berne, 1975).

Riklin, A. (ed.), *Handbuch Politisches System der Schweiz* (Berne, 1983).

Roberts, A., *Nations in arms: the theory and practice of territorial defence* (London, 1976).

Robinson, M., 'The role of the Irish parliament', *Administration*, 22 (1974).

Roche, D., 'John Leydon', *Administration*, 27 (1979).

Roche, R., 'The high cost of complaining Irish style: a preliminary examination of the Irish pattern of complaint behaviour and of its associated costs', *Irish Business and Administrative Research*, 4 (1982).

'The role of the Department of the Public Service', *Administration*, 27 (1979).

Rokkan, S., 'The growth and structuring of mass politics in Western Europe: reflections on possible models of explanation', *Scandinavian Political Studies*, 5 (1970).

Rose, R., *Northern Ireland: a time of choice* (London, 1976).

Rose, R., and Urwin, D., 'Persistence and change in western party systems since 1945', *Political Studies*, 18 (1970).

'Social cohesion, political parties and strains in regimes', *Comparative Political Studies*, 2 (1969).

Rosenberg, J.L., 'The 1941 mission of Frank Aiken to the United States: an American perspective', *IHS*, 22 (1980).

Roskill, S.W., *Churchill and the admirals* (London, 1977).

Ross, M., 'Comprehensiveness in regional policy', in B.R. Dowling and J. Durkan (eds.), *Irish economic policy* (Dublin, 1978).

Rothfels, H., 'Zeitgeschichte als Aufgabe', *Vierteljahrshefte für Zeitgeschichte*, 1 (1953).

Rothschild, J., *East Central Europe between the two world wars* (London, 1974).

Rottman, D., *et al.*, *The distribution of income in the Republic of Ireland* (ESRI, No. 109, 1982).

Ruane, F., 'The White Paper on industrial policy', *IBR* (1984).

Ruane, J., 'Needed theoretical developments from Irish rural studies: a review article', *Social Studies* 8 (1985).

Ruffieux, R., 'Changements et innovation dans la Suisse de l'après-guerre: quelques hypothèses de recherche', in *Cinq siècles de relations Franco-Suisses* (Neuchatel, 1984).

Ruin, O., 'Political science in Sweden', *Politologen*, 15 (1986).

Rumpf, E., and Hepburn, A.C., *Nationalism and socialism in twentieth-century Ireland* (Liverpool, 1977).

Ryan, Louden, 'Prospects for the '80s', in ESRI, *The economic and social state of the nation* (Dublin, 1982).

Ryan, Liam, 'Church and politics: the last twenty five years', *The Furrow*, 30 (1979).

'The Church now', *The Furrow*, 32 (1981).

'Urban poverty', in S. Kennedy, *One million poor* (Dublin, 1981).

Ryle Dwyer, T., *Irish neutrality and the USA 1939–47* (Dublin, 1977).

Eamon de Valera (Dublin, 1980).

Michael Collins and the Treaty (Dublin, 1981).

'Eamon de Valera and the Partition Question', in J.P. O'Carroll and J.A. Murphy (eds.), *De Valera and his times* (Cork, 1983).

Sacks, P.M., *Donegal Mafia: an Irish political machine* (London, 1976).

Sagarra, E., 'Dreissig Jahre Bundesrepublik – aus Irischer Sicht', in J. Haas-Heye, *Im Urteil des Auslands* (Munich, 1979).

Sandberg, L.G., 'The case of the impoverished sophisticate: human capital and Swedish economic growth before World War I', *Journal of Economic History*, 39 (1979).

Schmitt, D., *The irony of Irish democracy* (Lexington, 1973).

'Ethnic conflict in Northern Ireland: international aspects of conflict management', in M.J. Esman, *Ethnic conflict in the Western world* (London, 1977).

Schumann, W., and Haas, G. (eds.), *Deutschland im Zweiten Weltkrieg* (East Berlin, 1974).

Schweizerische Bibliographie für Statistik und Volkswirtschaft (Berne, 1937).

Schweizerisches Gesellschaft für Konjunkturforschung (ed.), *Kultur und Wirtschaft* (Zurich, 1963).

Scott, D., 'Adapting the machinery of central government', in D. Coombes (ed.), *Ireland and the European Communities: ten years of membership* (Dublin, 1983).

Scott, F.D., *Sweden: the nation's history* (Minneapolis, 1977).

Senghaas, D., *The European experience* (Coventry, 1986).

Senn, H., 'Schweizerische Dissuasionsstrategie im Zweiten Weltkrieg', in R. Bindschedler, H.R. Kurz, W. Carlgren and S. Carlsson (eds.), *Schwedische und Schweizerische Neutralität im Zweiten Weltkrieg* (Basel, 1985).

Shea, P., *Voices and the sound of drums* (Belfast, 1981).

Sheehan, J., 'Education and society in Ireland, 1945–70', in J.J. Lee (ed.), *Ireland 1945–70* (Dublin, 1979).

Sheehy, S.J., 'The Common Agricultural Policy and Ireland', in P.J. Drudy and D. McAleese (eds.), *Ireland and the European Community*, Irish Studies, 4 (Cambridge, 1984).

Shils, E., 'The intellectuals and the political development of the new states', *World Politics*, 12 (1960).

   The intellectuals and the powers and other essays: selected papers of Edward Shils, 1 (London, 1972).

   Center and periphery: essays in macrosociology: selected papers of Edward Shils 11 (London, 1975).

   Tradition (London, 1981).

Shklar, J., 'Let us not be hypocritical', *Daedalus*, 108 (1979).

Silverman, S.F., 'Agricultural organisation, social structure and values in Italy: amoral familism reconsidered', *American Anthropologist*, 70 (1968).

   '"Exploitation" in rural central Italy: structure and ideology', *Comparative Studies in Society and History*, 12 (1970).

Simpson, J., 'Economic development: cause or effect in the Northern Ireland conflict'? in J. Darby (ed.), *Northern Ireland: the background to the conflict* (Belfast, 1983).

Sinclair, T., 'The position of Ulster', in S. Rosenbaum (ed.), *Against Home Rule* (London, 1912; Kennikat edn, 1970).

Sinnott, R., 'Interpretations of the Irish party system', *EJPR*, 12 (1984).

Skodvin, M., 'Norwegian neutrality and the question of credibility', *Scandinavian Journal of History*, 2 (1977).

Smiley, D., 'Must Canadian political science be a miniature replica?', *Journal of Canadian Studies*, 9 (1974).

Smyth, D., *Diplomacy and strategy of survival. British policy and Franco's Spain, 1940–41* (Cambridge, 1986).

Smyth, W.J., 'Explorations of place', in J.J. Lee (ed.), *Ireland: towards a sense of place* (Cork, 1985).

Solow, R.M., 'Leif Johansen (1930–1982): a memorial', *Scandinavian Journal of Economics*, 85 (1983).

Southern, D., 'Germany', in F.F. Ridley (ed.), *Government and administration in Western Europe* (London, 1979).

Stephens, J., *The Insurrection in Dublin* (Dublin, 1965 edn).

Sterling, L., 'Introduction', *Social and Economic Studies*, 33 (1984).
Stewart, A.T.Q., *The Ulster crisis* (London, 1969).
The narrow ground; aspects of Ulster, 1609–1969 (London, 1977).
Sir Edward Carson (Dublin, 1981).
'The mind of Protestant Ulster', in D. Watt (ed.), *The Constitution of Northern Ireland* (London, 1981).
'History by committee', *Irish Times*, 2 August 1986.
Stokx, J., 'Belgian economic reforms 1982', *IBR* (1982).
Stolte-Heiskanen, V., and Heiskanen, I., 'Intellectual styles and paradigmatic changes in Finnish sociology and political science', in R. Alapuro, M. Alestalo, E. Haavio-Mannila and R. Väyrynen (eds.), *Small states in comparative perspective* (Oslo, 1985).
Stone, R., 'Discussion of M. Abramovitz, "Rapid growth potential and its realization: the experience of capitalist economies in the post-war world"', in E. Malinvaud (ed.), *Economic Growth and Resources*, 1, *The Major Issues* (London, 1979).
Stromberg, R.N., 'The intellectuals and the coming of war in 1914', *Journal of European Studies*, 3 (1973).
The Sunday Times Insight Team, *Ulster* (Harmondsworth, 1972).
Swedish Institute, *The Swedish economy. Facts and figures 1986* (Stockholm, 1986).
Symonds, R., *The British and their successors: a study in the development of the government services in the new states* (London, 1966).
Tansey, P., 'The Central Bank rules Finance', *Magill*, 3 (1979).
'Money matters', *Sunday Tribune*, 2 June 1985, 8 December 1985, 8 June 1986.
Taylor, P., *The distant magnet: European emigration to the USA* (New York, 1972).
Teeling, J., 'A symposium on increasing employment in Ireland', *JSSISI*, 21, (1975–6).
'The budget and the national economy', *IBR* (1958).
'The economy – some EEC comparisons', *IBR* (1982).
Thelen, D., 'The profession and the *Journal of American History*', *JAH*, 73 (1986).
Thompson, D., *Twentieth-century England* (Harmondsworth, 1965).
Thompson, W.I., *The imagination of an insurrection: Dublin, Easter 1916* (New York, 1967).
Thompson, R.S., 'The national development corporation: projects for a state investment company', *IBR* (1985).
Thorne, C., *Racial aspects of the Far Eastern War 1941–1945* (London, 1982).
'Societies, Sociology and the International', in W. Outhwaite and M. Mulkay (eds.) *Social theory and social criticism* (Oxford, 1987).
Thornley, D., 'Ireland: the end of an era?', *Studies* (1964).
'The Fianna Fáil party', *Irish Times*, 1 April 1965.
Thulstrup, A., 'Die schwedische Pressepolitik im Zweiten Weltkrieg', in R. Bindschedler, H.R. Kurz, W. Carlgren, and S. Carlsson (eds.), *Schwedische und Schweizerische Neutralität im Zweiten Weltkrieg* (Basel, 1985).

Thurston, T., 'A meeting of Ireland's two greatest natural resources', *Seirbhís Phoiblí*, 5 (1984).

Tierney, M., *Eoin MacNeill, scholar and man of action 1867–1945*, ed. F.X. Martin (Oxford, 1980).

Tilly, C., 'Reflections on the history of European state-making', in C. Tilly (ed.), *The formation of national states in Western Europe* (Princeton, 1975).

Tobin, F., *The best of decades: Ireland in the 1960s* (Dublin, 1984).

'Top level appointments in the civil service', *Administration*, 31 (1984).

Towey, T., 'The reaction of the British government to the 1922 Collins–de Valera pact', *IHS*, 22 (1980).

Townshend, C., *The British campaign in Ireland 1919–1921* (Oxford, 1978).

Political violence in Ireland: government and resistance since 1848 (Oxford, 1983).

'The Irish railway strike of 1920: industrial action and civil resistance in the struggle for independence', *IHS*, 21 (1979).

'Fifteen years on', *Times Literary Supplement*, 1 November 1985.

'Trends in the public finances', *IBR*, (1982).

Uhr, G.C., 'Economists and policy-making 1930–1936: Sweden's experience', *History of Political Economy*, 9 (1976).

Urwin, D.W., *From ploughshare to ballot box* (Oslo, 1980).

Utley, T.E., *Lessons of Ulster* (London, 1975).

Vaizey, J., 'The mind of republicanism', in D. Watt (ed.), *The Constitution of Northern Ireland* (London, 1981).

Valiulis, M.G., '"The man they could never forgive"! the view of the opposition: Eamon de Valera and the civil war', in J.P. O'Carroll and J.A. Murphy (eds.), *De Valera and his times* (Cork, 1983).

'The "army mutiny" of 1924 and the assertion of civilian authority in independent Ireland', *IHS*, 23 (1983).

Almost a rebellion: the Irish army mutiny of 1924 (Cork, 1985).

Van Amersfoort, H., and van der Wusten, H., 'Democratic stability and ethnic parties', *Ethnic and Racial Studies*, 4 (1981).

Vaughan, W.E. and Fitzpatrick, A.J., *Irish historical statistics: population, 1821–1971* (Dublin, 1978).

Vickery, K.P., '"Herrenvolk" democracy and egalitarianism in South Africa and in the US South', *Comparative Studies in Society and History*, 16 (1974).

Viney, E., 'Women in Rural Ireland', *Christus Rex*, 22 (1968).

Volkmann, H.E., 'Landwirtschaft und Ernährung in Hitler's Europa, 1939–45', *Militärgeschichtliche Mitteilungen* 1 (1984).

Walker, G., 'Previous plans: targets versus performance', in An Foras Forbartha, *Ireland in the year 2000: towards a national strategy* (Dublin, 1983).

Wall, M., 'Partition: the Ulster question (1916–1926)', in T.D. Williams (ed.), *The Irish struggle 1916–1926* (London, 1966).

Wallace, M., *Northern Ireland: 50 years of self-government (Newton Abbot, 1971)*.

British government in Northern Ireland: from devolution to direct rule (Newton Abbot, 1982).

Wallis, R. and Bruce, S., 'Sketch for a theory of conservative Protestant politics', *Social Compass*, 32 (1985).

Walsh, B.M., 'Economic growth and development, 1945–70', in J.J. Lee (ed.), *Ireland 1945–70* (Dublin, 1979).

'Ireland in the European Monetary System: the effects of a change in exchange rate regime', in M. de Cecco (ed.), *International economic adjustment: small countries and the European Monetary System* (Cambridge, 1983).

'Ireland's membership of the European Monetary System: expectations, out-turn and prospects', in P.J. Drudy and D. MacAleese (eds.), *Ireland and the European Community*; Irish Studies, 3 (Cambridge, 1984).

'Employment: a private sector strategy', *IBR* (1985).

'Youth unemployment: the economic background', *Administration*, 33 (1985).

Walsh, Dick, *The Party: Inside Fianna Fáil* (Dublin, 1986).

Walsh, J.J., *Recollections of a rebel* (Tralee, 1944).

Walsh, T., *Developing national potential in the new era* (Dublin, 1984).

Wangel, C.A., 'Verteidigung gegen den Krieg', in R.L. Bindschedler, H.R. Kurz, W. Carlgren and S. Carlsson (eds.), *Schwedische und schweizerische Neutralität im zweiten Weltkrieg* (Basel, 1985).

Ward, A.J., *Ireland and Anglo-American relations 1899–1921* (London, 1969).

Ward, C., 'The Background of the Department of Social Science, UCD', *UCD News*, October 1984.

Watson, G.J., 'Cultural identity: an Irish view', *Yale Review* (1986).

Whelan, N., 'Public service adaptation – its nature and requirements', *Administration*, 27 (1979).

'The Irish public service: its reform', *Administration*, 25 (1977).

Whitaker, T.K., *Interests* (Dublin, 1983).

'The finance attitude', *Administration*, 2 (1953).

'Staid na Tíre', *Administration*, 8 (1960).

'The civil service and development', in B. Chubb and P. Lynch (eds.), *Economic development and planning* (Dublin, 1969).

'Todhchaí eacnamaíoch agus shóisialta na hÉireann', *Central Bank of Ireland Quarterly Bulletin* (1971).

'An ceangal le sterling – ar cheart é a briseadh?', *Administration*, 24 (1976).

'From protection to free trade – the Irish experience', *Administration*, 24 (1976).

White, B., *John Hume* (Belfast, 1984).

'From conflict to violence: the re-emergence of the IRA and the Loyalist response', in J. Darby (ed.), *Northern Ireland: the background to the conflict* (Belfast, 1983).

Whyte, J.H., *Church and state in modern Ireland 1923–1970* (Dublin, 1971).

'Why is the Northern Ireland problem so intractable?', *Parliamentary Affairs*, 34 (1981).

'Church, state and society, 1950–70', in J.J. Lee (ed.), *Ireland 1945–70* (Dublin, 1979).

'How much discrimination was there under the Unionist regime, 1921–68?', in T. Gallagher and J. O'Connell (eds.), *Contemporary Irish Studies* (Manchester, 1983).

Wilding, R.W., 'The civil service in the modern state', *Studies*, 59 (1970).

Williams, Glanmor, 'Language, literacy and nationality in Wales', in Glanmor Williams, *Religion, language and nationality in Wales* (Cardiff, 1979).

Williams, Gwyn, *When was Wales?* (London, 1985).

Williams, T.D., 'A study in neutrality,' *The Leader*, 31 January – 25 April 1953.

'Neutrality', *Irish Press*, 27 June – 18 July 1953.

'Review of Fr Thomas Gilby, *A philosophy and theology of the state, Administration*, 1 (1953).

'Negotiations leading to the Anglo-Polish Agreement of 31 March 1939', *IHS*, 10 (1956).

'The historiography of World War II', *Historical Studies*, 1 (1958), reprinted in E.M. Robertson (ed.), *The origins of the Second World War* (London, 1971).

'The Risorgimento in retrospect: an Irish historian's view', in R.W.D. Edwards (ed.), *Ireland and the Italian Risorgimento* (Dublin, 1960).

'From the Treaty to the Civil War', in T.D. Williams (ed.), *The Irish struggle, 1916–1926* (London, 1966).

'The summing up', also in Williams (ed.), *The Irish struggle*.

'De Valera in power', in F. MacManus (ed.), *The years of the great test, 1926–39* (Cork, 1967).

'Conclusion', also in MacManus (ed.), *The years of the great test, 1926–39* (Cork, 1967).

'Ireland and the war', in K.B. Nowlan and T.D. Williams (eds.), *Ireland in the war years and after, 1939–51* (Dublin, 1969).

'Conclusion', also in Nowlan and Williams (eds.), *Ireland*.

'Irish foreign policy', in J.J. Lee (ed.), *Ireland 1945–70* (Dublin, 1979).

Wilson, T., 'Ulster and Éire', *Political Quarterly* 10 (1939), reprinted in W.A. Robson (ed.), *The political quarterly in the 1930s* (London, 1971).

'Manpower', in G.D. Worswick and P.H. Ady, *The British economy 1945–50* (Oxford, 1952).

'Devolution and partition', in T. Wilson (ed.), *Ulster under Home Rule* (London, 1955).

Wilson, W.A., *Folklore and nationalism in modern Finland* (London, 1976).

Winch, D., *Economics and politics* (London, 1972).

'The Keynesian revolution in Sweden', *Journal of Political Economy* (1966).

Winter, J.M., 'Britain's "lost generation" of the First World War', *Population Studies*, 31 (1976).

Wolfe, D.A., 'The rise and demise of the Keynesian era in Canada: economic policy 1930–1982', in M.S. Cross and G.S. Kealey (eds.), *Modern Canada: 1930–1980s* (Toronto, 1984).

Woodman, K., *Media control in Ireland 1923–1983* (Galway, 1986).

Worsthorne, P., 'Desmond Williams', *The Spectator*, 24 January 1987.

Wren, M.A., 'Dáil procrastinates while jobs evaporate', *Irish Times*, 5 March 1984.

Wright, F., 'Protestant ideologies and politics in Ulster', *European Journal of Sociology*, 14 (1973).

Wrigley, L., 'Ireland in economic space', in J.J. Lee (ed.), *Ireland: towards a sense of place* (Cork, 1985).

X, 'The nature of Irish politics', *Leader*, Christmas 1953.
Yonekawa, S., 'Recent writing on Japanese economic and social history', *Economic History Review*, n.s., 38 (1985).
Younger, C., *Ireland's civil war* (London, 1970).
Zeldin, T., *France, 1848–1945*, 2 (Oxford, 1977).
Zimmerman, J., 'Irish state sponsored bodies: the fractionalisation of authority and responsibility', *Seirbhís Phoiblí* (1986).

Addendum

Two sources listed as unpublished in the bibliography have been published while this work was in press. D.G. Bradley's thesis, 'The organization of agricultural labourers in Ireland, 1900–76', has now appeared as Dan Bradley, *Farm labourers: Irish struggle 1900–76* (Belfast, 1988), and the proceedings of the Royal Irish Academy conference on social science research in Ireland, 23 October 1986, are now published as L. O'Dowd (ed), *The state of social science research in Ireland* (Dublin 1988).

INDEX

A. E. (Russell, George), 172, 376
Aargauer Tagblatt, 607
Abortion Referendum, 653–7
academic culture, 618
academics, 395
Acheson, Dean, 308
Act of Union, 7
Acta Sociologica, 604
Adams, Gerry, 455
Administration, 341, 581, 585
Administrative change, 314, 573–4, 599
administrative culture, 547, 556, 605
administrative infra-structure, 230–5
adult suffrage, 283–4
advertising, 647
Advisory Economic Council, 416
Aer Lingus, 308
Aer Rianta, 190
Africa, 247
agrarianism, 181–3
agricultural labourer, 71, 115, 131, 159,
    181–2, 195, 285, 334, 378, 566, 567,
    649
agricultural machinery, 529
agricultural policy, 231, 633
agricultural prices, 94, 114–15, 171
Agricultural Research Institute, 582; *see*
    An Foras Talúntais.
agricultural slump, 491
Agricultural Wage Regulation Bill (1936),
    563
agriculture, 70, 94, 112–13, 117, 182,
    185, 255, 302, 345, 347, 350, 353,
    360–1, 500–1, 528
Agriculture and Technical Instruction,
    Department of, 91
Agriculture, Department of, 580, 635, 640
Aiken, Frank, 67, 144, 176, 222, 238–9,
    249, 252, 283, 287, 312–13, 322,
    337, 369–71, 388

air force, 236
Albania, 70, 76
Alberta, 287
Allardt, E., 600–1, 667
Alliance Party, 431, 443
amateurism, 93
ambiguity, 375, 673
America, *see* United States of America
American note, 251
American opinion, 43
American South, 4
amoral familism, 81
Amsterdam, 601
An Claidheamh Soluis, 20
An Foras Forbartha, 365
An Foras Talúntais, 622
An Foras Tionscail, 379
Ancient Order of Hibernians, 10
Andrews, C. S., 464, 618
Andrews, J. M., 257, 371, 411
Anglicisation, 133, 464, 661, 664, 666–7
Anglo-Irish, 1, 4–5, 75, 109, 170
Anglo-Irish Agreement (1938), 201,
    211–15
Anglo-Irish Agreement (Hillsborough
    Agreement) (1985), 456, 680ff
Anglo-Irish encounter, 467
Anglo-Irish Free Trade Agreement (1968),
    353, 404, 462
Anglo-Irish Trade Agreement (1948), 302,
    305
Anglo-Irish Treaty (1921), 47–55 *passim*,
    338, 685
anglophobia, 669
annuities, 178, 180, 186, 190, 214
anthropologists, 70, 669
anthropology, 584, 604, 619, 623
Anti-Christ, 45, 78
anti-communism, 181
anti-intellectualism, 563–77 *passim*, 620

anti-semitism, 78, 181, 183, 254
Antrim, 17, 74, 110, 148, 683
Aontacht Éireann, 460
Apprentice Boys, 420–1, 428, 437
archaeology, 620
Arensberg, C., 623, 651
Arigna, 74
Armagh, 45, 74, 142, 145, 148–9, 683
arms industry, 235
arms trial, 509
army, 76–7, 175–6, 228, 234–6, 242–4,
    269, 332, 429, 446, 459
Army Comrades Association, 178, 179
Army Council, 96
army mutiny, 96–105, *passim*
Army Volunteer Reserve, 180
Arnold, Bruce, 483
artisans, 183
Asia, 349
Asquith, H. H., 12–13, 15, 37
Association of Higher Civil Servants, 341
Association of Municipal Authorities, 273
Association Suisse d'organisation
    scientifique, 602–3
Athens, 561
Athlone, 560, 678
Atkins, Humphrey, 451–4
Aughrim, 204
Auschwitz, 266
Australia, 149, 299–301, 658
Austria, 114, 494, 519, 526, 601–2, 666
Austrian Institute for International Affairs,
    602
authoritarianism, 394, 659
Auxiliaries, 43

B Specials, 59, 61, 138, 420, 428–30, 441
balance of payments, 320, 322–5, 326–7,
    346, 349, 355–6, 358, 465, 467, 489,
    493, 500, 502, 520, 525, 625
Baldwin, S., 145, 151, 173
Balfour, Arthur, 44
Ballymurphy, 434
Banat, 79
Bandon, 74
bank deposits, 109
Bank of Ireland, 111
bankers, 184, 224, 579
Banking Commission (1927), 123;
    (1934–8), 199–200, 563–7, 624
banking policy, 287–8
banking system, 89, 199, 349
Banks, 287–8, 309, 490
Bann, 417
Bannside, 423, 426
Barbour, J. Milne, 8
barriers-to-entry, 538

Barrington, Ruth, 321n210
Barrington, T. J., 111, 121–3, 121n284,
    341, 550, 553, 585
Barry, Tom, 100
Barth Karl, 267
Barth, F., 604, 667
Barton, Robert, 48, 50
Basque, 664
Bastable, C. F., 576
Bates, Dawson, 139
Battle of the Atlantic, 447
Battle of Britain, 253
Battle of the Boyne, 204
Béal na Bláth, 63
Beattie, Desmond, 436
Beckett, J. C., 597
Beddy, J. P., 311, 529
Beere, Thekla, 551
begrudgery, 646–8
Belfast, 4–8, 10, 15, 59, 136, 139, 148–9,
    265n423, 392, 417, 422–3, 425, 429,
    434–5, 455, 660
Belfast Boycott, 59
Belfast Telegraph, 254, 416
Belgium, 66, 76, 114, 246, 280, 494
Belgian Congo, 370
Bell, 605
Beocheist, 607, 617
Berbers, 669
Berehaven, 212
Berner Tagblatt, 607
Bessarabia, 79
Beveridge Report, 373
Beveridge, W., 230, 261, 285
Bevin, Ernest, 249, 308
birth control, 71, 645, 656
Birthrates, 79, 515
Biscoe, Mr. 340
bishops, 385
Black and Tans, 43, 243, 269
Blackshirts, 183
Blaney, Neil, 82, 329, 409, 458–60, 495
Bleakely, D., 436
blind pensions, 125
Bloody Friday, 442
Bloody Sunday (1972), 440, 454, 461
Blowick, Joseph, 319
Blueshirts, 179–84 *passim*, 271
Blythe, E., 67, 74, 83, 97, 104, 107,
    119–20, 125–6, 134–5, 140–2, 146,
    156, 157, 168, 175, 177
Bodenstown, 168, 209, 221
Boer War, 6
Bogside, 428, 438, 440
Böhler, E., 607
Boland, F. H., 226–7, 246–7, 253, 265,
    303, 307–8, 369

Boland, Gerard, 152, 174, 205n132, 222–3, 238, 296, 329, 337, 408, 461
Boland, H. P., 106, 108, 395
Boland, Harry, 63
Boland, John, 555–6, 558–9, 559n161
Boland, Kevin, 205n132, 329, 410, 444, 458–60, 481
Böll, Heinrich, 266, 281
Bombay Street, 429, 432
Bonaparte-Wyse, A. M., 32
Bonjour, E., 603
Bórd na Gaeilge, 467
Bórd na Móna, 190
borrowing, 359, 470, 490
Boserup, E., 604
Boundary Commission, 51, 53, 60, 140–51, 178
Bovine TB, 522
Bowen, Elizabeth, 262
Brady, Conor, 678–9
Bratianu, I., 82
Bratten, Magnus, 550
Brennan Report, 364
Brennan, Joseph, 65, 74, 106–8, 121, 196, 199, 288, 313, 320, 324–5, 342, 347, 359, 571, 580, 618, 624–5
Brennan, Michael, 101, 175–6
Brennan, Séamus, 438
Bressand, Albert, 582
Brest-Litovsk, Peace of, 28
bribery, 163
Brighton, 455
Britain, 3, 21–2, 76, 82, 114, 173, 177, 187, 194, 201, 208–9, 211–12, 219, 220–1, 226, 230, 233, 236, 243, 245–8, 251–3, 260, 266, 269, 281, 300–2, 314, 352, 370, 378, 384, 463, 492, 524–5, 547, 568, 578, 653, 663, 679–87, *see* England
British Army, 18, 22, 31, 43, 244, 429, 433–4, 435–41, 445–6, 450
British Embassy, 461, 507
British influence, 87–91, 108, 122, 124, 198
British model, 192, 562, 622, 627
British 'offer' of unity (1940), 248–50
British opinion, 14, 43
British policy and War of Independence, 42–3
British standards, 349, 416, 430, 659–60
Broadcasting Act, Section 31, 477
Broadcasting Amendment Act (1976), 477
Brooke, Basil (Lord Brookeborough), 59, 257–9, 301, 333, 367, 404–5, 411–14, 416
Brosnan, Denis, 679

Browne, Dr Michael, Bishop of Galway, 267, 274, 316, 579
Browne, Noel, 307, 313–21, 398, 321n210
Brueghel, Peter, 645
Brugha, Cathal, 40, 48, 50–1, 63, 150
Brussels, 463, 474, 480, 491, 660
Bruton, John, 507
Buckingham Palace Conference (1914), 17
Buckley, Vincent, 661
Budget, 226: (1931), 157; (1931, Supplementary), 195; (1932), 168; (1936), 200; (1939), 216; (1947, supplementary), 288–9; (1950), 312; (1952), 322–5; (1957), 342; (1957), 351; (1972), 465–6; (1973), 470; (1975), 631; (1977), 471–2; (1978), 488; (1979), 491; (1981), 502; (1981, supplementary), 502, 507; (1982), 507
Building on Reality, 537, 554
Bukovina, 79
Bula Mine, 481
Bulgaria, 70, 76
bureaucracy, 84–5, 239, 257, 274–6, 281, 285–6, 292, *see* Civil Service
Burke, Dick, 508
Burke, Ellen, 162–3, 162n473
Burntollet, 422
business education, 131
business history, 634
businessmen, 121, 183, 261, 577, 668
Busteed, John, 188, 191, 193, 576, 580–1
Butler, Hubert, 268n439
Butler, W. F., 587
Butt, Isaac, 389
by-elections, (1925), 151; (1927) 155; (1939), 216; (1945), 319; (1947), 296; (1955), 328; (1965), 366; (1975), 480; (1976), 483; (1979), 495–6; (1980), 505; (1982), 508
Byrne, Dr Edward, Archbishop of Dublin, 66–7, 157

Cabinet Committee on family allowances, 278
Cairncross, Alec, 577
Callaghan, James, 430, 451
Cambridge, 616
Cambridge Journal, 606–7
Campaign for Social Justice, 420
Canada, 50, 149, 242, 300, 370, 517, 572, 622, 626
capital, 109, 225, 527
Capital Investment Advisory Committee, 343, 576
Capital-Output Ratio, 518

capitalism, 183, 271
Carlow, 120
Carlow-Kilkenny, 298, 543
Carrignavar, 74
Carroll, Charles, 582, 630, 642
Carson, Edward, 5–6, 9, 13, 16–17, 23,
    26, 35, 44, 59, 139, 163n477, 255,
    335, 371, 404
Carter, C. F., 577
Casement, Roger, 340
Cassel, Gustav, 200, 597–8, 606–7
Casti Connubii, 283
Castlebar, 161–2, 560
Catholic Association (Belfast), 10
Catholic Bulletin, 167, 427
Catholic Church, 42, 66, 75, 77–8, 90–1,
    136, 157–68 *passim*, 177, 203, 218,
    246, 267, 283–5, 362, 368, 395–6,
    578, 644, 650, 655–7
Catholic Ethic, 620–1
Catholic hierarchy, 39, 267–8, 314–18
Catholic Mind, 167, 427
Catholic self-image, 158
Catholic social thought, 285, 578–9
Catholics, 1–19 *passim*, 60–1, 411–57
    passim
Cavan, 45, 298
Ceannt, E., 24, 73
celibacy, 159
Censorship, 159–60, 253, 265–6
Censorship of Publications Act (1929), 158
Central Bank, 287–8, 313, 324, 354,
    466–7, 582, 602, 625
Central Statistics Office, 377, 575–6
centralisation, 547, 559, 678
centre and periphery, 74
Centre Party, 179
Chamberlain, Neville, 212, 255
Chandler, Alfred, 623
charisma, 372, 406, 599
chemical sector, 473
Chequers, 679–80
Chichester Clarke, James, 420, 424, 435
Childers, Erskine, 50, 63, 66
Childers, Erskine (President of Ireland),
    483
Children's Allowances, 277–85, 316
Christchurch, 340
Christian Brothers, 132
Christian Front, 273
Christianity, 283, 286–7
Christus Rex, 579
Chubb, Basil, 562, 626
Churchill, Lord Randolph, 46
Churchill, W. S., 26, 46, 91, 250, 264
cinema, 376, 386
Citizen Army, 30

civic culture, 643, 650, 657
civil service, 74, 89, 105, 108, 195–8, 275,
    364, *see* bureaucracy
Civil Service Commission, 107
Civil Service Economy Committee, 225,
    573–4
civil war, 62–4, 66–9, 93, 138, 171–2,
    184, 268, 335, 338
Clann na Poblachta, 295–6, 320, 327,
    336, 389
Clann na Talmhan, 72, 239–40, 242,
    298–9, 303, 319, 334, 543
Clare Champion, 35, 38–9, 540, 651
Clarke, Austin, 158
Clarke, Tom, 19–20, 24–5
Clarke, Mrs Tom, 223
Clarkson, J. K., 623
Clemence, Revd Gordon, 31–2
clergy, 76, 136, 159, 645
climate, 355, 391, 523
Clinton, Mark, 474–5
Clio, 318, 597
Clontarf, 229
Cluskey, Frank, 481, 486, 506
Coal–Cattle Pact, 201, 211
Cobh, 212
Codling, A., 106, 108
Coffin Point, 678–9
Colbert, Con, 73
Coleraine, 417
collaboration, 267
Colley, George, 361–2, 409, 458, 465,
    467–9, 475, 481, 488, 490–2, 494, 496
Collingwood, R. G., 594
Collins, Michael: and Easter Rising, 36;
    and Sinn Féin, 40; Minister for
    Finance, 42; Director of Intelligence in
    the Volunteers, 42; and Treaty,
    47–51, 106; and Boundary
    Commission, 53, 141–2, 148; and
    Civil War, 56ff; and Northern Ireland,
    59–62, 138; and Pact with de Valera,
    58; and Constitution (1922), 59;
    death, 63; appraisal, 63–6; potential
    Bonapartist?, 68; origins, 74; legacy,
    97–9; and 'apostles'; 97, memory of,
    101, 404
Comecon, 520
Commission of Inquiry into Army Mutiny,
    102, 104
Commission of Inquiry into the Civil
    Service (1932–5), 195–8, 275
Commission on Emigration, 380
Commission on Higher Education, 363,
    409, 587
Commission on Reconstruction and
    Development, 120

Commission on the relief of the sick and destitute poor, 24
Commission on Vocational Organisation 274ff, 283, 286, 316, 562, 578
Committee on Economic Planning (1942–5), 229–32, 277, 309
Committee on Family Allowances, 277
Committee on Government Organisation, 106
Committee on Industrial Organisation, 353, 401, 403
Committee of Inquiry into Workmen's Compensation, 126
Committee on Internal Security, 222
Committee on the Constitution (1966–7), 368–9, 409
Common Agricultural Policy, 463, 474–5, 490, 501
Commonwealth, 48, 178, 213, 215, 252, 299, 300–1
communism, 169, 181, 184, 218, 271, 284, 304, 308
Compton, Sir Edmund, 439
Conditions of Employment Act (1936), 195
Congested Districts Board, 121, 196
Congress of Irish Unions, 290
Connaught Tribune, 34
Connaught, 24, 185–6
Connell, Kenneth, 626
Connolly, James, 19, 24–5, 28, 30, 37, 41
conscription, 39–40
consensus, 403, 473, 478, 497–8
conservatism, 181, 330, 383, 394, 578, 624
Conservative Party, 12–13, 52, 143–4, 434
constituency boundaries, 59–60, 209, 293–9, 410, 481, 486, 545
Constitution (1922), 58–9, 77, 82–3, 87, 94, 144, 152, 154, 173, 209, 272
Constitution (1937), 201–11, 223, 249–50, 272, 288, 293, 338, 368, 464, 479, 653, 676, 679
Constitutional Law, 623
Consultants, 291–2, 623–6
Consumer Price Index, 466, 505, 520
contemporary history, 603, 677
contraception, 479, 498, 656; contraceptives, 203
Control of Manufactures Acts 190, 345
Conway, Cardinal William, 655
Cooney, Patrick, 480, 484
Cooper, B., 172
Cooper, Frank, 446
Cooper, Ivan, 422
Cooper-Whelan Report, 531
cooperativeness, 643

Córas Tráchtála, 379, 524, 532–3
Corcoran, Fr T. J., S. J., 134
Corish, Brendan, 388–9, 469, 481, 484, 476n53, 486
Cork By-Election (1965), 366
Cork City, 127, 193
Cork Examiner, 34, 217
Cork, 31, 73–4, 139
corporatism, *see* vocationalism
Corr, John A., 273
Corrigan, Mairéad, 452
corruption, 162–4, 273–4, 296, 310, 499, 536, 538, 559, 648
Cosgrave, Liam, 389, 459, 468–9, 475, 479–80, 482–6, 673
Cosgrave, W. T.:
  and Easter Rising, 36, 49
  and Treaty, 53
  elected Chairman of Provisional Government, 66
  uncle murdered in civil war, 67
  and army mutiny, 96–105 *passim*
  Acting Minister for Defence, 105
  and financial relations with Britain, 100
  and Fiscal Inquiry committee, 118
  and Ministers' and Secretaries Act, 120
  and Labour, 126–7, 139, 155
  and judicial system, 138
  and education, 129
  and local government, 139
  and Boundary Commission, 142ff
  and the London Agreement (1925), 151
  and death of Kevin O'Higgins, 154
  and oath of allegiance, 157
  and Catholic Church, 157, 160, 166–7
  and Dunbar-Harrison case, 162ff
  and Catholic press, 167
  and General Election (1932), 168
  and *Irish Press*, 168
  and electoral timing, 171
  as a state builder, 171–4
  and army, 175
  and Governor General, 177n11
  leader of Fine Gael, 179–80
  and austerity measures, 195
  and 1922 Constitution, 201–2
  resigns leadership of Fine Gael, 241
cosmopolitanism, 670
Costello, John A., 183, 299–301, 306, 309, 312, 317–18, 326, 332, 380, 388, 485
Coughlan, Paul, 535n72
Council of Europe, 301
Council of Ireland, 444, 449
county boundaries, 294–5
Cowan, Peadar, 300, 320
Coyne, Fr E. J., 275, 283

Craig, James (Lord Craigavon)
  as Carson's Lieutenant, 6
  Ulster Volunteer Force, 17
  as negotiator, 49
  and Treaty negotiations, 52
  becomes Ulster Unionist leader, 59
  and de Valera, 60, 141
  and Boundary Commission, 60
  and Collins, 61
  abolishes PR, 84
  and Education, 136–7
  and unity of the party, 138
  as party leader, 138, 257
  and courage, 138
  and corruption, 139
  and labour, 139
  and social services, 140
  and the Treasury, 140
  and British 'offer' of unity to Dublin,
    249–50
  health problems, 255
  death, 256
  and bureaucracy, 257
  and economic problems, 257
Craig, William, 418, 421–2, 435, 440–1,
  443, 449–50
Craigavon, 417
credit creation, 287
Cregan, Fr Donal, 587
Cremin, Con, 369
Criminal Justice Act (1970), 434
Criminal Law Amendment Act (1935), 203
criminology, 601, 604
Croke Park, 659
Cronin, Anthony, 607
Cronin, E., 180
Cullen, Louis, 585
Cumann na nGaedheal
  and anti-semitism, 78
  and local notables, 82
  and 1923 election, 94
  and electoral support, 111, 542–4
  and protectionism, 118
  and housing policy, 123
  and education, 129
  and Boundary Commission, 149
  and 1925 by-elections, 151
  and June 1927 election, 152
  and September 1927 election, 155
  and Farmer's Party, 155
  and red scare tactics, 156
  and Mayo vote, 164
  and 1932 election, 169–71
  and Army Comrades Association, 178
  and Fine Gael, 179
  and welfare policies, 187
  and 'proportionality' of seats, 210

Curragh Mutiny, 18
Currency Commission, 200; convertibility,
  358
Currie, Austin, 420
Curtis, Edmund, 587–8
Cusack, Séamus, 436
Custom and Excise duties, 111
Czechoslovakia, 77, 80, 246, 526, 669

Daalder, H., 86n125
D'Alton, Dean E. A., 162–4
D'Arcy, Dr, Bishop of Down, 11, 16, 27
D'Azeglio, M., 93
Dagens Nyheter, 606
Daily Express (Dublin), 29
Daily Express, 35
Dalton, C. F., 96
Daly, Edward, 73
Dancehalls, 159
Dargan, M. J., 553
Davidson, D., 597–8
Davitt, Michael, 392
D-Day, 251
de Fréine, Seán, 379
de Gaulle, Charles, 340, 352, 370–1, 449
de Paor, Liam, 607, 658, 660
de Valera, Eamon:
  and Easter Rising, 36, 38
  and Clare by-election (1917), 38
  elected President of Sinn Féin and Irish
    Volunteers (1917), 38
  imprisoned in 1918, 40
  in America (1919–20), 42
  escapes from Lincoln Jail (1919), 42
  and Truce (1921), 47
  and Treaty negotiations, 48
  and 'External association', 48
  as unifier, 48–50
  and document No. 2, 51
  and Boundary Commission, 53, 150
  struggle for Sinn Féin leadership, 54
  and Civil War, 57ff
  and Pact with Collins, 58
  and end of Civil War, 67
  rural background, 74
  and electoral system, 83
  imprisoned (1923), 94, 150
  and 1923 General Election, 95
  and the west, 126, 150
  and militarism, 150
  and murder of Kevin O'Higgins, 154
  and Oath of Allegiance, 154–5
  and the Church, 160, 160n464
  and Dunbar-Harrison case, 165
  and 1932 General Election, 176
  becomes Taoiseach and Minister for
    External Affairs (1932), 176

and unionists 177
and Eucharistic Congress, 177
and decency, 182
and Agricultural policy, 184, 231
and self-restraint, 184
and history, 185
and image of peasantry, 186
and self-sufficiency, 187, 215, 232–3
and the poor, 187
and a balanced economy, 191
and civil service, 198
and British market, 201
and 1937 Constitution, 201–11 *passim*,
    249–50
and 1922 Constitution, 202
and Northern Ireland, 204, 368
and women, 206
his childhood, 207
and his mother, 207
and image of family, 207
and constituency revision, 210
and 1938 Anglo–Irish Agreement,
    211–15
and historians, 211n258
and fear of European war, 212
and Neville Chamberlain 212
and Malcolm MacDonnald, 212, 246
and Commonwealth, 213–14, 252
and Britain, 213
and League of Nations, 213
and Partition, 214, 256
and revision of Treaty, 214–15
and stability, 215–16
and *Irish Press*, 218
and IRA, 219–24, 329
and IRA hunger strikes (1940), 222–3
and Offences against the State Act, 221
and Department of Finance, 229
and Committee on Economic Planning,
    229ff
and agricultural policy, 231
and National Government, 237
and cabinet changes, 237
as Minister for Education, 238,
    238n298
selects Lemass as Tánaiste, 239
and 1943 General Election, 239–40;
    (1944), 241
and 'Dream Speech' (1943), 241, 334
and Defence, 243
and death of Hitler, 244
and invasion fear, 245–6
and Munich, 246
and German expansion, 246
and Danzig, 246
and German invasion of Holland and
    Belgium, 246, 263

and British 'offer' of unity (1940), 248
and David Gray, 250–2
and Craig, 256–7
and reply to Churchill, 264
sends fire brigades to Belfast, 270
and cooperation with Allies, 264
and Vocationalism, 271ff
and Senate, 272
and charges of corruption in Senate
    elections, 273–4
and children's allowances, 277ff
and Trade Unions, 289, 402–3
and Clann na Poblachta, 296
and External Relations Act (1936), 300
and world tour, 301
and health policy, 314
and coalitions, 320
supported by Independents (1951), 320
and Mother and Child Scheme, 321
in opposition, 321
and 1952 budget, 324–5
and 1957 Cabinet, 329
resignation as Taoiseach (1959), 331
election as president (1959), 331
and Referendum on PR, 330–1
profile, 331–41
and emigration, 335, 379–80
and Irish language, 333, 333n21, 672
and Chancellor of the National
    University, 332
and Machiavelli, 332–3
and leadership style, 336ff
and *(First) programme for economic
    expansion*, 345, 352
and electoral triumphs, 366
and W. T. Cosgrave, 369
and Lemass, 372, 399
as chairman, 388
and national character, 399, 643
and electoral appeal, 540–2
and Alfred O'Rahilly, 564
and supply of statistics, 579
de Valera, Dr Eamon, 296
de Valera, Síle, 495, 500
de Valera, Vivion, 219, 322
de Wet, J., 35
de-rating of agricultural land, 111, 118,
    157
death rate, 70
Dedalus, Stephen, 669
Deeny, James, 314
Defence, Department of, 161, 222, 229,
    251, 268–9, 304
Defence of the Realm Act, 39
deflation, 325, 358
demand management, 346
Democratic Programme, 124, 127

Democratic Unionist Party, 427, 443, 456
Dempsey, J. F., 308, 551
Denison, E. F., 521
Denmark, 76, 111, 114, 235, 243, 263, 268, 370, 381, 494, 519, 524–5, 528, 530, 570, 604, 663–4
dependency ratio, 516
dependency syndrome, 560, 627–8
Derrig, T., 134, 238, 329, 337, 671
Derry Citizens' Action Committee, 422
Derry City, 141, 149, 204, 420, 422, 428, 436, 440, 459
Development, Ministry for, 416
Devlin, Bernadette, 422, 424, 453
Devlin Commission, 364, 409
Devlin, Liam St John, 364, 550, 642
Devlin Report, 548–53
Dignan, Dr John, Bishop of Clonfert, 285–6, 578
Dillon, James, 221, 242, 251, 277, 302–3, 306–7, 315, 319, 324, 374, 377, 385, 389, 572
Dillon, John, 32, 36, 40–1, 73, 387
Dingle, 668
direct rule, 441, 448, 452
dispensary service, 313
divorce, 157, 203, 368, 656
Dobruja, 79
Document No. 2, 51, 338
Doherty, Seán, 510
Dollymount Pier, 229
Donegal, 45, 145, 459–60
Donegal North East by-election (1976), 483
Donegal South West by-election (1980), 505
Donegan, Paddy, 482, 484
Donnelly, Eamon, 206
Donoghue, Denis, 419n36, 606
Dorr, Noel, 679
Douglas, Major, 287
Dowling, Brendan, 354–5, 630
Down, 142, 148–9, 453, 683
Downey, Dr Coadjutor Bishop of Ossory, 158
Downing Street Declaration, 430
drugs, 508
drunkenness, 645, 647
Dublin County Council, 273
Dublin Institute of Advanced Studies, 619
Dublin Lockout 1913, 110
Dublin, 30ff., 62, 124, 139, 181, 193, 218, 253, 293, 308, 327, 340, 410, 425, 461, 468–9, 481, 543–4, 560–2, 572, 579, 605, 620, 637, 654, 670
Dublin South West by-election (1976), 483
Duffy, Luke, 197–8

Dulanty, J. W., 201, 250
Dunbar-Harrison, L., 161, 163–4; case, 161–7, 166
Duncan, George, 199, 575–6, 580–1, 625
Dungannon, 420
Dunlaoghaire, 229, 368, 678
Durkan, Joe, 554

Easter Rising, 24–38 *passim*, 67, 369, 427
Eastern Region Development Organisation Report (1985), 637
Economic and Social History, 585
Economic and Social Research Institute, 365, 581–2, 622, 634
economic culture, 622
Economic Development, 342–8, 361, 373, 385, 554–5, 577, 581
Economic Development and Planning, Department of, 487, 503
economic history, 118, 585, 604
Economic Journal, 567
economic planning, 229, 305–6
economic war, 178–9, 181, 186, 190, 214, 259, 527
economics, 332, 620, 628
Economist, 216
Economists, 191–2, 261, 571–2, 575–7, 579–87, 596, 599, 600
Eden, Anthony, 371
Education, 42, 76, 90, 136–8, 143, 197–8, 361–4, 393–4, 573, 586–7, 603, 635, 640ff, 660, 677
Education Act (1923), 136; (1947), 412, 414
Education, Department of, 129, 224, 586, 641, 670
Edward VII, 202
Edwards, Owen Dudley, 341n43
Edwards, Robin Dudley, 588–97 *passim*, 620
EEC, 352, 453, 461–5, 472, 474–6, 489, 491, 493, 501, 516, 520, 553, 648, 660, 679
efficiency, 231, 275, 291–3, 303, 312–13, 352–3, 361, 392–3, 397, 403–4, 500, 504, 538, 558, 561
EFTA, 352, 520
elections (Senate), 273
Electoral Amendment Act (1927), 154
Electoral Amendment Bill (1947), 295
Electoral Bill (1935), 295
electoral system, 85, 540, 546
electricity, 305
electronics sector, 473, 534
emergency, 228, 232, 259, 261–2, 269
Emergency Powers Bill (1976), 482
emergency, state of, 221, 482

emigration, 71, 126, 134, 157, 159, 185, 187, 190, 201, 226–7, 260, 270, 288, 295, 303, 314, 323, 333, 335, 349, 351, 359–60, 365, 374–87, 390, 405, 513, 515, 539, 598, 644, 651, 665, 669, 678
Emmet, Robert, 270
Employer-Labour Conference, 401
employers, 649; employment, 185, 193–4, 216, 260
Engelbrecht division, 264
engineers, 637
England, 144–5, 181, 185, 188, 385, 419, 425, 439, 546, 629, 645, 669; *see* Britain
English, 660–70 *passim*
English example, 371; influence 220; 128n825; model, 404, 628
English Nationalists, 478
Enniskillen, 204
entrepreneurial ethos, 394
entrepreneurship, 110, 348, 535–6
enterprise, 347, 349, 350–1
envy, 644–8
Episcopalians, 2
Erhard, Ludwig, 371
ESB (Electricity Supply Board), 400
Esher, Lord, 14
Estonia, 70
ethical sense, 395
ethnicity, 604
Eton, 424
Eucharistic congress (1932), 168, 177
Eurodollar market, 358
Europe, 21, 200, 207, 220, 233, 242, 246, 252, 266, 282, 301, 546, 594, 633–4, 658–9
European Court, 439
European elections (1979), 453, 495
European Monetary System, 492–3, 501
Evans, Estyn, 585, 620, 626
evasion, 478, 673
Evelegh, R., 433
Ewart Biggs, Christopher, 482
Exchequer Bills, 287
Exchequer Borrowing Requirement, 488
expectations, 349, 378, 384, 386, 400, 472, 492–3
experts, 82, 93, 261, 291
exports, 114, 186–7, 190, 216, 356–7, 397, 403, 493, 527
External Affairs, Department of, 91, 246, 299, 301, 370, 377, 572, 633; *see* Foreign Affairs
external association, 49–50
factionalism, 79–81, 326n75

Fahey, Fr Denis, 78
Falls, 337, 429, 431–2, 434
family, 71, 159, 281, 283–4, 360, 649
Family Endowment, 284
Family Planning Act (1979), 498–9
famine, 158, 349, 374, 391, 655, 664–5
Fanning, C., 559n162
Fanning, Ronan, 632
farmers, 72, 112–18, 123, 131, 159, 179–80, 182–3, 186, 188, 225, 233, 239, 259, 302–3, 391, 394, 474, 490, 529–30, 542–3, 563, 578, 649; and taxation, 491–2
Farmers' Party, 155, 170, 179
Farrar-Hockley, General, 438
Farrell, Brian, 89, 278n31, 369n154, 387
Farrell, Michael, 422–4
fascism, 181–4, 254, 275–6
Faulkner, Brian, 416, 423–4, 431, 435, 437, 440–1, 443–4, 448–50
Fawsitt, D., 120
federalism, 143, 603
Feetham, Mr Justice Richard, 145–6, 148n411, 149
Fenians, 86, 161
Fennell, Desmond, 607
Ferguson, R. C., 123, 192, 575
Fermanagh, 45–6, 59–60, 142, 149, 257, 268, 416, 423
Fermanagh/Tyrone, 454
Fethard-on-Sea, 340
Fianna Fáil:
    and populism, 73, 182
    and national organisation, 82, 150–7 *passim*
    and Oath of Allegiance, 154–5
    and September 1927 general election, 155
    and the Church, 161, 177
    and censorship, 161
    and Mayo vote, 164
    and 1932 general election, 169–71
    and parliamentary apprenticeship, 176
    and ability to govern, 178
    and 1934 local elections, 179
    and 1933 general election, 179
    and constitutionalism, 180, 209
    and fascism, 182, 184
    and leadership, 182, 458–60
    and history, 183
    and economic policy, 184–201
    and welfare policies, 187
    and building industry, 193
    and social reform, 196
    and Civil Service, 198
    and 1937 general election, 209

and 'proportionality', 210
and 1938 general election, 215
as natural governing party, 215
and 1939 South Dublin city by-election,
216
and IRA, 168, 176–7, 219–24, 329,
460–1
and small farm ideology, 231
and National Government, 237
and 1943 general election, 240
and 1944 general election 241
and vocationalism, 271ff
and 1945 presidential election, 294
and 1947 local elections, 295
and 1948 general election, 297–8
and Clann na Poblachta, 296
and 1951 general election, 319
and 1954 general election, 326
and 1957 general election, 327
and Irish language, 333
and party system, 336
and 1961 general election, 365–6
and 1965 general election, 366–7
and 1969 general election, 410
and entry to the EEC, 465
and Northern Ireland, 467–8
and 1973 general election, 469
and RTE Authority, 477
and Conor Cruise O'Brien, 478
and 1977 general election, 483–4
and 1979 European elections, 495
and 1981 general election, 506
and 1982 Dublin West by-election, 508
and February 1982 general election,
507–8
and November 1982 general election,
510
and sources of electoral support, 542–5
and New Ireland Forum, 675ff
Finance, Department of, 106–7, 122, 135,
187, 214, 224–5, 230, 247, 257, 262,
275, 287–8, 290–2, 303, 305,
308–12, 322–5, 327, 343, 345–8,
364, 370, 377, 467, 470, 487, 507,
551, 563–77, 581, 624, 631–2, 672
Financial Times, 569
financiers, 183
Fine Gael, foundation, 179
and Presidency, 208
and university seats, 210
and 'proportionality', 210
and 1938 general election, 215
and neutrality, 237
and 1943 general election, 240
and 1944 general election, 241–2
and Vocationalism, 271
and 1945 presidential election, 294

and 1948 general election, 298
and inter-party government, 299
and the Republic, 300
and Mother and Child Scheme, 317
and 1951 general election, 319
and 1954 general election, 326
and 1957 general election, 327–8
and 1969 general election, 410
and 1972 budget, 465
and entry to the EEC, 465
and Offences against the State Act, 468
and 1973 electoral pact with Labour,
468,
and 1973 general election, 469
and 1977 general election, 484
and 1981 general election, 506
and February 1982 general election, 508
and 1982 Dublin-west by-election, 508
and November 1982 general election,
510
and sources of electoral support, 542–5
and New Ireland Forum, 675
Finland, 68–9, 76, 262, 381, 494, 511,
519–20, 523, 527–8, 600–1, 663–4
First Programme for Economic Expansion,
344–7, 354–5, 357, 359, 364, 386
First World War, 21ff, 41, 113, 514
Fiscal Inquiry Committee, 118–19, 121
fish, 523, 635
Fisher, J. R., 145–6
Fisher, Warren, 92
Fitt, Gerry, 431, 443, 453
Fitzgerald, Alexis, 380ff, 390
Fitzgerald, Desmond, 37, 156, 475
Fitzgerald, Garret, 343, 380, 456, 469,
475–6, 484–5, 506, 510, 539, 545,
606, 653–4, 679–80
Fitzgerald, Louis, 551
Flanagan, Oliver, 78, 183–4, 296–7
Flanders, 663–4
Flinn, Hugo, 225, 573–4
flour millers, 186
Fogarty, Michael, 581
Forde, General Robert, 438
Foreign Affairs, Department of, 461–3,
476, *see* External Affairs
foreign borrowing, 465, 471
foreign debt, 472, 500, 508, 515, 517
foreign investment, 122, 344, 358, 397,
473, 518, 535
forestry, 305, 523, 635
Foster, Roy, 652
Four Courts, 57, 62–3
fragmentation, 555, 595, 635
France, 76, 82, 114, 177, 234, 243, 245,
280–1, 565
Franco, F., 264

Frankfurt, 637
Free Presbyterian Church of Ulster, 426
free trade, 118–19, 344, 353
Freeman, T. W., 616, 626
Freeman's Journal, 29–30, 36, 57, 375
Freemasons, 78
Frisch, R., 599, 667

Gaelic Athletic Association, 80–1, 659
Gaelic League, 18, 135, 211, 673
Gaelicisation, 132
Gaeltacht, 123, 133, 186, 541, 673
Gaeltacht Commission, 134
Gaeltacht, Department of the 329
Gallagher, Frank, 217–19
Galtieri, General, 508
Galway, 73–4, 126, 217
Galway Harbour Commissioners, 204
Gárda Síochána, 88, 154, 218, 220, 234, 480
Geary, Patrick, 582
Geary, R. C., 377, 575–7, 581
Geldoff, Bob, 678
Gellner, E., 669
General Elections (1910), 12; (1918), 39–40; (1921), 47, 54, 59; (1922), 62; (1923), 94–5, 144, 151; (1923), 94–5, 151; (1925), 139; June 1927, 152, 336; (September 1927), 155, 168, 336; (1932), 168, 170, 184, 188–9; (1933), 168, 179; (1937), 202, 210; (1938), 215, 255; (1943), 240–1; (1944), 241; (1948), 296–9; (1951), 319–20; (1954), 326; (1957), 327–8; (1958), 413; (1961), 365; (1965), 366, 416; (1969), 410, 423–4; (1970 UK), 434; (1973), 442–3, 469; (1974 UK), 444; (1975), 448; (1977), 484; (1979 UK), 452; (1981), 506; (1982), 455, February 1982, 508; November 1982, 510
general strike, 445
generation change, 387–8
Geoghegan, J., 176
Geographical Association of Ireland, 585
Geographical Society of Ireland, 626
geography, 584–5, 625–6
George V, 47
George, David Lloyd, 37, 39, 42ff., 47, 49–50, 53–4, 60, 143, 449
German agent, 246
German Foreign Office, 633
German Plot, 40
Germany, 79, 177, 183, 201, 221, 235, 242–3, 247, 252–3, 263, 280–1, 413, 492, 530, 565–6, 616, 665
gerrymandering, 420

Gerschenkon, A., 601
Gibbons, Jim, 509
Gilmartin, Dr, Archbishop of Tuam, 162, 166
Girod, R., 603
Gladstone, W. E., 340
Glasgow, 669
Glenavy, Lord, 128, 188, 208
Glynn, Sir J., 162
Gold Standard, 110
Gough, Brigadier, 18
Government of Ireland Act, 43–4, 83, 137, 140
Gramsci, A., 649–50
Gray, A., 284
Gray, David, 250–2
graziers, 115, 186
Great Northern Railway, 229
great slump 156–7, 177, 526
Grebler, Leo, 566
greed, 644
Greenwood, Hamer, 43
Gregg, C. J., 105–7, 128
Gregory, Lady, 172
Gregory, T. S., 199
Gregory, Tony, 508
grievance, 267, 400, 648
Griffith, Arthur, 7, 38, 40, 48, 50, 52–4, 56ff, 63, 74–5, 100, 150, 162, 187–8, 191
Gross Domestic Product, 517
Gross National Product, 517
growth rates, 355, 514–15, 517
Guards; *see* Garda Síochána.
Guillebaud, C. W., 565
Guinan, Fr. J., 383
Guisan, H., 264

H-Block candidates, and 1981 general election, 506
Haberler, G., 601
Hadow Committee on Education, 129
Hagan, J., 160n464
Hales, Seán, 63, 66
Hall Report, 415
Hall Thompson, Colonel 412
Hand, G., 148n411
Hansson, Per Albin, 237, 264
Harkness, David, 677
Hartnett, Noel, 307
Harty, Dr, Archbishop of Cashel, 163, 167
Harvard, 651
Haughey, Charles, J., 367, 408–9, 458–61, 466, 481, 494, 498–510, 654
Hayden, Mary, 588
Hayek, F. von, 601
Hayes, Michael, 90, 107

Hayes, Roger, 408n277
Headlam, Maurice, 24, 92n147, 379
Health Act (1947), 315; (1953), 321;
    (1948), 412
Health and Social Services, Ministry of,
    416
Health and Social Welfare, Department of,
    314
Healy, John, 371, 646
Healy, Tim, 73, 177n11
Heaney, Séamus, 542
Hearne, John, 202
Heath, Edward, 434–5, 441, 444, 449
Heckscher, E., 597–8, 606, 667
hedonism, 656
Heffernan, M., 131
Hempel, Dr, E., 244, 246, 253, 264–5,
    267
Hendaye, 264
Henlein, K., 80
Henry VIII, 11
Henry, Dr, Bishop of Down and Conor, 10
hero, 181, 406–7
Herrema, T., 480
Herrenvolk, 4, 21, 59, 79, 596
Hertford College, Oxford, 567
Hewitt, C., 420n40
Hibernia, 410
Hiberno-English, 660
Hidden Ireland, 594
Higher Education Authority, 363, 409
higher education system, 621
Highlanders, 669
Hillery, Patrick, 361–2, 388, 461, 465,
    480
historians, 632–4, 638
historical evidence, 118
history, 224, 587–97
Hitler, 79, 181, 221, 242, 246–8, 251–2,
    264, 266, 268, 527
Hitler Shirts, 183
Hobson, Bulmer, 19
Hofer, W., 603
Hogan, G. P. S., 342, 344
Hogan, James, 184, 184n47, 587
Hogan, Patrick, 74, 97, 101, 112–13,
    115–17, 123, 184, 302–3, 345, 528
Holloway, J. C., 473
Holyhead, 384
home market, 530
Home Rule Act (1914), 37
Home Rule Bill (1912), 6–7, 16, 20
Home Rule Bill, Amendment (June 1914),
    17
Home Rule élite, 75
Home Rule Party, 12, 14–40 *passim*, 86,
    336, 375, 390

Home Rule within Home Rule, 15–16
Hooper, J., 126, 576
Hoselitz, B., 601
Hospital Sweepstake, 315
house searches, 433
housing, 124–5, 177, 193, 199, 212, 309,
    345, 364, 420, 508, 579
Hughes, Patrick, 105
Human Sciences, 603, 605
Hume, John, 422, 436, 543, 455, 675, 679
Hungary, 68, 70, 142, 526–7
hunger strike, 222, 454–6, 675
Hunt Report, 430
Hunt, Sir John, 430
Hurd, Douglas, 451
Hyde, Douglas, 211, 239, 669
hypocrisy, 135, 203, 263, 332, 447,
    651–2, 671

ideas, market for, 562–643 *passim*
identity, 82, 205, 426, 449, 456, 461, 605,
    621, 641–2, 653, 657–87
Imperial Conference (1926), 144, 154, 213
income distribution, 579
income tax, 109, 111, 195, 216, 236, 322
Independent Fianna Fáil, 460
Independent Orange Order, 4
Independents, 155, 170, 210, 215, 299,
    324, 326, 366, 506
India, 87, 300–1
individualism, 4
Industrial Credit Cooperation, 190, 225
Industrial Development Act (1945), 412
Industrial Development Authority, 309,
    343–5, 473–4, 530–6, 560, 635, 639
Industrial Efficiency Bill, 291–3, 310
Industrial Efficiency Bureau, 292
industrial labour force, 120
Industrial Policy, 473, 537–9, 554–5, 640,
    642
Industrial Relations Act, 290
Industry and Commerce, Department of,
    11, 120, 122ff, 127, 188ff, 226, 230,
    276–7, 310–11, 343, 473, 575, 580,
    635
infant mortality, 124, 256, 314
inferiority complex, 167, 172, 378–80,
    629, 660–1, 669–70
inflation, 280, 282, 313–14, 348, 466,
    470, 488–9, 492, 502, 526
information, 191–2, 574–7, 625
Inglis, Brian, 297n104, 320, 606
inheritance patterns, 645
instability, 69
Institute of Local, Regional and National
    Planning, Swiss Technical Institute,
    605

Institute of Public Administration, 338, 341, 621
integrity, 92
intellectual: imports, 622–30; inertia, 198; infra-structure, 235, 605, 634, 638, 670–1; integrity, 557; isolation, 260–1
intellectuals, 76
intelligence services, 244–5
interest groups, 537, 546, 550, 555, 621, 635, 640, 648, 657
interest rates, 501
Intergovernmental Conference, 456, 680
Intermediate Certificate Examination, 130
international relations, 585, 604
internment, 60, 220, 223, 329, 437, 450, 454
Investment in education, 361
Ireland Act (1949), 300
Iremonger, Val, 606
Irish Administrative System, 585
Irish Americans, 81, 252–3, 437
Irish Banking Review, 347–51, 378–9
Irish Bishops' Conference, 656
Irish Business and Administrative Review, 585
Irish Citizen Army, 19
Irish Congress of Trade Unions, 290, 538
Irish Convention, 39
Irish Distillers, 535
Irish Educational Studies, 585
Irish Farmers' Union, 181
Irish Geography, 585
Irish Independent, 29–30, 36, 151, 217, 295, 347, 365, 483, 607, 658
Irish jokes, 669
Irish Journal of Education, 585
Irish Labour History Society, 585
Irish language, 131–6, 204, 224–5, 230, 464, 658–74, 676
Irish Management, 393
Irish Management Institute, 403, 577
Irish Medical Association, 318, 321
Irish National League, 141
Irish National Liberation Army, 453
Irish National Productivity Committee, 401
Irish National Teachers' organisation, 134, 671
Irish News, 30
Irish Political Studies, 585, 598
Irish pound, 493
Irish Press, 166, 168, 170, 177, 207, 217–19, 254, 266, 322, 365, 377–8, 537, 541–2
Irish Republican Army, 42, 56–7, 78, 99, 151, 154, 157, 168, 176–81, 184, 214, 219–21, 235, 242–3, 256, 296, 327, 336, 415, 424, 431

Irish Republican Army Organisation, 96
Irish Republican Brotherhood, 20–2, 24–5, 100–2
Irish Shipping, 233
Irish Statesman, 605
Irish Studies in International Affairs, 585
Irish Sugar Company, 190
Irish Times, 29–30, 79–80, 95, 215, 217, 278, 335, 352, 359, 365, 405, 499, 606–7
Irish Trade Union Congress, 401
Irish Transport and General Workers Union, 115, 241, 290, 336
Irish Volunteers, 18, 22, 42, 336
Irishtown, 165
irredentism, 78–9
Isles Report, 415
Italy, 177, 183, 665

Jacobsson, Per, 199–200, 200n105, 624–5, 629
Japan, 266, 413, 491, 517, 634
jealousy, 645–8
Jews, 203, 254, 267, 394, 418, 665
John XXIII, Pope, 427
John Paul II, Pope, 653
Johnson, Harry, 566
Johnson, Thomas, 41, 172
Johnston, Joseph, 149, 580
Jones, Emrys, 626
Jones Hughes, T., 626
journalism, 572, 606–8
Joyce, James, 158
judiciary, 208, 332
Judiciary Committee, 128
Jurors Protection Act, 157
Justice, Department of, 48, 219, 222
Juvenal, 128

Katanga, 370
Kavanagh, Patrick, 159, 649
Keating, Justin, 410, 473, 481, 484, 486
Kee, Robert, 262n414
Kelleher, John, 427–8
Kenmare, 102
Kennedy, Hugh, 104–5, 128–9, 157
Kennedy, Kieran, 128–9, 157, 354–5, 581–2, 630
Kenny, Enda, 480
Kenny, Ivor, 394, 537, 554, 577
Kenny Report, 486
Kerry, 102, 126
Keyes, M. J., 309
Keynes, J. M., 200n107, 230, 232, 261, 566–7, 570, 575
Keynesianism, 312–13, 467, 502
Kiernan, T. J., 576, 608, 625

Kilbeggan, 296
Kilkenny People, 35
Killeen, Michael, 473–4, 530, 533, 535,
    560, 639
Killenaule, 74
Killorglin, 255
Kimball, S., 623, 651
King, Frank, 450
King, W. MacKenzie, 242, 338, 371
Kohn, Leo, 83, 623
Korean War, 323, 568, 570
Kuehn, Alfred, 351
Kuznets, Simon, 581, 583

laboratory facilities, 131
Labour Court, 290
Labour Party:
    and PR, 83–4
    and 1922 general election, 95, 542
    and 1923 general election, 95
    and 1927 general elections, 155
    and Mayo vote, 1932, 167
    and 1932 general election, 170–1
    and Fianna Fáil governments (1932,
        1937), 176–8, 211
    and 1937 general election, 179
    as 'natural ally' of Fianna Fáil, 182
    and Department of Finance, 200, 566
    and 1938 general election, 215
    and neutrality, 237
    and 1943 general election, 239–40
    splits, 240–1
    and 1944 general election, 241
    and 1948 general election, 298
    and inter-party government, 299
    and 1951 general election, 319–20
    and 1957 general election, 327
    and 1961 general election, 336
    and 1969 general election, 410
    and 1973 Pact with Fine Gael, 468
    and 1973 general election, 468
    and 'National Coalition', 469, 475
    and planning, 487
    and 1977 general election, 484
    and 1981 general election, 506
    and February 1982 general election, 508
    and November 1982 general election,
        510
    and National Development Corperation,
        536
    and Telesis, 555
    and liberal tendencies, 656
    and New Ireland Forum, 675
Labour Party (Britain), 256, 411
Labour relations, 289
Labour, Department of, 127
Lagan, 522

Lalor, P. J., 553
Land Act (1923), 71, 113
Land Annuities, 110, 145
Land Commission, 71
Land League, 86
land market, 646
land prices, 490–1
Land Rehabilitation Project, 303, 313
land war, 391
Lands, Department of, 231, 305
language shift, 605
Larkin, Jim, 19, 33, 95, 240, 290
Latin, 131
Latvia, 70
Laver, Michael, 544
law, 585
Law, Andrew Bonar, 12–13, 26, 44, 143
Lazersfeld, P., 602
The Leader, 182, 322, 325, 330, 367,
    373–4, 379, 398, 605–7, 617
League of Nations, 144, 156, 213, 527,
    567, 601
Leahy, Paddy, 550
'Learning by doing', 630–1
learning: capacity, 269, 627ff; from
    history, 396, 631–4; process, 668,
    684
Leaving Certificate Examination, 130–2,
    673
Leeds, 616
legal system, 127–9
Leinster Leader, 35
Leinster, 24, 185
Leitrim, 73–4
Leix-Offaly, 78, 296
Lemass, Eileen, 508
Lemass, Noel, 369
Lemass, Seán:
    and Easter Rising, 36
    in Four Courts, 63
    and organisational ability, 152
    Shadow Minister for Industry and
        Commerce, 156
    and anti-clericalism, 160–1
    and constitutionalism, 167, 180
    and the press, 168
    and 1932 general election, 169
    and Fianna Fáil's fitness for government,
        174
    and IRA, 176–7
    and protectionism, 177, 216
    Director of elections, 1932, 187
    and social and economic policy, 187–95
    and departmental leadership, 188
    and Department of Finance, 189, 230,
        232
    and John Leydon, 189

and de Valera, 189, 230, 372, 399,
  405–6
and agricultural policy, 231, 350–1, 373
and constituency revision, 210
and Ottawa Conference, 214
and efficiency, 217, 231, 291–3, 298,
  401
and war economy, 224ff
and Commnittee on Economic Planning,
  229ff
and Irish Shipping, 233
and Department of Supplies, 233, 237
and Seán MacEntee, 238, 322–4,
  324n227
appointed Tánaiste, 239
and British 'offer' of unity 1940, 249
and Commission on Vocational
  Organisation, 276
and children's allowances, 277ff
and working-class vote, 289
and exports, 290–1
and necessity, 293
and opportunity, 293
accused of corruption, 296
vindicated, 297
and Industrial Development Authority,
  312
in opposition, 321
and leadership of Fianna Fáil, 326
and leadership style 337, 406–8
succeeds de Valera, 341
and T. K. Whitaker, 343–4
and *(First) programme for economic
  expansion*, 345
and EEC, 352–70
and borrowing, 359
and educational policy, 361–3
and political inheritance, 365
as party leader, 366–7
and Northern policy, 367–9
tribute to W. T. Cosgrave, 369
and United Nations, 370
resigns as Taoiseach, 371
and sense of crisis, 372–3, 385, 400, 405
and industrialisation, 373
and emigration, 386
and nationalism, 387, 399
as chairman, 388
and performance principle, 390ff
and pragmatism, 397
and idealism, 398ff
and Labour Party, 398
and national character, 399
and socialism, 399
and capitalism, 399
and patriotism, 401
and trade unions, 401–2

and neo-corporatism, 402
and role of business, 402
and Second World War, 405
luck, 405–6
and Terence O'Neill, 411, 425
and search for enterprise, 528
and administrative reform, 548, 551–2,
  558
and economists, 580
Lenihan, Brian, 480
Lenin, 28
Leo XIII, Pope, 542
Lerner, Daniel, 88
Levi-Strauss, C., 652
Leydon, John, 74, 111, 118, 188–9,
  198–9, 229, 233, 237, 308, 311, 343,
  580
liberalism, 181
libraries, 131, 586
Lijphart, A., 601
Limerick, 63, 73, 78, 193
Lindahl, E., 597, 625, 667
linen, 139, 413
Lipset-Rokkan Model, 86
List, Frederick, 7
literacy, 76
Lithuania, 70
Little, P. J., 238, 637
Local Appointments Commission, 161–3
local Elections (1934), 179; (1947), 295
Local Government, 125, 136, 336,
  419–21, 424, 547, 559–62
Local Government, Department of, 222,
  273, 277, 284, 293–5, 299, 309
Local Government Act (1898), 106, 161;
  (1923), 132
Local Security Force, 234
localism, 80–1, 85, 546
location of industry, 192
Locke Distillery Tribunal, 296–7
Lockwood committee, 417
Lodge, David, 620
Logue, Cardinal, 39
London, 384, 629, 660, 679
London School of Economics, 199,
  200n105
London University, 342
Londonderry (county), 45, 152, 683
Londonderry, Lord, 136–7
loneliness, 637, 649
Long-term Recovery Programme, 305
Lough Swilly, 212
Loughnane, Bill, 509
lower middle class, 182–3
Loyalist strike (1974), 445–8; (1977), 451
Loyalists, 14, 17
luck, 391, 526–8

Lund, 598
Lurgan, 314
Lynch, Jack:
  as Minister for Education and the
    Gaeltacht, 329
  as Minister for Industry and Commerce,
    353
  and Report of Commission on the
    Constitution, 369
  as chairman, 388
  and electoral appeal, 406
  succeeds Lemass as Taoiseach, 409–10
  visits Stormont, 416
  and Northern Ireland, 429–30, 437,
    458–61, 480–1
  and 1969 general election, 410, 458
  and 1970 Cabinet crisis, 459
  and leadership style, 460, 479 and 1973
    general election, 467–9
  in opposition, 480
  and C. J. Haughey, 481
  and Constituency Boundary Review
    Commission, 482
  and nomination of Patrick Hillery as
    president, 482
  and 1977 general election, 483–4
  and economic policy, 487ff
  and 1979 by-elections, 495–6
  and death of Christy Ring, 545
  appraisal, 496–8
  resigns as Taoiseach, 496
  and de Valera, 497
  as party manager, 498
Lynchspeak, 429
Lynn Committee on Education, 129, 136,
  138
Lynn, Kathleen, 207
Lyon, Stanley, 191, 576
Lyons, Declan, 524
Lyons, F. S. L., 258

McAleese, Dermot, 533, 554, 582
Mac Amhlaoibh, Dónal, 384
MacAllister, R. A. S., 620
MacArdle, Dorothy, 270
MacBride, Maud Gonne, 296
MacBride, Major John, 74, 296
MacBride, Seán, 295, 299–301, 303–8,
  311, 317–18, 324–5, 327, 475–6, 523
McCann case, 11
McCarron, E. P., 198–9
McCartan, Patrick, 294
McCarthy, Charles, 643–4, 649
McCarthy, M. D., 575–6, 579, 581
McCreevy, Charles, 507, 509
McCullough, Denis, 20
MacDermot, Frank, 274

MacDermott, Seán, 20, 24–5, 30, 73
MacDonagh, Thomas, 24–5, 37, 73
MacDonald, Malcolm, 212–13, 245, 249,
  339
MacDonald, R., 173
McDowell, R. B., 615ff
Macedonia, 79
MacElligott, J. J., 74, 106, 108, 112, 120,
  156, 189, 192, 196, 200, 212, 224,
  227, 231–2, 261, 279–85, 287–8,
  308–9, 312, 320, 322, 324–5, 342,
  345, 347–8, 351, 359, 379, 405, 563,
  566–7, 571, 580–1, 624–5
MacEntee, Seán
  and Easter Rising, 26, 37
  and Catholic vote, 177
  as Minister for Finance, 189
  and civil service, 196, 275–6
  and economic history, 200
  and 1936 budget, 200
  and social conservatism, 200
  and Wolfe Tone, 209
  and *Irish Times*, 215
  and 1939 budget, 216,
  as Minister for Industry and Commerce,
    237
  and red scare tactics, 241, 298–9
  and Senate, 272–3
  and Children's Allowances, 279–87, 316
  and Dignan Plan, 285–6
  and trade unions, 290
  and constituency revision, 293–9
  and building activity, 309
  and Clann na Poblacta, 321–2
  and 1952 budget, 322–6, 345
  and Lemass, 322, 324, 324n227
  and leadership of Fianna Fáil, 326, 341
  and 1954 general election, 326
  as Minister for Health and Social
    Welfare, 329, 364
  and Congo, 370
  and Labour Party, 398
MacEoin, Seán, 294, 331, 370
McGarrigle, Pearse, 620
McGee case, 479
McGilligan, Patrick, 74, 104, 104n200,
  110, 121, 124, 127, 146, 156, 168,
  188, 286, 312–13, 326, 332, 342, 469
McGrath, J. J., 22
McGrath, Joseph, 96, 98–9, 102, 120,
  127, 151
McGrath, Patrick, 222–3
Machiavelli, 50, 332
Machlup, F., 601
MacHugh, Dr, Bishop of Down and
  Connor, 141
McKenna, Daniel, 236, 245n325

McKinsey's, 623–4
McKnight, Thomas, 7
MacMahon, Seán, 57, 96, 103
MacManus, M. J., 219
Macmillan, Harold, 414, 449
MacNeill, Eoin, 18–20, 22, 74, 129,
    132–4, 136, 144–5, 148–9, 587,
    595
MacNeill, James, 146, 177
McNeill, Randall, 5
McQuaid, Dr J. C., Archbishop of Dublin,
    316–18
McQuillan, Jack, 320
Macroom, 74
MacRory, Cardinal, 222, 254, 267
MacSharry, Ray, 500, 508
MacStiofáin, Seán, 433, 461
MacSwiney, Terence, 496
Maffey, Sir John, 250
Magaziner, Ira, 623
Magee College, 417
Maguire, Frank, 454
Maguire, Paddy, 649, 652
Maher, T. J., 495
Malvern Street Murders, 427
management, 292, 585, 603
management studies, 602
managerial infra-structure, 235
Managing the country better, 548
Manchester, 616
Manchester Guardian, 568
Mannix, Dr Daniel, archbishop of
    Melbourne, 155, 299
Mansergh, Nicholas, 145, 633
market, 392–3, 577; market research,
    292
Marrakesh, 669
marriage, 283–4; age, 360; rate, 70, 360,
    381, 515
Marshall Aid, 303–6
Mason, Roy, 451–2
Mater Hospital, 412
materialism, 158–9, 169, 271, 304, 317,
    425, 464, 522, 540–2, 651, 654
Matthews, Francis P., 302
Maudling, Reginald, 434
Maxwell, Sir John, 31
Maynooth, 422, 579, 584, 587, 626
Mayo, 73, 126, 161ff, 266, 646
Mayo County Council, 161
Mazzini, G., 674
Meade, James, 566
Meath, 543
media, 655, 660
medical profession, 76, 314–18, 385
mediocrity, 378–81, 405, 415, 499, 528,
    539, 562

Mediterranean, 349
Meenan, James, 580–2
Mellowes, Liam, 50, 56–7, 62–3, 66
Merseyside, 568
metropolis, 661
Meyrick, F. J., 118, 198
Mid-Ulster, 424
military bases, 50, 214, 245, 251–2,
    255–6, 302
military tribunal, 179–80
Miller, David, 14
Mills, Michael, 369
Milroy, Seán, 119
Minghetti, M., 79
ministerial responsibility, 282, 548
Ministers' and Secretaries Act, 105
minorities, 165
Mises, L. von, 601
missions, 395–6
Mitchell, G. F., 620
Mitchell, Jim, 507
mobility, 646
modern languages, 131
Moloney, Helena, 207
Molyneux, Jim, 450, 453
Monaghan, 45
Monahan, P., 127
monetary policy, 354
monetary reform, 183–4
Montague, John, 331, 649
Montegrano, 81
Montgomery, 422
Moody, T. W., 588–97 *passim*, 608, 620,
    626
Morahan, J. T., 163–4
morality, 158, 332, 619, 642–3, 645, 648,
    654
Morgenstern, O., 601
Morning Post, 145
Morrison, D., 455
Morrissey, Daniel, 308, 310
Moscow, 156
Moss, W., 623
Mother and Child Scheme, 313–22,
    578–9
motherhood, 206–7
motivation, 552
motor car salesmen, 385
Motu proprio, 11
Mountbatten, Louis, 455, 495
Mountjoy Jail, 222
Moylan, Seán, 231, 238, 329
Moynihan, Maurice, 74, 199, 202,
    245n325, 278–9, 306, 314, 337,
    466
Moynihan, Séan, 74, 199, 209
Mulcahy, Dónal, 586

Mulcahy, Richard, 37, 65–6, 74, 96,
　98–101, 105, 153, 173, 175, 241,
　299, 332, 388–9
Mullins, Tommy, 483
multinational companies, 518
Munich crisis, 234, 246
Munster, 24, 495
Murphy, John A., 497, 660, 670n505
Murphy, Kevin, 558
Murphy, M., 472
Murphy, T. J., 309
Murphy, William Martin, 19, 30
Murray, C. H., 467, 470, 472
Mussolini, B., 167, 181, 242, 272, 499
Myles na gCopaleen, 668; see O'Nolan
Myrdal, Gunnar, 571, 583, 597, 667

Napier, Oliver, 431
National Bank of Switzerland, 602
national character, 153, 403, 478, 493,
　501, 619, 643–57 passim, 673
National Coalition, 469
National Debt, 110, 199, 303, 517
National Defence Conference, 237
National Development Corperation,
　536–8
National Economic and Social Council,
　365, 404n269, 523, 560, 583
National Guard, 179
National Health Insurance Act (1933), 195
National Health Insurance Society, 285
national income, 118, 576, 625
National Industrial and Economic Council,
　365, 401, 583
National Institute for Higher Education,
　Dublin, 363
National Institute for Higher Education,
　Limerick, 363
National Labour Party, 241, 299
National League, 155
national psyche, 260, 264
national unity, 414
National University of Ireland, 204, 332,
　395, 467, 587, 616, 673
National University Women Graduates'
　Association, 207
National Vocational Council, 275
National Volunteers, 22
national wage agreements, 402, 466–7,
　471, 490, 502
nationalism, 10, 182, 477–9, 651, 657–8,
　661, 675–6
nationalist image of Ulster unionism, 19
nationalist Letter to President Wilson,
　1918, 41
Nationalist Party, 414, 431
NATO, 301, 684

natural law, 157–8
natural resources, 522ff
naval bases, 245
navy, 236
Nazism, 221, 247–8, 255, 265, 267, 269
Ne Temere, 11
Neary, Peter, 582
Neave, Airey, 453
negroes, 418
Netherlands, 76, 114, 246, 381, 494, 537,
　601, 663–4
Netherlands Central Bureau of Statistics,
　601
Netherlands School of Economics, 601
Neure Zürcher Zeitung, 569, 607
neutrality, 21–2, 40, 48, 213, 236, 242,
　244, 253, 258–70, 464, 543, 602,
　603, 605, 607, 659
New Deal, 169, 565
New Ireland Forum, 456, 596, 675, 680–1
New Order, 247, 253, 268
New York, 78, 207, 384
New Zealand, 300–1, 523
Ní Dhómhnaill, Nuala, 668
Niemba, 370
Nixon, Inspector, 138
non-conformity, 4
North Mayo, 151
Northern Ireland Act, 448
Northern Ireland Assembly, 442
Northern Ireland Civil Rights Association,
　420
Northern Ireland Committee of the Irish
　Congress of Trade Unions, 416
Northern Ireland Constitution Act, 441
Northern Ireland Constitutional Proposals,
　442
Northern Ireland Executive, 443–8
Northern Ireland Labour Party, 140, 301,
　413, 436
Northern Whig, 145
Norton amendment, 546
Norton, William, 223, 294, 388–9
Norway, 76, 235, 243, 263, 265, 268,
　381, 494, 511–19, 528, 599–600,
　604, 620, 663, 664–5
notionalism, 478
nuns, 76
Nurske, R., 604, 667

Ó Broin, Leon, 108, 608, 632, 670
Ó Buachalla, D., 177
Ó Cinnéde, Pádraig, 314
Ó Conaire, P., 164
Ó Dálaigh, C., 408, 482–3
Ó Fiaich, Cardinal Tomás, 655
Ó hAodha, Séamus, 101

Ó hEithir, Breandán, 607
Ó hEigeartaigh, D., 106n214, 176n6, 199
Ó hEocha, Colm, 617, 675
Ó hUigínn, Pádraig, 509
Ó Máille, Pádraig, 66
Ó Moráin, Mícheál, 329, 459–60
Ó Muirthuile, S., 96, 100
Ó Riordáin, S. P., 620
Ó Riordáin, Seán, 385, 607
Ó Tuathaigh, Gearóid, 387
O'Brien, Conor Cruise, 28, 268n439,
    369–70, 410, 476–9, 484, 486,
    509–10, 606–7
O'Brien, George, 112, 116–17, 119, 129,
    184, 199, 350, 350n88, 571, 576,
    580–1, 616
O'Brien, William (Labour), 41, 240–1,
    290
O'Brien, William, (Home rule), 15, 73, 79,
    168
O'Carroll, Dr Ffrench, 320
O'Carroll, J. P., 654n474
O'Casey, Seán, 26, 135, 158
O'Connell, Daniel, 75, 86, 371, 404, 665
O'Connor, Rory, 50–1, 57, 62, 66, 100
O'Connor, Seán, 362, 587
O'Donnell, Dr, Bishop of Raphoe, 15
O'Donoghue, Martin, 487–90, 503
O'Donovan Rossa, 27
O'Duffy, E., 67, 96, 102–4, 154, 175,
    179–80, 183–4, 184
O'Faolain, Sean, 263, 339, 594, 618,
    629
O'Flaherty, L., 158
O'Flanagan, Fr Michael, 17
O' Halloran, Michael, 74
O' Hegarty, P. S., 74
O' Higgins, Kevin: and Collins-de Valera
    Pact, 58; father murdered in Civil
    War, 67; denounces Mulcahy, 68;
    from Offaly, 74; and 1924 army
    mutiny, 96–105; as conservative
    revolutionary, 105; and
    protectionism, 118; and Democratic
    Programme 124; assassinated, 152;
    appraisal, 152–4; and 1926 Imperial
    Conference, 156
O'Higgins, T. F., 178
O'Higgins, Tom, 388
O'Keefe, P. D., 297n106
O'Kelly, M. J., 620
O'Kelly, Seán T., 41, 167, 169–70, 177,
    193, 198, 206, 209–10, 214, 222,
    229–30, 232, 238–9, 270, 279, 287,
    294, 330
O'Kennedy, Michael, 481, 508
O'Leary, Michael, 486, 506, 510

O'Loghlen, P. J., 200
O'Mahony, David, 581
O'Malley, Desmond, 461, 481, 508, 635
O'Malley, Donogh, 361–4, 480
O'Neill, Terence, 367–8, 414–9, 421–8,
    435
O'Nolan, Brian, 278; see Myles na
    gCopaleen
O'Nolan, Michael, 278n29
O'Rahilly, Alfred, 523, 564–6, 572,
    579–80
O'Reilly, Tony, 501
O'Shiel, K., 142ff, 146, 149
O'Sullivan, Gearóid, 57, 96
O'Sullivan, J. M., 132, 587–8
Oakeshott, M., 339
Oath of Allegiance, 50, 54, 59, 151–2,
    154, 157, 177
Oath to the Republic, 48
occupational structure, 70
OECD, 346, 361, 491, 494, 515–16, 525,
    559, 624, 639
OEEC, 305
Offences against the State Acts, 139, 221,
    223, 461, 468
Official IRA, 432, 453
Official Labour Party, 298
official mind, 276–7, 305–6, 341, 345,
    415, 535, 559, 573, 578, 580, 586,
    608, 625, 639–41, 671
Official Unionist Party, 443, 456, 682
Ohlin, B., 597, 606, 667
oil: crisis (1973), 468–70, 525; (1979),
    488, 500; exploration, 473
Old Age Pension Committee of Inquiry,
    125
old age pensions, 125, 140, 193, 225
Old IRA, 100
Oliver, John, 415, 419
OPEC, 470
Operation Motor Man, 442
Orange Order, 2, 10, 15, 254, 412, 414,
    422, 427–8, 437
Orangeism, 432
*Österreichische Zeitschrift für
    Politikwissenschaft*, 602
Ottawa, 299
Ottawa Conference (1932), 572
over-employment, 570
Oxford, 616
Oxford Union, 367–8

Paget, Sir Arthur, 18
Paisley, Ian, 4, 404, 423–4, 426–8, 435–6,
    443, 447, 449–50, 452–3, 505
Paisleyism, 427
papacy, 181

parades, 420
paranoia, 572, 681
Parliament Act (1911), 1
parliament and decision-making, 276
Parnell C. S., 75, 371, 387, 389–90, 404
partition, 43–7, 77, 80, 93, 214, 243, 245,
    253, 270, 300–1, 321, 375, 679, 682,
    684
party system, 85, 87, 336, 540, 545–6
patriarchy, 284
patriotism, 385, 402–3, 503, 541, 643
Patterson, Rev. Dr, 9
Peace Movement, 452
peace research, 601
Pearse, Patrick, 18–20, 24–6, 37, 41, 106,
    129–30, 133, 197, 394
Peillon, Michael, 585, 626
People's Democracy, 422–4
performance, 428, 604, 619, 621, 627,
    674, 678–9
performance principle, 390ff, 650
peripherality, 524, 604, 663, 668
perjury, 273, 645
Petty, William, 396
Phillips, W. A., 626
physical planning, 417
Pig Marketing Board, 255
Pilsudski, J., 76, 175
Pius XI, Pope, 170, 271
Pius XII, Pope, 285
Planning, 276, 343, 350, 401, 416, 487,
    625, 631, 677
Planning Bureau of the Netherlands, 601
Plunkett, Count, 38
Plunkett, John, 222
Plunkett, Joseph Mary, 24, 38, 222
Plunkitt, George Washington, 106
Poland, 70, 76–7, 80, 175, 526–7, 665–6
police, 220, 332; *see* Gárda Síochána,
    Royal Ulster Constabulary
political culture, 161ff, 171, 199, 224,
    254, 259, 335, 399, 406, 416, 440,
    478, 486, 493, 503, 547, 605, 655,
    676
political elites, 75
political leadership, 540
political science, 584, 599–600, 602–3,
    623
politicians, geographical origins, 73–4
politicisation, 86
Pollack, H. M., 140
Pompidou, Georges, 371, 461
poor law, 286, 313
Pope, the, 8–9, 11, 16, 45, 78, 414
Population, 71, 187, 232, 281, 349, 360,
    511–3, 572, 604, 631, 651
populism, 73, 182

Portlaoise, 480
proportional representation, 82ff, 546
possessing classes, 374, 376, 380, 385,
    644, 650
possessor ethos, 528; principle, 390ff, 517,
    645, 650
Postal Workers' Strike (1979), 492
Posts and Telegraphs, Department of, 477,
    553
potential, 539, 552, 621, 629, 678, 685
poverty, 159, 281, 285
Powell, Enoch, 453
power sharing, 437, 439, 443, 447–8, 450,
    452, 461, 681
practical men, 628, 672
Prendergast, Fr G., 162
Prendergast, Peter, 506
Prenter, Rev Dr Samuel, 9, 16
preparatory colleges, 133
Presbyterians, 2, 12, 418
presidency, 208, 211, 239
presidential election (1945), 270, 294;
    (1959), 331
pressure groups, 366, 402, 404n269, 486
price and wage controls, 233
prices, 185–6, 239, 289
Prices Commission 292
Primary Certificate Examination, 130
Prior, James, 451, 456
private enterprise, 190, 200, 277, 291,
    308, 310–11
Pro-Life Amendment Campaign, 653–4
Proclamation of the Republic (1916), 5,
    27, 30, 33, 38–9, 204, 208
Proclamation of the Ulster Provisional
    Government (1913), 5
professions, 131, 159, 316, 638
professors, 385
Progressive Unionists, 255
promotion, 107, 393, 395, 398, 476, 487,
    549, 556, 621, 646
propensity to import, 117–18, 528
property rights, 391
proportional representation, 84–5, 156
Protestant Ascendancy, 659
Protestant clergy, 136, 412
Protestant images of Catholics, 4, 9–11, 16
Protestant self-image, 14
Protestant Telegraph, 427
Protestant Unionist Party, 427
Protestant workers, 5, 414, 445
Protestants, 1–18 *passim*, 203–5, 211,
    250, 411–57 *passim*, 656, 661
providence, 380–3
provincialism, 661, 668
Provisional Government, 54, 57, 141,
    457

Provisional IRA, 432–8, 442, 449–55,
459, 461, 477, 480, 482, 484, 658
Public Administration, 585, 603–4
Public Capital Programme, 465
public morality, 107, 204, 332, 645
public myth, 648, 653
Public Safety Acts, 154, 157, 168, 177,
219–20
public sector trade unions, 470
Public Service Advisory Council, 550
Public Service, Department of the, 552–3,
553n136
Puritanism, 158
Pym, Francis, 443

Quadragesimo Anno, 271, 283
Quakers, 394
Queen's University Belfast, 414, 417, 422,
577, 584–5, 620, 626

RTE, 647
race, 46, 77, 144–5, 658, 661; racism,
2–3, 9–10, 20, 418–19, 453
Radio Eireann, 608
Raftery, Terry, 587
railway companies, 225, 638–9
rationing, 233–4, 288
reading, 616
Red Guards, 181
red scare, 156–7, 169, 241, 298–9, 410
Redmond, John, 7, 13, 15, 17–18, 23, 28,
31, 34, 37–40, 44, 46, 73, 204, 214,
249
Redmond, O. J., 279, 325, 342
Redmond, William, 155
Rees, Merlyn, 445–54
referendums: on 1937 Constitution,
210–11; on PR (1959) 330–1; (1968),
410; on EEC entry (1972), 465; on
voting age (1972), 468; on special
position of the Catholic Church
(1972), 468
regional commissioners, 267
regional planning, 196, 560
regional policy, 419
relatives assisting, 649
rentiers, 109–10, 127
Republican Clubs, 453
resistance to change, 548–50, 555–9
respectability, 159, 164, 222
Review of Economic Studies, 567
Reynolds, Albert, 500
rhetoric, 158, 458, 464, 490, 560, 605,
640, 679, 684
Richardson, Sir George, 17
ridicule, 646
Ring, Christy, 496

Riordan, E. J., 121
riots, 254
Roche, Stephen, 220–4
Rokkan, S., 86n123, 599–600, 604, 667
Romania, 70, 76–7, 527
Rome Rule, 45, 160
Roosevelt, F. D., 182, 251, 252, 264, 565
Roscommon, 38, 73
Roscommon Herald, 33, 35
Rosenstein Rodan, P., 601
Royal Air Force, 265
Royal Irish Academy, 467, 585
Royal Irish Constabulary, 110, 154
Royal Navy, 265
Royal Ulster Constabulary, 61, 88, 138,
421–3, 428–30, 434, 438, 441, 451
rugby, 659
rural electrification, 241
Russia, 79, 218, 262, 527
Ruth, G., 149
Ruttledge, Patrick J., 166, 214, 219, 222,
238, 277
Ryan, James, 37, 177, 184–5, 210, 214,
231–2, 239, 273, 314–15, 321, 329,
337, 343, 351, 388, 409, 580
Ryan, Louden, 343, 577, 581–2
Ryan, Richie, 469–73, 475, 481, 631

Salonica, 79
St Cyr, 340
St Laurent, Louis, 371
St Patrick's Training College, 587
Sands, Bobby, 454
Saothar, 585
savings, 288, 323
Schacht, Hjalmar, 565–6
Schieder, Theodor, 633
Schleswig Holstein, 142
scholarships, 132
School Attendance Act (1926), 131
School Medical Service, 313–14
Schumpeter, J. A., 601
Science, 131; scientific research, 292
Scotland, 412
*Second programme for economic
expansion*, 353
Second Vatican Council, 655
Second World War, 211–70 *passim*
Security, 349, 390ff
segregated education, 137–8
Seirbhís Phoiblí, 558, 560
self-deception, 269, 332, 426, 477, 652–3,
661–2
self-image, 426–7, 400, 447, 541, 560,
571, 617, 644, 648, 652
self-reliance, 269
self-respect, 262–4, 266–7, 674

self-sufficiency, 184, 186–7, 217, 232, 234–5
selfishness, 643, 657
Selma, 422
semi-state bodies, *see* state sponsored sector
Senate, 272
seniority, 549, 646
Serbia, 526
services sector, 117
Serving the country better, 559
sex, 158–9, 645
sexual morality, 656
Shankill, 170, 337
Shannon Scheme, 108, 112, 120–1
Shils, Edward, 76, 640
shipbuilding, 139, 413
Silesia, 79, 142
sin, 645, 650
Sinclair, Thomas, 5, 11
Sinn Féin, 7–8, 32, 38–44 *passim*, 75, 83, 94–5, 127, 141, 151–2, 154, 254, 327, 336, 389–90, 455–6, 596, 631, 675, 681
size, 524, 627, 629
Skelton, O., 622
Sloan, T. H., 4
Slovakia, 79
slums, 193, 281
Smiddy, T., 226, 232, 312
Smith, Paddy, 367, 388
Social Democratic and Labour Party, 431, 436, 439, 442–3, 449, 452–6, 675
social psychology, 603, 626
Social Research Committee, 621, 634
social science, 585, 598, 622, 628
social security, 285
social thought, 641, 667
socialism, 310, 422–4, 432, 579
Sociological Association of Ireland, 585
sociology, 584, 598–600, 602–4, 623, 626; sociologists, 579
Solemn League and Covenant, 6, 7, 12, 44
Solidarity, 643, 650–1
Solow, R. M., 620
Somme, 255, 447
South Dublin City, 216
South Dublin, 151
South Tipperary, 298
South Wall reclamation scheme, 229
Southern protestants, 82, 157
Southern unionists, 39, 128, 177, 215
sovereignty, 463
Soviets, 127
Spain, 263, 534
Special Powers Acts, 60, 289
spite, 354, 645–7

spoils system, 332
Spring, Dick, 510
stability, 72, 78–9, 82–3, 89–90, 93, 214, 224, 309, 313, 335–6, 381, 454, 479, 486, 540, 545, 651, 684
Stack, A., 48, 50
Stagg, Frank, 480
Stalin, 79, 264, 527
Stamboliski, A., 73
Standard, 167, 277, 283, 562
standard of living, 69, 513–14
Stardust fire, 505
state, 81, 205, 281, 283–6, 308, 315–16, 321
state capitalism, 182
state sponsored bodies, 84, 196, 332, 393, 400, 536, 577
Statistical Council, 579
Statistical Society, 574–5
statistics, 574, 602
Statistics Act (1926), 579
Statistics Branch, Department of Industry and Commerce, 191, 574
Statute of Westminster, 213
Steinmetz, S. R., 601
Stephens, E. M., 149
Stephens, James, 30–1
Stockholm Business School, 606
Stockholms Tidningen, 569, 606
Stockley, W., 618
Stormont, 88, 204, 255, 257, 329, 368, 411, 416, 426, 428, 430, 433, 435, 437, 678
Strasbourg, 660
strategic thinking, 631ff
Strategy and Structure, 624
strikes, 127
strokes, 392
Studies, 548
Sudetenland, 246–7
suicide, 599
Sunday Press, 344, 607
Sundbarg, G., 598
Sunningdale Agreement, 444–8
Supplies, Department of, 233, 261, 277, 573
Supreme Council of Defence, 98
Supreme Court, 290, 407–8, 479
Sweden, 76, 234–5, 237, 240, 244–5, 258, 260–5, 268, 370, 494, 511, 519, 523, 559, 569–70, 597–9, 600, 606–7, 624–5, 629, 663
Swedes, 665; Swedish language, 664
Swedish Journal of Economics, 598
Sweetman, Gerard, 326–8, 342, 345, 355, 388, 469, 475
Swiss Sociological Association, 603

Switzerland, 76, 84, 114, 234–5, 240, 243–4, 258, 261, 263–5, 381, 381n68, 494, 519, 528, 602–3, 607, 625, 629, 666

Tablet, 283
Tammany, 218
Tansey, Paul, 554
Taoiseach, Department of the, 301, 503–4, 574–5
Tariff Commission, 120, 122
tariffs, 7–8, 119–20, 353
Taxation, 186, 236, 240, 282, 285, 353–4, 356, 502, 519
tax protest, 492
Taylor, John, 453
Teacher Training Colleges, 394, 586
teachers, 76, 130, 133, 289
technical training, 292; education, 131; infra-structure, 235
technology, 628, 630, 638ff
Telesis Report, 504, 520, 531–7, 582, 623
television, 405, 421–2, 429, 464, 561, 639, 644, 647, 669
terms of trade, 325, 355–8, 465, 488, 520, 524–5
Teschen, 79
Thatcher, Margaret, 453, 455–6, 504, 679–80
The Accession of Ireland to the European Communities, 462–4
The future of Northern Ireland, 442
The Northern Ireland Constitution, 448
The Trend of External Trade, 323
The way forward, 508–9
Third programme for economic expansion, 353, 634
Thomas, J. H., 212
Thomas Davis Lectures, 608
Thompson, Geoffrey, 551
Thornley, David, 366, 410, 628
thought, 604, 630
Thrace, 79
Thurston, T., 556–7
Tierney, Michael, 274
The Times, 173
Times Literary Supplement, 565
Tinbergen, J., 601, 667
Tipperary, 73–4
Tipperary Star, 35
Tobin, Liam, 96, 100–1
Todd, J. E., 587, 620
tolerance, 163
Tone, Wolfe, 168, 209
top-level appointments committee, 556
tourist development, 308
town and country, 72–3

Trade Advisory Council, 291
Trade Loans Act (1924), 110, 112
Trade Union Act (1941), 290
trade unions, 89, 127, 182, 228, 280, 289, 401, 466, 470, 490, 492, 536, 572, 578
'traditional' Ireland, 643ff, 654–5, 657, 662
Tralee, 367
transfer pricing, 518, 535
Transylvania, 79
trasformismo, 79
Traynor, Oscar, 63, 222, 238
Treasury Bills, 287
Treaty of Accession to the EEC, 465
Treaty of Rome, 453, 464
Treaty Ports, 214
Trinity College Dublin, 47, 163, 165, 199, 204, 332, 363, 576, 580, 584–5, 587, 616ff., 626
Truce (July 1921), 47
Truman, Harry S., 302
Tuam, 162
tuberculosis, 314–15
tuberculosis authority, 412
Tulla, 170
Tully, Jaspar, 33, 35
Tully, Jim, 481, 484, 486, 631
Tullymander, 481–2
Turkey, 244
two nations theory, 14–15
Twomey, D., 74, 198, 580
Tyrie, Andy, 441
Tyrone, 45–6, 59–60, 142, 149, 268, 423

U-2, 659
Ukraine, 418
Ulster Black Shirt Movement, 254
Ulster Defence Association, 440–1
Ulster Defence Regiment, 430
Ulster Labour Unionist Association, 139
Ulster Loyalist Anti-Repeal Union, 12
Ulster Special Constabulary, see B Specials
Ulster Unionist Association, 139
Ulster Unionist Council, 6, 14, 444
Ulster Volunteer Force (1913), 17, 18, 20, 22, 26; (1966), 416, 427
Ulster Workers' Council, 445, 447
Ulsterisation, 450–1
Unemployment, 126, 139, 151, 164, 182, 190, 192, 201, 224–5, 254, 256, 260, 285, 288, 323, 333, 360–1, 412, 415, 465, 467, 470–1, 484, 489, 502, 505, 508, 515–16, 519, 539, 568, 570, 574, 602

Unemployment Assistance Acts, 186, 195, 284
unemployment benefits, 193
Unemployment Insurance Acts, 126
Uniforms Bill (1933), 180
Unionism, 1–18 *passim*, 43–7, 253–8, 411–57 *passim*, 675–96 *passim*
Unionist Association of Ireland, 12–13
Unionist Party of Northern Ireland, 448–9
United Ireland Party, 179
United Nations, 226, 369–71, 624, 680
United States of America, 71, 149, 187, 208, 218, 236, 241–3, 245, 251–3, 260–1, 266, 301, 378, 426, 454, 517, 565, 629–30, 646, 658, 665, 679, 684
United Ulster Unionist Council, 444, 448, 450
universities, 76, 130–2, 210, 261, 272, 363–4, 394–5, 563, 575, 586, 634, 646
University College Cork, 184, 188, 564, 576, 580, 584, 587, 619
University College Dublin, 99, 112, 134, 363, 575, 580, 582, 584, 587, 626
University College Galway, 584, 617, 619, 675
'University College Limerick', 620
University of Geneva, 603
University of Glasgow, 415
University of Zurich, 602
urbanisation, 182, 605, 657

Valiulis, M. G., 159n458
Vanguard Movement, 440
Vanguard Unionist Progressive Party, 443
Vatican, 260
Vienna, 669
Viking, 661
violence, 30, 44, 171–2, 179, 224, 335, 441, 443, 447, 645, 685
Vocational Education Act (1930), 132
vocationalism, 179, 181, 183, 271–7, 292
Volunteer Convention (1922), 57

Wages Standstill Order, 233
Wales, 412–13, 664, 673–4
Walsh, Brendan, 582
Walsh, Brian, 408
Walsh, J. J., 74, 119, 120, 149n415
Walshe, Joseph, 74, 246–8, 252–3
War of Independence, 42–3, 47–8, 243, 269
Ward, F. C., 314
Warnock, William, 248
Watt, S., 139
Webb, D. A., 615ff

Weimar, 184
welfare expenditure, 472
welfare state, 262
West, Harry, 416, 425, 436, 444, 449–50, 453, 455
West Belfast, 431
West Cork constituency, 294
West Mayo by-election (1975), 480
Westermarck, E., 667
Westminster model, 88
Wexford, 73–4, 185
Whale, John, 440
wheat, 185, 233
Whelan, Noel, 504, 531, 550
Whitaker, T. K., 279, 287, 309, 342–7, 350–1, 385, 388 405, 415, 466–7, 470, 472, 503, 548, 551, 554, 576–7, 581, 631, 672
White, Pádraic, 535
White Army, 181
White Paper on Full Employment (Britain), 230
Whitelaw, William, 439, 441–3, 449, 451
Whitley Councils, 108
Whyte, John, 204, 286
Wicklow People, 34–5
Wicksell, K., 597
Widgery Report, 440
widows' pensions, 195
Wigforss, E., 597–8
Wilkie, W., 252
Williams, Betty, 452
Williams, T. D., 146, 245n322, 318, 578–9, 590–2, 605–7, 633
Wilson, Harold, 421, 445–7
Wilson, Sir Henry, 62
Wilson, Thomas, 415, 418–19
Wilson, Woodrow, 41–2
Winter, General Ormonde, 42
women, 6, 34, 88, 94, 126, 207–8, 218, 239, 261, 375–7, 395–6, 452, 519, 647
Women's Right to Choose Group, 653
Woods, Tommy, 606
work ethic, 84, 394
Workers' Party, 508–9
Wright, Oliver, 430
Wrigley, Leonard, 519n24

Yeats, W. B., 296, 647
Young Ireland, 594
youth, 182
Yugoslavia, 70, 76–7, 80, 96, 175, 255, 527, 534

zero-sum, 420, 425, 682